BASIC ISSUES IN MEDIEVAL PHILOSOPHY

SELECTED READINGS PRESENTING THE INTERACTIVE DISCOURSES AMONG THE MAJOR FIGURES

edited by Richard N. Bosley & Martin M. Tweedale

broadview press

Canadian Cataloguing in Publication Data

Basic issues in medieval philosophy : selected readings presenting the interactive discourses among the major figures

Includes bibliographical references.
ISBN 1-55111-099-7

1. Philosophy, Medieval.   I. Bosley, Richard.
II. Tweedale, Martin, 1937-   .

B721. B37 1996   189   C96-932348-4

Broadview Press
Post Office Box 1243, Peterborough, Ontario, Canada K9J 7H5

in the United States of America:
3576 California Road, Orchard Park, NY 14127

in the United Kingdom:
B.R.A.D. Book Representation & Distribution Ltd.,
244A, London Road, Hadleigh, Essex SS7 2DE

Broadview Press gratefully acknowledges the support of the Canada Council, the Ontario Arts Council, and the Ministry of Canadian Heritage.

PRINTED IN CANADA

CONTENTS

CONTENTS

PREFACE

IN COMPILING AND EDITING THE TEXTS INCLUDED IN THIS VOLUME WE have aimed at producing a textbook for both introductory and more advanced courses in medieval philosophy. Two ideas governed the organization of the book: (1) that medieval philosophy is best studied as an interactive discussion or debate between thinkers working on very much the same problems despite often being widely separated both in time and locale; (2) that these discussions are often as much with the philosophers of ancient Greece as with authors in the medieval period. Consequently the student will find that this text is organized around nine large topics and that at the beginning of each topic there are one or more selections from ancient philosophy which were well known to medieval authors or at least were indirectly of great influence on them. The hope is that the student will see how the classical tradition in philosophy continued on throughout the middle ages and provided a touchstone unifying the many disparate writers who confronted it down through the centuries. Our intention, however, was not to compel the teacher to abandon a chronological ordering of assigned readings, if he or she so desires, but merely to organize the material in a way that would make evident to the student the interconnections between the various authors. This should be perfectly compatible with a chronological approach to the presentation of the material.

More than in most other presently available collections we have sacrificed breadth to depth. Some figures such as St. Bonaventure, Roger Bacon, Gersonides, John Buridan, *et al.*, who were certainly very important scholastics, are not represented. Instead we have given more than the usual amount of material from Averroes, Abelard, Duns Scotus, and William of Ockham. The traditional emphasis on philosophical work in western Christendom has been retained, although the reader will find a considerable body of material from the Islamic thinkers whose tradition of thought is worth a volume on its own. From the Jewish scholars we have included a substantial section of Maimonides' *Guide*, but again it cannot be said that justice has been done to that tradition.

We have not attempted major interpretive introductions to the materials presented, but tried to limit ourselves to facts about the philosophical and religious background against which they were written and without some knowledge of which those materials would not be very intelligible. Readers who are not fortunate enough to have access to an expert in the subject will find in these introductions enough to make their reading of the texts meaningful and interesting, but they might also want to consult some of the histories of medieval thought mentioned in the bibliography. Unfortunately, there is now no up-to-date history of the whole period available; The *Cambridge History of Later Medieval Philosophy*, however, is a reasonable guide to work done after 1100.

We have adjusted many of the translations given here to avoid the masculine gender bias which infects English often more than it does the original languages of the texts. But this has not been done where it would lead to oddness of construction or to too much of a clash with well-established formulations. Of course, sometimes the original text itself is very gender biased, and we have not tried to disguise that fact.

Our grateful thanks go to two of our very best students, Sophia Wong and Joni Petruskovich, who scaled the steep learning curve involved in using a scanner and thereby expedited our work by several months at least. Also thanks are due to Bernie Ohlhauser at Cooper Cameron Corporation for help with printing hard copies from our discs.

INTRODUCTION

MEDIEVAL PHILOSOPHY, AS WE DEFINE IT FOR THE PURPOSES OF THIS anthology, consists of works by thinkers who had allegiance to one or other of the three great monotheistic religions of the West, Judaism, Christianity, and Islam, and more or less took as their philosophical heritage the tradition of Greek philosophy emanating from Plato and Aristotle. The beginning of medieval philosophy is in fact best located in ancient times with the surprising ascendancy of Christianity to the status of the Imperial Religion during the reign of Constantine (c.320 C.E.); for it was then that Christian intellectuals, in an effort to make their faith more palatable to literate and sophisticated pagans and former pagans, as well as to defend it against pagan criticisms, sought the assistance of the Greek philosophical tradition.

Before that time Christians for the most part had been distinctly hostile to pagan philosophy in the belief that the way or ways of life that it proposed had been completely superseded by the way of Christ. Indeed, there was very good reason for Christians to feel that this philosophy would be much more of a hindrance than an aid to the acceptance of their creed. Greek philosophers for the most part had thought that the notion of a creation of the physical world a finite length of time ago was totally nonsensical. It broke the almost universally accepted rule that from nothing nothing comes. Neo-Platonism, the most widely accepted philosophy in the fourth century, held that the world was a logical result of an endless and completely necessary emanation from the first principle called the "One." Platonists also for the most part denied that this first principle had any knowledge of or concern with the particular things and events in the world of things that come to be and pass away, i.e. the temporal, physical world we experience ourselves to live in. Nor was there in the philosophical tradition much sympathy for any sort of personal immortality; at best some completely intellectual part of ourselves was supposed to survive our physical deaths. Doctrines of divine retributions for evil deeds and rewards for good lives were not taken very seriously among the educated. What was taken seriously was a doctrine of fate in which it was thought that what was going to happen to everyone had long since been determined and that chance and the possibility of choosing anything other than what one does choose were illusory.

On top of that, the theological doctrines that had developed during Christianity's first three centuries often appeared blatantly paradoxical to any philosophically minded person. The doctrine of the incarnation claimed that an all perfect, completely spiritual deity could make itself into a human being with a physical body and suffer just as humans did. Nothing could be more at odds with the Greek tradition of philosophical theology, which from the time of Xenophanes (sixth century B.C.E.) had tried to rid the deity of any attributes which indicated less than total perfection and bliss. Scarcely less acceptable to the philosophical mind was the strange doctrine of the Trinity in which God was three Persons but yet one completely non-complex entity (or non-entity for the neo-Platonists). Divisibility had long been conceived by the philosophical tradition as a source of corruption and hence philosophical theology had early on banned it from the deity. A final example is the doctrine of bodily resurrection. The Bible teaches that eventually the souls of the dead will have their bodies restored to them, or at least some sort of a body, one that is not subject to corruption. But the Platonist tradition had for centuries denigrated the body and thought that salvation lay in getting rid of it.

Although the Greek philosophical tradition contained plenty of competing lines of thought, by the time Christianity became an Imperial Religion only neo-Platonism with its cosmology of pure intellects eternally emanating from the "One" and utterly changeless in themselves, of heavenly spheres whose endless rotations gave motion to the heavenly bodies, and of a sublunary world of things that come to be and pass away where a sort of controlled chaos reigns, offered any hope of assistance to Christian apologists, and yet its divergence from Biblical Christianity was evident enough. No beginning of the world and hence no creation. No deity with freedom of choice let alone concern for particular earthly beings. No personal immortality. No salvation except for a hope that through concentration on abstract thought the soul might identify itself with its immortal intellectual part. No eventual everlasting *bodily* existence. The outlook for a rapprochement between Christianity and philosophy did not look promising at the start.

But somehow this rapprochement did occur, and despite the protests of a significant minority of thinkers down through the centuries it persisted right up to the end of the middle ages. In fact, we can place the end of medieval philosophy at whatever time this collaboration between Christian thought in the West and the ancient Greek philosophical tradition ceased to be significant. Already in the fourteenth century the rifts were widening and there were calls to retrieve Christian theology from the philosophy which it originally had given entry to as an assistant but had become increasingly subservient to in the later medieval period. Just as the ceasing of this collaboration can scarcely be dated with much precision, so we need not be too concerned with setting a definite date for the end of medieval philosophy, and in some circles it certainly persisted well into what historians call the modern period, i.e. after 1600.

In fact there were two quite separate encounters between the great monotheistic religions and the philosophy of Greece. There was the one we have just spoken of which occurred at the end of the ancient period and in which the basic dogmas of the Christian faith were defended with a more or less Platonist philosophy. This occurred in both the Greek speaking world and in the world in which Latin remained the language of the educated. From the former we have some selections from the author known as Dionysius (c.500) whose works became very influential throughout medieval Christendom; while from the Latin West there are extensive selections from St. Augustine of Hippo (354-430), whose heavily Platonized rendition of Christian doctrine became the standard authority for all later theologians in the West, as well as from Ancius Manlius Boethius (480-524), first minister to the Ostrogothic king Theodoric, whose translations of and commentaries on Aristotle's logic were to form the basis of secular education in the twelfth century revival of learning in western Europe.

The second encounter occurred within Islam and then spread to the Christian West from there. In the seventh and eighth centuries the ever victorious armies of Islam swept over the middle east and from there eastward through Persia and out on to the southern steppes of central Asia, as well as westward across North Africa and on up into Spain. At first there was little interest among the followers of Mohammed in the philosophical traditions of the lands they conquered, but in the ninth century, probably through contacts with Christians in Syria, Egypt and farther east, as well as centers of learning like Alexandria, a profound fascination with Greek philosophy, particularly Plato and Aristotle, took root and sparked a brilliant revival of both the Greek philosophical and scientific traditions. Although in the ninth and tenth centuries highly original atomistic and occasionalist doctrines flourished, a kind of Aristotelianism, heavily imbued with neo-Platonism, gradually came to dominate Islamic philosophic thought. The apogee of this movement is clearly Ibn Sina (Avicenna, 980-1037), whose masterful rendering of platonized Aristotelianism became a touchstone first for subsequent Islamic thinkers and then later for the Christian West once he came to its attention in the twelfth and thirteenth centuries.

But Greek thought posed much the same problems for the religion of Islam as it had for that of Christendom, and the orthodox reaction against it never permitted a reformulation of Islamic doctrine in pagan terms to the extent Christianity had. Further, Islamic philosophers did not feel the need constantly to defend and apologize for religious orthodoxy the way Augustine and Boethius had. Consequently they were free to adopt much more of the Aristotelian-Platonic world view than those earlier Christian thinkers. In fact, they often spoke quite condescendingly of the religious beliefs of the ordinary, uneducated Muslim and even of the picturesque language of the Koran. One very important and original thinker spoke out against these nominally Muslim philosophers and their philosophy, al-Ghazali (1058-1111). In a book called the *Incoherence* he attacked the supposed scientific status of Aristotelian philosophy and also pointed out its incompatibility with the commonly accepted beliefs of Islam. In the course of this polemic al-Ghazali threw skeptical doubts on the doctrine of natural causation as it was understood by the Aristotelians, thus cutting at the very heart of Aristotelian science.

The philosophical response to al-Ghazali was given its most complete form by Ibn Rushd (Averroes 1126-1198), who worked in Spain and North Africa at just the time learning was reviving in western Europe. In a book called *The Incoherence of the Incoherence* Ibn Rushd defended Aristotelianism against al-Ghazali's skepticism and also argued for the harmony of philosophy with true Islamic religion. But Ibn Rushd's Aristotle was quite different from Ibn Sina's. He had read, perhaps more carefully than any other person in history, the works of Aristotle and commented in detail on most of them. Out of that effort came an Aristotle largely purified of the platonizing that Ibn Sina had inherited. Ibn Rushd's work became widely relied on in thirteenth century Europe as the Christian scholastics struggled to understand what Aristotle had been saying. If Aristotle was "The Philosopher," Averroes was "The Commentator," so far as they were concerned.

The Christian West revived economically and culturally in the eleventh century, and the Church began a process of reforming itself at just the time that it split from the Eastern Orthodox Church centered on Byzantium and the remnants of the Greek eastern half of the old Roman Empire. Part of this reform involved educating the clergy, and for this purpose schools were formed in the vicinities of cathedrals and monasteries. The curriculum from the start included bits of what had once been taught in late ancient Roman schools, viz. grammar, logic, music, arithmetic, and rhetoric. Boethius' translations of Aristotle's logic and his commentaries on these were rediscovered and used extensively. In this way a modicum of ancient philosophy made its way into the educational process. In the late ancient world an introduction to Aristotle's *Categories* by the neo-Platonist (and anti-Christian) Porphyry, called the *Eisagoge*, had often been used to prepare the student for the full rigors and obscurities of the *Categories*. Boethius had translated and commented on this too, and these works also became school texts. It must be remembered that by the eleventh century hardly anyone in the Christian West knew Greek anymore, and even Latin had to be learned as a second language. Boethius' rendering of this ancient scholastic tradition into Latin was consequently of great service half a millennium after its author had died.

The Boethian texts were sufficient to give the early medieval scholastics a fairly good idea of one very central problem in ancient philosophy: the question of whether universals had any reality and if so, of what sort. It had been Plato, or perhaps his teacher Socrates, who had first emphasized the importance of the general characteristics of things for any scientific understanding of those things. Plato had promoted these characteristics into eternal immutable archetypes with their own existence independent of that of all the physical things the characteristics were originally thought to belong to. Aristotle directly opposed his teacher on this point, but, as any careful reader of Aristotle can verify, it was not at all clear from his writings what sort of status universals, i.e. these general characteristics, actually had. Boethius in his commentary on the *Eisagoge* attempted to resolve this problem by relying on a solution he says had been given by the earlier Aristotelian master, Alexander of Aphrodisias (c.200 C.E.). But Boethius' effort was itself not all that clear and resulted in the early scholastics developing a plethora of different lines on the subject. Perhaps the most subtle of these was that given by Peter Abelard (1079-1142) early in the twelfth century. His discussion, included in this anthology, leads into a profound investigation of the foundations of semantics and how language relates to reality.

It was just around the time when Abelard's work was coming to an end that the enormous body of learning that had been accumulating in the Islamic world began to enter the Christian West. This material eventually included virtually the whole corpus of still extant treatises by Aristotle as well as the commentaries on them by Averroes (Ibn Rushd) and much of the work of Avicenna (Ibn Sina). In this way Christian thinkers had for a second time to decide whether the Greek philosophical tradition, now accompanied by many Muslim additions (at this time western Christendom was in a state of more or less permanent conflict with Islam), was friend or foe, and for a second time the majority decided that it could be fairly safely relied on for assistance in clarifying and defending the faith. In the same way that in the eleventh century Anselm of Canterbury (1033-1109) had argued that the art of reasoning taught by ancient logical texts could usefully be deployed by the theologian, it was now gradually decided that most of Arabic-Aristotelian science and philosophy could be accepted without harm to the faith.

This admiration for Aristotle and Aristotelianism contrasted with the strong strain of neo-Platonic thought which had come down through the writings of the "Dionysius" mentioned above, i.e. someone in Syria around 500 C.E. who posed as the Dionysius whom *Acts* reports that St. Paul converted in Athens. This fictitious ascription came to be accepted from the sixth cerntury on and as a consequence these works, often very mystical in character, were given an authority they would not otherwise have enjoyed. They provided inspiration for a line of thought that is essentially outside the main stream of scholasticism and seeks a mystical union with God that lies well beyond the ambit of philosophy. (Some representative works from this tradition are found in Topic IX.)

The pinnacle of the acceptance of Aristotle by theologians is found in Thomas Aquinas (1225-1274). But even he knew that this could only go so far. One could not accept that the physical world had never had a beginning as did the Aristotelians. The possibility of personal immortality needed defending against the neo-Platonic tendencies of the Islamic thinkers. Christians had to reject the philosophical idea that this world is the only one God could possibly have created. But with exceptions like these Aquinas adopted and adapted the new learning for theological purposes and produced a very clear and synoptic demonstration of how this could be done in his *Summa Theologica*.

By the time Aquinas was working, the European university system had been created under the patronage of the Church. The earliest schools had developed in Italy and at Paris. Soon there was one at Oxford and many other cathedral cities of France. In the twelfth and thirteenth centuries, however, Paris was the pre-eminent center for theological and philosophical studies. Generally an administrative division was drawn between the faculty of theology and the faculty of arts, with the latter dealing exclusively with secular learning. All the prospective theologians had to pass through the arts curriculum before proceeding on to the study of theology, so they all increasingly were trained in the new science and philosophy entering from Islam. This had a huge impact on the way in which theology was carried out. More and more theological treatises became dominated by discussions of philosophical issues; Aristotle and Averroes were much more cited than the Bible or even St. Augustine. The new learning was in effect setting the theological agenda.

In addition, masters in the arts faculty who were not interested in proceeding onto theology became more and more enamoured of the Arabic-Aristotelian learning they were teaching. Soon some were taking Averroes's interpretation of Aristotle as completely authoritative and the science that it claimed to defend as the ultimate attainable by human reason operating without any divine revelation. In our anthology this movement, the "Averroists," is represented by Siger of Brabant (c.1235-1282), master of arts at Paris in the time of Aquinas. When this science conflicted with Christian doctrine, such thinkers were inclined simply to say that theology was none of their business and certainly they had no intention of denying any article of the faith. Their business was simply to render what the new learning, and hence unaided human reason, had to say.

At this point the ecclesiastical authorities, including the Pope, became alarmed. In 1270 and again in 1277 official condemnations were passed at Paris against numerous doctrines of the new science and philosophy in an attempt to curb its influence. (A selection of the theses condemned is given in these readings.) It is not clear how much of an effect these ecclesiastical interventions had, but certainly after 1277 we find theologians turning a much more critical eye on Arabic-Aristotelian philosophy and returning more to the Platonist views of St. Augustine. Aristotle and Averroes were still important authorities, but theologians were more ready to disagree with their views than before and to experiment with ideas which were definitely not Aristotelian in spirit. The result seems to have been the most original and sophisticated period in medieval scholasticism, a period which lasts at least up to the middle of the fourteenth century.

The condemnations of 1277 had another effect upon the course of dialectic and philosophical reasoning: while meaning to strengthen the understanding of God's omnipotence and filter out of philosophical thought neo-Platonist assumptions, the condemnations helped renew skeptical procedure; in effect a Trojan Horse was introduced into philosophical practice. How that potentiality for skepticism came about should be briefly explained.

There had been two ancient patterns of reasoning: according to the first of the two, if two things, A and B, are distinct, then they are separate. We call the pattern of reasoning from distinctness to separation the principle of separation. For example, if two atoms are distinct, they are separate - indeed separated by a void which surrounds each one. The principle of separation supports an atomistic outlook: the entities which make up reality are somewhat like letters of the alphabet: each one distinct and separate from any other one.

According to the second pattern, if two things, A and B, are distinct, they are separable; this pattern we call the principle of separability. The principle has skeptical import: for example, if any two distinct events are separable (at least by God's infinite power), then there is no necessary tie between them. But if there is no necessity, there is no certain or necessary knowledge of a connection between them.

Both the principle of separability and the principle of separation were denied by Plato and Aristotle. Plato suggests in his dialogue *Sophist* that the principle of separation would be the end of philosophy; for philosophy represents reality as if it were weaving a finely woven blanket whose threads, though remaining distinct, can be combined and associated together.

In the Islamic philosophical world reasoning in accordance with the principle of separability can be found in the work of al-Ghazali; he seems to be moved by the same spirit which moved Bishop Tempier, who oversaw the condemnations in Paris: saving and protecting an account of God's omnipotence against the philosophical strictures of the philosophers. In elevating God's omnipotence al-Ghazali places God at the center of the causal order but without the need of intermediary and second causes. It is as though God were the projector of a moving picture: elements of the picture do not produce or cause one another; they are separable (perhaps even, like the images of still slides, separate). They are rather caused by a single cause. Scholars call such a view Occasionalist.

After the condemnations of 1277 in Paris reasoning in accordance with the principle of separability can be found in the work of William of Ockham and Nicholas of Autrecourt. (Please see Section VII for relevant work included in this anthology.)

At this time the tensions between the philosophical and scientific tradition on the one hand and theology on the other were faced head on. A thinker like John Duns Scotus (1265-1308) revised the Aristotelian philosophy in order to accommodate better the doctrines of theology. A generation later his confrere in the Franciscan order, William of Ockham (1280-1349), viewed the conflict on a number of issues as irresolvable and resisted what he saw as innovations in philosophy. All this was accompanied by an increasing level of sophistication in logical analysis, which brought philosophy to a level of precision never before achieved in the West. The problem of universals was revisited in the light of the new texts of

Aristotle, Avicenna, and Averroes, but again nothing was definitively resolved. The logical and ontological basis of Aristotelian science thus remained in doubt.

In this milieu it is not surprising that skepticism had something of a revival. Augustineans like Henry of Ghent (d.1293) used Augustine's own skepticism about the possibility of human knowledge without divine assistance to undermine Aristotle's optimistically realist epistemology. The ultimate in this trend is reached with Nicholas of Autrecourt (fl.1340) who was ready to dispense with virtually the whole of Aristotelian science in favor of atomism and a world in which nothing ever passes out of existence. Not that he thought any such doctrines could be definitively proved; rather he claimed that in physical science and metaphysics only "probable" arguments are possible and in this case the most "probable" arguments show that Aristotle was wrong. Medieval scholastics were not yet ready to scuttle the whole Aristotelian enterprise; Nicholas's works were publicly burned.

Theology obviously played a very important role, then, in undermining the status of Arabic-Aristotelian science and philosophy in scholastic circles. To some extent this led to modifications and, some would say, improvements to that body of learning. Attempts to deal with the paradoxes of theology had an enlivening effect that prevented philosophers from taking too much of the philosophical tradition for granted, much in the way philosophical attempts in our own time to deal with the paradoxes of quantum physics have led to the questioning of both logical and metaphysical truisms. Having to accept the truth of the Trinity, or of divine foreknowledge of future contingents, or of the beginning of the world, forced the late scholastics to take a fresh look at the basic assumptions of the Aristotelian version of Greek philosophy in a way that had not ever been done before in the Christian West. There was no dramatic overthrow of the Arabic-Aristotelian doctrine, however. It was to form the basis of the arts curriculum well into the fifteenth century and beyond in many places. But the question of its usefulness to the Christian faith, or even compatibility with it, had been openly raised and would become even more of an issue as the medieval period drew to a close.

TOPIC I:

NECESSITY, CONTINGENCY, AND CAUSATION

TOPIC I

NECESSITY, CONTINGENCY, AND CAUSATION

IN THIS SECTION OF THE ANTHOLOGY THE READER WILL FIND ancient and medieval materials dealing with the topic of causation and necessity. The selections show thinkers at work clarifying the concepts of causation and necessity and also drawing out the implications of those concepts for related topics.

Medieval thinkers accepted the view of ancient philosophers that our understanding of the world can be and properly is articulated and systematized in terms of causation and necessity. There is no event without a cause. Further, a cause is not simply another event which precedes or is simultaneous with its effect. Every event has a cause which produces the event; the effect arises from its cause with necessity.

Medieval thinkers also tended to accept the Aristotelian view that there are four kinds of causes: material, efficient, formal, and final. Selection I.1.1. gives Aristotle's list and his brief explanations of these four kinds of causes. For example, if a full causal explanation is to be given of a table, we would mention wood as the material cause; the carpenter as the efficient cause; its use as the final cause; and its structure as the formal cause.

Medieval thinkers also accepted Aristotle's view that there are different senses in which things are said to be necessary. Selection I.1.2. gives Aristotle's summary of the various senses in which something can be said to be necessary. One of these, called relative necessity, is crucial to scientific understanding; for many effects are said to be necessary relative to their causes. Another sense in which something is necessary is that of hypothetical necessity, as when it is said that food is necessary for an animal to live.

It was commonly held that causes and effects are necessary in both senses: an effect is necessary relative to its cause, and a cause is hypothetically necessary for its effect. The use of the two notions of relational necessity articulate strict determinism: given a cause, one and only one effect can arise from it; given an effect, one and only one agent can be its cause.

Strict determinism has consequences which puzzle and disturb thinkers at two points: first regarding God and the world and then regarding human beings and their actions. In the first case the question arises whether God or the First Cause

3

(in the language of Avicenna) could have produced a different first effect. It would of course be granted that God is necessary for the world. Is the world also necessary relative to God as Creator and First Cause? As the following readings show, the question is answered differently: Avicenna answers the question in the affirmative; John Duns Scotus, in the negative.

If the world is necessitated by its First Cause, how do contingency and freedom arise? This question is taken up both in the readings of Topic I and of Topic IV. On the other hand, if the world begins as the realization of just one possibility (it being possible for God to create an infinite number of other worlds), how is God's potentiality for alternatives to be understood?

We remarked above that strict determinism has consequences which puzzle thinkers at two points. The second point concerns human beings and their actions. If any action of ours is necessary relative to a series of causes and effects - a series which begins at the beginning, - in what sense, if in any, can one be said to be a responsible agent? This question is taken up in selections of Topic IV. The point of mentioning it now is to notice the causal and modal language required for the question and, obviously, for its answers.

Strict determinism has been taken by many thinkers to be an extreme position; its opposing extreme would be the view that anything can bring about anything. An event would be purely contingent relative to a cause, provided that cause could equally give rise to many other events. If the world had a basis of pure potentiality, whatever is actual would be accidental. In that case there would be no science. For all science posits causation, and causation, as the ancient and medieval worlds saw things, requires necessity.

If there are to be both science and freedom, there must be a middle between the two extreme positions sketched above. The question which comes to occupy John Duns Scotus is this: given that there are contingency and freedom in human life, when and how do they arise? Cast an eye over the causal line from First Cause to human action: can contingency arise in the middle range (in the sublunary world, for example) without having arisen with the first act of the First Cause? Scotus gives a firm answer to the question: if there is contingency in the world at all, there was freedom at the beginning, and God could have created a different first effect. Although Scotus's answer becomes a commonplace after Leibniz, its initial exposition and defence required great logical power and originality.

I.1. ARISTOTLE

A GREAT DEAL OF MEDIEVAL PHILOSOPHY IS BASED UPON interpretations of the Aristotelian texts available at a given time. Arabic thinkers had a full Aristotelian corpus to refer to; early Latin thinkers before 1130 were restricted to parts of the organon. The following selections from Aristotle provided medieval thinkers with a basis for organizing and clarifying their notions of causation and necessity: selection **I.1.1.** defines the four causes; selection **I.1.2.** defines the various senses of the necessary, and selections **I.1.3.** and **I.1.4.** consider causation, first principles, and chance and spontaneity.

I.1.1. The four Causes (*Metaphysics* V.2)

We call a cause (1) that from which (as immanent material) a thing comes into being, e.g. the bronze of the statue and the silver of the saucer, and the classes which include these. (2) The form or pattern, i.e. the formula of the essence, and the classes which include this (e.g. the ratio 2:1 and number in general are causes of the octave) and the parts of the formula. (3) That from which the change or the freedom from change first begins, e.g. the man who has deliberated is a cause, and the father a cause of the child, and in general the maker a cause of the thing made and the change-producing of the changing. (4) The end, i.e. that for the sake of which a thing is, e.g. health is the cause of walking. For why does one walk? We say, "In order that one may be healthy." And in speaking thus we think we have given the cause. The same is true of all the means that intervene before the end, when something else has put the process in motion (as e.g. thinning or purging or drugs or instruments intervene before health is reached); for all these are for the sake of the end, though they differ from one another in that some are instruments and others are actions.

These, then, are practically all the senses in which causes are spoken of, and as they are spoken of in several senses it follows that there are several causes of the same thing, and in no accidental sense, e.g. both the art of sculpture and the bronze are causes of the statue not in virtue of anything else but *qua* statue; not, however, in the same way, but the one as matter and the other as source of the movement. And things can be causes of one another, e.g. exercise of good condition, and the latter of exercise; not, however, in the same way, but the one as end and the other as source of movement. – Again, the same thing is sometimes cause of contraries; for that which when present causes a particular thing, we sometimes charge, when absent, with the contrary, e.g. we impute the ship wreck to the absence of the steersman, whose presence was the cause of safety; and both – the presence and the privation – are causes as sources of movement.

I.1.2. Senses of the Necessary (*Metaphysics* V.5)

We call necessary (1) (a) that without which, as a condition, a thing cannot live; e.g. breathing and food are necessary for an animal; for it is incapable of existing without these; (b) the conditions without which good cannot be or come to be, or without which we cannot get rid or be freed of evil; e.g. drinking the medicine is necessary in order that we may be cured of disease, and a man's sailing to Aegina is necessary in order that he may get his money. (2) The compulsory and compulsion, i.e., that which impedes and tends to hinder, contrary to impulse and purpose. For the compulsory is called necessary (whence the necessary is painful, as Evenus says: "For every necessary thing is ever irksome"), and compulsion is a form of necessity, as Sophocles says: "But force necessitates me to this act." And necessity is held to be something that cannot be persuaded – and rightly, for it is contrary to the movement which accords with purpose and with reasoning. (3) We say that that which cannot be otherwise is necessarily as it is. And from this sense of 'necessary' all the others are somehow derived; for a thing is said to do or suffer what is necessary in the sense of compulsion only when it cannot act according to its impulse because of the compelling force – which implies that necessity is that because of which a thing cannot be otherwise; and similarly as regards the conditions of life and of good; for when in the one case good, in the other life and being, are not possible without certain conditions, these are necessary, and this kind of cause is a sort of necessity. Again, demonstration is a necessary thing because the conclusion cannot be otherwise, if there has been demonstration in the unqualified sense; and the causes of this necessity are the first premises, i.e. the fact that the propositions from which the syllogism proceeds cannot be otherwise.

Now some things owe their necessity to something other than themselves; others do not, but are themselves the source of necessity in other things. Therefore, the necessary in the primary and strict sense is the simple; for this does not admit of more states than one, so that it cannot even be in one state and also in another; for if it did, it would already be in more than one. If, then, there are any things that are eternal and unmovable, nothing compulsory or against their nature attaches to them.

I.1.3. Causation, Chance, and Spontaneity
(*Physics* II. 3-6)

Chapter 3

Now that we have established these distinctions, we must proceed to consider causes, their character and number. Knowledge is the object of our inquiry, and men do not think they know a thing till they have grasped the "why" of it (which is to grasp its primary cause). So clearly we too must do this as regards both coming to be and passing away and every kind of natural change, in order that, knowing their principles, we may try to refer to these principles each of our problems. In one way, then, that out of which a thing comes to be and which persists, is called a cause, e.g. the bronze of the statue, the silver of the bowl, and the genera of which the bronze and the silver are species.

In another way, the form or the archetype, i.e. the definition of the essence, and its genera, are called causes (e.g. of the octave the relation of 2:1, and generally number), and the parts in the definition.

Again, the primary source of the change or rest; e.g. the man who deliberated is a cause, the father is cause of the child, and generally what makes of what is made and what brings about change of what is changed.

Again, in the sense of end or that for the sake of which a thing is done, e.g. health is the cause of walking about. ("Why is he walking about?" We say: "To be healthy," and, having said that, we think we have assigned the cause.) The same is true also of all the intermediate steps which are brought about through the action of something else as means towards the end, e.g. reduction of flesh, purging, drugs, or surgical instruments are means towards health. All these things are for the sake of the end, though they differ from one another in that some are activities, others instruments.

This then perhaps exhausts the number of ways in which the term 'cause' is used.

As things are called causes in many ways, it follows that there are several causes of the same thing (not merely accidentally), e.g. both the art of the sculptor and the bronze are causes of the statue. These are causes of the statue *qua* statue, not in virtue of anything else that it may be only not in the same way, the one being the material cause, the other the cause whence the motion comes. Some things cause each other reciprocally, e.g. hard work causes fitness and vice versa, but again not in the same way, but the one as end, the other as the principle of motion. Further the same thing is the cause of contrary results. For that which by its presence brings about one result is sometimes blamed for bringing about the contrary by its absence. Thus we ascribe the wreck of a ship to the absence of the pilot whose presence was the cause of its safety.

All the causes now mentioned fall into four familiar divisions. The letters are the causes of syllables, the material of artificial products, fire and the like of bodies, the parts of the whole, and the premisses of the conclusion, in the sense of "that from which." Of these pairs the one set are causes in the sense of what underlies, e.g. the parts, the other set in the sense of essence – the whole and the combination and the form. But the seed and the doctor and the deliberator, and generally the maker, are all sources whence the change or stationariness originates, which the others are causes in the sense of the end or the good of the rest; for that for the sake of which tends to be what is best and the end of the things that lead up to it. (Whether we call it good or apparently good makes no difference.)

Such then is the number and nature of the kinds of cause.

Now the modes of causation are many, though when brought under heads they too can be reduced in number. For things are called causes in many ways and even within the same kind one may be prior to another: e.g. the doctor and the expert are causes of health, the relation 2:1 and number of the octave, and always what is inclusive to what is particular. Another mode of causation is the accidental and its genera, e.g. in one way Polyclitus, in another a sculptor is the cause of a statue, because being Polyclitus and a sculptor are accidentally conjoined. Also the classes in which the accidental attribute is included; thus a man could be said to be the cause of a statue or, generally, a living creature. An accidental attribute too may be more or less remote, e.g. suppose that a pale man or a musical man were said to be the cause of the statue.

All causes, both proper and accidental, may be spoken of either as potential or as actual; e.g. the cause of a house being built is either a house-builder or a house-builder building.

Similar distinctions can be made in the things of which the causes are causes, e.g. of this statue or of a statue or of an image generally, of this bronze or of bronze or of material generally. So too with the accidental attributes. Again we may use a complex expression for either and say, e.g., neither 'Polyclitus' nor a 'sculptor' but 'Polyclitus, the sculptor.'

All these various uses, however, come to six in number, under each of which again the usage is twofold. It is either what is particular or a genus,[1] or an accidental attribute or a genus of that, and these either as a complex or each by itself; and all either as actual or as potential. The difference is this much, that causes which are actually at work and particular exist and cease to exist simultaneously with their effect, e.g. this healing person with this being-healed person and that housebuilding man with that being-built house; but this is not always true of potential causes – the house and the housebuilder do not pass away simultaneously.

In investigating the cause of each thing it is always necessary to seek what is most precise (as also in other things): thus a man builds because he is a builder, and a builder builds in virtue of his art of building. This last cause then is prior; and so generally.

Further, generic effects should be assigned to generic causes, particular effects to particular causes, e.g. statue to sculptor, this statue to this sculptor; and powers are relative to possible effects, actually operating causes to things which are actually being effected.

This must suffice for our account of the number of causes and the modes of causation.

Chapter 4

But chance and spontaneity are also reckoned among causes: many things are said both to be and to come to be as a result of chance and spontaneity. We must inquire therefore in what manner chance and spontaneity are present among the causes enumerated, and whether they are the same or different, and generally what chance and spontaneity are.

Some people even question whether there are such things or not. They say that nothing happens by chance, but that everything which we ascribe to chance or spontaneity has some definite cause, e.g. coming by chance into the market and finding there a man whom one wanted but did not expect to meet is due to one's wish to go and buy in the market. Similarly, in other so-called cases of chance it is always possible, they maintain, to find something which is the cause; but not chance, for if chance were real, it would seem strange indeed, and the question might be raised, why on earth none of the wise men of old in speaking of the causes of generation and decay took account of chance; whence it would seem that they too did not believe that anything is by chance. But there is a further circumstance that is surprising. Many things both come to be and are by chance and spontaneity, and although all know that each of them can be ascribed to some cause (as the old argument said which denied chance), nevertheless they all speak of some of these things as happening by chance and

1. See glossary entry for 'species/genus.'

others not. For this reason they ought to have at least referred to the matter in some way or other.

Certainly the early physicists found no place for chance among the causes which they recognized – love, strife, mind, fire, or the like. This is strange, whether they supposed that there is no such thing as chance or whether they thought there is but omitted to mention it – and that too when they sometimes used it, as Empedocles[2] does when he says that the air is not always separated into the highest region, but as it may chance. At any rate he says in his *Cosmogony* that "it happened to run that way at that time, but it often ran otherwise." He tells us also that most of the parts of animals came to be by chance.

There are some who actually ascribe this heavenly sphere and all the worlds to spontaneity. They say that the vortex arose spontaneously, i.e. the motion that separated and arranged the universe in its present order. This statement might well cause surprise. For they are asserting that chance is not responsible for the existence or generation of animals and plants, nature or mind or something of the kind being the cause of them (for it is not any chance thing that comes from a given seed but an olive from one kind and a man from another); and yet at the same time they assert that the heavenly sphere and the divinest of visible things arose spontaneously, having no such cause as is assigned to animals and plants. Yet if this is so, it is a fact which deserves to be dwelt upon, and something might well have been said about it. For besides the other absurdities of the statement, it is the more absurd that people should make it when they see nothing coming to be spontaneously in the heavens, but much happening by chance among the things which as they say are not due to chance; whereas we should have expected exactly the opposite.

Others there are who believe that chance is a cause, but that it is inscrutable to human intelligence, as being a divine thing and full of mystery.

Thus we must inquire what chance and spontaneity are, whether they are the same or different, and how they fit into our division of causes.

Chapter 5

First then we observe that some things always come to pass in the same way, and others for the most part. It is clearly of neither of these that chance, or the result of chance, is said to be the cause – neither of that which is by necessity and always, nor of that which is for the most part. But as there is a third class of events besides these two events which all say are by chance – it is plain that there is such a thing as chance and spontaneity; for we know that things of this kind are due to chance and that things due to chance are of this kind.

Of things that come to be, some come to be for the sake of something, others not. Again, some of the former class are in accordance with intention, others not, but both are in the class of things which are for the sake of something. Hence it is clear that even among the things which are outside what is necessary and what is for the most part, there are some in connexion with which the phrase "for the sake of something" is applicable. (Things that are for the sake of something include whatever may be done as a result of thought or of nature.) Things of this kind, then, when they come to pass accidentally are said to be by chance. For just as a thing is something either in virtue of itself or accidentally, so may it be a cause. For instance, the housebuilding faculty is in virtue of itself a cause of a house, whereas the pale or the musical is an accidental cause. That which is *per se* cause is determinate, but the accidental cause is indeterminable; for the possible attributes of an individual are innumerable. As we said, then, when a thing of this kind comes to pass among events which are for the sake of something, it is said to be spontaneous or by chance. (The distinction between the two must be made later – for the present it is sufficient if it is plain that both are in the sphere of things done for the sake of something.)

Example: A man is engaged in collecting subscriptions for a feast. He would have gone to such and such a place for the purpose of getting the money, if he had known. He actually went there for another purpose, and it was only accidentally that

---

2. Philosopher in Greek Italy in the 5th century B.C.E. He had a theory that the species of animals now in existence are a selection from a much larger number of species that once existed and corresponded to all possible chance combinations of animal parts.

he got his money by going there; and this was not due to the fact that he went there as a rule or necessarily, nor is the end effected (getting the money) a cause present in himself – it belongs to the class of things that are objects of choice and the result of thought. It is when these conditions are satisfied that the man is said to have gone by chance. If he had chosen and gone for the sake of this – if he always or normally went there when he was collecting payments – he would not be said to have gone by chance. It is clear then that chance is an accidental cause in the sphere of those actions for the sake of something which involve choice. Thought, then, and chance are in the same sphere, for choice implies thought.

It is necessary, no doubt, that the causes of what comes to pass by chance be indefinite; and that is why chance is supposed to belong to the class of the indefinite and to be inscrutable to man, and why it might be thought that, in a way, nothing occurs by chance. For all these statements are correct, as might be expected. Things do, in a way, occur by chance, for they occur accidentally and chance is an accidental cause. But it is not the cause without qualification of anything; for instance, a housebuilder is the cause of a house; accidentally, a fluteplayer may be so.

And the causes of the man's coming and getting the money (when he did not come for the sake of that) are innumerable. He may have wished to see somebody or been following somebody or avoiding somebody, or may have gone to see a spectacle. Thus to say that chance is unaccountable is correct. For an account is of what holds always or for the most part, whereas chance belongs to a third type of event. Hence, since causes of this kind are indefinite, chance too is indefinite. (Yet in some cases one might raise the question whether any chance fact might be the cause of the chance occurrence, e.g. of health the fresh air or the sun's heat may be the cause, but having had one's hair cut cannot, for some accidental causes are more relevant to the effect than others.)

Chance is called good when the result is good, evil when it is evil. The terms 'good fortune' and 'ill fortune' are used when either result is of considerable magnitude. Thus one who comes within an ace of some great evil or great good is said to be fortunate or unfortunate. The mind affirms the presence of the attribute, ignoring the hair's breadth of dif-

ference. Further, it is with reason that good fortune is regarded as unstable; for chance is unstable, as none of the things which result from it can hold always or for the most part.

Both are then, as I have said, accidental causes – both chance and spontaneity – in the sphere of things which are capable of coming to pass not simply, nor for the most part and with reference to such of these as might come to pass for the sake of something.

Chapter 6

They differ in that spontaneity is the wider. Every result of chance is from what is spontaneous, but not everything that is from what is spontaneous is from chance.

Chance and what results from chance are appropriate to agents that are capable of good fortune and of action generally. Therefore necessarily chance is in the sphere of actions. This is indicated by the fact that good fortune is thought to be the same, or nearly the same, as happiness, and happiness to be a kind of action, since it is well-doing. Hence what is not capable of action cannot do anything by chance. Thus an inanimate thing or a beast or a child cannot do anything by chance, because it is incapable of choice; nor can good fortune or ill fortune be ascribed to them, except metaphorically, as Protarchus, for example, said that the stones of which altars are made are fortunate because they are held in honour, while their fellows are trodden under foot. Even these things, however, can in a way be affected by chance, when one who is dealing with them does something to them by chance, but not otherwise.

The spontaneous on the other hand is found both in the beasts and in many inanimate objects. We say, for example, that the horse came spontaneously, because, though his coming saved him, he did not come for the sake of safety. Again, the tripod fell spontaneously, because, though it stood on its feet so as to serve for a seat, it did not fall so as to serve for a seat.

Hence it is clear that events which belong to the general class of things that may come to pass for the sake of something, when they come to pass not for the sake of what actually results, and have an external cause, may be described by the phrase 'from spontaneity.' These spontaneous events are said to be from chance if they have the further characteristics of being the objects of choice and happening to agents capable of choice. This is indicated by the phrase 'in vain,' which is used when one thing which is for the sake of another, does not result in it. For instance, taking a walk is for the sake of evacuation of the bowels; if this does not follow after walking, we say that we have walked in vain and that the walking was vain. This implies that what is naturally for the sake of an end is in vain, when it does not effect the end for the sake of which it was the natural means – for it would be absurd for a man to say that he had bathed in vain because the sun was not eclipsed, since the one was not done for the sake of the other. Thus the spontaneous is even according to its derivation the case in which the thing itself happens in vain. The stone that struck the man did not fall for the sake of striking him; therefore it fell spontaneously, because it might have fallen by the action of an agent and for the sake of striking. The difference between spontaneity and what results by chance is greatest in things that come to be by nature; for when anything comes to be contrary to nature, we do not say that it came to be by chance, but by spontaneity. Yet strictly this too is different from the spontaneous proper; for the cause of the latter is external, that of the former internal.

We have now explained what chance is and what spontaneity is, and in what they differ from each other. Both belong to the mode of causation "source of change," for either some natural or some intelligent agent is always the cause; but in this sort of causation the number of possible causes is infinite.

Spontaneity and chance are causes of effects which, though they might result from intelligence or nature, have in fact been caused by something accidentally. Now since nothing which is accidental is prior to what is *per se*, it is clear that no accidental cause can be prior to a cause *per se*. Spontaneity and chance, therefore, are posterior to intelligence and nature. Hence, however true it may be that the heavens are due to spontaneity, it will still be true that intelligence and nature will be prior causes of this universe and of many things in it besides.

I.1.4. Science and the Accidental (*Metaphysics* VI)

Chapter 1

We are seeking the principles and the causes of the things that are, and obviously of things *qua* being. For there is a cause of health and of good condition, and the objects of mathematics have principles and elements and causes, and in general every science which is ratiocinative or at all involves reasoning deals with causes and principles, exact or indeterminate; but all these sciences mark off some particular being – some genus, and inquire into this, but not into being simply nor *qua* being, nor do they offer any discussion of the essence of the things of which they treat; but starting from the essence – some making it plain to the senses, others assuming it as a hypothesis they then demonstrate, more or less cogently, the essential attributes of the genus with which they deal. It is obvious, therefore, from such a review of the sciences, that there is no demonstration of substance or of the essence, but some other way of revealing it. And similarly the sciences omit the question whether the genus with which they deal exists or does not exist, because it belongs to the same line of thought to show what it is and that it is.

And since natural science, like other sciences, confines itself to one class of beings, i.e. to that sort of substance which has the principle of its movement and rest present in itself, evidently it is neither practical nor productive. For the principle of production is in the producer – it is either reason or art or some capacity, while the principle of action is in the doer – viz. choice, for that which is done and that which is chosen are the same. Therefore, if all thought is either practical or productive or theoretical, natural science must be theoretical, but it will theorize about such being as admits of being moved, and only about that kind of substance which in respect of its formula is for the most part not separable from matter. Now, we must not fail to notice the nature of the essence and of its formula, for, without this, inquiry is but idle. Of things defined, i.e. of essences, some are like snub, and some like concave.

And these differ because snub is bound up with matter (for what is snub is a concave nose), while concavity is independent of perceptible matter. If then all natural things are analogous to the snub in their nature e.g. nose, eye, face, flesh, bone, and, in general, animal; leaf, root, bark, and, in general, plant (for none of these can be defined without reference to movement – they always have matter), it is clear how we must seek and define the essence in the case of natural objects, and also why it belongs to the student of nature to study soul to some extent, i.e. so much of it as is not independent of matter. – That natural science, then, is theoretical, is plain from these considerations. Mathematics also is theoretical; but whether its objects are immovable and separable from matter, is not at present clear; it is clear, however, that it considers some mathematical objects *qua* immovable and *qua* separable from matter. But if there is something which is eternal and immovable and separable, clearly the knowledge of it belongs to a theoretical science, – not, however, to natural science (for natural science deals with certain movable things) nor to mathematics, but to a science prior to both. For natural science deals with things which are inseparable from matter but not immovable, and some parts of mathematics deal with things which are immovable, but probably not separable, but embodied in matter; while the first science deals with things which are both separable and immovable. Now all causes must be eternal, but especially these; for they are the causes of so much of the divine as appears to us. There must, then, be three theoretical philosophies, mathematics, natural science, and theology, since it is obvious that if the divine is present anywhere, it is present in things of this sort. And the highest science must deal with the highest genus, so that the theoretical sciences are superior to the other sciences, and this to the other theoretical sciences. One might indeed raise the question whether first philosophy is universal, or deals with one genus, i.e. some one kind of being; for not even the mathematical sciences are all alike in this respect, – geometry and astronomy deal with a certain particular kind of thing, while universal mathematics applies alike to all. We answer that if there is no substance other than those which are formed by nature, natural science will be the first science; but if there is an immovable substance, the science of this must be prior and must be first philosophy, and universal in this way, because it is first. And it will belong to this to consider being *qua* being – both what it is and the attributes which belong to it *qua* being.

Chapter 2

But since the unqualified term 'being' has several meanings, of which one was seen to be the accidental, and another the true (non-being being the false), while besides these there are the figures of predication, e.g. the "what," quality, quantity, place, time, and any similar meanings which 'being' may have; and again besides all these there is that which is potentially or actually: – since 'being' has many meanings, we must first say regarding the accidental, that there can be no scientific treatment of it. This is confirmed by the fact that no science – practical, productive, or theoretical – troubles itself about it. For on the one hand he who produces a house does not produce all the attributes that come into being along with the house; for these are innumerable; the house that is made may be pleasant for some people, hurtful to some, and useful to others, and different – to put it shortly – from all things that are; and the science of building does not aim at producing any of these attributes. And in the same way the geometer does not consider the attributes which attach thus to figures, nor whether a triangle is different from a triangle whose angles are equal to two right angles. – And this happens naturally enough; for the accidental is practically a mere name. And therefore Plato was in a sense not wrong in saying that sophistic deals with that which is not. For the arguments of the sophists deal, we may say, above all with the accidental; e.g. the question whether musical and lettered are different or the same, and whether musical Coriscus and Coriscus are the same, and whether everything which is, but is not eternal, has come to be, with the paradoxical conclusion that if one who was musical has come to be lettered, he must also have been lettered and have come to be musical, – and all the other arguments of this sort; the accidental is obviously akin to non-being. And this is clear also from arguments such as the following; of things which are in another sense there is generation and decay, but of things which are accidentally there is not. But still we must, as far as we can, say, regarding the accidental, what is its nature and from what cause it proceeds; for it will perhaps at the same time become clear why there is no science of it. Since, among things which are, some are always in the same state and are of necessity (nor necessity in the sense of compulsion but that which means the impossibility of being otherwise), and some are not of necessity nor always, but for the most part, this is the principle and this the cause of the existence of the accidental; for that which is neither always nor for the most part, we call accidental. For instance, if in the dog-days there is wintry and cold weather, we say this is an accident, but not if there is sultry heat, because the latter is always or for the most part so, but not the former. And it is an accident that a man is white (for this is neither always nor for the most part so), but it is not by accident that he is an animal. And that the builder produces health is an accident, because it is the nature not of the builder but of the doctor to do this, – but the builder happened to be a doctor. Again, a confectioner, aiming at giving pleasure, may make something wholesome, but not in virtue of the confectioner's art; and therefore we say it was an accident, and while there is a sense in which he makes it, in the full sense he does not make it. – For some accidental results sometimes tend to be produced by alien capacities, but to others there corresponds no determinate art nor capacity; for of things which are or come to be by accident, the cause also is accidental. Therefore, since not all things are or come to be of necessity and always, but the majority of things are for the most part, the accidental must exist; for instance a white man is not always nor for the most part musical, but since this sometimes happens, it must be accidental. If not, everything will be of necessity. The matter, therefore, which is capable of being otherwise than as it for the most part is, is the cause of the accidental. And we must take as our starting-point the question whether everything is either always or for the most part. Surely this is impossible. There is, then, besides these something which is fortuitous and accidental. But while what is for the most part exists, can nothing be said to be always, or are there eternal things? This must be considered later, but that there is no science of the accidental is obvious; for all science is either of that which is

always or of that which is for the most part. For how else is one to learn or to teach another? The thing must be determined as occurring either always or for the most part, e.g. that honey-water is useful for a patient in a fever is true for the most part. But one will not be able to state when that which is contrary to this happens, e.g. "on the day of new moon"; for then it will be so on the day of new moon either always or for the most part; but the accidental is contrary to this. We have stated, then, what the accidental is and from what cause it arises, and that there is no science which deals with it.

Chapter 3

That there are principles and causes which are generable and destructible without ever being in course of being generated or destroyed, is obvious. For otherwise all things will be of necessity, since that which is being generated or destroyed must have a cause which is not accidentally its cause. Will this be or not? – Yes if this happens; and if not, not. And this will happen if something else does. And thus if time is constantly subtracted from a limited extent of time, one will obviously come to the present. This man, then, will die by violence, if he goes out; and he will do this if he is thirsty; and he will be thirsty if something else happens; and thus we shall come to that which is now present, or to some past event. For instance, he will go out if he is thirsty; and he will be thirsty if he is eating something pungent; and this is either the case or not; so that he will of necessity die, or not die. And similarly if one jumps over to the past, the same account will hold good; for this – I mean the past condition – is already present in something. Everything, therefore, that is to be, will be of necessity, e.g. it is necessary that he who lives shall one day die; for already something has happened – e.g. the presence of contraries in the same body. But whether he dies by disease or by violence, is not yet determined, but depends on the happening of something else. Clearly then the process goes back to a certain starting-point, but this no longer points to something further. This then will be the starting-point for the fortuitous, and will have nothing else as cause of its coming to be. But to what sort of starting-point and what sort of cause we thus refer the fortuitous – whether to matter or to that for the sake of which or to the motive power, must be carefully considered.

Chapter 4

Let us dismiss the accidental; for we have sufficiently determined its nature. But since that which is in the sense of being true, or is not in the sense of being false, depends on combination and separation, and truth and falsehood together are concerned with the apportionment of a contradiction (for truth has the affirmation in the case of what is compounded and the negation in the case of what is divided, while falsity has the contradictory of this apportionment – it is another question, how it happens that we think things together or apart; by 'together' and 'apart' I mean thinking them so that there is no succession in the thoughts but they become a unity; for falsity and truth are not in things – it is not as if the good were true, and the bad were in itself false – but in thought; while with regard to simple things and essences falsity and truth do not exist even in thought): – we must consider later what has to be discussed with regard to that which is or is not in this sense; but since the combination and the separation are in thought and not in the things, and that which is in this sense is a different sort of being from the things that are in the full sense (for the thought attaches or removes either the "what" or quality or quantity or one of the other categories), that which is accidentally and that which is in the sense of being true must be dismissed. For the cause of the former is indeterminate, and that of the latter is some affection of the thought, and both are related to the remaining genera of being, and do not indicate any separate class of being. Therefore let these be dismissed, and let us consider the causes and the principles of being itself, *qua* being. (It was clear in our discussion of the various meanings of terms, that 'being' has several meanings.)

I.2. AVICENNA

AVICENNA (IBN SINA) WAS A GIFTED THINKER WHO BROUGHT LOGICAL and metaphysical acuity to the questions and problems which he addressed. The following four selections concern Avicenna's analysis of necessary and possible existence and his proof of a First Cause; the four selections are from "Ibn Sina on Necessary and Possible Existence."

It was Avicenna's view that whatever can be requires a cause to become actual; causal efficacy, in turn, requires necessity. The question arises for the student of Avicenna whether he is a strict determinist regarding the first levels of the being of the universe. He was certainly taken to hold this determinist position: nothing other than the first effect could have arisen from the First Cause nor could anything other than the First Cause have given rise to the first effect.

I.2.1. Two Kinds of Existents (*'Uyun al-masa'il*)

We say: Existents are of two kinds. In one of them, when the thing itself is considered, its existence is not necessary this is called "possible of existence." In the second, when the thing itself is considered, its existence is necessary; this is called "necessary of existence." If we suppose something possible of existence to be non-existent, no impossibility follows from that, so it cannot do without a cause for its existence. And if it does exist, it becomes necessary of existence by another thing; consequently it is something that is always possible of existence by itself and necessary of existence by another thing. This possibility is something that belongs either to what is everlasting or to what exists for a time but not all time.

Now it is inadmissible that possible things can continue in an infinite chain of causes and effects, or be in a circular relation; they must terminate in something necessary, which is the first existent. So when the necessary of existence by itself is supposed non-existent, an impossibility results. There is no cause for its existence, and it is inadmissible that its existence would be by another. It is the first cause for the existence of things, and consequently its existence is the most prior existence. It is free from all kinds of defect; its existence is therefore

complete. Consequently its existence is the most complete existence, free from causes such as matter, form, act and end, and it has no quiddity other than that it is necessary of existence; this is its individual nature. Consequently it has no genus[1] or differentia[2] or definition, and there is no demonstration of it, but it is the demonstration[3] of all things. Its existence by itself is without end or beginning, no privation is mixed with it, and its existence is not potential. Consequently it is not possible that it would not exist, it has no need of anything to provide its permanence, and it does not change from one state to another. It is one, in the sense that the reality that it has does not belong to any other thing.

I.2.2. Proof of the Necessary of Existence (from *al-Risala al-'arshiyya* in *Rasa'il Ibn Sina*)

The first principle: establishment of the necessary of existence

Know that every existent either has a cause for its existence or has no cause. If it has a cause, it is something possible, whether it is [referred to] before its existence, when we are supposing it mentally, or in the state of existence; for the possibility of existence of that whose existence is possible is

---

1 See glossary entry for 'species/genus.'
2 See glossary entry for 'specific difference.'
3 See glossary entry for 'demonstration.'

not annulled by its entry into existence. If it has no cause in any way for its existence it is necessary of existence.

If this doctrine is accepted as true, the proof that there is in existence an existent having no cause for its existence is as I shall state. This existent is either possible of existence or necessary of existence. If it is necessary of existence our problem concerning it is settled at once. If it is possible of existence, the possible of existence enters into existence only by a cause which makes its existence outweigh its non-existence. But if its cause too is possible of existence, and in like manner there is [a series of] possibles dependent on one another, then there will be no existent at all, because this existent which we supposed does not enter into existence unless it is preceded by an infinite [series of] existents, and that is impossible. Therefore possibles terminate in something necessary of existence.

The second principle: the unicity of the Exalted

***

***

The third principle: the denial of causes for Him

This is a consequence of the first principle. Know that the necessary of existence has no cause whatever. There are four kinds of causes: that from which the existence of the thing [arises], the efficient cause; that for whose sake the thing has existence, the final, perfecting cause; that in which the thing has existence, the material cause; and that in which the existence of the thing consists, the formal cause.

So we say: The demonstration – an obvious one – that He has no efficient cause is that if He had had a cause for existence He would have been a created being, while that cause would have been necessary of existence. So, if it is established that He has no efficient cause, this leads us to think that His quiddity[4] is His individual nature, i.e. His existence; and He is neither a substance[5] nor an accident.[6] And it is inadmissible that there should be two [such

beings], each one deriving existence from the other, or that He should be necessary of existence in one respect and possible of existence in another.

A proof that His quiddity is not distinct from Himself, but rather that His existence is unified in His reality: If His existence were not His reality itself, His existence would be an accident of His reality. But everything accidental is caused, and everything caused required a cause: and this cause would either be external to His quiddity or itself be His quiddity. If it were external, He would not be necessary of existence and not be free from an efficient cause. If the cause were the quiddity, then the cause must be fully existent in order for the existence of another thing to arise from it; but quiddity before existence has no existence, and if it had such a prior existence, it could do without a second existence. Then the question would come up again in connection with that [prior] existence: If it were accidental in the quiddity, where would it come from and be attached to it?

Thus it has been established that the individual nature of Him who is necessary of existence is His quiddity, that He has no efficient cause, and that necessity of existence is for Him what quiddity is for other things. And from this it is evident that the necessary of existence does not resemble other things in any respect, because the existence of all things apart from Him is other than [their] quiddity.

I.2.3. What is Possible of Existence is Necessary of Existence from something else (from *al-Najat*)

Explanation of the ideas of the necessary and the possible

The necessary of existence is that existent which cannot be supposed non-existent without the occurrence of an impossibility. The possible of existence is that which can be supposed non-existent or existent without the occurrence of an impossibility. The necessary of existence entails existence. The possible of existence is that which has no entailment of any kind, i.e. either of exis-

---

4 See glossary entry for 'quiddity.'
5 See glossary entry for 'substance.'
6 See glossary entry for 'accident.'

tence or of its absence. (This is what we mean in this context by "possible of existence," although by "possible of existence" may also be meant what is in potentiality, and "possible" is also predicated of everything that truly exists – as has been given in detail previously in the *Logic*.)

Next, the necessary of existence may be necessary by itself or not by itself. What is necessary of existence by itself is what is due to itself, not due to another thing, i.e. it is such a thing that from the supposition of its absence an impossibility follows. On the other hand, what is necessary of existence not by itself is such that if something other than it were postulated, it would become necessary of existence. As examples, 4 is necessary of existence not by itself but on the supposition of 2+2, and burning is necessary of existence not by itself but on the supposition of contact of a naturally active force with a naturally passive force, I mean of one which burns with one which is burned.

The necessary by itself cannot be necessary by another thing; The necessary by another thing is possible

It is inadmissible that one thing should be necessary of existence by itself and by another thing at the same time. For if the other thing were removed or its existence not considered, inevitably either the necessity of its existence would remain unaffected and thus not be the necessity of its existence by another thing, or the necessity of its existence would not remain and thus it would not be the necessity of its existence by itself.

Everything that is necessary of existence by another thing is possible of existence by itself, because the necessity of existence of what is necessary of existence by another thing is dependent on some connection and relation, and the consideration of the connection and relation is other than the consideration of the very thing itself which has the connection and relation. Then the necessity of existence is established only by consideration of this connection. So consideration of the thing itself alone must entail necessity of existence, or possibility of existence, or impossibility of existence. But it is inadmissible that it should entail impossibility of existence, because everything whose existence is impossibility by itself does not exist, even

by another thing. Nor can it be an existent that entails necessity of existence [by itself]; for we have said previously that, when something is necessary in its existence by itself, the necessity of its existence cannot be by another thing. So what remains is that by consideration of itself it is possible of existence, while by consideration of the injection of the connection with that other thing it is necessary of existence, and by consideration of the interruption of its connection with that other thing it is impossible of existence; but itself by itself, without condition, it is possible of existence.

What is not necessary does not exist

Thus it is now clear that everything necessary of existence by another thing is possible of existence by itself. And this is reversible, so that everything possible of existence by itself, if its existence has happened, is necessary of existence by another thing; because inevitably it must either truly have an actual existence or not truly have an actual existence – but it cannot not truly have an actual existence; for in that case it would be impossible of existence; so it remains that it truly has an actual existence. And in that case its existence is either necessary or not necessary. But that whose existence is not necessary is still possible of existence [only], and its existence has not been distinguished from its absence; and there is no difference between this state of it and the first state, because it was already possible of existence before its existence, and now it is in the same state as it was. So if it is postulated that now it has been made anew, a proper question can be asked about this state [of renewal]: Is it possible of existence or necessary of existence? If it were possible of existence, and if that state were also present previously in the thing's [pure] possibility, no new state would now have arisen. But if its existence is necessary and it is necessitated by something prior, the existence of a [new] state is necessary by this prior thing, and that state is nothing but the thing's emergence into existence; therefore its emergence into existence is necessary.

Further, everything possible of existence either has its existence by itself or has it due to some cause. If it is by itself, it is itself necessary of existence, not possible of existence. If it is by a cause, either its existence is necessary whenever the cause exists, or else it remains as it was before the existence of the cause, but this is impossible. Therefore its existence is necessary whenever the cause exists.

Thus everything possible of existence by itself is necessary of existence only by another thing.

Establishment of the necessary of existence

There is no doubt that there are existents, and every existent is either necessary or possible. If it is necessary, the existence of the necessary is at once verified, which was the conclusion sought. If it is possible, we shall show that the existence of the possible terminates in the necessary of existence. First we shall set forth some premises.

One of these is that it is not possible that all the things possible by themselves should simultaneously have an infinite number of causes possible by themselves. This is because all of them are either existent together or not existent together. If they are not existent together in infinite number simultaneously, but exist in a temporal series – we shall postpone discussion of this. If they are existent together and there is nothing necessary of existence among them, then inevitably their total insofar as it is that total, whether it is finite or infinite, is either necessary of existence by itself or possible of existence. So if it is necessary of existence by itself, but each of its units is possible, the necessary of existence would be composed of possibles of existence, which is absurd. And if it is possible of existence by itself, the total needs for existence something to bestow existence. This will be either external to the total or internal to it. If it is internal, either one unit will be necessary of existence, yet every one of them was [considered] possible, so this is absurd. Or this unit will be possible of existence and will be a cause for the existence of the total; but a cause of the total is primarily a cause for the existence of its parts, of which it is one, thus it will be a cause for the existence of itself. This is impossible; but even if it were true, it would in a way be the very conclusion sought; for everything sufficient to make itself exist is necessary of existence, yet it was [considered] not necessary of existence, which is absurd. What remains, then, is that it is external to the total, and it is not possible that it should be a possible cause, for we have assembled all causes

possible of existence within this total; therefore it is external to it and necessary of existence by itself. So now the possibles have terminated in a cause necessary of existence, and all possibles do not have an infinite number of possible causes.

I.2.4. Characteristics of the Necessary of Existence (from *al-Shifa: al-Ilahiyyat*)

The beginning of the statement on the necessary of existence and the possible of existence: that the necessary of existence has no cause, that the possible of existence is caused, and that the necessary of existence is not matched by another thing in its [mode of] existence and not dependent on another thing for that existence.

We return to our subject and say: Each one of these, the necessary of existence and the possible of existence, has its own properties. Thus we say: Things that are included in existence are subject to a rational division into two kinds. One of them is that which, when it is considered by itself, is not necessary in its existence. It is evident that its existence is also not impossible, otherwise it would not have been included in existence. This [kind of] thing is in the sphere of possibility. The other kind is that which, when it is considered by itself, has its existence of necessity.

So we say: The necessary of existence by itself has no cause, while the possible of existence by itself has a cause. The necessary of existence by itself is necessary of existence in all its aspects. It is not possible for the existence of the necessary of existence to be matched by another existence, so that each one of the two would be equal to the other in the necessity of its existence and they could be substituted for each other. It is inadmissible that its existence would be composed of any plurality whatever. It is also inadmissible that the reality which belongs to the necessary of existence should be shared in any way. Thus from these assertions of ours it follows that the necessary of existence is not relative, changeable, plural or sharing in respect to its [mode of] existence which is its unique property.

That the necessary of existence has no cause is evident. For, if the necessary of existence had a cause for its existence, its existence would be by that cause. But whenever the existence of a thing is by something [else], if it is considered by itself without another thing, an existence is not necessary for it; and whenever a thing is considered by itself without another thing, and an existence is not necessary for it, it is not necessary of existence by itself. It is clear, therefore, that if the necessary of existence by itself had a cause, it would not *be* necessary of existence by itself. So now it is evident that the necessary of existence has no cause.

And from this it becomes evident that it is inadmissible that anything could be both necessary of existence by itself and necessary of existence by another thing. For, if its existence were necessary by another thing, it would be inadmissible that it could exist without that other thing, and whenever it is inadmissible that it could exist without another thing it is impossible that its existence should be necessary by itself. [Conversely], if it were necessary by itself, it would then have happened, and necessitation from another would have had no effect on its existence; [whereas], when another thing has an effect on a thing in its existence, its [the latter's] existence is not necessary by itself.

Further, whenever anything considered by itself is possible of existence, both its existence and its non-existence are by a cause. For, if it exists, existence has happened to it in distinction from non-existence, and if it does not exist non-existence has happened to it in distinction from existence. Now inevitably each one of the two states happens to it either from another thing or not from another thing. But if it is from another thing, this other thing is the cause, while if it does not happen from another thing, it is necessary of existence by itself, not possible of existence by itself, as we had supposed. Thus it is clear that everything that has not existed and then exists is determined by something admissible other than itself. And the case is the same for non-existence.

This is because either the quiddity of the thing is sufficient for this determination or a quiddity is insufficient for it. Now if its quiddity is sufficient for either one of the two states so that it happens, and that thing is necessary in its quiddity through itself, and yet it was supposed not necessary, this is absurd. And if the existence of its quiddity is insufficient for it, but [it is] something to which the existence of itself is added, so that its existence must be due to the existence of another thing not itself, then this thing is its cause; therefore it has a cause. So, in sum, one of the two states is necessary for it not through itself but through a cause. The factor of existence comes by a cause which is a cause of existence, while the factor of non-existence comes by a cause which is the non-existence of the cause for the factor of existence, as you know.

We say: It is necessary that [the possible] becomes necessary by the cause, and in relation to it. For, if it were not necessary, upon the existence of the cause and being in relation to it it would still be [merely] possible, and it would be admissible that it would both exist and not exist, without being determined by one of the two states. And [even] while the cause existed it would need all over again the existence of a third thing by which existence would be determined for it rather than non-existence, or non-existence rather than existence; so that thing would be another cause, and the argument would go on to infinity. But [even] if it went on to infinity, in spite of that its existence would never have been determined for it, so an existence would never have happened to it. And this is impossible, not only because of the infinite series of causes (for in this context it is doubtful whether such an extension is impossible), but more because there does not exist *any* extension by which it can be determined, after it has been assumed as existing already. Therefore it has now been verified that everything possible of existence does not exist until it is necessary in relation to its cause.

I.3. ABELARD

The following selection comes from the end of Abelard's so-called *Theologia "Scolarium,"* a late work. The question which Abelard addresses is whether God can only do what he does do. Abelard's answer is worked out in an informal way – but in a way which anticipates the highly structured *Question* of the 13th century. His arguments and resolutions of objections make it clear, Abelard claims, that God can do or omit doing only those things which he does do or omits doing, and, further, that he can do them or omit doing them only in the way or at the time at which he does and not at any other. Abelard thus attributes to God a position held by some ancient philosophers (the Megarians), according to whom what can be is what is: what is, in turn, is what must be. It would seem, in terms used in the Introduction, that God's action is strictly determined and determining. This view echoes a certain view of perfection stemming from ancient Greek philosophy, namely that the path of actuality does not have side lanes, as it were, along which the actual could run. We should say rather that actuality exhausts potentiality. It is this view which, in selection **I.9.1.** and elsewhere, Duns Scotus sets out to refute.

I.3.1. That God can only do what He does do
(from *Theologia "Scolarium"* III)

I think it needs to be asked whether God can do more or better things than he does, or whether he even could in any way have stopped doing the things he is doing so that he never in fact did them. Whether we allow that he can or deny it we will likely face many worrisome problems. If we affirm that he can do more or fewer things or stop doing what he is doing, clearly we will greatly detract from his supreme goodness. Certainly it is argued that he can do only good things and only things which it is fitting for him to do and good for him to do.

Likewise it is also agreed that he can omit some things in the sense that he does not do them, only if they are things which it is fitting for him to omit or which it is good for him to omit. But to do and omit the same thing is not fitting to him, nor is it good. Certainly nothing admits of being done and being omitted at the same time, and what it is good to do cannot be good to omit, since the only contrary of good is bad. Neither can there be a valid reason why the same thing ought to be done and omitted. If, then, when it is good to do something it is not good to omit it, and God can do or omit only what it is good for him to do or omit, clearly it seems that he can only do or omit what he does do or does omit. For if it is good that he omit what he omits, then it is not good for him to do the same thing, and consequently he cannot do it.

Or if he omits what it is good for him to do and draws back from some things which should be done, who would not infer that he is sort of envious or hostile? Certainly he to whose will all things are equally subjected incurs no toil in making anything, just as it is written: "He has spoken and they have been done; he has commanded and they have been created."

It is clear, therefore, that there is a right and valid reason for whatever God does or omits, and consequently he only does or omits those things which he ought to and which it is proper for him to do or omit. If whatever he does he ought to do, it is right for him to do whatever he does, and doubtless he ought to do whatever he does. And if he ought to do it, clearly he cannot rightly omit doing it. Certainly everything which it is right to do it is wrong to omit, and whoever does not do what reason demands is at fault just as much as if they did that which does not agree with reason at all.

But perhaps you will say that just as that which he in fact does is right and good or reasonable, so also it might have been good or equally good if he had done something else and omitted what he in fact did. Further, if, when he had chosen this one thing, this other which he omitted doing would have been equally good, clearly there was no reason why he omitted this and chose the other. But, you will say, there was reason here, since, given it was not required that both of these be done and it was equally good for this as for that to be done, whichever of them would have been done it would have been done with reason.

But according to this reasoning clearly what was not done was just as much required to be done as what was done, and it was just as good for the former to be done as for the latter. But when it is good that something be done and there is a valid reason why it is to be done, clearly he who omits doing it, while realizing that of itself it ought to be done, acts irrationally. Thus we seem to slide back into the aforementioned difficulty.

But if you say of the one which was not done that it was good for it to be done only as long as the other was stopped, certainly by the same reasoning applied to the other which was done we should not allow unqualifiedly that it was good that it be done, since it has been allowed that it is just as good for the one to be done as for the other. And so does God do what it was not good to do? Away with that! If only that which he does is good for him to do, clearly he who can only do what it is good for him to do can only do what he does do.

It seems, then, that by the above reasoning God can do only what he does do, and can omit only what he does omit, since in fact in each case of something to be done or to be omitted he has a valid reason why he does it or omits it; nor can he, who is the height of reason, will or do anything which runs against what reason demands. Certainly no one can reasonably will or do what disagrees with reason.

It appears, then, from the above reasoning and citations, that God can only do what he sometimes does do. And yet if we claim that God can only do what he does do, we seem to face opposition from both arguments and authorities.

For who fails to know that this person who is going to be damned could be saved, or that this person who is good could become better than they will ever be, even though neither of these could occur except by way of God. For if this person who is going to be damned cannot at all be saved, neither can they do the things by which God would save them, and consequently they are not to be accused nor held to blame because they did not do those things which they were not able to do. Rather, the Lord did not rightly bid them do those things by which they would have been saved, since they were in no way able to do them.

But if they were able to be saved by the Lord through works which they might have done, who would doubt that God is able to save this person who nevertheless is never going to be saved? Is there any difference between that person's being saved by God and God's saving them? So, if it is possible for them to be saved by God, how could it not be possible for God to save them? For when the antecedent is possible, so also is the consequent, because the impossible in no way validly follows from the possible, although it is in fact agreed that from what is impossible the existence of the impossible follows. But who would deny that this person's being saved by God implies God's saving them, since in fact, as we said, for this person who is going to be damned to be saved by God is exactly the same as for God to save them? And so, since it is possible for this person who is going to be damned to be saved by God, who would deny that it is possible for God to save them?

Thus God can do what he in no way is going to do, and what we just now concluded is evidently completely false, namely that God can only do what at sometime he does do. Otherwise, thanks would not at all be owing to him for what he does since what he cannot omit he does more out of a necessary compulsion arising from his own nature than by having been drawn freely by a will for doing these things.

So far as I judge this, then, since God can only do what it is fitting for him to do and what he omits doing is not anything fitting for him to do, I truly think that he is only able to do what sometimes he does do, even though few people or none agree with this opinion of ours and it seems to disagree with the pronouncements of a number of saints and a little bit with reason as well. They say that this judgment detracts greatly from the divine excellence in that it says that he can only do what sometimes he does do and omit that which he does omit, since even we ourselves, who are far less powerful, can do or omit many things which we do not at all do or omit.

To them I reply that we ought not on account of this be judged more powerful or better, i.e. because we can do some things which he cannot do, like eat, walk, or even sin, things which are totally removed from the power of divinity and completely foreign to his dignity. In short, does it pertain to God to be able to do those things which he would never do or which are not in the least fitting for him to do? That we can do some things which we ought not to do is to be assigned more to our weakness than to our dignity; we would be totally better if we could do only those things which we ought to do and nothing shameful could be done by us. There is a reason why God has allowed us this power for doing wrong or sinning, namely that he, who is not at all able to sin, may appear more glorious by comparison to out weakness. And when we stop sinning, we attribute this not to our nature but to the assisting grace of him who arranges to his own glory not just good things but bad things as well.

There are those, too, who think God can do even those things which he does not do because it is certain that nothing can stop him if he were to want to do those things which he does not do. So it is said: "Who might stop his will?" So also the blessed Augustine says: "He is not called omnipotent because he can do all things but because whatever he wants to do he can do, nor can any effect of his will be obstructed." Thus whatever he wills necessarily he does when he wills it, because his will cannot in any way be deprived of its effect. But clearly by this reasoning of theirs we could say that under some sort of state of his will he could even sin or do something shameful, since it is in fact certain that nothing could stop his doing this if he willed to do that which he ought not. Besides, when they say here that he is called omnipotent because he can do whatever he wills, obviously they so associate his power and will that where his will is lacking his power is lacking too.

As for the objection given above that someone cannot be saved by God unless it is also the case that God can save them, the chief point to be made is that when we said that for someone to be saved by God and for God to save them are the same, saying that did not place enough constraints on us. Certainly for someone speaking to be silent is the same as for the one who is speaking to be silent, and yet perhaps it is not as possible for someone speaking to be silent as it is for the one who is speaking to be silent. Or again, although for that which is white to be black is the same as for whiteness and blackness to be at the same time in the same thing, it is nevertheless not just as possible for whiteness and blackness to be at the same time in the same thing as it is for that which is white to be black. What wonder, then, if we claim that for someone who is not going to be saved to be saved by God is the same as God's saving them, while not accepting that just as they are able to be saved by God so God is able to save them? Clearly when we say that they can be saved by God, we refer this possibility back to the capacity of human nature, as if we had said that human nature does not reject this, namely that it be saved, i.e. this nature is in itself so mutable that it admits of both its salvation and its damnation and presents itself to God as something that can be treated in either way. But when we say that God can save this person who is not going to be saved at all, we refer the possibility back to the nature of divinity so that we mean that the nature of God does not reject saving him. This is completely false. Obviously the nature of God totally rejects God's doing what detracts from his dignity and what is not in the least fitting for him to do.

Likewise, when we say that an utterance is audible, i.e. able to be heard by someone, and also that someone can hear the utterance, or that a field can be tilled by someone and also that someone can till the field, we refer the possibility to diverse items: in the one case to the nature of an utterance or a field, in the other case to the real nature or capacity of the one who is able to hear an utterance or till a field. Thus it is not necessary that whenever an utterance is audible, i.e. of itself suited to being heard by someone, someone is then suited to hearing it. Even if all humans in existence were deaf, or were totally non-existent, any utterance would have the nature which renders it audible to humans and nothing would have to be done to it to make it fit to be heard, even though no human exists yet who could hear it or is suited to hear it.

Finally, the traditional objection of philosophers that, since the antecedent is possible so also is the consequent, and the existence of the impossible follows from the impossible, is of no concern, if, as we said in the previous book, we understand the validity of their rules to be restricted to the natures of creatures. Thus when they say something is possible or impossible, they mean this in respect of the natures of creatures, i.e. they call possible only what no creature's nature rejects. But when we say that it is possible for God to do this or that, we relate 'possible' to the nature more of divinity than of creatures.

Also, even though for the judge to punish this person and for this person to be punished by the judge are the same, it need not be allowed that if it is right for the judge to punish the person it is also right for the person to be punished by the judge, since in fact this noun 'right' changes its signification in such cases just as 'possible' does. For when we say that it is right that the judge punish the person, we mean that the judge ought according to the law do this. But if we say that the person ought to be punished by the judge, we mean that the person deserves to be punished. It often happens that according to the letter of the law a judge ought to punish someone who nevertheless, so far as their own deserts go, ought not to be punished by the judge. For example, when some false witnesses, whom the judge is unable to refute, testify against some innocent person and under the law make the person seem responsible when they are not responsible, and make it be believed that the person is guilty when they are not. In this case, as we said, the judge ought to punish the person even though the person ought not to be punished by the judge, and it is right for the judge to do this even though it is not right, i.e. deserved, for the person to suffer that punishment. Therefore, – just as in this case, even though for the judge to punish the person is the same as for the person to be punished by the judge, it does not follow that since it is right for the judge to punish the person whom, as we said, according to the law he rightly punishes, so also it is right for that person to be punished by the judge, – for the very same reason, even though for someone to be saved by God is the same as for God to save them, it is no wonder that even where the former is possible the latter is not at all to be allowed to be possible.

From what has been said, I think, it is easy to refute what seems a possible objection to God's providence or his will in respect of creatures, so that, although he would not be able to be without those items which he has had in himself from all eternity, because that would not be fitting, still let us not propose that the things which have been forseen, or which he has willed are, therefore, not able not to be, i.e. that they happen from necessity. For even if he was not able to be without providence and also the course of events necessarily follows that providence, still it should not thereby be allowed that the things foreseen were not able not to exist. Or if we propose that he was not able to be without a will for creating the world, or a will for compassion, we are not thereby forced to allow that the world or the things that have been created were not able to have failed to be. In the former case, as we qualified it, 'possible' made reference to God's nature; in the latter case, to the natures of creatures. Thus, although God necessarily has from his own nature either providence of things or a good will in relation to them, because this is especially fitting for God, still it is not necessary that the nature of things – things which are completely able not to be – require that they be.

As for the last objection that no thanks are owing to God for those things which he does, since he is not at all able to omit them and acts more by some necessity than by will, this is totally trifling. For this nature or necessity of his goodness is not separate from his will, nor is it to be called compulsion, i.e. that by which even someone who is unwilling is compelled to do something. For even when we say that it is necessary for him to be immortal or that he is necessarily immortal, this necessity of the divine nature is not separated off from his will, since he wills to be that which it is necessary for him to be, i.e. which he is not able not to be. But if he necessarily did something in such a way that whether he was willing or unwilling he was forced to do it, then clearly no thanks are due him in this case.

But since his goodness is so great and his will is so much the best that it inclines him to doing this not in an unwilling way but spontaneously, he is all the more fully to be loved on account of his own nature and honored for this, the more this goodness of his belongs to him not accidentally but substantially and immutably. Indeed, the more he exists in a better way on account of this, the more firmly does he persist in it.

For would we not be grateful to someone who helped us if their piety were so great that when they saw us in great distress they could not keep themselves from helping, since their own piety itself compelled them to do it? For what is it for us to owe thanks to someone for received assistance other than for us to recognize that they genuinely deserve our thanks, i.e. should be praised for those things which their kindness made available to us?

The foregoing arguments and resolutions of objections make it clear to all, I think, that God can do or omit doing only those things which he does do or does omit, and he can do them or omit them only in the way or at the time that he does and not at any other.

I.4. AL-GHAZALI AND AVERROES

THE FOLLOWING SELECTIONS COME FROM AVERROES'S *Tahafut al-Tahafut*. The dialogue, which Averroes (Ibn Rushd) has in effect written between himself and al-Ghazali, is one of the great dialogues in the Western tradition, in the same league as the dialogue Leibniz wrote between himself and Locke. No less remarkable is the internal dialogue which al-Ghazali wrote in coming to grips with objections and answers which he can hear his adversaries making.

Our Anthology contains several selections from Averroes's *Tahafut al-Tahafut* (or: *the Incoherence of the Incoherence*); selection **I.4.1.** below concerns the question whether the philosophers (in particular Aristotle and Avicenna) have proved that the first cause is simple. Selection **I.4.2.** concerns the notions of necessity and causation. Al-Ghazali gives the world an early version of the sort of critique which David Hume was to write in the 18th century. The reader here has an opportunity to take the measure both of the depth of al-Ghazali's critique and of the success of Averroes's reply.

In two respects al-Ghazali and Averroes pass one another by. For they are dealing with what will eventually come to be recognized in the tradition as two distinct senses of the necessary. In an extended dialogue Averroes would acknowledge that al-Ghazali is right to allow the absolute contingency or (as Duns Scotus would say) the logical contingency of causal connection. For it is not self-contradictory to affirm the existence of an event and to deny the existence of a purported cause. But Averroes, for his part, tries to bring the discussion back to the relative necessity which he has from Aristotle: namely, to the necessity of events of this world relative to real powers. His strongest statement of this occurs in selection **I.4.1.** below:

> For true knowledge is the knowledge of a thing as it is in reality. And if in reality there only existed, in regard both to the substratum and to the Agent, the possibility of the two opposites, there would no longer, even for the twinkling of an eye, be any permanent knowledge of anything, since we suppose such an agent to rule existents like a tyrannical prince who has the highest power, for whom nobody in his dominion can deputize, of whom no standard or custom is known to which reference might be made. Indeed, the acts of such a prince will undoubtedly be unknown by nature, and if an act of his comes into existence the continuance of its existence at any moment will be unknown by nature.

The outlook of this paragraph was challenged not only by al-Ghazali; it was also to be challenged by John Duns Scotus, as selections in I.9 help make clear. Although al-Ghazali draws skeptical conclusions regarding the certainty and the necessity of natural science, Duns Scotus tries to save knowledge, both divine and human, while relaxing the requirement of absolute or logical necessity.

I.4.1. Whether the First Cause is simple (*Tahafut al-Tahafut*, The Eighth Discussion)

To refute their theory that the existence of the First is simple, namely that it is pure existence and that its existence stands in relation to no quiddity and to no essence, but stands to necessary existence as do other beings to their quiddity[1]

Ghazali says:
There are two ways of attacking this theory. The first is to demand a proof and to ask how you know this, through the necessity of the intellect, or through speculation and not by immediate necessity; and in any case you must tell us your method of reasoning. If it is said that, if the First had a quiddity, its existence would be related to it, and would be consequent on this quiddity and would be its necessary attribute, and the consequent is an effect and therefore necessary existence would be an effect, and this is a contradiction, we answer: This is to revert to the source of the confusion in the application of the term 'necessary existence'; for we call this entity 'reality' or 'quiddity' and this reality exists, i.e. it is not non-existent and is not denied, but its existence is brought into a relation with it, and if you like to call this 'consequent' and 'necessary attribute,' we shall not quibble about words, if you have once acknowledged that it has no agent for its existence and that this existence has not ceased to be eternal and to have no efficient cause; if, however, you understand by 'consequent' and 'effect' that it has an efficient cause, this is not true. But if you mean something else, this is conceded, for it is not impossible, since the demonstration proves only the end of a causal series and its ending in an existent reality; a positive quiddity, therefore, is possible, and there is no need to deny the quiddity.

If it is said: Then the quiddity becomes a cause for the existence which is consequent on it, and the existence becomes an effect and an object of the act, we answer: The quiddity in temporal things is not a cause of their existence, and why should it therefore be the cause in the eternal, if you mean by 'cause' the agent? But if you mean something else

by it, – namely that without which it could not be, let that be accepted, for there is nothing impossible in it; the impossibility lies only in the infinite causal series, and if this series only comes to a final term, then the impossibility – is cancelled; impossibility can be understood only on this point, therefore you must give a proof of its impossibility.

All the proofs of the philosophers are nothing but presumptions that the term has a sense from which certain consequences follow, and nothing but the supposition that demonstration has in fact proved a necessary existent with the meaning the philosophers ascribed to it. We have, however, shown previously that this is not true. In short, this proof of the philosophers comes down to the proof of the denial of attributes and of the division into genus and specific difference; only this proof is still more ambiguous and weak, for this plurality is purely verbal, for the intellect does allow the acceptance of one single existent quiddity. The philosophers, however, say that every existent quiddity is a plurality, for it contains quiddity and existence, and this is an extreme confusion; for the meaning of a single existent is perfectly understandable – nothing exists which has no essence, and the existence of an essence does not annul its singleness.

I say:
Ghazali does not relate Avicenna's doctrine literally as he did in his book *The Aims of the Philosophers*. For since Avicenna believed that the existence of a thing indicated an attribute additional to its essence, he could no longer admit that its essence was the agent of its existence out of the possibles; for then the thing would be the cause of its own existence and it would not have an agent. It follows from this, according to Avicenna, that everything which has an existence additional to its essence has an efficient cause, and since, according to Avicenna, the First has no agent, it follows necessarily that its existence is identical with its essence. And therefore Ghazali's objection that Avicenna assimilates existence to a necessary attribute of the essence is not true, because the essence of a thing is the cause of its necessary attribute and it is not possible that a thing should

---

1 See glossary entry for 'quiddity.'

be the cause of its own existence, because the existence of a thing is prior to its quiddity. To identify the quiddity and the existence of a thing is not to do away with its quiddity, as Ghazali asserts, but is only the affirmation of the unity of quiddity and existence. If we regard existence as an accidental attribute of the existent, and it is the agent which gives possible things their existence, necessarily that which has no agent either cannot have an existence (and this is absurd), or its existence must be identical with its essence.

But the whole of this discussion is built on the mistake that the existence of a thing is one of its attributes. For the existence which in our knowledge is prior to the quiddity of a thing is that which signifies the true. Therefore, the question whether a thing exists, either (1) refers to that which has a cause that determines its existence, and in that case its potential meaning is to ask whether this thing has a cause or not, according to Aristotle at the beginning of the second chapter of the *Posterior Analytics*; or (2) it refers to that which has no cause, and then its meaning is to ask whether a thing possesses a necessary attribute which determines its existence. And when by 'existent' is meant what is understood by 'thing' and 'entity,' it follows the rule of the genus which is predicated analogically, and whatever it is in this sense is attributed in the same way to that which has a cause and to that which has none, and it does not signify anything but the concept of the existent, and by this is meant "the true," and if it means something additional to the essence, it is only in a subjective sense which does not exist outside the soul except potentially, as is also the case with the universal. And this is the way in which the ancient philosophers considered the First Principle, and they regarded it as a simple existent. As to the later philosophers in Islam, they stated that, in their speculation about the nature of the existent *qua* existent, they were led to accept a simple existent of this description.

The best method to follow, in my opinion, and the nearest to strict proof, is to say that the actualization of existents which have in their substance a possible existence necessarily occurs only through an actualizer which is in act, i.e. acting, and moves them and draws them out of potency into act. And if this actualizer itself is also of the nature of the possible, i.e. possible in its substance, there will

have to be another actualizer for it, necessary in its substance and not possible, so that this sublunary world may be conserved, and the nature of the possible causes may remain everlastingly, proceeding without end. And if these causes exist without end, as appears from their nature, and each of them is possible, necessarily their cause, i.e. that which determines their permanence, must be something necessary in its substance, and if there were a moment in which nothing was moved at all, there would be no possibility of an origination of movement. The nexus between temporal existence and eternal can only take place without a change affecting the First through that movement which is partly eternal, partly temporal. And the thing moved by this movement is what Avicenna calls "the existence necessary through another," and this "necessary through another" must be a body everlastingly moved, and in this way it is possible that the essentially temporal and corruptible should exist in dependence on the eternal, and this through approach to something and through recession from it, as you observe it happen to transitory existents in relation to the heavenly bodies. And since this moved body is necessary in its substance, possible in its local movement, it is necessary that the process should terminate in an absolutely necessary existent in which there is no potency at all, either in its substance, or locally or in any of the other forms of movement; and that which is of this description is necessarily simple, because if it were a compound, it would be possible, not necessary, and it would require a necessary existent. And this method of proving it is in my opinion sufficient, and it is true.

However, what Avicenna adds to this proof by saying that the possible existent must terminate either in an existent necessary through another or in an existent necessary through itself, and in the former case that the necessary through another should be a consequence of the existent necessary through itself, for he affirms that the existent necessary through another is in itself a possible existent and what is possible needs something necessary-this addition, is to my mind superfluous and erroneous, for in the necessary, in whatever way you suppose it, there is no possibility whatsoever and there exists nothing of a single nature of which it can be said that it is in one way possible and in another way necessary in its existence. For the philosophers have proved that there is no possible whatsoever in the necessary; for the possible is the opposite of the necessary, and the only thing that can happen is that a thing should be in one way necessary, in another way possible, as they believed for instance to be the case with the heavenly body or what is above the body of the heavens, namely that it was necessary through its substance and possible in its movement and in space. What led Avicenna to this division was that he believed that the body of the heavens was essentially necessary through another, possible by itself, and we have shown in another place that this is not true. And the proof which Avicenna uses in dealing with the necessary existent, when this distinction and this indication are not made, is of the type of common dialectical notions; when, however, the distinction is made, it is of the type of demonstrative proof.

You must know further that the becoming of which the Holy Law speaks is of the kind of empirical becoming in this world, and this occurs in the forms of the existents which the Ash'arites call mental qualities and the philosophers call forms, and this becoming occurs only through another thing and in time, and the Holy Words: "Have not those who have disbelieved considered that the heavens and the earth were coherent, and we have rent them" and the Divine Words "then he straightened himself up to the sky which was smoke" refer to this. But as to the relation which exists between the nature of the possible existent and the necessary existent, this the Holy Law is silent, because it is too much above the understanding of the common man and knowledge of it is not necessary for his blessedness. When the Ash'arites affirm that the nature of the possible is created and has come into existence in time out of nothing (a notion which all the philosophers oppose, whether they believe in the temporal beginning of the world or not), they do not say this, if you consider the question rightly, on the authority of the law of Islam, and there is no proof for it. What appears from the Holy Law is the commandment to abstain from investigating that about which the Holy Law is silent, and therefore it is said in the Traditions: "The people did not cease thinking till they said: God has created this, but who has created God? And the Prophet said: "When one of you finds this, this is an act of pure faith," and in another version: "When one of you

finds this, let him read the verse of the Koran: Say, He, God is one. And know that for the masses to turn to such a question comes from the whisperings of Satan and therefore the prophet said: This is an act of pure faith."

Ghazali says:
The second way is to say that an existence without quiddity or essence cannot be conceived, and just as mere non-existence, without a relation to an existent the non-existence of which can be supposed, cannot be conceived, in the same way existence can be only conceived in relation to a definite essence, especially when it is defined as a single essence; for how could it be defined as single, conceptually differentiated from others, if it had not a real essence? For to deny the quiddity is to deny the real essence, and when you deny the real essence of the existent, the existent can no longer be understood. It is as if the philosophers affirmed at the same time existence and a non-existent, which is contradictory. This is shown by the fact that, if it were conceivable, it would be also possible in the effects that there should be an existence without an essence, participating with the First in not having a real essence and a quiddity, differing from it in having a cause, whereas the First is causeless. And why should such an effect not be imagined? And is there any other reason for this than that it is inconceivable in itself? But what is inconceivable in itself does not become conceivable by the denial of its cause, nor does what is conceivable become inconceivable because it is supposed to have a cause. Such an extreme negation is the most obscure of their theories, although they believe indeed that they have proved what they say. Their doctrine ends in absolute negation, and indeed the denial of the quiddity is the denial of the real essence, and through the denial of this reality nothing remains but the word 'existence,' which has no object at all when it is not related to a quiddity.

And if it is said: "Its real essence is that it is the necessary, and the necessary is its quiddity," we answer: The only sense of 'necessary' is 'causeless,' and this is a negation which does not constitute a real essence; and the denial of a cause for the real essence presupposes the real essence, and therefore let the essence be conceivable, so that it can be described as being causeless; but the essence cannot be represented as non-existent, since 'necessity' has no other meaning than 'being causeless.' Besides, if the necessity were added to the existence, this would form a plurality; and if it is not added, how then could it be the quiddity? For the existence is not the quiddity, and thus what is not added to the existence cannot be the quiddity either.

I say:

This whole paragraph is sophistry. For the philosophers do not assume that the First has an existence without a quiddity and a quiddity without an existence. They believe only that the existence in the compound is an additional attribute to its essence and it only acquires this attribute through the agent, and they believe that in that which is simple and causeless this attribute is not additional to the quiddity and that it has no quiddity differentiated from its existence; but they do not say that it has absolutely no quiddity, as he assumes in his objection against them. Having assumed that they deny the quiddity – which is false – Ghazali begins now to charge them with reprehensible theories.

He says:

If this were conceivable it would also be possible in the effects that there should be an existence without an essence, participating with the First in not having a real essence.

I say:

But the philosophers do not assume an existent absolutely without a quiddity: they only assume that it has not a quiddity like the quiddities of the other existents; and this is one of the sophistical fallacies, for the term 'quiddity' is ambiguous, and this assumption, and everything built upon it, is a sophistical argument, for the non-existent cannot be described either by denying or by affirming something of it. And Ghazali, by fallacies of the kind perpetrated in this book, is not exempt from wickedness or from ignorance, and he seems nearer to wickedness than to ignorance – or should we say that there is a necessity which obliged him to do this?

As to his remark, that the meaning of 'necessary existent' is 'causeless,' this is not true, but our expression that it is a necessary existent has a positive meaning, consequent on a nature which has absolutely no cause, no exterior agent, and no

agent which is part of it.

And as to Ghazali's words: "If the necessity were added to the existence, this would form a plurality; and if it is not added, how then could it be the quiddity? For existence is not the quiddity, and thus what is not added to the existence cannot be the quiddity either."

I say:

According to the philosophers necessity is not an attribute added to the essence, and it is predicated of the essence in the same way as we say of it that it is inevitable and eternal. And likewise if we understand by 'existence' a mental attribute, it is not an addition to the essence, but if we understand it as being an accident, in the way Avicenna regards it in the composite existent, then it becomes difficult to explain how the uncompounded can be the quiddity itself, although one might say perhaps: "In the way the knowledge in the uncompounded becomes the knower himself." If, however, one regards the existent as the true, all these doubts lose their meaning, and likewise, if one understands 'existent' as having the same sense as 'entity,' and according to this it is true that the existence in the uncompounded is the quiddity itself.

I.4.2. About the Natural Sciences (from the *Tahafut al-Tahafut*)

The denial of a logical necessity between cause and effect

Ghazali says:

According to us the connexion between what is usually believed to be a cause and what is believed to be an effect is not a necessary connexion; each of two things has its own individuality and is not the other, and neither the affirmation nor the negation, neither the existence nor the non-existence of the one is implied in the affirmation, negation, existence, and non-existence of the other, e.g. the satisfaction of thirst does not imply drinking, nor satiety eating, nor burning contact with fire, nor light sunrise, nor decapitation death, nor recovery the drinking of medicine, nor evacuation the taking of a purgative, and so on for all the empirical connexions existing in medicine, astronomy, the sciences, and the crafts. For the connexion in these things is based on a prior power of God to create them in a successive order, though not because this connexion is necessary in itself and cannot be disjoined – on the contrary, it is in God's power to create satiety without eating, and death without decapitation, and to let life persist notwithstanding the decapitation, and so on with respect to all connexions. The philosophers, however, deny this possibility and claim that that is impossible. To investigate all these innumerable connexions would take us too long, and so we shall choose one single example, namely the burning of cotton through contact with fire; for we regard it as possible that the contact might occur without the burning taking place, and also that the cotton might be changed into ashes without any contact with fire, although the philosophers deny this possibility. The discussion of this matter has three points.

The first is that our opponent claims that the agent of the burning is the fire exclusively; this is a natural, not a voluntary agent, and cannot abstain from what is in its nature when it is brought into contact with a receptive substratum. This we deny, saying: The agent of the burning is God, through His creating the black in the cotton and the disconnexion of its parts, and it is God who made the cotton burn and made it ashes either through the intermediation of angels or without intermediation. For fire is a dead body which has no action, and what is the proof that it is the agent? Indeed, the philosophers have no other proof than the observation of the occurrence of the burning, when there is contact with fire, but observation proves only a simultaneity, not a causation, and, in reality, there is no other cause but God. For there is unanimity of opinion about the fact that the union of the spirit with the perceptive and moving faculties in the sperm of animals does not originate in the natures contained in warmth, cold, moistness, and dryness, and that the father is neither the agent of the embryo through introducing the sperm into the uterus, nor the agent of its life, its sight and hearing, and all its other faculties. And although it is well known that the same faculties exist in the father, still nobody thinks that these faculties exist through him; no, their existence is produced by the First either directly or through the intermediation of the angels who are in charge of these events. Of this fact the philosophers who believe in a creator are quite convinced, but it is precisely with them

that we are in dispute.

It has been shown that coexistence does not indicate causation. We shall make this still more clear through an example. Suppose that a man blind from birth, whose eyes are veiled by a membrane and who has never heard people talk of the difference between night and day, has the membrane removed from his eyes by day and sees visible things, he will surely think then that the actual perception in his eyes of the forms of visible things is caused by the opening of his eyelids, and that as long as his sight is sound and in function, the hindrance removed and the object in front of him visible, he will, without doubt, be able to see, and he will never think that he will not see, till, at the moment when the sun sets and the air darkens, he will understand that it was the light of the sun which impressed the visible forms on his sight. And for what other reason do our opponents believe that in the principles of existence there are causes and influences from which the events which coincide with them proceed, than that they are constant, do not disappear, and are not moving bodies which vanish from sight? For if they disappeared or vanished we should observe the disjunction and understand then that behind our perceptions there exists a cause. And out of this there is no issue, according to the very conclusions of the philosophers themselves.

The true philosophers were therefore unanimously of the opinion that these accidents and events which occur when there is a contact of bodies, or in general a change in their positions, proceed from the bestower of forms who is an angel or a plurality of angels, so that they even said that the impression of the visible forms on the eye occurs through the bestower of forms, and that the rising of the sun, the soundness of the pupil, and the existence of the visible object are only the preparations and dispositions which enable the substratum to receive the forms; and this theory they applied to all events. And this refutes the claim of those who profess that fire is the agent of burning, bread the agent of satiety, medicine the agent of health, and so on.

I say:

To deny the existence of efficient causes which are observed in sensible things is sophistry, and he who defends this doctrine either denies with his tongue what is present in his mind or is carried away by a sophistical doubt which occurs to him concerning this question. For he who denies this can no longer acknowledge that every act must have an agent. The question whether these causes by themselves are sufficient to perform the acts which proceed from them, or need an external cause for the perfection of their act, whether separate or not, is not self-evident and requires much investigation and research. And if the theologians had doubts about the efficient causes which are perceived to cause each other, because there are also effects whose cause is not perceived, this is illogical. Those things whose causes are not perceived are still unknown and must be investigated, precisely because their causes are not perceived; and since everything whose causes are not perceived is still unknown by nature and must be investigated, it follows necessarily that what is not unknown has causes which are perceived. The man who reasons like the theologians does not distinguish between what is self-evident and what is unknown, and everything Ghazali says in this passage is sophistical.

And further, what do the theologians say about the essential causes, the understanding of which alone can make a thing understood? For it is self-evident that things have essences and attributes which determine the special functions of each thing and through which the essences and names of things are differentiated. If a thing had not its specific nature, it would not have a special name nor a definition, and all things would indeed be one, not even one; for it might be asked whether this one has one special act or one special passivity or not, and if it had a special act, then there would indeed exist special acts proceeding from special natures, but if it had no single special act, then the one would not be one. But if the nature of oneness is denied, the nature of being is denied, and the consequence of the denial of being is nothingness.

Further, are the acts which proceed from all things absolutely necessary for those in whose nature it lies to perform them, or are they only performed in most cases or in half the cases? This is a question which must be investigated, since one single action-and-passivity between two existent things occurs only through one relation out of an

infinite number, and it happens often that one relation hinders another. Therefore, it is not absolutely certain that fire acts when it is brought near a sensitive body, for surely it is not improbable that there should be something which stands in such a relation to the sensitive thing as to hinder the action of the fire, as is asserted of talc and other things. But one need not therefore deny fire its burning power so long as fire keeps its name and definition.

Further, it is self-evident that all events have four causes, agent, form, matter, and end,[2] and that they are necessary for the existence of the effects – especially those causes which form a part of the effect, namely that which is called by the philosophers matter, by the theologians condition and substratum, and that which is called by the philosophers form, by the theologians psychological quality. The theologians acknowledge that there exist conditions which are necessary for the conditioned, as when they say that life is a condition of knowledge; and they equally recognize that things have realities and definitions, and that these are necessary for the existence of the existent, and therefore they here judge the visible and the invisible according to one and the same scheme. And they adopt the same attitude towards the consequences of a thing's essence, namely what they call "sign," as for instance when they say that the harmony in the world indicates that its agent possesses mind and that the existence of a world having a design indicates that its agent knows this world. Now intelligence is nothing but the perception of things with their causes, and in this it distinguishes itself from all the other faculties of apprehension, and he who denies causes must deny the intellect.

Logic implies the existence of causes and effects, and knowledge of these effects can only be rendered perfect through knowledge of their causes. Denial of cause implies the denial of knowledge, and denial of knowledge implies that nothing in this world can be really known, and that what is supposed to be known is nothing but opinion, that neither proof nor definition exist, and that the essential attributes which compose definitions are void. The man who denies the necessity of any item of knowledge must admit that even this, his own

---

2 See selections I.1.1. and I.1.3.

affirmation, is not necessary knowledge.

As to those who admit that there exists, besides necessary knowledge, knowledge which is not necessary, about which the soul forms a judgement on slight evidence and imagines it to be necessary, whereas it is not necessary, the philosophers do not deny this. And if they call such a fact "habit," this may be granted, but otherwise I do not know what they understand by the term 'habit' – whether they mean that it is the habit of the agent, the habit of the existing things, or our habit to form a judgement about such things? It is, however, impossible that God should have a habit; for a habit is a custom which the agent acquires and from which a frequent repetition of his act follows, whereas God says in the Holy Book: "Thou shalt not find any alteration in the course of God, and they shall not find any change in the course of God." If they mean a habit in existing things, habit can only exist in the animated; if it exists in something else, it is really a nature, and it is not possible that a thing should have a nature which determined it either necessarily or in most cases. If they mean our habit of forming judgements about things, such a habit is nothing but an act of the soul which is determined by its nature and through which the intellect becomes intellect. The philosophers do not deny such a habit; but "habit" is an ambiguous term, and if it is analysed, it means only a hypothetical act; as when we say, "So-and-so has the habit of acting in such-and-such a way," meaning that he will act in that way most of the time. If this were true, everything would be the case only by supposition, and there would be no wisdom in the world from which it might be inferred that its agent was wise.

And, as we said, we need not doubt that some of these existents cause each other and act through each other, and that in themselves they do not suffice for their act, but that they are in need of an external agent whose act is a condition of their act, and not only of their act but even of their existence. However, about the essence of this agent or of these agents the philosophers differ in one way, although in another they agree. They all agree in this, that the First Agent is immaterial and that its

act is the condition of the existence and acts of existents, and that the act of their agent reaches these existents through the intermediation of an effect of this agent which is different from these existents and which, according to some of them, is exclusively the heavenly sphere, whereas others assume besides this sphere another immaterial existent which they call the bestower of forms.

But this is not the place to investigate these theories, and the highest part of their inquiry is this; and if you are one of those who desire these truths, then follow the right road which leads to them. The reason why the philosophers differed about the origin of the essential forms and especially of the forms of the soul is that they could not relate them to the warm, cold, moist, and dry, which are the causes of all natural things which come into being and pass away, whereas the materialists related everything which does not seem to have an apparent cause to the warm, cold, moist, and dry, affirming that these things originated through certain mixtures of those elements, just as colors and other accidents come into existence. And the philosophers tried to refute them.

Ghazali says:
Our second point is concerned with those who acknowledge that these events proceed from their principles, but say that the disposition to receive the forms arises from their observed and apparent causes. However, according to them the events proceed from these principles not by deliberation and will, but by necessity and nature, as light does from the sun, and the substrata differ for their reception only through the differentiations in their disposition. For instance, a polished body receives the rays of the sun, reflects them and illuminates another spot with them, whereas an opaque body does not receive them; the air does not hinder the penetration of the sun's light, but a stone does; certain things become soft through the sun, others hard; certain things, like the garments which the fuller bleaches, become white through the sun, others like the fuller's face become black: the principle is, however, one and the same, although the effects differ through the differences of disposition in the sub-

---

3 See glossary entry for 'element.'

stratum. Thus there is no hindrance or incapacity in the emanation of what emanates from the principles of existence; the insufficiency lies only in the receiving substrata. If this is true, and we assume a fire that has the quality it has, and two similar pieces of cotton in the same contact with it, how can it be imagined that only one and not the other will be burned, as there is here no voluntary act? And from this point of view they deny that Abraham could fall into the fire and not be burned notwithstanding the fact that the fire remained fire, and they affirm that this could only be possible through abstracting the warmth from the fire (through which it would, however, cease to be fire) or through changing the essence of Abraham and making him a stone or something on which fire has no influence, and neither the one nor the other is possible.

I say:

Those philosophers who say that these perceptible existents do not act on each other, and that their agent is exclusively an external principle, cannot affirm that their apparent action on each other is totally illusory, but would say that this action is limited to preparing the disposition to accept the forms from the external principle. However, I do not know any philosopher who affirms this absolutely; they assert this only of the essential forms, not of the forms of accidents. They all agree that warmth causes warmth, and that all the four qualities act likewise, but in such a way that through it the elemental fire and the warmth which proceeds from the heavenly bodies are conserved. The theory which Ghazali ascribes to the philosophers, that the separate principles[4] act by nature, not by choice, is not held by any important philosophers; on the contrary, the philosophers affirm that that which possesses knowledge must act by choice. However, according to the philosophers, in view of the excellence which exists in the world, there can proceed out of two contraries only the better, and their choice is not made to perfect their essences – since there is no imperfection in their essence – but in order that through it those existents which have an imperfection in their nature may be perfected.

As to the objection which Ghazali ascribes to the philosophers over the miracle of Abraham, such things are only asserted by heretical Muslims. The learned among the philosophers do not permit discussion or disputation about the principles of religion, and he who does such a thing needs, according to them, a severe lesson. For whereas every science has its principles, and every student of this science must concede its principles and may not interfere with them by denying them, this is still more obligatory in the practical science of religion, for to walk on the path of the religious virtues is necessary for human being's existence, according to them, not in so far as he is human, but in so far as he has knowledge; and therefore it is necessary for every human to concede the principles of religion and invest with authority the human who lays them down. The denial and discussion of these principles denies human existence, and therefore heretics must be killed. Of religious principles it must be said that they are divine things which surpass human understanding, but must be acknowledged although their causes are unknown.

Therefore, we do not find that any of the ancient philosophers discusses miracles, although they were known and had appeared all over the world, for they are the principles on which religion is based and religion is the principle of the virtues; nor did they discuss any of the things which are said to happen after death. For if a person grows up according to the religious virtues he becomes absolutely virtuous, and if time and felicity are granted to him, so that he becomes one of the deeply learned thinkers and it happens that he can explain one of the principles of religion, it is enjoined upon him that he should not divulge this explanation and should say, "All these are the terms of religion and the wise," conforming himself to the Divine Words, "But those who are deeply versed in knowledge say: we believe in it, it is all from our Lord."

Ghazali says:

There are two answers to this theory. The first is to say: We do not accept the assertion that the principles do not act in a voluntary way and that God

---

4 I.e. the separate forms or immaterial substances, which are all minds. See glossary entry for 'separate substance.'

does not act through His will, and we have already refuted their claim in treating of the question of the temporal creation of the world. If it is established that the Agent creates the burning through His will when the piece of cotton is brought in contact with the fire, He can equally well omit to create it when the contact takes place.

I say:

Ghazali, to confuse his opponent, here regards as established what his opponent refuses to admit, and says that his opponent has no proof for his refusal. He says that the First Agent causes the burning without an intermediary which He might have created in order that the burning might take place through the fire. But such a claim abolishes any perception of the existence of causes and effects. No philosopher doubts that, for instance, the fire is the cause of the burning which occurs in the cotton through the fire – not, however, absolutely, but by an external principle which is the condition of the existence of fire, not to speak of its burning. The philosophers differ only about the quiddity[5] of this principle – whether it is a separate principle, or an intermediary between the event and the separate principle besides the fire.

Ghazali says, on behalf of the philosophers:

But it may be said that such a conception involves reprehensible impossibilities. For if you deny the necessary dependence of effects or their causes and relate them to the will of their Creator, and do not allow even in the will a particular definite pattern, but regard it as possible that it may vary and change in type, then it may happen to any of us that there should be in his presence beasts of prey and flaming fires and immovable mountains and enemies equipped with arms, without his seeing them, because God had not created in him the faculty of seeing them. And a man who had left a book at home might find it on his return changed into a youth, handsome, intelligent, and efficient, or into an animal; or if he left a youth at home, he might find him turned into a dog; or he might leave ashes and find them changed into musk; or a stone changed into gold, and gold changed into stone.

And if he were asked about any of these things, he would answer: "I do not know what there is at present in my house; I only know that I left a book in my house, but perhaps by now it is a horse which has soiled the library with its urine and excrement, and I left in my house a piece of bread which has perhaps changed into an apple-tree." For God is able to do all these things, and it does not belong to the necessity of a horse that it should be created from a sperm, nor is it of the necessity of a tree that it should be created from a seed; no, there is no necessity that it should be created out of anything at all. And perhaps God creates things which never existed before; indeed, when one sees a man one never saw before and is asked whether this man has been generated, one should answer hesitantly: "It may be that he was one of the fruits in the market which has been changed into a man, and that this is that man." For God can do any possible thing, and this is possible, and one cannot avoid being perplexed by it; and to this kind of fancy one may yield *ad infinitum*, but these examples will do.

But the answer is to say: If it were true that the existence of the possible implied that there could not be created in man any knowledge of the non-occurrence of a possible, all these consequences would follow necessarily. But we are not at a loss over any of the examples which you have brought forward. For God has created in us the knowledge that He will not do all these possible things, and we only profess that these things are not necessary, but that they are possible and may or may not happen, and protracted habit time after time fixes their occurrence in our minds according to the past habit in a fixed impression. Yes, it is possible that a prophet should know in such ways as the philosophers have explained that a certain man will not come tomorrow from a journey, and although his coming is possible the prophet knows that this possibility will not be realized. And often you may observe even ordinary men of whom you know that they are not aware of anything occult, and can know the intelligible only through instruction, and still it cannot be denied that nevertheless their soul and conjecturing power can acquire sufficient strength to apprehend what the prophets apprehend in so far as they know the possibility of an event, but know that it will not happen. And if God interrupts the habitual course by causing this unusual event to happen this knowledge of the habitual is at the time of the interruption removed from their hearts and He no longer creates it. There is, therefore, no objection to admitting that a thing may be possible for God, but that He had the previous knowledge that although He might have done so He would not carry it out during a certain time, and that He has created in us the knowledge that He would not do it during that time.

I say:
When the theologians admit that the opposite of everything existing is equally possible, and that it is such in regard to the Agent, and that only one of these opposites can be differentiated through the will of the Agent, there is no fixed standard for His will either constantly or for most cases, according to which things must happen. For this reason the theologians are open to all the scandalous implications with which they are charged. For true knowledge is the knowledge of a thing as it is in reality. And if in reality there only existed, in regard both to the substratum and to the Agent, the possibility of the two opposites, there would no longer, even for the twinkling of an eye, be any permanent knowledge of anything, since we suppose such an agent to rule existents like a tyrannical prince who has the highest power, for whom nobody in his dominion can deputize, of whom no standard or custom is known to which reference might be made. Indeed, the acts of such a prince will undoubtedly be unknown by nature, and if an act of his comes into existence the continuance of its existence at any moment will be unknown by nature.

Ghazali's defence against these difficulties that God created in us the knowledge that these possibilities would be realized only at special times, such as at the time of the miracle, is not a true one. For the knowledge created in us is always in conformity with the nature of the real thing, since the definition of truth is that a thing is believed to be such as it is in reality. Therefore, if there is knowledge of

these possibles, there must be in the real possibles a condition to which our knowledge refers, either through these possibles themselves or through the agent, or for both reasons – a condition which the theologians call habit. And since the existence of this condition which is called habit is impossible in the First Agent, this condition can only be found in the existents, and this, as we said, is what the philosophers call nature.

The same congruity exists between God's knowledge and the existents, although God's knowledge of existents is their cause, and these existents are the consequence of God's knowledge, and therefore reality conforms to God's knowledge. If, for instance, knowledge of Zaid's[6] coming reaches the prophet through a communication of God, the reason why the actual happening is congruous with the knowledge is nothing but the fact that the nature of the actually existent is a consequence of the eternal knowledge, for knowledge as knowledge can only refer to something which has an actualized nature. The knowledge of the Creator is the reason why this nature becomes actual in the existent which is attached to it. Our ignorance of these possibles is brought about through our ignorance of the nature which determines the being or non-being of a thing. If the opposites in existents were in a condition of equilibrium, both in themselves and through their efficient causes, it would follow that they neither existed nor did not exist, or that they existed and did not exist at the same time, and one of the opposites must therefore have a preponderance in existence. And it is the knowledge of the existence of this nature which causes the actualization of one of the opposites. And the knowledge attached to this nature is either a knowledge prior to it, and this is the knowledge of which this nature is the effect, namely eternal knowledge, or the knowledge which is consequent on this nature, namely non-eternal knowledge. The attainment of the occult is nothing but the vision of this nature, and our acquisition of this knowledge not preceded by any proof is what is called in ordinary human beings a dream, and in prophets inspiration. The eternal will and eternal knowledge are the causes of this nature in existents. And this is the meaning of

---

6 'Zaid' is used as a name for whomever you please.

the Divine Words: "Say that none in the heavens or on the earth know the occult but God alone." This nature is sometimes necessary and sometimes what happens in most cases. Dreams and inspiration are only, as we said, the announcement of this nature in possible things, and the sciences which claim the prognostication of future events possess only rare traces of the influences of this nature or constitution or whatever you wish to call it, namely that which is actualized in itself and to which the knowledge attaches itself.

Ghazali says:

The second answer – and in it is to be found deliverance from these reprehensible consequences – is to agree that in fire there is created a nature which burns two similar pieces of cotton which are brought into contact with it and does not differentiate between them, when they are alike in every respect. But still we regard it as possible that a prophet should be thrown into the fire and not burn, either through a change in the quality of the fire or through a change in the quality of the prophet, and that either through God or through the angels there should arise a quality in the fire which limited its heat to its own body, so that it did not go beyond it, but remained confined to it, keeping, however, to the form and the reality of the fire, without its heat and influence extending beyond it; or that there should arise in the body of the person an attribute, which did not stop the body from being flesh and bone, but still defended it against the action of the fire. For we can see a man rub himself with talc and sit down in a lighted oven and not suffer from it; and if one had not seen it, one would deny it, and the denial of our opponents that it lies in God's power to confer on the fire or the body an attribute which prevents it from being burnt is like the denial of one who has not seen the talc and its effect. For strange and marvelous things are in the power of God, many of which we have not seen, and why should we deny their possibility and regard them as impossible?

And also the bringing back to life of the dead and the changing of a stick into a serpent are possible in the following way: matter can receive any form, and therefore earth and the other elements can be changed into a plant, and a plant, when an animal eats it, can be changed into blood, then blood can be changed into sperm, and then sperm can be thrown into the womb and take the character of an animal. This, in the habitual course of nature, takes place over a long space of time, but why does our opponent declare it impossible that matter should pass through these different phases in a shorter period than is usual, and when once a shorter period is allowed there is no limit to its being shorter and shorter, so that these potencies can always become quicker in their action and eventually arrive at the stage of being a miracle of a prophet.

And if it is asked: "Does this arise through the soul of the prophet or through another principle at the instigation of the prophet?" – we answer: Does what you acknowledge may happen through the power of the prophet's soul, like the downpour of rain or the falling of a thunderbolt or earthquakes, does that occur through him or through another principle? What we say about the facts which we have mentioned is like what you say about those facts which you regard as possible. And the best method according to both you and us is to relate these things to God, either immediately or through the intermediation of the angels. But at the time these occurrences become real, the attention of the prophet turns to such facts, and the order of the good determines its appearance to ensure the duration of the order of religion, and this gives a preponderance to the side of existence. The fact in itself is possible, and the principle in God is His magnanimity; but such a fact only emanates from Him when necessity gives a preponderance to its existence and the good determines it, and the good only determines it when a prophet needs it to establish his prophetic office for the promulgation of the good.

And all this is in accordance with the theory of the philosophers and follows from it for them, since they allow to the prophet a particular characteristic which distinguishes him from common people. There is no intellectual criterion for the extent of its possibility, but there is no need to declare it false when it rests on a good tradition and the religious law states it to be true. Now, in general, it is only the sperm which accepts the form of animals – and it receives its animal potencies only from the angels, who according to the philosophers, are the principles of existents – and only a human being can be created from the sperm of a man, and only a horse from the sperm of a horse, in so far as the actualization of the sperm through the horse determines the preponderance of the analogous form of a horse over all other forms, and it accepts only the form to which in this way the preponderance is given, and therefore barley never grows from wheat or an apple from a pear. Further, we see that certain kinds of animal are only produced by spontaneous generation from earth[7] and never are generated by procreation – e.g. worms, and some which are produced both spontaneously and by procreation like the mouse, the serpent, and the scorpion, for their generation can come also from earth. Their disposition to accept forms varies through causes unknown to us, and it is not in human power to ascertain them, since those forms do not, according to the philosophers, emanate from the angels by their good pleasure or haphazard, but in every substratum only in such a way that a form arises for whose acceptance it is specially determined through its own disposition. These dispositions differ, and their principles are, according to the philosophers, the aspects of the stars and the different relative positions of the heavenly bodies in their movements. And through this the possibility is open that there may be in the principles of these dispositions wonderful and marvelous things, so that those who understand talismans through their knowledge of the particular qualities of minerals and of the stars succeed in combining the heavenly potencies with those mineral peculiarities, and make shapes of these earthly substances, and seek a special virtue for them and produce marvelous things in the world through them. And often they drive serpents and scorpions from a country, and sometimes bugs, and they do other things which are known to belong to the science of talismans.

And since there is no fixed criterion for the principles of these dispositions, and we cannot ascertain their essence or limit them, how can we know that it is impossible that in certain bodies dispositions occur to change their phases at a quicker rhythm, so that such a body would be disposed to accept a form for the acceptance of which it was not prepared before, which is claimed to be a miracle? There is no denying this, except through a lack of understanding and an unfamiliarity with higher things and oblivion of the secrets of God in the created world and in nature. And he who has examined the many wonders of the sciences does not consider in any way impossible for God's power what is told of the wonders of the prophets.

Our opponents may say: "We agree with you that everything possible is in the power of God, and you theologians agree with us that the impossible cannot be done and that there are things whose impossibility is known and things which are known to be possible, and that there are also things about which the understanding is undecided and which it does not hold to be either impossible or possible. Now what according to you is the limit of the impossible? If the impossible includes nothing but the simultaneous affirmation and negation of the same thing, then say that of two things the one is not the other, and that the existence of the one does not demand the existence of the other. And say then that God can create will without knowledge of the thing willed, and knowledge without life, and that He can move the hand of a dead man and make him sit and write volumes with his hand and engage himself in sciences while he has his eye open and his looks are fixed on his work, although he does not see and there is no life in him and he has no power, and it is God alone who creates all these ordered actions with the moving of the dead man's hand, and the movement comes from God. But by regarding this as possible the difference between voluntary action and a reflex action like shivering is destroyed, and a judicious act will no longer indicate that the agent possesses knowledge or power. It will then be necessary that God should be able to bring about a change from one genus to another and transform the substance into an accident and knowledge into power and black into white and a voice into an odor, just as He is able to change the inorganic into an animal and a stone into gold, and it will then follow that God can also bring about other unlimited impossibilities."

The answer to this is to say that the impossible cannot be done by God, and the impossible consists in the simultaneous affirmation and negation of a thing, or the affirmation of the more particular with the negation of the more general, or the affir-

---

7 I.e., they are not produced by reproduction. This mistaken theory persisted through the middle ages.

mation of two things with the negation of one of them, and what does not refer to this is not impossible and what is not impossible can be done. The identification of black and white is impossible, because by the affirmation of the form of black in the substratum the negation of the form of white and of the existence of white is implied; and since the negation of white is implied by the affirmation of black, the simultaneous affirmation and negation of white is impossible. And the existence of a person in two places at once is only impossible because we imply by his being in the house that he cannot be in another place, and it cannot be understood from the denial that he is in another place that he can be simultaneously both in another place and in the house. And in the same way by will is implied the seeking of something that can be known, and if we assume a seeking without knowledge there cannot be a will and we would then deny what we had implied. And it is impossible that in the inorganic knowledge should be created, because we understand by inorganic that which does not perceive, and if in the organic perception was created it would become impossible to call it inorganic in the sense in which this word is understood.

As to the transformation of one genus into another, some theologians affirm that it is in the power of God, but we say that for one thing to become another is irrational; for, if for instance, the black could be transformed into power, the black would either remain or not, and if it does not exist any more, it is not changed but simply does not exist any more and something else exists; and if it remains existent together with power, it is not changed, but something else is brought in relation to it, and if the black remains and power does not exist, then it does not change, but remains as it was before. And when we say that blood changes into sperm, we mean by it that this identical matter is divested of one form[8] and invested with another; and it amounts to this, that one form becomes non-existent and another form comes into existence while the matter remains, and that two forms succeed one another in it. And when we say that water becomes air through being heated, we mean by it that the matter which had received the form of the

water is deprived of this form and takes another, and not the matter common to them but the attribute changes. And it is the same when we say that the stick is changed into a serpent or earth into an animal. But there is no matter common to the accident and the substance, nor to black and to power, nor to the other categories, and it is impossible for this reason that they should be changed into each other.

As to God's moving the hand of a dead man, and raising this man up, in the form of a living one who sits and writes, so that through the movement of his hand a well-ordered script is written, this in itself is not impossible as long as we refer events to the will of a voluntary being, and it is only to be denied because the habitual course of nature is in opposition to it. And your affirmation, philosophers, that, if this is so, the judiciousness of an act no longer indicates that the agent possesses knowledge is false, for the agent in this case is God; He determines the act and He performs it. And as to your assertion that if this is so there is no longer any difference between shivering and voluntary motion, we answer that we know this difference only because we experience in ourselves the difference between these two conditions, and we find thereby that the differentiating factor is power, and know that of the two classes of the possible the one happens at one time, the other at another; that is to say, we produce movement with the power to produce it at one time, and a movement without this power at another. Now, when we observe other movements than ours and see many well-ordered movements, we attain knowledge of the power behind them, and God creates in us all these different kinds of knowledge through the habitual course of events, through which one of the two classes of possibility becomes known, though the impossibility of the second class is not proved thereby.

I say:

When Ghazali saw that the theory – that with respect to everything things have no particular qualities and forms from which particular acts follow – is very objectionable, and contrary to com-

---

8 See glossary entry for 'form/matter.'

mon sense, he conceded this in this last section and replaced it by the denial of two points: first that a thing can have these qualities but that they need not act on a thing in the way they usually act on it, e.g. fire can have its warmth but need not burn something that is brought near to it, even if it is usually burnt when fire is brought near to it; secondly that the particular forms have not a particular matter in every object.

The first point can be accepted by the philosophers, for because of external causes the procession of acts from agents may not be necessary, and it is not impossible that for instance fire may sometimes be brought near cotton without burning it, when something is placed with the cotton that makes it non-inflammable, as Ghazali says in his instance of talc and a living being.

As to the point that matter is one of the conditions for material things, this cannot be denied by the theologians, for, as Ghazali says, there is no difference between our simultaneous negation and affirmation of a thing and our simultaneous denial of part of it and affirmation of the whole. And since things consist of two qualities, a general and a particular – and this is what the philosophers mean by the term *definition*, a definition being composed according to them of a genus and a specific difference[9] – it is indifferent for the denial of an existent which of its two qualities is denied. For instance, since human being consists of two qualities, one being a general quality, viz. animality, and the second a particular, viz. rationality, human remains human just as little when we take away his animality as when we take away his rationality, for animality is a condition of rationality and when the condition is removed the conditioned is removed equally.

On this question the theologians and the philosophers agree, except that the philosophers believe that for particular things the general qualities are just as much a condition as the particular, and this the theologians do not believe; for the philosophers, for instance, warmth and moisture are a condition of life in the transient, because they are more general than life, just as life is a condition of rationality. But the theologians do not believe this, and

so you hear them say: "For us dryness and moisture are not a condition of life." For the philosophers shape, too, is one of the particular conditions of life in an organic being; if not, one of two following cases might arise: either the special shape of the animal might exist without exercising any function, or this special shape might not exist at all. For instance, for the philosophers the hand is the organ of the intellect, and by means of it man performs his rational acts, like writing and the carrying on of the other arts; now if intelligence were possible in the inorganic, it would be possible that intellect might exist without performing its function, and it would be as if warmth could exist without warming the things that are normally warmed by it. Also, according to the philosophers, every existent has a definite quantity and a definite quality, and also the time when it comes into existence and during which it persists are determined, although in all these determinations there is, according to the philosophers, a certain latitude.

Theologians and philosophers agree that the matter of existents which participate in one and the same matter sometimes accepts one of two forms and sometimes its opposite, as happens, according to them, with the forms of the four elements,[10] fire, air, water, and earth. Only in regard to the things which have no common matter or which have different matters do they disagree whether some of them can accept the forms of others – for instance, whether something which is not known by experience to accept a certain form except through many intermediaries can also accept this ultimate form without intermediaries. For instance, the plant comes into existence through composition out of the elements; it becomes blood and sperm through being eaten by an animal and from sperm and blood comes the animal, as is said in the Divine Words: "We created man from an extract of clay, then We made him a clot in a sure depository" and so on till His words "and blessed be God, the best of creators." The theologians affirm that the soul of a human being can inhere in earth without the intermediaries known by experience, whereas the philosophers deny this and say that, if this were possible, wisdom would consist in the creation of a

9 See glossary entry for 'specific difference.'
10 See glossary entry for 'element.'

human being without such intermediaries, and a creator who created in such a way would be the best and most powerful of creators; both parties claim that what they say is self-evident, and neither has any proof for its theory. And you, reader, consult your heart; it is your duty to believe what it announces, and this is what God – who may make us and you into persons of truth and evidence – has ordained for you.

But some of the Muslims have even affirmed that there can be attributed to God the power to combine the two opposites, and their dubious proof is that the judgement of our intellect that this is impossible is something which has been impressed on the intellect, whereas if there had been impressed on it the judgement that this is possible, it would not deny this possibility, but admit it. For such people it follows as a consequence that neither intellect nor existents have a well-defined nature, and that the truth which exists in the intellect does not correspond to the existence of existing things. The theologians themselves are ashamed of such a theory, but if they held it, it would be more consistent with their point of view than the contradictions in which their opponents involve them on this point. For their opponents try to find out where the difference lies between what as a matter of fact the

theologians affirm on this point and what they deny, and it is very difficult for them to make this out – indeed they do not find anything but vague words. We find, therefore, that those most expert in the art of theological discussion take refuge in denying the necessary connexion between condition and conditioned, between a thing and its definition, between a thing and its cause and between a thing and its sign. All this is full of sophistry and is without sense, and the theologian who did this was Abu-l-Ma'ali.[11]

The general argument which solves these difficulties is that existents are divided into opposites and correlates, and if the latter could be separated, the former might be united, but opposites are not united and correlates therefore cannot be separated. And this is the wisdom of God and God's course in created things, and you will never find in God's course any alteration. And it is through the perception of this wisdom that the intellect of man becomes intellect, and the existence of such wisdom in the eternal intellect is the cause of its existence in reality. The intellect therefore is not a possible entity which might have been created with other qualities, as Ibn Hazm[12] imagined.

---

11 Juwaini, surnamed the Imam of the two Holy Towns, an Ash'arite and the teacher of al-Ghazali.
12 An important Islamic philosopher, 994-1064, who held an extreme view of God's powers.

I.5. ST. THOMAS AQUINAS

THE ROLE OF WHAT WAS CALLED RELATIVE NECESSITY IN THIS SECTION'S Introduction is evident in Aquinas's thinking about necessity and contingency in things. Things are necessary relative to God's intention to create them – somewhat as a trip to Banff is necessary relative to someone's intention to make the trip there. As Aquinas writes below, nothing prevents the non-necessary production of certain principles, for example an animal being composed of contraries. Relative to that constitution the death of an animal is necessary.

It would be consistent with Aristotle's modal logic and with the metaphysical and logical thinking of Avicenna to hold that every actual thing is necessary relative to a respect which can be traced to a respect in the First Cause, relative to which, therefore, the actual thing is necessary. For if C is necessary relative to some aspect or part of B and if B is necessary relative to some aspect or part of A, then C is necessary relative to some part or aspect of A.

If the First Cause is pure actuality, in what respect can the first effect be contingent? The traveller's trip to Banff is necessary relative to his decision, to be sure, but contingent relative to his power, strength and time; for he could have gone to Jasper instead. If the first effect is to be contingent in any respect whatsoever, it must be so relative to some aspect of the First Cause not included in the act of the divine will to create just this effect and no other. There must therefore be a distinction between the act of will and the power or capacity to will.

This difficulty is explored by Aquinas in selection **I.5.3.** below. It would seem to follow that there is potency in the will of God, which would consequently not be the substance of God, in which there is no potency.

I.5.1. How absolute Necessity can exist in Created Things (*Summa Contra Gentiles* II, 30)

Chapter 30

[1] Although all things depend on the will of God as first cause, who is subject to no necessity in His operation except on the supposition of His intention, nevertheless absolute necessity is not on this account excluded from things, so as to compel us to say that all things are contingent. (One might infer this from the fact that things have, with no absolute necessity, proceeded from their cause; for usually, in things, an effect is contingent which does not proceed from its cause necessarily.) On the contrary, there are some things in the universe whose being is simply and absolutely necessary.

[2] Such is the being of things wherein there is no possibility of not-being. Now, some things are so created by God that there is in their nature a potentiality to non-being; and this results from the fact that the matter present in them is in potentiality with respect to another form.[1] On the other hand, neither immaterial things, nor things whose matter is not receptive of another form, have potentiality to non-being, so that their being is absolutely and simply necessary.

[3] Now, if it be said that whatever is from nothing of itself tends toward nothing, so that in all creatures there is the power not to be – this clearly does not follow. For created things are said to tend to nothing in the same way in which they are from nothing, namely, not otherwise than according to the power of their efficient cause. In this sense,

---

1 See glossary entry for 'form/matter.'

then, the power not to be does not exist in created things. But in the Creator there is the power to give them being, or to cease pouring forth being into them, for He produces things not by a necessity of His nature, but by His will, as we have shown.

[4] Moreover, it is because created things come into being through the divine will that they are necessarily such as God willed them to be. Now, the fact that God is said to have produced things voluntarily, and not of necessity, does not preclude His having willed certain things to be which are of necessity and others which are contingently, so that there may be an ordered diversity in things. Therefore, nothing prevents certain things that are produced by the divine will from being necessary.

[5] Then, too, it pertains to God's perfection to have placed the seal of His own likeness upon created things, excluding only entities incompatible with the nature of created being; for it belongs to the perfect agent to produce its like as far as possible. But to be simply necessary is not incompatible with the notion of created being; for nothing prevents a thing being necessary whose necessity nevertheless has a cause, as in the case of the conclusions of demonstrations. Hence, nothing prevents certain things being produced by God in such fashion that they exist in a simply necessary way; indeed, this is a proof of God's perfection.

[6] Again. The more distant a thing is from that which is a being by virtue of itself, namely, God, the nearer it is to non-being; so that the closer a thing is to God, the further is it removed from non-being. Now, things which presently exist are near to non-being through having potentiality to non-being. Therefore, that the order of things be complete, those nearest to God, and hence the most remote from non-being, must be totally devoid of potentiality to non-being; and such things are necessary absolutely. Thus, some created things have being necessarily.

[7] And so we must bear in mind that if the universe of created things be considered as deriving from their first principle, then they are seen to depend on a will, and on no necessity of their principle, except a suppositional one, as we have said. On the other hand, if created things be considered in relation to their proximate principles, they are found to have absolute necessity. For nothing prevents the non-necessary production of certain principles on the supposition of which such and such an effect nevertheless follows necessarily; the death of this animal is an absolutely necessary consequence of its being composed of contraries, although it was not absolutely necessary for it to be composed of contraries. Similarly, the production of such and such natures by God was voluntary; but, having been so constituted, something having absolute necessity comes forth from them or exists as a result.

[8] In created things, however, there are diverse modes of necessity arising from diverse causes. For, since a thing cannot be without its essential principles, which are matter and form, whatever belongs to a thing by reason of its essential principles must have absolute necessity in all cases.

[9] Now, from these principles, so far as they are principles of existing there arises a threefold absolute necessity in things. *First*, through the relation of a thing's principles to its act of being. Since matter is by its nature a being in potentiality, and since that which can be can also not be, it follows that certain things, in relation to their matter, are necessarily corruptible – animals because they are composed of contraries, fire because its matter is receptive of contraries. On the other hand, form is by its nature act, and through it things exist in act; so that from it there results in some things a necessity to be. And this happens either because those things are forms not existing in matter, so that there is no potentiality to non-being in them, but rather by their forms they are always able to be, as in the case of separate substances;[2] or because their forms equal in their perfection the total potentiality of their matter, so that there remains no potentiality to another form, nor consequently, to non-being; such is the case with the heavenly bodies. But in things whose form does not fulfill the total potentiality of the matter, there still remains in the matter potentiality to another form; and hence in such things there is no necessity to be; rather, the power to be is in them the result of the victory of form over matter, as we see in the elements and

---

2 See glossary entry for 'separate substance.'

things composed of them. The form of an element does not embrace the matter in its total potentiality, for matter receives the form of one element only by being made subject to one of two contraries; but the form of a mixed body[3] embraces the matter according as it is disposed by a certain kind of mixture. Now, contraries, and all intermediaries resulting from the mixture of extremes, must have a common identical subject. The manifest consequence of this fact is that all things which either have contraries or are composed of contraries are corruptible, whereas things not of this sort are everlasting – unless they be corrupted accidentally, as forms which are not subsistent but which exist by being in matter.

[10] *Secondly*, from essential principles of things absolute necessity arises in them from the order of the parts of their matter or of their form, if it happens that in certain things these principles are not simple. For, since a human being's proper matter is a mixed body, having a certain temperament and endowed with organs, it is absolutely necessary that a human being have in himself each of the elements and humours and principal organs. Even so, if a human being is a rational mortal animal, and this is his nature or form, then it is necessary for him to be both animal and rational.

[11] *Thirdly*, there is absolute necessity in things from the order of their essential principles to the properties flowing from their matter or form; a saw, because it is made of iron, must be hard; and a human being is necessarily capable of learning.

[12] However, the agent's necessity has reference both to the action itself and the resulting effect. Necessity in the former case is like the necessity that an accident[4] derives from essential principles; just as other accidents result from the necessity of essential principles, so does action from the necessity of the form by which the agent actually exists; for as the agent actually is, so does it act. But this necessitation of action by form is different in the case of action that remains in the agent itself, as understanding and willing, and in action which

passes into something else, as heating. In the first case, the necessity of the action itself results from the form by which the agent is made actual, because in order for this kind of action to exist, nothing extrinsic, as a terminus for it, is required. Thus, when the power for sense perception is actualized by the sensible species,[5] it necessarily acts; and so, too, does the intellect when it is actualized by the intelligible species. But in the second case, the action's necessity results from the form, so far as the power to act is concerned; if fire is hot, it necessarily has the power of heating yet it need not heat, for something extrinsic may prevent it. Nor in this question does it make any difference whether by its form one agent alone suffices to carry out an action, or whether many agents have to be assembled in order to perform a single action – as, for example, many men to pull a boat – because all are as one agent, who is put in act by their being united together in one action.

[13] Now, the necessity in the effect or thing moved, resulting from the efficient or moving cause, depends not only on the efficient cause, but also on the condition of the thing moved and of the recipient of the agent's action; for the recipient is either in no way receptive of the effect of such action – as wool to be made into a saw – or else its receptivity is impeded by contrary agents or by contrary dispositions in the movable or by contrary forms, to such an extent that the agent's power is ineffective; a feeble heat will not melt iron. In order that the effect follow, it is therefore necessary that receptivity exist in the recipient,[6] and that the recipient be under the domination of the agent, so that the latter can transform it to a contrary disposition. And if the effect in the patient resulting from the agent's victory over it is contrary to the natural disposition of the recipient, then there will be necessity by way of violence, as when a stone is thrown upwards. But if the effect is not contrary to the natural disposition of its subject, there will be necessity not of violence, but of natural order; the movement of the heaven, for example, results from

---

3 I.e., a body composed of a mixture of elements.
4 See glossary entry for 'accident.'
5 See glossary entry for 'species.'
6 See glossary entry for 'agent/recipient.'

an extrinsic active principle,[7] and yet it is not contrary to the natural disposition of the movable subject, and hence is not a violent but a natural movement. This is true also in the alteration of lower bodies by the heavenly bodies, for there is a natural inclination in lower bodies to receive the influence of higher bodies. Such is the case, also, in the generation of the elements;[8] for the form to be engendered is not contrary to prime matter, which is the subject of generation, although it is contrary to the form that is to be cast aside; for matter existing under a contrary form is not the subject of generation.

[14] It is therefore clear from what we have said that the necessity which arises from an efficient cause in some cases depends on the disposition of the agent alone; but in others, on the disposition of both agent and patient. Consequently, if this disposition, according to which the effect follows of necessity, be absolutely necessary both in the agent and in the patient, then there will be absolute necessity in the efficient cause, as with things that act necessarily and always. On the other hand, if this disposition be not absolutely necessary, but removable, then from the efficient cause no necessity will result, except on the supposition that both agent and patient possess the disposition necessary for acting. Thus, we find no absolute necessity in those things that are sometimes impeded in their activity either through lack of power or the violent action of a contrary; such things, then, do not act always and necessarily, but in the majority of cases.

[15] The final cause[9] is responsible for a twofold necessity in things. In one way, necessity results from that cause inasmuch as it is first in the intention of the agent. And in this regard, necessity derives from the end in the same way as from the agent; for it is precisely so far as an agent intends an end that an agent acts. This is true of natural as well as voluntary actions. For in natural things the intention of the end belongs to the agent in keeping with the latter's form, whereby the end is appropriate to it; hence, the natural thing necessarily tends to its end in accordance with the power of its form; a heavy body tends toward the center according to

the measure of its gravity. And in voluntary things the will inclines to act for the sake of an end only so far as it intends that end, although the will, as much as it desires the end, is not always inclined to do this or that as means to it, when the end can be obtained not only by this or that means, but in several ways. Now, in another way, necessity follows from the end as posterior in actual being; and such necessity is not absolute, but conditional. Thus, we say that a saw will have to be made of iron if it is to do the work of a saw.

I.5.2. That God does not will other things in a necessary way (*Summa Contra Gentiles* I, 31)

Chapter 31

[1] But, if the divine will of necessity wills the divine goodness and the divine being, it might seem to someone that it wills of necessity other things as well, since God wills all other things in willing His own goodness, as was proved above. Nevertheless, if we consider the matter correctly, it appears that He does not will other things necessarily.

[2] For God wills other things as ordered to the end of His goodness. But the will is not directed to what is for the sake of the end if the end can be without it. For, on the basis of his intention to heal, a doctor does not necessarily have to give to a sick person the medicine without which the sick person can nevertheless be healed. Since, then, the divine goodness can be without other things, and, indeed, is in no way increased by other things, it is under no necessity to will other things from the fact of willing its own goodness.

[3] Furthermore, since the understood good is the object of the will, the will can will anything conceived by the intellect in which the nature of the good is present. Hence, although the being of any given thing is as such a good and its non-being an evil, the non-being of something can fall under the will (though not by necessity) because of some adjoined good that is preserved; since it is a good that something be, even though something else does not exist. Therefore, according to its own

7 See glossary entry for 'final cause.'
8 See glossary entry for 'element.'
9 See glossary entry for 'final cause.'

nature, the will cannot not will that good whose non-existence causes the nature of the good entirely to be lost. But there is no such good apart from God. According to its nature, therefore, the will can will the non-existence of anything whatever apart from God. But in God will is present according to its whole range, since all things in Him are universally perfect. God, therefore, can will the non-existence of anything whatever apart from Himself. Hence, it is not of necessity that things other than Himself exist.

[4] Moreover, God, in willing His own goodness, wills things other than Himself to be in so far as they participate in His goodness. But, since the divine goodness is infinite, it can be participated in in infinite ways, and in ways other than those by which it is participated in by the creatures that now exist. If, then, as a result of willing His own goodness, God necessarily willed the things that participate in it, it would follow that He would will the existence of an infinity of creatures participating in His goodness in an infinity of ways. This is patently false, because, if He willed them, they would be, since His will is the principle of being for things, as will be shown later on. Therefore, God does not necessarily will even the things that now exist.

[5] Again, the will of a wise man, by the fact of dealing with a cause, deals also with the effect that necessarily follows from the cause. For it would be foolish to wish the sun to be overhead and yet that it should not be daylight. But, as to an effect that does not follow of necessity from a cause, it is not necessary that someone will it because he wills the cause. Now, other things proceed from God without necessity, as will be shown later on. It is not necessary, therefore, that God will other things from the fact of willing Himself.

[6] Moreover, things proceed from God as artifacts from an artisan, as will be shown later on. But, although the artisan wishes to have the art, he does not necessarily wish to produce the artifacts. Neither, therefore, does God necessarily will that there be things other than Himself.

[7] We must therefore consider why it is that God necessarily knows things other than Himself, but does not necessarily will them, even though from

the fact that He understands and wills Himself He understands and wills other things. The reason is as follows. That he who understands should understand something arises from the fact that he is disposed in a certain way, since something is understood in act in so far as its likeness is in the one understanding. But that he who wills should will something arises from the fact that what is willed is disposed in a certain way. For we will something either because it is the end or because it is ordered to the end. Now, that all things be in God, so that they can be understood in Him, is necessarily required by the divine perfection; but the divine goodness does not necessarily require that other things exist, which are ordered to it as to the end. That is why it is necessary that God know other things, but not necessary that He will them. Hence, neither does God will all the things that can have an order[10] to His goodness; but He knows all things that have any order whatever to His essence, by which He understands.

I.5.3. Difficulties in the Concept of Will (*Summa Contra Gentiles* I, 82-83)

Chapter 82

[1] Awkward consequences seem to follow if God does not will necessarily the things that He wills.

[2] For, if with respect to certain objects the will of God is not determined to them, it would seem to be disposed to opposites. But every power that is disposed to opposites is in a manner in potency, since "to opposites" is a species of the contingent possible. Therefore, there is potency in the will of God, which will consequently not be the substance of God, in which there is no potency, as was shown above.

[3] If being in potency, as such, is of a nature to be moved, because what can be can not-be, it follows that the divine will is changeable.

[4] Furthermore, if it is natural to God to will something about His effects, it is necessary. Now there can be nothing unnatural in God, since there cannot be anything accidental or violent in Him, as was proved above.

---

10 See glossary entry for 'accidental vs. essential order.'

[5] Again, if what is open to opposites, being indifferently disposed, tends no more to one thing than to another unless it be determined by another, it is necessary either that God will none of the things towards which He is disposed to opposites, of which the contrary was proved above, or that God be determined to one effect by another. Thus, there will be something prior to Him, determining Him to one effect.

[6] But of these conclusions none necessarily follows. For to be open to opposites belongs to a certain power in a twofold way: in one way, from the side of itself; in another way, from the side of its object. From the side of itself, when it has not yet achieved its perfection, through which it is determined to one effect. This openness redounds to the imperfection of a power, and potentiality is shown to be in it; as appears in the case of an intellect in doubt, which has yet not acquired the principles from which to be determined to one alternative. From the side of its object, a certain power is found open to opposites when the perfect operation of the power depends on neither alternative, though both can be. An example is an art which can use diverse instruments to perform the same work equally well. This openness does not pertain to the imperfection of a power, but rather to its eminence, in so far as it dominates both alternatives, and thereby is determined to neither, being open to both. This is how the divine will is disposed in relation to things other than itself. For its end depends on none of the other things, though it itself is most perfectly united to its end. Hence, it is not required that any potentiality be posited in the divine will.

[7] Mutability, similarly, is not required. For, if there is no potentiality in the divine will, God does not thus prefer one of the opposites among His effects as if He should be thought as being in potency to both, so that He first wills both in potency and afterward He wills in act; rather, He wills in act whatever He wills, not only in relation to Himself but also in relation to His effects. The reason rather is that the object willed does not have a necessary order to the divine goodness, which is the proper object of the divine will; just as we call

enunciables,[11] not necessary, but possible when there is not a necessary order of the predicate to the subject. Hence, when it is said, *God wills this effect*, it is manifest that it is not a necessary enunciable but a possible one, not in the sense in which something is said to be possible according to some power, but in the sense in which the possible is that whose existence is neither necessary nor impossible, as the Philosopher teaches in *Metaphysics* v.[12] For example, for a triangle to have two equal sides is a possible enunciable, but not according to some power, since in mathematics there is neither power nor motion. The exclusion of the aforesaid necessity, therefore, does not take away the immutability of the divine will. This Sacred Scripture professes: "But the triumpher in Israel will not spare, and will not be moved to repentance."[13]

[8] However, although the divine will is not determined to its effects, we yet cannot say that it wills none of them, or that in order to will one of them it is determined by an exterior agent. For, since the apprehended good determines the will as its proper object, and the divine intellect is not outside God's will, because both are His essence, if God's will is determined to will something through the knowledge of His intellect, this determination of the divine will will not be due to something extraneous. For the divine intellect apprehends not only the divine being, which is God's goodness, but also other goods, as was shown above. These goods it apprehends as certain likenesses of the divine goodness and essence, not as its principles. And thus, the divine will tends to them as befitting its goodness, not as necessary to it. The same thing happens in the case of our own will. When it is inclined to something as absolutely necessary to the end, it is moved to it with a certain necessity; but when it tends to something only because of a certain befittingness, it tends to it without necessity. Hence, neither does the divine will tend to its effects in a necessary way.

[9] Nor, furthermore, is it necessary because of the foregoing to posit something unnatural in God. For His will wills itself and other things by one and the same act. But its relation to itself is necessary

11 I.e., what is sayable by a declarative sentence.
12 V, 12, 1019b30.
13 I *Kings* 15:29.

and natural, whereas its relation to other things is according to a certain befittingness, not indeed necessary and natural, nor violent and unnatural, but *voluntary*; for the voluntary need be neither natural nor violent.

Chapter 83

[1] From this we may infer that, although among His effects God wills nothing with absolute necessity, yet He does will something with the necessity of supposition.

[2] For it has been shown that the divine will is immutable. Now, if something is found in any immutable being, it cannot afterwards not be; for we say that a thing has moved if it is otherwise disposed now than it was previously. If, then, the divine will is immutable, assuming that it wills something, God must by supposition will this thing.

[3] Again, everything eternal is necessary. Now, that God should will some effect to be is eternal, for, like His being, so, too, His willing is measured by eternity, and is therefore necessary. But it is not necessary considered absolutely, because the will of

God does not have a necessary relation to this willed object. Therefore, it is necessary by supposition.

[4] Furthermore, whatever God could He can, for His power is not decreased, as neither is His essence. But He cannot now not will what He is posited as having willed, because His will cannot be changed. Therefore, at no time could He not will what He has willed. It is therefore necessary by supposition that He willed whatever He willed, and also that He wills it; neither, however, is absolutely necessary, but, rather, possible in the aforementioned way.

[5] Moreover, whoever wills something, necessarily wills whatever is necessarily required for it, unless there be a defect in him either because of ignorance or because he is led astray through passion from the right choice of that which leads to the intended end. This cannot be said of God. If God, then, in willing Himself wills something other than Himself, it is necessary that He will for this object whatever is necessarily required by it. Thus, it is necessary that God will the rational soul to exist supposing that He wills human being to exist.

I.6. SIGER OF BRABANT

THE FOLLOWING SELECTION FROM THE WRITINGS OF SIGER CONCERNS Aristotle's account of the necessary, selection **I.1.2.** above. The selection is drawn from Siger's lectures on Aristotle's *Metaphysics*.

I.6.1. Commentary on Necessity

[Aristotle says:] The necessary is said to be that without which something does not come about."[1]

In this part the Philosopher distinguishes the name 'necessary' which mentions a condition of a principle and a cause; since even its definition does not determine the subject-matter, it pertains, on that account, to the consideration of the philosopher. And in the first place [Aristotle] posits four modes; in the second, he reduces three of them to the fourth as to the primary mode.

The first mode is when something is said to be necessary for something because it is a co-cause for its being, as breathing is necessary for an animal because it is a co-cause for living. And that is necessary from a supposition. For it is not simply necessary for an animal to breathe but from this supposition: if it is to live.

The second mode is when something is said to be necessary either for acquiring some good or for being good or for removing something bad. For example, we say that drinking a relaxing medicine is necessary in order for someone not to suffer or to be sick; going to a certain place or square is necessary in order to receive money. This too is similarly necessary from the supposition of an end: for the end imposes necessity upon those things which exist for the end, as appears from *Physics* II 9. For this reason those things which exist for an end are necessary not simply but by supposing there either is or will be an end.

The third mode is that according to which the violent is said to be necessary and violence to be a kind of necessity; hence it is said that necessity makes one do something when that something implies violence. He explains what the violent is or what violence is when he says that it impedes and prohibits beyond impetus and intention, producing force, indeed being force.

Concerning this it should be understood that since there are two *per se* agencies, nature and setting something forth, and since every agent has some inclination to action, that inclination to function in natural agents is called impetus and what comes from setting something forth in agents is called intention. And again something is said to be impeded when something begins and stops after having begun; but something is said to be prohibited when it does not begin motion or action although intending it. So that which impedes and prohibits the intention of anyone brings violence to it; similarly he who impedes and prohibits a natural impetus is violating; the violating is not simply necessary but from a supposition, as in comparison with forcing.

Two corollaries can consequently be concluded. The first is that the necessary is painful and in another way conversely that what is painful is against the will and as such is necessary, as Sophocles says. The second is that necessity is not something to be inveighed against: for that is to be complained of and inveighed against which arises in accord with the will (not however as what must be nor when it must be nor in those things in which it must be, etc.). Necessity is something contrary to motion in accord with intention and is not to be complained against in so far as intention acts from violence and compelling necessity.

The fourth mode is that according to which what simply cannot be otherwise is said to be necessary. And this is the primary way in which something is necessary; the word 'necessary' fits this primary sense. And according to the definition of [this sense] of 'necessary' the other things are said to be necessary.

He then explains in what way the other modes of the necessary are reduced to this fourth mode. For

---

1 *Metaphysics* V, 5, 1015a20.

all things are said to be necessary because they cannot be otherwise: the violent is said to be necessary either in doing or in suffering because it is not possible to do or to suffer otherwise, for example according to impetus or intention, on account of being forced. And the same can be said in the second and the third modes: breathing is necessary for an animal to exist because there is no possibility otherwise unless through that being. Medication is similarly necessary lest someone suffer; for it is otherwise impossible to expel the disease.

Consequently, he reduces the necessary arising in various studies to the necessary in the fourth mode; for what is necessary *per se* is contained in it. From this he then concludes three corollaries. For he says that demonstration[2] is a necessary thing, namely as leading to a necessary conclusion which cannot be otherwise and this if it has been demonstrated simply. And this appears from the nature of the demonstration: for a demonstration is from necessary [premises] which simply cannot be otherwise. Therefore, since the conclusion follows from those premises necessarily, the conclusion will be similarly necessary. He consequently concludes three corollaries from this.

[*The first of three Corollaries*]

The first is that some of the necessary things have a cause of their necessity other than themselves and some do not. And this follows from what was just said; for the conclusion of a demonstration, since it is necessary, has its necessity from its premises or principles. But the principles are necessary of themselves. From which it follows that something is a first necessary thing: for since there are some things which of themselves can be and not be, they are never able to have being of themselves. Hence it is necessary, since they are, to have being from that which must be; for they cannot be without a cause sufficient for their being. But if that which must be must be from another, it is not a cause sufficient for being. Therefore if it is required necessarily to posit a cause sufficient for its own being, it is necessary for that to be necessary from itself and not from another. And this is the primary necessary being. It

follows that things capable of being and not being are reduced to that which must be of itself. For if not, there would not be anything which is a sufficient cause among things – which is impossible. There must therefore be a first necessary being among them.

[*The second Corollary*]

The second corollary is that the first and properly necessary being is simple.[3] For if it were not simple, it could exist in many ways; hence it could also be otherwise. Therefore, it would not be necessary in the primary mode. The first therefore follows.

Now that what is necessary in the primary way is entirely simple, can be verified in the following way. In a primary, necessary being there is no passive potentiality. For since act precedes potentiality simply (given that potency precedes act in the same subject), there is no potency from which something moves to act unless from a prior act. So if there were any passive potency in the first necessary being, then that potency would not become actual unless from some prior actuality. But it is impossible for there to be anything prior to the first necessary being. It is therefore impossible that there should be any passive potency in it. It is therefore simple.

For suppose it were composed of many parts. Then since every composite thing has at least a capacity for parts fitting together, since from many entities in actuality a unity does not arise, as is said in [the *Metaphysics* VII, 12], unless perhaps by bonding together, as with a house, there is some potentiality for union and bonding among those many parts. From this it follows that in every composite entity there is necessarily some potentiality. It follows there would be potency in the first being if it were composite. But this is impossible, as has already been shown. Therefore the primary, necessary being is altogether simple.

The same can be proved in the following way. In every being composed of many parts, when it becomes one thing from them, it is necessary for there to be a cause which puts them together and makes them one thing. Now the cause which puts

---

2 See glossary entry for 'demonstration.'
3 I.e., involves no composition of different components.

them together is the efficient cause of the composite being. The composite being, however, cannot be its own efficient cause. Therefore, every composite being has something else as its own productive cause. So since the first necessary being does not have an efficient cause of itself, (for then it would not be necessary in the primary way), it follows that it is not composed. It is therefore simple; for composition argues a cause and similarly potency, and potency being actual argues an efficient cause. Since composition argues a cause which composes many parts, it also argues an efficient cause. So since this cannot be found in the first being, neither can composition be found in it.

And again, it is universally true that what is more simple in any genus[4] is more noble. For if something is simple in any genus, then nothing in that genus is more so; hence nothing is nobler than it is in that genus. An example of this is that fire is [simply] hot; for fire is simple in the genus of hot things and thus is the finest of hot things. Therefore, everything simple in any genus is finer than something composite in that genus. That, therefore, which is most noble among all things universally and at the end of nobility is necessarily simple. So if it were composed, then there would be something simple from which it is composed; it would follow that it would be nobler than the other. But the primary, necessary being is the most noble among the other things, existing at the end of nobility. It is therefore the cause of all other things, as was shown before and the cause is universally more noble than the effect, as Proclus[5] proves. Hence it is altogether simple.

In addition to these reasons Aristotle gives a reason in this connection. He says that if it is not possible for what is primarily necessary to be in many ways, it is simple. From this he appears to suggest that if what is primarily necessary is composite, it would be changeable and able to be in many ways. And so whatever is composed [is not simple]; for if something composed can fail to be in many ways, Aristotle's reasoning would not hold. It should accordingly be understood that, if something is composed, it is changeable in so far as it fits the notion of the composite and, unless something else

prevents it, would be capable of dissolution, just as Aristotle seems to suggest. And this is clear; for the composite from many parts necessarily has a cause which fits the parts together; they would not otherwise become one thing. The component parts do not unify themselves. So with respect to themselves they are able to come apart unless something else prevents it. The notion of dissolution is not inconsistent with that of a composite considered as such, unless something else prevents it.

[The third Corollary]

The third corollary is that there is nothing either beyond the natural, i.e. violent, among things which are *per se* necessary and eternal. And this is apparent from the two preceding corollaries. For nothing can be added to a substance in so far as it is entirely simple; but everything violent in a thing is added to its substance. Indeed that which does not pertain to substance in a thing is added to it; but the violent does not pertain to substance. It follows that there can be nothing violent in something entirely simple. Now the first necessary being is entirely simple; therefore it is not possible for there to be anything violent in it.

The same conclusion is forthcoming from the first corollary: in so far as something must exist of itself, there is no state arising from something else. But the violent arises from something else, being something beyond the impetus and intention of that thing. It follows that it is not possible for the violent to exist in so far as something must exist of itself, as was shown before. Therefore, what is violent or beyond the natural does not exist in it.

And again in the third place this is apparent; for what is simply and primarily necessary cannot be otherwise and is unchangeable. But everything in which there is something violent is moveable and changeable and capable of being otherwise, for example by receiving violence. So in a primary sense and by itself it is necessarily not able to receive the violent nor what is beyond its nature.

---

4 See glossary entry for 'species/genus.'
5 Lived 410-485 C.E. Was the leader of the neo-Platonic school at the time.

Whether the definition of the necessary is well given as: impossible not to be

Since Aristotle defines 'necessary' by means of 'impossible to be otherwise' or 'impossible not to be,' it is asked whether 'necessary' is well defined. Avicenna has his doubts. And it seems that the definition is not well given. (1) Act universally precedes potentiality. But what must be is actual; hence everything eternal and necessary is pure act, as [Aristotle writes in *Metaphysics*] XII, 7. Now the possible to be is potential and is therefore posterior to the necessary. It follows that the impossible too, which is its privation, is posterior to the necessary. Therefore, the necessary is not well defined by means of it.

(2) It can again be argued in the same way as Avicenna does: the necessary signifies the force of being which is actual being without any potentiality. Now being is prior to non-being just as an entity is prior to non-entity. The necessary is therefore badly defined by means of *not to be*.

(3) Again, being is better known than non-being. Now the necessary signifies being since it signifies the force of being according to Avicenna. It is therefore better known than non-being. But what is better known is not to be defined by means of the less well known. It follows that non-being is not to be received into a definition of the necessary. Therefore, the necessary is not to be defined by means of 'impossible not to be,' whether because of 'impossible' or because of 'non-being.'

(4) Again, if 'impossible' is placed in a definition of the necessary, the definition will be circular; for 'impossible' would be defined by means of 'necessary'; the impossible would then be what it is necessary for it not to be. It would follow that the same thing would be defined by means of itself.

Aristotle intends the opposite here and in Book IV he expressly says that the sense of the necessary is impossible not to be.

[*Resolution of the Question*]

It should be said that there are five things which obtain with respect to the order of reason in understanding: in the first place, in relation to mind, is being; then non-being; in the third place the possi-

ble; in the fourth, the impossible, and finally the concept of the necessary or of things necessary. Now it is evident that being is first, as Avicenna says; for it is first of those things which come before our intellect. Next is non-being. Now in what way the others precede the necessary will come clear by resolving the arguments. And since the necessary is posterior to them, all of them can be posited in its definition. For this reason the definition is well given by means of 'impossible' and 'non-being.'

Avicenna thought that the necessary should be prior to the possible and the impossible and should therefore not be defined by means of either one of them. His reason has already been given: the necessary is the force of being and being is prior to any one of the others. He also says that all the ancient philosophers err in thus defining the necessary. He himself has nevertheless erred.

Now since it is argued that actuality precedes potentiality, it should be said that the actuality of any potentiality, in the order of reason, precedes the potentiality itself; indeed for this reason potentiality is defined by means of actuality, for example the visible as what is fit to be seen and the walkable as what can be walked. Still not every actuality precedes its potentiality in the order of reason, as in the above exposition; for the actuality of the necessary is immaterial and is even elevated above sensible things. But our cognition begins from sensible things. It is therefore not required that in the order of reason and in our cognition the necessary should be prior to the impossible which is found among sensible things. It should accordingly be understood, just as the Philosopher says in [*Metaphysics* II, 1] that, since things separated from matter are not known by us, this is not on their side but on ours; for in themselves they are known in a primary way; but since we receive nothing except from sense and sensible things, they are not known to us in a primary way. Thus the definition of the necessary, since it is separated from matter as such, is granted to be absolutely prior to the definition of the possible though not according to the order of our intellect; for the possible alone can be found among sensible things or maximally so, and since sensible things are prior according to the order of our intellect, to this extent too the definition of the possible is prior and consequently the definition of the impossible is prior to the definition of the necessary. And thus the necessary is well defined by means of them.

A similar reply can be made to the second argument: when it is said that the definition of being is prior to that of non-being, it is true that the definition of the being of anything is prior to that of the non-being opposed to it. Non-being is nevertheless able to be prior according to definition and better known than any particular determinate being and consequently better known than any determinate

non-being. But the necessary is not simply or universally that to which non-being is opposed but is rather some determinate being. Therefore it is absolutely and universally defined by means of non-being, and this is better known.

And when it is said in the third place that the definition will be circular, it should be said that this is not true; for he who defines the impossible by means of the necessary defines the prior by means of the posterior.

I.7. THE CONDEMNATION OF 1277

IN DECEMBER OF 1270 ETIENNE TEMPIER, THE BISHOP OF PARIS, condemned thirteen propositions concerning the necessity of events, the eternity of the world and limitations upon divine power and knowledge. Further steps were taken to fight the positions held by Aristotle, Avicenna, and Averroes, as well as positions of the Latin Averroists Siger of Brabant and Boethius of Dacia. On March 7, 1277, Bishop Tempier condemned 219 propositions, many of which are found below in selection **I.7.1.**

One effect of the condemnation is to expand an account of God's power. According to the account under siege God's power is in part defined by causal processes. An accepted part of that definition is the necessity of mediation: between God and a tree, there are many intermediate, causal links or second causes, as they were called. Number 69 below gives us that condemned proposition: "That God cannot produce the effect of a secondary cause without the secondary cause itself."

It is fair to say that the Condemnation of 1277 is a signpost of the road ahead: the waning of the influence of the mixture of Plato and Aristotle as formed into a metaphysical system by Avicenna and the waxing of a system of thought less necessitarian and less dependent upon philosophical reason. The hope of thinkers like Siger for independence between arts and theology was to have delayed fulfillment; the path of the future was to be laid, at least in part, by the work of Duns Scotus and William of Ockham. Much of Plato and Aristotle would nevertheless survive these changes (as the medical work of Avicenna was also to survive).

I.7.1. Extending God's Power

ERRORS IN PHILOSOPHY

On the Nature of Philosophy

1. That there is no more excellent state than to study philosophy. (40)[1]

2. That the only wise men in the world are the philosophers. (154)

3. That in order to have some certitude about any conclusion, man must base himself on self-evident principle. – The statement is erroneous because it refers in a general way both to the certitude of

apprehension and to that of adherence. (151)

4. That one should not hold anything unless it is self-evident or can be manifested from self-evident principles. (37)

5. That man should not be content with authority to have certitude about any question. (150)

6. That there is no rationally disputable question that the philosopher ought not to dispute and determine, because reasons are derived from things. It belongs to the philosopher under one or another of its parts to consider all things. (145)

7. That, besides the philosophic disciplines, all the sciences are necessary but that they are necessary only on account of human custom. (24)

---

1 The numbers enclosed in parentheses at the end indicate the original ordering.

On the Knowability of God

8. That our intellect by its own natural power can attain to a knowledge of the first cause. – This does not sound well and is erroneous if what is meant is immediate knowledge. (211)

9. That we can know God by His essence in this mortal life. (36)

10. That nothing can be known about God except that He is, or His existence. (215)

On the Nature of God

11. That the proposition, "God is being *per se* positively," is not intelligible; rather God is being *per se* privatively. (216)

12. That the intellect by which God understands Himself is by definition different from that by which He understands other things. – This is erroneous because, although the proper reason of His understanding is different in each case, the intellect is not other by definition. (149)

On divine Science

13. That God does not know things other than himself. (3)

14. That God cannot know contingent beings immediately except through their particular and proximate causes. (56)

15. That the first cause does not have science of future contingents. The first reason is that future contingents are not beings. The second is that future contingents are singulars, but God knows by means of an intellectual power, which cannot know singulars. Hence, if there were no senses, the intellect would perhaps not distinguish between Socrates and Plato, although it would distinguish between a man and an ass. The third reason is the relation of cause to effect; for the divine foreknowledge is a necessary cause of the things foreknown. The fourth reason is the relation of science to the known; for even though science is not the cause of the known, it is determined to one of two contradictories by that which is known; and this is true of divine science much more than of ours. (42)

On divine Will and Power

16. That the first cause is the most remote cause of all things. – This is erroneous if so understood as to mean that it is not the most proximate. (190)

17. That what is impossible absolutely speaking cannot be brought about by God or by another agent. – This is erroneous if we mean what is impossible according to nature (147)

18. That what is self-determined, like God, either always acts or never acts; and that many things are eternal. (52)

19. That an active potency that can exist without acting is mixed with passive potency. – This is erroneous if any operation whatsoever is understood here. (68)

20. That God of necessity makes whatever comes immediately from Him. – This is erroneous whether we are speaking of the necessity of coercion, which destroys liberty, or of the necessity of immutability, which implies the inability to do otherwise. (53)

21. That from a previous act of the will nothing new can proceed unless it is preceded by a change. (39)

22. That God cannot be the cause of a newly-made thing and cannot produce anything new. (48)

23. That God cannot move anything irregularly, that is, in a manner other than that in which He does, because there is no diversity of will in Him. (50)

24. That God is eternal in acting and moving, just as He is eternal in existing; otherwise He would be determined by some other thing that would be prior to Him. (51)

25. That God has infinite power, not because He makes something out of nothing, but because He maintains infinite motion. (62)

26. That God has infinite power in duration, not in action, since there is no such infinity except in an infinite body, if there were such a thing. (29)

On the Causation of the World

27. That the first cause cannot make more than one world. (34)

28. That from one first agent there cannot proceed a multiplicity of effects. (44)

29. That the first cause would be able to produce

an effect equal to itself if it did not limit its power. (26)

30. That the first cause cannot produce something other than itself, because every difference between maker and made is through matter. (55)

31. That in heavenly things there are three principles: the subject of eternal motion, the soul of the heavenly body, and the first mover as desired. – The error is in regard to the first two. (95)

32. That there are two eternal principles, namely the body of the heaven and its soul. (94)

On the Nature of the Intelligences

33. That the immediate effect of the first being has to be one only and most like unto the first being. (64)

34. That God is the necessary cause of the first intelligence, which cause being posited, the effect is also posited; and both are equal in duration. (58)

35. That God never created an intelligence more than He now creates it. (28)

36. That the absolutely first unmoved being does not move save through the mediation of something moved, and that such an unmoved mover is a part of that which is moved of itself. (67)

37. That the first principle is not the proper cause of eternal beings except metaphorically, in so far as it conserved them, for unless it was, they would not be. (45)

38. That the intelligences, or separated substances, which they say are eternal, do not have an efficient cause properly speaking, but only metaphorically, in so far as they have a cause conserving them in existence; but they were not newly-made, because then they would be mutable. (70)

39. That all the separated substances are coeternal with the first principle. (5)

40. That everything that does not have matter is eternal, because that which was not made through a change in matter did not exist previously; therefore it is eternal. (80)

41. That the separated substances, having no matter through which they would be in potency before being in act and being from a cause that always exists in the same manner, are therefore eternal. (72)

42. That God cannot multiply individuals of the same species without matter. (96)

43. That God could not make several intelligences of the same species because intelligences do not have matter. (81)

44. That no change is possible in the separated substances; nor are they in potency to anything because they are eternal and free from matter. (71)

45. That the intelligence is made by God in eternity because it is totally immutable; the soul of the heaven, however, is not. (83)

46. That the separated substances are the same as their essences because in them that by which they are and that which they are, is the same. (79)

47. That the science of the intelligence does not differ from its substance, for where there is no distinction between known and knower, there is no distinction of thing known either.

....

53. That an intelligence or an angel or a separated soul is nowhere. (218)

....

On the Heaven and on the Generation of lower Beings

64. That God is the necessary cause of the motion of the higher bodies and of the union and separation occurring in the stars. (59)

....

67. That the first principle cannot produce generable things immediately because they are new effects and a new effect requires an immediate cause that is capable of being otherwise. (54)

68. That the first principle cannot be the cause of diverse products here below without the mediation of other causes, inasmuch as nothing that transforms, transforms in diverse ways without being itself transformed. (43)

69. That God cannot produce the effect of a secondary cause without the secondary cause itself. (63)

70. That God is able to produce contraries, that is, through the medium of a heavenly body which occupies diverse places. (61)

....

76. That the intelligence moving the heaven influences the rational soul, just as the body of the heaven influences the human body. (74)

On the Eternity of the World

83. That the world, although it was made from nothing, was not newly-made, and, although it passed from nonbeing to being, the nonbeing did not precede being in duration but only in nature. (99)

84. That the world is eternal because that which has a nature by which it is able to exist for the whole future has a nature by which it was able to exist in the whole past. (98)

....

On the Necessity and Contingency of Things

93. That some things can take place by chance with respect to the first cause, and that it is false that all things are preordained by the first cause, because they would come about by necessity. (197)

94. That fate, which is the disposition of the universe, proceeds from divine providence, not immediately, but mediately through the motion of the higher bodies, and that this fate does not impose necessity upon the lower beings, since they have contrariety, but upon the higher. (195)

95. That for all effects to be necessary with respect to the first cause, it does not suffice that the first cause itself be not impedible, but it is also necessary that the intermediary causes be not impedible. – This is erroneous because then God could not produce a necessary effect without posterior causes. (60)

....

102. That nothing happens by chance, but everything comes about by necessity, and that all the things that will exist in the future will exist by necessity, and those that will not exist are impossible, and that nothing occurs contingently if all causes are considered. – This is erroneous because the concurrence of causes is included in the definition of chance, as Boethius says in his book *On Consolation.*[2] (21)

....

107. That God was not able to make prime matter save through the mediation of a heavenly body. (38)

---

2 1 V, prose 2.

I.8. HENRY OF GHENT

HENRY OF GHENT TAUGHT AT THE UNIVERSITY OF PARIS FROM 1276-92. He therefore comes just after the Condemnations of 1277 and during the period of the waning of the influence of Avicenna and Averroes and also of the Latin Averroists Siger of Brabant and Boethius of Dacia. Through the Condemnations philosophical notions that treated God and creation in purely philosophical ways were to be cast off in favour of accepted Christian terms. Henry of Ghent was one of the first to accept the challenge of rethinking the relevance of philosophy to theology and of reaffirming the essentials of revelation. It may perhaps be said that his contribution was two-fold: first, the reaffirmation of God's sovereignty as the supremely free and omnipotent creator. Henry rejected the necessitarianism and the strict determinism of Avicenna; he argued rather for the contingency of everything other than God: God does not need intermediaries; he can do anything, and whatever he does is through the freedom of his will. In thus preparing the way for Duns Scotus, Henry nevertheless keeps Avicenna's notion of being as the first object of knowledge.

I.8.1. The Finiteness of the World's Past
(*Quodlibet* VIII, qu. 9)

The species[1] essences of creatures, considered on their own, are all equally possible to be before receiving existence in some individual, for the species of the sun, considered on its own, is just as much a non-being as the species human being, and they equally have eternal existence in the divine knowledge. ...

Therefore, when the species are considered on their own, the species of the sun is not apt to be made by God in its one unique individual, the sun, before the species human being is made in some particular individual, for example in Adam. Likewise the individual which is this sun, taken on its own, is not apt to receive being from God before this individual which is this human, namely Adam, does. For every act of being belonging to a creature depends solely on the will of the creator; otherwise, God would not have been able to have made this human, Adam, before he made the sun. ...

Likewise, God himself, taken on his own, exists in a state that relates indifferently and equally to the alternatives of giving being first to the one species in its one unique individual or to the other species,

... for that he gives it to one and not to the other, or to one before giving it to the other, or gives it to them at the same time, all this proceeds entirely from the decision of his free will. If, then, God was able from eternity to have created the sun, so also he could have from eternity created this human Adam and no other human before him, so that he would be the origin of all other humans. ... Therefore, since in each circling or revolution of the sun either he or someone or some who had come from him would have been able to have engendered more and more humans, and since, given the sun was made from eternity, an infinity of solar revolutions have preceded the revolution the sun is now making, it follows that an infinity of humans have preceded the human engendered in the present revolution. Nevertheless, there would be a first human after whom and from whom all the others have come, as well as a last human who has come after all [the others] and after whom or from whom none have come. Consequently, even though there exists a single first end point and similarly a last one, there would be an infinity of humans in between. This is contrary both to nature and to reason.

For if an infinity of them had existed in between, we would never have gotten from the first end point

---

1 See glossary entry for 'species/genus.'

to the last. If, then, this is clearly false and impossible, that from which it follows is also false and impossible, namely that the first human, Adam, could have been made by God from eternity. Therefore, by a similar argument, it is false and impossible, on the above grounds, for it to have been possible for the sun to have been produced by God from eternity, and this is so even if not this sun [but some other]. ... The same argument works for any individual of any species, and consequently for any species, since a species is makeable only by the making of some individual of that species. Hence, neither was this whole world able to have been made by God from eternity, since it is constituted entirely of individuals belonging to species.

I argue for the same conclusion in a second way as follows: If the creature gets actual being from God, of itself it has possible being ...; for this reason, since unqualified being relates to possible unqualified being just as being from eternity relates to possible being from eternity, if a creature gets being from eternity from God, the creature of itself has possible being from eternity ... even though it does not in fact have being from eternity.

I ask then: Does the creature get the being from eternity it gets from God at exactly the same moment that it gets the possible being and not-being from eternity it gets from itself, or does it first get being from God rather than the reverse, or vice-versa? Not the first, because in that case there would be at the same moment in the same item opposed acts, namely being and not-being. Not the second, because according to Avicenna,[2] "what belongs to a thing on account of itself comes before what belongs to it from something else." The third, then, has to be the case, namely that creatures get from themselves possible being and not-being before they get being from God. ...

I ask: Do the possibility of being in existence and the possibility of not being in existence have being in the essence of a creature at the same moment or does one come earlier and the other later? Not at the same moment, because opposed potentials, according to The Philosopher and The Commentator [Averroes] in *De Caelo* I are completely unable to be at the same moment in the

same thing, just as is also the case for the opposed acts. For, as they say, if the potentials were there at the same moment ..., then it would be possible for the two opposed potentials to be realized in opposed acts, and thus from the assumption of the possible as a fact there would follow an impossible falsehood.

Therefore, in the essence of a creature either the possibility of being in existence precedes the possiblity of not being in existence, or vice versa, and this either by a precedence in nature or in time. But the possibility of being cannot come first in nature, because in nature not-being ... comes before being .... The possibility for not being, then, in nature comes before the possibility of being.

The question remains, which of these comes first in time? For if either one comes first in time, it follows that either this possibility [of being] precedes that one [of not being], or vice versa, or either can precede the other indifferently. This last alternative is impossible, because in that case the essence of the creature would relate in the same way to each of them, and just as it relates to those possibilities so it would relate to their acts. But the essence of a creature does not in fact relate in an equal way to the act of existing and to the act of not-existing, because it is inherently capable of getting its act of existing only from something else, while it gets its act of not existing from itself. ... But if the other [the possibility of being] came first in time, and this necessarily, ... then necessarily the existence of the creature would precede its not-being (and thus the creature would not be ... a non-being of itself in nature before it was a being on account of something else in some time; for anything that belongs to something earlier in nature is inherently going to belong to it earlier in time.) But this is impossible, because, as was said, what belongs to something of itself in nature comes before what belongs to it from something else. ...

Thus the second alternative [that the possibility of not-being precedes in time the possibility of being], must be the case, i.e. necessarily in the temporal being of a creature the possibility for not-being comes first, and consequently its not-being comes first not only in the order of nature but in the order of time as well. ... Therefore, we are left

---

2 *Metaphysics* VIII, 3.

with the conclusion that a creature is able to get being from something other than itself only if it has not-being (which belongs to it of itself) earlier in time. Thus there is no way it can be claimed that it is possible for it to be made from eternity; rather it has to be made in time.

I.9. JOHN DUNS SCOTUS

THE NECESSITARIAN LINE OF THINKING PRESENT IN THE ARISTOTELIAN neo-Platonic synthesis, and condemned in 1277 by Bishop Tempier, was one of Scotus's chief targets of criticism. This emerges here as well as in the selections from Scotus in Topics III and IV. Scotus thinks philosophy can show that there is a first efficient cause that is infinitely perfect, but he also believes that, if that first cause causes what it causes necessarily, there will be no contingency in the world. The "philosophers'" system leads to there being only one possible world – a result the philosophers themselves would have rejected at least for the part of the world where generation and destruction occur. These selections are usefully compared with those of Ockham's that follow, since Ockham criticizes Scotus, with regard to **I.9.2.**, on almost every point.

I.9.1. Proof of a First Cause (*Ordinatio* I, dist.2, pt.1, qu.1-2)

[This selection is part of Scotus's very elaborate proof of the existence of an infinite being; another part of it, the part concerned with the infinity of the First Cause, is found in selection **II.5.1.** Scotus emphasizes the distinction between essentially and accidentally ordered causes, giving on pp.117-8 a detailed differentiation of these. Another distinctively Scotist aspect of the discussion is the contrast between the realm of mere quidditative existence, i.e. of possible entities, and the realm of actual existents. Scotus realizes that after showing there is a first cause in the former further argument is needed to prove it actually exists.]

Now the first conclusion ... is this: Some being which can produce an effect is unqualifiedly first in the sense that it is neither something that can be produced nor something that is capable of producing in virtue of something other than itself.

Proof: Some being can be produced. Therefore, it is either produced by itself or by nothing or by something other than itself. Not by nothing, because what is nothing causes nothing. Also not by itself, for as Augustine points out in *On the Trinity* I,[1] nothing ever makes or begets itself.

Therefore, by something other than itself. Let this other be A. If A is first, in the sense explained above, then I have my intended conclusion. If it is not first, then it is a subsequent producer, either because it is producible by something else or because it is capable of producing in virtue of something else. (If you deny a negation, you get the affirmation.) Grant this other thing, and let it be B. Then we can argue of B just as we did of A. At this point we shall either proceed on to infinity where every [producer] comes after something prior to it, or we come to a stop with something that does not have anything prior to it. But an infinity in an ascending series is impossible; therefore it is necessary to have primacy, since what does not have anything prior to it is not subsequent to anything subsequent to itself, for a circular series of causes is absurd (since in such a series the same thing would be both prior to itself and subsequent to itself).

There are two objections to this argument: The first attacks the idea that there is a stop to the series of causes, because, according to those who philosophize, an infinity is possible in an ascending series; here they posit the example of the infinity of generations, where no generation is first and everyone follows another one; for, according to them, there is no absurdity in carrying the series of productions of the same sort of thing on to infinity.

---

1 c.1, PL 42, 820.

This series is, nevertheless, claimed by them not to be circular.

The second objection is that the argument seems to proceed from contingent premises and thus is not a demonstration.[2] That it proceeds from contingent premises is shown by the fact that the premises assume the existence of something that is caused, but anything that is caused exists contingently. (Also it proceeds from contingents because it proceeds from the notions of a producer and a produced, which are merely contingent terms.)

To exclude the first objection, I say that the philosophers do not claim that an infinity is possible in a series of essentially ordered causes[3] but only in causes that are accidentally ordered. This is clear from Avicenna's *Metaphysics* VI, c.5, where he speaks of an infinity of individuals within a species.

In order to make clearer what we intend to show, it has to be known what essentially ordered and accidentally ordered causes are. Here it should be noted that it is one thing to speak about *per se* causes and accidental causes, and quite another thing to speak about causes that are ordered *per se* or essentially and causes that are ordered accidentally. For in the first case there is just a relationship of one item to one item, i.e. of the cause to what it causes; and that is a *per se* cause which causes in virtue of its own nature and not in virtue of anything accidental to it. (For example, a subject is a *per se* cause of its own distinctive attribute;[4] and there are other cases like 'White pierces' and 'A builder builds.') That is an accidental cause which causes in the reverse way, for example 'Polycletus builds.' In the second case, there is a relationship of two causes to each other insofar as there is something caused by them.

Per se or essentially ordered causes differ from accidentally ordered causes in three respects. The first difference is that in essentially ordered causes the second depends on the first for its act of causing, while in accidentally ordered causes this is not the case, although the second may depend on the first for its existence or in some other way. (A son depends on his father for his existence but is not dependent on his father for the exercise of his causality, since the son can act just as well whether his father be living or dead.) The second difference is that in *per se* ordered causes the causality is of another type and rank, inasmuch as the higher cause is more perfect. But this is not the case in accidentally ordered causes. The second difference is a consequence of the first, since no cause in the exercise of its causality is essentially dependent on a cause of the same type as itself, for in the causation of anything one cause of a given type suffices. The third difference is that all *per se* and essentially ordered causes are simultaneously required for causation to be exercised; otherwise, some essential and *per se* causality would be lacking for the production of the effect. But in accidentally ordered causes this is not the case, because the simultaneity of these causes is not required for the exercise of causation. (This is because each has its own complete causality in respect of its effect without the others, for it suffices that each causes in succession, one after the other.)

From all this we propose to show that an infinity in the series of essentially ordered causes is impossible; secondly, that an infinity in the series of accidentally ordered causes is possible only if there is a stopping point in the series of essentially ordered causes; therefore, an infinity in essentially ordered causes is impossible in any case. Also, even if we deny that there is an essential order of causes, infinity is still impossible. Therefore, no matter what, there is necessarily and unqualifiedly a first productive cause. For the sake of brevity, let us call the first of these three assumptions A, the second B, and the third C.

Proof of A, i.e. that an infinity in the series of essentially ordered causes is impossible: First, because in the series of essentially ordered causes, where our opponent claims there is an infinity, a later member in the series depends for its causality on the first member. (This follows from the first difference [between essentially and accidentally ordered causes].) Consequently, if the series of causes were infinite in such a way that not just any later member of the series but any other as well

---

2 See glossary entry for 'demonstration.'
3 See glossary entry for 'accidental vs. essential order.'
4 See glossary entry for 'attribute.'

depended on a proximate and prior cause of itself, then the whole series of essentially ordered causes would depend on some cause which is not any member of that series, otherwise it would be a cause of itself. For the whole series of dependent causes would depend on something but not on any member of that series itself. And this I call a first productive cause. Thus, if the series is infinite, still it would depend on something which does not belong to that series.

Also, because then there would be an infinity of causes, i.e. essentially ordered ones, simultaneously acting. This follows from the third difference [between essentially and accidentally ordered causes]. (Given that an infinite series of essentially ordered causes concur in the production of some effect, and the third difference which states that all essentially ordered causes exist simultaneously, it follows that an infinity of causes work together at the same time to produce this effect.) This is something no philosopher claims.

Also, because what is prior is nearer to the beginning (see *Metaphysics* V[5]); therefore, where there is no beginning nothing is essentially prior.

Also, fourthly, it follows from the second difference [between essentially and accidentally ordered causes] that the higher cause is more perfect in its causality; therefore, what is infinitely higher is infinitely more perfect and thus possesses infinite perfection in its causality. Consequently, it is not something which causes in virtue of something else, since any such cause causes imperfectly by the fact that it is dependent for its causality on something else.

Also, fifthly, since being productive does not necessarily entail any imperfection, it can be in something without imperfection, for what does not include any imperfection can be posited among beings without imperfection. But if every cause is dependent on something prior to itself, no cause escapes imperfection. Therefore, an independent capacity to produce can belong to some nature, and that nature is unqualifiedly first. Therefore, it is possible to have an unqualifiedly first capacity for production. This is good enough, since later we will infer from this that, given such a first efficient cause is possible, it exists in reality. Thus we have

five arguments that show A.

B, viz. that an infinity in a series of accidentally ordered causes is only possible if there is a stopping point in the series of essentially ordered causes, is proved because, if an accidental infinity occurs, the members do not all occur at the same time, as is obvious, but rather just successively so that one comes after another as though it in some way flowed from the earlier. Nevertheless the later cause does not depend on the earlier for its causality, for it can cause just as well when the earlier does not exist as when it does. For example, a son produces a child just as well when his father is dead as when he is living. Such an infinite succession is only possible if there is a nature that lasts infinitely, on which the whole succession and every member of it depends. For nothing that is less than perfectly formed persists except by the power of some permanent entity which does not belong to that succession. This is because every successive member of that succession is of the same type, and no member of the succession can last as long as the whole succession does, for then it would not be a member of it. Rather, something essentially prior exists, for every member of the succession depends on it, and this dependence belongs to a different ordering from that by which it depends on the immediately preceding cause where the latter is a member of the succession. Therefore, whatever depends on an accidentally ordered cause depends more essentially on a *per se* cause which is essentially ordered. In fact, to deny the essential order is to deny the accidental order also, since accidents do not have any order save in virtue of what is fixed and permanent, so that, consequently, they are infinite in number. Thus B is shown.

C, viz. that even if the essential order is denied still an infinity is impossible, is shown as follows: From the first argument given above, viz. that nothing comes from nothing, it follows that there is some nature which is capable of producing. If the essential order of active causes is denied, that nature causes in virtue of nothing other than itself; and, even if it is found caused in some singular, still there will be some singular in which it is not caused, and that is what we wanted to show about this nature. Or, given that it is found caused in every singular, a contradiction follows immediately if we deny the existence of an essential order, because no nature under which there is an accidental ordering can be found caused in any singular unless it is caused in virtue of an essential ordering to some other nature.

Now we come to the second objection cited above, viz. that the argument relies on contingent premises and thus is not a demonstration (since I argue: Some nature is in fact produced; therefore, something is a producer.). I reply that it would be possible to argue as follows: Some nature is produced because some subject undergoes change, and thus the terminal result of the change begins to be in the subject, and thus this terminal result or composite is produced or effected.[6] Therefore, there is some efficient cause (on account of the nature of correlatives), and in that case the premise can in respect of truth be contingent although obvious. Nevertheless, it is possible to argue so as to prove the first conclusion [i.e. that some being which can produce an effect is unqualifiedly first] as follows: This is true: 'Some nature can be produced; therefore, some nature can produce.' Its antecedent is shown, because some subject can undergo change, since some entity is possible in the sense in which 'possible' rules out 'necessary.' Here the proof proceeds from necessary premises. In this case, the proof of the first conclusion concerns quidditative existence[7] or possible existence, but not actual existence. However, in the third conclusion we will show the actual existence of what for now we have shown only the possibility.

The second conclusion regarding the first producer is this: The first producer is unqualifiedly[8] uncausable. Proof: The first producer is unproducible while being independently capable of producing. This was shown earlier, because, if it had its capacity to cause from something else or were producible by something else, then there would be either an infinite regress, or a circle, or a stop to the series in something that is not producible while being independently capable of producing. This I call first, and, from what you have granted, it is clear that nothing else is first. Therefore, the further conclusion follows that, if this first cannot be produced, it cannot have any causes at all, because it can result from neither a final cause, nor a material cause, nor a formal cause.

The first inference, viz. that if it is unproducible it cannot be the result of a final cause, is shown because a final cause[9] causes only because it metaphorically moves the efficient cause to produce, for in no other way does the entity of the item caused by a final cause depend on that cause as on something prior. But we do not have a *per se* cause unless the caused item depends on it as on something essentially prior.

Now the other two inferences, viz. that if it is unproducible it can have no material or formal cause, are proved together at the same time, because what has no extrinsic cause has no intrinsic causes[10] either. This is because the causality of an extrinsic cause implies perfection without imperfection, while the causality of an intrinsic cause necessarily implies some attached imperfection, since the intrinsic cause is part of what it causes. Consequently, the character of an extrinsic cause is naturally prior to the character of an intrinsic cause. Once the prior is negated so also is the subsequent.

These same inferences are also proven by the fact that intrinsic causes are caused by extrinsic ones either in respect of their existence, or insofar as they cause the composite, or in both ways, for intrinsic causes do not of themselves without an agent make up a composite.

The third conclusion concerning the first being capable of producing is the following: The first being capable of producing exists in actuality and some nature that in fact actually exists is capable of producing in this way.

Proof: That whose own character rejects existing on account of something else is such that, if it is possible for it to exist, it is possible for it to exist on account of itself. But first being capable of produc-

---

6 See glossary entry for 'natural generation.'

7 I.e., merely having a quiddity. See glossary entry for 'quiddity.'

8 See glossary entry for 'qualified/unqualified.'

9 See glossary entry for 'final cause.' Scotus does not mean the last clause.

10 See glossary entry for 'intrinsic vs. extrinsic cause.'

ing has a character that unqualifiedly rejects existing on account of something else, as is clear from the second conclusion. Likewise, it is possible for it to exist, as is clear from the fifth proof of A, the first conclusion, which proof seems to prove less but at least shows this. However, the other proofs of A can be treated as concerned with the existence which this third conclusion claims is the case, and then they argue from contingent, though obvious, premises; or they can be treated as arguing from necessary premises and A is taken to be about a nature or quiddity or possibility. Thus, an unqualifiedly first being capable of producing can exist in virtue of itself. What does not in fact exist on account of itself cannot exist on account of itself; otherwise the non-existent would produce the existence of something, which is impossible, even apart from the fact that in that case the thing would cause itself and thus would not be entirely uncausable. [Consequently, an unqualifiedly first being capable of producing does in fact exist on account of itself.]

This last conclusion, viz. about the existence of a first being capable of producing, can be established in another way by the fact that it is absurd for the universe to lack what is the highest possible grade of being.

Once these three conclusions have been shown about the first being capable of producing, you should note a certain corollary, which is, as it were, contained in those three conclusions, viz. that not only is this first cause prior to all the others but for another to exist that is prior to it includes a contradiction. Thus insofar as it is first it exists. This is proved just as in the preceding argument, being uncausable is especially included in the character of such a first (this follows from the second conclusion); therefore, if it is possible for it to exist (because it does not contradict entity, as was proved by the first conclusion), it follows that it is possible for it to exist on account of itself, and thus it does exist on account of itself.

...

I propose three similar conclusions concerning the order of excellence. The first conclusion is that some excellent nature is unqualifiedly first in respect of perfection.

This is clear from the fact that an essential ordering exists among essences, for, as Aristotle says in *Metaphysics* VIII,[11] forms relate to each other in the way numbers do. That there is a stopping point in this ordering is proved by the five arguments above that proved there is a stopping point in the series of being capable of producing.

The second conclusion is that the supreme nature is uncausable. That is shown from the fact that it cannot have a final cause (as was shown earlier), and therefore it cannot be produced, and thus, even further, it cannot be caused. These two inferences have been proved in the second conclusion regarding being capable of producing. Again, we can prove that the supreme nature cannot be produced from the fact that every producible being has some essentially ordered cause, as was proved about B in the first conclusion concerning the first being capable of causing. But an essentially ordered cause exceeds its effect.

The third conclusion is that the supreme nature is something that actually exists, and it is shown by what we said before.

Corollary: For there to be some nature that is more excellent or superior to this one includes a contradiction. This is proved in the same way as the corollaries about the efficient and final causes were proven.

I.9.2. The First Cause causes contingently
(*Ordinatio* I, dist.2, pt.1, qu.1-2)

[In this selection Scotus argues that nothing will be contingently caused (in the way a free will causes one of its acts of willing) unless the very first cause of all (whose existence was proved in the previous selection) causes contingently. On Scotus's understanding of contingency a cause causes contingently if and only if at the moment it causes something it has the power to refrain from causing it *at that moment*, and this will be a point of controversy in Topics III and IV. At the end someone (Scotus himself?) has added a note explaining the way the philosophers would try to block Scotus's reasoning. Compare this with Siger of Brabant's discussion of determinism in selection **IV.5.1**.]

---

11 Ch.3, 1043b33.

Something is contingently caused, therefore the first cause causes contingently, therefore it causes by willing.

Proof of the first consequence: Any secondary cause causes insofar as it is moved by the first; therefore, if the first necessarily produces motion, any other cause is necessarily in motion and causes necessarily whatever it causes. Therefore, if some secondary cause produces motion contingently, also the first will produce motion contingently, because the secondary cause causes only in virtue of the first cause to the extent that it is moved by it.

Proof of the second consequence: There is no source for acting contingently except the will or something attendant on the will, because everything else acts out of the necessity of nature and thus not contingently. Therefore etc. [the first cause causes by willing].

[1] Against this argument we have the following objection, which also constitutes an argument primarily against the first consequence: In any event our will could cause something contingently, and thus it is not required that the first cause cause it contingently.

[2] Further, The Philosopher while conceding the antecedent, that something is contingently caused, denied the consequent, read as referring to willing, namely that the first cause causes contingently, by claiming that contingency occurs down below not because God wills contingently but on account of motion, which to the extent that it is regular is caused necessarily, but from its parts emerges irregularity and thus contingency.

[3] In opposition to the second consequence (if it causes contingently, it causes by willing), it does not seem to hold, because some items that are naturally moved can be stopped, and consequently the opposite of their normal effect can happen, contingently as well as violently.

To [1] we have to say that if God is in respect of our will the first mover or efficient cause, the same result follows for our will as for the other causes. Whether God immediately and necessarily puts it in motion, or something else does so immediately while being itself necessarily put in motion and so necessarily putting the will in motion (since this mover moves only in virtue of being itself in motion), – in either case it follows that the cause next to the will necessarily puts the will in motion, even if that item next to the will is the will itself.

Consequently, it wills necessarily and will be an item that necessarily wills. Another impossible result is that it necessarily causes whatever it causes.

To [2], I say that I do not mean by the word "contingent' whatever is non-necessary or non-everlasting, but rather that whose opposite can come to be when it comes to be. Hence I said "something is caused contingently," not "something is contingent." Now I say that The Philosopher cannot deny the consequent while saving the antecedent by recourse to motion, because, if that whole motion necessarily comes from its cause, any part of it is caused necessarily when it is caused, i.e. it is inevitably caused, in such a way that the opposite cannot at that moment be caused. Further, what is caused by any part of a motion is caused necessarily and inevitably. Therefore, either nothing comes to be contingently, i.e. avoidably, or the first cause causes immediately in such a way that it could also not cause.

To [3], I say that if some cause can stop that one, this is only on account of a higher cause, and so on right up to the first cause, and if it necessarily puts in motion the cause next to it there will be necessity right down to the last cause. Therefore, that cause stops the other one necessarily and consequently the other cause cannot cause naturally.

[To this text is interpolated the following note, perhaps by Scotus himself:]

Just as the first cause does everything out of causal necessity (as everyone claims, otherwise it would be a mutable cause), so also all other causes. This claim of his [i.e. of Scotus's] does not seem to be true, because with equal reason he could argue that there is nothing in things caused by chance and luck, and that just as everything is determined to come about relative to the first cause, so also relative to the other causes.

In replying to these things which he says, it can be said that the causes that are put in motion by the first cause do not so uniformly receive their motion that they produce motion of necessity in the same way as they were put in motion by the first cause. The expression 'same way' here indicates a mode belonging to God as a producer of motion, for they really are in motion in the same way that they are put in motion by the first, if the expression 'same way' refers to a mode of the moved causes. For a mode of the cause that produces motion is not always received by the moved cause; rather there the motion is received in accord with the mode of the recipient. Therefore, things are different for that motion from what they are for the first cause. [End of note.]

I.9.3. The Omnipotence of God (*Ordinatio* I, dist.42)

[Scotus thinks he has proved the existence of an infinitely powerful first cause (selection II.5.1.). But in this selection he realizes that even though such a cause can be shown to be able to bring about anything whose production is not logically impossible, it cannot be shown to be able to do this directly, i.e. without going through intermediary causes. But the Christian notion of omnipotence entails this, and the thesis that God required intermediary causes was condemned in 1277.]

Concerning the forty second distinction I ask: Is it possible by natural reason to prove that God is omnipotent?

[A. *Arguments for an affirmative answer*]

[1] Richard [of St. Victor], *On the Trinity* I:[12] "For all the things which we hold to by faith..." [Richard's text reads as follows: Thus in this work it is our intention to provide for the things we believe...not just probable arguments but also necessary ones, as well as to prepare lessons in our faith by unravelling and explaining the truth. For I believe without any doubt that there are not lacking both probable and necessary arguments for explaining anything which is necessarily the case, although it happens they have not yet been revealed by our efforts.]

[2] Besides, it is proved by reason that God has infinite power (see [Aristotle's] *Physics* VIII[13] and *Metaphysics* XII[14]). Now an infinite power is known to be omnipotent; therefore, etc.

Proof of the minor premiss: It is known that it is not possible to think without contradiction of some other power greater than an infinite power. But any power which is not omnipotent is such that a power greater than it can be thought without contradiction. (Proof: Omnipotence can be thought of without contradiction under the character of omnipotence; but that is thought of as greater than any other item which is not omnipotence.)

If you say that omnipotence cannot naturally be proved to be thinkable without contradiction, you can be countered as follows: It is true that among the things that exist there is omnipotence; therefore, any argument that tries to show the impossibility of omnipotence is fallacious. Every fallacious argument can be solved by the intellect relying on what is merely natural; therefore, such an intellect can by relying on what is merely natural know that nothing impossible follows from omnipotence, and it knows that that from which nothing impossible follows is possible. Therefore, it knows that the omnipotence of God is possible.

Moreover, from the above we can construct an argument that works through what is known through itself: If it is possible naturally to prove that omnipotence is possible (because not impossible), then naturally it is possible to prove it is necessary. For it is only able to exist if it is able to exist necessarily; but what is able to exist necessarily is necessary; therefore, etc.

[B. *Arguments for the negative reply*]

No philosophers when they use natural reason allow that God is omnipotent in the sense Catholics mean, no matter how much those philosophers consider God as an efficient cause. This is bolstered, since we find, as an article of faith in the Apostle's Creed, the following: "I believe in God, the Father omnipotent...."

[C. *Solution of the question*]

We can respond here by disambiguating the term 'omnipotent.' Either it means an agent which can

---

12 Ch.4, PL 196, 892.
13 Ch.10, 266a10-24. See selection **II.1.2.**
14 Ch.7, 1070a3-13. See selection **II.1.3.**

do everything possible either with or without an intermediary, and in this sense the active power of the first efficient cause is omnipotence inasmuch as it extends as either a proximate or a remote cause to every effect. Consequently, since it can be naturally shown that something is a first efficient cause (this was shown above in dist. 2),[15] it can naturally be inferred that it is omnipotent in this sense.

In another sense "omnipotent" is taken strictly in theology to mean what is able to produce any effect and anything that is possible (i.e. anything which neither is of itself necessary nor includes a contradiction), and this in such a way, I say, that it can do this immediately without the cooperation of any other causal agent. In this sense omnipotence is believed to hold of the first efficient cause but is not demonstrated to hold of it. For, even though the first efficient cause has in itself a causal efficacy more excellent that the power of any other effective cause, and also has in itself eminently[16] the effective power of any other cause (as was proven in distinction 2 where through this it was shown that it has infinite power), and this is the ultimate, as it were, to which natural reason can attain in the knowledge of God, still it does not seem that from this we can infer omnipotence in the second sense. This is because, even if it is true [that the first efficient cause has infinite power], still it is not clear to natural reason that what has in itself a more excellent causality, and has as well the causality of a secondary cause more excellently than that [secondary cause] has in respect of its own effect, could without an intermediary produce the effect immediately produced by the secondary cause. The ranking of lower to higher causes does not allow this, because, even if the sun had in itself a more excellent causality than a cow, or any other animal, has, it would still not be allowed that the sun can without any intermediary produce a cow in the way it can through the intermediary of cow acting as a cause produce a cow.

The philosophers would hold this mainly because they did not posit secondary causes that necessarily concur [with the first cause] in order to add some perfection to the effect but rather to add imperfection, as it were. Or rather [they reasoned] that the causality of the first cause is perfect when acting without an intermediary, and thus they claimed that it could not be the immediate cause of any imperfect effect. Consequently, some other less perfect causal agent would have to concur with the first, if the first cause were not to produce something by its own full power, but rather with that secondary causal agent produce a diminished and imperfect effect. I.e., by working through an intermediate and imperfect secondary cause it would not produce an effect as perfect as what it would produce if it acted without an intermediary.

Moreover, if the philosophers were not able by natural reason to show that God can cause contingently, how much more would they not be able to show that God could immediately produce any effect or anything which He can produce through other, intermediary secondary causes?

Besides, if they held as a sort of principle that "from nothing nothing comes to be" (at least in the case of generable and destructible things), it would not seem that God is omnipotent in the sense that he could totally produce some effect without the causal cooperation of any other cause.

Besides, if the philosophers claimed that God was an agent acting necessarily, as in fact many of them seemed to have thought and claimed, and then had they claimed that He was omnipotent in that second sense, they would have had to deny all causality to any secondary cause, which would be particularly absurd to them. For a cause that causes necessarily necessarily in any instant in which it is related to its effect causes and acts necessarily at that instant. Therefore, since a higher cause relates to the effect before the lower cause does, and is, according to what you have admitted, necessarily omnipotent, at that instant, then, it produces the whole effect. Consequently, in the next instant, when the secondary cause is related to the same effect, nothing is left to be caused, and thus a secondary agent or a secondary cause cannot cause anything.

From the above it is clear that the proposition, 'Whatever the first efficient cause can do along with a secondary cause, it can do by itself without any intermediary,' is not known in virtue of its

---

15 See selection I.9.2.
16 See glossary entry for 'eminence.'

terms, nor known by natural reason, but rather is only something we believe. For if that omnipotence, on which the above proposition depends, were known by natural reason, it would be easy for those philosophers to prove many truths and propositions which they themselves deny, and it would be easy for them to prove at least the possibility of many of the things we believe and they deny.

Omnipotence in this [second] sense, however, can be shown to be probably true and necessary, even though this cannot be entirely demonstrated. And it can be shown to be more probable than some other things we believe, for it is not absurd that some of the things we believe are more evident than others.

[D. Replies to the initial arguments]

To the authoritative text from Richard [of St. Victor] [A.1] I say that, even if there are necessary arguments that prove omnipotence and some other things we believe, still these are not evidently necessary and true. For example, the argument which proves the Trinity from the double production occurring within the divine being. For, even if the proof does proceed from necessary premises, those premises are not evidently necessary, since they are not known by the terms as we know them; nor is it possible to infer this doctrine from what is known immediately to us, as was said in dist.2, qu.2.

To the second [A.2] I say that, even given that by natural reason we can conclude that God has infinite power, this does not mean we can by natural reason conclude omnipotence in the strict sense.

When you say that nothing can be thought greater than an infinite power, this is true intensively; nevertheless, it does not seem to involve a contradiction to think of a power that is greater in the extensive sense of extending itself to more things. Or we might say that, even if it is not a contradiction to think of omnipotence, and omnipotence as such somehow exceeds an infinite power not thought of as omnipotence, still it is not naturally known that the power so thought of is omnipotence.

When the person arguing here says that it is

known that omnipotence in the strict sense can be thought of without contradiction, this is denied.

When it is argued that every argument which shows that the impossible follows from that is fallacious, to this it is said that it is fallacious, but it cannot be solved by natural reason. For the fallacy lies in the propositions that make up the argument and the fact that it has a false premiss, and, consequently, it can be solved only by the refutation of that premiss; but we cannot by natural reason know that it is something to be refuted, just as also we cannot know by natural reason that it is true.

But I argue against this as follows: Those propositions which by natural reason appear to be true and not to be refuted either appear to be true in virtue of their terms in the way immediate propositions do, or they appear to be inferred from such propositions. If the former, then we cannot be sure which immediate propositions are true and which are not; for ones that are unqualifiedly false appear nevertheless to it to be true in the way immediate propositions are true. In that case, there will be no sure principles which are like "doors in a house" (contrary to The Philosopher and The Commentator in *Metaphysics* II[17]) and concerning which error does not occur. If they appear to be true in the latter way (i.e. as inferred from the immediate terms), then I argue the following concerning that fallacious syllogism: The error lies either in the propositions that make it up or in the form. If the former, then it can be solved, because a false premiss that errs in what it says can be refuted; if the latter, then it can be solved by the art of logic. If it is said, however, that it errs in form and yet cannot be solved by natural reason, this seems absurd, because the intellect as included among the natural things has produced every art that deal with apparent syllogisms, whether well-formed or defective, and thus it is possible for the fallacy to be solved through the art designed for analysing the faults of any such syllogism and applying that art to the fallacious line of reasoning.

Consequently, I reply in a different way: Even if any fallacious line of reasoning that apparently deduces the impossible from the premiss which says that God is omnipotent, could be solved by the intellect and natural reason (whether the error lies

---

17 Ch.1, 993b4-5.

in the propositions making up the argument or in its form), and the intellect were able to know of any such false line of reasoning that it is solvable (taking this in the divided sense),[18] still it does not follow that it would know that God's omnipotence is not impossible. For the opposite of such knowledge exists, i.e. [the intellect] wonders whether this [God's omnipotence] is a primary opposition in virtue of the mutual rejection of the terms (in which case, nevertheless, it would be true that nothing more obviously impossible could follow from it), or it wonders whether from God's omnipotence can be inferred something impossible other than any of the things which have been inferred and thus whether the argument that infers that impossible conclusion is insoluble, even though the argument is not among those already made and which it knows how to solve.

Or we can give a general response to that argument (which is one that could be made for everything we believe), that we could work this line of argument on every possible proposition as well as on what we believe.

I.9.4. Impossibility (*Ordinatio* I, d.43)

[What makes something impossible in the sense that not even an omnipotent being could produce it? In this selection Scotus relies on the incompatibility between certain quiddities or formal characters which render them unable to exist together. Every non-complex entity is possible, but some combinations are not.]

Concerning the forty-third distinction, where the Master [Peter Lombard in his *Sentences*] disproves the views held by others, I ask whether the primary reason for the impossibility of a thing's being made lies on the side of God or on the side of the thing to be made.

Here is a proof that it is on the side of God: The Master argues in the next distinction, c.1, that the universe could have been made better, "because if it could not, then either this would be because it lacked no good, and then it would be God, or it

would be because it does lack something but it does not have the capacity to receive it." In the latter case, he argues that "it would have been made better if God had given it that capacity." And so I argue here: If something is unmakeable, then, if God gave it the capacity, it could be made. Therefore, in this sense it cannot be made because it has not been given the capacity; and, therefore, this impossibility seems primarily to derive from God, who is not able to give the capacity.

Against this is Anselm in *On the Fall of the Devil*, c.3: "God gave perseverance to the good angels, and as a consequence the good angels had it. But it was not because God did not give it to the bad angels that they did not have it; rather it was because the bad angels did not accept it," and this because they did not have the capacity.

I say ... that, even though the power God has directed toward Himself, i.e. some absolute perfection by which God is formally powerful, exists in God at the first instant of nature[19] (just as does any other unqualified perfection, for example, even though heat is an absolute form the power of heating things follows from it), nevertheless God does not have in virtue of that power, considered as omnipotence, an object which is primarily possible; rather it has such an object in virtue of the divine intellect, which produces it first in intelligible existence, and the intellect is not formally the active power in virtue of which God is said to be omnipotent. And then the thing that in the first instant of nature has been produced by the divine intellect with such an existence, i.e. intelligible existence, has in the second instant of nature in virtue of itself possible existence, because it does not formally reject being and of its own self it does formally reject having necessary existence derived from itself. The whole definition of omnipotence that corresponds to the notion of active power consists in those two points. Therefore, there is in the object no possibility which in some way comes before there is omnipotence in God, where we mean by 'omnipotence' some absolute perfection in God, just as no creature is prior to anything absolute in God. If, nevertheless, the thing is thought to be pos-

---

18 See glossary entry for 'composite and divided senses.' Scotus means that we can know not just that any false reasoning is solvable, but also of any false reasoning which we encounter we can know that it is solvable.
19 See glossary entry for 'instant of nature.'

sible before God by his omnipotence produces things, this is true; but its having that possibility is not unqualifiedly prior, but rather is produced by the divine intellect.

But now so far as impossibility is concerned, I say that this cannot primarily derive from God, but rather from the thing ... because it is impossible on account of its rejection of being made.

This I understand in the following way: What is unqualifiedly impossible includes incompossibles. These are incompossible in virtue of their own formal characters,[20] and their incompossibility takes its origin from the origin they have for their own formal characters. Therefore, there is this process: just as God by His own intellect produces the possible in possible existence, so He produces two items that exist formally, both in possible existence, and these "products" are formally incompossible in virtue of themselves, with the result that they cannot together be one item nor can some third item come from them. But they have formally from themselves this incompossibility which they have, and it takes its origin in some way from what produces them. Next, the impossibility of the whole construct that includes them follows from this incompossiblity they have, and from the impossibility of the construct in itself as well as from the incompossibility of its parts comes the impossibility of the construct for any agent. From this we reach the end of the process leading to the impossibility of the thing, for the final grade of incompossibility or impossibility is a negation in respect of any agent. Nor need there be any negative relation on the side of God; nor one on the side of anything else (and maybe it is just not anything in the nature of things), although the intellect can relate God, or any other agent, to that [impossible thing] through the negation of a relation.

Therefore, it follows that primary impossibility lies formally on the side of the impossible while having its origin in God. And given that it does derive from some origin, this does not mean that it derives from the negation of a possibility in God, but rather it derives from the divine intellect as its source, i.e. the source of its having that existence in which the parts formally reject each other, where this mutual rejection is the reason the whole com-

posed of those parts is unqualifiedly impossible.

From the above it is clear that the fantasy of those who seek the impossibility of some items in some single item, as it were, as though some single item, whether an intelligible or any sort of existent, might be of itself formally impossible in the way that God of Himself is formally necessary, is false. For nothing is a first of this sort in the realm of non-entity, nor is it even the case that the divine intellect is the reason for the possibility of an entity opposed to such a [first] non-entity, for not even the divine intellect is the exclusive reason for the possibility of what is opposed to nothing. ... Rather everything that is "unqualifiedly nothing" includes in itself the characters of several items in such a way that it is not primarily nothing on account of its own character, but on account of the characters of those items it is understood to include, i.e. because of the formal mutual rejection of the several included items. This character of mutual rejection derives from their formal characters, and this mutual rejection they get primarily from the divine intellect.

To the first argument: The Master's argument holds once we assume that the universe is able to have a capacity for greater perfection, because then it would be better made if it were given that capacity than it is made without that capacity, as though it were a capacity lots of other things had. Nevertheless, in an absolute sense the Master's argument does not hold up once it is denied that it was able to have been made better, just as it does not follow that fire, persisting as fire, could be made better if it were made with a capacity for intellect and will, once we grant that fire is not able to have that capacity. I say, then, to the form of the argument that God cannot give to nothing the capacity for receiving being made. But this is not the primary reason [it cannot be made]; rather the reason is that such an item cannot have such a capacity, and that reason derives from the formal mutual rejection of the parts, and further back to the divine intellect.

20 I.e., their quiddities.

I.9.5. Could God make things better than He does? (*Ordinatio* I, d.44)

[Compare this with Abelard's discussion of the same topic in selection I.3.1. Abelard talks as though there is a standard of what is good and right over and above God's will. In this selection Scotus denies that God could possibly act in an "unregulated" way, although he could do many things which do not accord with the rules he has in fact established. God's absolute power extends to all possibles, and no matter how he chooses he operates in a "regular" way. The distinction between God's "regulated power" (*potentia dei ordinata*) and his absolute power (*potentia dei absoluta*) became after Scotus the main way in which the regular behavior of nature was reconciled with divine omnipotence.]

Concerning the forty-fourth distinction, where the Master [Peter Lombard] treats the question of whether God was able to have made things better than he made them, I ask this question: Is God able to make things in a different way than He has ruled that they be made?

It seems that [He could] not: For then He would be able to make things in an unregulated way. The consequent is false; therefore, also the antecedent.

Against this: For things to be made differently that they have been made does not include a contradiction; neither is it necessary. Therefore, etc.

I answer: In everything that acts through an intellect and a will, and is able to act in conformity to right law and yet does not necessarily act in conformity to right law, one has to distinguish its regulated power from its absolute power. The reason for this is that it can act in conformity to that right law, and in that case it acts in accord with its regulated power (for it is regulated inasmuch as it is a principle of carrying out some things in conformity with right law), and it can also act outside of that law and contrary to it, and here we find its absolute power which goes beyond its regulated power. Consequently, not only in God but in every free agent which can act according to the dictates of right law and also outside of such a law or contrary to it, there is a distinction between its regulated power and its absolute power. Thus jurists say that

someone can *in fact* do something – here they speak of absolute power – or they can do it *in law* – here they speak of power regulated by law.

But when that right law, according to which things must be done in a regulated way, is not in the power of the agent, then its absolute power cannot go beyond its regulated power concerning certain objects without its acting with respect to them in an unregulated way. For, in relation to such an agent, it is necessary that that law remain in force, and in that case the action not in conformity with right law is neither right nor regulated, because such an agent is held to act in accord with the rule that it comes under. Hence, everything which comes under the divine law acts in an unregulated way, if it does not act in accord with that law.

But when the law and the rightness of the law is in the power of the agent in such a way that it is right only if it has been established, then in virtue of its freedom the agent can regulate things differently than that right law dictates. Nevertheless it can do this in a regulated way because it can establish another right law in virtue of which it acts in a regulated way. Neither does its absolute power then unqualifiedly go beyond its regulated power, because it would be regulated by the new law just as it was by the earlier one. Nevertheless, it does go beyond the regulated power that is in accord with just the earlier law, contrary to which or outside of which it operates. An example of this is a prince and his subjects, and the positive law.

By way of applying this, then, to the question at hand, I say that some general laws that dictate rightly have been put in place by the divine will and certainly not by the divine intellect as it precedes the act of the divine will (as was said in dist.38) because in those laws there is not found any necessity coming from the terms (for example, that every sinner will be damned), but only from the divine will that accepts it, which works according to the sort of laws which it has established (or it suffices here to say that these rules are established by the divine wisdom). But when the intellect sets such a law before the divine will, for example that everyone who is to be honored must first do some favor, that law is right law if it pleases the divine will; and so it is in the case of other laws.

Therefore, God, who is able to act in accord with those right laws as they have been put in place by Him, is said to act in accord with regulated power.

But inasmuch as he can do many things which are not in accord with the laws he has already put in place, but rather go outside them, He is said [to act] by his absolute power. Since God can do anything which does not involve a contradiction, and can act in any way which does not involve a contradiction (and there are many other such ways of acting), He is said in that case to act in accord with his absolute power.

Hence, I say that for Him to be able to do in a regulated way many other things, and for many other things to be able to be done in a regulated way – other, that is, than the things which are done in conformity to these laws – does not include a contradiction when the rightness of a law of the sort in virtue of which someone acts rightly and in a regulated way is in the power of the agent. Consequently, just as He can do otherwise, so He can set up another right law, and if this were set up by God it would be right, because no law is right except to the extent that it is set up by the divine will that accepts it. In this case His absolute power does not extend to anything other than what is brought about in a regulated way, if it is brought about. Certainly it would not be brought about in accord with this regulation, but it would be done in a regulated way in virtue of some other regulation, and that regulation the divine will would be able to set up in just the way that He is able to act.

We must also note what it means for something to be regulated and to be done in a regulated way, for this happens in two ways. In one way, by a general regulation. This pertains to the common law; for example, common law rules that everyone who is a sinner at the end is to be damned (just as if the king established that every murderer is to die). In a second way, by a particular regulation; i.e. in virtue of a particular judgment which the general law is not about, because the law is about universal causes. The law is not about particular causes, but a judgment, in accord with the law, of that which is against the law is (for example, that this murderer is to die).

I say, then, that God can act not only differently than has been ruled by a particular regulation, but also differently than has been ruled by a general regulation, or by the laws of justice. He can act in a regulated way because both the things which are outside that regulation and those which are contrary to that regulation are able to be done by God in a regulated way by his absolute power.

[An added note:] Further, it must be realized that "God is able to produce a thing different from the way He has decided." In the sense of a composition[21] it is false, for it signifies that the following is possible: 'God produces differently than the way he has decided.' In the sense of a division it is true, and in this case there are two categorical propositions[22] and the meaning is: God can do things in this way; He has not decided to do things in this way. Nevertheless, it does not follow that he acts in an unregulated way, as is clear from what was said.

Nevertheless, we speak of regulated power only in relation to the regulation of a general law, and not in relation to the regulation of a right law that concerns some particular. This is evident from the fact that it is possible for God to save someone He does not save, who in fact will die at the end in sin and will be damned. But it is not allowed that He can save a Jew who is already damned (nor is this impossible for God's absolute power, since it does not involve a contradiction). Therefore, in the same way that it is impossible to save the Jew who is already damned, it is possible to save the person [who will die at the end in sin and will be damned]. Therefore, He can save the latter by His regulated power (this is true), but he cannot save the former. This is certainly not in virtue of a particular regulation (which is, as it were, about just this doable or workable particular), but rather in virtue of a general regulation, because if He did save him that would be consistent now with right laws, which he has actually set up, concerning the salvation and damnation of individuals. For it is consistent with this: Someone bad at the end will be damned. (This is a law already put in place concerning who is to be damned.) This is because up to now he is not at the end a sinner but rather can be a non-sinner, especially while he is in this life. For God can by His grace intervene, just as if a king were to intervene to prevent someone from committing murder. But it is not consistent with particular law that He save the

21 See glossary entry for 'composite and divided senses.'
22 See glossary entry for 'composite and divided senses.'

71

Jew [who is already damned], for He can foreknow that the Jew is to be saved by His regulated power, but not regulated in this way, rather by absolute power if in this way. And the power will be regulated in some other way in accord with some other regulation, because it is possible for it to be brought about in accord with some other regulation.

[An inserted text:] Therefore, He can save the Jew by His absolute power, and He is able to save that sinner by His regulated power, even though he will not be saved. But He is not able by His absolute power to give blessedness to a stone, nor by His regulated power. From this it is evident where we speak of absolute power in God; it is where He can act against a general law, not against a particular law.

How the divine will can act in regard to particulars and in regard to right laws that are to be instituted without willing the opposite of what He now wills, was treated above in dist.39.

[*Replies to the arguments at the beginning*]

To the [first] argument it is clear that the inference is invalid, for if He made things in a different way from the way it has been ruled that they are to be made, this would not show that they were made in an unregulated way. This is because, if he had set up other laws by which they were to be made, they would be made by Him in a regulated way.

To the argument in favor of the opposite, I allow that it goes through for absolute power. But if this absolute power were the principle for doing something, it would be regulated by Him, but not according to a regulation previously put in place by Him, i.e. the same which He had before.

I.10. WILLIAM OF OCKHAM

ALTHOUGH OCKHAM, BEING A FAITHFUL CHRISTIAN, BELIEVES AS firmly as Scotus that there is a first cause on which all else depends and which causes contingently, he does not think this can be proved by natural reason. These selections show how Ockham thinks many of the arguments Scotus relied on in the previous set of selections fail to convince. Ockham argues, in particular, that it is not possible to prove by natural reason that God is the cause of things by acting contingently; for it is not possible to prove, from the perfection of the divine entity, that there are effects of that perfection which would not exist if God operated only by natural necessity. Somewhat like al-Ghazali, Ockham argues for the limits of human reason; the effect is not simply to distinguish and separate philosophy and religion but also, in widening that gap, to cultivate ground for the growth of skepticism (see Topic VII).

With respect to Scotus's attempt to prove the existence of a first efficient cause Ockham concludes (in selection **I.10.7.** below) that from a first production it cannot be sufficiently proven that there is no infinite regress in efficient causes such that each member of the series is caused successively by another *ad infinitum*.

I.10.1. Essentially ordered Causes (from *Quaestiones in libros Physicorum*, qu.134)

[In selection **I.9.1.** we found Scotus's explanation of the distinction of essentially ordered from accidentally ordered causes. Ockham here modifies Scotus's position to allow that the type of effect which in one instance is produced by a series of essentially ordered causes can in another instance be produced by just one of those causes. Nevertheless an *individual* effect produced by a series of essentially ordered causes could not have been produced by just one of them, on the general grounds that *numerically the same* effect as is produced by one agent could not be produced by another.]

Are essentially ordered causes necessarily required at the same time for producing an effect in respect of which they are essentially ordered causes?

[I] For an affirmative answer: There is a contradiction involved in saying that all these are essential causes of that effect and yet this same effect can be naturally produced when some of them are removed. This is because the following inference holds: An effect can naturally be produced without A; therefore A is not essentially required for its production; consequently, A is not an essential cause of the effect.

[II] For a negative answer: The sun whether working with a worm or without a worm produces a worm.

On this question Scotus says, in the second distinction of his first book [see selection **I.9.1.**], that it is necessary that one [cause] cannot act without another [cause].

But here are three conclusions against Scotus's view: The first is that an effect of the same species, which is produced at the same time by all [the causes], can sometimes be produced by one cause operating on its own. This is clear, because a worm generated by propagation and a worm generated by putrefaction are the same in species (this is obvious), and yet the worm that is produced by propagation is produced by all the essentially ordered causes operating at the same time, but the worm produced by putrefaction is produced by the sun without the action of any worm.[1]

If you say that then the particular cause is super-fluous, I say this is not the case, because it is not always possible for a universal cause to produce the effect without a particular cause. This arises from the fact that a determinate agent [does not always] determine for itself a definite effect in a given recipient,[2] even though it could produce by itself alone an effect of the same species as the effect which it produces by means of a particular cause.

The second conclusion is that sometimes a universal cause can produce on its own just as perfect an effect as it can operating at the same time with a particular cause. This is clear from the fact that, although a divisible effect is more perfect if caused by all those causes operating at the same time than if it is caused by one on its own, as is obvious in the case of heat caused by a fire and the sun working at the same time; nevertheless, when the effect is indivisible, in the way a substantial form[3] is, especially in the same part of matter, then it can be just as perfect when produced by one on its own as when produced by all working at the same time.

The third conclusion is that numerically the same effect[4] as is caused by all working at the same time cannot be caused by one on its own. This is clear from what will be said later on the subject of motion, viz. that a numerically single effect determines for itself a definite agent and a definite matter, in such a way that it is not possible for that effect to be produced by another agent. Consequently, numerically the same effect as is produced by all cannot be produced by just one, because all the causes necessarily concur for the production of that effect. Nevertheless, sometimes an effect of the same species can be produced by just one, as is clear in the case of worms.

Scotus was right if he is read as saying the above. Nevertheless, he himself has asserted the opposite, for according to him, if Adam had stayed in the state of innocence, those who have now been chosen [for salvation] would have been chosen, but

they would have had other fathers. Thus according to him varying the agent does not vary the effect, and, consequently, according to him numerically the same effect can have different equivocal causes,[5] so that numerically the same effect could be produced in the absence of one of those causes.

If you say that he intended that, if Adam had stayed [in innocence], those sons could, by the absolute power of God, have had other fathers, but not in accord with the order presently instituted, since he would then have decided to pass other laws – I answer that so understood I agree with what he has said.

Another way of saving Scotus is to say that it is true when we speak about the natural order that all the essentially ordered causes necessarily work together in maintaining an effect that is caused by them all at the same time, but not if it is caused by the first cause. But from this it follows that a human being is not an essentially ordered cause in the production of Socrates, because neither a singular human being nor the common human being[6] is, since without either of them Socrates can be saved and maintained.

As for the [first] argument at the beginning [I], I concede the conclusion, if we are speaking about numerically the same effect, but not if we are speaking of specifically the same effect.

As for the argument for the negative [II], I say that numerically the same effect is not produced and cannot naturally be produced by putrefaction as by propagation. Nor is it possible for this numerically the same effect which is produced by propagation to be produced naturally without the cooperation of its essentially ordered causes, although this could occur through the power of God.

I.10.2. Can it be proved that there exists a first productive Cause? (from *Quaestiones in libros Physicorum*, qu.135)

[In this selection Ockham sets out to refute the argument Scotus gave in selection I.9.1. for the exis-

---

1 See fn.7 of selection I.4.2.
2 See glossary entry for 'agent/recipient.'
3 See glossary entry for 'substantial form.'
4 See selections I.1.1. & 2. for discussion of numerical sameness.
5 See glossary entry for 'univocal production.'
6 I.e., the nature common to all human beings. Ockham holds, against Scotus, that this is not anything in extra-mental reality but only a concept in the mind. See selections VI.9.1 & 5.

tence of a first efficient cause. Basically Ockham argues that the series of causes could extend back infinitely without itself as a whole having a cause.]

Is it possible sufficiently to prove through production as opposed to conservation that there is a first efficient cause?

[A.1] For an affirmative answer: There is some being that can be produced, but not by itself; therefore by something else. Of that something else I ask just as before whether it is a first efficient cause or is able to be produced by something. There is no infinite regress here; therefore, etc.

[A.2] For a negative answer: In causes of the same type there is an infinite regress.

On this question Scotus argues the affirmative in dist. 2, qu.1 [see selection I.9.1.].

[B.1] His first proof is the following: The series of essentially ordered [causes and effects] is itself caused, and it is caused by something which is not a member of that series, otherwise the same thing would be a cause of itself.

[B.2] Secondly, the whole series of causes and effects is dependent, but not on any member of the series, otherwise the same thing would depend on itself.

[B.3] Thirdly, an infinity of essentially ordered causes would all be actually in existence at the same time, since all the essentially ordered causes work together at the same time to cause the effect. If, then, there were an infinity of them, it would follow etc.

[B.4] Fourthly, That is prior which is nearer the beginning; therefore where there is no beginning nothing is essentially prior.

[B.5] Fifthly, a higher cause is more perfect in causing; therefore, an infinitely higher cause is infinitely more perfect. But such a cause does not cause in virtue of something else; therefore, etc.

[B.6] Sixthly, being capable of producing does not imply imperfection. Therefore, it can be in something without any imperfection. But if it exists in nothing without dependence on something prior, it exists in nothing without imperfection. Therefore, the first being capable of producing is possible.

[B.7] Seventh, otherwise an infinity in accidentally ordered causes would be impossible, because this sort of infinity can not exist all at once but only successively, where one member comes after another in such a way that a secondary cause is caused by the first. But that secondary cause does not depend on the first for causation, since a son begets just as well when his father is dead as when he is alive. This sort of infinity can only exist on account of some nature that lasts infinitely, on which the whole succession and everything in it depends.

[B.8] Eighth, no deficiency in the way things are formed continues on in existence except by the power of something permanent which is not a member of that succession, because all the successive items are of the same type. Therefore, there is something essentially prior on which each member of the succession depends just as it would on a proximate cause, and which is not a member of the succession.

[B.9] Another person [evidently Walter Chatton] reinforces the first and second arguments as follows: I point to the whole plurality of all those things each of which is caused. For if that plurality is infinite, then the argument runs as follows: That plurality has an efficient cause, and that cause does not itself have another efficient cause; therefore, it is a first cause that is not caused. The first assumption is clear enough, because any member of that plurality is caused; therefore, the whole plurality is caused, because for the whole plurality to be caused is not anything other than for its members to be caused. The second assumption is, according to Scotus, clear, because the cause which precedes this whole plurality is not a member of that plurality, since otherwise it would not be a cause that precedes it and consequently not a cause that is not caused.

But these arguments are not sufficient to show their conclusion from production as opposed to conservation. I specifically object to the first [B.1], second [B.2], and last [B.9] arguments.

First, this is the argument which shows that God could not make a world which lasts forever into the future.[7] Suppose I point to the whole plurality of future days each of which has another that is subsequent to it in time. Then I argue as follows: That whole plurality has something that is subsequent to it in time, because any part of it has something subsequent to it in time. That thing subsequent to the whole plurality is the final thing, because it does

---

7 Ockham rightly assumes that Scotus would not accept this conclusion.

not have anything subsequent to it, since it is not a member of the plurality. Therefore, the view that there is an everlasting succession into the future involves a contradiction.

Secondly, it equally proves that a line is composed out of points and time out of instants. For let A be the first point of a line; then I point to the whole plurality of parts in the continuum each of which has a part in front of it that lies on the near side of point A. Then I argue as follows: That whole plurality of parts [has a part in front of it that lies on the near side of point A, but this part] does not have anything before[8] itself and beyond A, for otherwise that part would be a member of that whole plurality; therefore, this part has to be immediately after A. And it would not be divisible, because, if it were, one part of it would come before another part of it [and thus the latter part would be a member of the aforementioned plurality, contrary to the supposition]; therefore it is an indivisible that is right next to another indivisible.

Thirdly, the argument equally shows that it is not possible to continue to infinity in a series of acts that reflect back on themselves. Suppose I point to a whole plurality of acts each of which has another act subsequent to it. Then I argue as follows: That whole plurality of acts has an act subsequent to itself, because any act [that is a member of the plurality] has an act subsequent to itself, and this act [subsequent to the whole plurality] does not have another act subsequent to itself, since otherwise it would be a member of that plurality.

To the first [of Scotus's] arguments against my view [A.1] I concede that the series of caused things is caused. But someone relying on natural reason would challenge the inference, because that person would say that one caused thing is caused by another which is part of the plurality, and the latter is caused by still another that is part of the plurality, and so on to infinity. This is just as is the case, according to The Philosopher, in accidentally ordered causes and effects where one member is able to be caused by another, for example one human by another, and the latter is caused by still another, and so on to infinity. The opposite of this cannot be shown through production. Then it does

not further follow that "the same thing would be a cause of itself," because that whole plurality is not caused by any one cause; rather in that plurality one member is caused by another, and the other by still another.

To the second [of Scotus's arguments] [B.2] I say that production is not sufficient to prove that the whole series is dependent at the same time. This can only be shown from conservation, because a person who does not make any claim for conservation would say only that one member of that series depends on another member of the plurality, and the latter on still another, and so on to infinity, so far as production is concerned. Once one of these is made, it might not depend on anything, except something that conserves it, but in this case it is denied that there is such a conserver. And then it does not follow further that "otherwise the same thing would depend on itself," because the whole plurality does not depend on some one thing, but rather one member of it on another, and another on another.

To the third [B.3] I say that although everything that conserves something else, whether directly or through an intermediary, exists together with the thing it conserves, it is not the case that every producer of something, whether directly or through an intermediary, exists at the same time as what is produced. Consequently, it is possible for there to be an infinite regress in producers without there being an actual infinity. Hence, it was clear earlier [qu.134] that not all essentially ordered causes work together at the same time in order to cause something, although sometimes they do work together at the same time to conserve something.

To the fourth [B.4] I say that it is not possible from production alone to prove that something is essentially prior [to something else]; rather all that can be proved is that it is accidentally prior.

To the fifth [B.5], it was clear earlier[9] that a higher cause is not always in itself more perfect [than its effect]; rather, often it is less perfect.

To the sixth [B.6] I say that it is not posssible from production to prove sufficiently that being capable of producing does not entail imperfection, because from production alone it cannot be proved that

---

8 The text reads 'after' but this must be a mistake.
9 Qu. 133.

each thing capable of producing is not produced by another such thing, and so on to infinity.

To the seventh [B.7] I say that in accidentally ordered causes it is possible to have an infinity without there being some nature that lasts infinitely and on which the whole succession depends, for it is not possible from production to prove sufficiently that one human being cannot be produced by another as by a total cause. And then it could be said that one human totally depends on another, and the latter one on still another, and so on to infinity, but they do not depend on any thing that lasts infinitely. Nor can the opposite thesis be proved from production, although it can from conservation.

To the eighth [B.8] it can be said in the same way that that succession continues on because one member totally depends on some other member of the same type. Nor is it possible to prove from production or the whole succession that an infinite regress is possible only if there were some one permanent thing on which the whole infinity depends, for, so far as production is concerned, it suffices that in the genus of efficient causes one human being totally depends on another, and the latter on still another, and so on to infinity.

To the ninth [B.9] I concede that the whole plurality is caused, but not by some single cause. Rather, one is caused by one which is a member of the plurality, and another is caused by another which is a member of the same plurality, and so on. Consequently, I concede the first assumption and its proof when it is taken in the above sense, for nothing else can be sufficiently proven as following by natural reason from a first production. As for the second assumption I say that from a first production it is not sufficiently proved that the whole plurality of caused items is caused by something, and so on.

To the argument at the beginning [A.1] I say that it cannot from a first production be sufficiently proven that there is no infinite regress in efficient causes where each member of the series is caused successively by another. But from such a regress it does not follow that there is something that is actually infinite, as is clear from what was said.

I.10.3. Can it be proved that there exists a first Conserving Cause? (*Quaestiones in libros Physicorum*, qu.136)

[Ockham makes a distinction between what produces an effect, i.e. brings it into existence, and what conserves an effect, i.e. keeps it in existence. Both are efficient causes, but only in the latter type is an infinite regress impossible. Consequently, it can be shown that there is a first conserving cause of any effect. But in another place Ockham makes it clear that there can be no proof that there is only one such "first cause" for all effects, and this effectively undercuts treating such a first cause as the God of monotheistic faiths.]

Is it possible from conservation to prove sufficiently that there is a first efficient cause?

For a negative answer: To conserve is to produce; but from production it is not possible to prove there is a first efficient cause; therefore, neither [is it possible] from conservation.

Against the negative answer: All the causes that conserve an effect work together at the same time to conserve it. Therefore, if in causes that conserve something there were an infinite regress, there would be an infinity of things all actually existing at the same time. This is impossible; therefore, etc.

On this question I say, in brief, yes. This is proved by the fact that anything which is really produced by something is, as long as it stays in real existence, conserved by something – that much is clear. But this effect is produced – this is certain. Therefore, as long as it persists it is conserved by something. About that conserver I ask: Can it be produced by something else or not? If not, it is a first efficient cause just as much as it is a first conserver, because everything that conserves something is an efficient cause. But if that conserver is produced by something else, then it is conserved by something else, and of the latter I ask the same question as before. Consequently, either we have to go on to infinity or we have to stop with something which conserves but is in no way conserved, and such an efficient cause will be a first efficient cause. But there is in conservers no infinite regress, for otherwise an infinity of things would actually exist, which is impossible. This is because anything which conserves something else, whether directly or through an intermediary, exists at the same time with what it conserves, and, consequently, everything that is conserved actually requires everything that conserves it, but not everything that is produced actually requires everything that produces it, whether directly or through an intermediary. It follows that, although there can be an infinite regress in producers without an actual infinity, there cannot, nevertheless, be an infinite regress in conservers without an actual infinity.

But against this reasoning: It seems that that argument works just as well with a first production as with conservation. Argue this way: Something is produced. I ask of its producer: Either it is a producer that is not produced, and then we have our conclusion; or it is produced by something else, but this does not go on to infinity. Therefore, we reach a stopping point with some producer that is not produced. The assumption [that there is no infinite regress] is proved for essentially ordered [causes and effects in two ways]:[10] First, by the fact that in an essential ordering all the causes are required at the same time for the production of the effect; and thus, if there were an infinity of them, there would be an infinity actually existing. Secondly, by the fact that the whole plurality of caused things is itself essentially caused, and not by some member of that plurality, for then the same thing would cause itself; therefore, it is caused by something that is not caused and is outside the plurality of caused things. Likewise, in an accidental ordering it is clear that the whole plurality of caused things is actually caused, and not by some member of that plurality, for then in causing that whole plurality it would cause itself. Therefore, it is caused by something outside that plurality. And then, either that is the same not-caused thing [as was first in the essential ordering], and we have what we set out to prove; or it is caused by essentially ordered causes, and then we use the reasoning of the first part of this argument.

I answer that it is not possible, at least in accidentally ordered causes, and not even formally in essentially ordered ones, from first production alone to prove that there is not an infinite regress. To the first part of the above argument concerning the essential ordering, I say that, as was clear earlier [selection I.10.1], it is not the case that all essentially ordered causes work together in the first production of an effect. To both the parts that follow the first I say that the whole plurality, both in the essential ordering and in the accidental, is caused, but not by some one single thing, whether a member of that plurality or outside of it. Rather one member is caused by one which is a member of the plurality and another member by another, and so on to infinity. Nor is it possible from first production to prove sufficiently the opposite. In this case it does not follow that the same item causes the whole plurality, nor that the same item causes itself, because there is no one single item that is the cause of all.

To the argument at the beginning I say that from efficient causation, in the sense that a thing directly receives existence after non-existence, it is not possible to prove that there is a first efficient cause. But from efficient causation in the sense that a thing is continued in existence it is genuinely possible to prove this from conservation. Thus the answer to this question is clear.

I.10.4. Is God able to do Everything that it is possible for a Creature to do? (*Ordinatio* I, dist. 42)

[On this question Ockham agrees with the conclusion we saw Duns Scotus argue for in selection I.9.3. But Ockham does not accept all of the arguments that Scotus put forward. In particular Ockham does not agree that the philosophers introduced secondary causes between the first and its ultimate effects in order to allow for imperfection in those effects. Also Ockham turns, against Scotus himself, one of the arguments he used against the philosophers who took the first cause to cause from natural necessity. What Ockham thinks can be proved is that if God acts as a natural cause from necessity, then there must be some effects He cannot produce just by Himself. And since Ockham rejects Scotus's proof that God acts contingently (i.e. non-naturally) he does not see any way of showing that God is not such a natural cause.]

---

10 See selection **I.10.1.** for the notion of essentially ordered causes.

Concerning the forty-second distinction I ask: Is God able to do everything that it is possible for a creature to do?

For a negative answer: God cannot sin or die, but these are things that are possible for creatures. Therefore, etc.

For the opposite answer: God is omnipotent, but an omnipotent being can do everything. Therefore, etc.

In this question we first have to see whether it can be proved by natural reason that God can do, without any creature cooperating, anything that it is possible for a creature to do. Secondly, we must see whether this is something that must be believed.

On the first point:

It is said [by Duns Scotus] that it cannot be proved by natural reason. Four arguments are given for this conclusion. Of these two seem to me cogent, but the others do not seem to show their conclusion.

The *first* of these is the following: Although it can be proven by natural reason that God has infinite power, still it is not clear to natural reason that what has a more excellent causality and contains more excellently the causality of the secondary cause could without an intermediary produce the effect of the secondary cause, for the ranking of causes might not allow this. The Philosophers would hold this mainly because they did not posit secondary causes that necessarily concur [with the first cause] in order to add some perfection to the effect but rather to add imperfection, as it were, for they claimed that the first cause could not be the immediate cause of any imperfect effect. Consequently, some other less perfect causal agent had to concur [with the first], if the first cause were not to produce something by its own full power.

Besides [Scotus's *second* argument], if the philosophers were not able by natural reason to show that God can cause contingently, how much more would they not be able to show that God could immediately produce any effect or anything which He can produce through intermediary secondary causes?

Besides [Scotus's *third* argument], those [philosophers] held as a principle that "from nothing nothing comes to be"; therefore, at least in the case of generable and destructible things, it thus seems they would not have claimed that God is omnipotent in the sense that he could produce every effect without the cooperation of any cause.

Besides [Scotus's *fourth* argument], the philosophers claimed that God was an agent acting necessarily; therefore, had they claimed that He was omnipotent in that sense, they would have had to deny all causality to any secondary cause, which would be particularly absurd to them. This inference goes through, for a cause that causes necessarily at any instant in which it is related to its effect causes and acts necessarily at that instant. Therefore, since a higher cause relates to the effect before the lower cause does, and in this case is omnipotent in that sense, at that instant, then, it produces the whole effect. Consequently, in the next instant, when the secondary cause is related to the same effect, nothing is left to be caused, and thus a secondary agent or a secondary cause cannot cause anything.

The first of these arguments does not seem to show its conclusion. For philosophers did not claim that a secondary cause concurred [with the first] in order to have imperfection in the effect, as though the secondary cause added some imperfection to the effect. This is because, according to him [Scotus], The Philosopher claims that God is the cause of everything, and, therefore, He is the immediate cause of some effect as well as the total cause; otherwise we would have an infinite regress [of effects and causes]. But, according to him [The Philosopher], that effect is imperfect and God is infinitely more perfect than that effect. Therefore, according to the opinion philosophers hold, God is the immediate and total cause of some imperfect effect. Therefore, in the opinion of philosophers, God does not on account of the imperfection of the effect reject being the immediate cause of everything.

If it is said that, although the effect is imperfect in comparison to God, it is perfect in comparison with the other effects which on account of their imperfection are not able to be produced by God alone, [I reply as follows:] This does not seem to suffice to save the view, because, once we see that imperfection in general in the effect does not mean that God cannot produce the imperfect effect, it is necessary to give a specific reason why God rejects producing one imperfect effect more than some other.

This is bolstered by the following consideration:

God can be a total and immediate cause of many of the effects that are ranked according to more perfect and more imperfect; therefore, unless something else stands in the way, there seems to be no reason why He could not be the immediate cause of all imperfect effects. According to him [Scotus] the antecedent is clear enough, because only in that way can the first cause create anything, and thus everything that is created in the strict sense is made by God alone. But according to what he imputes to the view of The Philosopher there are many such items, and thus many such items are made by God alone. Consequently, his assumption, that according to the opinion of The Philosopher secondary causes concur with the first cause so that the first cause does not produce by the full force of its power and thus does not produce as perfect an effect as it can, is not true.

It is bolstered a second time as follows: In the case of natural causes we see that the same cause, without any other cause cooperating, produces many more perfect or more imperfect effects. For example, the sun produces in the same recipient several ranked effects.

The second argument seems to go through, or at least it is very probable, although that man [Scotus] seems to say the opposite in another place.[11] For in the other place he seems to want to show that there can be no contingency in things unless the first cause causes contingently. But it can be known by natural reason that there is contingency in things and that something acts contingently. Therefore, it can be known by natural reason, according to him, that the first cause acts contingently.

The third argument also seems effective, for, although according to some philosophers from nothing something may be made *from eternity*, still it seems to have been the opinion of philosophers that from nothing nothing is made *for the first time*. Consequently, they claimed that God does not cause everything without the cooperation of any other cause.

But the fourth argument when laid out in this way does not show its conclusion. The proof of the inference is not valid, for if it were it would follow that God could in no way co-act with a creature in the production of some effect. Proof of the infer-ence: if it is granted, as he argues, that God does co-act with a creature, then I argue as follows: The first causal agent, without which no effect can be produced, acts in any instant in which it is related to its effect. Therefore, since the first cause is related to the effect before the secondary cause is, and it causes at that instant, it follows that at that instant it produces the whole effect. Therefore, in the next instant, when the secondary cause is related to the effect, there is nothing left to be caused, and thus the secondary cause does not cause anything.

If it is said that this argument does not hold of the first cause since it causes freely, i.e. it can cause when it wants to cause, even though it does hold of a cause that causes necessarily, because such a cause necessarily causes at any instant in which it is related to the effect – [I reply that] this is not enough to make the point, because I accept that the first cause is something without which the secondary cause is not able to produce such an effect, and then I ask: Is the first cause related to that effect first or not? If it is, then it causes the effect at that moment, and then at that moment nothing remains to be caused. If it is not first, but rather it is related to the effect in the very same instant in which the secondary cause is related to the effect, and given that there is nothing more contradictory about two natural causes being related to the same effect at the same instant than about one natural cause and one free cause being so related to an effect, it follows that, not withstanding the primacy of the cause, even if God were a natural cause, He could concur and cause the same effect along with the secondary cause. Thus it seems that the same argument shows that no prior natural cause can concur with a secondary cause in the production of some effect. For I take any prior cause and any secondary cause subordinated to it, and I ask: Is that prior cause related to the effect before the secondary cause is, or not? If it is, then it causes in the first instant. And it certainly does not cause just part of the effect, because there is no more reason for it to cause one part rather than another, and, moreover, frequently the effect is indivisible and has no parts. Therefore, at the first instant it causes the whole effect, and therefore in the next instant there is nothing left to be caused. Consequently, it

---

11 See selection I.9.2.

is never the case that a secondary cause acts along with the first cause, and thus that argument does away with the essential order of causes.[12] But if that first cause does not relate to the effect before the secondary cause does, the same argument shows that the cause which is unqualifiedly first does not relate to the effect before the secondary cause does, and thus that priority [of what is unqualifiedly first] does not require us to deny that God is the immediate cause of everything.

[*Solution of the question:*]

So far as this article is concerned, I say that it cannot be demonstrated by natural reason that God can produce every effect immediately just by Himself, because it cannot be demonstrated by natural reason that God in fact causes everything just by Himself, for this is false and denied by everybody, both the philosophers and the saints, since everybody claims that there are secondary causes. Neither is it possible to prove that God acts or causes contingently whatever He causes. From those facts it follows that it cannot be shown by natural reason that God can cause everything immediately and just by Himself without the cooperation of any cause. This inference is clear enough, because any natural agent which is equally sufficient for producing many items necessarily either produces all of them or none. Therefore, given that God is a sufficient agent and one that causes naturally, then, if He relates equally to the items that can be produced (some by the intermediate action of second causes and others directly), either He will cause all of them necessarily or none of them. But obviously not all; therefore, none.

If it is said that God does not equally relate to all the items that can be produced, because some are produced through secondary intermediate causes and others not, [I say that] this reasoning is invalid, because if God just by Himself can produce the items He produces by secondary, intermediate causes, those secondary causes are not required for producing those items. So far as this is the case, then, He equally relates to those [produced by secondary, intermediate causes] and to the others that

are not produced by secondary, intermediate causes. Therefore, all are either equally produced by Him or equally not produced by Him. In fact, from this it follows that God necessarily produces either all producible items of the same type or none of them. The inference is clear enough, because a natural and sufficient cause that does not require something else for its effect produces either everything of the same type or none of that type. This is because there is no more reason for Him to produce one rather than another item of the same type since there is no ranking among items of the same type. Therefore, if God is a natural cause, there is no more reason for Him to produce this individual member of some most specific species rather than that one, and thus he produces either all of them or none.

I say, then, that there is no way for it to be the case that God is a natural cause and, nevertheless, at the same time He can produce every effect just by Himself without any other cause cooperating. Consequently, since it is not possible by natural reason to prove that God is a contingent cause, it is not possible by natural reason to prove that God can cause every producible effect just by Himself immediately.

Thus I say that the philosophers did not in order to add imperfection to the effect claim that necessarily secondary causes concur [with the first], since according to many of them [God] Himself is the cause of an imperfect effect. Rather the reason they claimed that secondary causes concurred was that they saw that an effect follows from its proximate secondary cause but it does not follow from a cause that is not proximate. The Philosopher touches on the reason in *On Generation [and Corruption]* II[13] in order to prove that the sun is a cause of things down here below. They claimed this also on account of the fact that, since God, according to them, is a natural cause, if He were able to produce some such effect without the cooperation of a secondary cause, it would follow that the effect would be produced by the pre-existent, sufficient cause before the secondary cause got near it, but we experience the opposite of this with our senses. Neither did they deny that He is the cause of every-

12 See I.10.6.
13 Ch.10, 336a33-b9.

thing, on account of the priority of the first cause to a secondary cause, because that would show that there is no essential order of causes in relation to the same effect produced immediately by both of those causes. This I reckon is unqualifiedly false. Thus it should not be imagined that at some instant the first cause is related to the effect and at the next instant the secondary cause is related to the same effect; rather [imagine that] at the very same instant they are as a whole related to the same effect.

And if someone says that the prior cause acts first, and therefore at that prior [instant] the secondary cause does not act, it should be said that, when this person says "the prior cause acts first," if they mean that the first cause acts at some instant at which the secondary cause does not act, what they say is unqualifiedly false, because they act together in the very same instant. But if it is meant that the prior cause is the more principal cause and is less limited and more perfect, this can be allowed, although perhaps not just by the meanings of the terms. But that is irrelevant to this question.

And if someone says that at least the first cause acts in something prior in which the secondary cause does not act, it should be said that it cannot strictly speaking be allowed, because nothing is there before other than the cause. Consequently, one must understand 'prior' to be a substantive meaning 'prior cause,' and then the sense of the claim that it acts in something prior is that it acts in some prior cause, which makes no sense, just as it makes no sense to say "a cause acts in a cause," for then we could just as well say that a secondary cause acts in a subsequent cause, which is nonsense.

This fantasy, then, of instants of nature[14] or of origin causes lots of errors and bad ways of talking. For example, suppose we were to argue as follows: A whole is prior to its own part because it is more perfect than the part; therefore, the whole exists in some instant in which its part does not exist; therefore, the whole exists without its own part, which is absurd. From this it is clear enough that this way of arguing is absurd.

From what we have said it is clear that it was not on account of this sort of priority that the philosophers denied that God is the cause of everything. But did the philosophers deny that God is the immediate cause of all effects although not the total? How much it was the intention of The Philosopher to draw this conclusion will become clear later. In any event, whatever the intention of The Philosopher was, I say that there is no effective argument, or even one that gives much of an appearance of efficacy, that can prove that God is not a cause that immediately concurs in the production of any effect. But this is something we will clarify in the second book.

Concerning the second article [whether it is to be believed that God can do everything a creature can do without the cooperation of any creature]:

It seems possible to hold as probable that God is a cause of any effect and is able just by Himself to cause every effect that can be produced. Nevertheless, neither part of this contradiction [i.e. the above proposition and its denial] can be fully proven by natural reason.

Nevertheless, here are some questions and difficulties for those views. One concerns the act of will by which someone hates God; [suppose God were to command this] then it would follow that someone could hate God without losing any merit [required for salvation], in fact could do it meritoriously. Another concerns the relation of efficient causation or action by which fire acts. I will clarify the first elsewhere. As regards the second I say that there is not the sort of relation of agent to recipient or produced item that humans commonly imagine there is. Rather, besides the cause all there is is the absolute product, and that is something God can make without any secondary cause cooperating.

Concerning the first argument, I deny this inference: 'God cannot sin nor die, but these are possible; therefore, He cannot do everything possible.' It is invalid in just the way the following inference is invalid: 'God can do every absolute and positive act just by Himself, but a meritorious act is that sort of act; therefore, God just by Himself can perform a meritorious act.' All such inferences commit the

---

14 See glossary entry for 'instant of nature.'
15 See glossary entry for 'fallacy of figure of speech.'

fallacy of "figure of speech,"[15] because in the first proposition one [term] is unqualifiedly absolute[16] while in the minor premiss it is connotative,[17] and where that happens we find the fallacy of "figure of speech." So it is in the inference we were discussing. "To sin" does not just mean the thing which is produced but also means some duty to perform the opposite of that which He does or omits. In the same way 'to die' does not mean just the destruction of some thing, but connotes as well the destruction of the very thing which is said to die. Consequently, although He can cause in some way the destruction of the thing which dies, He cannot Himself die.

I.10.5. Can God do things which He neither does do nor will do? (*Ordinatio* I, dist.43, qu.1)

[Ockham finds Scotus's arguments on this question in selection **I.9.2.** inconclusive. In particular Scotus's argument for the thesis that the first cause causes contingently can be successfully countered by the philosophers. But, of course, Ockham believes as much as Scotus that Christians must affirm that God can do things He does not do.]

Concerning the forty-third distinction I ask: Can God do things which He neither does do nor will do?

In this question we first have to assume that God is an efficient cause of things. Secondly, we must inquire whether it can be proven by natural reason that is a free and non-natural efficient cause. Thirdly, [we have to inquire] whether this is something we have to believe as a truth of the faith. Fourthly, we have to respond to the question on the basis of the above inquiries.

[Scotus's arguments:]

[I] Some [viz. Duns Scotus] prove the same conclusion [that God can do such things] but in a different way as follows:[18] Something is caused contingently; therefore, the first cause causes contingent-

ly. The inference is proved as follows: Any secondary cause causes to the extent that it is moved by the first cause; therefore, if the first cause puts things in motion necessarily, any of the other causes is moved necessarily and consequently any of them causes necessarily. Therefore, if any secondary cause causes contingently or puts things in motion contingently, the first will put things in motion contingently; for a secondary cause causes only in virtue of the first cause to the extent that it is moved by that first cause.

[II] Likewise the same inference is proven as follows: If the first cause necessarily relates to the cause next to it, call that B, then B is necessarily moved by the first cause. But in the same way in which it is moved by the first cause B puts in motion the [cause] next to it. Therefore, in putting C in motion B causes necessarily, and C likewise in putting D in motion, and by proceeding in this way through all the causes [we find that] nothing will exist contingently if the first cause causes necessarily.

[IIa] Besides, he [Scotus] argues as follows: A being that is absolute and necessary to the highest degree in which something can be thought to be necessary cannot not exist, no matter what thing other than itself is not in existence. God is necessary to the highest degree; therefore, it does not follow from the non-existence of any thing other than Him that He does not exist. But if He had a necessary relationship to the first caused item, and that caused item did not exist, then He would not exist. Therefore, etc.

[IIa1] The major premise is evident enough, because the more impossible does not follow from the less impossible, just as the more false does not follow from the less false. This is proven as follows: If the more false had a double reason to be false and the less false only a single reason, then, were we to eliminate from the more false one the reason for its falsity which the less false does not have, while the other reason remains in force, the more false one would be false and the less false one would not be false, since its reason for being false has been eliminated. And now the more false will

---

16 See glossary entry for 'absolute term.'
17 See glossary entry for 'connotative term.'
18 See selection **I.9.2.**

be false, and the less false will be true, and in that case the false would follow from the true.

[III] Besides, bad things are produced in the universe; therefore, God does not cause necessarily. The inference is proven as follows: An agent acting necessarily produces necessarily its effect, which it is able to produce in something capable of receiving it, to the extent it is able to produce it in that thing. The effect of the first [cause] is goodness and perfection; therefore, if it acts necessarily, it necessarily produces goodness in anything to the extent that the item capable of receiving it is able to receive. But what has as much goodness as it is capable of has no badness. Therefore, etc.

[IV] Besides, a cause acting necessarily acts to the full extent of its power. Therefore, if the first cause causes necessarily, it causes whatever it is able to cause; but it is able to cause of itself everything that can be caused; therefore, no secondary cause causes anything. This final inference is proven as follows: A prior cause naturally related to the caused before the subsequent cause does; therefore, at that prior [instant] it does the whole causing. The deduction proceeds the way it did in the preceding question [i.e. dist.42 (selection I.9.1.)].

[*Objections to Scotus's arguments:*]

But these arguments against the philosophers (for it is against them that they are brought forward) do not show their conclusion.

The first [i.e. **I** above] does not because the inference, 'Something is brought about contingently; therefore, the first cause causes contingently' cannot be clearly proven. For the philosophers would say that the contingency of an effect depends on the contingency of the action of some creature, for example the action of a necessarily required created will. Consequently, since according to them the created will necessarily concurs in the production of many effects, and thus causes with unqualified contingency no matter how much the other causes cause naturally, the effect will be produced contingently.

And when it is said [in **I** above] that a secondary cause causes only to the extent that it is moved by the first [cause], I ask you this: What is it for a secondary cause to act to the extent that it is moved by the first [cause]? Either [1] it is for the secondary cause to depend for its own existence on the first cause, or [2] it is for it to receive some influence

from the first cause by which it acts, or [3] it is for it not to be able to act unless the first cause co-acts.

If the first [1], it is clear that this inference is not valid: A secondary cause does not put something in motion except in so far as it is moved by the first cause; therefore, if the first cause puts things in motion necessarily, anything else [that is moved] is moved necessarily. For if the heavenly sphere preserved a will in existence and did this necessarily, the will would act just as contingently in that circumstance as it does now. This is clear enough from the fact that an agent that just preserves [something in existence] does not in any case necessitate acting [on the part of what it preserves]. Hence what does the preserving would no more necessitate necessarily than contingently. This is clear in the case of an agent equally disposed [toward two or more options], for it is all the same whether it acts necessarily or contingently.

This reasoning is bolstered by the following: No cause that conserves or produces another cause necessitates the other cause to act any more than does a cause that immediately cooperates with it and without which it is capable of nothing while once it is given it is capable of producing the effect. But such a cause does not necessitate some other cause to act. This is clear in the case of cognition, which is a natural cause, and without it the will cannot will, and yet in no case does it necessitate that the will not will contingently. Therefore, by like considerations, no matter how much God naturally and necessarily conserves the will, He would not necessitate it to act in such a way that the will would not be able freely to act and not to act.

If in the second sense [2] we understand that a secondary cause only puts things in motion to the extent that it is moved by the first cause, the reasoning has no force, because the will receives no such influence from the first cause, but rather it is itself a principle of acting.

Nor can this be understood in the third way [3], because then it is obviously false. The will cannot do anything without cognition, as was shown earlier, and cognition is a natural cause, and yet the will acts contingently.

From the above it is clear that the *second* proof [i.e. **II** above] of the inference does not hold, because it is unqualifiedly false that a subsequent cause puts things in motion in the same way in which it was put in motion by the prior cause.

Sometimes a subsequent cause is moved naturally by the prior cause, and yet it itself puts things in motion contingently. For example, the intellective soul is naturally moved by the object to an act of cognition, and yet it contingently moves itself to an act of willing.

Besides, the second argument does not seem to show its conclusion, because philosophers deny the major premise. They would say that from the negation of something other than the first cause follows the negation of the first cause in just the same way that from the existence of the first cause the existence of the effect follows. This would be the case on account of the naturalness that belongs to the first cause in respect of its acting.

Consequently, if there are ranks among impossibles, they would say that the more impossible does follow from the less impossible, because otherwise it would be necessary to reject many logical rules which are doubtless unqualifiedly necessary. For example, it is certain that it is valid to infer from one of two mutually co-extensive terms the other. Therefore, the following is a valid inference: 'A human being is not capable of laughing; therefore, a human being is not a human being.' Nevertheless, the consequent is more impossible than the antecedent. Likewise, once the conclusion is rejected the principle [from which it is deduced] is rejected, and yet the opposite of the principle is more impossible [than the opposite of the conclusion].

But to this line of reasoning it is said that it is irrelevant to the point we are discussing, because the conclusion is just part of the truth of the principle (where the principle has a sort of total truth), just as the singular is a part of the truth of the universal. But in the case of entities a caused being is not a sort of part of the entity of the cause, but rather is an entirely different entity dependent on the entity of the cause.

But this answer does not seem to be enough. On the one hand, this is because the truth of the conclusion is not part of the truth of the principle, but rather is a single truth unqualifiedly distinct from the truth of the principle. When truths relate in such a way that one can be known while the other is unqualifiedly unknown and vice versa, one is no more a part in respect of the other than vice versa.

But the conclusion can be known while the principle is unqualifiedly unknown, as is frequently obvious when we evidently know some conclusions and then go on to search for principles, and vice versa. Therefore, neither is a part in respect of the other. On the other hand, this is because the truth of a singular is not a part in respect of the truth of the universal, for one singular is no more a part in respect of its universal than any other singular is a part in respect of its universal. This is because something true is never part of what is false, except perhaps materially, which is not relevant to the question under discussion. But sometimes the singular is true and the universal false. Therefore, in this case the truth of a singular is not a part in respect of its universal. Therefore, never is the truth of a singular a part in respect of its own universal. Likewise, in the same way a conclusion is never part of the truth in respect of its premises, because sometimes the premises are true and the conclusion false. Likewise, the habits[19] of the principle and of the conclusion are unqualifiedly distinct habits, and neither is a part in respect of the other. In that same way one truth is not a part in respect of the other.

Moreover, the third argument [i.e. III above] fails to show the conclusion. For the argument assumes that God is an immediate and total efficient cause in respect of any effect; otherwise the argument is invalid. For, if it is not the total cause but rather the will concurs with it, then the effect would be produced only if the will co-acted. Therefore, when the will does not act, there can be guilt, not in God, but in the will. Likewise, if it is not an immediate cause, then it will do no more than preserve the will, and thus it will not produce anything in the will. Yet it will remain in the power of the will to produce and not to produce, and hence to sin or not to sin.

The final argument [i.e. IV above] fails to show the conclusion, because it is not possible by natural reason to prove against the philosophers either that God could just by Himself alone cause everything that is causable, or that He immediately concurs in the causing of everything causable. Nevertheless, it is necessary to prove both of these in order to prove that a secondary cause does noth-

---

19 I.e., the mental states of understanding the principle and the conclusion.

ing. Also this final deduction of the priority in acting of the first cause is invalid, as was shown in the preceding question, because, even if in fact the cause is in a way prior, still there is no prior instant in which it produces its effect before the secondary cause produces it.

[*Solution of the question:*]

To this article I say, then, that it is not possible to prove by natural reason that God is the cause of things by acting contingently, because it is not possible to prove that from the perfection of the divine entity do not follow many effects which otherwise would not exist in just the way that many effects follow from the perfection of the sun.

As for the second article I say that we must believe that God is a cause that acts contingently, because we must believe that God can cause immediately and totally those generable things. But if He were a natural cause, He would produce either everything or nothing, but both of these are obviously false. And thus it is obviously false that God is a natural cause of things other than Himself.

From the above it is clear that the solution of the question is that God can do things which he does not do, because a free cause acting contingently can do otherwise than it does, but God is such a cause; therefore, etc. Likewise, God can go on producing souls to infinity, because there He never has to stop at a certain number, and yet He does not go on producing souls to infinity but rather stops at a certain number.

[*Responses by the philosophers to Scotus's arguments:*]

To the other doctor's [i.e. Scotus's] first argument [i.e. I above] they would say that the following inference is not valid: Something is contingently brought about; therefore, the first cause acts contingently. They would say that the will is not moved immediately by God but is only preserved by Him, and therefore it is able to act contingently even though God acts necessarily, in just the way it acts contingently even though cognition necessarily co-acts.

They would make the same point to the second argument [i.e. II above] by saying that a secondary cause does not always put things in motion in the same way in which it is moved by the first cause.

To the other argument [i.e. IIa above] they would say that sometimes the non-being of the more necessary follows from the non-being of the less necessary. Likewise, the more impossible follows from the less impossible and the more false from the less false.

To the proof [Scotus gives, i.e. IIa1 above] I say that sometimes the more false has only one reason for falsity, but that reason is more false than the reason for the falsity of the less false. Likewise, given that [the more false] has two reasons for its falsity while the other has only one, still the proof is not valid, because the single reason for the falsity of the less false cannot in any way be eliminated, and thus that false item cannot be true, and consequently the false never follows from the true.

If you say that it can be eliminated in thought, I answer that if you eliminate it in thought by saying that it does not exist, your elimination of it is false. If you eliminate it without saying anything about the reason for the falsity, the false item will be just as false as before, because your considering it or not considering it is irrelevant to whether it is true or false.

To the other argument [i.e. III above] they would say that evil comes to be in the universe because God does not produce in the recipient[20] as much [goodness] as can be produced there. This can have two causes of its truth: either because it produces nothing in the recipient, or because it produces only with the concurrence of a will which concurs freely and contingently.

To the other argument [i.e. IV above] they would say that God is not able to cause everything that of itself can be caused. Or if it is said that the first cause contains the whole causality of the secondary cause and, therefore, can just by itself produce that effect, they would say that it contains the whole causality of the secondary cause only in the sense that it produces that whole secondary cause. But it is evident that sometimes what naturally produces a cause cannot immediately produce the

---

20 See glossary entry for 'agent/recipient.'

effect of that cause. For example, it is clear enough that the sun produces worms,[21] and yet the worm can produce some effects which the sun cannot. This is evident in lots of cases.

I.10.6. Does not being able to do the Impossible belong to God before not being able to be done by God belongs to the Impossible? (from *Ordinatio* I, dist.43, qu.2)

[Ockham here disagrees with the position Duns Scotus adopted in selection I.9.4. Ockham argues that the view that the divine intellect produces the creature in intelligible existence is incoherent. His ultimate conclusion is that God's inability to do the impossible is neither prior nor posterior explanatorily to the impossible's not being able to be done.]

Secondly, I ask: Does not being able to do the impossible belong to God before not being able to be done by God belongs to the impossible?

[*Scotus's view:*]

A different sort of reply is given [by Scotus, see selection I.9.4.] where the primary reason for the impossible does not lie on the side of God, but rather this item is unqualifiedly impossible because of its rejection of being made. This is explained as follows: What is unqualifiedly impossible includes incompossibles, which are incompossible on account of their own formal characters, and take the origin of their incompossibility from the origin they have for their own formal characters.

And then we get the following process: First the divine intellect produces a thing in intelligible existence at the first instant of nature;[22] at the second instant of nature the thing has through itself possible being. "And just as God by His intellect produces the possible in possible existence, so He produces both of the incompossibles which are included in the impossible as formally having possible existence; and these 'products' are of themselves formally incompossible, in such a way that that

they cannot together be one item, nor can some third item come from them. This incompossibility which they possess from themselves formally takes its origin from what produces them in possible being. And the impossibility of the whole signified item follows from that incompossibility of theirs. And then from that follows the impossibility in respect of any agent." At that point the whole process ends, but not in the negation of any possibility in God.

[*Arguments against Scotus's view:*]

Against some of the things said here it can be argued, first, that it does not seem right to say that the divine intellect produces creatures in intelligible existence. This is because what through some act receives no formal existence but is only denominated by an extrinsic denomination,[23] is not produced by such an act. But by the fact that it is thought of by God a creature receives nothing formal but is just denominated by an extrinsic denomination. In the same way an object of a created intellect is not produced by being thought of, but is just denominated by an extrinsic denomination. Therefore, creatures are not produced in such intelligible existence.

Besides, either the creature is produced in intelligible existence just by being thought of, or because before that it was nothing, or because before that it was not intelligible. Not the first, because in that case the divine essence would in fact be produced in intelligible existence when it is in fact thought of, and then anything which thinks of God would produce God in intelligible existence. Not the second either, because, even when a creature is thought of, it is nothing, although it is thought of. Nor the third, because before its own act of thinking the divine essence was not intelligible.

Besides, according to this man [i.e. Scotus], never is something produced in intelligible existence unless because something is produced in real existence. But according to him, when a creature is produced by the divine intellect, it is only produced in

---

21 It was mistakenly believed that maggots in rotting material were produced spontaneously by the sun and not by reproduction by insects.

22 See glossary entry for 'instant of nature.'

23 I.e., something which merely characterizes it as related to something else.

intelligible existence. Therefore, something else is produced in real existence, but in fact there is no such thing, as is clear from induction.[24]

Besides, when he says that at the first instant of nature [the creature] is produced in intelligible existence, and then in the second instant it has possible existence, I argue the contrary as follows: I take the first instant of nature in which the intellect precedes the intelligible existence of the creature and I ask: At that instant is the creature possible or not? If it is possible, then it is possible before it is produced in intelligible existence. If it is not possible, then it rejects existence.

Besides, when he says that the process comes to a stop in an impossibility in respect of any agent but without any corresponding relation in God, I argue the contrary as follows: Just as to every relation a creature in possible existence bears toward God there corresponds some relation God bears toward the creature in possible existence, so to the negation of a relation will correspond the negation of a relation God bears toward the impossible. Therefore, the process does not stop there.

If he were to say that to a relation a creature in possible existence bears toward God there does not correspond a relation that God bears [toward the creature], I argue the contrary as follows: The relation the creature in possible existence has is either a real relation or a relation of thought. It is not real, because it has no real basis. Therefore, it is a relation of thought which is made by the intellect relating the creature to God, which is what he in fact says. But the intellect is just as able to relate God to the creature as vice versa. Therefore, there can just as much be a relation God bears to the creature as vice versa; therefore, etc.

[*Solution of the question:*]

Consequently, I answer this question differently, by saying that in general to every relative item, as long as it is correctly picked out, there will correspond a correlative. Wherever we have a relative item that is relative in virtue of an active or passive power, or of a cause and an effect, there will always be at the

same time by nature something correlative to it. Consequently, since they are at the same time by nature mutually imply each other, neither is more the cause of the other than vice versa. Just as, because father and son are at the same time by nature (in the sense The Philosopher gives in *Categories*, the chapter on relation,[25] where he speaks of simultaneity of nature), it is no more the case that the son is a son because the father is a father than vice versa; nor does the son have a father because the father has a son any more than vice versa. Thus in all cases when we have a mutual entailment holding exclusively on account of the nature of correlatives, one proposition is not any more a cause of the other than vice versa.

And when it is asked whether not being able to make the impossible belongs to God before not being able to be made by God belongs to the impossible, I say that not being able to make the impossible does not belong to God before not being able to be made by God belongs to the impossible. Nor is it the case that not being able to be made belongs to the impossible before not being able to make the impossible belongs to God. I say the same thing about the affirmative cases: being able to make the possible or a creature does not belong to God before being able to be made by God belongs to the creature. Rather, they are at the same time by nature, i.e. something's being able to make does not come before something's being makeable, nor vice versa.

If it is said: Whatever a creature has it has from God; therefore it gets possible existence from God; but God does not get the ability to make from anything other than Himself. Now, something which belongs to a thing from itself belongs to it before what belongs to it from something else belongs to it. Therefore, being capable of making belongs to God before being makeable belongs to the creature, and hence they are not at the same time –

We have to say [to this] that whatever a creature has that is real as something inhering in it, it has from God as from a source. But it is not the case that whatever belongs to it in a predication is something it has from God as a source, except in the way

---

24 Ockham refers to the fact (for theologians) that in God nothing real is produced besides the second and third Persons, and clearly the production of intelligible existence does not depend on them.
25 Ch.7, 7b15-20.

that God also has such predication from God. Consequently, possible existence belongs to a creature in virtue of itself, but not really as something inhering in the creature; rather it is truly possible in virtue of itself, just as a human being is not an ass in virtue of itself. It follows that such arguments are valid only when they are about what really belongs to something, in the way that a whole has parts and accidents. It is not strictly correct to say that possible existence belongs to a creature; rather one ought more correctly to say that the creature is possible, not on account of something that belongs to it but because it can exist in reality.

I.10.7. Can God make a better world than this one? (*Ordinatio* I, dist.44)

[Ockham proceeds very carefully here because he finds that it is not provable one way or another whether the series of different types of worlds, "worlds different in species," each more perfect than the last, has a last, most perfect, member or extends on *ad infinitum*.]

Concerning the forty-fourth distinction I ask: Can God make a world better than this world?

[I] For the negative: What does not admit of more or less cannot be made better. But the world does not admit of more or less. Therefore, one world cannot be better than another. Therefore, etc. The minor premiss [the world does not admit of more or less] is clear enough because the world consists of substances and these do not admit of more or less.[26]

[II] Besides, by whatever reason God could make a world better than this world, by the same reason He could make a world better than that world, and so on *ad infinitum*. Consequently, He would be able to make an infinite world, which is impossible.

For the opposite view is the Master [Peter Lombard in his *Sentences* I, d.44, c.1] in the text [we are studying].

On this question we have to first see what the word 'world' means; secondly, what 'better' means;

thirdly, answer the question.

As for the first, I say that 'world' has two meanings: Sometimes it means the whole aggregate of created things, whether they be substances or accidents; sometimes it means a whole composed or aggregated from lots of items that are contained in one body as well as from the body containing them. And it has this latter sense in two ways, either as meaning exclusively the parts which are substances, or as meaning all the parts no matter what. But in this question 'world' has to be taken as meaning just the one universe which is composed, as it were, from parts that are substances, and not in the sense that it includes the accidents of the substances.

As for the second, I say that something can be better than something else either in virtue of an essential or substantial goodness, or in virtue of accidental goodness.

As for the third, we have to first see whether He could make a world that is better in virtue of essential or substantial goodness, and this in such a way that this world is distinct in species [from the one we have]. Secondly, whether He could make a better world that is distinct [from the one we have] only in number.[27] Thirdly, whether He could make a world that is better in virtue of accidental goodness.

As for the first, it is doubtful what to believe. For if we hold to the view that God can make a substance that is more perfect than any He has made, and we carry this to infinity (just in the way that a quality that can admit of more or less can increase to infinity in the sense that there is no point at which the increase stops), we have to say as a consequence that God can make a better world that is distinct in species, because he could make another substantial individual that is distinct in species and better than those He has already made.

On the other hand, if we hold that there is a stopping point in such a progression so that there is some most perfect substance which it is possible for God to make, the question is harder. If we hold to this view, both parts can be believed as probable, viz. that He can make another world distinct in species, [and that he cannot]. In favour of the for-

---

26 I.e., substances cannot be more, or less, the sort of substance they are. Ockham does *not* mean they could not be more, or less, in number.

27 For the notions of distinctness "in species" and "in number" see selections **V.1.1. & 2.**

mer part seems to be the view of Augustine and The Master [Peter Lombard] in the text[28] "God could have made a human being who neither was able to sin nor wished to sin." From this authoritative text I argue as follows: Whenever something belongs to some individual member of a most specific species, no individual of that same species rejects anything formally similar to it. But obviously being able to sin belongs to this human being here. Therefore, no individual of that human's species rejects sinning. But, according to Augustine, God can make a human being who rejects sinning. Therefore, such a human being would not be in the same most specific species with this human being here. Therefore, he would belong to another species, and consequently God could make an individual of a species other than those he has made, and consequently He could make a world of another species which for the same reason would be better.

If it is objected against this argument that its assumption is false, for being able to sin belongs to *this* human being here, and nevertheless *that* human being there – pointing to Christ – rejects being able to sin, notwithstanding the fact that he belongs to the same most specific species as does this human being who is able to sin –

And similarly, human being is a most specific species; therefore, there cannot be a human being of some other species than this human and who is able to sin –

The first of these does not show its conclusion, for although the divine Word[29] rejects being able to sin, still that nature which is united to the Word does not reject being able to sin, because if it were removed from the Word it would be able to sin. That nature belongs to the same most specific species as does this human being who can sin, but it is not of the same species as the Word which cannot sin.

Also the second does not show its conclusion, for 'human being' can have two meanings. In one sense it means anything composed out of a body and an intellectual nature. When 'human being' is taken in that sense, it is not a most specific species. Consequently, this human being who is made incapable by nature of sinning would not be of the same most specific species as this human being who can sin. In another sense, 'human being' means anything composed of a body and the sort of intellectual soul we have. When 'human being' is taken that way, it is a most specific species,[30] and then whoever is made incapable of sinning would not be a human being in this sense.

Also given we hold that there is a stopping point in the series of individuals that are distinct in species, we could hold that God could not make another individual distinct in species. For, if there is such a stopping point, there is a definite number of most specific species that are makeable by God, and consequently it is difficult to prove that some individuals of certain species are produced by God and some are not produced by God. Nor does there seem to be anything that harmonizes with this, except perhaps some authoritative text from the scriptures which it is difficult to find. On this view, God could not make another world distinct in species from this one.

There is a third way in which we can claim that there is such a stopping point. This is by supposing that of certain species there are some individuals that are producible by God that have not been produced and yet an individual of the highest species has been produced. For it does not seem likely that God would have produced individuals of lower species but not any of the highest, given there is a highest.

Augustine seems to be in favor of this when in *Confessions*[31] he says: "Lord, you have made two things, one near to yourself and one near to nothing." Just as it does not seem possible for something lower than prime matter[32] (which Augustine calls "near to nothing") to be made, so it does not seem possible for something more perfect than an angel (which Augustine calls "near to God") to be made.

Consequently it is clear enough that in this article

---

28 *Sentences* I, d.44,c.1,n.3, Augustine, *Literal Comments on Genesis* XI, c.7- 9. PL 34, 433.
29 I.e., Jesus Christ, who was a human being but could not sin.
30 See glossary entry for 'species/genus.'
31 XII, c.7; PL 32, 828.
32 See glossary entry for 'prime matter.'

there can be three opinions. I reckon it probable that God is able to make another world better than this one and distinct from this one in species, and do this in the strongest sense by making some things that are distinct in species and a greater number of species.

As for the second [article] I say that God can make a world better than this one as well as distinct just in number from this world. The reason for this is that God can produce an infinity of individuals of the same type as those that now exist. Therefore, God can produce as many individuals, and more, as have already been produced where those individuals would be of the same species as those already produced. But their production is not possible within the confines of this world. Therefore, he could produce them outside of this world and make out of them a single world, just as from those He has already produced He has made this world.

To the first argument at the beginning [I] I say that, although the world does not admit of more or less in the way accidental qualities admit of more or less, still one more perfect than this one can be made and this one can be added to. [This can happen] in the same way that an amount of water can be added to, and in the way that, when one small amount of water has been made, another one that is larger can be made. Consequently there can be a more perfect [world] in this way.

To the other [argument at the beginning, i.e. II], different people would reply in different ways. Those who say there is no stopping point in the series of individuals of different species (since for any given one a better can be made) would say that God could make a better world *ad infinitum*, but not an infinite world. This can happen in the same way that He is able to make an amount of water greater than any given amount of water, but not an infinite amount of water. Others would say that a world than which there is not able to be made a better could be made.

TOPIC II

IS THERE AN INFINITELY PERFECT BEING?

CHRISTIAN THEOLOGY WAS NOT SATISFIED WITH A GOD WHO WAS MERELY the most perfect and powerful of all the beings that in fact exist; it claimed that God was as perfect and as powerful as anything could possibly be. This led to the doctrine that in fact God is infinite in perfection and power, and that one of the great divides between the divine and the created realms is that the former is infinite and the latter finite. In ancient Greek thought infinity had usually not been thought of as a perfection and thus was rarely ascribed to the deity. Aristotle had argued that an actual infinity of items all existing simultaneously was self-contradictory, although he did allow for the infinite divisibility of the continuum and the infinity of past time required to ensure that motion never had a beginning. (See selection **III.1.1.**) It might be thought, then, that on this topic the incompatibility of the cosmological synthesis of the "philosophers" would have been seen to be clearly incompatible with Christian doctrine. But in fact Aristotle's discussion of the first mover, given below, was thought by many to show that what maintains motion over an infinite time must be infinite in power. Aristotle's strictures against infinity were thought to apply only to an "extensive" infinity, i.e. an infinity of spatial extension, and not to an "intensive" infinity, i.e. an infinite degree of some perfection or power.

Before Aristotle's *Physics* and *Metaphysics* were known to the western scholastics, Anselm had formulated an argument for the existence of something than which a more perfect being could not be thought without contradiction. Aquinas brushed this reasoning aside in favour of arguments grounded in causality. But to Duns Scotus it seemed to open a way to proving the infinite perfection of the deity, for surely anything with only finite perfection was something than which a more perfect being could be thought. All these discussions lead into the various puzzles surrounding infinity and should be compared in this regard with the selections by Duns Scotus and Ockham in topic **III**, where the coherence of an infinity of past time is called into question and then defended. The willingness of Christian thinkers to grant at least the logical possibility of an actual intensive infinity was, whether they knew it or not, a major break with Greek thought, and one that helped to open up possibilities for mathematics in later centuries.

In both Islamic and Christian thought the idea that the speculations of the "philosophers" could not be anything but inimical to the faith was never without its supporters. In the selections below we see Al-Ghazali pursuing this line and Averroes defending philosophy, and we also see William of Ockham rejecting the way Duns Scotus had tried to find support in Aristotle for Christian doctrine. As the condemnations at Paris in 1277 showed (see selection I.7) the tensions here were always threatening to erupt and spoil the hopes of those who wanted an accommodation between science and faith.

II.1. ARISTOTLE

IN TOPIC III WE FIND THAT ARISTOTLE BELIEVED THAT IT IS INCOHERENT to suppose that time and motion ever had a beginning or will ever have an ending. In this everlasting motion of the physical world he finds a feature which he argues can only be explained by positing some sustaining cause that is everlasting but without any motion at all. This he ultimately identifies with a mind that is eternally and continuously engaged in thinking, and which acts on the souls of the heavenly spheres as an object of desire. Although this "first mover" produces motion over an infinite length of time, it is not entirely clear whether Aristotle is proposing that it has infinite power or simply exists over an infinite length of time. The unclarity of the texts on this point led to considerable dissension among medieval commentators about how Aristotle understood the infinity of the first being.

II.1.1. Why there must be an eternal mover that is not itself in motion (*Physics* VIII, c.6, 258b10-260a19)

Since there must always be motion without intermission, there must necessarily be something eternal, whether one or many, that first imparts motion, and this first mover must not itself be in motion. Now the question whether each of the things that are not in motion but impart motion is eternal is irrelevant to our present argument; but the following considerations will make it clear that there must necessarily be some something, which, while it has the capacity of moving something else, is itself not in motion and exempt from all change, both qualified and accidental. Let us suppose, if you will, that in the case of certain things it is possible for them at different times to be and not to be, without any process of becoming and perishing (in fact it would seem to be necessary, if a thing that has no parts at one time is and at another time is not, that any such thing should without undergoing any change at one time be and at another time not be). And let us further suppose it possible that some principles that are not in motion but capable of imparting motion at one time are and at another time are not. Even so, this cannot be true of *all* such principles, since there must clearly be something that *causes* things that move themselves at one time to be and at another not to be. For, since nothing that has no parts can be in motion, everything which moves itself must have size, though

nothing we have said makes this necessarily true of every mover. So the fact that some things become and others perish, and that this is so continuously, cannot be caused by any one of those things that, though they are not in motion, do not always exist; nor again some be caused by some and others by others. The eternity and continuity of the process cannot be caused either by any one of them singly or by the sum of them, because this causal relation must be eternal and necessary, whereas the sum of these movers is infinite and they do not all exist together. It is clear, then, that though there may be countless instances of the perishing of movers that are not in motion, and though many things that move themselves perish and are succeeded by others that come into being, and though one thing that is not in motion moves one thing while another moves another, nevertheless there is something that comprehends them all, and that as something apart from each one of them, and this it is that is the cause of the fact that some things are and others are not and of the continuous process of change; and this causes the motion of the other movers, while they are the causes of the motion of other things. Motion, then, being eternal, the first mover, if there is but one, will be eternal also; if there are more than one, there will be a plurality of such eternal movers. We ought, however, to suppose that there is one rather than many, and a finite rather than an infinite number. When the consequences of either assumption are the same, we should always assume that things are finite rather than infinite in number, since in things constituted by nature that which is finite and that which is better ought, if possible, to be present rather than the reverse; and here it is sufficient to assume only one mover, the first of things not in motion, which being eternal will be the principle of motion to everything else.

The following argument also makes it evident that the first mover must be something that is one and eternal. We have shown that there must always be motion. That being so, motion must be continuous, because what is always is continuous, whereas what is in succession is not continuous. But further, if motion is continuous, it is one; and it is one only if the mover and the moved are each of them one, since in the event of a thing's being moved now by one thing and now by another the whole motion will not be continuous but successive.

Moreover a conviction that there is a first something that is not in motion may be reached not only from the foregoing arguments, but also by considering again the principles operative in movers. Now it is evident that among existing things there are some that are sometimes in motion and sometimes at rest. This fact has served to make it clear that it is not true either that all things are in motion or that all things are at rest or that some things are always at rest and the remainder always in motion; on this matter proof is supplied by things that fluctuate between the two and have the capacity of being sometimes in motion and sometimes at rest. The existence of things of this kind is clear to all; but we wish to explain also the nature of each of the other two kinds and show that there are some things that are always not in motion and some things that are always in motion. In the course of our argument directed to this end we establish the fact that everything that is in motion is moved by something, and that the mover is either not in motion or in motion, and that, if it is in motion, it is moved at each stage either by itself or by something else; and so we proceeded to the position that of things that are in motion, the principle of things that are in motion is that which moves itself, and the principle of the whole series is what is not in motion.

Further, it is evident from actual observation that there are things that have the characteristic of moving themselves, e.g. the animal kingdom and the whole class of living things. This being so, then, the view was suggested that perhaps it may be possible for motion to come to be in a thing without having been in existence at all before, because we see this actually occurring in animals: they are not in motion at one time and then again they are in motion, as it seems. We must grasp the fact, therefore, that animals move themselves only with one kind of motion, and that this is not strictly originated by them. The cause of it is not derived from the animal itself: there are other natural motions in animals, which they do not experience through their own instrumentality, e.g. increase, decrease, and respiration: these are experienced by every animal while it is at rest and not in motion in respect of the motion set up by its own agency; here the motion is caused by the environment and by many things that enter into the animal: thus in some cases the cause is nourishment – when it is being digested animals sleep, and when it is being distributed they awake and move themselves, the first principle for this motion being thus originally derived from outside. Therefore, animals are not always in continuous motion by their own agency: it is something else that moves them, something which itself is in motion and changing as it comes into relation with each several thing that moves itself. (Moreover, in all these things the first mover and cause of their self-motion is itself in motion by itself, though in an accidental sense: that is to say, the body changes its place, so that that which is in the body changes its place also and moves itself by leverage.) Hence we may be sure that if a thing belongs to the class of things not in motion which move themselves accidentally, it is impossible that it should cause continuous motion. So the necessity that there should be motion continuously requires that there should be a first mover that is not in motion even accidentally, if, as we have said, there is to be in the world of things an unceasing and undying motion, and the world is to remain self-contained and within the same limits; for if the principle is permanent, the universe must also be permanent, since it is continuous with the principle. (We must distinguish, however, between accidental motion of a thing by itself and such motion by something else, the former being confined to perishable things, whereas the latter belongs also to certain principles of heavenly bodies, of all those, that is to say, that experience more than one locomotion.)

And further, if there is always something of this

nature, a mover that is itself not in motion and eternal, then that which is first moved by it must also be eternal. Indeed this is clear also from the consideration that there would otherwise be no becoming and perishing and no change of any kind in other things, if there were nothing in motion to move them; for the motion imparted by what is not in motion will always be imparted in the same way and be one and the same, since what is not in motion does not itself change in relation to that which is moved by it. But that which is moved by something that, though it is in motion, is moved directly by what is not in motion stands in varying relations to the things that it moves, so that the motion that it causes will not be always the same; by reason of the fact that it occupies contrary positions or assumes contrary forms it will produce contrary motions in each several thing that it moves and will cause it to be at one time at rest and at another time in motion.

The foregoing argument, then, has served to clear up the point about which we raised a difficulty at the outset – why is it that instead of all things being either in motion or at rest, or some things being always in motion and the remainder always at rest, there are things that are sometimes in motion and sometimes not? The cause of this is now plain: it is because, while some things are moved by an eternal mover that is not itself in motion and are therefore always in motion, other things are moved by something that is in motion and changing, so that they too must change. But the mover that is not itself in motion, as has been said, since it remains simple and unvarying and in the same state, will cause motion that is one and simple.

II.1.2. The first Mover has no Size (*Physics* VIII, c.10, 266a10-267b26)

[There is no doubt here that Aristotle thinks that the fact that the first mover produces an endless motion in the heavenly bodies rules out its having any magnitude, i.e. size. But does his argument imply as well that the first mover has infinite power even if it has no size?]

We have now to assert that the first mover must be without parts and without size, beginning with the establishment of the premises on which this conclusion depends.

One of these premises is that nothing finite can cause motion during an infinite time. We have three things, the mover, the moved, and thirdly that in which the motion takes place, namely the time; and these are either all infinite or all finite or some – that is to say two of them or one of them – finite and some infinite. Let A be the mover, B the moved, and C infinite time. Now let us suppose that D moves E, a part of B. Then the time occupied by this motion cannot be equal to C; for the greater the amount moved, the longer the time occupied. If follows that the time F is not infinite. Now we see that by continuing to add to D I shall use up A and by continuing to add to E I shall use up B; but I shall not use up the time by continually subtracting a corresponding amount from it, because it is infinite. Consequently, the part of C which is occupied by all A in moving the whole of B, will be finite. Therefore, a finite thing cannot impart to anything an infinite motion. It is clear, then, that it is impossible for the finite to cause motion during an infinite time.

That in no case is it possible for an infinite force to reside in a thing of finite size, can be shown as follows: we take it for granted that the greater force is always that which in less time does an equal amount of work – heating, for example, or sweetening or throwing, or in general causing motion. Then that on which the forces act must be affected to some extent by the finite magnitude possessing an infinite force – in fact to a greater extent than by anything else, since the infinite force is greater than any other. But then there cannot be any time in which its action could take place. Suppose that A is the time occupied by the infinite power in the performance of an act of heating or pushing, and that AB is the time occupied by a finite power in the performance of the same act; then by adding to the latter another finite power and continually increasing the size of the power so added I shall at some time or other reach a point at which the finite power has completed the motive act in the time A; for by continual addition to a finite magnitude I must arrive at a magnitude that exceeds any assigned limit, and in the same way by continual subtraction I must arrive at one that falls short of any assigned limit. So we get the result that the finite force will occupy the same amount of time in performing the motive act as the infinite force. But this is impossible. Therefore, nothing finite can possess an infinite force. So it is also impossible for a finite force to reside in a thing of infinite size. It is true that a greater force can reside in a thing of lesser size; but then a still greater force will reside in a greater. Now let AB be an infinite magnitude. Then BC possesses a certain force that occupies a certain time, let us say the time EF, in moving D. Now if I take a magnitude twice as great as BC, the time occupied by this magnitude in moving D will be half of EF (assuming this to be the proportion): so we may call this time FG. That being so, by continually taking a greater magnitude in this way I shall never arrive at AB, whereas I shall always be getting a lesser fraction of the time originally given. Therefore, the force must be infinite; for it exceeds any finite force if the time occupied by the action of any finite force must also be finite (for if a given force moves something in a certain time, a greater force will do so in a lesser time, but still a definite time, in inverse proportion). But a force must always be infinite – just as a number or a size is – if it exceeds all definite limits. This point may also be proved in another way – by taking a thing of finite size in which there resides a force the same in kind as that which resides in the thing of infinite size, so that this force will be a measure of the finite force residing in the thing of infinite size.

It is plain, then, from the foregoing arguments that it is impossible for an infinite force to reside in a thing of finite size or for a finite force to reside in a thing of infinite size. But first it will be well to discuss a difficulty that arises in connexion with locomotion. If everything that is in motion with the exception of things that move themselves is moved by something, how is it that some things, e.g. things thrown, continue to be in motion when their mover is no longer in contact with them? If we say that the mover in such cases moves something else at the same time, e.g. the air, and that this in being moved is also a mover, then it will similarly be impossible for this to be in motion when the original mover is not in contact with it or moving it: all the things moved would have to be in motion when the original mover ceases to move them, even if, like the magnet, it makes that which it has moved capable of being a mover. Therefore, we must say that the original mover gives the power of being a mover either to air or to water or to something else of the kind, naturally adapted for imparting and undergoing motion; but this thing does not cease

simultaneously to impart motion and to undergo motion; it ceases to be in motion at the moment when its mover ceases to move it, but it still remains a mover, and so it causes something else consecutive with it to be in motion, and of this again the same may be said. The motion ceases when the motive force produced in one member of the consecutive series is at each stage less, and it finally ceases when one member no longer causes the next member to be a mover but only causes it to be in motion. The motion of these last two – of the one as mover and of the other as moved – must cease simultaneously, and with this the whole motion ceases. Now the things in which this motion is produced are things that admit of being sometimes in motion and sometimes at rest, and the motion is not continuous but only appears so; for it is motion of things that are either successive or in contact, there being not one mover but a number consecutive with one another. That is why motion of this kind takes place in air and water. Some say that it is mutual replacement; but the difficulty raised cannot be solved otherwise than in the way we have described. Mutual replacement makes all the members of the series move and impart motion simultaneously, so that their motions also cease simultaneously; but there appears to be continuous motion in a single thing, and therefore, since it cannot be moved by the same mover, the question is, what moves it?

Since there must be continuous motion in the world of things, and this is a single motion, and a single motion must be a motion of a thing with size (for that which is without size cannot be in motion), and of a single thing with size moved by a single mover (for otherwise there will not be continuous motion but a consecutive series of separate motions), then if the mover is a single thing, it is either in motion or not in motion; if, then, it is in motion, it will have to keep pace with that which it moves and itself be in a process of change, and it will also have to be moved by something; so we have a series that must come to an end, and a point will be reached at which motion is imparted by something that is not in motion. Thus we have a mover that has no need to change along with that which it moves but will be able to cause motion always (for the causing of motion under these conditions involves no effort); and this motion alone is regular, or at least it is so in a higher degree than any other, since the mover is never subject to any change. So, too, in order that the motion may continue to be of the same character, the moved must not be subject to change in relation to it. So it must occupy either the centre or the circumference, since these are the principles. But the things nearest the mover are those whose motion is quickest, and in this case it is the motion of the circumference that is the quickest; therefore, the mover occupies the circumference.

There is a difficulty in supposing it to be possible for anything that is in motion to cause motion continuously and not merely in the way in which it is caused by something repeatedly pushing (in which case the continuity amounts to no more than successiveness). Such a mover must either itself continue to push or pull or perform both these actions, or else the action must be taken up by something else and be passed on from one mover to another (the process that we described before as occurring in the case of things thrown, since the air, being divisible, is a mover in virtue of the fact that different parts of the air are moved one after another); and in either case the motion cannot be a single motion, but only a consecutive series of motions. The only continuous motion, then, is that which is caused by the mover that is not itself in motion, for it remains always invariable, so that its relation to that which it moves remains also invariable and continuous.

Now that these points are settled, it is clear that the first mover that is not itself in motion cannot have any size. For if has size, this must be either a finite or an infinite size. Now we have already proved in our course on *Physics* that there cannot be something with infinite size; and we have now proved that it is impossible for a thing of finite size to have an infinite force, and also that it is impossible for a thing to be moved by a thing of finite size during an infinite time. But the first mover causes a motion that is eternal and causes it during an infinite time. It is clear, therefore, that it is indivisible and is without parts and without size.

II.1.3. The Principle on which depend the Heavens and Nature (*Metaphysics* XII, c.6-7)

[In this selection Aristotle develops what he has said about a "first mover" in the previous selections into a true theology by describing the completely actualized and pleasant life of this mind which is always thinking of what is really the same as itself. He also adds the idea that God moves the first of the bodies that has motion as an "object of desire." This raises the question of whether God is just a final cause of motion rather than an efficient cause of it, and if so whether this account from the *Metaphysics* disagrees with that given in the preceding selections from the *Physics*.]

Chapter 6

Since there were three kinds of substance, two of them natural and one unmovable, regarding the latter we must assert that it is necessary that there should be an eternal unmovable substance. For substances are the first of existing things, and if they are all destructible, all things are destructible. But it is impossible that movement should either come into being or cease to be;[1] for it must always have existed. Nor can time come into being or cease to be; for there could not be a before and an after if time did not exist. Movement also is continuous, then, in the sense in which time is; for time is either the same thing as movement or an attribute of movement. And there is no continuous movement except movement in place, and of this only that which is circular is continuous.[2]

But if there is something which is capable of moving things or acting on them, but is not actually doing so, there will not be movement; for that which has a capacity need not exercise it. Nothing, then, is gained even if we suppose eternal substances, as the believers in the Forms[3] do, unless there is to be in them some principle which can cause movement; and even this is not enough, nor is another substance besides the Forms enough; for if it does not *act*, there will be no movement.

---

1 See selection **III.1.1**.
2 Aristotle thinks he has shown all this in *Physics* VIII, chs.7-9.
3 I.e., the "Forms" postulated by Plato which he thought to be changeless, everlasting substances outside the realm of things that come to be and perish. See passage from Plato's *Timaius* in selection **VI.1.1**.

Further, even if it acts, this will not be enough, if its substance is potentiality; for there will not be *eternal* movement; for that which is potentially may possibly not be. There must, then, be such a principle, whose very substance is actuality. Further, then, these substances must be without matter; for they must be eternal, at least if anything else is eternal. Therefore they must be actuality.

Yet there is a difficulty; for it is thought that everything that acts is able to act, but that not everything that is able to act acts, so that the potentiality is prior. But if this is so, nothing at all will exist; for it is possible for things to be capable of existing but not yet to exist. Yet if we follow the mythologists who generate the world form night, or the natural philosophers who say that all things were together, the same impossible result ensues. For how will there be movement, if there is no actual cause? Matter will surely not move itself – the carpenter's art must act on it; nor will the menstrual fluids nor the earth set themselves in motion, but the seeds and the semen must act on them.[4]

This is why some suppose eternal actuality – e.g. Leucippus[5] and Plato,[6] for they say there is always movement. But why and what this movement is they do not say, nor, if the world moves in this way or that, do they tell us the cause of its doing so. Now nothing is moved at random, but there must always be something present, e.g. as a matter of fact a thing moves in one way by nature, and in another by force or through the influence of thought or something else. Further, what sort of movement is primary? This makes a vast difference. But again Plato, at least, cannot even say what it is that he sometimes supposes to be the source of movement – that which moves itself; for the *soul* is later, and simultaneous with the heavens, according to his account.[7] To suppose potentiality prior to actuality, then, is in a sense right, and in a sense not; and we have specified these senses.

That actuality is prior is testified by Anaxagoras[8] (for his Mind is actuality) and by Empedocles[9] in his doctrine of love and strife, and by those who say that there is always movement, e.g. Leucippus.

Therefore chaos or night did not exist for any infinite time, but the same things have always existed (either passing through a cycle of changes or in some other way), since actuality is prior to potentiality. If, then, there is a constant cycle, something must always remain, acting in the same way. And if there is to be generation and destruction, there must be something else which is always acting in different ways. This must, then, act in one way in virtue of itself, and in another in virtue of something else – either of a third agent, therefore, or of the first. But it must be in virtue of the first. For otherwise this again causes the motion both of the third agent and of the second. Therefore, it is better to say the first. For it was the cause of eternal movement; and something else is the cause of variety, and evidently both together are the cause of eternal variety. This, accordingly, is the character which the motions actually exhibit. What need then is there to seek for other principles?

Chapter 7

Since this is a possible account of the matter, and if it were not true, the world would have proceeded out of night and "all things together" and out of non-being, these difficulties may be taken as solved. There is, then, something which is always in motion with an unceasing motion, which is motion in a circle; and this is plain not in theory but in fact. Therefore the first heavens must be eternal. There is therefore also something which moves them. And since that which is in motion and imparts motion is intermediate, there is a mover which moves without being in motion, being eternal, substance, and actuality. And the object of desire and the object of

---

4 It was Aristotle's view that the male semen acts on the fluids in the female womb, the ones the female discharges in her menstrual periods, in the same way that a seed acts on the earth so as to generate a new organism.
5 With Democritus the founder of Greek atomism in the 5th century B.C.E.
6 Aristotle's teacher who lived from 428 to 348 and founded the Academy where Aristotle studied for nearly twenty years.
7 I.e., the account he gives in the *Timaeus*. See selection VI.1.1.
8 Philosopher who taught for a while in 5th century B.C.E. at Athens and had the theory that "mind" (*nous*) sets all in motion.
9 Philosopher of the 5th century B.C.E. who worked in Sicily and was famous for his view that "love" and "strife" cause an endless cycle of cosmic mixing and separating.

thought move in this way; they move without being in motion. The primary objects of desire and of thought are the same. For the apparent good is the object of appetite, and real good is the primary object of wish.[10] But desire is consequent on opinion rather than opinion on desire; for the thinking is the starting-point. And thought is moved by the object of thought, and one side of the list of opposites is in itself the object of thought; and in this, substance is first, and in substance, that which is simple and exists actually. (The one and the simple are not the same; for 'one' means a measure, but 'simple' means that the thing itself has a definite nature.) But the good, also, and that which is in itself desirable are on this same side of the list; and the first in any class is always best, or analogous to the best.

That that for the sake of which[11] is found among the unmovables is shown by making a distinction; for that for the sake of which is both that *for* which and that *towards* which, and of these the one is unmovable and the other is not. Thus it produces motion by being loved, and it moves the other moving things. Now if something is moved it is capable of being otherwise than as it is. Therefore if the actuality of the heavens is primary motion, then in so far as they are in motion, in *this* respect they are capable of being otherwise, – in place, even if not in substance. But since there is something which imparts motion while being itself not in motion, existing actually, this can in no way be otherwise than as it is. For locomotion is the first of the kinds of change, and motion in a circle the first kind of locomotion; and this the first mover *produces*. The first mover, then, of necessity exists; and in so far as it is necessary, it is good, and in this sense a first principle. For the necessary has all these senses – that which is necessary perforce because it is contrary to impulse, that without which the good is

impossible, and that which cannot be otherwise but is *absolutely* necessary.

On such a principle, then, depend the heavens and the world of nature. And its life is such as the best which we enjoy, and enjoy for but a short time. For it is ever in this state (which we cannot be), since its actuality is also pleasure. (And therefore waking, perception, and thinking[12] are most pleasant, and hopes and memories are so because of their reference to these.) And thought in itself deals with that which is best in itself, and that which is thought in the fullest sense with that which is best in the fullest sense. And thought thinks itself because it shares the nature of the object of thought; for it becomes an object of thought in coming into contact with and thinking its objects, so that thought and object of thought are the same. For that which is *capable* of receiving the object of thought, i.e. the substance,[13] is thought. And it is *active* when it *possesses* this object. Therefore the latter rather than the former[14] is the divine element which thought seems to contain, and the act of contemplation is what is most pleasant and best. If, then, God is always in that good state in which we sometimes are, this compels our wonder; and if in a better this compels it yet more. And God *is* in a better state. And life also belongs to God; for the actuality of thought is life, and God is that actuality; and God's essential actuality is life most good and eternal. We say therefore that God is a living being, eternal, most good, so that life and duration continuous and eternal belong to God; for this *is* God.

Those who suppose, as the Pythagoreans[15] and Speusippus[16] do, that supreme beauty and goodness are not present in the beginning, because the beginnings both of plants and of animals are *causes*, but beauty and completeness are in the *effects* of these, are wrong in their opinion. For the seed comes from other individuals which are prior and com-

---

10 By 'wish' Aristotle means a rationally arrived at desire for something.

11 I.e., the "final cause." See entry for this in glossary.

12 Aristotle means to refers to the activities of being awake, perceiving, and thinking, as opposed to the mere potentiality for these.

13 Here Aristotle means the form abstracted from the matter, if what is being thought of is the "substance" of a material thing.

14 I.e., the activity rather than the mere capacity.

15 Members of the school established in southern Italy in the 6th century B.C.E. by the mysterious figure of Pythagoras, who mixed religious cult with a devotion to mathematics.

16 Succeeded Plato as head of the Academy from 348 to 339.

plete, and the first thing is not seed but the complete being, e.g. we must say that before the seed there is a man, – not the man produced from the seed, but another from whom the seed comes.

It is clear then from what has been said that there is a substance which is eternal and unmovable and separate from sensible things. It has been shown also that this substance cannot have any magnitude, but is without parts and indivisible.[17] For it produces movement through infinite time, but nothing finite has infinite power. And, while every magnitude is either infinite or finite, it cannot, for the above reason, have finite magnitude, and it cannot have infinite magnitude because there is no infinite magnitude at all. But it is also clear that it is impassive and unalterable; for all the other changes are posterior to change of place. It is clear, then, why the first mover has these attributes.

---

17 See preceding selection, i.e. *Physics* VIII, c.10.

II.2. ST. ANSELM

IN THIS FAMOUS PASSAGE ANSELM TRIES TO SHOW THAT ONCE GOD IS defined as that than which a greater cannot be thought it becomes self-contradictory to deny the existence of God.

II.2.1. The Being "a greater than which cannot be thought" (from *Proslogion*, ch.1-4)

Chapter 1

.... O Lord, I acknowledge and give thanks that You created in me Your image so that I may remember, contemplate, and love You. But this image has been so effaced by the abrasion of transgressions, so hidden from sight by the dark billows of sin, that unless You renew and refashion it, it cannot do what it was created to do. Lord, I do not attempt to comprehend Your sublimity, because my intellect is not at all equal to such a task. But I yearn to understand some measure of Your truth, which my heart believes and loves. For I do not seek to understand in order to believe but I believe in order to understand. For I believe even this: that I shall not understand unless I believe.

Chapter 2

Therefore, Lord, Giver of understanding to faith, grant me to understand – to the degree You deem best – that You exist, as we believe, and that You are what we believe You to be. Indeed, we believe You to be something than which nothing greater can be thought. Is there, then, no such nature as You, for the Fool has said in his heart that God does not exist?[1] But surely when this very Fool hears the words "something than which nothing greater[2] can be thought," he understands what he hears. And what he understands is in his understanding, even if he does not understand [judge] it to exist. Indeed, for a thing to be in the understanding is different from understanding [judging] that this thing exists. For when an artist envisions what he is about to paint, he has it in his understanding, but he does not yet understand [judge] that there exists what he has not yet painted. But after he has painted it, he has it in his understanding and he understands [judges] that what he has painted exists. So even the Fool is convinced that something than which nothing greater can be thought exists at least in his understanding; for when he hears of this being, he understands [what he hears], and whatever is understood is in the understanding. But surely that than which a greater cannot be thought cannot be only in the understanding. For if it were only in the understanding, it could be thought to exist also in reality – which is greater [than existing only in the understanding]. Therefore, if that than which a greater cannot be thought existed only in the understanding, then that than which a greater *cannot* be thought would be that than which a greater *can* be thought! But surely this conclusion is impossible. Hence, without doubt, something than which a greater cannot be thought exists both in the understanding and in reality.

Chapter 3: God cannot be thought not to exist.

Assuredly, this being exists so truly [really] that it cannot even be thought not to exist. For there can be thought to exist something whose non-existence is inconceivable; and this thing is greater than anything whose non-existence is conceivable. Therefore, if that than which a greater cannot be thought could be thought not to exist, then that than which a greater cannot be thought would not be that than which a greater cannot be thought – a contradiction. Hence, something than which a

---

1 Psalm 13:1; 52:1 (14:1; 53:1).
2 By 'greater' Anselm means 'better,' 'more perfect,' 'more excellent.'

greater cannot be thought exists so truly [really] that it cannot even be thought not to exist.

And You are this being, O Lord our God. Therefore, Lord my God, You exist so truly [really] that You cannot even be thought not to exist. And this is rightly the case. For if any mind could conceive of something better than You, the creature would rise above the Creator and would sit in judgment over the Creator – an utterly preposterous consequence. Indeed, except for You alone, whatever else exists can be conceived not to exist. Therefore, You alone exist most truly [really] of all and thus most greatly of all; for whatever else there is does not exist as truly [really] as You and thus does not exist as much as do You. Since, then, it is so readily clear to a rational mind that You exist most greatly of all, why did the Fool say in his heart that God does not exist? Why indeed except because he is foolish and simple!

Chapter 4: How the Fool said in his heart what cannot be thought.

Yet, since to say something in one's heart is to think it, how did the Fool say in his heart what he was not able to think, or how was he unable to think what he did say in his heart ? Now, if he really – rather, since he really – both thought [what he did] because he said it in his heart and did not say it in his heart because he was unable to think it, then there is not merely one sense in which something is said in one's heart, or is thought. For in one sense an object is thought when the word signifying it is thought, and in another when what the object [i.e., its essence] is understood. Thus, in the first sense but not at all in the second, God can be thought not to exist. Indeed, no one who understands what God is can think that God does not exist, even though he says these words [viz. "God does not exist"] in his heart either meaninglessly or else bizarrely.[3] For God is that than which a greater cannot be thought. Anyone who comprehends (*bene intelligit*) this, surely understands (*intelligit*) that God so exists that He cannot even conceivably not exist. Therefore, anyone who understands that this is the manner in which God exists[4] cannot think that He does not exist.

I thank You, good Lord, I thank You that what at first I believed through Your giving, now by Your enlightening I so understand that even if I did not want to believe that You exist, I could not fail to understand [that You exist].

---

3 Literally: "either without any signification or with some strange signification."
4 Literally: "that God exists in this manner..."

II.3. AL-GHAZALI AND AVERROES

II.3.1. Can we prove that the First Being is incorporeal? (from *The Incoherence of the Incoherence* [*Tahafut al-Tahafut*])

[Ghazali holds that once the philosophers have allowed that there are everlasting physical bodies that never had a beginning of their existence they have no basis for a proof that the first cause is not itself one of these bodies. (Aristotle attempted such a proof in selection II.1.2. above.) Averroes tries to defend the philosophers, i.e. those who have adopted the neo-Platonic/Aristotelian cosmology, against this charge.]

The Ninth Discussion

To refute their [i.e. the philosophers'] proof that the First is incorporeal Ghazali says:

There is a proof only for him who believes that body is only temporal, because it cannot be exempt from what is temporal and everything that is temporal needs a creator. But you, when you admit an eternal body which has no beginning for its existence, although it is not exempt from temporal occurrences, why do you regard it as impossible that the First should be a body, either the sun, or the extreme heaven, or something else?

If the answer is made "Because body must be composite and divisible into parts quantitatively, and into matter and form conceptually, and into qualities which characterize it necessarily so that it can be differentiated from other bodies (for otherwise all bodies in being body would be similar) and the necessary existent is one and cannot be divided in any of these ways" we answer: We have already refuted you in this, and have shown that you have no proof for it except that a collection is an effect, since some of its parts require others, and we have argued against it and have shown that when it is not

impossible to suppose an existent without a creator, it is not impossible to suppose a compound without a composing principle and to suppose many existents without a creator, since you have based your denial of plurality and duality on the denial of composition and your denial of composition on the denial of a quiddity[1] distinct from existence, and with respect to the last principle we have asked for its foundation and we have shown that it is a mere presumption.

And if it is said: "If a body has no soul, it cannot be an agent, and when it has a soul, well, then its soul is its cause, and then body cannot be the First," we answer: Our soul is not the cause of the existence of our body, nor is the soul of the sphere[2] in itself a cause of its body, according to you, but they are two, having a distinct cause; and if they can be eternal, it is possible that they have no cause.

And if the question is asked, "How can the conjunction of soul and body come about?", we answer: One might as well ask how the existence of the First comes about; the answer is that such a question may be asked about what is temporal, but about what is eternally existent one cannot ask how it has come about, and therefore, since body and its soul are both eternally existent, it is not impossible that their compound should be a creator.

I say:

When a man has no other proof that the First is not body than that he believes that all bodies are temporal, how weak is his proof, and how far distant from the nature of what has to be proved! – since it has been shown previously that the proofs on which the theologians build their statement that all bodies are temporal are conflicting; and what is more appropriate than to regard an eternal composite as possible, as I said in this book when speaking of the Ash'arites,[3] i.e. in saying that

---

1 See glossary entry for 'quiddity.'

2 A reference to the souls of the heavenly spheres, which in the cosmology the philosophers accepted were living beings.

3 An early school of Islamic thinkers who followed Al-Ashari (tenth century) and adopted such philosophically heterodox views as atomism and the belief that only God really has causal power.

according to them an eternal body is possible, since in the accidents there is some eternal element, according to their own theory, for instance, the characteristic of forming a compound; and therefore their proof that all bodies are temporal is not valid, because they base it exclusively on the temporal becoming of the accidents. The ancient philosophers do not allow for the existence of a body eternal through itself, but only of one eternal through another, and therefore according to them there must be an existent eternal through itself, through which the eternal body becomes eternal. But if we expound their theories here, they have only a dialectical value, and you should therefore instead ask for their proofs in their proper place.

And as to Ghazali's refutation of this, and his words, we answer: "We have already refuted you in this, and we have shown that you have no proof for this except that a collection is an effect, since some of its parts require others."

I say:

He means that he has discussed this already previously, and he says that the philosophers cannot prove that the existent necessary through itself is not a body, since the meaning of 'existent necessary through itself' is 'that which has no efficient cause,' and why should they regard an eternal body which has no efficient cause as impossible – and especially when it should be supposed to be a simple body, indivisible quantitatively or qualitatively, and in short an eternal composite without a composing principle? This is a sound argument from which they cannot escape except through dialectical arguments. But all the arguments which Ghazali gives in this book either against or on behalf of the philosophers or against Avicenna[4] are dialectical through the equivocation of the terms used, and therefore it is not necessary to expatiate on this.

And as to his answer on behalf of the Ash'arites that what is eternal through itself does not need a cause for its eternity, and that when the theologians assume something eternal through itself and assume its essence as the cause of its attributes, this essence

does not become eternal because of something else,

I say:

It is a necessary consequence to be held up against Ghazali that the Eternal will be composed of a cause and an effect, and that the attributes will be eternal through their cause, i.e. the essence. And since the effect is not a condition for its own existence, the Eternal is the cause. And let us say that the essence which exists by itself is God and that the attributes are effects; then it can be argued against the theologians that they assume one thing eternal by itself and a plurality of things eternal through another, and that the combination of all these is God. But this is exactly their objection against those who say that God is eternal through Himself and the world eternal through another, namely God. Besides, they say that the Eternal is one, and all this is extremely contradictory.

And as to Ghazali's statement that to assume a compound without the factor which composes it, is not different from assuming an existent without a creator, and that the assumption either of a single existent of this description or of a plurality is not an impossible supposition for the mind, all this is erroneous. For composition does not demand a composing factor which again itself is composed, but there must be a series leading up to a composing factor composing by itself, just as, when the cause is an effect, there must finally be a cause which is not an effect. Nor is it possible, by means of an argument which leads to an existent without a creator, to prove the oneness of this existent.

And as to his assertion that the denial of the quiddity implies the denial of the composition, and that this implies the assertion of composition in the First, this is not true. And indeed the philosophers do not deny the quiddity of the First, but only deny that it has the kind of quiddity which is in the effects, and all this is a dialectical and doubtful argument. And already previously in this book we have given convincing arguments, according to the principles of the philosophers, to prove that the First is incorporeal, namely that the possible leads to a necessary existent and that the possible does not proceed from the necessary except through the

4 See entry for 'Avicenna' in the biographical sketches.

mediation of an existent which is partly necessary, partly possible, and that this is the body of the heavens and its circular motion; and the most satisfactory way of expressing this according to the principles of the philosophers is to say that all bodies are finite in power, and that they only acquire their power of infinite movement through an incorporeal being.

Ghazali answering the objection which infers that according to the philosophers the agent is nothing but the sphere, composed of soul and body, says: If it is answered: "This cannot be so, because body in so far as it is body does not create anything else and the soul which is attached to the body does not act except through the mediation of the body, but the body is not a means for the soul in the latter's creating bodies or in causing the existence of souls and of things which are not related to bodies," we answer: "And why is it not possible that there should be amongst the souls a soul which has the characteristic of being so disposed that both bodies and incorporeals are produced through it? The impossibility of this is not a thing known necessarily, nor is there a proof for it, except that we do not experience this in the bodies we observe; but the absence of experience does not demonstrate its impossibility, and indeed the philosophers often ascribe things to the First Existent which are not generally ascribed to existents, and are not experienced in any other existent, and the absence of its being observed in other things is not a proof of its impossibility in reference to the First Existent, and the same holds concerning the body and its soul."

I say:

As to his assertion that bodies do not create bodies, if by 'creating' is understood producing, the reverse is true, for a body in the empirical world can only come into being through a body, and an animated body only through an animated body, but the absolute body does not come into being at all, for, if it did, it would come into being from non-existence, not after non-existence. Individual bodies only come into being out of individual bodies and

through individual bodies, and this through the body's being transferred from one name to another and from one definition to another, so that for instance the body of water changes into the body of fire, because out of the body of water is transformed the attribute through which the name and definition of water is transferred to the name and definition of fire, and this happens necessarily through a body which is the agent, participating with the becoming body specifically or generically in either a univocal[5] or an analogical way; and whether the individual special corporeality in the water is transformed into the individual special corporeality of the fire is a problem to be studied.

And as to Ghazali's words:
But the body is not a means for the soul in the latter's creating bodies or in causing the existence of souls,

I say:

This is an argument which he builds on an opinion some of the philosophers hold, that the bestower of forms on inanimate bodies and of souls is a separate substance,[6] either intellect or a separate soul, and that it is not possible that either an animated body or an inanimate body should supply this. And if this opinion is held and at the same time it is assumed that heaven is an animated body, it is no longer possible for heaven to supply any of the transitory forms, either the soul or any other of these forms. For the soul which is in the body only acts through the mediation of the body, and that which acts through the mediation of the body can produce neither form nor soul, since it is not of the nature of the body to produce a substantial form,[7] either a soul or any other substantial form. And this theory resembles that of Plato about forms separate from matter, and is the theory of Avicenna and others among the Muslim philosophers; their proof is that the body produces in the body only warmth or cold or moisture or dryness, and only these are acts of the heavenly bodies according to

---

5 See glossary entry for 'univocal production.'
6 See glossary entry for 'separate substance.'
7 See glossary entry for 'substantial/accidental form.'

them. But that which produces the substantial forms, and especially those which are animated, is a separate substance which they call the giver of forms. But there are philosophers who believe the contrary and affirm that what produces the forms in the bodies is bodies possessing forms similar to them either specifically or generically, those similar specifically being the living bodies which produce the living bodies of the empirical world, like the animals which are generated from other animals, whereas those forms produced by forms generically similar, and which are not produced from a male or a female, receive their lives according to the philosophers from the heavenly bodies, since these are alive. And these philosophers have non-empirical proofs which, however, need not be mentioned here.

And therefore Ghazali argues against them in this way: And why is it not possible that there should be among the souls a soul which has the characteristic of being so disposed that both bodies and incorporeals are produced through it?

I say:

He means: "Why should it not be possible that there should be among the souls in bodies souls which have the characteristic of generating other animate and inanimate forms?" And how strange it is that Ghazali assumes that the production of body out of body does not happen in the empirical world, whereas nothing else is ever observed.

But you must understand that when the statements of the philosophers are abstracted from the demonstrative[8] sciences they certainly become dialectical, whether they are generally acknowledged, or, if not, denied and regarded as strange. The reason is that demonstrative statements are only distinguished from statements which are not demonstrative, by being considered in the genus of science which is under investigation. Those statements which can be subsumed under the definition of this genus of science, or which comprise in their definition this genus of science, are demonstrative, and those statements which do not seem to fulfil these conditions are not demonstrative. Demonstration is only possible when the nature of

this genus of science under investigation is defined, and the sense in which its essential predicates exist is distinguished from the sense in which they do not, and when this is retained in mind by keeping to that sense in every statement adopted in this science, and by having the identical meaning always present in the mind. And when the soul is convinced that the statement is essential to this genus or a necessary consequence of its essence, the statement is true; but when this relation does not enter into the mind, or when it is only weakly established, the statement is only an opinion, and is not evident. And therefore the difference between proof and convincing opinion is more delicate than the appearance of a hair and more completely hidden than the exact limit between darkness and light, especially in theological questions which are laid before the common people, because of the confusion between what is essential and what is accidental. Therefore we see that Ghazali, by relating the theories of the philosophers in this and others of his books and by showing them to people who have not studied their works with the necessary preparation the philosophers demand, changes the nature of the truth which exists in their theories or drives most people away from all their views. And by so doing he does more harm than good to the cause of truth. And God knows that I should not have related a single one of their views, or regarded this as permissible, but for the harm which results from Ghazali's doings to the cause of wisdom; and I understand by 'wisdom' speculation about things according to the rules of the nature of proof.

Ghazali says, on behalf of the philosophers: "If it is said that the highest sphere, or the sun, or whatever body you may imagine, possesses a special size which may be increased or decreased, and this possible size needs for its differentiation a differentiating principle and can therefore not be the First," we answer: "By what argument will you refute the man who says that this body must have the size it possesses for the sake of the order of the universe, and this order could not exist if this body were smaller or larger, since you philosophers yourselves affirm that the first effect determines the size of the highest sphere because all sizes are equivalent in relation to the essence of the first effect, but certain

---

8 See glossary entry for 'demonstration.'

sizes are determined for the sake of the order which depends on them and therefore the actual size is necessary and no other is possible; and all this holds just as well when no effect is assumed. Indeed, if the philosophers had established in the first effect, which is according to the philosophers the cause of the highest sphere, a specifying principle, as for instance the will, a further question might be put, since it might be asked why this principle willed this actual size rather than another, in the way the philosophers argued against the Muslims about their theory of the relation between the temporal world and the Eternal Will, an argument which we turned against them with respect to the problems of the determination of the direction of the heavenly movement and of the determination of the points of the poles. And if it is clear that they are forced to admit that a thing is differentiated from a similar one and that this happens through a cause, it is unessential whether this differentiation be regarded as possible without a cause or through a cause, for it is indifferent whether one puts the question about the thing itself and asks why it has such-and such a size, or whether one puts the question about the cause, and asks why it gave this thing this special size; and if the question about the cause may be answered by saying that this special measure is not like any other, because the order depends on it exclusively, the same answer may be made about the thing itself, and it will not need a cause. And there is no escape from this. For if the actual size which has been determined and has been realized were equivalent to the size which has not been realized, one might ask how one thing comes to be differentiated from a similar one, especially according to the principle of the philosophers who do not admit a differentiating will. If, however, there is no similar size, no possibility exists, and one must answer: 'This has been so from all eternity, and in the same way therefore as, according to the philosophers, the eternal cause exists.' And let the man who studies this question seek help from what we said about their asking about the eternal will, a question which we turned against them with respect to the points of the poles and the direction of the movement of the sphere. It is therefore clear that the man who does not believe

in the temporal creation of the bodies cannot establish a proof that the First is incorporeal."

I say:

This indeed is a very strange argument of Ghazali's. For he argues that they cannot prove another creator than the heavenly body, since they would have to give an answer by a principle in which they do not believe. For only the theologians accept this principle, since they say that heaven receives the determinate size it has, to the exclusion of other sizes it might have, from a differentiating cause, and that the differentiating principle must be eternal. He either attempted to deceive in this matter or was himself deceived. For the differentiation which the philosophers infer is different from that which the Ash'arites[9] intend, for the Ash'arites understand by 'differentiation' the distinguishing of one thing either from a similar one or from an opposite one without this being determined by any wisdom in the thing itself which makes it necessary to differentiate one of the two opposite things. The philosophers, on the other hand, understand here by the differentiating principle only that which is determined by the wisdom in the product itself, namely the final cause, for according to them there is no quantity or quality in any being that has not an end based on wisdom, an end which must either be a necessity in the nature of the act of this being or exist in it, based on the principle of superiority. For if, so the philosophers believe, there were in created things a quantity or quality not determined by wisdom, they would have attributed to the First Maker and Creator an attitude in relation to His work which may be only attributed to the artisans among His creatures, with the intention of blaming them. For when one has observed a work with respect to its quantity and quality, and asked why the maker of this work chose this quantity or this quality to the exclusion of all other possible quantities and qualities, there is no worse mistake than to answer "Not because of the intrinsic wisdom and thoughtfulness in the product itself, but because he willed it," since according to this view all quantities and qualities are similar with respect to the end of this product, which in fact the maker

9 See fn.3 above.

produced for its own sake, namely for the sake of the act for whose purpose it exists. For indeed every product is produced in view of something in it which would not proceed from it, if this product had no definite quantity, quality and nature, although in some products an equivalent is possible. If any product whatever could determine any act whatever, there would exist no wisdom at all in any product, and there would be no art at all, and the quantities and qualities of the products would depend on the whim of the artisan and every man would be an artisan. Or should we rather say that wisdom exists only in the product of the creature, not in the act of the Creator? But God forbid that we should believe such a thing of the First Creator;

on the contrary, we believe that everything in the world is wisdom, although in many things our understanding of it is very imperfect and although we understand the wisdom of the Creator only through the wisdom of nature. And if the world is one single product of extreme wisdom, there is one wise principle whose existence the heavens and the earth and everything in them need. Indeed, nobody can regard the product of such wonderful wisdom as caused by itself, and the theologians in their wish to elevate the Creator have denied Him wisdom and withheld from Him the noblest of His qualities.

II.4. ST. THOMAS AQUINAS

AMONG THE MEDIEVAL SCHOLASTICS, AQUINAS WAS ONE OF THE most determined supporters of accommodation between Christian faith and Aristotelian philosophy. While recognizing that there were some points of conflict, as in the question of the eternity of the world (see topic **III**), he generally tried to show how a great deal of Christian doctrine about God, the world, and human beings, could receive considerable support, if not outright demonstration, through the sciences that Aristotle had created and which had been furthered by the tradition of the "philosophers." In the following selections we find him rejecting the Anselmian proof of the existence of God in favour of arguments which take their starting points from easily observed facts about the world and reason along causal lines, in the way Aristotle and Avicenna had pioneered.

II.4.1. God's existence is not self-evident to us
(*Summa Theologiae* Ia, qu.2, art.1)

[In this question Aquinas briefly states what he takes to be the force of Anselm's argument (see **II.2.1** above) and replies to it near the end of the selection.]

Is God's existence self-evident?

On this first article we proceed as follows:

[1] It seems that God's existence is self-evident, for we call those things self-evident the knowledge of which is naturally in us, as is clear in the case of first principles. But "the knowledge of God's existence is naturally implanted in everybody," as [St. John] Damascene[1] says in the beginning of his book [*On the orthodox faith*]. Therefore, that God exists is self-evident.

[2] Besides, we call those things self-evident which are known as soon as the terms are known, which is what The Philosopher attributes to the first principles of demonstrations.[2] For as soon as one knows what a whole is and what a part is, one knows that every whole is greater than its part. But

once one understands what is signified by this name 'God,' one realizes that God exists. For this name signifies that than which a greater cannot be signified. But what exists in reality and in the intellect is greater that what exists just in the intellect, and consequently, once this name 'God' is understood, it immediately exists in the intellect, and then it follows that it also exists in reality. Therefore, that God exists is self-evident.

[3] Besides, That truth exists is self-evident, because whoever denies that truth exists concedes that truth exists. For if truth does not exist, it is true that truth does not exist; but if there exists something true, it must be the case that truth exists. Now God is truth itself. "I am the way, the truth, and the life."[3] Therefore, that God exists is self-evident.

But against the above: No one can think the opposite of what is self-evident, as The Philosopher makes clear in discussing the first principles of a demonstration. But it is possible to think the opposite of the proposal that God exists, since according to the *Psalms*.[4] "The fool has said in his heart: God does not exist." Therefore, that God exists is not self-evident.

---

1 The leader of the Christian community in Damascus in the 8th century.
2 See glossary entry for 'demonstration.'
3 *John* 14, 6.
4 13 (14), 1; 52 (53), 1.

Reply: It should be said that something happens to be self-evident in two senses: in one sense, it is self-evident in itself but not to us, and in another sense it is self-evident in itself and to us. For a proposition is self-evident in virtue of the fact that its predicate is included in the definition of the subject. For example, 'A human being is an animal,' for 'animal' is in the definition of 'human being.' Therefore, if everybody knows in respect of the predicate and the subject what it is, that proposition will be self-evident to everybody. This is obvious in the case of first principles of demonstrations, since their terms are certain general items which no one fails to know, for example, being and non-being, whole and part, and the like. But given that there are some people who do not know in respect of the predicate and the subject what it is, the proposition will certainly be self-evident in itself, but it will not be to those people who do not know the predicate and subject of the proposition. Thus it can happen, as Boethius notes, that some items are "common conceptions of the soul" and self-evident "just to the wise; for example, 'Incorporeal things do not exist in a place.'"

I say, then, that this proposition 'God exists,' is self-evident in itself, since the predicate is the same as the subject; for God is His own existence, as will be clear later. But, because we do not know in respect of God what He is, it is not self-evident to us. Rather it needs to be demonstrated through things which are more known to us but less known in their nature; i.e. it has to be demonstrated through [His] effects.

To the first [1], then, it should be said that knowing that God exists is naturally implanted in us in the form of some general notion and under a certain vague term, i.e. we know this insofar as God is the complete happiness of a human being. For human beings naturally desire complete happiness, and what human beings naturally desire they know. But this does not amount to unqualifiedly knowing that God exists, just as to know someone coming is not to know Peter, even though Peter is the person who is coming. For many people think that the perfect good, which is complete happiness, is wealth, or pleasures, or something else.

To the second [2], it should be said that perhaps the person who hears this name 'God' does not understand it to signify something than which a greater cannot be thought, since some people have

believed that God is a body. But given that everyone does understand the name 'God' to signify what was said, namely that than which a greater cannot be thought, still it does not follow from this that the person thinks that what is signified by that name exists in the real world; rather [it follows] only [that the person thinks it exists] in the intellect's apprehension of it. Only if it is given that something than which a greater cannot be thought exists in reality, can it be argued that it does exist in reality; but this is not given by those claiming that God does not exist.

To the third [3] it should be said that the existence of truth in general is self-evident, but that the first truth exists is not self-evident to us.

II.4.2. The five Ways (*Summa Theologiae* Ia, qu.2, art.3)

[In this famous question Aquinas briefly sketches the main ways in which he thought philosophy could prove the existence of God. The reader of this selection should bear in mind that since Aquinas envisions himself as arguing with the philosophical tradition he assumes that the world as a whole and the motions of the heavenly bodies in it had no beginning but had existed forever. In other words time extends back into the past infinitely. Since Christian orthodoxy claims that the world as a whole did have a beginning a finite time ago, Aquinas does not actually believe this assumption, but he also does not believe that the world's having had a beginning can be proved (see selection III.5.2.). If he could have proved that, then the existence of God as the creator of that world would have followed in short order given the usual principles of metaphysics which dictate that everything that comes into being must have had a cause with sufficient perfection to produce it. Instead, Aquinas works on the assumption that the philosophers will accept, namely the eternity of the world, from which it is much harder to prove God's existence. Consequently, the proofs below do not try to show that the world or motion was begun by God, since the assumption is that they had no beginning. Rather, Aquinas is arguing that motion and other things require something that maintains them and which is itself not in motion nor even part of the physical order. The first three ways, in particular, need to be read in this dialectical context.

The reader also needs to be aware that Aquinas believes he can back up the claim that the being whose existence he proves here is the God of monotheistic religion with arguments he gives elsewhere; those arguments show that there is only one such being and that it is eternal, supremely perfect, infinite in power, all-knowing, and beneficent.]

Does God exist?

In the third article we proceed as follows:

[1] It seems that God does not exist, because if one of two contraries were infinite it would totally destroy the other. But by the name 'God' we understand what is an infinite good. If, then, God existed, we would not find any evil existing. But we do find evil in the world. Therefore, God does not exist.

[2] Besides, what can be accounted for by a few principles is not to be accounted for by more. But it seems that all the things which we find in the world can be accounted for by other principles on the supposition that God does not exist. For natural things are traced back to the principle which is their nature, while things that result from purpose are traced back to the principle which is human reason or will. There is, then, no necessity for claiming that God exists.

But against the above: In *Exodus* [3.14] we find God saying, "I am who am."

Reply: It should be said that it is possible to prove that God exists in five ways:

The **first** and more evident way is one which is based in motion. For it is obvious and apparent to the senses that some things in this world are in motion. But everything which is in motion is moved by something else. For something is in motion only in virtue of the fact that it has a potential for that toward which it is moving. But something moves something by being actual. Now, something can be taken from potency into act only by something actual. For example, something actually hot, like a fire, makes a piece of wood, which is potentially hot, be actually hot, and in so doing it moves and

alters the stick. However, it is not possible that one and the same item is simultaneously actual and potential in respect of the same thing; rather this can only occur in respect of different things. For what is actually hot cannot at the same time be potentially hot; rather it is at that time potentially cold. Therefore, it is impossible that one and the same thing be both mover and moved in respect of the same motion, or that it put itself in motion. Thus it is necessary that everything which is in motion is moved by something else. Then, if that by which it is moved is itself in motion, it is necessary that it too be moved by something else. But there can be no infinite regress here, because, if there were, there would not be a first mover and consequently neither any other mover, since secondary movers only move things in virtue of the fact that they themselves are moved by the first mover. For example, a stick will not move anything unless because it is moved by a hand. Therefore, we have to arrive at some first mover which is not moved by anything, and this everybody thinks is God.

The **second** way derives from the notion of an efficient cause.[5] For in the realm of things perceivable by the senses we discover that there is an ordering of efficient causes. Nevertheless, we do not find there, nor is it possible, that something is an efficient cause of itself, because if it were it would exist before itself, which is impossible. Moreover, there cannot be an infinite regress in efficient causes, for in every case of efficient causes in an ordered series the first is the cause of the intermediary and the intermediary is the cause of the last (allowing that the intermediary can be several causes or just one). Now if the cause is taken away, so is the effect. Therefore, if in these efficient causes there was no first, there would not be the last nor the intermediary. But if there is an infinite regress in efficient causes there will be no first efficient cause, and thus there will not be the final effect nor any intermediary efficient causes, which is obviously false. Therefore it is necessary to posit a first efficient cause, which everybody calls 'God.'

The **third** way is based in possibility and necessity and runs as follows: Among things we discover some for which both existing and not existing are

---

5 The notion of efficient causation is extensively explored in the selections under topic I.

possible, since some things are found to be generated and destroyed and as a result to exist and not to exist. But it is impossible that everything which exists is of this sort, because that for which not existing is possible, at some time does not exist. If then everything is such that not existing is possible for it, at some time there was nothing really existing.[6] But if this were true, then right now there would be nothing, since what is not in existence begins to exist only in virtue of something which exists. If, then, there was nothing in existence, it was impossible for anything to begin to exist, and thus there would be nothing now, which is obviously false. Therefore, it is not the case that all beings are possible ones; rather, there must be something in reality that is necessary. Now every necessary thing either has its necessity caused by something else, or not. Nor is it possible to have an infinite regress in necessary things whose necessity has a cause, just as neither in efficient causes, as was shown. Therefore, we must posit something which is necessary through itself and does not have its necessity caused by something else, but which is a cause of necessity in other things. [And this everybody says is God.]

The **fourth** way is based in the degrees which we find in things. For in things we find that something is more or less good and true and noble, and so on for other cases of this sort. But different things are said to be more or less by the fact that they vary in their nearness to something which is a maximum. For example, that is more hot which comes closer to what is maximally hot. There is, then, something which is most true, most good, and most noble, and as a result is maximally a being; for, according to *Metaphysics* II,[7] the things that are maximally true are maximally beings. Now, "what is a maximum in some genus is the cause of everything in that genus," for example, "fire which is maximally hot is the cause of everything that is hot," as he says in that same book.[8] Therefore, there is something which is the cause of existence, and goodness, and every perfection in all things, and this we say is God.

The **fifth** way is based in the governance of things. For we see that some things which lack cognition, viz. natural bodies [i.e. the elemental bodies], function for an end. This is evident from the fact that they always or very frequently function in the same way and end up resulting in what is best. From this it is clear that it is not by chance but by purpose that they arrive at the end. But now those things which lack cognition do not tend towards an end unless they are directed by something with knowledge and intelligence, just as the arrow is directed by the archer. Therefore, there is some intelligent being who directs all natural things to an end, and this being we say is God.

To the first [1], then, we should say what Augustine says in *Enchiridion*: "Since He is the highest good, God would never permit anything bad in his works if He were not omnipotent and good to the point of making even out of evil something good." It belongs then to the infinite goodness of God that He allows evil to exist and from it brings forth good.

To the second [2], it should be said that, since a nature functions for a determinate end under the direction of some higher agent, it is necessary that the things which come to be by nature are also traced back to God as to a first cause. Likewise, also the things that come to be by purpose have to be traced back to some higher cause which is not human reason or will, for the latter are changeable and subject to failure, and everything subject to motion and capable of failure must be traced back to some first principle that is immobile and necessary through itself, as was shown.

II.4.3. A Being which just is its own Existence
(from *On Being and Essence*, ch.4)

Whatever does not belong to the thought of an essence or quiddity[9] is something which comes from outside and makes a composition with the essence, because no essence can be thought of without the things which are parts of it. Now, every

---

6 To appreciate this inference it is particularly important to realize that Aquinas assumes, for the purposes of argument, that time extends back into the past infinitely.

7 c.1, 993b30.

8 c.1, 993b25.

9 See glossary entry for 'quiddity.'

essence or quiddity can be thought of without anything being thought about its existence. For I can think of what a human being is, or what a phoenix is, and yet not know whether they have existence in the real world. It is clear, therefore, that existence is other than essence or quiddity.

There is perhaps an exception to this if there exists a thing whose quiddity is its existence. And there can be only one such thing, and it would be first, because it is impossible to plurify a something except either by the addition of some difference, as the nature of the genus is multiplied in its species, or by the reception of a form into diverse matters, as the nature of the species is multiplied in diverse individuals, or by this: that one is absolute and the other is received in something; for example, if there were a separated heat, it would by virtue of its very separation be other than heat which is not separated. Now, if we posit a thing which is just existence, such that the existence itself is subsistent, this existence would not receive the addition of a difference because it would no longer be just existence, but existence plus some form. And much less would it receive the addition of matter because it would no longer be a subsistent existence, but a material existence. Whence it remains that such a thing, which is its own existence, cannot be but one.

It follows that it is necessary that in any thing other than this one its existence is other than its quiddity, or its nature, or its form. Consequently, it is necessary that in the intelligences[10] existence is something besides the form, and this is why it was said that an intelligence is form and existence.

Now, whatever belongs to something is either caused by the principles of its nature, as the ability to laugh in human beings, or comes from some extrinsic principle, as light in the air from the influence of the sun. But it cannot be that the very existence of a thing is caused by the form or quiddity of that thing – by 'cause' here I mean an efficient cause – because then something would be its own cause, and would bring itself into existence, which is impossible. It is therefore necessary that every thing of the sort whose existence is other than its nature has its existence from something else. And because every thing which exists by virtue of something else is led back to that which exists by virtue of itself as to its first cause, it is necessary that there be some thing which is the cause of the existence of all things in virtue of the fact that it is just existence. Otherwise, there would be an infinite regress of causes, since every thing which is not just existence has a cause of its existence, as has been said. It is clear, therefore, that an intelligence is form and existence, and that it gets existence from the first being, which is just existence. And this is the first cause, which is God.

---

10 See glossary entry for 'intelligence.'

II.5. JOHN DUNS SCOTUS

For Duns Scotus the best definition of God was 'infinite being'; hence any proof of the existence of God had to be a proof of the existence of a being with infinite power. Below Scotus explores two possible ways of constructing such a proof.

II.5.1. The first efficient Cause has infinite Power
(from *Ordinatio* I, dist.2, pt.1, qu.1-2)

[The first of these ways depends on Aristotle's arguments given above in selections **II.1.2** and **II.1.3**, i.e. arguments which assume we have proved that there is a first mover that keeps the motion of the heavenly spheres going forever. Scotus explores these without apparently reaching any firm conclusion as to whether such arguments suffice for his purposes.]

... I argue for the infinity [of God] in four ways. The first is through efficient causation, and here the conclusion is shown in two ways, first by the fact that God is the first efficient cause of everything...

[A.] The Philosopher touches on this first way through causality in *Physics* VIII[1] and in *Metaphysics* XII,[2] where he argues that since [the first efficient cause] puts things into an infinite motion it must have infinite power.

[A.1] This argument is strengthened in respect of its antecedent as follows: The conclusion follows just as much given that it *can* impart to things an infinite motion as given that it *does* impart to things an infinite motion. This is because it is just as necessary for it actually to exist as it is for it to be able to exist (this is clear from the first argument[3] relating to its existing from itself). Therefore, even though it does not give things an infinite motion, in the way Aristotle thinks, still, if we take the antecedent as meaning that so far as it itself is concerned it can put things into [an infinite] motion, we have a true antecedent and one that is

equally sufficient to show our conclusion.

The inference is proven as follows: If it gives things an infinite motion in virtue of itself and not by the power of something else, then it has not received this putting things in motion in this way from something else, but rather it has in its own active power the whole of its effect all at once, because it has it independently. But what has in its power all at once an infinite effect is infinite; therefore etc.

[A.2] The first inference can be strengthened in another way as follows: The first mover has all at once in its power all the effects which it is possible to produce by motion. But these are infinite, given that the motion is infinite. Therefore, etc.

Against these claims of Aristotle's:
[B.1] Whatever is to be said about the antecedent, the first inference [A.1] does not seem to be validly proven. Not in the first way [where the antecedent posits that the first mover does in fact cause an infinite motion], because a greater duration adds nothing to perfection. A whiteness which persists for one year is no more perfect than if it had persisted for just one day; therefore, a motion that lasts for whatever time you want is not a more perfect effect than a motion which lasts just one day. Consequently, from the fact that an agent has in its own active power all at once the production of an infinite motion, we cannot conclude that there is any greater perfection in this case than in any other, just that the mover puts things in motion over a longer time and in virtue of itself. Thus we would have to prove that the eternity of the agent

---

1 ch.10. See selection **II.1.2**.
2 ch.7. See selection **II.1.3**.
3 See selection **I.9.1**, pp.59-63.

implied its infinity, for otherwise the latter could not be inferred from the infinity of the motion. Then in regard to the form of the argument, the last proposition of this strengthening of it [i.e. that the first mover is infinite] is denied, unless it just means that the first mover has infinite duration.

The second strengthening of the inference [A.2] is also disproved, since we cannot conclude to a greater intensive perfection merely from the fact that an agent, if it remains in existence long enough, can produce successively any number whatsoever of the same species. For what it can do at one time in one such case it can by the same power do in a thousand such cases if it stays in existence for a thousand times. However, according to the philosophers, who assumed only a finite number of species, the only infinity possible is the numerical one [as opposed to an infinity of things each different in species] of effects producible by motion (i.e. of things that are generable and destructible). Hence from the fact that it can produce successively an infinite number of effects the intensive infinity of the agent no more follows than if it could produce only two, since according to the philosophers only a numerical infinity is possible.

Now, if someone would prove that an infinity of species is possible, arguing that some of the motions of the heavenly bodies are incommensurable and thus they can never return to the same arrangement as they once had even if they lasted for an infinite time, and that infinite, specifically distinct arrangements of heavenly bodies would cause an infinity of generable things differing in species – whatever one is to say about this proposal in itself, it is irrelevant to what The Philosopher means, since he would deny the infinity of species.

[C.] The final probable interpretation advanced in favor of The Philosopher's reasoning is the following: Anything which is able to produce at the same time a number of things each of which requires some perfection peculiar to it, can be inferred to be more perfect the more such things it can produce. Thus it seems we must concede that, if the first agent could cause at the same time an infinity of effects, its power would be infinite. Consequently, if

the first agent has a power for causing an infinity of things at the same time, insofar as it of itself could produce them at the same time even though the nature of the effects does not allow for it, still the infinity of its power could be inferred. This last inference is proved by the fact that what can cause both white and black is not less perfect because they cannot be caused at the same time; for this non-simultaneity comes from their mutual rejection and nor from any deficiency in the agent, since the agent would have at the same time power in respect of both if they were of themselves compossible.

Therefore, the major premiss is the following: Any agent that has a power in virtue of which it can, to the extent that this depends on what it is of itself, produce an infinity of things at the same time, even though the incompossibility of the effects prevents their existing all at once, has an infinite power. The first agent is of this sort; therefore, etc. The major premiss has already been explained above, because in a cause which, so far as it itself is concerned, can produce things at the same time a greater number of such things implies a greater perfection; therefore, an infinity of things which it can, so far as it itself is concerned, produce implies that it has an infinite power. The minor premiss [i.e. that the first agent is this sort of cause] is proved by the fact that, if the first agent had formally at the same time all causal power, it would be infinite even though it would not be possible for all causables to exist at the same time, since so far as it itself is concerned it could produce an infinity of things at the same time. Also, the more things it can produce at the same time the greater its power intensively. Therefore, if it has all causal power even more perfectly than if it had it formally, even more its intensive infinity would follow. But it does have in a more excellent way than if it had it formally[4] all the causal power of any thing to the full extent that that power is in that thing.

Therefore, even though I believe that omnipotence in the strict sense that theologians mean is only believed and is not proven by natural reason, as will be stated in distinction 42,[5] still it can be proven naturally that there is an infinite power

---

4 See glossary entry for 'eminence.'
5 See selection I.9.3.

which, so far as it itself is concerned, has all at once all causal power and could at the same time produce an infinity of effects if they were producible at the same time.

[D.] If you object [to C]: The first agent, even though it has more excellently all the causal power belonging to a secondary cause which is in that secondary cause, still cannot of itself produce the effects of all the secondary causes, because, when we speak of this more excellent way of having the power, it is not clear that it could be the total and proximate cause of all the effects in the absence of any secondary causes. And thus the minor is not evident, viz. that the first agent could of itself produce an infinity of effects. – This poses no obstacle, because what is required for it to be a total cause would not make it any more perfect than it is now when it has what is required to be the first cause.

This is, first of all, because those secondary causes are not required for perfection in causing things, otherwise the effect that is further from the first cause would be the more perfect since it would require a more perfect cause. But if secondary causes are needed in addition to the first cause, the reason, according to the philosophers is the imperfection of the effect; i.e. the first cause could along with some imperfect cause cause an imperfect effect which, according to them, it could not immediately cause.

This is also because, according to Aristotle, the totality of all perfections exists more excellently in the first agent than if their very formalities[6] existed in it, were that possible. This is proved by the fact that the secondary cause which is next to the first cause gets its total causal perfection from the first alone; therefore, the first cause has that total perfection more excellently than does the secondary cause which has it formally. The inference is clear enough, since the first cause is the total and equivocal cause[7] of that secondary cause. Likewise, ask the same question about the third cause either in relation to the second or in relation to the first. If in relation to the first, what we wanted to show follows. If in relation to the second, it follows that the

second eminently contains the total perfection which exists formally in the third. But its containing in this way the perfection of the third is something the second gets from the first, as we showed above. Therefore, the first has to contain the perfection of the third more excellently than does the second, and so on for all the others right on down to the last. For this reason, in my judgment, it seems that Aristotle's argument about an infinite substance (taken from *Physics* VIII and *Metaphysics* XII and presented above) can show that the first cause possesses eminently the total causal perfection of everything and does so more perfectly than if it had formally the causality of everything, were that possible.

[E.] In addition to this proof which from the infinity of the effects which the first agent, so far as it itself is concerned, can produce at the same time, infers the infinite power of the first, a like proof can be drawn from the infinity of causes as follows: If the first were able to have formally in itself all the secondary causalities along with the causality of the first, then, so far as it itself is concerned, it would have infinite power in some way; therefore, much more will it be infinite if it has all those secondary causalities more excellently than if it had them formally.

[F.] It is possible to reply to these two proofs [i.e. D & E] of Aristotle's inference as follows:

[F.1] To the first [D.] , I concede that where each of several items requires its cause to have either formally or virtually[8] some peculiar perfection, what is able to produce more of these is more perfect than what is able to produce fewer, because at least it would have virtually more of those formal perfections which would be distinctive of the greater number of effects. But that which has virtually more formal perfections is infinite in perfection. But where, either at the same time or successively, the cause can produce more effects of which it is not required that each has its own peculiar perfection which must exist formally or virtually in its cause, from the greater number the greater perfec-

6 See glossary entry for 'formality.'
7 See glossary entry for 'univocal production.'
8 See glossary entry for 'virtual existence.'

tion cannot be inferred. Thus the philosophers would say to this proposal that the first agent, so far as it itself is concerned, can produce an infinity but only a numerical infinity which is finite in respect of specific natures. However, it is only a distinction of specific natures in effects that requires different formal or virtual perfections in the cause, not a distinction in number.

[F.2] This point can be applied to the second proof [E.], because secondary causes are not infinite in species, according to Aristotle; therefore, it cannot be inferred from the fact alone that something has the power of all these that it is intensively infinite.

[G.1] Against the first of the above points [F.1] : What can produce at the same time more things is more powerful than what can produce fewer whether those items are of different species or of the same species; therefore, what can produce at the same time an infinity of things is infinite and possesses infinite power.

[G.2] Against the second of the above points [F.2]: If all the secondary causalities were formally in the first cause, in it there would be a virtual infinity, at least an extensive one. Therefore, if they are in it eminently, there will be some infinity there. But it will not be an extensive infinity, because that does away with excellence; for this reason they exist there as a unit. Therefore, in this case there will be an infinity that is not extensive; therefore, intensive.

[H.1] To the first of these remarks [G.1]: We should deny the antecedent and say that simultaneity does nothing to improve the case for a greater power. For example, if an infinity of bodies were arranged on a sphere at the right distance around a certain fire, the fire would act on all at the same time just as much as it now acts on the finite number of parts of a spherical body surrounding it.

[H.2] To the second of these remarks [G.2] : By that reasoning the sun, in fact any everlasting cause which can produce successively an infinity of individuals, would be infinite. Therefore, although this reasoning seems probable, it is in fact sophistical, because it seems that the proposition on which the argument rests is in itself false, viz. this one:

"Whatever items possess in themselves extensive infinity imply some virtual infinity if they are to be possessed more excellently." This is false, because they can be possessed more excellently by a finite, equivocal cause. Also the conclusion cannot be reached by that proposition, because in a situation where they have no infinity they do not exist eminently in a relationship to the infinity of them. For it is false that eminence creates a unity and does away with the extensive material infinity which existed. Also, this argument does not in any event conclude to a formal intensive infinity, because a finite formality is sufficient to contain eminently a material and extensive infinity.

[I.] In addition to this way of efficient causation, some argue that it has an infinite power because it creates, for any power that can bridge an infinite distance between terms of a relation (like that between something and nothing) is infinite. But the divine power exhibits this ability in creation. However, the antecedent is only something that is to be believed, and it is true that in the case of creation in the real order non-existence sort of precedes temporally existence, i.e. the real existence of the creature. Whereas if we take creation as Avicenna does in *Metaphysics* V,[9] in the sense that non-existence precedes existence merely by a priority of nature,[10] then it is sufficiently proven that at least the first nature after God is from Him and not from itself, nor does it get its being once something has already been put in place. Therefore, it is created. For, if there is a first being capable of producing, anything other than it gets its whole existence from that first being, otherwise there would be something that followed it which did not depend on it, and thus it would not be the first being capable of producing. But anything which gets its whole existence from something in such a way that through its own nature it has existence after non-existence is created; therefore, etc. But if we take it in this sense that there is something prior in nature to both non-existence and existence, we do not have there the terms of a change which that power causes, nor does being brought about in this sense require being changed.

9 Actually VI, ch.2.
10 See glossary entry for 'order of nature.'

Whatever is to be said of the antecedent of this argument, the inference remains unproven. This is because, when between the terms of a relation there is no intervening distance but rather those terms themselves are said to stand apart just by reason of how they relate to each other, the amount of the distance is the same as that of the greater term. For example, God is at an infinite distance from a creature, not because of any intervening distance between the terms of the relation but because of the infinity of one of the terms. Therefore, contradictories do not stand apart in virtue of something that mediates between them (because contradictories are immediately related in such a way that no matter how little something departs from one term it immediately falls under the other), but rather they stand apart on account of the terms themselves. In this case, then, the distance is just as great as is the term which is the more perfect; this latter is finite; therefore, etc.

This reasoning is bolstered by the fact to have total power over the positive term of a distance of this sort is to have power over the distance or the transition from one term into the other. Therefore, infinity follows from power over that transition only if it follows from total power over its positive term. That term is finite, and, therefore, power over the transition to that term does not imply demonstratively an infinite, active power.

Still the common saying that "contradictories are infinitely distant" can be understood in the sense of 'indeterminately.' For just as no distance is too small to produce a contradiction, so also none is too large, even if it were greater than the maximum possible, to make it be the case that the terms were not contradictories. Therefore, this distance is infinite in the sense that it is not determined to any size, great or small. Consequently, the consequent about an infinite power no more follows from such an infinite distance than it does from a minimal distance, since even in the latter the distance is infinite in the above sense. And what does not follow from the antecedent does not follow from the consequent either. (Contradictories, then, are at the greatest distance and in the greatest opposition to each other, but privatively and indeterminately. Positively, howev-

er, the greatest distance is between contraries, as is clear from *Metaphysics* X[11]).

II.5.2. The Infinity of the most excellent Being
(from *Ordinatio* I, dist.2, qu.1-2)

[Scotus has argued earlier in this question that there is a most perfect being, that it is identical with the first efficient cause, and that there is only one such being. Here he argues that it must be infinite in its perfection. In the course of his discussion he revises Anselm's reasoning (selection **II.2.1**) to bolster his own arguments. In the next selection we find Ockham's critique of this whole enterprise.]

Is there among beings something which exists and is actually infinite?

[Scotus argues in four ways for an affirmative answer. What follows is the fourth of those ways.]

[1] Again, in the fourth way what we proposed is shown by the way of excellence. I argue as follows: It is incompatible with a most excellent being that there is something more perfect [than it] (as was shown above). But it is not incompatible with a finite being that there be something more perfect [than it] . Therefore, etc.

The minor premiss [that it is not incompatible with a finite being that there be something more perfect than it] is shown because entity does not reject the infinite, but an infinite is greater than any finite.

[2] Here is another way of arguing for this; it amounts to the same. What does not reject being intensively infinite is supremely perfect only if it is infinite, because if it is finite it can be exceeded or excelled since it does not reject being infinite. Entity does not reject infinity; therefore, the most perfect being is infinite.

The minor premiss in this argument [that entity does not reject infinity] , which was assumed in the preceding argument, does not seem capable of being proved *a priori*, because just as contradictories contradict in virtue of their own notions and that they contradict cannot be shown through anything clearer, so terms that do not reject each other lack rejection on account of their own notions and the only way of proving they do not reject each other is to explicate their natures. "Being" is not explicated by anything better known than itself, and the infinite we understand through the finite. (I explain it in the commonly accepted way as follows: the infinite is what exactly exceeds any given finite item by no finite proportion, but rather exceeds it beyond any such assignable proportion.)

[2.1] Nevertheless, what we proposed can be persuasively argued for. Just as we ought to allow as possible anything whose impossibility does not show up, so also we should allow as compatible items whose incompatibility does not show up. No incompatibility shows up here because finiteness does not belong to the notion of being, nor does it appear from the notion of being that it is an attribute necessarily co-extensive with being. One or the other of these has to be the case if there is to be the aforesaid rejection of one by the other, for the primary attributes of being and those necessarily co-extensive with being seem well enough known to belong to it.

[2.2] Here is another persuasive argument: Quantity does not reject the infinite by its mode, i.e. by taking it part after part. Therefore, neither does entity reject the infinite by its mode, i.e. by all-at-once perfection of being.

[2.3] Further, if quantity of power is unqualifiedly more perfect than quantity of bulk, why will infinity be possible in bulk but not in power? That if it is possible it is actual is evident from the third conclusion above concerning primacy as an efficient cause,[12] and will be proved below as well.

[2.4] Further, because the mind, whose object is being, finds nothing incompatible when it thinks of something infinite; rather it seems the most perfect of thinkable items. Now it is surprising that a contradiction of this sort concerning the mind's primary object is not evident to any mind, although a discord in sounds quickly offends the sense of hearing. For if what is in disagreement immediately offends perception, why is it that no mind naturally rejects an infinite thinkable item as something not in agreement with but destructive of the mind's own primary object.

[2.5] Using the above we can strengthen that argument of Anselm's in his *Proslogion* [c.5] [13] about the highest thinkable good so that the description of it is understood as follows: God is that item thought without contradiction than which a greater cannot be thought without contradiction. It is clear that we have to add 'without contradiction,' for that the knowledge or thought of which includes a contradiction is said to be non-thinkable, since we have then two opposed thinkables in no way making a single thinkable, because neither is a determination of the other.

This highest item thinkable without contradiction can exist in reality.

[2.5.1] First, this is shown for quidditative[14] being, because the mind most of all comes to a rest in thinking of such a thinkable; therefore, the notional content of the first object of the mind, i.e. of being, is found in that thinkable, and there to the greatest extent.

[2.5.2] Next we argue further that it is in the sense of existing. The highest thinkable does not exist just in a mind thinking of it, for, if it did, then it would be able to exist, because it is a possible thinkable, and not able to exist, because its notional content rejects being from some cause (as was clear above in the second conclusion of the way of efficient causation). Therefore, the thinkable which exists in reality is greater than that which exists only in a mind. This is not to be understood to mean that one and the same item if it is thought of is a greater thinkable if it actually exists [than if it does not]; rather it means that something which exists is greater than anything which exists only in the mind.

[2.5.3] Or we might strengthen it in another way as follows: What exists is a greater thinkable, i.e. more perfectly knowable, because it is visible or apprehensible by an intuitive[15] mental act of apprehension. What does not exist, neither in itself nor

---

12 See selection I.9.1.
13 See selection II.2.1.
14 Scotus means that we can show there is a quiddity of this sort, apart from the question of whether it really exists. See glossary entry for 'quiddity.'
15 See glossary entry for 'intuitive vs. abstractive cognition.'

in something more noble to which it adds nothing, is not visible. But the visible is more perfectly knowable than what is not visible and only apprehensible abstractively. Therefore a most perfectly knowable thing exists. (The difference between intuitive and abstractive mental acts of apprehension, and how the intuitive is the more perfect, will be treated in dist.3 and in other places where it is relevant.)

II.6. WILLIAM OF OCKHAM

ON MANY QUESTIONS OCKHAM ARGUED THAT CHRISTIAN THEOLOGY could not get support from the cosmological science of the "philosophers" in the way that many of his predecessors, Aquinas and Duns Scotus included, thought it could. In these selections he argues that view for the thesis that there is a first cause with infinite power, i.e. an entity which Christians could treat as God. His intent is not to cast doubt on Christian doctrine but to widen the gap between it and what can be scientifically shown.

II.6.1. Why the first efficient Cause cannot be proved to have infinite Power (*Quodlibet* VII, qu.11)

[Ockham rejects the idea that the mere fact that the first cause could (or even in fact does) produce an infinity of effects successively over time can show that that cause has infinite power. Scotus's claim (see selection **II.5.1**) that the first cause, so far as it itself is concerned, could produce an infinity of effects all at once is rejected on the grounds that such a simultaneous infinity is impossible.]

Is it possible by the way of efficient causation to prove sufficiently that God is intensively infinite?

[1] For an affirmative answer: An infinity of effects argues an infinite cause; but the effects which are producible by God could be infinite; therefore, etc.

[2] For a negative answer: The sun can produce an infinity of effects, and yet the sun is finite.

[3] On this question Scotus holds in his second distinction[1] the affirmative answer.

[3.1] He proves it first as follows. A cause which has of itself by its own active power infinite effects is itself infinite. But a cause which can of itself cause an infinite motion is that sort of cause; therefore, etc. The minor premiss is obvious. The major is shown by the fact that every effect is contained in its cause either formally or eminently.[2] But an infin-

ity of effects are not contained formally in the first cause; therefore, they are contained eminently. But this could not be the case if the first cause were not infinite. Therefore, etc.

[3.2] His second proof goes as follows: An agent which can produce more effects is more perfect[3] than one that can only produce fewer; therefore, one that can produce an infinity of effects has infinite power; but God is of that sort; therefore, etc.

[3.3] His third proof goes as follows: A cause which can produce an infinity of effects simultaneously is itself infinite. But if the first cause had formally the causal powers of all possible causes, it could, so far as it itself is concerned, produce an infinity of effects at the same time. But right now it does contain the causal powers of all causes more perfectly than if it had formally the causal powers of all causes at the same time, since it now contains them in a more excellent way. Therefore, right now it has infinite power.

[3.3.1] This reasoning is bolstered by the fact that, whenever a greater number implies a greater perfection than does a lesser number, infinity implies an infinite perfection. But being able to produce more effects at the same time is a mark of greater perfection than being able to produce fewer effects [at the same time] ; therefore, etc.

[3.4] His fourth proof goes as follows: A first efficient cause to which no secondary cause adds any amount of perfection is infinite, because otherwise the opposite would follow. For example, since lower causes add to the sun some perfection in acting, it

---

1 See selection **II.5.1**.
2 See glossary entry for 'eminence.'
3 See glossary entry for 'perfection.'

follows that the sun is intensively finite. But to the first cause no secondary cause adds any perfection in acting. Therefore the first cause is infinite. The minor is proved by the fact that, if the secondary causes did add some perfection to the first cause, then the more secondary causes worked together the more perfect the effect would be. This is clear from *Metaphysics* VII.[4] But God's first effect is the most perfect effect, viz. an intelligence[5] or something of that sort. Therefore, secondary causes do not add any perfection to the first cause.

[3.4.1] This reasoning is bolstered by the fact that a first cause to whose final power and causality secondary causes add some perfection in causing cannot alone without the secondary causes cause as perfect an effect as it can with the secondary causes, since its causal power is not as great as the sum of its own causal power and the causal power of the secondary causes. Therefore, if what is apt to come from secondary causes and the first acting together, is more perfect when it comes from the first alone, the secondary cause adds nothing to the perfection of the first. But everything finite adds some perfection to anything finite. Therefore, the first cause is infinite.

[3.4.2] It is bolstered again by the fact that the intuitive knowledge[6] of any creature is apt to be generated by that creature as by a proximate and secondary cause. Therefore, if this knowledge belongs to some intellect without the action of the object (which is a secondary cause only by the power of a prior cause) and belong to it more perfectly than if it were generated by both the prior and the secondary cause together, that prior cause is infinite, since the lower cause adds nothing to it in causing. Such a prior cause is God's essence, since just by its presence to the divine intellect, with no lower object helping out, intuitive knowledge exists of any lower object. Therefore, no other object adds perfection to it in causing, and consequently it is infinite in knowability; therefore, in entity. (See *Metaphysics* II.[7])

[4] Against Scotus's opinion:

[4.1] A mover with intensively infinite power can produce motion in an instant. But God cannot do this; therefore, etc. The major premiss is proved because at the end of *Physics* VIII[8] it is proved that, if there existed an infinite power in matter, it would cause motion in an instant. But an infinite power which is outside of matter has only as much power as it would if were in matter; therefore, etc. The minor premiss is proved by the fact that [motion in an instant] includes a contradiction, viz. that the motion would not be a motion, and the movable item would be located simultaneously in all the parts of space in which it is in motion.

[5] I say, then, that it is not possible by the way of efficient causation to show that God is intensively infinite. The reason for this has been stated in the first question of *Quodlibet* III. Seek it there.

[What follows is the relevant portion of that question:]

On this question I say first that from the assumption that God is an efficient cause of everything it is not possible to prove sufficiently that God is infinite in strength, for from a finite number of effects or even from a finite number of effects producible at the same time it is not possible to prove the infinity of the cause. But any effect producible by God is finite; also all the effects producible at the same time by God are finite. Therefore, the infinity of God cannot be shown from the efficient causation of them. ...

... I concede that he can produce an infinity of things successively. But beyond that I say that to have the power to produce an infinity of things successively is not to have an infinite power, for otherwise the sun and an angel would be infinite since they both have the power to produce an infinity of things successively. But to have the power to produce an infinity of things all at the

---

4 c.8-9, 1033a24-1034b19.

5 See glossary entry for 'intelligence.'

6 See glossary entry for 'intuitive vs. abstractive cognition.'

7 c.1, 993b30-31.

8 c.10. See selection **II.1.2.**

same time is to have an infinite power. But God does not have such a power since it involves a contradiction.

... I concede that God does contain virtually[9] and at the same time an infinity of effects that are successively producible, because this is nothing other than to be able to produce an infinity of effects successively. But to contain things in this way is not to have infinite power, for in this way one small fire virtually contains an infinity of effects.

... This is a correct inference: God can produce an infinity of things so far as He Himself is concerned; therefore, God can produce an infinity of things. It is valid because the phrase 'so far as He Himself is concerned' is not a determination which lessens or subtracts from what it determines. Also this is a good inference: God can produce an infinity of things; therefore, an infinity of things can be produced by God. The consequent includes a contradiction. Consequently, I say that neither of Himself nor by anything else can God produce an infinity of things.

If you say that God does not of Himself reject this, I say that He does. I, nevertheless, say that it is consistent with my position that, if an infinity of things were producible all at the same time, God would be able to produce them all at the same time. But the antecedent involves a contradiction, and thus nothing can be demonstratively proven from that antecedent; rather it can only be inferred in the way that anything at all can be inferred from what is impossible.

[End of passages from *Quodlibet III*, qu.1]

[Replies to Scotus's arguments:]

[6.1] To the first [3.1] I say first of all that to say that a cause has in its own active power all its effects etc. is not a proper way of speaking, because in reality it no more has in itself the effect before it produces it than after. Otherwise, in producing the effect it would lose some thing intrinsic to itself. Rather, I understand this saying as follows: the cause of itself has a power for producing all its effects. In that sense

it can be said to the argument that the major premiss is false, unless it refers to an effect that is intensively infinite. But in that case the minor is false.

[6.1.1] As for the proof of the major premiss, where it is understood to refer to an infinity of effects or an extensively infinite effect, it can be said that, even though the first mover contains an infinity of effects more excellently than they exist in themselves, since it is a nature that is more excellent than any of those numerically infinite effects, it is not on account of this necessary that the first mover be intensively infinite. Rather, it suffices that it be something finite that is more noble than any of those [effects] and that it have infinite duration so that it can successively produce that infinity.

[6.2] To the second [3.2] it can be said that every agent of itself would be able to produce an infinity of effects if it had infinite duration. Consequently, the antecedent is true only if we understand it to refer to effects which are many in species, not just in number.[10] Understood in that way, the antecedent does not show the conclusion, because natural reason does not see that the first being can produce effects that vary infinitely in species. Also maybe even if we grant that it could produce an infinity of species it still does not follow that He is intensively infinite; it is possible to have this sort of multiplication of species to infinity in number and yet never arrive at a species that has twice the perfection of the first species that was given. This occurs by always adding to the second to get the third an amount that is only half of what was added to the first to get the second, and so on to infinity, as clearly happens in the division of the continuum.

[6.2.2] But against this reply: In acts that reflect back on each other there is an infinite regress, and always the subsequent is more perfect than the prior, and they differ in species.

I answer... [Ockham's reply is missing.]

[6.3] To the third [3.3] , I concede that, if the first cause formally and distinctly had the causal power of all possible causes, it would be infinite. But that antecedent includes a contradiction, viz. that it is possible and it is not possible for it to produce

---

9 See glossary entry for 'virtual existence.'
10 The notions of "one in number" and "one in species" are defined by Aristotle in selections V.1-2.

something. This is because, if it were able to produce something, that producible would have really and formally pre-existed in the first cause, and, consequently, it would not be produced nor could it be produced. Thus the antecedent includes a contradiction.

[6.3.1] And when it is further claimed that the first cause right now contains the causal power of all causes more perfectly than if it had them at the same time formally, this can be denied even though it can be conceded for any particular causal power whatsoever. This inference is invalid: It contains the causal power of this cause more perfectly (i.e. it is a more perfect form and is able to cause it) than if it had it really, and so on for each individual case; therefore, it contains the causal powers of all causes more perfectly than if it had them formally. The reasoning commits the fallacy of "figure of speech" by moving from many definite cases to one, just as if we were to argue as follows: This dollar [*denarius*] is more valuable than this penny [*obolum*] , and than that, and so on for each individual case; therefore, it is more valuable than all the pennies taken together.

[6.3.2] To the bolstering [3.3.1] we have given an answer earlier in *Quodlibet* III, qu.1.

[What follows is the relevant section of this earlier question.]

I say that the general proposition 'Where a numerical plurality implies greater perfection than just one, there infinity implies infinite perfection,' is true for items which are of the same type, but it is not true, neither in respect of its first part nor in respect of the second, for items which are of different types. Example: If one person can carry only one stone at a time while another person can carry four stones of the same weight or greater at the same time, the second person would be more perfect than the first. Consequently, if some person could carry an infinity of stones at the same time, they would have infinite power, since in this case the stone carriers are all of the same species. But this inference does not hold: A single human being can only carry one stone at a time, while a horse can carry six of the same or greater weight at the same time; therefore, a horse is more perfect than a human being. Nor does this follow: A human

being, while standing and not falling, can only carry two stones at the same time; but a tree, while standing and not falling, can carry ten stones at the same time; therefore, the tree is more perfect than the human being. The reason for this is that in this case the things doing the carrying are of different types.

If you say: If an ass or a horse were able to carry an infinity of stones at the same time, they would have infinite perfection; therefore, this proposition holds for things which are of different types just as much as for things of the same type – I answer: It is true that the horse would have infinite perfection, because you could find another horse which was not able to carry an infinity of stones, and a third that was able to carry no more than ten at the same time. In these cases one is always more perfect than the other, and those horses are of the same type. But if it were possible for there not to be any horse which could carry fewer stones, then it would not be possible to prove the infinity of the horse through the proposition, 'Where a numerical plurality etc.'

Likewise the minor premiss seems to be false. First, because it has a false implication, viz. that there is an efficient cause which can only make one thing, for it is impossible that there be an efficient cause which cannot make several individuals of the same type. Also, because the ability to make three or four does not imply a greater perfection etc., since a small fire in virtue of the same power can make one fire or four fires, or, in fact an infinity of fires at the same time if that many combustible things were equally near it. Consequently, the ability to produce more things does not in this way imply a greater perfection. But if there were two fires, and one of these were able at one moment to produce a single fire equally perfect with it, while the second fire was able at the same time to produce two fires, one of which was equally perfect with the first fire and the other more perfect, then the second of the two original fires would be more perfect than the first.

In brief, then, that proposition ['Where a numerical plurality implies a greater perfection than just one etc.'] holds universally for things which are of the same type in the aforesaid way, but it does not hold universally for things which are of different types. Thus I concede that, if God were of the same type as other created agents and were able to produce all at once an infinity of things excelling themselves in perfection, then it would be possible to prove that God was infinite in strength, whether the members of that infinity were of the same type or of different types. I also concede that if He were able to produce an infinity of things all at the same time, it would follow in the way that anything follows from what is impossible that he would have infinite power. But the antecedent involves a contradiction.

[End of passage from *Quodlibet* III, qu.1]

[6.4] To the fourth [3.4] it can be said that for a secondary cause to add perfection to the first cause can be understood in two senses. In one sense it means that the aggregate of the first cause and the secondary cause is more perfect than the first cause alone. In another sense it means that the aggregate is more powerful in doing things than is the first cause on its own, and this in respect of any of its effects whatsoever. In the first sense the major premiss [A first cause to which a secondary cause adds no perfection is infinite.] is true, because whenever a finite thing is added to a finite thing the result is a more perfect whole. But in this sense the minor premiss [To the first cause no secondary cause adds any perfection in acting.] is false, and his proof of it does not work on this understanding of that premiss. In the second sense, the major premiss is false and the minor true.

[6.4.1] As to the proof of the major premiss which talks about the sun, I say that perhaps some effect immediately produced by the sun without any secondary cause might be more noble that all the effects it produces one after another with the helps of secondary causes. For example, according to the philosophers, the second intelligence,[11] without any mediating secondary cause, is the cause of the third intelligence, and that effect is nobler than all its [other] effects, no matter what secondary causes work together with it.

[6.4.2] To the first bolstering [3.4.1] , I say that the major premiss should be denied when given the

first sense, as is clear from what was said.

And when through this he proves that the causal power of the first cause would be lessened, I say that, according to philosophers, it is true in respect of many secondary effects, since, according to them, God cannot cause light to exist in air without some other luminous thing acting as a secondary agent. Nevertheless, it does not follow that He could not on His own make another more noble effect, namely the unqualifiedly first effect.[12]

Likewise the proposition which is assumed in the argument, viz. that any finite thing adds some perfection to any finite thing, could be shown to be true if it referred to an additional perfection in being; but then in that sense it does not help show what was to be shown. But if it refers to an additional perfection in doing anything whatsoever, then it does help show the desired conclusion, but it is false, as is evident from the above.

[6.4.3] To the other bolstering [3.4.2] which speaks of intuitive knowledge I say that, if that major premiss [If intuitive knowledge belongs to some intellect without the action of the object etc.] is read as referring to a caused intuition, it is true. And then, when we maintain the same meaning, if it is argued that this intuitive knowledge is apt to be caused more perfectly in the divine intellect by the first cause alone through the presence of its essence, the philosophers will deny that proposition.

What he cites as support, viz. that in God the intuition of a creature is more perfect than in a created intellect, is not relevant to showing the conclusion, because the intuition God has is not caused and is not of the same type as our intuition. Hence, the argument would only go through if it proved that a caused intuition of a creature is made more perfectly by God on His own than by God and a creature acting together. But this it does not prove, since The Philosopher denies it. Therefore, etc.

[7] To the argument at the beginning [1] I say that an infinity of effects produced all at the same time does imply an infinite cause, an infinity of effects producible successively does not. Now the effects

---

11 In neo-Platonic cosmology the "intelligences" were ordered according to their causal proximity to the "One," i.e. the source of all being. The "second intelligence" would have been produced directly by the first, which in turn would have been the direct effect of the ultimate source.

12 I.e., the "first intelligence."

brought about by God do not have the first sort of infinity, only the second.

II.6.2. Why it cannot be proven that the most perfect Being is infinite in Perfection (*Quodlibet* VII, qu.15)

[This selection responds to the arguments Scotus gave in selection **II.5.2**, including his attempt to bolster Anselm's argument in *Proslogion* 2, i.e. selection **II.2.1.**]

Can it be evidently shown by the way of excellence that God is intensively infinite?

[1] That it can:
What does not reject intensive infinity is not perfect in the highest degree unless it is infinite; otherwise it could be exceeded. But entity does not reject intensive infinity; therefore the most perfect being, which is God is infinite.

[2] In opposition:
It cannot be evidently shown that God is the most excellent being; therefore it cannot be shown by the way of excellence that he is infinite.

[3] On this question Scotus adopts the affirmative answer in his second distinction.[13]
  [3.1] His first proof runs as follows: It is incompatible with the most excellent being for there to be something more perfect than it; but it is not incompatible with any finite being for there to be something more perfect than it; therefore the most excellent being is not finite.
  The major premiss is obvious.
  [3.1.1] The minor premiss is proved as follows: Entity does not reject being infinite. But if there cannot be a being more excellent than every finite being, entity rejects the infinite. Therefore the finite does not reject there being something more perfect than it.
  [3.1.1.1] The major of this subsidiary syllogism is proved as follows: If entity rejected the infinite *per*

se, this would be for either of two reasons. Either the opposite of the infinite is *per se* included in the concept of a being, which is false, because in that case we could not think of *being* without also thinking of *finite*; or the opposite of infinite is an attribute[14] necessarily co-extensive with *being*, which is not true, because once the subject is known the attribute is known right away, but when *being* is known *finite* does not occur right away.
  [3.1.1.2] This is bolstered by the fact that the sensory powers, which are less cognitive than the mind, immediately perceive a disagreement in their object, as is clear in the case of hearing sounds. Therefore, if entity, the mind's object, rejected infinity, the mind would notice that incompatibility right away and naturally reject it, but this is clearly false.
  [3.2] A second proof runs as follows: According to Anselm's argument in *Proslogion*, c.2,[15] that than which a greater cannot be thought without contradiction is infinite. But God is that sort of thing; therefore etc. [God is infinite] .
  [3.2.1] If you say that that does not exist in reality nor does such a being exist, against you is the following: The mind most of all comes to rest in the highest of thinkables; therefore, the notional content of the mind's primary object, namely *being*, most of all exists in that highest of thinkables.
  [3.2.2] Besides, if that highest of items thinkable without contradiction exists just in the mind thinking of it, then that highest item is able to exist, since it can be thought to exist without contradiction, and is also not able to exist, because its notional content rejects being from something else. Therefore, what exists in reality is a greater thinkable than what exists only in the mind. I do not mean here that one and the same item is greater by the fact that it exists, but that something which exists is a greater thinkable than anything which exists only in the mind.
  [3.2.3] Besides, what is apprehensible by an intuitive act[16] of mental apprehension or is visible is more perfectly knowable than the non-visible and only apprehensible abstractively. But what exists is

---

13 See selection **II.5.2.**
14 See glossary entry for 'attribute.'
15 See selection **II.2.1.**
16 See glossary entry for 'intuitive vs. abstractive cognition.'

intuitively visible, while what does not exist is only abstractively apprehensible; therefore, the most perfect of thinkables exists.

[3.3] A third proof runs as follows: What does not reject intensive infinity is perfect in the highest degree only if infinite, for otherwise it could be exceeded. But entity does not reject intensive infinity; therefore, the most perfect being is infinite.

[3.3.1] This is bolstered as follows: Quantity does not reject the infinite, where we take part after part; therefore, neither does entity reject it in its own mode of perfection existing all at once.

[3.3.2] It is bolstered secondly as follows: Quantity of power is unqualifiedly more perfect than quantity of bulk. Therefore, if infinity is possible in the quantity of bulk it will be possible in the quantity of a power, and if it is possible it is actual.

[4] Nevertheless, I hold the opposite view, both because it cannot be adequately shown that God is the most excellent being, and because he can be the most excellent being in the sense that nothing is better or more excellent than he, and still be finite; nor is it possible to show the opposite evidently.

[5] I reply to Scotus's arguments:

[5.1] To the first [3.1] I say that philosophers disambiguate the major premiss [It is incompatible with the most excellent being for there to be something more perfect than it.] according to composition and division,[17] just as 'It is impossible for someone sitting to be walking' is true in the composite sense. In that sense the major premiss means this: This proposition, 'There is something more perfect than the most excellent being' is impossible. But then the syllogism is invalid, just as this one is:

It is impossible for anyone sitting to be walking.

It is not impossible for anyone with healthy feet to be walking.

Therefore, no one with healthy feet is sitting.

where the major premiss is read in the composite sense.

But if the major premiss is interpreted in the divided sense, then there has to be a further disambiguation as regards the incompatibility, because something can reject there being a greater than it either by reason of its quantity insofar as it is so much, or by reason of its nature insofar as it is of such a nature. An example: Eternal motion rejects there being something greater than it insofar as it is so much, but not insofar as it is of such a nature, because the whole motion is of the same nature as its part but clearly the part does not reject there being a greater motion.

On this point I say that according to the philosophers the major premiss is true in the divided sense where we mean an incompatiblity due to the nature inasmuch as it is a nature of a certain sort. For just as by his nature inasmuch as it is a nature of a certain sort God rejects being from something else, so also he rejects there being something greater than him. But when we mean the incompatiblity due to quantity inasmuch as he is so much, according to the philosophers we have to deny the major. When we take the major in the first sense, where the incompatibility is due to the nature, it is true in the divided sense, but taken in the same way the minor premiss [It is not incompatible with any finite being for there to be something more perfect than it.] is false.

[5.1.1] As for his proof [3.1.1] , when he says, "Entity does not reject the infinite," this can be understood in two senses. In one sense it means that no being rejects being infinite. This is false, because God rejects there being something greater [than him] and consequently, according to the philosophers, God rejects being infinite. In another sense it can mean that a being insofar as it is does not reject the infinite. This is true, and on this reading the proof and its reinforcement about disagreement go ahead; but not on the first reading, for otherwise it could be proven that no being rejects being infinite an infinite number of times.

[5.2] To the second [3.2] , I say that according to the philosophers the minor premiss [God is that than which a greater cannot be thought without contradiction.] has to be denied.

[5.2.1] To the first proof [3.2.1] I say that for something to be the highest of thinkables can have two senses: either by a true thought, or by a

---

17 See glossary entry for 'composite and divided senses.'

thought that does not include a contradiction. Not every thought that does not include a contradiction is a true thought; for example, no contradiction is involved in thinking of me as being above the stars.

In the first sense, it is true that the mind most of all comes to rest in the highest of thinkables, and in that the notional content of *being* exists most of all. But it is possible to think without any contradictions, by a false and made-up thought, of something greater than that highest [of thinkables] .

In the second sense of 'highest of thinkables,' according to the philosophers the following has to be denied: that the mind most of all comes to rest in the highest of items thinkable by a thought that does not include a contradiction. This is because according to the philosophers something greater than God can be thought without contradiction, but the mind more comes to rest in a true thought of God himself than in a false and made-up thought of something greater that is thought.

[5.2.2] To the second proof [3.2.2], I say that according to the philosophers the highest of items thinkable by a thought that does not include a contradiction does not exist in reality, because for such a highest item to exist is incompatible with God. Further, I say that what exists in reality is not a greater item thinkable by a thought that does not include a contradiction than what is merely in the mind. But it is a greater item thinkable by a true thought. Consequently, the argument does not show that such a highest of thinkables exists than which a greater cannot be thought by a thought that does not include a contradiction.

[5.2.3] To the bolstering argument [3.2.3] I say that it only shows that the most perfect item thinkable by a true thought exists, and the philosophers allow that. Nevertheless, something greater than it can be fictively thought by a thought that does not include a contradiction.

[5.2.4] If you say: What then does Anselm's argument in *Proslogion* 2[18] prove, where he tries to show that that than which a greater cannot be thought exists in reality?

I answer: Something's being that than which a greater cannot be thought has two senses: In one sense it means that nothing which can be thought is in fact greater. In another sense it means that it is not possible for something to be thought which would be greater if it existed. In the first sense Anselm's argument proves its conclusion. Formulated as follows, 'Nothing which does not exist in reality is in fact greater than what exists in reality; therefore, that than which a greater cannot be thought exists in reality,' the inference certainly holds good, on the assumption that in existing things the series of one thing greater than another does not go to infinity. Further, if that than which a greater cannot be thought exists in reality, since everybody agrees that the greatest of the items which are thought is God, it follows that God exists in reality.

[5.3] To the third proof [3.3] I say that if the minor premiss [Entity does not reject intensive infinity.] is read as follows, 'A being insofar as it is a being does not reject intensive infinity,' it is true, as was said earlier. But in that case the conclusion does not follow from the premisses. On the other hand, if the minor premiss is read as follows, 'No being rejects intensive infinity for any reason,' it is false, as was earlier said.

[5.3.1] To the first reinforcing argument [3.3.1] one possible reply is that a being insofar as it is a being does not reject intensive infinity, but God does reject it insofar as he is this being. Another possible reply is that a successive infinity is not similar to an intensive infinity in persistent[19] things.

[5.3.2] To the second reinforcing argument [3.3.2] , I say that in the quantity of a bulk the reason for the possibility of going to infinity is division and imperfection, as is clear in *Physics* III, comment 60. But an intensive infinity requires a additional amount of perfection;[20] God cannot be increased in perfection this way; therefore, he is not infinite.

[6] The reply to the argument at the beginning [1] is clear from what has been said.

---

18 See selection II.2.1.

19 See glossary entry for 'successive being.'

20 The idea of infinity here is Aristotle's (*Physics* III, c.6 207a7-8): "That is infinite of which it is always possible to take some part outside, when we take according to quantity" (trans. by E. Hussey).

II.6.3. Aristotle did not intend to prove the Infinity of the first Cause (*Quodlibet* VII, qu.17)

[Aristotle's arguments in selections **II.2.2** & 3 were often taken to show that the first mover has infinite power since it imparts motion over an infinite extent of time. Ockham tries to show both that such arguments are uncompelling and that in fact Aristotle did not intend to reach this conclusion but only to show that the first mover is not spatially extended.]

Do The Philosopher's proofs in Physics VIII[21] *and in* Metaphysics XII[22] *show that God is intensively infinite?*

[1] For an affirmative answer: In *Physics* VIII he shows that the first mover does not have size by arguing as follows: If it has size, then either it is infinite in size or it is finite in size. Not the former, because nothing is like that, as is clear from *Physics* III;[23] not the latter, because an infinite power cannot exist in a thing of finite size. Therefore, either he is referring to intensive finitude and infinity, and then we have what we set out to show; or extensive finitude and infinity in respect of temporal duration, in which case his assumption is false, since in a thing with size a power is able to last for an infinite time, as is clear in the case of the heavenly bodies.

[2] For a negative answer: Those arguments only show that God makes things move over an infinite time. But a finite incorporeal power can do this, as long as it lasts for an infinite time. Therefore, it proves only that God lasts for an infinite time.

[3] On this question Scotus in his second distinction[24] answers affirmatively.

[3.1] His first proof runs as follows: The first mover makes things move with an infinite motion; therefore, it has an intensively infinite power. Even

though the antecedent here is in fact false, still it is certain that the first mover can make things move with an infinite motion. And then, given that from making things move with an infinite motion follows an infinite power, the same follows if it has the power of making things move with an infinite motion. This inference is shown in many ways, and we have replied to those arguments in the preceding questions.[25]

[3.2] His second proof runs as follows: At the end of *Physics* VIII[26] it is shown that if the first mover were in matter it would make things move in an instant. This would not at all be true if God were not intensively infinite.

[4] But I hold the opposite, that those arguments show only that God has infinite duration. The reason for this is that an active power that cannot wear down or be destroyed in itself can through the same power cause an effect and make it continue, nor is it the case that a greater power is required for making the effect to continue a thousand years than a single day, as long as there is no cause acting against it and diminishing the power. This is clear from that famous proposition, 'Given active and receptive factors[27] are disposed in the same way, other things being equal, the same effect will result and will be continued.' But there is nothing acting against God; therefore, etc.

[5. Replies to Scotus's arguments:]

[5.1] To the first [3.1] I say that this inference is not valid: God makes things move with an infinite motion; therefore, He is intensively infinite. Nor is this the way The Philosopher argues. Rather The Philosopher means to show that the first mover does not have size, but rather is unpartitionable. He argues as follows: No intensively finite power in a body can make things move for an infinite time; but the first mover moves the heavens with a motion that lasts for an infinite time; therefore, the first

21 c.10. See selection **II.1.2.**
22 c.7. See selection **II.1.3.**
23 c.4,5, 204a1-206a8.
24 See selection **II.5.1.**
25 See selection **II.6.1.**
26 c.10, 266a24-266b6. See selection **II.1.2.**
27 See glossary entry for 'agent/recipient.'

mover is not a power in a body, and consequently does not admit of partition and is indivisible. The minor premiss is obvious from what was already said. He proves the major premiss by first assuming from *Physics* III[28] that every power in a body is intensively[29] finite, and then he argues as follows: If a power in a body moves something mobile over a certain time by using its full power, part of that power or mover will move part of the mobile thing over a shorter time. But the ratio of the first time to the second is in proportion to the ratio of the first mover to the second and of the first mobile thing to the second in each motion. Also the ratio of the one mover to the other, and of the mobile thing which is a part to the mobile thing which is the whole, is finite in each case of motion. Therefore, the ratio of the times is finite, and consequently each time, both the partial time and the total time, is finite. And thus it is clear that no intensively finite power existing in a body can make things move over an infinite time.

He does not prove this general conclusion: No intensively finite power can make things move over an infinite time. Rather he only proves that no intensively finite power *existing in a body* can do this. This is clear from what The Commentator[30] says in comment 78, viz. that it is possible to have a part of the mover which moves a part of the thing moved from the fact that the mover which is a power in a body can be divided. And later he says, "It should be noted that the conditional propositions which Aristotle puts forward here are propositions that are true of the heavenly body, since it was given that its motive powers are forms in matter." And right after that he says, "For all this follows from the claim that the heavenly body is a form" in matter.

[5.2] To the second [3.2] I say first that The Philosopher shows there that if any mover that moves things with a motion that lasts over an infinite time were in matter, that mover would have an intensively infinite action and be infinite in strength, as is said in *On the substance of the sphere*, ch.3.[31] This is because every active power existing in a body has, according to The Philosopher, a contrary; consequently, if it were finite in strength, at some point in time it would be destroyed by the action of this contrary. And from this it follows that if the mover had an action which was infinite in duration, it would have infinite strength, since in every case of a finite power existing in matter the part has less power for lasting than does the whole.

If you say that the same conclusion seems to follow for a separated[32] mover that moves things with a motion that lasts for an infinite time, viz. that it is intensively infinite – I answer: It does not follow, because a mover outside of matter does not have a contrary that destroys and diminishes its power; rather it is indestructible and does not admit of wearing down. Therefore, it can move things over an infinite time even though it is intensively finite.

Secondly, he shows that, if there were an intensively infinite mover in matter, it would make things move in an instant, so that something would make the movement from a very remote location to another in an instant, a movement which would be normally produced by a finite mover over a stretch of time. For example, this mover would be able to make some mobile thing which is right now here be in Rome without being in between. But it cannot make this movement be successive and in an instant, because that includes a contradiction. And, therefore, I say that this movement from one location to another is not a motion, but rather an immediate shift. This is what The Philosopher means to show, and nothing more. And in the same way I allow that God, even though He is a mover outside of matter, can on account of his intensive infinity make a body which is in London immediately come to be in Rome without its ever being in between.

[6.1] But there is a problem with regard to the first conditional which was put forward in order to prove the major premiss [see above, 5.1], namely, 'if

---

28 c.4,5, 204a1-206a8.
29 The text has 'extensively,' but this seems to be a mistake.
30 I.e., Averroes in his commentary on Aristotle's *Physics*.
31 A work by Averroes.
32 See glossary entry for 'separate substance.'

a power in a body [moves something mobile over a certain time by using its full power, part of that power or mover will move part of the mobile thing over a shorter time],' because this seems opposed to what is explained at the end of *Physics* VII, comment 36, where it is shown that if a mover moves something mobile over a certain time, half of the mover will move half the mobile thing over the same time. Therefore, if parts of the mover and the moved are taken in the same proportion, the part of the mover will not move the part of the mobile thing over either a shorter or a longer time than the whole moves the whole.

[6.2] Besides, from what was said it follows that the ratio of the one time to the other time in the motions of the whole and the part varies directly with the ratios of the one mover to the other and of the one mobile thing to the other in each motion. But it is certain that if parts of both the mover and the moved are taken in equal proportions, the ratio of them to their wholes is the same; therefore, the time taken by one motion is the same or equal to the time taken by the other motion.

[7.1] To the first problem [6.1] I answer that some things are possible for motion in general in so far as it is a motion which are not possible in any definite matter, for example infinite speed, just as The Commentator says in *Physics* VI, comment 15; and the same holds for movers and mobile things. Accordingly, I say that what is explained at the end of *Physics* VII about the ratio of whole to part in moving are attributed to a mover and a mobile thing in so far as they are mover and mobile thing. But in the matter under discussion the objection is taken to hold because of some of the definite matter in which [the mover and the mobile thing exist] .

And the reason why a part moves a part over a shorter time than the whole moves the whole is that the whole is the sort of thing whose natural perfection consists in the conjunction of its parts, both its qualitative as well as its quantitative ones. This is what is meant when, in *Physics* VI, comment 91, it is said that "the action of any entity is perfected by its limited quantity and quality, just as is the case in artificial entities." This is especially so in perfect

things. Something similar to this is said in *On the Heaven*, comment 94, and in *Metaphysics* V, comment 21. Consequently, when such a whole is divided, the part does not last as long as the whole, as is obvious in the case of worms, and as a result the part does not impart as much motion to something mobile of an equal proportion. For we see that in the case of animate things the more they are perfect the more they require the unity of their quantitative parts in order to exist.

To the main point at issue I say that, if the mover of the heaven were the form of the heaven and extended throughout it, then the heaven would be the most perfect animate thing. And, if the power of the mover were divided by the division of its subject, the part would last for a shorter time than the whole, and consequently it would move the mobile thing proportioned to it over a shorter time than the whole does, just in virtue of the fact that it does not last as long. Thus The Commentator in *Physics* VIII, comment 78, says that "the conditional propositions which Aristotle asserted here are propositions true of the heavenly body, since it has been asserted that its motive powers are forms in matter, and on account of this its act is perfected only when the parts of that matter are joined together in a bounded closeness."

[7.2] To the second problem [6.2] I say that that proposition should be read as speaking of a ratio of whole to part not in respect of a quantitative ratio but rather in respect of length of duration. For a quantitative ratio amounts to a ratio of motions in respect of speed and slowness, since, if a certain amount of power makes things move in a certain amount of time, twice that amount of power will make things move in half that time, other things being equal, as is explained in *Physics* VII.[33] That ratio is not relevant to the question here. But the second ratio amounts to a ratio of motions in respect of how long they last, and this is relevant.

Then to the minor premiss I say that, if the quantitative ratios of the part of the mover and the part of the moved to their respective wholes are the same, it follows that the motions are equal in speed, other things being equal. But it does not follow that the time consumed by the motion of the

33 c.5, 249b27-250b7.

part is equal to that consumed by the motion of the whole, since a partial motive power more quickly fails than does the power of the whole. But if the ratios of the parts are the same in respect of duration, then it follows that the times are in the same ratio and that the time consumed by the motion of the part is equal to the time consumed by the motion of the whole. But in the case under discussion the parts are not proportioned to each other in this way.

Thus the whole basis for this dictum lies in the assumption that the whole and the part are proportioned to each other in length of duration in such a way that they last or not equally. The reason for this is that, if a part is of finite duration, it has a contrary, and consequently the whole too has a contrary, and so is destructible.

[8] To the argument at the beginning [1] I say that it shows that the first mover is not infinite in size, because nothing is like that, nor is it finite in size, because it makes things move over an infinite time, as was explained above in responding to the first argument.

And further, when it is asked about infinity, I say that he means an infinity in respect of duration. And I say that, even if the sun were able to last for an infinite time, still, if its mover is in the sun as a form extended throughout matter, it would not be able to make things move with an infinite motion, for the reason given above.

TOPIC III

COULD THE WORLD BE ETERNALLY EXISTENT?

MANY ANCIENT THINKERS, INCLUDING PLATO AND ARISTOTLE, thought that not everything comes to be in time; some things are eternal, i.e. they have had no beginning but have been in existence for an infinite amount of time. Plato had held this to be true at least of the Forms or Archetypes on which everything is modelled and of the underlying material substratum of the physical world. Aristotle thought that the heavenly bodies, the earth, and all the species of natural substances had been in existence forever with no beginning. The chief philosophical advantage of such theories is that they avoid unanswerable questions about what brought things into existence. If they never came into existence, there is no question to answer.

Nevertheless, some thinkers thought that the physical universe, even though it had had no beginning of its existence, required a cause of its existence (but not of its coming-into-existence). Plotinus and the neo-Platonists generally, whose system came to be widely accepted among the philosophically minded in late antiquity, theorized that the whole spatio-temporal world, despite never having come into existence, depended for its existence on a non-temporal, eternal realm of "Intellects" or "Intelligences," i.e. minds, that existed apart from any matter. These in turn had "emanated" in a totally necessary fashion from a source of all existence the neo-Platonists called the "One." The physical world too, in its general features, was a necessary result of the Intelligences on which it depended. What was contingent were some of the particular things of the physical world, those that did come into existence and pass away during the course of time. Also a major distinction was made in the physical world between the heavenly bodies and things in the sub-lunary world. The former existed forever without every coming into being and everything that happened to them was necessitated. But among the latter there is coming-into-being and there are events which occur without having been necessitated to occur.

(The neo-Platonists often drew a distinction between what is strictly speaking eternal and what is merely everlasting, i.e. without beginning or end. To be "eternal" in this sense is not to be in time at all, and thus to be utterly changeless. In medieval discussions this usage is occasionally adhered to, but more often we find "eternal" being applied to what lasts forever as well. It is in this latter sense that the question arises as to whether the physical world is eternal.)

In medieval times some neo-Platonic writings were wrongly ascribed to Aristotle, and as a result Aristotle himself was supposed to have held a theory of emanation of Intelligences and of the efficient causation of the whole universe by an eternal first cause. (See the first topic.) What Aristotle in fact did hold was that time had had no beginning, and then, because he thought that time was impossible without motion, he concluded that motion too is without a beginning, i.e. there has never been a time when things in the world began to move. (This conception of time is quite different from the one modern physics deploys, where the space-time continuum is something explanatorily prior to motion.) Aristotle also believed that the motions of the heavenly bodies never had a start and would never come to an end. Nevertheless, he thought these motions did require an efficient cause, something that kept them going endlessly, and that this cause did this in a completely necessary fashion.

This synthesis of Aristotelian and neo-Platonic cosmology had great prestige among literate people in late antiquity and throughout the middle ages in both Islam and Christendom. Its status as science was roughly equivalent to that of astrophysics in our own day. Yet it was clearly not in accord with the traditional teachings of either of those religions nor of the Jewish faith from which they had both sprung. The monotheistic religions taught that the whole universe apart from God had been brought into being by God a finite length of time ago, and that in doing this God operated of his own free will and was not necessitated into this creation. He *contingently* produced the world, and He could have produced quite a different world, or even no world at all. The stage was set here for a major conflict between religious faith and the "scientific" views of the "philosophers," i.e. those who taught as received wisdom some version of the Aristotelian/neo-Platonic synthesis.

Within this overall dispute between traditional religion and philosophy we find a sub-debate developing over whether a universe with no beginning was something that even *could* be created by God. If contingency is built right into the definition of creation, it could well seem that accepted philosophical principles just ruled out the creation of an eternal world. If there is contingency, then there is the possibility of not-existing; but if this possibility were there for an infinite time surely at some point it would be realized, and thus the world would have gone out of existence at some point in the past, and thus it would not be eternal. On the other hand, God is supposedly omnipotent and can produce by His will anything whose production is not self-contradictory. The philosophers themselves claim that an eternal world is produced by the first cause, so they at least cannot think its production involves any contradiction, and hence God could produce it by His free will. The debate on this issue compelled the late Christian scholastics like Henry of Ghent, Duns Scotus, and William of Ockham, to sharpen their notions of what was involved in necessary and contingent causation. A number of the selections under this topic focus on that debate and are thus a natural sequel to much of the discussion under topic I.

Another facet to this topic is the subject of infinity, which has already been explored in topic II when the infinity of the first cause was the issue. Many challenging puzzles arise both when we try to understand the infinite divisibility of the continuum and the infinite length of time. There were many thinkers who thought that in fact the world could not be eternal simply because there was a barely hidden contradiction in the very notion of an infinitely long past time. The thinkers we deal with here all reached the conclusion that in fact no such contradiction exists, but in the course of dispelling the supposed difficulties we see them at work constructing a theory of the infinite which in the end would lay the groundwork for the sophisticated mathematical theories of modern times.

Finally, the reader should be aware of how these thinkers react to a situation in which arguments on neither side of a question are completely conclusive. Maimonides, the great Jewish rabbi of the 12th century, is particularly aware of this problem. Can arguments which are not completely conclusive nevertheless give some rational support to one side rather than the other? Can one argument be more conclusive than another? When no argument is completely conclusive is it reasonable to rely simply on authority? These are questions which arise in any age about some issues, and they have never been very satisfactorily resolved.

III.1. ARISTOTLE

ALL MEDIEVAL DISCUSSIONS OF THE ETERNITY OF THE WORLD AND OF whether motion did or could have had a beginning start from the text from the *Physics* presented below. To the "philosophers" it seemed to prove that the physical world and the motions of the heavenly bodies could not have had a beginning, but rather existed before any moment of time no matter how far back in the past. This thesis did away with the need for any account of how the whole physical world began; the assumption that it had begun was simply rejected. All the three great monotheistic religions that dominated the medieval world, Judaism, Islam, and Christianity, shared the creation story of *Genesis* and assumed that there was a mystery about how the world began that could only be answered by reference to something eternal existing outside that world. Conflict between these religions and the main stream of Greek philosophical thought was thus inevitable on this issue.

III.1.1. Did Motion ever have a Beginning? Will it ever end? (*Physics* VIII, ch.1)

Was there ever a coming-to-be of motion before which it had no being, and is it perishing again so as to leave nothing in motion? Or are we to say that it never had any coming-to-be and is not perishing, but always was and always will be? Is it in fact an immortal never-failing property of things that are, a sort of life as it were to all naturally constituted things?

Now the *existence* of motion is asserted by all who have anything to say about nature, because they all concern themselves with the construction of the world and study the question of coming-to-be and perishing, which processes could not come about without the existence of motion. But those who say that there is an infinite number of worlds, some of which are in process of coming-to-be while others are in process of perishing, assert that there is always motion (for these processes of coming-to-be and perishing of the worlds necessarily involve motion), whereas those who hold that there is only one world, whether everlasting or not, make corresponding assumptions in regard to motion. If then

it is possible that at any time nothing should be in motion, this must come about in one of two ways: either in the manner described by Anaxagoras,[1] who says that all things were together and at rest for an infinite period of time, and that then Mind introduced motion and separated them; or in the manner described by Empedocles,[2] according to whom the universe is alternately in motion and at rest – in motion, when Love is making the one out of many, or Strife is making many out of one, and at rest in the intermediate periods of time – his account being as follows:

> Since One hath learned to spring from Manifold,
> And One disjoined makes Manifold arise,
> Thus they Become, nor stable is their life;
> But since their motion must alternate be,
> Thus have they ever Rest upon their round.

for we must suppose that he means by 'alternate' that they change from the one motion to the other. We must consider, then, how this matter stands; for the discovery of the truth about it is of importance, not only for the study of nature, but also for the investigation of the First Principle.

---

1 Lived in the fifth century B.C.E. and taught in Athens. Plato in the *Phaedo* portrays him as attracting the attention of the young Socrates who was disappointed to find that despite his crediting the beginning of all motion to Mind he did not try to explain things by showing that they were all arranged in the best possible way.
2 Lived in Italy and Sicily in the fifth century B.C.E. Was famous for his doctrine of an endless cycle of coming together and separating out of the basic elements of the world, viz. earth, air, fire and water, under the alternate influence of Love and Strife.

Let us take our start from what we have already laid down in our course on physics. Motion, we say, is the actuality of the movable in so far as it is movable. Each kind of motion, therefore, necessarily involves the presence of the things that are capable of that motion. In fact, even apart from the definition of motion, everyone would admit that in each kind of motion it is that which is capable of that motion that is in motion; thus it is that which is capable of alteration that is altered, and that which is capable of local change that is in locomotion; and so there must be something capable of being burned before there can be a process of being burned, and something capable of burning something before there can be a process of burning. Moreover, these things also must either have a beginning before which they had no being, or they must be eternal. Now if there was a coming-to-be of every movable thing, it follows that before the motion in question another change or motion must have taken place in which that which was capable of being moved or of causing motion had its coming-to-be. To suppose, on the other hand, that these things were in being throughout all previous time without there being any motion appears unreasonable on a moment's thought, and still more unreasonable, we shall find, on further consideration. For if we are to say that, while there are on the one hand things that are movable, and on the other hand things that cause motion, there is a time when there is a first mover and a first moved, and another time when there is no such thing but only something that is at rest, then this thing must previously have been in process of change; for there must have been some cause of its rest, rest being the privation of motion. Therefore, before this first change there will be a previous change. For some things cause motion in only one way, while others can produce either of two contrary motions; thus fire causes heating but not cooling, whereas it would seem that knowledge may be directed to two contrary ends while remaining one and the same. Even in the former class, however, there seems to be something similar; for a cold thing in a sense causes heating by turning away and retiring, just as one possessed of knowledge voluntarily makes an error when he uses his knowledge in the reverse way. But at any rate all things that are capable of affecting and being affected, or of causing motion and being moved, are capable of it not under all conditions, but only when they are in a particular condition and approach one another; so it is on the approach of one thing to another that the one causes motion and the other is moved, and when they are present under such conditions as rendered the one motive and the other movable. So if the motion was not always in process, it is clear that they cannot have been in a condition such as to render them capable respectively of being moved and of causing motion, but one or other of them needed change; for in what is relative this is a necessary consequence: e.g. if one thing is double another when before it was not so, one or other of them, if not both must have changed. It follows, then, that there will be a change previous to the first.

(Further, how can there be any before and after without the existence of time? Or how can there be any time without the existence of motion? If, then, time is the number of motion or itself a kind of motion, it follows that, if there is always time, motion must also be eternal. But so far as time is concerned we see that all with one exception are in agreement in saying that it is uncreated; in fact, it is just this that enables Democritus[3] to show that all things cannot have had a coming-to-be; for time, he says, is uncreated. Plato alone asserts the creation of time, saying that it is simultaneous with the world, and that the world came into being. Now since time cannot exist and is unthinkable apart from the *now*, and the *now* is a kind of middle-point, uniting as it does in itself both a beginning and an end, a beginning of future time and an end of past time, it follows that there must always be time; for the extremity of the last period of time that we take must be found in some *now*, since in time we can take nothing but *nows*. Therefore, since the *now* is both a beginning and an end, there must always be time on both sides of it. But if this is true of time, it is evident that it must also be true of motion, time being a kind of attribute of motion.)

---

3 Lived in the late 5th and early 4th centuries B.C.E. With Leucippus he was a founder of the ancient Greek atomist school of philosophers of nature. His system rigorously eschewed all forms of teleology in the explanation of things in favour of strict materialism.

The same reasoning will also serve to show the imperishability of motion: just as a coming-to-be of motion would involve, as we saw, a change previous to the first, in the same way a perishing of motion would involve a change subsequent to the last; for when a thing ceases to be in motion, it does not therefore at the same time cease to be movable – e.g. the cessation being burned does not involve the cessation of the capacity of being burned, since a thing may be capable of being burned without being burned – nor, when a thing ceases to be a mover, does it therefore at the same time cease to be motive. Again, the destructive agent will have to be destroyed when it has destroyed, and then that which has the capacity of destroying *it* will have to be destroyed afterwards, for being destroyed is a kind of change. If, then, this is impossible, it is clear that motion is eternal and cannot have existed at one time and not at another; in fact, such a view can hardly be described as anything else than fantastic.

And much the same may be said of the view that such is how things naturally are and that this must be regarded as a principle, as would seem to be the view of Empedocles when he says that the constitution of the world is of necessity such that Love and Strife alternately predominate and cause motion, while in the intermediate period of time there is a state of rest.[4] Probably also those who, like Anaxagoras, assert a single principle would hold this view. But that which holds by nature and is natural can never be anything disorderly; for nature is everywhere the cause of order. Moreover, there is no ratio in the relation of the infinite to the infinite, whereas order always means ratio. But if we say that there is first a state of rest for an infinite time, and then motion is started at some moment, and that the fact that it is this rather than a previous moment is of no importance, and that it involves no order, then we can no longer say that it is nature's work; for if anything is of a certain character naturally, it either is so invariably and is not sometimes of this and sometimes of another character (e.g. fire, which travels upwards naturally,

does not sometimes do so and sometimes not) or there is a ratio in the variation. It would be better, therefore, to say with Empedocles and anyone else who may have maintained such a theory as his that the universe is alternately at rest and in motion; for in a system of this kind we have at once a certain order. But even here the holder of the theory ought not only to assert the fact; he ought also to explain the cause of it, i.e. he should not make any mere assumption or lay down any unreasoned axiom, but should employ either inductive or demonstrative reasoning. The Love and Strife postulated are not in themselves causes, nor is it of the essence of either that it should be so, the essential function of the former being to unite, of the latter to separate. If he is to go on to explain this alternate predominance, he should adduce cases where such a state of things exists, as he points to the fact that among mankind we have something that unites human beings, namely Love, while on the other hand enemies avoid one another. Thus from the observed fact that this occurs in certain cases comes the assumption that it occurs also in the universe. Then, again, some argument is needed to explain why the predominance of each lasts for an equal period of time. But it is a wrong assumption to suppose universally that we have an adequate first principle in virtue of the fact that something always is so or always happens so. Thus Democritus reduces the causes that explain nature to the fact that things happened in the past in the same way as they happen now; but he does not think fit to seek for a principle to explain this "always"; so, while his theory is right in so far as it is applied to certain individual cases, he is wrong in making it of universal application. Thus, a triangle always has its angles equal to two right angles, but there is nevertheless an ulterior cause of the eternity, whereas principles are external and have no ulterior cause. Let this conclude what we have to say in support of our contention that there never was a time when there was not motion and never will be a time when there will not be motion.

---

4 Aristotle understands Empedocles to have thought that when Love has completed its work and all the elements are thoroughly mixed there is a moment of rest before Strife begins its work of separating them. Likewise, once Strife has finished the work of separation there occurs another moment of rest before the cycle starts again.

III.2. ST. AUGUSTINE

ALTHOUGH, LIKE ARISTOTLE, AUGUSTINE THOUGHT TIME IS DEPENDENT on motion, he did not accept that it requires the motion of anything physical like the stars or other heavenly bodies. Nor did he find difficulty in the idea that time was created when something with motion was created even though such creatures have not existed for an infinity of past time, but rather had a beginning of their existence. However, the very notion of time itself he did find problematic.

III.2.1. What is Time? (*Confessions* XI, chs.12-28)

Chapter 12: What God did before the creation of the world

Behold, I answer to him who asks, "What was God doing before He made heaven and earth?" I answer not, as a certain person is reported to have done facetiously (avoiding the pressure of the question), "He was preparing hell," said he, "for those who pry into mysteries." It is one thing to perceive, another to laugh – these are things I answer not. For more willingly would I have answered, "I know not what I know not," than that I should make him a laughing-stock who asks deep things, and gain praise as one who answers false things. But I say that Thou, our God, art the Creator of every creature; and if by the term "heaven and earth" every creature is understood, I boldly say that before God made heaven and earth, He made not anything. For if He did, what did He make unless the creature? And would that I knew whatever I desire to know to my advantage, as I know that no creature was made before any creature was made.

Chapter 13: Before the times created by God, times were not

But if the roving thought of anyone should wander through the images of bygone times, and wonder that Thou, the God Almighty, and All-creating, and All-sustaining, the Architect of heaven and earth, didst for innumerable ages refrain from so great a work before Thou wouldst make it, let him awake and consider that he wonders at false things. For whence could innumerable ages pass by which Thou didst not make, since Thou art the Author and Creator of all ages? Or what times should those be which were not make by Thee? Or how should they pass by if they had not been? Since, therefore, Thou art the Creator of all times, if any time was before Thou madest heaven and earth, why is it said that Thou didst refrain from working? For that very time Thou madest, nor could times pass by before Thou madest times. But if before heaven and earth there was no time, why is it asked, What didst Thou then? For there was no "then" when time was not.

Nor dost Thou by time precede time; else wouldest not Thou precede all times. But in the excellency of an ever-present eternity, Thou precedest all times past, and survivest all future times, because they are future, and when they have come they will be past; but Thou art the same, and Thy years shall have no end.[1] Thy years neither go nor come; but ours both go and come, that all may come. All Thy years stand at once since they do stand; nor were they when departing excluded by coming years, because they pass not away; but all these of ours shall be when all shall cease to be. Thy years are one day, and Thy day is not daily, but to-day; because Thy to-day yields not with to-morrow, for neither doth it follow yesterday. Thy to-day is eternity; therefore didst Thou beget the Co-eternal, to whom Thou saidst, "This day have I begotten Thee."[2] Thou hast made all time; and before all times Thou art, nor in any time was there not time.

---

1 *Psalm* 102:27.
2 *Psalm* 2:7; *Heb.* 5:5.

Chapter 14: Neither time past nor future, but the present only, really is

At no time, therefore, hadst Thou not made anything, because Thou hadst made time itself. And no times are co-eternal with Thee, because Thou remainest forever; but should these continue, they would not be times. For what is time? Who can easily and briefly explain it? Who even in thought can comprehend it, even to the pronouncing of a word concerning it? But what in speaking do we refer to more familiarly and knowingly than time? And certainly we understand when we speak of it; we understand also when we hear it spoken of by another. What, then, is time? If no one ask of me, I know; if I wish to explain to him who asks, I know not. Yet I say with confidence, that I know that if nothing passed away, there would not be past time; and if nothing were coming, there would not be future time; and if nothing were, there would not be present time. Those two times, therefore, past and future, how are they, when even the past now is not, and the future is not as yet? But should the present be always present, and should it not pass into time past, truly it comes into existence because it passes into time past, how do we say that even this is, whose cause of being is that it shall not be — namely, so that we cannot truly say that time is, unless because it tends not to be?

Chapter 15: There is only a moment of present time

And yet we say that time is long and time is short; nor do we speak of this save of time past and future. A long time past, for example, we call a hundred years ago; in like manner a long time to come, a hundred years hence. But a short time past we call, say, ten days ago: and a short time to come, ten days hence. But in what sense is that long or short which is not? For the past is not now, and the future is not yet. Therefore let us not say, "It is long"; but let us say of the past, "It has been long," and of the future, "It will be long." O my Lord, my light, shall not even here Thy truth deride humans? For that past time which was long, was it long when it was already past, or when it was as yet present? For then it might be long when there was that which could be long, but when past it no longer was; wherefore that could not be long which was not at

all. Let us not, therefore, say, "Time past has been long"; for we shall not find what may have been long, seeing that since it was past it is not; but let us say that present time was long, because when it was present it was long. For it had not as yet passed away so as not to be, and therefore there was that which could be long. But after it passed, that ceased also to be long which ceased to be.

Let us therefore see, O human soul, whether present time can be long; for to thee is it given to perceive and to measure periods of time. What wilt thou reply to me? Is a hundred years when present a long time? See first, whether a hundred years can be present. For if the first year of these is current, that is present, but the other ninety and nine are future, and therefore they are not as yet. But if the second year is current, one is already past, the other present, the rest future. And thus, if we fix on any middle year of this hundred as present, those before it are past, those after it are future; wherefore a hundred years cannot be present. See at least whether that year itself which is current can be present. For if its first month be current, the rest are future; if the second, the first has already passed, and the remainder are not yet. Therefore neither is the year which is current as a whole present; and if it is not present as a whole, then the year is not present. For twelve months make the year, of which each individual month which is current is itself present, but the rest are either past or future. Although neither is that month which is current present, but one day only: if the first, the rest being to come, if the last, the rest being past; if any of the middle, then between past and future.

Behold, the present time, which alone we found could be called long, is abridged to the space scarcely of one day. But let us discuss even that, for there is not one day present as a whole. For it is made up of four-and-twenty hours of night and day, of which the first has the rest future, the last has them past, but any one of the intervening has those before it past, those after it future. And that one hour passes away in fleeting particles. Whatever of it has flown away is past, whatever remains is future. If any portion of time be conceived which cannot now be divided into even the minutest particles of moments, this only is that which may be called present; which, however, flies so rapidly from future to past, that it cannot be extended by any delay. For if it be extended, it is divided into the past and future; but the present has no space. Where, therefore, is the time which we may call long? Is it future? Indeed we do not say, "It is long," because it is not yet, so as to be long; but we say, "It will be long." When then will it be? For if even then, since as yet it is future, it will not *be* long, because what may be long is not as yet; but it shall be long, when from the future, which as yet is not, it shall already have begun to be, and will have become present, so that there could be that which may be long; then does the present time cry out in the words above that it cannot be long.

Chapter 16: Time can only be perceived or measured while it is passing

And yet, O Lord, we perceive intervals of times, and we compare them with themselves, and we say some are longer, others shorter. We even measure by how much shorter or longer this time may be than that; and we answer that this is double or treble, while that is but once, or only as much as that. But we measure times passing when we measure them by perceiving them; but past times, which now are not, or future times, which as yet are not, who can measure them? Unless, perchance, any one will dare to say, that that can be measured which is not. When, therefore, time is passing, it can be perceived and measured; but when it has passed, it cannot, since it is not.

Chapter 17: Nevertheless there is time past and future

I ask, Father, I do not affirm. O my God, rule and guide me. Who is there who can say to me that there are not three times (as we learned as boys, and as we have taught boys), the past, present, and future, but only present, because those two are not? Or are they also; but when from future it becomes present, comes it forth from some secret place, and when from the present it becomes past, does it retire into anything secret? For where have they who have foretold future things seen these things, if as yet they are not? For that which is not cannot be seen. And they who relate things past could not relate them as true, did they not perceive them in their mind. Which things, if they were not, they could in no wise be discerned. There are therefore things both future and past.

Chapter 18: Past and future times cannot be thought of but as present

Suffer me, O Lord, to seek further; O my Hope, let not my purpose be confounded. For if there are times past and future, I desire to know where they are. But if as yet I do not succeed, I still know, wherever they are, that they are not there as future or past, but as present. For if there also they be future, they are not as yet there; if even there they be past, they are no longer there. Wheresoever, therefore, they are, whatsoever they are they are only so as present. Although past things are related as true, they are drawn out from the memory – not the things themselves, which have passed, but the words conceived from the images of the things which they have formed in the mind as footprints in their passage through the sense. My childhood, indeed, which no longer is, is in time past, which now is not; but when I call to mind its image, and speak of it, I behold it in the present, because it is as yet in my memory. Whether there be a like cause of foretelling future things, that of things which as yet are not, the images may be perceived as already existing, I confess, my God, I know not. This certainly I know, that we generally think before on our future actions, and that this premeditation is present; but that the action on which we premeditate is not yet, because it is future; which when we shall have entered upon, and have begun to do that which we were premeditating, then shall that action be, because then it is not future, but present.

In whatever manner, therefore, this secret preconception of future things may be, nothing can be seen, save what is. But what now is not future, but present. When, therefore, they say that things future are seen, it is not themselves, which as yet are not (that is, which are future); but their causes or their signs perhaps are seen, which already are. Therefore, to those already beholding them, they are not future, but present, from which future things conceived in the mind are foretold. these conceptions again now are, and they who foretell those things behold these conceptions present before them. Let now so multitudinous a variety of things afford me some example. I behold daybreak; I foretell that the sun is about to rise. That which I behold is present; what I foretell is future – not that the sun is future, which already is; but his rising, which is not yet. Yet even its rising I could not predict unless I had an image of it in my mind, as now I have while I speak. But that dawn which I see in the sky is not the rising of the sun, although it may go before it, nor that imagination in my mind; which two are seen as present, that the other which is future may be foretold. Future things, therefore, are not as yet; and if they are not as yet, they are not. And if they are not, they cannot be seen at all; but they can be foretold from things present which now are, and are seen.

Chapter 19: We are ignorant in what manner God teaches future things

Thou, therefore, Ruler of Thy creatures, what is the method by which Thou teachest souls those things which are future? For Thou hast taught Thy prophets. What is that way by which Thou, to whom nothing is future, dost teach future things; or rather of future things dost teach present? For what is not, of a certainty cannot be taught. Too far is this way from my view; it is too mighty for me, I cannot attain unto it;[3] but by Thee I shall be enabled, when Thou shalt have granted it, sweet light of my hidden eyes.

Chapter 20: In what manner time may properly be designated

But what now is manifest and clear is, that neither are there future nor past things. Nor is it fitly said, "There are three times, past, present and future"; but perchance it might be fitly said, "There are three times; a present of things past, a present of things present, and a present of things future." For these three do somehow exist in the soul, and otherwise I see them not: present of things past, memory; present of things present, sight; present of things future, expectation. If of these things we are permitted to speak, I see three times, and I grant there are three. It may also be said, "There are three times, past, present and future," as usage falsely has it. See, I trouble not, nor gainsay, nor reprove; provided always that which is said may be understood, that neither the future, nor that which is past, now is. For there are but few things which we speak properly, many things improperly; but what

we may wish to say is understood.

Chapter 21: How time may be measured

I have just now said, then, that we measure times as they pass, that we may be able to say that this time is twice as much as that one, or that this is only as much as that, and so of any other of the parts of time which we are able to tell by measuring. Wherefore, as I said, we measure times as they pass. And if any one should ask me, "Whence dost thou know?" I can answer, "I know, because we measure; nor can we measure thing that are not; and things past and future are not." But how do we measure present time, since it has not space? It is measured while it passes; but when it shall have passed, it is not measured; for there will not be aught that can be measured. But whence, in what way, and whither does it pass while it is being measured? Whence, but from the future? Which way, save through the present? Whither, but into the past? From that, therefore, which as yet is not, through that which has no space, into that which now is not. But what do we measure, unless time in some space? For we say not single, and double, and triple, and equal, or in any other way in which we speak of time, unless with respect to the spaces of times. In what space, then, do we measure passing time? Is it in the future, whence it passes over? But what yet we measure not, is not. Or is it in the present, by which it passes? But no space we do not measure. Or in the past, whither it passes? But that which is not now, we measure not.

Chapter 22: He prays God that He would explain this most entangled enigma

My soul yearns to know this most entangled enigma. Forbear to shut up, O Lord my God, good Father – through Christ I beseech Thee – forbear to shut up these things, both usual and hidden, from my desire, that it may be hindered from penetrating them; but let them dawn through Thy enlightening mercy, O Lord. Of whom shall I inquire concerning these things? And to whom shall I with more advantage confess my ignorance than to Thee to whom these my studies, so vehemently kindled

---

3 *Psalm* 139:6.

towards Thy Scriptures, are not troublesome? Give that which I love; for I do love, and this hast Thou given me. Give, Father, who truly knowest to give good gifts unto Thy children.[4] Give, since I have undertaken to know, and trouble is before me until Thou dost open it.[5] Through Christ, I beseech Thee, in His name, Holy of Holies, let no man interrupt me. For I believed, and therefore do I speak.[6] This is my hope; for this do I live, that I may contemplate the delights of the Lord.[7] Behold, Thou hast made my days old,[8] and they pass away, and in what manner I know not. And we speak as to time and time, times and times – "How long is the time since he said this?" "How long the time since he did this?" and, "How long the time since I saw that?" and, "This syllable has double the time of that single short syllable." These words we speak, and these we hear; and we are understood, and we understand. They are most manifest and most usual, and the same things again lie hid too deeply, and the discovery of them is new.

Chapter 23: That time is a certain extension

I have heard from a learned man that the motions of the sun, moon, and stars constituted time, and I assented not. For why should not rather the motions of all bodies be time? What if the lights of heaven should cease, and a potter's wheel run round, would there be no time by which we might measure those revolutions, and say either that it turned with equal pauses, or, if it were moved, at one time more slowly, at another more quickly, that some revolutions were longer, others less so? Or while we were saying this, should we not also be speaking in time? Or should there in our words be some syllables long, others short, but because those sounded in a longer time, these in a shorter? God grant to humans to see in a small thing ideas common to things great and small. Both the stars and luminaries of heaven are for signs and for seasons, and for days and years.[9] No doubt they are; but nei-

ther should I say that the circuit of that wooden wheel was a day, nor yet should he say that therefore there was no time.

I desire to know the power and nature of time, by which we measure the motions of bodies, and say (for example) that this motion is twice as long as that. For, I ask, since 'day' declares not the stay only of the sun upon the earth, according to which day is one thing, night another, but also its entire circuit from east even to east – according to which we say, "So many days have passed" (the nights being included when we say "so many days," and their spaces not counted apart) – since, then, the day is finished by the motion of the sun, and by his circuit from east to east, I ask, whether the motion itself is the day, or the period in which that motion is completed, or both? For if the first be the day, then would there be a day although the sun should finish that course in so small a space of time as an hour. If the second, then that would not be a day if from one sunrise to another there were but so short a period as an hour, but the sun must go round four-and-twenty times to complete a day. If both, neither could that be called a day if the sun should run his entire round in the space of an hour; nor that, if, while the sun stood still, so much time should pass as the sun is accustomed to accomplish his whole course in from morning to morning. I shall not therefore now ask, what that is which is called day, but what time is, by which we, measuring the circuit of the sun, should say that it was accomplished in half the space of time it was wont, if it had been completed in so small a space as twelve hours; and comparing both times, we should call that single, this double time, although the sun should run his course from east to east sometimes in that single, sometimes in that double time. Let no person then tell me that the motions of the heavenly bodies are times, because, when at the prayer of one the sun stood still in order that he might achieve his victorious battle, the sun stood still, but time went on. For in such space of time as

---

4 *Matthew* 7:11.
5 *Psalm* 73:16.
6 *Psalm* 116:10.
7 *Psalm* 27:4.
8 *Psalm* 39:5.
9 *Genesis* 1:14.

was sufficient was that battle fought and ended.[10] I see that time, then, is a certain extension. But I do see it, or do I seem to see it? Thou, O Light and Truth, wilt show me.

Chapter 24: That time is not a motion of a body which we measure by time

Dost Thou command that I should assent, if any one should say that time is the motion of a body? Thou dost not command me. For I hear that no body is moved but in time. This Thou sayest; but that the very motion of a body is time, I hear not; Thou sayest it not. For when a body is moved, I by time measure how long it may be moving from the time in which it began to be moved till it left off. And if I saw not whence it began, and it continued to be moved, so that I see not when it leaves off, I cannot measure unless, perchance, from the time I began until I cease to see. But if I look long, I only proclaim that the time is long, but not how long it may be; because when we say, "How long," we speak by comparison, as, "This is as long as that," or, "This is double as long as that," or any other thing of the kind. But if we were able to note down the distances of places whence and whither comes the body which is moved, or its parts, if it moved as in a wheel, we can say in how much time the motion of the body or its part, from this place to that, was performed. Since, then, the motion of a body is one thing, that by which we measure how long it is another, who cannot see which of these is rather to be called time? For, although a body be sometimes moved, sometimes stand still, we measure not its motion only, but also its standing still, by time; and we say, "It stood still as much as it moved"; or, "It stood still twice or thrice as long as it moved"; and if any other space which our measuring has either determined of imagined, more or less, as we are accustomed to say. Time, therefore, is not the motion of a body.

Chapter 25: He calls on God to enlighten his mind

And I confess unto Thee, O Lord, that I am as yet ignorant as to what time is, and again I confess

unto Thee, O Lord, that I know that I speak these things in time, and that I have already spoken of time, and that very "long" is not long save by the stay of time. How, then, know I this, when I know not what time is? Or is it, perchance, that I know not in what wise I may express what I know? Alas for me, that I do not at least know the extent of my own ignorance! Behold, O my God, before Thee I lie not. As I speak, so is my heart. Thou shalt light my candle; Thou, O Lord my God, wilt enlighten my darkness.[11]

Chapter 26: We measure longer events by shorter in time

Doth not my soul pour out unto Thee truly in confession that I do measure times? But do I thus measure, O my God, and know not what I measure? I measure the motion of a body by time; and the time itself do I not measure? But, in truth, could I measure the motion of a body, how long it is, and how long it is in coming from this place to that, unless I should measure the time in which it is moved? How, therefore, do I measure this very time itself? Or do we by a shorter time measure a longer, as by the space of a cubit the space of a crossbeam? For thus, indeed, we seem by the space of a short syllable to measure the space of a long syllable, and to say that it is double. Thus we measure the spaces of stanzas by the spaces of the verses, and the spaces of the verses by the spaces of the feet, and the spaces of the feet by the spaces of the syllables, and the spaces of long by the spaces of short syllables; not measuring by pages (for in that manner we measure spaces, not times), but when in uttering the words they pass by, and we say, "It is a long stanza because it is made up of so many verses; long verses because they consist of so many feet; long feet, because they are prolonged by so many syllables, a long syllable, because double a short one." But neither thus is any certain measure of time obtained; since it is possible that a shorter verse, if it be pronounced more fully, may take up more time than a longer one, if pronounced more hurriedly. Thus for a stanza, thus for a foot, thus for a syllable. Whence it appeared to me that time

---

10 *Joshua* 10:12-14.
11 *Psalm* 18:28.

is nothing else than extension; but of what I know not. It is wonderful to me, if it be not of the mind itself. For what do I measure, I beseech Thee, O my God, even when I say either indefinitely, "This time is longer than that"; or even definitely, "This is double that?" That I measure time, I know. But I measure not the future, for it is not yet; nor do I measure the present, because it is extended by no space; nor do I measure the past, because it no longer is. What, therefore, do I measure? Is it times passing, not past? For thus had I said.

Chapter 27: Times are measured in proportion as they pass by

Persevere, O my mind, and give earnest heed. God is our helper; He made us, and not we ourselves.[12] Give heed, where truth dawns. Lo, suppose the voice of a body begins to sound, and does sound, and sounds on, and lo! it ceases – it is now silence, and that voice is past and is no longer a voice. It was future before it sounded, and could not be measured, because as yet it was not; and now it cannot, because it no longer is. Then, therefore, while it was sounding, it might, because there was then that which might be measured. But even then it did not stand still, for it was going and passing away. Could it, then, on that account be measured the more? For, while passing, it was being extended into some space of time, in which it might be measured, since the present has no space. If, therefore, then it might be measured, lo! suppose another voice has begun to sound, and still sounds, in a continued tenor without any interruption, we can measure it while it is sounding; for when it shall have ceased to sound, it will be already past, and there will not be that which can be measured. Let us measure it truly, and let us say how much it is. But as yet it sounds, nor can it be measured, save from that instant in which it began to sound, even to the end in which it left off. For the interval itself we measure from some beginning to some end. On which account, an utterance which is not yet ended cannot be measured, so that it may be said how

long or how short it may be; nor can it be said to be equal to another, or single or double in respect of it, or the like. But when it is ended, it no longer is. In what manner, therefore, may it be measured? And yet we measure times; still not those which as yet are not, nor those which no longer are, nor those which are protracted by some delay, nor those which have no limits. We, therefore, measure neither future times, nor past, nor present, nor those passing by; and yet we do measure times.

Deus Creator omnium [God, Creator of all]; this verse of eight syllables alternates between short and long syllables. The four short, then, the first, third, fifth and seventh, are single in respect of the four long, the second, fourth, sixth and eighth. Each of these has a double time to every one of those. I pronounce them, report on them, and thus it is, as is perceived by common sense.[13] By common sense, then, I measure a long by a short syllable, and I find that it has twice as much. But when one sounds after another, if the former be short the latter long, how shall I hold the short one, and how measuring shall I apply it to the long, so that I may find out that this has twice as much, when indeed the long does not begin to sound unless the short leaves off sounding? That very long one I measure not as present, since I measure it not save when ended. But its ending is its passing away. What, then, is it that I can measure? Where is the short syllable by which I measure? Where is the long one which I measure? Both have sounded, have flown, have passed away, and are no longer; and still I measure, and I confidently answer (so far as is trusted to a practised sense), that as to space of time this syllable is single, that double. Nor could I do this, unless because they have passed, and are ended. Therefore do I not measure themselves, which now are not, but something in my memory, which remains fixed.

In thee, O my mind, I measure times. Do not overwhelm me with thy clamor. That is, do not overwhelm thyself with the multitude of thy impressions. In thee, I say, I measure times; the impression which things as they pass by make on thee, and which, when they have passed by, remains, that I

---

12 *Psalm* 100:3.
13 By "common sense" Augustine does not mean what we nowadays call common sense, but rather an aspect of our faculty of sense perception. See entry for 'common sense' in glossary.

measure as time present, not those things which have passed by, that the impression should be made. This I measure when I measure times. Either, then, these are times, or I do not measure times. What when we measure silence, and say that this silence has lasted as long as that utterance lasts? Do we not extend our thought to the measure of an utterance, as if it sounded, so that we may be able to declare something concerning the intervals of silence in a given space of time? For when both the voice and tongue are still, we go over in thought poems and verses, and any discourse, or dimensions of motions; and declare concerning the spaces of times, how much this may be in respect of that, not otherwise than if uttering them we should pronounce them. Should any one wish to utter a lengthened sound, and had with forethought determined how long it should be, that person has in silence surely gone through a space of time, and, committing it to memory, he begins to utter that speech, which sounds until it be extended to the end proposed; truly it has sounded, and will sound. For what of it is already finished has surely sounded, but what remains will sound; and thus does it pass on, until the present intention carry over the future into the past; the past increasing by the diminution of the future, until, by the consumption of the future, all be past.

Chapter 28: Time in the human mind, which expects, considers, and remembers

But how is that future diminished or consumed which as yet is not? Or how does the past, which is no longer, increase, unless in the mind which enacts this there are three things done? For it both expects, and considers, and remembers, that that which it expects, through that which it considers may pass into that which it remembers. Who, therefore, denies that future things as yet are not? But yet there is already in the mind the expectation of things future. And who denies that past things are now no longer? But, however, there is still in the mind the memory of things past. And who denies that time present wants space, because it passes away in a moment? But yet our consideration endures, through which that which may be present

may proceed to become absent. Future time, which is not, is not therefore long; but a "long future" is "a long expectation of the future." Nor is time past, which is now no longer, long; but a long past is "a long memory of the past."

I am about to repeat a psalm that I know. Before I begin, my attention is extended to the whole: but when I have begun, as much of it as becomes past by my saying it is extended in my memory; and the life of this action of mine is extended both ways between my memory, on account of what I have repeated, and my expectation, on account of what I am about to repeat; yet my consideration is present with me, through which that which was future may be carried over so that it may become past. The more this is done and repeated, by so much (expectation being shortened) the memory is enlarged, until the whole expectation be exhausted, when that whole action being ended shall have passed into memory. And what takes place in the entire psalm, takes place also in each individual part of it, and in each individual syllable: this holds in the longer action, of which that psalm is perchance a portion; the same holds in the whole life of a person, of which all the actions of the person are parts; the same holds in the whole age of the children of mankind, of which all the lives of persons are parts.

III.2.2. How Creatures have always been but are not co-eternal with God (*On the City of God*, XII, ch.15)

For my own part, indeed, as I dare not say that there ever was a time when the Lord God was not Lord, so I ought not to doubt that humans had no existence before time, and were first created in time. But when I consider what God could be the Lord of, if there was not always some creature, I shrink from making any assertion, remembering my own insignificance, and that it is written, "what person is he that can know the counsel of God? or who can think of what the will of the Lord is? For the thoughts of mortal people are timid, and our devices are but uncertain. For the corruptible body presseth down the soul, and the earthly tabernacle weigheth down the mind that museth upon many things."[14] Many things certainly do I muse upon in

14 *Wisdom* 9:13-15.

this earthly tabernacle, because the one thing which is true among the many, or beyond the many, I cannot find. If, then, among these many thoughts, I say that there have always been creatures for Him to be Lord of, who is always and ever has been Lord, but that these creatures have not always been the same, but succeeded one another (for we would not seem to say that any is co-eternal with the Creator, an assertion condemned equally by faith and sound reason) I must take care lest I fall into the absurd and ignorant error of maintaining that by these successions and changes mortal creatures have always existed, whereas the immortal creatures had not begun to exist until the date of our own world, when the angels were created; if at least the angels are intended by that light which was first made, or, rather, by that heaven of which it is said, "In the beginning God created the heavens and the earth."[15] The angels, at least did not exist before they were created; for if we say that they have always existed, we shall seem to make them co-eternal with the Creator. Again, if I say that the angels were not created in time, but existed before all times, as those over whom God, who has ever been Sovereign, exercised His sovereignty, then I shall be asked whether, if they were created before all time, they, being creatures, could possibly always exist. It may perhaps be replied, Why not *always*, since that which is in all time may very properly be said to be "always"? Now so true is it that these angels have existed in all time that even before time was they were created; if at least time began with the heavens, and the angels existed before the heavens. And if time was even before the heavenly bodies, not indeed by hours, days, months, and years – for these measures of time's periods which are commonly and properly called times, did manifestly begin with the motion of the heavenly bodies, and so God said, when He appointed them, "Let them be for signs, and for seasons, and for days, and for years"[16] – if, I say, time was before these heavenly bodies by some changing movement, whose parts succeeded one another and could not exist simultaneously, and if there was some such movement among the angels which necessitated the existence of time, and that

they from their very creation should be subject to these temporal changes, then they have existed in all time, for time came into being along with them. And who will say that what was in all time, was not always?

But if I make such a reply, it will be said to me, How, then, are they not co-eternal with the Creator, if He and they always have been? How ever can they be said to have been created, if we are to understand that they have always existed? What shall we reply to this? Shall we say that both statements are true? that they always have been, since they have been in all time, they being created along with time, or time along with them, and yet that also they were created? For, similarly, we will not deny that time itself was created, though no one doubts that time has been in all time; for if it has not been in all time, then there was a time when there was no time. But the most foolish person could not make such an assertion. For we can reasonably say there was a time when Rome was not; there was a time when Jerusalem was not; there was a time when Abraham was not; there was a time when mankind was not, and so on: in fine, if the world was not made at the commencement of time, but after some time had elapsed, we can say there was a time when the world was not. But to say there was a time when time was not, is as absurd as to say there was a human being when there was no human being; or, this world was when this world was not. For if we are not referring to the same object, the form of expression may be used, as, there was no other human when this human was not. Thus we can reasonably say there was another time when this time was not; but not the merest simpleton could say there was a time when there was no time. As, then, we say that time was created, though we also say that it always has been, since in all time time has been, so it does not follow that if the angels have always been, they were therefore not created. For we say that they have always been, because they have been in all time; and we say they have been in all time, because time itself could nowise be without them. For where there is no creature whose changing movements admit of succession, there cannot be time at all. And consequently, even if they have always existed, they were created; neither, if they have always existed, are they therefore co-eternal with the Creator. For He has always existed in unchangeable eternity; while they were created, and are said to have been always, because they have been in all time, time being impossible without the creature. But time passing away by its changefulness, cannot be co-eternal with changeless eternity. And consequently, though the immortality of the angels does not pass in time, does not become past as if now it were not, nor has a future as if it were not yet, still their movements, which are the basis of time, do pass from future to past; and therefore they cannot be co-eternal with the Creator, in whose movement we cannot say that there has been that which now is not, or shall be that which is not yet. Wherefore, if God always has been Lord, He has always had creatures under His dominion – creatures, however, not begotten of Him,[17] but created by Him out of nothing; nor co-eternal with Him, for He was before them though at no time without them, because He preceded them, not by the lapse of time, but by His abiding eternity. But if I make this reply to those who demand how He was always Creator, always Lord, if there were not always a subject creation; or how this was created, and not rather co-eternal with its Creator, if it always was, I fear I may be accused of recklessly affirming what I know not, instead of teaching what I know. I return, therefore, to that which our Creator has seen fit that we should know; and those things which He has allowed the abler people to know in this life, or has reserved to be known in the next by the perfected saints, I acknowledge to be beyond my capacity. But I have thought it right to discuss these matters without making positive assertions, that they who read may be warned to abstain from hazardous questions, and may not deem themselves fit for everything. Let them rather endeavor to obey the wholesome injunction of the apostle, when he says, "For I say, through the grace given unto me, to every person that is among you, not to think of themselves more highly than they ought to think; but to think soberly, according as God hath dealt to every person the measure of faith."[18] For if an infant receive nourishment suited to its strength, it becomes capable, as it grows, of taking more; but if its strength and capacity be overtaxed, it dwindles away in place of growing.

---

17 Augustine alludes here to the dogma that the second Person of the Trinity was "begotten" by the first Person. This kind of "generation" of genuinely eternal beings Augustine contrasts with "creation."
18 *Titus* 1:2-3.

III.3. AL-GHAZALI AND AVERROES (IBN RUSHD)

ONE OF THE PHILOSOPHIC DOCTRINES OF THE "PHILOSOPHERS" WHICH Al-Ghazali viewed as unproven was that the world had had no beginning of its existence even though it was causally dependent on God. In his *Incoherence of the Philosophers (Tahafut al-Falasifah)* he argued that the case for a temporal creation of the world was at least as strong as that for this thesis of the philosophers. Averroes, who in the twelfth-century world of Islamic Spain defended Aristotelian philosophy against religious attacks, wrote a reply called *The Incoherence of the Incoherence (Tahafut alTahafut)* from which this selection is taken.

III.3.1. **Is the Doctrine of the "Philosophers" as regards the Production of the World coherent?**

The aim of this book is to show the different degrees of assent and conviction attained by the assertions in [Al-Ghazali's book] *The Incoherence of the Philosophers,* and to prove that the greater part has not reached the degree of evidence and of truth.

THE FIRST DISCUSSION

Concerning the Eternity of the World

Ghazali, speaking of the philosophers' proofs for the eternity of the world, says:
The philosophers say: It is impossible that the temporal should proceed from the absolutely Eternal. For it is clear – if we assume the Eternal existing without, for instance, the world proceeding from Him, then, at a certain moment, the world beginning to proceed from Him – that it did not proceed before, because there was no determining principle for its existence, but its existence was pure possibility. When the world begins in time, a new determinant either does or does not arise.

If it does not, the world will stay in the same state of pure possibility as before; if a new determinant does arise, the same question can be asked about this new determinant, why it determines now, and not before, and either we shall have an infinite regress or we shall arrive at a principle determining eternally.

I say:

This argument is in the highest degree dialectical and does not reach the pitch of demonstrative proof.[1] For its premises are common notions, and common notions approach the equivocal,[2] whereas demonstrative premises are concerned with things proper to the same genus. For the term 'possible' is used in an equivocal way of the possible that happens more often than not, of the possible that happens less often than not, and of the possible with equal chances of happening, and these three types of the possible do not seem to have the same need for a new determining principle. For the possible that happens more often than not is frequently believed to have its determining principle in itself, not outside, as is the case with the possible which has equal chances of happening and not happening. Further, the possible resides sometimes in the agent, i.e. the possibility of acting, and sometimes in the recipient,[3] i.e. the possibility of receiving, and it does not seem that the necessity for a determining principle is the same in both cases. For it is well known that the possible in the recipient needs

1 See glossary entry for 'demonstration.'
2 "Common notions" are very general concepts which apply across several or all the Aristotelian categories. Averroes' point is that they resist being given a single unambiguous definition that holds for all their applications.
3 See glossary entry for 'agent/recipient.'

a new determinant from the outside; this can be perceived by the senses in artificial things and in many natural things too, although in regard to natural things there is a doubt, for in most natural things the principle of their change forms part of them. Therefore, it is believed of many natural things that they move themselves, and it is by no means self-evident that everything that is in motion has a mover and that there is nothing that moves itself. But all this needs to be examined, and the old philosophers have therefore done so. As concerns the possible in the agent, however, in many cases it is believed that it can be actualized without an external principle, for the transition in the agent from inactivity to activity is often regarded as not being a change which requires a principle; e.g. the transition in the geometer from non-geometrizing to geometrizing, or in the teacher from non-teaching to teaching.

Further, those changes which are regarded as needing a principle of change can sometimes be changes in substance, sometimes in quality, or in quantity, or in place. In addition, 'eternal' is predicated by many of the eternal-by-itself and the eternal-through-another. According to some, it is permissible to admit certain changes in the Eternal, for instance a new volition in the Eternal, according to the Karramites,[4] and the possibility of generation and corruption which the ancients attribute to primary matter, although it is eternal. Equally, new concepts are admitted in the possible intellect[5] although, according to most authors, it is eternal. But there are also changes which are inadmissible, especially according to certain ancients, though not according to others.

Then there is the agent who acts of his will and the agent which acts by nature, and the manner of actualization of the possible act is not the same for both agents, i.e. so far as the need for a new determinant is concerned. Further, is this division into two agents complete, or does demonstration lead to an agent which resembles neither the natural agent nor the voluntary agent of human experience?

All these are multifarious and difficult questions which need, each of them, a special examination, both in themselves and in regard to the opinions the ancients held about them. To treat what is in reality a plurality of questions as one problem is one of the well-known seven sophisms, and a mistake in one of these principles becomes a great error by the end of the examination of reality.

Ghazali says:
There are two objections to this. The first objection is to say: Why do you deny the theory of those who say that the world has been created by an eternal will which has decreed its existence in the time in which it exists; that its non-existence lasts until the moment it ceases and that its existence begins from the moment it begins; that its existence was not willed before and therefore did not happen, and that at the exact moment it began it was willed by an eternal will and therefore began? What is the objection to this theory and what is absurd in it?

I say:
This argument is sophistical: although it is not allowable for him to admit the possibility of the actual effect being delayed after the actual cause, and in a voluntary agent, after the decision to act, he regards it as possible that the effect should be delayed after the will of the agent. It is possible that the effect should be delayed after the will of the agent, but its being delayed after the actual cause is impossible, and equally impossible is its being delayed after a voluntary agent's decision to act. The difficulty is thus unchanged; for he must of necessity draw one of these two conclusions: either that the act of the agent does not imply in him a change which itself would need an external principle of change, or that there are changes which arise by themselves, without the necessity of an agent in whom they occur and who causes them, and that therefore there are changes possible in the Eternal without an agent who causes them. And his adversaries insist on these two very points: (1) that the act of the agent necessarily implies a change and that each change has a principle which causes it; (2) that

---

4 A sect named after Muhammed Ibn Karram of Khorasan (9th century). They said that God is a substratum for new accidents, and that nothing comes into existence in the world without being preceded by new accidents in God, e.g., new volitions.

5 See entry in glossary for 'possible/passive intellect.'

the Eternal cannot change in any way. But all this is difficult to prove.

The Ash'arites[6] are forced to assume either a first agent or a first act of this agent, for they cannot admit that the disposition of the agent, relative to the effect, when he acts is the same as his disposition, when he does not act. This implies therefore a new disposition or a new relation, and this necessarily either in the agent, or in the effect, or in both. But in this case, if we posit as a principle that for each new disposition there is an agent, this new disposition in the first agent will either need another agent, and then this first agent was not the first and was not on his own account sufficient for the act but needed another, or the agent of the disposition which is the condition of the agent's act will be identical with the agent of the act. Then this act which we regarded as being the first act arising out of him will not be the first, but his act producing the disposition which is the condition of the effect will be anterior to the act producing the effect. This, you see, is a necessary consequence, unless one allows that new dispositions may arise in the agents without a cause. But this is absurd, unless one believes that there are things which happen haphazardly and by themselves, a theory of the old philosophers who denied the agent, the falsehood of which is self-evident.

In Ghazali's objection there is a confusion. For our expressions 'eternal will' and 'temporal will' are equivocal, indeed contrary. The empirical will is a faculty which possesses the possibility of doing equally one of two contraries and then of receiving equally one of the two contraries willed. For the will is the desire of the agent towards action. When the agent acts, desire ceases and the thing willed happens, and this desire and this act are equally related to both the contraries. But when one says, "There is a Willer who wills eternally one of two contraries in Himself," the definition of the will is abandoned; we have transferred its nature from the possible to the necessary. If it is objected that in an eternal will the will does not cease through the presence of the object willed, (for as an eternal will has no beginning, there is no moment in it which is specially determined for the realization of the object willed),

we answer: This is not obvious, unless we say that demonstrative proof leads to the existence of an agent endowed with a power which is neither voluntary nor natural, which, however, the Divine Law calls 'will,' in the same way as demonstrative proof leads to middle terms between things which seemed at first sight to be contrary, without being really so, as when we speak of an existence which is neither inside nor outside the world.

Ghazali answers, on behalf of the philosophers:
The philosophers say: This is clearly impossible, for everything that happens is necessitated and has its cause, and as it is impossible that there should be an effect without a necessitating principle and a cause, so it is impossible that there should exist a cause of which the effect is delayed, when all the conditions of its necessitating, its causes and elements are completely fulfilled. On the contrary, the existence of the effect, when the cause is realized with all its conditions, is necessary, and its delay is just as impossible as an effect without a cause. Before the existence of the world there existed a Willer, a will, and its relation to the thing willed. No new willer arose, nor a new will, nor a new relation to the will – for all this is change. How then could a new object of will arise, and what prevented its arising before? The condition of the new production did not distinguish itself from the condition of the non-production in any way, in any mode, in any relation. On the contrary, everything remained as it was before. At one moment the object of will did not exist; everything remained as it was before, and then the object of will existed. Is not this a perfectly absurd theory?

I say:
This is perfectly clear, except for one who denies one of the premises we have laid down previously. But Ghazali passes from this proof to an example based upon convention, and through this he confuses this defence of the philosophers.

Ghazali says:
This kind of impossibility is found not only in the necessary and essential cause and effect but also in

---

6 The Ash'arites were followers of Al-Ash'ari (873-935) who claimed that God is the only real cause of anything. Created things appear to have causal power only because of the regularity in the way God chooses to bring things about.

the accidental and conventional. If a man pronounces the formula of divorce against his wife without the divorce becoming irrevocable immediately, one does not imagine that it will become so later. For he made the formula through convention and usage a cause of the judgement, and we do not believe that the effect can be delayed, except when the divorce depends on an ulterior event, e.g. on the arrival of tomorrow or on someone's entering the house, for then the divorce does not take place at once, but only when tomorrow arrives or someone enters the house; in this case the man made the formula a cause only in conjunction with an ulterior event. But as this event, the coming of tomorrow and someone's entering the house, is not yet actual, the effect is delayed until this future event is realized. The effect only takes place when a new event, i.e. entering the house or the arrival of tomorrow, has actually happened. Even if a man wanted to delay the effect after the formula, without making it dependent on an ulterior event, this would be regarded as impossible, although it is he himself who lays down the convention and fixes its modalities. If thus in conventional matters such a delay is incomprehensible and inadmissible, how can we admit it in essential, rational, and necessary causal relations? In respect of our conduct and our voluntary actions, there is a delay in actual volition only when there is some obstacle. When there is actual volition and actual power and the obstacles are eliminated, a delay in the object willed is inadmissible. A delay in the object willed is imaginable only in decision, for decision is not sufficient for the existence of the act; the decision to write does not produce the writing, if it is not, as a new fact, accompanied by an act of volition, i.e. an impulse in the man which presents itself at the moment of the act. If there is thus an analogy between the eternal Will and our will to act, a delay of the object willed is inadmissible, unless through an obstacle, and an antecedent existence of the volition is equally inadmissible, for I cannot will to get up tomorrow except by way of decision. If, however, the eternal Will is analogous to our decision, it does not suffice to produce the thing decided upon, but the act of creation must be accompanied by a new act of volition, and this brings us again to the idea of a change. But then we have the same difficulty all over again. Why does this impulse or volition or will or whatever you choose to call it happen just now and not before? There remain, then, only these alternatives: either something happening without a cause, or an infinite regress. This is the upshot of the discussion: There is a cause the conditions of which are all completely fulfilled, but notwithstanding this the effect is delayed and is not realized during a period to the beginning of which imagination cannot attain and for which thousands of years would mean no diminution; then suddenly, without the addition of any new fact, and without the realization of any new condition, this effect comes into existence and is produced. And this is absurd.

I say:
This example of divorce based on convention seems to strengthen the argument of the philosophers, but in reality it weakens it. For it enables the Ash'arites to say: In the same way as the actual divorce is delayed after the formula of divorce till the moment when the condition of someone's entering the house, or any other, is fulfilled, so the realization of the world can be delayed after God's act of creation until the condition is fulfilled on which this realization depends, i.e. the moment when God willed it. But conventional things do not behave like rational. The Literalists, comparing these conventional things to rational, say: This divorce is not binding and does not become effective through the realization of the condition which is posterior to the pronouncement of the divorce by the divorcer, since it would be a divorce which became effective without connexion with the act of the divorcer. But in this matter there is no relation between the concept drawn from the nature of things and that which is artificial and conventional.

Then Ghazali says, on behalf of the Ash'arites:
The answer is: Do you recognize the impossibility of connecting the eternal Will with the temporal production of anything, through the necessity of intuitive thought or through a logical deduction, or, to use your own logical terminology, do you recognize the clash between these two concepts through a middle term[7] or without a middle term?

---

7 See glossary entry for 'middle term.'

If you claim a middle term – and this is the deductive method – you will have to produce it, and if you assert that you know this through the necessity of thought, why do your adversaries not share this intuition with you? For the party which believes in the creation of the world in time through an eternal Will includes so many persons that no country can contain them and no number enumerate them, and they certainly do not contradict the logically minded out of obstinacy, while knowing better in their hearts. A proof according to the rules of logic must be produced to show this impossibility, as in all your arguments up till now there is only a presumption of impossibility and a comparison with our decision and our will; and this is false, for the eternal Will does not resemble temporal volitions, and a pure presumption of impossibility will not suffice without proof.

I say:

This argument is one of those which have only a very feeble persuasive power. It amounts to saying that one who claims the impossibility of delay in an effect, when its cause with all its conditions is realized, must assert that he knows this either by a syllogism or from first principles; if through a syllogism, he must produce it – but there is none; if from first principles, it must be known to all, adversaries and others alike. But this argument is mistaken, for it is not a condition of objective truth that it should be known to all. That anything should be held by all does not imply anything more than its being a common notion, just as the existence of a common notion does not imply objective truth.

Ghazali answers on behalf of the Ash'arites:

If it is said, "We know by the necessity of thought that, when all its conditions are fulfilled, a cause without effect is inadmissible and that to admit it is an affront to the necessity of thought," we answer: "What is the difference between you and your adversaries, when they say to you, 'We know by the necessity of thought the impossibility of a theory which affirms that one single being knows all the universals, without this knowledge forming a plurality in its essence or adding anything to it, and without this plurality of things known implying a plurality in the knowledge'?" For this is your theory of God, which according to us and our science is quite absurd. You, however, say there is no analogy

between eternal and temporal knowledge. Some of you acknowledge the impossibility involved, and say that God knows only Himself and that He is the knower, the knowledge and the known, and that the three are one. One might object: The unity of the knowledge, the knower, and the known is clearly an impossibility, for to suppose the Creator of the world ignorant of His own work is necessarily absurd, and the Eternal – who is far too high to be reached by your words and the words of any heretics – could, if He knows only Himself, never know His work.

I say:

This amounts to saying that the theologians do not gratuitously and without proof deny the admitted impossibility of a delay between the effect and its cause, but base themselves on an argument which leads them to believe in the temporal creation of the world, and that they therefore act in the same way as the philosophers, who only deny the well-known necessary plurality of knowledge and known, so far as it concerns their unity in God, because of a demonstration which, according to them, leads them to their theory about Him. And that this is still more true of those philosophers who deny it to be necessary that God should know His own work, affirming that He knows only Himself. This assertion belongs to the class of assertions whose contrary is equally false. For there exists no proof which refutes anything that is evidently true, and universally acknowledged. Anything that can be refuted by a demonstrative proof is only supposed to be true, not really true. Therefore, if it is absolutely and evidently true that knowledge and known form a plurality, both in the visible and in the invisible world, we can be sure that the philosophers cannot have a proof of this unity in God; but if the theory of the plurality of knowledge and known is only a supposition, then it is possible for the philosophers to have a proof. Equally, if it is absolutely true that the effect of a cause cannot be delayed after the causation and the Ash'arites claim that they can advance a proof to deny it, then we can be absolutely sure that they cannot have such a proof. If there is a controversy about questions like this, the final criterion rests with sound understanding which does not base itself on prejudice and passion, when it probes according to the signs and rules by which truth and mere opinion are logically distinguished. Likewise, if two people dispute about a sentence and one says that it is poetry, the other that it is prose, the final judgement rests with the sound understanding which can distinguish poetry from prose, and with the science of prosody. And as, in the case of metre, the denial of him who denies it does not interfere with its perception by him who perceives it, so the denial of a truth by a contradictory does not trouble the conviction of the men to whom it is evident. This whole argument is extremely inept and weak, and Ghazali ought not to have filled his book with such talk if he intended to convince the learned.

Drawing consequences which are irrelevant and beside the point, Ghazali goes on to say:
But the consequences of this argument cannot be overcome. And we say to them: How will you refute your adversaries, when they say the eternity of the world is impossible; for it implies an infinite number and an infinity of unities for the spherical revolutions, although they can be divided by six, by four, and by two. For the sphere of the sun revolves in one year, the sphere of Saturn in thirty years, and so Saturn's revolution is a thirtieth and Jupiter's revolution – for Jupiter revolves in twelve years – a twelfth of the sun's revolution. But the number of revolutions of Saturn has the same infinity as the revolutions of the sun, although they are in a proportion of one to thirty and even the infinity of the sphere of the fixed stars which turns round once in thirty-six thousand years is the same as the daily revolution which the sun performs in twenty-four hours. If your adversary says that this is plainly impossible, in what does your argument differ from his? And suppose it is asked: Are the numbers of these revolutions even or uneven or both even and uneven or neither even nor uneven? If you answer, both even and uneven, or neither even nor uneven, you say what is evidently absurd. If, however, you say 'even' or 'uneven,' even and uneven become uneven and even by the addition of one unit and how could infinity be one unit short? You must, therefore, draw the conclusion that they are neither even nor uneven.

I say:
This too is a sophistical argument. It amounts to saying: In the same way as you are unable to refute our argument for the creation of the world in time,

that if it were eternal, its revolutions would be neither even nor uneven, so we cannot refute your theory that the effect of an agent whose conditions to act are always fulfilled cannot be delayed. This argument aims only at creating and establishing a doubt, which is one of the sophist's objectives.

But you, reader of this book, have already heard the arguments of the philosophers to establish the eternity of the world and the refutation of the Ash'arites. Now hear the proofs of the Ash'arites for their refutation and hear the arguments of the philosophers to refute those proofs in the wording of Ghazali!

If you imagine two circular movements in one and the same finite time and imagine then a limited part of these movements in one and the same finite time, the proportion between the parts of these two circular movements and between their wholes will be the same. For instance, if the circular movement of Saturn in the period which we call a year is a thirtieth of the circular movement of the sun in this period, and you imagine the whole of the circular movements of the sun in proportion to the whole of the circular movements of Saturn in one and the same period, necessarily the proportion between their wholes and between their parts will be the same. If, however, there is no proportion between two movements in their totality, because they are both potential, i.e. they have neither beginning nor end but there exists a proportion between the parts, because they are both actual, then the proportion between the wholes is not necessarily the same as the proportion between the parts – although many think so, basing their proof on this prejudice. For there is no proportion between two magnitudes or quantities which are both taken to be infinite. When, therefore, the ancients believed that, for instance, the totality of the movements of the sun and of Saturn had neither beginning nor end, there could be no proportion between them, for this would have implied the finitude of both these totalities, just as this is implied for the parts of both. This is self-evident. Our adversaries believe that, when a proportion of more and less exists between parts, this proportion holds good also for the totalities, but this is only binding when the totalities are finite. For where there is no end there is neither 'more' nor 'less.' The admission in such a case of the proportion of more and less brings with it another absurd consequence, namely that one infinite could be greater than another. This is only absurd when one supposes two things actually infinite, for then a proportion does exist between them. When, however, one imagines things potentially infinite, there exists no proportion at all. This is the right answer to this question, not what Ghazali says in the name of the philosophers.

And through this are solved all the difficulties which beset our adversaries on this question, of which the greatest is that which is habitually formulated in this way: If the movements in the past are infinite, then no movement in the actual present can take place unless an infinite number of preceding movements is terminated. This is true, and acknowledged by the philosophers, once granted that the anterior movement is the condition for the posterior movement's taking place, i.e. once granted that the existence of one single movement implies an infinite number of causes. But no philosopher allows the existence of an infinite number of causes, as accepted by the materialists, for this would imply the existence of an effect without cause and a motion without mover. But when the existence of an eternal prime mover had been proved, whose act cannot be posterior to his being, it followed that there could as little be a beginning for his act as for his being; otherwise his act would be possible, not necessary, and he would not be a first principle. The acts of an agent who has no beginning have a beginning as little as his existence, and therefore it follows necessarily that no preceding act of his is the condition for the existence of a later, for neither of them is an agent by itself and their sequence is accidental. An accidental infinite, not an essential infinite, is admitted by the philosophers; nay, this type of infinite is in fact a necessary consequence of the existence of an eternal first principle. And this is not only true for successive or continuous movements and the like, but even where the earlier is regarded as the cause of the later, for instance the human who engenders a human like himself. For it is necessary that the series of temporal productions of one individual human by another should lead upwards to an eternal agent, for whom there is no beginning either of his existence or of his production of human out of human. The production of one human by another *ad infinitum is* accidental, whereas the relation of before and after in it is essential. The agent who has no beginning either for his existence or for those acts of his

which he performs without an instrument, has no first instrument either to perform those acts of his without beginning which by their nature need an instrument. But since the theologians mistook the accidental for the essential, they denied this eternal agent; the solution of their problem was difficult and they believed this proof to be stringent. This theory of the philosophers is clear, and their first master Aristotle has explained that, if motion were produced by motion, or element by element, motion and element could not exist. For this type of infinite the philosophers admit neither a beginning nor an end, and therefore one can never say of anything in this series that it has ended or has begun, not even in the past, for everything that has an end must have begun and what does not begin does not end. This can also be understood from the fact that beginning and end are correlatives. Therefore, one who affirms that there is no end of the celestial revolutions in the future cannot logically ascribe a beginning to them; for what has a beginning has an end and what has no end has no beginning, and the same relation exists between first and last; i.e., what has a first term has also a last term, and what has no first term has no last term, and there is in reality neither end nor beginning for any part of a series that has no last term, and what has no beginning for any of its parts has no end for any of them either. When, therefore, the theologians ask the philosophers if the movements which precede the present one are ended, their answer is negative, for their assumption that they have no beginning implies their endlessness. The opinion of the theologians that the philosophers admit their end is erroneous; for they do not admit an end for what has no beginning. It will be clear to you that neither the arguments of the theologians for the temporal creation of the world of which Ghazali speaks, nor the arguments of the philosophers which he includes and describes in his book, suffice to reach absolute evidence or afford stringent proof. And this is what we have tried to show in this book. The best answer one can give to him who asks where in the past is the starting-point of His acts, is: The starting-point of His acts is at the starting-point of His existence; for neither of them has a beginning.

And here is the passage of Ghazali in which he sets forth the defence of the philosophers against the argument built on the difference in speed of the celestial spheres, and his refutation of their argument.

Ghazali says:

If one says, "The error in your argument consists in your considering those circular movements as an aggregate of units, but those movements have no real existence; for the past is no more and the future not yet. "Aggregate" means units existing in the present, but in this case there is no existence."

Then he says to refute this:

We answer: Number can be divided into even and uneven; there is no third possibility, whether for the numbered permanent reality, or for the numbered passing event. Therefore, whatever number we imagine, we must believe it to be even or uneven, whether we regard it as existent or nonexistent. If the thing numbered vanishes from existence, our judgement of its being even or uneven does not vanish or change.

This is the end of his argument. But this argument – that the numbered thing must be judged as even or uneven, whether it exists or not – is only valid so far as it concerns external things or things in the soul that have a beginning and an end. For of the number which exists only potentially, i.e. which has neither beginning nor end, it cannot truly be said that it is even or uneven, or that it begins or ends; it happens neither in the past nor in the future, for what exists potentially falls under the law of non-existence. This is what the philosophers meant when they said that the circular movements of the past and the future are non-existent. The upshot of this question is: Everything that is called a limited aggregate with a beginning and an end is so called either because it has a beginning and end in the world exterior to the soul, or because it is inside, not outside, the soul. Every totality, actual and limited in the past, whether inside or outside the soul, is necessarily either even or uneven. But an unlimited aggregate existing outside the soul cannot be other than limited so far as it is represented in the soul; for the soul cannot represent unlimited existence. Therefore, also this unlimited aggregate, as being limited in the soul, can be called even or uneven; in so far, however, as it exists outside the soul, it can be called neither even nor uneven. Equally, past aggregates which are considered to exist potentially outside the soul, i.e. which have no beginning, cannot be called even or uneven unless they are looked upon as actual, i.e. as having

beginning and end. No motion possesses totality or forms an aggregate, i.e. is provided with a beginning or an end, except in so far as it is in the soul, as is the case with time. And it follows from the nature of circular movement that it is neither even nor uneven except as represented in the soul. The cause of this mistake is that it was believed that, when something possesses a certain quality in the soul, it must possess this quality also outside the soul, and, since anything that has happened in the past can only be represented in the soul as finite, it was thought that everything that has happened in the past must also be finite outside the soul. And as the circular movements of the future are regarded by the imagination as infinite; for it represents them as a sequence of part after part. Plato and the Ash'arites believed that they might be infinite, but this is simply a judgement based on imagination, not on proof. Therefore, those who believe – as many theologians have done – that, if the world is supposed to have begun, it must have an end, are truer to their principles and show more consistency.

Ghazali says after this:

And we say moreover to the philosophers: According to your principles it is not absurd that there should be actual units, qualitatively differentiated, which are infinite in number; I am thinking of human souls, separated through death from their bodies. These are therefore realities that can neither be called even nor uneven. How will you refute the person who affirms that this is necessarily absurd in the same way as you claim the connection between an eternal will and a temporal creation to be necessarily absurd? This theory about souls is that which Avicenna accepted, and it is perhaps Aristotle's.

I say:

This argument is extremely weak. It says, in brief, "You philosophers need not refute our assertion that what is a logical necessity for you is not necessary, as you consider things possible which your adversaries consider impossible by the necessity of thought. That is to say, just as you consider things possible which your adversaries consider impossible, so you consider things necessary which your adversaries do not consider so. And you cannot bring a criterion for judging the two claims." It has already been shown in the science of logic that this is a weak rhetorical or sophistical kind of argument. The answer is that what we claim to be necessarily true is objectively true, whereas what you claim as necessarily absurd is not as you claim it to be. For this there is no other criterion than immediate intuitive apprehension, just as, when one person claims that a line is rhythmical and another denies it, the criterion is the intuition of sound understanding.

As for the thesis of a numerical plurality of immaterial souls, this is not a theory acknowledged by the philosophers; for they regard matter as the cause of numerical plurality and form as the cause of congruity in numerical plurality. And that there should be a numerical plurality without matter, having one unique form, is impossible. For in its description one individual can only be distinguished from another accidentally, as there is often another individual who participates in this description, but only through their matter do individuals differ in reality. And also this: The impossibility of an actual infinite is an acknowledged axiom in philosophical theory, equally valid for material and immaterial things. We do not know of any one who makes a distinction here between the spatial and the non-spatial, with the single exception of Avicenna. I do not know of any other philosopher who affirms this; it does not correspond with any of their principles, and it makes no sense. For the philosophers deny the existence of an actual infinite equally for material and for immaterial things, as it would imply that one infinite could be greater than another. Perhaps Avicenna wanted only to satisfy the masses, telling them what they were accustomed to hear about the soul. But this theory is far from satisfactory. For if there were an actual infinite, and if it were divided in two, the part would equal the whole; e.g. if there were a line or a number actually infinite in both directions, and if it were divided in two, both the parts and the whole would be actually infinite; and this is absurd. All this is simply the consequence of the admission of

an actual and not potential infinite.

Ghazali says:
If it is said, "The truth lies with Plato's theory of one eternal soul which is only divided in bodies and returns after its separation from them to its original unity," we answer: This theory is still worse, more objectionable and more apt to be regarded as contrary to the necessity of thought. For we say that the soul of Zaid is either identical with the soul of Amr or different from it; but their identity would mean something absurd, for everyone is conscious of his own identity and knows that he is not another, and, were they identical, their knowledge, which is an essential quality of their souls and enters into all the relations into which their souls enter, would be identical too. If you say their soul is unique and only divided through its association with bodies, we answer that the division of a unity which has no measurable volume is absurd by the necessity of thought. And how could the one become two, and indeed a thousand, and then return to its unity? This can be understood of things which have volume and quantity, like the water of the sea which is distributed into brooks and rivers and flows then back again into the sea, but how can that which has no quantity be divided? We seek to show by all this that the philosophers cannot shake the conviction of their adversaries that the eternal Will is connected with temporal creation, except by claiming its absurdity by the necessity of thought, and that therefore they are in no way different from the theologians who make the same claim against the philosophical doctrines opposed to theirs. And out of this there is no issue.

I say:
Zaid and Amr[8] are numerically different, but identical in form.[9] If, for example, the soul of Zaid were numerically different from the soul of Amr in the way Zaid is numerically different from Amr, the soul of Zaid and the soul of Amr would be numerically two, but one in their form, and the soul

---

8 These names do not refer to any particular real persons but are used to designate any two people whatsoever.
9 Identical in form because they are of the same species. Averroes' idea is that the soul of a person is just the form which makes them be of a certain most specific species, viz. human being. This form is the same for all members of that species. There would not be different human souls except for the fact that this form gets numerically diversified by being in different batches of matter.

would possess another soul. The necessary conclusion is therefore that the soul of Zaid and the soul of Amr are identical in their form. An identical form inheres in a numerical, i.e. a divisible, multiplicity, only through the multiplicity of matter. If then the soul does not die when the body dies, or if it possesses an immortal element, it must, when it has left the bodies, form a numerical unity. But this is not the place to go deeper into this subject.

His argument against Plato is sophistical. It says in short that the soul of Zaid is either identical with the soul of Amr or different from it; but that the soul of Zaid is not identical with the soul of Amr and that therefore it is different from it. But 'different' is an equivocal term, and 'identity' too is predicated of a number of things which are also called 'different.' The souls of Zaid and Amr are one in one sense and many in another; we might say, one in relation to their form, many in relation to their substratum. His remark that division can only be imagined of the quantitative is partially false; it is true of essential division, but not of accidental division, i.e. of those things which can be divided, because they exist in the essentially divisible. The essentially divisible is, for example, body; accidental division is, for instance, the division of whiteness, when the bodies in which it is present are divided, and in this way the forms and the soul are accidentally divisible, i.e. through the division of the substrate. The soul is closely similar to light: light is divided by the division of illuminated bodies, and is unified when the bodies are annihilated, and this same relation holds between soul and bodies. To advance such sophistical arguments is dishonest; for it may be supposed that he is not a man to have overlooked the points mentioned. What he said, he said only to flatter the masses of his times, but how far removed is such an attitude from the character of those who seek to set forth the truth! But perhaps the man may be forgiven on account of the time and place in which he lived; and indeed he only proceeded in his books in a tentative way.

Since these arguments carry no evidence whatsoever, Ghazali says:

We want to show by all this that the philosophers cannot shake the conviction of their adversaries that the eternal Will is connected with temporal creation, by claiming its absurdity by the necessity of thought, and that therefore they do not distinguish themselves from the theologians, who make the same claim against the philosophical doctrines opposed to theirs. And out of this there is no issue.

I say:

When someone denies a truth of which it is absolutely certain that it is such-and-such, there exists no argument by which we can come to an understanding with him; for every argument is based on known premises about which both adversaries agree. When each point advanced is denied by the adversary, discussion with him becomes impossible, but such people stand outside the pale of humanity and have to be educated. But for him who denies an evident truth, because of a difficulty which presents itself to him there is a remedy, truth, because he is lacking in intelligence, cannot be taught anything, nor can he be educated. It is like trying to make the blind imagine colors or know their existence.

Ghazali says:

The philosophers may object: This argument (that the present has been preceded by an infinite past) can be turned against you. For God before the creation of the world was able to create it, say, one year or two years before He did, and there is no limit to His power; but He seemed to have patience and did not create. Then He created. Now, the duration of His inactivity is either finite or infinite. If you say finite, the existence of the Creator becomes finite; if you say infinite, a duration in which there is an infinite number of possibilities receives its termination. We answer: Duration and time are, according to us, created, but we shall explain the real answer to this question when we reply to the second proof of the philosophers.

I say:

Most people who accept a temporal creation of the world believe time to have been created with it. Therefore his assertion that the duration of His inactivity was either limited or unlimited is untrue. For what has no beginning does not finish or end. And the opponent does not admit that the inactivity has any duration at all. What one has to ask them about the consequences of their theory is: Is it possible, when the creation of time is admitted, that the term of its beginning may lie beyond the real time in which we live? If they answer that it is not possible, they posit a limited extension beyond which the Creator cannot pass, and this is, in their view, shocking and absurd. If, however, they concede that its possible beginning may lie beyond the moment of its created term, it may further be asked if there may not lie another term beyond this second. If they answer in the affirmative – and they cannot do otherwise – it will be said: Then we shall have here a possible creation of an infinite number of durations, and you will be forced to admit – according to your argument about the spherical revolutions – that their termination is a condition for the real age which exists since them. If you say what is infinite does not finish, the arguments you use about the spherical revolutions against your opponents your opponents will use against you on the subject of the possibility of created durations. If it is objected that the difference between those two cases is that these infinite possibilities belong to extensions which do not become actual, whereas the spherical revolutions do become actual, the answer is that the possibilities of things belong to their necessary accidents and that it does not make any difference, according to the philosophers, if they precede these things or are simultaneous with them, for of necessity they are the dispositions of things. If, then, it is impossible that before the existence of the present spherical revolution there should have been infinite spherical revolutions, the existence of infinite possible revolutions is equally impossible. If one wants to avoid these consequences, one can say that the age of the world is a definite quantity and cannot be longer or shorter than it is, in conformity with the philosophical doctrine about the size of the world. Therefore, these arguments are not stringent, and the safest way for him who accepts the temporal creation of the world is to regard time as of a definite extension and not to admit a possibility which precedes the possible; and to regard also the spatial extension of the world as finite. Only, spatial extension forms a simultaneous whole; not so time.

Ghazali expounds a certain kind of argument attributed to the philosophers on this subject against the theologians when they denied that the impossibility of delay in the Creator's act after His existence is known by primitive intuition.

[*Ghazali says:*]

How will you defend yourselves, theologians, against the philosophers, when they drop this argument, based on the necessity of thought, and prove the eternity of the world in this way, saying that times are equivalent so far as the possibility that the Divine Will should attach itself to them is concerned; for what differentiates a given time from an earlier or a later time? And it is not absurd to believe that the earlier or the later might be chosen when on the contrary you theologians say about white, black, movement, and rest that the white is realized through the eternal Will although its substrate accepts equally black and white. Why, then, does the eternal Will attach itself to the white rather than to the black, and what differentiates one of the two possibles from the other for connexion with the eternal Will? But we philosophers know by the necessity of thought that one thing does not distinguish itself from a similar except by a differentiating principle, for if not, it would be possible that the world should come into existence, having the possibility both of existing and of not existing, and that the side of existence, although it has the same possibility as the side of non-existence, should be differentiated without a differentiating principle. If you answer that the Will of God is the differentiating principle, then one has to inquire what differentiates the Will, i.e. the reason why it has been differentiated in such or such way. And if you answer: One does not inquire after the motives of the Eternal, well, let the world then be eternal, and let us not inquire after its Creator and its cause, since one does not inquire after the motives of the Eternal! If it is regarded as possible that the Eternal should differentiate one of the two possibles by chance, it will be an extreme absurdity to say that the world is differentiated in differentiated forms which might just as well be otherwise, and one might then say that this has happened by chance in the same way as you say that the Divine Will has differentiated one time rather than another or one form rather than another by chance. If you say that such a question is irrelevant, because it refers to anything God can will or decide, we answer that this question is quite relevant, for it concerns any time and is pertinent for our opponents to any decision God takes.

We answer: The world exists, in the way it exists, in its time, with its qualities, and in its space, by the

Divine Will and will is a quality which has the faculty of differentiating one thing from another, and if it had not this faculty, power in itself would suffice. But, since power is equally related to two contraries and a differentiating principle is needed to differentiate one thing from a similar, it is said that the Eternal possesses besides His power a quality which can differentiate between two similars. And to ask why will differentiates one of two similars is like asking why knowledge must comprehend the knowable, and the answer is that 'knowledge' is the term for a quality which has just this nature. And in the same way, 'will' is the term for a quality the nature or rather the essence of which is to differentiate one thing from another.

The philosophers may object: The assumption of a quality the nature of which is to differentiate one thing from a similar one is something incomprehensible, nay even contradictory, for 'similar' means not to be differentiated, and 'differentiated' means not similar. And it must not be believed that two blacks in two substrates are similar in every way, since the one is in one place and the other in another, and this causes a distinction; nor are two blacks at two times in one substrate absolutely similar, since they are separated in time, and how could they therefore be similar in every way? When we say of two blacks that they are similar, we mean that they are similar in blackness, in their special relation to it, not absolutely. Certainly, if the substrate and the time were one without any distinction, one could not speak any more of two blacks or of any duality at all. This proves that the term 'Divine Will' is derived from our will, and one does not imagine that through our will two similar things can be differentiated. On the contrary, if someone who is thirsty has before him two cups of water, similar in everything in respect to his aim, it will not be possible for him to take either of them. No, he can only take the one he thinks more beautiful or lighter or nearer to his right hand, if he is right-handed, or act from some such reason, hidden or known. Without this the differentiation of the one from the other cannot be imagined.

I say:
The summary of what Ghazali relates in this section of the proofs of the philosophers for the impossibility of a temporal proceeding from an eternal agent is that in God there cannot be a will.

The philosophers could only arrive at this argument after granting to their opponents that all opposites – opposites in time, like anterior and posterior, as well as those in quality, like white and black – are equivalent in relation to the eternal Will. And also non-existence and existence are, according to the theologians, equivalent in relation to the Divine Will. And having granted their opponents this premise, although they did not acknowledge its truth, they said to them: It is of the nature of will that it cannot give preponderance to one thing rather than to a similar one, except through a differentiating principle and a cause which only exist in one of these two similar things; if not, one of the two would happen by chance – and the philosophers argued for the sake of discussion, as if they had conceded that, if the Eternal had a will, a temporal could proceed from an eternal. As the theologians were unable to give a satisfactory answer, they took refuge in the theory that the eternal Will is a quality the nature of which is to differentiate between two similar things, without there being for God a differentiating principle which inclines Him to one of two similar acts; that the eternal Will is thus a quality like warmth which gives heat or like knowledge which comprehends the knowable. But their opponents, the philosophers, answered: It is impossible that this should happen, for two similar things are equivalent for the willer, and his action can only attach itself to the one rather than to the other through their being dissimilar, i.e. through one's having a quality the other has not. When, however, they are similar in every way and when for God there is no differentiating principle at all, His will will attach itself to both of them indifferently and, when this is the case – His will being the cause of His act – the act will not attach itself to the one rather than to the other, it will attach itself either to the two contrary actions simultaneously or to neither of them at all, and both cases are absurd. The philosophers, therefore, began their argument, as if they had it granted to them that all things were equivalent in relation to the First Agent, and they forced them to admit that there must be for God a differentiating principle which precedes Him, which is absurd. When the theologians answered that will is a quality the nature of which is to differentiate the similar from the similar, in so far as it is similar, the philosophers objected that this is not understood or meant by the idea of will. They therefore appear to reject the principle which they granted them in the beginning. This is in short the content of this section. It waves the argument from the original question to the problem of the will; to shift one's ground, however, is an act of sophistry.

Ghazali answers in defence of the theological doctrine of the Divine Will:
There are two objections: First, as to your affirmation that you cannot imagine this, do you know it by the necessity of thought or through deduction? You can claim neither the one nor the other. Your comparison with our will is a bad analogy, which resembles that employed on the question of God's knowledge. Now God's knowledge is different from ours in several ways which we acknowledge. Therefore it is not absurd to admit a difference in the will. Your affirmation is like saying that an essence existing neither outside nor inside the world, neither continuous with the world nor separated from it, cannot be understood, because we cannot understand this according to our human measure; the right answer is that it is the fault of your imagination, for rational proof has led the learned to accept its truth. How, then, will you refute those who say that rational proof has led to establishing in God a quality the nature of which is to differentiate between two similar things? And, if the word 'will' does not apply, call it by another name, for let us not quibble about words! We only use the term 'will' by permission of the Divine Law. It may be objected that by its conventional meaning 'will' designates that which has desire, and God has no desire, but we are concerned here with a question not of words but of fact. Besides, we do not even with respect to our human will concede that this cannot be imagined. Suppose two similar dates in front of a man who has a strong desire for them, but who is unable to take them both. Surely he will take one of them through a quality in him the nature of which is to differentiate between two similar things. All the distinguishing qualities you have mentioned, like beauty or nearness or facility in taking, we can assume to be absent, but still the possibility of the taking remains. You can choose between two answers: either you merely say that an equivalence in respect to his desire cannot be imagined – but this is a silly answer, for to assume it is indeed possible – or you say that if an equivalence

is assumed, the man will remain for ever hungry and perplexed, looking at the dates without taking one of them, and without a power to choose or to will, distinct from his desire. And this again is one of those absurdities which are recognized by the necessity of thought. Everyone, therefore, who studies, in the human and the divine, the real working of the act of choice, must necessarily admit a quality the nature of which is to differentiate between two similar things.

I say:
This objection can be summarized in two parts: In the first Ghazali concedes that the human will is such that it is unable to differentiate one thing from a similar one, in so far as it is similar, but that a rational proof forces us to accept the existence of such a quality in the First Agent. To believe that such a quality cannot exist would be like believing that there cannot exist a being who is neither inside nor outside the world. According to this reasoning, will, which is attributed to the First Agent and to human beings, is predicated in an equivocal way, like knowledge and other qualities which exist in the Eternal in a different way from that in which they exist in the temporal, and it is only through the prescription of the Divine Law that we speak of the Divine Will. It is clear that this objection cannot have anything more than a dialectical value. For a proof that could demonstrate the existence of such a quality, i.e. a principle determining the existence of one thing rather than that of a similar, would have to assume things willed that are similar; things willed are, however, not similar, but on the contrary opposite, for all opposites can be reduced to the opposition of being and not being, which is the extreme form of opposition; and opposition is the contrary of similarity. The assumption of the theologians that the things to which the will attaches itself are similar is a false one, and we shall speak of it later. If they say: We affirm only that they are similar in relation to the First Willer, who in His holiness is too exalted to possess desires, and it is through desires that two similar things are actually differentiated, we answer: as to the desires whose realization contributes to the perfection of the essence of the willer, as happens with our desires, through which our will attaches itself to the things willed – those desires are impossible in God; for the will which acts in this way is a longing for perfec-

tion when there is an imperfection in the essence of the willer; but as to the desires which belong to the essence of the things willed, nothing new comes to the willer from their realization. It comes exclusively to the thing willed, for instance, when a thing passes into existence from non-existence, for it cannot be doubted that existence is better for it than non-existence. It is in this second way that the Primal Will is related to the existing things, for it chooses for them eternally the better of two opposites, and this essentially and primally. This is the first part of the objection contained in this argument.

In the second part he no longer concedes that this quality cannot exist in the human will, but tries to prove that there is also in us, in the face of similar things, a will which distinguishes one from the other; of this he gives examples. For instance, it is assumed that in front of a man there are two dates, similar in every way, and it is supposed that he cannot take them both at the same time. It is supposed that no special attraction need be imagined for him in either of them, and that nevertheless he will of necessity distinguish one of them by taking it. But this is an error. For, when one supposes such a thing, and a willer whom necessity prompts to eat or to take the date, then it is by no means a matter of distinguishing between two similar things when, in this condition, he takes one of the two dates. It is nothing but the admission of an equivalence of two similar things; for whichever of the two dates he may take, his aim will be attained and his desire satisfied. His will attaches itself therefore merely to the distinction between the fact of taking one of them and the fact of leaving them altogether; it attaches itself by no means to the act of taking one definite date and distinguishing this act from the act of leaving the other (that is to say, when it is assumed that the desires for the two are equal); he does not prefer the act of taking the one to the act of taking the other, but he prefers the act of taking one of the two, whichever it may be, and he gives a preference to the act of taking over the act of leaving. This is self-evident. For distinguishing one from the other means giving a preference to the one over the other, and one cannot give a preponderance to one of two similar things in so far as it is similar to the other – although in their existence as individuals they are not similar since each of two individuals is different from the other by reason of

a quality exclusive to it. If, therefore, we assume that the will attaches itself to that special character of one of them, then it can be imagined that the will attaches to the one rather than the other because of the element of difference existing in both. But then the will does not attach itself to two similar objects, in so far as they are similar. This is, in short, the meaning of Ghazali's first objection. Then he gives his second objection against those who deny the existence of a quality, distinguishing two similar objects from one another.

Ghazali says:
The second objection is that we say: You in your system also are unable to do without a principle differentiating between two equals, for the world exists in virtue of a cause which has produced it in its peculiar shape out of a number of possible distinct shapes which are equivalent; why, then, has this cause differentiated some of them? If to distinguish two similar things is impossible, it is irrelevant whether this concerns the act of God, natural causality, or the logical necessity of ideas. Perhaps you will say: the universal order of the world could not be different from what it is; if the world were smaller or bigger than it actually is, this order would not be perfect, and the same may be asserted of the number of spheres and of stars. And perhaps you will say: The big differs from the small and the many from the few, in so far as they are the object of the will, and therefore they are not similar but different; but human power is too feeble to perceive the modes of Divine Wisdom in its determination of the measures and qualities of things; only in some of them can His wisdom be perceived, as in the obliquity of the ecliptic in relation to the equator, and in the wise contrivance of the apogee and the eccentric sphere. In most cases, however, the secret is not revealed, but the differences are known, and it is not impossible that a thing should be distinguished from another, because the order of the world depends on it; but certainly the times are absolutely indifferent in relation to the world's possibility and its order, and it cannot be claimed that, if the world were created one moment later or earlier, this order could not be imagined; and this indifference is known by the necessity of thought.

We answer: Although we can employ the same reasoning against your argument in the matter of different times, for it might be said that God creat-

ed the world at the time most propitious for its creation, we shall not limit ourselves to this refutation,
but shall assume, according to your own principle,
a differentiation in two points about which there
can be no disagreement: (1) the difference in the
direction of spherical movement; (2) the definite
place of the poles in relation to the ecliptic in
spherical movement. The proof of the statement
relating to the poles is that heaven is a globe, moving on two poles, as on two immovable points,
whereas the globe of heaven is homogeneous and
simple, especially the highest sphere, the ninth,
which possesses no stars at all, and these two
spheres move on two poles, the north and the
south. We now say: Of all the opposite points,
which are infinite, according to you philosophers,
there is no pair one could not imagine as poles.
Why then have the two points of the north and
south pole been fixed upon as poles and as immovable; and why does the ecliptic not pass through
these two poles, so that the poles would become the
opposite points of the ecliptic? And if wisdom is
shown in the size and shape of heaven, what then
distinguishes the place of the poles from others, so
that they are fixed upon to serve as poles, to the
exclusion of all the other parts and points? And yet
all the points are similar, and all parts of the globe
are equivalent. And to this there is no answer.

One might say: Perhaps the spot in which the
point of the poles is, is distinguished from other
points by a special quality, in relation to its being
the place of the poles and to its being at rest, for it
does not seem to change its place or space or position or whatever one wishes to call it; and all the
other spots of the sphere by turning change their
position in relation to the earth and the other
spheres and only the poles are at rest; perhaps this
spot was more apt to be at rest than the others.

We answer: If you say so, you explain the fact
through a natural differentiation of the parts of the
first sphere; the sphere, then, ceases to be homogeneous, and this is in contradiction with your principle, for one of the proofs by which you prove the
necessity of the globular shape of heaven, is that its
nature is simple, homogeneous, and without differentiation, and the simplest shape is the globe; for
the quadrangle and the hexagon and other figures
demand a salience and a differentiation of the
angles, and this happens only when its simple
nature is added to. But although this supposition of

yours is in contradiction with your own theory, it
does not break the strength of your opponents'
argument; the question about this special quality
still holds good, namely, can those other parts
accept this quality or not? If the answer is in the
affirmative, why then is this quality limited to a few
only of those homogeneous parts? If the answer is
negative, we reply: The other parts, in so far as they
constitute bodies, receiving the form of bodies, are
homogeneous of necessity, and there is no justification for attributing this special quality to this spot
exclusively on account of its being a part of a body
and a part of heaven, for the other parts of heaven
participate in this qualification. Therefore its differentiation must rest on a decision by God, or on
a quality whose nature consists in differentiating
between two similars. Therefore, just as among
philosophers the theory is upheld that all times are
equivalent in regard to the creation of the world,
their opponents are justified in claiming that the
parts of heaven are equivalent for the reception of
the quality through which stability in position
becomes more appropriate than a change of position. And out of this there is no issue.

I say:
This means in brief that the philosophers must
acknowledge that there is a quality in the Creator
of the world which differentiates between two similars, for it seems that the world might have had
another shape and another quantity than it actually has, for it might have been bigger or smaller.
Those different possibilities are, therefore, equivalent in regard to the determination of the existence
of the world. On the other hand, if the philosophers say that the world can have only one special
shape, the special quantity of its bodies and the
special number of them it actually has, and that
this equivalence of possibilities can only be imagined in relation to the times of temporal creation –
since for God no moment is more suitable than
another for its creation – they may be told that it is
possible to answer this by saying that the creation
of the world happened at its most propitious
moment. But we, the theologians say, want to show
the philosophers two equivalent things of which
they cannot affirm that there exists any difference
between them; the first is the particular direction of
the spherical movement and the second the particular position of the poles, relative to the spheres;

for any pair whatever of opposite points, united by a line which passes through the centre of the sphere, might constitute the poles. But the differentiation of these two points, exclusive of all other points which might just as well be the poles of this identical sphere cannot happen except by a quality differentiating between two similar objects. If the philosophers assert that it is not true that any other place on the sphere might be the seat for these poles, they will be told: such an assertion implies that the parts of the spheres are not homogeneous and yet you have often said that the sphere is of a simple nature and therefore has a simple form, viz. the spherical. And again, if the philosophers affirm that there are spots on the sphere which are not homogeneous, it will be asked how these spots came to be of a heterogeneous nature; is it because they are a body or because they are a celestial body? But the absence of homogeneity cannot be explained in this way. Therefore, Ghazali says just as among philosophers the theory is upheld that all times are equivalent in regard to the creation of the world, the theologians are justified in claiming that the parts of heaven are equivalent in regard to their serving as poles, and that the poles do not seem differentiated from the other points through a special position or through their being in an immovable place, exclusive of all other places. This then in short is the objection; it is, however, a rhetorical one, for many things which by demonstration can be found to be necessary seem at first sight merely possible. The philosophers' answer is that they assert that they have proved that the world is composed of five bodies: a body neither heavy nor light, i.e. the revolving spherical body of heaven and four other bodies. two of which are earth, absolutely heavy, which is the centre of the revolving spherical body, and fire, absolutely light, which is seated in the extremity of the revolving sphere; nearest to earth is water, which is heavy relatively to air, light relatively to earth; next to water comes air, which is light relatively to water, heavy relatively to fire. The reason why earth is absolutely heavy is that it is furthest away from the circular movement, and therefore it is the fixed centre of the revolving body; the reason why fire is absolutely light is that it is nearest to the revolving sphere; the intermediate bodies are both heavy and light, because they are in the middle between the two extremes, i.e. the farthest point and the nearest. If there were not a revolving body, surely there would be neither heavy nor light by nature, and neither high nor low by nature, and this whether absolutely or relatively; and the bodies would not differ by nature in the way in which, for instance, earth moves by nature to its specific place and fire moves by nature to another place, and equally so the intermediary bodies. And the world is only finite, because of the spherical body, and this because of the essential and natural finiteness of the spherical body, as one single plane circumscribes it. Rectilinear bodies are not essentially finite, as they allow of an increase and decrease; they are only finite because they are in the middle of a body that admits neither increase nor decrease, and is therefore essentially finite. And, therefore, the body circumscribing the world cannot but be spherical, as otherwise the bodies would either have to end in other bodies, and we should have an infinite regress, or they would end in empty space, and the impossibility of both suppositions has been demonstrated. He who understands this knows that every possible world imaginable can only consist of these bodies, and that bodies have to be either circular – and then they are neither heavy nor light, or rectilinear – and then they are either heavy or light, i.e. either fire or earth or the intermediate bodies; that these bodies have to be either revolving, or surrounded by a revolving periphery, for each body either moves from, towards, or round the centre; that by the movements of the heavenly bodies to the right and to the left all bodies are constituted and all that is produced from opposites is generated; and that through these movements the individuals of these four bodies never cease being in a continual production and corruption. Indeed, if a single one of these movements should cease, the order and proportion of this universe would disappear, for it is clear that this order must necessarily depend on the actual number of these movements – for if this were smaller or greater, either the order would be disturbed, or there would be another order – and that the number of these movements is as it is, either through its necessity for the existence of this sublunary world, or because it is the best.

Do not ask here for a proof for all this, but if you are interested in science, look for its proof, where you can find it. Here, however, listen to theories which are more convincing than those of the theologians and which, even if they do not bring you complete proof, will give your mind an inclination to lead you to proof through scientific speculation. You should imagine that each heavenly sphere is a living being, in so far as it possesses a body of a definite measure and shape and moves itself in definite directions, not at random. Anything of this nature is necessarily a living being; i.e. when we see a body of a definite quality and quantity move itself in space, in a definite direction, not at random, through its own power, not through an exterior cause, and move in opposite directions at the same time, we are absolutely sure that it is a living being, and we said only "not through an exterior cause" because iron moves towards a magnet when the magnet is brought to it from the outside – and besides, iron moves to a magnet from any direction whatever. The heavenly bodies, therefore, possess places which are poles by nature, and these bodies cannot have their poles in other places, just as earthly animals have particular organs in particular parts of their bodies for particular actions, and cannot have them in other places, e.g. the organs of locomotion, which are located in definite parts. The poles represent the organs of locomotion in animals of spherical form, and the only difference in this respect between spherical and non-spherical animals is that in the latter these organs differ in both shape and power, whereas in the former they only differ in power. For this reason it has been thought on first sight that they do not differ at all, and that the poles could be in any two points on the sphere. And just as it would be ridiculous to say that a certain movement in a certain species of earthly animal could be in any part whatever of its body, or in that part where it is in another species, because this movement has been localized in each species in the place where it conforms most to its nature, or in the only place where this animal can perform the movement, so it stands with the differentiation in the heavenly bodies for the place of their poles. For the heavenly bodies are not one species and numerically many, but they form a plurality in species, like the plurality of different individuals of animals where there is only one individual in the species. Exactly the same answer can be given to the question why the heavens move in different directions: that, because they are animals, they must move in definite directions, like right and left, before and behind, which are directions determined by the movements of animals, and the only

difference between the movements of earthly animals and those of heavenly bodies is that in the different animals these movements are different in shape and in power, whereas in the heavenly animals they only differ in power. And it is for this reason that Aristotle thinks that heaven possesses the directions of right and left, before and behind, high and low. The diversity of the heavenly bodies in the direction of their movements rests on their diversity of species, and the fact that this difference in the directions of their movements forms the specific differentia of their species is something proper to them. Imagine the first heaven as one identical animal whose nature obliges it – either by necessity or because it is for the best – to move with all its parts in one movement from east to west. The other spheres are obliged by their nature to have the opposite movement. The direction which the body of the universe is compelled to follow through its nature is the best one, because its body is the best of bodies and the best among the moving bodies must also have the best direction. All this is explained here in this tentative way, but is proved apodictically in its proper place. This is also the manifest sense of the Divine Words, "There is no changing the words of God," and "There is no altering the creation of God." If you want to be an educated man, proceeding by proof, you should look for the proof of this in its proper place.

Now if you have understood all this, it will not be difficult for you to see the faults in Ghazali's arguments here about the equivalence of the two opposite movements in relation to each heavenly body and to the sublunary world. On first thoughts it might be imagined that the movement from east to west might also belong to other spheres besides the first, and that the first sphere might equally well move from west to east. You might as well say that the crab could be imagined as having the same direction of movement as a human being. But, as a matter of fact, such a thought will not occur to you about humans and crabs, because of their difference in shape, whereas it might occur to you about the heavenly spheres, since they agree in shape. He who contemplates a product of art does not perceive its wisdom if he does not perceive the wisdom of the intention embodied in it, and the effect intended. And if he does not understand its wisdom, he may well imagine that this object might have any form, any quantity, any configuration of its parts, and any composition whatever. This is the case with the theologians in regard to the body of the heavens, but all such opinions are superficial. He who has such beliefs about products of art understands neither the work nor the artist, and this holds also in respect of the works of God's creation. Understand this principle, and do not judge the works of God's creation hastily and superficially – so that you may not become one of those about whom the Koran says: "Say, shall we inform you of those who lose most by their works, those who erred in their endeavour after the life of this world and who think they are doing good deeds?" May God make us perspicacious and lift from us the veils of ignorance; indeed He is the bounteous, the generous! To contemplate the various actions of the heavenly bodies is like contemplating the kingdom of heaven, which Abraham contemplated, according to the words of the Koran: "Thus did we show Abraham the kingdom of heaven and of the earth, that he should be of those who are sure." And let us now relate Ghazali's argument about the movements.

Ghazali says:

The second point in this argument concerns the special direction of the movement of the spheres which move partially from east to west, partially in the opposite direction, whereas the equivalence of the directions in relation to their cause is exactly the same as the equivalence of the times. If it is said: If the universe revolved in only one direction, there would never be a difference in the configuration of the stars, and such relations of the stars as their being in trine, in sextile, and in conjunction would never arise, but the universe would remain in one unique position without any change; the difference of these relations, however, is the principle of all production in the world – we answer: Our argument does not concern the difference in direction of movement; no, we concede that the highest sphere moves from east to west and the spheres beneath it in the opposite direction, but everything that happens in this way would happen equally if the reverse took place, i.e. if the highest sphere moved from west to east and the lower spheres in the opposite direction. For all the same differences in configuration would arise just as well. Granted that these movements are circular and in opposite directions, both directions are equivalent; why then

is the one distinguished from the other, which is similar to it? If it is said: as the two directions are opposed and contrary, how can they be similar? – we answer: this is like saying "since before and after are opposed in the existing world, how could it be claimed that they are equivalent?" Still, it is asserted by you philosophers that the equivalence of times, so far as the possibility of their realization and any purpose one might imagine in their realization is concerned, is an evident fact. Now, we regard it as equally evident that spaces, positions, situations, and directions are equivalent so far as concerns their receiving movement and any purpose that might be connected with it. If therefore the philosophers are allowed to claim that notwithstanding this equivalence they are different, their opponents are fully justified in claiming the same in regard to the times.

I say:

From what I have said previously, the speciousness of this argument and the way in which it has to be answered will not be obscure to you. All this is the work of one who does not understand the exalted natures of the heavenly bodies and their acts of wisdom for the sake of which they have been created, and who compares God's knowledge with the knowledge of ignorant man.

Ghazali says:

If it is said: As the two directions are opposed and contrary, how can they be similar? – we answer: this is like saying, "Since before and after in the existing world are opposed, how could it be claimed that they are equivalent?" Still, it is asserted by you philosophers that the equivalence of times so far as the possibility of their realization, and any purpose one might imagine in their realization is concerned, is an evident fact. Now, we regard it as equally evident that spaces, positions, situations, and directions are equivalent so far as concerns their receiving the movement and any purpose that might be connected with it.

I say:

The falsehood of this is self-evident. Even if one should admit that the possibilities of human existence and non-existence are equivalent in the matter out of which humans have been created, and that this is a proof for the existence of a determin-

COULD THE WORLD BE ETERNALLY EXISTENT?

ing principle which prefers the existence of humans to their non-existence, still it cannot be imagined that the possibilities of seeing and not seeing are equivalent in the eye. Thus no one can claim that the opposite directions are equivalent, although he may claim that the substratum for both is indifferent, and that therefore out of both directions similar actions result. And the same holds good for before and after: they are not equivalent, in so far as this event is earlier and that event later; they can only be claimed to be equivalent so far as their possibility of existence is concerned. But the whole assumption is wrong: for essential opposites also need essentially opposite substrata and a unique substratum giving rise to opposite acts at one and the same time is an impossibility. The philosophers do not believe that the possibilities of a thing's existence and of its non-existence are equivalent at one and the same time; no, the time of the possibility of its existence is different from the time of the possibility of its non-existence, time for them is the condition for the production of what is produced, and for the corruption of what perishes. If the time for the possibility of the existence of a thing and the time for the possibility of its non-existence were the same, that is to say in its proximate matter, its existence would be vitiated, because of the possibility of its non-existence, and the possibility of its existence and of its non-existence would be dependent only on the agent, not on the substratum.

Thus he who tries to prove the existence of an agent in this way gives only persuasive, dialectical arguments, not apodictic proof. It is believed that Farabi[10] and Avicenna[11] followed this line to establish that every act must have an agent, but it is not a proof of the ancient philosophers, and both of them merely took it over from the theologians of our religion. In relation, however, to the temporal creation of the world – for him who believes in it – before and after cannot even be imagined, for before and after in time can only be imagined in relation to the present moment, and as, according to the theologians, there was before the creation of the world no time, how could there be imagined something preceding the moment when the world

was created? A definite moment cannot be assigned for the creation of the world, for either time did not exist before it, or there was an infinite time, and in neither case could a definite time be fixed to which the Divine could attach itself. Therefore, it would be more suitable to call this book *Incoherence* without qualification rather than *The Incoherence of the Philosophers,* for the only profit it gives the reader is to make him incoherent.

Ghazali says:
If, therefore, the philosophers are allowed to claim that, notwithstanding this equivalence, they are different, their opponents are fully justified in claiming the same in regard to times.

I say:
He wants to say: If the philosophers are justified in claiming a difference in the direction of movement, the theologians have the right to assert a difference in times, notwithstanding their belief in their equivalence. This is only a verbal argument, and does not refer to the facts themselves, even if one admits an analogy between the opposite directions and the different times, but this is often objected to, because there is no analogy between this difference in times and directions. Our adversary, however, is forced to admit that there is an analogy between them, because they are both claimed to be different, and both to be equivalent! These, therefore, are one and all only dialectical arguments.

Ghazali says:
The second objection against the basis of their argument is that the philosophers are told: "You regard the creation of a temporal being by an eternal as impossible, but you have to acknowledge it too, for there are new events happening in the world and they have causes. It is absurd to think that these events lead to other events *ad infinitum,* and no intelligent person can believe such a thing. If such a thing were possible, you need not acknowledge a creator and establish a necessary being on whom possible existences depend. If, however, there is a limit for those events in which their

---

10 Al-Farabi (870-950). He was one of the earliest of Islamic thinkers to make extensive use of Aristotle and neo-Platonic thought.
11 I.e., Ibn-Sina (980-1037). See biographical entry under 'Avicenna' in this volume.

sequence ends, this limit will be the eternal and then indubitably you too acknowledge the principle that a temporal can proceed from an eternal being."

I say:

If the philosophers had introduced the eternal being into reality from the side of the temporal by this kind of argument, i.e. if they had admitted that the temporal, in so far as temporal, proceeds from an eternal being, there would be no possibility of their avoiding the difficulty in this problem. But you must understand that the philosophers permit the existence of a temporal which comes out of a temporal being *ad infinitum* in an accidental way, when this is repeated in a limited and finite matter when, for instance, the corruption of one of two things becomes the necessary condition for the existence of the other. For instance, according to the philosophers it is necessary that human should be produced from human on condition that the anterior human perishes so as to become the matter for the production of a third. For instance, we must imagine two humans of whom the first produces the second from the matter of a human who perishes; when the second becomes a human himself, the first perishes, then the second human produces a third human out of the matter of the first, and then the second perishes and the third produces out of his matter a fourth, and so we can imagine in two matters an activity continuing ad infinitum, without any impossibility arising. And this happens as long as the agent lasts, for if this agent has neither beginning nor end for his existence, the activity has neither beginning nor end for its existence, as it has been explained before. And in the same way you may imagine this happening in them in the past: When a human exists, there must before him have been a human who produced him and a human who perished, and before this second man a human who produced him and a human who perished, for everything that is produced in this way is, when it depends on an eternal agent, of a circular nature in which no actual totality can be reached. If, on the other hand, a human were produced from another human out of infinite matters, or there were an infinite addition of them, there would be an impossibility, for then there could arise an infinite matter and there could be an infinite whole. For if a finite whole existed to which things

were added *ad infinitum* without any corruption taking place in it, an infinite whole could come into existence, as Aristotle proved in his *Physics*. For this reason the ancients introduce an eternal absolutely unchanging being, having in mind not temporal beings, proceeding from it in so far as they are temporal, but beings proceeding from it as being eternal generically, and they hold that this infinite series is the necessary consequence of an eternal agent, for the temporal needs for its own existence only a temporal cause. Now there are two reasons why the ancients introduce the existence of an eternal numerically unique being which does not suffer any change. The first is that they discovered that this revolving being is eternal, for they discovered that the present individual is produced through the corruption of its predecessor and that the corruption of this previous individual implies the production of the one that follows it, and that it is necessary that this everlasting change should proceed from an eternal mover and an eternal moved body, which does not change in its substance, but which changes only in place so far as concerns its parts, and approaches certain of the transitory things and recedes from certain of them, and this is the cause of the corruption of one half of them and the production of the other half. And this heavenly body is the being that changes in place only, not in any of the other kinds of change, and is through its temporal activities the cause of all things temporal; and because of the continuity of its activities which have neither beginning nor end, it proceeds from a cause which has neither beginning nor end. The second reason why they introduce an eternal being absolutely without body and matter is that they found that all the kinds of movement depend on spatial movement, and that spatial movement depends on a being moved essentially by a prime mover, absolutely immobile, both essentially and accidentally, for otherwise there would exist at the same time an infinite number of moved movers, and this is impossible. And it is necessary that this first mover should be eternal, or else it would not be the first. Every movement, therefore, depends on this mover and its setting things in motion essentially, not accidentally. And this mover exists simultaneously with each thing moved, at the time of its motion, for a mover existing before the thing moved – such as a human producing a human – sets in motion only accidentally, not essentially; but the mover who is the condition of a human's existence from the beginning of his production till its end, or rather from the beginning of his existence till its end, is the prime mover. And likewise its existence is the condition for the existence of all beings and the preservation of heaven and earth and all that is between them. All this is not proved here apodictically, but only in the way we follow here and which is in any case more plausible for an impartial reader than the arguments of our opponents.

If this is clear to you, you certainly are in no need of the subterfuge by which Ghazali in his argument against the philosophers tries to conciliate them with their adversaries in this matter; indeed these artifices will not do, for if you have not understood how the philosophers introduce an eternal being into reality, you have not understood how they settle the difficulty of the rise of the temporal out of the eternal; they do that, as we said, either through the medium of a being eternal in its essence but generable and corruptible in its particular movements, not, however, in its universal circular movement, or through the medium of what is generically eternal – i.e. has neither beginning nor end in it acts.

Ghazali answers in the name of the philosophers:
The philosophers may say, "We do not consider it impossible that any temporal being, whatever it may be, should proceed from an eternal being, but we regard it as impossible that the first temporal should proceed from the eternal, as the mode of its procession does not differ from that which precedes it, either in a greater inclination towards existence or through the presence of some particular time, or through an instrument, condition, nature, accident, or any cause whatever which might produce a new mode. If this therefore is not the first temporal, it will be possible that it should proceed from the eternal, when another thing proceeds from it, because of the disposition of the receiving substratum, or because the time was propitious or for any other reason."

Having given this reply on the part of the philosophers, Ghazali answers it: This question about the actualization of the disposition, whether of the time and of any new condition which arises in it, still holds good, and we must either come to an infinite regress or arrive at an eternal being out of which a first temporal being proceeds.

I say:
This question is the same question all over again as he asked the philosophers first, and this is the same kind of conclusion as he made them draw then, namely that a temporal proceeds from an eternal, and having given as their answer something which does not correspond with the question, i.e. that it is possible that a temporal being should proceed from the Eternal without there being a first temporal being, he turns the same question against them again. The correct answer to this question was given above: the temporal proceeds from the First Eternal, not in so far as it is temporal but in so far as it is eternal, i.e. through being eternal generically, though temporal in its parts. For according to the philosophers an eternal being out of which a temporal being proceeds essentially is not the First Eternal, but its acts, according to them, depend on the First Eternal; i.e. the actualization of the condition for activity of the eternal, which is not the First Eternal, depends on the First Eternal in the same way as the temporal products depend on the First Eternal and this is a dependence based on the universal, not on individuals.

After this Ghazali introduces an answer of the philosophers, in one of the forms in which this theory can be represented, which amounts to this: A temporal being proceeding from an eternal can only be represented by means of a circular movement which resembles the eternal by not having beginning or end and which resembles the temporal in so far as each part of it is transient, so that this movement through the generation of its parts is the principle of temporal things, and through the eternity of its totality the activity of the eternal.

Then Ghazali argues against this view, according to which in the opinion of the philosophers the temporal proceeds from the First Eternal, and says to them: Is this circular movement temporal or eternal? If it is eternal, how does it become the principle for temporal things? And if it is temporal, it will need another temporal being and we shall have an infinite regress. And when you say that it partially resembles the eternal, partially the temporal, for it resembles the eternal in so far as it is permanent and the temporal in so far as it arises anew, we answer: Is it the principle of temporal things, because of its permanence, or because of its arising anew? In the former case, how can a temporal proceed from something because of its permanence?

And in the latter case, what arises anew will need a cause for its arising anew, and we have an infinite regress.

I say:

This argument is sophistical. The temporal does not proceed from it in so far as it is eternal, but in so far as it is temporal; it does not need, however, for its arising anew a cause arising anew; for its arising anew is not a new fact, but is an eternal act, i.e. an act without beginning or end. Therefore its agent must be an eternal agent, for an eternal act has an eternal agent, and a temporal act a temporal agent. Only through the eternal element in it can it be understood that movement has neither beginning nor end, and this is meant by its permanence, for movement itself is not permanent, but changing.

III.4. MOSES MAIMONIDES

FAMILIAR AS HE WAS WITH BOTH ISLAMIC AND GREEK THOUGHT ON the question of whether the physical world was created, Moses Maimonides was well placed to evaluate whether the findings of natural science and astronomy proved that there was no creation from nothing (*creatio ex nihilo*), contrary to what his Jewish faith had proclaimed for centuries. His conclusion is that they do not, and that, in fact, the theory of *creatio ex nihilo* has less difficulty handling certain astronomical phenomena than do the theories which claim the physical universe has existed from all eternity, although neither it nor the others are capable of being demonstratively proven. At the end of these selections Maimonides is drawn into a discussion of the proper scientific method for handling disputes about questions that do not admit of being demonstratively settled either way. Thirteenth and fourteenth century Christian scholastics were well aware of Maimonides' work and perhaps more influenced by it than their references to him would indicate. At any rate, there is hardly a better summary of the issues involved in this question than the one Maimonides gave in his famous work, *The Guide for the Perplexed*, from which these selections are taken.

III.4.1. Arguments of the Mutakallemim purporting to show that the Universe was created out of nothing (*The Guide for the Perplexed*, pt. 1, ch.74)

In this chapter will be given an outline of the proofs by which the Mutakallemim[1] attempt to demonstrate that the universe is not eternal. You must of course not expect that I shall quote their lengthy arguments *verbatim*; I only intend to give an abstract of each proof, to show in what way it helps to establish the theory of the *creatio ex nihilo*[2] or to confute the eternity of the universe, and briefly to notice the propositions they employed in support of their theory. If you were to read their well-known and voluminous writings, you would not discover any arguments with which they support their view left unnoticed in the present outline, but you might find there greater copiousness of words combined with more grace and elegance of style;

frequently they employ rhyme, rhythm, and poetical diction, and sometimes mysterious phrases which perhaps are intended to startle persons listening to their discourses, and to deter those who might otherwise criticize them. You would also find many repetitions; questions propounded and, as they believe, answered, and frequent attacks on those who differ from their opinions.

The First Argument

Some of the Mutakallemim thought that by proving the creation of one thing, they demonstrated the *creatio ex nihilo* in reference to the entire universe. E.g., Zaid,[3] who from a small molecule had gradually been brought to a state of perfection, has undoubtedly not effected this change and development by his own efforts, but owes it to an external agency. It is therefore clear that an agent is required

---

1 The school of Islamic theologians which originated in the ninth century in response to the introduction of Aristotelian philosophy to Islamic thinkers. They accepted the role of reason in interpreting the faith and attempted to defend by reason orthodox Islamic doctrines against the arguments of Aristotle and other Greek philosophers as well as those Islamic thinkers who largely adopted the philosophic ideas of Aristotle and neo-Platonism.
2 I.e., creation out of nothing, a formula which summarized the doctrine of creation common to Islam, Judaism, and Christianity.
3 Zaid serves here as a proper name for whatever person you choose.

for such organization and successive transmutation. A palm-tree or any other object might equally be selected to illustrate this idea. The whole universe, they argue, is analogous to these instances. Thus you see how they believe that a law discovered in one thing may equally be applied to everything.

The Second Argument

This argument is likewise based on the belief that the proof by which the creation of one thing is demonstrated, holds good for the *creatio ex nihilo* in reference to the whole universe. E.g., a certain individual, called Zaid, who one time was not yet in existence, subsequently came into existence; and if it be assumed that Amr, his father, was the cause of his existence, Amr himself must likewise have passed from non-existence into existence; suppose then that Zaid's father unquestionably owed his origin to Khaled, Zaid's grandfather, it would be found that Khaled himself did not exist from eternity, and the series of causes could thus be carried back to infinity. But such an infinite series of beings is inadmissible according to the theory of the Mutakallemim, as we have shown in our discussion of the eleventh proposition.[4] In continuing this species of reasoning, you come to the first human being, who had no parent, viz. Adam. Then you will of course ask, whence came this first human? If, e.g., the reply be given that he was made out of earth, you will again inquire, "Whence came that earth?" "Out of water." "Whence came the water?" The inquiry would be carried on, either *ad infinitum,* which is absurd, or until you meet with a something that came into existence from absolute non-existence; in this latter case you would arrive at the real truth; here the series of inquiries ends. This result of the question proves, according to the opinion of the Mutakallemim that the whole universe came into existence from absolute non-existence.

The Third Argument

The atoms of things are necessarily either joined together or separate, and even the same atoms may at one time be united, at another disunited. It is therefore evident that the nature of the atoms does not necessitate either their combination or their separation; for if they were separate by virtue of their nature they would never join, and if they were joined by virtue of their nature, they could never again be separated. Thus there is no reason why atoms should rather be combined than separate, or *vice versa,* why rather in a state of separation than of combination. Seeing that some atoms are joined, others separate, and again others subject to change, they being combined at one time and separated at another, the fact may therefore be taken as a proof that the atoms cannot combine or separate without an agent. This argument, according to the opinion of the Mutakallemim, establishes the theory that the universe has been created from nothing. You have already been told, that those who employ this argument rely on the first proposition of the Mutakallemim with its corollaries.[5]

The Fourth Argument

The whole universe is composed of substance and accidents; every substance must possess one accident or more, and since the accidents are not eternal, the substance, the substratum of the accidents, cannot be eternal; for that which is joined to transient things and cannot exist without them is itself transient. Therefore, the whole universe has had a beginning. To the objection that the substance may possibly be eternal while the accidents, though in themselves transient, succeed each other in an infinite series, they reply that, in this case, an infinite number of transient things would be in existence, an eventuality which, according to their theory, is impossible.

This argument is considered by them the best and safest, and has been accepted by many of them as a strict proof. Its acceptance implies the admission of

---

4 This disscussion is not included in these selections.

5 The "first proposition" is basically the atomist theory that everything physical is composed of indestructible units of matter. Some of the early Mutakallemim adopted this view in opposition to Aristotle's insistence on the infinite divisibility of matter.

the following three propositions, the object of which is well understood by the philosophers.

(1) An infinite series of things, of which the one succeeds when the other has ceased to exist, is impossible.

(2) All accidents have a beginning. Our opponent, who defends the theory of the eternity of the universe, can refute this proposition by pointing to one particular accident, namely to the circular motion of the sphere;[6] for it is held by Aristotle that this circular motion is eternal, and, therefore, the spheres which perform this motion are, according to his opinion, likewise eternal. It is of no use to prove that all other accidents have a beginning; for our opponent does not deny this; he says that accidents may supervene on an object which has existed from eternity, and may follow each other in rotation. He contents himself with maintaining that this particular accident, viz. circular motion, the motion of the heavenly sphere, is eternal, and does not belong to the class of transient accidents. It is therefore necessary to examine this accident by itself, and to prove that it is not eternal.

(3) The next proposition which the author of this argument accepts is as follows: Every material object consists of substance and accidents, that is to say, of atoms and accidents in the sense in which the Mutakallemim use the term. But if a material object were held to be a combination of matter and form, as has been proved by our opponent, it would be necessary to demonstrate that the primal matter and primal form are transient, and only then the proof of the *creatio ex nihilo* would be complete.

The Fifth Argument

This argument is based on the theory of Determination, and is made much of by the Mutakallemim. It is the same as the theory which I explained in discussing the tenth proposition.[7] Namely, when they treat either of the universe in general, or of any of its parts, they assume that it can have such properties and such dimensions as it actually has; that it may receive such accidents as in reality are noticed in it, and that it may exist in such

a place and at such a time as in fact is the case; but it may be larger or smaller, may receive other properties and accidents, and come to existence at an earlier or a later period, or in a different place. Consequently, the fact that a thing has been determined in its composition, size, place, accident and time – a variation in all these points being possible – is a proof that a being exists which freely chooses and determines these divers relations; and the circumstance that the universe or a part of it requires a being able to make this selection, proves that the universe has been created *ex nihilo*. For there is no difference which of the following expressions is used: "to determine," "to make," "to create," "to produce," "to originate," or "to intend"; these verbs have all one and the same meaning. The Mutakallemim give a great many examples, both of a general and a special character. They say it is not more natural for earth to be under water than to be above water; who then determined its actual position? Or, is it more natural that the sun is round than that it should be square or triangular; for all qualities have the same relation to a body capable of possessing them. Who, then, determined one particular quality? In a similar way they treat of every individual being; when, e.g., they notice flowers of different colors, they are unable to explain the phenomenon, and they take it as a strong proof in favor of their theory; they say, "Behold, the earth is everywhere alike, the water is alike; why then is this flower red and that one yellow? Some being must have determined the color of each, and that being is God. A being must therefore exist which determines everything, both as regards the universe generally, and each of its parts individually. All this is the logical consequence of the tenth proposition. The theory of determination is moreover adopted by some of those who assume the eternity of the universe, as will be explained below. In conclusion, I consider this to be the best argument; and in another part I shall more fully acquaint you with the opinion I have formed concerning the theory of Determination.

---

6 I.e., the heavenly sphere which carries around the fixed stars.

7 The tenth proposition is that everything that is conceived by the imagination is admitted by the intellect to be possible.

The Sixth Argument

One of the modern Mutakallemim thought that he had found a very good argument, much better than any advanced hitherto, namely, the argument based on the triumph of existence over non-existence. He says that, according to the common belief, the existence of the universe is merely possible; for if it were necessary, the universe would be God – but he seems to forget that we are at issue with those who, whilst they believe in the existence of God, admit at the same time the eternity of the universe. The expression "A thing is possible" denotes that the thing may either be in existence or not in existence, and that there is not more reason why it should exist than why it should not exist. The fact that a thing, the existence of which is possible, actually does exist – although it bears the same relation to the state of existence as to that of non-existence – proves that there is a Being which gave the preference to existence over non-existence. This argument is very forcible; it is a modified form of the foregoing argument which is based on the theory of Determination. He only chose the term "preference" instead of "determination," and instead of applying it to the properties of the existing being he applies it to "the existence of the being itself." He either had the intention to mislead, or he misunderstood the proposition, that the existence of the universe is possible. Our opponent who assumes the eternity of the universe, employs the term "possible," and says, "the existence of the universe is possible" in a sense different from that in which the Mutakallemim applies it, as will be explained below. Moreover, it may be doubted whether the conclusion, that the universe owes its origin to a being which is able to give preference to existence over non-existence, is correct. For we may apply the terms "preference" and "determination" to anything capable of receiving either of two properties which are contrary or opposed to each other; and when we find that the thing actually possesses one property and not the other, we are convinced that there exists a determining agent. E.g. you say that a piece of copper could just as well be formed into a kettle as into a lamp; when we find that it is a lamp

or a kettle, we have no doubt that a deciding and determining agent had advisedly chosen one of the two possible forms; for it is clear that the substance of copper existed, and that before the determination took place it had neither of the two possible forms which have just been mentioned. When, however, it is the question whether a certain existing object is eternal, or whether it has passed from non-existence into existence, this argument is inadmissible; for it cannot be asked who decided in favor of the existence of a thing, and rejected its non-existence, except when it has been admitted that it has passed from nonexistence into existence; in the present case this is just the point under discussion. If we were to take the existence and the non-existence of a thing as mere objects of imagination, we should have to apply the tenth proposition[8] which gives prominence to imagination and fiction, and ignores the things which exist in reality, or are conceived by the intellect. Our opponent, however, who believes in the eternity of the universe, will show that we can imagine the non-existence of the universe as well as we can imagine any other impossibility. It is not my intention to refute their doctrine of the *creatio ex nihilo;* I only wish to show the incorrectness of their belief that this argument differs from the one which precedes; since in fact the two arguments are identical, and are founded on the well known principle of determination.

The Seventh Argument

One of the modern Mutakallemim says that he is able to prove the creation of the universe from the theory put forth by the philosophers concerning the immortality of the soul. He argues thus: If the world were eternal, the number of the dead would necessarily be infinite, and consequently an infinite number of souls would coexist, but it has long since been shown that the coexistence of an infinite number of things is positively impossible.

This is indeed a strange argument! One difficulty is explained by another which is still greater! Here the saying, well known among the Aralneans,[9] may be applied: "Your guarantee wants himself a guarantee." He rests his argument on the immortality

8 See fn.7.
9 Syrians who spoke Aramaic.

of the soul, as though he understood this immortality, in what respect the soul is immortal, or what the thing is which is immortal! If, however, he only meant to controvert the opinion of his opponent, who believed in the eternity of the universe, and also in the immortality of the soul, he accomplished his task, provided the opponent admitted the correctness of the idea which that Mutakallem formed of the philosopher's view on the immortality of the soul. Some of the later philosophers explained this difficulty as follows: The immortal souls are not substances which occupy a locality or a space, and their existence in an infinite number is therefore not impossible. You must bear in mind that those abstract beings which are neither bodies nor forces dwelling in bodies, and which in fact are ideals, are altogether incapable of being represented as a plurality unless some ideals be the cause of the existence of others, and can be distinguished from each other by the specific difference that some are the efficient cause and others the effect; but that which remains of Zaid[10] [after his death] is neither the cause nor the effect of that which is left of Amr, and therefore the souls of all the departed form only one being as has been explained by Ibn Bekr Ibn al-Zaig,[11] and others who ventured to speak on these profound subjects.

It should be noted that whoever endeavors to prove or to disprove the eternity of the universe by these arguments of the Mutakallemim, must necessarily rely on one of the two following propositions, or on both of them; namely on the tenth proposition, according to which the actual form of a thing is merely one of many equally possible forms, and which implies that there must be a being capable of making the special selection; or on the eleventh proposition which rejects the existence of an infinite series of things coming successively into existence. The last-named proposition is demonstrated in various ways, e.g., they advert to a class of transient individuals and to a certain particular date. From the theory which asserts the eternity of the universe, it would follow that the individuals of

that class up to that particular date are infinite in number; a thousand years later the individuals of that class are likewise infinite in number; the last number must exceed the previous one by the number of individuals born in those thousand years, and consequently one infinite number would be larger than another. The same argument is applied to the revolutions of the heavenly sphere, and in like manner it is shown that one infinite number of revolutions would be larger than another; the same result is obtained when revolutions of one sphere are compared with those of another moving more slowly; the revolutions of both spheres [though unequal] would be infinite in number. Similarly they proceed with all those accidents which are subject to destruction and production; the individual accidents that have passed into non-existence are counted and represented as though they were still in existence, and as though they were things with a definite beginning; this imaginary number is then either increased or reduced. Yet all these things have no reality and are mere fictions. Abu Nazar Alfarabi,[12] in criticizing this proposition, has exposed all its weak points, as you will clearly perceive when you study his book on the changeable beings earnestly and dispassionately.

III.4.2: Different views on the Eternity of the Universe among those who believe God exists (*The Guide for the Perplexed,* pt.2, ch.13-14)

Chapter XIII

Among those who believe in the existence of God, there are found three different theories as regards the question whether the Universe is eternal or not.

First theory: Those who follow the Law of Moses, our Teacher, hold that the whole universe, i.e., everything except God, has been brought by Him into existence out of non-existence. In the beginning God alone existed, and nothing else; neither angels, nor spheres,[13] nor the things that are con-

---

10 See above, fn.3.
11 Ibn Bajja (Avempace) who lived in Moslem Spain and died in 1138.
12 One of the earliest Islamic thinkers to be heavily influenced by Aristotle and neo-Platonism. Lived ca. 870-950 C.E.
13 I.e., the heavenly spheres on which, according to the astronomy of the day, were placed the heavenly bodies, viz. stars, sun and moon.

182

tained within the spheres existed. He then produced from nothing all existing things such as they
are, by His will and desire. Even time itself is
among the things created; for time depends on
motion, i.e., on an accident in things which move,
and the things upon whose motion time depends
are themselves created beings, which have passed
from non-existence into existence. We say that God
existed before the creation of the universe,
although the verb "existed" appears to imply the
notion of time; we also believe that He existed an
infinite space of time before the universe was created; but in these cases we do not mean time in its
true sense. We only use the term to signify something analogous or similar to time. For time is
undoubtedly an accident, and, according to our
opinion, one of the created accidents, like blackness and whiteness; it is not a quality, but an accident connected with motion. This must be clear to
all who understand what Aristotle has said on time
and its real existence.[14]

The following remark does not form an essential
part of our present research; it will nevertheless be
found useful in the course of this discussion. Many
scholars do not know what time really is, and men
like Galen[15] were so perplexed about it that they
asked whether time has a real existence or not; the
reason for this uncertainty is to be found in the circumstance that time is an accident of an accident.[16]
Accidents which are directly connected with material bodies, e.g., color and taste, are easily understood, and correct notions are formed of them.
There are, however, accidents which are connected
with other accidents, e.g., the splendor of color, or
the inclination and curvature of a line; of these it is
very difficult to form a correct notion, especially
when the accident which forms the substratum for
the other accident is not constant but variable. Both
difficulties are present in the notion of time: it is an
accident of motion, which is itself an accident of a
moving object; besides, it is not a fixed property;
on the contrary, its true and essential condition is,

not to remain in the same state for two consecutive
moments. This is the source of ignorance about the
nature of time.

We consider time a thing created; it comes into
existence in the same manner as other accidents,
and the substances which form the substratum for
the accidents. For this reason, viz., because time
belongs to the things created, it cannot be said that
God produced the universe *in the beginning*.
Consider this well; for he who does not understand
it is unable to refute forcible objections raised
against the theory of *creatio ex nihilo*. If you admit
the existence of time before the Creation, you will
be compelled to accept the theory of the Eternity of
the Universe. For time is an accident and requires a
substratum.[17] You will therefore have to assume
that something [besides God] existed before this
universe was created, an assumption which it is our
duty to oppose.

This is the first theory, and it is undoubtedly a
fundamental principle of the Law of our teacher
Moses; it is next in importance to the principle of
God's unity. Do not follow any other theory.
Abraham, our father, was the first that taught it,
after he had established it by philosophical
research. He proclaimed, therefore, "the name of
the Lord the God of the Universe" (*Genesis.* 21:33);
and he had previously expressed this theory in the
words, "The Possessor of heaven and earth" (*ibid.*
14:22).

Second theory: The theory of all philosophers
whose opinions and works are known to us is this:
It is impossible to assume that God produced anything from nothing, or that He reduces anything to
nothing; that is to say, it is impossible that an object
consisting of matter and form[18] should be produced
when that matter is absolutely absent, or that it
should be destroyed in such a manner that that matter be absolutely no longer in existence. To say of
God that He can produce a thing from nothing or
reduce a thing to nothing is, according to the opin-

---

14 Cf. selection III.1.1.

15 A physician and scientist who lived from 129 to about 199 C.E. and wrote a number of philosophic treatises in Greek
which were well respected in the medieval Islamic world.

16 See glossary entry for 'accident.'

17 See glossary entry for 'substratum.'

18 See glossary entry for 'form/matter.'

ion of these philosophers, the same as if we were to say that He could cause one substance to have at the same time two opposite properties, or produce another being like Himself, or change Himself into a body, or produce a square the diagonal of which be equal to its side, or similar impossibilities. The philosophers thus believe that it is no defect in the Supreme Being that He does not produce impossibilities, for the nature of that which is impossible is constant – it does not depend on the action of an agent, and for this reason it cannot be changed. Similarly there is, according to them, no defect in the greatness of God, when He is unable to produce a thing from nothing, because they consider it as one of the impossibilities. They therefore assume that a certain substance has coexisted with God from eternity in such a manner that neither God existed without that substance nor the latter without God. But they do not hold that the existence of that substance equals in rank that of God; for God is the cause of that existence, and the substance is in the same relation to God as the clay is to the potter, or the iron to the smith; God can do with it what He pleases; at one time He forms of it heaven and earth, at another time He forms some other thing. Those who hold this view also assume that the heavens are transient, that they came into existence, though not from nothing, and may cease to exist, although they cannot be reduced to nothing. They are transient in the same manner as the individuals among living beings which are produced from some existing substance, and are again reduced to some substance that remains in existence. The process of genesis and destruction is, in the case of the heavens, the same as that of earthly beings.

The followers of this theory are divided into different schools, whose opinions and principles it is useless to discuss here; but what I have mentioned is common to all of them. Plato holds the same opinion. Aristotle says in his *Physics* that according to Plato the heavens are transient. This view is also stated in Plato's *Timaios*. His opinion, however, does not agree with out belief; only superficial and careless persons wrongly assume that Plato has the same belief as we have. For whilst we hold that the heavens have been created from absolutely nothing, Plato believes that they have been formed out of something. This is the second theory.

Third theory: viz., that of Aristotle, his followers, and commentators. Aristotle maintains, like the adherents of the second theory, that a corporeal object cannot be produced without a corporeal substance. He goes, however, farther, and contends that the heavens are indestructible. For he holds that the universe in its totality has never been different, nor will it ever change: the heavens, which form the permanent element in the universe, and are not subject to genesis and destruction, have always been so; time and motion are eternal, permanent, and have neither beginning nor end; the sublunary world, which includes the transient elements, has always been the same, because the primary matter is itself eternal, and merely combines successively with different forms; when one form is removed, another is assumed. This whole arrangement, therefore, both above and here below, is never disturbed or interrupted, and nothing is produced contrary to the laws or the ordinary course of nature. He further says, though not in the same terms, that he considers it impossible for God to change His will or conceive a new desire; that God produced this universe in its totality by His will, but not from nothing. Aristotle finds it as impossible to assume that God changes His will or conceives a new desire, as to believe that He is non-existing, or that His essence is changeable. Hence it follows that this universe has always been the same in the past, and will be the same eternally.

This is a full account of the opinions of those who consider that the existence of God, the First Cause of the universe, has been established by proof. But it would be quite useless to mention the opinions of those who do not recognize the existence of God, but believe that the existing state of things is the result of accidental combination and separation of the elements, and that the universe has no ruler or governor. Such is the theory of Epicurus[19] and his school, and similar philosophers, as stated by Alexander [of Aphrodisias];[20] it

---

19 Founder of the Epicurean school who taught in Athens at the end of the 4th century B.C.E. In large measure he adopted the atheistic atomism of Democritus who had taught about a century before.
20 Leading member of the Peripatetic (Aristotelian) school in late antiquity. He was working around 200 C.E.

would be superfluous to repeat their views, since the existence of God has been demonstrated whilst their theory is built upon a basis proved to be untenable. It is likewise useless to prove the correctness of the followers of the second theory in asserting that the heavens are transient, because they at the same time believe in the eternity of the universe, and so long as this theory is adopted, it makes no difference to us whether it is believed that the heavens are transient, and that only their substance is eternal, or the heavens are held to be indestructible, in accordance with the view of Aristotle. All who follow the Law of Moses, our Teacher, and Abraham, our Father, and all who adopt similar theories, assume that nothing is eternal except God, and that the theory of *creatio ex nihilo* includes nothing that is impossible, whilst some thinkers even regard it as an established truth.

After having described the different theories, I will now proceed to show how Aristotle proved his theory, and what induced him to adopt it.

Chapter XIV

It is not necessary to repeat in every chapter that I write this treatise with the full knowledge of what you have studied; that I therefore need not quote the exact words of the philosophers; it will suffice to give an abstract of their views. I will, however, point out the methods which they employ, in the same manner as I have done when I discussed the theories of the Mutakallemim.[21] No notice will be taken of the opinion of any philosopher but that of Aristotle; his opinions alone deserve to be criticized, and if our objections or doubts with regard to any of these be well founded, this must be the case in a far higher degree in respect to all other opponents of our fundamental principles.

I now proceed to describe the methods of the philosophers.

First method: According to Aristotle, motion, that is to say, motion *par excellence*, is eternal. For if the motion had a beginning, there must already have been some motion when it came into existence, for transition from potentiality into actuality, and from non-existence into existence, always implies motion; then that previous motion, the cause of the motion which follows, must be eternal, or else the series would have to be carried back ad *infinitum*. On the same principle he maintains that time is eternal, for time is related to and connected with motion: there is no motion except in time, and time can only be perceived by motion, as has been demonstrated by proof. By this argument Aristotle proves the eternity of the universe.

Second method: The first substance common to the four elements[22] is eternal. For if it had a beginning it would have come into existence from another substance; it would further be endowed with a form, as coming into existence is nothing but receiving form. But we mean by "first substance" a formless substance; it can therefore not have come into existence from another substance, and must be without beginning and without end; hence it is concluded that the universe is eternal.

Third method: The substance of the spheres contains no opposite elements; for circular motion includes no such opposite directions as are found in rectilinear motion. Whatever is destroyed, owes its destruction to the opposite elements it contains. The spheres contain no opposite elements;[23] they are therefore indestructible, and because they are indestructible they are also without beginning. Aristotle thus assumes the axiom that everything that has had a beginning is destructible, and that everything destructible has had a beginning; that things without beginning are indestructible, and indestructible things are without beginning. Hence follows the eternity of the universe.

Fourth method: The actual production of a thing is preceded in time by its possibility. The actual change of a thing is likewise preceded in time by its possibility. From this proposition Aristotle derives the eternity of the circular motion of the spheres.

21 See selection **III.4.1.**
22 I.e., earth, air, fire and water. See glossary entry for 'element.' By the "first substance" here Maimonides refers to a material substratum common to those elements.
23 The four elements oppose each other by the opposition of warm vs. cold, or fluid (wet) vs. dry, or both. See glossary entry for 'element.'

The Aristotelians in more recent times employ this proposition in demonstrating the eternity of the universe. They argue thus: When the universe did not yet exist, its existence was either possible, or necessary, or impossible. If it was necessary, the universe could never have been non-existing; if impossible, the universe could never have been in existence; if possible, the question arises, What was the substratum of that possibility? for there must be in existence something of which that possibility can be predicated. This is a forcible argument in favor of the eternity of the universe.

Some of the later schools of the Mutakallemim imagined that they could confute this argument by objecting that the possibility rests with the agent, and not with the production. But this objection is of no force whatever; for there are two distinct possibilities, viz., the thing produced has had the possibility of being produced before this actually took place; and the agent has had the possibility of producing it before he actually did so. There are, therefore, undoubtedly two possibilities: that of the substance to receive a certain form, and that of the agent to perform a certain act.

These are the principal methods, based on the properties of the universe, by which Aristotle proves the eternity of the universe. There are, however, other methods of proving the eternity of the universe. They are based on the notions formed of God, and philosophers after Aristotle derived them from his philosophy. Some of them employed the following argument:

Fifth method: If God produced the universe from nothing, He must have been a potential agent before He was an actual one, and must have passed from a state of potentiality into that of actuality – a process that is merely possible, and requires an agent for effecting it. This argument is likewise a source of great doubts, and every intelligent person must examine it in order to refute it and to expose its character.

Sixth method: An agent is active at one time and inactive at another, according as favorable or unfavorable circumstances arise. The unfavorable circumstances cause the abandonment of an intended action. The favorable ones, on the other hand, even produce a desire for an action for which there has

not been a desire previously. As, however, God is not subject to accidents which could bring about a change in His will, and is not affected by obstacles and hindrances that might appear or disappear, it is impossible, they argue, to imagine that God is active at one time and inactive at another. He is, on the contrary, always active in the same manner as He is always in actual *existence*

Seventh method: The actions of God are perfect; they are in no way defective, nor do they contain anything useless or superfluous. In similar terms Aristotle frequently praises Him, when he says that Nature is wise and does nothing in vain, but makes everything as perfect as possible. The philosophers therefore contend that this existing universe is so perfect that it cannot be improved, and must be permanent; for it is the result of God's wisdom, which is not only always present in His essence. but is identical with it.

All arguments in favor of the eternity of the universe are based on the above methods, and can be traced back to one or other of them. The following objection is also raised against *creatio ex nihilo:* How could God ever have been inactive without producing or creating anything in the infinite past? How could He have passed the long infinite period which preceded the Creation without producing anything, so as to commence, as it were, only yesterday, the creation of the universe? For even if you said, e.g., that God created previously as many successive worlds as the outermost sphere could contain grains of mustard, and that each of these worlds existed as many years, considering the infinite existence of God, it would be the same as if He had only yesterday commenced the creation. For when we once admit the beginning of the existence of things after their non-existence, it makes no difference whether thousands of centuries have passed since the beginning, or only a short time. Those who defend the eternity of the universe find both assumptions equally improbable.

Eighth method: The following method is based on the circumstance that the theory implies a belief which is so common to all peoples and ages, and so universal, that it appears to express a real fact and not merely an hypothesis. Aristotle says that all people have evidently believed in the permanency and stability of the heavens; and thinking that these were eternal, they declared them to be the habitation of God and of the spiritual beings or angels. By thus attributing the heavens to God, they expressed their belief that the heavens are indestructible. Several other arguments of the same kind are employed by Aristotle in treating of this subject in order to support the results of his philosophical speculation by common sense.

III.4.3. That the Universe is eternal has not been proven (The Guide for the Perplexed, pt.2, ch. 16-19)

Chapter XVI

In this chapter I will first expound my view on this question and then support it by argument – not by such arguments as those of the Mutakallemim,[24] who believe that they have proved the *creatio ex nihilo*. I will not deceive myself, and consider dialectical[25] methods as proofs; and the fact that a certain proposition has been proved by a dialectical argument will never induce me to accept that proposition, but, on the contrary, will weaken my faith in it, and cause me to doubt it. For when we understand the fallacy of a proof, our faith in the proposition itself is shaken. It is therefore better that a proposition which cannot be demonstrated be received as an axiom, or that one of the two opposite solutions of the problem be accepted on authority. The methods by which the Mutakallemim proved the *creatio ex nihilo* have already been described by me, and I have exposed their weak points. As to the proofs of Aristotle and his followers for the eternity of the universe, they are, according to my opinion, not conclusive; they are open to strong objections, as will be explained. I intend to show that the theory of the creation, as taught in Scripture, contains nothing that is impossible; and that all those philosophical arguments which seem to disprove our view contain weak points which make them inconclusive, and render the attacks on

our view untenable. Since I am convinced of the correctness of my method, and consider either of the two theories – viz., the eternity of the universe, and the creation – as admissible, I accept the latter on the authority of Prophecy, which can teach things beyond the reach of philosophical speculation. For the belief in prophecy is, as will be shown in the course of this treatise, consistent even with the belief in the eternity of the universe. When I have established the admissibility of our theory, I will, by philosophical reasoning, show that our theory of the creation is more acceptable than that of the eternity of the universe; and although our theory includes points open to criticism, I will show that there are much stronger reasons for the rejection of the theory of our opponents.

I will now proceed to expound the method by which the proofs given for the eternity of the universe can be refuted.

Chapter XVII

Everything produced comes into existence from non-existence; even when the substance of a thing has been in existence, and has only changed its form, the thing itself, which has gone through the process of genesis and development, and has arrived at its final state, has now different properties from those which it possessed at the commencement of the transition from potentiality to reality, or before that time. Take, e.g., the human ovum as contained in the female's blood when still included in its vessels; its nature is different from what it was in the moment of conception, when it is met by the semen of the male and begins to develop; the properties of the semen in that moment are different from the properties of the living being after its birth when fully developed. It is therefore quite impossible to infer from the nature which a thing possesses after having passed through all stages of its development, what the condition of the thing has been in the moment when this process commenced; nor does the condition of a thing in this moment show what its previous condition has

---

24 See selection III.4.1, fn. 1.

25 In Aristotelian logic, dialectic deals with arguments which, while providing some support for belief in their conclusions, do not in fact render those conclusions certain. Maimonides here takes an unusually negative attitude toward such "proofs."

been. If you make this mistake, and attempt to prove the nature of a thing in potential existence by its properties when actually existing, you will fall into great confusion; you will reject evident truths and admit false opinions. Let us assume, in our above instance, that a man born without defect had after his birth been nursed by his mother only a few months; the mother then died, and the father alone brought him up in a lonely island, till he grew up, became wise, and acquired knowledge. Suppose this man had never seen a woman or any female being; he asks some person how human beings have come into existence, and how they have developed, and receives the following answer: "Human beings begin their existence in the womb of an individual of their own class, namely, in the womb of a female, which has a certain form. While in the womb they are very small; yet they have life, move, receive nourishment, and gradually grow, till they arrive at a certain stage of development. They then leave the womb and continue to grow till they are in the condition in which you see them." The orphan will naturally ask: "Did these persons, when they lived, moved, and grew in the womb, eat and drink, and breathe with their mouths and their nostrils? Did they excrete any substances?" The answer will be, "No." Undoubtedly he will then attempt to refute the statements of that person, and to prove their impossibility, by referring to the properties of a fully developed person, in the following manner: "When any one of us is deprived of breath for a short time they die, and cannot move any longer. How then can we imagine that any one of us has been inclosed in a bag in the midst of a body for several months and remained alive, able to move? If any one of us would swallow a living bird, the bird would die immediately when it reached the stomach, much more so when it came to the lower part of the belly; if we should not take food or drink with our mouth, in a few days we should undoubtedly be dead; how then can a human being remain alive for months without taking food? If any person would take food and would not be able to excrete it, great pains and death would follow in a short time, and yet I am to believe that a human being has lived for months without that function! Suppose by accident a hole were formed in the belly

of a person, it would prove fatal, and yet we are to believe that the navel of the foetus has been open! Why should the foetus not open the eyes, spread forth the hands and stretch out the legs, if, as you think, the limbs are all whole and perfect." This mode of reasoning would lead to the conclusion that human beings cannot come into existence and develop in the manner described.

If philosophers would consider this example well and reflect on it, they would find that it represents exactly the dispute between Aristotle and ourselves. We, the followers of Moses, our Teacher, and of Abraham, our Father, believe that the universe has been produced and has developed in a certain manner, and that it has been created in a certain order. The Aristotelians oppose us, and found their objections on the properties which the things in the universe possess when in actual existence and fully developed. We admit the existence of these properties, but hold that they are by no means the same as those which the things possessed in the moment of their production; and we hold that these properties themselves have come into existence from absolute non-existence. Their arguments are therefore no objection whatever to our theory; they have demonstrative force only against those who hold that the nature of things as at present in existence proves the creation. But this is not my opinion.

I will now return to our theme, viz., to the description of the principal proofs of Aristotle, and show that they prove nothing whatever against us, since we hold that God brought the entire universe into existence from absolute non-existence, and that He caused it to develop into the present state. Aristotle says that the primary matter[26] is eternal, and by referring to the properties of transient beings he attempts to prove this statement, and to show that the primary matter could not possibly have been produced. He is right; we do not maintain that the primary matter has been produced in the same manner as a human being is produced from the ovum, and that it can be destroyed in the same manner as a human is reduced to dust. But we believe that God created it from nothing, and that since its creation it has its own properties, viz., that all things are produced of it and again

---

26 I.e., the material substratum common to the elements.

reduced to it, when they cease to exist; that it does not exist without form; and that it is the source of all genesis and destruction. Its genesis is not like that of the things produced from it, nor its destruction like theirs; for it has been created from nothing, and if it should please the Creator, He might reduce it to absolutely nothing. The same applies to motion. Aristotle founds some of his proofs on the fact that motion is not subject to genesis or destruction. This is correct; if we consider motion as it exists at present, we cannot imagine that in its totality it should be subject, like individual motions, to genesis and destruction. In like manner Aristotle is correct in saying that circular motion is without beginning, in so far as seeing the rotating spherical body in actual existence, we cannot conceive the idea that that rotation has ever been absent. The same argument we employ as regards the law that a state of potentiality precedes all actual genesis. This law applies to the universe as it exists at present, when everything produced originates in another thing; but nothing perceived with our senses or comprehended in our mind can prove that a thing created from nothing must have been previously in a state of potentiality. Again, as regards the theory that the heavens contain no opposites [and are therefore indestructible], we admit its correctness; but we do not maintain that the production of the heavens has taken place in the same way as that of a horse or ass, and we do not say that they are like plants and animals, which are destructible on account of the opposite elements[27] they contain. In short, the properties of things when fully developed contain no clue as to what have been the properties of the things before their completion. We therefore do not reject as impossible the opinion of those who say that the heavens were produced before the earth, or the reverse, or that the heavens have existed without stars, or that certain species of animals have been in existence, and others not. For the state of the whole universe when it came into existence may be compared with that of animals when their existence begins; the heart evidently precedes the testicles, the veins are in existence before the bones; although, when the animal is fully developed, none

of the parts is missing which is essential to its existence. This remark is not superfluous, if the scriptural account of the Creation be taken literally; in reality, it cannot be taken literally, as will be shown when we shall treat of this subject.

The principle laid down in the foregoing must be well understood; it is a high rampart erected round the Law, and able to resist all missiles directed against it. Aristotle, or rather his followers, may perhaps ask us how we know that the universe has been created; and that other forces than those it has at present were acting in its creation, since we hold that the properties of the universe, as it exists at present, prove nothing as regards its creation? We reply, there is no necessity for this according to our plan; for we do not desire to prove the creation, but only its possibility; and this possibility is not refuted by arguments based on the nature of the present universe, which we do not dispute. When we have established the admissibility of our theory, we shall then show its superiority. In attempting to prove the inadmissibility of *creatio ex nihilo,* the Aristotelians can therefore not derive any support from the nature of the universe; they must resort to the notion our mind has formed of God. Their proofs include the three methods which I have mentioned above, and which are based on the notion conceived of God. In the next chapter I will expose the weak points of these arguments, and show that they really prove nothing.

Chapter XVIII

The first method[28] employed by the philosophers is this: they assume that a transition from potentiality to actuality would take place in the Deity itself, if He produced a thing only at a certain fixed time. The refutation of this argument is very easy. The argument applies only to bodies composed of substance – the element that possesses the possibility [for change] – and form; for when such a body does not act for some time, and then acts by virtue of its form, it must undoubtedly have possessed something potential that has now become actual, and the transition can only have been effected by some external agent. As far as corporeal bodies are con-

27 See glossary entry for "element."
28 This is the *fifth method* found in selection III.4.2.

cerned, this has been fully proved. But that which is incorporeal and without substance does not include anything merely possible; everything it contains is always in existence. The above argument does not apply to it, and it is not impossible that such a being acts at one time and does not act at another. This does not imply a change in the incorporeal being itself nor a transition from potentiality to actuality. The Active Intellect[29] may be taken as an illustration. According to Aristotle and his school, the Active Intellect, an incorporeal being, acts at one time and does not act at another, as has been shown by Abu-Nasr[30] in his treatise on the intellect. He says there quite correctly the following: "It is an evident fact that the Active Intellect does not act continually, but only at times." And yet he does not say that the Active Intellect is changeable, or passes from a state of potentiality to that of actuality, although it produces at one time something which it has not produced before. For there is no relation or comparison whatever between corporeal and incorporeal beings, neither in the moment of action nor in that of inaction. It is only by homonymy that the term "action" is used in reference to the forms residing in bodies, and also in reference to absolutely spiritual beings. The circumstance that a purely spiritual being does not effect at one time that which it effects at another, does not necessitate a transition from potentiality to actuality; such a transition is necessary in the case of forces connected with bodies. It might, perhaps, be objected that our argument is, to some extent, a fallacy; since it is not due to anything contained in the Active intellect itself, but to the absence of substances sufficiently prepared for its action, that at times it does not act; it does act always when substances sufficiently prepared are present, and, when the action does not continue, it is owing to the absence of substances sufficiently prepared, and not to any change in the Intellect. I answer that it is not our intention to state the reason why God created at one time and not at anoth-

er; and, in referring to the Active Intellect as a parallel, we do not mean to assert that God acts at one time and not at another, in the same manner as the Active Intellect, an absolutely spiritual being, acts intermittently. We do not make this assertion, and, if we did, the conclusion would be fallacious. What we infer, and what we are justified in inferring, is this: the Active Intellect is neither a corporeal object nor a force residing in a body; it acts intermittently, and yet whatever the case may be why it does not always act, we do not say that the Active Intellect has passed from a state of potentiality to that of actuality; or that it implies the possibility [for change], or that an agent must exist that causes the transition from potentiality to actuality. We have thus refuted the strong objection raised by those who believe in the eternity of the universe; since we believe that God is neither a corporeal body nor a force residing in a body, we need not assume that the creation, after a period of inaction, is due to a change in the Creator Himself.

The second method[31] employed in proving the eternity of the universe is based on the theory that all wants, changes, and obstacles are absent from the essence of God. Our refutation of this proof, which is both difficult and profound, is this. Every being that is endowed with free will and performs certain acts in reference to another being, necessarily interrupts those acts at one time or another, in consequence of some obstacles or changes. E.g., a person desires to have a house, but he does not build one, because he meets with some obstacles: he has not the materials, or he has the materials, but they are not prepared for the purpose on account of the absence of proper instruments; or he has materials and instruments, and yet does not build a house, because he does not desire to build it since he feels no want for a shelter. When changed circumstances, as heat or cold, impel him to seek a shelter, then he desires to build a house. Thus changed circumstances change his will, and the will, when it

---

29 In Aristotle's thought the active or agent intellect actualizes intelligible forms in the human mind and is treated as the immortal part of the human soul. Later Aristotelians came to view it as a single immaterial substance on its own which influenced all the various individual human minds. See Aristotle's *De anima* III, 5.

30 I.e., Alfarabi. See selection **III.4.1**, fn.12. It is doubtful that Alfarabi has interpreted Aristotle correctly here, for in *De anima* Aristotle explicitly says that the active intellect is always active. What is clear is that Alfarabi takes the second of the views of the Active Intellect mentioned in the preceding footnote.

31 This is the *sixth method* found in selection **III.4.2**.

meets with obstacles, is not carried into effect. This, however, is only the case when the causes of the actions are external; but when the action has no other purpose whatever than to fulfill the will, then the will does not depend on the existence of favorable circumstances. The being endowed with this will need not act continually even in the absence of all obstacles, because there does not exist anything for the sake of which it acts, and which, in the absence of all obstacles, would necessitate the action: the act simply follows the will. But, some might ask, even if we admit the correctness of all this, is not change imputed in the fact that the will of the being exists at one time and not at another? I reply thus: The true essence of the will of a being is simply the faculty of conceiving a desire at one time and not conceiving it at another. In the case of corporeal beings, the will which aims at a certain external object changes according to obstacles and circumstances. But the will of an absolutely spiritual being which does not depend on external causes is unchangeable, and the fact that the being desires one thing one day and another thing another day, does not imply a change in the essence of that being, or necessitate the existence of an external cause [of this change in the desire]. Similarly, it has been shown by us that if a being acted at one time and did not act at another, this would not involve a change in the being itself. It is now clear that the term "will" is homonymously[32] used of human will and of the will of God, there being no comparison whatever between God's will and that of a human being. The objection is refuted, and our theory is not shaken by it. This is all we desire to establish.

The third method[33] employed in proving the eternity of the universe is this: whatever the wisdom of God finds necessary to produce is produced automatically by that fact alone. But this wisdom, being His Essence, is eternal, and that which results from His wisdom must be eternal.

This is a very weak argument. As we do not understand why the wisdom of God produced nine spheres, neither more nor less, or why He fixed the number and size of the stars exactly as they are; so we cannot understand why His wisdom at a certain time caused the universe to exist, while a short time before it had not been in existence. All things owe their existence to His eternal and constant wisdom, but we are utterly ignorant of the ways and methods of that wisdom, since, according to our opinion, His will is identical with His wisdom, and all His attributes are one and the same thing, namely, His Essence or Wisdom. More will be said on this question in the section on Providence.[34] Thus this objection to our theory falls likewise to the ground.

There is no evidence for the theory of the eternity of the universe, neither in the fact cited by Aristotle of the general consent of the ancient peoples when they describe the heavens as the habitation of the angels and of God,[35] nor in the apparent concurrence of scriptural texts with this belief. These facts merely prove that the heavens lead us to believe in the existence of the Intelligences,[36] i.e. Forms[37] and angels, and that these lead us to believe in the existence of God; for He sets them in motion, and rules them. We will explain and show that there is no better evidence for the existence of a creator, as we believe, than that furnished by the heavens; but also according to the opinion of the philosophers, as has been mentioned by us, they give evidence that a being exists that sets them in motion, and that this being is neither a corporeal body nor a force residing in a body.

Having proved that our theory is admissible, and not impossible, as those who defend the eternity of the universe assert, I will, in the chapters which follow, show that our theory is preferable from a philosophical point of view, and expose the absur-

32 See glossary entry for 'homonymous.'
33 This is the *seventh method* found in selection III.4.2.
34 Not included in these selections.
35 See the *eighth method* found in selection III.4.2.
36 I.e., the eternally existent, immaterial minds of neo-Platonic cosmology, whose reality was accepted by many thinkers during the middle ages both in Islam and Christendom.
37 The reference is probably to the Forms postulated by Plato and which Plotinus and his neo-Platonist followers effectively replaced with the Intelligences. But it may refer to the "separated forms" Aristotle believed in. See glossary entry for 'form/matter.'

dities implied in the theory of Aristotle.

Chapter XIX

It has been shown that according to Aristotle, and according to all who defend his theory, the universe is inseparable from God; He is the cause, and the universe the effect; and this effect is a necessary one; and as it cannot be explained why or how God exists in this particular manner, namely being one and incorporeal, so it cannot be asked concerning the whole universe why or how it exists in this particular way. For it is necessary that the whole, the cause as well as the effect, exist in this particular manner, it is impossible for them not to exist, or to be different from what they actually are. This leads to the conclusion that the nature of everything remains constant, that nothing changes its nature in any way, and that such a change is impossible in any existing thing. It would also follow that the universe is not the result of design, choice, and desire; for if this were the case, they would have been non-existing before the design had been conceived.

We, however, hold that all things in the universe are the result of design, and not merely of necessity; He who designed them may change them when He changes His design. But not every design is subject to change; for there are things which are impossible, and their nature cannot be altered, as will be explained. Here, in this chapter, I merely wish to show by arguments almost as forcible as real proofs, that the universe gives evidence of design; but I will not fall into the error in which the Mutakallemim[38] have so much distinguished themselves, namely, of ignoring the existing nature of things or assuming the existence of atoms, or the successive creation of accidents, or any of their propositions which I have tried to explain, and which are intended to establish the principle of divine selection.[39] You must not, however, think that they understood the principle in the same sense as we do, although they undoubtedly aimed

at the same thing, and mentioned the same things which we also will mention, when they treated of divine selection. For they do not distinguish between selection in the case of a plant to make it red and not white, or sweet and not bitter, and determination in the case of the heavens which give them their peculiar geometrical form and did not give them a triangular or quadrilateral shape. The Mutakallemim established the principle of determination by means of their propositions, which have been enumerated above.[40] I establish this principle only as far as necessary, and only by philosophical propositions based on the nature of things. But before I begin my argument, I will state the following facts: Matter is common to things different from each other; there must be either one external cause which endows this matter partly with one property, partly with another, or there must be as many different causes as there are different forms of the matter common to all things. This is admitted by those who assume the eternity of the universe. After having premised this proposition, I will proceed with the discussion of our theme from an Aristotelian point of view, in the form of a dialogue.

We: You have proved that all things in the sublunary world have one common substance; why then do the species of things vary? why are the *individuals* in each species different from each other?

Aristotelian: Because the composition of the things formed of that substance varies. For the common substance[41] at first received four different forms, and each form was endowed with two qualities, and through these four qualities the substance was turned into the elements of which all things are formed. The composition of the elements takes place in the following manner: First they are mixed in consequence of the motion of the spheres, and then they combine together; a cause for variation arises then in the variation of the degree of heat, cold, moisture, and dryness of the elements which

---

38 See selection III.4.1, fn.12.

39 I.e., the "theory of determination" or "preference" mentioned in the fifth and sixth arguments of selection III.4.1.

40 But not in any selection in this volume.

41 I.e., the prime matter which is a substratum common to the elements. See glossary entry for 'element.'

form the constituent parts of the things. By these different combinations things are variously predisposed to receive different forms; and so on. Each generic form finds a wide sphere in its substance both as regards quality and quantity; and the individuals of the classes vary accordingly. This is fully explained in natural science. It is quite correct and clear to all who readily acknowledge truth, and do not wish to deceive themselves.

We: Since the combination of the elements prepares substances and enables them to receive different forms, what has prepared the first substance and caused one part of it to receive the form of fire, another part the form of earth, and the parts between these two the forms of water and of air, since one substance is common to all? Through what has the substance of earth become more fit for the form of earth, and the substance of fire more fit for that of fire?

Ar.: The difference of the elements was caused by their different position; for the different places prepared the same substance differently, in the following way: the portion nearest the surrounding sphere[42] became more rarified and swifter in motion, and thus approaching the nature of that sphere, it received by this preparation the form of fire. The farther the substance is away from the surrounding sphere towards the center, the denser, the more solid, and the less luminous it is; it becomes earth; the same is the cause of the formation of water and air. This is necessarily so; for it would be absurd to deny that each part of the substance is in a certain place; or to assume that the surface is identical with the center, or the center with the surface. This difference in place determined the different forms, i.e., predisposed the substance to receive different forms.

We: Is the substance of the surrounding sphere, i.e., the heavens, the same as that of the elements?

Ar.: No; the substance is different, and the forms are different. The term "body" is homonymously used of these bodies below and of the heavens, as

has been shown by modern philosophers. All this has been demonstrated by proof.

But let now the reader of this treatise hear what I have to say. Aristotle has proven that the difference of forms becomes evident by the difference of actions. Since, therefore, the motion of the elements is rectilinear, and that of the spheres circular, we infer that the substances are different. This inference is supported by natural science. When we further notice that substances with rectilinear motion differ in their directions, that some move upward, some downward, and that substances which move in the same direction have different velocities, we infer that their forms must be different. Thus we learn that there are four elements. In the same way we come to the conclusion that the substance of all the spheres is the same, since they all have circular motion. Their forms, however, are different, since one sphere moves from east to west, and another from west to east;[43] and their motions have also different velocities. We can now put the following question to Aristotle: There is one substance common to all spheres; each one has its own peculiar form. "Who thus determined and predisposed these spheres to receive different forms? Is there above the spheres any being capable of determining this except God? I will show the profundity and the extraordinary acumen which Aristotle displayed when this question troubled him. He strove very hard to meet this objection with arguments, which, however, were not borne out by facts. Although he does not mention this objection, it is clear from his words that he endeavours to show the nature of the spheres, as he has shown that of the things in the sublunary world. Everything is, according to him, the result of a law of Nature, and not the result of the design of a being that designs as it likes, or the determination of a being that determines as it pleases. He has not carried out the idea consistently, and it will never be done. He tries indeed to find the cause why the sphere moves from east and not from west; why some spheres move with greater velocity, others with less velocity, and he finds the cause of these differences in their different positions in reference to the uppermost

---

42 I.e., the outermost of all the heavenly spheres, which surrounds the whole universe.
43 The latter sort are required in the Ptolemaic system to explain the "retrograde" motion of some of the planets.

sphere. He further attempts to show why there are several spheres for each of the seven planets, while there is only one sphere for the large number of fixed stars. For all this he endeavours to state the reason. so as to show that the whole order is the necessary result of the laws of Nature. He has not attained his object. For as regards the things in the sublunary world, his explanations are in accordance with facts, and the relation between cause and effect is clearly shown. It can therefore be assumed that everything is the necessary result of the motions and influences of the spheres. But when he treats of the properties of the spheres, he does not clearly show the causal relation, nor does he explain the phenomena in that systematic way which the hypothesis of natural laws would demand. For let us consider the spheres: in one case a sphere with greater velocity is above a sphere with less velocity, in another case we notice the reverse; in a third case there are two spheres with equal velocities, one above the other. There are, besides, other phenomena which speak strongly against the hypothesis that all is regulated by the laws of Nature, and I will devote a special chapter to the discussion of these phenomena.[44] In short, there is no doubt that Aristotle knew the weakness of his arguments in tracing and describing the cause of all these things, and therefore he prefaces his researches on these things as follows: "We will now thoroughly investigate two problems, which it is our proper duty to investigate and to discuss according to our capacity, wisdom, and opinion. This our attempt must not be attributed to presumption and pride, but to our extraordinary zeal in the study of philosophy; when we attempt the highest and grandest problems, and endeavour to offer some proper solution, everyone that hears it should rejoice and be pleased."[45]

So far Aristotle. This shows that he undoubtedly knew the weakness of this theory. How much weaker must it appear when we bear in mind that the science of astronomy was not yet fully developed, and that in the days of Aristotle the motions of the spheres were not known so well as they are at present. I think that it was the object of Aristotle in attributing in his *Metaphysics* one Intelligence to

every sphere, to assume the existence of something capable of determining the peculiar course of each sphere. Later on I will show that he has not gained anything thereby; but now I will explain the words, "according to our capacity, wisdom, and opinion," occurring in the passage which we quoted. I have not noticed that any of the commentators explain them. The term "our opinion" refers to the principle that everything is the result of natural laws, or to the theory of the eternity of the universe. By "our wisdom" he meant the knowledge of that which is clear and generally accepted, viz., that the existence of every one of these things is due to a certain cause, and not to chance. By "our capacity" he meant the insufficiency of our intellect to find the causes of all these things. He only intended to trace the causes for a few of them; and so he did. For he gives an excellent reason why the sphere of the fixed stars moves slowly, while the other spheres move with greater velocity, namely, because its motion is in a different direction [from that of the uppermost sphere]. He further says that the more distant a sphere is from the eighth sphere the greater is its velocity. But this rule does not hold good in all cases, as I have already explained. More forcible still is the following objection: There are spheres below the eighth that move from east to west. Of these each upper one, according to this rule, would have a greater velocity than the lower one; and the velocity of these spheres would almost equal that of the ninth sphere. But astronomy had, in the days of Aristotle, not yet developed to the height it has reached at present.

According to our theory of the creation, all this can easily be explained; for we say that there is a being that determines the direction and the velocity of the motion of each sphere; but we do not know the reason why the wisdom of that being gave to each sphere its peculiar property. If Aristotle had been able to state the cause of the difference in the motion of the spheres, and show that it corresponded as he thought to their relative positions, this would have been excellent, and the variety in their motions would be explained in the same way as the variety of the elements, by their relative position between the center and surface; but this is

---

44 Not included in the selections in this volume.
45 From *On the Heavens (De Caelo)* II, 291b24-28. The translation given by Maimonides is not all that accurate.

not the case, as I said before.

There is a phenomenon in the spheres which more clearly shows the existence of voluntary determination; it cannot be explained otherwise than by assuming that some being designed it: this phenomenon is the existence of the stars. The fact that the sphere is constantly in motion, while the stars remain stationary, indicates that the substance of the stars is different from that of the spheres. Abu-nasr[46] has already mentioned the fact in his additions to the *Physics* of Aristotle. He says: "There is a difference between the stars and the spheres; for the spheres are transparent, the stars are opaque; and the cause of this is that there is a difference, however small it may be, between their substances and forms." So far Abu Nasr. But I do not say that there is a small difference, but a very great difference; because I do not infer if from the transparency of the spheres, but from their motions. I am convinced that there are three different kinds of substance, with three different forms, namely: (1) Bodies which never move of their own accord; such are the bodies of the stars; (2) bodies which always move, such are the bodies of the spheres; (3) bodies which both move and rest, such are the elements. Now, I ask, what has united these two bodies, which, according to my opinion, differ very much from each other, though, according to Abu Nasr, only a little? Who has prepared the bodies for this union? In short, it would be strange that, without the existence of design, one of two different bodies should be joined to the other in such a manner that it is fixed to it in a certain place but does not combine with it. It is still more difficult to explain the existence of the numerous stars in the eighth sphere; they are all spherical; some of them are large, some small; here we notice two stars apparently distant from each other one cubit; there a group of ten close together; whilst in another place there is a large space without any star. What determined that the one small part should have ten stars, and the other portion should be without any star? And the whole body of the sphere being uniform throughout, why should a particular star occupy

the one place and not another? The answer to these and similar questions is very difficult, and almost impossible, if we assume that all emanates from God as the necessary result of certain permanent laws, as Aristotle holds.

But if we assume that all this is the result of design, there is nothing strange or improbable; and the only question to be asked is this: What is the cause of this design? The answer to this question is that all this has been made for a certain purpose, though we do not know it; there is nothing that is done in vain, or by chance. It is well known that the veins and nerves of an individual dog or ass are not the result of chance; their magnitude is not determined by chance; nor is it by chance, but for a certain purpose, that one vein is thick, another thin; that one nerve has many branches, another has none; that one goes down straight, while another is bent; it is well known that all this must be just as it is. How, then, can any reasonable person imagine that the position, magnitude, and number of the stars, or the various courses of their spheres, are purposeless, or the result of chance? There is no doubt that every one of these things is necessary and in accordance with a certain design; and it is extremely improbable that these things should be the necessary result of natural laws, and not that of design.

The best proof for design in the universe I find in the different motions of the spheres, and in the fixed position of the stars in the spheres. For this reason you find all the prophets point to the spheres and stars when they want to prove that there must exist a divine being. Thus Abraham reflected on the stars, as is well known; Isaiah[47] exhorts to learn from them the existence of God, and says, "Lift up your eyes on high, and behold who hath created these things?" Jeremiah [calls God] "the maker of the heavens"; Abraham calls Him "the God of the heavens";[48] [Moses], the chief of the Prophets, uses the phrase explained by us, "He who rideth on the heavens."[49] The proof taken from the heavens is convincing; for the variety of things in the sublunary world, though their sub-

46 I.e., Alfarabi. See selection **III.4.1**, fn.12.
47 xl.26.
48 *Genesis*, 24:7.
49 *Deuteronomy*, 33:26.

stance is one and the same, can be explained as the work of the influences of the spheres, or the result of the variety in the position of the substance in relation to the spheres, as has been shown by Aristotle. But who has determined the variety in the spheres and the stars, if not the will of God? To say that the Intelligences[50] have determined it is of no use whatever; for the Intelligences are not corporeal, and have no local relation to the spheres. Why then should the one sphere in its desire to approach the Intelligence, move eastward, and another westward? Is the one Intelligence in the east, the other in the west? or why does one move with great velocity, another slowly? This difference is not in accordance with their distances from each other, as is well known. We must then say that the nature and essence of each sphere necessitated its motion in a certain direction, and in a certain manner, as the consequence of its desire to approach its Intelligence. Aristotle clearly expresses this opinion. We thus have returned to the part from which we started; and we ask, Since the substance of all things is the same, what made the nature of one portion different from another? Why has this sphere a desire which produces a motion different from that which the desire of another sphere produces? This must have been done by an agent capable of determining. We have thus been brought to examine two questions: (1) Is it necessary to assume that the variety of the things in the universe is the result of design, and not of fixed laws of Nature, or is it not necessary? (2) Assuming that all this is the result of design, does it follow that it has been created after not having existed, or does *creatio ex nihilo* not follow, and has the being which has determined all this done always so? Some of those who believe in the eternity of the universe hold the last opinion. I will now begin the examination of these two questions, and explain them as much as necessary in the following chapters.

III.4.4. The view that God has produced the Universe from all Eternity and how it is to be evaluated (*The Guide for the Perplexed*, part 2, chs.2 1-23)

Some of the recent philosophers who adhere to the theory of the eternity of the universe hold that God produces the universe, that He by His will designs and determines its existence and form; they reject, however, the theory that this act took place at one certain time, and assume that this always has been the case, and will always be so. The circumstances that we cannot imagine an agent otherwise than preceding the result of its action, they explain by the fact that this is invariably the case in all that we produce; because for agents of the same kind as we are, there are some moments in which they are not active, and are only agents potentially; they become agents when they act. But as regards God there are no moments of non-action, or of potentiality in any respect; He is not before His work, He is always an actual agent. And as there is a great difference between His essence and ours, so is also a great difference between the relation of His work to Him and the relation of our work to us. They apply the same argument to will and determination; for there is no difference in this respect whether we say He acts, wills, designs, or determines. They further assume that change in His action or will is inadmissible. It is therefore clear that these philosophers abandoned the term "necessary result," but retained the theory of it; they perhaps sought to use a better expression, or to remove an objectionable term. For it is the same thing, whether we say in accordance with the view of Aristotle that the universe is the result of the first cause, and must be eternal as that cause is eternal, or in accordance with these philosophers that the universe is the result of the act, design, will, selection, and determination of God, but it has always been so, and will always be so; in the same manner as the rising of the sun undoubtedly produces the day, and yet does not precede it. But when we speak of design we do not mean it in this sense; we mean to express by it that the universe is not the "necessary result" of God's existence, as the effect

---

50 See glossary entry for 'intelligence.'

is the necessary result of the efficient cause; in the latter case the effect cannot be separated from the cause; it cannot change unless the cause changes entirely, or at least in some respect. If we accept this explanation we easily see how absurd it is to say that the universe is in the same relation to God as the effect is to the efficient cause, and to assume at the same time that the universe is the result of the action and determination of God.

Having fully explained this subject, we come to the question whether the cause, which must be assumed for the variety of properties noticed in the heavenly beings, is merely an efficient cause, that must necessarily produce that variety as its effect, or whether that variety is due to a determining agent, such as we believe, in accordance with the theory of Moses our Teacher. Before I discuss this question I will first explain fully what Aristotle means by "necessary result"; after that I will show by such philosophical arguments as are free from every fallacy why I prefer the theory of *creatio ex nihilo*. It is clear that when he says that the first Intelligence is the necessary result of the existence of God, the second Intelligence the result of the existence of the first, the third of the second [and so on], and that the spheres are the necessary result of the existence of the Intelligences, and so forth, in the well-known order which you learned from passages dealing with it, and of which we have given a summary in this part[51] – he does not mean that the one thing was first in existence, and then the second came as the necessary result of the first; he denies that any one of these beings has had a beginning. By "necessary result" he merely refers to the causal relation; he means to say that the first Intelligence is the cause of the existence of the second; the second of the third, and so on to the last of the Intelligences; and the same is also the case as regards the spheres and the prime matter; none of these preceded another, or has been in existence without the existence of that other. We say, e.g., that the necessary result of the primary qualities

are roughness [and] smoothness, hardness [and] softness, porosity and solidity; and no person doubts that heat, cold, moisture, and dryness are the causes of smoothness and roughness, of hardness and softness, porosity and solidity, and similar qualities, and that the latter are the necessary result of those four primary qualities.[52] And yet it is impossible that a body should exist with the primary qualities without the secondary ones; for the relation between the two sets of qualities is that of causality, not that of agent and its product. Just in the same way the term "necessary result" is used by Aristotle in reference to the whole universe, when he says that one portion is the result of the other, and continues the series up to the first cause as he calls it, or first Intellect, if you prefer this term. For we all mean the same, only with this difference, that according to Aristotle everything besides that being is the necessary result of the latter, as I have already mentioned; while, according to our opinion, that being created the whole universe with design and will, so that the universe which had not been in existence before, has by His will come into existence. I will now begin in the following chapters my proofs for the superiority of our theory, that of *creatio ex nihilo*.

Chapter XXII

Aristotle and all philosophers assume as an axiom that a simple element can only produce one simple thing, while a compound can produce as many things as it contains simple elements; e.g., fire combines in itself two properties, heat and dryness; it gives heat by the one property, and produces dryness by the other; an object composed of matter and form produces certain things on account of its matter, and others on account of its form, if [both matter and form] consist of several elements. In accordance with this axiom, Aristotle holds that the direct emanation from God must be one simple Intelligence, and nothing else.[53]

---

51 I.e., in an earlier chapter not included in these selections.
52 In Aristotle's theory of the elements the two oppositions, hot vs. cold, and dry vs. wet, are the basis for the four elements: earth, air, fire and water. See glossary entry for 'element.'
53 The theory of emanation is not in fact one Aristotle held. It was developed by Plotinus in the third century C.E. and became part of the neo-Platonic synthesis which he taught. Some of Plotinus's writings were ascribed to Aristotle in both Islam and Christendom during the middle ages.

A second axiom assumed by him is this: Things are not produced by other things at random; there must be some relation between cause and effect. Thus accidents are not produced by accidents promiscuously; quality cannot be the cause of quantity, nor quantity of quality; a form cannot emanate from matter, nor matter from form.

A third axiom is this: A single agent that acts with design and will, and not merely by the force of the laws of nature, can produce different objects.

A fourth axiom is as follows: An object, whose several elements are only connected by juxtaposition, is more properly a compound than an object whose different elements have entirely combined; e.g., bone, flesh, veins, or nerves, are more simple than the hand or the foot, that are a combination of bone, flesh, veins, and nerves. This is very clear and requires no further explanation.

Having premised these axioms, I ask the following question: Aristotle holds that the first Intelligence is the cause of the second, the second of the third, and so on, till the thousandth, if we assume a series of that number. Now the first Intellect is undoubtedly simple. How then can the compound form of existing things come from such an Intellect by fixed laws of nature, as Aristotle assumes? We admit all he said concerning the Intelligences, that the further they are away from the first, the greater is the variety of their compounds, in consequence of the larger number of the objects comprehensible by the Intelligences; but even after admitting this, the question remains: By what law of nature did the spheres emanate from the Intelligences? What relation is there between material and immaterial beings? Suppose we admit that each sphere emanates from an Intelligence of the form mentioned; that the Intelligence, including, as it were, two elements, in so far as it comprehends itself and another thing, produces the next Intelligence by the one element, and a sphere by the other; but the question would then be how the one simple element could produce the sphere, that contains two substances and two forms, namely, the substance and the form of the sphere, and also the substance and the form of the star fixed in

that sphere. For, according to the laws of nature, the compound can only emanate from a compound. There must therefore be one element, from which the body of the sphere emanates, and another element, from which the body of the star emanates. This would be necessary even if the substance of all stars were the same; but it is possible that the luminous stars have not the same substance as the non-luminous stars;[54] it is besides well known that each body has its own matter and its own form. It must now be clear that this emanation could not have taken place by the force of the laws of nature, as Aristotle contends. Nor does the difference of the motions of the spheres follow the order of their positions; and therefore it cannot be said that this difference is the result of certain laws of nature. We have already mentioned this (ch. xix).[55]

There is in the properties of the spheres another circumstance that is opposed to the assumed laws of nature; namely, if the substance of all spheres is the same, why does it not occur that the form of one sphere combines with the substance of another sphere, as is the case with things on earth, simply because their substance is fit [for such changes]? If the substance of all spheres is the same, if it is not assumed that each has a peculiar substance, and if, contrary to all principles, the peculiar motion of each sphere is no evidence for the special character of its substance, why then should a certain form constantly remain united with a certain substance? Again, if the stars have all one substance, by what are they distinguished from each other? Is it by forms? Or by accidents?

Whichever be the case, the forms or the accidents would interchange, so that they would successively unite with everyone of the stars, so long as their substance [being the same] admits the combinations [with every one of the forms or the accidents]. This shows that the term substance, when used of the spheres or the stars, does not mean the same as it signifies when used of the substance of earthly things, but is applied to the two homonymously. It further shows that every one of the bodies of the spheres has its own peculiar form of existence dif-

---

54 All the heavenly bodies including the sun, the moon, the planets, as well as the "fixed stars" are called stars here. It was recognized that at least the moon did not give off its own light but reflected the light of the sun.
55 See the preceding selection.

ferent from that of all other beings. Why then is circular motion common to all spheres, and why is the fixed position of the stars in their respective spheres common to all stars? If we, however, assume design and determination of a creator, in accordance with His incomprehensible wisdom, all these difficulties disappear. They must arise when we consider the whole universe, not as the result of free will, but as the result of fixed laws of nature: a theory which, on the one hand, is not in harmony with the existing order of things, and does not offer for it a sufficient reason or argument; and, on the other hand, implies many and great improbabilities. For, according to this theory, God, whose perfection in every respect is recognised by all thinking persons, is in such a relation to the universe that He cannot change anything; if He wished to make the wing of a fly longer, or to reduce the number of the legs of a worm by one, He could not accomplish it. According to Aristotle, He does not try such a thing, and it is wholly impossible for Him to desire any change in the existing order of things; if He could, it would not increase His perfection; it might, on the contrary, from some point of view, diminish it.

Although I know that many partial critics will ascribe my opinion concerning the theory of Aristotle to insufficient understanding, or to intentional opposition, I will not refrain from stating in short the results of my researches, however poor my capacities may be. I hold that the theory of Aristotle is undoubtedly correct as far as the things are concerned which exist between the sphere of the moon and center of the earth. Only an ignorant person rejects it, or a person with preconceived opinions of his own, which he desires to maintain and to defend, and which lead him to ignore clear facts. But what Aristotle says concerning things above the sphere of the moon is, with few exceptions, mere imagination and opinion; to a still greater extent this applies to his system of Intelligences, and to some of his metaphysical views; they include great improbabilities, [promote] ideas which all nations consider as evidently corrupt, and cause views to spread which cannot be proved.

It may be asked why I have enumerated all the doubts which can be raised against the theory of Aristotle; whether by mere doubts a theory can be overthrown, or its opposite established? This is certainly not the case. But we treat this philosopher exactly as his followers tell us to do. For Alexander[56] stated that when a theory cannot be established by proof, the two most opposite views should be compared as to the doubts entertained concerning each of them, and that view which admits of fewer doubts should be accepted. Alexander further says that this rule applies to all those opinions of Aristotle in *Metaphysics* for which he offered no proof. For those that followed Aristotle believed that his opinions are far less subject to doubt than any other opinion. We follow the same rule. Being convinced that the question whether the heavens are eternal or not cannot be decided by proof, neither in the affirmative nor in the negative, we have enumerated the objections raised to either view, and shown how the theory of the eternity of the universe is subject to stronger objections, and is more apt to corrupt the notions concerning God [than the other]. Another argument can be drawn from the fact that the theory of the creation was held by our Father Abraham, and by our Teacher Moses.

Having mentioned the method of testing the two theories by the objections raised against them, I find it necessary to give some further explanation of the subject.

Chapter XXIII

In comparing the objections raised against one theory with those raised against the opposite theory, in order to decide in favor of the least objectionable, we must not consider the number of the objections, but the degree of improbability and of deviation from real facts [pointed out by the objections]; for one objection may sometimes have more weight than a thousand others. But the comparison cannot be trustworthy unless the two theories be considered with the same interest, and if you are predisposed in favor of one of them, be it on account of your training or because of some advan-

---

56 Alexander of Aphrodisias, whose interpretative work on Aristotle around 200 C.E. revived the peripatetic school of philosophy in late antiquity.

tage, you are too blind to see the truth. For that which can be demonstrated[57] you cannot reject, however much you may be inclined against it; but in questions like those under consideration you are apt to dispute [in consequence of your inclination]. You will, however, be able to decide the question, as far as necessary, if you free yourself from passions, ignore customs, and follow only your reason. But many are the conditions which must be fulfilled. First you must know your mental capacities and your natural talents; you will find this out when you study all mathematical sciences, and are well acquainted with Logic. Secondly, you must have a thorough knowledge of natural science, that you may be able to understand the nature of the objections. Thirdly, you must be morally good. For if a person is voluptuous or passionate, and, loosening the reins, allows his anger to pass the just limits, it makes no difference whether he is so from nature or from habit, he will blunder and stumble in his way, he will seek the theory which is in accordance with his inclinations. I mention this lest you be deceived; for a person might some day, by some objection which he raises, shake your belief in the theory of the creation, and then easily mislead you; you would then adopt the theory [of the eternity of the universe] which is contrary to the fundamental principles of our religion, and leads to "speaking words that turn away from God." You must rather have suspicion against your own reason, and accept the theory taught by two prophets who have laid the foundation for the existing order in the religious and social relations of mankind. Only demonstrative proof should be able to make you abandon the theory of the creation; but such a proof does not exist in nature....

---

57 I.e., given a strict logical proof from self-evident axioms and definitions, as in mathematics. See glossary entry for 'demonstration.'

III.5. ST. THOMAS AQUINAS

IN SOME WAYS AQUINAS ADOPTED THE POSITION OF MAIMONIDES, whose *Guide* he knew well. He does not believe it is possible to give strict proofs for either the affirmative or negative reply to the question of whether the physical world has existed from eternity. But he departs from Maimonides on the question of whether God could have created a world that had no beginning to its existence. He thinks it is sufficient to prove the affirmative answer to this question that it be shown simply that there is no explicit or implicit contradiction in such an idea.

III.5.1. That it is not necessary for Creatures to have existed always (*Summa Contra Gentiles* or *On the Truth of the Catholic Faith*, bk.II, ch.31)

[1] It remains for us to show from the foregoing that it is not necessary for created things to have existed from eternity.

[2] For, if the existence of the whole universe of creatures, or of any single creature, is necessary, then its necessity must be derived either from itself or from something else. But it cannot owe its necessity to itself; for we proved above[1] that every being must derive its existence from the first being. But anything whose being is not self-derived cannot possibly have necessary existence from itself, because that which necessarily is cannot not-be; so, whatever of itself has necessary existence is for that reason incapable of not being; and it follows that it is not a non-being, and hence is a being.

[3] But, if the creature's necessity of which we speak is derived from something other than itself, then this must be from some extrinsic cause; for whatever is received within a creature owes its being to another. An extrinsic cause, however, is either an efficient or a final[2] one. Now, from the efficient cause it follows that the effect exists necessarily when the agent necessarily acts; for it is through the agent's action that the effect depends on the efficient cause. Consequently, if the agent need not act in order to produce the effect, then it is not absolutely necessary for the effect to be. God, however, acts out of no necessity in the production of creatures, as we have shown.[3] Therefore, it is not absolutely necessary for the creature to be, as concerns necessity dependent on the efficient cause. Nor is it necessary as regards dependence on the final cause. For the means to an end derive necessity from the end only so far as without them the end either cannot be – life cannot be preserved without food – or cannot well be – as a journey without a horse. Now, as we have shown in Book I, the end of God's will, whereby things came into being, cannot be anything else than His own goodness.[4] But the divine goodness does not depend on creatures, either as to being, since it is necessarily existent in virtue of itself, or as to well-being, since it is by itself absolutely perfect. (All these points have been previously[5] demonstrated.) Therefore, it is not absolutely necessary for a creature to exist; nor, then, is it necessary to maintain that a creature always existed.

[4] Consider, also, that nothing proceeding from a will is absolutely necessary, except when it chances to be necessary for the will to will it. But, as we have shown,[6] God brings creatures into being not through a necessity of His nature, but volun-

---

1 See *SCG* II, ch. 15. Not included in these selections.
2 See glossary entry for 'final cause.'
3 See *SCG* II, ch. 23. Not included in these selections.
4 *SCG* I, ch. 75-80. Not included in this volume but see selection **I.5.2.**
5 *SCG* I, ch. 13 and 28. Not included in these selections.
6 See *SCG* II, ch. 23. Not included in these selections.

tarily. Nor, as proved in Book I, does He necessarily will the existence of creatures.[7] Hence, it is not absolutely necessary for the creature to be, and therefore neither is it necessary for creatures to have existed always.

[5] Moreover, we proved above[8] that God's action is not outside Himself, as though passing from Him and terminating in the created thing, in the way in which heat issues from fire and terminates in wood. On the contrary, His act of will is identical with His action; and things are as God wills them to be. But it is not necessary that God will a creature to have existed always, for indeed, as we proved in Book I, it is not necessary that God will a creature to be at all.[9] Hence, it is not necessary for a creature to have always been.

[6] Then, too, a thing does not proceed necessarily from a voluntary agent except because of something due. But, as we have shown above,[10] it is not by reason of any debt that God brings the creature into being, if the universal production of creatures be considered absolutely. Therefore, God does not of necessity produce the creature. Nor, then, is it necessary that God should have produced the creature from eternity because He Himself is eternal.

[7] Also, we have just shown[11] that absolute necessity in created things results not from a relation to a first principle which is of itself necessarily existent, namely, God, but from a relation to other causes whose existence is not essentially necessary. But the necessity arising from a relation to that which is not of itself necessarily existent does not make it necessary for something to have always existed; if a thing runs, it follows that it is in motion, yet it is not necessary for it to have always been in motion, because the running itself is not essentially necessary. There is, therefore, no necessity that creatures should have existed always.

III.5.2. That God could have created an eternal World (*On the Eternity of the World*)

[1] If we suppose, in accord with Catholic faith, that the world has not existed from eternity but had a beginning of its duration, the question arises whether it could have existed forever. In seeking the true solution of this problem, we should start by distinguishing points of agreement with our opponents from points of disagreement.

If the question is phrased in such a way as to inquire whether something besides God could have existed forever, that is, whether a thing could exist even though it was not made by God, we are confronted with an abominable error against faith. More than that, the error is repudiated by philosophers, who avow and demonstrate that nothing at all can exist unless it was caused by Him who supremely and in a uniquely true sense has existence.

However, if we inquire whether something has always existed, understanding that it was caused by God with regard to all the reality found in it, we have to examine whether such a position can be maintained. If we should decide that this is impossible, the reason will be either that God could not make a thing that has always existed, or that the thing could not come to be, even though God were able to make it. As to the first alternative, all parties are agreed that God could make something that has always existed, because of the fact that His power is infinite.

[2] Accordingly our task is to examine whether something which has always existed could possibly have been made. If we reply that this is impossible, our answer is unintelligible except in two senses or because there are two reasons for its truth: either because of the absence of passive potentiality, or because of incompatibility in the concepts involved.

The first sense may be explained as follows. Before an angel was made, an angel could not have

---

7 *SCG* I, ch. 81. Not included in this volume but see selections **I.5.2-3.**
8 See *SCG* II, ch. 9 and 23. Not included in these selections.
9 *SCG* I, ch. 81. Not included in this volume but see selections **I.5.2-3.**
10 See *SCG* II, ch. 28. Not included in these selections.
11 *SCG* II, ch. 30. See selection **I.5.1.**

come to be, because no passive potentiality is at hand prior to the angel's existence, since the angel was not made out of pre-existing matter. Yet God could have made the angel, and could also have caused the angel to come to be, because in fact He has made angels and they have come to be. Understanding the question in this way, we must simply concede, in accordance with faith, that a thing caused by God cannot always exist, because such a position would imply that a passive potentiality has always existed, which is heretical. However, this does not require the conclusion that God cannot bring it about that always some being comes to be.

Taken in the second sense, the argument runs that something cannot be so made because the concepts are incompatible, in the same way as affirmation and denial cannot be simultaneously true; yet certain people assert that even this is within God's power. Others contend that not even God could make such a thing, because it is nothing. However, it is clear that He cannot bring this about, because the power by which it is supposed to be effected would be self-destructive. Nevertheless, if it is alleged that God is able to do such things, the position is not heretical, although I think it is false, just as the proposition that a past event did not take place involves a contradiction. Hence Augustine, in his book against Faustus, writes as follows: "Whoever says, 'If God is omnipotent, let Him bring it about that what has been made was not made,' does not perceive that what he really says is this: 'If God is omnipotent, let Him bring it about that what is true is false for the very reason that it is true.'"[12] Still, some great masters have piously asserted that God can cause a past event not to have taken place in the past; and this was not esteemed heretical.

[3] We must investigate, therefore, whether these two concepts are logically incompatible, namely, that a thing has been caused by God and yet has always existed. Whatever may be the truth of the matter, no heresy is involved in the contention that God is able to bring it about that something caused by Him should always have existed. Nevertheless I believe that, if the concepts were to be found incompatible, this position would be false.

However, if there is no contradiction in the concepts, not only is it not false, but it is even possible; to maintain anything else would be erroneous. Since God's omnipotence surpasses all understanding and power, anyone who asserts that something which is intelligible among creatures cannot be made by God, openly disparages God's omnipotence. Nor can anyone appeal to the case of sin; sins, as such, are nothing.

The whole question comes to this, whether the ideas, to be created by God according to a thing's entire substance, and yet to lack a beginning of duration, are mutually repugnant or not. That no contradiction is involved, is shown as follows. A contradiction could arise only because of one of the two ideas or because of both of them together; and in the latter alternative, either because an efficient cause must precede its effect in duration, or because non-existence must precede existence in duration; in fact, this is the reason for saying that what is created by God is made from nothing.

[4] Consequently, we must first show that the efficient cause, namely God, need not temporally precede His effect, if that is what He Himself should wish.

In the first place, no cause producing its effect instantaneously need precede its effect temporally. Now God is a cause producing His effect, not by way of motion, but instantaneously. Therefore He need not temporally precede His effect. The major premise is clear from induction, based on all instantaneous changes, such as illumination, and the like. It can also he demonstrated by reasoning. In any instant in which a thing is asserted to exist, the beginning of its action can likewise be asserted, as is evident in all things capable of generation; the very instant in which fire begins to exist, it emits heat. But in instantaneous action, the beginning and the end of the action are simultaneous, or rather are identical, as in all indivisible things. Therefore, at any moment in which there is an agent producing its effect instantaneously, the terminus of its action can be realized. But the terminus of the action is simultaneous with the effect produced. Consequently no intellectual absurdity is implied if we suppose that a cause which produces its effect instantaneously does not precede its

---

12 *Contra Faustum*, XXVI, 5 (PL, 42, 481).

effect temporally. There would be such an absurdity in the case of causes that produce their effects by way of motion, because the beginning of motion must precede its end. Since people are accustomed to think of productions that are brought about by way of motion, they do not readily understand that an efficient cause does not have to precede its effect temporally. And that is why many, with their limited experience, attend to only a few aspects, and so are overhasty in airing their views.

This reasoning is not set aside by the observation that God is a cause acting through His will, because the will, too, does not have to precede its effect temporally. The same is true of the person who acts through his will, unless he acts after deliberation. Heaven forbid that we should attribute such a procedure to God!

[5] Moreover, the cause which produces the entire substance of a thing is no less able to produce that entire substance than a cause producing a form is in the production of the form; in fact, it is much more powerful, because it does not produce its effect by educing it from the potentiality of matter as is the case with the agent that produces a form.[13] But some agent that produces only a form can bring it about that the form produced by it exists at the moment the agent itself exists, as is exemplified by the shining sun. With far greater reason, God, who produces the entire substance of a thing, can cause His own effect to exist whenever He Himself exists.

Besides, if at any instant there is a cause with which the effect proceeding from it cannot co-exist at that same instant, the only reason is that some element required for complete causality is missing; for a complete cause and the effect caused exist together. But nothing complete has ever been wanting in God. Therefore an effect caused by Him can exist always, as long as He exists, and so He need not precede it temporally.

Furthermore, the will of a person who exercises his will suffers no loss in power. But all those who undertake to answer the arguments by which Aristotle proves that things have always had existence from God for the reason that the same cause always produces the same effect,[14] say that this consequence would follow if He were not an agent acting by His will. Therefore, although God is acknowledged to be an agent acting by His will, it nevertheless follows that He can bring it about that what is caused by Him should never have been without existence.

And so it is clear that no logical contradiction is involved in the assertion that an agent does not precede its effect in duration. As regards anything that does imply logical contradiction, however, God cannot bring it into being.

[6] We now proceed to inquire whether logical contradiction is latent in the position that a created thing was never without existence. The reason for doubting is that, since such a thing is said to have been made from nothing, non-existence must seemingly precede its existence in the temporal order. The absence of any contradiction is shown by Anselm in the eighth chapter of his *Monologium*, where he explains how a creature may be said to have been made from nothing. "The third interpretation," he states, "according to which something is said to have been made from nothing, is reasonable if we understand that the thing was, indeed, made, but that there is nothing from which it was made. In a like sense we may say that, when a man is saddened without cause, his sadness arises from nothing. In this sense, therefore, no absurdity will follow if the conclusion drawn above is kept in mind, namely, that with the exception of the supreme essence all things that exist were made by it out of nothing, that is, not out of something."[15] According to this explanation, then, it is clear that no order is established between what was made and nothing, as though what is made would first have to be nothing, and would afterward be something.

[7] To proceed further, let us suppose that the order alluded to above, namely, relationship to nothingness, remains asserted, so that the sense is this: the creature is made from nothing [ex nihilo] that is, it is made after nothing. The term "after" unquestionably connotes order. But order is of various kinds; there is a temporal order and an order

---

13 See glossary entry for 'form/matter.'

14 *Physics*, III, 4 (203b 27-30).

15 *Monologium*, 8 (PL, 158, 156; ed. Schmidt, I, 23).

of nature.[16] If, therefore, the distinctive and the particular do not follow from the common and the universal, it will not be necessary, just because the creature is said to exist subsequent to nothingness, that it should first have been nothing, in the temporal order, and should later be something. It is enough that in the order of nature it is nothing before it is a being; for that which befits a thing in itself is naturally found in it before that which it merely has from another. But a creature does not have existence except from another; regarded as left simply to itself, it is nothing; prior to its existence, therefore, nothingness is its natural lot. Nor, just because nothingness does not precede being in duration, does a thing have to be nothing and being at the same time. For our position is not that, if the creature has always existed, it was nothing at some time. We maintain that its nature is such that it would be nothing if it were left to itself; just as, if we say that the air was always illuminated by the sun, we must hold that the air has been made luminous by the sun. And because everything that comes into being comes from what is not contingent, that is, from that which does not happen to exist along with that which is said to become, we must assert that the air was made luminous from being not luminous or from being dark; not in the sense that it was ever non-luminous or dark, but in the sense that it would be such if it were left to itself alone. And this is brought out more clearly in the case of stars and planets that are always being illuminated by the sun.

[8] Thus it is evident that the statement that something was made by God and nevertheless was never without existence, does not involve any logical contradiction. If there were some contradiction, it is surprising that Augustine did not perceive it, as this would have been a most effective way of disproving the eternity of the world; and indeed he brings forward many arguments against the eternity of the world in the eleventh and twelfth books of *De civitate Dei*;[17] yet he completely ignores this line

of argumentation. In fact, he seems to suggest that no logical contradiction is discernible here. Thus in Book X, chap. 31 of *De civitate Dei*, he says of the Platonists: "They found a way of accounting for this by explaining that it was not a beginning of time but a principle of subordination. They point out that if a foot had always, from eternity, been planted in the dust, there would always be a footprint underneath, and no one would doubt that the footprint had been made by someone stepping there; and yet the foot would not be earlier than the print, although the print was made by the foot. In the same way, they continue, the world and the gods created in it have always existed, since He who made them has always existed, and nevertheless they were made."[18] Augustine never charges that this is unintelligible, but proceeds against his adversaries in another way. He also says, in Book XI, chap. 4: "They who admit that the world was made by God, yet do not wish it to have a beginning in time but only a beginning of its creation, so that it was always made in some sense that is scarcely intelligible, do indeed say something."[19] How and why this is scarcely intelligible, was touched on in the first argument.[20]

[9] Another surprising thing is that the best philosophers of nature failed to discern this contradiction. In the fifth chapter of the same book, Augustine, writing against those who were mentioned in the preceding reference, remarks: "Our present discussion is with those who agree with us that God is incorporeal and is the Creator of all natures, with the exception of His own." And, regarding the latter, he adds, further on: "They surpassed all other philosophers in prestige and authority."[21] The same situation emerges if we carefully consider the position of those who held that the world has always existed; for in spite of this they teach that it was made by God, and perceived no logical inconsistency in this doctrine. Therefore they who do descry such inconsistency with their hawk-like vision are the only rational

---

16 See glossary entry for 'order of nature.'
17 *De civitate dei*, XI, cc. 4-6; XII, cc.
18 *Ibid.*, X, 31 (*PL*, 41, 311).
19 *Ibid.*, XI, 4 (*PL*, 41, 319).
20 Cf. no. 4 above.
21 *De civitate dei*, XI, 5 (*PL*, 41, 320 f.).

beings, and wisdom was born with them!

[10] Yet, since certain authorities seem to be on their side, we have to show that the foundation furnished by these authorities is fragile. Damascene, for instance, in the eighth chapter of the first book, observes: "What is brought to existence from non-existence is not of such a nature as to be co-eternal with Him who is without beginning and exists forever."[22] Similarly Hugh of St. Victor[23] says, in the beginning of his book, *De sacramentis*: "The ineffable power of omnipotence could not have anything co-eternal with it, so as to have aid in creating."[24]

The minds of these authorities and of others like them is clarified by what Boethius says in the last book of the *Consolation*: "Certain people, when they learn about Plato's view that this world did not have a beginning in time and is to have no end, wrongly conclude that the created world is thus made co-eternal with its Creator. But it is one thing to be carried through an endless life, which is what Plato attributed to the world, and quite another to embrace the whole presence of endless life all at once, which is manifestly proper to the divine mind."[25]

[11] Hence it is clear that the difficulty feared by some does not follow, that is, that the creature would be on a par with God in duration. Rather we must say that nothing can be co-eternal with God, because nothing can be immutable save God alone. The statement of Augustine in *De civitate Dei*, XII, chap. 15, is to the point: "Since the flight of time involves change, it cannot be co-eternal with changeless eternity. Accordingly, even though the immortality of the angels does not run on in time, and is not past as though it were no longer present, or future as though it had not yet arrived, yet their movements, by which successive times are traversed, do change over from the future into the past. And therefore they cannot be co-eternal with the Creator, in whom we cannot say that any movement has occurred that no longer endures, or that any will occur that has not yet taken place."[26] He speaks in like vein in the eighth book of his commentary on Genesis: "Because the nature of the Trinity is absolutely changeless, it is eternal in such a way that nothing can be co-eternal with it."[27] And he utters similar words in the eleventh book of the *Confessions*.[28]

[12] They also bring in arguments which philosophers have touched on, and then undertake to solve them. One among them is fairly difficult; it concerns the infinite number of souls: if the world has existed forever, the number of souls must now be infinite. But this argument is not to the purpose, because God could have made the world without human beings and souls; or He could have made human beings at the time He did make them, even though He had made all the rest of the world from eternity. Thus the souls surviving their bodies would not be infinite. Besides, no demonstration has as yet been forthcoming that God cannot produce a multitude that is actually infinite.

There are other arguments which I forbear to answer at the present time. A reply has been made to them in other works.[29] Besides, some of them are so feeble that their very frailty seems to lend probability to the opposite side.

22 St. John Damascene, *De fide orthodoxa*, I, 8 (PG, 94, 814).
23 German theologian, born in 1096, who headed the school of the abbey of St. Victor from 1133 to his death in 1141.
24 Hugh of St. Victor, *De sacramentis*, I, 1 (PL, 176, 187).
25 Boethius, *De consolatione philosophiae*, V, pr. 6 (PL, 63, 859). See selection **IV.2.1**.
26 *De civitate dei*, XII, 15 (PL, 41, 364). See selection **III.2.2**.
27 *De Genesi ad litteram*, VIII, 23 (PL, 34, 389).
28 *Confessiones*, XI, 30 (PL, 32, 826).
29 See, for example, the previous selection.

III.6. HENRY OF GHENT

IN THESE SELECTIONS HENRY ARGUES THAT WHAT IS CREATED IN THE strict sense of the term, which implies being produced by a will acting freely, must have had a beginning to its existence. It will be clear in reading this section that several different theories have to be carefully distinguished: (1) The view of most of the philosophers that the world is dependent for its existence on an eternal first cause but that cause produced the world necessarily and hence the world has been in existence from eternity. (2) The view of a minority of ancient philosophers that the world as a whole has been in existence from eternity but has had no cause at all. (3) A view of the sort which Aquinas thought involved no contradiction but which Henry does think involves contradiction, viz. that God has through His free will created a world *out of nothing* that has no beginning to its existence. (4) The view of all three major religions that God has in fact created through His free will *out of nothing* a world that has had a beginning, and where no stand is taken on the question of whether God could have created a world without a beginning. (5) The view of some theologians that the very idea of a temporal world that has had no beginning involves implicit contradictions. Henry's view should not be confused with this last position.

III.6.1. That a created thing cannot have existed from eternity (from *Quodlibet* I, qu.7 & 8)

Was it possible for a creature to have existed from eternity? Is having existed from eternity incompatible with being a creature?

On this question there was the opinion of philosophers that it was possible for a creature to have existed from eternity and that the nature of a creature does not reject this [eternal existence]. Along with this they held the view that, even though a creature does not get actual being from itself, still when we consider its creator we find the creature was not able not to be, and this in such a way that it was not able to begin to be nor will it ever be able to stop being. Avicenna says this in his *Metaphysics*[1]: In some case, he says, a cause is the cause of the existence of what it causes although earlier the caused item did not exist. This happens

when the cause is not through its own essence a cause of the caused item but through some definite relationship which it has to it and the cause of that relationship is motion. Thus, as he says, when some thing was through its own essence the cause of the existence of some other thing, it will always be a cause as long as it has existence, and consequently it absolutely prevents the [caused] thing from not existing. Among the wise this is what is meant by creation.

Thus those philosophers claimed that God is the cause of creatures not by a decision of his will but by the necessity of his nature. Ambrose[2] says this in *Hexameron* I[3]: "Some gentiles maintained that the world is co-eternal with God like a little shadow of divine power." Although they granted that God is the cause of the world, they claimed he was not a cause in virtue of his will and decision but rather in the way a body is the cause of a shadow and a light of radiance. Thus if the light had been from eternity so also would the radiance, accord-

---

1 Bk. VI, 2.
2 St. Ambrose (c.333-397), Bishop of Milan.
3 ch.5, no.18.

ing to what Augustine says with another example given in his comments on *John*, sermon 36[4]: "Let there be a face situated over water. Is it not situated there along with its image? As soon as it begins to exist there along with it at the same time begins to exist its image. It has not preceded its image in being there but exists there with its image, and yet the image results from it, not it from the image. Therefore, they are co-temporal. If the face always exists there, so too does the face's image."

This position of philosophers is clearly heretical in that they say God was not able not to have caused a creature nor is he able to allow it to go into nothing after it once has existence. This means that the creature was not able to have had non-being temporally before having being, nor can it have non-being after being. Thus even if they say that by will God created the world and conserved it in being, they do not mean that he does this by a will that is free both to do and not to do, but by a will that is immutably immutable and coincides with the necessity of his nature. For the catholic faith expressly holds that it is by God's free will that at some time the creature began to be and always will last, and also that by God's free will which decides things from eternity the creature was able never to have existed and after it has been made it is able to fall back into non-being.

***

But now what about the original question? Does a creature so reject having existed from eternity that God was not able to have made it from eternity? For if it was able to have been from eternity and God was able to make from eternity whatever does not reject being made, God was able to have made a creature from eternity.

The Philosophers who claim in the above way that the world has existed from eternity and thus was able not only to exist from eternity but also to have gotten its being from God from eternity, also would say that the creature has always been made by God and has not had from God any beginning of its duration, so that in some scarcely intelligible sense they claim that the world was made by God but

never had from him a coming-to-be of this making. Thus Augustine, in *On the City of God* X, ch.31, says: "If the foot had always been in the dust from eternity, always under it would have been the imprint, and nevertheless no one would doubt that that imprint was made by the shoe." No one, indeed, would doubt it was made by the shoe, but they might doubt it came to be while not doubting it was made. For the imprint in the dust came to be only by a pressing down of the parts of the dust which necessarily is some motion or change that is finite and before which the foot was not in the dust and the parts of the dust presented an even surface. But after that change by which the imprint comes to be and is generated by the pressing down of the previously evenly arranged parts, given the foot stays forever in the dust, it can forever conserve that imprint, allowing that the imprint can only be conserved while the foot is present, just as the shape of a signet ring cannot be conserved in water without the presence of the ring.

A better analogy is the one the philosophers give for the world having been from God from eternity: If the sun had existed from eternity, it would have produced a ray of light existing from eternity, or in the way a body casts a shadow or a face produces its image. For from the fact that the sun produces its ray of light by a necessity of its nature, if the sun had existed from eternity, from eternity it would have produced the ray as something existing on its own.

Consequently, if God had produced the created world in this way, it would be necessary to claim that he produced it from eternity. For the ray would have existed of necessity and have been able to exist from eternity in the same way the sun itself does, except that the sun itself does not causally get its being from the ray but rather vice versa, the ray from the sun. And in the same way that the sun would never have gotten from God its own coming-into-being but would always have been fixed as existing in its own made-being, so also that ray, except that the ray would get its made-being from the sun, which gets its from itself. Thus the existence of creatures dependent on God would be nothing more than a continuous, everlasting conservation of them in their made-being without any

---

4 *Sermo* 117. ch.9, n.12.

preceding coming-into-being, in just the way that the existence of that ray dependent on the sun would just be a continuous, everlasting conservation of it in its own made-being without any preceding coming-into-being. Alternatively, the existence of the creature would just be its continuously coming into being, so that simultaneously and eternally would exist its coming-into-being and its made-being, just as, according to some, happens in the case of the sun's ray, i.e. it has existence only in continuously coming into being whenever it exists.

Now to get down to the question at hand, we should realize that common to all the philosophers as well as believers was the opinion that a creature, insofar as it is a creature, has only a shared-in being and thus does not get it from itself but from something else, which something else has its own being through its essence.

But concerning the non-being of a creature it is thought that there were two opinions: One is that of certain philosophers who say that a creature gets its being from something else in such a way that it nevertheless does not get non-being from itself or from the nature of its essence, and this neither really nor in respect of an idea of it. This means that the production of the Son from the Father in God would be just like the production of a creature by God, except that the Son has his being in the same substance as the Father while the creature has its in a different substance. This view is absurd, since no substance is of its own nature different from non-being except the one which is being itself through its essence, not through sharing. For only this being-of-itself is absolutely [different] from non-being.

Thus there is another opinion that the creature, since it gets its being from something else, has that being in such a way that it has non-being to the extent that it is of itself and is its own nature.

On this matter we find different views among some philosophers and believers. To have non-being of itself can be understood in two ways. In one way it is a matter merely of how things are grasped in the mind and means that the essence of the creature is understood as not being before it is

understood as being. In another way, it means that in itself really that essence is a non-being temporally before it gets being from something else.

Following the first way some philosophers used to claim that a creature has non-being before being not at all in respect of the thing itself, but rather its non-being can precede its being only in the mind. In this way Avicenna calls creation having being from something else after non being. He says this in the sixth book of his *Metaphysics*[5]: "Among the wise 'creation' means to give being after absolute non-being. For something caused insofar as it exists in itself is like what does not exist, but that it exists belongs to it insofar as it relates to its cause. Now what belongs to a thing in virtue of its idea belongs to it by essence, not temporally, before what belongs to it from something else. Thus every caused being is a being after non-being by posteriority of essence."

Following the second way catholics claim that a creature has non-being before being, in such a way that in the thing itself, not just in the mind, it could have non-being before being. It is in this way of understanding the nature of a creature and production by God, i.e. not by a necessity of his nature but by free will, that we should read our question, namely, whether the creature rejects having been from eternity, and therefore whether God could not have produced it from eternity or could have.

Some say that the creature does not reject this, but nevertheless God has produced the creature in time and this resulted merely from God's will "whose cause should not be sought," because to seek that would be to seek a cause for that for which there is no cause, as Augustine says.[6] These people also say that it is to be taken only on faith that creatures have not always existed and it cannot be demonstratively proven[7] because the quiddity of a creature abstracts from all temporal duration.

It is certainly true that given the way the philosophers speak about the nature of a creature and say it has being from God, it is not possible to prove that a creature has begun, and the texts of the saints agree with this. But it is certainly possible,

5 ch.2.
6 *De div. quaest. 83*, qu.28.
7 See glossary entry for 'demonstration.'

given how catholics speak of the nature of creature and say it has being from God, to show a creature has begun, once we assume certain things which right reason requires us to assume, as will now be shown.

Their argument [which concludes that demonstrative proof is not possible] is invalid because, even though the quiddity of a thing taken absolutely abstracts from the here and now, still its actual existence or its existing as an effect does not always abstract from the here and now. Thus, even though the quiddity[8] of an eclipse of the moon abstracts from the here and now and thus when it is taken in that unqualified way it cannot be proved, still its actual existence does not abstract from the here and now and thus can indeed be proved to be here and now. Consequently, even though the quiddity of a creature and the being it has which is entailed by its essence cannot be proven, still its being of actual existence can in fact be shown to have been new to it insofar as it is shown that the created world can have being as an effect only after its non-being precedes in temporal duration. And this is to prove that the created world began to be.

***

That this holds necessarily can be made evident as follows: A creature, which of itself is a non-being in the sense that neither formally nor by causation does it get its being from the nature of its own essence, does not just get its being from something else in the way in which in God the Son gets it from the Father,[9] or in the way the ray gets it from the sun (given both are eternal and the ray has of itself non-being only as it is in the mind, as was said before); but rather the creature acquires its being in such a way that God not only serves as the cause for its being in made-being but also makes it to be out of non-being, and this is called creation. For if God had given the creature existence only in made-being and had not made it in any other sense, there would be no difference between the way, in God, the Father gives being to the Son and the way God gives it to a creature, except that in the former case the Son is given being in the substance of the Father while in the latter the creature receives it in a different substance, as we said above. Since every transition of making something from not-being is a transmutation and the transmutation is natural when it works with a pre-existent subject, an act of creation – even if it is not a true transmutation, like the one which is natural, because creation goes from not-being into being – is a sort of mutation (not a motion) like the action by which a thing acquires being by natural generation.[10] The only difference is that generation is out of matter while creation is out of nothing.

For this reason in the sixth book of his *Metaphysics* Avicenna says, "We find that there are some items which are always due to a cause without matter and there are some which are due to something intermediate. It is appropriate then that we call everything which is not out of pre-existing matter created, not generated." Now every transmutation which is a sudden action has an indivisible duration, not a successive one, rather it lacks succession and duration both on the side of what comes before and on the side of what comes after. Therefore, the creation by which anything acquires being cannot be from eternity. Also the action by which the thing acquires being necessarily precedes the action by which occurs the conservation which continues the thing's existence into later moments of time. Therefore, although the thing afterwards can be conserved in its existence so that on account of the continuation of the act of conserving it does not cease to exist, nevertheless, on account of the simpleness of the creation by which it acquires being, in the direction of what came before it can exist only if it begins to exist after not existing.

From the above it is clear how stupidly some people talk who say that by the same action God creates and conserves a thing, just as the sun by the same action causes and conserves light in a medi-

---

8 See glossary entry for 'quiddity.'
9 According to orthodox theology the Son (i.e. the second Person of the Trinity) is *necessarily* generated by the Father (the first Person) and thus co-eternal with the Father.
10 See glossary entry for 'natural generation.'

um. For if the sun had being from itself and not-being did not in any way belong to it from its own nature, while the nature of the light radiating from it had of its own nature being after non-being, even though the conservation [of the light] would be a continuous process of coming-to-be, still it would be necessary for some coming-to-be to come earlier in which it first received being. Consequently, positing the sun to exist from eternity and not of itself to have not-being requires positing its light-ray to exist in the same way from eternity and not to have being after not-being except in the mind (and maybe not even there), or to say that the sun produces the ray not by any necessity of its nature but by free will.

It also seems to be a major difficulty that the being of the creature, although it is substantial, persistent being,[11] is always in a continuous process of coming-to-be, even though it can persist only in the presence of its cause. Now in the generation of natural things we find that the particular agent, since it is a cause only of the thing's coming-to-be – this is because it does not have in itself the definitive content of the whole species – causes through its species something similar to itself in matter and once that is generated its action stops and it does not go on to conserve it in being. But we also find in the generation of natural things that a universal agent, which does have in itself the definitive content of the whole species, for example a celestial body or its mover, is such that (in view of the difference between an act of generation and an act of conservation) if it first generates the thing by itself directly, and once it is generated conserves it afterwards, its action of generation is different from its conserving. Having found all this to be the case as regards generation, we ought likewise to conclude it for creation.

***

Thus we must absolutely say that, since a creature, just by the fact that it is a creature, has been made from nothing by God acting voluntarily, it cannot exist from eternity on pain of contradiction, because by being posited with no beginning it is posited to get a being for itself that is not acquired from something else out of not-being, while by being a creature it is posited that it gets for itself a being acquired from God out of not-being.

Perhaps someone will say that it is not part of the definition of a creature *qua* creature that it have acquired being in the sense that it has to have not-being temporally before it has being (although in my estimation this has already been sufficiently proven); rather what is part of that definition is that it is *possible* for it to have had acquired being. Thus, just as what has from eternity been predestined[12] to be going to be was able from eternity not to have been predestined to be going to be or to have been predestined not to be going to be, so even if the world had from eternity being from God, and thus did not have an acquired being, nevertheless, because it was not by any necessity of his nature or of an immutable will coinciding with his nature that the world had being from him from eternity, the world was able not to have had being from him and thus was able to have had acquired being from God, in the same way our faith says is now the case in fact.

But in opposition to this Aristotle says that what is, when it is, necessarily is,[13] so that at the time at which it is, there is no potential for it not to be, neither on the side of the entity itself nor on the side of some efficient cause, because there is no potential for this, since it would require making contradictories exist simultaneously. Likewise, for what was, at the time at which it was, it is necessary that it was; also for what will be, at the time at which it will be, it is necessary that it will be. Thus in none of these ways is there a potential for the opposite at the time that the act is given. Rather, if there is a

---

11 See glossary entry for 'persistent being.'
12 Predestination is the act whereby God selects someone to be saved and to live everlastingly in heaven.
13 *De Int.* 9. See selection **IV.1.1.**

potential for the opposite, this is a potential for some other time at which the act can be stopped because it is contingent. In this sense, although what is, when it is, necessarily is, still it is not absolutely necessary, because there was a potential at a preceding time through which that act was able to be stopped, and on account of this the act was able not to be at the time at which it is. Likewise, what was, when it was, necessarily was. Nevertheless, it was not absolutely necessary, because there was a potential at a preceding time by which that act was able to be stopped and on account of this the act was able at that time absolutely to have not been. Likewise, what will be, when it will be, necessarily will be. Nevertheless, it will not be absolutely necessary, because there was, or is, or will be a potential before that future event by which that act will be able to be stopped, and on account of this it will be able absolutely not to be going to be.

If, then, something was at some time and there never was a preceding potential by which its act of being at the time at which it was was able to be stopped, it was absolutely necessary, because there was no potential at all, neither one belonging to the existent thing nor one belonging to the efficient cause, by which it was able to be stopped from having been at that time. But if something always had being from eternity, there was never a preceding potential, neither belonging to the existing thing nor belonging to some efficient cause, by which its act of being could be stopped at some moment if we go backward in time. Therefore, it is absolutely necessary for it always to have been. If, then, the world creature is posited to have always had being from God and from eternity, it is absolutely necessary that it have been always and from eternity. And if this is the case, there was never from eternity – neither on God's part nor on the part of the thing – a potential by which it was able at some time not to have been. Thus the world creature, on the supposition that it had being from God from eternity, not only never started to have acquired being from God at some initial moment in time, but also *could* in no way ever have started to have acquired being from God at some initial moment of time. This is unqualifiedly false and impossible, since our faith in claiming that at some

time the world was made new by God holds the opposite.

It is, then, not only unqualifiedly false but even impossible that the creation of the world has being from God from eternity so that never does it have acquired being from him even though it was possible for it to acquire it. Rather, either it is necessary to claim that it has started to have acquired being from God and God afterwards conserves the world, so that it is completely unable to have being from him in some different way, as the preceding proof showed, or it is necessary to claim, supposing the world to have non-acquired being from God from eternity, that it is not possible for the world not to get being from him and so it was never possible for it to start to acquire being from him nor will it ever be possible that it is permitted to fall into not-being, as the last proof showed.

Without doubt this was the view and mind of the philosophers on the eternity of the world, namely that the world creature never had acquired being, since, as they thought, it did not of its own nature have not-being, except merely in the mind, and thus, even though it had being from God as from a first cause, nevertheless it always had and always will have being from him from eternity. Nor did they think it less impossible for the world creature to be able at some time not to be going to be than for it at some time not to have been. Thus it was a principle for them that a creature does not get its own non-existence from its own nature and essence even if it were abandoned to itself (as though *per impossibile*); and thus it does not have of itself the possibility for not-being, but rather it is impossible for it not to be so far as it itself is concerned.

Moreover, there is for the impossible no potential which releases it and brings it back to the possible by bringing it all the way back to actuality. On account of a principle of this sort, they claimed that no agent can make the world creature not be or not have been, and in this way they claimed that the world gets its being from God from eternity but has never been made by him, except in the broad sense of 'making' where it is equivalent to creation in the sense Avicenna gives to the act of creation (discussed above), but not in the sense catholics explain it, i.e. a making of the world as consisting of new things. Consequently, they have claimed that the world gets its being from God in such a way that God could not have not given it being nor could he take being away from it, since on their view the world gets its being from God merely by the necessity of his nature or by a will bound to the necessity of the immutability of his nature, not a will that is free to give being and not to give it.

***

Therefore, we who are compelled by the truth itself of our faith to hold that the world creature has acquired its being from God in time, and that no creature has from itself and of its own nature being, but rather gets it from God alone, and this being is acquired because the creature has of its own nature not-being, as the first proof above shows, must first destroy the philosophers' basic premiss by saying that every creature, inasmuch as it is a creature, gets from its own nature taken unqualifiedly its not also existing in reality unless it gets being from something else. For if we were to say that its existence comes from its own nature, necessarily we would have to allow all the other points that are inferred by them about the eternity and indestructibility of the world. Once we have denied that basic premiss, we can say that the world gets acquired being for itself from God, but not from eternity. In fact, if it had its being from God from eternity it would not have acquired being from God nor would it be possible for it to acquire it, and vice versa, as was said. We can, and we ought, to say as a result that the world gets being from God by no necessity, neither of God's nature nor of God's will.

From the above it is clear that what was said above against our position is unqualifiedly false, namely that supposing the world to have had being from God from eternity, we can still claim that the world from eternity was able not to have had being from God, and that God from eternity was able [to give] to the world acquired being, so that what we mean by calling a creature 'a creature' is not that it has acquired being but that it is able to acquire being

from God, and it is suited to acquiring it even though from eternity it has from God non-acquired being. For these are totally incompatible, as was said.

As for what was argued by the analogy with predestination – namely that what has from eternity been predestined to be going to be was able from eternity not to be predestined to be going to be or to be predestined not to be going to be, so likewise with a creature even though it is posited to have had being from eternity from God, nevertheless this is compatible with its from eternity having been able not to have being from God and thus its from eternity having been able to get acquired being from him at some time – to this we have to say that the cases are not similar, because 'getting being from God' does not mean something that is relative to some definite moment of time or duration, in the way that 'being predestined by God' does mean this on account of the prefix 'pre.' Only that is predestined whose existence is preceded by the predestination itself, because only what begins to be at some determinate moment of time is predestined, and thus, since there is no necessity in its beginning to be at that moment, along with the fact that it is predestined to be going to be at that moment it is also true that it was able not to be going to be at that moment.

Further, what was able not to be going to be in reality was able to be predestined by God not to be going to be, or not predestined to be going to be, because predestination, even if it is eternal, always accords with the condition of the predestined thing. This is[14] because 'predestined to be going to be' refers to some thing belonging to a divine act in respect of some determinate time, in respect of which the thing can exist otherwise than it does. On the other hand, 'to get being from God' refers to some thing belonging to a divine act without any respect to some determinate time. 'To get being from God from eternity' refers entirely to an act that extends over every moment and every finite stretch of time, so that in respect of no determinate time is it possible for it to be otherwise than it is;

14 Reading *id est* for *ideo*.
15 *Physics* III, 4, 203b30.

rather in respect of the infinite eternity in which it exists it lacks the possiblity of being otherwise than it is, as was clearly shown above.

From this it is obvious that what is from eternity predestined to be going to be was able not to be predestined to be going to be, or predestined not to be going to be. Rather what gets being from God from eternity was not able from eternity to get not-being from him nor in any way to get acquired being, as was explained earlier through what The Philosopher correctly and beautifully says,[15] namely that in everlasting things, which always exist, being and possibility do not differ.

III.6.2. Contradictions involved in the view that God makes eternal things (*Quodlibet* VIII, qu.9)

[This selection can be found as **I.8.1.** on pp. 56-8.]

III.7. JOHN DUNS SCOTUS

On the question which Henry of Ghent and Thomas Aquinas reached opposite conclusions, viz. whether God could have freely created a world that had no temporal beginning, Scotus takes no position himself, but is content to show that Henry's arguments for the negative (see **III.6.**) have no force and that the arguments of Aquinas (see **III.5.2.**) and others are inconclusive. Given Scotus' claim elsewhere (see selection **IV.6.1.**) that a free will such as God's has at the moment it is willing one thing the power to will at that same moment the opposite, it is perhaps surprising that Scotus has not adopted the affirmative answer, for that view would seem to open the door to the contingency even of an eternally existent act of production.

III.7.1. Arguments on both sides and their Refutations (*Ordinatio II*, dist.1, qu.3)

Thirdly, I ask: Is it possible for God to produce something other than himself with no beginning?

[A.] That it is:

[A.1] The Philosopher in *Physics* I¹ proves that matter is ungenerated and indestructible – otherwise there would be an infinite series of materials. Therefore either matter was not produced or it was produced with no beginning, which answers the question. Or if it was not produced, at least some form was produced in it, and one with no beginning since matter never existed without form.

[A.2] According to The Philosopher in *Physics* VIII² [c.1] and *Metaphysics* XII [c.6] time has no beginning. His proof seems to go as follows: If it did have a beginning, time could have existed before it existed or could be before it would be; but 'before' marks a temporal difference; thus there was time before time was.

[A.3] In *De Generatione* [*et Corruptione*] I [c.3] The Philosopher says that the generation of one item is the destruction of another. Therefore, there never was some original first generation, and consequently with no beginning it has been the case

that there have been some generable items.

[A.4] A cause that is not something that acts through motion and is not stoppable, can have an effect coeval with it, as is clear in the created realm. Therefore, etc.

[B.] In opposition to this:

[B.1] Augustine in *To Felicianus*³ gives a definition of 'creature' saying: "Something is a creature in virtue of the fact that its substance is produced out of not-being into being by the will of the omnipotent God." If then being produced from not-being is part of what it means to be a creature, it is impossible for a creature to be produced with no beginning.

[B.2] Any reason for God's having been able to have produced one item with no beginning will show he could have produced another and so on until it shows that an actual infinite number could have been produced. Also he would have been able to put together all the bulks that resulted to produce an infinite mass. But [Aristotle's] *Physics* III [c.5] shows that both infinite masses and infinite numbers are impossible.

[C.] The first opinion:

[C.1] God was able to produce something other

---

1 Ch.9.
2 Ch.1. See selection **III.1.1.**
3 Ps. Aug., *De unitate trinitate contra Felicianum arianum*, ch.7.

than himself with no beginning because it cannot be proven that he was not able to have done this (i.e. to have produced something other than himself with no beginning). It cannot be proven either through an intrinsic middle term[4] or through an extrinsic one.

It cannot be proven through an extrinsic middle term because that term is the will of God and it cannot be known, nor can there be any argument, why God wishes for something to be more with a beginning than without.

Nor can it be proven through an intrinsic middle term, i.e. through the quiddity of the makeable item itself, because a quiddity abstracts away from the here and now, so there is no way of proving anything about the here and now.

[C.2] That anything else is from God is an article of faith. Therefore, it does not help either the believers or the unbelievers to have proofs of this; rather it seems dangerous. So far as believers are concerned, having them would seem to eliminate the merit involved in faith. So far as unbelievers are concerned, they would then be able to argue that we believe such things on account of arguments and thus have no faith; and further, if the arguments seemed to them sophistical (as they do seem to some believers), the unbelievers could wonder whether we believed on account of sophisms of that sort.

[C.3] Augustine in *De Trinitate* VI, 4: "If fire were eternal, the radiance it causes would be eternal, and be co-eternal with it."

From this it seems we can argue effectively for this opinion, because Augustine's consequence is a natural one,[5] otherwise it would be of no use in proving the co-eternity of the Son with the Father, against Arius.[6] But the consequence holds only because the cause and effect here are perfect examples of such. Thus, just as in this case necessary co-temporality is inferred from a perfect example of a cause that acts naturally, so the possible co-tempo-

rality of a limited effect with its unlimited cause can be inferred where we have a perfect example of a cause that acts voluntarily. This is because the only difference there seems to be between a natural agent and a free agent is that one acts naturally and the other contingently, but there is no difference in what they can do or not do, since whatever a natural agent can do the free agent can do too – the difference is solely in the way they cause what they cause.

There are several ways of bolstering this argument:

[C.3.1] Any perfection found in a secondary cause which results from any positive feature of the cause – this feature being the perfection – is in the primary cause as it is a cause. But in some secondary cause it is a perfection to have an effect co-temporal with itself. Consequently, if it were eternal or an effect co-eternal with its cause, that perfection would be in the cause. Therefore, etc.

[C.3.2] Another way of deducing this, and it amounts to the same as the above, is the following: According to Ambrose in *On the Incarnation of the Word*,[7] the way in which it is caused does not formally affect what is caused. But if God had naturally and necessarily caused [what he causes], he would have been able to cause an effect co-temporal and co-eternal with himself; therefore, if he caused in a voluntary way, even though he would not cause necessarily, he would still be able to cause an effect co-temporal with Himself.

[C.3.3] Supposing someone says that Augustine referred to an immanent radiance of the fire that is not formally caused by the fire, we can cite against this Augustine's own words[8]: "The radiance produced and emitted by it."

[C.3.4] The same view is found in his sermon 36 *On John*,[9] where he speaks of a bush and its reflection in water. It is certain that if there were such a reflection it would be caused and produced by the bush.

---

4 See glossary entry for 'middle term.'

5 I.e., depends for its validity simply on the existence of natural necessity.

6 Arius was a Christian living in Alexandria in the 4th century. He formulated a doctrine of the trinity which denied that the second and third Persons of the trinity share the same substance as the Father and in effect treated them as creatures. This doctrine was declared heretical by church councils but persisted among some Gothic peoples well into the middle ages.

7 *De Incarn.*, ch.9, n.102.

8 *loc. cit.*

9 *Sermo* 117, ch.9, n.12.

[C.4] Anything which limitation does not reject, a creature (as long as we mean by 'a creature' 'some entity') does not reject. But the limitation of a creature does not reject any duration whatsoever, because what lasts one day is no more imperfect than what lasts ten years. Thus, an infinite duration would not seem to posit any greater perfection in a creature than would a shorter duration, and, consequently, it would not reject having always been in existence without any beginning.

[C.5] Any creature, to the extent that it exists of itself, tends toward not-being in the same way that it is a non-being to the extent that it exists of itself and from nothing. Therefore, just as with some creatures there is no contradiction involved in their always tending toward not-being and yet always existing (as is obvious in the case of angels and souls), so no contradiction is involved in their being able always to have been and yet, to the extent that they exist of themselves, always to have had not-being.

[C.6] In *On the City of God* X, c.31, Augustine says that "if a foot were eternally in some dust there would always have been an imprint under it, and still no one would doubt that the imprint had been made by the shoe; nor would one be earlier than the other even if one had been made by the other."

[C.7] In the same place he says that "in a scarcely intelligible way" philosophers have said that the world was made but does not have a beginning of its temporal duration. Therefore, if this way is "scarcely intelligible" it is intelligible, and so no contradiction is involved in something's always having been without any beginning.

[C.7.1] This is bolstered by the fact that it seems unlikely that such famous philosophers, who so carefully sought truth and so clearly defined their terms, would not see a contradiction if it were actually there implicit in the terms.

[C.7.2] That there is no contradiction here is also reinforced by the philosophers, because not just the natural philosophers consider the four causes, but also metaphysicians, and they consider them under a prior and more general concept. Thus being an efficient cause extends to more things than those that move or even change, and consequently it is possible to give being without motion. Therefore, the first efficient cause can give being without giving new being, because it can give being without doing it through motion or change.

[C.8] Motion is an effect that is co-temporal and co-eternal with the first mover itself. Therefore, there can be some product or effect of the first efficient cause that is co-eternal and co-temporal with it.

[D.] The second opinion:

[D.1] In opposition to the above it is argued that for something other than God to have existed without any beginning does involve a contradiction because of anything that is produced it is at some time true, or will be at some time true, to say that it is produced, since even of the Son of God who was produced in eternity we can say truly that he is produced in eternity. Thus a creature either is always produced as long as it is or is sometimes produced but not always. If the latter, then in that instant in which it is produced in this way it first gets existence, and this answers the question [by showing it had a beginning]. If the former, then the creature is continuously coming into being, but that seems absurd since then it would be a non-permanent entity.[10]

[D.1.1] It also seems that then [i.e. if the creature is always being produced] being created and being conserved would not differ.[11] This result is disproved in two ways:

[D.1.1.1] To be created is to be produced from not-being, but to be conserved presupposes the being of the thing, and thus to be created is not to be conserved.

[D.1.1.2] A particular agent produces but does not conserve. Therefore where both producing and preserving co-incide in the same item, they are different from each other.

[D.1.2] To the above argument we can add that a creature has acquired being and consequently has being after not-being.[12] If it did not, it would have being without acquisition, as does the Son of God,

---

10 I.e., a "successive" being. See entry for 'successive being' in glossary.
11 Cf. Henry of Ghent's argument in selection III.6.1, pp.207ff, p.208.
12 Cf. Henry of Ghent's argument in selection I.8.1, pp. 56-58.

although it would not have the very same being as has that from which it would have acquired its being [in contrast to the Son of God, who does].

[D.2] In [Aristotle's] *Peri hermenias* I[13] it says, "Everything which is, when it is, necessarily is." Therefore, it can not be only because a power precedes its being which can prevent its being. But if something existed from God through eternity, no power preceded its being from God; therefore, it was not able not to be from God.[14]

[D.2.1] To this it is objected that a predestined[15] person can be saved or not saved; therefore, likewise for what has been made from eternity it is possible for it to have existed and not to have existed.[16]

[D.2.1.1] Reply: Predestination relates to a thing outside for some given moment of time at which in fact the thing is able not to be and so not to be predestined, since predestination relates to the thing's nature. But to give something being from eternity relates to a power for infinite eternity where there is no power directed toward the opposite and thus none for the opposite of the act of giving being.

This is reinforced by what is said in [Aristotle's] *Physics* III [c.4]: "In the realm of everlasting things to be is no different than being able to be."[17] Also in [his] *Metaphysics* IX [c.8], the last chapter: "Nothing that always exists has potential."

[D.3] Further, and thirdly, elsewhere[18] he [Henry of Ghent] argues for the same conclusion as follows: Any species has an equal potential for being when it is compared to God, the giver of being. Therefore, just as the sun could have existed from eternity, so also an ass, i.e. a complete one able to reproduce. Then from that ass all the other asses which have existed could have been engendered right up to this one that is now engendered. Now I ask whether all those were then finite or infinite. If finite, then the whole time extending from that time to this one would have been finite. If infinite, then even though the end points are given the intermediate ones would have been able to be actually infinite, which is absurd.

[D.4] Further he [Henry] argues as follows[19]: From eternity for a creature it is possible for it to be and possible for it not to be. If, then, it is posited in being, it has acquired this being. Therefore its own not-being preceded its new or acquired being.

[D.5] Further, in favor of this opinion it is argued that, if the world could have existed from eternity without any beginning, there would have been an infinity of souls that have minds.

[D.6] Besides, it is counter to the definition of a quantitative infinite for it to be able to be exceeded or for it to be taken as a whole. (This is clear from the definition in [Aristotle's] *Physics* III [c.6] where Aristotle says that the infinite is not that of which nothing further is to be taken but that for which there is always something further to be taken no matter how many of its parts have been taken.) But if the world had been able to have existed from eternity without any beginning, an infinity would have been able to be exceeded as well as taken to be as a whole, because to the infinity [of time] which has gone before and is now taken there are continuous additions. Therefore it is impossible for the world to have existed from eternity.

Neither does the reply have any force which says that the infinity would have been potential and forever in going-to-be-taken being, not in taken being. This is because the intellect's dividing is irrelevant to the question of whether the infinite is actually taken, since it is impossible for a future infinity to have been taken sometime even though there would be no intellect which would divide the parts of that infinite time.

[D.7] Further, it is argued that the part would be greater than its whole, because, let A be noon today and B be noon tomorrow. Now, if on either side of A there can be an infinite time, the same will hold for the past in respect of B and the future in respect of B. Thus, anything the past relative to B is greater than, also the future relative to B is greater than. But the past relative to B is greater than the past relative to A, just as any whole is greater than its part,

---

13 *De Int.* 9. See selection **IV.1.1**.
14 Cf. Henry of Ghent's argument in selection **III.6.1**, pp.207-8.
15 See glossary entry for 'predestination.'
16 Cf. Henry of Ghent's argument in selection **III.6.1**, p.210.
17 Cf. Henry of Ghent's argument in selection **III.6.1**, p.211.
18 Cf. selection **I.8.1**.
19 Cf. *ibid.*

and thus the past relative to B is greater than the future relative to A [since past relative to A = future relative to A]. Therefore, the future relative to B, which is equal to the past relative to B, would be greater than the future relative to A, and so a part would be greater than its whole.

[E.] Replies to the arguments in favor of the first opinion [i.e. the arguments of C], from the point of view of those holding the second opinion:

Those who accept this conclusion [that a contradiction is involved in God's making something other than himself without any beginning] and do so in the strongest way by saying that no matter what type of thing you mean the same impossibility is found (allowing that in some types, for example, successive beings,[20] it seems that everything taken is finite even though the whole is infinite when we take one part after another) answer the arguments for the first opinion as follows:

[E.1] To the first [C.1]: Although it cannot be naturally known whether God's will is directed to this or that, still it can be naturally known that it is not directed toward what is of itself unwillable from the fact that it includes a contradiction, and consequently the impossibility that the divine will is directed toward what has no meaning.

But given the above, we have to claim non-willableness for the object, just as we claimed incompatibility in *Ordinatio* I, d.43.[21] And then to the argument that quiddity is not a middle for proving existence, we say that even if that is true, still a creature can be a middle for demonstrating the beginning of its existence.

[E.1.1] In opposition to this: The middle by which beginning of existence is to be demonstrated cannot be the quiddity, according to them, therefore it is existence.

And then it seems this argument fails in two ways: First by committing the fallacy of the consequent,[22] because in the minor premise "existence" does not mean actual existence. Secondly, because the premiss in which existence is attributed to a stone, will be contingent, and thus the demonstration will not

be a highly probable argument, but rather a sophistical one.

[E.1.2] Nevertheless, to the argument [C.1] it can be replied that, even though quiddity relates contingently to actual existence or non-actual (and thus is not a middle for demonstrating absolute existence nor some absolute condition of existence), still some quiddity can reject some condition of existence and thus can be a middle for demonstrating that existence under such a condition does not belong to that of which it is the quiddity. For example, the quiddity of a stone, even though it does not include in itself existence, still rejects of itself existing uncreated, and thus from the definition of this quiddity it can be concluded that it does not have uncreated being, nor does it have everlasting being.

So, from the point of view of the second opinion, we have to say in answer to the question that a stone rejects existing forever, and thus from the quiddity of a stone it can be demonstrated that it does not have everlasting being. And from this we further show, not absolutely that it has new being, but that if it exists, it has new being – which answers the question.

[E.1.3] The argument also, it seems, fails in another way by committing the fallacy of the consequent.[23] For this is a non-sequitur: "The opposite of this cannot be demonstrated; therefore, this is possible." Rather it commits the fallacy of the consequent. For primary impossibles are items that are impossible in virtue of their terms, just as their opposites, the primary necessaries, are necessary in virtue of their terms, and, even though these latter, the opposites of the former, are not able to be demonstrated (since they are primary truths), still it does not follow that the former are possible. Rather, [to get a valid inference] it is necessary to add to the antecedent (i.e. to "the opposite cannot be demonstrated") that the opposite is not a primary necessary nor known in virtue of its terms. Perhaps this is what some would deny [by saying that the opposite is a primary necessary and known in virtue of its terms] even though the necessity due

---

20 Like a day whose parts succeed one another in time. See glossary entry for 'successive being.'
21 See selection **I.9.4.**
22 See glossary entry for 'fallacy of consequent.'
23 See glossary entry for 'fallacy of consequent.'

to the terms is hidden and not evident to any mind that conceives the terms in a confused way.

[E.2] To the second [C.2], it can be said that if there are some necessary arguments in favor of what is believed, it is not dangerous to put them forward, neither on account of the believers nor on account of the unbelievers.

[E.2.1] It is not dangerous so far as believers are concerned, for the catholic doctors who with arguments sought after the truth of their beliefs and strove to understand what they believed did not by this intend to destroy the merit of faith. Rather Augustine and Anselm believed that they meritoriously worked to understand what they believed, in line with *Isaiah* 7 (according to another translation), "Unless you have believed you will not understand." For while believing they sought to understand by arguments what they had believed. As for the question of whether demonstrations, given we can have them, take away faith or not, see book III of this work on the incarnation.[24]

[E.2.2] Neither is it dangerous so far as the unbelievers are concerned. Given we could have necessary arguments, even if these could not prove the actual fact, i.e. the article of faith, but did show the possibility of the fact, these would be useful against unbelievers, because they might somehow persuade them not to resist such beliefs as impossible. But it would be dangerous to put forth sophisms as demonstrations against unbelievers, since this would be to expose the faith to derision; likewise in all other subjects, even ones to which faith is indifferent, like geometry, it is dangerous to put forth sophisms as though they were demonstrations. For it is better for an ignorant person to know they do not know than on account of sophisms to think they know. But those who oppose this argument claim that they do not put forth sophisms but rather necessary arguments and true demonstrations, and thus they are not creating any pre-conceptions against the faith (neither as

regards the believers nor as regards the unbelievers); rather they are strengthening the faith with arguments of this sort.

[E.3] To the third [C.3], although we speak in several senses of something being for different reasons, I say here that in one and the same consequence there can be several reasons why the inference is necessary and so several *loci*[25] in the antecedent. Wherever one of these reasons or one of these *loci* can be found, a similar sort of inference can be found and run. An example: 'A human being runs; therefore, an animal runs' validly follows by means of the *locus* "from the species,"[26] as well as from a more general *locus*, namely the *locus* "from a subjective part,"[27] because the consequence is valid not only wherever there is an inference from species to genus, but also wherever there is an argument from a subjective part to a whole. We could find other examples where several reasons for inferring coincide, but this is enough to make our point.

Thus I say this follows: 'There is fire in this now and it is not blocked; therefore, there is light.' The *locus* is "from a naturally causing cause, not blocked"; not just this, though, but also this consequence can hold on account of a more general reason in the antecedent, namely from the reason of something that produces naturally and is not blocked. For it is not just what causes naturally and is not blocked that has a caused item or effect coeval with it ([Aristotle's] *Physics* II [c.8]), but also what produces naturally has a product coeval with it, as is clear from the second argument.[28] Therefore, wherever we find a like reason for inferring, the consequence will be necessary and natural not just in virtue of the specific reason but also in virtue of the general one.

So I say that the example [viz. that if fire were eternal, the radiance it causes would be eternal] actually makes my point. If fire's being implies that radiance is emitted by reason of being a natural producer, then the consequence is valid even

---

24 *Ordinatio* III, dist.24.

25 See glossary entry for '*loci (topoi)*.'

26 I.e., one can infer from what is true of a species what is true of some members of the genus.

27 I.e., from what is true of a subjective part of some term one can infer what is true of some of the subjective whole. The subjective whole is just the total extension of a term; the subjective part a proper sub-class of that extension.

28 "Production" here is taken as a term covering both efficient causation and the generation of the second and third Persons of the trinity from the Father, which is not taken to be a case of causation. The "second argument," then, is Augustine's proof of the co-eternity of the Son with the Father.

though the antecedent is impossible and incompatible, and the consequent likewise. Therefore, wherever we have this reason for inferring we will have a valid and necessary consequence, no matter what holds for the antecedent and the consequent. This is so in the case of The Father and The Son, since The Father is a natural producer in respect of the Son; consequently in the other case the similar consequence will be valid and necessary.

[E.3.1] From the above it is clear how to reply to the bolstering argument [C.3.1] that no perfection is denied to the first cause which can exist in a secondary cause. But to be able to have an unqualifiedly necessary effect is not one of the perfections of a secondary cause; rather no secondary cause has this (as was said in dist.8 of the first book[29]), although some secondary causes have it in a qualified way. For to cause with unqualified necessity includes a contradiction, and thus no secondary cause has it. Nor is it from this that Augustine argues as though from what is impossible (and infers something or other in respect of fire); rather he argues it from the more general reason (namely from the reason of what produces), which does not include a contradiction, and this suffices for his argument.

[E.3.2] This same point makes clear how to reply to that other argument [C.3.2], "that different ways of causing do not formally affect what is caused." This is true of the "different ways of causing" which are able to belong to a cause in some causation; but if one way of causing is possible and another impossible, what is caused by the possible way will be other than what is caused by the impossible way. Just as from the impossible the impossi-

ble follows, and even by a natural consequence, so I say that by a natural consequence it follows that if it caused naturally it would cause necessarily (and even co-eternally). But this way of causing contradicts God's causing freely, while the other way of causing – namely, freely – is compatible with the cause and thus does not destroy the compatibility of the antecedent and the consequent.

[E.4] To the fourth [C.4], someone speaking for the second opinion might say that to exist forever does include some unlimitedness, because it includes being made equal to God in some respect (namely, in unlimitedness of duration), which cannot happen without unlimitedness [in every other respect], because something cannot be made equal to God in one respect but not in some other.

But this comes to nothing, since today co-exists with God and is not on account of that equated with the eternity with which today co-exists. Also this eternity, as co-exisiting with this day, is infinite and independent, while the creature, like today co-existing with eternity, is finite and dependent, and thus not equated with it.

Consequently, it has to be said that to be forever implies some unlimitedness in the creature, and therein lies the incompatibility. But why there is this incompatibility and this unlimitedness anyone would explain by the basic argument which they produce for themselves.

[E.5] To the fifth [C.5], a reply is given by arguing the opposite: Just as a creature cannot actually tend toward not-being and nevertheless always be going to be, so it is not able actually to have been after not being and nevertheless always have been. (According to this view it belongs to the notion of

---

29 The following comes from Scotus's discussion of the necessity and contingency of causes in *Ordinatio* I, d.8, last paragraph:

...I say that in creatures there is no unqualifiedly necessary natural connection between a cause and what it causes, nor does any secondary cause cause in an unqualifiedly natural way or in an unqualifiedly necessary way, but rather only qualifiedly. The former assertion is evident because everything depends on the relationship of the first cause to what it causes. Likewise, no secondary cause causes without what it causes being co-caused by the first cause, and the first cause's causing is naturally prior to the proximate cause's causing. Now the first cause only causes contingently, and consequently a secondary cause causes in an unqualifiedly contingent way, since it depends on the first cause's causation which is unqualifiedly contingent.

The latter assertion, i.e. the one about qualified necessity, is evident, because many natural causes, so far as it is a question solely of them, cannot not cause their effects, and thus the necessity here is qualified, i.e. it is a necessity so far as it is a question solely of them, and not an unqualified necessity. For example, fire, so far as it is a question solely of it, cannot not radiate heat; nevertheless, absolutely it is able not to radiate heat, since it would not if God did not cooperate, as is clear and was made clear by the three boys in the oven [*Daniel* 3, 49-50].

a creature not just to have had a tendency toward not-being before being but also to have actually had not being before being.)

[E.6] To the authoritative text [C.6], I say that in this text from *On the City of God*, bk.X, Augustine does not give his own opinion but rather that of philosophers, whom he begins by mentioning when he says, "For they ask the following: If a foot were in dust from all eternity, etc." In fact for a foot to have always been in dust and to have caused a print in the dust involves a contradiction, because local motion is required for a print to be caused by the pressing of a foot into dust; consequently, some such motion would have had no beginning, which contradicts the very definition of motion as being between opposites.

[E.7] To the one about what is "scarcely intelligible" [C.7], I say that the mind can apprehend contradictories, even at the same time (otherwise no mind would say they were contradictories), which is clear in general from The Philosopher's argument in *De anima* II [c.2], where he proves concerning the common sense[30] and the other particular senses that no sense relates terms unless it apprehends both. To be apprehended in this way is to be scarcely understood in the sense in which we say that we understand what we believe to be true and do not understand what we do not believe to be true even though we apprehend it.

We can reply in another way by saying that if we mean by 'intelligible' what the mind can give assent to and in this sense what the philosophers said was scarcely intelligible, it can be explained that in a general sense it was intelligible, but not in itself and in a particular sense. For it was intelligible with assent to it as meaning something that produces, but not as meaning something that causes. To understand causing merely by understanding the meaning of 'producing' is to understand causing in an incomplete way, just as to understand human being merely by understanding the meaning of 'animal' is to understand human being in an incomplete way.

Or in a third way it can be said (and perhaps this

is Augustine's view) that hidden contradictories, as long as the contradiction evident in them is not perceived, can in some way be apprehended by the mind, but not with certitude. Thus the contradiction here, if there is one, is hidden from the philosophers and could scarcely be understood by them.

[E.7.1] To what is added about the philosophers [C.7.1] it can be said that they agreed to many hidden contradictions. For example, they generally denied that there is a first cause that causes contingently, and yet they claimed that there is contingency in beings and some things come about contingently. But the view that some things come about contingently and the first cause causes necessarily, involves a contradiction, as was deduced in dist.8 of the first book[31] as well as in dist.39,[32] and was touched on a little in the preceding question.

[E.7.2] To what is added about the four causes [C.7.2] (which are considered by the metaphysician), and shows that the mind can abstract an idea of an efficient cause apart from movement and change, I say that not everything which can be abstracted in idea (or in virtue of the mind's consideration of it) can necessarily be separated in reality from what the mind abstracts it from. Thus it does not follow that there is in reality some efficient cause that neither moves nor changes.

[F.] Replies to the arguments in favor of the second opinion, from the point of view of those holding the first:

Those who hold the first opinion rely mainly on the fact that no contradiction is found between the terms 'other than God' and 'existing forever,' and secondly on the fact that the arguments which seem to prove the contradiction involve special cases, and thus even if they do prove the contradiction for some special cases they do not prove it of everything that is other than God, and thirdly on the fact that some of the arguments seem to work just as much for what can come to be in the future as for what is past, although no one denies the possibility of an endless future, whether we mean the coming

---

30 See glossary entry for 'common sense.'
31 See fn. 29 above, and selection I.9.2.
32 See selection IV.6.1.

to be of something non-successive or of something successive.[33] These people, I say, argue against the opinion [D] which says there is a contradiction and reply to its arguments.

[F.1] To the first [D.1] [the reply is] that some creature was able always to have been produced, namely an angel, whose existence is in the *aevum*.[34]

And if you say that this creature is made at some point, they would concede that it is made at an instant of the *aevum*, and [then they would say] that when it is it is always being made and produced. When you infer "therefore it would be successive," this does not follow, because the Son of God is always generated and yet he is not something successive but rather perfectly persistent, because the instant in which he is generated always remains.[35] Likewise, these people would say that the same now remains and in it the angel persists and receives being. Consequently, there is no succession since successive items always get their being one part after another.

[F.1.1] To the other argument [D.1.1] about preserving and creating, the reply will be clear from what we will say on the first question about the *aevum*.

***

[What follows are the relevant portions of *Ordinatio* II, dist.2, p.1, qu.1, where Scotus evaluates two views on how the duration of an angel's existence is measured. One holds that there is formally in the angel's existence a succession and the other holds there is no succession there. The first passage cites Augustine as favouring the former view, but in the second passage Scotus argues that Augustine's statement can be read as consistent with the latter view as well.]

In favour of this opinion [that there is succession in the actual existence of an angel] are four arguments:

First, in virtue of conservation. The argument is based on the authoritative text from Augustine's *Literal Commentary on Genesis*, bk.VIII, ch.19,[36] where he says that just as it is not the case that air has been made transparent by the sun but rather it is made transparent (otherwise the air would stay transparent after the sun went away[37]), so does a creature relate to God.

Further, in the same work, bk.IV, ch.14,[38] he says that God does not relate to a creature as a builder relates to a house.

From the above it is argued as follows: If it is not the case that a creature vis-a-vis God has been made to be by him but rather is sort of formally in a process of being made, then always it is formally put in being by God, and so, just as it persists continuously, so there is continuously a creation of it into being by God.

This is bolstered by the fact that to conserve is not just not to destroy, but is some positive action of God's (otherwise someone who does not close the window would be said to conserve the light; also to annihilate[39] would be a positive action, which is false, because to annihilate is not to act); therefore, to conserve is to act.

This is also clear from the fact that in its own being no creature is independent since it is not a pure act. Thus it depends continuously for its being on its cause, and not just on a cause which gave it being and now does not, for then to conserve would be merely to have acted earlier and now not to destroy.

If after all the above is granted, [you say] that God in preserving does something positive to a creature but not by any continuous action (because in this case there is no form by which the continuation of the action could be assigned) nor,

---

33 See glossary entry for 'successive being.'

34 See glossary entry for '*aevum*.' Although Augustine does not use this term, the idea can be found in selection III.2.2.

35 The generation of the 2nd and 3rd Persons of the Trinity occurs in eternity where there is, so to speak, only one instant, the eternal "now."

36 *De Gen. ad litt.* VIII, 12, n.26.

37 In Aristotelian physics darkness is due to the air's no longer facilitating sight as a medium between the eye and its object. In this sense when dark air is not "transparent."

38 *Op. cit.*, c.12, n.22.

39 See glossary entry for 'annihilation.'

either, by different actions, but rather always by the same action – the following argues against you: This causation, formally and ultimately, does not give what it is possible not to have even when the causation is given. (I prove this as follows: The cause causing by this causation is an ultimate cause directed to bringing the effect into being; therefore, if it is possible for that effect not to be even when that cause exists, it does not seem that the causation here involves the ultimate cause of the effect.) But even when the causation by which the angel is made to be is given, it is possible for the angel not to have being tomorrow. Therefore, it will not have being tomorrow formally by that causation, and thus it has being by some other causation.

If you say that from the first causation it does not get being plus co-existence with tomorrow; rather for this it is required that that future time exist, and then once the future exists the reason for the future is the reason the angel co-exists with it – the following argues against you: That is the way it is in eternity, which does not have co-existence with time insofar as it is an existence, but rather since time exists it co-exists with it. Thus, if this were the reason, the *aevum* would not differ from eternity. Likewise, it is not just that the angel can not have being in the future when the causation of the future is not given; rather it is possible for it not to have the basis of that co-existence, i.e. absolute existence. Therefore, it does not get this absolute existence from co-existence of that sort.

To the first [i.e. the argument based in the text from Augustine] I say that both ways conserve what Augustine says. The first way says that a creature always and equally essentially depends on God, so that the conservation of the thing is a sort of continuous causation or an infinite series of causations, and consequently God always actually causes the thing in the same way he caused it in the first moment (although we call the causation occurring at the first moment creation, and it occurring at the other moments conservation.) Likewise, the second position, since it sees no reason for the continuation of the causation (since there is no continued form) nor sees much reason for a distinction (since it sees no distinction either in what causes or what is caused insofar as they are the formal terms of the relation), says that a single action always persisting in respect of the creature is a creation insofar as it is understood as co-existing with the first temporal *now*, i.e. the temporal *now* that was immediately preceded by the not-being of the item caused, and that same action persisting is called conservation insofar as it co-exists with the other parts of time that do not immediately follow after the not-being [of the item caused] but rather after the being previously obtained at those parts of time. In this sense the action is a continuation of what was sort of previously obtained, not by any relation to not-being (where there is no earlier and later), but by a relation to the parts of time with which it co-exists.

But Augustine's intentions aside, there seems to be a problem for the argument developed there, namely that it is by different causations that the thing has being with different *nows*, because that whose opposite seems compatible with some causation is not completely obtained by that causation.

I reply: That proposition has to be disambiguated according to composition and division.[40] In the composite sense it is true and means that that whose opposite exists simultaneously with a certain causation is not itself completely obtained by that causation. But in the divided sense it is false because it is possible even for that causation itself not to be although the causation by which the thing ultimately has its being has been posited. Thus even though the causation of the angel is posited, it is still possible divisively (that causation posited) for that angel not to be, but it is not possible conjunctively.[41]

The above shows how to reply to the following similar argument: It cannot be the case simultaneously both that an angel is created and is annihilated; therefore to be created and to be conserved are not the same, since when it is conserved

---

40 See glossary entry for 'composite and divided senses.'
41 Scotus means that this could be true: The causation of the angel exists and the angel retains a possibility for not-existing. But this could not be true: The causation of the angel exists but the angel does not exist.

it can be annihilated, but not when it is created.

I reply: Just as it cannot be the case simultaneously in the composite sense that an angel is created and annihilated, so neither can it be the case simultaneously in the composite sense that it is conserved and annihilated. But in the divided sense it can be the case regarding an angel that there is at some time creation or conservation and nevertheless at that moment it is possible for the angel not to be (and thus it is possible for there to be annihilation). This is like what was said on the subject of God's predestining and his foreknowledge,[42] namely that in the divided sense there is a potential for one of two opposites even though the other is still there, but not that there is a potential for one of the opposites to exist at the same time the other one is still there.

***

[F.1.2] To what is added about the acquired being [D.1.2], they grant that it has acquired being because it does not have a being which of itself is formally necessary, but nevertheless it does not seem that it is acquired after not-being, because acquisition, like reception, seems to require no more than that it not get from itself what it is said to acquire, whether that acquired item is new or old.

[F.2] To the second [D.2] concerning The Philosopher's claim in *De Interpretatione* II [c.9] that everything which is, when it is, necessarily is, the reply is clear from dist. 41 of the first book[43] where this objection is put forward in order to prove that [a thing] does not exist contingently in that moment at which it exists, since [if it did], its opposite would be able to exist then. From this it is clear that what was assumed is false; rather in that moment and at that moment in which it exists and at which it exists it exists contingently, just as we argued and determined in that distinction. I say the same about a cause, for a cause does not cause to the extent that it temporally precedes its effect; rather it is a cause to the extent that it precedes its

effect in nature. Thus if every cause at the instant at which it causes causes necessarily and not contingently, then every cause causes necessarily and none cause contingently.

[F.3] To the third [D.3], it can be denied that in every species whatsoever there is an equal possibility for eternity and everlastingness, because the contradiction does not evidence itself equally for every species, and therefore the possibility is not similar.

Or if we grant about the ass that it could have been produced from eternity, and was able to reproduce, and consequently from it there could have been all the asses that have been engendered right down to this one, when you ask whether they would have been finite or infinite, it is denied that they are infinite; rather they would have been finite. And when you infer that therefore the whole duration, from the production of the ass right up to this ass would have been finite, the consequence is denied. For even if that ass were produced from eternity, still it was not able to have engendered from eternity, because generation necessarily includes, in the case of creatures, that there is change between opposite terms (namely, privation and form), and whatever is between opposites that follow on each other cannot be everlasting.

And if you say that then it would have had to have refrained from reproducing for an infinite time even though it was made complete and capable of reproduction, which seems absurd, I answer: The ass would not have been made from eternity more complete for reproducing than God for causing, and yet according to you God has to have refrained from causing A for a sort of imagined infinity so that there would be a contradiction involved in his having caused something and a sort of imagined past infinity not having preceded that. But in the case of God's causing, i.e. in the case of giving total being to what has being in itself it does not seem so necessary for newness to be included as it does in the case of reproduction which involves going from privation[44] to form. Therefore, it is not absurd, given the ass had to reproduce, that it refrained for an imagined infinity from that action which neces-

---

42 See selection **IV.6.1**.
43 The reference here actually seems to be to dist.39, which is included in selection **IV.6.1**.
44 See glossary entry for 'privation.'

sarily includes that something new exists, when you claim God necessarily refrained from an action which you do not show formally includes newness.

[F.4] To the fourth [D.4] I say that the whole argument for those potentials seems otiose and to go wrong in lots of ways. Nevertheless, if we speak about potential in the way he [Henry of Ghent] does at the end of his argument, it has to be concluded according to him that the potential for not being necessarily precedes the potential for being, and thus his argument, the one about contrary potentials (which he gets from The Philosopher in On the Heaven I [c.12]), ought to be interpreted as about potentials that are incompatible in respect of their acts. And then if a potential for not being necessarily precedes a potential for being, being necessarily precedes not-being, because a potential for not being never exists, on this understanding of it, except in something where being has preceded it.

We have to realize here that in the strict sense of potential, i.e. as something prior to an act, the subject for immediate opposites is never in potential to both opposites at once, because then it would have neither of them actually, and thus they would not be immediate opposites in respect of that same subject. Of these [opposites] it is true to say that the potential for one never exists without the actuality of the other. This is not to say that the act is receptive of that potential, rather only the subject receives that potential just as only it receives its act. (For if act A were prior to the potential for B on account of being receptive of it, then it would also be prior to B itself because in one and the same subject the potential is prior by nature to the act. But by an equally good argument B is prior to the potential for A, and thus the same item is both prior and posterior to the same.) But the potential for one necessarily goes along with the act of the other, on account of the immediation of the acts [i.e. they are immediate opposites].

To the question I say that [the creature] was from eternity under a potential for being and under a potential for not being, but first it was under a potential for being (i.e. in fact this was true), because it was under not-being and so not under a potential for not being. But if it had been from eter-

nity, it would always have been under a potential for not being and never under a potential for being but rather under the actuality of being. But if you do not speak of a potential as existing prior to the act but rather as though it were a sort of subject, and you assume the essence not to be related this way to being [i.e. as being a potential for being] unless it is under not-being, the assumption is false and was disproved above.

Setting aside then the talk of potentials, the argument in brief seems to rest on the point that opposites which belong to the same thing in the order of nature[45] cannot belong to the same thing at the same moment in the temporal order, because what is prior in nature is prior temporally. Therefore, being and not-being, since they belong to a stone in the order of nature, cannot belong to it at the same moment in time; nor is it the case that it makes no difference which precedes the other, rather necessarily not-being precedes temporally its being; and thus it cannot always have existed. That not-being belongs to it in nature before being does is shown by the fact that not-being applies to the stone of itself, while being applies to it not of itself but on account of something else.

To this I say that two opposites do not belong at the same moment in the order of nature to the same thing, when we speak sort of positively about the order of nature (as we do when we say that in human being animal comes before rational, and in the composite of substance and accident the substance comes before the accident); rather [they belong at the same moment when we speak of the order of nature] sort of privatively, i.e. the one would belong if it were not blocked. This sense has been explained in the preceding question in the course of explaining Avicenna's view. Using this sense I say that what belongs earlier in nature to something does not have to belong to it earlier in time, for what does not get to be something from itself can be helped out by some positive cause which gives it something which it does not get from itself, and thus it would earlier in time get the opposite of that which it gets from itself.

---

45 See glossary entry for 'order of nature.'

***

[What follows is the relevant section of qu.2, where Scotus explains 'priority of nature':]

The phrase 'priority of nature' I understand as follows: Something can be said positively to be prior in nature where it belongs to something earlier and the entity is earlier than that which is said to belong to the subject later in nature. For example, *animal* and *rational* in human being, and substance and accident in an accidental composite.

In another sense one item is said to be prior in nature to another sort of privatively or potentially, on account of the elimination of one or the other or the exclusion of one or the other, since it belongs to the subject once the other cause is excluded. This does not in fact belong to what it is said primarily to belong to, but it would belong to it if it were not blocked by something else. For example, suppose it is said that in matter privation[46] is naturally prior to form. This does not mean that the two are in the matter at the same time but in such a way that the privation is there before the form is, but rather that the privation as such can be said to be prior by nature and in the matter by nature before the form is because the privation would always have belonged to the matter if it had not received the form by the action of some agent. Thus for having the privation it suffices to have just the matter with the negation or privation of the extrinsic cause, but for having the form an extrinsic cause is required. Nevertheless, the privation is not part of the definition of the matter, just as neither is the form, and both cannot exist in the matter at the same time.

***

This reply is evidently applicable in other cases. Consider the argument which tries to prove that God cannot create matter under a form, because matter is deprived earlier in nature than it is informed, because it is on account of itself that it is deprived and on account of something else that it is informed, and therefore form can exist in matter only if unformed matter has preceded it in time. But this argument is inconclusive, because matter is not on account of itself positively deprived but only privatively, since it also does not get the form from itself but from something else (as from an engenderer or a creator), while it by itself, without any other positive cause, suffices for it itself to be deprived. Therefore, it would always be deprived if it were not for some positive cause that blocks the continuation of its privation. Nevertheless, since the positive cause can block the privation of the matter right from the beginning of its existence by giving it a being which is always not deprived, it does not necessarily follow from such a priority of nature that there is a priority in time.

[F.5] To the other [D.5] concerning the infinity of souls, I reply: Whatever cannot be made by God in one day because it includes a contradiction would also not be able to be done in an infinity of past time (if that had been), and for the same reason. For in this day there are infinite moments (in fact there is such an infinity in one hour of one day) in any of which he could create a soul just as he could in any one day of the whole of infinite time if that existed (for it would not have been necessary for him to take a rest from one day to the next to create one soul after another). Thus, if in the infinite moments of this day he is not able to create infinite souls (because this is not something doable), neither was he able to have created infinite souls in the infinite days of the whole of past time.

If you say that the moments of this day have not actually existed in the way the infinite past days have, your reply is insufficient, because just as the infinite instants of the infinite days in which he created existed potentially according to you (in the same way an "indivisible" is in the continuum[47] and not in actuality), because none of these were actually the end point of the whole time, so also is it the case with the infinite moments of this day. Therefore, the infinity of the instants of this day, or of this hour, seems to be equal to the infinity of the infinite instants of infinite days, and from that what I proposed seems to follow. Nevertheless, some philosophers allow that it is not impossible to have an infinity in accidentally ordered things, as is

---

46 See glossary entry for 'privation.'
47 See glossary entry for 'continuum.'

clear in Avicenna's *Metaphysics* VI, the chapter on causes [c.2].

[F.6] To the argument [D.6] concerning the passage through the infinite, it seems to disprove the everlastingness of successive entities.[48] But according to those who hold this opinion the reason for impossibility in successive entities is not like that for impossibility in persistent entities,[49] because even though persistent entities (any of them) can be measured by time in virtue of their motions, they are nevertheless posited as being measured by the *aevum* in virtue of their own substantial being. Consequently to posit a persistent entity as existing without any beginning does not seem to posit that something infinite has been accepted.

The reason [for the impossibility] of a successive infinite is reinforced by imagining a line in reverse. Suppose some line were extended as though to infinity, then starting from this point A it would not be possible to traverse the line. Therefore, also it seems that in reverse, by imagining the line as extending into the past, it would not be possible that it reach right up to A.

[F.7] To the last argument [D.7] it can be said that equal, greater, and less belong only to the quantity of finite magnitudes, because 'how much' is divided by finite and infinite before equal or unequal apply to it, for it belongs to a greater quantity to exceed, to a smaller one to be exceeded, and to an equal quantity to be commensurate with [what it is equal to]. All of these seem to imply finitude. Therefore, it would be denied that one infinity is equal to another infinity, because equal and unequal, greater and less, are differences of finite quantity, not of infinite quantity.

[G.] Replies to the original arguments [A & B] for both sides.

[G.1] To the first original argument [A.1], I grant that matter is ungenerated and incorruptible, but from that it does not follow that it is everlasting, because although there is no matter from which it comes to be, the whole of it is produced. This production is not generation, because generation and destruction belong to composites, not to incomplex items.

[G.2] To the second [A.2], concerning the everlastingness of time, I say it is invalid because otherwise we could infer that what puts things in motion is not able not to be in motion. (The reply to this is in the preceding question.)

***

[What follows is the relevant section of qu.2.]

To the original argument, I say that the first cause can immediately produce some new effect without any newness in the cause itself. This is clear from the following example: If it were given that the sun always is in itself equally radiant and some clear medium is created next to it, the sun will start to illuminate that medium in such a way that there will be nothing new in the sun which is the reason for that new illumination. Also, if it were possible for it of itself to posit the clear medium and illuminate it by causing light in it, then it could produce into being this whole, the illuminated medium, without any newness in itself.

If you say: This would not be possible if the agent were a natural one existing in the same condition, because in that case it would always produce in the same way; therefore the example is not what is required to show what you propose – I reply: It is true that this example was good for showing that newness in the effect does not require newness to be posited in the cause even though it was not good for showing that a total cause acting naturally could have a new effect, because such an agent, if there were such, would always act in the same way in respect of its effect. But a free agent can by the same old act of will produce a new effect at that time when it wills that effect to be new. For it is not necessary that if it wills everlastingly and it is not able to start willing, therefore it wills [what it wills] for all time, just as it is not necessary in my case that if I now will something that then I will it for now; rather I can will it for tomorrow, and even though the same act of will remains without any change on the part of my will I can cause that new thing tomorrow, which is when I will it for.

---

48 See glossary entry for 'successive being.'
49 See glossary entry for 'persistent being.'

And when it is argued against this by the following argument: Some new relationship naturally must precede in the producer in regard to the produced but not vice versa – I say (just as we said in dist.35 of bk.I and many times elsewhere) an absolute[50] item in the cause immediately follows on an absolute item in the effect, while in the effect there primarily follows a relation to the cause. And then, if there is some relation of cause to effect, that relation to the effect is the final one, and sometimes does not exist at all. When, then, it is said that because the cause gives being, therefore the effect receives being, and not vice versa, I say that if the word "because" implies a reduplication of a relation in the cause or some new reality in the cause (whether relative or absolute), the proposition is false. But if it implies the reduplication of the primary act of the cause which naturally precedes what is caused, the proposition is true in this sense, for something absolute in the cause naturally precedes what is caused.

And if you say: It does not cause just because the absolute item is there, because that absolute item is there even when it is not causing – I say that in that moment when it causes it causes in virtue of being naturally prior[51] to that action [of causing], and so nothing is understood [to be prior] besides that absolute item from which the caused item gets its being. Consequently, nothing can be meant by the fact that it causes except that it is prior, and this in relation to any moment. The idea is wrong which says that the cause always seems to be indeterminate right up to the instant when it causes, and at that point some relation which determines it to the effect is first required on the cause's part. This is false, for that same absolute item which in the cause preceded both in nature and in time the produced effect or caused item, is in the cause as naturally prior at the moment at which it causes. It is now causing in virtue of the same absolute item in virtue of which it was earlier ready to cause and not in virtue of some extra item, whether absolute or relative.

***

As for the remarks about what is "before," I say that the argument goes through only for an imagined "before," or in the way eternity is "before" – which amounts to nothing. It is just like saying outside the universe there is nothing where either "outside" is denied to be or we affirm something only of an imagined "outside."

[G.3] To the third [A.3], about *De generatione* I. Although the proposition, "the destruction of one item is the generation of another," is in some sense probable (I say it is true to the extent that no natural agent tends of itself to destroy something but rather incidentally destroys what is incompatible with what it does tend toward of itself, i.e. the item generated), nevertheless this does not entail that the process of generating is everlasting, since the final destruction can coincide with the final generation, for example when all mixed things are resolved into their elemental constituents.[52] At that point there will be a stop to both generation and destruction, even though that final destruction is not an annihilation.

Nevertheless, The Philosopher assumes along with that proposition another one, namely that any such generable item is again destructible and its destruction is the generation of something else – but this is not true.

But if we argue about the past, we have to read the proposition as meaning that the generation of one item is the destruction of another, and this is not so true as the former reading when we consider the tendencies natural agents have of themselves. For a generator happens to destroy because of the incompatibility of the item to be destroyed with the item which the generator tends toward. It is able to produce the form which it tends toward only in pre-existent matter and that pre-existent matter is usually sustaining a form which is incompatible with the form which the generator tends toward, and consequently it has to destroy the pre-existent composite item in order to generate what it tends toward.[53] Even granted that this entails that no gen-

50 See glossary entry for 'absolute.'
51 See glossary entry for 'order of nature.'
52 See glossary entry for 'element.'
53 See glossary entry for 'natural generation.'

eration produces the whole [of what it produces], the eternity of the thing does not follow. When the whole is produced it is not required that part of it pre-exist under some incompatible form and its production need not be the destruction of some other entity but merely the destruction of nothing or exclusively of a non-being. Then there is no need for another production to have preceded this first one because the *terminus a quo* of the latter was the *terminus ad quem* of some production, since there is no production that produces nothing.

[G.4] To the fourth [A.4], about the succession due to motion where it is said that an agent that does not cause through motion and is not stoppable can have an effect coeval with it, it would be said that this major premiss is true when the cause and the effect can have a single sort of essence. But where they cannot have a single sort of essence, but rather the priority in nature of the cause necessarily requires its priority in time in respect of the effect, the major premiss is false. But this is how it is in the matter in question.

[G.5] To the first argument in opposition [B.1], I say that either this is not a definition of 'creature' but rather some description which Arius[54] (against whom Augustine is arguing) would accept because

he said that the Son of God at sometime did not exist, and then it suffices for Augustine's purposes to accept this definition or description as granted against him and from the negation of the description in the case of the Son of God (something granted by Arius) to infer against him that the Son is not a creature.

Or if this is a definition of 'creature,' and a definition in the strict sense of 'creature in so far as it is a creature,' this does not mean it is a definition of anything other than God (for example of angel or human being), because it would be said that this definition just happens to belong to what it is to be a creature. If we were given a definition of 'has a beginning' and in fact everything other than God has a beginning, then everything other than God is a creature would not follow, rather there would be a fallacy of accident[55] because of the extraneousness of the middle term in respect of the third term insofar as it is related to the first term. For not everything that an accident rejects is rejected by the subject to which that accident happens to belong.

[G.6] To the second [B.2], about infinity in plurality and in magnitude, the reply was given earlier in replying to the argument about the actual infinity of souls.

---

54 See fn.6.
55 See glossary entry for "fallacy of accident."

III.8. WILLIAM OF OCKHAM

Although on the surface Ockham's treatment of this question, which Aquinas, Henry, and Scotus have debated in the preceding selections, seems to reach much the same indecisive result that Scotus came to, in fact Ockham's outlook is much different. In agreeing with Henry and against Scotus that a cause cannot at the very instant it is causing something have the potential not to cause it at that instant, Ockham in effect makes impossible the *contingent* production of an eternal being. As in the selections in topic IV (divine foreknowledge of contingents) the disagreement comes down to conflicting intuitions about what genuine contingency in the world requires. Also noteworthy here is the much fuller treatment Ockham gives of apparent problems with infinities and the continuum.

III.8.1. Could God make a World that has existed from Eternity? (*Quaestiones Variae*, qu.3)

Could the world have existed by divine power from eternity?

[A] I say that it is possible to answer either way and neither answer can be completely disproved. Nevertheless, since the world's having existed from eternity does not seem to include an obvious contradiction (although Henry of Ghent says the opposite, as will be clear later), I shall first put forward those of the arguments showing that it could not have existed from eternity which make a stronger case for the conclusion.

[A.1] The first argument is that an infinity would actually have been gone through, since an infinity of revolutions would have actually been gone through, because in this case there would be no first revolution, rather for any given revolution there would be another before it *ad infinitum*. Therefore, since all these revolutions have actually occurred in the past, it follows that an infinity of them have actually occurred in the past.

[A.2] The second argument is that in this case there would be an actual infinity, because if an infinity of revolutions have been gone through, and we assume that in each revolution, i.e. in each day,

God creates a single human being, (for according to The Philosopher and The Commentator there was no first human being), i.e. that he creates each day a single intellective soul, it follows then that there would be an infinity of souls actually existing, since the destruction of the soul does not follow from the destruction of the human being. Thus something other than God would be actually infinite in perfection,[1] since the totality of souls would be, and this seems absurd.

[A.3] The third argument is that an infinity would actually be exceeded. This is because, according to you, an infinity of solar revolutions have actually occurred in the past. But, since there are more lunar revolutions than solar, it follows that the lunar revolutions are in their infinity greater in number than the solar. But what is exceeded is not infinite. Therefore, the infinite is not infinite, from the fact that it is exceeded.

[A.4] Further, I take today's revolution and I ask: Is there some revolution which is infinitely distant from today's, or not? If not, then all the revolutions taken together will not be infinite.

[A.4.1] This is bolstered by the fact that, just as in continuously existing persistent[2] entities when a finite one is added to a finite one the result is just something finite and not at all something infinite, so in continuously existing successive entities[3] a

---

1 See glossary entry for 'perfection.'
2 Contrasted with "successive" entities. See glossary entry for 'persistent being.'
3 See glossary entry for 'successive being.'

finite revolution added to a finite revolution, from which it is only finitely distant, would never result in anything other than what is finite. But if some revolution is infinitely distant from today's revolution, I then ask the following about the revolution which immediately follows that revolution that is infinitely distant: Is it infinitely distant from today's revolution or not? If it is not, then neither is the one that precedes it infinitely distant from today's revolution, and from that it follows that between those two revolutions there is only a finite distance. If it is infinitely distant from today's revolution, by the same argument it will follow that the one which immediately follows it, i.e. this second one, will be infinitely distant, and likewise the one after that, and so on right up to yesterday's revolution. Consequently, yesterday's revolution will be infinitely distant from today's, which is obviously false. This is because the series in accidentally ordered things exists in just the same way as it does in essentially ordered things.[4]

[A.5] Besides, if this were the case, it would follow that a part of a whole would be greater than the whole. I show this as follows: Let a be the whole of past time ending at today's beginning, and let b be the whole of future time starting from today's beginning. Also let c be the whole of past time ending at today's end, and let d be the whole of future time starting from today's end. Then I argue as follows: a and b are equals, because the whole of past time ending at today's beginning and the whole of future time starting from today's beginning are equal. Therefore, a is greater than c. The antecedent is true by hypothesis, because both a and b are infinite times. The inference I show as follows: a is equal to b by the hypothesis, and b is greater than d because the whole of future time starting from today's beginning is greater than the whole of future time starting from today's end. Therefore, a, which is equal to b, is greater than d, since if one of two equals is greater than a third the other equal will also be greater than the third. Further, d is equal to c, because the whole of past time ending at today's end is equal to the whole of

future time starting from today's end, since both are infinite. If, then, a is greater than d, as was shown, it follows that a will be greater than c, since it is greater than something equal to c. But a is a part of c, since the whole of past time ending at today's beginning is a part of the whole of past time ending at today's end. Therefore, it follows that a part of a whole is greater than the whole, which seems absurd.[5]

[A.6] Further, there are as many revolutions after today's revolution as there are before it. This is certainly something The Philosopher means to say. But it is impossible for all the future revolutions to be gone through and for all these to be a whole, since there is an infinity of them. Therefore, it is impossible for all the revolutions before today's to have been gone through, given that there is an infinity of them. Then from the fact that they all have actually been gone through it follows that they are actually finite.

[Henry of Ghent's arguments (see selections **III.6.1.** & **2.**):]

[A.7][6] That the world's having existed from eternity involves a contradiction is shown as follows: What of itself and of its own nature is a non-being in such a way that it is neither formally nor by causation a being is not only produced by something else in respect of its made-being, in the way a ray would get its existence from the sun if the sun were eternal, but also is produced by something else in respect of its coming-into-being, since no transition from one of two contradictories to the other can come to be without mutation. But the world in so far as it is a creature is of this sort, especially when we speak about creation in the way believers do, i.e. when a creature is produced in this way by God its non-being precedes its being, and not just by nature or in thought as the philosophers said, but rather it precedes it in reality; otherwise, the creature would not really be made from nothing, the opposite of which the faith maintains. Therefore, the creature is produced by God, not

---

4 See glossary entry for 'accidental vs. essential order.'
5 In brief: $a=b$, $b>d$, thf $a>d$; $d=c$, thf $a>c$, where a is part of c.
6 See selection III.6.1., pp396 ff.

just in respect of made-being as the Son is produced by the Father in God,[7] but also in respect to coming-into-being. However, the act of creation is indivisible in respect of temporal duration and lacks all succession and duration either in the direction of what came before or in the direction of what comes after, since it is an instantaneous and non-complex change. Therefore, creation cannot exist from eternity, because in that case it would have duration in the direction of what came before, when in fact it does not. Here, then, is the contradiction: if the creature had existed from eternity, it would not have aquired being after not-being, but rather it would always have had just made-being. But from the fact that it is a creature it is implied that it has acquired being after not-being, and this is a contradiction.

[A.7.1][8] This reasoning is bolstered by the fact that, when something belongs to something of its own nature, it is impossible that its opposite belongs to that thing at the same time, for otherwise contradictories would be true at the same time. But, according to all the saints and philosophers, a creature is of itself a non-being. Therefore, on that ground it is not able to have being; consequently it must have it on some other ground.

[A.8] If someone says that it is not part of the definition of a creature that it have being after not-being in the sense that the not-being temporally precedes the being, but rather it is said to have being after not-being because God could have not made the creature from eternity just as much as he could have made it from eternity, and thus the not-being of the creature does not necessarily precede its being, except in virtue of thought or nature and not temporally –

[A.8.1][9] Against this: According to The Philosopher, everything which is necessarily is when it is, in the sense that at the time at which it is there is no potential for its not being, neither on the part of the thing itself nor on the part of its efficient cause; otherwise, contradictories could be true at the same time. In the same way, it is true of that which was, that at the time at which it was,

necessarily it was. Likewise, it is true of that which will be, that at the time at which it will be, necessarily it will be. Thus in none of these cases is there a potential for the opposite at the very same time in which the act is given. If there is a potential for the opposite, this will occur at some earlier point where that act can be prevented, and thus the principle that everything which is, necessarily is when it is, is not absolutely necessary. But if the world had existence from eternity, there would never have been an antecedent potential by which the world's act of existing could have been prevented at some instant. Therefore, if it had existed from eternity, it would with absolute necessity have existed from eternity and in no way contingently.

[A.8.2] Besides, if not-being precedes being just in virtue of the nature, I ask: Was the creature, then, in that prior state really a non-being or a being? If the former, then we get our conclusion that not-being precedes being in reality. If the latter, then the creature was before it was.

[A.8.3] Likewise, what belongs to something naturally belongs to it really. This is clear by induction. If, then, not-being belongs to a creature from its nature, it belongs to it really. And it does not belong to it when it is, so it must belong to it before that.

These are the stronger arguments, I think, for showing that a creature rejects having existed from eternity.

[B] But despite these arguments it does not seem that there is any obvious contradiction involved in a creature's having existed from eternity, nor any obvious incompatibility arising either from God or from the creature.

[B.1] If you say that, when we speak of creation in the sense that Christians use, there is an incompatibility, since in this sense the non-existence of the creature really precedes its existence temporally, and, if it had existed from eternity, it would not really precede that existence –

I say that, when we speak of creation in this sense,

---

7 A reference to the production of the second and third Persons of the trinity, something which occurs in eternity, not in time.
8 See selection III.6.1., p.397.
9 *Ibid.*, p.401.

there is no sense in asking whether what necessarily is produced after not existing temporally is able to be produced without [having not existed] temporally. Obviously this involves a contradiction. But our question here is this: Could that which is produced in such a way that its non-existence really precedes its existence (and temporally, as the believers claim by faith) be produced, without any incompatibility, in such a way that its non-existence does not temporally precede its existence? In this sense, there does not seem to be any obvious contradiction arising either from God or from the creature, although the arguments opposing this are not easy to solve in such a way that those hearing them will be satisfied. Consequently, I say that if God can make whatever does not include a contradiction, He was able to have made the world from eternity.

[C.] To the opposing arguments:

[C.1] To the first [A.1], I answer that following the approach I am taking we should allow that an infinity of revolutions has actually been gone through, just as the argument deduces. This should be accepted not as an absurdity that destroys the premiss but as something that in fact follows.

[C.2] To the second [A.2], I allow that there could be an infinity of actual souls, and that there could be an infinity of actual perfections other than God, but from this it does not follow that something other than God has infinite perfection, because those souls cannot [all together] amount to some single thing.

If you say that at least it must be allowed that something outside of God has as many perfections as God has, I do allow this because a human being has a greater number of perfections that God has, since God formally has just one, the one perfection which is His essence. But if we mean by the words ['has a greater number of perfections'] 'has virtually,'[10] then He does have a greater number of perfections, because he can create a human being, an ass, and so on.

[C.3] To the third [A.3], I allow that an infinity would be exceeded just as the argument shows, and that one infinity is greater than another infinity in just the way the lunar revolutions exceed the solar revolutions.

[C.4] To the other [A.4] I say that no revolution is infinitely distant from today's revolution, for this is a single universal proposition whose every singular instance is true, since neither this [revolution is infinitely distant] nor that one, and so on *ad infinitum*. And when it is further asserted, "therefore, all of them taken together are finite," the inference is invalid. We find a counter-example in the parts of the continuum,[11] where no part is infinitely distant from any given part of the continuum, where we mean by a distance something which exists through parts of the same size; for between no parts [of the continuum] do we find an infinity of parts of the same size. Nevertheless, it does not follow that "therefore, all the parts of the continuum are finite." The reason is that that inference is only valid where there is a definite order of the parts such that we find there a first, a second, and a third, none of which is part of the other. We do not find such an order in the continuum nor in revolutions.

[C.4.1] To the bolstering argument [A.4.1], I say that just as in a persistent continuum when any finite and limited part is added to another the result is something finite and not infinite, and yet in that continuum there actually exists an infinity of parts outside their cause, so also when any revolution is added to another the result is something finite, and yet all the revolutions taken together are infinite.

[C.4.1.1] Suppose you argue this way: No matter what revolution you take, some revolution will be infinitely distant from it, because this is a universal proposition everyone of whose individual instances is true. Therefore, from today's revolution some revolution is infinitely distant; therefore, some revolution is infinitely distant from today's revolution. I accept this, and then I run the argument given earlier [in A.4.1] about the revolution that immediately follows [and draw the conclusion that today's revolution is infinitely distant from yesterday's].

To this I answer as follows: The same argument can be made about the parts of a continuum. For every part of the continuum there is a smaller part. This is a universal proposition everyone of whose

---

10 See glossary entry for 'virtual existence.'
11 See glossary entry for 'continuum.'

singular instances is true, for there is some part smaller than this part, and some part smaller than that part, and so on for each individual case. Therefore, there is some part that is smaller than any part of the continuum. Then I ask of that part: Is it the smallest or is there some other smaller [than it]. If it is the smallest, then it is indivisible. If there is another smaller [than it], then that original part is not smaller than any part of the continuum.

Consequently, I say that both arguments commit the "fallacy of figure of speech,"[12] because the mode of supposition is changed from a term with *merely confused* supposition,[13] where there is no descent [to the singular instances], to a term with *determinate* supposition, where there is such a descent.

***

[Above Ockham has used technical terms which he defines in his *Summa Logicae*, p.I, c.70, when he explains personal supposition. Below we translate the relevant passages (which the editors of Ockham's *Quaestiones Variae* have helpfully included as a footnote).]

Personal supposition can first be divided into *discrete* supposition and *common* supposition. *Discrete* supposition occurs where a proper name of something or a demonstrative pronoun, taken in a significative way [i.e. not as standing for itself], stands for something. Such supposition renders the proposition singular. For example: 'Socrates is a human being,' 'This human being is a human being,' and so on. ...

Common personal supposition occurs when a general term stands for something. For example: 'A human being is running,' 'Every human being is an animal.'

Common personal supposition is divided into *confused* and *determinate*. *Determinate* supposition occurs when there is a descent to singular instances through a disjunction. For example, this is a valid inference: 'A human being is running;

therfore, either this human being is running, or that one [is running], and so on for each case. ...' Every personal supposition of a common term which is not determinate is a case of *confused* personal supposition. And this is divided into *merely confused* supposition and *confused and distributive* supposition. *Merely confused* personal supposition occurs when a general term stands for something personally and there is no descent to the singular instances by way of a disjunction where no change has been made in the other term of the proposition; rather the descent occurs by way of a proposition with a disjunctive predicate, and that can be inferred from any given singular instance. For example, in this proposition, 'every human being is an animal,' 'animal' has *merely confused* supposition, because there is no descent under 'animal' to the instances it covers by way of a disjunction. I.e., this is not a good inference: 'Every human being is an animal; therefore, every human being is this animal, or every human being is that other animal' and so on for each case. Nevertheless, there is descent to a proposition with a disjunctive predicate involving the singular cases, for the following is a good inference: 'Every human being is an animal; therefore, every human being is this animal or that animal or that one' and so on for each case. The consequent here is a categorical proposition composed of the subject term 'human being' and the predicate 'this animal or that animal or' (so on for each case). ...

Confused and distributive supposition occurs when there is in some way a conjunctive descent, given that the term covers a number of things and cannot be formally inferred from any one. For example, in 'every human being is an animal' the subject term has *confused and distributive* supposition, for this is a good inference: 'Every human being is an animal; therefore, this human being is an animal, and that human being is an animal' and so on for each case. Also this is not formally a good inference: 'this human being (where we point to anyone whosoever) is an animal; therefore, every human being is an animal.'

---

12 See glossary entry for 'fallacy of figure of speech.'
13 See glossary entry for 'supposition.'

***

Likewise there is also a change from a term with *confused and distributive* supposition into one with *merely confused* supposition. For in this proposition, 'For any given revolution there is some [revolution] infinitely distant from it,' the phrase 'some revolution' in the predicate has *merely confused* supposition, because this is not a good inference: 'For any given revolution there is some revolution infinitely distant from it; therefore, for any given revolution this revolution is [infinitely] distant from it or that [revolution is infinitely distant from it].' This inference commits the "fallacy of the consequent".[14] Rather it is the case that in the consequent [of the original argument], when we infer, 'Therefore, some revolution is infinitely distant from any given [revolution],' the word 'revolution' has *determinate* supposition for this one or for that one. Consequently, there is a descent under that term with that supposition by saying: 'Therefore, this revolution is infinitely distant from any given revolution, or that one [is],' and thus we find here the "fallacy of figure of speech" on account of the different modes of supposition given to the same term occurring in the predicate of one proposition and in the subject in the other.

Similarly, in the first proposition [of C.4.1.1] the word 'revolution' (taken as being in the subject when it is said, 'For any given revolution there is some [revolution] which is infinitely distant from it'), has *confused and distributive* supposition on account of the universal sign [i.e. 'any'] which is added to it in the subject, and consequently there is descent under it. [I.e. we can infer, 'For this revolution there is some revolution infinitely distant from it, and for that revolution,' etc.] But in the consequent it has *merely confused* supposition, i.e. when we say, 'Therefore, some revolution is infinitely distant from any given revolution,' and thus there is no descent under it. [I.e. we cannot infer, 'Some revolution is infinitely distant from this revolution, and some revolution is infinitely distant from that revolution,' etc.] It follows that all arguments of this sort commit the fallacy of figure of speech in the fourth mode.

If you ask whether these propositions, 'Some revolution is infinitely distant from today's revolution,' 'From today's revolution some [revolution] is infinitely distant,' should be allowed, I say that the first of these should be unqualifiedly denied, because the word 'revolution' occurring in the subject has *determinate* supposition and stands for this revolution or for that, and therefore the proposition is unqualifiedly false, because neither this one nor that one are infinitely distant from today's revolution. But the second should be unqualifiedly allowed, because the word 'revolution' occurring in the predicate has *merely confused* supposition and does not *determinately* stand for this revolution or for that one.

Also if you say, "If this is true, 'From today's revolution some revolution is infinitely distant,' then I accept that and run the original argument," I answer that you cannot accept that, because there is no descent under the phrase 'some revolution' that occurs in the predicate. The similar arguments about the parts of the continuum should be resolved in the same way.

[C.1.2] Another and better way to respond is to say that a general term in the predicate never has *confused* supposition except when a universal sign occurs in the subject, or some term in virtue of which the subject has *confused and distributive* supposition. Therefore, perhaps both of these propositions, 'Some revolution is infinitely distant from today's revolution' and 'From today's revolution some revolution is infinitely distant,' are false, because in them the word 'revolution,' both when occurring in the subject and when occurring in the predicate, stands *determinately* for this or that revolution. But this is not the case in these propositions, 'Some revolution is infinitely distant from any revolution' and 'From any revolution some [revolution] is infinitely distant.'

If in addition to what was said above it is said that in any continuum there is an actual infinity[15] of parts each of which includes its own perfection, and therefore any continuum has an intensively infinite perfection, it can be said in reply that, if in the continuum there were an actual infinity of parts none of which is part of the other, in such a

---

14 See glossary entry for 'fallacy of consequent.'
15 See glossary entry for 'infinity.'

way that there would be a first, second and third that are actually distinct, then the argument would be valid. But in a continuum this is not the case, because there it is always the case that the parts of two things that result from a division are parts of the things that resulted from the first division. This always holds, and thus there is no first part in a continuum which is prior to the others, for, let any part be given, it is then divisible into a prior part. Consequently, the argument does not go through.

But even so the argument seems to work, because a continuum can be divided into two halves, and one of these halves into two other halves, and so on *ad infinitum*. Also those halves resulting from the divisions are really and totally distinguished from each other in such a way that none is part of some other. Since, then, according to you there is an actual infinity of such halves in the continuum, it follows that there is in the continuum an infinity of parts none of which is part of some other, and thus they will be of infinite perfection.

Consequently, I say that, although in any continuum there is an actual infinity of parts and an actual infinity of perfections of which none is the other (in the way just described), nevertheless, because all those perfections are the sort which result in a single finite perfection, it does not follow that the continuum has infinite perfection, no more than this follows: 'The continuum has an infinity of partial sizes; therfore, it has infinite size.'

Also if you ask how it is possible to think that there is an infinity of parts and perfections in something and nevertheless the composite whole does not have infinite perfection, I answer that in anything where we find an infinity of parts of the same size so that we get a first part which cannot be the second or the third, and in the same way we get a second and a third, it can be argued that the thing composed of an infinity of such parts has infinite perfection. But where there is just an infinity of parts in virtue of proportion or of the same proportion, the second of which is always a part of the first, and we do not get some part which of its own nature is more first than second, nor vice versa, we do not have a good argument from the infinity of such parts to the infinity of the thing composed of them. Nor should one seek a reason for this other

than that the nature of such a thing is like that.

[C.4.3] Some objections to the preceding:

[C.4.3.1] Suppose you say that according to The Philosopher the parts in a continuum exist potentially, not actually.

[C.4.3.2] Further, if the world had existed from eternity and an infinity of revolutions had actually been gone through, and God on each day had made a single division of the continuum, the continuum would have been actually divided into an infinity of parts, and there would be one division of the past into an actual infinity and another infinite division of the future, which could never exist without an infinity of perfection.

[C.4.3.3] Further, according to The Philosopher, in anything we find a natural minimum, for example a minimal bit of flesh. Therefore, this bit of flesh does not have an infinity of parts.

[C.4.4] Replies to these objections:

[C.4.4.1] To the first [C.4.3.1] I answer that The Philosopher says that they exist potentially because they are not actually separated. But he does not mean that they exist potentially in the sense in which the Antichrist's soul now, when it is nothing, exists potentially, for if they existed potentially in that sense they could never make up the continuum. Therefore, he means that they are something outside of their cause. But they exist potentially because no part of the continuum is some separated whole existing by itself.

[C.4.4.2] To the other [C.4.3.2] I allow that the continuum would have been divided into an actual infinity of parts, given the hypothesis, and that there would exist a division into an actual infinity of parts and that those parts would then be divisible *ad infinitum*, and this is not compatible with division down to an infinity of indivisible parts. But from this it does not follow that the whole continuum made up of those parts has infinite perfection; the reasons for this have been stated above.

[C.4.4.3] To the other [C.4.3.3] I say that there is no natural minimum in the sense of something that cannot always be divided into ever smaller parts *ad infinitum* while retaining the same natural form.[16] It is, for example, clear in the case of flesh that there is no minimal bit of flesh which cannot be divided into a smaller bit, because every bit of

16 See glossary entry for 'form/matter.'

flesh, no matter how small, can be divided into a smaller bit *ad infinitum*, at least by divine power. As for The Philosopher I say that he means that there is a natural minimum and a minimal bit of flesh which can naturally exist by itself and withstand outside agents tending to destroy it (for example, cold and heat, air or water, etc.), so that if there were a smaller bit of flesh it would not be able naturally to withstand outside agents and immediately, on account of its lack of power, would give way to its destruction, in which the form of flesh would be destroyed and a new form, of air or something else, would be induced. But God can suspend the actions of outside agents and preserve the flesh from destruction while always dividing it into ever smaller bits *ad infinitum;* and in that case the division will never stop at a minimal part of flesh, nor, on account of His suspension of the action of outside agents and His preservation of the flesh from destruction, will any part divided off or going to be divided off give way to destruction. If such parts were left to themselves without any special preservation, and the outside agents were not prevented from engaging in their actions, they would immediately give way to destruction.

[C.5] To the next original argument [A.5] I say that that argument is based on something false, viz. that all infinities are equal, which is falsely assumed in the hypothesis. For it was clear earlier that an infinity of solar revolutions have been gone through, given that the world has existed from eternity, and likewise for the lunar revolutions. Nevertheless there are more lunar revolutions than solar revolutions. Therefore, given the hypothesis, it ought to be allowed that one infinity is greater than another and is exceeded by an infinity. Consequently, one infinity is not equal to another, and this holds whether one gone-through infinity is compared to another or to an infinity that is going to be gone through. For it is obvious that if the world had existed from eternity the whole of past time ending at today's beginning would be actually infinite, and likewise the whole of past time ending at today's end. Nevertheless, the whole of past time ending at today's end would be greater than the time ending at today's beginning, at least it would be one day greater. Similarly I say that the whole of past time ending at today's beginning and the whole of future time starting from today's beginning are not equal; rather one is greater than the

other. But which one is greater and which one is smaller it is difficult or impossible for us to tell. Since, then, that whole deduction is based on the proposition that all infinites are equal, which is false, as was shown, it is obvious that it does not follow that a part is greater than its whole.

[C.6] To the next [A.6] I say that there are not just as many future revolutions as past ones, given the hypothesis without any qualifications. Rather either there are more or fewer, as is clear from what was just said. But given that there are just as many, then I say that all the future revolutions are not able to be gone through, because they are infinite. This is because it is generally true that an infinity which at some time is yet to be gone through can never actually be gone through. Neither can we ever get the last member of such an infinity, which is because we must always accept what it means for it to be infinite. But an infinity which at no time was to be gone through, but rather was always already gone through, can be gone through not withstanding its infinity. Thus, from the fact that something which at some time was to be gone through has been gone through, it follows that it is finite. But if something has been gone through which never was to be gone through, then it need not be finite but can be infinite. But now, if the world had existed from eternity, all the past revolutions would never have been something to be gone through, because at no instant of time would this proposition have been true: 'All these revolutions (pointing to all the past revolutions) are to be gone through.' Therefore, the conclusion does not follow.

[Replies to Henry of Ghent's arguments:]

[C.7] To the first of Henry's arguments [A.7] I say that it fails in two ways.

[C.7.1] The first is that it accepts that a creature is a non-being in virtue of its own nature, so that, according to him, it is necessary that on the side of the thing the creature's non-being precedes its being. For it is obvious that this is false, 'A creature is a non-being in virtue of its own nature,' for if it were true no power could make it a being. And if some authorities say that a creature is of itself a non-being, I say that by such assertions they really mean denials, i.e. they mean to say that a creature is not in virtue of its own nature a being nor does it get being [from its own nature]. This is because the creature does not get being from itself but rather from something else. This is made clear in my *Reportatio* where it treats of the known being that a creature has from eternity, and in my *Ordinatio* on a similar question. Then this is not a good inference: 'A creature is not from itself a being; therefore, it rejects having existed from eternity,' because it could have existed in virtue of something else from eternity.

If you say, just as he seems to say, that opposites which in the natural order belong to the same thing cannot belong to it at the same time on account of their opposition, but being and not-being in the natural order belong to a creature because naturally the creature is a non-being before it is a being, therefore etc. – I answer in the same way that Scotus does, and correctly,[17] that this argument would show that matter could not be produced at the same time that it is produced under a form, for by the order of nature privation[18] and form belong to matter and by nature the matter is under the privation before it is under the form. Therefore, I say, just as Scotus says, that the proposition in question is true for positive opposites where both of them are positive, but it is not true for those opposites where one is positive and the other privative. This is because, if there were some positive opposites which belonged to something in the order of nature, both of them would really have to belong to it, and consequently they could not belong to it at the same time on account of their formal incompatibility. Therefore, such opposites belong to it earlier and later in time. But if of the opposites one were negative and the other positive and they belonged to something in the order of nature, the negative one would not have to belong to it really, but rather it would belong to it really unless it were prevented by an outside agent that produced the other positive opposite. It is in this way that non-being naturally belongs to a creature, because it does not cause itself to be a being, but rather God does. Consequently, it is not necessary that a creature is really a non-being at some time before it is a being, and as a result opposites of this sort do not have to belong to the thing in the temporal order, as do positive opposites, nor at the same time. The whole reason for this is that the negative term does not have to belong to the thing really, and thus it does not belong to it earlier in time, nor at the same time as does the positive opposite.

[C.7.2] It fails in another way because he claims that it is necessary for creation and conservation to be distinguished in respect of any creature. This is because whoever would claim that the world had existed from eternity would say that the world had never been created, in the sense of creation where it connotes a negation which immediately preceded the being of the thing, since this sort of preceding of the negation did not exist on the side of the thing. Neither is its coming-into-being in any way distinguished from its made being, and always it got its made being and its being conserved from God, but never its coming-into-being or its being created, as distinct from its conservation.

[C.7.2.1] Suppose you say the following: If the world had existed from eternity, still it would have been produced by God. This occurs, then, either by creation, and in that case I have what I wanted to prove, and that creation will take place in an indivisible measure [of time], or by an absolute change, which should not be claimed.

[C.7.2.2] Besides, from the fact that the world has crossed from one contradictory to another because from not-being to being, it cannot come into being without a change, and this cannot exist without a measure.

[C.7.3.1] I answer the first [C.7.2.1] by saying there is an equivocation on the term 'creation.' For if you mean by it the total production of something by some efficient cause, then in this sense the world would have been created even if it were eternal, and in this sense you are now created by God. Such a creation does not have any measure, either divisible or indivisible. And in this sense creation does not differ from conservation, because a thing is always said to be created in this sense as long as it is being conserved. Consequently, if the world had existed from eternity, it would from eternity have been created in this sense and preserved.

In another sense 'creation' is taken to signify the thing produced while connoting that the negation of that thing really comes first. It is in this sense

---

17 See selection **III.7.1**, p.433.
18 See glossary entry for 'order of nature.'

that Christians speak of creation. In this sense it is distinguished from conservation, as was made clear in the second book of my *Questions on the Sentences*. Taken in this sense creation has a divisible or indivisible measure and can have both actually or potentially according as the thing can be created in an instant or over a length of time. If we speak this way, the coming-into-being of a creature is distinguished from its made-being, in the same way that creation is distinguished from conservation. But if the world had existed from eternity, it would not have been created in this sense by a creation of that sort; consequently the argument does not work.

[C.7.3.2] To the other [C.7.2.2] I say that if the world had existed from eternity there would not have been a real transition from one contradictory into the other, because it would never have really been under non-being; rather always it would have been under being, since always it would have been a being and never a non-being. Consequently, there would not have been in this case some change measured by any measure, divisible or indivisible, because such a change only occurs when something first is not and then later is, and that is not the case here given the hypothesis.

[C.8] To the next [A.8] [I say that] it is clear from the above how non-being belongs to a creature in virtue of its own nature. When the authorities say affirmatively. "A creature is a non-being [of itself]," they mean to make negative claims, viz that the creature is not of itself a being. Thus if the world had existed from eternity, it would never have been a non-being. Consequently, these contradictories, being and not-being, would not really belong to it either at the same instant of time or at different instants, because one would always belong to it, viz. being, and the other would never belong to it, viz. not-being.

[C.8.1] To the next [A.8.1] I say that this proposition, 'Everything which is necessarily is when it is,' is incorrectly employed, since it is not asserted by The Philosopher in *De Interpretatione* I.[19] Rather The Philosopher says that the following proposition is necessary: 'Everything which is is when it is,' for this cannot be false. In like fashion the following proposition is necessary: 'Everything which

was was when it was,' and likewise this one: 'Everything which will be will be when it will be.' When the proposition is understood in the way in which it is usually understood it is false, because every singular instance is false, with the exception of God. For this is false: 'Socrates when he is, necessarily is,' since for a temporal proposition [i.e. with a temporal subordinate clause] to be true or necessary requires that both parts of it be true or necessary at the same time.

Here we have to know what the differences are among a conditional proposition, a causal proposition and a temporal proposition. For the truth of a conditional proposition it is required that the antecedent not be able to be the case or to be true without the consequent. But it is not required that either the antecedent or the consequent be in fact true. Consequently, this conditional is true, 'If Socrates exists, Socrates exists,' whether or not Socrates exists. This is because all that is meant is a relationship between the antecedent and the consequent, i.e. the relationship of not being able to be true without the consequent.

For the truth of a causal proposition there is required not only this relationship in which the antecedent cannot be true without the consequent, but also that both parts are in fact true and the antecedent is the cause of the consequent. Example: For this causal proposition to be true, 'Because you are running you are moving,' it is required that the antecedent, 'you are running,' be true only if the consequent, 'you are moving,' is true, and that 'you are running' is a cause of 'you are moving,' and that both 'you are running' and 'you are moving' are in fact true. Therefore, if you are not running, the causal proposition will not be true, but rather will be false on account of a false implication.

But for the truth of a temporal proposition is required the factual truth of both parts at the same time as that for which the temporal proposition is said to be true; otherwise it is not true. Consequently, if one or the other part is false, the temporal proposition is false on account of a false implication.

As for the case under discussion, this temporal proposition, 'Socrates when he is, or while he is, necessarily is,' has a false part, viz. this, 'Socrates necessarily is,' and this holds whether Socrates is or is not. Consequently, this temporal proposition, 'Socrates when he is, necessarily is,' is false, and the same holds for any positive, created case. But in the case of God the temporal proposition is true and necessary, i.e. when we say 'God, when He is, necessarily is,' because 'God is' is true and also 'God necessarily is' is true and for the same time.

If you say that 'Everything which is, necessarily is when it is' is true by a conditioned necessity rather than an absolute necessity, I answer that this is illogical. This is because the proposition is no more necessary by a conditioned necessity than by a categorical[20] necessity, since every proposition which is necessary is absolutely necessary. Those who correctly interpret this proposition think that some necessary propositions are conditional or temporal and others are simply categorical and neither conditional nor temporal. An example of the former: This conditional proposition is necessary, 'If Socrates exists, Socrates exists,' or 'If Socrates runs, Socrates moves.' An example of the second: This categorial proposition is necessary, 'God is good and wise' and so on for others. Therefore they think, if they think correctly, that when some conditional or temporal proposition is necessary but not one or the other of its parts, then it is necessary by a conditioned necessity. For example, this conditional is necessary, 'If Socrates runs, Socrates moves,' but neither 'Socrates runs' nor 'Socrates moves' is true, and thus the whole is said to be necessary by a conditioned necessity. But it would be more proper to speak here of the necessity of a conditional than of a conditioned necessity, for this conditional is absolutely necessary since it can never be false. In the same way the necessity of a categorical proposition is the necessity of a categorical and not a categorical necessity.

[C.8.1.1] Further, I say that there is no potential for the opposite, namely that this conditional be false, 'If Socrates exists, Socrates exists,' either at the instant in which Socrates exists or at an earlier or at a later time, for it is never able to be false. This is because, whether or not Socrates exists, as long as this proposition is formed by the mind it is true.

Suppose you say that if Socrates exists at instant a, he is not able not to exist at a. This inference is then necessary: 'Therefore, if Socrates exists at a, necessarily he exists at a.' But not absolutely; therefore, conditionally.

Further, he was able not to have existed at a. Either, then, he has at a the potential for not existing at a, or he had it earlier. The first is ruled out on account of the contradiction involved; therefore, the second alternative holds, and then the argument goes through.

I answer as before that when we understand that this conditional is necessary, 'If Socrates exists at a, Socrates exists at a' and similarly this one, 'If Socrates exists at a, Socrates is not able not to exist at a,' I concede these and say that those conditionals are absolutely necessary, not conditionally, and yet both parts of the conditional are contingent.

Also I allow that Socrates was able not to have existed at a. When you ask, "Was he, then, at a able not to have existed at a, or before a?", I say that it was before a. Also it can be said that it is true, given the hypothesis, that the world has existed from eternity and that this proposition is now necessary, 'The world has existed from eternity,' because this would now be true and is never able to be false. Nevertheless, it was able to have been false, in the way that any true proposition about the past is necessary and yet was able to have been false. But he supposes that this proposition, 'The world has existed from eternity,' given the hypothesis, is not necessary. What he supposes is false, given the hypothesis.

[C.8.1.2] Also it can be said that if the world had existed from eternity, God would have produced the world necessarily, just as the Philosophers said, and not contingently. This is because, once it is given that the world has existed from eternity, he was not able not to have produced the world, because he was not able before eternity, since there is nothing before it, nor in eternity on account of the contradiction that would involve. Therefore, he has produced it necessarily.

If you say that God does nothing necessarily outside of Himself, this is now in fact true, even though that is compatible with the claim that He was able to have done something outside Himself

20 See glossary entry for 'categorical proposition.'

necessarily, and he would have done just that given the hypothesis. On this approach, then, given the hypothesis, the proposition, 'The world has existed from eternity' is absolutely necessary, since it is neither false nor able to be false.

Then to the question, 'Did it have at *a* a potential for not existing, or before *a*?' I answer that if by *a* you indicate some instant of time, then I say that before *a* it was able not to have existed at *a*. If by *a* you indicate eternity, then I say that neither at *a* was the world able not to have existed at *a*, on account of the contradiction involved, nor before *a*, because nothing is really before *a*. But if we held that the world's being produced by God contingently was compatible with its having been produced from eternity, we would have to say, it seems, that on account of this the world was able not to have existed at *a* because God was able earlier in nature[21] or in idea not to have produced the world at *a*, since His will had the alternatives of producing it at *a* or not produing it [at *a*].

[C.8.2] To the next [8b] I say that, if it is allowed that the creature had not-being by nature before it had being, in the good sense that concerns what it is in virtue of its own nature, then it first was a non-being, i.e. it did not exist before it actually did exist. I say, then, further that that way of arguing about what is earlier ought not to be allowed in this case nor ever, except when earlier and later correspond to distinct measures, as is made clear in several places in my *Ordinatio* and *Reportatio*. Seek it there. But in this case, given the hypothesis, the creature's not-being did not have any measure in reality; therefore, etc.

[C.8.2.1] Another response is that there is no pri-

ority of nature between the creature's not-being and its being, when we speak as do The Philosopher and The Commentator in *Metaphysics* V [c.11][22] when they say that that is called prior which can be separated from the later, but not vice versa. But in this case being can be separated from not-being in the same way that not-being can be separated from being. In fact this is necessarily the case on account of their opposition. Consequently, properly speaking we find priority of this sort only between disparate positive terms, not between mutually incompatible positive terms. This is because opposites can be mutually separated just as can opposites one of which is positive and the other is privative; in fact they are separated in this way.

[C.8.3] To the bolstering [A.8.3] I say that a positive term which belongs to something naturally, belongs to it really. This is not so in the case of negative and privative terms; rather they belong it really unless an outside agent prevents them, as is the case here. This is clear enough from what has been said already.

[D] However, persons who want to hold the opposite, namely that the world rejects having existed from eternity, can easily respond to the objections that are usually brought against their view, with this exception: they cannot point to any obvious contradiction [involved in the world's having existed from eternity]. Consequently, those who take this approach should adopt it more on account of the arguments derived from facts about what we can sense, as Scotus does,[23] (these arguments were presented earlier), than on account of some contradiction that is involved, for it seems that the world's

---

21 See glossary entry for 'order of nature.' We know from selection **IV.7.1.** that Ockham rejected the idea of distinct instants of nature that are simultaneous in time.
22 1019a1-3.
23 Ockham apparently refers here to a passage from Scotus's *Reportata Parisiensia* II, dist.1, qu.4 (pp.538-548 in the Vives edition of Scotus's *Opera Omnia* XXII). On p.545a we find the following: "Thirdly it is said that even if the world were eternal, it would not follow that an infinity of human beings had come earlier, because God could create human beings in some other way than by generation, and then there would not have to be another one before this one *ad infinitum*. But this reply is more against the philosophers, and against what can be sensed, since if natural reason necessarily concludes more the non-everlastingness of the world than its everlastingness, then the philosophers who rely on natural reason ought more to posit that; if what can be sensed more proves the case for everlastingness, then they ought to go along with what seems to be the case on the basis of what is sensed and more posit that. But the philosophers say that human beings can only exist by generation, because to a philosopher it is just as absurd for God to have created a first human as for Him to have created a second or a third. Therefore, the philosopher claims that in all cases the generation of one item is the destruction of some other, and that humans were only produced by natural reproduction."

having existed from eternity does not include any contradiction.

[D.1] But against this appoach there are some arguments.

[D.1.1] The first of these is that, according to Ambrose in *On the Trinity*, God has been God from eternity, because 'God' is the name of a nature and a power.

[D.1.2] Further, many propositions have been true from eternity, for this was true from eternity, 'Two and four are six,' according to Augustine in *On the Immortality of the Soul*. This holds for many other propositions which were not God, and therefore were something other than God.

[D.1.3] Besides, given the existence of an efficient cause that is sufficient and is not thwartable, the effect can exist; but God was from eternity a cause of this sort in respect of the world; therefore, etc.

[D.1.4] Besides, no agent acting without any succession necessarily precedes its effect temporally. This is clear in the case of the sun, which immediately, as it were, illuminates things. Also in the case of an angel, who immediately, as it were, can think. But God has produced, or at least was able to produce, the world without any succession; therefore, etc.

[D.1.5] Besides, in the case of things produced instantaneously the agent can exist at the same time as its effect, for an agent that produces instantaneously can exist along with the beginning of its action, since in any instant in which the thing is given the beginning of its action can be given. But in an instantaneous action the principle, the beginning, the terminus of the coming-into-being, and the made-being all exist at the same time. Therefore, the proposition assumed before is evident. But God has produced the world instantaneously; therefore, etc.

[D.1.6] Besides, let *a* be the first instant of the existence of the world, and suppose the world only lasts for an instant. Then let *b* be the last instant of the world's not-existing. Now I ask: Are *a* and *b* one instant or two? If they are one, then contradictories are true at the same instant, since in the same instant the world exists and does not exist. If they are two instants, and between any two such

instants there is a length of time, and that length of time is divisible into an infinity of prior parts, then the world existed over an infinity of times before the first instant of its existence. Therefore, we reach the conclusion that there was no first instant of its existence, and consequently it has existed from eternity.

The same argument holds for a first instant of something which actually lasts for only an instant. We should then ask: Does it exist in the same instant in which it does not exist? In that case contradictories are true at the same time. Or does it exist in one instant and not exist in another? In that case there is between those two an intervening time, *and in that time the thing would neither exist, for it only exists for an instant, nor not exist, since the first instant of its not-existing comes after that time.* [24]

[D.1.7] Besides, infinity does not seem to be any reason for its not having been able to exist from eternity, because the length of time from the present instant into a future without an end is just as great as that from the present instant into a past without a beginning. But the world is capable of the infinity involved in persisting infinitely into the future. Therefore, it was capable of the other infinity involved in not having had a beginning.

[D.1.8] Besides, God could have created an angel before He created the world, and perhaps He in fact did [create an angel] before He created time. But only eternity exists before time; therefore, He could have created an angel from eternity.

[D.1.9] Besides, the "now" of time exists together with the "now" of eternity; but the "now" of eternity has no beginning; therefore, neither does the "now" of time.

[D.1.10] Besides, this is true from eternity. 'A human being is an animal'; also this, 'An angel is a substance.' These were not God; therefore, etc.

[D.1.11] Besides, what was able to come into being before every assigned instant and before every instant it is possible to assign, could have come into being from eternity, since before the first assigned instant and before every instant which can be thought of as assigned there exists only eternity and infinite duration. But God could have made the

---

24 The Latin text for the bit between the asterisks is faulty. We have reconstructed the apparent line of thought while remaining as close to the text as possible.

world in this way; therefore, etc.

To this are added the examples of a fire if it were eternal, and of heat and brilliance, of the sun and its radiance, of the body opposed to the sun, if it were eternal, as well as of the shadow and of the foot standing from eternity in the dust and its imprint.

[D.1.12] Besides, God can do whatever does not involve a contradiction. But the world's having existed from eternity does not involve a contradiction; therefore etc.

TOPIC IV

DETERMINISM, FREE WILL, AND DIVINE FOREKNOWLEDGE

THE SET OF PROBLEMS DEALT WITH IN THESE SELECTIONS HAS A VERY ancient lineage. Aristotle had already in the fourth century B.C.E. confronted thinkers who wanted to claim that all that happens in the world happens necessarily, i.e. there had never been a time at which it had been possible for the world to work out in a different way than it has and in fact will. They had an argument to prove this from the principle that every proposition, even those about the future, is either true or false (the principle of bi-valence), which Aristotle grapples with in our first selection. The Stoics later adopted a view of fate based on the idea that everything that comes to be must have a sufficient cause of itself in what precedes it, and the ancient neo-Platonists came to believe that God from his position outside time has knowledge of the whole course of events in the temporal realm including what to us is yet to come. Everyone agrees that some features of the future are inevitable, but it is not just these inevitabilities that are fated or are known by a supra-temporal deity; how those matters which we ordinarily take to be up to chance or to the free choices of agents (called "future contingents") will turn out was also considered by these thinkers to fall within the scope of either fate or divine foreknowledge or both.

On these questions Christian thinkers were caught by apparently contradictory demands. On the one hand, it seemed necessary to ascribe knowledge of everything, including future contingents, to God if His perfection and omnipotence were to be maintained; on the other hand, the freedom of human choices had to be defended against the determinist Stoic line if God's rewarding the righteous and punishing the evil doers could be seen as just. But how could there be knowledge of matters about the future which were not in fact yet determined? Here Boethius took up the Platonist line that since God is outside of time He can, so to speak, in the one moment of eternity gaze upon the whole course of events through all of time including the future and thus know everything which, from our point of view within time, is going to happen, even though much that is going to happen has not been determined to be going to be by what has already occurred, i.e. it is still contingent. This doctrine seems to imply that right now some propositions about future contingents are true and some false, and they all have one or the other of these truth values. But by an argument advanced by Aristotle (in **IV.1.1.**) it seems that from that admission alone the necessity of everything about the future follows. Medieval theologians who adopted Boethius' proposal had somehow to defeat this argument, and such efforts elicited some of the most sophisticated of the scholastics' discussions of the modalities of possibility, necessity, and contingency.

In the second half of the thirteenth century dissatisfaction with Boethius's way of handling the problem came to the fore. Siger of Brabant, writing from a strictly philosophical point of view, argued (in **IV.5.1.**) that divine foreknowledge of the future was not compatible with a world left undetermined by both its own past and divine decisions. Duns Scotus (in **IV.6.1.**) based divine foreknowledge in God's knowledge on His own will, but contingency was protected by the freedom of that will itself. Scotus denied that from a philosophical point of view God's creative causation of the world should be viewed as a case of necessary causation;[1] rather God's perfection is guaranteed only if we view Him as capable at the same moment of choosing not to create what He in fact chooses to create. This sort of freedom for opposites, Scotus argued, is compatible with divine immutability, i.e. the impossibility of God's ever changing in any way.

In the final selection, William of Ockham, writing in the generation after Scotus during the first quarter of the fourteenth century, rejects both the Boethian and Scotist approaches, and, in fact, comes close to admitting that the problem is intractable. But he at least sketches a way in which outright contradiction can, he believes, be avoided. Perhaps no other theological doctrine forced the Christian thinkers into a more searching and critical examination of their philosophic heritage than did this one concerning divine foreknowledge. It brought to light how trying to combine the idea of an immutable, omnipotent, and all-knowing deity with the cosmology of necessary first causes necessarily causing everything else leads to perhaps insuperable problems for a belief in freedom both for the deity and for lesser beings such as ourselves.

---

1 See selection **III.7.1.**

IV.1. ARISTOTLE

THE FOLLOWING SELECTION, CHAPTER 9 OF ARISTOTLE'S
On Interpretation, was available throughout the medieval period. This work,
together with Boethius's two commentaries on it, formed part of the core of
medieval curricula. The question arose for medieval thinkers whether it was
Aristotle's intention to say that many statements concerning future events are neither true nor false, since the events they describe are not yet determined to be
going to occur.

IV.1.1. Determinism and the Truth of future contingent Statements (*On Interpretation* 9)

With regard to what is and what has been it is necessary for the affirmation or the negation to be true or false. And with universals[1] taken universally it is always necessary for one to be true and the other false, and with particulars too, as we have said; but with universals not spoken of universally it is not necessary. But with particulars that are going to be it is different.

For if every affirmation or negation is true or false it is necessary for everything either to be the case or not to be the case. For if one person says that something will be and another denies this same thing, it is clearly necessary for one of them to be saying what is true – if every affirmation is true or false; for both will not be the case together under such circumstances. For if it is true to say that it is white or is not white, it is necessary for it to be white or not white; and if it is white or is not white, then it was true to say or deny this. If it is not the case it is false, if it is false it is not the case. So it is necessary for the affirmation or the negation to be true. It follows that nothing either is or is happening, or will be or will not be, by chance or as chance has it, but everything of necessity and not as chance has it (since either he who says or he who denies is saying what is true). For otherwise it might equally well happen or not happen, since what is as chance has it is no more thus than not thus, nor will it be.

Again, if it is white now it was true to say earlier that it would be white; so that it was always true to say of anything that has happened that it would be so. But if it was always true to say that it was so, or would be so, it could not not be so, or not be going to be so. But if something cannot not happen it is impossible for it not to happen; and if it is impossible for something not to happen it is necessary for it to happen. Everything that will be, therefore, happens necessarily. So nothing will come about as chance has it or by chance; for if by chance, not of necessity.

Nor, however, can we say that *neither* is true – that it neither will be nor will not be so. For, firstly, though the affirmation is false the negation is not true, and though the negation is false the affirmation, on this view, is not true. Moreover, if it is true to say that something is white and large, both have to hold of it, and if true that they will hold tomorrow, they will have to hold tomorrow; and if it neither will be nor will not be the case tomorrow, then there is no "as chance has it." Take a sea-battle: it would *have* neither to happen nor not to happen.

These and others like them are the absurdities that follow if it is necessary for every affirmation and negation either about universals spoken of universally or about particulars, that one of the opposites be true and the other false, and that

---

1 See glossary entry for 'universal vs. particular.' Here Aristotle refers to three types of propositions: (1) a universal categorial proposition, e.g. 'Every human being has hair,' and its denial, 'Not every human being has hair'; (2) a particular categorial proposition, e.g. 'Some human being has hair,' and its denial, 'No human being has hair'; and (3) indefinite propositions like 'Human beings have hair,' and the denial 'Human beings do not have hair.' Aristotle thought in the case of the last both the proposition and its denial could be true.

nothing of what happens is as chance has it, but everything is and happens of necessity. So there would be no need to deliberate or to take trouble (thinking that if we do this, this will happen, but if we do not, it will not). For there is nothing to prevent someone's having said ten thousand years beforehand that this would be the case, and another's having denied it; so that whichever of the two was true to say then, will be the case of necessity. Nor, of course, does it make any difference whether any people made the contradictory statements or not. For clearly this is how the actual things are even if someone did not affirm it and another deny it. For it is not because of the affirming or denying that it will be or will not be the case, nor is it a question of ten thousand years beforehand rather than any other time. Hence, if in the whole of time the state of things was such that one or the other was true, it was necessary for this to happen, and for the state of things always to be such that everything that happens happens of necessity. For what anyone has truly said would be the case cannot not happen; and of what happens it was always true to say that it would be the case.

But what if this is impossible? For we see that what will be has an origin both in deliberation and in action, and that, in general, in things that are not always actual there is the possibility of being and of not being; here both possibilities are open, both being and not being, and consequently, both coming to be and not coming to be. Many things are obviously like this. For example, it is possible for this cloak to be cut up, and yet it will not be cut up but will wear out first. But equally, its not being cut up is also possible, for it would not be the case that it wore out first unless its not being cut up were possible. So it is the same with all other events that are spoken of in terms of this kind of possibility.

Clearly, therefore, not everything is or happens of necessity: some things happen as chance has it, and of the affirmation and the negation neither is true rather than the other; with other things it is one rather than the other and as a rule, but still it is possible for the other to happen instead.

What is, necessarily is, when it is; and what is not, necessarily is not, when it is not. But not everything that is, necessarily is; and not everything that is not, necessarily is not. For to say that everything that is, is of necessity, when it is, is not the same as saying unconditionally that it is of necessity. Similarly with what is not. And the same account holds for contradictories: everything necessarily is or is not, and will be or will not be; but one cannot divide and say that one or the other is necessary. I mean, for example: it is necessary for there to be or not to be a sea-battle tomorrow; but it is not necessary for a sea-battle to take place tomorrow, nor for one not to take place – though it is necessary for one to take place or not to take place. So, since statements are true according to how the actual things are, it is clear that wherever these are such as to allow of contraries as chance has it, the same necessarily holds for the contradictories also. This happens with things that are not always so or are not always not so. With these it is necessary for one or the other of the contradictories to be true or false – not, however, this one or that one, but as chance has it; or for one to be true *rather* than the other, yet not *already* true or false.

Clearly, then, it is not necessary that of every affirmation and opposite negation one should be true and the other false. For what holds for things that are does not hold for things that are not but may possibly be or not be; with these it is as we have said.

IV.2. BOETHIUS

The following selection is from Boethius's book *The Consolation of Philosophy*. The book is written as a dialogue between Boethius, who is in prison awaiting execution, and the personification of philosophy, who comes to give Boethius consolation. Philosophy deepens Boethius's understanding of causation and necessity, and explains how to God in eternity all events, past, present, and future are present at once. It is not then required that the temporal world be deterministic, i.e. that the past determine all that will happen in the future, for God to know all that will happen in the future. The idea that God surveys from eternity the whole of time is one Boethius has borrowed from the Platonists and was destined to be the dominant solution to the problem among Western scholastics, unless challenged by Duns Scotus and others in the late 13th century.

IV.2.1. How can God know everything about the Future? (Book V of the *Consolation*)

I

She finished speaking, and was going to turn the course of her speech to deal with and explain some other questions; then I said: "Your exhortation is right indeed and very worthy of your authority, but what you said just now about providence, that it was a question involving many others, I know from experience. For I want to know whether you think chance is anything at all, and if so, what?"

"I am hastening," she replied, "to make good my promise and open the way to you by which you may be brought back to your homeland. But these things, though they are very useful to know, are yet a little aside from the path we have set ourselves, and it is to be feared you may not be able to last out to the end of the direct road if you are tired by going down by-paths."

"There is really no need," I said, " for you to be afraid of that. For I shall find it a resting-place, to understand these things, which I most delight in. At the same time, since every side of your argument would be set up in undoubted credibility, nothing that follows from it would be doubted."

"I will grant your wish," she said then; and at once began thus: "If indeed someone were to define chance as an event produced by random motion and not by any chain of causes, then I assert that chance is nothing at all, and I judge that apart from signifying the subject-event it refers to, it is a sound entirely empty of meaning. For what place can be left for randomness where God constrains all things into his order? For that nothing comes from nothing is a true opinion, which none of the ancients ever contested, but they laid it as it were as a foundation of all arguments about nature, though they applied it not to the creative principle but to the material subject to it. But if something were to arise from no causes, that will seem to have arisen from nothing; and if this cannot be, then even chance cannot even possibly exist, of such a kind as we have just now defined.

"Why then," I said, "is there nothing which can rightly be called chance or fortuitousness? Or is there something, although it is hidden from common men, to which these names belong?"

"My Aristotle," she said, "defined it in his *Physics* II[1] in an argument brief and close to the truth."

"How?" I asked.

"Whenever," she said, "something is done for the sake of some given end, and another thing occurs, for some reason or other, different from what was intended, it is called chance: as, for example, if a

---

1 See selection I.1.3.

man digging in the ground in order to till his field were to find he had dug up a quantity of gold. Now this is indeed believed to have happened by chance, but it does not come from nothing; for it has its proper causes, and their unforeseen and unexpected coming together appears to have produced a chance event. For if the man tilling his field were not digging the ground, and if the man who put it there had not hidden his money in that particular spot, the gold would not have been found. These are therefore the causes of that fortuitous profit, which is produced by causes meeting one another and coming together, not by the intention of the doer of the action. For neither he who hid the gold, nor he who worked the field, intended that money to be found, but as I said, where the one buried it the other happens and chances to have dug. We may therefore define chance as the unexpected event of concurring causes among things done for some purpose. Now causes are made to concur and flow together by that order which, proceeding with inevitable connexion, and coming down from its source in providence, disposes all things in their proper places and times."

I Verse

Among the crags of the Achaemenian cliffs, where turned in flight
The fighting Parthian's arrows pierce his pursuers breast,
The Tigris and Euphrates rise from one spring,
Next they separate and their waters divide;
Herodotus, Strabo and Pliny knew.
If they should come together, into one course brought back again,
If all that the water of each stream bears should flow into one,
Their ships would meet, as will treetrunks torn up by the river,
And their mingled waters in chance paths will twist and turn.
Yet these chance wanderings the very slopes of the land
And the downflowing nature of the slipping stream control.
So too that chance which seems slack-reined to roam
Endures its own bridle, and itself moves by law.

II

"I see that," I said, "and I agree it is as you say. But in this close-linked series of causes, is there any freedom of our will, or does this chain of fate also bind even the motions of people's minds?"

"Freedom there is," she said, "for there could not be any rational nature, did not that same nature possess freedom of the will. For that which can by its nature use reason, has the faculty of judgement, by which it determines everything; of itself, therefore, it distinguishes those things which are to be avoided, and those things that are to be desired. Now what a man judges is to be desired, that he seeks; but he runs away from what he thinks is to be avoided. And therefore those who have in themselves reason have also in them freedom to will or not to will, but this freedom is not, I am sure, equal in all of them. For heavenly, divine substances possess penetrating judgement, an uncorrupted will, and the ability to achieve what they desire. But human souls must indeed be more free when they preserve themselves in the contemplation of the divine mind; less free, however, when they slip down to the corporeal, and still less free when they are bound into earthly limbs. But their ultimate servitude is when, given over to vice, they have lapsed from the possession of the reason proper to them. For when from the light of the highest truth they have lowered their eyes to inferior, darkling things, at once they are befogged by the cloud of unknowing, they are disturbed by destructive affections, by giving in and by consenting to which they strengthen that servitude which they have brought upon themselves, and are in a way made captive by their freedom. Yet that regard of providence which looks forth on all things from eternity, sees this and disposes all that is predestined to each according to his deserts."

II Verse

That Phoebus shining with pure light
"Sees all and all things hears,"
So Homer sings, he of the honeyed voice;
Yet even he, with the light of his rays, too weak,
Cannot burst through
To the inmost depths of earth or ocean.
Not thus the Maker of this great universe:
Him, viewing all things from his height,

No mass of earth obstructs,
No night with black clouds thwarts.
What is, what has been, and what is to come,
In one swift mental stab he sees;
Him, since he only all things sees,
The true sun could you call.

III

Then I said: "See, I am again confused, with a still more difficult doubt."

"What is that?" she asked. "Tell me, for I already guess what troubles you."

"It seems," I said, "much too conflicting and contradictory that God foreknows all things and that there is any free will. For if God foresees all and cannot in any way be mistaken, then that must necessarily happen which in his providence he foresees will be. And therefore if he foreknows from all eternity not only the deeds of human beings but even their plans and desires, there will be no free will; for it will be impossible for there to be any deed at all or any desire whatever except that which divine providence, which cannot be mistaken, perceives beforehand. For if they can be turned aside into a different way from that foreseen, then there will no longer be firm foreknowledge of the future, but rather uncertain opinion, which I judge impious to believe of God. For neither do I agree with that argument according to which some believe that they can solve this knotty question. For they say that a thing is not going to happen because providence has foreseen that it will be, but rather to the contrary, that since something is going to be, it cannot be hidden from divine providence, and in this way the necessity slips over to the opposite side. For, they say, it is not necessary that those things happen which are foreseen, but it is necessary that those things that will happen are foreseen; as if indeed our work were to discover which is the cause of which, foreknowledge of future things' necessity, or future things' necessity of providence, and as if we were not striving to show this, that whatever the state of the ordering of causes, the outcome of things foreknown is necessary, even if that foreknowledge were not to seem to confer on future things the necessity of occurring. For indeed, if anyone sit, then the opinion that thinks that they sit must be true; and conversely also, if the opinion about any person be true, that they sit, then they must be sitting. There is thus a necessity in both cases: in the latter, they must be sitting, but in the former, the opinion must be true. But a person does not sit because the opinion about them is true, but rather that opinion is true because that someone is sitting happened first. So that although the cause of truth proceeds from the one part, yet there is in both a common necessity. Obviously the same reasoning holds with regard to providence and future events: for even if the reason they are foreseen is that they are future events, yet they do not happen simply because they are foreseen; and yet nevertheless things either must be foreseen by God because they are coming, or happen because they are foreseen, and that alone is enough to destroy the freedom of the will. But now how upside-down it is that it should be said that the cause of eternal foreknowledge is the occurrence of temporal things! But what else is it, to think that God foresees future things because they are going to happen, than to think that those things, once they have happened, are the cause of his highest providence?

"Furthermore, just as when I know that something is, then that necessarily is so, so when I know something will be, then that necessarily will be so; and so it happens that the occurrence of a thing foreknown cannot be avoided.

"Lastly, if a man think a thing to be otherwise than it is, that is not only not knowledge, but it is a mistaken opinion very different indeed from the truth of knowledge. And therefore if something is future in such a way that its occurrence is not certain or necessary, how will it be possible for it to be foreknown that it will occur? For just as real knowledge is unmixed with falsity, so that which is grasped by knowledge cannot be otherwise than as it is grasped. For the real reason why knowledge lacks any falsehood is that every single thing must necessarily be just as knowledge comprehends it to be. Well then, how does God foreknow that these uncertain things shall be? For if he thinks those things will inevitably occur which it is yet possible may not occur, he is mistaken, which it is not only impious to think but still more impious to say aloud. But if he sees that those future things are just as indeed they are, so that he knows that they can equally either happen or not happen, what sort of foreknowledge is this, that grasps nothing certain, nothing stable? Or how does it compare with that ridiculous prophecy of Tiresias?[2] – 'Whatever

I say will either happen or not?' And in what will divine providence be better than the opinions of humans, if it judges in the way humans do those things to be uncertain the occurrence of which is uncertain?

But if in him, the most certain fount of all things, there can be nothing uncertain, then the occurrence is certain of those things which he firmly foreknows will be. And therefore there is no freedom in human intentions or actions, which the divine mind, foreseeing all without mistaken error, binds and constrains to one actual occurrence. This once accepted, it is clear what a great collapse of human affairs follows! For it is vain to propose for good and evil persons rewards or punishments which no free and voluntary act of their minds has deserved. And that very thing will seem most unjust of all which now is judged most just, that either the wicked are punished or the good rewarded, since they have not been brought by their own wills but driven by the certain necessity of what shall be to one or other end. And therefore there would be no vices nor virtues, but rather a mixed-up and indistinguishable confusion of all deserts, and – than which nothing more wicked can be conceived! – since the whole ordering of things proceeds from providence and nothing is really possible to human intentions, it follows that even our vices are to be referred to the author of all things good. And therefore there is no sense in hoping for anything or in praying that anything may be averted; for what even should any man hope for or pray to be averted when an inflexible course links all that can be desired? And so that sole intercourse between humans and God will be removed, that is, hope and prayer for aversion (if indeed at the price of a proper humility we deserve the inestimable return of God's grace), and that is the only way in which humans seem able to converse with God and to be joined by the very manner of their supplication to that inaccessible light, even before they receive what they seek. Now if these things, once the necessity of what shall be is admitted, be thought to have no power, how should we be able to be joined and cleave to him, the highest principle of all things? So it will necessarily follow, as you sang a little while ago, that human kind would, torn apart and disjoined, in pieces fall from their origin."

III Verse

What cause discordant breaks the world's compact?
What god sets strife so great
Between two truths,
That those same things which stand, alone and separate,
Together mixed, refuse to be so yoked?
Or is there no such discord between truths,
And do they ever each to other firmly cleave,
But is it the mind, eclipsed by the body's unseeing parts,
That cannot recognize, by its suppressed light's fire,
The world's fine fastenings?
But why does it blaze with so great love
To find the hidden characters of truth?
Does it know what it anxiously seeks to know?
But who is there labours to know known things?
Yet if it does not know, why then in blindness seek?
For who would long for anything he knows not of,
Or who could follow after things unknown,
Or how discover them? Who could in ignorance recognize
The form of what he found?
Or, when it perceived the highest mind,
Did it know at once the whole and the separate parts?
Now, clouded and hidden by the body's parts,
It is not totally forgetful of itself,
And the whole it keeps, losing the separate parts.
Therefore whoever seeks the truth
Is of neither class: for he neither knows
Nor is altogether ignorant of all,
But the whole he keeps, remembers and reflects on,
All from that height perceived goes over once again,
That he might to those things he has preserved
Add the forgotten parts.

---

2 In Greek mythology Tiresias was a human who was struck blind for having spied on the goddess Athena. In her pity Athena gave him knowledge of all things past and all things to come.

IV

Then she said: "That is the old complaint about providence, one powerfully dealt with by Cicero[3] when he was classifying kinds of divination, and a matter for a very long time and deeply investigated by yourself; but it has so far been by no means sufficiently carefully or steadfastly developed by any of you. The cause of this obscurity is that the movement of human reasoning cannot approach the simplicity of divine foreknowledge; if that could by any means be conceived, no doubt whatever will remain. And I shall try to make clear and explain this only when I have first considered those things by which you are now troubled. For I ask, why do you think that explanation of those solving the problem less than effectual which, since it considers that foreknowledge is not the cause of any necessity for future events, thinks the freedom of the will not at all restricted by foreknowledge? For you, surely, do not produce proof of the necessity of future things other than from the fact that those things that are foreknown cannot not happen? Then if foreknowledge imposes no necessity on future things, which you did indeed admit a little while ago, what is the reason why the outcome of those things dependent on the will should be forced to end in a certain result? Now for the sake of argument, that you may see what follows, let us suppose that there is no foreknowledge. In such a case, those things that depend upon the will would not be forced into any necessity, would they?"

"Not at all."

"Again, let us suppose that there is foreknowledge, but that it enjoins no necessity on things; there will remain, I think, that same freedom of the will, whole and absolute. But foreknowledge, you will say, although it does not constitute a necessity for future things, of their happening, yet it is a sign that they will necessarily come to be. In this way, then, even had there been no foreknowledge, it would be agreed that the outcome of future things is necessary; for every sign only points to what is, but does not cause to be what it signifies. Wherefore it must first be demonstrated that nothing happens except of necessity, that foreknowledge may be seen to be the sign of that necessity; otherwise, if there is no necessity, nor then will foreknowledge be able to be a sign for that which does not exist. But it is agreed that a proof supported by firm reasoning must be drawn not from signs nor from arguments fetched from outside the subject, but from relevant and necessary causes.

"But how could it be that those things should not happen which are foreseen to be future? Just as if we were to believe that those things which providence foreknows will happen were not going to happen, and did not rather think that although they do happen, yet they have of their nature no necessity that they must happen. Which you may easily gather from this: for many things, while they are happening, we look at set out before our eyes, as for example those things which charioteers are watched doing in guiding and turning their teams, and other things of a similar kind. Now surely no necessity compels any of these things to happen as it does?"

"Not at all; for the exercise of skill would be useless if all things moved under compulsion."

"Therefore, things which, while they are happening, lack any necessity of being so, these same things, before they happen, are future without any necessity. And therefore there are some things going to happen the occurrence of which is free from all necessity. For I do not think that any person would say this, that those things which are happening now were not 'going to happen' before they happened; therefore of these, even foreknown, the occurrence is free. For just as knowledge of present things introduces no necessity into those things which are happening, so the foreknowledge of future things introduces none into those things which are to come.

"But this, you say, is exactly what is in doubt, whether there can be any foreknowledge of those things which do not have necessary outcomes. For these two (foreknowledge and not-necessary outcomes) seem to be incompatible, and you think that if things are foreseen, necessity is a consequence, and if there is no necessity, they cannot be foreknown at all, and nothing can be grasped by knowledge except what is certain. But if those things which are of uncertain outcome are foreseen as if they were certain, that is really the obscurity

---

3 Roman statesman, orator, and student of Greek philosophy. Lived 106-43 B.C.E.

of opinion, not the truth of knowledge; for you believe thinking things to be other than as they are to be alien to the integrity of knowledge.

"The cause of this mistake is that each thinks that all that he knows is known simply by the power and nature of those things that are known. Which is altogether otherwise: for everything which is known is grasped not according to its own power but rather according to the capability of those who know it. For that this may become clear by a brief example the same roundness of a body sight recognizes in one way and touch in another; the former sense remaining at a distance looks at the whole at once by the light of its emitted rays, while the latter, being united and conjoined to the round body, going right round its circuit, grasps the roundness by parts.

"A human being himself also, sense, imagination, reason and intelligence look at in different ways. For sense examines the shape set in the underlying matter, imagination the shape alone without the matter; while reason surpasses this too, and examines with a universal consideration the specific form[4] itself, which is present in single individuals. But the eye of intelligence is set higher still; for passing beyond the process of going round the one whole, it looks with the pure sight of the mind at the simple Form[5] itself. And herein the greatest consideration is to be given to this: for the higher power of comprehension embraces the lower, while the lower in no way rises to the higher. For neither can sense attain to anything outside matter, nor does imagination look at universal specific forms, nor reason grasp the simple Form: but the intelligence, as it were looking down from above, by conceiving the Form distinguishes all the things subject to that Form, but only because of the way it comprehends the Form itself, which could not be known to anything else. For it knows the reason's universal,[6] and the imagination's shape, and what is materially sensible, but without using reason, imagination or the senses, but by the one stroke of the mind, Formally, so to speak, looking forth on all these things together. Reason, too, when it

regards some universal, without using imagination or the senses grasps the imaginable and sensible aspects. For reason it is which defines the universal it has conceived thus: man is a rational, bipedal animal. And although this is a universal idea, at the same time no-one is ignorant that it is an imaginable and sensible thing which the reason is considering, not by means of imagination or sense, but in its rational conceiving. Imagination also, although it has taken its beginning of seeing and forming shapes from the senses, yet with sense removed surveys all sensible things not by a sensible manner of examining them but by an imaginative one. Do you therefore see that in knowing, all these use their own capability rather than that of those things which are known? Nor is this wrong: for since every judgement is the act of one judging, it must be that each performs his task not from some other's power but from his own."

IV Verse

Sometimes the Porch[7] has brought into the world
Some very obscure old philosophers,
Such as think sensible images from bodies outside
    themselves
Are impressed upon men's minds;
As at times with swiftly-moving stylus
Men are used to print the blank space of a page
Which has no marks
With impressed letters.
But if the mind, with the strength of its proper
    motions,
Nothing unfolds,
But merely passive lies
Subject to other bodies' marks,
And like a mirror but reflects
The empty images of things,
Whence then this all-discerning common concept's strength
In the minds of men? What power singulars perceives,
Or what power all things known divides?
Things thus divided what collects again,

---

4 See glossary entries for 'form/matter,' and 'species/genus.'
5 See glossary entry for 'Form.'
6 See glossary entry for 'universal vs. particular.' See Topic **VI**.
7 I.e., the Stoic philosophers.

And taking either way in turn
Now lifts its head to highest things
And now to lowest things descends,
Then to itself returning
Falsehood refutes with truth?
This is an efficient cause
More powerful by far
Than that which passively receives
Only the impressed marks on things material.
Yet there precedes,
To stir and move the powers of the mind,
Emotive movement in the living body,
As when light strikes the eyes,
Or a cry in the ears resounds.
Then the mind's wakened power,
Calling upon these forms it holds within
To similar motions,
Applies them to the marks received from without
And joins those images
To the forms hidden within.

V

"Now if in perceiving corporeal things, although qualities presented from without affect the apparatus of the senses, and the emotive movement of the body precedes the activity of the active mind, a movement which calls forth upon itself the action of the mind and stirs up the forms previously lying at rest within; if, I say, in perceiving corporeal things, the mind is not marked by that movement, but of its own power judges that movement, which is a quality of the body, then how much the more do those things which are quite separate from all bodily affections, in the act of judgement not follow things presented from without, but set in motion the action of the mind to which they belong! And so on this principle many kinds of knowledge belong to different and diverse substances. For sense alone without any other kind of knowledge belongs to living things that do not move, such as are sea shells and such other things as feed clinging to rocks; but imagination belongs to beasts that move, which seem already to have in them some disposition to flee or to seek out things. But reason belongs only to human kind, as intelligence only to the divine. So it is that that kind of knowledge is better than the rest which of its own nature knows not only its own object but the subjects of other kinds of knowledge also.

"What, then, if sense and imagination gainsay reasoning, saying that that universal which reason thinks she perceives, is nothing at all? For that which is the object of sense and imagination cannot, they say, be universal; therefore either the judgement of reason is true, and there is nothing sensible, or, since they know that many things are objects of the senses and imagination, reason's concept is empty, since she thinks of that which is sensible and singular as if it were some kind of universal. Further, if reason rejoins to this that she does indeed see both the object of sense and the object of imagination under the aspect of their universality, but that they cannot aspire to the knowledge of universality since their knowledge cannot go beyond corporeal shapes, but we must give credence rather to the more firm and perfect judgement concerning the knowledge of things: in this sort of argument, then, should we not, we who have in us the power of reasoning as well as those of imagination and sense, should we not rather judge in favor of reason's case?

"It is similar when human reason thinks that the divine intelligence does not see future things except in the same manner as she herself knows them. For this is how you argue: if any things seem not to have certain and necessary occurrences, those things cannot be certainly foreknown as going to occur. Therefore, of these things there is no foreknowledge, and if we think there is foreknowledge in these matters, there will be nothing which does not happen from necessity. Now if just as we have a share in reason, so we could possess the judgement belonging to the divine mind, then just as we have judged that imagination and sense ought to give way to reason, so we should think it most just that human reason should submit to the divine mind. Wherefore let us be raised up, if we can, to the height of that highest intelligence; for there reason will see that which she cannot look at in herself, and that is, in what way even those things which have no certain occurrence a certain and definite foreknowledge yet does see, neither is that opinion, but rather the simplicity, shut in by no bounds, of the highest knowledge.

V Verse

In what diversity of shapes do living things traverse the lands!

For some are long in body and sweep the dust
And draw a continuous furrow, moved by their
    belly's power;
There are those the lightness of whose wandering
    wings beats on the winds
And floats in the spaces of the ether far with flight
    so smooth;
These others delight to press their footprints in
    the ground, and with their steps
To cross green fields, or pass beneath the woods.
And all these, though you see they differ in their
    various forms,
Yet their downturned faces make their senses
    heavy grow and dull.
Only the race of men lift high their lofty heads
And lightly stand with upright bodies, looking
    down so on the earth.
And (unless, being earthly, you are stupidly
    wrong) this shape tells you,
You who with upright face do seek the sky, and
    thrust your forehead out,
You should also bear your mind aloft, lest weight-
    ed down
The mind sink lower than the body raised above.

VI

"Since, then, as was shown a little while ago, every-thing which is known is known not according to its own nature but according to the nature of those comprehending it, let us now examine, so far as is allowable, what is the nature of the divine sub-stance, so that we may be able to recognize what kind of knowledge his is. Now that God is eternal is the common judgement of all who live by reason. Therefore let us consider, what is eternity; for this makes plain to us both the divine nature and the divine knowledge. Eternity, then, is the whole, simultaneous and perfect possession of boundless life, which becomes clearer by comparison with temporal things. For whatever lives in time pro-ceeds in the present from the past into the future, and there is nothing established in time which can embrace the whole space of its life equally, but tomorrow surely it does not yet grasp, while yester-day it has already lost. And in this day to day life

you live no more than in that moving and transito-ry moment. Therefore whatever endures the condi-tion of time, although, as Aristotle thought con-cerning the world,[8] it neither began ever to be nor ceases to be, and although its life is drawn out with the infinity of time, yet it is not yet such that it may rightly be believed to be eternal. For it does not simultaneously comprehend and embrace the whole space of its life, though it be infinite, but it possesses the future not yet, the past no longer. Whatever therefore comprehends and possesses at once the whole fullness of boundless life, and is such that neither is anything future lacking from it, nor has anything past flowed away, that is rightly held to be eternal, and that must necessarily both always be present to itself, possessing itself in the present, and hold as present the infinity of moving time.

"And therefore those are not right who, when they hear that Plato thought this world neither had a beginning in time nor would have an end, think that in this way the created world is made co-eter-nal with the Creator. For it is one thing to be drawn out through a life without bounds, which is what Plato attributes to the world, but it is a different thing to have embraced at once the whole presence of boundless life, which it is clear is the property of the divine mind. Nor should God seem to be more ancient than created things by some amount of time, but rather by his own simplicity of nature. For this present nature of unmoving life that infi-nite movement of temporal things imitates, and since it cannot fully represent and equal it, it fails from immobility into motion, it shrinks from the simplicity of that present into the infinite quantity of the future and the past and, since it cannot pos-sess at once the whole fullness of its life, in this very respect, that it in some way never ceases to be, it seems to emulate to some degree which it cannot fully express, by binding itself to the sort of present of this brief and fleeting moment, a present which since it wears a kind of likeness of that permanent present, grants to whatsoever things it touches that they should seem to be. But since it could not be permanent,[9] it seized on the infinite journeying of time, and in that way became such that it should

---

8 See selection **III.1.1.**
9 See glossary entry for 'persistent being.'

continue by going on a life the fullness of which it could not embrace by being permanent. And so if we should wish to give things names befitting them, then following Plato we should say that God indeed is eternal, but that the world is perpetual.

"Since then every judgement comprehends those things subject to it according to its own nature, and God has an always eternal and present nature, then his knowledge too, surpassing all movement of time, is permanent in the simplicity of his present, and embracing all the infinite spaces of the future and the past, considers them in his simple act of knowledge as though they were now going on. So if you should wish to consider his foreknowledge, by which he discerns all things, you will more rightly judge it to be not foreknowledge as it were of the future but knowledge of a never-passing instant. And therefore it is called not prevision (*praevidentia*) but providence (*providentia*), because set far from the lowest of things it looks forward on all things as though from the highest peak of the world. Why then do you require those things to be made necessary which are scanned by the light of God's sight, when not even humans make necessary those things they see? After all, your looking at them does not confer any necessity on those things you presently see, does it?"

"Not at all."

"But if the comparison of the divine and the human present is a proper one, just as you see certain things in this your temporal present, so he perceives all things in his eternal one. And therefore this divine foreknowledge does not alter the proper nature of things, but sees them present to him just such as in time they will at some future point come to be. Nor does he confuse the ways things are to be judged, but with one glance of his mind distinguishes both those things necessarily coming to be and those not necessarily coming to be, just as you, when you see at one and the same time that a man is walking on the ground and that the sun is rising in the sky, although the two things are seen simultaneously, yet you distinguish them, and judge the first to be voluntary, the second necessary. So then the divine perception looking down on all things does not disturb at all the quality of things that are present indeed to him but future with reference to imposed conditions of time. So it is that it is not opinion but a knowledge grounded rather upon truth, when he knows that something is going to happen, something which he is also aware lacks all necessity of happening.

"If at this point you were to say that what God sees is going to occur cannot not occur, and that what cannot not occur happens from necessity, and so bind me to this word 'necessity,' I will admit that this is a matter indeed of the firmest truth, but one which scarcely anyone except a theologian could tackle. For I shall say in answer that the same future event, when it is related to divine knowledge, is necessary, but when it is considered in its own nature it seems to be utterly and absolutely free. For there are really two necessities, the one simple, as that it is necessary that all men are mortal; the other conditional, as for example, if you know that someone is walking, it is necessary that he is walking. Whatever anyone knows cannot be otherwise than as it is known, but this conditional necessity by no means carries with it that other simple kind. For this sort of necessity is not caused by a thing's proper nature but by the addition of the condition; for no necessity forces him to go who walks of his own will, even though it is necessary that he is going at the time when he is walking. Now in the same way, if providence sees anything as present, that must necessarily be, even if it possesses no necessity of its nature. But God beholds those future events which happen because of the freedom of the will, as present; they therefore, related to the divine perception, become necessary through the condition of the divine knowledge, but considered in themselves do not lose the absolute freedom of their nature. Therefore, all those things which God foreknows will come to be, will without doubt come to be, but certain of them proceed from free will, and although they do come to be, yet in happening they do not lose their proper nature, according to which, before they happened, they might also not have happened.

"What then does it matter that they are not necessary, since on account of the condition of the divine knowledge it will turn out in all respects like necessity? Surely as much as those things I put before you a moment ago, the rising sun and the walking man: while these things are happening, they cannot not happen, but of the two one, even before it happened, was bound to happen, while the other was not. So also, those things God possesses as present, beyond doubt will happen, but of them the one kind is consequent upon the necessity of things, the other upon the power of those doing them. So therefore we were not wrong in saying that these, if related to the divine knowledge, are necessary, if considered in themselves, are free from the bonds of necessity, just as everything which lies open to the senses, if you relate it to the reason, is universal, if you look at it by itself, is singular.

"But if, you will say, it lies in my power to change my intention, I shall make nonsense of providence, since what providence foreknows, I shall perhaps have changed. I shall reply that you can indeed alter your intention, but since the truth of providence sees in its present both that you can do so, and whether you will do so and in what direction you will change, you cannot avoid the divine prescience, just as you could not escape the sight of an eye that was present, even though of your own free will you changed to different courses of action. What then will you say? Will the divine knowledge be changed by my disposition, so that, since I want to do this at one time and that at another, it too alternates from this kind of knowledge to that? Not at all. For the divine perception runs ahead over every future event and turns it back and recalls it to the present of its own knowledge, and does not alternate, as you suggest, foreknowing now this, now that, but itself remaining still anticipates and embraces your changes at one stroke. And God possesses this pre-

sent instant of comprehension and sight of all things not from the issuing of future events but from his own simplicity.

"In this way that too is resolved which you suggested a little while ago, that it is not right that our future actions should be said to provide the cause of the knowledge of God. For the nature of his knowledge as we have described it, embracing all things in a present act of knowing, establishes a measure for everything, but owes nothing to later events. These things being so, the freedom of the will remains to mortals, inviolate, nor are laws proposing rewards and punishments for wills free from all necessity unjust.

"There remains also as an observer from on high foreknowing all things, God, and the always present eternity of his sight runs along with the future quality of our actions dispensing rewards for the good and punishments for the wicked. Nor vainly are our hopes placed in God, nor our prayers, which when they are right cannot be ineffectual. Turn away then from vices, cultivate virtues, lift up your mind to righteous hopes, offer up humble prayers to heaven. A great necessity is solemnly ordained for you if you do not want to deceive yourselves, to do good, when you act before the eyes of a judge who sees all things."

IV.3. ST. ANSELM

ANSELM'S APPROACH TO THE SAME PROBLEM THAT TROUBLED BOETHIUS in the preceding selection shows his emphasis on the clarification of concepts and the careful discrimination of the ambiguities that infect our ways of speaking. In other words, with the logician's tools Anselm believes he can show how there is no real contradiction between freedom of the will and divine foreknowledge. That appearance of such a contradiction is a result merely of unclear and misleading language.

IV.3.1. The Harmony of Foreknowledge and Free Will (from *The Harmony of the Foreknowledge, the Predestination, and the Grace of God with free Choice*)

With the help of God I shall try to set forth in writing what He will deign to reveal to me concerning these three controversies in which free choice seems to be incompatible with (1) the foreknowledge, (2) the predestination, and (3) the grace of God.

First Controversy: Foreknowledge and Free Choice

I

Admittedly, free choice and the foreknowledge of God seem incompatible; for it is necessary that the things foreknown by God be going to occur, whereas the things done by free choice occur without any necessity. Now, if these two are incompatible, then it is impossible that God's all-foreseeing foreknowledge should coexist with something's being done by freedom of choice. In turn, if this impossibility is regarded as not obtaining, then the incompatibility which seems to be present is completely eliminated.

Therefore, let us posit as existing together both God's foreknowledge (from which the necessity of future things seems to follow) and freedom of choice (by which many actions are performed, we believe, without any necessity); and let us see whether it is impossible for these two to coexist. If this coexistence is impossible, then some other impossibility arises from it. For, indeed, an impossible thing is one from which, when posited, some other impossible thing follows. Now, on the assumption that some action is going to occur

without necessity, God foreknows this, since he foreknows all future events. And that which is foreknown by God is, necessarily, going to occur, as is foreknown. Therefore, it is necessary that something be going to occur without necessity. Hence, the foreknowledge from which necessity follows and the freedom of choice from which necessity is absent are here seen (for one who rightly understands it) to be not at all incompatible. For, on the one hand, it is necessary that what is foreknown by God be going to occur; and, on the other hand, God foreknows that something is going to occur without any necessity.

But you will say to me: "You still do not remove from me the necessity of sinning or the necessity of not sinning. For God foreknows that I am going to sin or foreknows that I am not going to sin. And so, if I sin, it is necessary that I sin; or if I do not sin, it is necessary that I do not sin." To this claim I reply: You ought to say not merely "God foreknows that I am going to sin" or "God foreknows that I am not going to sin" but "God foreknows that it is without necessity that I am going to sin" or "God foreknows that it is without necessity that I am not going to sin." And thus it follows that whether you sin or do not sin, in either case it will be without necessity; for God foreknows that what will occur will occur without necessity. Do you see, then, that it is not impossible for God's foreknowledge (according to which future things, which God foreknows, are said to occur of necessity) to coexist with freedom of choice (by which many actions are performed without necessity)? For if this coexistence were impossible, then something impossible would follow. But no impossibility arises from this coexistence.

Perhaps you will claim: "You still do not remove

the constraint of necessity from my heart when you say that, because of God's foreknowledge, it is necessary for me to be going to sin without necessity or it is necessary for me to be not going to sin without necessity. For *necessity* seems to imply coercion or restraint. Therefore, if it is necessary that I sin willingly, I interpret this as indicating that I am compelled by some hidden power to will to sin; and if I do not sin, [I interpret this as indicating that] I am restrained from willing to sin. Therefore, it seems to me that if I sin I sin by necessity, and if I do not sin it is by necessity that I do not sin."

2

And I [reply]: We must realize that we often say "necessary to be" of what is not compelled-to-be by any force, and "necessary not to be" of what is not excluded by any preventing factor. For example, we say "It is necessary for God to be immortal" and "It is necessary for God not to be unjust." [We say this] not because some force compels Him to be immortal or prohibits Him from being unjust, but because nothing can cause Him not to be immortal or can cause Him to be unjust. Similarly, then, I might say: "It is necessary that you are going to sin voluntarily" or "It is necessary that, voluntarily, you are not going to sin" – just as God foreknows. But these statements must not be construed to mean that something prevents the act of will which shall not occur, or compels that act of will which shall occur. For God, who foresees that some action is going to occur voluntarily, foreknows the very fact that the will is neither compelled nor prevented by anything. Hence, what is done voluntarily is done freely. Therefore, if these matters are carefully pondered, I think that no inconsistency prevents freedom of choice and God's foreknowledge from coexisting.

Indeed, (if someone properly considers the meaning of the word), by the very fact that something is said to be *foreknown*, it is declared to be going to occur. For only what is going to occur is foreknown, since knowledge is only of the truth. Therefore, when I say "If God foreknows something, it is necessary that this thing be going to occur," it is as if I were to say: "If this thing will occur, of necessity it will occur." But this necessity neither compels nor prevents a thing's existence or nonexistence. For because the thing is presumed to

exist, it is said to exist of necessity; or because it is presumed not to exist, it is said to not-exist of necessity. [But our reason for saying these things is] not that necessity compels or prevents the thing's existence or nonexistence. For when I say "If it will occur, of necessity it will occur," here the necessity follows, rather than precedes, the presumed existence of the thing. The sense is the same if we say "What will be, of necessity will be." For this necessity signifies nothing other than that what will occur will not be able not to occur at the same time.

Likewise, the following statements are equally true: (1) that some thing did exist and does exist and will exist, but not out of necessity, and (2) that all that was, necessarily was, all that is, necessarily is, and all that will be, necessarily will be. Indeed, for a thing to be past is not the same as for a past thing to be past; and for a thing to be present is not the same as for a present thing to be present; and for a thing to be future is not the same as for a future thing to be future. By comparison, for a thing to be white is not the same as for a white thing to be white. For example, a staff is not always necessarily white, because at some time before it became white it was able not to become white; and after it has become white, it is able to become not-white. But it is necessary that a white staff always be white. For neither before a white thing was white nor after it has become white can it happen that a white thing is not-white at the same time. Similarly, it is not by necessity that a thing is temporally present. For before the thing was present, it was able to happen that it would not be present; and after it has become present, it can happen that it not remain present. But it is necessary that a present thing always be present, because neither before it is present nor after it has become present is a present thing able to be not-present at the same time. In the same way, some event – e.g., an action – is going to occur without necessity, because before the action occurs, it can happen that it not be going to occur. On the other hand, it is necessary that a future event be future, because what is future is not able at the same time to be not-future. Of the past it is similarly true (1) that some event is not necessarily past, because before it occurred, there was the possibility of its not occurring, and (2) that, necessarily, what is past is always past, since it is not able at the same time not to be past.

Now, a past event has a characteristic which a present event or a future event does not have. For it is never possible for a past event to become not-past, as a present event is able to become not present, and as an event which is not necessarily going to happen has the possibility of not happening in the future. Thus, when we say of what is going to happen that it is going to happen, this statement must be true, because it is never the case that what is going to happen is not going to happen. (Similarly, whenever we predicate something of itself, [the statement is true]. For when we say "Every human is a human," or "If he is a human, he is a human," or "Every white thing is white," or "If it is a white thing, it is white": these statements must be true because something cannot both be and not be the case at the same time.) Indeed, if it were not necessary that everything which is going to happen were going to happen, then something which is going to happen would not be going to happen – a contradiction. Therefore, necessarily, everything which is going to happen is going to happen; and if it is going to happen, it is going to happen. (For we are saying of what is going to happen that it is going to happen.) But ["necessarily" here signifies] subsequent necessity, which does not compel anything to be.

3

However, when an event is said to be going to occur, it is not always the case that the event occurs by necessity, even though it is going to occur. For example, if I say "Tomorrow there will be an insurrection among the people," it is not the case that the insurrection will occur by necessity. For before it occurs, it is possible that it not occur even if it is going to occur. On the other hand, it is sometimes the case that the thing which is said to be going to occur does occur by necessity – for example, if I say that tomorrow there will be a sunrise. Therefore, if of an event which is going to occur I state that it must be going to occur, [I do so] either in the way that the insurrection which is going to occur tomorrow is, necessarily, going to occur, or else in the way that the sunrise which is going to occur tomorrow is going to occur by necessity. Indeed, the insurrection (which will occur but not by necessity) is said necessarily to be going to occur – but only in the sense of subsequent necessity. For we

are saying of what is going to happen that it is going to happen. For if the insurrection is going to occur tomorrow, then – necessarily – it is going to occur. On the other hand, the sunrise is understood to be going to occur with two necessities: (1) with a preceding necessity, which causes the event to occur (for the event will occur because it is necessary that it occur), and (2) with a subsequent necessity, which does not compel anything to occur (for because the sunrise is going to occur, it is – necessarily – going to occur).

Therefore, when of what God foreknows to be going to occur we say that it is necessary that it be going to occur, we are not in every case asserting that the event is going to occur by necessity; rather, we are asserting that an event which is going to occur is, necessarily, going to occur. For something which is going to occur cannot at the same time be not going to occur. The meaning is the same when we say "If God foreknows such-and-such an event" – without adding "which is going to occur." For in the verb "to foreknow" the notion of future occurrence is included, since to foreknow is nothing other than to know the future; and so if God foreknows some event, it is necessary that this event be going to occur. Therefore, from the fact of God's foreknowledge it does not in every case follow that an event is going to occur by necessity. For although God foreknows all future events, He does not foreknow that all of them are going to occur by necessity. Rather, He foreknows that some of them will occur as the result of the free will of a rational creature.

Indeed, we must note that just as it is not necessary for God to will what He does will, so in many cases it is not necessary for a human to will what they do will. And just as whatever God wills must occur, so what a human wills must occur – in the case, that is, of the things which God so subordinates to the human will that if it wills them they occur and if it does not will them they do not occur. For since what God wills is not able not to occur: when He wills for no necessity either to compel the human will to will or to prevent it from willing, and when He wills that the effect follow from the act of human willing, it is necessary that the human will be free and that there occur what it wills. In this respect, then, it is true that the sinful deed which a human wills to do occurs by necessity, even though the human does not will it by necessity. Now, with respect to the human will's sin when it wills to sin: if someone asks whether this sin occurs by necessity, then they must be told that just as the will does not will by necessity, so the will's sin does not occur by necessity. Nor does the human will act by necessity; for if it did not will freely, it would not act – even though what it wills must come to pass, as I have just said. For since, in the present case, to sin is nothing other than to will what ought not [to be willed]: just as willing is not necessary, so sinful willing is not necessary. Nevertheless, it is true that if a man wills to sin, it is necessary that he sin – in terms, that is, of that necessity which (as I have said) neither compels nor prevents anything.

Thus, on the one hand, free will is able to keep from willing what it wills; and, on the other hand, it is not able to keep from willing what it wills – rather, it is necessary for free will to will what it wills. For, indeed, before it wills, it is able to keep from willing, because it is free. And while it wills, it is not able not to will; rather, it is necessary that it will, since it is impossible for it to will and not to will the same thing at the same time. Now, it is the will's prerogative that what it wills occurs and that what it does not will does not occur. And the will's deeds are voluntary and free because they are done by a free will. But these deeds are necessary in two respects: (1) because the will compels them to be done, and (2) because what is being done cannot at the same time not be done. But these two necessities are produced by freedom-of-will; and the free will is able to avoid them before they occur. Now, God (who knows all truth and only truth) sees all these things as they are – whether they be free or necessary; and as He sees them, so they are. In this way, then, and without any inconsistency, it is evident both that God foreknows all things and that many things are done by free will. And before these things occur it is possible that they never occur. Nevertheless, in a certain sense they occur necessarily; and this necessity (as I said) derives from free will.

4

Moreover, that not everything foreknown by God occurs of necessity but that some events occur as the result of freedom-of will can be recognized from the following consideration. When God wills or causes something, He cannot be denied to know what He wills and causes, and to foreknow what He shall will and shall cause. ([It makes no difference here] whether we speak in accordance with eternity's immutable present, in which there is nothing past or future, but in which all things exist at once with out any change (e.g., if we say only that He wills and causes something, and deny that He has willed or has caused and shall will or shall cause something), or whether we speak in accordance with temporality (as when we state that He shall will or shall cause that which we know has not yet occurred).) Therefore, if God's knowledge or foreknowledge imposes necessity on everything He knows or foreknows, then He does not freely will or cause anything (either in accordance with eternity or in accordance with a temporal mode); rather, He wills and causes everything by necessity. Now, if this conclusion is absurd even to suppose, then it is not the case that everything known or foreknown to be or not to be occurs or fails to occur by necessity. Therefore, nothing prevents God's knowing or foreknowing that in our wills and actions something occurs or will occur by free choice. Thus, although it is necessary that what He knows or foreknows, occur, nevertheless many events occur not by necessity but by free will – as I have shown above.

Indeed, why is it strange if in this way something occurs both freely and necessarily? For there are many things which admit of opposite characteristics in different respects. Indeed, what is more opposed than coming and going? Nevertheless, when someone moves from one place to another, we see that his movement is both a coming and a going. For he goes away from one place and comes toward another. Likewise, if we consider the sun at some point in the heavens, as it is hastening toward this same point while always illuminating the heavens: we see that the point to which it is coming is the same point from which it is going away; and it is constantly and simultaneously approaching the point from which it is departing. Moreover, to those who know the sun's course, it is evident that in relation to the heavens, the sun always moves from the western sector to the eastern sector; but in relation to the earth, it always moves only from east to west. Thus, the sun always moves both counter to the firmament and – although more slowly [than the firmament] – with the firmament. This same phenomenon is witnessed in the case of all the planets. So then, no inconsistency arises if (in accordance with the considerations just presented) we assert of one and the same event (1) that, necessarily, it is going to occur (simply because it is going to occur) and (2) that it is not compelled to be going to occur by any necessity – except for the necessity which (as I said above) derives from free will.

Now Job says to God with reference to man: "You have established his end, which cannot be escaped." On the basis of this verse someone might want to prove – in spite of the fact that sometimes someone does seem to us to cause his own death by his own free will – that no one has been able to hasten or delay the day of his death. But this objection would not tell against that, which I have argued above. For since God is not deceived and sees only the truth – whether it issues from freedom or from necessity – He is said to have established immutably with respect to Himself something which, with respect to man, can be altered before it is done. This is also what the Apostle Paul says about those who, in accordance with [God's] purpose, are called to be saints: "Whom He foreknew He predestined to become conformed to the image of His Son, so that His Son would be the firstborn among many brethren. And whom He predestined, these He also called. And whom He called, these He also justified. And whom He justified, these He also glorified." Indeed, within eternity (in which there is no past or future but is only a present) this purpose, in accordance with which they have been called to be saints, is immutable. But in these men this purpose is at some time mutable because of freedom of choice. For within eternity a thing has no past or future but only a present; and yet, without inconsistency, in the dimension of time this thing was and will be. Similarly, that which within eternity is not able to be changed is proved to be, without inconsistency, changeable by free will at some point in time before it occurs. However, although within eternity there is only a present, nonetheless it is not the temporal present, as is ours, but is an eternal present in which the whole of time is contained. For, indeed, just as present time encompasses every place and whatever is in any place, so in the eternal present the whole of time is encompassed at once, as well as whatever occurs at any time. Therefore, when the apostle says that God foreknew, predes-

tined, called, justified, and glorified His saints, none of these actions is earlier or later for God; rather everything must be understood to exist at once in an eternal present. For eternity has its own "simultaneity" wherein exist all things that occur at the same time and place and that occur at different times: and places.

But in order to show that he was not using these verbs in their temporal sense, the same apostle spoke in the past tense of even those events which are future. For, temporally speaking, God had not already called, justified, and glorified those who He foreknew were still to be born. Thus, we can recognize that for lack of a verb [properly] signifying the eternal present, the apostle used verbs of past tense; for things which are temporally past are altogether immutable, after the fashion of the eternal present. Indeed, in this respect, things which are temporally past resemble the eternal present more than do things which are temporally present. For eternally present things are never able not to be present, just as temporally past things are never able not to be past. But all temporally present things which pass away do become not-present. In this manner, then, whenever Sacred Scripture speaks as if things done by free choice were necessary, it speaks in accordance with eternity, in which is present immutably all truth and only truth. Scripture is not speaking in accordance with the temporal order, wherein our volitions and actions do not exist forever. Moreover, just as when our volitions and actions do not exist, it is not necessary that they exist, so it is often not necessary that they ever exist. For example, it is not the case that I am always writing or that I always will to write. And just as when I am not writing or do not will to write, it is not necessary that I write or will to write, so it is not at all necessary that I ever write or will to write.

A thing is known to exist in time so differently from the way it exists in eternity that at some point the following statements are true: (1) in time something is not present which is present in eternity; (2) in time something is past which is not past in eternity; (3) in time something is future which is not future in eternity. Similarly, then, it is seen to be impossible to be denied, in any respect, that in the temporal order something is mutable which is immutable in eternity. Indeed, being mutable in time and being immutable in eternity are no more opposed than are not existing at some time and always existing in eternity – or than are existing in the past or future according to the temporal order and not existing in the past or future in eternity. For, indeed, the point I am making is not that something which always exists in eternity never exists in time, but is only that there is some time or other at which it does not exist. For example, I am not saying that my action of tomorrow at no time exists; I am merely denying that it exists today, even though it always exists in eternity. And when we deny that something which is past or future in the temporal order is past or future in eternity, we do not maintain that that which is past or future does not in any way exist in eternity; instead, we are simply saying that what exists there unceasingly in its eternal-present mode does not exist there in the past or future mode. In these cases no contradiction is seen to raise an obstruction. Thus, without doubt and without any contradiction, a thing is said to be mutable in time, prior to its occurrence, although it exists immutably in eternity. [In eternity] there is no time before it exists or after it exists; instead, it exists unceasingly, because in eternity nothing exists temporally. For there exists there, eternally, the fact that temporally something both exists and – before it exists – is able not to exist (as I have said).

It seems to me to be sufficiently clear from what has been said that free choice and God's foreknowledge are not at all inconsistent with each other. Their consistency results from the nature of eternity, which encompasses the whole of time and whatever occurs at any time. But since we do not in all respects have free choice, we must consider where and what that freedom of choice is which we believe a man always to have, and what that choice itself is. For choice and the freedom in terms of which the choice is called free are not identical. We speak of freedom and of choice in many cases – as, for example, when we say that someone has the freedom to speak or not to speak and that whichever of these he wills lies within his choice. Likewise, in many other instances we speak of a freedom and of a choice which are not always present or else are not necessary to us for the salvation of our souls. However, the present investigation is being conducted only with respect to that choice and that freedom without which a human, after once being able to use them, cannot be saved. For many people

lament because they believe that free choice is of no avail for salvation or condemnation, but that as a result of God's foreknowledge only necessity [determines salvation or condemnation]. Therefore, since after a human being has reached the age of understanding, he is not saved apart from being just: the choice and the freedom which are under discussion must be dealt with in terms of where the seat of justice is. Accordingly, first justice must be exhibited, and next this freedom and this choice.

Indeed, any justice whatever (whether great or small) is uprightness-of-will kept for its own sake. And the freedom [which is under discussion] is the ability to keep uprightness-of will for its own sake. I regard myself as already having set forth these definitions with clear reasoning – the first one in the treatise which I wrote *On Truth*, and the second in the treatise which I composed *On this very Freedom*. In the latter, I also showed how this freedom is present in a man inseparably and naturally, even though he does not always use it. Moreover, [I showed] that it is so powerful that as long as a man wills to use it nothing is able to remove from him the aforementioned uprightness (i.e., justice) which he has. By contrast, justice is not a natural possession; in the beginning it was separable from the angels in Heaven and from men in Paradise. And even now in this life [it is separable], not by necessity but by the autonomous willing of those who possess it. Now, since it is evident that the justice by which someone is just is uprightness-of-will, which (as I have said) is present-in someone only when he wills what God wills for him to will: it is evident that God is not able to remove this uprightness from him against his will; for God cannot will this removal. Moreover, neither can God will for one who possesses uprightness to desert it unwillingly as the result of some compelling force. (Indeed, [were that the case] God would will for him not to will that which He wills for him to will – which is impossible). Therefore, it follows that in this manner God wills that an upright will be free for willing rightly and for keeping this uprightness. And when the upright will is able [to do] what it wills, it does freely what it does. Hence, we can also recognize very clearly that both a will and its action are free – without its being the case that God's foreknowledge is incompatible therewith, as was demonstrated above.

Let us now posit an example in which there appears an upright (i.e., a just) will, freedom of choice, and an actual choice. And [let us consider] both how the upright will is attacked so that it deserts uprightness, and how the upright will keeps uprightness by means of free choice. [Let us suppose that] someone desires to cling to the truth because he discerns that it is right to love the truth. Surely, he already has an upright will and uprightness-of will. But the will is distinguishable from the uprightness by which it is upright. Now, [suppose that] another man approaches and threatens the first man with death unless he tells a lie. We see that it is now within this man's choice whether to relinquish his life for the sake of uprightness-of-will or to relinquish uprightness for the sake of his life. This choice – which can be called a judgment – is free; for reason, by means of which uprightness is understood, teaches that this uprightness ought always to be cherished for its own sake, and that whatever is extended in order [to induce] the for-saking of uprightness ought to be despised. Moreover, it is the prerogative of the will to reject and to elect in accordance with what rational discernment teaches. For to this end, especially, will and reason have been given to rational creatures. Therefore, the will's choice to desert uprightness is not compelled by any necessity, even though the man is beset by the obstacle of death. For although it is necessary either to relinquish his life or his uprightness, no necessity determines which one of these he keeps or relinquishes. Assuredly, the will alone here determines what he keeps; and where only the will's choosing is operative, there the force of necessity accomplishes nothing. Now, someone who is not under the necessity of deserting the uprightness-of-will which he possesses is obviously not lacking in the ability, or freedom, to keep uprightness. For this ability is always free. For this is the freedom which I have defined as the ability to keep uprightness-of-will for its own sake. In terms of this freedom both the choice and the will of a rational nature are called free.

Since God is believed to foreknow or know all things, we are now left to consider whether His knowledge derives from things or whether things derive their existence from His knowledge. For if God derives His knowledge from things, it follows that they exist prior to His knowledge and hence do not derive their existence from Him; for they can only exist from Him in accordance with His knowledge. On the other hand, if all existing things derive their existence from God's knowledge, God is the creator and the author of evil works and hence is unjust in punishing evil creatures – a view we do not accept.

Now, this issue can easily be resolved provided we first recognize that the good which is identical with justice is really some thing, whereas the evil which is identical with injustice lacks all being. (I have presented this solution very clearly in the treatise on *The Fall of the Devil* and in the short work which I entitled *The Virgin Conception and Original Sin*. For injustice is neither a quality nor an action nor a being but is only the absence of required justice and is present only in the will, where justice ought to be. And every rational nature as well as any of its actions is called just or unjust in accordance with a just or an unjust will. Indeed, every quality and every action and whatever has any being comes from God, from whom all justice and no injustice is derived. Therefore, God causes all the things which are done by a just or an unjust will, viz., all good and evil deeds. Indeed, in the case of good deeds He causes what they are [essentially] and the fact that they are good; but in the case of evil deeds He causes what they are [essentially] but not the fact that they are evil. Now, for anything to be just or good is for it to be something; but it is not the case that for a thing to be unjust or evil is for it to be something. For, indeed. to be good or just is to have justice, and having this is something; but to be evil or unjust is to lack the justice which one ought to have, and it is not the case that this lack is something. For justice is something, but injustice is nothing, as I have said.

But there is another kind of good, which is called benefit; and its opposite is the evil which is detriment. In some cases (e.g., blindness) this evil is nothing; in other cases (e.g., pain) it is something. When this evil is something, we do not deny that God causes it, because (as is read) He is the one who "causes peace and creates evil." For He creates detriments by means of which He tries and purifies the just as well as punishing the unjust. Therefore, with regard only to that evil which is identical with injustice and by virtue of which a man is called unjust: assuredly, this evil is never something. And it is not the case that for a thing to be unjust is for it to be something. And even as God does not cause injustice, so He does not cause something to be unjust. Nevertheless, He does cause all actions and movements, because He causes the things by which, from which, through which, and in which they are produced; and, unless God grants it, nothing has any power to will or to do anything. Moreover, the act of willing – which is sometimes just, sometimes unjust, and which is nothing other than using the will and the power-to-will which God bestows – is, with respect to the fact that it is, something good and is derivative from God. Indeed, when willing exists rightly, it is something good and just; but when it does not exist rightly, then solely in virtue of the fact that it does not exist rightly, it is evil and unjust. However, existing rightly is something, and it is from God; but not existing rightly is not something and is not from God. Now, when someone uses his sword or his tongue or his ability-to-speak, the sword or the tongue or the ability-to-speak is not one thing when its use is correct and something different when its use is incorrect. Similarly, the will, which we use for willing (even as we use reason for reasoning), is not one thing when someone uses it rightly and something different when he uses it wrongly. Now, the will is that in virtue of which a substance or an action is called just or unjust; and when the will is just, it is not any more or any less that which it is essentially than when it is unjust. Thus, then, in the case of all good wills and deeds God causes both what they are essentially and the fact that they are good; but in the case of all evil wills and deeds, He does not cause the fact that they are evil but causes only what they are essen-

tially. For even as the being of things comes only from God, so their rightness comes only from Him. Now, the absence of this uprightness about which I am speaking – an absence which is identical with injustice – is found only in the will of a rational creature, who ought always to have justice. But why does a creature not have the justice which it always ought to have, and how is it that God causes good things only by means of His goodness and causes evil things only through the fault of human beings and the Devil? And how does a human, under the guidance of grace, do good works by free choice and do evil by the working only of an autonomous will? "And what part does God have, blamelessly, in evil works, and does man have, laudably, in good works, so that nevertheless the good deeds of man are clearly seen to be imputed to God and the evil works to man?"

By the gift of God [the answers] will become more evident, it seems to me, when we shall take up [the topic of] grace and free choice. But for now I will say only that an evil angel does not have justice because he abandoned it and did not subsequently receive it again. On the other hand, a human is deprived of justice because in his first parents he cast it away and subsequently either did not receive it again or else, having received it again, rejected it anew. I think that by the assistance of God's grace I have shown – provided the points I have made are weighed carefully – that the coexistence of free choice and God's foreknowledge is not impossible, and that there can be no objection which is not answerable.

IV.4. ST. THOMAS AQUINAS

THE FOLLOWING SELECTION COMES FROM AQUINAS'S *SUMMA Theologiae* Ia, question 14 article 13. The selection shows the masterful suppleness of Aquinas's style in resolving problems through appropriate distinctions. For example, the proposition, "Everything known by God necessarily is the case," can be disambiguated by means of a distinction, the understanding of which Abelard had helped perfect: the proposition can be taken *de re* or *de dicto*. If it is read as *de re*, it has a divided sense, is false, and means, "Every thing which God knows is necessary." Read as *de dicto* it has a composite sense, is true, and means, "This *dictum*, that what is known by God is the case, is necessary." As the reader will see, the distinction is of considerable help in resolving the puzzles discussed below.

IV.4.1. Does God's Knowledge extend to Future Contingents? (*Summa Theologiae* Ia, qu.14, art.13)

On the thirteenth question we proceed as follows:

[1] It seems that God's knowledge does not extend to future contingents, for a necessary cause results in a necessary effect. But God's knowledge is the cause of what he knows, as was said above [art.8]. Since, then, his knowledge itself is necessary, it follows that the items known are necessary. Thus God's knowledge does not extend to contingents.

[2] Further, in every conditional where the antecedent is absolutely necessary, the consequent is absolutely necessary, for the antecedent relates to the consequent just as premises to a conclusion. But where the premises are necessary, any conclusion that follows has to be necessary, as is shown in the *Posterior Analytics* [I,6]. The following is a true conditonal: If God knew that this was going to be, this will be, because his knowledge extends only to truths. But in this conditional the antecedent is absolutely necessary, both because it is eternal and because it says something about the past. Therefore, the consequent is absolutely necessary. Therefore, whatever is known by God is necessary, and so God's knowledge does not extend to contingents.

[3] Further, everything God knows necessarily is the case, because even for us everything we know necessarily is the case, and yet God's knowledge is more certain than our knowledge. But no future contingent necessarily is the case. Therefore, no future contingent is known by God.

But, in opposition to this, we have these words:[1] "He who has shaped each of their hearts separately understands all their works," i.e. all the works of human beings. But the works of human beings are contingents, since they are subject to free will. Therefore, God knows future contingents.

Reply: We have to say that, as was shown above [art.9], since God knows everything, not just actual things but also things that are in his own power or the power of a creature, and some of these are contingent matters about what is future for us, it follows that God knows future contingents.

To make this clear we have to note that something can be thought of as contingent in two senses: in one sense, in itself, in virtue of the fact that it is already actual. In this sense it is not thought of as future but as present, not as contingently poised to go either way but as determined to one way. On

---

1 *Psalm* 32 (33):15.

account of this it can fall infallibly under a sure cognition like the sense of sight, as when I see that Socrates is sitting. In another sense something can be thought of as contingent on account of how it is in its cause. In this sense it is thought of as future and as contingent and not yet determined to one way, since a contingent cause relates to opposite [effects]. In this sense, a contingent is not something of which there can be certain knowledge. Thus whoever knows a contingent effect only through its cause has of that effect only a conjectural knowledge. But God knows all contingents not just as they are in their causes, but also as each of them actually is in itself.

Further, even though contingents come to be actually in succession, God knows contingents as they are in their own being, not successively, as we do, but all at once. This is because his knowledge is measured by eternity, just as also his being is, and eternity as a whole that exists all at once surrounds the whole of time, as was said above.[2] Thus everything which exists in time is present to God from eternity, not just in the sense that he has present to himself the definitive notions of things, as some say, but because his gaze falls over everything from eternity inasmuch as they are in his present.

From the above it is clear that contingents are infallibly known by God insofar as by their presence they fall under the divine sight, and yet they are future contingents in relation to their proximate causes.

To [1], then, we have to say that, even though the supreme cause is necessary, still its effect can be contingent on account of its contingent proximate cause. For example, the germination of a plant seed is contingent on account of its proximate cause, even though the motion of the sun, which is the first cause, is necessary. Likewise, the items known by God are contingent on account of their proximate causes, even though God's knowledge, which is the first cause, is necessary.

To [2], we have to say that some say that the antecedent, 'God knew this future contingent' is not necessary but contingent, because even though it is in the past tense it implies a relation to the future. But this does not do away with the necessity, since what had the relation to the future necessarily had it, even though the future thing sometimes does not follow.

Others say that this antecedent is contingent because it is composed out of a necessary and a contingent, just as the following *dictum* is contingent, that Socrates is a white human. But this too comes to nothing, for when we say, "God knew something to be a future contingent," the contingent item given there is only like the object of the verb and not like a main part of the proposition. Consequently, its contingency or necessity makes no difference to whether the whole proposition is necessary or contingent, true or false. For it can be true that I said a human being is an ass,[3] just as I said Socrates is running or God exists; like reasoning holds for necessity and contingency.

Consequently, we have to say that the antecedent is absolutely necessary. Some say that it nevertheless does not follow that the consequent is absolutely necessary, for the antecedent is a remote cause of the consequent and the latter is contingent on account of its proximate cause. But this comes to nothing, for the conditional would be false if its antecedent were a necessary remote cause and the consequent a contingent effect; for example, if I had said, "If the sun is in motion, the herbs will germinate."

We have to say, then, something else, namely that when we find in the antecedent something concerning an act of the soul, the consequent has to be read as referring not to the way something is in itself but to the way something is in the soul. For the being of a thing in itself is something other than the being of the thing in the soul. For example, if I say, "If the soul apprehends something, that something is immaterial," we have to read that as meaning that the item apprehended is immaterial as it exists in the mind, not as it exists in itself. Likewise, if I say, "If God knew something, that something will be," the consequent is to be read as about the thing as it falls under divine knowledge, i.e. as it is in its own presentness. And in that sense it is necessary, just as the antecedent is too, because "everything which is,

2 Ia,qu.10, art.2 ad4.
3 I.e., even though what I say is false, that I said it is true.

when it is, necessarily is," as is said in *De Interpretatione* [9].[4]

To [3], we have to say that we know successively in time things which are actualized temporally; but God knows them in eternity, which is beyond time. Consequently, we, knowing future contingents as future contingents, cannot be certain about them; but God can be since his intellectual apprehension is in eternity beyond time. It is like this: those who go down a road do not see those who are following them, but someone who from a height sees the whole road sees all the travelers on the road at once. Therefore, what we know must also be necessary in virtue of what it is in itself, because the items which in themselves are future contingents we cannot know. But the items which God knows must be necessary in virtue of the way they fall under divine knowledge, as was said. But they are not absolutely necessary when they are considered as in their own causes.

Thus this proposition, 'Everything known by God necessarily is the case,' is commonly disambiguated. It can be *de re* or *de dicto*.[5] If it is read as *de re*, it has a divided sense, is false, and means, 'Every thing [*res*] which God knows is necessary.' Read as *de dicto* it has a composite sense, is true,

and means, 'This *dictum*, that what is known by God is the case, is necessary.'

Some object to this and say that this disambiguation is [only] in order when we deal with forms that are separable from their subject, for example, if I say, "A white item is possibly black." This clearly is false when read *de dicto* and true when read *de re*, for the thing which is white can be black, but the *dictum*, "A white item is black," can never be true. Where we deal with forms that are inseparable from their subject this sort of disambiguation is not in order. For example, if I say, "For a black crow it is possible to be white," since in this case both senses are false. But being known by God is inseparable from the thing, because what is known by God cannot not be known.

This objection would be in order if by 'known' I meant some disposition inhering in the subject [that is known]. But since it means an act of a knower, even though the thing itself that is known is always known, something can be attributed to it in virtue of itself which is not attributed to it insofar as it falls under the act of being known. For example, being material is attributed to a stone in virtue of itself, but is not attributed to it in virtue of its being apprehensible by the mind.

---

4 See selection **IV.1.1.**
5 See glossary entry for "de re/de dicto."

IV.5. SIGER OF BRABANT

THE FOLLOWING SELECTION IS A SHORT TREATISE OF SIGER'S. THE Treatise shows Siger to have been an acute reader of the philosophy of Averroes. Siger makes a promising attempt to find a middle between strict determinism and total contingency. Contingency arises because some causes inferior to the first, but through which the first must work, are stoppable by interfering factors.

IV.5.1. How Contingency arises in the World (*On the Necessity and the Contingency of Causes*)

Your question is not unworthy of perplexity, whether it is necessary for all future things to come to be before they are; concerning both present and past things too: whether it was necessary for them to come to be before they came to be.

[A] Now it seems so.

[A.1] Every effect which arises arises from a cause with respect to which the existence of the effect is necessary, as Avicenna says; indeed, the proposition can be proved. For if some effect arises from a cause and if, when the cause is posited, it is possible for the effect both to be and not to be posited, then that cause is an entity in potency towards producing an effect, and it would lack some factor which would take it from potentiality to actuality such that the factor would make it a cause in actuality. Whence it is necessary for every cause which actually causes its effect to be such that when it is posited, its effect is necessarily posited. And if that cause is the effect of another, the same is argued concerning it. For it comes to be from such a cause: when it is posited, the effect which is also a cause is posited necessarily. One thus proceeds to the First Cause of all things. Whence all effects seem to proceed from their causes in such a way that it is necessary for them to come to be before they do come to be.

[A.2] Further, in present things there is a cause of all of those things which afterwards will come to be, such that all future events will come to be from present events with or without an intermediate term, whether one or many, a greater or a lesser number. But if there is a necessary cause among present events for those things which will arise, the proposition is proved. If not and from present events future things are able both to be and not to be, then there is no cause of future [things] among present [conditions], unless as matter. Whence nothing future will arise which does not have a necessary cause among present conditions; or if something does arise, matter by itself without an agent will actuate itself. So there must be a necessary cause among present conditions for all future events. It can be argued in the same way with respect to things which took place previously.

[A.3] Further, everything that happens either arises from a cause which by itself necessitates the effect and which cannot be impeded or arises from a cause which is by itself effective for the most part but which nevertheless can be impeded or arises from a cause to which cofactors come. And concerning future happenings which arise from a cause of the first type it is clear that their coming about is necessary. For the coming about from a cause which for the most part [exists] in that disposition in which the cause is not impeded is necessary, such that whenever that cause is posited in such a disposition, it is necessary to posit the effect too. Such is also true of an effect which arises from an accidental cause. For such a cause taken to be in a state in which it is a cause necessary for its effect brings about its effect of necessity. And if anyone should say that there does not apply to that cause the accident in virtue of which it causes of necessity, in as much as the accident is not necessary, let it be argued as before: with respect to a cofactor or with respect to that cause which requires a cofactor it is true that since there is some effect, it arises from a cause which exists in one of the three mentioned modes, and thus the arising of that effect which depends upon a cofactor will be necessary as before.

[A.4] Further, Aristotle and his Commentator [Averroes], in *Metaphysics* VI 3[1] say that if there were no accidental being, all things would be necessary, and this appears to be so. For a cause for the most part would be necessary unless something happens to it. Now however, the truth is that nothing is simply an accidental being. For consider an effect, related to some particular cause, which effect results from it *per accidens*, namely by the co-occurrence of another agent, either through the intervention of a contrary or from the weakness of matter which accompanies the agent (these cofactors nonetheless related to a higher cause which extends over many consequences); from this as from a cause by itself the cofactors can be found to be united. No co-occurrences would apply to that higher cause. And if all things were necessary, if there were no accidental being, as Aristotle says and as we have seen, there would be no unqualified accidental being, as has been said and as will come clear when we resolve the question: it will then be seen that all effects have some *per se* cause from which they necessarily follow, given that by *some cause* one means that some effects proceed from an accidental cause and some from a cause for the most part. But, as can be seen, this is to relate both to some necessary cause.

[A.5] Further, every effect which has a present or a past cause from which it necessarily follows arises of necessity, as Aristotle holds in *Metaphysics* VI 3. But every future effect has a present cause from which it necessarily follows; proof of the proposition is divine providence. For if A will come to be, it has been foreseen by God that A will come to be, and this is by infallible providence; for it is not possible for divine providence to be mistaken. Therefore, A follows from such a cause necessarily.

[A.6] Further, the proposition can be argued from the same basis more efficaciously: whenever some conditional is true, the consequent is necessary upon the assumption of the antecedent. But this conditional is true: if it has been foreseen that A will come to be, A will come to be absolutely (not adding to the consequent that it will come to be necessarily or contingently). But if the antecedent is already true, the consequent is necessarily to be.

[A.7] Further, it is asked in just the following way: How can there be an infallible providence of a fallible thing, since these two seem not to be consistent? For if the order of things or of a cause, in relation to some effect, is fallible, then the account of the order of that cause in relation to its effect (that is, providence) will be fallible. For if this – B's coming to be from A or that B will come to be from A – if this is itself fallible, although not failing, then reason or intellect which projects that B will come to be from A is fallible. And the same mode of deficiency arises and can be argued in the same way with respect to that divine foreknowledge of future events which precedes the future events. For in the three ways in which the argument has been made concerning providence it can also be made concerning foreknowledge, as comes clear to anyone who exerts himself. Of course divine foreknowledge of future events and providence are different: for divine foreknowledge of future events – under reason as foreknowledge – pertains to the divine intellect insofar as it grasps those future things absolutely; providence, however, since it is a part of prudence which concerns the future – the providence of future events pertains to the divine intellect not only insofar as it grasps them absolutely but also insofar as it is practical. Whence, it belongs to the foreseeing to describe the foreseen. Providence and foreknowledge agree in that both are infallible.

[Arguments against]

[B.1] Aristotle holds, in *Metaphysics* VI 3, that not everything arises from necessity, and he holds, in the same place, that some causes are such that sometimes, when they are posited, they cause their effects and sometimes not. His intention is therefore plain, namely to deny that all things happen of necessity, when he says in the same place that not all future things do happen of necessity, for example how a living being will die. Something has already taken place: that contraries can be found in the body from which death will come to be of necessity. But although one must die of old age or by force, it has not yet been determined or is not yet

---

1 1027a29-33; see selection I.1.4.

present how one must die, as was said above.

[B.2] Further, Aristotle's intention is also clear in *On Interpretation* 9[2] where he holds that not everything arises of necessity, since then it would not be required either to deliberate or to bother about things. Therefore, etc.

We divide the resolution of this question into four parts. In the first certain things should be seen concerning the order of causes in relation to effects. Second, in what way some thinkers have strayed from this order believing that all things happen necessarily on account of the connection of causes and the disposition of the universe. Third, in what way those people have made mistakes thus going wrong and in what way the question can be resolved. Fourth and last, the arguments of those opposing the truth must be resolved from the truth thus determined.

I

Concerning the first part it should be understood that five orders of causes to things caused can be found, and this according to the intention of the philosophers. The first order is that the First Cause, being the cause of all being, is the cause of the first intellect:[3] *per se*, immediate, necessitating and when posited, Its first effect is posited at the same time. And this I say according to the intention of the philosophers. I say that It is its cause *per se*; for the First Cause causes nothing *per accidens*, since nothing is able to concur with It; for then It would not be the cause of the whole being of Its effect. Indeed the causal order is not one of accidents one after another. I say that It is its immediate cause since that is Its first effect. It is indeed a necessitating cause of it in that a *per se* cause, which cannot be subjected to an impediment nor causes through an intermediate, stoppable cause, is a cause which necessitates Its effect. Thus does the First Cause stand to the first effect, and besides this, I say that that is necessary which always is at the same time as its caused effect.

Now nothing prevents certain present causes being necessary for their future effects in that they

are a cause of those effects by an intermediate motion and through an ordering of motion which causes a posteriority in duration. But since the First Cause causes Its first effect not by an ordering of motion nor by intermediate motion and since It is a necessitating cause above that first effect, they will exist simultaneously with respect to duration.

The second order is that the First Cause is the cause of the separate intelligences, both of the spheres and their motions and generally of things which are not generated. A cause, I am saying, *per se* and necessitating and which has its being simultaneously with effects of this kind. And this should be explained in the same way as that in which the relation was explained between the First Cause and Its first effect. But in one respect this order falls short of the earlier order, namely in that the First Cause is not the cause of the previously mentioned things unless according to some order and not immediately the cause of all of them, since nothing follows immediately from one simple thing unless it is itself one; nor do many things follow unless by means of a certain order. But it is irrelevant to the argument to consider according to what order the aforementioned things proceed. The First Cause is not only the cause of whatever of the aforementioned things you like *per se* (the mentioned mode of causality being understood) but also of the connection which happens to arise among them such that this one has its being with that one.

The third order is that the First Cause is the cause of the moon now being in such a place, the sun in such a place and similarly concerning other stars. And the First Cause is the cause of those things *per se* and necessarily, not immediately nor in that when It is posited, these effects are also posited in that the First Cause does not cause the situations mentioned except through the order of motion which effects a posteriority. Yet none the less it follows necessarily from the existence of the First Cause that the sun will then come to be in such a place and the moon in such a place and similarly concerning other stars. And it can be proved, as before, that It is a necessary cause. For It is an essential cause of this, since It is first, and not subject to anything joining It; for It is not fit to be

2 See selection **IV.1.1.**

3 I.e., intelligence. See glossary entry for 'intelligence.'

impeded nor does It cause Its effects through any intermediate causes which are preventable. The mover peculiar to any given star is the cause of the things foretold in the stars *per se* and immediate and necessary, although it is not such that when it is posited, the effect is posited too. Even the First Cause is a cause *per se*, necessitating, not immediate nor such that when It is posited, the effect of any given contingent connection or separation among the celestial stars should be posited in such a way that all these things would necessarily come to be at a time determined by the First Cause. And thus Aristotle well says[4] that, supposing something does arise by accident from celestial bodies, nevertheless nothing happens fortuitously and by accident among them, since whatever arises among them does so from causes *per se* and necessary, as has been seen: but such a thing does not happen fortuitously. For no mover peculiar to them is the cause of the combination or separation among celestial bodies but there is a higher cause which does the uniting; for what does not fall under an order of a lower cause (as also under its causality) falls under the order of a higher cause. For the order of any cause extends only as far as its causality extends. Whence it is the First Cause, and not movers peculiar to them, that orders combinations and separations among the stars.

The fourth order of causes arises because celestial things cause something in things down below, but they do this in different ways. Sometimes one of the celestial constellations causes something down below as a cause that is *per se*, necessary, immediate and simultaneous with the effect; sometimes it does this as a cause that is *per se* and necessary, but not simultaneous with the effect since it causes through a mediating motion; also sometimes it causes but not as an immediate cause; sometimes a sphere causes something here below as a cause that is *per se* and works in most cases since celestial constellations are apt to be stopped by the weakness of matter; and sometimes it causes through a cofactor. But that the celestial body causes something down below through a cofactor – where the cofactor presents an impediment to the celestial constellation (we take 'cofactor' here in its unqualified sense as being some disposition of the matter or some coun-

teracting factor here below), is traced back to something celestial as its cause; but the coincidence of the accident with the celestial constellation is not [traced back to something celestial], even though, none the less, this coincidence is traced back to a higher cause, for whatever happens in the celestial realm, and however the celestial things come together, has a unifying cause, as we saw. Since every disposition of matter is traced back to something celestial, in unifying celestial things the [higher cause] makes the disposition of matter caused by one constellation coincide with that other constellation, whether that disposition is simultaneous with its cause, or caused by it later, or stays around after its cause is gone. Therefore, in comparison to divine causes, which cause things in the celestial realm, celestial causes of things down below are deficient in that they cause something through a cofactor and can be stopped; this is not true of the divine causes.

The fifth and last order of causes arises because particular causes down below, whose causal influence does not extend very far, cause some of their effects *per se* and necessarily, some *per se* and in most cases, and some through cofactors. Those that have *per se* causality more frequently cause not in a necessary way but in most cases, since these causes are particularly subject to change. Nevertheless, the cofactors down below, whether they are two coincident causes, or counteracting and blocking agents, or some dispositions of matter, are found to be ordered and to have in the realm of higher causes a *per se* cause of their coincidence. For these factors down below are caused by higher things; and, consequently, the coincidence of two of them is caused either by one thing in the celestial realm or by several. In the former case there is a *per se* cause of them in the celestial realm; in the latter case there is one in the divine realm, as appears from what was said earlier. But these particular causes are deficient in comparison to celestial bodies inasmuch as celestial causes, even though they may be stopped from having their effect by the weakness of matter, are, nevertheless, not able to be affected and moved in themselves in the way lower causes can. Also cofactors here below, which have among particular causes no cause of their

---

4 *Physics* II, 4.

coincidence, sometimes are found to coincide on account of something in the celestial realm, because celestial causes extend further than do the particular causes down below.

II

From the foregoing appears the second of the propositions set out above, namely that which leads some thinkers into error, thinking that all future events which arise come to be necessarily before they are and similarly too concerning present and past events before they come to be. For every effect, in relation to the First Cause, arises from It as from a cause *per se* for the effect, since nothing joins that cause for producing its effect. Therefore, too, the effect arises from It as from a cause which cannot be prevented. For no cause is capable of being prevented unless an impediment is able to join or to come to it. From this one can argue thus: every effect which arises from a cause *per se* which cannot be stopped takes place necessarily; but everything which takes place, in relation to the First Cause of its taking place, arises from It as from an unstoppable, *per se* cause, as has already been explained. Therefore, everything which arises, before it exists, is necessarily to come to be from the existence of the First Cause, which is a cause *per se* and unable to be prevented from the futurity of any effect which arises in its own time.

Now there is a clarification of this argument, because Aristotle[5] would have it that there are two things which make it be that not everything comes to be necessarily. One is that some things arise from a *per se* cause but nevertheless stoppable, and these are not necessary. For example, if someone by eating certain pungent things should die, it is nevertheless not necessary that by eating pungent things he should die. The other is that some things are accidents which according to Aristotle[6] are not necessary: for example, in digging a grave one finds a treasure.

Now if effects which, relative to some particular cause, arise from it as from a stoppable cause, but relative to the First Cause arise from It as from a *per se* cause not subject to anything which impedes

Its power from bringing about the effect at a determined time, then effects of this sort, arising from a particular cause effective for the most part nevertheless arise necessarily relative to the First Cause. And even if those things which are accidents are considered in themselves and in relation to certain particular causes, they can always be found to have a uniting and ordering cause, as was seen earlier, such that accidents of this sort arise too from a cause which is *per se* and unstoppable. So notwithstanding such accidents all things would arise necessarily from their causes.

This is what moves some Parisian professors (others saying other things) against the teaching of their master Aristotle. For example, they say certain future things, which we have called contingencies in relation to certain of their causes, do not arise necessarily from them nor is it necessary that they come to be from those causes before they exist, even though they are in a future relation to the First Cause from which all intermediate causes exist and act right up to the effect, whether in relation to the whole connection of causes or the whole condition of existing things – it is necessary that these things come to be from the existence of the First Cause, from the connection of causes or from the condition of existing things. All things which come to be, before they are, are such that it is absolutely true to say that all things which come to be, before they are, have something in the condition of existing things from which it is necessary for them to come to be.

III

The third of the propositions laid out above is to be considered now, namely in what way those people go wrong who think in the way already mentioned. And this is because, although the First Cause is not a stoppable cause or one to which an impeding accident [can] join, It Itself, however, produces lower effects through intermediate causes and not immediately; although these intermediate causes receive from the order of the First Cause that whereby they produce their effects, even then the fact that they have not been stopped would never-

---

5 *Metaphysics* VI, 3.
6 *Metaphysics* VI, 2. See selection **I.1.4.**

theless not arise unless they were in their nature stoppable. Therefore, although the First Cause is not stoppable, It nevertheless produces an effect through a stoppable cause. Accordingly this effect, even in relation to the First Cause, will not necessarily come to be before it is. For even if all co-occurring events have an ordering and uniting cause, that cause, as is obvious and the reason for which will appear, is nevertheless not such as to make all accidents necessary such that some among them would not be rare but all those which are frequent would rather be necessary.

Now it would be required, if all things were to arise necessarily, that future events should not arise from the First Cause through stoppable, intermediate causes and not only that their first cause is not stoppable. It is also required that there be no accident among things unless it has a *per se* unifying and ordering cause not just any you like but one which prohibits its being rare such that, as Aristotle holds,[7] if the accidental did not exist, everything would be necessary, it being understood that the elimination of the accidental in relation to the First Cause does not make everything necessary; it is required that there be an elimination of the accidental impediment in relation to particular causes through which, as intermediaries, the First Cause works. And so if one values truth, one will find Aristotle holding two things in the sixth book of the *Metaphysics*:[8] one is that if all future events arise necessarily, all events would arise from *per se* causes not capable of being impeded. The other is that the rare accident would not exist. These two aforementioned things in truth accompany one another.

From these [considerations] we can briefly resolve the question along with Aristotle[9] by saying that those future events alone arise necessarily which arise from a *per se* cause which is not capable of being impeded and not alone from the First Cause but from a near [cause]. And because not all future events are like that, but some of them are accidents, some of them indeed arise from impedible causes (even if they have not been impeded), therefore not all events arise necessarily. And this is apparent. If

one attends [to the matter], some future event is said to arise necessarily not only because it will arise thus and not otherwise, but because it is not able to arise otherwise than as it arises. But a future event is not said to be unable to be otherwise than it will be unless because its cause is already present in such a way that not only will it not be other than [a cause] from which an effect arises of this sort, but because in its nature it is such that it is not possible for it to be other than [a cause] from which the effect arises. And because not all things which will arise will arise thus from their cause, therefore not everything will arise necessarily. Indeed it is required that if everything which will come to be will be necessarily, any given thing among present [things] would have a certain cause which cannot be impeded and from which a future effect of that sort would arise immediately or through intermediate future causes which also cannot be impeded – just as in a living being the cause of future death is present and which cannot be impeded from that effect.

We therefore say that many future effects [will arise] contingently and not necessarily even by referring them to the whole connection of causes or the disposition of present [conditions], or even to the First Cause. For even if a cause not impeded or under the privation of some future impediment should be contained within the disposition of present [conditions] or within the whole connection of causes, nevertheless the cause is not contained in them as a necessary [cause which is] unchangeable and unimpedible, unable to be otherwise. This would not even be the case if that which would move or impede or make the present cause of a future contingency otherwise were not to exist in the disposition of present events or in the connection of causes. Even the First Cause, being a cause which is not impedible, nevertheless causes by means of an impedible cause, as has been said. Nor is it necessary for future contingencies to arise with respect to divine providence, since it has been seen from the order and connection of causes and the disposition of present [conditions] that it is not necessary for many things to come to be which will

7 *Metaphysics* I, 2.
8 VI, 2-3.
9 *Metaphysics* VI, 3.

come to be. Whence by the reason and mind of its order and connection of causes in relation to their effects [necessity does not arise]. Indeed divine providence is nothing other than the practical reason of the aforementioned order and connection.

But at this point three doubts arise concerning what has been said. The first is in what way these propositions can hold at the same time: "the First Cause is a cause not able to be impeded with respect to any future event which will arise" and nevertheless "that effect proceeds from It by means of causes which can be impeded." For if the means and instruments can be impeded from their effect, then the First Cause too will be capable of being impeded from Its effect – through those intermediaries.

The second doubt arises because, even if a cause, which is said to be a cause for the most part, is capable of doing other than to produce its effect, the cause nevertheless, taken *per se* and absolutely and as not having been impeded, is not able to do other than to produce its effect. For thus a cause produces its effect, namely insofar as it has not been impeded. It therefore seems that the effect proceeds from its cause by necessity.

The third doubt is how it is that not all co-occurrences have a necessary concomitance, since they all have a *per se* and ordering cause, as was said earlier. For the flowering of this and of that tree, which considered by themselves are co-occurrences, have a necessary or at least a frequent concomitance because of the fact that they have a *per se* cause which unifies and conjoins them. But if all co-occurrences which have the definition of accident – considered in themselves and related to certain particular causes – are found to be resolved into and ordered by higher causes, why will it not be that there is necessary concomitance for all such things? And we ask this because, given that there are certain stoppable causes from which something will come to be according to an accident: if an accidental impediment should be something among necessary things from a uniting and ordering cause, the necessity of futurity would not be lifted among those things which arise as they arise, even though

some things indeed will come to be from causes which are sometimes impeded, since the concourse of impediments will come to be necessarily.

The first of these doubts can be resolved [in the following way]. [The following two propositions] do not stand together at the same time: "the First Cause is a necessitating cause of any effect which will arise" and "some effect is produced through intermediate, stoppable causes." But for the First Cause to be an unstoppable cause is not for It to necessitate any effect which arises, but rather for It to be a cause to which no impediment outside Its order can come. It follows from the fact that the First Cause is not stoppable that no future event is able to arise outside Its order. And so, if one part of a contradictory pair (future and contingent) were only to fall under the order of the First Cause (such that the other one were not able to fall under another order – as does happen with some particular causes), then that future event would happen of necessity.

What is said, however, does not obtain because there is no such particular causal order. Therefore, from a particular and proximate cause a future contingency does not arise necessarily; for it is possible for the emergence of that future event to happen otherwise and beyond the order of its cause. Indeed, from the First Cause that future event does not arise necessarily; for although, concerning the emergence of that future event, it is not possible for it to happen otherwise than according to the order of the First Cause (in this that It is not a stoppable cause), nevertheless that future event does not alone fall under Its order but its opposite can too; in respect of the First Cause the emergence of the future contingent is thus not necessary.

In reply to the second doubt one should understand, as Aristotle says in the first book of *De Caelo*,[10] that he who is sitting, while he is sitting, has power to stand. But he who is sitting, while he is sitting, does not have power to stand while sitting. And to this point it is said in *On Interpretation*[11] that what is, when it is, must be; not, however, this: what is must be. Thus even a

---

10 I, 12.
11 Chapter 9; 19a22. See selection **IV.1.1**.

cause for the most part which has not been impeded, even when it has not been impeded, [is such that] it is possible that the effect should not arise from it, even if it is not possible [taken in a combined sense as illustrated above] that when a cause for the most part has not been impeded, the effect should not arise from it.

Since necessity is a certain impossibility of being otherwise, it appears that there is a certain necessity in the emergence of an effect from a stoppable cause, namely because a cause for the most part, existing in a disposition in which it can cause its effect and has not been stopped, is not in a potential state for not causing the effect – being thus disposed. And unless there were such necessity, nothing would arise from such causes. It is this necessity which Avicenna understood when he said that every effect with respect to its cause is necessary. This, however, is not simple necessity, nor is it of any particular present thing. For a cause for the most part is then stoppable when it has not been stopped and has the potency for an effect not to come to be from it, even if it does not have the potency for being stopped, not being stopped.

But some thinkers not perceiving the different kinds of necessity mentioned above fall into diverse errors. For some – who take cognisance of the fact that a cause, not stopped and existing generally in a condition sufficient for causing its effect, is not in a potential state for not causing the effect, standing thus, – have said that everything arises necessarily. It is already clear how they go wrong. Others, in order to avoid this error, fall into another [error] saying that a cause, existing in that condition in which it is able to cause its effect, would not in any way be a cause which necessitates its effect, since then deliberation and free will would be destroyed.

Now the distinction between kinds of necessity mentioned before resolves this ignorance of such people. If everything were to arise necessarily – that is, from unstoppable causes – it would be useless to deliberate how to stop certain future effects, as if, for example, the ingesting of a certain drug were an unstoppable cause of death, it would be useless to seek medical advice. Now even this – the cause in producing its effect is a cause unstoppable and necessary – would destroy free will; for then all our willing would be caused by a cause which our will would not be able to resist. But this – the ingesting of a drug, not stopped, is not in a poten-

tial state for not causing death – does not remove the usefulness of medical advice. But one does not seek medical advice so that the ingesting of a drug, which has not been stopped, will not induce death but rather because the ingesting of the drug, which has not been stopped, was stoppable so that at another time with the help of medicine [the effect] of the said ingestion can be stopped and death not induced.

This however obtains: for the will always to be moved to its willing by a cause existing in that condition in which it is fit to move the will and for the will to exist in a condition in which it is fit thus to be moved, is not to destroy free will, in that nothing moves the will unless it is stoppable from motion – even if it has not then been stopped when it moves the will. So one needs to consider that the freedom of the will is not to be understood in its operation to be such that the will is the primary cause of its willing or of its operating, capable of moving towards opposites, not moved by something prior. For the will is not moved to willing unless from some act of comprehension. Even this is not freedom of the will: when the will itself exists in that disposition in which it is fit to be moved to some act of willing and when it moves, existing in a disposition in which it is fit to move, the will need not then be moved or should have the capacity of not being moved, being thus disposed and the agent being thus disposed; for this is impossible. But freedom of the will consists in this that although the will is found to be moved by certain things at certain times, when such factors which move the will have not been impeded, the nature of the will is such that whichever of those factors can move the will are able to be impeded from their motion. This happens to the will against sensuous appetite because the will wills from the judgment of reason; sensuous appetite, however, is activated from the judgment of sense. But [things are such that] we are born with determinate judgment of sense concerning the pleasant and the painful, determinately feeling these things as pleasant and those as painful. Now on account of this fact the sensuous appetite does not freely pursue or flee whatever [it perceives]. However, we are not in this way born with determinate judgment concerning good and bad; but it is possible to go both ways, and because of this things are such in the will too.

In reply to the third proposition one should say that those accidents are necessary which have a single cause and none of which can arise except from a cause from which effects arise one after another. Indeed they are not proper accidents, as in the example given earlier: when this tree is in bloom, another is also in bloom. But it is nonetheless possible for those things which happen together from a uniting cause to arise from diverse causes and also for one of them not to arise from the cause of the other; the co-occurrence of such things is not necessary. It is as if at the time a creditor wants to go to the market-place, the debtor too wants [to go there] for the same reason (perhaps because of crop-failure). Now since it is possible for this to arise from different causes and one of them is not from the cause of the other (happening as if they should be from one cause) – because of this it is not necessary that by the creditor wanting to go to the market-place so too does the debtor. And since an accident does not have a proximate, uniting cause unless *per accidens*, a remote cause, which is God, does not introduce necessity into the co-occurrence of accidents. On just this point Aristotle well says[12] that an accident is not a true being but, as it were, in name only, nor a true unity and that there is no cause of its own generation. Hence, when any two things concur in being *per accidens*, it is true that they have a uniting cause. But just as it happens to them to be united, so it happens to them to be from a single cause, since it is possible for one of them to be found with its own cause apart from that of the other. This therefore holds: a being for the most part does not arise of necessity, as that someone consuming pungent substances should die. Those things which are accidental are not necessary, as that in digging a grave one discovers a treasure. It is this that makes it true that not all future things are necessary but only those which arise from causes which are not stoppable and among present conditions have such a cause as future death has in the body of an animal presently living.

IV

In reply to the first argument [A.1] in opposition it should be said that the cause of an effect [which arises] for the most part, taken by itself, does not necessitate its effect; even taken as not having been stopped it remains stoppable and does not necessitate its effect. But it is true that a cause for the most part taken as not having been impeded and as in a state in which such a cause acts does not have the potentiality for not causing its effect, not being impeded and standing in that relation. And Avicenna thus understands that every effect in respect to its cause is necessary – which necessity, as was seen earlier, is only that according to which whatever is is necessary when it is. And the reason is that a cause for the most part, taken not to have been impeded, although at one time it was capable of being stopped so as not to produce its effect, nevertheless when it has not been stopped, it does not have such potentiality that the effect is able not to be posited – given that the cause is not impeded and that a cause for the most part is an actual cause causing its effect, nothing is required beyond the removal of an obstruction nor is anything else required which would essentially take it from potency to act, since when it is stopped, it is not a cause in potency unless accidentally.

In reply to the second argument [A.2] it should be said in the same way that a future contingent effect which will come about does not only have a cause in the state of present factors which is, as it were, a material cause, but also a cause in actuality, nevertheless not a cause from which that future effect will necessarily be. And this is clear. For it is possible for a cause with or without an intermediate term, whether through one or many, to reside in a state of present factors and not to be impeded. And as has been seen, it is thus not necessary in relation to its effect nor is there a cause only as matter requiring something that makes it an actual cause. It follows that that argument is deficient which supposes that if a future effect does not have among present conditions just a cause which is a material cause, then there presently exists already some cause of that effect which has not been impeded and which is necessary.

In the same way the third argument [A.3] can be resolved, as would appear to anyone who well considers these things.

---

12 *Metaphysics* VI, 2.

In reply to the fourth argument [A.4] it should be said that the following proposition 1. requires another, 2.:

1. everything will arise necessarily in relation to the First Cause and in relation to the whole connection of causes and the condition of present events;

2. there is no being *per accidens*, and not just in relation to the First Cause; not only would the First Cause be a cause which is not stoppable, but there could not even be an accidental impediment in relation to intermediate causes through which the First Cause produces its effects, as was said before.

In reply to the other [argument] concerning providence [A.5] it should be known that some thinkers have said the following: everything that will come to be will necessarily come to be on account of reasons touched upon in the three arguments concerning divine providence laid out above. But they are in error. For divine providence does not impose necessity upon things – something which comes clear thus: divine providence is nothing other than practical reason or intellect of the order and connection of causes in relation to their effects. And if this order and connection does not impose necessity upon all future events but only on those which arise from causes which cannot be prevented, then the account of that connection does not impose necessity either, since if causes which the head of a family preordains towards some end do not necessarily bring that end about, then neither does reason or the providence of the head of a commonwealth.

Because of this other thinkers have said that through divine providence it can be foreseen concerning some future event not only that it will arise but also in what way it will arise, namely according to the condition of its proximate cause, contingently or necessarily. And so concerning the emergence of future contingents they say that it is necessary that such things should come to be – nevertheless contingently. But this discussion can be understood in three ways. In one way it is so under-

stood not that future events of this kind will come to be necessarily but rather that in the emergence of future events of this kind it is necessary that there is contingency such that, if they will come to be, it is necessary that they do so contingently; and this is true. But this is not what they mean to say when they say that it is necessary that future events of this kind would come to be, nevertheless contingently. For their intention is to posit necessity and infallibility in the emergence of future events of this kind by virtue of the fact that through infallible providence it has been foreseen concerning them that they would arise. And on that account their discourse can be understood in a second way as saying that it is necessary that future events of that sort will come to be – nevertheless contingently – that certain future events will come to be contingently in relation to some one of their causes which is stoppable and that it should nevertheless be necessary that they will arise in relation to providence and the whole connection of causes. And this is to say that they will come to be absolutely necessarily, even if they would be contingencies in some respect; but, as has been seen before, that all future events are necessary even with respect to the whole connection of causes, is false.

In a third way it can be understood that they mean to say that there is absolute contingency even with respect to divine providence and the connection of causes and not only in respect to a certain cause. But then their discourse implies opposites which cannot stand at the same time. For [these two propositions] do not stand at the same time: that it is necessary that A comes to be and that A comes to be contingently. They do not say such things unless – because of the infallibility of divine providence – they place infallibility and necessity in the emergence of all future events. But, as was said before, if the connection, order, and disposition of present events do not impose necessity upon all future events, then neither does the practical intellect of that order and disposition.

But one should attend carefully to the fact that, if it is preconceived, concerning any future event which we have called contingent, that it will come to be, and if preconceived through this conception which is of that event in itself and not in another and through its own proper account and through an infallible conception, whether the conception be divine or some other, then that future event would be necessary. Therefore, because some [thinkers] assimilate the divine intellect, whereby it is known concerning some future event that it will come to be, with their own, and positing the first intellect as infallible, they have to say all future things are necessary, just as Averroes does say in *Metaphysics* VI, namely that according to what is said in *Legal Examples,* everything has been written and what has been written must pass into actuality – because of this all future events are necessary. For *Legal Examples* accepts [the supposition] that in the divine intellect there is a conception of everything that will take place – will itself be – and a conception by which those things are conceived in themselves and not in another and through a proper account. For *Legal Examples* accepts [the proposition] that everything has been written in a book; by "written in a book" Averroes means what some [thinkers] mean when they speak of divine foreknowledge, providence or predestination which is a part of providence or the book of life.

But one should notice that neither the present nor the future or the emergence of future events is conceived by the divine intellect by means of a conception of them in themselves but rather by a conception whereby something is conceived in another. For the aforementioned things do not have any conception in God unless a conception which is of itself and is God's substance. But regarding such an infallible and always true conception of future events it is not required that it impose necessity upon future events in such a way that one should say concerning some future contingency that it has not been foreseen and preconceived by God that it would come to be, since nothing is foreseen and preconceived by God unless it is true. Now however, as Aristotle holds in *On Interpretation* [9], although it is true that a sea battle either will or will not be, you cannot divide and say either one truly. Now if it is true that a sea battle will be, then a sea battle being would be necessary, as he draws out in the same place.

On the other hand, if it sounds hard to some people's ears to say that this is not preconceived by

God, then it should be said, as was said before, that since this event itself, A, which is to be, does not have a concept in God unless one which is of divine substance, indeed is the divine substance itself – even such a concept of the event A itself which will come to be is of the event in some other immutable being, although that A will arise would be mutable and imposes no necessity upon A towards its taking place.

From [these considerations] one should reply to the first argument [A.1] by conceding the major premise, namely that a future effect which has a present cause from which it necessarily follows will arise of necessity, and by denying the minor which takes it that everything which will happen has a present cause from which events necessarily follow. And when it is argued on behalf of the minor premise "Because it has been foreseen concerning them that they will arise," the argument can be denied, as has been said, and it can be asserted that it has not been foreseen that A will arise since neither would this be true.

On the other hand, it should be said, even if it were foreseen that A will arise (and by an infallible providence), that it is nonetheless fallible that A will come to be – [fallible] in that this providence and infallible concept of A itself is not of the event in itself but in an immutable other. Now in the divine mind mutable things have an immutable science and fallible future events too have an infallible foreknowledge and providence.

To the second argument concerning providence [A.6] one should reply by means of the same [procedure] – either by denying the antecedent (namely that it has been foreseen that A will come to be) for the reason given or by setting aside the consequence whereby it is said that if it has been foreseen that A will be, then A will be. For if it does not follow from the state of present conditions and from the connection of causes that A will come to be – for then the future event would necessarily arise from them – then neither [does it follow] from the existence of the First Cause, since the First Cause is not in a position to cause that event unless through intermediate causes; further, if from things previously said it does not follow that A will arise, then neither [does it follow] from a providence which the event has in God, since the providence which it has in God is God. Another reason too is that since it is not necessary for some effect to follow from ordained causes, neither [does it follow] from the practical reason of that order.

The following escapes [them] that if it has been foreseen that A will arise, A itself will arise. This happens because the providence of A's arising is understood by the similarity to our minds and to our foreseeing concerning some future event that it will be.

To the third argument from providence [A.7] it should be said that just as an immutable science can be in God of some mutable subject in this respect that the science is not known which is of its subject in itself but in relation to something immutable, so too there can be an infallible providence of a future, fallible event. It should nevertheless be noted that although A's coming to be is fallible, the event of A's coming to be is nevertheless not able to arise outside the order of the First Cause; but even its being able not to arise is not outside its own order.

If it should be argued from divine foreknowledge of future events or from predestination, we should speak in the same way as we have spoken of divine providence.

And here end the six problems and one question, and this has been determined by Master Siger of Brabant.

IV.6. JOHN DUNS SCOTUS

IN THIS SELECTION SCOTUS REJECTS THE SOLUTION OFFERED BY
Boethius and argues that God knows the future by knowing His own will, a will
which is a contingent cause in the radical sense that even when it is willing something, it has the potential to will the opposite *at that very instant*. In this contingency lies the freedom of both divine and human will. The reader should refer
back to selections **I.9.1.-2.** where Scotus argued that the first cause must be a contingent cause if there is to be contingency at all. Also note how Scotus's ideas on
contingency contrast totally with those of Siger of Brabant in the preceding selection.

In the discussion of the divine will below in section [5.5] the reader needs to
bear in mind that orthodox theology allows that God can only have one single
eternal act of willing, since God is entirely simple and immutable. Scotus, therefore, has to hold that God can will different things even though He cannot have a
different act of willing.

IV.6.1. How God can know Future Contingents by knowing His own Will (*Ordinatio* I, dist.38 & 39)

[1] In the second part of the thirty-eighth distinction the Master[1] treats of the infallibility of divine
knowledge, and in the thirty-ninth distinction he
treats of the immutability of divine knowledge.
Therefore, in respect of this subject matter in so far
as divine knowledge relates simply to the existences
of things, I ask five questions:

[1.1] First, does God have determinate knowledge
of everything in respect of all their conditions of
existence?

[1.2] Second, does He have certain and infallible
knowledge of everything in respect of all their conditions of existence?

[1.3] Third, does He have immutable knowledge
of everything in respect of every condition of existence?

[1.4] Fourth, does He necessarily know every condition of the existence of everything?

[1.5] Fifth, can some contingency on the side of
the things in existence co-exist with the determinacy and certitude of His knowledge?

[2 Initial arguments]

[2.1] To the first question I argue no:

[2.1.1] Because, according to the Philosopher in
his *Perihermenias* II,[2] in future contingents there is
no determinate truth, – therefore neither is there
determinate knowability. Therefore, neither does
the intellect have determinate knowledge of them.

This argument is reinforced by his own proof in
that same text: Because then neither deliberation
nor taking trouble would be needed. It seems this is
so. If there is some determinate knowledge of some
future contingent, neither taking trouble nor deliberation is needed because whether we deliberate or
not, this thing will occur.

[2.1.2] Besides, if God's power were limited to
one member [of a contradictory pair] it would be
imperfect, because if God were able to do this in
such a way that he was not able to do the opposite,
His power would be limited and he would not be
omnipotent. Therefore, in like fashion, if he knew
one member in such a way that he did not know the
other, he would be limited in respect of knowledge
and not omniscient.

[2.2] To the second question I argue that no:

[2.2.1] Because this inference holds: God knows

---

1 Peter Lombard, bishop of Paris, 1150-52, wrote a work called *Sentences* which became a standard text for 13th-centu-
ry students of theology.
2 See selection **IV.1.1.**

that I am going to sit tomorrow. I will not sit tomorrow. Therefore, God is deceived. Therefore, by like reasoning, this inference holds: God knows that I am going to sit tomorrow. I can not-sit tomorrow. Therefore, God can be deceived.

That the first holds is obvious, because he who believes what is not the case in reality is deceived. From this I prove that [the second] consequence holds, because just as from two *de inesse*[3] premisses follows a *de inesse* conclusion, so from one *de inesse* premiss and one *de possibili*[4] follows a conclusion *de possibili*.

[2.2.2] Besides, if God knows that I am going to sit tomorrow, and it is possible for me not to sit tomorrow, assume it is a fact that I will not sit tomorrow; it follows that God is deceived. But from assuming that what is possible is a fact, the impossible does not follow. Therefore, it will not be impossible for God to be deceived.

[2.3] To the third question I argue that no:

[2.3.1] There can be no transition from a contradictory to a contradictory without some change, because if there is no change there does not seem to be any way by which what was first true is now false. Therefore, if God when He knows A is able not to know A, this would seem to be the case in virtue of some possible change, and a change in that very A as it is known by God, since nothing has being if not in God's knowledge. Consequently, a change in A cannot occur without a change in God's knowledge – which is what we proposed.

[2.3.2] Besides, whatever is not A but can be A can begin to be A, because it seems unintelligible that the affirmation opposed to a negation which is the case can be the case without beginning to be the case. Therefore if God does not know A but can know A, He can begin to know A; therefore He can be changed into knowing A.

[2.3.3] Besides, there is this third argument: If God does not know A but can know A, I ask what is this power? Either it is passive, and then it is in respect of a form[5] and it follows that there is change; or it is active, and it is clear that it is nat-

ural because the intellect *qua* intellect is not free but rather something that acts naturally. Such a power can act after not acting only if it is changed. Therefore, as before, it follows that there is change.

[2.4] To the fourth question I argue that yes:

[2.4.1] Because God immutably knows A, therefore necessarily. (By A understand 'the Antichrist is going to exist.') Proof of this consequence: First, because the only necessity posited in God is the necessity of immutability. Therefore whatever is in Him immutably is in Him necessarily.

Second, because everything immutable seems to be formally necessary, just as everything possible – in the sense opposed to 'necessary' – seems to be mutable, for everything possible in this sense does not exist in virtue of itself and can exist in virtue of something else. But for it to exist after not existing (either in the order of duration or in the order of nature), does not seem to be possible without some mutability; therefore etc.

[2.4.2] Besides, whatever can exist in God, can be the same as God, and consequently can be God. But whatever can be God, of necessity is God, because God is immutable; therefore whatever can be in God, of necessity is God. But to know A, can be in God; therefore of necessity it is God, and consequently He knows A necessarily without qualification.

[2.4.3] Besides, every unqualified, i.e. absolute, perfection[6] of necessity belongs to God. To know A is an unqualified perfection, since otherwise God would not be imperfect if He did not know A formally, because He is imperfect only by lacking some unqualified perfection.

[2.5] To the fifth question I argue no:

[2.5.1] Because this inference holds: God knows A. Therefore, A will necessarily be the case.

The antecedent is necessary. Proof of the consequence: A rational act is not lessened by the subject matter it relates to, just as saying is not lessened if it relates to this, 'that I say nothing,' for this inference holds: I say that I say nothing. Therefore, I say

---

3 I.e., a proposition which simply asserts that a predicate holds of a subject.
4 I.e., a proposition which asserts only that a predicate *could* hold of a subject.
5 I.e., it would have to receive a form. See glossary entry for 'agent/recipient.'
6 See glossary entry for 'absolute perfection.'

something. Therefore, by similar reasoning, since God's knowing is necessary without qualification, it is not lessened in that necessity by the fact that it relates to something contingent.

[2.5.2] Besides, everything known by God to be going to be will necessarily be; A is known by God to be going to be; therefore, etc. The major premiss is true in as much as it is *de necessario*,[7] because the predicate of necessity belongs to the subject. The minor is without qualification *de inesse*, because it is true for eternity. Therefore, there follows a conclusion *de necessario*.

[3 In opposition to the above]

[3.1] *Hebrews* 4: "All things are bare and open to His eyes." Also the gloss on this. (Seek it out.) Therefore, He has determinate and certain knowledge of everything in respect of everything knowable in them. Also He has immutable knowledge, as is obvious, since nothing in Him is mutable.

[3.2] In opposition on the fourth question: If God necessarily knew A, then A would be necessarily known; and if necessarily known, then necessarily true. The consequent is false, therefore the antecedent is.

[3.3] In opposition on the fifth question: Being is divided into the necessary and the contingent; therefore, the intellect, when it apprehends beings in respect of their own peculiar aspects, apprehends this one as necessary and that one as contingent (otherwise it would not apprehend them as being those sorts of beings), and consequently that knowledge does not do away with the contingency of what is known.

[4 Others' opinions]

[4.1] As regards these questions, the certitude of divine knowledge, of everything in respect of all conditions of existence, is posited on account of ideas which are posited in the divine intellect, and this on account of their perfection in representing, because they represent the things of which they are not just in respect of themselves but in respect of every aspect and relationship. Thus they are in the divine intellect sufficient reason not just for simply apprehending the ideated items but also for apprehending every union of them and every mode of those ideated items that pertains to their existence.

Against [this opinion]: The concepts involved in apprehending the terms of some complex[8] are not sufficient to cause knowledge of that complex unless it is apt to be known in virtue of its terms. A contingent complex is not apt to be known in virtue of its terms, because if it were it would be not only necessary but also primary and immediate.[9] Therefore, the concepts involved in apprehending the terms, however perfectly they represent those terms, are insufficient to cause knowledge of the contingent complex.

Besides, ideas only naturally represent what they represent, and they represent it under the aspect by which they represent something. This is proved by the fact that ideas are in the divine intellect before every act of the divine will, in such a way that they exist there in no way through an act of that will; but whatever naturally precedes an act of the will is purely natural. I take, then, two ideas of terms which are represented in them, ideas of human and of white, for example. I ask: Do those ideas of themselves represent the composition of those extremes,[10] or the division,[11] or both? If only the composition, then God knows that composition (and in a necessary way), and as a consequence He in no way knows the division. Argue in the same way if they represent only the division. If they represent both, then God knows nothing through them, because to know contradictories to be simultaneously true is to know nothing.

Besides, there are ideas of possible items in the same way there are ideas of future items, because between possibles that are not going to be and those that are going to be a difference exists only by an act of the divine will. Therefore, an idea of a future item no more represents it as necessarily going to be than does the idea of a possible item.

Besides, an idea of a future item will not represent

---

7 I.e., a proposition which asserts that its predicate *must* hold of the subject.
8 See glossary entry for 'complex.'
9 I.e., not provable from other more self-evident propositions.
10 I.e., the proposition 'A human is white.'
11 I.e., the proposition 'A human is not white.'

something as existing any more at this instant than at some other.

[4.2] Another opinion is that God has certain knowledge of future contingents through the fact that the whole flow of time and all things which are in time is present to eternity.

[4.2.1] This is shown – through the fact that eternity is limitless and infinite, and as a consequence just as what is limitless is present to every place all at once, so the eternal is present to the whole of time all at once.

This is explained by the example of a stick fixed in water: Even if the whole of the river flows past the stick and thus the stick is present sucessively to every part of the river, still the stick is not limitless in respect of the river, since it is not present to the whole all at once. Therefore, by the same reasoning, if eternity were something standing still (as was the stick) past which time flowed in such a way that only one instant of time would ever be present to it all at once (just as only one part of the river was present to the stick all at once), eternity would not be limitless in respect of time.

[4.2.2] This point is reinforced by the following consideration: The "now" of eternity when it is present to the "now" of time is not co-equal to it; therefore, when it is present to that now it goes beyond it. But it would go beyond it, when it is present to that "now," only if it were all at once present to another "now."

[4.2.3] It is also reinforced by this: If the whole of time could exist in external reality all at once, the "now" of eternity would be present to the whole of time all at once. But even though on account of its succession time is opposed to existing all at once, this detracts not at all from the perfection of eternity. Therefore now eternity itself is equally present to the whole of time and to anything existing in time.

This is reinforced by another example, that of the center of a circle. If we let flowing time be the circumference of a circle and the "now" of eternity be the center, no matter how much flow there was in time the whole flow and any part of it would always be present to the center. In this way, then, all things, no matter what part of time they exist in

(whether they are in this "now" of time or are past or future), are all present in respect of the "now" of eternity. In this way what is in eternity on account of such a co-existence sees those things presently, just as I can see presently what in this very instant I see.

I argue against this opinion: First, I turn back against them what they claimed about limitlessness. Given that a place can increase continuously *ad infinitum* (and this occurs in such a way that just as time is in continuous flux so God increases and increases the place in a process of becoming), still God's limitlessness would be to Him a ground for co-existing with some place (in some "now") only if it were an existing place. For God by His limitlessness co-exists only with what is in Him, even though he could cause a place outside the universe and then by His limitlessness He would co-exist with it. If, then, limitlessness is a ground for co-existing only with an actual place and not with a potential one (because it does not exist), by like reasoning eternity will be a ground for co-existing only with something existent. This is what is argued for when we say, "What is not can co-exist with nothing," because 'co-exist' indicates a real relation,[12] but a relation whose basis[13] is not real is itself not real.

Again, if an effect has being in itself in relation to a primary cause, it unqualifiedly is in itself, because there is nothing in relation to which it has truer being. Thus what is said to be something in relation to the primary cause can unqualifiedly be said to be such. Therefore, if something future is actual in relation to God, it is unqualifiedly actual. Therefore it is impossible for it to be later posited in actuality.

Besides, if my future sitting is now present to eternity (not just in respect of the entity it has in knowable being but also that which it has in the being of existence), then it is now produced in that being by God, for only that has being from God in the flow of time which is produced by God with that being. But God will produce this sitting [of mine] (or the Antichrist's soul – it is all the same); therefore, that which is already produced by Him will again be

12 See glossary entry for 'real relation.'
13 See glossary entry for 'basis of a relation.'

produced in existence, and thus twice it will be produced in existence.

Besides, this position does not seem to help with the problem it was supposed to solve, viz. having certain knowledge of the future. First, because this sitting, besides the fact that it is present to eternity as being in some part of time, is itself future in itself in virtue of the fact that it is future and is going to be produced by God. I ask: Does He have certain knowledge of it? If yes, then this is not because it is already existent, but rather in virtue of the fact that it is future. And we must say that this certitude is through something else, something that suffices for every certain apprehension of the existence of this thing. If he did not know it with certitude as future, then he produces it without previously apprehending it. But he will apprehend it with certitude when he has produced it. Therefore, he knows things done, in a different way than he knows things going to be done, which is counter to what Augustine says in *Super Genesim*, 7.

Secondly, because the divine intellect obtains no certitude from any object other than its own essence, for otherwise it would be cheapened. Hence even now the divine intellect does not have certitude about my action which has actually occurred in such a way that that action of itself causes certitude in the divine intellect, for it does not move His intellect. Therefore, in the same way all temporal things, given they are in their existence present to eternity in virtue of those existences they have, do not cause in the divine intellect certitude of themselves. Rather certain knowledge of the existence of these must be obtained through something else, and this something else suffices for us.

Besides, these people propose that the eternal life of an angel is completely simple and co-exists with the whole of time; therefore an angel, which is in eternal life, is present to the whole flow of time and to all the parts of time. Therefore, it seems, according to this account of theirs, that an angel can naturally know future contingents.[14]

[4.3] A third position says that although some things are necessary in relation to divine knowledge, it, nevertheless, does not follow that they are not able to be contingent in relation to their proximate causes.

[4.3.1] This derives some support from Boethius in the last chapter of book in of his *Consolation*,[15] where he says the following: "If you were to say that what God sees is going to occur cannot not occur, and that what cannot not occur happens from necessity, and so bind me to this word 'necessity' I shall say in answer that the same future event, when it is related to divine knowledge, is necessary, but when it is considered in its own nature it seems to be utterly and absolutely free" etc.

[4.3.2] In favor of this it is also argued that it is possible for imperfection to exist in an effect on account of its proximate cause but not on account of its remote or prior cause, – for example there is deformity in an act on account of the created will but not in as much as it is due to the divine will. Consequently, sin is not traced back to God as its cause, but rather is only imputed to the created will. Therefore, even though necessity would belong to things to the extent that it is from God's side – who is the remote cause –, it is nevertheless possible for contingency to be in them on account of their proximate causes.

Against this: We argued in dist. ii,[16] and showed there through the contingency of things that God thinks and wills, because there can be no contingency in some cause's causation of its effect unless the first cause relates contingently to the cause next to it or to its effect.

In brief, this is shown from the fact that where we have a cause which in so far as it is in motion produces motion, if it is necessarily in motion it will necessarily produce motion. Consequently, where we have a secondary cause which produces something in so far as it is moved by a primary cause, if it is necessarily moved by the primary cause it will necessarily move the cause next to it or produce its effect. Therefore the whole hierarchy of causes, right down to the final effect, will produce the effect necessarily if the relationship of the primary cause to the cause next to it is necessary.

Further, a prior cause naturally relates to its effect

---

14 But this was supposed to belong solely to God, according to orthodox theology.
15 See selection **IV.2.1.**
16 See selection **I.9.1.**

before a posterior cause; consequently in the case of the prior cause if it has a necessary relationship to the effect, it will give it necessary being. But in the second instant of nature[17] the proximate cause cannot give it contingent being, since it is already supposed to have from the primary cause a being that rejects contingency. Neither can you say that in the same instant of nature these two causes give caused being, because on that being cannot be based the necessary relationship to the cause that perfectly gives being as well as a contingent relationship to some other cause.

Further, whatever is produced by posterior causes could be immediately produced by the primary cause; and in that case it would have the same entity it now has, and then would be contingent just as it is now contingent. Therefore, even now it has its contingency from the primary cause and not just from a proximate cause.

Further, God has produced many things immediately – for example he created the world and now creates souls – and yet all these he produced contingently.

[5] In answering these questions we must proceed as follows: First, we must see how there is contingency in things, and, secondly, how the certitude and immutability of God's knowledge of these things is compatible with their contingency.

[5.1] In regard to the first I say that this disjunction, necessary or possible, is an attribute of being,[18] where I mean a convertible attribute in the way many such items are unlimited in respect of beings. But convertible attributes of being – are immediately said of being, because being has an unqualifiedly simple concept and, therefore, there cannot be a middle[19] between it and its attribute, because there is no definition of either that could serve as a middle.

Also if it is a non-primary attribute of being, it is difficult to see what might be prior to it and serve as a middle whereby the attribute could be proved of being, since neither is it easy to see a ranking in the attributes of being. And even if we did appre-

hend such a ranking, the propositions taken from the attributes as premises would not seem to be much more evident than the conclusions.

But in disjunct attributes once we suppose that the less noble one belongs to some being, we can conclude that the more noble one belongs to some being, even though the whole disjunction cannot be proved of being. For example, this follows: 'If some being is finite, then some being is infinite' and 'if some being is contingent, then some being is necessary,' because in these cases the more imperfect one cannot belong to some particular being unless the more perfect one, on which the less perfect depends, belongs to some being.

But it does not seem possible in this way for the more imperfect member of such a disjunction to be shown. For it is not the case that, if the more perfect is in some being, necessarily the more imperfect is in some being (unless the disjunct members are correlative, like cause and caused). Consequently the disjunction 'necessary or contingent' cannot be proved of being by some prior middle. Also the part of the disjunction which is 'contingent' cannot be shown of anything from the assumption that 'necessary' belongs to something. Thus it seems that 'Some being is contingent' is primarily true and not demonstrable *propter quid*.

Thus The Philosopher, when he argues against the necessity of future events,[20] reasons not to something that is more impossible than the hypothesis, but to something more obviously impossible to us, namely that there is no need either to deliberate or take trouble.

Therefore, those who deny such obvious facts need either punishment or sense perception, because, according to Avicenna in *Metaphysics* I, those who deny a first principle should be either flogged or burned until they allow that being burned is not the same as not being burned, being flogged not the same as not being flogged. So also those who deny that some being is contingent ought to be tortured until they allow that it is possible for them not to be tortured.

17 See glossary entry for 'instant of nature.'
18 See glossary entry for 'attribute.'
19 See glossary entry for 'middle.'
20 In selection **IV.1.1.**

[5.3] Assuming then that it is obviously true that some being is contingent, we must inquire how contingency can be preserved in beings. I say (on account of the first argument that was made against the third opinion [4.3], which is further explicated in dist. 2 in the question "Concerning God's being") that we can maintain the contingency of some cause only if we propose that the first cause immediately causes in a contingent way, and if we do this by positing in the first cause a perfect causality, just as the catholics propose.

The primary being causes through its intellect and will; and if a third executive power other than those is proposed, this will not help answer the question, because if it ideates and wills necessarily, it produces necessarily. Therefore, we must seek this contingency in the divine intellect or in the divine will.

But not in the intellect as it has its first act before every act of the will, because whatever the intellect ideates in this way it ideates merely naturally and by a natural necessity, and thus there can be no contingency in its knowing something which it knows or in ideating something which it ideates by such a primary ideation.

[5.4] Consequently we must seek contingency in the divine will. In order to see how it is to be posited there we must first see how it is in our will, and there three questions arise: (1) In respect of what does our will have freedom? (2) How does possibility or contingency follow from this freedom? (3) Concerning the logical distinction of propositions, how is possibility in respect of opposites expressed?

[5.4.1] As to the first question I say that the will, in so far as it is a first actuality, is free in respect of opposite acts. Also it is free, when those opposite acts mediate, in respect of opposite objects toward which it tends, and further in respect of opposite effects which it produces.

The first freedom necessarily has some imperfection attached to it, because of the passive potentiality and mutability of the will. The third freedom is not the second, because even if *per impossibile* it brought about nothing outside, still, in so far as it is will, it can freely tend toward objects. But the middle character of freedom has no imperfec-

tion, but rather is necessary for perfection, because every perfect power can tend toward everything which is apt to be an object of such a power. Therefore, a perfect will can tend toward everything which is apt to be willable. Therefore, the freedom that has no imperfection, in so far as it is freedom, is in respect of opposite objects toward which it tends, to which, as such, it happens that it produces opposite effects.

[5.4.2] As regards the second [question] I say that along with that freedom goes an obvious potential for opposites. For although this is not a potential for at the same time willing and not willing (since that is nothing), still it is a potential for willing after not willing, or for a series of opposite acts.

In all mutable things it is obvious that there is this potential for a series of opposites in them. Nevertheless there is another not so obvious potential that involves no temporal series. For if we suppose that a created will exists for just one instant, and in that instant has this willing, it does not then necessarily have it.

Proof: If in that instant it had it necessarily, since it is a cause only in that instant when it causes it, it is unqualifiedly the case that the will, when it causes, necessarily causes. For in this case it is not a contingent cause because it pre-existed before that instant in which it causes (and then as pre-existing it was able to cause or not to cause). Just as this being, when it is, is necessary or contingent, so a cause, when it causes, causes necessarily or contingently. Therefore, from the fact that in that instant it non-necessarily causes this willing it follows that it causes it contingently. There is, then, without any temporal series this potential of the cause for the opposite of that which it causes. There is then this potential which is real and, as a first actuality,[21] naturally prior[22] to the opposites which as second actualities are naturally posterior. For a first actuality, considered in that instant in which it is naturally prior to its second actuality, so posits that second actuality in existence, as its contingent effect, that, as naturally prior, it can equally posit some other opposite in existence.

Along with this real active potential, which is naturally prior to that which it produces, goes a logi-

---

21 See glossary entry for 'first/second actuality.'
22 See glossary entry for 'order of nature.'

cal potential amounting to a non-repellency of terms. For to the will as a first actuality, even when it is producing this willing, the opposite willing is not repellent. This is both because it is a contingent cause in respect of its effect and consequently the opposite sort of effect is not repellent to it, and because in as much as it is a subject, it relates contingently to the act in as much as that act informs it, since to a subject the opposite of its *per accidens* accident[23] is not repellent.

Therefore, along with the freedom of our will, in so far as it tends toward opposite acts, goes a potential both for opposites in a temporal series and for opposites at the same instant. I.e., either one can be in existence without the other, and the second potential is a real cause of the act in such a way that it is naturally prior to the logical potential. But the fourth potential, viz. for simultaneous opposites does not go along with that [real potential]; for that [fourth one] is nothing.

[5.4.3] From the answer to that second question [5.4.2] the third is clear, i.e. the disambiguation to be made in respect of the proposition, 'A will that is willing A is able not to will A.' In composite sense[24] it is false, since then it signifies the possibility of this complex: 'A will that is willing A does not will A.' In the divided sense it is true since then it signifies the possibility for opposites in temporal series, since a will that is willing at time A is able not to will at time B.

But if we interpret the proposition as uniting *de possibili* the terms at the same instant, for example as this proposition: 'A will that is not willing something at A is able to will it at A,' again it should be disambiguated in respect of composition and division: in the composite sense it is false, i.e. it is false that there is a possibility that it is at the same time willing at A and not willing at A; the divided sense is true, i.e. it is true that to the will to which willing at A belongs not willing at A is able to belong – but the not willing does not exist at the same time [as the willing], rather the not willing [belongs to the will] because then the willing does not belong to it.

In order to understand this second distinction, which is the more obscure, I say that the composite sense there is a single categorical proposition[25] whose subject is 'A will that is not willing at A' and whose predicate is 'willing at A,' and then this predicate is attributed possibly to this subject to which it is repellent. Consequently, to it belongs impossibly what is denoted to belong to it possibly. In the divided sense there are two categorical propositions ascribing to the will two predicates; in one of these propositions, which is *de inesse*, the predicate 'not willing A' is ascribed to the will (this categorical proposition is understood as being there through an implicit composition); in the other categorical proposition, which is *de possibili*, willing A is possibly ascribed [to the will]. These two propositions are found to be true because they signify their predicates to be attributed to the subject at the same instant, and clearly it is true that not willing A belongs to that will at the same instant as possibility for the opposite of A, just as though *inesse* were signified along with the proposition *de possibili*.

Here is an example of this sort of disambiguation: 'Every man who is white is running.' Given that every white man (and not black or in-between) is running, it is true in the composite sense, false in the divided sense. In the composite sense there is a single proposition with a single subject determined by 'white'; in the divided sense there are two propositions attributing two predicates to the same subject. Similarly this proposition, 'A man who is white is necessarily an animal,' in the composite sense is false, because the predicate does not necessarily belong to that whole subject, while in the divided sense it is true because two predicates are asserted to be said of the same subject, one necessarily and the other absolutely and without necessity, and both do belong and both of those categorical propositions are true.

But against this second disambiguation it is argued in three ways that it is not logical and that there is at some instant no potential for the opposite of what is the case at that instant. First, through the proposition asserted in *Perihermenias* II: 'Everything which is, when it is, necessarily is.'

---

23 See glossary entry for 'accident.'
24 See glossary entry for 'composite and divided senses.'
25 See glossary entry for 'categorical proposition.'

Secondly by the following rule governing the "obligatory" art:[26] 'If something false and contingent is supposed about the present moment, it must be denied to be the case.' He proves this rule as follows: "What is supposed must be sustained as true; therefore it must be sustained for some instant at which it is possible. But it is not a possible truth for the instant at which it is supposed because if it were possible for that instant, then it could be true through motion or through change. But in neither way could it be true, because motion does not occur in an instant and change to the opposite of what is the case does not occur in an instant, because then change and its terminal state would exist at the same time."

Further, and thirdly: If at some instant there is a potential for something whose opposite is in fact the case, either that potential exists with its act or before its act. Obviously, not with the act. But not before the act either, because then that potential would be for an act at an instant other than the one at which that potential is a fact.

[Responses to these objections]
To the first [5.1] I answer that that proposition of Aristotle's can be either categorical or hypothetical just as also this one: 'For an animal to run if a man runs is necessary.' Taken as a conditional this obviously has to be disambiguated according as 'necessary' can mean the necessity of the consequence or the necessity of the consequent. [27] In the first sense it is true; in the second, false. In its sense as a categorical proposition this whole 'to run if a man runs' is predicated of animal with the mode of necessity, and this categorical proposition is true, because the predicate so determined necessarily belongs to the subject, although not the predicate absolutely. Consequently, to argue from the predicate taken absolutely is to commit the fallacy of "qualifiedly and unqualifiedly."[28]

So I say here that if this proposition is interpreted as a temporal hypothetical,[29] necessarily either it

denotes the necessity of concomitance or the necessity of the concomitant.[30] In the former case it is true; in the latter, false. But if it is interpreted as categorical, then 'when it is' does not determine the composition implicit in 'which is' but rather the principal composition signified by the final 'is.' And then it declares that this predicate 'is when it is' is said of the subject 'which is' with the mode of necessity, and so the proposition is true, but it does not follow that therefore it necessarily is. Such an inference would commit the fallacy of "qualifiedly and unqualifiedly" in some other part. Therefore, no true sense of this proposition declares that for something to be, in the instant in which it is, is necessary, but only that it is necessary with the qualification 'when it is.' This is compatible with its being unqualifiedly contingent in that instant in which it is, and consequently with its opposite being able to be the case in that instant.

To the second [5.2]: The rule is false and the proof invalid, because, although what is supposed should be sustained as true, still it can be sustained for that instant while not denying that instant to be one for which it is false, because (contrary to what the proof intimates) this inference does not hold: 'This is false for this instant; therefore it is impossible.' And when the opponent says, "If it can be true at the moment at which it is false, either it can be found true at that instant [or could be true through motion or change]," I say that neither alternative is the case, because that possibility for its truth is not a possibility for a temporal series (where one occurs after the other), but is a potential for the opposite of what in fact belongs to something, in so far as it is naturally prior to that act.

To the third [5.3] I say that the potential is before the act, not temporally "before" but "before" by the ordering of nature, since what naturally precedes that act, as it naturally precedes the act, could exist with the opposite of that act. Then we

---

26 See glossary entry for "obligation.'
27 See glossary entry for 'necessity of consequence/consequent.'
28 See glossary entry for "qualified and unqualified.'
29 See glossary entry for 'hypothetical proposition.'
30 In a temporal hypothetical of the form 'When p, q,' q is the "concomitant" and the whole hypothetical expresses a "concomitance." When the mode of necessity is added, a composite/divided sense ambiguity arises, just as with conditions where it leads to the distinction of "necessity of the consequence" and "necessity of the consequent."

must deny that every potential is "with its act or before its act" where 'before' indicates temporal priority. It is true where 'before' indicates priority of nature.

There is a fourth objection to this. This inference holds: If it is possible to will A at this instant, and not will A at this instant, then it is possible not to will A at this instant. [The reason is that] from a proposition *de inesse* follows that proposition *de possibili*. And then it seems to follow that it is possible to will A and not to will A at the same time for the same instant.

To this I answer, following the Philosopher in *Metaphysics* IX, that what has a potential for opposites so acts as it has the potential for acting, but it is not the case that a mode is applied to the potential"s term, rather than to the potential itself, as it has the potential for acting. This is because I have at the same time a potential for opposites but I do not have a potential for opposites at the same time.

Then I say that this inference does not hold: It is possible to will this at A and it is possible to nill[31] this at A; therefore, it is possible to will and to nill [this] at A. [The reason is that] it is possible for there to be a potential for each of two opposites disjunctively at some instant, even if not for them both at once. This is because as there is a possibility for one of them so there is for the not-being of the other, and, conversely, just as there is a possibility for the other so there is for the not-being of the first. Therefore, there is not a possibility at the same time for this and that opposite, because a possibility for simultaneity exists only where there is a possibility for both to occur at the same instant, which is not implied by the fact that for that instant there is a potential for both divisively. An example of this shows up in persisting things: This does not follow: This body can be in this place at instant A, and that body can be in the same place at instant A; therefore, those two bodies can be in the same place at instant A. For the first body can be there in such a way that the second body cannot be there, and vice-versa. Thus this does not follow: If there is a potential for each at the same instant or place, then there is a potential for both. This fails every time

each of the two excludes the other. Thus also this does not follow: I can carry this stone for the whole day (i.e., it is something that is carryable by my strength), and I can carry that stone for the whole day; therefore I can carry both stones at once. [The reason is that] here each of the items for which there is divisively a potential excludes the other. Moreover, simultaneity can never be inferred from just the sameness of that one instant or place; rather it is required to have besides this the conjunction of the two which are said to be at the same time, in respect of a third item.

[5.5] Following what has been said about our will we must look into some matters concerning the divine will. First, in respect of what does it have freedom? Secondly, what is contingency in the willed items? (As for the logical disambiguation, it is the same in this case as in the former.)

[5.5.1] As for the first, I say that the divine will is not indifferent to different acts of willing and nilling, because this did not exist in our will apart from imperfection of the will. Also our will was free for opposite acts, in order to be free for opposite objects, because of the limitation of each act in respect of its object. Consequently, given the absence of limitation on one and the same willing of diverse objects, it is not necessary in order to have freedom in respect of opposite objects to posit freedom in respect of opposite acts. Also the divine will itself is free in respect of opposite effects, but this is not its primary freedom, just as also it is not in us. Therefore, there remains that freedom which is of itself a perfection and possesses no imperfection, namely a freedom in respect of opposite objects, so that just as our will can by different willings tend toward different willed items, so the divine will can by a single, simple, unlimited willing tend toward any willed items whatsoever. This is so in such a way that if the will or that willing were of just one willable item, and not able to be of the opposite even though it is of itself willable, this would constitute an imperfection in the will, just as was argued earlier as regards our will.

And even though in us the will can be distinguished as it is receptive and operative and productive (for it is productive of acts, and it is that by

---

which what has it operates formally by willing, and it is receptive of its own willing), freedom seems to belong to it in so far as it is operative, i.e. in so far as what has it formally can through it tend toward an object. Therefore, in this way freedom is posited in the divine will *per se et primo*[32] in so far as it is an operative power, even though it is neither receptive nor productive of its willing. Nevertheless, some freedom can be saved in it in so far as it is productive, for although production into existence does not necessarily accompany its operation (since the operation is in eternity while production of existence is in time), still its operation is necessarily accompanied by production into willed being. In that case this power of the divine will does not produce primarily as it is productive but rather qualifiedly, i.e. into willed being, and this production goes along with it as it is operative.

[5.5.2] As to the second article I say that the divine will takes for its object necessarily only its own essence. Thus to anything else it relates contingently in such a way that it can be of the opposite, and this when we consider it as it is naturally prior to the tendency toward that opposite. Not only is it naturally prior to its own act (as a willing) but also [it is prior] in so far as it is willing, because just as our will, as naturally prior to its own act, elicits that act in such a way that it can in the same instant elicit the opposite, so the divine will, in so far as it is naturally prior to its one sole willing, tends toward the object contingently by such a tendency that in the same instant it can tend toward the opposite object.

And this is the case both by a logical potential, which amounts to a non-repellency of terms (as we said of our will), and by a real potential, which is naturally prior to its act.

[5.6] Now that we have looked into the contingency of things so far as their existence is concerned, and this by considering it in respect of the divine will, it remains to look into the second principal question, how the certitude of knowledge is compatible with this. This can be explained in two ways: In one way by the fact that the divine intellect, in seeing the determination of the divine will, sees that this will

be the case at time A, because that will determines that it is going to be at that time; for the intellect knows that the will is immutable and unthwartable. Or in another way: Since the above way seems to posit a process of inference in the divine intellect (as though it infers that this is going to be from the intuition of the will's determination and immutability), it can be explained in a different way that the divine intellect presents simples[33] of which the union in reality is contingent, or, if it presents a complex, it presents it as neutral to it. The will, in choosing one part, namely the conjunction of these for some "now" in reality, makes to be determinately true this complex, 'This will be at time A.' Given this exists as determinately true, the essence is the reason by which the divine intellect apprehends that truth, and this occurs naturally, in as much as it is on the side of the essence, in such a way that just as it naturally apprehends all necessary principles as though before the act of the divine will (because their truth does not depend on the act and they would be known by the divine intellect if *per impossibile* there was no willing), so the divine essence is the reason for knowing them in that prior moment, because then they are true. Certainly those truths, nor even their terms, do not move the divine intellect to apprehending such a truth, because otherwise the divine intellect would be cheapened, since it would receive its evidence from something other than its own essence. Rather the divine essence is the reason for knowing simples and complexes alike. But at that point there are no contingent truths because at that point there is nothing by which they might have determinate truth. But once the determination of the divine will is given, then they are true in that second instant and the reason for the intellect's apprehending those which are now true in the second instant, and would have been known in the first if they had been true in the first instant, is the same as it was in the first. An example: Just as if in my power of vision a single act that always exists were the reason for seeing an object, and if, by something else being present, now this color is present, and now that, my eye would see now this, now that and yet by that same act of sight there will only be a difference in

---

32 See glossary entry for 'essential-in-the-first-mode.'
33 As opposed to "complex," i.e., propositions. See glossary entry for 'complex.'

the priority and posteriority of seeing on account of the object being presented earlier or later; so also, if one color were naturally made to be present and another freely, there would not be formally in my vision some difference so that on its side the eye would not naturally see both, and yet it would be able to see one contingently and the other necessarily, in as much as one is present to it contingently and the other necessarily.

By both of these ways the divine intellect is asserted to know the existence of things, and it is clear on both that there is a determination of the divine intellect to the existent to which the divine will is determined, and there is the certitude of infallibility because the divine will can be determined only if the intellect determinately apprehends what the will determines, and there is immutability, because both the will and the intellect are immutable.

This responds to the first three questions [1.1, 1.2, and 1.3]. Nevertheless, the contingency of the object known is compatible with all these, because the will that determinately wills this wills it contingently (see the first article [5.4]).

As for the fourth question [1.4], it seems perhaps that we should disambiguate this proposition, 'God necessarily knows A,' in respect of composition and division. In the sense of a composition the proposition indicates the necessity of the knowledge as it holds of that object [A]; in the sense of a division it indicates the necessity of the knowledge taken absolutely [i.e. without any relation to anything], a knowledge which, nevertheless, does hold of that object. In the first sense the proposition is true; in the second, false.

Nevertheless, such a disambiguation does not seem logical. For when an act holds of an object, there does not seem to be a need to distinguish between the act taken absolutely and the act as it holds of the object. For example, if I were to say that 'I see Socrates' it is to be disambiguated into a sense which is about the seeing as it holds of Socrates and a sense which is about the seeing taken absolutely. And just as there is no distinction needed in this case of an assertoric [i.e. non-modal] proposition, so neither does there seem to be a need for a distinction in the case of the modal proposition. Rather it just seems to be necessary if the act holds of the object necessarily. Consequently, it seems we should unqualifiedly deny 'God necessar-

ily knows A,' on the grounds that the predicate determined in that way does not necessarily belong to that subject, although without a determination does belong [necessarily].

It is objected against this that a rational act is not diminished by the material it holds of. For there is just as much an unqualified saying when it holds of my saying nothing as when it holds of my saying something. Consequently 'I am saying' follows just as much from 'I am saying that I am saying nothing' as it does from 'I am saying that I am sitting.' Therefore in the case of God knowing is not diminished by the material it holds of so that there is not an equal necessity.

Reply to this: Even though it is not so diminished that it has only a qualified existence, still it may not have its necessity as it is signified to hold of the matter (even though in itself it has necessity). This is the case if the act is in itself especially powerful in respect of diverse objects. For example, if I had an act of speaking that was the same as its motive power and that act was able to relate contingently to different objects, then, even if I necessarily had the act just as I necessarily had the power, still I would not necessarily have the act as it relates to such an object; rather there can be necessity of the saying by itself with contingency in respect of its object, and yet the saying of that object would exist unqualifiedly and would not be a qualified saying.

[6] To the principal arguments in order:

[6.1.1] To the first in respect of the first question [2.1.1], I say that truth in future matters is not similar to truth in present or past matters. In present and past matters truth is determinate in such a way that one of the terms is posited. In this sense of "posited" it is not in the power of the cause that it be posited or not posited, because, although it is in the power of a cause as it is naturally prior to its effect to posit or not to posit the effect, it is not as the effect is now understood to be posited in being. But for the future determination is not of this sort, because, although for some intellect one part is determinately true, and one part is even true in itself, determinately, even though no intellect apprehends it, still it is determinate in such a way that it is in the power of the cause to posit the opposite for that instant. This indeterminacy suffices for deliberation and taking trouble. If neither part were future it would not be necessary either to take trouble or to deliberate. Therefore, that one part is future while the other can come about does not prevent deliberation and taking trouble.

[6.1.2] To the second [2.1.2], I say that for knowledge to be of one part in such a way that it *cannot* be of the other does posit imperfection in that knowledge. Likewise in the will positing it to be of one in such a way that it *cannot* be of the other willable object [attributes imperfection to it]. But for knowledge to be of one in such a way that it is of the other (and likewise for the will) *posits* no imperfection, just as a power is in determinate actuality for one opposite, the one it produces, and not for the other. But there is this dissimilarity between a power, on the one hand, and knowledge and will on the other: A power seems to be said to be for just one opposite since it *can* only be directed toward that, while knowledge and will [are of one opposite] in such a way that they merely know or will that. But if we treat these in a similar way, the determination is equal in both cases, because any of them is actually of one opposite and not both. Also any of them can be directed to either, but for the power to be for something seems to signify a *potential* relationship of it to that something, while for knowledge or will to be of something seems to signify an *actual* relationship to that same item. Nevertheless, nothing wrong follows if we treat the cases similarly, because then just as knowing relates to knowledge and willing to will, so producing (but not being able to produce) relates to power, and just as being able to produce relates to power so being able to know to knowledge and being able to will to will.

[6.2.1] To the first argument regarding the second question [2.2.1], I say that, although from two premisses *de inesse* follows a conclusion *de inesse* (not syllogistically, though, since what we have here is a non-syllogistic string of expressions that can be analysed into several syllogisms),[34] still from one premiss *de inesse* and one *de possibili* a conclusion *de possibili* does not follow either syllogistically or necessarily. The reason is that to be deceived is to think that a thing is in a way different from what it is at that time for which it is believed to be. All this is included in the two premisses *de inesse*, one of which signifies that he believes this and the other of

which denies that this [i.e. what is believed] is the case, and for the same instant; consequently the conclusion about being deceived follows. But in the other case it is different, since the premiss *de inesse* affirms one opposite for that instant, while the premiss *de possibili* affirms a potential for the other opposite, and not for the same instant conjunctively but rather disjunctively. Therefore, it does not follow that at some instant there can be conjoined in reality the opposite of what is believed [and the belief]; and, therefore, the possibility of deception, which includes that conjunction, does not follow. For a like reason the conclusion in a syllogism that mixes the *de contingenti* with the *de inesse* follows only where the major premiss is unqualifiedly *de inesse*.

This response is evidenced by the fact that if we argue from the opposite of the conclusion and the premiss *de possibili*, we do not infer the opposite [of the premiss *de inesse*] but of this premiss taken *de necessario*. Thus in order to infer the conclusion the major premiss must be really the same as that proposition *de necessario*. For this does not follow: God cannot be deceived, and A can not be going to be; therefore God does not know that A is going to be. Rather this follows: Therefore, he does not necessarily know that A is going to be.

This is evident because, if my intellect always kept up with change in things so that while you are sitting I think that you are sitting and when you stand up I think that you are standing up, I cannot be deceived, and yet from these propositions: "You could be standing at time A, and I cannot be deceived" there follows only this: "Therefore, I do not necessarily know that you are sitting at time A."

So in the matter under discussion: Although the divine intellect does not follow reality as an effect follows its cause, there is still a concomitance there, since as the thing is able not to be so the divine intellect is able not to know, and thus it never follows that the divine intellect apprehends a thing otherwise than it is. Consequently, the things required for deception can never exist at the same time; rather just as the known thing is able not to be, so God is able not to know it, and if it will not be, he will not know it.

---

34 See glossary entry for 'syllogism.'

[6.2.2] To the second [2.2.2] regarding the positing of the possible in being, I say that from such a positing by itself there never follows something impossible. Nevertheless the proposition *de inesse*, to the extent that some proposition *de possibili* is posited, can be repellent to something to which the *de possibili* proposition when posited in being is not repellent, since an antecedent can be repellent to something to which the consequent is not repellent. Then from the antecedent and what it is repellent to it there can follow something impossible, which does not follow from the consequent plus that same proposition, which is not incompatible with it. It is no wonder if an impossible proposition follows from incompatible ones, because, according to the Philosopher in *Prior Analytics* II, in a syllogism composed of opposites an impossible conclusion follows.

I say then that given this proposition 'It is possible for me not to sit' is posited in being, from it alone nothing impossible follows. But from it and this other proposition, viz. 'God knows that I will sit' there follows something impossible, viz. that God is deceived. This impossibility does not follow from the impossibility of what is posited in being, nor even from some incompatibility which is in it absolutely, but rather from it and something else at the same time, which is impossible.

Neither is it absurd that what is impossible follows from something *de inesse* in as much as something *de possibili* is posited as something *de inesse*, because, although 'It is possible for me to stand' is compatible with 'I am sitting,' still the former taken *de inesse*, in as much as it is posited, is repellent to the latter *de inesse*, and from those two taken *de inesse* something incompatible follows, viz. 'What is standing is sitting.' Nor does this follow: 'Therefore, the *de possibili* proposition that was posited in being was false.' Rather either it was false, or some other, along with which its *de inesse* form was taken, is incompatible with its *de inesse* form.

[6.3.1] To the first argument regarding the third question [2.3.1], I concede the major premiss, that there is no transition without change. But in the minor I say that there is no transition, nor can there be any, because transition implies a temporal series so that one opposite comes after the other. No such can exist in this case; for just as he cannot both know and not know at the same time, so also that

he sometimes knows and sometimes does not know are not able to co-exist at the same time. But without this transition from opposite to opposite there is no change.

And if you ask: "At least if he is able not to know B, which he knows, something would be different – what is that?," I say that it is B in *esse cognito*. But it would not exist differently than it did earlier, but rather differently than it exists now, so that 'differently' would not indicate a temporal succession of one opposite after the other opposite but rather that the one opposite can be present in the same instant in which the other is present. This is not sufficient for mutation.

[6.3.2] To the second [2.3.2]: This consequence is not valid: 'What does not know A can know A; therefore, it can begin to know A.' This is the case when there is a potential in something naturally prior for the opposite of the posterior at that same instant at which and in which the posterior contingently exists, just as is the case in what we are discussing. In creatures, where there is potentiality for opposites in temporal succession, the consequence holds only on account of matter. [In the divine case] although this would not be, still there would be the possibility for each of them at one instant.

[6.3.3] To the third [2.3.3], it can be conceded, so far as this argument is concerned, that this power for opposites is an active power, for example, that the divine intellect, in so far as it is actual by its essence and infinite by its actual ideation, is an active power in respect of any objects whatsoever which it produces in *esse intellecto*.

And when the argument says, "Therefore it can act with respect to something in respect of which it was not acting before only if it is changed," I say that the consequence is not valid when the thing acting requires an object in respect of which it acts. For example, in created agents it is not required that an agent which acts for the first time be changed, if for the first time the receptor on which it acts comes near to it. Thus it is in what we are discussing. The divine will, when it determines that some object shown to it by the intellect is going to be, makes such a complex be true and thus intelligible by the fact that it is present to the intellect as an object. And just as the will can make this willed item and not make it, so that item can be true and not true and thus is able to be known and not known by that natural intellect. This is not because of some contingency which is prior in that natural agent, but rather because of the contingency on the side of the object, which is contingently true by the act of the will that makes it true.

If you object that still this cannot be without change at least in the ideated object (just as the coming close of a natural receptor to a natural agent can only occur by change in the receptor, and perhaps in the agent itself as it comes close), – I answer that that object is not changed in that being because it cannot be under opposites in temporal succession. Nevertheless it is contingently in that being and this contingency is on the side of the will that produces it in such being. And this contingency of the will can exist without change in the will, as was explained in the first article of the solution [5.4].

[6.4] To the arguments concerning the fourth question: [2.4]

[6.4.1] In response to the first [2.4.1] I deny the consequence. To the first proof I say that even if there is in God no necessity other than the necessity of immutability (i.e. it is none other than the fourth of those modes of necessity assigned by the Philosopher, according to which it means that "it does not happen to exist differently," since the other modes of necessity involve imperfection, for example the necessity of compulsion, etc.) still there we do not have just the necessity of immutability in the sense that immutability is of itself necessity, because immutability eliminates only a possible temporal succession of opposite on opposite, but unqualified necessity eliminates absolutely the possibility of the opposite and not just the temporal succeeding of that opposite. And this does not follow: 'An opposite cannot succeed its opposite; therefore, the opposite cannot occur.'

To the second proof I say that although everything with being of existence which it is possible to be going to be is mutable, where we treat creation, as does Avicenna, to be a mutation, even from the eternal, nevertheless in *esse intellecto* or *volito*[35] (which is qualified[36] being) it is not necessary that every possibility which is repellent to necessity of

itself formally implies mutability. This is because this being is not real being, but is reduced to the real being of something necessary of itself. On account of the necessity of this other item there can be no mutability here, and yet the of-itself necessity attaching to this other does not belong to it formally, and so it is not of itself formally[37] necessary, because it does not have the being of that term to which it really relates. Nevertheless, it is not mutable either, because in virtue of this diminished being it relates to an immutable term, and mutation in something that occurs in virtue of its relation to something else cannot occur without mutation in that something else.

[6.4.2] To the second argument [2.4], I say that something can be in God in two ways, either formally, or subjectively in the way logically any predicate is said to be in its subject. In the first way, I concede the major that everything of that sort is God and necessarily the same as God. In the second way I do not concede the major, since, for example, a relative appellation can be in God in as much as God is said to be "Lord" in virtue of time, and yet that appellation does not signify something the same as God (so that necessarily it is the same as God or is God Himself), because then it would not be in virtue of time.

Now, I say that for God to know B is, in as much as it is knowing absolutely, for him to know formally, but in as much as it is of this term B it is in God only in the second way. For the knowing is of this term since that known item has a relation to divine knowledge, and because of this some relative appellation is in God as a predicate in a subject.

[6.4.3] To the third, I say that no unqualified perfection[38] in God depends on a creature, nor does it even with unqualified necessity require a creature in any sort of being. Consequently, for God to know B, where we understand the knowing not just absolutely but also as it relates to B, is not an unqualified perfection. Then I say that the major premiss of this argument is true for the perfection of that knowledge taken absolutely, but then the minor is false and the proof of it proves only that

---

35 See glossary entry for '*esse objectivum*.'
36 See glossary entry for 'qualified/unqualified.'
37 I.e., is not a feature directly belonging to it.
38 See glossary entry for 'absolute perfection.'

unqualified perfection necessarily implies that there is [knowing] of such an object, since it necessarily follows that it has such a relation to such an unqualified perfection. Nevertheless, unqualified perfection is not in him either in virtue of such a relation something else bears to him nor from the relative appellation that belongs to him.

[6.5] To the arguments concerning the fifth question:

[6.5.1] To the first, I say that the antecedent is not unqualifiedly necessary. And when it is argued that "a rational act is not lessened by its subject matter," my reply is the one given in response to the argument put up against the solution of this question.[39]

[6.5.2] To the second: That mixed syllogism is valid only if the minor is unqualifiedly de inesse, and this means that it is not just true for all time but that it is necessarily true. Perhaps we have to think of 'per se' as being implicit in the middle term (it is sufficient for what is proposed that it be required to be necessarily true). That this is required is clear in this case: 'Everything at rest necessarily is not in motion. A stone at the center of the earth is at rest. Therefore, necessarily the stone is not in motion.' The conclusion does not follow even though the minor is always true – and yet not necessarily true. So it is in what we are considering. For although the minor de inesse is always true, it is not necessarily true; for God is able not to know A just as he is able not to will A, because of contingency, which primarily is in the will and then in the object secondarily, and in virtue of this it is concomitantly in the intellect, as was explained before.

[7] To the arguments for the second opinion: [4.2]

[7.1] To the first [4.2.1] I allow that the limitless is present to every place, but not to every actual and potential place (as was argued in the first argument against this opinion), and thus neither will eternity on account of its infinity be present to some nonexistent time. From this it is clear what to say about the example of the stick and the river. Since the stick does not have that whereby it could be present to all parts of the water, it is not unlimited in respect of them. But the "now" of eternity does

have, in so far as it is considered on its own, that whereby it would be present to all parts of time if they were. The other example about the center and the circumference similarly argues the opposite. If we imagine a straight line with two terminal points, A and B, and let A be held fixed while B is moved around (just as with a compass one point is held fixed and the other moved), B as it is moved around causes a circumference according to the geometers' imagination, who imagine the flowing point to cause a line. Given this, if nothing were to remain of the circumference by B's flow, but rather in the circumference there is only that point (in such a way that whenever that point ceases to be somewhere nothing of that circumference is then there), then the circumference is never present at the same time to the center, but rather only some point of the circumference is present to the center. Nevertheless, if that whole circumference were there at the same time, the whole would be present to the center. So it is here. Since time is not a static circumference but a flowing whose circumference is only an actual instant, nothing of it will be present to eternity (which is like the center) except that instant which is like the point. Nevertheless, if per impossibile it were proposed that the whole of time was in existence at once, that whole would be at the same time present to eternity as to a center.

[7.2] Through the above it is clear what to say to the other argument [4.2.2]. When it is said that the "now" of eternity as co-existing with the "now" of time is not equal to it, that is true, because the "now" of eternity is formally infinite and thus formally goes beyond the "now" of time. But it does not do this by co-existing with another "now." For example, the limitlessness of God, though present to this universe, is not equal to this universe, and thus formally goes beyond it; nevertheless He is somewhere only in this universe.

[7.3] Through this same point it is clear what to say to the remaining argument [4.2.3]. If the whole of time existed all at once, eternity would encompass it, and so I concede that eternity as it is of itself has an infinity sufficient to encompass the whole of time if that whole existed all at once. But no matter how much limitlessness is posited on the side of one term, on account of which it can co-

39 See end of [5.5].

exist with no matter how much is posited in the other term, since co-existence indicates a relation between two terms (and thus requires both), from the limitlessness of one term we can infer co-existence only with that in the other term which exists.

[7.4] Thus all these arguments rely on something that is insufficient, namely the limitlessness of eternity. From that the co-existence which indicates a relation to something else follows only if we are given something in the other term which can be a term of co-existence with that basis. A non-being cannot be such, yet all of time save the present is a non-being.

All the authoritative texts of the saints, which seem to signify that all things are present to eternity, must be interpreted as about presence in the sense of knowable. And here 'knowable' refers not just to abstractive knowledge[40] (as a non-existent rose is present to my intellect by a species),[41] but to true intuitive knowledge, because God does not know what has occurred in a different way than what is going to occur, and thus what is going to occur is just as perfectly known presently by the divine intellect as what has occurred.

[8] Replies to the arguments for the third opinion [4.3]

[8.1] To the first argument for the third opinion [4.3.1]: Boethius immediately explains himself in that place, for he immediately disambiguates there in respect of the necessity of the consequent and the necessity of the consequence. Using this I concede that contingents that are related to divine knowledge are necessary by a necessity of the consequence (i.e. this consequence is necessary: 'If God knows this is going to be, this will be'), nevertheless they are not necessary by an absolute necessity nor by a contingent necessity.

[8.2] To the other for the third opinion [4.3.2], I say that contingency is not just a la.ck or defect of entity (as is the deformity of a sinful act); rather contingency is a positive mode of being (just as necessity is another mode), and a positive being which is in an effect comes more principally from the prior cause. Thus this does not follow: 'Just as deformity comes to the act itself from a secondary cause and not from the primary cause, so also contingency.' Rather contingency is from the first cause before it is from a second cause. On account of this no caused item would be formally contingent unless it were caused contingently by the first cause, just as we showed above [4.3.2, reply].

40 See glossary entry for "intuitive vs. abstractive cognition."
41 See glossary entry for "species."

IV.7. WILLIAM OF OCKHAM

WRITING WITH SCOTUS'S TEXT BEFORE HIM (I.E. THE PREVIOUS selection) Ockham sets out to show the incoherence of Scotus's position. He argues that Scotus's view of contingency is self-contradictory and that his view that God knows the future by knowing His own will does not save human freedom. Ockham comes near to giving up on the problem but thinks that the orthodox theological view can at least be saved from outright contradiction by carefully distinguishing propositions that are genuinely about the present or past from those that appear to be but are really about the future. For example, the proposition which says that 'The Antichrist will come' was true yesterday, is really in part an assertion about the future to the effect that the Antichrist will come. Such a proposition is, then, not subject to the rule that a true past-tense proposition is now and always will be *necessarily* true. Evidently, Ockham would have us treat the proposition that God knew that the Antichrist will come, in this way, i.e. though true it is not necessarily true, but could be false.

IV.7.1. Why Scotus's Solution will not work
(*Ordinatio* I, dist. 38)

Distinction 38

Regarding the thirty-eighth distinction I ask whether God has determinate and necessary knowledge of all future contingents.

[1] [It seems] that He does not. For that which is not determinately true in itself is determinately true for no one, but a future contingent is not determinately true in itself; therefore [a future contingent is determinately true for no one]. Consequently it is not determinately true for God. Then I argue as follows.

That which is not determinately true is not known by God with determinate knowledge, but a future contingent is of that sort, as has been shown; therefore [a future contingent is not known by God with determinate knowledge]. It seems, moreover, that He does not have necessary knowledge of all future contingents. Or, if He has necessary knowledge of some future contingent, then I argue as follows: God has necessary knowledge; therefore [what is known] is necessary. Further,

therefore, 'A is true' is necessary. But if 'A is true' is necessary, what is known is not contingent. Consequently, A is not a future contingent, which is counter to the hypothesis.

[2] On the contrary, "all things are naked and open to His eyes"; therefore, all things are known by God. But nothing is known except with determinate knowledge. Therefore God has determinate knowledge of all things. Again, it seems that He has necessary knowledge. For there is one single knowledge in God; therefore God's knowledge of necessaries and of contingents is one and the same. But God's knowledge of necessaries is necessary; therefore God's knowledge of future contingents is necessary. Consequently God has necessary knowledge of contingents.

[3] Regarding the question it is said[1] that although it cannot be proved *a priori,* it must nevertheless be maintained that there are future contingents. On this supposition [viz., that there are future contingents], it is said that contingency in things can be preserved only if the first cause, which acts through the [divine] intellect and will, causes contingently – and this while perfect causality is posited in the

---

1 By Scotus in the preceding selection.

first [cause], as Catholics posit it. Thus this contingency must be sought either in the divine intellect or in the divine will. But not in the divine intellect, because whatever the intellect understands it understands merely naturally. Consequently it must be sought in the divine will. He [Scotus] says that in order to understand this one must see, first, in relation to what things our will is free, and second, in what way possibility or contingency follows from that freedom. As to the first point, it is said that the will, insofar as it is first actuality, is free as regards opposite acts; and by means of those opposite acts it is free as regards opposite objects, which it foretells: and further, [it is free] as regards opposite effects, which it produces. The first freedom necessarily has a certain imperfection associated with it – viz., the passive potentiality and mutability of the will. The second freedom however, is without any imperfection, even if the will cannot have the third freedom.

Regarding the second point, it is said that an evident capacity for opposites accompanies that [first] freedom. For although there is no capacity for willing and not willing at one and the same time (for that is nothing at all), nevertheless there is in [the will] a capacity for willing after not willing, or for a succession of opposite acts. In [connection with] these [opposite acts], however, there is another [capacity], not evident in this way, [and] without any succession. For if we suppose that there is a created will that exists at only one instant, and that at that instant it has this or that volition, then it does not necessarily have it at first. For if at that instant it had the volition necessarily (since it is a cause only at that instant when it caused the volition), then, absolutely, the will, when it caused the volition, would cause it necessarily. For it is not now a contingent cause because it pre-existed before the instant at which it causes and pre-existing then could either cause or not cause. For just as this or that being, when it is, is then either necessary or contingent, so a cause, when it causes, causes then either necessarily or contingently. Therefore, whatever this willing causes at that

instant, and causes not necessarily, it causes contingently. Therefore, this capacity to cause the opposite of that which it does cause is without succession. And this real capacity is a naturally prior[2] capacity (as of first actuality)[3] for opposites – [opposites] that are naturally posterior (as of second actuality). For first actuality, considered at that instant at which it is, is naturally prior to second actuality. Thus [first actuality] contingently posits [second actuality] in reality as its effect, so that as naturally prior it could equally posit the opposite in reality.

On the basis of these remarks some things are said about the divine will. First, what its freedom is. And it is said that the divine will is not free as regards the distinct acts of willing and nilling.[4] But because of the limitlessness of volition [the divine will] is free as regards opposite objects, and that is [its] first [freedom]. In addition to that there is a freedom as regards opposite effects, and the divine will is free [in that respect] insofar as it is operative, not insofar as it is productive or receptive of its volition.

Second, in relation to what things the divine will is free. And it is said that it relates necessarily to no object but its own essence. Therefore it relates contingently to anything else, so that it can be [related] to the opposite – and this while it is considered as naturally prior intending the object, not only as the will is naturally prior to its act, but also insofar as it is willing [its act]. For our will, as naturally prior to its act, elicits that act in such a way that it could at one and the same instant elicit its opposite. In the same way the divine will, insofar as volition itself alone is naturally prior to such an intention *(tendentia)*, intends the object contingently in such a way that at the same instant[5] it could intend the opposite object. And this [is] as much by virtue of a logical capacity – i.e., the compatibility *(non-repugnantia)* of the terms (as he said earlier regarding our will) – as by virtue of the real capacity – i.e., [the will's being] naturally prior to its act.

But how is the certainty of the divine knowledge consistent with such contingency? It is said that

---

2 See glossary entry for 'order of nature.'
3 See glossary entry for 'first/second actuality.'
4 I.e., willing that something not be the case.
5 See glossary entry for 'instant of nature.'

this can be posited in two ways. In one way by this means, that the divine intellect seeing the determination of the divine will sees that x will be at t, since the will determines that it will be at t; for [the divine intellect] knows that the will is immutable and unimpedable. He [Scotus] says that it can be posited in another way. For the divine intellect either presents [to itself] simples, the union of which is contingent in reality; or if it presents to itself complexity, it presents it as neutral with respect to itself, and the will choosing one part – viz., a conjunction of these [simples] for something [that is] now in reality – makes "x will be at t" determinately true. Insofar as this exists determinately [in the divine] essence, however, it is for the divine intellect a basis for understanding that truth – and this naturally, insofar as [this understanding] is based upon the [divine] essence. [The divine intellect] understands all necessary principles naturally, as if before the act of the divine will (since their truth does not depend upon that act and they would be understood even if, *per impossibile*, [the divine will] were not willing). Thus, the divine essence is the basis for [the divine intellect's] cognizing these things at that prior [instant], since they are true then. Not, indeed, that those truths move the divine intellect, nor [are] their terms even [required] for the apprehending of such truth. But the divine essence is the basis for cognizing such complexes as well as simples.

But then [at that prior instant those complexes] are not true contingents, since there is nothing in virtue of which they have determinate truth then. Once the determination of the divine will has been posited, however, they are already true, and at that second instant the [divine] essence will be the basis for cognizing them.

The following sort of example is offered. Suppose that one act, always actualized in my visual capacity, is the basis for my seeing an object, and that, as a result of another [act of presenting], now this color is present, now that. [In that case] my eye will see now this, now that, but by means of one and the same [act of] vision. The only difference will be in the priority of seeing, because of an object's having been presented earlier or later; and if one color were present naturally and another freely, there would be no formal difference in my vision. For its part, indeed, the eye would see both naturally and yet would see one contingently and the other nec-

essarily, insofar as the one is present contingently and the other necessarily.

If it is posited that the divine intellect cognizes the existence of things in both those ways, it is clear that in both ways there is a determination of the divine intellect with respect to the existent thing in relation to which the divine will is determined. And [there is] the certainty of infallibility, since the will cannot be determined without the intellect determinately apprehending that which the will determines. And [the divine intellect cognizes] immutably, since the intellect and the will are immutable. And the contingency of the cognized object is consistent with these [claims], since the will, willing something determinately, wills it contingently.

[4] One can argue against this view:

[4.1] First, against the claim that a nonevident capacity for opposites – i.e., for opposites without succession – accompanies the first freedom, for this does not seem true. The reason is that a capacity that can be actualized by no capacity, not even by an infinite [capacity], is not to be posited. But this nonevident capacity can be actualized by no capacity, since if it were actualized the will would will something at t and not will it at t, and so contradictories would evidently be true at one and the same time.

Suppose it is said that if it is actualized, 'the will willed x at t' is no longer true, nor even 'the will wills x at t,' since from the very fact that the will does not will x at t it follows that 'the will wills x at t' is not true.

On the contrary, it is generally conceded by philosophers and theologians that God cannot make what is past not to be past without its afterwards always being true to say that it was past. Therefore, since by hypothesis 'the will wills x at t' is now determinately true and consequently ['the will willed x at t'] will always be true afterwards and 'the will does not will x at t' never was true, after t 'the will did not will x at t,' always is impossible. Furthermore, now afterwards it is true to say that 'the will does not will x at t' could not have been true at the instant at which its opposite was true, even though it was true earlier, since frequently a true proposition becomes impossible.

Suppose it is said that that [nonevident] capacity could be actualized, since [the will] can cease to will x at t.

I answer that this does not hold good, since *this* capacity for opposites is evident and with succession. For at one instant 'the will wills *x* at *t*' will be true, and at another instant 'the will does not will *x* at *t*' will be true. But that both are true at the same instant as a result of any capacity whatever is absolutely impossible. In the same way it is impossible that 'a created will wills *x* at *t*' is true at first and that 'a [created] will never willed *x* at *t*' is true afterwards. And so with respect to creatures it is universally true that there never is a capacity for opposite objects without succession any more than for opposite acts. Indeed, by one and the same argument it can be "proved" that there is a capacity of a created will for opposite acts without succession and for opposite objects. But his argument does not come to a successful conclusion, and yet it must be conceded that the will, when it causes, causes contingently.

But there can be two causes of this truth. It is said to cause contingently either (a) because it is possible that at one and the same instant it is true to say that [the will] does not cause (and this is impossible, because having posited that it is causing at some instant it is impossible that it is not causing at that same instant), or (b) because it can cease from the act at another instant, freely, without any variation occurring in itself or another, and not as a result of the cessation of another cause, so that at *another* instant it is not causing, not that at that *same* instant it is not causing. And the will does cause contingently in that way.

[Causing] in that way it is not a natural cause, however, for a cause acting naturally always acts, unless it is changed or something new happens to it, either because some cause ceases to cause or in some other way. Even if none of these is the case, the will can cease from the act in virtue of its freedom alone.

As to the form of the argument, I maintain that at the instant at which [the will] causes it causes contingently and not necessarily. But it does not follow from this that this capacity of a cause for the opposite of what it causes is [a capacity] for its opposite without succession. For it is impossible that [such a capacity] should be actualized by any capacity

whatever. But there is a capacity for its opposite, a capacity that can be actualized in succession. For I take [as an example] heat heating wood. That heat can *not* heat, and this capacity [for not heating] can be actualized by the destruction of the agent of the heat, or by the removal of the patient, or by the interposition of an impediment, or by the withdrawal of a coacting cause (suppose that God does not will to coact with it),[6] or by the full actualization *(perfectionem)* of the end product (since fully actualized heat is produced in such a way that a more fully actualized [heat] cannot be produced by that same heat). Besides these ways [in which a natural cause can cease from causing an act], there is one additional way in which a created will can cease from causing an act – viz., all by itself – even though none of the aforementioned things is lacking but all are posited, and this and nothing else is the will causing contingently.

From this it is clear that it is inconsistent to say that the divine will as naturally prior posits its effect in reality at *t* in such a way that it can *not* posit it in reality at the same instant. For there are no such instants of nature as he [Scotus] imagines, nor is there in the first instant of nature such an indifference as regards positing and not positing. Rather, if at some instant it posits its effect in reality, it is impossible by means of any capacity whatever that both the instant occurs and [the effect] does not occur at that instant, just as it is impossible by means of any capacity whatever that contradictories are true at one and the same time.

I maintain, therefore, that in general there is never a capacity by means of which opposites are verified without succession. Indeed, it is impossible that God should have an object in view and not have it in view, unless either there is at least some succession in actuality or it coexists (and in that case there would be a change in everything else).

[4.2] [One can argue,] moreover, against what he says about the determination of the divine will: first, that the principal conclusion is not true. For when something is determined contingently, so that it is possible that it never was determined, one cannot have certain and infallible evidence as a result of such a determination. But the divine will is

6 It was Ockham's view that God is a partial immediate cause of all the effects which are not brought about by Him alone.

304

determined in such a way that it is still possible that it never was determined. Therefore one cannot have certain and infallible evidence as a result of such a determination, as a consequence of which (ex *quo*) it can simply never have been. And so it seems that the determination of the divine will, if it occurred, would produce too little.

Moreover, however much the certainty of [God's] knowledge can be preserved by the determination of the [divine] will in respect of all effects produced by the will, and even in respect of all effects, of natural causes with which the divine will coacts, still it does not seem that the certainty of [God's knowledge in respect of] future acts of a created will itself can be preserved by that determination. For if the divine will is determined in respect of all things, I ask whether or not the determination or production of a created will necessarily follows that determination. If so, then a created will acts naturally just as does any natural cause. For when the divine will exists as determined to one of [two] opposites, it is not in the power of any natural cause not to coact, and also when it is not determined a natural cause does not coact. In the same way, when the divine will exists as determined, a created will would coact, nor would it have it in its power not to coact, and consequently no act of a created will would be imputable to [that will] itself. If, however, the determination of a created will does not necessarily follow the determination of the divine will, then the determination of the divine will does not suffice for knowing whether an effect will be posited, but the determination of a created will is required, which is not yet or [at any rate] was not from eternity. Therefore God did not from eternity have certain cognition of future contingents as a result of the determination of the divine will.

Moreover, however much a created will is determined to one or the other part [of a contradiction] and however much the [divine] intellect sees that determination, nevertheless since our will can cease from that determination and not be determined, the [divine] intellect does not have certain cognition of that part. Therefore seeing the determination of a [created] will, a will that can *not* be determined to that part, does not suffice for certain cognition of that part.

Moreover, his claim that at the first instant the divine intellect presents simples [to itself], and that the divine will afterwards chooses one part, and that the intellect thereafter has evident cognition of that part, does not seem to be true. For there is no process or priority or contradiction in God such that the divine intellect at one instant does not have evident cognition of future contingents and at another instant does have [such cognition of them]. For to say that the divine intellect receives any perfection from something else would be to posit an imperfection [in the divine intellect].

[5] Therefore as regards the question I say that it is to be held indubitably that God knows all future contingents certainly and evidently. But to explain this clearly and to describe the way in which He knows all future contingents is impossible for any intellect in this [present] condition.

[5.1] And I maintain that the Philosopher would say that God does not know some future contingents evidently and certainly, and for the following reason. What is not true in itself cannot be known at a time at which it is not true in itself. But a future contingent absolutely dependent on a free capacity is not true in itself, since no reason can be given in accord with [that description of] it why the one part is true rather than the other. And so either both parts are true or neither [is true], and it is not possible that both parts are true; therefore neither is true. Consequently neither is known.

This argument does not come to a successful conclusion, according to the Philosopher's way [of thinking], except as regards those [future contingents] that are in the power of a will. But it does not hold good in connection with those that are not in the power of a will but depend absolutely on natural causes – e.g., that the sun will rise, and thus also as regards others [of that sort]. This is because a natural cause is determined for one part [of a contradiction], and no natural causes can be impeded except by a free cause. Nevertheless, they can be impeded by it in respect of one determined effect though not in respect of any and every [effect].

[5.2] This argument notwithstanding, it must nevertheless be maintained that God has evident cognition of all future contingents. But I do not know how to describe the way [in which He has it].

Still, it can be said that God Himself, or the divine essence, is a single intuitive cognition[7] as much of Himself as of all things creatable and uncreatable – [a cognition] so perfect and so clear that it is also evident cognition of all things past, future, and present. Thus just as our intellect can have evident cognition of some contingent propositions from our intuitive intellective cognition of the extremes[8] [of those propositions], so the divine essence itself is a cognition by which is known not only what is true (both necessary and contingent) regarding the present but also which part of a contradiction [involving future contingents] will be true and which will be false. And perhaps this is not as a result of the determination of His will. But even if it is supposed, *per impossibile,* that the divine cognition, existing as perfect as it now is, is neither the total nor the partial efficient cause of contingent effects, there would still be the cognition by which it would be evidently known by God which part of a contradiction will be true and which will be false. And this would not be because future contingents would be present to Him to be cognized either by means of ideas or by means of reasons, but by the divine essence itself or the divine cognition, which is the cognition by which it is known what is false and what is true, what was false and what was true, what will be false and what will be true.

This conclusion, although it cannot be proved *a priori* by means of the natural reason available to us, nevertheless can be proved by means of the authorities of the Bible and the Saints, which are sufficiently well known. But I pass over those things at present.

In the view of certain scholars *(artistis),* however, it must be known that although God knows regarding all future contingents which part will be true and which false, still 'God knows that this part will be true' is not necessary. Indeed, it is contingent to such an extent that although 'God knows that this part of the contradiction will be true' is true, it is still possible that it will never have been true. And in that case there is a capacity for its opposite without any succession, since it is possible that it will

never have been. But it is different in the case of a created will, since after a created will will have performed some act it is not possible that it is afterwards true to say that it never performed such an act.

Regarding *de possibili* propositions I maintain, as do others, that the proposition 'it is possible that God willing that A will be wills that it will not be' and others like it must be distinguished with respect to composition and division.[9] In the sense of composition it is indicated that this is possible: 'God willing that A will be does not will that A will be,' and this is impossible, since it includes a contradiction. In the sense of division it is indicated that God willing that A will be can not will that A will be, and that is true.

And suppose one says "suppose that it is posited in reality (and it is not impossible that that should happen); as a consequence 'God wills that A will be' and 'God does not will that A will be' hold good at one and the same time." In that case I maintain that when that possible [proposition] has been posited in reality an impossible [proposition] does not follow. But it must not be posited in reality in this way: 'God willing that A will be does not will that A will be.' Rather, it must be posited in reality in this way: 'God does not will that A will be.' And when that has been posited in reality nothing impossible follows, for only this follows: 'God never willed that A will be.' And that is not impossible but contingent, just as its contradictory – 'God wills that A will be' – always was contingent.

On the basis of the preceding remarks one can respond to the question [as follows]. God has determinate knowledge of future contingents because He knows determinately which part of a contradiction will be true and which false. But that He has [necessary] knowledge of future contingents can be understood in two ways; either that the knowledge by which future contingents are known is necessary, or that that knowledge is known necessarily. I maintain that God has necessary knowledge of future contingents in the first way, for there is one single cognition in God that is

---

7 See glossary entry for 'intuitive vs. abstractive cognition.'
8 See glossary entry for 'extremes.'
9 See glossary entry for 'composite and divided senses.'

a cognition of complexes[10] and of non-complexes, of necessaries and of contingents, and universally of all things imaginable. And that knowledge is the divine essence itself, which is necessary and immutable. That God has necessary knowledge of future contingents is understood in the second way as follows: that God necessarily knows this future contingent. It is not to be granted that He has necessary knowledge in that way, for just as it contingently will be, so God contingently knows that it will be.

In response to the first principal [argument] [1] it can be said that one or the other part of the contradiction is determinately true, so that it is not false but is contingently true. Therefore it is true in such a way that it can be false and can never have been true.

And suppose one says that a proposition true at some time of the present has [corresponding to it] a necessary proposition about the past – e.g., if 'Socrates is seated' is true at some time, 'Socrates was seated' will be necessary ever afterwards; therefore if 'A is true' is true now (A being such a contingent proposition), 'A was true' will always be true and necessary. In that case it must be said that when such a proposition about the present is equivalent to a proposition about the future or depends on the truth of a future [proposition], it is not required that a necessary proposition about the past correspond to the true proposition about the present. And this is the case in the matter under discussion.

In response to the second [principal argument] it is clear that 'God has necessary knowledge of A' does not follow unless 'has necessary knowledge' is taken in the second way. Therefore God necessarily knows A. But when 'has necessary knowledge' is taken in the first way the consequence does not hold good.

The response to the argument in opposition is clear from the preceding remarks.

---

10 See glossary entry for 'complex.'

TOPIC V:

IDENTITY AND DISTINCTION

TOPIC V

IDENTITY AND DISTINCTION

DURING THE COURSE OF MEDIEVAL PHILOSOPHY DOCTRINES ABOUT HOW things are identical or distinct became ever more sophisticated until in the late middle ages these doctrines were among the most elaborate of all the scholastic philosophic endeavors. The impulse for this work, like so many other topics surveyed in this anthology, had origins both in ancient Greek philosophy and in the demands of Christian theology. In his dialogue *Theaetetus* Plato had explored several ways in which perceiving something and knowing something are distinct, and in many other dialogues Plato had Socrates ask whether all the supposedly different virtues were really the same as knowledge and the same as each other. No doubt because of his training under Plato, in both his early logical treatise the *Topics* and in his later work in the *Metaphysics*, Aristotle laid out different ways in which items can be the same and distinct. Often we find him distinguishing sameness and distinctness "in being" from sameness and distinctness "in number" so that items the same in number might nevertheless be distinct in being. This doctrine found many applications in the whole of Aristotle's work. But what made the topic crucial for Christian thinkers was the paradoxical theological dogma of the divine Trinity. According to this doctrine God was three Persons, the Father, the Son and the Holy Spirit, and although each of these was the same as God's essence, and that essence was a completely undivided and non-complex entity, they were not the same as each other. The important logical principle that items each of which are identical with a third item are identical with each other seemed to be contradicted in this case.

The attempt to defend the doctrine of the Trinity against such obvious difficulties led to a very careful examination of exactly what is being said when we say x is the same as y, or x is distinct from y, and, following Aristotle, the medieval thinkers, beginning with Boethius, found that we say such things in a number of different ways. One of the most astute of these efforts was Peter Abelard's, but like so many of the philosophical efforts to arrive at some non-paradoxical reading of the Trinity Abelard's did not find favour with the church authorities and was condemned. Scholastic theologians had to tread very carefully in this area. Although few were willing to come right out and say the doctrine is philosophically indefensible (here Ockham is an exception), every attempt at providing a coherent way of understanding it seemed to fall either into the Sabellian heresy, where there is no real distinction between the Persons, or into the Arian heresy where one is confronted with three ranked deities.

The modern student, who perhaps has little interest in the doctrine of the Trinity itself, will still find the logical and philosophical analyses of identity and distinction sophisticated and interesting. The Trinity raises, for example, the issue of whether things really distinct have to be really separable, for certainly the Persons of the Trinity are not really separable in the sense that one could possibly exist without the others. In the later medieval period we find Duns Scotus trying to defend a form of distinction which is mind-independent and yet does not require that the things distinguished be separable. Ockham challenged this, and the debate between them divided the scholastics right to the end of the medieval period.

Certainly this whole topic has not disappeared from the philosophical agenda; witness debates in this century over proposals that mental entities are the same as physiological ones, that items of ordinary experience are identical with the unfamiliar entities of theoretical science, and that persons are the same as their bodies, or their minds, or certain four-dimensional entities extended through time. Reflection on scholastic ideas may well lead to interesting insights into these modern problems, or at least break the hold of various modern assumptions that lead to apparent paradox.

V.1. ARISTOTLE

V.1.1. Senses of 'same' (*Topics* I, ch.7)

[In this selection Aristotle first explains the difference between numerical sameness, where there is a single individual thing referred to, and sameness in species or genus, where there is more than one individual involved, but all the individuals belong to the same species or genus. Following that, he divides numerical sameness into cases where the different terms referring to the same individual have the same definition, or are related such that one is a "property," i.e. distinctive feature, of the other, or are related such that one is an accident of the other.]

First of all we must determine the number of ways we talk of sameness. Sameness would be generally regarded as falling, roughly speaking, into three divisions. We generally apply the term numerically or specifically or generically – numerically in cases where there is more than one name but only one thing, e.g. doublet and cloak; specifically, where there is more than one thing, but they present no differences in respect of their species, as one human and another, or one horse and another; for things like this that fall under the same species are said to be specifically the same. Similarly, too, those things are called generically the same which fall under the same genus, such as a horse and a man. It might appear that the sense in which water from the same spring is called the same water is somehow different and unlike the senses mentioned above; but really such a case as this ought to be ranked in the same class with the things that in one way or another are called the same in view of unity of species. For all such things seem to be of one family and to resemble one another. For the reason why all water is said to be specifically the same as all other water is because of a certain likeness it bears to it, and the only difference in the case of water drawn from the same spring is this, that the likeness is more emphatic: that is why we do not distinguish it from the things that in one way or another are called the same in view of unity of species.

It seems that things numerically one are called the same by everyone with the greatest degree of agreement. But this too is apt to be rendered in more than one sense; its most literal and primary use is found whenever the sameness is rendered by a name or definition, as when a cloak is said to be the same as a doublet, or a two-footed terrestrial animal is said to be the same as a human; a second sense is when it is rendered by a distinguishing feature, as when what can acquire knowledge is called the same as a human, and what naturally travels upward the same as fire; while a third use is found when it is rendered in reference to some accident, as when the creature who is sitting, or who is musical, is called the same as Socrates. For all these are meant to signify numerical unity. That what I have just said is true may be best seen where one form of appellation is substituted for another. For often when we give the order to call one of the people who are sitting down, indicating that person by name, we change our description whenever the person to whom we give the order happens not to understand us; they will, we think, understand better from some accidental feature; so we bid them call to us the person who is sitting or conversing – clearly supposing ourselves to be indicating the same object by its name and by its accident.

V.1.2. Senses of 'One' (*Metaphysics* V, ch.6)

[Things which are *prima facie* different might nevertheless be one single thing in a variety of ways, which Aristotle attempts to explain here. Comparison with the preceding selection shows that these are closely related to the modes of sameness. It follows, of course, that a thing which is in some way one thing, might in other ways be many things. The idea of things which are "many things" will play an important role in the discussion found in topic VI of what sort of reality universals have.]

We call one (1) that which is one by accident, (2) that which is one by its own nature. (1) Instances of the accidentally one are Coriscus and musical, and musical Coriscus (for it is the same thing to say "Coriscus" and "musical," and "musical

Coriscus"), and musical and just, and musical Coriscus and just Coriscus. For all these are called one by accident, just and musical because they are accidents of one substance, musical and Coriscus because the one is an accident of the other; and similarly in a sense musical Coriscus is one with Coriscus, because one of the parts in the formula is an accident of the other, i.e. musical is an accident of Coriscus; and musical Coriscus is one with just Coriscus, because both have parts which are accidents of one and the same subject. The case is similar if the accident is predicated of a class or of any universal term, e.g. if one says that human is the same as musical human; for this is either because musical is an accident of human, which is one substance, or because both are accidents of some individual, e.g. Coriscus. Both, however, do not belong to the person in the same way, but one doubtless as genus and in the substance, the other as a state or affection of the substance.

The things, then, that are called one by accident, are called so in this way. (2) Of things that are called one in virtue of their own nature some (a) are so called because they are continuous, e.g. a bundle is made one by a band, and pieces of wood are made one by glue; and a line, even if it is bent, is called one if it is continuous, as each part of the body is, e.g. the leg or the arm. Of these themselves, the continuous by nature are more one than the continuous by art. A thing is called continuous which has by its own nature one movement and cannot have any other; and the movement is one when it is indivisible, and indivisible in time. Those things are continuous by their own nature which are one not merely by contact; for if you put pieces of wood touching one another, you will not say these are one piece of wood or one body or one continuum of any other sort. Things, then, that are continuous in any way are called one, even if they admit of being bent, and still more those which cannot be bent, e.g. the shin or the thigh is more one than the leg, because the movement of the leg need not be one. And the straight line is more one than the bent; but that which is bent and has an angle we call both one and not one, because its

movement may be either simultaneous or not simultaneous; but that of the straight line is always simultaneous, and no part of it which has magnitude rests while another moves, as in the bent line.

(b) Things are called one in another sense because the substratum does not differ in kind; it does not differ in the case of things whose kind is indivisible to the sense. The substratum[1] meant is either the nearest to, or the furthest from, the final state. For, on the one hand, wine is said to be one and water is said to be one, *qua* indivisible in kind; and, on the other hand, all juices, e.g. oil and wine, are said to be one, and so are all things that can be melted, because the ultimate substratum of all is the same; for all of these are water or air.

(c) Those things are called one whose genus[2] is one though distinguished by opposite differentiae; and these are all called one because the genus which underlies the differentiae is one (e.g. horse, human, and dog are one, because all are animals), and in a way similar to that in which the matter is one. These are sometimes called one in this way, but sometimes it is the higher genus that is said to be the same (if they are *infimae species* of their genus) – the genus above the proximate genera, e.g. the isosceles and the equilateral are one and the same figure because both are triangles, but they are not the same triangles.

(d) Two things are called one, when the formula which states the essence of one is indivisible from another formula which shows the essence of the other (though in itself every formula is divisible). Thus even that which has increased or is diminishing is one, because its formula is one, as, in the case of planes, is the formula of their form. In general those things, the thought of whose essence is indivisible and which cannot be separated either in time or in place or in formula, are most of all one, and of these especially those which are substances.[3] For in general those things that do not admit of division are one in so far as they do not admit of it, e.g. if something *qua* human does not admit of division, it is one human; if *qua* animal, it is one animal; if *qua* magnitude, it is one magnitude. – Now most things are called one because they do or

---

1 See glossary entry for 'substratum.'
2 See glossary entry for 'species/genus.'
3 See glossary entry for 'substance.'

have or suffer or are related to something else that is one, but the things that are primarily called one are those whose substance is one, – and one either in continuity or in form or in formula; for we count as more than one either things that are not continuous, or those whose form is not one, or those whose formula is not one.

(e) While in a sense we call anything one if it is a quantity and continuous, in a sense we do not unless it is a whole, i.e. unless it has one form; e.g., if we saw the parts of a shoe put together anyhow, we should not call them one all the same (unless because of their continuity); we do this only if they are put together so as to be a shoe and have thereby some one form. This is why the circle is of all lines most truly one, because it is whole and complete.

What it is to be one is to be a beginning of number; for the first measure is the beginning, for that by which we first know each class is the first measure of the class; the one, then, is the beginning of the knowable regarding each class. But the one is not the same in all classes. For here it is a quarter-tone, and there it is the vowel or the consonant; and there is another unit of weight and another of movement. But everywhere the one is indivisible either in quantity or in kind. That which is indivisible in quantity and *qua* quantity is called a unit if it is not divisible in any dimension and is without position, a point if it is not divisible in any dimension and has position, a line if it is divisible in one dimension, a plane if in two, a body if divisible in quantity in all – i.e. in three dimensions. And, reversing the order, that which is divisible in two dimensions is a plane, that which is divisible in one a line, that which is in no way divisible in quantity is a point or a unit, – that which has not position a unit, that which has position a point. Again, some things are one in number, others in species, others in genus, others by analogy; in number those whose matter is one, in species those whose formula is one, in genus those to which the same figure of predication[4] applies, by analogy those which are related as a third thing is to a fourth.[5] The latter kinds of unity are always found when the former are, e.g. things that are one in number are one in

species, while things that are one in species are not all one in number; but things that are one in species are all one in genus, while things that are so in genus are not all one in species but are all one by analogy; while things that are one by analogy are not all one in genus.

Evidently "many" will have uses corresponding to those of "one"; some things are many because they are not continuous, others because their matter – either the proximate matter or the ultimate – is divisible in kind, others because the formulae which state their essence are more than one.

V.1.3. How the Motion of the Agent is the same as the Motion in the Recipient, yet different (from *Physics* III, ch.3, 202a12-b22)

[Here Aristotle explains how things which are different in definition or in what they are can nevertheless be numerically the same. His example is the actualization of an agent and the actualization of the thing the agent acts on (the "recipient"); both are a single motion existing in the thing acted on. Toward the end Aristotle states a very important principle, viz. that items which are numerically the same thing need not have all their characteristics in common if they differ in what they are. One cannot then automatically infer from the numerical sameness of A and B, and the assumption that A has property P, that B also has property P.]

The solution of the difficulty is plain: motion is in the movable. It is the fulfillment of this potentiality by the action of that which has the power of causing motion: and the actuality of that which has the power of causing motion is not other than the actuality of the moveable; for it must be the fulfillment of *both*. A thing is capable of causing motion because it *can* do this; it is a mover because it actually *does* it. But it is on the moveable that it is capable of acting. Hence there is a single actuality of both alike, just as one to two and two to one are the same interval, and the steep ascent and the steep descent are one – for these are one and the same, although their definitions are not one. So it is with the mover and the moved.

---

4 I.e., a category. See glossary entry for 'category.'
5 Aristotle's most frequent examples are drawn from biology. Thus the roots of a plant might be called its "mouth" because they perform for the plant the same function of taking in nutrients that mouths perform for animals.

This view has a dialectical difficulty. Perhaps it is necessary that there should be an actuality of the agent and of the recipient. The one is acting and the other is what is acted on; and the outcome and end of the one is an action, that of the other a reception. Since, then, they are both motions, we may ask: *In* what are they, if they are different? Either both are in what is acted on and moved, or the acting is in the agent and the being acted on is in the recipient. (If we ought to call the latter also 'acting,' the word would be used in two senses.)

Now, in the latter case, the motion will be in the mover, for the same account will hold of mover and moved. Hence either *every* mover will be moved, or, though having motion, it will not be moved.

If, on the other hand, both are in what is moved and acted on – both the acting and the being acted on, (e.g. both teaching and learning, though they are two, in the learner), then, first, the actuality of each will not be present *in* each, and, a second absurdity, a thing will have two motions at the same time. How will there be two alterations of quality in *one* subject towards *one* form? The thing is impossible: the actualization will be one.

But (someone will say) it is contrary to reason to suppose that there should be one identical actualization of two things which are different in kind. Yet there will be, if teaching and learning are the same, and acting and being acted pm. To teach will be the same as to learn, and to act the same as to be acted on – teachers will necessarily be learning everything they teach, and the agent will be acted

on. It is not absurd that the actualization of one thing should be in another. Teaching is the activity of a person who can teach, yet the operation is performed in something – it is not cut adrift from a subject, but is of one thing while in another.

There is nothing to prevent two things having one and the same actualization (not the same in being, but related as the potential is to the actual). Nor is it necessary that the teacher should learn, even if to act and to be acted on are one and the same, provided they are not the same in respect of the account which states their essence (as raiment and dress), but are the same in the sense in which the road from Thebes to Athens and the road from Athens to Thebes are the same, as has been explained above. For it is not things which are in any way the same that have all their attributes the same, but only those where what it is to be the one is the same as what it is to be the other. But indeed it by no means follows from the fact that teaching is the same as learning, that to learn is the same as to teach, any more than it follows from the fact that there is one distance between two things which are at a distance from each other, that being here at a distance from there and being there at a distance from here are one and the same. To generalize, teaching is not the same as learning, or acting as being acted on, in the full sense, though they belong to the same subject, the motion; for the actualization of the former in the latter and the actualization of the latter through the action of the former differ in definition.

V.2. BOETHIUS

BOETHIUS AT THE BEGINNING OF THIS SELECTION BORROWS NOTIONS FOUND
in the preceding selections from Aristotle, but quickly moves on to theology,
claiming that God is pure form and thus not a subject for attributes and hence not
capable of being composed of many distinct things. Nevertheless the Christian
doctrine of the Trinity demands that in God there are three Persons, each of
which is God even though they are in some way different from each other.
Boethius does not explain here how this can be. The selection more states the
problem than gives any solution to it.

For the purposes of this and other selections the following summary of the doctrine of the Trinity will suffice. The divine essence is itself an entirely simple entity, admitting of no sort of composition. Nevertheless, this essence is common to
three "Persons" in that they are each the same as that essence although not the
same as each other. There is an order among these Persons. The first Person, "the
Father," is in no way a result of anything; the second Person, "the Son," is "generated" by the Father, but is just as eternal as the Father and otherwise equal to
the Father; the third Person, "the Holy Spirit," "proceeds" from both the Father
and the Son, but is just as eternal and perfect as the other two. The "production"
of the second and third Persons is not at all a temporal process but more akin to
a mere logical ordering where what is posterior logically requires what is prior,
but not vice versa, the way a set requires its members but the members do not
require the set. The production of these Persons is also an entirely necessary fact,
in contrast to God's creation of the world which depends on a free decision of
God's will.

V.2.1. Sameness and Difference in the Trinity
(from *On the Trinity*)

I

There are many who claim as theirs the dignity of
the Christian religion; but that form of faith is
most valid and only valid which, both on account
of the universal character of the rules and doctrines
through which the authority of that same religion
is perceived, and because its form of worship has
spread throughout almost all the world, is called
catholic or universal. The belief of this faith concerning the unity of the Trinity is as follows: The

Father they say is God, the Son is God, the Holy
Spirit is God. Therefore, Father, Son, and Holy
Spirit are one God, not three Gods.

The cause of this union is absence of difference.
Difference cannot be avoided by those who add to
or take from the unity, as for instance the Arians,[1]
who by graduating the Trinity according to merit
break it up and convert it to plurality. For the principle of plurality is otherness; for apart from otherness plurality is unintelligible.

In fact, the diversity of three or whatever number
of things lies in genus or species or number; for as
often as 'same' is said, so often is 'diverse' also
predicated. Now sameness is said in three ways: in

---

1 I.e., the followers of Arius, a fourth century prelate in Alexandria whose doctrine of the Trinity was declared heretical
since it denied that the three Persons shared the same substance. Arianism was the dominant form of Christianity in
Boethius's day among the Ostrogoths who ruled northern Italy as nominally part of the Roman Empire.

genus, e.g. a human is the same as a horse because they have the same genus, animal; in species, e.g. Cato is the same as Cicero because they have the same species, human being; in number, e.g. Tully and Cicero because he is one in number.[2] Similarly 'diverse' too is said in genus, species and number.

Now numerical difference is caused by variety of accidents; for three humans differ neither by genus nor species but by their accidents, for even if we mentally separated from them all their accidents the places for each of them would still be diverse and in no way could we make them one place, since two bodies cannot occupy one single place and that place is an accident. Thus those three are many in number because their accidents make them many.

II

Come, then, let us begin and consider each several point, as far as it can be grasped and understood; for as has been wisely said,[3] in my opinion, it is a scholar's duty to try to formulate his belief about each thing according as it actually is.

Since there are three theoretical sciences – (1) natural science dealing with things in motion that have not been abstracted (i.e. *anupexairetos*) (for it is concerned with forms conjoined to matter,[4] forms which cannot actually be separated from bodies, bodies which are in motion, those with earth moving downward, those with fire moving upward, and these forms take on the motion of the matter to which they are conjoined); (2) mathematics dealing with motionless things that have not been abstracted (for it investigates the forms of bodies without the matter and thus without the motion, forms which being in matter cannot be separated from those bodies); (3) theology dealing with motionless things that have been abstracted and are separable (for God's substance is without either matter or motion) – in natural science, then, we shall be bound to use scientific, in mathematics, systematical, in theology intellectual concepts. In theology we should not be diverted to play with imaginations, but rather apprehend that form which is pure form and no image, which is very being and the source of being.

For all being is dependent on form. A statue is not called a likeness of an animal on account of the bronze which is its matter, but on account of the form whereby that likeness is impressed upon it. And the bronze itself is not called bronze because of the earth which is its matter, but because of the form of bronze. Likewise earth is not called earth by reason of unqualified matter (*apoion hylen*) but by reason of dryness and weight, which are forms. So nothing is said to be because of its matter, but because of its distinctive form.

But the divine substance is form without matter, and is therefore one single item and is that which it is. Other things are not that which they are, for each thing has its being from the things of which it is composed, that is, from its parts. It is this and that, that is, its parts taken together; it is not this or that, where each part is taken separately. Since an earthly human, for example, consists of body and soul, that human is body and soul, but not body or soul, where each is taken separately; therefore, the human is not that which it is.

That, on the other hand, which does not consist of this and that, but is only this, is truly that which it is, and is altogether beautiful and stable because it does not depend on anything. Wherefore, that is truly one in which is no number, in which there is nothing besides that which it is. Nor can it become a subject for something, for it is a form and forms cannot be subjects. For if other forms, like humanity, are subjects for accidents, each of them does not sustain accidents through the fact that it exists, but through the fact that it has matter as its subject. For when the matter which is the subject for humanity sustains any accident, humanity itself seems to sustain it. But a form which is without matter will not be able to be a subject for something, nor indeed to be in matter, else it would not be a form but an image. For from those forms which are outside matter have come those forms which are in matter and produce a body. We misname those that are in bodies when we call them forms, since they are mere images; for they only resemble those forms which are not existent in matter. Therefore, in the

---

2 'Tully' and 'Cicero' are alternative names of the great Roman statesman Marcus Tullius Cicero, 106-43 B.C.E.

3 Cicero, *Tusc.*, v.7, 19.

4 See glossary entry for 'form/matter.'

divine substance there is no difference, no plurality arising out of difference, no multiplicity arising out of accidents, and accordingly no number either.

III

Now God differs from God in no respect, for there is no distinction through either accidents or substantial differences[5] existing in a subject. But where there is no difference, there is no sort of plurality and accordingly no number; here, therefore, is unity alone. For although we mention God three times when we name the Father, the Son, and the Holy Spirit, these three unities do not produce a plurality of number just from the fact that they are, if we think of numerable things and not of number itself. For in this case the repetition of ones does make a number; but in the sense of number which means countable things, the repetition and plurality of ones do not by any means produce numerical difference in the objects counted.

For there are two kinds of number: one with which we count and the other which consists in countable things. For indeed, an item that is one is a thing; unity is that by which we call a thing one. Again, two items belong to the class of things, like humans or stones; not so duality; duality is merely that whereby two humans or two stones are made [to be two]. Similarly for the rest. Therefore, in the case of that number by which we count, the repetition of ones makes plurality; but the repetition of ones does not produce plurality in the sense of a number of things, as, for example, if I say of one and the same thing, "one sword, one brand, one blade."[6] For one sword can be known under several different words, for this is more an iteration of ones rather than a counting, just as if we were to say

"brand, blade, sword," we would have a sort of repetition of the same thing rather than a counting of different things. It is just as though I said "sun, sun, sun," in which case I would not have produced three suns, but only have said sun several times of the one sun.

So then if God be said three times of Father, Son, and Holy Spirit, the threefold predication does not result in plural number. The risk of that, as has been said, threatens only those who distinguish them [the Persons] according to merit. But Catholic Christians, allowing no difference of merit in God, and positing that He really is a form and is other than that which is something,[7] rightly regard the statement "the Father is God, the Son is God, the Holy Spirit is God, and this Trinity is one God," not as a counting of different things but as a repetition of one and the same thing, like the statement, "Blade and brand are one sword" or "Sun, sun and sun are one sun."

Let this be enough for the present to establish my meaning and to show that not every repetition of ones produces number and plurality. Still in saying "Father, Son, and Holy Spirit" we are not using them as though they meant the same. A brand and a blade both are each other and are the same; but although Father, Son and Holy Spirit are the same, they are not each other. This point deserves a moment's consideration. For to those who ask, "Is the Father the Son Himself?" Catholics answer "Not at all." Again, "Is the one the same as the other?" They deny it. There is not, therefore, complete indifference between them. Thus number does come in, number which, as we explained above, results from a diversity of subjects. We will briefly debate this point when we have done examining how particular predicates can be applied to God.

---

5 See glossary entry for 'specific difference.'
6 The Latin terms here are roughly synonymous.
7 Hence God cannot be a subject of attributes; see above p. 17.

V.3. ABELARD

ABELARD HERE WRESTLES WITH THE PROBLEM WHICH FACED BOETHIUS in the preceding selection, namely how the Persons can differ from each other even though they are the same as the divine essence. There must be some difference otherwise there would be no distinction. But how can this differentiation occur without allowing that there are in God things that are not God, i.e. without making God a subject of accidents in a way that violates His simplicity?

V.3.1. How to have many Persons in one God
(from *Christian Theology* [*Theologia Christiana*] bks.III & IV)

The cult of the Christian faith immovably holds, vigorously believes, always asserts, and truly professes that the one God is three Persons, the Father, the Son, and the Holy Spirit – I say just one god and in no way several gods, one creator of all things both visible and invisible, one origin, one good, one Lord and disposer of all, one eternal being, and one omnipotent being. In everything it preaches and believes in only the singleness of unity, except in what pertains to the distinction of the three Persons, i.e. of the Father, of the Son, and of the Holy Spirit, where alone it professes plurality or multiplicity or diversity, even though in all other matters, as we said, it preserves unity.

We certainly speak of three Persons, Father, Son, and Holy Spirit, diverse from each other by their distinguishing features, but not of three gods or lords. In this way we profess unity in all except the multiplicity of Persons, allowing that no one of these Persons is any one of the others and each in itself is fully God and Lord, so that (following here the assertion of the blessed Jerome when he wrote "On Faith" for Pope Damasus) [we say that] except for the words which indicate the distinguishing features of the Persons, whatever is said of one Person can be interpreted as something all three are fully worthy of having. For the Father is neither the Son nor the Holy Spirit, nor is the Son Himself the Holy Spirit, but the Father is God, the Son is God, and the Spirit is God. This does not mean that there are three or several gods; rather there is just one god consisting eternally and immutably of three Persons. Thus also there is one creator and one lord, and likewise in the other cases. Neither

does it affect the truth of what we assert if we say one god of the three Persons singly or of them all together, since it is equally the case that each of the three is one and the same god as the other two and that the three together, i.e. the Trinity itself, is one god, one lord, etc.

There is, then, of these three Persons completely one and the same substance and totally individual and simple essence, utterly one power, one glory, one majesty, one reason, one will, and the same undivided activity. They are one and the same in all things except what pertains to the differences between the distinguishing features in virtue of which they exist in perpetual diversity from each other, so that the distinguishing feature of one Person never flows over into another Person nor is ever shared in by the other Person. Otherwise, it would not be a distinguishing feature but rather a shared one.

It is distinctive of the Father to exist from just himself, not from anything else, and to generate or have generated eternally the Son who is co-eternal with him. And it is distinctive of the Son to be generated or to have been generated eternally from the Father alone, not created nor made, and not proceeding but simply generated. And it is distinctive of the Holy Spirit to proceed from the Father together with the Son, but not to be created, nor made, nor generated, but simply proceeding. Hence the distinction of the three Persons from each other is in virtue of the distinguishing features of each.

* * * *

There is certainly just one and the same thing in each of the Persons, one essentially individual substance and completely simple essence to which belong the three distinguishing features in which the diversity of the Persons consists, and not some numerical multiplicity of things, since there is just one singular and completely indivisible thing. Hence we say the Trinity is holy and individual, since there is in it no multiplicity of things but only a diversity of distinguishing features. It follows, then, that the three Persons are co-equal to each other in all things, just as they are also co-eternal with each other, because items which have completely the same singular and individual essence cannot have any difference in rank.

****

We must rely here on a great and very subtle distinction lest the identity of the singular substance and the individual unity of the essence block the diversity of Persons and falling into the error of Sabellius[1] we profess only one Person, just as only one god, and lest the diversity of the Persons block the singularity of the substance and falling into the cesspit with Arius[2] we assert that there are three gods just as there are three Persons, rather than that God is completely one in the singularity of his substance and triune in the separateness of the three Persons.

****

The greatest problem of all, I think, is this: How are we to think of there being a diversity of Persons in so much unity of an individual and totally undifferentiated substance, when we do not seem to be able to find any mode of difference distinguished by philosophers in terms of which we might be able to explain this diversity of the Persons?

****

Now let us remove that first obstacle they [certain "pseudo-dialecticians," whom Abelard does not identify] erect to the differentiation of the Persons of one and completely the same essence, namely

that the type of differentiation needed here seems unknown both to philosophers and to everyone else.

Porphyry in his discussion of differences distinguished types of differences, and the fact that among these types is not found the type of difference we have between the Persons in God poses no problem for us. In that place he treats only of differences that consist in forms, i.e. where distinct things stand apart from each other by diverse forms or the same thing changes by forms, one after the other, coming to exist in it. But there are no forms in God. Still, we do not any the less say that God differs from creatures, just because in his treatise on 'Difference'[3] Porphyry has not listed this difference. There are many other types of difference besides those Porphyry distinguishes which we are forced to allow.

In order to pursue these types more fully and carefully we must distinguish in how many and what ways 'same,' as well as 'diverse,' are used, especially since the crux of the whole controversy hangs on the identity of the divine substance and the diversity of the Persons, nor can the controversy itself be ended unless we show that this identity is not contrary to that diversity. To do this more carefully we have to set out in advance, as we said, in how many ways 'same' is used and in how many 'diverse.'

Each taken by itself seems, perhaps, to be used in five or more ways. For something is said to be the same or one with something (1) in respect of essence or number, (2) the same in distinguishing feature, (3) the same in definition, (4) the same in likeness, (5) the same as meaning unchanged. Turning to the contrary, we use 'diverse' in just as many ways, or perhaps even in more.

We say that something is essentially the same with something where they have numerically the same essence, in the sense that this and that are numerically the same essence. For example, a blade and a sword[4] are numerically the same essence, or a substance and a body, or an animal and a human, or even Socrates, and a white item is the same in

---

1 3rd century Christian Roman prelate who treated the three Persons as merely three manifestations of the divine essence.
2 4th century Christian in Alexandria whose doctrine that the second and third Persons of the Trinity are not identical with the divine essence and inferior to the first became one of the most widespread of the early Christian heresies.
3 From Porphyry's *Isagoge* (see selection **VI.3.1.**).
4 The Latin words for 'blade' and 'sword' are pretty much synonymous.

number as a hard item. For it is true that a substance is this body, or this animal, although not every substance is. Clearly all these, i.e. those which are essentially the same, are said to be the same in number, because, since the essence of each is the same, the number of things cannot in them be multiplied nor can the counting of things in virtue of their separateness be continued, i.e. saying of them "one, two" etc. For number exists only in separate essences, i.e. in those which are so completely diverse that not only is the one not the other but also one does not belong to the other, nor does something belonging to one belong to the other, i.e. one is not a quantitative part of the other nor do they share a part that is the same in both.

Something is said to be the same with something in distinguishing feature when the one shares the distinguishing feature of the other, as when a white item shares the distinguishing feature of a hard item, or a hard of a white. For a white item shares in hardness, which is the distinguishing feature of a hard item, that is to say a white item is hard; or conversely a hard item shares in the distinguishing feature of a white item.

Some items are essentially the same even though they are distinguished by their distinguishing features. This occurs where their properties remain so completely unmixed that the property of one is not at all shared by the other, even though each has completely the same substance numerically. For example, in this waxen image the wax, i.e. the material itself, and the enmattered item are the same in number, even though here the matter itself and the enmattered item do not have their distinguishing features in common. For the matter itself of the waxen image is not enmattered (i.e. [we do not say] this wax is made of wax), nor is the enmattered item itself matter in this case (i.e. [we do not say] the waxen image is the matter of the waxen image), since nothing equal[5] to itself is in any way constitutive of or naturally prior [to itself]. Thus the matter of the waxen image and the item enmattered in wax are unmixed in their distinguishing features, even though they are numerically the same essence. The very matter of the waxen image and

the enmattered item itself, i.e. the wax itself and the waxen image itself, are the same wax, namely this wax. But the enmattered item in this case is in no way matter, nor is the matter enmattered, although it is the thing which is enmattered. It pertains to the distinguishing feature of matter to precede the enmattered item which comes from it, while it pertains to the distinguishing feature of the enmattered item to follow and to be posterior.

Thus the distinguishing feature of matter is that priority in accord with which something is made materially from it, while the distinguishing feature of the enmattered is the converse posteriority. Therefore, the distinguishing features are unmixed by predication, although the items distinguished, as I might call them, are predicated mixedly of the same thing. Certainly it is one thing to predicate a form, another to predicate the formed item itself, i.e. the very thing serving as a subject for the form. For if I say, "The waxen image is prior to the wax, i.e. has priority in respect of the wax," then I link it [to something] and I predicate a form, and what is said is false. But if I say, "The waxen image is something prior to the wax, i.e. it is some *thing* prior to the wax," then I link it [to something] and I predicate a formed item; and now the proposition is true, since that image is a body which is prior to the wax. Likewise, Socrates does not have continuousness, i.e. he is not continuous, although he is a continuous thing, namely this body.

Since we have shown what items are diverse by distinguishing features, it is clear by contrariety what items are the same by agreement in distinguishing features.

Besides these, i.e. those which we say are the same essentially, or the same in distinguishing features, there are some which are the same in definition, like a blade and a sword,[6] or Marcus and Tullius,[7] and generally any items that have exactly the same definition. For not only is a blade a sword and a sword a blade, but also it is a sword from the very fact that it is a blade, and conversely, so that they are to be delimited by the same definition, since the one has the same expressed and distinctive being as the

---

5 Reading 'par' here for 'pars.'
6 See fn. 2.
7 Both names refer to Cicero.

other. It is in this sense that Boethius uses 'same' in *Topics* I,[8] where he says that a question about definition is about 'same,' as when we ask, "Is the useful the same as the honorable?" and he says that "things whose definitions are the same are the very same things, and things whose definitions are diverse are diverse things."

Here I mean by a definition what as a whole expresses the force and distinguishing feature of the defined item and neither goes beyond in any way the sense of the noun nor falls short of it, as, for example, when someone defines 'body' by saying it is a corporeal substance, not by saying it is a colored substance. For, although this definition 'colored substance' belongs to all and only bodies, just as does the former, still it does not express the force and sense of this noun 'body' in the way the former does. For the noun 'body' does not entail colour, which is an accident of body, in the way it entails corporeity, which is substantial to the body. Neither does this definition ['colored body'] display what the distinguishing feature of body demands from the very fact that it is a body, in the way that the former [definition, 'corporeal substance,'] does. Thus when we say that a blade and a sword are the same in definition it is as if we said: A blade and a sword are the same essence in such a way that from the mere fact that it is a blade it is required that it be a sword, and conversely, so that not only are the blade and the sword the same essence but also being a blade and being a sword are entirely the same. Therefore, those items are said to be the same in definition which are so attached that not only is the one the other, but the fact that it is the one demands that it be the other, and conversely. Certainly substance and body, or white item and hard item, cannot be said to be the same in this way, although they are the same essentially. Thus all items which are the same in definition are the same essentially, but not conversely.

* * * *

Also we say that whatever items are apart from each other in the sense that one is not the other are essentially diverse from each other. For example, Socrates is not Plato nor is Socrates' hand Socrates.

We say that any disparate items are essentially diverse, since the essence of the one is not the essence of the other, even though it belongs to the essence of the other, as a hand belongs to a man, or a wall to a house. Therefore, just as Socrates is essentially something other than Plato, so Socrates' hand [is essentially something other] than Socrates, and any part [is essentially something other] than its whole. It is in this sense that we say that one thing is simple and another composite, since that which is simple is not the composite item itself, even though it belongs to the composite item. Thus we call essentially diverse all those items which are so removed from each other that the one is not the other.

Even Porphyry himself explicitly inserts this difference into the sphere of common items, namely where he shows that a completely general item and a completely specific item differ in this, that the completely general item never becomes the completely specific nor does the completely specific become the completely general.

But of the items which are essentially diverse, some are also diverse in number, some not. Certainly we say that those items are diverse in number which are separate from each other by the whole quantity of their essence, so that not only is the one not the other but also neither is part of the other nor has the same part in common with it. Thus all and only those items are different in number which are separate by the whole quantity of their essence, whether they differ from each other only in number, like Socrates and Plato, or also in species, as this human and this horse, or even in genus as this human and this whiteness, or differ from each other by any form whatsoever whether that form be a difference in the wide sense, i.e. a separable accident like sitting, or is a difference in the strict sense, i.e. an inseparable accident like curvature of the nose, or is a difference in an even stricter sense, i.e. a substantial difference like rationality, where a substantial difference does not just make something be "another," i.e. in some way diverse, but also makes it be "something else," i.e. diverse substantially and in species. Only these [i.e. items that are diverse in number] are in the strict sense called 'several' and

---

8 *De differentiis topicis* I.

'many,' because strictly speaking 'several' and 'many' pertain to number and are used in virtue of number.

Therefore, there are some items which are essentially diverse which are not numerically different, as, for example, a house and its wall, and any complete whole and its own part. God Himself is said to differ from creatures in respect of both the above types of diversity, i.e. both essentially and numerically. We also use 'diverse' in this sense when we deny that there are diverse pairs in a triplet. For even though a third unit makes a single pair with either of the other two units, and the one pair is not the other, still we refuse to call them diverse pairs, since they are not separate by the whole capacity or content of their essence, since they share a unit. Also when we say that someone owns just a house, i.e. a house and nothing else diverse from the house, we take 'diverse' to mean numerically rather than essentially. For the person who owns a house also owns a wall which is not the house. But although the wall is essentially diverse from the house to which it belongs, it is not numerically diverse [from the house], since it is included in the very quantity of the house.

It is to be noted that, although everything essentially the same with something is numerically the same with it, and conversely; nevertheless, not everything essentially diverse from something is numerically diverse from it, as we taught above. Any part is certainly essentially diverse from its whole, but not numerically diverse. Neither, perhaps, is it numerically the same, unless perhaps someone uses 'numerically the same' negatively to mean not numerically diverse. For if a part were said to be numerically diverse from its whole, 'Socrates' would have to be allowed to be predicated of numerically different items, since this whole composed of the hand and the rest of the body is Socrates and also the rest of the body minus the hand must be said to be Socrates, i.e. to be vivified by this soul. This has been developed more fully by us elsewhere in treating of the category of substance.

Those items are diverse in definition which cannot be delimited by the same definition of sense, i.e. which are such that they do not mutually require each other, even though the same thing is both, as in the case of a substance and a body, or a white item and a hard item. For it does not follow from the fact that it is a substance that it is a body, nor from the fact that it is white that it is hard, since the one is able to exist without the other and does not of itself require the other.

* * * *

Certainly we often say in place of 'the same or diverse in definition' 'the same *status*[9] or diverse *status*,' and we say this *status* is that one only where this thing is completely the same in definition with that one, and this *status* is not that one only where this thing is not completely the same with that one in its expressed being, i.e. in totally the same definition.

* * * *

Also when we say, "One artisan is a painter, another a carpenter, another etc.," we speak of 'one' and 'another' in respect of effects or functions, since the noun 'artisan' belongs to something on account of an activity or a function, and not in respect of persons, since it may be that at sometime the same person has both functions.

But when your Aristotle says in *Peri hermenias* I[10] that spoken as well as written words are not the same for all but different for different people, he says this in respect of the function of signifying, and this belongs to spoken and written words not in respect of the vocal production of utterances, because, although the vocal production of utterances is natural to all, not everybody recognizes the function of signifying; rather it holds only for those who know the imposition of the utterances. Also later when in *Peri hermenias* II[11] he says that there is one utterance and many affirmations, or when Priscian says[12] that many nouns coincide in a single

---

9 The term 'status' is a term of art for Abelard. It figures importantly in his theory of universals (see selection **VI.6.1.**, p.378-92), and can be thought of as meaning roughly the same as the English word 'property' taken in its broad logical sense. The plural and singular forms of 'status' are the same.

10 *De Interpretatione* 1, 16a5.

11 *De Interpretatione* 8, 18a17-26.

utterance, 'many' or 'diverse' are used in respect of that function of signifying the different thoughts which have to be agreed upon if they are to be called affirmations or nouns. He speaks of a single utterance on account of the vocal production itself and the form of the sound, not on account of the function, since the noun 'utterance' in fact applies on account of the quality of the sound and not on account of the function of signifying.

In this way, then, 'same' and 'diverse' frequently change their significations on account of the juxtaposition of subjects, as is often the case with other words, for example, when I say, 'good cithara player' and 'good human being,' or 'simple utterance' and 'simple proposition,' or 'true definition' and 'true sentence.'

I think I have distinguished carefully enough for the present purposes in how many ways 'same' or 'diverse' are used, so that now it is easy to explain in what consists the diversity of the Persons who are in God, whose substance is completely the same. By 'same' I mean essentially and numerically the same, just as the substance of a blade and a sword, or of this human and this animal, is the same. The Persons, i.e. the Father, the Son, and the Holy Spirit, are diverse from each other in a way like that in which those items are diverse which are diverse in definition or in distinguishing feature, i.e. by the fact that, although completely the same essence which is God the Son or God the Holy Spirit is God the Father, still one item is distinctive of God the Father, i.e. inasmuch as the essence is the Father, and another distinctive of the Son, and still another of the Holy Spirit.

* * * *

Nevertheless, when we hear distinguishing features spoken of, we must not interpret this in such a way that we think there are some forms in God; rather we speak of distinguishing features as distinctive items, i.e. in the way Aristotle says that not being in a subject, or not admitting more and less, or having no contrary, are common to every substance. By these commonnesses which he assigns he does not mean any forms; in fact, he assigns these common-

nesses more in order to take away something than to posit something. In this very way we say that subsisting through itself is distinctive of substance because for a substance to exist requires only this; and we say that not having forms is distinctive of an unformed thing, for example to God Himself, and lacking parts is distinctive of simple things. We do not seem to posit any forms by this, but rather, in fact, to take away all forms and parts. But if someone understands some forms in these cases too, it is certain that they are in no way things diverse from the very substances they belong to. And it is in this way that we say this is distinctive of the Father, that is distinctive of the Son, and that of the Holy Spirit.

* * * *

The objection – since anything which exists is either a substance or a form, how can there be said to be many items if there are not many substances or many forms or many combinations of the two? – has already been silenced by our having denied completely that God is many, because although there are many Persons it does not necessarily follow that there are many full stop, since a multiplicity does not genuinely arise except where there are separate essences that are numerically diverse. From the acceptance that God is many to the extent that there is a diversity of distinguishing features or definitions, as we explained, it does not follow that we can proceed by division as follows: If God is many in this way, then he is either many substances, which means numerically diverse, or many forms, etc. Certainly the same soul, or any substance, is many by definitions, but it nevertheless does not follow that it is many substances or etc. If it were many in number, then doubtless we could proceed with this division.

* * * *

This objection is refuted in many ways because, although each of the three Persons is God or a substance and one Person is not some other, nevertheless it does not follow that they are many gods or substances. For it is not necessary that when a noun of singular number is said of each of some items

---

12 *Inst. Gram.*II, 5.

individually that the plural [of that noun] be said of the same items taken all together. For, although Plato is the brother of one person and Socrates the brother of another, and consequently it is allowed that Plato is a brother and Socrates is a brother, it is not necessary to allow that Plato and Socrates are brothers, i.e. something we say only to indicate that they are brothers to each other. Also, although both this whiteness and that whiteness[13] exist, still we do not say that because of them there are diverse colors, since they are not specifically different colors.

Also suppose there are two people standing by me when I produce the utterance 'human,' and each understands by this 'mortal, rational animal.' Then, certainly the essence of the one person's idea is diverse from the essence of the other person's. Each of those essences is an idea, but we do not speak, therefore, of many ideas, since they do not conceive of diverse items in diverse ways. And even though many nouns and many affirmations coincide in a single utterance, and moreover every affirmation and every noun is an utterance or an essence, still we do not speak on account of that of many utterances or many essences.

* * * *

Moreover, in a single human, or in a single piece of wood or in a single pearl, there are many parts so diverse from each other that the one is not the other, and these parts, when other parts have been cut away or removed, are said to be humans or pieces of wood or pearls. Each of these parts before the cutting away was a human or a piece of wood or a pearl, for our performing the separation does not confer anything substantial on that which remains or on that which has been removed which it did not have before, because, when a hand has been cut off, that which then stays a human was also staying a human before the amputation, although it was hidden as a part in the human who was the whole. Likewise, if a foot is cut off, the remainder is a human, and it was a human even before that amputation, since then too it had the definition of human by the fact that even then it was an animal, since it was animate and sensory, as well as rational and mortal, in the same way as it is

now. Therefore, although before all amputations there were many parts in one human each of which was a human, still there were not for this reason many humans in one human, because we do not speak of many humans unless they live by many souls.

So, if when there are essentially diverse things each of which is an idea or a human, we nevertheless do not for that reason speak of many ideas or many humans, so much the more ought we not to speak of many gods or many substances even though each of the Persons, of whom the essence is completely the same, is God or is a substance. For, although each of the three grammatical persons which are in Socrates is Socrates and is a human – since he who speaks is a human and Socrates, as well as he to whom someone speaks or about whom someone speaks – we do not on account of that speak of three Socrateses or three humans, for the three persons here, i.e. he who speaks, he to whom someone speaks, and he about whom someone speaks, have the same essence. For the same reason, although each of the three Persons who are in God is one essence, is God, or a substance, it is not on this ground necessary to say they are three gods or three substances, because often, as we noted above, utterances vary their signification as a result of items juxtaposed to them, for example, the word 'three' and many others. Certainly we say that the same person is three artisans in virtue of their knowledge of three functions, but we do not as a result say the person is three humans.

* * * *

But here we encounter the greatest obstacle, because the Persons in God seem to be essentially separate from each other, since in fact the one is not the other, which is not so in the case of grammatical persons. To this we must answer that the former Persons are no more separate essentially than are the latter, since of the former as of the latter there is completely one and the same essence. In comparison to this unity, i.e. the unity of the divine essence, we ought not call any corporeal or spiritual creature one, since the former unity in no way admits any diversity or parts or forms and cannot

---

13 Substituting here 'whiteness' ('albedo') for 'color' ('color').

change in any respect. In his *De Trinitate*[14] Boethius says that "that is truly one in which there is no number and nothing in it that is something over and above that which it is."

Thus the philosophers were right when they wanted to call it a monad, i.e. a unity, rather than a "one." But even though there is in the Persons no separateness from each other in essence, still it is not necessary to say, "The Father is the Son, or the Holy Spirit" or "The Son is the Holy Spirit," because, even if someone might be able to attach a valid sense to these words, namely that the same essence which is the Father is also the Son and the Holy Spirit, in the usage of the holy fathers the sense is completely false. It is as though we said that the Person who generates is the Person generated or the Person who proceeds from both. This is to say that both Persons have the same distinguishing feature, so that both Persons are delimited and expressed by the same definition, which is altogether false.

Certainly, although the *status*[15] capable of laughing and the *status* capable of sailing are the same in number and moreover of whatever 'capable of laughing' is said also 'capable of sailing' is said, nevertheless we do not say that the one *status* is the other *status*, i.e. capable of laughing is the same in definition as capable of sailing, since the noun 'capable of laughing' means something other than what the noun 'capable of sailing' means, even though completely the same thing is subject through denotation to both nouns, namely human itself to which both 'capable of laughing' and 'capable of sailing' assign a distinctive item.

Therefore, just because we do not speak of the same or diverse *status* except in respect of an expressed and complete definition or distinguishing feature, it is necessary that, when we say the one *status* is the other, we show that the one thing is completely the same in expressed distinguishing feature with the other. So also in the divine Persons, where the whole diversity looks to their distinguishing features and not to the number of things, the one cannot be said truly to be the other as long as there is some diversity of distinguishing features expressed by nouns diverse in sense, just as happens

in the case of these Persons. 'God the Father' certainly means something; 'God the Son,' something else; and 'God the Holy Spirit,' something else again. God the Father has one distinguishing feature, viz. that he generates God the Son; God the Son has another distinguishing feature, viz. that he is generated by him; and God the Spirit has still another distinguishing feature, viz. that he proceeds.[16]

Thus whoever says of God, "The Father is the Son," does not make a simple assertion, i.e. one which shows merely an identity of essence, as if they had said, "This which is the Father is the Son." Rather they express as well a unity of distinguishing features, as if they said, in fact, that the distinguishing feature of the one is the same as that of the other, which is just as if they had said that the one *status* is the other in all those items which get expressed by nouns diverse in sense. This is altogether false, even though both Persons have the same essence.

* * * *

Let us put before our eyes a waxen image and let us consider in it that very nature of wax, i.e. the waxen substance itself, out of which, according to the philosophers, the image is made as an enmattered item out of matter, even though the same essence is the wax itself and the waxen image, so that the wax and the image can be associated with each other even by predication, and we can say the waxen image is it. But we do not then any the less say that the waxen image is made out of wax, and that the wax is not made out of the waxen image; and the wax itself is the matter of the waxen image, not that the waxen image is the matter of the wax itself or of the waxen image.

Again, we say that the waxen image is enmattered out of the wax itself, but not that the wax or the image is enmattered out of the waxen image. Here we must note that if we take those nouns which are said absolutely and not relatively of the wax and the waxen image, it is permitted that they be joined to each other in a true predication because of the identity of the substance of the wax and the waxen

---

14 *On the Trinity* 2 (see selection V.2.1., p.317-19).
15 See fn. 9 above.
16 For an explanation of the doctrine of the Trinity see introduction to selection V.2.1.

image; for example, when the wax is yellow and the image is straight, it is true[17] that the yellow item is straight, and conversely. But[18] if we take those names which are said relatively to each other in respect of the generation or formation of the wax image from wax – for example, 'matter' and 'the enmattered,' or 'the forming' and 'the formed,' or 'the cause' and 'the effect,' or 'the generating' and 'the generated' – they are not allowed to be associated with each other by predication in respect of their distinguishing features, as when we say here that the matter is the enmattered, or the enmattered is the matter, etc.

* * * *

Thus for the same reason we are not allowed to say that matter is enmattered by itself or the enmattered is its own matter, or the constituent is constituted out of itself or is posterior to itself or generates itself, even though in these cases the matter is essentially the same as the enmattered, for example this bronze is the same as this statue, and the constituent the same as the constituted, and the prior the same as the posterior, and the generating the same as the generated – for an analogous reason, I say, also in the divine Persons the Father is not the Son, i.e. God the Father is not engendered from himself, and neither is the Son the Father, i.e. God the Son is not his own generator. This would be to say that the divine power is from itself or the divine wisdom is from itself. Rather the wisdom is only from itself as that power, as was discussed, just as the image is from the wax. The image is not from itself, nor is the wax from itself or from the image, although the wax is the same as the image just as the Father is the same as the Son, i.e. in respect of substance, not in respect of distinguishing feature or definition. Also the omnipotent God himself is wise, or kind, and conversely. And just as in that [earlier] case that which is matter is that which is enmattered out of it, – for example, the wax is the waxen image and conversely – but that matter is nevertheless not enmattered out of itself nor is the enmattered its own matter, so also in this case that which the Father is that which is the Son, and conversely, but the Father is nevertheless not the Son, nor conversely. Clearly in the one case there is a predication of the substance, as when we say it is that which is enmattered or that which is the Son; but in the other case there is a predication of distinguishing feature, as when we say it is enmattered or is the Son. The substance is the same but the distinguishing features are unmixed.

---

17 Substituting 'true' ('*verum*') for 'one' ('*unum*').
18 Substituting 'but' ('*vero*') for 'true' ('*vera*').

V.4. JOHN DUNS SCOTUS

IN THIS SELECTION SCOTUS ATTEMPTS TO EXPLAIN HOW ITEMS CAN be distinct and yet not distinct in such a way that one could exist without the other. We have here a doctrine of distinction without separability. He defines here two such kinds of distinction, the formal distinction and the adequate distinction. Both are closely related to Aristotle's distinctness in definition or being (see selection V.1.3.). With these Scotus hopes to give a coherent and non-heretical account of the Trinity.

The reader will confront here the view that what distinguishes one Person from another is the presence or absence of a "relation of origin." These relations are simply those of being generated by the Father and proceeding from the Father and the Son. Apparently the Persons are distinguished not by items intrinsic to them, but by their relations to each other — a fairly paradoxical doctrine in itself, but not one questioned here.

V.4.1. Qualified and unqualified Distinctions
(from *Reportata parisiensia* I, dist.33, qu.2.)

Does the simplicity of a divine Person reject every sort of real distinction whatsoever of the items that make up that Person?

[1] It seems that it does not, because it does not violate the simplicity of a Person that that Person has the essence and a relation,[1] and these bear a real distinction since the essence is not the relation nor vice versa.

For Augustine says in *De Trinitate* V, ch.5,[2] that "whatever is said in virtue of the substance is not said in virtue of the relation." Also in *De Trinitate* VII, ch.4,[3] "What is said on account of the relation is not said in virtue of the substance; consequently" etc.

[2] For the opposite view: [Augustine in] *On the Trinity* VI, ch.4[4]: "Thus God is simple because He is whatever He has, with the exception of that to which He is said to bear a relation." But the essence has a relation which is in it, and it does not bear a relation to that. Therefore, the essence is the relative property, and consequently in a Person there will not be a real distinction since in a Person there exists only the essence and the relation.

* * * *

[3] I answer the question, then, by saying that it is consistent with the simplicity of a divine Person that the relation is distinguished from the essence not just by an act of the intellect, as though the relation were nothing, but not that it is also distin-

---

1 The "essence" is God's essence and the relation is a "relation of origin," i.e. one of the relations which distinguish one of the Persons from the others. In the orthodox theology of the day it was held that the first Person of the Trinity, The Father, "begets" the second Person, The Son, and then The Father and The Son together produce the third Person, The Spirit, who is said to "proceed" from the first two Persons. This does not reflect a process that takes place over time, but rather an eternally existent ordering of prior to posterior. Since the Son is the only Person "begotten" by the Father, this relation differentiates Him from the others. Similarly, The Father is the only Person to "beget" something, and The Spirit is the only Person that "proceeds" from both the others. The divine essence, on the other hand, is something common to all the Persons.
2 PL 42, 914.
3 PL 42, 927.
4 PL 42, 927.

guished *ex natura rei*[5] so that the relation is a reality other than the reality of the essence.

But then it seems that the relation is nothing, since from the fact that it is distinguished from the essence not by thought alone and yet is not a reality other than that essence, it seems in no way to be distiguished from it, for between a real being and a being of thought[6] there is no intermediate.

I say that the essence and the relation are distinguished in such a way that before every act of intellect this property is *qualifiedly*[7] distinguished from the essence.

[3.1] But the qualified real distinction of items can be understood in two ways:

[3.1.1] In one way the determination 'qualified' refers to the reality, and in this way the earlier opinions[8] intended the essence and the relation to be *qualifiedly* distinguished, because 'relative reality' does not mean a reality unqualifiedly, rather it means it with the determination of 'relative' added to 'reality,' as says the first opinion. Also the second opinion says that 'relation' means some other mode supervening on the essence; but it is not a mode *unqualifiedly*, rather it is a mode of such a thing. It is not in this way that I claim that the essence and the relation are *qualifiedly* really distinguished. Otherwise, the sense of the claim would be that the distinction of the essence and the relation is a distinction of *qualified* realities, which is absurd because the essence is unqualifiedly a thing since it is formally[9] infinite.

[3.1.2] In another way this determination 'qualifiedly' can be applied to the distinction so that the sense of the claim is that the essence and the relation *ex natura rei*[10] are *qualifiedly* distinguished. In this sense it is true that the distinction of the essence and the relation belongs to an *unqualified* thing and the distinction is *qualified*. How this can be understood I explain as follows: For some items to be *unqualifiedly* distinguished four conditions must be met:

[3.1.2.1] The first is that the distinction be between items that are in actuality and not merely in potentiality, for items which exist potentially in matter are not unqualifiedly distinguished, since they are not in actuality.

[3.1.2.2] The second is that it be between items which have formal being, not just virtual being the way effects are virtually[11] in their cause and do not exist formally.[12]

[3.1.2.3] The third is that it be between items which do not have confused being, as do the extremes in an intermediate mixture;[13] rather it must be of items which have distinct being through their own peculiar actualities.

[3.1.2.4] The fourth condition, which by itself is sufficient to render a distinction complete, is that the distinction is a non-identity, as is evident through the Philosopher, *Metaphysics* V, ch.9,[14] where he says 'diverse' and 'distinct' are [opposed to][15] 'same.'

---

5 Literally: "from the nature of the thing." Scotus means that the distinction is there in the real world independently of thought about the items distinguished.
6 See glossary entry for 'being of thought.'
7 See glossary entry for 'qualified/unqualified.' Scotus tries in this selection to apply such a contrast to the predicates 'is distinct' and 'is the same.'
8 The views mentioned here have not been included in this selection.
9 The expression 'formally' is used here to rule out being infinite merely by real identity with something infinite. In general something is "formally" X when it possesses X-ness as its own property and is not X merely by some relation to something else that genuinely possesses X-ness.
10 See fn. 5.
11 X is "virtually" P just in case X can cause something to be P. See glossary entry for 'virtual existence.'
12 I.e., has its own real existence.
13 A mixture whose own properties are a sort of mean between those of its constituents.
14 1018a11.
15 The Latin text seems faulty at this point.

[3.1.3] Those items, then, are completely distinguished which in virtue of their actual, distinctive, and determinate being are not the same unqualifiedly. Those items are qualifiedly distinguished which do not have non-identity unqualifiedly but only a qualified non-identity. Further, the diversity we get when all of the first three conditions are met but identity is preserved is a qualified distinction.

[3.2] Now, the essence and the relation meet the first three conditions for they have neither potential, nor virtual, nor confused [being], but rather actual, formal, distinctive, and determinate [being], since the essence is as completely in accord with all of the first three conditions as it would be if nothing were there but it, and likewise paternity[16] is as completely there as it would be if nothing else were there besides it. Nevertheless, they do not meet the fourth condition, which is sufficient for complete distinction, i.e. non-identity, because they do not have unqualified non-identity, but only a qualified non-identity, which accords with the first three conditions, since so far as those three conditions are concerned they are distinguished. For they are unqualifiedly the same, since one of them, namely the essence, is formally infinite, but the infinite is the same as any being compatible with it. To be in some way completed, or actualized, is rejected by this [infinite] being, because if some other perfection were added to it, this further item would be compatible with it and consequently it would not be unqualifiedly infinite. But the relation of origin is compatible with it, since it comes out of its abundance, as was clear above.[17] Therefore, the relation is the same as it by a most complete identity, as if it were in no way distinguished from it, and thus their non-identity is only a qualified one, and consequently their distinction is a qualified non-identity.

Moreover, the distinction of the essence and the relation can be called a distinction *ex natura rei*[18] because they have a qualified non-identity just as if *ex natura rei* each had its own peculiar actual and determinate existence without the other.

[3.3] But how can there be a qualified non-identity of the essence and the relation? I answer that in this case there are two sorts of non-identity – formal non-identity and adequate non-identity – and each is a qualified non-identity, because they can exist at the same time with unqualified identity. For the essence and the relation have the first sort of non-identity, i.e. formal non-identity, since the relation is not formally the essence nor vice versa. Items are said not to have formal identity when one does not belong to the essential-in-the-first-mode[19] concept of the other, in the way a definition or the parts of a definition belong to the concept of what is defined, but rather neither is included in the formal character of the other, even though they are really the same. It is just in this way that being and one are said to be the same in *Metaphysics* IV, ch.2,[20] for the formal character of being does not belong to the essential concept of one, since one is an attribute[21] of it, and an attribute does not belong to the formal concept of its subject, and yet they are really the same, as The Philosopher and Commentator show in that same place. But now if the essence and the relation in God were defined, neither would fall into the definition of the other, except as something added. Therefore, the essence does not belong to the formal concept of paternity, nor vice versa. Rather they differ formally and have a formal, quidditative[22] non-identity. Also the formal character of the essence is [an absolute being while that of paternity is] a directed-toward-something-else being,[23] which beings differ quidditatively, and yet it does not follow from this formal non-identity that one is not unqualifiedly the same as

---

16 I.e., the distinctive feature of the Father.

17 In a previous question not included in this selection.

18 See fn. 5.

19 See glossary entry for 'essential-in-the-first-mode.' An "essential-in-the-first-mode concept" is the concept definitive of what it is the concept of.

20 1003b23.

21 See glossary entry for 'attribute.'

22 I.e., in respect of what it is to be them. '*Quid*' in Latin means 'what?' See glossary entry for 'quiddity.'

23 Because it is a relation, namely the relation of "begetting" the Son.

the other. This is evident in the case of being and its attributes,[24] and also in the case under discussion on account of the infinity of one of the two terms.

Further, the essence and the property are not the same by an adequate identity, which belongs to items neither of which goes beyond the other; rather each is exactly the other, neither more nor less, as in the case of a definition and what is defined. Items are said to be the same by a non-adequate identity where one of them goes beyond the other, or the unity of the one goes beyond the unity of the other, as is the case with animal in relation to human. But the essence and the property are not adequately the same, because one does go beyond the other and vice versa. But the going beyond of one in respect of the other, and thus the term 'non-adequately,' can be understood in two ways:

[3.3.1] In respect of predication and non-convertibility,[25] and in this way animal and human are inadequately the same, because animal is predicated of more items than human is.

[3.3.2] In respect of power and perfection,[26] and in this way human goes beyond animal, and form goes beyond matter.[27]

Property transcends the essence in the first way, because it is predicated formally of more items than the essence is. For, according to Damascene[28] in book I, ch.4,[29] of *De Fide Orthodoxa*, the essence is only common to the three Persons by a real commonness; but property, as we showed earlier, in as much as it is abstracted from any one of the three properties, viz. paternity, filiation, and procession, is common to them by a conceptual commonness, and is predicated of them formally and *in quid*.[30]

Thus property is not adequately the same as the essence in respect of predication. But conversely the essence goes beyond property in respect of power and perfection. It is clear, then, that the essence goes beyond the property, because it is formally infinite while the property is not, since it [i.e. the property] is not the same as it [i.e. the essence] by an adequate identity. But this does not prevent their being able to be unqualifiedly and absolutely the same.

In creatures we find that some of them are unqualifiedly the same but not by an adequate identity. For although a faculty of the soul is unqualifiedly the same as the soul itself in which it exists, it is not adequately the same as it, because it is not the whole soul in respect of its faculties; otherwise one faculty would be based in some other faculty, for example the intellect in the will, just as it is based in the soul's essence.

Also if it were not the case that many items which are not adequately the same are unqualifiedly the same, it would follow that an accidental form like whiteness would be really composite. For if the character of color, from which we get the generic[31] character, were some reality other than that from which we get the character of the specific difference[32] of whiteness, then whiteness would be composed from two realities, which is generally denied. Therefore, in whiteness these two are one reality, and yet neither is adequately the essential reality of whiteness, otherwise one or the other would be superfluous. Thus this color in whiteness and in blackness is of the same character, and is not adequately whiteness nor blackness; as having the same character it precedes both differences, because the individuals do not belong to a genus of a different character. Nevertheless, the differences

---

24 In scholastic metaphysics *being* was considered to have at least these three attributes necessarily co-extensive with it: *one, true, good.*

25 Terms are "convertible" when they are necessarily mutually co-extensive.

26 "Perfection" involves fullness of being, so that the more properties a term implies of anything it is said of the more perfection it would indicate as belonging to that thing. See glossary entry for 'perfection.'

27 See glossary entry for 'form/matter.'

28 St. John Damascene (c.a.675-749), a Greek theologian who led the Christian community in Damascus in the early eighth century when the city had already fallen under Islamic control. He is one of Scotus's favorite patristic authorities.

29 Actually ch.8.

30 I.e., in respect of what (*quid*) they are.

31 See glossary entry for 'species/genus.'

32 See glossary entry for 'specific difference.'

of the species, i.e. of whiteness and of blackness, are of a different character.

[3.4] From what we have said certain corollaries follow:

[3.4.1] From the fact that because the property persists in the Person as having its own formal character also the essence persists in the formal character of the essence, and vice versa, it follows that each possesses what is implied by its own formal character; for example, the essence has directed-toward-itself being, while the relation has directed-toward-something-else being.

[3.4.2] Again, since there is not a formal identity of the essence to the relation, nor vice versa, it is not then required that whatever formally belongs to one belongs to the other. For example, if the Father unqualifiedly relates to the Son, it is not required that it [so] relate as the essence.

[3.4.3] Again, because the essence and the property are not adequately the same, it is not required that one property be the same as another, even though they are the same as the essence. This is because when two items are related to something in virtue of its unlimited being in respect of them and yet those related items are not that something adequately, it is not then required that those two are the same as each other even though they are the same as the third. An example: God is here with someone and God is at Rome with that person who is there, but this person who is here and he who is at Rome are not together with each other. Similarly, God is now with Socrates, who exists now, and will be simultaneously with the future Antichrist; therefore, it follows that the future and the past will be together with[33] each other. But the past and the future are not together with each other. So it is in what we are discussing. The divine essence is formally infinite; therefore, it is not necessary, if one property is the same as the essence and another one is likewise, that on account of this they are the same as each other, since the cause of

their identity is absolutely taken away from the third item.

[3.5] Augustine in *De Trinitate* VII, ch.3, toward the end,[34] agrees with what we have said: "Every nature which is spoken of as relative is something besides relative." And on account of this he infers toward the beginning of ch.3: "On account of this, if the Father is not something directed-toward-itself it is not completely the case that it is spoken of as relative to something else." And this holds not just on account of an act of thinking. Therefore, over and above all operation of an intellect, in addition to the relation it bears, it is something directed-toward-itself. Again, in the same place: "Not on account of this is the Word wise, but rather on account of this the Word is God by identity." Therefore, the Word is not formally God or wisdom, because on this approach they are distinguished by their formal characters.

[3.6] For here is the ordering of unities in God:

[3.6.1] First there is the unity of the essence.

[3.6.2] After this unity come the formal distinction of essence and property, which is a unity of identity. And this distinction is such that some distinction of thought can precede it, but it is not presupposed by the distinction of essence and property, because a distinction which is *ex natura rei*[35] or real never necessarily presupposes a distinction of thought, just as also a real unity does not presuppose a unity of thought.

[3.6.3] After the *qualified* or formal distinction of essence and relation, comes the distinction of the Persons, which necessarily presupposes the distinction *ex natura rei* of essence and property, because, since the essence and property constitute the Person as real, if they were not in some way really distinguished, as was said, the Person would only be a being of thought. This distinction, moreover, of the property from the essence is qualified and *ex natura rei*, as we said. The expression 'qualified'

---

33 Instead of 'be together with' the Vives text mistakenly has 'be the same as.'
34 Actually ch.1 (PL 42, 935).
35 See fn. 5.

does not indicate an imperfection, because it says that that has a distinction or a qualified non-identity on account of the infinity of one of the two terms. For if one were unqualifiedly distinguished from the other, neither would be unqualifiedly infinite, because the infinity of one of the terms takes away the non-identity and unqualified distinction of those items. This is the case, then, because the infinity is not adequate, not even in respect of predication, as was clear earlier.

[4. Responses to the original arguments:]

[4.1] To the first [1] the response is clear from what has been said. When it is said: "Whatever is said in virtue of the substance is not said in virtue of the relation," I say that the phrase 'in virtue of' indicates essentiality-in-the-first-mode, because what is of itself merely absolute indicates no relation in virtue of its own formal thought. Augustine understands that 'what is in virtue of substance does not indicate a relation' is true in such a way that it means that the one does not belong to the formal concept of the other in the first mode. Thus they are formally, and qualifiedly, distinguished; but they are not unqualifiedly distinguished, on account of the infinity of one of the two terms, a term which is the same as anything compossible with it.

[4.2] To the authoritative text from Augustine that argues the opposite [2], the response is clear, viz. that God on account of his simplicity is whatever he has, excepting that to which he is said to be related by a most true identity, but not adequately and formally, as was clear earlier. For although human and animal are the same by a most true identity, they are not the same adequately and formally, because the character of human is drawn from the specific difference, i.e. from rationality, while the character of animal is drawn from the sensitive soul. This same point is clear too in the case of being and one, whiteness and color, where a true identity co-exists with the formal distinction, although it is not an adequate identity either in respect of convertibility or in respect of power and perfection.

V.5. WILLIAM OF OCKHAM

V.5.1. No Formal Distinction without Real Distinction (from his *Ordinatio* I, distinction ii, qu.3)

[This selection is part of Ockham's extended critique of Scotus's position on the reality of universals (see selections **VI.8.1-2.**). Scotus maintained that in an individual member of a species there were entities corresponding, on the one hand, to its common nature and, on the other hand, to what differentiated it as an individual distinct from the other individuals in that species, i.e. its individuating or "contracting" difference. These entities, he maintained were formally distinct but not absolutely really distinct, although the formal distinction exists in the things themselves independently of any thought of them (*ex natura rei*). Here Ockham argues that such a distinction makes no sense.]

[1] It is this Doctor's[1] intention that besides numerical unity[2] there is a real unity less than numerical unity, which belongs to this nature which is in some way universal. Thus the contractible nature can first be compared to the singular itself, secondly to numerical unity, thirdly to universal being, and fourthly to the unity less than numerical unity.

If it is compared to the singular itself, he then proposes this opinion, that the nature is not of itself *this* but rather is *this* through something added. And secondly he proposes that the added factor is not a negation (qu.2)[3], nor is it some accident (qu.3), nor actual existence (qu.4), nor matter (qu.5). Thirdly, that the added factor is in the genus

of substance and is intrinsic to the individual. Fourthly, that the nature is naturally prior to the contracting factor.

Thus he says:[4] "Every partial or total entity belonging to a genus is of itself indifferent to that entity or to that, in such a way that as a quidditative[5] entity it is naturally prior to that entity as it is *this*. And, since it is naturally prior, just as being *this* does not belong to it of itself so it does not in virtue of its own character reject its opposite. Also, just as a composite does not include that entity by which it is *this* composite, so matter in so far as it is matter does not include the entity by which it is *this* matter; the same holds for form.[6] Therefore, this entity is neither matter nor form nor the composite in so far as any of these is a nature. Rather it is the ultimate reality of the being which is the matter, and of the being which is the form, and of the being which is the composite. In just the way that any common but determinable item, however much it is a single thing, can still be distinguished into several formally distinct realities, of which one is not formally the other, so here the one is formally the entity of the singular and the other is formally the entity of the common nature. Neither can these entities be a thing and a thing, as can the reality from which we take the genus and the reality from which we take the difference and from both of which sometimes is taken the specific reality. Rather in the same item (whether in a part of it or the whole of it) there are always formally distinct realities belonging to the same thing."

---

1 I.e., John Duns Scotus's.

2 I.e., the unity of an individual which keeps it from being common to other individuals. See selection **V.1.1.**

3 The references here are to Scotus's *Ordinatio* II, dist. 3. qus. 1-6. Portions of qus. 1 and 6 are found in selections **VI.8.1-2.**

4 See selection **VI.8.2.**, [5.] .

5 See glossary entry for 'quiddity.'

6 See glossary entry for 'form/matter.'

* * *

[2] We can argue against this opinion in two ways:

[2.1] First, it is impossible in creatures for some items to differ formally without being really distinguished. Therefore, if the nature is in some way distinguished from the contracting difference, they must be distinguished either as a thing and a thing, or as a being of thought[7] and a being of thought, or as a real being and a being of thought. But he himself denies the first, and likewise the second. Therefore, we are left with the third; therefore, the nature which is in some way or other distinguished from the individual is only a being of thought.

The antecedent is clear, because if the nature and that contracting difference are not the same in every way, something can be truly affirmed of the one but denied of the other. But in creatures the same item cannot be both truly affirmed and truly denied of the same thing. Therefore, they are not one thing.

The minor premiss is evident because, if it were not true, every way of proving a distinction of things in creatures would fail, since contradiction is the most powerful way of proving a distinction of things. Thus if in creatures completely the same item can be truly denied and truly affirmed of the same thing (or of the same item standing for the same thing), no real distinction can be proved to exist in them. This is confirmed because all contradictories equally reject each other. But the rejection between being and not-being is so great that, if A is and B is not, it follows that B is not A. Therefore, it is the same for any contradictories whatsoever.

If someone says: Of primary contradictories it is true that they happen to prove real non-identity, but this does not occur with other contradictories –

Against: A syllogistic form holds equally in all subject matters; therefore, this is a good syllogism:[8]

Every A is B

C is not B

Therefore, C is not A.

Consequently it is just as true of A and not-A that if this is A and this is not A, then this is not this, as it is true that if this is and this is not, this is not this. Therefore, it is likewise in the proposed case: if every individual difference is of itself peculiar to some individual and the nature is not of itself peculiar to some individual, it follows that the nature is not the individual difference, and this holds really.

If someone says that this argument is invalid because the divine essence is the Son, the Father is not the Son, but yet the Father is the essence –

This answer is insufficient because just as it is an exception that in God three things are a thing one in number so that the thing one in number is each of those three things and yet any one of those three is not the other, so it is an exception beyond all understanding that this does not follow: The essence that is one in number is the Son; the Father is not the Son; therefore, the Father is not the essence. Thus this exception should be posited only where the authority of sacred scriptures requires it. Thus this sort of consequence ought never to be denied in creatures because there no authority of sacred scriptures requires it, since in creatures there is no single thing that many things are in the sense that each of them is it.

If someone says that an inference of this sort is good if both premisses are taken without any determination, and then it rightly follows:

Every individual difference is peculiar to some individual.

The nature is not peculiar.

Therefore, the nature is not really the individual difference.

But then the minor is false. Such an inference does not hold universally if it is taken exclusively under some definite syncategorematic[9] determination, like 'of itself' and 'through itself.'

---

7 See glossary entry for 'being of thought.'
8 See glossary entry 'syllogism.'
9 See glossary entry for 'syncategorematic term.'
10 See glossary entry for 'categorical proposition.'
11 Modal adverbs are words like 'necessarily' or 'possibly' which modify the connection between subject and predicate. A modal proposition is one where such an adverb is operative.

This reply is invalid, because just as both in categorical[10] and in modal[11] propositions there is a uniform syllogistic form – and likewise there is a syllogistic form that is mixed from these – so there are uniform and mixed syllogistic forms for propositions taken with other syncategorematic determinations, for example 'through itself,' 'in so far as,' and the like. Consequently, there is just as much a syllogistic form in this case:

Every human being is *per se* an animal.

No stone is *per se* an animal.

Therefore, no stone is *per se* a human being, and consequently in general no stone is a human being.

as there is in this case:

Every animal is of necessity a substance.

No accident is of necessity a substance.

Therefore, no accident is of necessity an animal.

Likewise here is a good mixed syllogism:

Every human being is *per se* an animal.

No white item is an animal.

Therefore, no white is a human being.

Therefore, in the same way this will be a good syllogism:

Every individual difference is *per se* peculiar to some individual.

The nature is not *per se* peculiar.

Therefore, the nature is not an individual difference.

And likewise this will be a good syllogism:

No individual difference is really common.

The nature is really common.

Therefore, the nature is not really the individual difference.

And since the premises are true so will the conclusion be true.

This is bolstered by the fact that just as always from propositions in the mode of necessity follows a categorical conclusion, so from propositions with the mark of *per-se*ness follows a categorical conclusion. This is because '*per se*' means 'necessary.' Therefore, just as this follows formally and syllogistically:

The nature necessarily is communicable.

The contracting difference necessarily is not communicable.

Therefore, the contracting difference is not the nature.

so also this follows:

The nature is *per se* communicable to many.

The contracting difference is not *per se* communicable to many.

Therefore, the contracting difference is not the nature.

Neither is it valid to say that the conclusion is true, i.e. that the contracting difference is not the nature although it is not really distinguished from it, because this follows: They are not distinguished really and both are things; therefore, they are really the same and so one is really the other, and further one is the other. Consequently, the predication of one of the other is true. The next to last consequence holds because 'really' is neither a subtracting nor a diminishing determination, just as neither is 'formally,' and consequently to infer from something taken with that determination something taken on its own is a formal consequence according to the Philosopher's rule in *Peri Hermenias* II.

The whole preceding argument is bolstered, for

just as this syllogism is governed by the rule of "*dici de nullo*" – [12]

No difference is common.

The nature is common.

Therefore, the nature is not a difference.

so also this is governed by the rule of "*dici de nullo*":

No difference is *per se* common.

The nature is *per se* common.

Therefore, the nature is not a difference.

---

12 The rule of "*dici de nullo*" is just simply that a universal negative proposition is true if and only if "the predicate is removed from everything of which the subject is said," to use Ockham's own words in his *Summa Logicae*.

TOPIC VI:

UNIVERSALS AND PARTICULARS

TOPIC VI

UNIVERSALS AND PARTICULARS

AN ANCIENT VIEW NOURISHED THE DIALECTICAL SKILLS OF MEDIEVAL thinkers. The view is that both particulars, such as this horse and that dog, and also universals, such as the species horse and the species dog, exist and are real. This ancient view tended to be accompanied by the thesis that particulars are objects of perception and that universals are objects of knowledge. Universals are what science is all about. Such a package of related views can be found in the dialogues of Plato and in the works of Aristotle.

A view which posits the extra-mental existence of universals is called *realist*; the view which denies this existence for universals in favour of the existence of particulars is called *nominalist*. The dominant view of both the ancient and the medieval worlds tended to posit the existence of universals; the questions which attracted close attention are how they exist and how they are related to particulars. It seems to have been Plato's view that universals (or Forms or Ideas, as they are called in various dialogues) are distinct and separable from particulars. A particular shares or participates in a universal and thereby acquires a nature and characteristics.

Plato's view led to difficulties which Aristotle was by no means reticent to explore. In order to escape some of the difficulties Aristotle seems prepared to make universals dependent upon particulars for their existence. In other places, Aristotle writes as though universals do not exist outside the soul.

In the dialogue *Timaios* Plato presents a view, through the mouth of a Pythagorean, that the Demiurge, the creator of the world, looked to Forms in fashioning a spatial, temporal world. The view posits two things which would not be acceptable to theologians of the three revealed religions. The first is that the Forms are eternal and external to the creator; the second is the eternity of matter out of which a creator creates. In terms of Aristotle's Four Causes, discussed in Topic I, this means that two of the four causes are independent of the creator. Such a view is evidently inconsistent with a posit of God's omnipotence. We shall return to the synthesis between the Greek and religious traditions in a moment.

On the path to his Christian conversion Augustine accepted a ride from the Platonist or neo-Platonist vehicle of dialectical reasoning; this reasoning affirms the primal reality and knowability of universals and especially of number. Universals, after all, are what science is all about. Regarding their knowability there are three orders of argumentation: the first order concerns universals; the second order concerns things purely in time, and the third concerns things in time and in space. Put differently, the first order of argumentation concerns the existence and the nature of universals; the second concerns the existence and nature of temporal individuals, and the third concerns material objects.

The first two orders of arguments have commonly been taken to reach the highest degree of certainty and necessity. For example, it is easiest to prove the existence of certain universals such as Truth and Existence. Thomas Aquinas records one of the shortest and most compelling proofs concerning a universal: Truth exists; if not, this is true, that there is no truth; but then what is true would not be true. Since this is impossible, Truth necessarily exists. It should be equally easy to prove the necessary existence of Existence itself, as Avicenna tries to do. A proof parallel to that just given for Truth would be: if Existence did not exist, there would be something which Existence is not, namely Existence. But Existence cannot possibly fail to be itself; therefore, Existence exists. And in the first part of his *Proslogion* Anselm tries a short and economical proof of the existence of Goodness (for an introduction to this proof and the proof itself please see Topic II). It stands to reason that the closer the universals are to enabling the discourse of reason, the shorter the proofs; for how long can the life of discourse be in doubt when the doubter is actually doubting? Long before Descartes in the 17th century, St. Augustine, in the 5th century, argues that the doubter, in doubting, knows of his own existence.

The next set of proofs which admit of certainty concern Time and some things in time: especially things which exist in the Now and are immediately present to the mind. It was suggested above that the soul doubting its own existence in the Now discovers the doubter's contradiction and can therefore assert its own existence.

The third and last set of arguments concern spatial, temporal things. Just how and why the provability of their existence and nature became doubtful, is a question to be taken up in Topic VII on skepticism. We return to the question of the synthesis between religion and philosophy.

Plato sometimes writes as though Forms exist neither in time nor in space. Perhaps for this reason Aristotle thought that a Form could not be an efficient cause. Plato's *Timaios* evidently thinks so too; for the creator looks to formal causes for doing the best he can in creating a world, like a painter who paints well but whose painting is not as beautiful as his model is who presents herself in eternal light.

We remarked above that the *Timaios* view is inconsistent with a posit of God's omnipotence. For how could God be omnipotent if God relies upon matter for the creation of a world and upon Forms for giving the world shape and form? The question is answered in the negative; further, steps are taken to forestall the question and its difficulties: God creates matter out of nothing.

And what of the great universals such as Goodness, Truth, and Existence, as well as the Cardinal Virtues Wisdom, Courage, Moderation, and Justice? A jealous God would clear the skies of any co-eternal entities, particularly those offering the formal cause of goodness, truth, being, wisdom, and justice. But if God makes them His own, like a Greek god devouring the children of his competitor, does God pass outside Time or are the universals rather brought inside Time? Answering this question calls for the brilliant negotiation between the partners in the marriage. The terms of synthesis are not liberal: there can be only one master in the house; only one reality at home.

Looking back at the terms of synthesis it becomes clear that the language of universals is preserved; several of the names of universals become the names of the resident power and reality. The names of the universals are in effect appended, like conquered titles, to the Lord and Master: God in Heaven, Goodness, Truth, Being, Justice, Wisdom.

Many of the old names remain in dialectical use. When dialectic has finished its course of reasoning and has concluded that Truth necessarily exists, the name *Truth*, excusing itself from further philosophical duty, leaves the stage and allows the true owner of the name to show Himself: God. Ancient philosophical dialectic has become a stage mask; when it has played its old play, the mask may be lifted and put down; pure light shines behind it.

Here are three examples of what we mean to suggest by the idea of re-assigning names in creating the philosophical masks of God; the first example comes from St. Augustine's *The City of God*; the second, from Anselm's *Proslogion*, and the third from Aquinas's *Summa Theologica*. Augustine writes:

> There is then one sole good, which is simple, and therefore unchangeable; and that is God. By this Good all good things were created; but they are not simple, and for that reason they are changeable. They are, I say, created, that is to say, they are made, not begotten. For what is begotten by the simple Good is itself equally simple, identical in nature with its begetter: and these two, the begetter and the begotten, we call the Father and the Son; and these two, with their Spirit, are one God. (Book XI, Chapter 5)

The second example comes from Anselm's famous ontological proof [selection **II.1.1**]: having shown the necessity of that than which nothing greater can be conceived Anselm removes the philosophical mask: "Something than which a greater cannot be thought exists so truly then that it cannot be even thought not to exist; and You, Lord our God, are this being."

And the third example comes from the Five Ways of Aquinas [selection **II.4.2**]: having concluded that it is necessary to arrive at a first mover, moved by no other, Aquinas further says, "And this everyone understands to be God."

What then is the effect of using the old names? Can one have the names of such powerful parts of the language of reason without being avenged for the theft and the deception of the mask? If God is to be a creator, God must be in time; and yet, if God is Goodness or Being or Wisdom or Justice or all of them melted down into one, it would seem that God is not in time. Of course, it would not do to bite the bullet and to say that God is both in time and not in time.

Such difficulties were to be resolved by placing God in time, but in a special way. The details of resolving difficulties in this way are explored in another section (Topic III); they are mentioned now only in the context of outlining the changes in the fortunes of a theory of universals. And one further matter before charting the fate of universals. In contemplating his sins in *The Confessions* Augustine could hardly avoid entering upon a profound meditation - or perhaps rather conversation with God about Time [selection III.2.1.]. Is God Time itself, Goodness, and Being? Augustine does not make the suggestion, to be sure; his meditation is nevertheless a force for placing time as firmly in Mind as the great universals are identified with God. But for God Time is the Now; from within that Now all things in time are somehow beheld. (For a brilliant discussion of this please see John Duns Scotus in Topic IV.)

To say that universals are in the mind of God as ideas, is really to set aside a realist theory of universals (eternal, outside time and space, and independent of mind) and to take up a conceptualist theory.

The ancient Greek legacy, combined with theology, was certainly confusing and would naturally have invited a thinker with the power, for example, of Abelard to think the whole project of universality through again. An emerging nominalist view, like Abelard's, brings in its wake a re-thinking of the nature of human knowledge and a close study of grammar and syntax. For if universality is to be accounted for by language, it falls to the nominalist philosopher to account for the possibility of *predication*: How is generality possible? How is it possible to say the same thing of many things? The study of grammar is given new depth and power and naturally overlaps with the study of logic.

Many of the selections to follow are concerned with the status of genus and species. The sciences of nature evidently require clear understanding of them. A remarkable development in the thought of Abelard is to account for universality in the use of language and not necessarily by looking to universals which exist independently of thought and language. For example, in selection VI.6.1. Abelard remarks "Universals in a way signify diverse things by naming, not by establishing an idea that arises from them but one that pertains to individuals. Thus this expression 'human being' both names individuals on account of a common cause, viz. that they are human beings, and for this reason it is said to be universal, and establishes a certain common idea pertaining to the individuals of which it grasps a common similarity."

The following selections explore this project.

VI.1. PLATO

In the following selection – from Plato's dialogue *Timaios* – Plato has a Pythagorean character Timaios account for the world; the creator of the world looks to eternal forms for doing the best he can in creating a fine world. In terms of Aristotle's Four Causes we can say that three of the causes of the world are external to the creator: matter, as material cause; form, as formal cause, and goodness, as final cause. The creator is therefore an efficient cause. This picture of a creator as limited in at least three ways is dissolved in the course of medieval philosophy.

The *Timaios* was one of the few Platonic works available in the West during the middle ages. The cosmological vision recorded there captured the imagination of both ancient and medieval thinkers. It provided a way of seeing the physical world as an imperfect copy of something non-physical, namely its eternal pattern or archetype. Rational thought should, then, strive to form some notion of this archetype if it is truly to understand why things are the way they are. Plato talks here only of the archetype for the world as a whole, but he himself in other places, as well as many of his followers, referred to Forms for all the various types of things that there are. Things in the physical world are instances of types that reflect such Forms. Scientific classification should try to bring itself into congruence with this pre-ordained discussion of things. Few thinkers in the middle ages entirely escaped the assumption implied by this vision.

VI.1.1. A World based on Archetypes (from the *Timaios* 27-39; 51-52)

THE DISCOURSE OF TIMAIOS

Prelude: Nature and Scope of Physics

TIMAIOS. That, Socrates, is what all do who have a grain of sense: always, at the start of any undertaking, great or small, they call upon a god. We here are about to discourse on the universe and describe how (if at all) it began to exist; so unless we are completely out of our minds we too must invoke gods and goddesses, praying that all we say may be pleasing to them and in consequence satisfactory to ourselves. Let that then be sufficient invocation of the deities; the appeal to our own powers must be that you may most readily learn and I may most clearly expound my views on the subject before us.

In the first place, I think, we must draw the following distinction: What is that which is always real and has no becoming, and what is that which is always becoming and is never real? That which is apprehensible by thought with a rational account is the thing that is always unchangeably real; whereas that which is the object of belief together with irrational sensation is the thing that becomes and passes away, but never has real being. Again, everything that becomes must of necessity do so by the agency of some cause; without a cause nothing can come to be. Whenever the maker of an object looks to that which is always unchanging and uses a model of that kind in fashioning the form and quality of his work, all that he thus accomplishes must be good; but if his eyes are set upon something that has come into existence and uses a generated model, the object thus fashioned will not be good. So as regards the whole Heaven or World – let us call it by whatever name fits it best – we must begin by asking that fundamental question which has to be asked about everything: Has it always existed, without any source of becoming; or has it come to be, starting from some principle? It has come to be; for it is visible and tangible and possessed of a body, and all such things are sensible; and sensibles, being apprehended by belief with the aid of sensation, are, as we saw, things that become and can be generated. And that which becomes, we said, must necessarily do so by the agency of some cause. To discover the maker and father of this universe would be hard enough; and having discovered him, it would be absolutely impossible to declare him to all men. Let us, however, go back to that question about the world: After which of the models did its artificer construct it – after that which is always in the same unchanging state, or after that which has come to be? Well, if this world is good and its maker is good, evidently he looked to the eternal; but if otherwise (an impious hypothesis), his eyes were upon that which has come to be. It is clear to everyone then that he looked to the eternal; for the world is the best of all things which have become, and he the best of all causes. So having come to be in this way, the world has been constructed on the model of that which is apprehensible by rational discourse and understanding and is always in the same state.

Further, on the strength of these premises the world must inevitably be a likeness of something. Now no matter with what subject we have to deal, it is most important to begin at the natural beginning. Therefore in dealing with a copy and its model we must make this distinction: an account is of the same order as the things it expounds – an account of what is abiding and stable and discoverable by reason will itself be abiding and unchangeable in so far as it is possible for an account to be incontrovertible and irrefutable; it must never fall short of that; while an account of what is fashioned after the likeness of that other, but is only a likeness, will itself be likely, standing to accounts of the former kind in a proportion – as truth is to belief so is reality to becoming. Therefore, Socrates, do not be surprised if in dealing with a great many matters touching the gods and the generation of the universe we prove unable to supply accounts that are always in all respects self-consistent and perfectly exact. We ought indeed to be only too glad if we manage to provide accounts that are inferior to none in likelihood, remembering that both I who speak and you who judge are merely human creatures, so that it behooves us to be content with the probable account and refrain from seeking beyond it.

SOCRATES. Excellent, Timaios! Of course we must accept it as you suggest; we have certainly listened to your prelude with admiration. So now please go right ahead and develop your main theme.

The Works of Reason

Motive of Creation (29D-30C)

TIM. Let us then state for what reason becoming and the universe were framed by their constructor. He was good; and in the good no jealousy in respect of anything ever arises. Being devoid of jealousy, therefore, he desired that all things should approach as near as possible to being like himself. We shall most surely be right in accepting from men of understanding that this is the supremely valid principle of becoming and of world order. Desiring then that all things should be good and, so far as possible, nothing incomplete, the god took over all that is visible – not at rest, but in discordant and chaotic motion – and brought it from disorder into order, deeming that the latter state was in every way the better.

Now it was not, nor can it ever be, conceivable that the supremely good should do anything but what is best. Taking thought, therefore, he found that among things that are by nature visible none that is without intelligence will ever be better than one that is rational, when each is taken as a whole, and further that intelligence cannot be present in anything other than soul. Because of this reasoning, when he constructed the universe he fashioned reason within soul and soul within body, to the end that the work he was accomplishing might be of its nature as excellent and perfect as possible. Thus then, in accordance with the likely account, we must declare that this world came to be, by the god's providence, in very truth a living creature endowed with soul and reason.

The Model Used by the Demiurge (30C-31A)

This being premised, we must now ask the following question: What was the living creature in whose likeness he constructed the world? We cannot allow that it was any that ranks only as a species; for no copy of that which is incomplete can ever be good. Let us rather say that the world resembles most closely that Living Creature of which all other living creatures, severally and in their families are parts. For that embraces and contains within itself all the intelligible living creatures, just as this world contains ourselves and all other creatures that have been fashioned as visible things. For the god, desiring to make it most closely resemble that intelligible thing that is best and in all respects complete, constructed it as a single visible living creature, containing within itself all living things whose nature is of the same order.

Only One World (31A-B)

Have we, then, been correct in calling it one Heaven, or would we have spoken more truly of many and indeed of an infinite number? One it must be called, if we are to hold that it was made according to its pattern. For that which embraces all the intelligible living creatures there are, could never be one of a pair, because then there would have to be yet another Living Creature embracing them both, and they would be parts of it; and thus our universe would be more correctly described as a likeness, not of them, but of that other which would embrace them. Therefore, in order that this world might resemble the complete Living Creature in respect of its uniqueness, its maker did not fashion two worlds nor an indefinite number. No, this Heaven has come to be and is and shall be hereafter one and unique.

Body of the World

It Consists of Four Primary Bodies (31B-32C)

Now that which comes to be must be corporeal, and therefore visible and tangible; but nothing can be visible without fire, or tangible without something solid, and nothing is solid without earth. Hence the god, when he began to construct the body of the universe, set about making it of fire and earth. Two things alone, however, cannot be properly conjoined without a third; for there must be some bond between then tying them together. Now the best of all bonds is that which makes itself and the things it conjoins a unity in the fullest sense; and it is of the nature of a continued geometrical proportion to effect this most perfectly.

For whenever, of three numbers, [32] the middle one between any two that are either cubes or squares is such that, as the first is to it, so is it to the last, and conversely as the last is to the middle, so is the middle to the first, then since the middle becomes first and last, while the last and first become middle, it follows that all will come to play the same part in relation to one another, and will thereby all form a unity.

Now if it had been required that the body of the universe should be a plane surface with no depth, a single mean would have sufficed to connect its fellows and itself; in fact, however, the world was to be solid in form, and solids are always conjoined not by one mean, but by two. Accordingly the god set water and air between fire and earth, and made them so far as possible proportional to one another, so that as fire is to air, so is air to water, and as air is to water, so is water to earth; and thus he constructed the frame of a world visible and tangible.

For these reasons and from such elements, four in number, the body of the universe was brought into being, coming into concord by means of proportion; and from these it acquired Amity, so that coming into unity it became indissoluble by any agent other than him who bound it together.

It Contains the Whole of Those Four Elements (32C-33B)

Now the frame of the world took up the whole of each of those four primary bodies; its constructor made it consist of *all* the fire and water and air and earth, leaving no part or power of any one of them outside it. This was his purpose: first, that it might be to the fullest extent a living creature whole and complete, of complete parts; next that it might be single, nothing being left over out of which such another might come into being; and further that it might be secure from age and sickness. For he perceived that when hot things and cold and all things having strong powers beset a composite body and assail it from without, they doom it to untimely dissolution and cause it to waste away by subjecting it to sickness and age. For this reason, and so considering, he fashioned it into a single whole compound of all the above-mentioned wholes complete and free from age and sickness.

It is a Rotatory Sphere Devoid of Organs and Limbs (33B-34A)

For shape he gave it that which suited and was akin to its nature; and the fitting shape for the living creature that was going to embrace within itself all living creatures would be the figure that comprises in itself all the figures that there are. He therefore turned it, as on a lathe, rounded and spherical, with its extremities equidistant in all directions from centre to extremity – the most perfect and uniform of all figures, for he deemed uniformity to be infinitely better than its opposite. And all round on the outside he made it perfectly smooth, for several reasons. It had no need of eyes, for nothing visible was left outside; nor of hearing, since there was nothing outside to be heard. There was no surrounding air to call for respiration, nor again did it need any organ whereby to receive food into itself or to excrete it again when drained of its juices. For nothing went out or came into it from anywhere, because there was nothing: it was designed to supply its own waste as food for itself and to act and be acted upon entirely by itself and within itself; for its constructor thought it would be better self-sufficient rather than dependent on other things.

It needed neither hands with which to grasp or defend itself, nor feet or anything that would serve as support; so he saw no need to equip it with these unwanted limbs. For he assigned to it the motion proper to its bodily form, namely that one of the seven which belongs especially to reason and intelligence; he therefore caused it to turn uniformly in the same place and within its own bounds, and made it revolve round and round; he withheld the other six motions and fashioned it free of their wanderings. And since for this revolution it had no need of feet, he made it without legs or feet.

The World-Soul

Summary. Transition to the World-Soul (34A-B)

All of this, then, was devised by the ever-existent god for the god who was one day to be. According to this plan he made it smooth and uniform, everywhere equidistant from its centre, a body whole and complete compounded of complete bodies. And in the midst thereof he set a soul and extended it throughout the whole, and also wrapped its

body round with soul on the outside; and so he established one world alone, round and revolving in a circle, solitary but able by virtue of its excellence to keep itself company, needing no other acquaintance or friend but sufficient unto itself. For all these reasons the world he brought into being was a blessed god.

Soul Prior to Body (34B-C)

Now although this soul comes later in the account we are now attempting, the god did not make it younger than the body; for when he united them he would not have allowed the elder to be ruled by the younger. Human nature partakes largely of the casual and random, which becomes apparent in our speech; but the god made soul elder than the body and prior in birth and excellence, to be the body's mistress and ruler.

Composition of the World-Soul (35A)

The things of which he constructed soul and the manner of its composition were as follows: First, between the indivisible Existence, which remains always in the same state, and the divisible Existence that becomes in bodies, he compounded a third form of Existence out of both. Second, in the case of Sameness and in that of Difference, he also on the same principle fashioned a compound intermediate between that kind of them which is indivisible and the kind that is divisible in bodies. Then, third, taking the three, he blended them all into one form, compelling the nature of Difference, hard though it was to mingle, into union with Sameness, and mixing them together with Existence.

Its Division into Harmonic Intervals (35B-36B)

Having thus made a unity of the three, he divided this whole into a suitable number of parts, each part being a blend of Sameness, Difference and Existence. And here is how he began the division:

First he took one portion [1] from the whole, and next a portion [2] double of this; the third [3] half as much again as the second, and three times the first; the fourth [4] double of the second; the fifth [9] three times the third; the sixth [8] eight times the first; and the seventh [27] twenty-seven times the first.

Next he proceeded to fill up both the double and the triple intervals, cutting off further parts from the original mixture and placing them between the terms, so that within each interval there were two means, the one [harmonic] exceeding the one extreme and being exceeded by the other by the same fraction of the extremes, the other [arithmetical] exceeding the one extreme by the same number whereby it was exceeded by the other.

These links produced intervals of 3/2 and 4/3 and 9/8 within the original intervals. And he went on to fill in all the intervals of 4/3 [fourths] with the interval 9/8 [the tone], leaving over in each a fraction. This remaining interval of the fraction had its terms in the numerical proportion 256 : 243 [semitone approx.]. By this time the mixture from which he was cutting off these portions was all spent.

Construction of the Circles of the Same and the Different and of the Planetary Circles (36B-D)

He then split this whole fabric lengthwise into two halves; and making the two intersect one another at the centres in the form of a cross +, he bent each round into a circle, making each meet itself at a point [B] opposite to that [A] where they had been laid together. He then included them in the motion that revolves in the same place, and made the one the outer, the other the inner circle. The outer movement he named the movement of the Same; the inner, the movement of the Different. He caused the movement of the Same to revolve to the right by way of the side; the movement of the Different to the left by way of the diagonal.

And he gave supremacy to the revolution of the Same and uniform, for he left it single and undivided; but the inner revolution he split in six places into seven unequal circles, severally corresponding to the double and triple intervals, of each of which there were three. And he arranged that these circles should move in opposite directions to one another; while in speed three should be similar, but the other four should differ in speed from one another and from the three, though moving according to ratio.

Body of the World Fitted to its Soul (36D-E)

When the whole structure of the soul had been completed to its maker's mind, he next began fashioning within it all that is corporeal, brought the two together and fitted them centre to centre. And the soul, being woven throughout from the centre to the farthest heaven and enveloping the latter on the outside, revolving within her own limit, made a divine beginning of unceasing and intelligent life for all time.

Discourse in the World-Soul (36E-37C)

Whereas the body of the heaven has been created visible, the soul is invisible, and, by virtue of sharing in reason and harmony, is the best of things brought into being by the most excellent of entities intelligible and eternal. Inasmuch then as the soul has (a) been blended of Sameness, Difference and Existence, those three ingredients, and (b) has been divided and bound together in due proportion, and (c) revolves upon herself, it follows that whenever she makes contact with anything which has dispersed existence or with anything whose existence is indivisible, she is set in motion throughout herself [B] and tells in what respect exactly, and how, and in what sense, and when, it happens that something is qualified as either the same of different with respect to any given thing, whatever it may be, with which it is the same or from which it differs, either as regards things that become or as regards things that are forever changeless.

Now whenever discourse that is alike true, whether it concerns that which is different or that which is the same, being carried on without speech or sound within the self-moved, is about that which is sensible, and the circle of the Different, moving aright, reports its message throughout its entire soul – then there arise judgments and beliefs that are firm and true. But whenever discourse is concerned with the rational, and the circle of the Same, spinning smoothly, declares it, the result must be rational understanding and knowledge. And if anyone calls that in which these two come to exist by any name other than 'soul,' he will be speaking anything rather than truth.

Time, the Moving Likeness of Eternity (37C-38C)

When the father who had engendered it saw it in motion and alive, a shrine brought into being for the everlasting gods, he rejoiced and, being well pleased, he conceived the idea of making it still more like its model. Accordingly, as that model is the ever-existent Living Being, he set about making the universe also like it, as far as possible, in that respect. Now the nature of the Living Being was eternal, a character with which it was impossible fully to endow a generated thing. But he planned to make it as it were a moving likeness of eternity; and, at the same time that he set in order the Heaven, he made, of eternity that abides in unity, an ever-flowing likeness moving according to number – that to which we have given the name Time.

Before the Heaven came into being there were no days and nights, months and years; but he designed that they should now come to be simultaneously with the framing of the Heaven. They are all parts of Time, and "was" and "shall be" are forms of time; we are wrong when we thoughtlessly transfer them to eternal being. We say that it was and is and shall be; but "is" alone really belongs to it and describes it truly; "was" and "shall be" are properly applicable to becoming, which proceeds in time, for both are motions. But that which is ever and unchangeably in the same state cannot be becoming older or younger by the passage of time, nor can it ever become so; neither can it now have been or be on the way to becoming so; and in general it cannot be subject to any of the conditions that Becoming attaches to the moving things of sense, these having come into being as forms of time, which reflects eternity and revolves according to number. Moreover we make statements such as "what is past *is* past," "what happens now *is* happening now," and again "what will happen *is* what will happen" and "the non-existent *is* non-existent"; yet not one of these expressions is correct. But this, perhaps, may not be the right moment for a detailed discussion of these matters.

At all events, Time came into being simultaneously with the Heaven, in order that, as they were brought into being together, so they might be dissolved together if ever their dissolution should occur. And it is made after the pattern of the ever-enduring nature, in order that it may resemble that pattern as closely as possible; for the pattern is something that has being for all eternity, whereas the Heaven has been and is and shall be perpetually throughout time.

The Planets as Instruments of Time (38C-39E)

By virtue, therefore, of this scheme and purpose of the god with a view to the genesis of Time, in order that Time might be brought into being, Sun and Moon and five other stars – "planets" (i.e. wanderers) as they are called – were made for the definition and preservation of the numbers of Time. Having made a body for each of them, the god placed them in the circuits in which the revolution of the Different was moving – seven bodies in seven circuits; the Moon in the circuit nearest the Earth; the sun in the second above the Earth; the Morning Star [Venus] and the one called sacred to Hermes [Mercury] in circles revolving so as, in point of speed, to run their race with the Sun, but endowed with the tendency contrary to his; whereby the Sun, the star of Hermes and the Morning Star alike overtake and are overtaken by one another. As for the remainder, if one were to explain where he enshrined them and for what reasons, the account (though no more than subsidiary) would prove a heavier task than that which it subserved. Later perhaps, at our leisure, these points may receive the attention they deserve.

To resume: when each of the beings that were to co-operate in producing Time had attained the motion suitable to it, and when, as bodies bound together with living bonds, they had become living creatures and learnt their appointed task, then they began to revolve by way of the motion of the Different (which was aslant crossing the movement of the Same and subject to it), some moving in greater circles more slowly, some in lesser circles more rapidly.

So because of the movement of the Same, those which revolved more rapidly appeared to be overtaken by those which travelled more slowly, though actually overtaking them. For the movement of the Same, which gives all their circles a spiral twist because they have two distinct forward motions in opposite directions, caused the body which departs most slowly from itself – the swiftest of all movements – to appear to be keeping pace with it most closely.

...

This being so, we must agree that there is, firstly, the unchanging Form, ungenerated and indestructible, which neither receives anything else into itself from elsewhere nor itself enters into anything else anywhere, invisible and otherwise imperceptible – that, in fact, which thinking has as its object.

Secondly, there is that which has the same name and is similar to that Form; is sensible; is generated; is perpetually in motion, coming to be in a certain place and again departing from it; apprehensible by belief involving perception.

Thirdly, there is Space, which is everlasting, not admitting of destruction; affording a situation for all things that come into being, but itself apprehended without the senses by a kind of bastard reasoning, and scarcely an object of belief. This

indeed is what we behold as in a dream and say that anything that is must of necessity be in some place and occupy some room, and that what is not somewhere on earth or in heaven is nothing. Because of this dreaming state we prove unable to bestir ourselves and draw all these and other kindred distinctions (even in the case of the waking and truly existing nature), and thus to state the truth: namely that, whereas for an image – since not even the very principle on which it has come into being belongs to that image, but it is the ever-moving semblance of something else – it is proper that it should come to be *in* something, clinging to its existence as best it may on pain of being nothing at all; on the other hand, that which has real being enjoys the support of the exactly true account, which declares that, so long as two things are different, neither can ever come to be in the other in such a way that the two should become at once both one and the same thing and also two.

VI.2. ARISTOTLE

IN THE FOLLOWING SELECTIONS ARISTOTLE SETS AND DEFINES MANY
of the terms for the discussions, in the middle ages, of the problem of universals.
Aristotle calls "universal" whatever is said of or apt to be said of many things. (If
x is "said of" *y*, then the proposition '*y* is *x*' is true.) He never denies there are
such things, but he is aware of the problems of treating them as each "one in number" in the way those Platonists do who hold that Plato's Forms are universals.
The selections below amply show both the framework for discussion and the
array of problems Aristotle bequeathed to his successors when it came to discussing the ground for regarding things as arranged in a hierarchy of types.

VI.2.1. Categories and the things there are
(*Categories* 2-5)

[This selection covers texts which were among the
most familiar to medieval logicians. In them we
find the famous doctrine of ten categories, or highest genera. Does Aristotle here try to give a universal classification scheme or does he attempt a classification of words or meanings? Disagreement on
this question was an important part of discussions
of universals in the middle ages. We also encounter
Aristotle's definition of 'substance' as an ultimate
subject, a definition he himself was forced to
retreat from when in his *Metaphysics* he saw that
this would mean that only prime matter was a substance.]

Chapter 2

Of things that are said, some involve combination
while others are said without combination.
Examples of those involving combination are:
human being runs, human being wins; and of those
without combination: human being, ox, runs,
wins.

Of things there are: (a) some are *said of* a subject
but are not *in* any subject. For example, human
being is said of a subject, the individual human
being, but is not in any subject. (b) Some are in a
subject but are not said of any subject. (By 'in a
subject' I mean what is in something, not as a part,

and cannot exist separately from what it is in.) For
example, the individual knowledge-of-grammar is
in a subject, the soul, but is not said of any subject;
and the individual white is in a subject, the body
(for all colour is in a body), but is not said of any
subject. (c) Some are both said of a subject and in
a subject. For example, knowledge is in a subject,
the soul, and is also said of a subject, knowledge-
of-grammar. (d) Some are neither in a subject nor
said of a subject, for example, the individual
human being or the individual horse – for nothing
of this sort is either in a subject or said of a subject.
Things that are individual and numerically one are,
without exception, not said of any subject, but
there is nothing to prevent some of them from
being in a subject – the individual knowledge-of-
grammar is one of the things in a subject.

Chapter 3

Whenever one thing is predicated of another as of
a subject, all things said of what is predicated will
be said of the subject also. For example, human
being is predicated of the individual human being,
and animal of human being; so animal will be
predicated of the individual human being also – for
the individual human being is both a human being
and an animal.

The differentiae of genera[1] which are different
and not subordinate one to the other are themselves different in kind. For example, animal and

1 See glossary entry for 'species/genus.'

352

knowledge: footed, winged, aquatic, two-footed, are differentiae of animal, but none of these is a differentia of knowledge; one sort of knowledge does not differ from another by being two-footed. However, there is nothing to prevent genera subordinate one to the other from having the same differentiae. For the higher are predicated of the genera below them, so that all differentiae of the predicated genus will be differentiae of the subject also.

Chapter 4

Of things said without any combination, each signifies either substance or quantity or qualification or a relative or where or when or being-in-a-position or having or doing or being-affected. To give a rough idea, examples of substance are human being, horse; of quantity: four-foot, five-foot; of qualification: white, grammatical; of a relative: double, half, larger; of where: in the Lyceum, in the market-place; of when: yesterday, last-year; of being-in-a-position: is-lying, is-sitting; of having: has-shoes-on, has-armour-on; of doing: cutting, burning; of being-affected: being cut, being-burned.

None of the above is said just by itself in any affirmation, but by the combination of these with one another an affirmation is produced. For every affirmation, it seems, is either true or false; but of things said without any combination none is either true or false (e.g. human being, white, runs, wins).

Chapter 5

A *substance* – that which is called a substance most strictly, primarily, and most of all – is that which is neither said of a subject nor in a subject, e.g. the individual human being or the individual horse. The species in which the things primarily called substances are, are called *secondary substances*, as also are the genera of these species. For example, the individual human being belongs in a species, human being, and animal is a genus of the species; so these – both human being and animal – are called secondary substances.

It is clear from what has been said that if something is said of a subject both its name and its definition are necessarily predicated of the subject. For example, human being is said of a subject, the individual human being, and the name is of course

predicated (since you will be predicating human being of the individual human being), and also the definition of human being will be predicated of the individual human being (since the individual human being is also a human being). Thus both the name and the definition will be predicated of the subject. But as for things which are in a subject, in most cases neither the name nor the definition is predicated of the subject. In some cases there is nothing to prevent the name from being predicated of the subject, but it is impossible for the definition to be predicated. For example, white, which is in a subject (the body), is predicated of the subject; for a body is called white. But the definition of white will never be predicated of the body.

All the other things are either said of the primary substances as subjects or in them as subjects. This is clear from an examination of cases. For example, animal is predicated of human being and therefore also of the individual human being; for were it predicated of none of the individual humans it would not be predicated of human being at all. Again, colour is in body and therefore also in an individual body; for were it not in some individual body it would not be in body at all. Thus all the other things are either said of the primary substances as subjects or in them as subjects. So if the primary substances did not exist it would be impossible for any of the other things to exist.

Of the secondary substances the species is more a substance than the genus, since it is nearer to the primary substance. For if one is to say of the primary substance what it is, it will be more informative and apt to give the species than the genus. For example, it would be more informative to say of the individual human being that he is a human being than that he is an animal (since the one is more distinctive of the individual human being while the other is more general); and more informative to say of the individual tree that it is a tree than that it is a plant. Further, it is because the primary substances are subjects for all the other things and all the other things are predicated of them or are in them, that they are called substances most of all. But as the primary substances stand to the other things, so the species stands to the genus: the species is a subject for the genus (for the genera are predicated of the species but the species are not predicated reciprocally of the genera). Hence for this reason too the species is more a substance than the genus.

But of the species themselves – those which are not genera – one is no more a substance than another: it is no more apt to say of the individual human being that he is a human being than to say of the individual horse that it is a horse. And similarly of the primary substances one is no more a substance than another: the individual human being is no more a substance than the individual ox.

It is reasonable that, after the primary substances, their species and genera should be the only other things called secondary substances. For only they, of things predicated, reveal the primary substance. For if one is to say of the individual human being what he is, it will be in place to give the species or the genus (though more informative to give human being than animal); but to give any of the other things would be out of place – for example, to say white or runs or anything like that. So it is reasonable that these should be the only other things called substances. Further, it is because the primary substances are subjects for everything else that they are called substances most strictly. But as the primary substances stand to everything else, so the species and genera of the primary substances stand to all the rest: all the rest are predicated of these. For if you will call the individual human being grammatical, then you will call both a human being and an animal grammatical;[2] and similarly in other cases.

VI.2.2. Universals and Particulars (*On Interpretation* Chapter 7)

[At the beginning of this selection Aristotle gives the definition of 'universal' (and 'particular') that was to be accepted (and variously interpreted) by all the medieval thinkers.]

Chapter 7

Now of actual things some are universal, others particular (I call universal that which is by its nature predicated of a number of things, and particular that which is not; human being, for instance, is a universal, Callias a particular). So it must sometimes be of a universal that one states that something holds or does not, sometimes of a particular. Now if one states universally of a universal that something holds or does not, there will be contrary statements (examples of what I mean by 'stating universally of a universal' are: every human being is white – no human being is white). But when one states something of a universal but not universally, the statements are not contrary (though what is being revealed may be contrary). Examples of what I mean by 'stating of a universal not universally' are: a human being is white – a human being is not white; human being is a universal but it is not used universally in the statement (for 'every' does not signify the universal but that it is taken universally). It is not true to predicate a universal universally of a subject, for there cannot be an affirmation in which a universal is predicated universally of a subject, for instance: every human being is every animal.

I call an affirmation and a negation *contradictory* opposites when what one signifies universally the other signifies not universally, e.g. every human being is white – not every human being is white, no human being is white – some human being is white. But I call the universal affirmation and the universal negation contrary opposites, e.g. every human being is just – no human being is just. So these cannot be true together, but their opposites may both be true with respect to the same thing, e.g. not every human being is white – some human being is white.

VI.2.3. The Problem of Universals (from *Metaphysics* III, 4)

[The next two selections are "aporematic"; i.e. they set up a problem or problems that Aristotle hopes later to resolve. Here Aristotle shows that no matter whether we answer the question 'Are there things apart from individual things?' yes or no, we are in difficulty. The affirmative answer leads to genera that exist apart from species. The negative answer gives scientific thought nothing to focus on.]

---

2 I.e., knowledgeable about grammar.

Chapter 4

There is a difficulty connected with these, the hardest of all and the most necessary to examine, and to this our argument has now brought us. If, on the one hand, there is nothing apart from individual things, and the individuals are infinite in number, how is it possible to get knowledge of the infinite individuals? For all things that we know, we know in so far as they have some unity and identity, and in so far as some attribute belongs to them universally. But if this is necessary, and there must be something apart from the individuals, it will be necessary that the genera exist apart from the individuals, – either the lowest or the highest genera; but we found by discussion just now that this is impossible.

Further, if we admit in the fullest sense that something exists apart from the concrete thing, whenever something is predicated of the matter, must there, if there is something apart, be something corresponding to each set of individuals, or to some and not to others, or to none? If there is nothing apart from individuals, there will be no object of thought, but all things will be objects of sense, and there will not be knowledge of anything, unless we say that sensation is knowledge.

Further, nothing will be eternal or unmovable; for all perceptible things perish and are in movement. But if there is nothing eternal, neither can there be a process of coming to be; for that which comes to be, and that from which it comes to be, must be something, and the ultimate term in this series cannot have come to be, since the series has a limit and nothing can come to be out of that which is not.

Further, if generation and movement exist there must also be a limit; for no movement is infinite, but every movement has an end, and that which is incapable of completing its coming to be cannot be in process of coming to be; and that which has completed its coming to be must be as soon as it has come to be.

Further, since the matter exists, because it is ungenerated, it is *a fortiori* reasonable that the substance, that which the matter is at any time coming to be, should exist; for if neither substance nor matter is, nothing will be at all. And since this is

impossible there must be something besides the concrete thing, viz. the shape or form. But again if we are to suppose this, it is hard to say in which cases we are to suppose it and in which not. For evidently it is not possible to suppose it in all cases; we could not suppose that there is a house besides the particular houses. – Besides this, will the substance of all the individuals, e.g. of all humans, be one? This is paradoxical, for all the things whose substance is on this view one would be one. But are they many and different? This also is unreasonable. At the same time, how does the matter become each of the individuals, and how is the concrete thing these two elements?

Again, one might ask the following question also about the first principles. If they are one in kind only, nothing will be numerically one,[3] not even unity-itself and being-itself. And how will it be possible to know, if there is not to be something common to a whole set of individuals? But if there is a common element which is numerically one, and each of the principles is one, and the principles are not as in the case of perceptible things different for different things (e.g. since this particular syllable is the same in kind whenever it occurs, the elements of it are also the same in kind; only in kind, for these also, like the syllable, are numerically different in different contexts), – if the principles of things are not one in this sense, but are numerically one, there will be nothing else besides the elements; for there is no difference of meaning between 'numerically one' and 'individual.' For this is just what we mean by the individual, the numerically one, and by the universal we mean that which is predicable of the individuals. Therefore it is just as, if the elements of articulate sound were limited in number, all the literature in the world would be confined to the ABC, since there could not be two or more letters of the same kind.

VI.2.4. Are first Principles Universals? (from *Metaphysics* III, 6)

[Here Aristotle refers to "thises" and "suches." The former is anything which has numerical unity, i.e. is paradigmatically just one thing. A "such" is something that lacks that sort of unity. Aristotle here

---

3 Cf. selection **V.1.2.**

says that what is common to many must be of the latter sort.]

Chapter 6

We must not only raise these questions about the first principles, but also ask whether they are universal or what we call individuals. If they are universal, they will not be substances; for everything that is common indicates not a "this" but a "such," but substance is a "this." – And if we can actually posit the common predicate as a single "this," Socrates will be several animals – himself and human being and animal, if each of these indicates a "this" and a single thing. – If, then, the principles are universals, these results follow; if they are not universals but of the nature of individuals, they will not be knowable; for the knowledge of anything is universal. Therefore if there is to be knowledge of the principles there must be other principles prior to them, which are universally predicated of them.

VI.2.5. Substance and Universals (from *Metaphysics* VII)

[In this selection Aristotle attacks any view which treats universals as substances, either the substances of physical individuals or separated substances like Plato's Forms.]

Chapter 13

Let us again return to the subject of our inquiry, which is substance. As the substrate and the essence and the compound of these are called substance, so also is the universal. About two of these we have spoken; about the essence and about the substrate, of which we have said that it underlies in two senses, either being a "this" – which is the way in which an animal underlies its attributes – , or as the matter underlies the complete reality. The universal also is thought by some to be in the fullest sense a cause, and a principle, therefore let us attack the discussion of this point also. For it seems impossible that any universal term should be the name of a substance. For primary substance is that kind of substance which is peculiar to an individual, which does not belong to anything else; but the universal is common, since that is called universal which naturally belongs to more than one thing. Of which individual then will this be the substance? Either of all or of none. But it cannot be the substance of all; and if it is to be the substance of one, this one will be the others also; for things whose substance is one and whose essence is one are themselves also one.

Further, substance means that which is not predicable of a subject, but the universal is predicable of some subject always.

But perhaps the universal, while it cannot be substance in the way in which the essence is so, can be present in this, e.g. animal can be present in human being and horse. Then clearly there is a formula of the universal. And it makes no difference even if there is not a formula of everything that is in the substance; for none the less the universal will be the substance of something. Human being is the substance of the individual human being in whom it is present; therefore the same will happen again, for a substance, e.g. animal, must be the substance of that in which it is present as something peculiar to it. And further it is impossible and absurd that the "this," i.e. the substance, if it consists of parts, should not consist of substances nor of what is a "this," but of quality; for that which is not substance, i.e. the quality, will then be prior to substance and to the "this." Which is impossible; for neither in formula nor in time nor in coming to be can the attributes be prior to the substance; for then they would be separable from it. Further, in Socrates there will be a substance in a substance, so that he will be the substance of two things. And in general it follows, if human being and such things are substances, that none of the elements in their formulae is the substance of anything, nor does it exist apart from the species or in anything else; I mean, for instance, that no animal exists apart from the particular animals, nor does any other of the elements present in formulae exist apart. If, then, we view the matter from these standpoints, it is plain that no universal attribute is a substance, and this is plain also from the fact that no common predicate indicates a "this," but rather a "such." If not, many difficulties follow and especially the "third man."[4]

The conclusion is evident also from the following consideration – that a substance cannot consist of substances present in it actually (for things that are thus actually two are never actually one, though if they are potentially two, they can be one, e.g. the double line consists of two halves – potentially; for the actualization of the halves divides them from one another; therefore if the substance is one, it will not consist of substances present in it); and according to the argument which Democritus[5] states rightly; he says one thing cannot come from two nor two from one; for he identifies his indivisible magnitudes with substances. It is clear therefore that the same will hold good of number, if number is a synthesis of units, as is said by some; for two is either not one, or there is no unit present in it actually.

The consequence of this view involves a difficulty. If no substance can consist of universals because a universal indicates a "such," not a "this," and if no composite substance can be composed of actual substances, every substance would be incomposite, so that there would not even be a formula of any substance. But it is thought by all and has been previously stated that it is either only, or primarily, substance that can be defined; yet now it seems that not even substance can. There cannot, then, be a definition of anything; or rather in a sense there can be, and in a sense there cannot. And what we say will be plainer from what follows.

Chapter 14

It is clear also from these very facts what consequences confront those who say the Ideas are substances and can exist apart, and at the same time make the Form consist of the genus and the differentiae. For if the Forms exist and animal is present in human being and horse, it is either one and the same in number, or different. (In formula it is clearly one; for he who states the formula unfolds the same formula in either case.) If there is a human being-in-himself who is a "this" and exists apart, the parts of which he consists, e.g. animal and two-footed, must indicate a "this" and be things existing apart and substances; therefore animal too must be of this sort.

Now if animal, which is in the horse and in human being, is one and the same, as you are one and the same with yourself, how will the one in things that exist apart be one, and how will this animal escape being divided even from itself?

Further, if it is to share in two-footed and many-footed, an impossible conclusion follows; for contrary attributes will belong at the same time to it although it is one and a "this." If it does not, what is the relation implied when one says the animal is two-footed or has feet? But perhaps these are put together and are in contact, or are mixed. Yet all these are absurd.

But suppose the Form to be different in each species. Then there will be practically an infinite number of things whose substance is animal; for it is not by accident that human being has animal for one of its elements. Further, animal-in-itself will be many. For the animal in each species will be the substance of the species; for it is not dependent on anything else; if it were, that other would be an element in human being, i.e would be the genus of human being. And further all the elements of which human being is composed will be Ideas. Now nothing can be the Idea of one thing and the substance of another; this is impossible. Each, then, of the Ideas present in the species of animals will be the ideal animal. Further, from what will these Ideas be derived; how will they be derived from the ideal animal? Or how can an Idea of animal whose essence is simply animal exist apart from the ideal animal? Further, in the case of sensible things both these consequences and others still more absurd follow. If, then, these consequences are impossible, clearly there are not Forms of sensible things in the sense in which some maintain their existence.

4 The "third man" is an argument which runs as follows: Assume the universal human being is a single thing. Surely human being is a rational animal; in fact this is a definition. But anything that is a rational animal is a human being (by definition). Therefore human being is a human being. But not any of the individual human beings, since they are particulars and not universals. So there must be a human being which is not one of the particular human beings, which is absurd, given the assumption that it is a single thing.
5 Fifth-century B.C.E. Greek philosopher who with Leucippus founded the atomist school.

VI.3. PORPHYRY

The *Isagoge* of Porphyry was set at the beginning of Aristotle's logic as an introduction. Plotinus had urged Porphyry to write an introduction which could help the student master Aristotle's logical works, taken to be a preparation for a full understanding of the philosophy of Plato and Aristotle. Porphyry's short introduction was a subject of commentary throughout the middle ages.

VI.3.1. The five "Predicables" (from *Isagoge*)

Since, Chrysaorius, to teach about Aristotle's Categories it is necessary to know what genus and difference are, as well as species, property, and accident, and since reflection on these things is useful for giving definitions, and in general for matters pertaining to division and demonstration, therefore I shall give you a brief account and shall try in a few words, as in the manner of an introduction, to go over what our elders said about these things. I shall abstain from deeper enquiries and aim, as appropriate, at the simpler ones. For example, I shall beg off saying anything about (a) whether genera and species are real or are situated in bare thoughts alone, (b) whether as real they are bodies or incorporeals, and (c) whether they are separated or in sensibles and have their reality in connection with them. Such business is profound, and requires another, greater investigation. Instead I shall now try to show you how the ancients, the Peripatetics among them most of all, interpreted genus and species and the other matters before us in a more logical fashion.

On genus

It seems that neither 'genus' nor 'species' is said in a single sense. For (a) the collection of things related somehow to one thing and to one another is called a "genus." In accordance with this meaning, the Heraclids are called a genus because of their being derived from one person – that is to say, from Heracles, and because of the multitude of people who somehow have a kinship to one another derived from him and are called by a name that separates them from other genera.

(b) In another sense too the origin of each person's birth, whether the one who begot him or the place in which he was born, is called his "genus." For in this way we say that Orestes has his genus from Tantalus, but Hyllus from Heracles, and again that Pindar is Theban by genus, but Plato Athenian. For the country is a kind of origin of each person's birth, just as his father is. This latter sense of the word seems to be a common one. For those who come down from the race of Heracles are called Heraclids, and those from Cecrops, together with their kin, are called Cecropides. The origin of each person's birth was above called a "genus," and after these the multitude of things that come from one origin, like the Heraclids. Dividing that group off and separating them from others, we said the whole collection of Heraclids is a genus.

(c) In yet another way, that to which a species is subordinated is called a "genus." Perhaps this is said because of the similarity with the former senses. For such a genus is also a kind of origin for the things under it, and seems also to include the whole multitude contained under it.

Now although 'genus' is said in these three ways, discussion among philosophers concerns the third. They describe this sense and set it out by saying that a genus is what is predicated, with respect to what the thing is, of several things differing in species. For example, animal. For among predicates, some are said of one thing only, for example individuals like 'Socrates,' and 'he' and 'this.' Others are said of several things, such as genera, species, differences, properties, and common accidents, although not accidents that are proper to something. An example of genus is 'animal'; an example of species, 'human being'; an example of difference, 'rational'; an example of property, 'risible'; examples of accident, 'white,' 'black,' 'sitting.'

Genera then differ from what are predicable of one thing only, since genera are given as being predicated of several. Again, among what are predicable of several, genera differ from species because species, even though they are predicated of several, are yet not predicated of what differ in species but only in number. For 'human being,' which is a species, is predicated of Socrates and Plato, who do not differ from one another in species but only in number. But 'animal,' which is a genus, is predicated of human being and ox and horse, which differ from one another also in species, not just in number.

Again, genus differs from property because property is predicated of only the one species it is the property of and of the individuals under the species, as 'risible' is predicated only of human being and of particular human beings. But genus is predicated not only of one species but of several differing species.

Again, genus differs from difference and from common accidents because even though differences and common accidents are predicated of several things differing in species, yet they are not predicated with respect to what the thing is. For when we ask about the respect in which these are predicated, we say they are predicated not with respect to what the thing is but rather with respect to what manner of thing it is. For to the question what manner of thing a human being is, we say "rational." And to the question what manner of thing a crow is, we say "black." ('Rational' is a difference, and 'black' an accident.) But when we are asked what a human being is, we answer "animal." (The genus of human being was 'animal.')

So the fact that genus is said of many things distinguishes it from individuals, which are predicated of one alone, while its being predicated of what differ in species distinguishes genus from what are predicated as species or as properties. And its being predicated with respect to what a thing is separates it from differences and common accidents, each of which is predicated of what it is predicated of, not with respect to what the thing is but with respect to what manner of thing it is or in what disposition. Thus the given outline of the notion of genus is neither too broad nor too narrow.

On species

(a) 'Species' is said of each thing's form. As has been said: "First a species worthy of sovereignty." (b) What is under a given genus is also called a species. In this sense we usually call 'human being' a species of 'animal' ('animal' being the genus), 'white' a species of 'colour,' and 'triangle' a species of 'figure'. Now if in giving an account of the genus we mentioned the species – by saying "predicated with respect to what the thing is, of several things differing in species" – and we call "species" what is under the given genus, then we must acknowledge that since both genus is the genus of something and species is the species of something, each of the other, both must be used in the definitions of both. Therefore, they give the following account of species: (c) Species is what is arranged under the genus and is what the genus is predicated of with respect to what the thing is. Again: (d) Species is what is predicated, with respect to what the thing is, of several things differing in number. The last account is of the most specific species and of what is only a species, whereas the others [(a)-(c)] are also of species that are not most specific ones.

This statement can be clarified as follows: In each category some things are most general and again others most specific, and yet others are between the most general and the most specific. The most general is that above which there is no other genus that transcends it. The most specific is that after which there is no other, subordinate species. What are between the most general and the most specific are all the others. These, the same things, are both genera and species, taken in relation to one or the other.

Let us clarify the above statement for just one category. 'Substance' itself is a genus. Under this is 'body,' and under 'body' 'animate body,' under which 'animal,' under 'animal' 'rational animal,' under which 'human being.' Under 'human being' are 'Socrates' and 'Plato' and the particular human beings. Of these, 'substance' is the most general and the one that is only a genus. 'Human being' is the most specific and the one that is only a species. 'Body' is a species of 'substance' but a genus of 'animate body.' 'Animate body' is a species of 'body' but a genus of 'animal.' Again, 'animal' is a species of 'animate body' but a genus of 'rational animal.' 'Rational animal' is a species of 'animal' but a genus of 'human being.' Now 'human being' is a species of 'rational animal,' but no longer a genus of particular human beings. Instead it is a species only. Everything prior to individuals and predicated immediately of them is a species only, no longer a genus. Therefore, just as 'substance,' being the highest, was a most general genus because there is nothing prior to it, so too 'human being,' being a species after which there is no species or any of what can be cut up into species, but only individuals (for Socrates and Plato and this white thing are individuals), is a species only, both the last species and, as we say, the "most specific."

What are in between are species of what is prior to them, but genera of what comes after. Thus they stand in two relations, (a) the one to things prior to them, in virtue of which relation they are said to be species of those things, and (b) the other to things after them, in virtue of which relation they are said to be genera of those things. The two extremes each have one relation only. For the most general genus has (b) the relation to things under it, since it is the highest genus of them all. But it no longer has (a) the relation to things prior to itself, since it is highest, both as the first origin and, as we said, that above which there is no other genus that transcends it. The most specific species also has one relation only, (a) the one to things prior to itself, of which it is a species. But it does not have the other relation, (b) to things after it, even though it is called a species of individuals. Rather it is called a species of individuals because it includes them, and again it is called a species of what are prior to it because it is included by them. Thus they define the most general genus as (i) that which, although it is a genus, is not a species, and again, as (ii) that above which there is no other genus that transcends it. The most specific species they define as (i) that which, although it is a species, is not a genus, and (ii) that which, although it is a species, we cannot divide further into species, and as (iii) that which is predicated, with respect to what the thing is, of several things differing in number. What are between the two extremes they call "subordinate" genera and species. Each of them they hold to be both a

genus and a species, taken in relation to the one extreme or the other. The genera prior to the most specific species, going up to the most general genus, are called both species and subordinate genera. For example, Agamemnon, from Atreus, from Pelops, from Tantalus, and in the end from Zeus. Now as for genealogies, they lead up to one thing – to Zeus, let us say – to the origin in most cases. But with genera and species this is not so. For being, as Aristotle says,[1] is not one common genus of all things; neither are all things "homogeneous" in accordance with one highest genus. Instead let us posit the ten first genera as ten first principles, as in the Categories. If then one calls all things "beings," he will do so equivocally Aristotle says, but not univocally. For if being were one genus common to all, all things would be called "beings" univocally. But since there are instead ten first genera, the community among them is in name only, not at all in a definition that goes with that name. Therefore, the most general genera are ten. The most specific species are of a certain number too, surely not infinite. But individuals, which come after the most specific species, are infinite. That is why Plato exhorts us[2] to stop after going down from the most general to the most specific, to go down through the intermediary levels and to divide by differences. He tells us to leave the infinite [individuals] alone. For there is no knowledge of them. So in going down to the most specific species we must proceed by division through a multitude. But in going up to the most general genera we must gather the multitude into one. For species (and genus even more) is a combination of many things into one nature. By contrast particulars and singulars always divide the one into a multitude. The many human beings are one by participation in the species, but the one common human being, the species, is made several by its individuals. For the individual is always divisive, but what is common combines and unites. Now given what each of genus and species is, and given that whereas the genus is one the species are several (for the division of a genus is always into several species), the genus is always predicated of the species, and all the higher things are predicated of those beneath them. But the species is predicat-

1 *Metaphysics* III. 3, 998b22.
2 *Philebus*, 16c-18d, *Politicus*, 262a-c.

ed neither of the genus immediately above it nor of higher ones. For it does not go both ways. Either equals must be predicated of equals, like hinnibility[3] of horses, or else greaters of lessers, like animal of human being. But lessers are never predicated of greaters. For you must never say animal is a human being, as you may say human being is an animal. Whatever the species is predicated of, the genus of that species will of necessity be predicated of them too, and the genus of the genus, on up to the most general genus. For if it is true to say Socrates is a human being, human being an animal, animal a substance, then it is also true to say Socrates is an animal and a substance. Thus since the higher are always predicated of the lower, the species will be predicated of the individual, the genus both of the species and of the individual, and the most general genus both of the genus or genera – if there are several, intermediary subordinate genera – and also of the species and of the individual. For the most general genus is said of all the genera and species and individuals under it, while the genus prior to the most specific species is said of all the most specific species and of individuals, and what is only a species is said of all the individuals. But the individual is said of only one of the particulars. Socrates is called an individual, and so is this white thing and the one who is approaching, the son of Sophroniscus (if Socrates is his only son). Such things are called individuals because each of them consists of characteristics the collection of which can never be the same for anything else. For the characteristics of Socrates cannot be the same for any other particular.

But the characteristics of human being – I mean, of human being in general – are the same for several things, or rather for all particular human beings insofar as they are human beings. The individual then is included under the species and the species under the genus. For the genus is a kind of whole and the individual a part, while the species is both a whole and a part, although a part of one thing and the whole not of another thing but rather in other things. For the whole is in the parts. (38) Therefore, we have discussed genus and species,

what a most general genus is, what most specific species are, which genera are the same as species, what individuals are, and in how many ways 'genus' and 'species' are said.

On difference

'Difference' is said broadly, strictly, and most strictly. In the broad sense one thing is said to "differ" from another when it is distinguished in any way by an otherness, either from itself or from something else. For Socrates is said to differ from Plato by an otherness. And he is said to differ from himself as a child and as a grown human being, as doing something or as having stopped doing it. Indeed, he always differs from himself in such othernesses of disposition.

In the strict sense one thing is said to "differ" from another when the one differs from the other by an inseparable accident. An inseparable accident is, for example, greenness of the eyes, hookedness of the nose, or a hardened scar from a wound.

In the strictest sense one thing is said to "differ" from another when it is distinguished by a specific difference. For example, human being is distinguished from horse by a specific difference: the quality rational.

In general, every difference when added to something varies it. But differences in the broad and the strict senses only make it otherwise, whereas differences in the strictest sense make it other.[4] For some differences make a thing otherwise, while others make it other. The ones that make it other are called "specific" differences, whereas those that make a thing otherwise are called just "differences." For when the difference "irrational" comes to animal, it makes it other. But the difference "being moved" makes a thing only otherwise than resting. Hence the former makes it other; the latter only makes it otherwise. It is in accordance with the differences that make a thing other that there arise the divisions of genera into species, and that definitions are given, since definitions are made up of a genus and such differences. But it is in accordance with differences that only make a thing oth-

---

3 I.e., ability to neigh.
4 Socrates as a child is "otherwise" than he is as a grown human being, but he is "other" than a horse. In the former case numerical identity is preserved; in the latter it is not.

erwise that mere othernesses and changes of disposition arise.

So beginning again from the top, we must say that
among differences some are separable and others
inseparable. Being moved and resting, being
healthy and being ill, and any differences like these,
are separable, whereas being green-eyed, or snub-
nosed, or rational or irrational are inseparable.

Among inseparable differences some belong
essentially, some by accident. Rational belongs
essentially to human being, and mortal and being
capable of knowing do too. But being hook-nosed
or snub-nosed belongs by accident and not essentially. Differences that belong essentially are included in the definition of the substance and make the
thing other, but those that belong by accident are
not included in the definition of the substance .
Neither do they make the thing other, but rather
otherwise.

Those that belong essentially do not admit of
more and less, but those that belong by accident,
even if they are inseparable, acquire an intension
and remission.[5] The genus is not predicated more
and less of whatever it is a genus of, and neither are
the differences of the genus, by which it is divided.
For these differences are what complete the definition of each, and the being of each thing is one and
does not admit of either a remission or an intension. But being hook-nosed or snub-nosed, or
being colored in such and such a way, are intended
and remitted.

Thus we have seen three species of "difference."
Some are (a) separable, while some are inseparable.
Again of the inseparable ones some are (b) essential
and others (c) by accident. Again among essential
differences there are some in accordance with
which we divide genera into species, and some in
accordance with which the divided genera are
"specified." For instance, given that all the differences that belong to animal by themselves are: animate and sensate, rational and irrational, mortal
and immortal, the difference 'animate and sensate'
is constitutive of the substance animal (for animal
is animate, sensate substance), but the difference
'mortal and immortal,' and the difference 'rational
and irrational' are divisive differences of animal
(for we divide genera into species by means of

them). These divisive differences of the genera are
completing and constituting differences of the
species. For animal is partitioned both by the difference rational and irrational, and again by the
difference mortal and immortal. The differences
mortal and rational are constitutive of human
being, while the differences rational and immortal
are constitutive of god, and the differences irrational and mortal are constitutive of irrational animals. So too, since the difference animate and inanimate and the difference sensate and insensate are
divisive of the highest substance, therefore the differences animate and sensate, taken together with
substance, complete the genus animal, whereas the
differences animate and insensate complete the
genus plant. Thus while the same differences taken
one way are constitutive and in another way are
divisive, they are all called "specific" differences.

The main usefulness of these inseparable differences that belong essentially – but not of inseparable differences that belong by accident, and still less
of separable differences – is for the divisions of
genera and for definitions. They define differences
by saying: Difference is that by which the species
surpasses the genus. For human being has more
than animal: he also has rational and mortal.
Animal is not none of these, since if it were, where
would the species get their differences? But neither
does animal have them all, since then the same
thing will have opposites at the same time. Rather,
as they think, it potentially has all the differences of
things under it but none of them actually. In this
way, neither does anything come from non-beings
nor will opposites belong to the same thing at the
same time.

They also define it like this: Difference is what is
predicated, with respect to what manner of thing
each is, of several things differing in species. For
'rational' and 'mortal,' when predicated of human
being, are said with respect to what manner of
thing human being is, not with respect to what he
is. If we are asked what human being is, it is strict
to say "an animal." But when we inquire what manner of animal, the strict reply we shall give is "a
rational and mortal one." Just as things consist of
matter and form, or have a structure analogous to
matter and form – for instance a statue is made up

of matter (the bronze) and form (the shape) – so too the specific human being in common consists of an analogue of matter (the genus) and of form (the difference). The whole, rational-mortal-animal, is human being – just as for the statue.

They also describe such differences as follows: Difference is what naturally separates what are under the same genus. For rational and irrational divide human being from horse, which are under the same genus animal.

They describe them also like this: Difference is that by which each thing differs. For human being and horse do not differ according to genus, for both we and the irrational animals are mortal animals. But when rational is added, it divides us from them. Both we and the gods are rational, but when mortal is added it divides us from them. In working through the facts about difference, they do not say difference is just anything that separates things under the same genus, but rather whichever of such factors contributes to the being of such a thing, and what is a part of what the thing was to be. The aptitude for sailing is not a difference of human being even if it is a property of human being. For we might say some animals have an aptitude for sailing whereas others do not, and we might separate the former from the others. But the aptitude for sailing does not contribute to completing the substance, and is not a part of that substance, but only a "fitness" of it for sailing, since it is not like what are strictly called "specific" differences. Specific differences then are the ones that make another species and the ones taken up into what a thing was to be. So much then about difference.

On Property

They divide property in four ways: (a) What belongs accidentally (i) to one species only, even if not to all of it, as practicing medicine or doing geometry does to human being. (b) What belongs accidentally (ii) to all of a species, even if not to it alone, as being a biped does to human being. (c) What belongs (ii) to all of a species and (i) to it alone and at the same time, as growing grey-haired in old age does to human being. (d) The fourth kind of property: that in which belonging (i) to only one species, (ii) to all of it, and (iii) always, all go together, as risibility does to human being. For even if he is not always laughing he is nevertheless

called "risible," not because he always is laughing but because he has an aptitude for laughing. This aptitude always belongs to him innately, as hinnibility does to a horse. They say that these are properties in the proper sense, because it goes both ways: If a horse then hinnibility, and if hinnibility then a horse.

On Accident

Accident is what comes and goes without the destruction of the substrate. It is divided into two kinds. One kind of accident is separable and the other is inseparable. Thus sleeping is a separable accident, whereas being black is an inseparable accident of the crow and the Ethiopian. Nevertheless a white crow and an Ethiopian who has lost his color can be conceived without the destruction of the substrate. They also define accident as follows: Accident is what admits of belonging or not belonging to the same thing, or what is neither a genus nor a difference nor a species nor a property, but always has its reality in a substrate. All the proposed terms have been defined – that is to say, 'genus,' 'species,' 'difference,' 'property,' and 'accident.' We must now say what common features belong to them, and what are the properties of each.

On the community among the five words

Being predicated of several things is common to all of them. But genus is predicated of species and of individuals, and so is difference, whereas species is predicated only of the individuals under it. Property is predicated of the species it is the property of, and of the individuals under the species. Accident is predicated of species and of individuals. For 'animal' is predicated of horses and oxen, which are species, and of this horse and this ox, which are individuals. 'Irrational' is predicated of horses and oxen, and of particulars. A species, such as 'human being,' is predicated of particulars only. A property, such as risibility, is predicated both of human being and of particular men. 'Black,' which is an inseparable accident, is predicated of the species of crows and of the particulars, whereas being moved, which is a separable accident, is predicated of human being and of horse – primarily of the individuals, and in a secondary sense of the species that include the individuals.

On the community between genus and difference

Including species is common to genus and differ- ence. For the difference also includes species, even if not all that genera do. Rational, even though it does not include irrational things as animal does, nevertheless includes human being and god, which are species.

VI.4. BOETHIUS

AT THE BEGINNING OF THE PREVIOUS SELECTION FROM HIS *ISAGOGE*
Porphyry declined to tackle "deeper" questions concerning the ontological status
of universals, particularly genera and species. Here Boethius, in one of the
ancient texts that most influenced later medieval thought in the Christian West,
first develops an argument to show that universals are nothing at all and the
thoughts of them are empty and useless. Then he proceeds to refute this argument
by explaining the line taken by later Peripatetics, although at the end, good
Platonist that we was, Boethius distances himself from that solution.

VI.4.1. The "deeper Questions"

"On the subject of genera and species," he
[Porphyry] says, "I shall at present decline to say
whether they subsist or are given in mere bare
thoughts, and whether as subsistents they are corporeal or incorporeal, and whether they are separate from sensible items or given in sensible items as
existing in and around them. For topics of this sort
are very deep and demand a long inquiry."

I omit the deeper questions, he [Porphyry] says, in
order not to upset readers' initial efforts by having
them pay attention to these matters at the wrong
time. But so that the reader will not overlook them
altogether and think there is nothing more hidden
here than what Porphyry himself had said, he
introduces the very topic whose treatment he has
promised to delay. By not at all treating the topic
obscurely and exhaustively he avoids overwhelming
the reader with obscurities and yet enables the
reader, strengthened by knowledge, to understand
what it is that could rightly be inquired about.

The inquiries he promises not to say anything
about are both very useful as well as mysterious.
Many learned men have attempted them but few
have resolved them. The first of them is the following: Everything the mind thinks of either is something that exists as part of the nature of things, and
this the mind grasps and describes for itself by an
account of it, or is something that does not exist,
and this the mind pictures to itself by an empty
mental image. Therefore we ask of which sort is a
thought of a genus or of one of the others [i.e. of a
species, difference, property or accident]? Do we
think of species and genera as things which exist

and from which we take a true thought? Or do we
delude ourselves by forming for ourselves in vain
mental activity things that do not exist?

If we establish that they do exist, and if we say the
thought of them is drawn from things that do exist,
then another, greater and more difficult inquiry
engenders a question, since there appears to be the
greatest difficulty in discerning and thinking of the
nature of a genus itself. For since everything that
exists is necessarily either corporeal or incorporeal,
genus and species will have to be in one of these
groups. Of which sort, then, is what is called a
genus? Is it corporeal or rather incorporeal? There
will be no careful consideration of what it is, if we
do not know in which of these sorts it is to be
placed.

But even when this question has been resolved,
there still remains some uncertainty. For given we
say that genera and species are incorporeal, something remains to besiege and detain our capacity
for thought, viz. whether they subsist in and
around bodies themselves or seem to be incorporeal items that subsist apart from bodies. Obviously,
there are two forms of incorporeal items. Some can
exist apart from bodies and exist in their own
incorporeality as separate from bodies, like God,
the mind, and the soul. Others, although they are
incorporeal, cannot exist apart from bodies, for
example, lines, planes, numbers and particular
qualities. Although we declare them to be incorporeal because they are not at all extended in three
dimensions, nevertheless they exist in bodies in
such a way that they cannot be torn away or separated from them, and if they were separated from
bodies they would in no way continue to exist.

Although Porphyry, finding these inquiries hard, declined to resolve them, let me, nevertheless, take them up in such a way that I neither leave the reader's mind troubled about them, nor I myself spend time and effort on what lies beyond my list of tasks. First, then, I shall set out a few points that underlie the uncertainty involved in the inquiry and then try to untie that same knot of the problem and explain it.

Genera and species either exist and subsist, or are formed by the intellect and mere mental activity. But genera and species cannot exist. This is grasped from the following considerations: Everything that is common to several items at one time cannot be *one* item. What is common belongs to many items chiefly when one and the same thing is *as a whole* in many items at one time. For no matter how many species there are, their genus is one item in all of them, not in the sense that each single species sort of plucks off some part of it, but rather in the sense that at one and the same time each of the species has the whole genus. From this it follows that the genus which is posited as a whole in several particular [species] at one and the same time cannot be *one* item. For it cannot be the case that although it is a whole in several things at one time, nevertheless in itself it is one in number. And if it is the case that a genus cannot be *one* item, then it is utterly nothing. For every thing that is is because it is *one* item. The same can be said about species.

But even if genera and species do exist, but each is a multiple item and not one in number, there will be no last genus. Rather it will have another genus placed above it, and this will include that multiplicity by means of the word expressing its one name. For just as several animals require a genus, since they have something similar but are not the same, so also, since a genus, which is in many items and thus a multiple item, has its own likeness because it is a genus, and is not a single item since it is in many, another genus must be sought for this genus. And when it has been discovered, by the same line of argument as used above still a third genus is tracked down. And so the argument must go on to infinity, since there is no end to the process of discovering.

If a genus is one in number, it cannot be common to many. For if one thing is common, either (1) it is common in virtue of its parts, and then it is not

common as a whole, but rather each of its parts belongs to its own particular; or (2) it is common in that over the course of time it is used by different owners, as is a well or a fountain, or a slave or a horse; or (3), as a theatre or show is common to all who watch it, it is common to all at one time but not so as to constitute the substance of the items it is common to. But a genus cannot be common to its species in any of these ways, for it has to be common in such a way that it is in the particulars both as a whole and at one time, and it must be able to constitute and form the substance of the items which it is common to.

Therefore, if it is neither *one* item, since it is common, nor a multiple item, since another genus must be sought for its multiplicity, it seems that a genus does not exist at all, And we will have to think the same of the others [i.e. species, differences etc.] as well.

Given that genera, species and the others are grasped only by thoughts, then, since every thought arises from a subject thing, either as that thing itself is or as that thing itself is not, a thought which concerns no subject is empty, for a thought cannot arise from no subject. If the thoughts of genera, species and the others come from subject things in such a way that those things are thought of as they are, then not only have they been posited by the thought but they are also established in the truth of things. And again it must be asked what is their nature, which is what the above inquiry was tracking down. If the thoughts of genera and the others are drawn from things but in such a way that those things are subjects for the thoughts not as those things themselves are, then those thoughts must be empty, since they are drawn from the things but not as the things themselves are, for that is false which is thought differently from the way the things are.

So, then, since it is neither the case that genera and species exist nor that when they are thought of there is a true thought of them, there can be no doubt that all this effort in discussing the aforesaid five items [genus, species, difference, property, accident, i.e. the five predicables] should be laid aside, since the inquiry is neither about things which exist nor even about things of which it is possible to think articulately anything true.

At present the above is the problem as regards

what we have been considering, and we resolve it in accord with Alexander[1] by the following reasoning. For we say that not every thought which is from a subject but not as that subject itself is must be viewed as false and empty. For false opinion, as opposed to thinking, occurs only in what comes to be through composition. If someone puts together and joins in thought what nature does not allow to be joined, no one fails to know that the result is false. For example, if someone joins in the imagination a horse and a man so as to make up a centaur. But if this occurs through division and abstraction, even though the thing does not exist in the way in which it is thought, still that thought is not at all false. For there are many items which have their existence in others, and from these others either they cannot be separated or if they were separated from them they would in no way subsist.

The following familiar example may make this clear to us. A line is something in a body, and it owes to the body that which it is, i.e. it retains its being through the body. This is shown as follows: If it were separated from the body, it would not subsist. For who has ever perceived by any sense a line separated from a body? But when the mind takes into itself from the senses confused things mixed with bodies, it distinguishes them by its own power and mental activity. For the senses transmit to us with the bodies all the incorporeal things of this sort that have their being in bodies. But the mind, which has the power both to put together what is separate and dissolve what is composite, so distinguishes what is transmitted by the senses as confused and joined with bodies that it may look into and see the incorporeal nature by itself without the bodies in which it concretely exists. For incorporeal items that are mixed with bodies have different properties even when separated from bodies. Consequently, genera, species and the others are found in incorporeal things as well as corporeal ones. If the mind discovers these in incorporeal things, it immediately has a thought of a genus of incorporeal items; but if it has observed genera and species of corporeal things, it removes, in its usual way, from the bodies the nature of incorporeal items and views that as alone and pure, as it is in itself the form itself. In this way when the mind receives items mixed up with bodies, by dividing it looks at and considers the incorporeal items.

Consequently, let no one say that, since the line cannot exist apart from bodies, we think of the line falsely when we grasp it mentally as though it existed apart from bodies. For not every thought which grasps subject things differently from the way those things themselves are is to be considered false. Rather, as we said above, the thought which does this in a composition is false, as when joining a human being and a horse it judges the result to be a centaur. Not only is that thought not false which brings this about by divisions, abstractions, and removals from the things in which they are, it is, in fact, the only thought which can discover what is true about the property of something. Therefore, things of this sort exist in corporeal and sensible items, but they are thought of apart from sensible items so that their nature can be perceived and their property understood.

For this reason when a genus or a species is considered, a likeness of it is gathered from the particulars in which they exist, for example a likeness of humanness from the particular humans who are dissimilar to each other. This likeness when considered by the mind and perceived in a true way becomes a species. Again, a likeness formed from the different species, which likeness can exist only in those species or in their particulars, makes up a genus.

Thus these [genera and species] exist in particulars but are thought of as universals. A species should not be considered anything but the mental activity that is gathered from the substantial likeness of individuals that are numerically dissimilar, while a genus is the mental activity gathered from a likeness of species.

But when this likeness is in particulars it becomes sensible; when in universals, intelligible. Likewise, when it is sensible it persists in singulars; when it is thought of, it becomes universal. Therefore, they subsist in and around sensibles, but are thought of as apart from bodies. For nothing prevents two things in the same subject being different in definition, as, for example, a convex and a concave line. Although these things are delimited by different

1 Alexander of Aphrodisias, who worked in the late 2nd and early 3rd centuries C.E., revived the Peripatetic school with his commentaries on Aristotle.

367

definitions and the thoughts of them are different, still they are always found in the same subject; for it is the same line that is concave that is convex. And so it is with genera and species, i.e. while there is a single subject for singularity and universality, still it is universal in one way, when it is thought of, and singular in another, when it is sensed in those things in which it has its existence.

Given these determinations, every problem, I think, is solved. For while the genera and species themselves exist in one way, they are thought of in another. They are incorporeal, but when joined to sensible items they subsist in sensible items. They are thought of as subsisting on their own and not as having their existence in other items.

But Plato held not only that genera, species and the others are thought of as universals but also that they subsist apart from bodies. Aristotle, on the other hand, held that they are thought of as incorporeal and universal but subsist in sensibles. I have not deemed it fitting to judge between these views, for that belongs to a deeper philosophy. We have followed closely Aristotle's view, not because we especially agree with it, but because this book was written to accompany the *Categories*, of which Aristotle is the author.

VI.5. GARLANDUS COMPOTISTA

THE AUTHOR OF THIS ELEVENTH-CENTURY WORK INTERPRETS THE doctrine of predicables and categories as dealing with utterances, i.e., the physical sounds produced in speech. He re-writes Porphyry so as to make such an interpretation coherent. He also uses a notion of signification where a term signifies whatever it is true of, while allowing that terms that signify the same things might differ in mode of signifying. This has some odd results which its author does not hold back from embracing.

VI.5.1. The Predicables are just Utterances (from *Dialectica*)

BOOK I: NON-COMPLEX UTTERANCES

1. *On the five predicables*

a. Genera

'Genus' has three senses. (1) It is a collection of items that relate to some one thing and to each other, as for example the genus of Romans relate to Romulus. (2) Or it is an origin of generation. We call that an origin of generation which is either the father of a single generation, as, for example, Jupiter was the ultimate father of Tantalus, Pelops, Atreus and Agamemnon, or the place in which someone produced a generation as, for example, Thebes where Cadmus produced many children. But philosophers do not speak of either of these sorts of genera.

(3) The third sense, which philosophers use, is defined as follows: A genus is what is predicated of many items differing in species in respect of what they are. The phrase 'what is predicated' differentiates genera from those items which are not predicated, i.e. from things (as opposed to utterances), which do not get placed in propositions. The phrase 'differing in species' differentiates them from completely specific species, which are not predicated of many items differing in species but items differing only in number. The phrase 'in respect of what they are,' i.e. the what-question, differentiates them from all the items which are predicated in respect of what the item is like or how

it relates. Consequently the above description of a genus is valid.

The phrase 'of many items differing in species' should be taken to mean that those many items differ *from each other* in respect of their species; for example, this human and this ass differ from each other in respect of 'human,' and 'ass.' The phrase 'from each other' must be understood here if we are to avoid the absurdity of having a completely specific species possibly being shown to be a genus, for a completely specific species like 'human' is predicated of many differing in species in respect of what they are, namely of 'Socrates' and 'Plato'; but 'Socrates' and 'Plato' do not differ *from each other* in respect of their species, i.e. in respect of 'human.'

Here we find the following sophism:

What is not a human is a human. Is this the case?

If what is not a genus is a genus, also what is not a human is a human. But what is not a genus is a genus. Is this the case?

If a completely specific species, like 'human,' is a genus, also what is not a genus is a genus. But a completely specific species is a genus. Is this the case?

If it accords with the definition of 'genus,' it also is a genus. This must be qualified with the phrase 'in so far as it is the definition of 'genus,' for otherwise the inference fails, since, given that there are different ways in which the definition of genus can be explained, a completely specific species can accord with an improper explanation of the definition and still not be a genus.

On the assumption that the whole was so qualified argue as follows: But a completely specific species does accord with the definition of genus; for example, 'human' does, for 'human' is predicated of many items differing in species in respect of what they are, namely of 'Socrates' and 'Plato,' who differ in respect of their species, i.e. 'human,' from individual asses. Therefore, a completely specific species is a genus; therefore, what is not a genus is a genus, and what is not a human is a human.

The phrase 'in species' has to be interpreted as meaning 'in respect of their own species.' Otherwise, it will not help to read in as understood the phrase 'from each other,' for even with the qualification 'from each other' inserted still a completely specific species will accord with the definition of 'genus' as long as 'in species' is not interpreted as meaning 'in respect of their own species.' For example, 'human' is a completely specific species and is rightly predicated of many items differing from each other, i.e. of 'Socrates' and 'Plato.' I mean of the 'Socrates' and 'Plato' that stay in their own species, 'human.' If someone added 'from each other' and then later did not interpret 'in species' as having the meaning it has in the definition of genus, they would face the same absurdity we mentioned before.

Therefore, clearly this proposition, 'If a completely specific species accords with the definition of "genus," it also is a genus,' has to be qualified, for unless it accords with it, the inference fails, and later we will have to see under what interpretation a genus accords with that definition or description. If we are not careful in interpreting it, we will end up faced with absurdity. For the definitions of those utterances which are genera, for example 'sensate, animate substance,' the definition of 'animal,' accord then with this definition [of 'genus'], for this is predicated as answering the what-question of many items differing in species.

Also, just as this definition accords with the definition of 'genus,' so the definition of 'genus' accords with itself. For this utterance 'genus,' which is used to define 'species,' falls under [the category of] relation and is called a genus and is predicated as answering the what-question of many items differing in species, for example other genera. Likewise for its own definition. If, then, the definition of 'genus' is predicated as answering the what-question of many items differing in species in the same way the item it defines is, it is called a genus too. Therefore, what is not a genus is a genus, for no definition is a genus.

To evade this absurdity we have to be careful in interpreting the definition of 'genus.' For this reason the phrase 'in respect of what they are' should be interpreted as follows: Let the utterance which is predicated of many items differing in species stay in this name, i.e. be signified by this name 'what'; in other words, let the utterance which is predicated of many items differing in species be the type, because this utterance 'what' to us designates type utterances. For this reason if someone so interprets 'in respect of what they are' as meaning what answers a what-question and adds nothing further, they will face the absurdity of 'sensate, animate substance' being a genus. For this phrase 'sensible, animate substance' is correctly predicated of many items differing from each other in respect of their species, for example of 'this human' and 'this ass.' Also it correctly answers the what-question, for to someone who asks 'What is Socrates?' we can correctly answer; 'a sensate, animate substance.' Nevertheless, a phrase does not admit of being called a genus. Thus to avoid absurdity qualifications of the definition of 'genus' are required.

Genus is divided into its species as follows: Some genera are completely generic genera, others are subalternate genera. This can be seen better by taking a single category as an example. We call this utterance 'substance' along with the utterances placed under it a category because there the genus is predicated of its species and all the higher items of lower items.

We have to realize that in any category there is a single completely generic genus and several completely specific species and some other utterances which are called subalternate genera and subalternate species. Also there is the completely generic, which is the higher genus, and the completely specific species which are lower species. We have to realize, too, that just as the completely generic genus cannot be a species, so neither can the completely specific species be genera. The ones which lie between the completely generic and the completely specific are all called subalternate genera and subalternate species, as long as they have the same nature. The phrase 'the same nature' is inserted to exclude the differences which come in between, because they are not of the same nature as the genera and species.

Thus those items which lie between the completely generic and the completely specific are said to be subalternate, because they are found under some while others are found under them. They are called genera in respect of the items beneath them; species, in respect of those above them.

All of this is clear in the case of this category [viz. substance]: Some substances are bodies, others non-bodies. Some animate bodies are animals, others insensate bodies. Some animals are rational animals, others irrational. Some rational animals are humans, others gods. Notice that 'substance,' which is the higher utterance, is completely generic, while 'human' and 'god,' which are lower species, are called completely specific species. 'Animal,' 'body,' and the others that lie in between are for the aforesaid reason subalternate genera and subalternate species. For 'body' is a subalternate utterance because it takes its origin from 'substance' itself and this other utterance, 'animate body,' is found under it. It is called a species in relation to 'substance,' which is its genus, and a genus in relation to this utterance 'animate body,' which utterance is its species. Thus also for the others which lie in between the completely specific items and the completely generic one.

Some say that individuals belong to the category; others deny this completely. Those who say they do not belong to the category rely on the argument that individuals cannot be predicated in the strict sense of 'predicated,' that is they cannot be predicated of anything beneath themselves, and thus they cannot belong to the category. The others rely on the argument that even though they cannot be predicated in the strict sense, nevertheless, they fall under all the higher items and thus really do belong to the category.

We look at it differently and say that in one respect they do belong to the category and in another they do not. On the one hand, we say they unworthily belong to the category because they fall under all the higher items; on the other hand, we deny that they worthily belong, because they are not predicated of anything in the strict sense. I say

that something is predicated in the strict sense when either a genus is predicated of a species and of individuals or a species of individuals.

So much for genera.

b. Species

'Species' has two senses, one in respect of things, the other in respect of utterances. In things the form of anything is called a species, because it is through its form that anything is inspected. It is species in respect of utterances that philosophers talk about and it is defined as follows: A species is a type of individuals that falls under a genus. The phrase 'type of individuals' is used here to exclude all those utterances which are not types, whether they are predicated in answering the what-question or not. Here definitions are excluded, since even if they are predicated an answering the what-question, still they are not genuine types, because they are neither genera nor species. Also excluded are differences, distinctive features, and other accidents which are neither predicated as answering the what-question nor are genuine types. But since a genus is a genuine type, in order to exclude it the phrase 'that falls under a genus' is added, because no genus insofar as it is a genus falls under a genus, but rather it does this insofar as it is a species. Consequently this definition of species is elegant and universally convertible, for every species is a type of individuals that falls under a genus and every type of individuals that falls under a genus is a species.

Another definition, which holds only for completely specific species is the following: A species is what is predicated as answering the what-question for many items differing in number. But here we need to add 'only in number'; otherwise, any genus would accord with it, since a genus, like 'animal,' is correctly predicated as answering the what-question of many items differing in number, but not of many differing only in number, because they also differ in species.

I mean by 'number' a collection of accidents distinctive of something; these are called a number because they are enumerated in something. For example, in Garlandus are enumerated those accidents by which he differs from other people and which are distinctive of him. Even if these are enumerated in someone else, still completely the same

UNIVERSALS AND PARTICULARS

ones or the same ranking will not exist in someone else, because they will belong to that person more intensely or to a lesser extent. These, I say, are the accidents that belong to Garlandus: 'dark,' 'curly-haired,' 'handsome,' 'humble,' 'lovable,' 'of ordinary height.'

'Species' is divided as follows: Some species are completely specific; others are subalternate.

So much for species.

c. Differences

What follows concerns differences. First, the broad sense of 'difference' is divided to reach the philosophical notion of difference. Thus some differences are separable; others are inseparable. The separable differences are the transitive utterances which happen to belong to things generally, for example 'white' and 'black' and like utterances which happen to belong to things generally, belonging now to me and now to others.

Of inseparable differences some are differences in a strict sense, others are differences in an even stricter sense. Something that happens to belong to something inseparable, like blindness to the eyes, is called a difference in the strict sense. Specific differences, i.e. those which are constitutive of a species, like 'mortal' and 'immortal' and the like, are called differences in an even stricter sense. These are the ones the philosophers treat and define as follows: A difference is that by which a species goes beyond its genus. This description is complete and is convertible with 'specific difference' when it is interpreted as follows: A difference is the utterance drawn from the genus, as 'mortal' is drawn from 'animal,' by which the species that is constituted from that genus and from that utterance drawn from it goes beyond [its genus], i.e. the species is united with this utterance in addition to its genus. I say it is united with it, because the utterance which is drawn from the genus and which with it is constitutive of the species always follows the species it is constitutive of. This is clear in the following example: The utterance 'mortal' is drawn from the genus 'rational animal,' and united with that is constitutive of the species 'human.' And that utterance follows the species in all cases, for if something is a human it is mortal. But it does not always follow the genus, since it is not true that every rational animal is mortal. Thus the species

goes beyond the genus in this, because it has the difference constitutive of itself more than the genus does, since the difference accompanies the species in every case, but not the genus. Thus anything that is a difference is that by which a species goes beyond its genus, and anything which is that by which a species goes beyond its genus is a difference.

There are some definitions of 'difference' which belong not just to specific differences; for example: A difference is that by which particulars differ from each other.

We must realize that every specific difference is both divisive and constitutive or completing. It is divisive in relation to the genus which it divides, for example: some animals are rational, others irrational. It is constitutive in relation to the species which along with its genus it is constitutive of, for example: 'rational' and 'mortal' united with animal are constitutive of 'human.' Consequently, differences are said to be completing, because, where there is a shortage of utterances which are called species, they joined with their genus complete the species which has not been invented and are used in place of it. For example, immediately under 'animal' no non-complex utterance has been invented which is said to be its species; rather the difference 'rational' united with 'animal' completes that species which has not been invented, i.e. it is used in place of it and the difference joined with the genus is called a species. Thus when I say: 'Some animals are rational animals, others are irrational animals,' this is a genuine division of a genus into species only to the extent that it means: 'Some animals are a's, others are b's,' where 'a' and 'b' would be immediate species of 'animal.'

This should be enough about differences.

d. Properties

'Property' has four senses: (1) That which is predicated of only one species even if not universally, as for example 'physician' is predicated of 'human'; (2) that which is predicated of only one species both universally and at some time, as for example 'growing gray' is predicated of a human if the person survives into old age; (3) that which is universally predicated of some species even if it is not predicated of that one only, as for example 'bipedal' is predicated not only of 'human' but of 'chicken' too; (4) that which is predicated universally of only one species and of that at all times and convertibly, as for example 'Every human is capable of laughing' and 'Every item capable of laughing is a human.' Only these last properties are said to be properties in the strict sense.

When it is said that 'physician' is a property only of the species which is 'human,' a sophism arises as follows:

Some human is not a human. Is this the case?

If no physician is a human, also some human is not a human. But no physician [is a human]. Is this the case?

If no human is a physician, also no physician is a human. But no human [is a physician]. Is this the case?

If no animal is a physician, also no human is a physician. But no animal is a physician. Is this the case?

If the utterance 'physician' in no way applies to 'animal,' also no animal is a physician. But 'physician' [in no way applies to 'animal']. Is this the case?

If the utterance 'animal' is a species, also 'physician' in no way applies to it. If someone allows that proposition, assume it and draw the conclusion. But if someone wants to deny it, you can prove it to be true as follows:

If being a physician belongs to no species other than 'human,' then this proposition is true: 'If 'animal' [is a species, also 'physician' in no way belongs to it.]' But to no [species other than 'human' does 'physician' apply]. Is this the case?

If 'physician' applies only to the species 'human,' also it applies to no other species. But 'physician' applies only to the species 'human.' Is this the case?

If the Book says it, it is true. Thus draw your conclusion by going right back to the beginning.

Solution: If you interpret it in the sense the Book[1] uses, then this inference is false: If 'physician'

applies only to the species 'human,' also it applies to no other species. For the Book uses the phrase 'only the species 'human'' merely to exclude species opposed to 'human,' not to exclude 'animal.' Wherever someone mentions to you the phrase 'only the species' in the treatise on properties, qualify it in this same way.

So much for properties.

e. Accidents

It remains to define 'accident' as follows: An accident is what belongs to and is absent from a subject without involving the destruction of the subject. Even inseparable accidents, which never seem to depart from their subject, as for example a human is always capable of laughter and a crow is always black, seem to be covered by this description if it is correctly interpreted. Let us say, then, that an accident is what belongs to something and is absent from something, i.e. that utterance is called an accident which belongs to a subject, i.e. to a substantive utterance, in other words it applies to it by co-signification, and is absent from it, i.e. it is far away from that substantive utterance, in mode of signifying, because it does not signify substantially as that does – or it is absent from it, i.e. is far away from the substantive utterance to which it applies in the sense that it is not given in its definition and nevertheless the definition is no less valid. This is what is meant by the phrase 'without involving the destruction of the subject,' i.e. without involving the definition of the substantive utterance. The definition is here called the destruction of the subject because, if the definition itself is destroyed, that destroys the subject, i.e. the substantive utterance the definition constitutes.

Putting this altogether we get the following: That utterance is called an accident which co-signifies, in a way indicative of belonging, with a substantive utterance and which can fail to be in its definition, i.e. the definition of the substantive utterance, even though that substantive utterance retains existence. For example, 'capable of laughing' is not found in the definition of 'human,' which is 'mortal, rational animal.'

We should realize that some accidents are predi-

---

1 I.e., Porphyry's *Isagoge*.

cated of only one species and of just some of the individuals in that species, for example 'shoemaker' and 'leather-worker,' which apply only to humans. Some are predicated of only one species and of all the individuals in it, like 'capable of laughing.' Some are predicated of only some species and of only some individuals in those species, for example 'white' and 'black.' And some are predicated of all the species existing in one branch of substances and of all the individuals in those species, for example 'colored,' which accident is predicated of 'body' and everything that falls under 'body.'

So much for these matters.

2. On the Ten Categories[2]

Now we must speak about the ten categories. But since categorial utterances are genera and species, we have to see whether we must treat of them in the way we did above in the treatise on genus and species or in some other way. It turns out that we will treat of these same utterances in a different way than we did before, because there we treated them only in so far as they were genera and species, whereas here we will treat of them in so far as they are subjects or items existing in subjects; in other words, in this treatise we intend to reveal what utterances are basic in respect of other utterances, i.e. which sustain the others, and what ones require a basis, i.e. are sustained by others.

[There follow three sections on a. univocals, b. equivocals, and c. denominatives, which have been omitted in this selection.]

d. Substances

Some substances are first, others second. Substantial individuals like 'some human' are called first substances; substantial species, like 'human,' and genera are called second substances. We must realize that 'this human,' 'Socrates,' and 'some human' are correctly called individuals, but 'Socrates' is more worthy [of being called an individual], because 'this human' designates only what

is present and 'some human' designates both that and that, since it is directed toward all humans. But 'Socrates' designates something both when it is present and when it is absent, and is specifically, i.e. in virtue of its imposition, directed to just one item.

Individuals, then, are called first substances because it is they that first of all sustain accidents and because of them accidents are attributed to second substances. For example, if Socrates is white also a human is white; but this does not convert, i.e. we cannot infer that if a human is white then Socrates is white.

We must realize too that individuals are more worthy than species and genera of being called substances[3] for another reason, namely that they are ranked under all higher items. For the same reason we can see in the case of second substances that the species more than the genus is called a substance both because it receives accidents from the first substances more immediately than does the genus, and because in the category in question it is found under more utterances than is the genus.

No substances, neither the first nor the second substances, admit of more and less. This is not to be interpreted as something that seems contrary to what was just said, namely that a first substance is more a substance than a species or a genus is, and a species is more a substance than a genus is. There is no real opposition here, because, where it is said that no substance admits of more and less, that is to be interpreted as meaning that no substance, i.e. substantial utterance, admits of more or less, i.e. it is not intensified or diminished. For example, 'human' applies equally to Socrates and to Plato, for Socrates is not more a human than Plato. Likewise other substantial utterances are not intensified or diminished. But where it is said that one substance is more a substance than some other substance, this means that this utterance 'substance' applies to one substantial utterance more than to some other for a variety of reasons, namely those which were mentioned earlier.

Thus unless those two rules are interpreted as we suggested, or in some other way that does not make them seem contrary to each other, we will get the following sort of argument for this absurd conclusion:

---

2 See selection **VI.2.1.**, ch4.

3 *Substantia*, i.e. items that are *under* something.

The thing which is called human is not called animal. Is this the case?

If that which is called a completely specific species is not called a species, also that which is called human is not called animal. This follows from its likeness to a similar case, because if in the one case what is designated by the species is not designated by the genus, neither will it be in the other case.

Now resume the argument: But that which is called a completely specific species is not called a species. Is this the case?

If this utterance 'human,' i.e. a completely specific species of substance, is not a species, also that which is called a completely specific species is not a species. But this utterance 'human' [is not a species]. Is this the case?

No species admits of more and less, but 'human' admits of more and less. Is this the case?

If it is more a substance than 'animal' and less than 'Socrates,' then it admits of more and less. But it is more a substance than 'animal,' according to Aristotle in the *Categories*,[4] who says that an individual is more a substance than a species and a species more than a genus. Therefore, 'human' admits of more and less; therefore, it is not a species. And if this completely specific species 'human' is not a species, neither is that which is human an animal.

Solution: The proposition which reads, 'No species admits of more and less,' has to be qualified as follows: Either it is said to admit of more and less in respect of its co-signification with something, i.e. in respect of its own self, i.e. in such a way that it applies to its significates by co-signifying in a more or less way, or it admits of more and less in its own designation, i.e. some noun applies to it in a more or less way, as, for example, this utterance 'human' is more called a substance than 'animal' is and less than 'Socrates' is. If, then, when I say, "No species admits or more and less," I mean that no species admits of more and less in its own

designation, the proposition is false. But if I mean that [no] species admits more and less in respect of its co-signification with something, then the proposition will be true and the assumption [of the sophistical reasoning, viz. that 'human' admits of more and less] will be false when it is interpreted in that same way.

Further: Utterances in the category of substance are not called contraries. We must realize that no individuals besides individual substances admit of contraries. For example, 'Socrates' at different times admits of 'white' and 'black.' But this individual of the sentence which in its designation is the sentence 'Socrates is sitting' does not, while remaining a single individual, admit of the contraries 'true' and 'false,' although the sentence 'Socrates is sitting' is true when he sits and false when he stands up, because this individual which is this sentence will be an individual either of a true sentence or of a false sentence. If it is an individual of a true sentence, it will always be true; if an individual of a false sentence, it will always be false. But if it is said to be an individual of both a true and a false sentence, then it will not stay a single individual but will be like two individuals.

We should not neglect to remark that the utterance 'substance,' in its role as a completely generic genus, signifies everything whatsoever that there is. But this seems absurd to some, who argue as follows: If 'substance,' insofar as it is a completely generic genus, signifies everything, also it signifies itself insofar as it is a completely generic genus, and this is absurd.

But we see nothing absurd in allowing that 'substance' signifies itself, just as there is no absurdity when a given species signifies itself as well as its genus, and a given individual signifies itself as well as its species and genus, even the most generic genus itself. 'Body' is a species that signifies itself and its genus. We prove this as follows:

'Air' is a species of 'body,' and 'air' signifies the utterance 'body' as well as the utterance 'substance'; therefore, 'body,' the genus of 'air,' signifies itself as well as 'substance,' the completely generic genus, because whatever a species, insofar as it is a species and in its role as a species, signifies, its genus signifies as well.

---

4 See **VI.2.1.**, ch.5.

Also the individual 'this air' signifies itself. This is proved as follows:

What is signified by a species is signified by some individual of that species. If 'air' is a species of this individual 'this air,' also 'air' signifies this articulation 'this air.' Therefore, this articulation 'this air' is signified by some individual of 'air'; therefore by 'this air.' Also this individual 'this air' signifies as well this articulation 'air,' i.e.[5] its species, and the articulation 'body,' i.e. its genus, as well as the articulation 'substance,' i.e. its completely generic genus.

Thus we say that the completely generic genus 'substance,' insofar as it is a completely generic genus, signifies itself, because every completely generic genus signifies itself. This is to be seen in each case and should be proved of one case so that it may be better seen in the others.

Question: Does the completely generic genus 'substance' signify itself? Whatever is signified by a species is signified by the completely generic genus for that species. But this utterance 'substance' is designated by the species 'body'; therefore, it is designated by its completely generic genus 'substance.' 'Substance' then is designated by 'substance.' The first proposition, however, is false, unless we read in there: 'insofar as it is a species of that completely generic genus.'

But perhaps when you take up this line of reasoning, someone objects that 'body,' insofar as it is a species of 'substance,' does not signify the utterance 'substance.' For if insofar as it is a species of 'substance' it signified that, then every species of 'substance' would signify its completely generic genus [viz. 'substance']; therefore, 'human' would, which would be absurd.

But there is no force to this objection, since when you say, "Whatever the species, insofar as it is a species of that completely generic genus, signifies also the completely generic genus itself signifies," you do not interpret the phrase 'insofar as it is a species' to mean 'on account of its being a species,' because then it would be false to assume: "But 'body,' insofar as it is a species of 'substance,' signifies itself," given this means that it is on account of its being a species of substance that it signifies itself. For if it signified 'substance' itself on

account of its being a species of 'substance,' then likewise these two species 'animal' and 'human' would signify the utterance 'substance,' which would be absurd. But the phrase 'insofar as it is a species of "substance"' is to be interpreted as meaning 'in its role as a species,' i.e. 'in virtue of the imposition by which it was imposed on it to be and stay a species.' In this sense the proposition will be true which says, 'Whatever is signified by a species, insofar as it is a species, is signified by that species' completely general genus,' and also the assumption is true which is, 'But "body," insofar as it is a species of it, signifies "substance," i.e. in virtue of this that it was imposed as an acknowledged species of it.' You can then conclude with certainty that 'substance' signifies itself insofar as it is a completely generic genus.

Thus we have qualified the proposition with the phrase 'insofar as it is a species' because otherwise the principle would fail in the case of species which go beyond their genus in signification, in some other role than that which they have by being imposed as acknowledged species. For example, when I say, "Some animals are humans; others are non-humans," 'non-human,' which is a sort of species of 'animal,' goes beyond what is signified by 'animal' in a role other than that which it has by being imposed as an acknowledged species of 'animal,' for it signifies non-animals as well.

Just as it was proved that 'substance' signifies itself, so it can be proved of all the other completely generic genera. Briefly, then, let us show this in each case by the same argument we used to show it of 'substance.'

'Quantity' signifies itself. Is this the case? 'Utterance' is a species of 'quantity' and signifies 'quantity' in virtue of its imposition as an acknowledged species of it. Therefore, 'quantity' signifies itself.

'Quality' signifies itself. Is this the case? 'Figure' is a species of 'quality' and signifies 'quality' in virtue of its imposition. Therefore, 'quality' signifies itself.

'Relation' signifies itself. Is this the case? 'Figure' is a species of 'quality' and signifies

---

5 Reading *scilicet* for *secundum*.

'relation' in virtue of its imposition. Therefore, 'relation' signifies itself.

'Place' signifies itself. Is this the case? 'To be at Rome' is a species of 'place' and this utterance 'to be at Rome' designates place. Therefore, 'place' signifies itself.

'Time' signifies itself. Is this the case? 'Yesterday' is a species of 'time' and 'to be yesterday' signifies 'time.' Therefore, 'time' signifies itself.

'To be positioned' signifies itself. Is this the case? 'Imposed' is a species of 'to be positioned,' and this utterance 'imposed' signifies 'to be positioned.' Therefore, 'to be positioned' signifies itself.

'Having' signifies itself. Is this the case? 'Having signification' is a species of 'having' and 'having signification' signifies 'having.' 'Having,' then, signifies itself.

'Doing' signifies itself. Is this the case? 'Designating' is a species of 'doing,' and 'designating' is imposed on 'doing.' Therefore, 'doing' is imposed on itself.

Does 'being acted on' signify itself? 'Being articulated' is a species of 'being acted on,' and 'being articulated' is imposed on 'being acted on.' 'Being acted on,' then, [is imposed on] its own self.

We have to realize that all completely general genera signify the same items, but in different ways. If, therefore, this completely general genus 'substance' signifies the utterance 'quality,' which is another completely general genus, as well as all the other completely general genera, it is necessary that they all signify each other. All the completely general genera, I say, signify the same items in different ways, because 'substance' signifies the thing which merely is, i.e. the pure being of the thing. 'Quantity' signifies the same thing as 'measured,' i.e. as a quantity, i.e. as it is quantified, whether small or big. 'Quality' signifies the same item as a mere quality, i.e. as what is qualified, i.e. whether it is white or black or receives some other qualitative utterance. 'Relation' signifies the same thing as being reciprocally related, i.e. inasmuch as the thing receives some utterance that relates to another utterance, just as 'created' relates to 'creator.' 'Place' signifies the same item inasmuch as it is in a place. 'Time,' inasmuch as it is in a time. 'Having,' as possessing. 'Doing,' as acting. 'Being acted on,' as undergoing something.

We must realize too that every completely general genus signifies all the utterances placed under it. This is proved as follows: Any completely general genus signifies everything, and the utterances placed under any completely general genus are part of everything. Thus any completely general genus signifies the utterances placed under it.

When I say that every completely general genus signifies all things, I do not mean to imply that all the nouns denoting those things are placed under those completely general genera; rather I intend that only some are, as we can see in the following case: This completely general genus 'substance' signifies everything; therefore, it signifies a house, i.e. the thing which is called 'house.' Nevertheless, this utterance 'house' is not placed under 'substance,' a noun denoting that thing, as a categorial utterance is, but rather [what it designates] is designated by other utterances which are placed under 'substance.' For example, the thing which is called 'house' is designated by the utterances 'this substance,' 'this body,' as well as by those utterances placed under 'substance' that designate it by its parts, like 'stone,' 'wood,' 'earth.'

Here ends the treatise on substance.

VI.6. ABELARD

ABELARD STUDIED AND TAUGHT AT PARIS AND ELSEWHERE IN FRANCE in the early twelfth century before all of Aristotle's Logic had been recovered in western Europe. He knew Aristotle's *Categories, De Interpretatione (Peri ermenias)*, and Boethius's commentaries on these as well as on Porphyry's *Isagoge*, and later Aristotle's *Topics* but little else of the ancient doctrines in logic. Consequently, his acute mind was free to engage the subject in a more original way than were most of the later scholastics. Certainly his treatment of univerals is very un-Aristotelian and resembles more ancient Stoic doctrines, which it seems he could not have been aware of. Also it owes much to the school of logicians represented by Garlandus (previous selection) with its identification of predicables with utterances.

Although few authors after 1150 cite Abelard, his rejection of the idea that logic basically treats of "real" entities instead of words and sentences was without doubt influential in steering later scholastics away from the realist view. The position that logic is basically a *scientia sermonum*, science of words, found many supporters right to the end of the medieval period and beyond.

VI.6.1. The Existence and the Nature of Universals (from *Logica Ingredientibus, Gloss on Porphyry*)

[This selection comes from Abelard's gloss on Porphyry and takes up the earlier commentary of Boethius, Selection **VI.4.1.** above.

We remarked in the introduction to this topic that for very powerful theological reasons universals are re-conceived as entities either in time alone or in both time and space. It is inevitable that a theory of concepts or names will come to the fore in an attempt to explain and account for the facts of predication. The following selection from Abelard shows the shape of the new effort. By means of great dialectical skill Abelard demolishes attempts to make sense of universals as real temporal or spatial things. How could a spatial object conceivably fulfill the demands of a universal and be in several particulars without being spatially divided? Abelard gives arguments which he takes to show why things either individually or collectively cannot be called universal, i.e. said to be predicated of many. It remains for him to ascribe universality to utterances alone.]

Boethius says there are three [questions] which are obscure and useful and although taken up by many philosophers have been solved by few. The first is as follows: Do genera and species subsist or are they posited only [in the mind]? Which is the same as asking whether they have true being or exist only in opinion.

If it is conceded that they truly are, the second question is whether they are corporeal or incorporeal, and the third, whether they are separate from sensibles or are given in them. For there are two species of incorporeal things: some, like God and the soul, can persist in their incorporeal existence over and above sensibles; others can in no way be without those sensibles they are in, as, for example, a line cannot be without its subject body.

There are other questions too about the same things which are similarly difficult. For example, the question of the common cause of the imposition of a universal noun, which is that in respect of which diverse things agree. Or the question about the idea associated with a universal noun, through which no thing seems to be conceived (nor does a universal word seem to deal with any thing); and many other difficult questions.

In this way we can explain the words 'and concerning related matters' by adding a fourth question, viz. whether it is necessary for genera and species, as long as they are genera and species, to have some thing subject by nomination, or given that the named things have been removed from the signification of the idea, is the universal still able to exist; for example can this noun 'rose' [exist] when there are no roses to which it is common? But on these questions we will argue more carefully later.

But now let us go back to the previous questions, as we promised, and carefully look into and solve them. And since [Boethius] notes that genera and species are universals and through them he touches generally on the nature of universals, let us here distinguish the properties distinctive of universals as opposed to singulars and inquire whether these belong only to words or also to things.

Aristotle defines a universal as follows in the *On Interpretation*:[1] "What is naturally suited to be predicated of many." Porphyry also defines a singular, i.e. an individual, as "what is predicated of only one."[2] Authority seems to ascribe [universality] to both things and expressions. Aristotle himself seems to ascribe it to things when right before his definition of 'universal,' he says, "Since of things some are universals, others are singulars, I say that a universal can be predicated of many, but a singular cannot." Also Porphyry, when he wants to construct a species from a genus and a difference, assigns these to the nature of things. From this it is clear that things themselves are contained under the noun 'universal.'

Nouns are also called universals. So Aristotle says, "A genus determines a quality of a substance, for it signifies a certain quale." And Boethius in his book on division says, "It is useful to know that a genus is a single likeness of many species which points out the substantial agreement of all those species." Signifying and pointing out belong to expressions; being signified, to things. Also Boethius says, "The word 'noun' is predicated of many nouns and is in a way a species containing individuals under itself." But it is not properly said to be a species, since it is not a substantial but is rather an accidental word. But without doubt that is a universal with which the definition of universal

agrees. This shows that also expressions are universals, since only they are held to be the predicate terms of propositions.

But since both things and expressions seem to be called universals, we have to ask how the definition of 'universal' can be applied to things, for no thing nor any collection of things seems to be predicated of many one at a time, which is the property a universal must have. For even if this people or this hour or Socrates are said of all their parts at once, no one says they are fully universals, since they are not predicated of singulars. But a single thing is predicated much less of many than a collection is. Therefore, let us hear how either a single thing or a collection is called a universal and let us put down all the opinions of everyone.

Some understand a universal thing in such a way that they find in things diverse by reason of forms essentially the same substance which is the material essence of the singulars in which it is and which in itself is one and is diverse only by reason of the forms of its inferiors. If it happened to be separated from these forms there would be utterly no differences between things, i.e. the things are separate from one another only by diversity of the forms, since they have completely the same essential matter. For example, in individual humans differing in number there is the same substance of human being which here is made Plato by these accidents and there is made Socrates by those accidents. Porphyry especially seems to assent to this when he says: "By participation in the species many humans are one, but in particulars what is one and common is many." Again: "Individuals are said to be of this sort since each of them consists of properties the collection of which is not in another."

Likewise, in individual animals differing in species they propose one and the same essential substance of animal, which they draw into diverse species by means of the reception of diverse differences, just as I may make from this wax both a statue of a human being and a statue of a cow by fitting different forms to what remains completely the same essence. But the cases differ in that the same wax does not make up these statues at the same time, whereas this is conceded to the universal

1 See selection **VI.2.2**.
2 See selection **VI.3.1**.

because the universal is common in such a way, as Boethius says, that at one and the same time the whole [universal] is in diverse things materially constituting their substance. And although in itself it is universal, it is also singular by reason of the accidental forms without which it naturally subsists in itself. Apart from them in nature a universal in no way actually persists, but rather the singular. The incorporeal and insensible is understood in the simplicity of its universality, but the corporeal and sensible actually subsists by reason of its accidents. Also according to Boethius singulars subsist and universals are understood.

This is one of two opinions. Although the authorities seem to give it much assent, natural science finds it in all ways repugnant. For if essentially the same thing is present in singulars although occupied by diverse forms, that which is affected by these forms has to be that which is occupied by them, so that the animal formed by rationality has to be the animal formed by irrationality, and thus the rational animal has to be the irrational animal. Consequently contraries will be simultaneously present in the same thing. But in no way do we have contraries where they are present in entirely the same essence at the same time. This would be the case even if the thing were sometimes white and sometimes black, just as it is sometimes white and sometimes hard. For not even contraries of a different type, like relatives and most others, can belong to the same thing at the same time. Thus Aristotle in "Relation," where he shows large and small to be in the same thing at the same time but in different ways argues by this that they are not contraries.

But perhaps it will be said that according to this opinion rationality and irrationality are not less contraries because they are found in the same thing, i.e. in the same genus or in the same species, unless they are also grounded in the same individual. But this also is shown: rationality and irrationality are, indeed, in the same individual because they are in Socrates. They are simultaneously in Socrates because they are simultaneously in Socrates and Brunellus. But Socrates and Brunellus are Socrates. Socrates and Brunellus are indeed Socrates, because Socrates is Socrates and

Brunellus, and this because Socrates is Socrates and Socrates is Brunellus. It is shown as follows that, according to this opinion, Socrates is Brunellus: Whatever is in Socrates other than the forms of Socrates is that which is in Brunellus other than the forms of Brunellus. But whatever is in Brunellus other than the forms of Brunellus is Brunellus. Whatever, then, is in Socrates other than the forms of Socrates is Brunellus. But if this is the case, since Socrates is that which is other than the forms of Socrates, then Socrates himself is Brunellus.

That what we assumed above is true, viz. that whatever is in Brunellus other that the forms of Brunellus is Brunellus, is obvious from this: The forms of Brunellus are not Brunellus since then accidents would be substances; neither are the matter and forms of Brunellus together Brunellus, since then it would be necessary to admit that a body and a non-body are a body.

There are those who in confusion complain only about the words of the proposition, "A rational animal is an irrational animal," not about its sense. They say that certainly it is both, but this is not properly stated by these words, since the thing, even though it is one and the same, is called rational for one reason and irrational for another, i.e. it is called such on account of opposed forms. But then those forms which completely adhere to it at the same time have no opposition. Nor do they complain about these propositions: "A rational animal is a mortal animal" and "A white animal is a walking animal," although it is not in as much as it is rational that it is mortal nor in as much as it is white that it walks. Rather they accept them as completely true because one and the same animal has both at once, although for diverse reasons. Otherwise, they would have to agree that no animal is a human being since nothing is a human being in as much as it is an animal.

Moreover, according to this theory there are only ten essences of all things, viz. the ten highest genera, for in each category[3] we find only one essence, which is diversified, as we said, only by the forms of what is below it and would not have any variety without them. Thus just as all substances are completely the same so also are all qualities, all quantities, etc. Since Socrates and Plato have in them-

3 See glossary entry for 'category.'

selves the things of each category and they are themselves completely the same, all the forms of one belong to the other and they [i.e. the forms] are not in themselves essentially diverse, just as the substances to which they adhere are not. So the quality of one is not diverse from the quality of the other; they are both qualities. They are not any more diverse on account of the nature of qualities than on account of the nature of substance, because there is one essence of their substance just as there is one essence of their qualities. Likewise quantity makes no difference since it is the same, nor do any of the other categories. It follows that there cannot be any difference from the forms, which are not any more diverse in themselves than are the substances.

Further, how many substances would we think there were if the only diversity there were was the diversity of forms, since the subject substances would remain completely the same? We do not say that Socrates is numerically plural just because he receives several forms. Also, it will not do to maintain, as they wish, that individuals are made by their accidents. For if individuals draw their being from accidents, then the accidents are naturally prior to them, just as differences are prior to the species which they draw into being. For just as human being is separated out by the formation of a difference, so they call something Socrates on account of its reception of accidents. Thus Socrates can no more exist over and above his accidents than human being can over and above differences. Consequently, he is not the underlying support for these accidents just as neither is human being the underlying support for the differences. But if accidents are not in individual substances as in subjects, certainly they are not in universals as in subjects. For [Aristotle] shows that whatever things are in second substances as in subjects are always in first substances as in subjects. This shows that the opinion which holds that completely the same essence is present in diverse things at the same time is utterly devoid of reason.

Others, who hold a different opinion about universality and pay more attention to the sense of 'thing,' say that individual things are not diverse from each other just by forms but are distinct in

their essences. Also in no way is that which is in one in another whether it is matter or form; neither are these things less able to subsist in their own distinct essences when apart from forms, for their particular distinctness, in virtue of which this is not that, results not from forms but is a consequence of a diversity of essence. Likewise the forms themselves are in themselves diverse from each other; otherwise the diversity of forms would proceed *ad infinitum*, since it would be necessary to account for the diversity of forms by positing other forms. Porphyry noted such a difference between the most general and the most specific when he said: "A species does not ever become a highest genus nor a genus a lowest species," as if he had said: They differ in that the essence of the latter is not the essence of the former. Thus the division of the categories comes not from some forms but by the diversity of distinctive essences. But since they want all things to be so different from each other that none share with any other the same essential material or the same essential form, and yet they want to retain universal things, they say that the things which are distinct are the same; not essentially the same, of course, but indifferently. For example, they say that the individual humans which in themselves are distinct are the same in human being, i.e. they do not differ in the nature of humanness. And the same things which they say are singulars in virtue of distinctness they say are universals in virtue of indifference and similarity.

But there is distinction here too. For some claim that the universal is only the collection of several things. They do not call Socrates or Plato a species, but rather they say that all humans collected at once is that species which is human being and all animals taken at once is that genus which is animal, and so forth. Boethius seems to agree with them:[4] "A species is thought to be only a thought collected from the substantial likeness of individuals, and a genus from the likeness of species." For when he says "collected from a likeness," he means collecting several. Otherwise in no way would they have a predication of several or a containing of many in a universal thing, and there would not be any fewer universals than there would be singulars.

Others say that not just the collected humans but

4 See selection VI.4.1.

also the individuals in as much as they are humans are a species. When they say that the thing which is Socrates is predicated of many, they speak figuratively as if they had said: Many are the same as it, i.e. agree with it, or it agrees with many. They posit just as many species as individuals in respect of the number of things, and likewise with genera. But as the likeness of natures they assign a smaller number to universals than to singulars. Certainly all humans are in themselves both many on account of personal separateness and one on account of the likeness of humanness. And they maintain that things are different from themselves in terms of distinctness and similarity. For example, Socrates in as much as he is a human being is separated from himself in as much as he is Socrates. One and the same thing could not be its own genus or species unless it had some difference of its own from itself; for relative terms are opposed to one another at least in some respect.

Now let us undercut the theory given earlier about the collection, and let us inquire how the whole collection of humans which is called one species can be predicated of many so that it is a universal. If it were conceded that it is predicated of different things via its parts in that its individual parts are fitted to them, this does not show that there is present here the commonness of a universal, because the universal ought to be, according to Boethius, wholly in each. And on account of this it is different from what is common via its parts in the way that a field whose different parts are different items is common.

Besides, we could also say Socrates of many via his different parts, and thus it would be a universal. Further, any several humans taken together could be called a universal since the definition of universal would fit them. Even the definition of species would fit them, so that the whole collection of humans would include many species. Likewise we could call any collection of bodies and spirits a single universal substance, so that since the whole collection of substances is one highest genus, when any one of these is taken away while the others remain, we would have many highest genera in substances.

But perhaps it can be said that no collection which is included in a highest genus is a highest genus. But I object that if after one substance has been separated out the remaining collection is not a highest genus and yet the universal substance remains, it will have to be a species of substance and have an *equal* species under the same genus. But what can be opposed to it when a species of substance either is contained directly in it or shares with it the same individuals, as rational animal, mortal animal do?

Further every universal is naturally prior[5] to its own individuals, but a collection of any things relates as an integral whole to the individuals from which it is constructed and is naturally posterior to them. Further, between a whole and a universal, Boethius says in *Divisions*, there is this difference: a part is not the same as the whole but a species is always the same as its genus. But how could the whole collection of humans be the multitude of animals?

It remains now to object to those who say that each individual in that it agrees with others is universal and who allow that the same items are predicated of many, not in that many are essentially them, but because many agree with them. But if to be predicated of many is the same as agreeing with many, how is it that we say an individual is predicated of only one, since there is nothing which agrees with only one thing? Also how does being predicated of many constitute a difference between universal and singular, since Socrates agrees with many in exactly the same way as a human being agrees with many? Certainly a human being insofar as he is a human being and Socrates insofar as he is a human being agrees with others. But neither a human being insofar as he is Socrates nor Socrates insofar as he is Socrates agrees with others. Therefore, whatever a human being has Socrates also has, and in the same way.

Besides, since human being which is in Socrates and Socrates himself are conceded to be completely the same things, there is no difference of the latter from the former. For no thing is diverse from itself at one and the same time, because whatever it has in itself it has and in entirely the same way. Thus Socrates while white and literate is not in virtue of these diverse from himself, although he

5 See glossary entry for 'order of nature.'

has diverse things in himself, for he has both these and in entirely the same way. He is not in one way of himself literate and another way white, just as it is not one thing which of itself is white and another literate.

Also when they say that Socrates and Plato agree in human being, how is that to be understood when it is agreed that all humans differ from each other both in matter and in form? For if Socrates agrees with Plato in the thing which is human being, but no thing is human being other than Socrates himself or some other human being, he will have to agree with Plato either in himself or in someone else. But in himself he is diverse from Plato and likewise in another since he is not the other.

There are those who understand agreeing in human being negatively as if it were said: Socrates does not differ from Plato in human being. But we could also say that he does not differ from Plato in stone since neither is a stone. Then we note no greater agreement between them in human being than in stone, unless perhaps there is an earlier proposition, as though we said: They are human being because they do not differ in human being. But this cannot be since it is altogether false that they do not differ in human being. For if Socrates does not differ from Plato in the thing which is human being, neither does he in himself. For if he differs in himself from Plato, since he is the thing which is human being, certainly he will differ from Plato in the thing which is human being.

Now that we have given the arguments why things either individually or collectively cannot be called universal, i.e. said to be predicated of many, it remains to ascribe universality to utterances alone. So just as grammarians call some nouns common and others proper, so dialecticians call some simple expressions universal, some particular, i.e. singular. A word is universal when it is apt to be predicated of many individually on account of its establishment, like the noun 'human being' which is conjoinable to particular names of humans in virtue of the nature of the subject things to which it is applied. A singular word is one which is predicable of only one, like 'Socrates,' since it is taken to be a name of only one.

For if you take an equivocal item, you have not one word but many words in respect of signification. According to Priscian one utterance may give expression to many nouns. Thus when we say that a universal is what is predicated of many, this 'what' indicates not just the simplicity of the expression in respect of the distinctness of word strings but also the unity of the signification in respect of the distinction of equivocals.

Now that we have shown what the 'that which' means in the definition of 'universal,' there are the two elements of the definition that follow, viz. 'to be predicated' and 'many,' to be carefully considered.

To be predicated is to be conjoinable to something truly by the force of assertion of a substantive verb[6] in the present tense, as for example 'human being' can be truly joined via a substantive verb to diverse things. Also verbs like 'runs' and 'walks' when predicated of many have the force of a substantive verb in respect of linking. Thus Aristotle in II *Peri Ermenias* says, "Where there happens to be no 'is,' as where we have 'runs' and 'walks,' it is the same as if 'is' were added." Also: "There is no difference between 'A human being walks' and 'A human being is a walking thing.'"

'Of many' collects nouns in respect of the diversity of things named. Otherwise Socrates would be predicated of many since we say: This human being is Socrates, this animal is [Socrates], this white [is Socrates], or this musician [is Socrates]. Although these nouns are diverse in their ideas, they have entirely the same subject thing. But note that the conjoining in construction which the grammarian attends to is different from the conjoining of predication which the dialectician considers. According to the force of construction 'human being' and 'stone' and any noun in the nominative case are just as conjoinable by 'is' as 'animal' and 'human being,' so far as we are concerned with setting forth an idea rather than showing the state of a thing. The conjoining in construction is good just as often as it sets forth a complete sense, whether it is the case or not. But the conjoining of predication, which we are talking about here, pertains to the nature of things and to pointing out the truth of their state. Thus if someone says: 'A human being is a stone,' he has made from 'human being' and

---

6 I.e., some form of the verb 'to be.'

'stone' a construction with an acceptable sense which he wished to set forth, nor has he committed any grammatical vice. And although so far as the force of assertion is concerned 'stone' is here predicated of 'human being' (in which sense the term 'predicate' is construed so that even false categorical propositions[7] have predicates), still in the nature of things 'stone' is not predicable of 'human being.' It is only this sense of predication that we use when we define 'universal.'

And it does not at all seem that the universal is what is appellative[8] nor the singular what is a proper noun. Rather each exceeds the other and is exceeded by the other. The classes of appellative and proper nouns include not just nominative cases but oblique cases as well, but these latter are not predicated and thus are excluded by the definition of 'universal.' The oblique cases Aristotle does not even consider to be nouns (rather he calls them cases of nouns), because they are less necessary for declarative sentences, which are according to Aristotle the sole object of his speculation at that point, i.e. of dialectical consideration. And just as not all appellative or proper nouns are to be called universals or singulars, so also conversely. For the class of universals contains not only nouns but also verbs and infinite nouns.[9] The definition Priscian[10] gives of 'appellative' does not seem to fit the latter, viz. infinite nouns.

Now that we have assigned 'universal' and 'singular' by definition to expressions, let us carefully inquire into the properties of universal expressions. About these universals some questions have been raised because there are problems especially as to their signification, since they do not seem to have any subject thing nor to establish any valid idea. There do not seem to be any things to which universal nouns are applied, since all things subsist distinctly in themselves and do not agree, as we showed, in any thing which would serve as that in virtue of which universal nouns are applied. So since it is certain that universals are not applied to things on account of the difference of their discreteness, for then they would be singular rather

than common, and neither can they name things as agreeing in some thing, since there is no thing in which they agree, universals do not seem to draw in any signification of things, especially when they do not establish any idea of a thing.

Thus in *Divisions* Boethius says that this expression 'human being' creates a problem as regards its idea. When it is heard, he says, "the mind of the hearer is throw into confusion and led into errors. For unless someone defines the matter by saying 'Every human being walks' or 'Some human being walks' and designates this human being, given such should happen to be the case, the idea the hearer has will not have anything to understand rationally." For since 'human being' is applied to singulars on account of one and the same cause, viz. that they are mortal rational animals, this commonness of its application prevents anyone from understanding it like the noun 'Socrates' which is understood to be of just one person and thus is said to be singular. In a common noun like 'human being' neither Socrates nor some other human being nor the whole collection of humans is rationally understood via the force of the utterance. Nor is Socrates, even in so far as he is a human being, indicated by this noun, as some want to say. For even if Socrates alone were sitting in this house and for him alone this proposition were true: 'A human being is sitting in this house,' still in no way does the proposition mention Socrates by the subject noun 'human being' not even in so far as he is a man; for otherwise we could reasonably gather from the proposition that sitting belonged to him, and we could infer from the fact that a human being is sitting in this house that Socrates is sitting in it. Likewise, no other human being can be understood through this noun 'human being,' and neither can the whole collection of human beings, since the proposition can be true of only one. Thus it seems that neither 'human being' nor any other universal word signifies anything, since it establishes an idea of no thing. And neither does it seem that there can be an idea which does not have a subject thing which it grasps. Thus Boethius in his

---

7 See glossary entry for 'categorical proposition.'
8 I.e., denotes many items.
9 I.e., nouns which are formed by negating a positive noun, e.g. 'non-animal.'
10 Grammarian working in Byzantium around 500 C.E.

Commentary says: "Every idea is made from a subject thing either as the subject thing itself is or as it is not. An idea cannot be made from no subject thing." Therefore universals seem to be totally divorced from signification. But this is not the case. Universals in a way signify diverse things by naming, not by establishing an idea that arises from them but one that pertains to individuals. Thus this expression 'human being' both names individuals on account of a common cause, viz. that they are human beings, and for this reason it is said to be universal, and establishes a certain common idea pertaining to the individuals of which it grasps a common similarity.

But now let us carefully inquire into those matters which we have briefly touched on, viz. what is this common cause in virtue of which a universal noun is imposed and what does an idea of a common similarity of things grasp, and whether a word is said to be common on account of a common cause in which things agree or on account of a common conception or on account of both together.

First, let us consider the common cause. Individual humans who are separate from each other while they differ both in their own essences and in their own forms, as we noted above when inquiring into the nature of a thing, nevertheless agree in this, that they are human beings. I do not say they agree in a human being, since a human being is not any thing unless a distinct human. Rather I say in being a human being. Being a human being is not a human being nor any thing if we consider the matter carefully, just as not being in a subject thing is not anything and neither is not receiving contrariety or not receiving more or less, i.e. what Aristotle says all substances agree in. As we showed above, there cannot be any agreement in a thing. If there is some agreement of things, we must understand it in such a way that it is not some thing for Socrates and Plato to be similar in being a human being, just as it is not for a horse and an ass in not being human beings, in virtue of which both are called non-human being. For diverse individual things to agree is for them to be or not to be the same, for example, to be a human being or white or not to be a human being or not to be white. But it seems absurd for us to understand the agreement of things in such a way that it is not some thing, as though we were uniting in nothing things which exist when we say that they agree in the *status* of

human being, that is in this: that they are human beings. But we mean merely that they are humans and do not differ at all in this regard, i.e. not in as much as they are humans, although we call on no essence. We call the *status* of human being its being a human, which is not a thing. We also say that this is the common cause of the application of the noun to singulars in as much as they agree with each other. Often we call by the noun 'cause' items which are not any things, as when we say: He was whipped because he did not want to come to court. Not wanting to come to court, which is given as a cause, is no essence. Also we can call the *status* of human being the things themselves now established by the nature of human being, i.e. the things whose common likeness he conceived who applied the word [to them].

Now that we have shown what is the signification of a universal (i.e. that it is of things by naming) and pointed out the common cause of its imposition, let us show what are the ideas which they establish. And first let us examine the nature of all ideas.

Both sensings and ideas belong to the soul, and this is their difference: sensings are exercised only through corporeal instruments and perceive only bodies or what is in bodies, as for example, seeing perceives a tower or its visible qualities. An idea does not need a corporeal instrument and it need not have a subject body to which it refers. Rather it is associated with the likeness of the thing which the soul constructs for itself and into which it directs its action of understanding. Thus given that the tower is destroyed or taken away, the sensing which dealt with it ceases to exist, but the idea remains as long as a likeness of the thing is retained by the soul.

But just as the sensing is not the thing sensed toward which the sensing is directed, so neither is the idea the form of the thing which it grasps. Rather the idea is a certain action of the soul, and the form toward which it is directed is a certain imaginary and made-up thing which the soul constructs for itself when and as it wants, like those imaginary cities seen in sleep or the form for constructing a structure which the builder conceives as the likeness and model of the thing to be constructed, and which we cannot call either a substance or an accident.

Yet some say this is the same as the idea, in other

words that the made-up tower which I conceive when the tower is absent and I think of as high, four-sided and sitting in a wide field is the same as the idea of the tower. Aristotle seems to agree with them when in the *Peri ermenias* he calls the passions of the soul, which they call ideas, likenesses of things.

We say that an image is the likeness of a thing, although one can still say that in a sense the idea is a likeness in that it grasps that which is properly called a likeness of the thing. But we were correct in saying that it is diverse from that [likeness]. For I ask whether this four-sidedness and this height are true forms of the idea which is directed toward the likeness of the quantity of the tower and of its shape. Certainly true four-sidedness and true height belong only to bodies. From a made-up quality neither an idea nor any true essence can be formed. Thus it must be that just as the quality is made-up so is the substance that is its subject. Perhaps also the image in a mirror which seems to appear as a subject of seeing can be said to be nothing in fact, since often in the white surface of the mirror a quality of contrary color appears.

The question arises: when the soul simultaneously senses and thinks of the same thing, for example a stone, does the idea then deal with the image of the stone or do the idea and the sensing simultaneously deal with the stone itself? It seems more reasonable that then the idea does not require an image, since the reality of the substance is present to it. If someone says that where there is a sensing there is no idea, we do not agree. Often it happens that the soul perceives one thing and thinks of another, as is readily apparent to students who with open eyes perceive what is present and think of other things about which they are writing.

Now that we have investigated the general nature of ideas let us distinguish the ideas of universals and singulars. Certainly they are different in that the idea of a universal noun grasps a common and confused image of many, but the idea generated by a singular expression takes a quasi-singular form proper to one thing, i.e. relating to only one particular subject. Thus when I hear 'human being' a certain likeness arises in my soul which so relates to individual humans that it is common to all and distinctive of none. But when I hear 'Socrates' a certain form arises in my soul which expresses a likeness of a definite particular subject. Thus through

this word 'Socrates,' which induces in the soul a form proper to one, a certain thing is indicated and described. But in the case of 'human being,' whose idea relies on a form common to all, there is the commonness of confusion, so that we understand what belongs to all. Thus 'human being' is not correctly said to signify Socrates nor any other [human being], since no one is picked out by the force of the noun, although it still names individuals. But 'Socrates,' and any singular noun, not only names but also determines a subject thing.

But the question arises how the ideas of universals have subject things since according to Boethius, as we mentioned above, every idea has a subject thing. Certainly we must note that Boethius introduces this in that sophistical argument by which he shows that the idea of a universal is empty. Thus nothing prevents construing this not to be the truth and interpreting him as avoiding falsity in showing the arguments of others. Also we can say that the thing subject to an idea is either the true substance of the thing, as when the idea is simultaneous with a sensing, or, when the thing is absent, the conceived form of the thing, whether that form is common, in the way we said, or proper. I say "common" in as much as it retains a likeness to many, although in itself it is considered as one thing. For just as in order to show the nature of every lion we can make one picture which is proper to and representative of none of them, so also another which denotes something distinctive can be made to distinguish any one of them, for example, if it were painted as limping or mutilated or injured by the spear of Hercules. Thus just as some figures are painted as common to things, others as singular, so also some are conceived as common, others as distinctive.

It is not absurd to wonder about this form to which an idea is subject whether the noun also signifies it. That it does seems to be confirmed by both authority and reason. In I *Constructiones* Priscian, after he has demonstrated the common application of universals to individuals, seems to add on some other signification of a common form. He says:

> These [nouns] by which genera and species are shown to be of the nature of things can also be proper to general and special forms of things, which are established as intelligible in

the divine mind before they show up in bodies.

Here he treats God as a builder constructing something and who preconceives in his mind a model form of the thing to be constructed. This is then said to proceed into a body since the real thing is constructed in its likeness. He is correct in ascribing this common conception to God rather than to humans, because those generic or specific states of nature are works of God not of a builder; thus human being, soul, and stone are works of God, but a house or a sword a work of a human being. Thus these natures, house and sword, are not works like those, nor are their words substances but rather accidents, and thus they are neither genera nor lowest species. Thus it is correct to ascribe abstracted conceptions of this sort to the divine mind, not the human, for humans, who know things only through the senses, hardly ever arrive at a simple understanding of this sort. The sensibleness of accidents prevents their conceiving the natures of things in a pure way. But God, to whom all things He has made are by themselves obvious and who knew them before they were, distinguishes the individual *status* in them. To Him, who has only true understanding, there is no impediment of sense. This we learn by experience, for after *thinking* about a city we have not seen, when we come to it we discover it to be different than we thought it to be.

So also, I believe, it is the case with the intrinsic forms which do not come to the senses (like rationality, mortality, fatherhood, sitting) that we have opinion [rather than understanding]. Nevertheless, any names of any existents, taken in themselves, generate an idea rather than an opinion, because the inventor intends to apply them on account of certain natures or properties, even if he does not know how to think correctly of a nature or property of a thing. Priscian says these common conceptions are general or specific because general or specific nouns indicate them to us. He says these universals are like proper names of these conceptions. Although they have a confused signification as regards the named essences, they immediately direct the mind of the hearer to that common conception just as proper names do to the one thing which they signify. Porphyry, too, when he says that some are established in virtue of matter and form, others in the likeness of matter and form, seems to have had this conception when he speaks of "in the likeness of matter and form," a topic to be treated more fully in its place. Also Boethius when he says that a genus or species is a thought gathered from the likeness of many seems to have understood this same common conception. Some think Plato was of this opinion, namely that he would call those common ideas which he places in *nous*[11] genera and species. Perhaps it is on this matter that Boethius recalls Plato to have disagreed with Aristotle, i.e. where Boethius says that Plato wanted genera, species etc. not just to be understood as universals but also to exist and subsist over and above bodies, as if he had said that Plato understood these common conceptions which he established separate from bodies in the *nous* to be universals. In saying this he probably did not mean by "universal" common predication, as Aristotle does, but rather a common likeness of many, for that conception does not seem to be predicated of many in any way like a noun which is fitted to each of several items. There is another way, too, of interpreting Boethius when he says that Plato thought universals subsisted outside sensibles so that there is no disagreement between the opinions of the philosophers. When Aristotle says that universals always subsist in sensibles, he is speaking as regards the actual, for that nature which is animal and which is designated by a universal noun and thus is metaphorically said to be a universal, is found actually only in a sensible thing. But Plato thinks the nature subsists in itself, i.e. it retains its being even when not a subject of sense, and in virtue of its natural being it is referred to by a universal noun. Thus what Aristotle denies as regards the actual, Plato, the investigator of natural science, assigns to a natural fitness, and thus there is no disagreement between them.

Also reason seems to agree with those authorities who apparently think that common conceived forms are designated by universal nouns. What is it to be conceived through nouns if not to be signified by them? But certainly once we treat them [the

11 *nous* = mind.

forms] as different from ideas, there has now come to be a third signification for nouns besides the thing and the idea. And even if this does not have the backing of authority, still it is not contrary to reason.

Now let us answer the question that we promised to discuss above, viz. whether the commonness of universal nouns is judged to be due to a common cause of application or on account of a common conception or both. Nothing prevents its being due to both, but that common cause which is understood to pertain to the nature of things seems to have the greater force.

Also we must discuss what we noted above, viz. that the ideas of universals are made by abstraction, and how they can be alone, bare and pure and yet we do not say they are empty.

And first as to abstraction. We have to realize that, although matter and form are always mixed together, the reasoning faculty of the soul has the power to think about matter by itself, to consider form alone, and to conceive of both as mixed together. The first two occur by abstraction, which abstracts something from joined items so that it can consider its nature. The third is by conjunction. For example, the substance of this human being is both body and animal and human being and clothed with infinite forms. When I attend to this substance in its material essence with all its forms removed I have an idea through abstraction. Also when I attend in it only to the corporeality which I join to substance, here also I have an idea which is by conjunction in respect of the former, which attended only to the nature of substance, and which is by abstraction in respect of the forms other than corporeality, since I do not attend to any of them, like life, sensibility, rationality, whiteness.

But ideas of this sort made by abstraction may seem false and empty because they perceive a thing in a way different from that in which it subsists. For since they attend to matter or form by itself and in separation, and yet none of these subsists in separation, they certainly seem to conceive of the thing differently from the way it is, and therefore they seem to be empty. But this is not so. For if someone understands a thing in a way different from the way it is, so that he attends to it in a nature or property which it does not have, he certainly has an empty idea. But this does not happen in abstraction. When I attend only to this human being in the nature of substance or of body, but not of animal or of human being or of grammarian, certainly I understand only what is in him, although I do not attend to everything that he has. And when I say that I attend to him only in respect of that which he has, the 'only' refers to the attending and not to the mode of subsisting; otherwise the idea would be empty. For he – the thing here – does not have only this, but he is only attended to as having this. He is said to be understood in a way that is different from the way in which he exists, not in the sense that he is understood to be some type different from what he is, as was said above, but differently in this sense, that the mode in which he is understood is different from the mode in which he subsists. For this thing is understood apart from another but not as apart, although it does not exist apart. And matter is perceived purely and form simply, although the former does not exist purely nor the latter simply. The purity and the simplicity are reduced to the understanding of the thing not to its subsisting and are modes of understanding not of subsisting. Even senses often act divisively as regards what is composite. For example, given a statue that is half gold and half silver I can discern separately the conjoined gold and silver by noting the gold and then the silver by itself. In this case I perceive conjoined things divisively but not as divided. Thus also the idea attends to things divisively, not as divided; otherwise it would be empty.

Perhaps also that idea can be valid which considers conjoined items as divided in one way and conjoined in another, and conversely. For both the conjunction and division of things can be understood in two ways. For we say that some things are conjoined to each other by some similarity, like these two humans in that they are humans or are literate, and some are conjoined by an apposition or aggregation, like form and matter or wine and water. It [the idea] conceives things thus joined as diverse in one way and as conjoined in another. Thus Boethius ascribes this power to the soul: by its rational faculty it can compound the disjoint and resolve the compounded, in neither case excluding the nature of the thing but rather perceiving only that which is in the nature of the thing. Otherwise we would not have reason but only opinion, i.e. if the understanding deviated from the state of the thing.

And here this question arises about the foresight

of a builder: Is it empty when it holds up for the soul the form of a future work but there is as yet no thing itself? And if we agree that God had this foresight before he constructed his works, are we compelled to say that it is empty? But if someone says that it is empty as regards its effect in the sense that God had not fulfilled what he foresaw, it is false that this foresight is empty. But if he says that it is empty because it does not accord with the future state of things, then, although we shrink from these terrible words, we cannot find fault with their sense. For it is true that when the future state of the world did not yet exist materially He was disposing of that future in His mind. But we do not customarily say that a thought or foresight of something is empty unless it is lacking in effect, nor do we say that we think in vain unless we will not complete those works. Therefore, changing the words around, we do not call a foresight empty which does not think in vain but rather conceives what does not yet materially exist as subsisting, for that is natural to all foresights. Certainly foresight of the future, memory of the past, and understanding of the present are properly called thought. But if someone calls "deceived" someone who in thinking of the future thought of a future state as though it were now existing, he who thought that the other must be called "deceived" is rather the one who is deceived. He who foresees the future is deceived only if he believes that to be the case now which he foresees. For a conception of a non-existent thing does not make one deceived, only if faith is added is there deception. Even if I think of a rational raven but do not believe there is such, I am not deceived. So also one who foresees does not think that that exists because he thinks of it as already existing; rather he thinks of it as present so that he can at present posit it in the future. Every conception of the soul is as if of the present. If I consider Socrates either in as much as he was a boy or in as much as he will be an old man, I join to him as if present youth or oldness, because I attend to him presently in respect of a past or future property. Yet no one says this memory is empty because it attends to something conceived as present in respect of the past. But we will have more to say about this in the section on the *Peri ermenias*.

The question about God is more genuinely solved by saying that His substance, which alone is unchangeable and simple is not changed by any

conceptions of things or other forms. For although human words customarily presume to speak about the creator as though He were a creature when they say that he foresees or understands, still nothing in Him ought to be understood as diverse from Himself, nor can either the intellect or any other form be such. Thus every question about an idea belonging to God is superfluous. If we speak the truth more precisely, we will say that seeing the future is for Him nothing other than for Him who is in Himself true reason not to hide the future.

But now having said a lot about the nature of abstraction, let us return to the ideas of universals, which always have to be made by abstraction. When I hear 'human being' or 'whiteness' or 'white,' I do not note from the force of the noun all of the natures or properties which are in the subject things, but through 'human being' I have a conception, confused rather than discrete, of animal, rational and mortal, but not of any later accidents. For ideas of singulars are also produced by abstraction, as for example when we say 'this substance,' 'this body,' 'this white.' For through 'this man' I attend only to the nature of human being but concerning a definite subject; but through 'human being' I attend to that same nature simply and in itself, not concerning some man.

Thus it is correct to say that the ideas of universals are alone, bare and pure: they are alone in being apart from sense because they do not perceive a thing as sensible; and they are bare in being abstracted from either all or some forms; they are pure as a whole in respect of discreteness, because no thing, whether matter or form is indicated in them, and on account of this we said earlier that they are confused conceptions in this way.

With this preface let us proceed to a solution of the questions raised by Porphyry about genera and species. We can easily do this now that we have clarified the nature of all universals.

The first was this: Do genera and species subsist, i.e. do they signify some truly existent items or are they posited only in the idea etc., i.e. are they posited in an empty opinion without a thing like these nouns 'chimera,' 'goat-stag,' which do not generate a definite idea. The answer to this is that in fact they signify by nomination truly existent things, viz. those same things which singular nouns signify, and in no way are they given in an empty opinion. Nevertheless, in a certain way they are present through an idea which is alone, bare and pure, just as we explained. And nothing stands in the way of one who interprets in a different way certain expressions in the question giving a different answer as though he were to say: You ask whether they are posited in the idea alone etc. This can be understood in such a way that it is true, as we explained above. And the expressions can be taken in completely the same way by both the answerer and the questioner, and then a single question is not made through the opposites of the earlier members of these two dialectical questions: Are they or are they not, and are they posited alone, bare and pure or not?

The same thing can be said to the second question, which is whether these subsistents are corporeal or incorporeal, i.e. since it is conceded that they signify subsistents do they signify some subsistents which are corporeal or some which are incorporeal. Certainly everything which is, as Boethius says, is either corporeal or incorporeal, whether we understand these names 'corporeal' and 'incorporeal' for a substantial body and for a non-body, or for that which can be perceived by the bodily sense, like man, wood, whiteness, or for what cannot, like soul, justice. 'Corporeal' can also be understood as meaning discrete, as though the question were: Given they signify subsistents, do they signify discrete or non-discrete ones? For he who rightly investigates the truth of things attends not just to what can be truly said, but to whatever can be thought to be the case. Thus even if it is certain to someone that only discrete items subsist, still since there can be the opinion that other items exist, it is proper to ask about them too. And this last meaning of 'corporeal' seems more in line with the sense of the question, i.e. the question is about discrete or non-discrete items. But perhaps when Boethius says that everything which is is either corporeal or incorporeal, 'incorporeal' is superfluous, since no existent is incorporeal, i.e. non-discrete. Neither does anything about the order of the questions seem to show anything, except perhaps that just as 'corporeal' and 'incorporeal' in another signification divide subsistents, so also in this case it seems as though the questioner meant to say: I see that some existents are called corporeal and some incorporeal. Which of these do we call those things which are signified by universals? To this we answer: In one way corporeals, i.e. items discrete in

their own essence and incorporeals in respect of the noting of a universal noun, because they name them not discretely or determinately but confusedly, as we showed enough earlier. Thus those universal nouns are said to be both corporeal in respect of the nature of the things and incorporeal in respect of the mode of signification, because even if they name discrete things, still they do not name discretely and determinately.

The third question, whether they are posited in sensibles etc., assumes that they are incorporeal, for the incorporeal admits in a way of division into what is in sensibles and what is not, as we noted earlier. And universals are said to subsist in sensibles, i.e. to signify an intrinsic substance that exists in a thing which is sensible on account of exterior forms, and although they signify this substance which actually subsists in the sensible thing, they point it out as naturally separate from the sensible thing, as we explained above in connection with Plato. Thus Boethius says that genera and species are understood, but do not exist, over and above sensibles; i.e. the things of genera and species are attended to by the mind in respect of their own nature over and above all sensibleness, because given all sensible forms by which they come to the senses are removed they can truly subsist in themselves. For we concede that all genera and species exist in sensible things. But because the ideas of them are always said to be apart from sense, they do not seem to be in sensible things in any way. Thus it is reasonable to ask whether they can ever be in sensibles; and the answer is that some are in sensibles, but they naturally persist as over and above sensibleness, as we said.

In the second question we can interpret 'corporeal' and 'incorporeal' to mean sensible and insensible, so that the order of the questions is better. Because, as we said, ideas of universals are said to be apart from sense, it is rightly asked whether they are sensibles or insensibles. And after we answer that some of them are sensible as to the nature of things while also being insensible in their mode of signifying, for the sensible things which they name do not designate in the way they are sensed, i.e. as discrete, and neither through this demonstration of them does sense find them, there remains the question of whether they refer only to sensibles or signify something else as well. The answer to this is that they signify both sensibles and at the same time that common conception which Priscian ascribes especially to the divine mind.

And concerning what is like them. Here as noted above, we understand a fourth question. The solution is that we do not want in any way to say that there are [not] universal nouns when they are not predicable of many nor common to any things because their things have been destroyed, like the noun 'rose' when no roses are left, because although it lacks nomination still it signifies an idea, otherwise this would not be a proposition: 'There is no rose.'

Rightly such questions are asked about universals but not about singulars, for there are no such problems with the meaning of singulars. Their mode of signifying obviously agrees well with the state of the things. Just as they are discrete in themselves, so they are signified discretely by singulars, and their ideas are of a definite thing, which is not the case with universals. Besides, since universals do not signify things as discrete, neither do they seem to signify them as agreeing, for there is no thing in which they agree, as we showed earlier. Thus because there are so many problems with universals, Porphyry chose to treat of them alone, excluding singulars as obvious enough by themselves, although sometimes he treats of them incidentally in order to deal with other things.

We must note, too, that although the definition of universal or genus or species includes only expressions, nevertheless often these nouns are transferred to their things; for example, when a species is said to be composed of a genus and a difference, i.e. the thing of the species from the thing of the genus. For when we open the nature of expressions in respect of their signification we deal both with expressions and with things, and frequently nouns of the former are transferred to those of the latter. Thus especially treatises in logic and in grammar are ambiguous on account of these metaphors and lead many into error who do not distinguish correctly either the property of imposition of nouns or the abuse of metaphor.

In his commentaries Boethius, in particular, creates this confusion by metaphors, and especially in his inquiry into these questions, so much so, in fact, that it seems right to give up what he calls genera and species. Let us then briefly run over his questions and apply the aforesaid opinion as is neces-sary. Thus in the investigation of these questions in order better to solve the matter he upsets things with some sophistical questions and arguments, and through them he teaches us how to explain things later. He puts forward a difficulty of such a sort that every concern with and inquiry into genera and species must be put off, as though he said: Genera and species cannot be said to be what they seem to be, viz. words, either in virtue of the signification of things or in virtue of ideas. In regard to the signification of things he shows that a thing, whether single or multiple, is never found to be universal, i.e. predicable of many, just as he carefully explains and we have proved above.

That a single thing is not universal and thus neither a genus nor a species he argues first as follows: Everything that is one is one in number, i.e. discrete in its own proper essence; but genera and species which must be common to many cannot be one in number and consequently are not single. But because against the assumption someone can say that there are things one in number which are common, he argues away such confusion as follows: Everything that is one in number and common is common either by its parts, or wholly by succession of times, or wholly at the same time but in such a way that it does not constitute the substance of those things to which it is common. He removes all those modes of commonness from both genera and species by saying that they are common in such a way that wholly at the same time they are in singulars and constitute their substance. Certainly universal nouns are not shared via their parts by the diverse things which they name; rather they are wholly and completely nouns of singulars at one and the same time. They can also be said to constitute the substances of those things to which they are common either in that by metaphor they signify things constituting others, as animal names something in horse or human being which is their matter and even the matter of individual men, or in that they are said to make up a substance because in a way they come into their sense, and thus they are said to be substantial to them, for certainly 'human being' notes this whole which is animal, rational and mortal.

After Boethius has shown that the single thing is not a universal, he proves the same of what is multiple by showing that a multitude of discrete things in not a species or a genus. And he destroys the opinion by which someone can say that all substances collected together are the genus substance and all humans the species human being, as if he were to say: If we propose that every genus is a multitude of substantially agreeing things, then any such multitude will naturally have another above it, and that other will again have another and so on ad infinitum, which is absurd. Thus it has been shown that universal nouns do not seem to be universal in virtue of the signification of things, whether of a single thing or of a multiple thing, since they do not signify any universal thing, i.e. any thing predicable of many.

That they should not be called universals in virtue of the signification of an idea he argues as follows: He shows sophistically that this idea is empty because it is otherwise than the thing subsists, since it exists by abstraction. The knot of this sophism he resolves sufficiently, and we have carefully done so above. But he did not think the other part of the argument where he showed that no thing is universal needed an explanation, because it was not sophistical. For he understands 'thing' to mean thing and not expression, because the common expression, although it is like a single thing in its essence, is common by nomination in that it refers to many, and it is in virtue of this reference, not in virtue of its essence, that it is predicable of many. Still it is the multitude of these things that causes the universality of the noun, for, as we noted above, only what contains many is universal. The thing in itself does not have the universality which it nevertheless confers on the expression, and certainly it is not owing to the thing that the expression has signification. Also a noun is deemed appellative on account of there being many things, although we do not say that things either signify or are appellative.

VI.6.2. Universals and Signification (from *Logica Petitioni Sociorum*)

[The problem in this selection is to say what it is I ideate (think of) when I ideate a human being without thinking of any particular human being. Abelard argues that there does not need to be any thing that I am thinking of in this case, just as when I want a hood, there does not need to be any thing that I want, although, of course, it is true that I want something.]

At this point three matters concerning these universals come up for investigation, namely what signification and ideation they have, what knowledge they produce, and how they have an appropriate application.

Often it is asked about the signification and ideation, which these universal nouns have, what things they manage to signify. For when I hear this noun 'human being,' which is common to many things it equally relates to, I ask what thing I ideate by it. If we answer, as we must, that human being itself is ideated, another question follows: How might this be true if this human being or some other human being is not ideated, since every human being is this man or that human being or some other. For just as they say, "When a human being is sensed, it is necessary that this human being or that human being is sensed because of the fact that every human being is this man or that man," so also it is argued for ideation by analogy with sensing.

Besides 'human being' indicates nothing other than 'some human being.' Thus he who ideates human being clearly ideates some human, and thus he ideates this human being or that human being, which seems completely false.

To this we must answer, I think, that if we want to reason correctly and carefully attend to the sense of each sentence, we encounter no difficulty. For when we say "Human being is thought of," the sense is that someone through an ideation conceives of human nature, i.e. he attends to such an animal. Hence if afterwards he goes on as follows: "But every human being is this one or some other; therefore he conceives of this one or some other," he does not go on correctly. Rather we have to speak as follows: Every ideation that ideates human being ideates this or that man. Then obviously we keep the same middle term, and we correctly go on to the joining of the extreme terms. But the assumption is false.

Likewise when we say, "I want a hood," and every hood is this or that hood, it still does not follow that I want this or that hood. Rather we would have to speak as follows: "I want a hood, and everyone who wants a hood wants this or that hood." The argument would then proceed correctly in like fashion.

It is not, therefore, necessary that if I ideate human being I consequently ideate this human being or that human being, since there are innumerably many other concepts in which human nature is considered, but indifferently, without, i.e., any definiteness of the person, for example the simple conception itself that belongs to this noun 'human being' or to this noun 'white' by itself. These are, nevertheless, valid, because through their ideations many items can be validly considered. Thus it is with the ideation associated with 'every human being,' which applies to all humans, because by the ideation associated with it we can validly consider each human being and signify some being the human being has. For example, if I say, "Plato is a human being," by the ideation of the predicate noun I declare and expose a being Plato has. Thus the predicated utterance Boethius calls the higher ranking part of the proposition in virtue of privilege, and he calls it declarative because in virtue of its ideation it declares what each thing is, but according to him what each thing is is not apprehended by the total ideation, and consequently he says that declaration also becomes consideration. Now that we have explained the signification, i.e. both of things and of ideations, let us explain what knowledge they produce.

We must say, then, that all separate things are opposed in number, for example Socrates and Plato. Also these same items agree in virtue of something, namely in virtue of the fact that they are human beings. But I do not say that they agree in virtue of Socrateity or Platoneity, nor in virtue of some thing which they share between them; but I do say that they agree in virtue of something, i.e. they have some agreement in virtue of the fact, namely, that they are human beings. Thus if I say, "I want something," and someone asks, "What do you want?" to this I will answer very correctly: "A golden castle," because when I said, "I want something," I said I had some want, and when he said, "What do you want?" he asked what want I had, and I then specified that want for him. Since things of necessity agree and differ among themselves in this fashion, it has been necessary in order to produce this knowledge to invent words which specify separate things as well as signify the agreement of things. For according to Plato useful and necessary knowledge consists in noting these two, i.e. the agreement and the difference of things.

Having noted their knowledge let us see how they have an appropriate application. For, if we want to show that something belongs to or is absent from

all humans, we cannot do this using particular nouns, both because of their instability (now they have substance, now they do not) and because of their infinity, because, according to Plato, of an infinity no sure knowledge is possessed. Thus it is necessary to invent universals in order to do what singulars cannot do.

The objection concerning the superfluousness of the application of universal nouns that they do not seem to produce knowledge but rather confusion, since, according to Boethius, through a universal noun no thing is attended to (for as often as the utterance is said without determination it produces a question in the intellect etc.) has no force. Even though they are universal they produce knowledge and certitude, although they do not eliminate from the hearer every question which can arise in his mind, just as neither do singulars. For when I say, "Socrates runs," I do not indicate how he runs or how much he runs. So also when I say, "A human being runs," I indicate human nature, which he was not aware of, although that does not tell him what human being, nor do I eliminate all the questions which he has. For Boethius says this: "A hearer does not have anything which he rationally ideates by this spoken expression 'human being.'" This is both true and false. For if he understands it as asserting something about the substance of the noun, viz. that there is no thing of which the hearer has an ideation, it is true. But if as asserting something about the substance of the verb, viz. that the hearer has no ideation, it is false. The case is similar to these questions: What are you ideating? What do you know? If taken about the substance of the noun it means: What thing is it of which you have an ideation? Then one has to answer by mentioning a definite particular subject of which one has an idea. If taken as about the substance of the verb, it means: What ideation do you have? Likewise the question, 'What do you want?' has two senses: What thing is it of which you have a want? or: What want do you have? But that this question, 'What do you want?' has this sense, What want do you have?, is clear from the fact that even when there exists no golden castle, I can truly answer, "I want a golden castle," i.e. I have such a want. Likewise one can answer to "What are you ideating?" "I am ideating a chimera," even when nothing is a chimera. Therefore, when I ideate a chimera, even if there is no thing which I ideate, still I ideate something.

VI.6.3. What Propositions signify (from *Logica Ingredientibus, Gloss on De Interpretatione*)

[In the previous selection Abelard referred to what things have in common as a "status" and said it was "no thing." This unusual doctrine should be read in the light of what Abelard here says about "*dicta*," i.e. what propositions say. Sentences and their nominalizations are not treated as referring to anything and the sentences in which they take the subject position grammatically are "impersonal," i.e. do not from a logical standpoint have any subject at all. This position should be compared with the way Abelard talks about *status* in his *Theologia Christiana*, selection V.3.1.]

But we do not hold that propositions signify either just ideas or things themselves; rather [we say that] along with a signification of ideas they have another signification, which is completely nothing, for example, for Socrates to be a human, or not to be [a human]. Thus we hold that two items are signified by a proposition, namely an idea which it generates of things and besides that something which it proposes and says, namely, for a human to be an animal, or not to be [an animal]. These latter, i.e. for a human to be an animal, or not to be [an animal], are in no way any essences, neither one single essence nor several, as we will show later.

But now let us first show that not just ideas are designated by propositions but also some other items, regardless of whether they are things or are altogether nothing as we claim. When we say that some consequence in some proposition or other[12] is necessary, the reason we can call it necessary must lie not in its essence, which is transitory, but rather in its signification, i.e. in virtue of its signification. But the proposition's idea does not have in itself any necessity, since it is a transitory action. Consequently, there has to be something else the proposition signifies on account of which it can be said to be necessary. For example, since we allow that this consequence, "If there is a rose, there is a flower" is always true and necessary, even when the things are destroyed, we have to see what reason

there is to judge the signification to be necessary. But in things there is no necessity, since, even given they are totally destroyed, what the consequence says, i.e. that if this is that is, is no less necessary.

But perhaps it will be said that the things, even when destroyed, are in some way in a certain necessity of connection which they have to each other, and that in virtue of this relationship of connection the things are said by the consequence to follow [one on the other]. But first let us ask what this relationship is in virtue of which the consequence signifies the things and the things themselves are said to be necessary. If it is something, it is either those very things, the rose and the flower, or it is something else. If it is those very things, then, when we say that those things in that relationship are necessary, we are calling them necessary in themselves, which is false since they are transitory. If by this relationship we mean some property in the things, then they do not remain necessary in that either, because, when they do not exist at all, they do not have that property or any other. Therefore, since we judge the proposition to be necessary on account of its signification, and this necessity cannot be derived from either the ideas or the things, something other than those must be designated [by the consequence].

For this reason we allow that the *dictum* [i.e., what is *said* by the proposition] of any given proposition is not any thing at all, not even several things. Perhaps this is obvious in consequences and in negative propositions, which are true even when the things are totally destroyed, because even then we can correctly say that 'This is not that' is true or necessary. But it does not seem so obvious in affirmative [propositions] like 'Socrates is a human,' which can in no way be true unless the thing persists. Thus perhaps in such cases the things themselves will seem to be signified by the proposition. But then clearly 'Socrates is Socrates' will designate the one Socrates, just as does the noun 'Socrates,' and in the same way. 'Socrates' certainly signifies him in virtue of his being Socrates, and yet it does not *say* that he is Socrates in the way 'Socrates is Socrates' does. Thus in its *dictum* the proposition has this difference from the noun: the proposition *says* Socrates is Socrates, which is not some essence, but 'Socrates' does not *say* this, even

---

12 Abelard refers here to a conditional proposition that asserts an entailment.

though it names Socrates in virtue of his being Socrates.

Furthermore, if propositions did not have some signification besides the significations of things and of ideas, 'running Socrates' and 'Socrates runs' would not in any way be different in sense.

Moreover, when in attributing necessity to a consequence we say that that which the antecedent says cannot exist without that which the consequent says, the attribution cannot hold either in virtue of the idea or in virtue of things. For example, when we say, "If there is not a body, there is not a human"[13] it is not true to say that the one idea cannot be without the other nor that the things of the former cannot be without the things of the latter. But it cannot happen that it is as the first says, unless it is as the second says.

Therefore, just as nouns and verbs have a twofold signification, namely of things and of ideas, so also we allow that a proposition's [signification] is two-fold, namely of an idea composed out of the ideas of the parts, and of its *dictum*, which is like a thing for the proposition, even though it is really no essence at all. It is especially in virtue of these *dicta* that [propositions] are judged true or false, or opposed, or necessary, or possible, because it is their *dicta* that are true or false, or opposed to each other, or necessary, or possible. For example, for Socrates to be a human, or not to be a stone, is true, and for him not to be a human and to be a stone is false, i.e. in reality it is such that he is a human or is not a stone, and in reality it is not such that he is not a human and is a stone.

Aristotle clearly indicates that propositions are to be called true or false on account of their *dicta* when in the chapter on 'prior'[14] he says: "Necessarily, a sentence is called true or false depending on whether the thing exists or does not." He too calls the dicta of propositions their things, when he says in the same place that the thing is the cause of the truth of the proposition; for example, that Socrates is a human and that he is not a stone are the causes why the propositions that so assert

are true. Also he refers[15] to the *dicta* of propositions as what are classified as affirmations and negations, or as items opposed to each other. For example, according to Boethius[16] for Socrates to sit is opposed to for Socrates not to sit, and in virtue of these *dicta*, he says, the affirmation and negation always divide true and false whether in fact the things are or are not, because it is always the case that of the items which are said by an affirmation and a negation that divide[17] one is in reality and the other is not. Thus also when in [*De Interpretatione* 8] he explains the distinguishing feature of a contradiction, he says that necessarily always one part of the contradiction is true and other false, because necessarily in reality it always happens that one or the other of their *dicta* either exists or does not exist. If the items which are said by an affirmation and a negation were things, it would not be true that always one exists and the other does not exist. Clearly the negation does not contain any thing other than what the affirmation contains, since they have to be made from essentially the same [things].

Further: If it were the things themselves that are said by propositions, when we say, "If there is a human, there is an animal," and by assumption establish the negation of the consequent, 'But there is not an animal,' which is the case given the things have been destroyed, we do not posit some things but rather we allow that it is as the negation says. Now if the negation said the things themselves, to allow that it is as the negation says we would have to allow the things themselves to exist. Consequently, the negation could not be true, i.e. say what is in reality, unless the things were, even though people would more say the negation is true when the things are destroyed.

Moreover, if when we say, "If Socrates is, Socrates is a human," we joined together in necessity the things themselves, I do not see how this would differ in sense from saying, "If Socrates being, Socrates being a human"; and since we negate propositions in respect of their senses by the

---

13 The text is corrupt here, and the translation is conjectural at this point.

14 *Categories* 12, 14b14-21.

15 *Categories* 10, 12b6-10.

16 In his commentary on the *Categories* (PL 272C).

17 I.e., are logical contradictories.

destruction of the consequent and the antecedent, by the whole proposition which denies Socrates to be an animal or Socrates to be Socrates we would clearly deny two things or one thing. But I have no idea what would be meant by negating Socrates and a human or himself.

Moreover, if 'Socrates is a human' signifies Socrates and a human, so that it treats of these, when we say, "For Socrates to be a human, or to be an ass, is true," i.e. "That Socrates is a human, or an ass, is in reality," we join by the verb 'is,' which is predicated, to the things themselves their being in reality, so that we in fact say that Socrates and human, the things themselves, are in reality.[18] But what is that which is in reality except the things themselves? If so, then certainly when we say, "For Socrates to be an ass is true," i.e. "is in reality," it is as if we said that Socrates and an ass are things [in reality], which is true. And thus the proposition which proposes that, namely "For Socrates to be an ass is true," is true.

So true is it that the items which are said by propositions are not any things that, when we say that Socrates and Plato agree in being human or in being a substance, if we take this as referring to things, no things will be able to be assigned as those in which they agree, just as we taught in our discussion of Porphyry.[19]

Further, when we say, "From the fact that he is a human Socrates is rational, but from the fact that he is an animal, he is not rational," if by 'to be human' we mean the thing 'human' refers to and by 'to be an animal' the thing 'animal' refers to, then clearly it follows that if he has this from [to be] a human he has the same from [to be] an animal, because if the nature of human confers this on him so also does the nature of animal, because the human itself is an animal.

Moreover, when we say, "For the living to be dead is possible," it is false. Therefore, the presence in sentences of 'to be' or 'not to be' turns those sentences toward such *dicta* as can be said to be absolutely nothing.

But it is objected: Given the *dicta* of propositions

are nothing, how is it that propositions happen to be true on account of them, for how can those items which are or are able to be absolutely nothing be called a cause? But a person is hanged on account of a theft they performed which is now nothing, and a person dies because they do not eat, and are damned because they do not act rightly. Yet not eating and not acting rightly are not any essences. Thus Augustine, speaking to Paul and Eutropius in his book *On Nature and Grace*[20] when he would say that sin is no essence and yet it corrupts a substance, uses as an example abstaining from food, which is not a substance, i.e. not eating is not, because it is not any essence, and nevertheless it kills and weakens a substance, since on account of not eating someone may languish and die.

But it is also said that when it is ordered of someone that they make a fire, or not make a fire, since certainly to make a fire, or not to make a fire, is nothing, that which is nothing is injoined,[21] i.e. the person is given an order for that which is not anything. The lighting of the fire, for the sake of which the order was given, is certainly not as yet a good action which the impious is ordered to do, nor ever will be; nevertheless, the order does not cease for that reason nor is the God unjust who punishes or damns for that which never is anything.

We should note too that when we say, "I order you to make a fire," and the order is for making a fire, which, i.e. the making of the fire, we take to be forever nothing, still it is not ordered that someone make the making of a fire, but only that they make a fire.

But if someone were to say that whoever orders the making of a fire orders nothing, since making a fire is not something, certainly there can be a valid sense where an order is given for that which is not anything. But the grammatical construction which reads, "He commands nothing," makes no sense, just as it would amount to nothing to say, "I order fire making." Often utterances which have completely the same signification are not substitutable in the same grammatical construction, for example 'feed on' and 'eat,' which are used intransitively

---

18 Reading here '*in re*' for '*unum*.'
19 See selection **VI.6.1.**, pp. 3ff.
20 PL 44, 291.
21 Reading *iniungitur* for *coniungitur* ('conjoined').

with different cases.[22] Also 'lack' and 'do not have' amount to the same, but it is one thing to say, "I do not have every cloak," and another to say, "I lack every cloak," i.e. "I have no cloak." Likewise, although 'for Socrates to run' and 'Socrates runs' mean the same, still they admit of use in different grammatical constructions; because, if I say, "For Socrates to run, or to walk, is possible, or true," this is an acceptable construction, but it is not acceptable to say, "Socrates runs is possible," or if I say, "If Socrates runs, Socrates walks," this is acceptable, but if I say, "If for Socrates to run, for Socrates to walk," we have nothing.

Moreover, 'nothing' can be said affirmatively of the *dictum* of a proposition, i.e. I say affirmatively that it is nothing, but negatively that it is not something. What wonder, then, if when I say impersonally, "For Socrates to run happens," I cannot say "Nothing happens"? For impersonal verbs are not joined to infinitive verbs in the way they are joined to nouns.

Here I must say something, as I promised, about this impersonality of declarative sentences. First, we have to say that although propositions signify their *dicta* by proposing them, still these propositions do not establish ideas. For nouns and verbs as well as sentences signify their ideas, but these ideas do not go on to establish other ideas. In this way propositions both propose their *dicta* and establish ideas composed out of the ideas belonging to the parts.[23] Consequently, through propositions it is necessary not that the *dicta* be thought of but that the things be grasped in the idea. On the other hand, the name '*dictum*' itself – for example, if I say "this *dictum*" – establishes a certain non-complex idea of the *dictum*, just as does any noun as regards its thing. Consequently, the name '*dictum*' admits of being used in a personal declarative sentence, as, for example, when I say, "This *dictum* is something, or is not anything." But if the subject in a sentence contains a *dictum* while not establishing an idea of it, as, for example, if I say, "For Socrates

to run is true, or possible," the sense is impersonal, and it is this whole which is true or possible. This is just like when 'it has come,' or 'it pleases,'[24] is used impersonally in a sentence, and then that sentence contains nothing personally, since it has no subject of which it establishes an idea, as we said. Therefore, just as we say that 'It has come to the church'[25] is an impersonal declarative sentence, so also is 'To come to the church is possible.'

****

At this point we must not neglect to ask whether these definitions of 'affirmation' and 'negation' [where an affirmation is a declarative sentence which affirms something of something, and a negation one which takes something away from something] cover all cases of affirmations and negations. If we accept that they do, then we still have to ask in the case of impersonal declarative sentences what we join to what, or what we take away – for example, when we say, "It is come to the church," or "It happens that this is, or is not."

But perhaps someone says that 'It has come to the church' is not a proposition unless I add 'by some.' And if I say, "It is come by some, or by these, to the church," then I arrive at a proposition meaning either 'they come,' i.e. 'some come to the church' or 'they have come,' where 'is come' and 'it has come' are predicated and 'by these,' or 'by some,' is the subject. Likewise, when we say, "It tires me" or "It grieves me," the pronoun serves as subject while the verbs are predicated. Then, since persons are added to the impersonal verbs, clearly there is no doubt that these amount to propositions. Since in a grammatical construction they can be associated in a general way with all persons and are not restricted to just one person but equally admit of being joined both with all persons and numbers (we can say: "It tires me, him, us, you, them" and "It is run by me, by you, by them, by us, by you [pl.], by them"), we do not call these impersonal.

---

22 In Latin the expression translated as 'feed on' takes an object in the ablative case, while the word translated as 'eat' takes the accusative.

23 I.e., to the noun and the verb.

24 Latin expresses these without any subject noun by using simply the verbs '*ventum est*' and '*placet,*' whereas English uses the referentless 'it.'

25 This sentence is used by Quintillian to begin a discussion of the church and in that place could be translated as 'Now we come to the church.'

Also if someone takes the 'it is run' mentioned by Priscian and analyses it into 'a running occurs,' when we say, "It is run to the church," it seems that 'it is run' functions as both subject and predicate, as if we said, "A running is to the church," in virtue of the fact that it [the running] is directed toward the church. For all verbs seem to possess the force of the substantive verb,[26] as, for example, 'walks' means 'is walking' and thus 'is run' means 'a running is.' Consequently, also on this analysis 'It is run by them' means that they are runners.

But perhaps to the above it will have to be objected that, since 'is run' [in latin 'curritur'] is a non-composite word, it does not possess the single composite idea without which a predication cannot occur. Earlier in his work Aristotle has denied that anything signifies this idea without being composite, and he has totally affirmed that the idea possessed by a declarative sentence is not completed by a noun or a verb uttered by itself. Besides, a verb is supposed to signify the signified property not in essence but in attachment, as we found out in solving the question about 'runs.'[27] But 'A running is' does not indicate the attaching of a running, just as neither does 'A human is' indicate the attaching of a human; nor is any sense which we intend produced when someone says, 'It is run by them,' i.e., 'A running is by them.' Consequently, 'It is run' in no way produces a proposition unless 'by some' is understood; nor does 'it has been run,' nor 'it is come,' nor 'it has come,' nor any other such impersonal expressions which get joined to cases [of nouns] or to persons, if the cases are not added or at least understood.

But what are we going to say in the other cases where [the verbs] occur completely impersonally and do not get used with cases but only with infinitival expressions, which likewise are impersonal, as, for example, when I say, "For a human to run, or not to run, comes about, occurs, or happens"? Also many nouns[28] admit of a grammatical structure of this sort, i.e. they are used with infinitival verbs, for example, 'possible,' 'impossible,' 'necessary,' 'true,' 'false,' and sometimes 'good' or 'bad' or 'useful' or

'decent,' as in 'To run, or not to run, is good.' There are several other nouns as well which like those three[29] can be used both personally and impersonally. For just as we say, "For a human to run is good, or is not good," so also we say, "To run, or not to run, is good."

We now have to inquire what it is in declarative sentences of this sort that is predicated and of what it is predicated, and what in the meaning of the sentence is joined to what. Priscian, in *Constructions* II where he tells us that of all the moods of a verb only the infinitival verb gets used with a substantive verb [the copula], says that both the infinitival verb and the finite verb serve in place of the very name of the thing. For, he says, when I say, "To read is good," I mean nothing other than 'A reading is good.' In that case there is certainly no question what is predicated and what serves as subject, because then 'to read' is accepted in place of a noun used personally.

But what will be the case if it is taken impersonally as having the force of a verb, as when we say, "To read dialectic is good," where now 'to read' cannot be taken as having the force of a substantive noun to which an accident is joined and which contains reading as attaching. Likewise, when we say, "Not to read is good" or "For a human to be, or not to be, is good," we have to ask what is it we link to what. For when I say that 'good' derives from 'goodness,' we have to ask what it is we attribute goodness to or say to be good.

If we say, "Socrates reads dialectic is good," clearly 'Socrates reads dialectic' is used personally, and to it 'good' is linked by the third person verb 'is,' just as though we had said, "That is good which is Socrates reads dialectic." But in that case, since Socrates reads dialectic is not anything, the proposition which links 'good' to it is false.

In order, then, to preserve the impersonality of the grammatical construction as well as its truth, we say, "For Socrates to read dialectic is good," and the sense is this: 'There comes about something good on account of the fact that Socrates reads dialectic.' But here 'comes about' is impersonal and

---

26 I.e., the verb 'to be' used as a copula.

27 The text has 'is run,' but the reference is almost certainly to Abelard's view that the simple verb 'runs' implicitly contains the copula and amounts to 'is a running one.'

28 In ancient and medieval grammar the category of noun included adjectives as well as what we would call nouns.

29 An apparent slip. Abelard has given us four such words.

does not contain the signification of any accident, just as neither does the substantive verb when it is used impersonally, for example in this passage from Priscian:[30] "There is [the time] when Aeoles takes the digamma to mean nothing."

Consequently, if someone asks, "What happens?" when we say, "Something good to be happens" that person fails to produce a grammatical construction, because it is wrong to join what is like a nominative case noun to an impersonal [word] to which it cannot be associated without an infinitive. To avoid the fallacy of accident[31] we should say, "What to be comes about?" Likewise if someone says, "To read tires me," you cannot ask, "What tires me?", but rather [you should ask], "To do what tires me?", so that the construction is impersonal. Certainly 'for me to read' or 'for me to do' no more have personal signification than do complete sentences, for no mood of a verb makes a sentence have personal signification.

Consequently, just as this whole sentence 'Socrates reads' or 'for Socrates to read' does not have personal signification, so neither does 'For Socrates to be a reader' have it in the way 'Socrates [who is] reading' or 'Socrates [who is] being a reader,' which get joined to personal verbs, have it. Therefore, when we say impersonally, "For me to read comes about," if someone says, "What comes about?" or says, "Something comes about" or "Nothing comes about," the construction is totally ill-formed since personal [nouns] are joined to impersonal [verbs]. It is just like when we say, "It is run by him" and someone asks, "What is run?", or we say, "It has been run by him" and someone asks "What has been run?" or says "Something has been run" or "Nothing [has been run]," there cannot be any grammatical construction here nor any saying of anything.

When, then, I analyse 'For me to read is good' into 'Something good to be comes about from the fact that I read,' you cannot ask "What comes about?" or "From what comes about some good?" Clearly the nominative form 'What' cannot be joined to 'comes about,' nor can 'some good,' because those [nouns] are personal while that [verb] is impersonal. Likewise, if someone says,

"For me to read is something, or is not something," and 'to read' is used with the force of the infinitival mood, it is wrong to link it to 'is' or 'something,' since they are personal. But if I take it as meaning 'My reading is something,' or I use 'for me to read' as the name of the proposition's *dictum*, just as if we said, 'this proposition's *dictum*,' the construction can be well-formed, whether true or not, because then you have personal subjects and predicate nouns with a verb in between. Likewise, when I say, "For Socrates to read is possible," and I create an impersonal sense, if someone asks, "What is possible?" the construction is ill-formed. This holds too if someone says, "Something, or nothing, is possible," because 'is possible' is used impersonally, just as 'it is come' is, and the sense is the following: 'That Socrates reads is able to happen.' It cannot be the case here that [the expression] 'that Socrates reads' is a personal phrase, and 'is able' is used here impersonally in place of 'is possible' and does not indicate any form. (We will talk about this in discussing modal propositions.)

Modes, however, do not take grammatical well-formedness away from the sentences which assert some subject for them. Thus Aristotle in discussing modal sentences says 'possible' and the other modes are predicated and 'to be' and 'not to be' are made the subjects so far as the grammatical constructions are concerned. This is just like the way in which he calls modes predicates with respect to the construction, but not with respect to the meaning. Thus when Aristotle defined 'affirmation' and 'negation' as what asserts something of something, or something away from something, he was referring to the terms of the grammatical construction, which terms are sometimes personal and sometimes impersonal. The meaning of what he says, then, is the following: An affirmation is a declarative sentence which by linking, i.e. affirming, asserts one term of another; a negation is one which by taking away, i.e. denying, asserts [something away from something] – and this whether the linking or taking away occurs personally or impersonally. It occurs personally if one thing is essentially linked to something, as when we say that this is that, or is essentially taken away, as when I say

---

this is not that.

It also happens that sometimes infinitive verbs too are linked to personal verbs, and then there is no subject-place in the construction, but rather there is the place of the qualifier,[32] for example, if I say, "I want to read a book" or "I am able to read [a book]." In this case if I infer [from the above], 'I want something, or I am able something, or not,' the construction is totally ill-formed, because without the infinitive these words fail to make a complete sentence.

Therefore, some verbs as well as some subjects are personal, like 'I see a wall'; some are impersonal, like 'I want to see a wall'; clearly, 'wall' refers by naming to a thing, [and 'see' refers to] vision about which I say that it belongs to me, but 'to see a wall' does not refer to some thing in virtue of which I might show that vision belongs to me. Consequently, if, when I say, "I want to see a wall," someone asks in respect of what is a will said to belong to me, I cannot mention a personal[33] qualification of anything, but I can, nevertheless, mention the following qualification: 'I have a will for seeing a wall,' i.e. '[I have a will] that I see a wall.'

Thus no complete sentence taken as a whole says personally any subject thing, i.e. has any subject thing. But some phrases which are not complete sentences do have [subject things], as 'white human' and 'running human' have the thing which is human, while others do not, like 'for Socrates to run,' 'for a human to be white.' No proposition, then, has personally some subject thing. Some propositions are put together out of impersonal terms, like 'For Socrates to run happens, or is possible' etc., and some out of personal terms, like 'A human is an animal, or is not' or 'A white human runs, or does not.' Consequently, the former can be said to be impersonal both in respect of themselves and in respect of their terms, while the latter are personal in respect of their terms.

---

32 I.e., the direct object.
33 The text has 'impersonal' but this would contradict Abelard's point.

VI.7. AVICENNA

Philosophers who depend upon Aristotle for their conception of a universal understand that a universal is something which can be predicated of many. What is said of this and that is that each is a horse; we do not say what this is by saying, "This is horseness." And yet it remained a standard way of referring to universals – at least in the dialogues of Plato – to use an abstract noun such as "horseness." Although horseness is not a horse, horseness, it would seem, is a universal. In the selection immediately below Avicenna means to clarify the notion of universality.

Both of these selections are translated from the Latin rendering of Avicenna's works which began appearing in western Europe in the late twelfth century. Hence, even though Avicenna (Ibn Sina) lived and worked a full century before Abelard (fl. 1120), they are here placed after the selections from Abelard's writings. This reflects the fact that Avicenna's ideas had little impact on the Christian West before 1200.

VI.7.1. The Nature of Universals (from *First Philosophy* V)

[An essence is not of itself universal, or singular. It is a universal, i.e. predicable of many, only once it is thought in abstraction. This conception of universality as an accident of some essence was adopted by many late scholastics, including Duns Scotus.]

I say, then, that 'universal' has three senses: (1) Something is called universal because it is actually predicated of many items, for example *human being*. (2) An intention[1] is called universal when it is possible for it to be predicated of many, even if none of these items actually exist, for example, the intention of a seven-sided house. This is universal because its nature can be predicated of many; it is not necessary that those many items exist nor even some one of them. (3) An intention is called universal when nothing prevents its being thought to be predicated of many, because if something did prevent [its being predicated of many] it would prevent this by a cause by which this is proven. Sun and earth are examples, for so far as the idea of them is concerned the fact that sun and earth are thought

does not prevent its being possible for their intention to be found in many. This is only prevented if we bring in an argument by which it may be known that this is impossible. And then this will be impossible because of an extrinsic cause, not because of the imagination of them.

All of these senses agree in this much: what is universal is something which in thought it is not impossible to predicate of many. The logical universal and whatever is similar to it must have this feature. Thus a universal, just from being a universal, is something, and from being something to which universality happens to belong it is something else. Thus one of the aforesaid terms is signified by 'universal' just because it has been made a universal, for, since it is *human being* or *horse*, the intention here, which is humanity or horseness will be something else outside the intention of universality.

For the definition of horseness is outside the definition of universality, and universality is not contained in the definition of horseness. Horseness has a definition which does not require universality; rather universality happens to belong to it. Consequently, horseness itself is just mere horseness. In itself it is neither many nor one, existent

---

1 See glossary entry for 'intention.'

neither in sensibles nor in the soul, neither potential nor actual in such a way that this is contained within the essence of horseness; rather [it is what it is in itself] from the fact that it is mere horseness.

***

Animal can be considered on its own [*per se*] even though it exists with something other than itself, for its essence is with something other than itself. Therefore its essence belongs to it on its own. Its existing with something other than itself is something which happens to it or something which goes along with its nature, for example *this* animality and humanity. Therefore, this consideration precedes in being both the animal which is individual on account of its accidents, and the universal which is in these sensible items and is intelligible, just as the non-composite precedes the composite and as the part the whole. For from this being it is neither a genus nor a species nor an individual, nor one nor many; rather from this being it is merely *animal* and merely *human being*.

But doubtless being one or many goes along with this, since it is impossible for something to exist but not be one or the other of these, although they go along with it extrinsically.

***

Thus, just as *animal* in existing has many modes, so also in the intellect. In the intellect it is the abstracted form of *animal* in virtue of the abstraction we have talked of earlier, and in this mode it is said to be an intelligible form. And in the intellect the form of *animal* exists in such a way that in the intellect by one and the same definition it agrees with many particulars. On account of this, one form in the intellect will be related to a multiplicity, and in this respect it is universal. [It is a universal] because it is a single intention in the intellect whose comparison does not change no matter which animal you take, i.e. when you first represent the form of any of these in your imagination, if later the intellect strips away the accidents from its intention, you will acquire in the intellect this very form. Therefore, this form is what you acquire by stripping away from animality any individual imagination taken from its external existence, even though it does not have external existence, rather

the imagination abstracts it. ... Thus common things in a way have existence outside and in a way do not. But that a thing one and the same in number is predicated of many, i.e. predicated of this individual in such a way that this individual is it, and likewise this [other] individual, is obviously impossible.

VI.7.2. The Essences of things (from Avicenna's *Logic*)

[An essence has two modes of existence, in the mind and in material singulars, also is just simply what it is apart from modes of existence. Avicenna, in effect, tries to have Plato's Forms without attributing a special eternal existence to them.]

The essences of things either are in the things themselves or are in the intellect. Thus they have three relationships: One relationship of an essence exists in as much as the essence is not related to some third existence nor to what follows on it in virtue of its being such. Another is in virtue of its existing in these singulars. And another is in virtue of its existing in the intellect. And then there follow on it accidents which are distinctive of this sort of existence. For example, supposition [i.e. standing for things], predication, universality and particularity in predicating, essentiality and accidentality in predicating, and others which you will get to know later. But in the items which are outside there is no essentiality or accidentality at all; neither is there some complex or non-complex item, neither proposition nor argument, nor anything else like these.

***

Let us take an example of a genus: *animal* is in itself something. And it is the same whether it is sensible or is apprehended in the soul by thought. But in itself it is neither universal nor singular. For if it were universal in itself in such a way that animality from the fact that it is animality is universal, no animal could possibly be singular; rather every animal would be universal. But if *animal* from the fact that it is *animal* were singular, it would be impossible for there to be more than one singular, viz. the very singular to which animality is bound, and it would be impossible for another singular to be an animal....

Generality is called a logical genus, which means what is predicated of many items of different species in answer to the question 'What?'. It does not express or designate something because it is *animal* or something else. Just as a white item is in itself something thought of, but that it is a human being or a stone is outside its idea but follows on that, and is thought to be one, so also the logical genus. But the natural genus is *animal* according as it is *animal*, which is suited to having the comparison of generality added to its idea. For when the idea is in the soul it becomes suited to having generality understood of it. Neither the idea of Socrates nor the idea of *human being* has this aptitude. ...

But if some one of the species is a genus, it has this not from its generality which is above it, but from those items which are under it. But the natural genus attributes to that which is under it its name and definition from its own naturalness, i.e. from the fact, for example, that *animal* is *animal*, and not from the fact that it is a natural genus, i.e. something which once it has been thought of tends to become a genus from the fact that it is the way it is. For it is impossible that the latter [i.e. the genus] not have what is beneath the former [i.e. the species].

And generally when it is said that the natural genus gives to that which is under it its name and definition, this is not really true except by accident. For it does not give this from the fact that is a natural genus, just as also it did not give it its being a logical genus, since it gave it only a nature which is apt to be a natural genus. This nature by itself is not a natural genus just as it is not a logical genus.

But if a natural genus means only the primary nature on its own [*per se*] which is suited to generality, and natural genus is not understood as we understand it, then it is correct to say that a natural genus attributes its name and definition to that which is under it. And then *animal* is really a natural genus only because it is mere *animal*.

An individual does not become an individual until outside properties, either shared or unshared, are joined to the nature of the species and this or that particular matter is designated for it. However, it is impossible for properties apprehended by thought to be added to the species, no matter how many they are, because in the end they will not succeed in showing the individuating intention on account of which an individual is created in the intellect. For if you say that Plato is tall, a beautiful writer, and so on, no matter how many properties you add still they will not describe in the intellect the individuality of Plato. For it is possible that the intention which is composed from all of them is possessed by more than one item and shows you only that he exists, and is a pointing to the individual intention. For example, if we said that he is the son of this person and at a given time is a tall philosopher, [and] it happened at that time that no one else had those properties, and you happened to know this appearance, then you would know his individuality just as you would know that which is sensible if it were pointed out to you with a finger. For example, if Plato were pointed to at the third hour. For then his individuality would be determined for you, and this would be a case of pointing out his individuality to you. ...

And the difference which there is between *human being* which is a species and *individual human being*, which latter is common not just in name but also by being predicated of many, is this: We say that the idea of *human being*, which is a species, is that it is *rational animal*. And what we say of *individual human being* is that that nature taken together with an accident which happens to belong to it is joined to some designated matter. It is just as though we said 'a certain human being,' i.e. 'some rational animal.' Thus *rational animal* is more common than that, for sometimes it is in the species, sometimes in the individual, i.e. in this one named item. For the species is *rational animal* just as the individual rational animal is rational animal.

***

VI.8. JOHN DUNS SCOTUS

IN THESE SELECTIONS WE SEE SCOTUS STARTING FROM THE AVICENNIAN notion of an essence or nature and proceeding to a theory of how, on the one hand, such a nature gets to be a universal, and, on the other hand, how it gets to be an individual.

VI.8.1. Natures are not of themselves individuated
(*Ordinatio* II, dist.iii, pt.1, qu.1)

[Scotus treats universality as a "second intention," i.e. it belongs to something only in so far as that something is thought of, i.e. is a "first intention." But the nature which is thought of has a real existence in extra-mental reality where it is "contracted" to various individuals.]

As regards the third distinction we must inquire into the personal distinction in the angels. But in order to get a view of that distinction in them we first have to inquire into the individual distinction in material substances. Different people have said different things about this and as a consequence they have differed on the matter of a plurality of individuals in the same species of angel. So that we may see distinctly what each of the different opinions thinks the question is regarding the distinction or indistinction of material substance, I am going to pose separate questions for each of the different ways of approaching the matter; and first:

Is it on account of itself, i.e. on account of its own nature, that a material substance is individual or singular?

[1] In favor of an affirmative answer: In *Metaphysics* VII[1] the Philosopher shows – against Plato – that "the substance of any thing whatsoever is peculiar to that of which it is the substance and does not belong to anything else," therefore, etc. Therefore a material substance in virtue of its

own nature, everything else left aside, is peculiar to that in which it exists, and this in such a way that in virtue of its own nature it cannot belong to anything else. Therefore, in virtue of its own nature it is individual.

[2] Against this: [2.1] Whatever belongs to something in virtue of its own essential character belongs to it in any instance; therefore, if the nature of stone were of itself *this*, no matter what item the nature of stone is in, that nature would be *this* stone. The consequent here is absurd when we speak of determinate singularity, as we are in this question.

[2.2] Moreover, what of itself possesses one of a pair of opposites will of itself reject the other opposite. Therefore, if a nature were of itself one in number,[2] it would reject numerical multiplicity.

[3] Here it is said that just as a nature of itself is formally a nature so also it is of itself singular, and this in such a way that there is no need to seek a cause of its singularity other than the cause of the nature, as if the nature were a nature before (temporally or naturally)[3] it was a singular and then were contracted to make a singular by something arriving in it.

[3.1] This is shown by an analogy: Just as a nature of itself has true being outside the soul but has being in the soul only in virtue of something else, i.e. in virtue of the soul itself (the reason for this is that true being belongs to it unqualifiedly, but being in the soul is its being qualifiedly),[4] so uni-

---

1 Ch.13, 1038b10-11. See selection **VI.2.5.**
2 See selections **V.1.1-3**, for the notion of something 'one in number.'
3 See glossary entry for 'order of nature.'
4 See glossary entry for 'qualified/unqualified.'

versality belongs to a thing only in virtue of its qualified being, namely being in the soul. Singularity, on the other hand, belongs to a thing in virtue of its true being and thus belongs to it of itself and unqualifiedly. Therefore, we should seek a cause for why a nature is universal and we have to propose the intellect as this cause. But we need not seek some cause for why a nature is singular, i.e. a cause, other than the nature of the thing, that acts as an intermediary between it and its singularity. Rather the same causes which cause the unity of the thing also cause its singularity. Therefore, etc.

[4] Against this proposal it is argued as follows:

[4.1] The object insofar as it is the object is naturally prior to the act itself, and, according to you, as prior the object is of itself singular, because this is always the case with a nature when it is not considered as qualified or in respect of the being which it has in the soul. Therefore an intellect that ideates that object under the character of a universal ideates it under a character opposed to its own character, because as it precedes that act it is determined of itself to the opposite of that character, i.e. of that character of a universal.

[4.2] Moreover, what has a real unity, peculiar to it and sufficient for it, but less than a numerical unity, is not of itself one by a numerical unity (i.e. is not of itself *this*). But the nature existing in this stone has a real and sufficient unity peculiar to it, and one less than numerical unity. Therefore etc.

The major is self-evident because nothing is of itself one by a unity greater than the unity sufficient for it. For if its own peculiar unity, which is due to something of itself, were less than numerical unity, numerical unity would not belong to it from its own nature and in virtue of itself. Otherwise just from its own nature alone it would have both a greater and lesser unity. But these when taken as about the same item and in respect of the same item are opposed, because a multiplicity opposed to the greater unity can co-exist without contradiction with the lesser unity, but this multiplicity can-

not co-exist with the greater unity because it rejects it; therefore etc.

Proof of the minor: If there is no real unity of the nature less than singularity and every unity other than the unity of singularity, and which belongs to a specific nature, is less than a real unity, then there will be no real unity less than numerical unity. The consequent is false as I will prove in five or six ways. Therefore etc.

[4.2.1] The first way runs as follows: According to the Philosopher in *Metaphysics* X,[5] "In every genus there is one primary item which is the standard and measure for everything which belongs to that genus." This unity of the primary measure is real, because the Philosopher shows[6] that the primary character of a measure belongs to one item, and explains through ranking how in every genus that to which the character of measuring belongs is one. But this unity belongs to something insofar as that item is primary in its genus; therefore it is real, because the items that are measured are real and they are really measured, but a real being cannot be really measured by a being of thought.[7] Therefore this unity is real.

Further, the unity is not numerical because there is no singular in a genus which is the measure of all the items in that genus. For, according to the Philosopher in *Metaphysics* III,[8] "in individuals of the same species it is not the case that this one is prior and that one posterior."

Although the Commentator explains[9] the notion of something prior that constitutes something posterior, this makes no difference to the minor premiss, because The Philosopher there intends to give as the reason why Plato posited a separated character for a species but not in the case of a genus, that there is in species an essential ranking on account of which the posterior can be reduced to the prior; and therefore, according to him it is not necessary to posit the idea of a genus through participation in which the species are what they are, but rather only the idea of a species to which all the other species are reduced. On the other hand, according

---

5 Ch.1, 1052b18.
6 *Ibid.* 19-24.
7 See glossary entry for 'being of thought.'
8 Ch.3, 999a12-13.
9 Averroes, Comment 11 on *Meta*.III.

to Plato and according to The Philosopher who relates this, in individuals there is no such ranking whether or not one constitutes another. Therefore etc. Thus it is the Philosopher's intention here to agree with Plato that among individuals of the same species there is no essential ranking. Therefore no individual is through itself a measure of the items in its own species; consequently no numerical or individual unity [is such a measure].

[4.2.2] Further I show in a second way that that same consequent is false, because, according to the Philosopher in *Physics* VII,[10] comparison takes place within an indivisible species because in that case there is a single nature, but not in a genus because a genus does not have that sort of unity.

This difference of unities is not due to thought, because the concept of the genus is one in number in the same way as the concept of the species is; otherwise, no concept would be said *in quid*[11] of several species (and thus no concept would be a genus), but rather just as many concepts would be said of species as there are concepts of species, and so in each predication the same item would be predicated of itself. Likewise the unity of the concept or of the non-concept is irrelevant there to the intention of the Philosopher, i.e. to the question of whether there is comparison or not. Consequently, the Philosopher means there that the specific nature is one by the unity of the specific nature, but he does not mean that it is one by a numerical unity, because comparison does not occur in the case of numerical unity. Therefore, etc.

[4.2.3] Further, in a third way, according to The Philosopher in *Metaphysics* V, (the chapter about relation),[12] same, similar and equal are based on one in such a way that, although similarity has for its basis[13] a thing in some qualitative genus, the relation is real only if it has a real basis and a real proximate character of being based. Therefore, the unity which is required of the basis of the relation of similarity is real; but it is not a numerical unity, because nothing one and the same is similar or equal to itself.

[4.2.4] Further, in a fourth way, for a single real

opposition there are two real primary terms; but contrariety is a real opposition. This is clear because one really corrupts or destroys the other even when every operation of the intellect has been excluded; this occurs only because they are contraries. Therefore each primary term of this opposition is real and one by some real unity; but not by a numerical unity, because then exclusively *this* white would be the primary contrary to *this* black, or exclusively *that* white to *that* black, which is absurd because then there would be just as many primary contrarieties as there are contrary individuals. Therefore etc.

[4.2.5] Further, in a fifth way, for a single action of a sense there is an object that is one in virtue of some real unity; but not a numerical unity. Therefore, there is some other real unity than numerical unity.

Proof of the minor premiss: A power that apprehends an object in this way, i.e. insofar as it is one by this unity, apprehends it insofar as it is distinct from anything which is not one by this unity. But a sense does not apprehend an object insofar as it is distinct from anything which is not one by that numerical unity. This is clear because no sense discerns that this ray of sunlight numerically differs from some other ray, and yet they are diverse on account of the sun's motion. If all common sensibles, for example diversity of location or situation, were eliminated, and if through divine power two quantities were put in existence at the same time and these were completely similar and equal in whiteness, sight would not discern that there were two whites there. Yet if it apprehended one or the other of them insofar as that item were one by a numerical unity, it would apprehend that item insofar as it is one item *distinct* by a numerical unity.

On this point it can also be argued that the primary object of a sense is one in itself by some real unity, because just as an object of this power, insofar as it is an object, precedes the intellect, so also in respect of its real unity it precedes every action of the intellect.

But this argument is not as conclusive as the pre-

10 Ch.4, 249a3-8.
11 See glossary entry for '*in quid*.'
12 Ch.15, 1021a9-12.
13 See glossary entry for 'basis of a relation.'

ceding, for one can propose that some primary object, as it is adequate to a faculty, is something common, abstracted from all particular objects, and thus it has only the unity of commonness to those several particular objects. At any rate, this proposal does not seem to deny that the single object of a single act of sensing necessarily has a real unity that is less than numerical unity.

[4.2.6] Further, in a sixth way, if every real unity is numerical, then every real diversity is numerical. But the consequent is false, because every numerical diversity, insofar as it is numerical, is equal, and thus all things would be equally distinct. Then it follows that the intellect would no more be able to abstract something common from Socrates and Plato than from Socrates and a line, and every universal would be a pure fabrication of the intellect.

The first consequence [that if every real unity is numerical, then every real diversity is numerical] is shown in two ways: First, one and several, same and diverse, are opposites (see *Metaphysics* X, ch.5).[14] But one of a pair of opposites is said just as often as the other one is said (see *Topics* I).[15] Therefore, to any unity corresponds its own peculiar diversity.

Secondly, each of the terms of any diversity is in itself one, and it is diverse from the other term in the very same way by which it is one in itself, so that the unity of one term seems to be through itself the reason for the diversity of the other term.

This conclusion is defended in another way. If in this thing there is only a real numerical unity, then any entity there is in that thing is of itself one in number. Therefore this and that are primarily diverse in virtue of every entity in them, because they are diverse items that in no way agree in some *one* item.

It is also defended in this way: Numerical diversity is for this singular not to be that singular, given the entity of both terms. But such unity necessarily belongs to either term.

[4.2.7] Further: Even if no intellect existed, fire would generate[16] fire and destroy water, and there would be some real unity between the generator and the generated in virtue of a form on account of which there would be univocal generation.[17] For the intellect that considers it does not make the generation be univocal; rather it apprehends it to be univocal.

[5] To the question, then, I concede the conclusions of those arguments, and I say that a material substance is not on account of its own nature *this* of itself, because, as the first argument proves [4.1], if it were, the intellect would not be able to ideate it under an aspect opposed [to *this*] without ideating its object under an aspect of ideation that conflicts with the character of such an object.

Also, as the second argument [4.2] with all its proofs deduces, there is some real unity in things, apart from all operations of the intellect, which is less than numerical unity or the unity proper to a singular, and this unity belongs to the nature in virtue of itself. In virtue of this unity that is peculiar to the nature as it is a nature, the nature is indifferent to the unity of singularity; therefore, it is not of itself one by that unity, i.e. by the unity of singularity.

How to understand this can in some way be seen from the remark of Avicenna in *Metaphysics* V, ch.1[18] where he maintains that "horseness is just horseness; it is not of itself either one or many, either universal or particular." I read this as meaning: It is not of itself one by a numerical unity nor many by a plurality opposed to that unity; neither is it actually universal, i.e. in the way that something is universal when it is an object of the intellect, nor is it of itself particular. For although it is never really apart from some of these, of itself, nevertheless, it is not any of them, but rather is naturally prior to them all.

In virtue of its natural priority it is what something is and by itself an object of the intellect, and by itself as such it is studied by the metaphysician and is expressed through a definition. Propositions that are true in the first mode are true by reason of

---

14 Actually ch.3, 1054b22-23.
15 Perhaps *Topics* II, 7, 113a34.
16 See glossary entry for 'natural generation.'
17 See glossary entry for 'univocal production.'
18 *Philosophia Prima (sive Metaphysica)*, vol.2, p.228. (See selection **VI.7.1**.)

a quiddity[19] taken in this way, because nothing is said *per se* in the first mode[20] of a quiddity unless it is essentially included in it, insofar as it is abstracted from all those items which are naturally posterior to it.

But not only is the nature itself of itself indifferent to being in the intellect and in the particular, and consequently to being universal and particular or singular, but also when it has being in the intellect it does not have universality primarily in virtue of itself. For although it is ideated under universality as under a mode of ideating it, still universality is not part of its primary concept, because it is not a metaphysician's concept but a logician's, for, according to him [Avicenna], the logician studies second intentions[21] that are applied to first intentions. Therefore, the primary ideation is of the nature as not ideated along with some mode, neither a mode which belongs to it in the intellect nor one which belongs to it outside the intellect, even though universality is the mode of ideating that ideated item, but it is not a mode that is itself ideated.

And just as the nature is not of itself universal in virtue of that being, but rather universality happens to that nature in virtue of the first character of it in virtue of which it is an object, so also in things outside where the nature exists with singularity the nature is not of itself determined to that singularity; rather it is naturally prior to the character that contracts it to that singularity, and insofar as it is naturally prior to that contracting factor it is not repellent to it to be without that contracting factor. And just as the object in the intellect in virtue of *that* entity of it and universality has true intelligible being, so also in reality the nature has in virtue of *that* entity true real being outside the soul, – also in virtue of *that* entity it has a unity proportional to itself which is indifferent to singularity in such a way that it does not of itself conflict with that unity which is given with any unity of singularity.

This is what I mean by saying that the nature has a real unity that is less than numerical unity. And although it does not of itself have it in such a way that it is within the definition of the nature (since "horseness is just horseness," according to Avicenna in *Metaphysics* V),[22] still that unity is an attribute peculiar to the nature in virtue of its primary entity, and consequently it is not of itself *this* either intrinsically or in virtue of the entity peculiar to it that is necessarily included in the nature itself in virtue of its primary entity.

[6] But against this there seem to be two objections:

[6.1] One arises because this view seems to propose that a universal is something real in things, which runs counter to what the Commentator [Averroes] says in *De Anima* I, comment 8: "The intellect produces universality in things in such a way that it exists only through the intellect." Thus it is just a being of thought. For that nature, as it exists in this stone and yet is naturally prior to the singularity of the stone, is, according to what was said, indifferent to this singular and to that one.

[6.2] Further, Damascene[23] says in chapter 8 [of *De Fide Orthodoxa*]: "We have to realize that it is one thing to consider something as it is in reality, another to consider it as it is in reason and thought. Therefore, and more specifically, in all creatures the separation of substrates is considered to be in reality (for Peter and Paul are considered to be separate in reality), but commonness and linkage [of predicate to subject] are considered by reason and thought as in the intellect alone (for we apprehend by the intellect that Peter and Paul are of a single nature and have one common nature)"; "For these substrates are not in each other; rather each is set apart on its own, i.e. is separated as a thing." Later he says: "But the reverse is the case in the holy and super-substantial Trinity, for there, a single common item is considered to be in reality," "while later the division is considered to be in thought."

---

19 See glossary entry for 'quiddity.'
20 See glossary entry for 'essential-in-the-first-mode.'
21 See glossary entry for 'intention.'
22 See fn. 18.
23 St. John Damascene, who in the 8th century led the Christian community in Damascus when it was already under Moslem rule.

[7. Replies]

[7.1] To the first objection [6.1] I say that the actual universal is what has an indifferent unity in virtue of which it is the same in its proximate potential for being said of any *suppositum*[24] whatsoever, since, according to the Philosopher in *Posterior Analytics* I,[25] "the universal is what is one in many and of many." For nothing, no matter what unity it has, is such in reality that in virtue of that precise unity it has a proximate potential in respect of every *suppositum* for a predication that says *this* is *this*. This is because, although there is something that exists in reality which does not reject being in a singularity other than the one in which it is, still it cannot be truly said of any item beneath it that it is it. This is possible only for an object which is the same in number and actually before the intellect. Certainly this, as an object of the intellect, has even a numerical unity of an object, and in virtue of this it is the same item predicable of every singular by saying that *this* is *this*.

From this it is clear how to refute the remark that the agent intellect produces universality in things by the fact that of every item which is what something is and exists in the imagination it can be said that it does not reject being in something else, and by the fact that the intellect strips bare this item existing in the imagination. For no matter where it exists before it has objective being[26] in the intellect, whether in reality or in the imagination, whether it has certain existence or existence inferred by argument (and so such a nature is not by means of some light, but rather always of itself, something which does not reject being in something else), still it is not such that being said of anything belongs to it by a proximate potential, rather it is such by a proximate potential only when it exists in the possible intellect.[27]

Therefore, there is in reality a common item which is not of itself this, and consequently it of itself does not reject being *not-this*. But such a common item is not actually universal, because it lacks that indifference in virtue of which the complete universal is universal, i.e. in virtue of which as

the same item by some identity it is predicable of any individual in such a way that any one of them is it.

[7.2] To the second objection from Damascene [6.2] I say that there is not in creatures a common item that is really one in the way in God there is a common item that is really one. For in God the common item is singular and individual, since the divine nature itself of itself is *this*, and it is obvious that no universal in creatures is really one in that way. To propose otherwise would be to propose that some individual created nature was predicated of many individuals by a predication that says *this* is *this*, just as we say that the Father is God and the Son is the same God.

Nevertheless, there is in creatures something common that is one by a real unity but a unity less than numerical unity. Certainly this common item is not so common that it is predicable of many, although it is so common that it does not reject being in something other than that in which it is.

Thus it is clear in two ways how the authority [i.e. Damascene] is not against me. First, because he talks of the unity of singularity in God, and in this sense not only the created universal is not one but neither in creatures is the common item one.

Secondly, because he speaks of a common predicable, not just of the common item that is in fact determined [to an individual] even though it does not reject being in something else. Such a common item can be posited as real only in creatures.

[8] From what has been said it is clear how to reply to the principal argument [1]: The Philosopher refutes the fiction he credits to Plato, namely that this human being who exists *per se* and who is posited as an Idea is through itself universal to every human being, because "every substance that exists *per se* is peculiar to that of which it is [the substance]," i.e. either it is of itself peculiar or it is made peculiar by something that contracts it, and once the contracting factor is given it cannot belong to something else, although it does not of itself reject belonging to something else.

---

24 See glossary entry for '*suppositum*.'
25 Ch.4, 73b26-33.
26 See glossary entry for '*esse objectivum*.'
27 See glossary entry for 'passive or possible intellect.'

This gloss is also true when we use 'substance'[28] in the sense in which it means a nature. Then it follows that an Idea will not be the substance of Socrates because it is not the nature of Socrates, because it is neither of itself peculiar to Socrates nor made peculiar to Socrates so that it is only in him – rather according to him [Plato] it is also in something else.

But if 'substance' is taken for primary substance, then it is true that any substance is of itself peculiar to that of which it is [the substance], and then it follows much more that the Idea, which he claims is a substance that exists *per se*, cannot in that sense be the substance of Socrates or of Plato. But the first alternative suffices for what we have said.

[9] In response to the defense of the opinion [3]: It is clear that commonness and singularity do not relate to a nature in the way being in the intellect and true being outside the soul do, because commonness belongs to the nature as outside the intellect, as does singularity. Commonness belongs to the nature of itself, while singularity belongs to the nature through something in reality that contracts it. But universality does not belong to the thing of itself.

Therefore I allow that we do need to seek a cause of universality, but we do not need to seek a cause of commonness other than the nature itself. And given there is commonness in the nature itself in virtue of its own entity and unity, we necessarily need to seek a cause of the singularity, which adds something further to the nature to which it belongs.

VI.8.2. What makes a Substance individual (from *Ordinatio* II, dist.3, qu.6)

[Here Scotus explains as best he can the sort of entity which he believes "contracts" the common nature to an individual. He treats it as analogous to a specific difference. The whole theory is attacked by Ockham in selection **VI.9.1**.]

[1] Therefore in answer to the question I say that yes [a material substance is individual on account of some positive entity that of itself determines a nature to singularity].

[1.1] For this I add the following argument: Just as unity in general is itself a consequence of entity in general, so any sort of unity is of itself a consequence of some entity. Therefore unqualified unity, such as is the unity of the individual which we have often described above as that which rejects division into several subjective parts[29] and which rejects not being *this*, i.e. a signed item, if it exists in beings (which everyone supposes), is of itself a consequence of some *per se* entity. But it is not a consequence of the *per se* entity of the nature, because that has its own *per se* real unity, just as was proven in the resolution of the first question. Therefore, it is a consequence of some other entity that determines that [nature], and this [other entity] with the entity of the nature produces something that is one *per se*, for the whole possessing this unity is complete of itself.

[1.2] Again, every difference of differences[30] ultimately leads back to something primarily different (otherwise there would be no point at which we stop finding differences). But individuals are different in the strict sense because they are different beings with something the same. Therefore their differences lead back to some items which are primarily different. Moreover, these primarily diverse items are not the nature in this and the nature in that, because that by which items agree formally is not the same as that by which they differ really, although what is really distinct can be the same as what really agrees. For being distinct is quite different from being that by which something is primarily differentiated, and consequently likewise for unity. Therefore besides the nature in this and in that there are some items that are primarily different by which this and that differ (one of them in this and another in that). These cannot be negations – see the second question; nor can they be accidents – see the fourth question. Therefore they will be some positive entities that of themselves determine the nature.

---

28 See glossary entry for 'substance.'
29 I.e., "parts" which it could be predicated of in the way 'animal' is predicated of 'rabbit,' 'goose,' 'cow,' etc.
30 See selection **VI.3.1.**, pp. 5ff.

[2] Against the first argument [1.1] it is objected that if there is some real unity less than numerical unity, it belongs to something that is either in numerically the same item or is in something else. Not to something in numerically the same item, because whatever is in numerically the same item is one in number; not to something in two items because in them there is nothing that is really one, since that feature is exclusive to the case of the divine *supposita* (as we explained in discussing above what John Damascene said).[31]

[3] I answer: Just as was said on this subject in the resolution of the first question, the nature is naturally prior to *this* nature and its own distinctive unity, consequent on the nature as a nature, is naturally prior to its unity as *this* nature, and it is under this character that there is metaphysical consideration of the nature, a definition is assigned to it and we have *per se* in the first way[32] propositions. Therefore in the same item that is one in number there is some entity on which is consequent a unity that is less than numerical unity, and it is real. That to which such a unity belongs is not formally of itself one item by a numerical unity. I allow, then, that a real unity does not belong to something that exists in two individuals but rather [to something that exists] in one.

[4] And when you object: "Whatever is in numerically the same individual is numerically the same,"

[4.1] I answer first by citing an analogous and clearer case: This argument is invalid: Whatever is in a single species[33] is one in species. Therefore, color in whiteness is one in species. Therefore, color does not have a unity less than the unity of a species. For, just as we said elsewhere (namely in book I, the question about attributes,[34] before the resolution of the principle argument about attributes, by way of resolving the first point of doubt) that something can be called alive denominatively,[35] as a body is, or *per se* in the first way, as a human

being is (also in this way a surface is called white denominatively while a white surface is called white *per se* in the first way, because the subject includes the predicate), so I say that a potential which is restricted by an actual item, is informed by that actual item, and through that is informed by the unity consequent on that actuality or that act is one by that actual item's own unity, but it is one this way denominatively. It is not, however, this way one of itself, not in the first way, nor through an essential part. Therefore, color in whiteness is one in species, but it is not one of itself, not *per se*, nor primarily, but rather only denominatively. The specific difference, however, is primarily one because it primarily rejects being divided into items that are many in species. Whiteness is one in species *per se*, but not primarily, because it is one in species by something intrinsic to itself, i.e. by the difference. Thus I allow that whatever is in this stone is one in number either primarily, or *per se*, or denominatively. Primarily [one in number], perhaps, is that by which such a unity belongs to this composite. *Per se* [one in number] is this stone, of which that is a part which is primarily one by this unity. Only denominatively [one in number] is that potential which is perfected by this actual item and which sort of denominatively relates to its actuality and unity.

[4.2] Further by explaining this resolution: What this entity is in virtue of which the perfect unity exists can be explained by analogy with the entity from which we get the specific difference.[36] Certainly the specific difference, or the entity from which we get the specific difference can be related to that which is beneath it, or to that which is above it, or to that which is on its own level.

[4.2.1] In the first way [i.e. as related to what is beneath it], the specific difference and the specific entity reject being divided into items essentially many in species or nature, and in virtue of it the whole of which that entity is a *per se* part rejects such division. Likewise in the case we propose, this

---

31 See previous selection [7.2].
32 See glossary entry for 'essential-in-the-first-mode.'
33 See glossary entry for 'species/genus.'
34 *Ord*.I, d.8, n.214 (Balic IV, p.271).
35 See glossary entry for 'denominative term.'
36 See glossary entry for 'specific difference.'

individual entity primarily rejects being divided into any subjective parts whatsoever, and in virtue of it the whole of which that entity is a part rejects such division. The only difference between these cases lies in this, that the unity of the specific nature is less than that unity [of the individual], and for that reason the former unity does not exclude every division into subjective parts but only that division which is of essential parts. The latter unity, however, excludes all division. This sufficiently confirms what we proposed, for, given that any unity less than that unity [of the individual] has its own entity on which it is of itself consequent, it seems unlikely that this most perfect unity would not have its own entity on which it is consequent.

[4.2.2] When we relate the specific nature to what is above it, I say that the reality from which we get the specific difference is actual in relation to the reality from which we get the genus or generic character. This is the case in such a way that the one reality is not formally the other; otherwise, in the definition there would be redundancy because the genus alone (or the difference alone) would suffice for the definition, since it would indicate the whole entity of the defined.

Nevertheless, sometimes the restricting item is different from the form from which we get the generic character, namely, when the species adds some thing over and above the nature of the genus. Sometimes, however, it is not another thing but only another formality or another formal concept of the same thing. On account of this some specific differences have concepts that are not unqualifiedly simple, for example those we get from the final abstraction of the form. (In dist. 3 of book I we spoke of this distinction among specific differences, how some specific differences include being and some do not.)

The reality of the individual is similar to the specific reality in this respect: it is a sort of act that determines the reality of the species, which is a sort of possible and potential item. But it is dissimilar in this respect: we never get it from an added form; rather we get it exclusively from the final reality of the form. Also it is dissimilar in this respect: the specific reality establishes the composite of which it is a part in quidditative being, because it is a quidditative entity; this reality of the individual, however, is primarily diverse from all quidditative entity.

This is shown by the fact that when we apprehend any quidditative entity (speaking now of limited quidditative entity), we find it is common to many and it does not reject being said of many items each of which is it. Therefore, this entity, which of itself is an entity different from a quiddity or a quidditative entity, cannot establish the whole of which it is a part in quidditative being, but rather in some other sort of being.

Also since in the works of the Philosopher quiddity is frequently called 'form' (This is clear in *Metaphysics* V, the chapter on 'cause,'[37] as well as in many other places; also in *Metaphysics* VII, the chapter on parts of a definition,[38] he says, "in any items where there is no matter the what-it-is is the same as that of which it is [the what-it-is]. As we will explain, he speaks here of matter and form.) and in his works 'material' means whatever has a restricted quiddity (Also Boethius in his little book *On the Trinity*[39] claims that no form can be the subject of an accident, because a form is said *in quid* of anything else. Also if humanity is a subject, this belongs to it not insofar as it is a form. Certainly humanity is not the form of one or the other part of the composite, i.e. of the form or of the matter; rather it is the form of the whole composite that has a restricted quiddity or in which there is a restricted quiddity.) – given this, every specific reality establishes [the whole of which it is a part] in formal being since in quidditative being, and the reality of the individual establishes [the whole of which it is a part] exclusively in material being, i.e. in restricted being. From this follows the logical distinction that the one is essentially formal, the other material, because the latter establishes [the whole of which it is a part] in the character of a subject while the former establishes [the whole of which it is a part] exclusively in the character of a predicable, and a formal predicate has the character of a form while a subject has the character of matter.

---

37 Ch.2, 1013a26-28.
38 Ch.11, 1037a32-b5.
39 Ch.2, (PL64,1250).

[4.2.3] Thirdly, when we relate the specific difference to what is on the same level as it, i.e. to another specific difference, we find that although sometimes it can be non-primarily diverse from another, as is the entity which we get from the form, still the ultimate specific difference is primarily diverse from another, i.e. the one which has an unqualifiedly simple concept [is primarily diverse]. In this regard I say that the individual difference resembles the specific difference of the ultimate sort, because every individual entity is primarily diverse from any other.

From this it is clear how to answer the following objection: This [individual] entity and that [individual] entity are either of the same sort or not. If they are, then some entity can be abstracted from them, and this will be specific. Then of this entity we will have to ask what restricts it to this entity and that entity. If we say it is restricted of itself, then with equal reason we could have stopped with the nature of a stone; if we say it is restricted by something else, then we have an infinite regress. If they are of different sorts, then also the item they are a constituent of will be of different sorts and thus will not be individuals of the same species.

I answer: Ultimate specific differences are primarily diverse, and therefore from them nothing that is *per se* one item can be abstracted. But from this it does not follow that the items they are a constituent of are primarily diverse and not of some one type. For that some items are equally differentiated can be understood in two ways: either that they are equally incompatible, i.e. that they cannot belong to the same thing, or that they equally lack agreement in anything. In the first sense it is true that differentiated items are just as diverse as the very items that differentiate them, for the differentiating items cannot be incompatible without the differentiated items being incompatible. In the second sense it is universally impossible [for the differentiated items to be just as diverse as the items that differentiate them] because the differentiated items not only include the differentiating items but something else as well which is a sort of potential in respect of the distinguishing items, and yet the distinguishing items in it have nothing in common.

As regards individual entities I answer, just as for the primarily diverse differences, that they are primarily diverse, i.e. they have nothing the same in common, and yet it is not necessary for the differentiated items to be unqualifiedly differentiated. Still, just as those [individual] entities are incompatible, so also are the individuals having those entities.

[5] And if you ask me what is this individual entity from which we get the individual – is it matter or form or a composite?

I answer: Every partial or total quidditative entity, belonging to a genus is of itself indifferent as a quidditative entity to this entity and to that, in such a way that as a quidditative entity it is naturally prior to that entity as it is *this*. And since it is naturally prior, just as being *this* does not belong to it so it does not in virtue of its own character reject its opposite. Also, just as a composite does not insofar as it is a nature include its own entity by which it is formally *this*, so neither does the matter insofar as it is a nature include its own entity by which it is *this* matter, nor does the form insofar as it is a nature include its own. Therefore, this entity is neither matter nor form nor the composite insofar as any of these is a nature. Rather it is the ultimate reality of the being which is the matter or which is the form or which is the composite. In just the way that any common but determinable item, however much it is a single thing, can still be distinguished into several formally distinct[40] realities of which one is not formally the other, so here the one is formally the entity of the singular and the other is formally the entity of the nature. Neither can these two realities be a thing and a thing, as can the reality from which we take the genus and the reality from which we take the difference and from both of which is taken the specific reality. Rather, in the same item (whether in a part of it or the whole of it) there are always formally distinct realities belonging to the same thing.

VI.8.3. Is a Universal something in things? (from *Quaestiones Subtillisimae super Libros Metaphysicorum Aristotelis*, lib. VII, qu.18)

[In this question Scotus defends the real existence

---

40 Formal distinction is explained by Scotus in selection V.4.1.

of a "common" nature, i.e. something which is not of itself one in number, but through various "individual realities" is "contracted" to individuals.]

Is a universal[41] *something in things?*

[1] This question can be treated first by arguing against the position of Plato, who, according to Aristotle,[42] posited Ideas on account of the formal entity of things..., and on account of scientific knowledge, since it is only about necessary items while singulars are corruptible; and also on account of generation,[43] since more is needed than the particular generator.

If this view proposes that an idea is some substance apart from motion and from accidental accidents,[44] which has nothing in itself except the separated specific nature complete to the extent that it can be complete, and which perhaps has in itself attributes of the species (otherwise nothing would be known about it), this view cannot be validly disproved, because such a singular having such a nature does not seem to be rejected by the notion of unqualified entity.

And neither does Aristotle unqualifiedly disprove it. Rather in so far as it is viewed as incorruptible he argues against it at the end of book X.[45] But here in book VII he argues not its impossibility but its lack of necessity. For here he argues against Ideas as follows: Nothing which is not obvious is to be posited by philosophers without necessity. There is no necessity in the reasons for positing Ideas; therefore, they should simply not be posited. That it is not necessary on account of entity or knowledge he argues in [Ch 6 of] *Metaphysics* VII, which begins: "Moreover is that which is a what...."

But if someone further proposes that this idea is formally universal in such a way that it is predicated as identical with this corruptible item by a predication which says this is this, immediately a contradiction arises, because numerically the same item is the quiddity[46] of many different items and

yet is outside them (for otherwise it would not be incorruptible).

[2] Setting aside this approach we can treat the question by following the view Aristotle takes in speaking of the universal. We find here two opposed opinions:

[2.1] The first is that the universal is in things. There are three arguments for this:

[2.1.1] The first of these is that the universal is that which is naturally suited to be said of many. But a thing naturally suited to be said of many is so *of itself*. If it were not, that suitability would be contrary to it and could not be conferred on it, at least not by the intellect, for then the intellect could give Socrates such a suitability.

[2.1.2] Moreover, the universal, about which we are speaking, is predicated of a thing, for example of a singular, by a predication that says this is this, for example, 'Socrates is a human.' But it is impossible for something to be predicated of a thing and not be in things.

[2.1.3] Also, a "what" taken completely absolutely[47] is a true thing, because it is a principle and a cause, as we see in *Metaphysics* VII, the last chapter [ch.17]. But when taken absolutely it is a universal. Proof: What is taken absolutely is expressed by a definition; but definitions are only of universals.

[2.2] The way this is posited is as follows: As was said in the question on individuation, in a thing with the grade of limitation by which it is *this* singular, there is also a nature limited by that grade. This nature is not only intelligible without that grade but is also prior in the thing; and as such it does not reject being in something else, because as prior in this way it is not as a result limited to *this*. Therefore, as prior in this way it is universal.

[2.3] Against this view there are three ways of arguing.

[2.3.1] First, as follows: The universal is a numerically single object of the intellect and is under-

---

41 See glossary for a definition of the term.
42 *Meta.*I,6 987b1-11, 9 991b3-9; XIII,4 1078b12-17.
43 See glossary entry for 'natural generation.'
44 See glossary entry for 'accident.'
45 Cf.1059a10-14.
46 See glossary entry for 'quiddity.'
47 See glossary entry for 'absolute.'

stood by numerically one act of understanding. This occurs in such a way that the intellect in attributing it to different singulars attributes numerically the same object conceived many times as a predicate of different subjects by saying this is this. But it seems to be impossible that something which is in things is numerically the same intelligible item and is attributed as such to different items.

This reasoning is bolstered because even *this* nature as prior to its limiting grade, if it were understood, would be correctly attributed to only one item. For *this* concept is not correctly attributed to another singular, but rather there is another concept of another nature which is in the other [singular].

[2.3.2] Secondly, an attribute[48] of a subject belongs to whatever its subject belongs to under the character by which it is the subject [of that attribute]. Therefore, if human belongs to Socrates under that thought by which human is truly universal, Socrates is truly universal. This reasoning does not involve the fallacy of accident since the middle term stays the same.

[2.3.3] Thirdly, it would follow that the senses would have as their *per se* objects universals. For, as was said in the question on the intellectual apprehension of the singular, although nature does not cause motion unless it is *this* nature, it does not cause motion in as much as it is *this* nature. Also it follows that if every universal is of itself actually in things, it is completely superfluous to propose an agent intellect.[49]

[2.4] Against the way of positing this view: It follows that there would be as many universals as singulars, because any nature in any individual has this assigned character of a universal; and there is no nature other than those of individuals, as the first argument above showed. Thus any nature is a universal and there is none [other than those of individuals].

Also in the predication of a universal of a singu-lar the same item would be predicated of itself.

[2.5] The other opinion is that the universal is only in the intellect. In support of this: the authority of the Commentator in *De Anima* I:[50] The intellect makes the universality in things, otherwise the agent intellect would not seem to be necessary. This point is bolstered by the fact that the agent intellect is not a productive power, and therefore does not cause anything outside the intellect. Also Boethius, speaking about unity and 'one':[51] "Everything which is is one in number." In support of this there is the argument that "the universal is one in many and of many" (*Posterior Analytics* I).[52] It includes essentially, then, a relationship with *supposita*,[53] as a predicable is related to a subjectible. But such a relationship is not in the things, but only in an intellect relating them.

For this view and the mode of proposing it we have the authority of Avicenna in *Metaphysics* V, ch.2,[54] where he intends that the intelligible form is singular in relation to the soul and forms in different intellects are different. But the same form is universal in respect of individuals outside the mind.

[2.6] Against this opinion:

[2.6.1] The object naturally precedes the act. Therefore, the universal naturally precedes the ideation when it is ideated. But it is actually in the intellect only by an ideation. This is bolstered by the fact that if the object, as object and as prior to the ideation, were not universal, it could not be related by the intellect to the many items outside the mind.[55]

To these points it can be said that although the object is prior by nature to the act, still this need not be in the object necessarily, especially when it is a matter not of the mode of the known but of a mode under which it is known, and especially if the object exists only at the same time as the act, as Avicenna claims of the universal.

But, contrary to this, it would follow that if no one were thinking there would not be an actual uni-

---

48 See glossary entry for 'attribute.'
49 See glossary entry for 'agent or active intellect.'
50 Averroes, comm.18, AOAC Supp.II, 161F.
51 See selection **VI.4.1**.
52 Ch.1 71a7.
53 See glossary entry for '*suppositum*.'
54 See selection **VI.7.1**.
55 The following 2 paragraphs are out of place in the Wadding/Vives edition.

versal, and thus habitual[56] scientific knowledge would not be of an actually universal object.

Furthermore, in so far as the object is prior to the act it is not ideated under this mode; therefore, it is ideated either under no mode or under the opposite mode, for since it is an object it determines some mode for itself.

[2.6.2] Moreover, the subject of scientific knowledge, in so far as it is a subject, precedes the ideation. But as such it is universal, because as a subject it is primarily such in its relationship to its own distinctive attribute; and if it is this primarily, then [that attribute is said] of everything [that falls under that subject], and thus there can be scientific knowledge of it.

This is bolstered as follows: Just as a first principle, which is a universal proposition, can be conceived as prior to the complex act, so its term outside the mind under that character by which it is its term, can be conceived as prior to the incomplex act of ideation. But the term within the first principle is universal, because it can be taken universally.

[2.6.3] Thirdly, universality would be a condition of what is a being in the intellect, just as *true* is. Thus the former would weaken the sense of 'being' just as the latter does. Thus some scientific knowledge would be no more of the universal than of the true.

[2.6.4] Against the mode of proposing this view: This intelligible form is subjectively[57] in the soul and really in it; if the universal is in the intellect, it will seem to be there as an object known is in the knower. These modes of being are different; therefore, etc. And thus the arguments already given disprove this opinion.

[3] Concerning the solution of this question:

[3.1] First we must distinguish the senses of 'universal,' for it is taken or can be taken in three ways: It can be taken for a second intention[58] which is a certain relation of thought in the predicable directed to that of which it is predicable. The noun 'universal' signifies this relation concretely just as 'universality' does abstractly.

In another sense 'universal' is taken for that which is denoted by that intention, which is a thing of first intention, for second intentions are applied to first intentions. In this sense it can be taken in two ways: In one way for that which is denoted by this intention as a sort of remote subject. In another way, for the near subject. In the first way a nature taken absolutely is called universal, because it is not of itself a *this*. and thus it is not contrary to it of itself to be said of many. In the second way only that is universal which is actually indeterminate in such a way that numerically one intelligible is sayable of every *suppositum*. This is the complete universal.

The second opinion [2.5] can be interpreted as about the first sense, because that relationship which is a second intention, belongs to the object only as it is in an intellect that is relating [it to something]. The first opinion [2.1] can be interpreted as about the second sense, for the nature is not of itself a *this*. But the first opinion does not posit a complete universal because it is not sufficiently indeterminate, since it is not contrary to determination, but sort of deprived of it or contradictory to it.

The second opinion does not speak of the complete sort of universal either, since the question is difficult. Rather it speaks of a certain intention naturally posterior to the complete sort [or universal]. For the indetermination which is sort of contrary [to determination] and by which human being is indeterminate in such a way that when quidditatively conceived it belongs to every human being, naturally precedes that second intention which is logical universality or a relationship to many.

[4] Therefore, it remains to see whether the universal taken in the third sense is primarily in the intellect.

[4.1] Just as we can speak of two ways of being in, so we can speak in two ways of being in the intellect objectively. In one sense we speak of it as habitual, in another as actual whether in the primary act or in the secondary act.[59] In the first sense

---

56 See glossary entry for 'habit.'
57 I.e., in it as in a subject, as opposed to being in it objectively, i.e., as the object of some psychological act or state.
58 See glossary entry for 'intention.'
59 See glossary entry for 'first/second actuality.'

it is there when it is there as immediately motivating to an ideation. In the second sense, when it is actually ideated. According to Avicenna's position, these are simultaneous, although the first is prior in nature. For although he does not propose that an intelligible species[60] by which an object is present in the first sense remains in the intellect even while the intellect is not actually ideating, still the present object as a motivator is prior in nature to the actual ideation. For the first precedes the ideation as its cause; the second follows or accompanies it.

To someone else who denies the intelligible species it is not clear how these two beings can be distinct, since according to him an object in the intellect has no being except by way of an act of ideation. Thus it does not have the first sort of being at all, and in no way does it move the intellect. Nevertheless, [Avicenna] holds the contrary of this.

There is a third approach that is common and which says that the first being precedes temporally and naturally the second and stays on without it in the way those propose who maintain that the intelligible species remains without the act. For it seems absurd to deny to the intellect (in as much as it is a created intellect) the retention after the act of its peculiar object, when this capacity is found in the senses. And although the intellect is joined to phantasms,[61] I ask what is the intrinsic perfection of the intellect? For in so far as it is an intellect it accidentally happens to it that it is joined to phantasms; and although it would be less perfect if not joined to phantasms, still it would not, to be sure, be a different type of power. Therefore, just as a separated intellect is intrinsically retentive, so also ours, although less so.

[4.2] To the question as posed in this section I say that the universal spoken of in the third sense is not necessarily in the intellect in the second way, i.e. it is not as though such a being belonged to it necessarily. This the arguments [2.6] against the second opinion prove. But necessarily it is in the intellect in

the first way, i.e. universality would not belong to it if this did not accompany the object. This is proved by the first argument [2.3.1] against the first position. But what is the cause of this indeterminacy by which the object when it has this first being in the intellect is completely universal?

I answer that not just the thing [is the cause], for in it there is not that much indeterminacy, as the first argument proves. And not the possible intellect[62] either, for it does not more indeterminately receive than the object is productive.

In every nature (as Aristotle argues in *De Anima* III,[63] text commentary 17 & 18),[64] given something which is made into everything, there is something which makes everything. I.e., generally in all of nature to any passive power there corresponds an active power; and if it is not extrinsic, then it is intrinsic in the same nature. Therefore, since we experience that there is some intellect in us which is made universal (i.e. to which belongs something through which the object is present as a universal), there must be something active. And this is not outside the mind (as has been argued); therefore, it is within.

Therefore, the agent intellect in conjunction with a nature which is in some way indeterminate of itself is the whole effective cause of the object in the possible intellect in respect of its first being. And this is the case as regards the complete indetermination of the universal. And just as there is no reason why what is warm makes things warm other than the existence of an appropriate power, likewise there is no other cause why the agent intellect in conjunction with the nature makes the object exist in this way. Therefore, a nature has a remote potency toward the determination of singularity and toward the indetermination of a universal. And just as it is joined to singularity by its producer, so it is joined to universality by the thing as an agent in conjunction with an agent intellect. It is in this way that Avicenna is correctly interpreted when he says (*Metaphysics* V, ch.1)[65] that a nature of itself is

---

60 See glossary entry for 'species.'
61 See glossary entry for 'phantasm.'
62 See glossary entry for 'passive or possible intellect.'
63 Ch.5 430a10-14.
64 I.e., Averroes's commentary.
65 *Philosophia Prima (sive Metaphysica)* II, 228. See selection **VI.7.1.**

neither universal nor particular, but only a nature. It is this second form of indeterminacy which the third argument [2.1.3] along with its supporting arguments proves, not the indeterminacy of a universal, because this lesser indeterminacy saves similarity, contrariety, etc. And in this way we speak of a 'what.' This indeterminacy is privative; the other greater one is a contrary universality.

[4.3] As for the second part of the question: Is it in things? I answer that being in the intellect in the first way or the second is only to have a relation of thought[66] to the intellect. But that which is in things does in fact have this relation; therefore, that which is universal is in things.

This is bolstered as follows: Otherwise in knowing something about universals we would not know anything about things but only about our concepts. Neither would our opinion change from true to false on account of a change in the existence of a thing. Thus a universal can be in things in such a way that it is the same nature which is determinate by being in existence through a grade of singularity and which is indeterminate by being in the intellect, i.e. by having a relation to the intellect of known to knower. And just as these two beings occur together accidentally in the same nature and each can be without the other, so also the determinacy and indeterminacy we spoke of. And from this we see that it is not necessary that what is universal be in things, although it can, but it is necessary that it be in the intellect.

---

66 See glossary entry for "relation of thought."

VI.9. WILLIAM OF OCKHAM

THESE SELECTIONS SHOW THE BASIC FEATURES OF OCKHAM'S
"nominalism," i.e. the approach he shared with Garlandus and Abelard in which
universality belongs to something only in virtue of its having a certain sort of signification. Having cleared away Scotus's view that there are in extra-mental reality "common natures," Ockham proceeds to treat universals as signs which exist
in the mind as acts of thinking of things. Spoken and written signs get their signification by being subordinated to the mental signs, which, in Ockham's view,
compose a mental language grounding overt language. In this way Ockham coun-
ters the tendency among some scholastics to treat logic as a kind of ontology
rather than a science of meanings.

VI.9.1. Universals and Distinction (from *Ordinatio*
I, dist.ii, qu.3)

[In the following selection Ockham argues against
the sort of posit of universals which Duns Scotus
makes; Ockham also conducts a searching examination of Scotus's way with the making of distinctions. He finds that even given Scotus's formal distinction the view that there is in every individual a
common nature contracted to the individual by an
individuating difference is incoherent.]

... I ask: Is something which is universal and univocal really outside the soul and in reality distinct
from the individual although not really distinct? ...

To this question it is said [by Duns Scotus] that in
things outside the soul the nature is really the same
with the difference that contracts it to a determinate individual, but it is distinct formally. Of itself
it is neither universal nor particular, but in things it
is incompletely universal while it is completely universal in virtue of its existence in the intellect. ...

[Ockham argues against Scotus's view in two ways.
The first amounts to an attack on the "formal distinction" and is found in selection **V.5.1**. What follows is his second mode of argument.]

In a second way we can argue against the aforesaid
opinion that it is not true even given that there is
such a distinction.

[1] First as follows: Whenever one of a pair of
opposites really belongs to something in such a way
that that something is really characterized by it,
whether it belongs to it of itself or through something else, as long as this state of affairs persists
unchanged, the other opposite will not really
belong to it, but rather will be absolutely denied of
it. But according to you every thing outside the soul
is really singular and one in number, although some
items are of themselves singular and some only by
something added. Therefore, no thing outside the
soul is really common or one by a unity opposed to
the unity of singularity. Therefore, there is not really any unity besides the unity of singularity.

[1.1] If someone says that these two unities are
not really opposed, and in the same way singularity and community are not really opposed, [we say],
against this reply: If they are not really opposed to
each other, then there is no opposition from which
it can be concluded that on the side of reality they
cannot belong primarily to the same item.
Therefore, it cannot be sufficiently concluded that
the same item, which is the same in all ways, is not
one both by that unity and by this, and that the
same item, the same in all ways, is both singular
and common.

Further, whenever consequents reject each other
the antecedents also reject each other. But the following consequences hold: A is common or one by
a lesser unity; therefore, a multiplicity opposed to
the greater unity, i.e. numerical multiplicity, can co-

exist with A.

Also, A is one by the greater unity; therefore, the opposed multiplicity, i.e. numerical multiplicity cannot co-exist with A. But the following reject each other: A numerical multiplicity can co-exist with A; a numerical multiplicity cannot co-exist with A. Therefore, these reject each other: A is one by the lesser unity; A is one by the greater unity. But according to you this is true: A is one by the greater unity, because you say that the nature is one in number. Therefore, this is false: A is one by the lesser unity, always taking A for the very nature you say is always one by a lesser unity. And if the nature is not one by the lesser unity, much less anything else will be.

The assumption is granted by him who says: "A multiplicity opposed without contradiction to the greater unity can co-exist with the lesser unity, but this multiplicity cannot co-exist with the greater unity, because it rejects it."

If someone says that this form of arguing is invalid because blackness co-exists with human being but blackness does not co-exist with white, and nevertheless a human being is white and A is a human being and is white: This has no force because when we give the same meaning to 'co-exist' one or the other of the propositions is false. If we give 'co-exist' an actual sense then it is false that blackness co-exists with Socrates given Socrates is white. If we give it a potential sense, then it is false that blackness does not co-exist with white, because blackness can co-exist with white in the sense that a white can be black or have blackness. Thus although blackness rejects whiteness it does not reject that which is white and consequently does not reject white because these two terms 'white' and 'that which is white' convert.[1]

Further, his saying that "a multiplicity opposed without contradiction to the greater unity can co-exist with the lesser unity" seems to contradict his other statement that the nature and the individual difference do not really differ, because, when two items are really the same, whatever by divine power one of them can really be the other can be as well. But this individual difference cannot be numerically many really distinct items; therefore, neither can

the nature which is really the same with that contracting difference be really many items. Consequently, neither can it be some thing other than that contracting difference; and thus the nature is not without contradiction compatible with a numerical multiplicity.

This reasoning is bolstered by the fact that every item that is really universal, whether it is completely universal or not, is really common to many (or at least can be really common to many); but no thing is really common to many; therefore, no thing is universal in any way. The major is obvious because a universal is distinguished from a singular in that the singular is determined to one item, but the universal is indifferent to many in that way in which it is universal. The minor is obvious because no item that is really singular is common to many, but every thing, according to them, is really singular; therefore, etc. Likewise, if some thing referred to by human being is common to many, it is either the nature which is in Socrates or the nature which is in Plato, or some third nature different from these. It is not the nature of Socrates, because from the fact that it is really singular it cannot be in Plato. Neither is it the nature of Plato, for the same reason. And it is not a third nature because no such thing exists outside the soul, since according to them every thing outside the soul is really singular.

It is bolstered in a second way by the fact that what cannot be communicated to many even by divine power is not really common. But no thing we can point to can be communicated to many by divine power because it is really singular. Therefore, no thing is really and positively common.

[1.2] If someone says that this nature rejects being in many but it does not reject it of itself but on account of something added with which it makes one item by a real identity, I argue against this as follows: This non-rejection is of itself not positive and consequently that commonness is not positive in such a way that it is something common, but only negative, and consequently there is no positive unity besides just numerical unity.

Further, I can attribute this sort of lesser negative unity to the individual grade, because it is certain-

---

1 I.e., are necessarily co-extensive.

ly not of itself, *per se*, and *per se primo modo*,[2] one in number. Thus if we take non-rejection to be of itself and *per se*, in the sense in which it is opposed to belonging to something *per se primo modo*, this will be true: 'This individual difference does not of itself reject being in many' or 'It does not of itself reject being one by a unity less than numerical unity,' because its opposite is false, i.e. that that individual difference is *per se primo modo* one in number, according to them.

[2] In this way I argue secondly as follows: If the nature were common in this way, it would follow that there would be as many species and genera as there are individuals, since the nature of Socrates is a species and for the same reason the nature of Plato. Then I argue: Whenever some items are really many and each of them can be said to be a species, then there are many species. But this is how it is in the case proposed; therefore, etc.

This is bolstered by the fact that on the multiplication of the proximate subject follows the multiplication of the attribute.[3] But according to him this lesser unity is an attribute of the nature. Therefore, just as the nature is really multiplied so is the attribute – since it is real – really multiplied. Consequently, just as there are really two natures in Socrates and Plato, so there will be really two lesser unities. But this lesser unity either is commonness or is inseparable from commonness, and consequently from the common item. Therefore, these are two common items in Socrates and Plato, and consequently two species. Consequently, Socrates would be under one common item and Plato under another; thus, there will be just as many common items – even most general genera – as there are individuals, which seems absurd.

If someone says that the thing is not completely universal but rather is that only in virtue of being considered by the intellect, I argue against this reply: I ask about what is immediately characterized as a universal: Is it exclusively a true thing outside the soul, or is it exclusively a being of thought,[4] or is it an aggregate of a real being and a being of thought? If the first, we have our conclusion that the singular thing is simply a complete universal. This is against their own saying because according to them there is nothing outside the soul that is not really singular. Consequently, the same thing which is really singular is common; and no more one than the other. Therefore, there are as many singulars as there are complete universals.

If the second, it follows that no *thing* is universal, neither completely nor incompletely, neither actually nor potentially, because what divine power cannot bring to completion and act so that it is of some sort is neither potentially nor incompletely of such a sort. And this is true where we do not have something which by being reduced to one act remains in potential to another, as in the division of the continuum[5] *ad infinitum*, or something which is in potential to contradictories, which is not the case in what we are considering. Therefore, if exclusively a being of thought is completely a universal, and actually a universal, and a thing outside the soul is in no way these, it follows that a thing outside the soul is in no way universal, no more one than another.

If the third, we have the conclusion, because always the multiplication of the whole or of the aggregate follows on the multiplication of any part. Therefore, if the complete universal is an aggregate of a thing and a being of thought, there will be as many such aggregates as there are things outside the soul each of which is a part of a whole aggregate. Thus we reach the conclusion that there will be as many most general genera as there are individuals.

Further, just as the universal is one item in many and belonging to many and predicable of them, so the common item is one in many and belonging to many and predicable of them. But according to them this suffices to make something completely universal. Therefore, every common item has whatever is required to make something completely universal and consequently to make something a species or a genus. But according to them, as we

---

2 See glossary entry for 'essential-in-the-first-mode.'
3 See glossary entry for 'attribute.'
4 See glossary entry for 'being of thought.'
5 See glossary entry for 'continuum.'

noted, commonness belongs to a nature of itself outside the intellect; therefore, also being completely universal belongs to it of itself outside the intellect. Consequently, from what was proved above, that there are as many common items as there are individuals, it follows that there are as many most general genera in reality as there are individuals.

This is bolstered by the fact that if that nature which is in Socrates is truly common, then, since when Socrates is destroyed anything essential to him is destroyed, it follows that something common will be truly destroyed and annihilated. But it is certain that there remains something common of which an individual remains. From this sort of contradiction, according to them, we can infer a real distinction. Therefore, one of these common items is not really the other, and consequently when they are they are many.

If someone says that the nature is not common because it is made peculiar to Socrates by the contracting difference I argue against this reply as follows: According to you this commonness belongs to the nature outside the intellect. I ask, then, for what does 'nature' stand there: Either for a real being or for a being of thought. You cannot say the second because this would include a contradiction. If it stands for a real being, either it stands for a real being which is singular or for some real being which is not really singular. If the first, then it is not common and consequently is not of itself common. If the second, then there is some thing outside this soul which is not really singular; but they deny this, saying that the nature is really one in number and singular.

[3] Thirdly, I argue as follows: The humanity in Socrates and the humanity in Plato are really distinguished; therefore, each of them is really one in number, and consequently neither is common.

If someone says that these natures are distinct only by added differences, just as some of them are one in number only by an added difference, and thus neither of them is of itself singular but rather is of itself common, I argue against this reply as follows:

Every thing is distinguished from every other

thing from which it is essentially distinguished either by its own self or by something intrinsic to it. But the humanity which is in Socrates is essentially distinguished from the humanity which is in Plato. Therefore, it is distinguished from it either by its own self or by something intrinsic to it, and not, therefore, by something extrinsic added to it. The major is clear because it is nonsense to say that Socrates is distinguished from that ass essentially by Plato.

Likewise, to be the same and diverse follow on being immediately; therefore, nothing is the same as or diverse from something by something extrinsic. Likewise, according to the Philosopher and the Commentator, *Metaphysics* IV,[6] every being is one item by its essence and not by some added factor; therefore nothing is one in number by some added factor; therefore, the nature which is in Socrates, if it is one in number, will be one in number by its own self or by something essential to it.

Likewise, if the nature is one in number, then it is not common, and consequently it is not of itself common, because that determination 'of itself' is not a determination that subtracts or diminishes. Therefore, to infer from the unqualified negation of a determinable the negation of the determinable with that determination is valid. Therefore just as this follows: 'Socrates is not a human being; therefore, he is not necessarily a human being,' so it follows 'The humanity which is in Socrates is not common; therefore, it is not of itself common.'

This reasoning is bolstered by the fact that whenever something is said to belong to something of itself not positively but negatively (for example, when we say that a creature is of itself not a being and that matter is of itself deprived, which like are all false by the meanings of the words but are true if taken as equivalent to certain negatives, for example these: 'Matter is not of itself informed,' 'A creature is not of itself such a being'), although it is not necessary that it actually belong to that which of itself it is said to belong to, nevertheless it can belong to it unqualifiedly, at least by divine power; for example, a creature can be not a being and matter can be deprived. Therefore, likewise the humanity which is in Socrates can be common to many human beings. The consequent is impossible and

---

6 Ch.2, 1003b24; Averroes, comment 3.

therefore so is the antecedent.

Proof of the falsity of the consequent [i.e. that the humanity in Socrates can be common to many human beings]: When some items are the same really it is impossible for one of them to be really the same as something which the other is not really the same as. This is true in creatures and it is even true in a way in the case of God, because although it is not true to say that the Father is the Son, despite the identity of both the Father and the Son with the divine essence, still it is true to say that the Father is that which is the Son. Therefore, since the humanity which is in Socrates is really the same as the contracting difference, if the humanity which is in Socrates can be really the same as the contracting difference in Plato, it follows that this contracting difference and that contracting difference can be one thing, and consequently some one item can be Socrates and Plato, which involves a contradiction.

Further, whatever is distinguished on the side of reality from something else that does not belong to its own formal concept can be intuitively seen[7] without the other item, according to this doctor, who even proposes that the divine essence can be seen without the Persons. Therefore, the humanity which is in Socrates can be intuitively seen without the contracting difference and in the same way the humanity which is in Plato can be seen intuitively without a contracting difference. Consequently, since those humanities are distinguished by place and subject, such an intellect can distinguish one from the other apart from all contracting differences. This would not be possible if they were exclusively distinguished by their contracting differences; therefore, they are numerically distinguished by their own selves.

This is bolstered by the fact that such an intellect can form a negative proposition of this sort by saying "This is not this," and it can know that that is true; therefore, that thing by its own self is not the other thing.

The reasoning is bolstered because according to this doctor items that are mutually compatible or mutually reject each other are mutually compatible or mutually reject each other because of their own formal characters. Therefore, by the same argument whatever items are distinguished or are the same are distinguished or are the same because of their own formal characters. Therefore, if these humanities, the ones belonging to Socrates and Plato, are really distinguished, they are distinguished by their very own formal characters and not by any added items. Consequently each of these of itself, without anything added, is really distinguished from the other. The assumption holds because he says the following: "We should note that just as mutually rejecting items reject each other on account of their own characters, so non-mutual rejection or compatibility is on account of the compossibles' own characters."[8]

If it is said that when you say "these humanities" in 'these humanities are really distinguished' you include those contracting differences, because they are "these" only through those contracting differences; and thus they are distinguished by their formal characters, since those differences belong to the formal characters of those humanities in such a way that were those differences taken away only an indistinct humanity would remain, I argue against this reply as follows:

Whenever some items are distinguished in any way on the side of reality, a term can be established which stands exclusively for one and not for the other. Otherwise there could not be any true proposition marking the distinction of the one from the other. Therefore, I establish this term 'A' as standing exclusively for that which in Socrates is distinguished formally and not really from the contracting difference, because according to you there is something in Socrates which is formally distinguished from the contracting difference even though it is really the same with that difference and thus is really singular. Also I establish this term 'B' as standing exclusively for that which is formally distinguished from the contracting difference in Plato, even though it is really the same as that contracting difference. Then I ask: Are A and B really the same, or not. If they are, then as long as they are left unvaried they are in no way distinguished really, and consequently there is something indistinct really in Socrates and Plato, which is some-

---

7 See glossary entry for 'intuitive vs. abstractive cognition.'
8 Scotus, *Ord.* I, d.2, p.2, q.1-4 (377 in Balic vol. II). See selection I.9.4.

thing they deny, because they say that there is in Socrates and Plato no item that is really the same and indistinct. If they are not really the same, then they are really distinguished, and this by their own formal characters. But these do not include the contracting differences, *ex hypothesi*, and thus we reach the conclusion that they are distinguished by their own selves.

Further, according to you this is true: 'A really rejects the contracting difference of Plato.' Therefore, it rejects it by its own character, and therefore it is really distinguished from it by its own character. Therefore, it is really distinguished by its own self, and this numerically because it is not distinguished in species or genus. Therefore, by its own self it is one in number.

If someone says that when any items mutually reject each other, or are compatible, they mutually reject each other, or are compatible, either by their own characters or by something really the same as them, [I reply that] this is invalid, because, as is clear according to this doctor, he speaks in this place not only of mutual rejection and compatibility of really distinct items but also of mutual rejection and compatibility of items which are only formally distinguished or are compatible, for example of the divine essence and a divine relation.[9] Therefore, A and B will be distinguished by their own selves or will be really the same even when those differences are taken away. But they are not really the same, because if they were they would never be able to be really distinguished. Therefore, they are distinguished really by their own selves.

[4] Fourthly, I argue as follows: If the contracted nature were really distinct from every contracting grade, the nature would of itself be one in number, just as was shown in the first question. Therefore, since this nature is not less one item on account of its real identity with the contracting difference, it follows that it will of itself be one in number.

This is bolstered by the fact that the nature loses nothing of its unity by being really the same as what is one to the highest degree. Therefore, no less will it be of itself one by being really the same as

the individual difference than if it were really distinguished from the individual difference.

This is bolstered by the fact that, according to this doctor, whatever ordering some items would have if they were really distinct that same ordering they possess where they are distinguished in any way although not really. But if the contracting difference and the nature were really distinguished, they would possess the ordering of two items each of which would be of itself one in number, and one would be of itself a potentiality and the other an act. Therefore, they will have a like ordering where they are distinguished formally.

This confirmation is more obvious when it concerns the nature of a genus in respect of specific differences,[10] because if the nature of color were not really the same as the specific difference of whiteness, and the nature of color were not really the same as the difference of blackness, and yet those natures were distinguished by themselves, they would have an ordering of more perfect and more imperfect. Therefore, when now they are not really distinguished from specific differences but are really distinguished from each other, they will have by their own selves the same ordering. This would not be possible if they were not distinguished by their own selves, because it is a contradiction for some items by their own selves to relate to each other as more perfect and more imperfect where they are not by their own selves distinguished, since what are perfect and imperfect are necessarily distinguished. Therefore, if now these specific natures relate to each other by an ordering of more perfect and more imperfect they will be distinguished by their own selves.

[5] Fifthly, it would follow that that grade would be equally as communicable[11] as the nature; in fact, it is communicated to several universals whereas the nature rejects this in respect of individual differences. Therefore, the individual grade is not less communicable than the nature.

[6] Sixthly, because that difference and that nature are either of the same character or of different

---

9 See selection V.4.1.

10 See glossary entry for 'specific difference.'

11 I.e., able to be common.

characters. If of the same character, then one is no more singular than the other. If they are of different characters, I argue to the contrary: Items which are one thing in creatures are not of different characters; but the individual difference and the contracted nature are one thing; therefore, etc.

Likewise, there is a greater, or equal, similarity and agreement between items which are one thing than between items which are really distinguished. Therefore, more or equally they can agree in properties and attributes, as long as they are all equally simple or composite. Therefore, if the individual grade contracting the nature of human being and the individual grade contracting the nature of ass agree in the attribute of being of itself *this*, equally will the individual grade and the nature, which is the same really as that grade, be able to agree in the same attribute.

Likewise, A and B, which are really the same, are not less of the same character than A and D if they are really distinguished. But the nature which is in Socrates and the nature which is in Plato, which are really distinguished, are of the same character; therefore, much more will the nature of Socrates and the contracting difference be of the same character.

Likewise, then Socrates would include something of a character different from anything which is in Plato. This is false, because then Socrates and Plato would not be unqualifiedly of the same character.

[7] In the seventh place, if the nature were so contracted exclusively by a contracting difference only formally distinct from it, equally we could posit a real univocity,[12] i.e. of some real item univocal on the side of reality to God and to creatures, just as it is possible to posit such a univocity in respect of any individuals in creatures. The consequent is contrary to them, since they say elsewhere that in just this one case there is some concept univocal to God and to creatures but not something on the side of reality. The consequence holds because such a univocity is to be denied if there would follow a composition in God of something contracted and something contracting. But no composition follows

if we use the formal distinction, because items which are only formally distinguished are not combined, as is clear in the case of the divine essence and a relation. Therefore, the divine simplicity does not reject univocity.

This is bolstered by the fact that there is no more reason for these formally distinct items to be combined than for others, although these are more distinguished than others, because by what reason grades are posited in the formal distinction by the same reason grades are posited in combinations out of formally distinct items.

This is bolstered by the fact that just as when some items are really distinguished, whether more or less, if they make up something one *per se* there is no more reason for these to combine than those, even though these are less really distinguished than those, so also if some items are formally distinguished and make up something one *per se*, there is no more reason for these to combine than those. Therefore, either all formally distinct items making up or constituting something one *per se* combine, or none do.

VI.9.2. The Distinction of First and Second Intentions (from *Quodlibet* IV, qu. 35)

[In this selection Ockham rejects the idea (held by Scotus among others) that "intentions" or concepts have mere "objective being," rather than full real being. Ockham holds that it suffices to save knowledge and thought to think of intentions as just the acts of thought themselves. Then, since these acts are real, and really distinct (and not just distinguished by thought), the various intentions are real and really distinct. (The reader is referred to Topic V for clarification of the ideas of sameness and distinctness.)]

Are first and second intentions[13] really distinguished?

That they are not: Beings of thought[14] are not really distinguished. But both first as well as second intentions are merely beings of thought. Therefore, etc.

In opposition to this: First and second intentions

---

12 See glossary entry for 'univocity.'
13 See glossary entry for 'intention.'
14 See glossary entry for 'being of thought.'

are things but not the same thing. Therefore they are distinct things and, consequently, are really distinguished.

In this question we first have to see what a first intention and what a second intention is. Then secondly, we answer the question.

As to the first, I say that both 'first intention' and 'second intention' can be taken in two senses, a broad sense and a narrow sense. In the broad sense, every intentional sign existing in the soul which does not signify exclusively intentions or concepts in the soul or other signs is called a first intention. This holds whether 'sign' means what can in a proposition stand for something and be a part of the proposition (i.e. the categorematic terms)[15] or 'sign' means what is not able to stand for something nor to be the subject or predicate of a proposition when it is used significatively (i.e. the syncategorematic terms).[16]

In this sense, not just mental categorematic terms which signify things which are not signs but also mental syncategorematic terms, both verbs and conjunctions and the like, are called first intentions. Examples: In this sense not just the concept of human being, a concept which signifies all singular humans (which humans themselves signify nothing) and can stand for those humans and be part of a proposition, and the concept of whiteness, and the concept of color, etc., are called first intentions, but also syncategorematic concepts like these: if, nevertheless, not, while, as well as is, runs, reads and the like are called first intentions. This is because the latter, even though they do not when taken on their own stand for things, still when conjoined to other terms they make them stand for things in different ways. For example, in this proposition 'Every human is running' 'every' makes 'human' stand for and be distributed for all humans, and yet this sign 'every' on its own signifies nothing since it signifies no thing outside the mind nor any intention of the soul.

In the strict sense what gets called a first intention is exclusively a mental noun suited to be the subject or predicate of a proposition and to stand for a thing which is not a sign; for example, the concepts

of human being, of animal, of substance, of body, in brief every mental noun which naturally signifies the singular things which are not signs.

Likewise, in the broad sense, what gets called a second intention is a concept of the soul which signifies not just the intentions of the soul which are the natural signs of things, i.e. the first intentions in the strict sense, but can signify also items that by convention signify mental signs like mental syncategorematic terms. In this sense perhaps all we have are verbal expressions corresponding to second intentions.

In the strict sense, however, a concept which exclusively signifies first intentions that naturally signify, for example genus, species, difference and others of this sort, is called a second intention. Just as the concept of human being is predicated of all humans by saying "This human being is a human being," "That human being is a human being," and so on for each case, so a general concept which is a second intention is predicated of first intentions which stand for things, as when we say "Human being is a species," "Ass is a species," "Whiteness is a species," "Animal is a genus," "Body is a genus," "Quality is a genus," and this in the way one noun is predicated of different nouns by saying "'Human being' is a noun," "'Whiteness' is a noun." These second intentions thus signify first intentions naturally and stand for them in a proposition just as first intentions signify things naturally and can stand for them.

As for the second task, some say that first and second intentions are certain made-up beings which only exist objectively in the mind[17] and nowhere subjectively.

In opposition to this: When a proposition is verified for things, if two things suffice for its truth it is redundant to posit another third thing. But all propositions such as the following, 'A human being is thought of,' 'A human being is a subject,' 'A human being is a predicate,' 'A human being is a species,' 'An animal is a genus,' and the like, on account of which it is claimed that there are such made-up items, are verified for things and two

15 See glossary entry for 'categorematic term.'
16 See glossary entry for 'syncategorematic term.'
17 See glossary entry for 'esse objectivum.'

things suffice, or at least true and really existing things suffice for verifying them all. Therefore, etc.

The assumption is evident, for, given there is knowledge of a human being in the mind, it is impossible that this proposition is false, 'A human being is thought of.' Likewise, given the intention of *human being* in general and the intention of *subject* in general, once this mental proposition 'Human being is a subject' in which one intention is predicated of another, is formed, necessarily this proposition, 'Human being is a subject' is true without there being any made-up item; therefore, etc.

Besides, such a made-up item prevents knowledge of the thing; therefore, it should not be posited on account of knowledge. The assumption is evident, because this [made-up item] is neither a cognition, nor the whiteness outside that is known, nor both together, but rather it is some third intermediate item between the knowledge and the thing. Therefore if that made-up item is thought of, the thing outside is not thought of. Then when I form this mental proposition, 'God is three and one,' I am not thinking of God in himself but of that made-up item, which view seems absurd.

Besides, for the same reason God in thinking of other things would be thinking of such made-up items. Thus from eternity there was a creation of as many made-up beings as there are able to be different intelligible things, and these existed so necessarily that God was unable to destroy them, which seems false.

Besides, such a made-up item need not be posited in order to have a subject and a predicate in a universal proposition, because the act of thinking of something suffices for this, since that made-up entity is just as singular both in being and in representing as is the act. This is clear from the fact that one made-up item can be destroyed while some other one persists, just as with the acts. Either the made-up item depends essentially on the act, or not. If it does, then, when by one act's ceasing the one made-up item is destroyed, still the [other] made-up item persists in the other act, and consequently there are two singular made-up items just as there are two acts. If it does not depend on this singular act, then neither does it depend essentially on any act of that type, and thus that made-up item will persist in

objective being without there being any act, which is impossible.

Besides, there is no contradiction involved in God's making a universal cognition without such a made-up item, because cognition does not essentially depend on such a made-up item. But it is a contradiction for there to be posited in the mind a thinking which is not a thinking of anything; therefore, it need not be posited on account of thinking of what is common.

Therefore, I say that both first intentions and second intentions are truly acts of thinking, because by acts can be saved anything that is saved by having made-up items, and in virtue of the fact that the act is a likeness of the object, it can signify and stand for things outside, can be a subject and a predicate in a proposition, can be a genus, a species, etc., just as well as the made-up item can.

From that it is clear that first intentions and second intentions are really distinguished, because a first intention is an act of thinking that signifies things which are not signs, while a second intention is an act that signifies first intentions. Therefore, they are distinguished.

How to reply to the argument at the beginning is clear from what has been said, namely that both first and second intentions are truly real beings, because they are truly qualities existing subjectively[18] in the mind.

VI.9.3. The Synonymy of Concrete and Abstract Nouns (from *Quodlibet* V, qu.10)

[In this selection we encounter a case where theological doctrine forces Ockham to adopt a view which from a purely philosophical perspective he would judge implausible. If it were not for the incarnation of the second Person of the Trinity as a human being, Ockham would say that 'human being' and its abstract correlate 'humanness' signified exactly the same things in the same way. Since Ockham, in contrast to Scotus, does not believe in a human nature common to all humans and in some way distinct from each of them, he feels free to treat 'humannness' as a count noun and say that Socrates is a humanness as well as a human being. Only in the case of the incarnation must a distinc-

---

18 I.e., as features really belonging to the mind, not items which exist only objectively.

tion be made between the human being and its humanness, for in that case what is a human being, the second Person, is not of itself a human being but only "assumes" humanness.]

Are 'human being' and 'humanness' synonymous[19] *nouns according to the truth of the faith?*

That they are not synonyms:
When two terms are synonyms, if a proposition in which one term is found is true the proposition in which the other term is found will be true. But this is true, 'Humanness can be assumed,'[20] as is this, 'Humanness has been assumed,' but this is not true, 'A human being has been assumed,' nor is this, 'A human being can be assumed'; therefore etc.

In opposition to this:
Any items which signify entirely the same and stand for the same in the same grammatical and logical mode of signifying are synonyms. But 'human being' and 'humanness' are of this sort; therefore, etc.

Here we must first say what nouns are synonyms and then, secondly, reply to the question.

As for the first, I say that the noun 'synonym' has two senses, a strict sense and a broad sense. In the strict sense those nouns are called synonyms which everybody who uses them intends without qualification to use for the same item and in the same mode of signifying; for example, 'Marcus' and 'Tullius'[21] are synonymous nouns.

In the broad sense those nouns are called synonyms which unqualifiedly signify the same in all modes and in the same mode of signifying, in such a way that one signifies nothing in some mode which is not signified in the same mode of signifying by the other, even though not everyone who uses them believes they signify the same; rather those who are mistaken think that one signifies something which the other does not. For example, someone might believe that this noun 'God' refers to one whole item and 'deity' to a part of it.

As for the second, I say that according to the truth of theology 'human being' and 'humanness' are not synonymous nouns, neither in the strict sense nor in the broad sense. The reason for this is that these nouns signify distinct things and stand for distinct things, and one of these nouns signifies a thing which the other neither does signify nor can signify. For the noun 'human being' truly stands for the Son of God and signifies the Son of God; the noun 'humanness' does not stand for the Son of God nor can it stand for the Son of God, no more than does this noun 'whiteness.' For this reason we have to grant this, 'The Son of God is a human being,' and this has to be denied, 'The Son of God is humanness.' Consequently, since it is not the case that everything which the one refers to is referred to in the same way by the other, they are not synonymous nouns.

The assumption that these nouns do not signify the same is clear from their nominal definitions. The following is the definition of 'humanness': A humanness is a single nature composed of a body and a soul of the sort that includes a mind. Also that noun does not connote that the nature that includes a mind is supported by a divine Person nor that it is not so supported, and therefore it always stands for that nature. On account of this it can never stand for the Son of God, since the Son of God cannot be that nature.[22]

On the other hand, this noun 'human being' is defined as follows: A human being is a single nature composed of a body and a soul that includes a mind which is not supported by any underlying subject. Or, a human being is some underlying subject supporting such a nature that includes a mind. One or the other of these descriptions is verified for every human being, for this is true, 'Socrates is a nature composed of a body and a soul that includes a body and is not supported by any underlying subject.' Also this is true, 'The Son of God is an underlying subject supporting a nature that includes a mind and is the term on which that nature depends.' From this it is evident that those nouns ['human being' and 'humanness'] do not signify

---

19 See glossary entry for 'synonymy.'
20 The reference is to the Son of God assuming humanity in the incarnation.
21 Both are proper names of Cicero.
22 The Son *has* that nature and also has a divine nature. He is not the same as his human nature.

completely the same.

From the above some conclusions follow: The first is that, although the following must be granted, 'A human being is humanness,' nevertheless the following is false, 'Every human being is humanness,' and the following is true, 'Some human being is not humanness.'

This is shown as follows: If neither of these nouns, 'human being' and 'humanness,' includes in its meaning some syncategorematic term,[23] we have to grant this proposition, 'A human being is a humanness,' because it is an indefinite proposition which has a true singular instance, namely the proposition 'Socrates is a humanness,' for in that proposition the subject and predicate cannot stand for distinct things, rather they stand for the same thing. Nevertheless the following is false, 'Every human being is a humanness,' because it has this false singular instance, 'This human being is a humanness,' where we point to the Son of God. These two subcontraries[24] are both true at once: 'A human being is a humanness,' 'A human being is not a humanness.'

The second conclusion is that, on this view, the following propositions ought to be granted: 'The abstract is predicated of the concrete' and vice versa; for example, 'A human being is a humanness' and 'A humanness is a human being.' Likewise the abstract is correctly affirmed and denied of the concrete when it is taken particularly [i.e. as quantified by 'some'], and vice versa, but not when the concrete term is taken universally [i.e. as quantified by 'every' or 'all']. For example, the following must be granted: 'Some human being is a humanness,' 'Some human being is not a humanness.' Likewise, it is true that a concrete term of this sort is affirmed and denied successively of numerically the same item; for example the following is now true, 'This humanness which is Socrates is a human being.' If that humanness were assumed by some divine Person, then the following would be false, 'This humanness is a human being.' This is because the noun 'human being' only stands for this humanness when it is not united [to a subject].[25] Since sometimes it can be united and sometimes not, sometimes it stands for it and sometimes it does not. On account of this sometimes the concrete is predicated of this sort of abstract; sometimes it is not.

To the argument at the beginning I say that according to the truth of faith they are not synonymous nouns, as is evident from the above.

Nevertheless, in place of the first argument I say that just as we have to grant in virtue of the meaning of the terms this proposition, 'A humanness can be assumed by a divine Person,' so also this has to be granted, 'A human being can be assumed by a divine Person,' and this is so equally whether the subject is taken to cover what exists or what is able to exist. Nevertheless, while granting 'A humanness is assumed' we have to deny 'A human being is assumed by a divine Person,' since the latter includes an obvious contradiction. This is clear from the nominal definition of the term 'human being,' which is that it is a nature inclusive of mind that is not supported by any underlying subject. Then, if 'A human being is assumed' were true, that nature would be supported by an underlying, divine subject, and thus it would follow that that nature would at the same time be supported and not be supported, which is an obvious contradiction.

If you say: According to you this is true, 'A human being can be assumed by a divine Person.' Let that be posited in actuality; then this will be true, 'A human being is assumed,' or 'An underlying subject is assumed,' if an underlying subject can be assumed.

---

23 See glossary entry for 'syncategorematic term.'

24 Subcontraries are propositions which cannot both be false but can both be true. In the traditional "square of opposition" a particular affirmative proposition and its corresponding particular negative proposition were considered to be subcontraries, e.g. 'Some wall is white,' 'Some wall is not white.' Ockham here treats "indefinite" propositions (those lacking an explicit quantifier applied to the subject term) as equivalent to particular ones, i.e. those beginning with the quantifier 'some' or its equivalent.

25 The humanness is united to a subject just when there is something distinct from the humanness which possesses it. Ockham holds that this occurs only in the case of the Son of God assuming humanness in the incarnation. In all other cases the subject of humanness, i.e. the human being, is not distinct from the humanness itself.

I reply: The consequence is invalid because either that proposition, taken in the divided sense,[26] cannot be posited in actual being or it must be posited in being in another way. Example: this is true, 'A white item can be black,' and yet if it is posited in actual being as 'A white item is black,' it is impossible. Consequently, either it cannot be posited in actual being, or if it can it should be posited in actual being as 'Socrates is black,' given 'white item' stands for Socrates. In the case we were considering it is like that. This proposition, 'A human being, or human underlying subject, can be assumed by a divine Person,' ought not to be posited in actual being as 'An underlying subject is assumed,' but rather as 'Socrates is assumed' or 'This human nature is assumed,' where we point to that nature that 'underlying subject' stands for; otherwise, it cannot be posited in actual being.

VI.9.4. Is a Universal a Singular? (from *Quodlibet* V, qu.12)

[To a scholastic to say a universal is a singular sounds self-contradictory; the two terms are thought of as opposites. Through skillful distinguishing of senses of 'singular' Ockham shows how a universal can be a singular so far as its reality is concerned, but not in respect of its signification.]

Is a universal a singular?

That it is not: Every universal is predicated of many; the singular is predicated of just one; therefore, etc.

In opposition to this: Everything which is is singular; a universal is; therefore, it is singular.

First I disambiguate the term 'singular'; then, secondly, I shall reply to the question.

As for the first, I say that according to The Philosopher 'singular,' 'individual,' 'underlying subject' are co-extensive nouns. This, I say, holds for logicians, even though according to theologians the term 'underlying subject' is restricted to substances while 'individual' and 'singular' apply to accidents.

Now from the point of view of logic 'singular' and 'individual' have three senses. In one sense that is said to be singular which is numerically one thing and not many things.[27] In another sense, a thing outside the soul, which is one and not many, and is not a sign of anything, is said to be singular. In a third sense a sign of just one item, which sign is called a discrete term, is said to be singular.

The first two parts of this division are obvious. The third part is proved because Porphyry says that an individual is predicated of only one item.[28] This cannot be read as referring to a thing that exists outside the soul, for example Socrates, because a thing outside the soul is neither predicated nor subjected [i.e. made a subject] (as we said in another *Quodlibet* [III, qu.12]), and consequently it is read as referring to some exclusive sign which is predicated of only one item that stands not for itself but for the thing.

Besides, logicians say that the underlying subjects of a general term are of two sorts, those that are *per se* and those that are incidentally such subjects. Example: The underlying subjects *per se* of this general term 'white item' are 'this white item' and 'that white item'; the incidental underlying subjects are 'Socrates' and 'Plato.' Here they cannot refer to the Socrates who is outside the soul, because he is not a sign of anything. Since in speech a thing outside the soul cannot be an underlying subject of a common term, neither *per se* nor incidentally, 'underlying subject' has to be read as meaning a term for just one item. It is then said to be an underlying subject because a general term is predicated of it, but of it as standing for its significate, not for itself.

Then underlying subjects of this sort for a general term are of two kinds. Some are *per se*, for example demonstrative pronouns combined with the general term – in the case of the general term 'white item' these are 'this white item,' 'that white item.' The underlying subjects that are incidental are proper nouns, like 'Socrates,' 'Plato.'

There is this major difference between these underlying subjects: Where we have two opposed

---

26 See glossary entry for 'composite and divided senses.'
27 See selections **V.1.1-2**.
28 See selection **VI.3.1**.

terms it is impossible for one of them to be truly predicted of a *per se* underlying subject of the other; for example, this is impossible, 'This white item is black.' But the one opposite can be correctly predicated of the incidental subject of the other, although it is not yet one of the underlying subjects for that first opposite. For example, if Socrates is white, this is nevertheless possible, 'Socrates is black.' This is because the same item can be an incidental underlying subject of two opposites, although not a *per se* underlying subject. Therefore, etc.

As for the second article, I say that a universal is a singular and an individual in the first sense, since it really is a single singular quality of the mind and is not several qualities. But in the second sense it is not a singular, because no universal is in any way a thing outside the soul. Likewise, a universal is not a singular in the third sense, because a universal is a natural or conventional sign common to many and not just to one.

The reply to the arguments at the beginning is obvious from the above.

VI.9.5. Is every Universal a Quality of the Mind?
(from *Quodlibet* V, qu.13)

[Ockham's view is that universals are "qualities" of the mind in that they are acts of thinking of things. Here he disarms a number of spurious objections to this claim by skillful use of the logical terminology of supposition.]

Is every universal a quality of the mind?

That it is not: Substance, which is a most generic genus, is not a quality of the mind; therefore, not every universal is a quality of the mind. The assumption is obvious, because [substance] is predicated univocally[29] and *in quid*[30] of a substance; therefore it is not a quality.

In opposition to this: A universal exists only in the soul, and not objectively, as was shown earlier;[31] therefore, [it exists there] subjectively. Therefore, it is a quality of the mind.

To this question I say that it is. The reason for this is that, as will become evident, a universal is not something outside the soul. Also it is certainly not nothing. Therefore, it is something in the soul, and not just objectively, as was shown earlier; therefore, [it is in the soul] subjectively and consequently is a true quality of the mind.

But in opposition to this [we have the following arguments]: [1] Given this [that every universal is a quality of the mind], all categories[32] will be accidents, and consequently some accident would be higher than substance.[33]

[2] Further, one and the same item is not predicated of different categories, and consequently quality is not common to all the categories.

[3] Further, it follows that one and the same item is higher than itself, because, according to this opinion, all universals are in the genus of quality as its species and individuals. Consequently, the category of quality is common to all universals, and consequently the category of quality is common to itself, and thus one and the same item is higher than itself.

[4] Further, given this we have to grant that one and the same item signifies itself and stands for itself, because in the proposition 'Every universal is a being' the word 'being' personally stands[34] for all universals, and consequently it stands for this universal which is 'being,' and so 'being' stands for itself.

Likewise, inasmuch as it stands personally [for something] it stands just for what it signifies and it stands for itself, because otherwise this universal proposition would be false, 'Every universal is a

29 See glossary entry for 'univocity.'
30 I.e., it says of the item of which it is predicated what kind of thing that item is.
31 See selection **VI.9.2.**
32 See glossary entry for 'category.' Also see selection **VI.2.1.**
33 I.e., would be so general as to include all substances in its extension.
34 A term "personally stands" for items in what we would call its "extension." For example, 'animal' personally stands for the things which in fact are animals.

being,' because it would have one singular instance which is false [viz.: 'Being' is a being.]; therefore, one and the same item [viz. 'being'] signifies itself.

[5] Further, it follows that one and the same item is both higher and lower in respect of the same item, because this universal 'being' is higher than the categories, and also lower, since it is one individual in the genus of quality; therefore, etc.

[Replies to these objections:] To the first [1] of these I grant that all universals are accidents, but not all are signs of accidents; rather some universals are signs only of substances, and these accidents make up the category of substance; other accidents make up the other categories. I grant further that some accident, which is a sign only of substances, is of itself higher than any substance. This is no more absurd than saying that some utterance is a name of several substances or signifies many substances.

To the other [2] I say that one and the same item is not predicated of different categories when those categories stand [for something] personally and significatively. But when they stand [for something] materially or simply,[35] it is not absurd for one and the same item to be predicated of different categories.

Hence, if in the proposition 'Substance is a quality' the subject stands materially or simply, the proposition is true, and likewise for 'Quantity is a quality.' But if [those subjects] stand [for something] personally, then [the propositions] are not true. Thus, just as these two propositions, 'Substance is an utterance,' 'Quantity is an utterance,' are true if the subjects stand [for something] materially or simply and not significatively, so it is in the case we are considering.

To the other [3] I say that one and the same item is not both higher and lower than itself, because for something to be higher than something else

requires that those items be distinct and that the higher signify more items than the lower. Accordingly, I say that not all universals are of themselves lower than the common item 'quality,' even though all universals are qualities, because this universal 'quality' is one quality, and yet it is not lower than 'quality' but rather just is itself.

But if you say: It follows at least that 'spiritual, mental quality' is in more and higher than any category because it is predicated of all the categories, while no category is predicated of all the categories; therefore etc. –

I reply: 'spiritual, mental quality' is not predicated of all the categories when they are used significatively and personally, but rather of them only when they are used to refer to signs. Consequently, it does not follow that 'quality' is in more or higher than any category, for items are higher or lower from the fact that one of them when used significatively is predicated of more items than is the other when used significatively. This does not hold for 'quality,' which is a universal. Nevertheless some items, like the concept 'being,' are predicated of more items than is any category.

To the other [4], I say that we must grant this conclusion: One and the same item signifies itself; one and the same item stands for itself; one and the same item is predicated univocally of itself. The case is just like this proposition, 'Every utterance is a being,' where the subject stands for every utterance and thus stands for this utterance 'utterance,' and signifies it and is predicated univocally of it.

To the other [5], I say that the same difficulty we have here arises for this noun 'word' and this noun 'noun,' because the noun 'word' is one of the items contained under 'noun,' since the noun 'word' is a noun and not every noun is this noun 'word.' Nevertheless, this noun 'word' is in a way higher than all nouns and, as a result, than this noun 'noun,' because this noun 'noun' is a word, but not

---

35 For a word to stand for something *materially* is for it to stand for the very verbal expression which it is, for example 'red' in the sentence 'Red is a word of one syllable.' For a word to stand for something *simply* is for it to stand for the mental sign that it substitutes for and from which it derives its meaning, for example 'red' in the sentence 'Red is a color concept.'

every word is a noun. Thus one and the same item is both lower and higher than the same item.

Accordingly, I say on behalf of both [that 'being' is both higher than the categories and lower than they] that the argument would go through if in all the propositions used to express the conclusion the terms stood for items in a uniform way. But in what was proposed this is not the case, because 'being,' when it is predicated of the categories, stands [for something] personally, not simply nor materially. But in the sense in which it is an individual quality it stands [for something] materially and simply. Once we take both 'being' and 'quality' significatively,[36] 'being' is unqualifiedly higher because it signifies more items. And in this sense it is not lower than quality, nor is it an individual quality. But if we say that something is lower than something else where the former stands [for something] in some way or other and the latter is predicated of it as well as of many other items, then, even though the latter is not predicated of the former when it stands [for something] in some other way (especially if the latter is taken universally), it can be granted that one and the same item is both higher and lower in respect of the same item. But in that case 'higher' and 'lower' are not opposites but rather disparates.

To the arguments at the beginning the replies are obvious from what has already been said.

VI.9.6. Is a Category made up of things outside the Mind or of Concepts of Things? (from *Quodlibet* V, qu.23)

[Ockham here resolutely carries through his program of treating Aristotle's logic as basically about mental signs. It is interesting to see how much he returns to the view of Garlandus (selection VI.5.1.), although there is no evidence that he ever read Garlandus's work. The only major difference is that whereas Ockham's signs are in the mind,

Garlandus's were restricted to verbal utterances.]

Is a category made up of things outside the mind or of concepts of things?

That it is made up of things is shown as follows: A category is made up not only out of universals but also out of individuals; but according to The Philosopher in *Categories* [c.5],[37] who says that a substance, which exists in the strict and primary sense, is neither said of a subject nor present in a subject, individuals are individuals outside the soul. What he says there must concern things outside the soul, because every concept, whether exclusively of one item or common [to many] is in a subject, because it is a quality, and it is said of a subject.

In opposition to this: A category is predicated truly of anything contained under it; but it is not predicated of any *thing*, because a thing outside is neither the subject of a proposition nor the predicate. Therefore, etc.

Here we first have to interpret the question; secondly we must see what it is to be in a category; thirdly [we must reply] to the question.

As for the first, I say, just as was said earlier,[38] 'category' has two senses. In one sense it refers to a primary and most common predicable in a categorical hierarchy. In another sense it refers to a single grouping or to the whole arrangement of predicables arranged according to higher and lower in a categorical hierarchy. In this question 'category' is read in the second sense, not the first.

As for the second, I say, as was said earlier,[39] that 'to be in a category' has two senses.

In one sense it refers to what is pointed to by a pronoun of which is predicated truly the category. In this sense only singular substances outside the soul are in the category of substance, while all universals, both genera and species as well as differences, are most definitely in the genus of quality, since where the demonstrative pronoun points to any universal this will be true: 'This is a quality.'[40]

In another sense 'to be in a category' refers to

---

36 I.e., personally.
37 See selection VI.2.1.
38 *Quodlibet* V, qu.21.
39 *Ibid.*
40 See previous selection.

what is in a category in the sense that of it, significatively used, is predicated the category, significatively used. In this sense some universals are in the category of substance, and some are in the category of quality. For in this proposition 'A human being is an animal' or 'A human being is a substance,' the word 'human being' does not stand for itself but for what it signifies,[41] since if it stood for itself this would be false, 'A human being is a substance,' and this true, 'A human being is a quality,' just as if this utterance 'human being' stood for itself, this would be false, 'Human being is a substance' and this true 'Human being is an utterance and a quality.'

As for the third, I say a category in the second sense is exclusively made up out of concepts and in no way out of things outside the soul which are not signs (this last I say to allow for spoken and written nouns). I show this in several ways: First, as follows: Substance, according to Aristotle, is divided into first and second substances[42] as into the items out of which the category is made up. But this is not a general division among some things which are outside the soul nor among any things of which 'substance' is predicated (where the things stand for themselves), because this proposition is false, 'A second substance is a substance.' This is obvious, because whatever is universally denied of every item immediately contained under some common item is universally denied of that common item. But 'second substance' is denied of everything immediately contained under 'substance'; therefore, 'second substance' is universally denied of substance. Consequently, this is true, 'No second substance is a substance,' and likewise this, 'No substance is a second substance.' What was assumed [viz. that 'second substance' is denied of everything immediately contained under 'substance'] is evident from the fact that this is true, 'No corporeal substance is a second substance,' and likewise this, 'No incorporeal substance is a second substance,' That these are true is clear by applying the same rule: Whatever is denied universally etc., because in virtue of this rule this is true, 'No animate body is a second substance,' and likewise this, 'No inani-

mate body is a second substance.' That these are true is clear by the same rule, because this is true, 'No sensory body is a second substance,' and likewise this, 'No non-sensory body is a second substance.' That these are true is proved by the same rule, for this is true, 'No rational animal is a second substance,' and likewise this, 'No non-rational animal is a second substance.' That the first of these is true is shown by the fact that this is true, 'No human being is a second substance,' because any of its singular instances [e.g. Socrates is not a second substance] is true. Consequently, this is unqualifiedly true, 'No substance is a second substance,' and consequently this is true, 'No second substance is a substance.'

Therefore, this division must be of a noun into less common nouns, so that the division amounts to this: Of nouns referring to substances outside the soul some are nouns exclusively designating one singular substance, for example 'Socrates,' and these nouns or concepts are called first substances by The Philosopher, and some are nouns common to many substances, and those concepts he calls second substances. These The Philosopher later divides into genera and species, which are not things outside the soul but rather are true qualities or concepts in the soul. Therefore, since the category is made up out of first and second substances and these are concepts and nouns, the category is made up out of concepts.

Further, The Philosopher in *Categories*[43] says that every substance seems to signify some this, and it is doubtless true that according to him any first substance signifies some this. But a particular substance existing outside the soul does not signify some this, because that substance is signified. Therefore The Philosopher treats first substances as names of singular substances, and even more definitely he treats second substances as nouns and concepts; therefore, etc.

Further, in the *Categories* Aristotle claims that a category is made up out of non-complex items, as was noted earlier, and propositions are made out of these non-complex items. But propositions are not made up out of things outside the soul but rather

---

41 On Ockham's theory a term signifies the items it *personally* stands for, i.e., the items in its extension.
42 See glossary entry for 'substance.' Also see selection **VI.2.1**.
43 Ch.5, 3b10-12.

out of concepts. Therefore, etc.

Further, in the *Categories*[44] Aristotle says that all the other items either are said of primary substances serving as subjects or are in substances. But in that place he does not mean by a subject a singular substance existing outside the soul and standing under accidents, because he says second substances are said and predicated of first substances serving as subjects. But no proposition is made up out of substances outside the soul; therefore, a first substance, which is a subject for a second substance is a name or a concept in the soul.

Further, Damascene in his *Logic*[45] says that utterances are brought together in the category of substance.

Accordingly, I say that just as a category written in a book is made up out of written words and a category expressed in speech is made up out of utterances, so a category in the mind is made up out of concepts and in no way out of things outside, since a category, just like a proposition, has just three ways of being: in the mind, in writing, in speech.

To the arguments at the beginning I say that Aristotle sometimes treats an individual as a singular thing outside the soul, sometimes as a name exclusively of that thing. But the individual which is a subject and the lowest item in a category is not the first sort of individual, since a proposition is not made up out of things outside the soul, but rather is the second sort of individual.

---

44 Ch.5, 2b4-5.
45 St. John Damascene, *Dialectica*, c.46. Damascene led the Christian community in 8th-century Damascus.

TOPIC VII

SKEPTICISM

TWO FORMS OF SKEPTICISM WERE CULTIVATED IN ANCIENT GREEK philosophy: pyrrhonian skepticism (named after its founder Pyrrho, 365/360-275/270 B.C.E.) and academic skepticism which arose in Plato's Middle Academy (third century B.C.E.). It was characteristic of pyrrhonian skepticism to exhibit competing positions and conflicting arguments on two sides of a question, both sides being shown to be equally powerful. The consequence of a dispassionate appreciation of the debate would be to suspend judgment and to allow - but with peace of mind - that one cannot resolve the disagreement.

We have all had experience of the basic situation: a high school debate in which the affirmative side argues for the death penalty for capital offense and in which the negative side argues against the death penalty. A pyrrhonian skeptic would not assume the possibility of the position of a judge who is not already party to the dispute; for there is no point of view from which one can judge, with the full evidence of experience, what punishment a capital offense deserves in reality: some communities go this way; other communities, that way.

In remaining neutral the skeptic does not become cynical; the skeptic, after all, lives in a community. Pyrrho himself returned to his home and, along with his sister, attended to religious duties. The pyrrhonian skeptic may remain a seeker (something implied by uses of the Greek word *skepticos*).

It may strike the reader that the medieval Question (*quaestio*), of which the anthology gives many splendid examples, has the first part of the skeptical methodology: the setting forth of competing arguments and the claims of authority. The Question, unlike a skeptical treatise (if a Pyrrhonian skeptic could finish a treatise), passes through two further stages: a middle part which provides material for a resolution and a final part which resolves the question and dissolves the force of the arguments on the wrong side of the debate. Some questions, without the aid of Revelation, read like the work of a pyrrhonian skeptic: Thomas Aquinas thinks natural reason cannot resolve the question as to whether the world has an infinite past.

Pyrrhonian skepticism underwent a powerful development with the so-called skeptical tropes of Aenesidemus and of Agrippa; of particular interest here are three of the tropes of Agrippa: opposition and conflict, infinite regression, and circularity. The role of opposition is to show the futility of a dogmatic attempt to resolve conflict; the role of the trope of infinite regression is to show how hopeless the attempts of the dogmatists are to ground their beliefs and to provide them with an absolute foundation, and the role of the trope of circularity is that two things needing one another cannot give adequate support for one another. It would be as if my word is supported by yours and yours by mine. We could both be failing to tell the truth.

Although pyrrhonian skepticism seems not to have had any direct influence upon medieval thinkers whose works are represented in this anthology, they realized the intuitive force (perhaps by natural reason) of the tropes of Agrippa. Conflict must be resolved; arguments and proof need a starting point and foundation; circularity is a sign of a fallacious argument. We shall return to the challenge of skepticism in the form of meeting the skeptical tropes in a moment.

Academic skepticism arose with Arcesilaus (316/315-242/241 B.C.E.) who was head of the Academy in the mid third century. It differs from pyrrhonian skepticism in that it makes a firmer denial of the possibility of knowledge. In selection **VII.1.1.** Augustine explores a central tenet of academic skepticism.

The form of skepticism which does arise in the middle ages is somewhat tied to the elevation of philosophical interpretations of God's omnipotence. According to the interpretation sanctioned in the 1277 Condemnation, God can do anything which does not involve a logical contradiction. An effect of this interpretation is that the only limit to possibility is the self-contradictory. The area of things possible for God is widened as far as it could logically be.

A beneficiary of that interpretation is the principle of separability, according to which, if any two things, A and B, are distinct, they are separable. The principle is at work in the thought of al-Ghazali; in al-Ghazali's case the principle of separability is used to show that there is no necessary connection between cause and effect. Al-Ghazali writes (see selection **I.4.2.**):

Now what according to you is the limit of the impossible? If the impossible includes nothing but the simultaneous affirmation and negation of the same thing, then say that of two things the one is not the other, and that the existence of the one does not demand the existence of the other. And say then that God can create will without knowledge of the thing willed, and knowledge without life, and that He can move the hand of a dead man and make him sit and write volumes with his hand and engage himself in sciences while he has his eye open and his looks are fixed on his work, although he does not see and there is no life in him and he has no power, and it is God alone who creates all these ordered actions with the moving of the dead man's hand, and the movement comes from God.

Here it is implied that difference between two things A and B, given God's power, is sufficient for their mutual separation. And in the hands of skeptics this reasoning has this form: a difference is sufficient for logical possibility; the logical possibility of a separation between And B is enough for their separability.

Analogous reasoning is also in the thought of William of Ockham; he writes:

> Furthermore, if [essence and existence] were two things, then no contradiction would be involved if God preserved the essence of a thing in the world without its existence, or vice versa, its existence without its essence; both of which are impossible.
>
> We have to say, therefore, that essence and existence are not two things. On the contrary, the words *thing* and *to be* signify one and the same thing, but the one in the manner of a noun and the other in the manner of a verb. (*Summa totius logicae*, III, II, C. xxvii)

The skepticism which infects our ordinary judgments about the causal relation between, for example, fire and the burning of paper, is limited to human judgment; the beneficiary of this skepticism is belief in the omnipotence of God who is to be acknowledged as the only true cause and agent of our experience. But how long can religious belief remain immune to the spread of skepticism? The history of skepticism tends to show that the spread of skepticism is difficult if not possible to limit.

The principle of separability, together with the 1277 interpretation of God's omnipotence, is a force for one of two extreme positions: that of disconnected pluralism and that of congested monism. The first is a condition which the skeptic allows we may well be in: we live in a world of disparate items, ignorant (despite appearances) as to how those items are united and form a coherent whole, if they can. The second condition, that of monism, is a desperate refuge of a dogmatist, dissolving differences into a single and simple reality.

In contrasting pyrrhonian and academic skepticism the point was made above that the academic skeptic is, in certain but central moments of their skepticism, indistinguishable from a dogmatist who is as certain of his ignorance as the positive dogmatist is of his knowledge. But extremes are sometimes closer to one another than either is to the middle way.

As Western skepticism takes shape in ancient Greece and in the middle ages of Europe there is a striking difference between the skepticism articulated by the great Buddhist philosopher Nagarjuna (second century B.C.E.): using Ockham's example Nagarjuna would argue that existence and essence can be neither the same nor different; Ockham shows in the argument cited that there can be no difference; Nagarjuna would go on to show that they cannot be the same either. Therefore, since there is neither sameness nor otherness, there is no reality of essence and existence.

We have written of skepticism somewhat as if it were a disease, perhaps like the Black Plague, which proved difficult if not impossible to contain. The image, from the point of view of the skeptic, is not agreeable. A better image would perhaps be a fire started in a forest by lightning: it can have a beneficiary role, clearing out excess underbrush and making room for new life. On this view the dogmatist and the skeptic need one another to protect each from extremes which are like diseases causing the decline of philosophical culture.

VII.1. ST. AUGUSTINE

IT WAS REMARKED IN THE INTRODUCTION THAT THERE IS A CRUCIAL difference between pyrrhonian and academic skepticism; the first would have us suspend judgment; the second is really negative dogmatism, asserting, as it does, that one knows nothing. The selection following takes up the question of the coherence of academic skepticism. The academic holds that there is such a thing as the wise person; can we then turn around and say this wise person knows nothing?

VII.1.1. Arguments against Academic Skepticism
(*Against the Academics*, Bk.II, 11-13, & III, 1-8)

[This selection takes the form of a dialogue between Augustine and his friends Licentius, Trygetius and Alypius.]

BOOK TWO

Chapter 11
The "Probable"

Though the following day dawned no less pleasant and peaceful, we could scarcely get away from domestic preoccupations. The greater part of it had already passed, especially in the writing of letters, when, with barely two hours remaining, we went to the meadow. The weather was really unusually fair and inviting, and we decided that we should not allow even the little time that was left, to be wasted. When, therefore, we had come to the tree where we usually sat, and had settled down, I said: "I would like you young men, since we are not to embark on anything serious to-day, to rehearse for me how Alypius yesterday answered the little question that upset you."

To this Licentius remarked: "It is so short that it takes no effort to recall it; but as for its being an easy question, that is for you to demonstrate. Indeed, as far as I can see, once the matter at issue had been clarified, it did not allow you to raise a dispute about words."

"Have you all," I said, "sufficiently appreciated the point and force of this?"

"Yes, I think I have," said Licentius. "But please explain it a little. I have indeed often heard you say that it is a disgrace for disputants to haggle about words, when no difference about the subject matter remains; but this is too fine a point that I should be asked to explain it."

"Listen then," I said, "to what is meant. The Academics call that the 'probable' or 'what-is-like-truth' which can induce us to act while we withhold our assent. I say 'while we withhold assent,' inasmuch as we do not judge that what we do is true, or think that we know it, but we do it all the same. As for example, if a man were to ask us if, since last night was so bright and clear, today's sun would rise with the same cheerful mien, I think we would say that we did not know, but that we thought so. 'The things, then,' says the Academic, 'that I have decided to describe as "probable" or "what-is-like-truth," are all of such kind. If you wish to call them by another name, I make no objection. I am quite satisfied if you have grasped well what I mean, that is to say, what things I have in mind in using these terms: the wise man should not be an artificer of words, but an inquirer into realities.' Do you now grasp fully how those silly toys, with which I was trying to arouse your interest, have been dashed from my hands?"

When both replied that they had understood, and kept looking at me in anticipation of what I would reply to them, I said: "What do you think? Was Cicero,[1] whose words I have just quoted, so poor a

---

1 Cicero: 106-43 B.C.E.; Roman statesman, orator, and philosopher; he considered himself an Academic. He is the source of Augustine's knowledge of skepticism in Plato's Academy of the middle period.

Latinist that he used unsuitable terms for the things he had in mind?"

Chapter 12

To this Trygetius replied: "Indeed, since the matter is obvious, we do not think that we should provoke any dispute about words. So, think rather of what you will reply to Alypius who has relieved us, but whom now you want to attack again."

"A moment, please," Licentius said in turn, "something is dawning upon me. I am beginning to see that that argument of yours should not so easily have been disposed of." He was silent for a while, lost in thought. Then he said: "Nothing, I submit, seems more absurd than that a person who does not know what truth is, should say that he follows 'what-is-like-truth.' Nor does that comparison of yours disconcert me. For if I were asked whether, judging by the evening sky, there will be no rain on the morrow, I am right in replying that it does not seem likely. I do in fact know some truth. I know, for instance, that this tree cannot at a moment's notice turn into silver; and many other facts like this I can truly say that I know without being over-confident, and I note that like these are those things which I call 'what-is-like-truth.' But you, Carneades,[2] or any other Greek pest, to say nothing of our own brood – for why should I hesitate to desert to the side of him whose captive I am by right of victory? – you, I say, whence do you get this 'what-is-like-truth,' since you say that you know no truth whatever? 'But I could not get another name for it,' says Carneades. Why, then, do we bother to discuss anything with one who does not even know how to express himself?"

"I am not a man," said Alypius, "who fears deserters. Much less so the great Carneades. I do not know whether it is through boyish or youthful levity that you judged it proper to assail him with insults rather than with some weapon. But in support of his teaching, whose point of departure was always the probable, this will be quite sufficient to silence you for the present, the fact, namely, that we are so far removed from the discovery of truth that you yourself can be instanced as a telling argument against yourself.[3] By one little question you were so shaken in your position that you were at a complete loss as to where you should stand. But let us postpone this and your knowledge, which you have just avowed was communicated to you regarding this tree, to another time. For, although you have now chosen another side, nevertheless I shall take pains to explain to you what I said shortly before. We had not got as far, I think, as the question as to whether or no truth could be found; I was of the opinion, however, that this at least should be decided right at the threshold of my defence – a point where I had seen you prostrate and exhausted – namely, whether one should not seek 'what-is-like-truth,' or the 'probable,' or whatever else it can be called, which the Academics hold to be enough. It is of no interest to me if you seem to your self to be even now an excellent discoverer of truth. Afterwards, if you are thankful for my coming to your rescue now, you may, perhaps, teach me what you know."

Chapter 13

What was the Real Teaching of the New Academy?

Here I intervened because Licentius, his face flushed with shame, was cowed by the onset of Alypius: "Alypius, you have preferred to speak in every way but the way we ought to when we engage in debate with these boys who do not know how to speak."

Alypius replied: "Since I as well as everybody else have known for a long time, and now by your own profession you give evidence enough of the same, namely, that you are an expert in speaking, I wish you would first explain the use of this investigation of yours. It is either irrelevant, as I think, and it would be much more irrelevant to reply to it, or, if you decide that it is to the point, in which case it is too difficult for me to explain, then heed my earnest plea: do not weary of being my teacher."

"You remember," I said, "that I promised yesterday to treat of those words later. And now yonder sun reminds me to put away again in their boxes the

2 Skeptical philosopher who lived from 214-129 B.C.E. and founded the so-called "New Academy."
3 Cf. Cicero's *Academica*, 2.71.

toys which I set before the boys – especially since I take them out for the sake of ornament rather than to sell them. But before darkness, ever the advocate of the Academics, prevents writing, I would like it to be fully agreed between us to-day as to what question we shall attack the first thing in the morning. Accordingly, tell me, please, do you think that the Academics had a definite teaching about truth and were opposed to imparting it indiscriminately to minds ignorant or uncleansed, or that their thoughts were really at one with the tenor of their disputations?"

He replied: "I shall not rashly assert what their mind on the matter was. In so far as one can gather this from their books, you know better what words they are accustomed to use for the expression of their opinion. If you ask me what I think myself, I reply that I think that truth has not yet been discovered. I add, too – a point on which you were questioning me in connection with the Academics – that I think that it cannot be found, not only because of my ingrained conviction which you have observed in me practically from the start, but also on the authority of great and outstanding philosophers, to whose opinions we are somehow induced to submit, whether through our own mental impotence, or because of the keenness of their minds, which, we are forced to believe, cannot possibly be surpassed."

"This is exactly what I wanted," I said. "I was afraid lest if we should see eye to eye, our debate would be a stunted affair; for there would be nobody who would compel us to treat the matter from the other side so that it might be thrashed out by us as well as we can.[4] Therefore, in case this had happened, I was prepared to ask you to defend the Academics on the lines that, in your opinion, they not only argued that truth could not be discovered, but also that they were convinced of this.

"The point, therefore, at issue between us is whether or no their arguments make it probable that nothing can be perceived and that one should not assent to anything. If you demonstrate that they do this, I shall gladly yield. But if I can demonstrate that it is much more probable both that the wise man can arrive at truth, and that one should not always withhold one's assent, you will have no

excuse, I think, for refusing to come over to my side."

He and all that were present agreed to this, and as the shadows of evening were already falling about us, we returned to the house.

BOOK THREE

WISDOM AND KNOWLEDGE
Chapter 1

Man's Need of Truth

When on the day following that on which we had finished the discussion contained in the second book, we had taken our places in the baths – for the day was too disagreeable to go to the meadow – I began as follows: "I take it that you all have noted well the points which we have decided to take up in the problem that we are discussing. But before I take up my own role, which is to explain those points, I would like you to show your good will and listen to a few remarks not irrelevant to our subject – remarks which have to do with our hopes, our life, and our principles. It is our business, neither trivial nor unnecessary, but rather, in my opinion, most necessary and of the greatest importance, to seek with all our strength for truth. Alypius and myself are in agreement about this. For all philosophers believed that the wise man, as they conceived him, had found truth; but the Academics declared that their wise man must try with his utmost efforts to find it, and that in fact he does so conscientiously, except that, since truth is either hidden in obscurity or because of confusion does not stand out clearly, he follows as a guide in action that which seems to him to be probable and 'like-the-truth.'

"The same conclusion was reached in your own recent discussion. Thus one of you contended that happiness for man lay in the finding of truth, and the other was satisfied that merely seeking for truth constituted happiness. Accordingly, none of us has any doubt that we should attend to the seeking of truth above everything else. Let us consider, then, how, for example, we may judge ourselves to have spent yesterday. Of course, you were free to give

4 Cf. *ibid.*, 2. 65.

your time to your studies. For instance, you, Trygetius, spent the time pleasantly reading the poems of Virgil, and Licentius applied himself to poetic composition, to which he is so much given that it was especially for his sake that I decided to bring up this topic. It is high time that philosophy should take and hold a greater part in his mind than poetry or any other subject.

Chapter 2

Is Man Independent of Fortune?

"But, tell me, did you not feel sorry for us? We had gone to bed on the previous evening with the intention of dealing with practically nothing else but our postponed discussion when we should arise. The urgency, however, of matters that had to be taken care of about the place was such, that we were completely taken up by them and we had barely two hours at the close of day in which to give ourselves time to breathe. Hence, it has always been my opinion that, whilst the *wise* man indeed needs nothing, he needs much help from fortune to *become* wise. But perhaps Alypius holds a different view."

Alypius replied: "I do not know as yet what you think to be the province of fortune. If you believe that fortune's help is necessary for the contemning of fortune herself, then I am with you in that belief. But if you believe that it is her function to provide only those bodily necessities which cannot be had without her favour, then I do not agree. For either the person who does not yet possess wisdom, but is desirous of it, can procure the things we deem necessary for life, even if fortune be adverse and unwilling, or we must admit that she dominates the whole life of the wise man – since the wise man himself, too, cannot dispense with the need of bodily necessities."

"You say, then," I replied, "that he who is seeking wisdom needs fortune, but you deny that this is so for the wise man?"

"To say the same thing over again has its advantages," he said, "so I in turn ask you if you think that fortune helps towards the contemning of herself. If you think so, then I do say that he who seeks

wisdom is in great need of assistance from fortune."

"I do think so," I answered. "It is by her help that he becomes such as can contemn her. And this is not absurd: when we are infants we need a mother's breasts, and by them it is brought about that later on we can live and be strong without them."

"It is clear to me," he said, "that if there is no disagreement in our minds in conceiving them, our opinions agree; though a person might think that he should argue the point that it is not breasts or fortune, but some other thing that helps us to contemn fortune or breasts."

"It is a simple matter," I said, "to give another comparison. For instance, a man cannot cross the Aegean, even if he wants only to get to the other side, without a ship or some other means of transport, or, so that I might not seem to avoid mention of the method evolved by Daedalus[5] himself, some device constructed for this purpose, or some preternatural power. When he has made the crossing, he is ready to throw away and contemn whatever brought him across. So, too, whoever wishes to arrive at the safe and tranquil land and haven of wisdom, seems to me to have fortune's help in his purpose. I shall give but one example of what I mean: he cannot be wise, if he be blind and deaf; and blindness and deafness are in the power of fortune. Once he has achieved this purpose, though he should be considered to be still in need of certain things pertaining to the health of his body, it is evident, nevertheless, that such things are not necessary so that he be wise, but only that he should continue to exist among men."

"Nay, more," said Alypius, "if he be blind and deaf, he will, in my opinion, rightly contemn the acquisition of wisdom and that life itself, for which wisdom is sought."

"Nevertheless," I said, "since life itself during our days on earth is in the power of fortune, and only a living person can become wise, must we not admit that we need her favour in order to reach wisdom?"

"But," he replied, "since wisdom is necessary to those only who are alive, and if life be taken away no need for wisdom remains, I do not fear fortune as far as the continuation of life is concerned. For it is because I live that I desire wisdom, and it is not

---

5 Figure in Greek legend famous for his mechanical contrivances.

because I desire wisdom that I wish to live. If fortune, then, takes my life away, she takes away the reason for my seeking wisdom. There is no reason, therefore, why I should either desire the favour, or fear the interference of fortune in becoming wise. But perhaps you have other considerations to offer."

I asked: "You do not think, then, that he who is seeking for wisdom can be prevented by fortune from becoming wise, if one suppose that she does not deprive him of his life?"

"No, I do not," he replied.

Chapter 3

The Difference between the Wise Man and the Philosopher

"I would like you," I said, "to tell me briefly what you think to be the difference between the wise man and the philosopher."

"In my opinion," he said, "the wise man differs in no way from the philosopher except that the wise man in a certain way possesses those things which can only be longed for – however eagerly – by the philosopher."

"Now, then," I asked, "what are these things? For my part, I see no difference except that one knows wisdom, and the other wants to know."

"If," he said, "you give us a simple definition of knowledge, your point already becomes more clear."

"No matter how I define it," I replied, "all are agreed that there cannot be knowledge of what is not true."

"In my remark," he said, "I purposed to limit that question for you, in order to prevent an unconsidered concession of mine from allowing your oratory to gallop unrestrained over the plains of this cardinal question."

I replied: "To be sure, you have left me no galloping space at all! Indeed, if I mistake not, we have arrived at that for which I have been striving all the time – the end. For if, as you stated so acutely and truly, there is no difference between the philosopher and the wise man except that the former loves, the latter possesses, wisdom – for which reason you did not hesitate to use the term proper here, 'possession'; and since no one can possess wisdom in his mind, if he has not learned anything; and since no

one can learn anything, if he does not know anything; and since no one can know what is not true: therefore, the wise man knows truth, for you yourself have just admitted that he has wisdom, that is to say, its 'possession,' in his mind."

"I may," he said, "seem to be impertinent, but I do wish to deny that I admitted that the wise man has the 'possession' of the power of inquiring into divine and human things. I do not see why you should think that it is not the 'possession' of discovered probabilities that he has."

"Do you concede to me," I asked, "that no one knows what is not true?"

"Certainly," he replied.

"Assert, if you can," I said, "that the wise man does not know wisdom."

"But why," said he, "do you in this way restrict the whole question? Could he not believe that he has grasped wisdom?"

"Give me your hand," I said, "If you recall, this is the point which I said yesterday that I would prove; and now I am happy that it was not I who expressed this conclusion, but that you offered it to me spontaneously on your own. For I said that between the Academics and myself there was this difference, that while they thought it probable that truth could not be perceived, I believed that, though I myself had not yet found it, it could be found by the wise man. You now, when pressed by my question as to whether or no the wise man did not know wisdom, reply: 'He thinks that he knows.'"

"Well," he asked, "what follows from that?"

"This," I replied, "that if he thinks that he knows wisdom, he does not think that the wise man cannot know anything. Or, if wisdom is nothing, then say so."

"I should indeed believe," he replied, "that we had arrived at our final objective, but that suddenly, as we joined hands, I realized that we are very far apart and separated by a long distance. For, obviously, the only point at issue between us was, whether or no the wise man could arrive at the perception of truth. You asserted that he could. I denied it. But I do not think that I have now conceded to you anything except that the wise man can believe that he has achieved the wisdom of probabilities. That wisdom I understood to be concerned with the investigation of things human and divine. We are, I take it, agreed on that."

"You will not," I said, "evolve a method of escape by involving the issue! For the moment, it would seem to me, you are arguing merely to try your skill. You know well that these young men can scarcely as yet follow subtle and acute reasoning. You abuse, then, the ignorance of your jury. It is a case of your saying as much as you like simply because no one will protest. Now, a few moments ago, when I was questioning you as to whether or no the wise man knew wisdom, you said that he believed that he knew. But he who believes that the wise man knows wisdom, certainly cannot believe that the wise man knows nothing. Such a proposition is impossible, unless a man dares to say that wisdom is nothing. From this it follows that in this your view is identical with mine. For my view that the wise man knows something, is, I believe, also yours, since you believe that the wise man believes that he knows wisdom."

He replied: "I think that you wish to exercise your powers just as much as I do. I am surprised at that, for you have no need of any practice in this matter at all. I may, of course, still be blind in seeing a difference between 'believing-one-knows' and 'knowing,' and between the wisdom bound up with investigation, and truth itself. I do not see how these opinions expressed by each of us can be squared with one another."

As we were being called to lunch, I said: "I am not displeased that you should be so obstinate. Either both of us do not know what we are talking about, and we must, therefore, take steps to avoid such a disgrace; or this is true of only one of us, and to leave him so and neglect him, is equally disgraceful. We shall, however, have to meet again in the afternoon; for, just when I thought that we had finished, you began to indulge in fisticuffs with me."

They all laughed at this and we departed.

Chapter 4

The Wise Man Knows Truth

When we returned, we found Licentius, whose thirst for Helicon could never be quenched, eagerly trying to think out verses. For he had quietly arisen without having had anything to drink, in the mid-dle of lunch, even though this was over almost as quickly as it had begun. I remarked to him: "I certainly hope that some day you will realize your heart's desire and master poetry. Not that I take such pleasure in the art; but I see that you are so obsessed by it that you cannot escape from this infatuation except through tiring of it, and this is a common experience when one has reached perfection. And another thing, since you have a good voice, I would prefer that you would ply our ears with your verses than that you should sing, like poor little birds that we see in cages, from those Greek tragedies words which you do not understand. But I suggest that you go, if you wish, and drink something and then return to our school, provided the *Hortensius*[6] and philosophy still mean something to you. To her you have already dedicated the tender first fruits of your mind in your recent discussion – a discussion which inflamed you even more than does poetry for the knowledge of great and truly fruitful things. But while I endeavour to bring you back to the circle of those studies by which the mind is developed, I fear lest it become a labyrinth to you, and I almost repent of having held you back from your first impulse."

Licentius blushed and went away to drink. He was very thirsty. Moreover, he could thus avoid me, who seemed likely to have more and sharper things to say to him.

When he had come back, I began as follows, while all paid close attention: "Alypius, can it be that we disagree on a matter which to me seems really very evident?"

"It is not surprising," he said, "if what you say is manifest to you should be obscure to me. After all, many things evident enough in themselves can be more evident to some than to others; so, too, some things obscure in themselves can be still more obscure to some people. For, believe me, that if this matter is evident to you, there is some one else to whom it is even more evident, and still another person to whom it is more obscure than it is to me. But I beg you to make what is evident still more evident, so that you may cease to regard me as a diehard in argument."

"Please, listen closely," I said, "and do not bother for the moment to reply to my question. Knowing

---

6 A philosophical dialogue written by Cicero in his later years.

you and myself well, I feel that with a little attention my point will become clear and one of us will quickly convince the other. Now, then, did you not say or, perhaps, I did not hear rightly – that the wise man thought that he knew wisdom?"

He said that this was so.

"Let us," I said, "forget about the wise man for the moment. Are you yourself wise or are you not?"

"I am anything but that," he replied.

"But," said I, "do give me your own personal opinion about the Academic wise man. Do you think that he knows wisdom?"

He replied: "Is thinking that one knows the same as, or different from, knowing? I am afraid lest confusion on this point might afford cover to either of us."

"This," I said, "has become what they call a Tuscan argument: for this is the name they gave to an argument when instead of answering a difficulty, a man proposes another. It was this that our poet – let us win the attention of Licentius for a moment – in his *Eclogues* judged fairly to be rustic and downright countryish: when one asks the other, where the heavens are no more than three ells broad, the other replies:

In what lands do flowers grow engraved with the names of kings?[7]

"Please, Alypius, do not think that we can allow ourselves that merely because we are on the farm! At least, let these little baths serve you as a reminder of the decorum that is expected in places of learning. Kindly answer my question: Do you think that the Academic wise man knows wisdom?"

"Not to lose ourselves," he replied, "parrying words with words – I think that he thinks that he knows wisdom."

"Therefore," I said, "you think that he does not know wisdom? I am not asking you what you think the wise man thinks, but if you think that the wise man knows wisdom. You can, I take it, say either yes or no, here and now."

"I do wish," he returned, "that the matter were either as easy for me as it is for you, or as difficult for you as it is for me; and that you were not so insistent, and put such great store in these points. For, when you asked me what I thought about the Academic wise man, I replied that in my opinion it seemed to him that he knew wisdom: I did not wish to assent rashly that I knew, or, what would be just as rash, say that he knew."

"I shall be greatly obliged," I said, "if you will be good enough, first, to answer the question I put to you, and not those that you yourself put to yourself. Secondly, you may disregard for the moment what satisfaction I expect to receive from this: I know that you are as interested in it as in your own expectations. Obviously, if I deceive myself by this line of questioning, I shall promptly come over to your side and we shall finish the dispute. Finally, banish the anxiety which I note is somehow gripping you, and pay close attention, so that you will have no trouble in understanding what I want you to reply.

"Now, you said that you did not give your assent or denial – but this is just what you should do with my question – for the reason that you did not wish to state rashly that you knew what you did not know. As if I were to ask you what you know, and not what you think! And now I ask the same question more plainly – if, indeed, I can ask it any more plainly: is it, or is it not, your opinion that the wise man knows wisdom?"

"If it is possible," he replied, "to find a wise man such as reason conceives of, I can believe that he knows wisdom."

"Reason, therefore," I said, "indicated to you that the wise man is such that he knows wisdom. So far you are right. You could not have properly held any other opinion.

"And now I ask you if the wise man can be found. If he can, then he can also know wisdom and our discussion is finished. But if you say that he cannot be found, then the question will be, not if the wise man knows anything, but rather if any one can be a wise man. Answering this in the affirmative, we must take leave of the Academics, and go over this point with you as far as we can, and with great care and attention. For the Academics maintained, or rather opined, at one and the same time that the wise man could exist, but that, nevertheless, man could not attain to knowledge. Therefore, they actually claimed that the wise man knows nothing. But you believe that he knows wisdom, which cer-

7 Virgil, *Ecl.* 3. 104-107.

tainly is not identical with knowing nothing. For we are agreed, as are all the ancients and even the Academics themselves, that no one can know what is not true. Accordingly, there remains now that you either maintain that wisdom is nothing, or admit that the wise man as described by the Academics is such as is unknown to reason, and then, dropping that question, agree to investigate if man can possess such wisdom as is conceived by reason. For there is no other wisdom which we should, or can, rightly call by that name."

Chapter 5

The Question of Assent

"Even though I should concede," he said, "what you are so anxiously striving for, namely, that the wise man knows wisdom, and that between us we have discovered something which the wise man can know, nevertheless, I do not at all think that the whole case of the Academics has been undermined. Indeed, I notice that they can fall back on a stronghold that is by no means weak, and that their line of retreat has not been cut off. They can still withhold assent. In fact, the very point in which you think they have been vanquished, helps their cause. For they will say that it is so true that nothing can be known and that assent must be withheld from everything, that even this their principle of not being able to know anything, which practically from the very beginning until you came along, they had maintained as probable, is now wrested from them by your argument. Your argument may be in fact invincible or may seem so to me in my stupidity, but as before, so now, it cannot dislodge them, when they can still with confidence assert that even now assent must be withheld from everything. It is possible, they will say, that perhaps some day they themselves or some one else will discover some argument which can be urged with point and probability against this second principle of theirs also. They would have us notice that their behaviour is illustrated and mirrored, so to speak, by that of Proteus[8] who, it is said, could be caught only by means which invariably did not result in his capture. His pursuers were never sure that what they

had was still he, unless some divinity informed them. May that divinity be present to us, and may he deign to show us that truth for which we strive so hard! I, too, shall then confess, even if the Academics do not agree – though I think they will – that they have been overcome."

"Good!" I said, "that was all I wanted. For, look, I beg you, at all the great gains I have made! First, we can say that the Academics are so far vanquished that they have now no defence left except the impossible. Indeed, who could in any way understand or believe that a man who is beaten, by the very fact that he has been beaten, boasts that he has won? And so, if we have any further dispute with them, it is not on the score of their assertion that nothing can be known, but on the score of their maintaining that one must not assent to anything.

"Consequently, we are now in agreement. For both they and I believe that the wise man knows wisdom. But they advise, all the same, that assent should not be given to this. They say that they *believe* only, but do not at all *know*. As if I should profess that I *know*! I say that I also *believe* this. If they do not know wisdom, then they, and I with them, are stupid. But I think that we should approve of something, namely, truth. I ask them if they deny this, that is to say, if they declare that one must not assent to truth. They will never say this; but they will maintain that truth cannot be found. Consequently, in this I am to a great extent at one with them in so far as both of us do not object, and, therefore, necessarily agree, to the proposition that one must assent to truth.

"'But who will indicate truth for us?' they ask. On that point I shall not trouble to dispute with them. I am satisfied since they consider it no longer probable that the wise man knows nothing. Otherwise, they would be forced to maintain a most absurd proposition, that either wisdom is nothing, or the wise man does not know wisdom.

Chapter 6

Truth Revealed only by a Divinity

"You, Alypius, have told us who it is that can point

8 Son of Poseidon, god of the sea. He eluded capture by changing rapidly from one form to another.

out truth – and I must take pains to disagree with you as little as possible. You remarked that only some divinity could reveal truth to human beings. Your words were brief but full of piety. There has been nothing in our discussion which has given me more delight, nothing more profound, nothing more probable, and, provided, so I trust, that divinity be present to us, nothing more true. With what profound understanding and sensitiveness to what is best in philosophy did you direct our attention to Proteus! Proteus, of whom you all know, is introduced as a symbol of truth. You will see, young men, from this that the poets are not entirely despised by philosophy. Proteus, as I say, plays in poetry the role of truth which no one can hold if, deceived by false representations, he slackens or lets loose the bonds of understanding. It is these representations which, because of our association with corporeal things, do their best to fool and deceive us through the senses which we use for the necessities of this life, even when we have already grasped truth and hold it, so to speak, within our hands.

"Here, then, is the third blessing which has come upon me, and I cannot find words to express how highly I value it. I find my most intimate friend agreeing with me not only on probability as a factor in human life, but also on religion itself – a point which is the clearest sign of a true friend; for friendship has been rightly and with just reverence defined as 'agreement on things human and divine combined with goodwill and love.'"

Chapter 7

Augustine's Refutation of the New Academy

"Nevertheless, lest the arguments of the Academics should seem somewhat to cloud the issue, or we ourselves seem to some to dispute arrogantly the authority of highly learned men, among whom Tullius[9] especially must always have weight with us, I shall with your leave first put forward a few considerations against those who would believe that the arguments referred to stand in the way of truth. Then I shall show why, as it seems to me, the Academics concealed their real doctrine. Now, then, Alypius, although I see that you are entirely

on my side, nevertheless take a brief for them for a few moments, and answer my question."

"Since," he replied, "you have, as they say, got off on the right foot to-day, I shall not do anything to hinder your complete victory. I shall with the greater confidence attempt to defend their side, seeing that the task is one imposed by yourself. All the same, I would prefer you, if you find it convenient, to achieve the result you aim at rather by means of an uninterrupted discussion than by this questioning, lest, although already your prisoner, I should be tormented, as being in fact an unyielding enemy, by the rack of all your detailed arguments. Such cruelty is not at all in accordance with your humanity!"

And so I, when I noticed that the others, too, wanted this, began, as it were, anew. "I shall do as you wish," I said, "although I had hoped that after my toil in the rhetoric school, I should find some rest in this light armour – that is, I should conduct these enquiries by question and answer rather than by exposition – nevertheless, since we are so few and it will not be necessary for me to raise my voice beyond what is good for my health, and since I have also wished that the pen should, so to speak, guide and control my discourse – also on account of my health, lest I become more excited mentally than is good for my body – listen, then, to my opinion, given to you, as you wish, in continuous exposition.

"In the first place, however, let us examine a point about which the enthusiastic supporters of the Academics are very boastful. There is in the books which Cicero wrote in support of them a certain passage that to me seems seasoned with rare wit, while some think it a passage of great power and conviction. It would be hard to imagine that any man should not be impressed by what is there written:

Everybody of every other school that claims to be wise, gives the second place to the wise man of the Academy. It is inevitable, of course, that each claims the first place for himself. From this one can conclude with probability that the Academic rightly judges himself as holding the first place, since in the judgment of all the others he holds the second.

9 I.e., M. Tullius Cicero.

Suppose, for example, that there is a Stoic wise man present. It was against the Stoics especially that the Academics felt called upon to pit their wits. If Zeno[10] or Chrysippus[11] be asked who is the wise man, he will reply that it is the man whom he himself has described. But Epicurus[12] or some other adversary will deny this, and maintain that his own representative rather, one who is as skilled as a bird-catcher in catching pleasure, is the wise man. The fight is on! Zeno shouts, and the whole Porch[13] is in uproar: man was born for nothing else but virtue; she draws souls to herself merely by her grandeur, without resorting to the bait of any external advantage and, as it were, of a pandering reward; the pleasure vaunted by Epicurus is a thing received in common by beasts and by them alone; to pitch out man – and the wise man! – into such company is abominable.

But over against this, Epicurus, like another Bacchus, calling from his Gardens a horde to aid him, who, though drunk, yet look for someone whom in their Bacchic frenzy, they can tear to pieces with their long nails and savage fangs, and exploiting the popular approval of pleasure and an easy-going and quiet life, maintains passionately that without pleasure nobody could appear to be happy.

Should an Academic chance upon their quarrel, he will listen to each side as it attempts to win him over to itself. But if he joins one side or the other, he will be shouted down by the side he is leaving in the lurch, as crazy, ignorant, and reckless. Accordingly, when he has given an attentive ear now to this side, now to that, and is asked his opinion, he will say that he is in doubt. Now ask the Stoic, which is the better – Epicurus who declares that the Stoic is talking nonsense, or the Academic who gives the verdict that he must give further consideration to a matter of such moment – and no one doubts but that the Academic will be preferred. And next turn to Epicurus and ask him which he prefers – Zeno by whom he is called a beast, or

Arcesilaus who tells him: "Perhaps what you say is true, but I shall have to look into the matter more closely." Is it not clear that Epicurus will decide that the whole Porch is crazy, and that in comparison with them, the Academics are unassuming and judicious people?"

"Quite similarly, regarding practically all the other philosophical sects Cicero treats his readers to what we might call a delightful piece of theatre. He shows, as it were, that there is none of those sects which, having of necessity put itself in the first place, does not proclaim that it allots the second place to the one which it sees is not in opposition to, but merely undecided about, its own position. On that point I shall not oppose them in any way or deprive them of any glory."

Chapter 8

"Some people, to be sure, may think that in this passage Cicero was not poking fun, but rather that because he was appalled by the levity of these Greeklings, he purposed to dig up and collect some of their banalities and rantings. But if I wished to join issue with such pretence, could I not easily show how much less an evil it is to have no knowledge than to be incapable of receiving any? Thus it happens that if this petty boaster of the Academics offers himself as a pupil to the various sects, and none of them succeeds in convincing him of what it thinks it knows, they will then all come together with a will and make a mockery of him. For now each of them will judge that every other adversary has not indeed learnt anything, but that the Academic is *incapable* of learning anything. After that he will be driven from one school after the other not with the rod, which would cause him a little more shame than hurt, but by the clubs and cudgels of the men of the mantle. For there will be no trouble in calling in the help of the Cynics, as one would call in Hercules, to overcome the common scourge.

"And if I, who may be more easily allowed to do

---

10 Zeno of Citium, founder of the Stoic school. Lived from c. 336-264 B.C.E.
11 Systematized Stoic doctrine. Lived from 281-208 B.C.E.
12 Founder of the Epicurean school. Born at Samos in 342 and opened a school in Athens in 307 B.C.E.
13 "Stoa" means porch in Greek.

so, seeing that though I practise philosophy I am not yet wise, wish to compete with the Academics for the contemptible glory that is theirs, how can they halt me? Suppose that an Academic and myself together came upon the conflict of philosophers described before. Let all be present. Let them expound their opinions briefly in the time allowed. Ask Carneades his opinion. He will reply that he is in doubt. Promptly each will prefer him to all the others; that is to say, all will prefer him among all the others – truly a distinction great and remarkable!

"Who would not like to achieve a like distinction? And so, when I am asked my opinion, I, too, shall give the same answer. I shall be equally commended. That is to say, the glory which the wise man is reaping is of the sort that equates him with the blockhead! But suppose the latter easily beats him in his distinction: will not the Academic be put to shame? As he is trying to slip off from the trial, I shall pull him back – for stupidity surpasses itself in craving for a victory of this kind. Holding him tight, I shall tell the judges something which they do not know, and say: 'Gentlemen, there is this much in common between this fellow and myself, that neither of us knows which of you follows truth. But we have also individual opinions of our own, about which I ask you to enter a judgment. I, for my part, am uncertain, although I have heard your expositions, as to where truth is, for the simple reason that I do not know which of you is the wiser. But this fellow denies that even the wise man knows anything, even wisdom itself, to which he owes it that he is called wise!'

"Can anybody fail to see who will win the palm? If my opponent admits my charge, I shall best him in glory. But if he blushes for shame and confesses that the wise man does know wisdom, then my opinion carries the day."

VII.1.2. Internal Knowledge (from *City of God*, Book XI, ch.xxvi)

[This selection contains a famous argument against skepticism extended even to one's own existence; Augustine writes:

Well, if I am mistaken, I exist. For a man who does not exist can surely not be mistaken either, and if I am mistaken, therefore I exist. So, since I am if I am mistaken, how can I be mistaken in believing that I am when it is certain that if I am mistaken I am.

Avicenna was later to advance an analogous argument of the "flying man": suppose a grown person, created suddenly and possessing all his powers. Even if his eyes are covered and he is suspended in empty space, having no sensory experience of the world nor of his body and its parts, would nevertheless know that he exists. And still later Descartes would become famous for his argument that in doubting one would know the existence of the doubting, conscious that one is doubting. Descartes, like Augustine, means to protect two things from the extending hand of skepticism: the existence of the I and the existence of God.]

Chapter XXVI

On the image of the most high Trinity that in a certain fashion is found in human nature even before a man has attained bliss

We too as a matter of fact recognize in ourselves an image of God, that is of this most high Trinity, even if the image is not equal to Him in worth, but rather very far short of being so. The image is not co-eternal and, to sum the matter up briefly, it is not formed of the same substance as God. Yet it is nearer to him in the scale of nature than any other thing created by him, although it still requires to be reshaped and perfected in order to be nearest to him in its likeness to him also. For we both are and know that we are, and we love our existence and our knowledge of it. Moreover, in these three statements that I have made we are not confused by any mistake masquerading as truth. For we do not get in touch with these realities, as we do with external objects, by means of any bodily sense. We know colours, for instance, by seeing them, sounds by hearing them, odours by smelling them, the taste of things by tasting them, and hard and soft objects by feeling them. We also have images that closely resemble these physical objects, but they are not material. They live in our minds, where we use them in thinking, preserve them in our memory, and are stimulated by them to desire the objects themselves. But it is without any deceptive play of my imagination, with its real or unreal visions, that I am quite certain that I am, that I know that I am, and that I love this being and this knowing.

Where these truths are concerned I need not quail before the Academicians when they say: "What if you should be mistaken?"[14] Well, if I am mistaken, I exist. For a man who does not exist can surely not be mistaken either, and if I am mistaken, therefore I exist. So, since I am if I am mistaken, how can I be mistaken in believing that I am when it is certain that if I am mistaken I am. Therefore, from the fact that, if I were indeed mistaken, I should have to exist to be mistaken, it follows that I am undoubtedly not mistaken in knowing that I am. It follows also that in saying that I know that I know, I am not mistaken. For just as I know that I am, so it holds too that I know that I know. And when I love these two things, I add this same love as a third particular of no smaller value to these things that I know. Nor is my statement, that I love, a mistake, since I am not mistaken in the things that I love; yet even if they were illusions, it would still be true that I love illusions. For on what grounds could I rightly be blamed or prevented from loving illusions, if it were a mistaken belief that I love them? But since these things are themselves true and certain who can doubt that, when they are loved, the love itself is also true and certain? Furthermore, it is as true that there is no person who does not wish to be as that there is no person who does not wish to be happy. For how can a person be happy if he is nothing?[15]

VII.1.3. Can we know there is something above Human Reason? (from *On Free Choice*, II iii 7 – xv 39)

[The first of the two selections below is from St. Augustine's dialogue *On Free Choice*. The dialogue is between Augustine and his friend Evodius.]

Augustine: Let us discuss these three questions, if you please, and in this order. First, how it is manifest that God exists. Secondly, whether all good things, in so far as they are good, are from him. Lastly, whether free will is to be counted among the good things. When these questions have been answered it will, I think, be evident whether free will has been rightly given to man. First, then, to begin with what is most obvious, I ask you: "Do you exist?" Are you perhaps afraid to be deceived by that question? But if you did not exist it would be impossible for you to be deceived.

Evodius: Proceed to your other questions.

Aug. Since it is manifest that you exist and that you could not know it unless you were living, it is also manifest that you live. You know these two things are absolutely true.

Ev. I do.

Aug. Therefore this third fact is likewise manifest, namely, that you have intelligence.

Ev. Clearly.

Aug. Of these three things which is most excellent?

Ev. Intelligence.

Aug. Why do you think so?

Ev. To exist, to live and to know are three things. A stone exists but does not live. An animal lives but has not intelligence. But he who has intelligence most certainly both exists and lives. Hence I do not hesitate to judge that that is more excellent, which has all these qualities, than that in which one or both of them is absent. That which lives, thereby exists, but it does not follow that it has also intelligence. That is a life like that of an animal. That which exists does not necessarily have either life or intelligence. Dead bodies must be said to exist but cannot be said to live. Much less can that which has not life have intelligence.

Aug. We gather, therefore, that of these three things a dead body lacks two, an animal one, and human beings none.

Ev. That is true.

Aug. And of these three things that is most excellent which human beings have along with the other two, that is intelligence. Having that, it follows that he has both being and life.

---

14 For the principles on which the Academicians based their scepticism, see esp. Cicero, *Academica Priora* 2.13.40-42.
15 See *De Moribus Ecclesiae Catholicae* 1.3.4; *De Trinitate* 13.20.25; *Confessions* 10.21.31.

Ev. I am sure of that.

Aug. If, now, we could find something which you could unhesitatingly recognize not only as existing but also as superior to our reason, would you have any hesitation in calling it, whatever it may be, God?

Ev. Well, I should not without hesitation give the name, God, to anything that I might find better than the best element in my natural composition. I do not wish to say simply that God is that to which my reason is inferior, but that above which there is no superior.

Aug. Clearly so, for it is God who has given to your reason to have these true and pious views of him. But, I ask, supposing you find nothing superior to our reason save what is eternal and unchangeable, will you hesitate to call that God? You realize that bodies are mutable; and it is evident that life which animates the body is not without mutability by reason of its varying affections. Even reason is proved to be mutable, for sometimes it strives to reach the truth and sometimes it does not so strive. Sometimes it reaches the truth and sometimes it does not. If without the aid of any bodily organ, neither by touch nor by taste nor by smell, neither by the ears nor the eyes, but by itself alone reason catches sight of that which is eternal and unchangeable, it must confess its own inferiority, and that the eternal and unchangeable is its God.

Ev. This I will certainly confess to be God than whom there is nothing superior.

Aug. Very well. It will be enough for me to show that there is something of this nature which you will be ready to confess to be God; or if there be something higher still that at least you will allow to be God. However that may be, it will be evident that God exists when with his aid I have demonstrated to you, as I promised, that there is something above reason.

Ev. Then proceed with your demonstration as you promise.

Aug. I shall do so. But I first ask you this. Is my bodily sense identical with yours, or is mine mine and yours yours only? If the latter were not the case I should not be able to see anything with my eyes which you also would not see.

Ev. I admit that at once, though while each of us has severally the senses of sight, hearing and the rest, your senses and mine belong to the same class of things. For one man can both see and hear what another does not see or hear, and with any of the other senses can perceive what another does not perceive. Hence it is evident that your sense is yours alone and mine mine alone.

Aug. Will you make the same reply about the interior sense?

Ev. Exactly. My interior sense perceives my perceiving, and yours perceives yours. Often someone who sees something will ask me whether I also see it. The reason for asking simply is that I know whether I see or not, and the questioner does not know.

Aug. Has each of us, then, his own particular reason? For it can often happen that I know something when you do not know it, and I know that I know it, but you cannot know that.

Ev. Apparently each of us has his own private rational mind.

Aug. But you cannot say that each of us has his own private sun or moon or stars or the like, though each of us sees these things with his own particular sense of sight?

Ev. No, of course I would not say that.

Aug. So, many of us can see one thing simultaneously, though our senses, by which we perceive the object we all see together, are our own. In spite of the fact that my sense and yours are two different things, what we actually see need not be two different things, one of which I see, while you see the other. There is one object for both of us, and both of us see it simultaneously.

Ev. Obviously.

Aug. We can also hear one voice simultaneously, so that, though my hearing is not your hearing, there are not two voices of which you hear one and I another. It is not as if my hearing caught one part of the sound and yours another. The one sound, and the whole of it, is heard by both of us simultaneously.

Ev. That, too, is obvious.

Aug. But notice, please, what is to be said about the other senses. It is pertinent to the present discussion to observe that the case with them is not quite the same as with sight and hearing, though it is not entirely different. You and I can breathe the same air and feel its effects by smelling. Likewise we can both partake of one piece of honey, or some other food or drink, and feel its effects by tasting. That is to say, there is one object, but we each have our own senses. You have yours and I have mine. So while we both sense one odour and one taste, you do not sense it with my sense nor I with yours, nor with any sense that we can have in common. My sense is entirely mine and yours yours, even though both of us sense the same odour or the same taste. In this way these senses some what resemble sight and hearing. But there is this dissimilarity, which is pertinent to the present problem. We both breathe the same air with our nostrils, and taste one food. And yet I do not breathe in the same particles of air as you do, and I consume a different portion of food from that consumed by you. When I breathe I draw in as much air as is sufficient for me, and when you breathe you draw in as much as is sufficient for you, but both of us use different parts of air. If between us we consume one food, the whole of it is not consumed either by you or by me, as we both hear the whole sound of a word spoken, or see the whole object offered to our sight simultaneously. One part of a drink must pass into your mouth and another into mine. Do you understand?

Ev. I admit that is all clear and certain.

Aug. Do you think the sense of touch is comparable to the senses of sight and hearing in the fashion we are now discussing? Not only can we both feel one body by touching it, but we can both feel not only the same body but the same part of it. It is not as in the case of food where both of us cannot consume the whole of it when we both eat it. You can touch what I touch and touch the whole of it. We do not touch each one a different part but each of us touches the whole.

Ev. So far, I admit that the sense of touch resembles the first two senses, sight and hearing. But I see there is this difference. We can both simultaneously at one and the same time see or hear the whole of what is seen or heard. No doubt we can both touch simultaneously the whole of one object, but in any one moment we can only touch different parts. The same part we can only touch at different times. I cannot touch the part you are touching unless you move away your hand.

Aug. You are most vigilant. But here is another thing you ought to notice, since there are some things which both of us can feel, and others which we must feel severally. Our own senses, for example, we must feel each for himself. I cannot feel your sense nor you mine. But in the case of corporeal things, that is, things we perceive with the bodily senses, when we cannot both perceive them together but must do so severally, it is due to the fact that we make them completely ours by consuming them and making them part of ourselves, like food and drink of which you cannot consume the same part as I do. It is true that nurses give infants food which they have chewed, but the part which has been squeezed out and been swallowed, can not be recalled and used to feed the child. When the palate tastes something pleasant it claims a part, even if only a small part, which it cannot give up, and does with it what is consonant with corporeal nature. Were this not so no taste would remain in the mouth when what had been chewed was put out. The same can be said of the part of the air which we draw into our nostrils. You may breathe in some of the air which I breathe out, but you cannot breathe that part which has gone to nourish me, for I cannot breathe it out. Physicians sometimes bid us take medicine through our nostrils. I alone feel it when I breathe it in and I cannot put it back again by breathing out, so that you may breathe it in and feel it. All sensible things, which we do not destroy and take into our systems when we sense them, we can perceive, both of us, either at the same time or at different times, one after the other, in such a way that the whole or the part which I perceive can also be perceived by you. I mean such things as light or sound or bodily objects which we do not destroy when we use and perceive them.

Ev. I understand.

Aug. It is therefore evident that things which we perceive with the bodily senses without causing them to change are by nature quite different from our senses, and consequently are common to us both, because they are not converted and changed into something which is our peculiar and almost private property.

Ev. I agree.

Aug. By "our peculiar and private property" I mean that which belongs to each of us alone, which each of us perceives by himself alone, which is part of the natural being of each of us severally. By "common and almost public property" I mean that which is perceived by all sentient beings without its being thereby affected and changed.

Ev. That is so.

Aug. Now consider carefully, and tell me whether anything can be found which all reasoning beings can see in common, each with his own mind and reason; something which is present for all to see but which is not transformed like food and drink for the use of those for whom it is present; something which remains complete and unchanged, whether they see it or do not see it. Do you perhaps think there is nothing of that kind?

Ev. Indeed, I see many such, but it will be sufficient to mention one. The science of numbers is there for all reasoning persons, so that all calculators may try to learn it, each with his own reason and intelligence. One can do it easily, another with difficulty, another cannot do it at all. But the science itself remains the same for everybody who can learn it, nor is it converted into something consumed like food by him who learns it. If anyone makes a mistake in numbers the science itself is not at fault. It remains true and entire. The error of the poor arithmetician is all the greater, the less he knows of the science.

Aug. Quite right. I see you are not untaught in these matters, and so have quickly found a reply. But suppose someone said that numbers make their impression on our minds not in their own right but rather as images of visible things, springing from our contacts by bodily sense with corporeal objects, what would you reply? Would you agree?

Ev. I could never agree to that. Even if I did perceive numbers with the bodily senses I could not in the same way perceive their divisions and relations. By referring to these mental operations I show anyone to be wrong in his counting who gives a wrong answer when he adds or subtracts. Moreover, all that I contact with a bodily sense, such as this sky and this earth and whatever I perceive to be in them, I do not know how long it will last. But seven and three make ten not only now but always. In no circumstances have seven and three ever made anything else than ten, and they never will. So I maintain that the unchanging science of numbers is common to me and to every reasoning being.

Aug. I do not deny that your reply is certainly most true. But you will easily see that numbers are not conveyed to us by our bodily senses if you consider that the value of every number is calculated according to the number of times it contains the number one. For example, twice one is called two; thrice one is called three; ten times one is called ten, and every number receives its name and its value according to the number of times it contains the number one. Whoever thinks with exactitude of unity will certainly discover that it cannot be per-

ceived by the senses. Whatever comes into contact with a bodily sense is proved to be not one but many, for it is corporeal and therefore has innumerable parts. I am not going to speak of parts so minute as to be almost unrealizable; but, however small the object may be, it has at least a right-hand part and a left-hand part, an upper and a lower part, a further and a nearer part, one part at the end and another at the middle. We must admit that these parts exist in any body however small, and accordingly we must agree that no corporeal object is a true and absolute unity. And yet all these parts could not be counted unless we had some notion of unity. When I am seeking unity in the corporeal realm and am at the same time certain that I have not found it, nevertheless I know what I am seeking and failing to find, and I know that I cannot find it, or rather that it does not exist among corporeal things. When I know that no body is a unity, I know what unity is. If I did not know what unity is, I could not count the plurality of parts in a body. However I have come to know unity, I have not learned it from the bodily senses, for by them I can know only corporeal objects, and none of them, as we have proved, is a true unity. Moreover, if we do not perceive unity with any bodily sense, neither do we perceive any number, of the kind at any rate which we discern with the intellect. For there is none of them which is not a multiple of unity, and unity cannot be perceived by the bodily senses. The half of any body, however small, requires the other half to complete the whole, and it itself can be halved. A body can be divided into two parts but they are not simply two. [They may in turn be further sub-divided.] But the number two consists of twice simple unity, so that the half of two, that is, simple unity, cannot be sub-divided by two or three or any other number whatever, because it is true and simple unity.

Following the order of the numbers we see that two comes next to one, and is found to be the double of one. The double of two does not immediately follow. Three comes first and then four, which is the double of two. Throughout the numerical series this order extends by a fixed and unchangeable law. After one, which is the first of all numbers, two follows immediately, which is the double of one. After the second number, that is, two, in the second place in order comes the double of two. In the first place after two comes three and in the second place four, the double of two. After the third number, three, in the third place comes its double, for after three four comes first, five second, and in the third place six, which is the double of three. Similarly the fourth number after the fourth is its double; five, six, seven, and in the fourth place eight, which is the double of four. And throughout the numerical series you will find the same rule holds good from first to last. The double of any number is found to be exactly as far from that number as it is from the beginning of the series. How do we find this changeless, firm and unbroken rule persisting throughout the numerical series? No bodily sense makes contact with all numbers, for they are innumerable. How do we know that this rule holds throughout? How can any phantasy or phantasm yield such certain truth about numbers which are innumerable? We must know this by the inner light, of which bodily sense knows nothing.

By many such evidences all disputants to whom God has given ability and who are not clouded by obstinacy, are driven to admit that the science of numbers does not pertain to bodily sense, but stands sure and unchangeable, the common possession of all reasoning beings. Many other things might occur to one that belong to thinkers as their common and, as it were, public property, things which each beholder sees with his own mind and reason, and which abide inviolate and unchangeable. But I am glad that the science of numbers most readily occurred to you when you had to answer my question. For it is not in vain that the holy books conjoin number and wisdom, where it is written, "I turned and [inclined] my heart to know and consider and seek wisdom and number."[16]

Now, I ask, what are we to think of wisdom itself? Do you think that individual men have wisdoms of their own? Or is there one wisdom common to all, so that a man is wiser the more he participates in it?

Ev. I do not yet know what you mean by wisdom. I observe that men judge variously of what deeds or words are wise. Soldiers think they are acting wisely in following their profession. Those who despise military service and give all their care and labour to agriculture think themselves wise. Those who leave all these things aside or reject all such temporal concerns and devote all their zeal to the search for truth, how they can know themselves and God, judge that this is the chief task of wisdom. Those who are unwilling to give themselves to the life of leisure for the purpose of seeking and contemplating truth, but prefer to accept laborious cares and duties in the service of their fellows and to take part in justly ruling and governing human affairs, they too think themselves to be wise. Moreover, those who do both of these things, who live partly in the contemplation of truth and partly in laborious duties, which they think they owe to human society, those think they hold the palm of wisdom. I do not mention the sects innumerable, of which there is none which does not put its own members above all others and claim that they alone are wise. Since we are now carrying on this discussion on the understanding that we are not to state what we merely believe but what we clearly understand, I can make no answer to your question, unless in addition to believing I also know by contemplation and reason what wisdom is.

Aug. Surely you do not suppose that wisdom is anything but the truth in which the chief good is beheld and possessed? All those people whom you have mentioned as following diverse pursuits seek good and shun evil, but they follow different pursuits because they differ as to what they think to be good. Whoever seeks that which ought not to be sought, even though he would not seek it unless it seemed to him to be good, is nevertheless in error. There can be no error when nothing is sought, or when that is sought which ought to be sought. In so far as all people seek the happy life they do not err. But in so far as anyone does not keep to the way that leads to the happy life, even though he professes to desire only to reach happiness, he is in error. Error arises when we follow something which does not lead to that which we wish to reach. The more a person errs in his way of life, the less is he wise, the further he is from the truth in which the chief good is beheld and possessed. Everyone is happy who attains the chief good, which indisputably is the end which we all desire. Just as it is universally agreed that we wish to be happy, it is similarly agreed that we wish to be wise, because no one is happy without wisdom. For no one is

---

16 *Ecclesiastes* 7:25.

happy except by the possession of the chief good which is beheld and possessed in the truth which we call wisdom. Before we are happy the notion of happiness is stamped upon our minds; that is why we know and can say confidently without any hesitation that we want to be happy. Likewise, even before we are wise we have the notion of wisdom stamped upon our minds. For that reason each of us, if asked whether he wants to be wise, will, without any groping in the dark, answer that, of course, he does.

Perhaps we are now agreed as to what wisdom is. You may not be able to express it in words, but if you had no notion in your mind of what it is you would not know that you want to be wise, and that you ought to want to be wise. That, I am sure you will not deny. Suppose, then, that we are agreed as to what wisdom is, please tell me whether you think that wisdom too, like the science of numbers, is common to all reasoning beings. Or, seeing that there are as many minds as there are persons, and I cannot observe anything that goes on in your mind, nor you what goes on in mine, do you suppose that there are as many wisdoms as there can be wise people?

Ev. If the chief good is one for all people, the truth in which it is seen and possessed, that is, wisdom, must be one and common to all.

Aug. Have you any doubt that the chief good, whatever it may be, is one for all people?

Ev. I certainly have, because I see that different persons rejoice in different things as if they were their chief good.

Aug. I wish there were no more doubt about the nature of the chief good than there is about the fact that without it, whatever it may be, no one can become happy. But that is a big question and demands a long discourse, so let us suppose that there are just as many "chief goods" as there are different things sought by different people under the impression that they are "chief goods." Surely it does not follow that wisdom is not one and common to all because the good things which people see in it and choose are manifold and diverse? If you think it does, you might as well doubt whether the light of the sun is one light because there are many diverse things which we see by means of it. Of these each one chooses at will something to enjoy looking at. One person likes to behold a high mountain and rejoices to look at it. Another prefers the plain, another a hollow valley, or green woods, or the wavy expanse of the sea. Some one may like all these or some of them whose united beauty contributes to the pleasure of looking at them. The things which people see by the light of the sun and choose for enjoyment are many and various, but the light is one in which each person sees what he enjoys looking at. So, although there are many diverse good things from among which each may choose what he likes, and seeing and possessing it and enjoying it, may rightly and truly constitute it his own chief good, nevertheless it may be that the light of wisdom in which these things can be seen and possessed is one light common to all wise persons.

Ev. I admit it may be so, and that there is nothing to prevent there being one wisdom common to all, though there are many various chief goods. But I should like to know whether it is so. To admit that something may be is not exactly the same as to admit that it is.

Aug. Meantime we have established that there is such a thing as wisdom, but we have not yet determined whether it is one and common to all, or whether individual wise persons have their particular wisdoms just as they have their particular souls or minds.

Ev. That is so.

Aug. We hold it as settled that there is such a thing as wisdom, or at least that there are wise persons, and also that all people want to be happy. But where do we see this? For I have no doubt at all that you see this and that it is true. Do you see this truth in such a way that I cannot know it unless you tell me what you think? Or could I see this truth, just as you understand it, even if you did not tell me?

Ev. I do not doubt that you too could see it even if I did not want you to.

Aug. Is not one truth which we both see with our different minds common to both of us?

Ev. Clearly.

Aug. Again, I believe you do not deny that people should strive after wisdom. You admit that that is true?

Ev. I have no doubt about that.

Aug. Here is another truth which is one and common to all who know it, though each one sees it with his own mind and not with mine or yours or any other man's. Can we deny that, since what is seen can be seen in common by all who see it?

Ev. We cannot deny it.

Aug. Again, take such propositions as these: People ought to live justly; the worse ought to be subjected to the better; like is to be compared with like; each person should be given his due. Don't you admit that these statements are absolutely true and stable, to be shared by you and me and all who see them?

Ev. I agree.

Aug. The same would be true of these statements: The incorrupt is better than the corrupt, the eternal than the temporal, the inviolable than the violable?

Ev. Undeniably.

Aug. Could anyone claim truths of that kind as his own private truths, seeing they are unchangeably present for all to contemplate who have the capacity to contemplate them?

Ev. No one could claim any one of them as his own, for not only are they true but they are equally common property to all.

Aug. And again, who denies that the soul ought to be turned from corruption and converted to incorruption, in other words not corruption but incorruption ought to be loved? Who, confessing that that is true, does not also understand that it is unchangeably true and can be understood in common by all minds which have the capacity to understand it?

Ev. Most true.

Aug. Will anyone doubt that a life which no adversity can drive from a certain and honourable opinion is better than one which is easily broken and overwhelmed by temporal disadvantages?

Ev. Who can doubt it?

Aug. I shall ask no more questions of that kind. It is sufficient that you see as I do that these rules and guiding lights of the virtues, as we may call them, are true and unchangeable, and singly or all together they stand open for the common contemplation of those who have the capacity to behold them, each with his own mind and reason. This you admit is quite certain. But I do ask whether you think these truths belong to wisdom. For I am sure you think that he who has acquired wisdom is wise.

Ev. I most certainly do.

Aug. Could the person who lives justly so live unless he saw how to apply the principles of subordinating the inferior to the superior, joining like to like, and giving to each his due?

Ev. He could not.

Aug. Would you deny that he who sees this sees wisely?

Ev. I would not.

Aug. Does not he who lives prudently choose incorruption and perceive that it is preferable to corruption?

Ev. Clearly.

Aug. If he makes what no one doubts is the right choice as to the goal towards which he should direct his mind, can it be denied that he has made a wise choice?

Ev. I could not deny it.

Aug. When he directs his mind to what he has wisely chosen, again he does it wisely?

Ev. Most certainly.

Aug. And if by no terrors or penalties can he be driven from what he has wisely chosen and towards which he has wisely directed his mind, again there is no doubt that he acts wisely?

Ev. There is no doubt.

Aug. It is therefore abundantly evident that these rules and guiding lights of virtue, as we have called them, belong to wisdom. The more a man uses them in living his life, and the more closely he follows them, the more wisely does he live and act. Everything that is wisely done cannot rightly be said to be done apart from wisdom.

Ev. That is perfectly true.

Aug. Just as the rules of numbers are true and unchangeable, and the science of numbers is unchangeably available for all who can learn it, and is common to them all, so the rules of wisdom are true and unchangeable. When you were asked about them one by one you replied that they were true and evident and open to the common contemplation of all who have the capacity to examine them.

Ev. I cannot doubt it. But I should very much like to know whether wisdom and numbers are contained within one class of things. You mentioned that they were linked together in the Holy Scriptures. Or is one of them derived from the other or contained within the other? For example, is number derived from wisdom or is it contained in wisdom? I should not dare to suggest that wisdom is derived from number or is contained in it. For I know many arithmeticians or accountants, or whatever they are to be called, who count perfectly and indeed marvellously, but somehow very few of them have wisdom, perhaps none. So wisdom strikes me as being far more worthy of respect than arithmetic.

Aug. You mention a matter which has often made me wonder, too. When I consider in my mind the unchangeable science of numbers and the recondite sanctuary or region, or whatever other name we are to give to the realm and abode of numbers, I find myself far removed from the corporeal sphere. I find possibly some vague idea but no words adequate to express it, and so in order to say something I return wearily to these numbers which are set before our eyes and call them by their wonted names. The same thing happens when I am thinking as carefully and intently as I can about wisdom. And so I greatly marvel that though wisdom and number are alike in being mysteriously and certainly true, and are linked together by the testimony of Scripture which I have quoted, I say I marvel greatly that number is so contemptible to the majority of people, while wisdom is precious. To be sure it may be because they are one and the same thing. On the other hand it is also written in Scripture of Wisdom that "she reaches from one end of the world to the other with full strength and ordereth things graciously" (Wisdom 8:1). Perhaps it is called number from its potency to reach with strength from end to end, and is properly called wisdom because it graciously ordereth all things. For both are functions of wisdom alone.

Wisdom has given numbers even to the smallest and most remote of things, and all bodies have their own numbers. But it has not given to bodies the power to be wise, nor even to all souls, but only to rational souls, in which, as it were, it has taken up its abode from whence it ordereth all things, even the smallest to which it has given numbers. Now we have no difficulty in judging corporeal things as things which belong to a lower order, and the numbers they bear stamped upon them we see are also lower than we are. Therefore we hold them in contempt. But when we begin to consider them from another angle we discover that they transcend our minds and abide unchangeably in the truth. And because few can be wise and many fools can count, people admire wisdom and despise numbers. But learned and studious men, the further they are removed from earthly corruption, behold the more clearly in the light of truth both numbers and wisdom, and hold both to be precious. By comparison with truth they prize neither gold nor silver nor the other things over which people strive,

indeed they even come to think of themselves as of little account.

There is no need to be surprised that people think little of numbers and value wisdom highly, because counting is easier than being wise. You see how they set a higher value on gold than on the light of a candle, compared with which gold is a ridiculous thing. But a vastly inferior thing is more highly honoured because any beggar can light himself a candle, and only a few possess gold. Far be it from me to suggest that compared with numbers wisdom is inferior. Both are the same thing, but wisdom requires an eye fit to see it. From one fire light and heat are felt as if they were "consubstantial," so to speak. They cannot be separated one from the other. And yet the heat reaches those things which are brought near to the fire, while the light is diffused far and wide. So the potency of intellect in which dwells wisdom causes things nearer to it to be warm, such as rational souls. Things further away, such as bodies, it does not affect with the warmth of wisdom, but it pours over them the light of numbers. Probably you will find that obscure, but no similitude drawn from visible things can be completely adapted to explain an invisible thing so as to be understood by everybody. Only take note of this which is sufficient for the problem we have in hand, and is clear enough to humbler kinds of mind such as ours. Though it cannot be made crystal-clear to us whether number is part of wisdom or is derived from wisdom or vice versa, or whether both names can be shown to designate one thing, it is at least evident that both are true and unchangeably true.

Accordingly, you will never deny that there is an unchangeable truth which contains everything that is unchangeably true. You will never be able to say that it belongs particularly to you or to me or to any man, for it is available and offers itself to be shared by all who discern things immutably true, as if it were some strange mysterious and yet public light. Who would say that what is available to be shared by all reasoning and intelligent persons can be the private property of any of them? You remember, I dare say, our recent discussion about the bodily senses. Those things with which we both make contact by means of our eyes or ears, colours and sounds which you and I see or hear together, do not belong to our actual eyes or ears, but are common to both of us so that we may alike perceive them. So you would never say that those things which you and I behold in common, each with his own mind, belong to the actual mind of either of us. You would not say that what the eyes of two persons see belongs to the eyes of one or the other of them. It is a third thing towards which both direct their regard.

Ev. That is most clear and true.

Aug. Do you, then, think that this truth of which we have already spoken so much and in which we behold so many things, is more excellent than our minds, or equal to our minds, or inferior? If it were inferior we should not use it as a standard of judgment, but should rather pass judgment on it, as we do on bodies which are inferior to our minds. For of them we often say not only that it is so or is not so, but that it *ought to be so* or not so. Similarly with our minds we know not only that it *is* thus or thus, but often also that it *ought to be* thus or thus. We judge of bodies when we say this is not so white as it ought to be, or not so square and so on. Of minds we say this one is not so capable as it ought to be, or it is not gentle enough or eager enough, according to our moral standard. All these judgments we make according to those inward rules of truth, which we discern in common. But no person passes any judgment on these rules. One may say the eternal *is* superior to the temporal, or seven and three *are* ten, but no one says these things *ought to be so.* Knowing simply that they are so one does not examine them with a view to their correction but rejoices to have discovered them. If, then, truth were the equal of our minds, it too would be mutable. Our minds sometimes see more sometimes less, and so confess their mutability. But truth abiding steadfast in itself neither advances when we see more, nor falls short when we see less. Abiding whole and uncorrupt it rejoices with its light those who turn to it, and punishes with blindness those who turn from it. We pass judgment on our minds in accordance with truth as our standard, while we cannot in any way pass judgment on truth. For we say of our mind it understands less than it ought, or it understands exactly as it ought; and a mind approaches the proper standard of intelligence as it is brought nearer to unchangeable truth, and becomes able to cleave to it. Hence if truth is neither inferior to nor equal to our mind it must be superior and more excellent.

I promised, if you remember, to show you some-thing superior to the human mind and reason. There it is, truth itself. Embrace it if you can. Enjoy it. Delight in the Lord and he will grant you the petitions of your heart. What do you ask for more than to be happy? And what is more happy than to enjoy unshakable, unchangeable truth which is excellent above all things? Men exclaim that they are happy when they embrace the beautiful bodies, deeply longed for, of their wives or even of harlots, and shall we doubt that we are happy in the embrace of truth? People exclaim that they are happy when with throats parched with heat they find a fountain flowing with pure water, or being hungry, find a copious meal all ready prepared, and shall we deny that we are happy when truth is our meat and drink? We are wont to hear the voices of people proclaiming that they are happy if they lie among roses or other flowers and enjoy scented ointments, and shall we hesitate to call ourselves happy when we are inspired by truth? Many place happiness in music, vocal and instrumental, flutes and strings. When they are without music they consider themselves unhappy; when they have it, they are transported with joy. Shall we, when the harmonious and creative silence of truth steals, so to speak, noiselessly over our minds, seek the happy life elsewhere, and fail to enjoy that which is ours now and securely. People delight in the sheen of gold and silver, gems and colours. They delight in the brightness and pleasantness of visible light as it appears in fire or in the sun, moon and stars. When no trouble or want comes to rob them of that pleasure they think themselves happy, and therefore wish to live for ever. Shall we fear to place the happy life in the light of truth?

Nay, since the chief good is recognized to be truth and is possessed when truth is possessed, and truth is wisdom, in wisdom let us discern the chief good and possess it and enjoy it. He is happy indeed who enjoys the chief good. Truth points out all the things that are truly good, and intelligent persons, according to their capacity, choose one or more of them in order to enjoy them. People, for example, find pleasure in looking at some object which they are glad to behold in the light of the sun. Those among them who are endowed with strong healthy eyes love to look at nothing better than at the sun itself, which sheds its light upon the other things which delight weaker eyes. So a strong and vigorous mental vision may behold many true and changeless things with certain reason, but directs its regard to the truth itself whereby all things are made clear, and, cleaving to the truth and forgetting, as it were, all other things, it enjoys them all together in the truth. Whatever is pleasant in other true things is pleasant also in truth itself.

Here in is our liberty, when we are subject to truth. And Truth is our God who liberates us from death, that is, from the condition of sin. For the Truth itself, speaking as Man to men, says to those who believe in him: "If ye abide in my word ye are truly my disciples, and ye shall know the truth and the truth shall make you free" (John 8:31-32). No soul enjoys a thing with liberty unless it also enjoys it with security.

But no one is secure in the possession of goods which he can lose against his will. Truth and wisdom no one can lose unwillingly. From them there can be no spatial separation. What is called separation from truth and wisdom is a perverse will which loves lower things. No one wills anything involuntarily. Here is something which we can all enjoy equally and in common. Here there is no straitness, no deficiency. She receives all her lovers, being grudging to none, shared by all in common but chaste to each. None says to another: "Stand back that I too may approach," or "Remove your hand that I too may touch." All cleave to the same wisdom. All are brought into contact with it. Nothing is consumed as in the case of food, and you cannot drink so as to prevent me from drinking too. From that common store you can convert nothing into your private possession. What you take remains unharmed for me to take also. I do not have to wait for you to breathe out what you have breathed in that I may then breathe it in. Nothing ever belongs to one person or to any group of people as a private possession. The whole is common to all at one and the same time.

Truth, therefore, is less like the things we touch or taste or smell, and more like the things we hear and see. For every word is heard as a whole by all who hear it and by each one at the same time. And every sight offered to the eyes is exactly the same for all who see it, and is seen by all at the same time. But though there is similarity there is also a great difference. A whole word is not spoken all at once. It is extended over a period of time, one syllable being pronounced first and another after it.

Every visible sight varies with the place from which it is seen, and is nowhere seen in its totality. And certainly all these things can be taken from us whether we will or no, and there are difficulties in the way of our enjoying them. Even supposing someone could sing sweetly for ever, those who were eager to hear him would come as rivals. They would get packed closely together, and the more there were of them they would strive for seats, each one anxious to get nearer to the singer. And when they heard him no one would be able to retain permanently what was heard. They would hear nothing but transient fugitive sounds. If I wanted to look at the sun and had the power to do so without being dazzled, nevertheless it would forsake me when it set, or it might be veiled in cloud, and for many other causes I might unwillingly lose my pleasure in seeing the sun. And supposing I had the power and pleasure of eternally seeing the light and hearing music, what great advantage would I have, seeing that even beasts could share it with me? But the beauty of truth and wisdom, so long as there is a persevering will to enjoy it, does not exclude those who come by any packed crowd of hearers. It does not pass with time or change with locality. It is not interrupted by night or shut off by shadow, and is not subject to the bodily senses. To all who turn to it from the whole world, and love it, it is close at hand, everlasting, bound to no particular spot, never deficient. Externally it suggests, internally it teaches. All who behold it, it changes for the better, and by none is it changed for the worse. No one judges it, and no one without it judges aright. Hence it is evident beyond a doubt that wisdom is better than our minds, for by it alone they are made individually wise, and are made judges, not of it, but by it of all other things whatever.

You admitted for your part that if I could show you something superior to our minds you would confess that it was God, provided nothing existed that was higher still. I accepted your admission and said it would be sufficient if I demonstrated that. If there is anything more excellent than wisdom, doubtless it, rather, is God. But if there is nothing more excellent, then truth itself is God. Whether there is or is not such a higher thing, you cannot deny that God exists, and this was the question set for our discussion. If you are influenced by what we have received in faith from the holy discipline of

Christ, that there is the Father of Wisdom, remember that we also received in faith that there is one equal to the eternal Father, namely Wisdom who is begotten of him. Hence there should be no further question, but we should accept it with unshakable faith. God exists and is the truest and fullest being. This I suppose we hold with undoubting faith. Now we attain it with a certain if tenuous form of knowledge. This is sufficient for the question in hand, so that we can go on to explain other pertinent questions; unless you have any opposition to offer.

Ev. I accept what you have said with incredible and inexpressible joy, and I declare it to be absolutely certain. I declare it in my mind where I hope to be heard by the truth itself, and where I hope to cleave to truth. For I confess that it is not only good, but the chief good and the beatific good.

VII.2. HENRY OF GHENT

IN THE FOLLOWING SELECTION HENRY DRAWS OUT AN IMPLICATION OF a position taken by thinkers of the middle ages concerning the universals called transcendentals: the one, the true, the good. In the Introduction to Topic VI it was observed that the universals Being, Truth, and Goodness are in effect identified with God. Unlike Plato's *Timaios,* which distinguishes the eternal Forms and the Demiurge, the Christian position places the Forms as paradigms and exemplars in the Divine Mind. Platonists thought that human knowledge requires a recollection of universals; this recollection, with the help of a teacher or a dialectician such as Socrates, otherwise depends only upon human reason and the use of sensory experience available to everyone. But if to recall a Form which supports or helps constitute knowledge as to the true nature of objects of perception is to apprehend an exemplar in the mind of God, it would seem that one would need to know God. Once this implication of the Christian position and its modification of Platonism becomes explicit, it would seem to be evident that all knowledge rests upon knowledge of God (something made explicit again in modern philosophy by Descartes).

The Christian position, articulated and made explicit in such ways, is an invitation to skepticism. First, the existence of God and the knowability of the content of God's mind must be proved, if anything else is capable of proof. And yet the history of skepticism shows how cunning the skeptic has proved to be, carrying the techniques of skepticism into the fabric of the theologians' and the philosophers' proofs for the existence of God.

In the following selection Henry tries to limit the skeptical thrust to *judgments* (what he calls "combining and dividing" are affirmative and negative judgments, respectively) about what a thing truly is. Mere apprehensions of things can be true in that what is apprehended is indeed truly something, even if we cannot be sure about what it truly is. The reason such judgments cannot be sure, at least not without special divine assistance, is that all such judgments require comparison with an "exemplar," but when we are left to our own natural capacities, the only exemplars available to us are the "species" or likenesses created through sense experience in our own minds, and these are far too changeable to be a basis for certainty. Only apprehension of the divine, immutable exemplars could provide that. To make his point here Henry deploys some classic skeptical arguments including a version of the trope which says we have no certain way of distinguishing dreams from waking experience. Henry's line will come in for some severe criticism from Duns Scotus in selection VII.4.1.

VII.2.1. Knowledge requires Divine Illumination of the Mind (*Summa Quaestionum Ordinarium*, art. 1, qu.2)

Is it possible for a human being to know something without divine illumination?

To this it must be said that, when it is a question of any items that are knowable in an order where always the subsequent is known by knowing the preceding, if we can get knowledge of the first in this ordering just by relying on what is merely natural and without any special divine illumination, we can likewise in the same way get knowledge of all the subsequent items. For if a human being by relying on what is merely natural without any special divine illumination can arrive at a knowledge of the first principles of a speculative science, likewise they can by relying on what is merely natural without any special illumination arrive at knowledge of all the conclusions that follow from the principles. For even though the knowledge of the principles is a sort of illumination in respect of the knowledge of the conclusions, still if a human being can, by relying on what is merely natural, arrive at that knowledge, we would not say that a special divine illumination was involved in knowing the conclusions through those principles.

But if, where it is a question of some knowable items ordered to each other, the first of these cannot be arrived at by a human being relying on what is merely natural but rather requires a special divine illumination, then in the same way none of those which come afterwards can [be arrived at by a human being relying on what is merely natural], for subsequent items are only known by way of the first.

Now, it is doubtless true that in some cases of knowable items the first cannot be apprehended or known by relying on what is merely natural but rather only by relying on a special divine illumination. So it is with those that are of themselves and unqualifiedly articles of the faith. Consequently, in their case we must unqualifiedly and absolutely grant that it is not possible for a human being to know anything by relying on what is merely natural but rather only by relying on a special divine illu-mination in virtue of which here below such matters are decided.

But some want to extend this mode of knowing to all knowable items. They say that no true item can be known by a human being by relying on what is merely natural without any special divine illumination being added to the natural one. They think Augustine held this view in all his books where he teaches that anyone sees a true item in the first truth, or in the eternal rules, of in the eternal light, as he says in *On the City of God XI, c.* 10: "Let it be said without absurdity that the soul is illumined by the light of simple divine wisdom, just as the corporeal air is illumined by a corporeal light."

Those who say this detract a great deal from the worth and perfection of the created intellect. For, since any natural thing complete in its own form must have some natural action or function of its own, it can by relying on what is merely natural attain by that action or function the good natural to it, as is obvious in all the other natural things. So says Damascene[1] in *Sentences I:* "Items which have different natures also have different functions, for it is impossible for a substance to be deprived of its natural function." Also in his book *On the Dual Nature and Will of Christ*, c.4: "It is impossible for a nature to exist apart from its own natural prop-erties, for example, living, reason, possessing a will. What does not reason is not a human being, for a human being that does not reason, neither well nor badly, is not something that gets to exist."

Since, then, to know and to think are most of all the intellect's own peculiar functions, as is said in *De Anima I*, no function at all can belong to the intellect by relying on what is merely natural if knowing cannot, and in that case the intellect would be the most inferior of creatures, which is absurd. As The Philosopher says in *On Heaven and Earth* II,[2] a thing that is good by a full and whole goodness does not need any function by which it is good, and it is the completely first cause from which every other thing obtains its goodness. These other things consequently must have a function of their own and by which they are moved in them-selves to share in the divine being of the first cause to the extent that they can. For everything desires

---

1 St. John Damascene, leader of the Christian community in 8th century Damascus.
2 Aristotle, *De Caelo* II, 12.

this, and whatever acts in virtue of the cause of that acts in virtue of its nature.

At this point someone might say in favor of the aforementioned view [that nothing is known without reliance on a special divine illumination] that it is certainly true that thinking of and knowing a true item is a function natural to and distinctive of the intellect and the human soul and through that the soul acquires its goodness, yet for that is required a special illumination on account of that act's excellence and worth, even though other things perform their actions by relying on what is merely natural. This fact about them is due to the imperfection of their actions, and consequently it is not absurd for one thing to require more for performing its more perfect action while another thing requires less for performing its less perfect action.

To say this is completely absurd and takes away a lot from the worth of the rational soul. For given that other, lesser things can by relying on what is merely natural perform a function that is appropriate to and in proportion to their nature, it is absurd to deny this to the rational soul, i.e. to claim that, although the rational soul would not be able, by relying on what is merely natural, to perform a highly excellent function that goes beyond its nature, it would not even be able to do this in respect of any function in agreement with and in proportion to its own nature. For it is totally absurd to claim that God made the human soul as one of the natural things but did not furnish it with the natural tools by which it could perform some natural function it necessarily has, while He did furnish these instruments to the other, lesser things. For God even much less than nature does anything in vain, or fails to provide to any thing what is necessary for it. Now the function natural to and distinctive of the human soul is nothing other than to know or apprehend. Therefore, it must absolutely be granted that a human being can by its soul and without any special divine illumination know or apprehend something, and it can do this by relying on what is merely natural. To say the opposite takes away a lot from the worth of the soul and of human nature.

However, when I say "by relying on what is merely natural," I do not mean to exclude the general influence of the first intelligence[3], which is the primary agent in every intellectual and cognitive action. Just as in the case of the first mover which is a cause of motion wherever we find any natural thing in motion, the general influence which assists in apprehension does not prevent its being the case that that apprehension can be said to come about by relying on what is merely natural. Since human beings in apprehending anything that they apprehend naturally have that influence assisting them, it has to be said that the apprehension they get through that influence of all the things subsequent to that influence is acquired by relying on what is merely natural.

Thus if we take "knowing" in a broad sense as applying to any sure apprehension of a thing, then it includes even sensory apprehension, as we said in the preceding question. So far as the senses and sure sensory cognition are concerned, it is clear that we must say without qualification and absolutely that knowing and apprehension by a sure sensory cognition occur, as was shown in the previous question, and this happens by relying on what is merely natural, which is what is relevant to this question. This is because the sensible objects of the senses merely by some natural necessity affect the senses and through these objects all subsequent sensible objects also affect both the exterior and interior senses by a natural necessity.

So far as the intellect and intellective cognition are concerned — it is this sort of cognition that is called "knowing" in the strict sense — we have to make a distinction. For even though Augustine in his 83 *Questions* says that nothing is known except what is true, still it is one thing to know concerning a creature what is true in it and something else to know its truth, and accordingly the cognition by which the thing is apprehended is one thing and that by which its truth is apprehended is something else. For every cognitive faculty that apprehends through its own cognition a thing as having existence on its own outside the apprehender apprehends what is true in it. But it does not by that apprehend the thing's truth. For even the senses of sub-human animals apprehend about a thing what is true in it, for example a true human, a true stick, a true stone, and especially the distinctive objects of these senses concerning which these senses are necessarily true. Nevertheless, they do not apprehend or have cognition of the truth of anything, and consequently they cannot judge what is in the thing by its truth; for example, of a human being that it is a true human being, or of a color that it is a true color.

Accordingly, a created thing can have two sorts of intellective cognition. One is that by which it knows or apprehends, by a simple thought exclusively that which is a thing; the other is that by which it knows and apprehends by a thought that combines or divides, the truth of that very thing. In the first sort of cognition our intellect completely follows the senses, and nothing is conceived in the intellect which was not previously in the senses. Consequently, such an intellect, insofar as it is of this sort, can certainly be true when it conceives or apprehends a thing just as it in fact is (in the same way as the senses which the thought follows from [can be true]) even though it does not conceive or think of the truth itself of the thing by intuiting in a sure judgement what the thing is, for example, that it is a true human being or a true color.

The explanation for this has two sides, one concerning the intellect itself, the other, the item that can be thought of. On the side of the intellect the explanation is that the intellect does not grasp truth in a non-complex thought but rather only by combining and separating, as The Philosopher says in *Metaphysics* VI and will get explained below. Thus, just as a sense is said to be true when it takes in a thing just as it in fact is but not by taking in its truth, so also a non-complex thought that derives from a true sense is called true in virtue of taking in the thing just as it in fact is, but not by taking in its truth. On the side of the item that can be thought of, the explanation is that the intention[4] of the thing by which it is that which it is is one thing, that by which it is called true is something else. This is so even though they are always together in any thing, and they are co-extensive since every being is true and vice versa. For, just as the first proposition in *On Causes*[5] says, the first creat-

ed thing is being, and consequently the first intention that the intellect can take in is the character of being which it can think of without thinking of any other intention applicable to a being. This is because the [intention of being] includes none of these others in itself, while it is included in all the others.

For even though the intention of being (which is in virtue of itself the object of the intellect) is thought of only under the aspect of a true item, this does not mean that being true by the fact that it is a character under which we think of being is an object of the intellect in the way being is. For the character of truth is the character of intelligibility found in anything whatsoever, but the object is a true being, or a true good, and likewise for the other intentions of things.

It is just because the intention of being is included in all the other intentions of things, both universals and particulars, (for what is not a being is nothing), that The Commentator [i.e. Averroes] holds the view about the first proposition from *On Causes* that being has a stronger adherence to the thing than do the other intentions which are in the thing. Now, after the intention of being, the universal intentions of one, true, and good are closest to the thing. They are this in different ways and in a certain order, because any thing that exists under the intention of being can be thought of in three ways. First, it can be thought of as having determinate being in its own nature by which, in virtue of its form, it is unseparated in itself while being separated from everything else; in this way the intention of one belongs to it. For any thing whatsoever is one by the fact that it is formally unseparated in itself and is separated from anything else. As The Philosopher says in *Metaphysics* III, something is one which exists all alone by itself.

Secondly, to the extent that its own being means that it represents an exemplar of what it is, the intention of true belongs to it, for anything is true just to the extent that it contains in itself its representing its exemplar.

Thirdly, to the extent it has an end for which it is,

---

4 The term "intention" refers to what is meant by some expression and is an object of thought. The intention itself, however, can be something that exists independently of being thought of. Here it means the character the thing has which renders it what it is. See glossary entry for 'intention.'

5 A treatise commonly taken in the middle ages to be by Aristotle but is in fact by the 5th-century C.E. neo-Platonist Proclus.

the intention of good belongs to it, for anything is good just to the extent that it relates to an end which is good.

Therefore, since true means an intention of a thing relating it to its exemplar, it is not a primary intention but rather a secondary one, while being means a primary and absolute intention of the thing. Consequently, that which in reality is a being and is true can certainly be apprehended by the intellect without its apprehending the thing's intention of truth, for the intention of truth in a thing cannot be apprehended except by apprehending its conformity to its exemplar. The intention of being, on the other hand, is apprehended in the absolute thing without involving any real relation. However, in the second sort of cognition where the truth of the thing itself is known or apprehended, and without which perfect human cognition of the thing does not exist, the cognition and judgment of the intellect completely surpasses the cognition and judgment of the senses, because, as we said, the intellect apprehends the truth of a thing only by combining and separating, and this the senses are unable to do. Consequently, such an intellect can apprehend the thing in a way the senses cannot. Neither can the act of intellect which is a thought of what is non-complex do this, i.e. it cannot apprehend by a sure judgment that it is such and such in the real truth of things, for example that it is a true human being or true color and the like. The question can now be restated as about this [second] way of knowing and apprehending something with the intellect by which the truth of the thing is known (which is knowing in the strict sense) as follows: Can a human being by relying on what is merely natural know something without any special divine illumination?

When the question is put this way it must be said that the truth of a thing can only be apprehended by a cognition of the conformity of the thing apprehended to its own exemplar, because, as Augustine says in *On True Religion:* "True items are true just to the extent that they are similar to the one principal [true item]." Also Anselm in *On Truth* says: "Truth is the conformity of the thing to

its own truest exemplar." And in the same book: "What truly is is to the extent that it is what is there."

Secondly, [it must be said] that there are two sorts of exemplars of a thing, and the truth of a thing gets apprehended by a human in two ways depending on which sort is involved. This accords with Plato in the first chapter of the *Timaios* where he speaks of two sorts of exemplar, one made and worked on, one everlasting and immutable. The first sort of exemplar of a thing is its universal species[6] existing in the soul, through which the soul acquires cognition of all the items that exemplar stands for, and it is caused by the thing. The second exemplar is the divine art that contains the ideal characters of all things. About this second sort Plato says that god set up the world in just the way an artisan makes a house on the basis of an exemplar of art in his mind; but he does not say this about the first sort.

When human beings look at the first sort of exemplar, we have to realize that they can look at it in two ways: (1) as at an apprehended object depicted outside the apprehender, for example by looking at the image of a human drawn on a wall for the purpose of apprehending a human being; (2) as at a means of apprehending depicted in the apprehender in the way that a species of sensible items is depicted in the sense and a species of items that can be thought of in the intellect. In the first way it is impossible to apprehend the truth of a thing by looking at its exemplar; rather all that one gets in an imaginary apprehension of the sort that the person's faculty of imagination might have by chance formed for them. This is the sense in which a person would be astonished if a person whom they had never seen but whose image they have were to meet them, as Augustine says in *On the Trinity* VIII, ch.2.[7] Also, by that imaginary apprehension taken from the drawn image, as long as the person whose image it was had a name, it would be possible to arrive at an estimative judgment about the person whose image it was, if that person were encountered, and then, first, to apprehend the thing's truth from seeing the thing itself in its own

---

6 A species here is a likeness of something. This use of the term "species" should not be confused with that in which it means a class of things that falls under some genus. See glossary entry for "species."

7 Actually ch.5.

distinctive form and next to judge from that apprehension whether the image of it was a true image corresponding to it. This is what is meant when we read that queen Candace had near her an image depicting Alexander before she ever saw him, and she knew him immediately when she did see him, even though he was pretending to be someone else.

In the second way, i.e. by looking at an exemplar taken from the thing itself (for example, at a means of apprehending residing in the apprehender himself), it is certainly possible for the truth of the thing itself in some way to be apprehended by forming a concept in the mind of the thing that conforms to that exemplar. It is in this way that Aristotle posited that knowledge of things and cognition of truth is acquired by humans relying on what is merely natural and that such an exemplar of natural, changeable things is acquired from the things through the sense serving as the first principle of the arts and sciences, as he says at the beginning of the *Metaphysics:* "Now, an art comes to be when from many items experienced by the mind we arrive at a single universal notion for similar things." See *Posterior Analytics* II:[8] "Out of the senses clearly we get memory, and from memory repeated many times, experience, and from experience the universal existing in the soul as a one over and above the many, which is the beginning of art and science." Augustine agrees with this when in *On the Trinity XI*, ch.3, he says: "Once the species of the body which is sensed by the bodily senses is taken away, there remains in memory a likeness of it and with this the will again changes the faculty of mind so that it is formed inside by the likeness, just as by a body a sensible object was formed on the outside." Also, as he says in book VIII, ch.5: "We think of the things we do not see through the general or specific cognitions of things which we are either naturally born with or have gathered from experience." Thus we know of anything we encounter whether it is an animal or not by the universal cognition we have acquired from different species of animals, and we know of anything we encounter whether it is an ass or not by the specific cognition of ass.

What is utterly impossible, however, is that by this sort of exemplar which we acquire in ourselves we have a completely sure and infallible knowledge of truth. For this there are three reasons. The first concerns the thing from which an exemplar of this sort is abstracted. The second concerns the soul in which an exemplar of this sort is received. The third concerns the exemplar itself, which comes from the thing and is received in the soul.

The first reason is that such an exemplar necessarily has some aspect of changeability from the fact that it is abstracted from a changeable thing. It is on these grounds that The Philosopher, because natural things are more changeable than mathematical ones, claims that the mathematical sciences have more certainty than do the natural sciences through their universal species, and this is only because of the changeability of the species of them existing in the soul. Augustine treats this way what he takes to be the cause of uncertainty in the sciences of natural and sensible things in his *83 Questions, qu.9*, where he says that genuine truth is not to be sought from the bodily senses, and that it is very much in the interests of our salvation to be warned to turn away from this world and zealously to turn toward God in the truth which is understood and grasped in the mind within, which truth always persists as the same nature.

The second reason is that the human soul, being changeable and receptive of error cannot by anything that has a changeability equal to or greater than its own be set right so as not to fall into error but rather to persist in the correctness of truth. Every exemplar, however, which the soul receives from natural things, since it is an inferior grade of nature to the soul, necessarily has a changeability equal to or greater than the soul's. Therefore, this exemplar cannot set the soul right so that it persists in infallible truth. This is the argument Augustine uses in *On True Religion*, where he proves that the immutable truth by which the soul has sure knowledge is above the soul in this way: Since the law of all arts is completely immutable while the human mind which we grant can see such a law is able to undergo change and error, it is clear enough that there is above our mind a law which is called truth and which alone suffices for setting our changeable and wayward mind right on the path of infallible cognition. Our mind does not judge this law but rather through it judges of everything else, for what is inferior to the mind is what the mind judges rather than what it uses to judge something else, as he explains in the same place.

The third reason is that an exemplar of this sort, since it is an intention and a sensible species of the thing abstracted from mental images, has a likeness to the false as well as to the true in such a way that it itself does not enable one to determine which it is. For in the case of images of sensible things that we have in sleep or in delirium we judge the images to be the things themselves and when awake and healthy we also make judgments about the things themselves. But genuine truth is not perceived unless it can be distinguished from what is false. Therefore, it is impossible to get sure knowledge and sure cognition of the truth by relying on such an exemplar; and, consequently, if it is to acquire sure knowledge of the truth, the mind must turn away from the senses and sensible things, and from all intentions no matter how universal and abstracted away from sensible things they are, and turn toward the unchangeable truth that exists above the mind where there is no image of what is false from which that truth cannot be distinguished, as Augustine says in 83 *Questions,* where he lays out this argument.

Therefore, genuine truth, as was said, can be grasped only by reference to an eternal exemplar. But we should note that genuine truth can be known by looking on this exemplar in two ways: in one way by looking on it as an apprehended object exemplified in the seeing itself, because it certainly tests the image which contemplates the exemplar, as Augustine says in *Against the Academics* III, ch.30; in another way by looking on that exemplar as a mere means of knowing. In the first way we know that an image of Hercules is a true image of him by seeing Hercules, and in noticing the correspondence of the image to the exemplar, we know that it is true image of it. In this way the truth of any creature made by reference to the exemplar is apprehended as perfectly as possible once its exemplar is seen. Consequently, since every creature is an image of a divine exemplar, the truth of what any

creature is is apprehended as truly and perfectly as possible by seeing directly the divine essence. Augustine says as much in *On the City of God* XI: "The holy angels through the very presence of unchangeable truth know the creature itself better in that way (as in the art by which it has been made) than they know those creatures in themselves."

It follows that not only is an image apt to be apprehended through the exemplar as from something that is prior to it,[9] but also, conversely, the exemplar is apt to be apprehended through the image as from something subsequent to it. Thus Augustine teaches us through creatures what sort of art there is of a divine exemplar, when he says in *On Job* II "Humans notice a wonderful work of art and wonder at the skill of the artist. They are stunned by what they see and love what they do not see. If, then, human skill gets praised on account of some great work of art, you can see what sort of skill God has, i.e. the Word of God. Observe this work of art which is the world; see what the Word has made and know what that Word is like."

From the fact that a knowledge of all creatures, gathered from this world, functioning as a single perfect image of that divine art, which is so much more perfect, can exist in creatures, philosophers have claimed that there can be a perfect apprehension of God to the extent that this is possible by relying on what is merely natural, as we will see below. A human being, however, cannot by relying on what is merely natural with no special illumination attain to such a cognition of a divine exemplar, nor can a human being attain that in this life by the general light of grace.[10]

But given that genuine truth may be known by looking on the divine exemplar as a means of knowing, we see that Plato claimed that every truth is known in this way by looking at the eternal exemplar. Accordingly, Augustine, bringing in here the authority of Cicero, says in his letter to Disoscorus: "Observe how Cicero shows very clearly in many ways that Plato possessed a wisdom that was not human but rather obviously divine." From this we can see that it is in a sense human to have established on the basis, to be sure, of this wisdom

---

9 In Latin, *a priori* and *a posteriori,* where what is prior is that whose existence is the cause of or a prerequisite for what is subsequent.

10 I.e., the grace which God gives to anyone whom He wills to save.

that is completely unchangeable and always stays the same truth, the end of the good, the causes of things, and a trust in reasoning, and that the Platonists were opposed to the Epicureans and Stoics who tried to establish the end of the good, the causes of things, and a trust in reasoning, on the basis of the nature of the body or the soul.

Nevertheless, errors about morals, about the nature of things, and about the way of investigating truth had persisted right up into Christian times, which errors we now see have ceased. From this we can see that even the Platonist philosophers themselves, having changed a few things which Christian learning disproved, had to bow their righteous necks to the single invincible king, Christ, who commanded, and what they used to fear to profess was believed.

Augustine followed Plato's view on this matter when at the end of *Against the Academics* he says: "No one doubts that we were driven to learning by the twin forces of authority and reason. Consequently, it is certain that I shall never depart from the authority of Christ, for I find no authority more compelling. But what must be pursued by highly subtle reasoning, as long as it is not opposed to our holy books, I am confident is something for me to inquire into, for I am the sort of person who, with Plato, desires to apprehend what is true not by belief alone but also by understanding." This is a view which he holds in all his books and which we hold as well when we say that no one can have any sure and infallible cognition of genuine truth without looking to the exemplar of the uncreated light and truth.

VII.3. SIGER OF BRABANT

SIGER OF BRABANT TAUGHT IN PARIS BUT, UNLIKE MANY OF HIS famous contemporaries, he remained within the Faculty of Arts. He did not become a theologian and may, perhaps without exaggeration, be said to be a medieval version of a modern professor of philosophy who separates philosophy from religion. His point of departure is the texts of Aristotle understood in the neo-Platonic framework of his period. Within that framework he had much more to fear from religious dogmatism than from a skepticism which had not yet taken shape. As far as ordinary perceptual judgments go, the mind can rest content and find a beginning in ordinary sense experience. As Siger argues below, it is not necessary for us first to answer sophistical arguments in order to ground sense judgments.

VII.3.1. Some Judgments are to be trusted (Book IV, Question 22, *Quaestiones in Metaphysicam*)

Whether, among contrary judgments, one is more to be trusted than another.

I answer yes. A judgment of any given sense is not to be trusted equally. For one should not equally trust sight concerning sweetness, if one judges by color, as one would trust taste; one would accordingly dismiss a judgment based on sight and follow a judgment based on taste. One should not even equally trust sight concerning its proper object and concerning some subject of it.[1]

One should similarly not trust states of sleeping and of being awake. Nor should magnitudes be believed to be such as they are judged to be. Nor should things be judged or believed to be as they are imagined to be. And again, one should not equally trust a healthy and an unhealthy sense.

If it is asked why it is certain that things are more apt to be as one sense judges than as another, it should be said: that something is sweet and is not qualified in a contrary way, is not known for any other reason than that it is sensed by taste not to be sour. By this means it is to be believed, not by any other, that the object is sweet. It follows that if someone seeks to know that this is sweet through some other means than through sense, he is asking for a reason at the beginning of reason. But a reason is not to be sought at the beginning of reason; such

a reason cannot accept anything determinately true by certitude. For, unless there is something primary and known *per se* which is believed because it is sensed as such, nothing after is able to be certain.

It follows that something else is not to be sought among all cognitions which verifies that cognition; it is rather necessary to stop with first propositions which are known through themselves. But for knowing these propositions an understanding of their terms is required and here cognition finally turns to sense. What is sensed, because it is sensed, is known and not through anything else. To that which is said to be known through itself someone is able to say verbally that there is an opposite but cannot mentally sense it. The mind may well hesitate concerning sophistical arguments, namely concerning their resolution, but still no one hesitates as to whether that is white which looks white, even though the mind can hesitate concerning some subject as to whether what looks white is snow or flour. Not only does a human being not doubt that what he sees as white he does see as white; but it is also the case that what a human being sees as white he does not doubt is white, whatever that thing is, whether snow or flour; concerning that question he may well err and doubt. But insofar as someone does not doubt one should not seek something else offering verification.

Indeed, if someone seeks to understand by reason that something is sweet just as it is sensed, either reason will not be efficacious or, if it is, it will pro-

---

1 Siger follows the teaching of Aristotle's *On the Soul* and distinguishes a proper object of a sense (or an object peculiar to the sense) – colour, for example, and something coloured, snow.

ceed from something such that it will be known to be such because it is sensed to be such.

It follows that something will be judged to be sweet because it is warm as well as moist or of the same temperature, and something will be known to be warm or moist by sense. And if there is a sense contrary to that sense, the opposing sense is not to be trusted. So concerning the sweet one would set aside a judgment of sight and follow one of taste. So it is not true that something appears to one just as it appears to another [sense] with respect to contrary judgments; for something sweet does not appear to the sense of sight just as something sour appears to the sense of taste. For then one would not dismiss a judgment of sight when he is tasting something if he believed both equally. Nor is every judgment of sense uncertain, although a sense does not always judge in the same way concerning some one sensible. But about its own sensible object the judgment of a sense is always the same, and thus some judgements of sense are certain.

Here there seems to be an objection: unhealthy taste which judges something to be sour, when it is healthy, judges it to be sweet.

It is true that taste can judge a subject of sweet in different ways, as for example wine: either because of a change of the subject of sweet itself, as of the wine, or because of a change in the body of the person tasting or because of a different disposition of the medium. But concerning sweetness, when there has been a sense or sensation of sweetness, the sense never changes its judgment. For as *De anima* II says,[2] a sense senses its object and its sensation, and even if there can be deception in the first case, there nevertheless cannot be any in the second; indeed just how someone senses so he takes himself to sense, and as something appears to him so he takes himself to sense. It is in this way that some people[3] explicate Aristotle: they say that the sense concerned with sweetness does not change its judgment so that it does not judge the thing to be such as it senses it to be. But from this it seems that a sense always makes the same judgment concerning sweetness. And for this to be true, namely that there is always the same judgment, it is necessary that a sense always judges

as sweetness is and not as it appears.

To this point it should be said that when unhealthy taste senses something sweet, such as wine, but judges that it is sour, the judgment of taste has not been made from the sweet thing but from sourness which prevails. So it does not change its judgment about sweetness when there has been sweetness but when taste has a tongue infected with sourness, there is no sense of sweetness but rather of sourness.

In a similar way one opinion is more to be trusted than another among contrary opinions; for example that opinion is more to be trusted which has been taken from things known *per se* to the intellect and from sensibles with respect to which a judgment of sense arises without error. (Science is understood at the moment as falling under the notion of opinion.) Hence it is true that what the wise take for granted is more to be trusted. But who is wise is not something known *per se*, given that the wise are the measure of things; still things are rather the measure of the wise. For it is more certain that we take the measure of someone as wise than that we measure the thing itself from the judgment of the wise. So if it is not known whether someone is wise unless through the fact that he judges concerning things as they are, then it is one and the same thing to judge someone to be wise as to judge just how things are. And just as many kinds of error arise concerning things by trusting popular testimony, so too there is error in believing that someone is wise if this is believed by means of popular testimony. In this way, by following popular testimony sophists are regarded as wise men and in fact are not only sophists. For some sophists are in fact not sophists since they are are ignorant of the sophistical art.

So when it is said that one's opinion appears just as much to be the case to that person as someone else's opinion appears to them to be the case, this is not true. For he who has an opinion inferred from probabilities, if he is able to have his opinion inferred from things known *per se*, dismisses the earlier opinion – something that would not happen if he equally believed both. So by means of demonstration[4] one is able to return to science after false statements.

---

2 Aristotle, *De anima*, II, 6(418a11ff).
3 Cf. Thomas Aquinas, *On the Metaphysics* IV, lect. 14, no. 703.
4 See the glossary entry for 'demonstration.'

VII.4. JOHN DUNS SCOTUS

SCOTUS HERE ARGUES THAT HENRY OF GHENT'S VIEW (see **VII.2.1.**) leads to the skepticism of the Academics; if we adopt Henry's view of what is required for knowledge of truth, not even divine illumination will be able to secure it for us. He then proceeds to show how without any special divine assistance our minds can know four classes of truths. (Like all the theologians of his day Scotus would have granted that all natural functionings require the kind of general divine cooperation which maintains the natural order in existence.) One of these classes consists of self-evident principles, i.e. the axioms on which all scientific knowledge ultimately rests. Scotus explains (pp. 478-479) that the terms of such propositions necessarily and evidently relate to each other so as to make the proposition immutably true and known to anyone grasping the terms. (Compare this discussion with selection **I.9.4.**)

Another class consists of propositions about what is the natural cause of what and involves a certain kind of inductive reasoning based on the experience of one sort of thing causing another in various circumstances. A third class are the propositions about our own acts, which Augustine emphasized in selection **VII.1.2.** and many other places. The final class is made up of propositions about the particulars which we seem to perceive with our senses. Scotus even tries to disarm the notorious skeptical trope about not being sure whether we are dreaming or awake (pp. 484-485).

Although in all this Scotus defends our natural capacity for genuine knowledge, he retains the Augustinian theory of divine exemplars as the ultimate source for all knowledge. Even though we do not in this life directly apprehend the divine mind, we do have apprehension of some of the natures which the divine mind has originally apprehended, and these natures move our minds in virtue of that divine intellect which gives those natures their intelligible being (pp. 489-490). None of this, however, is meant to deny that our access to these natures is, as Aristotle claimed, by abstraction from sensible phantasms carried out by our "active intellects" so as to produce intelligible species in our "passive intellects"; Scotus has in this way cleverly welded Christianized Platonism to the epistemology of Aristotle's *De Anima*.

VII.4.1. Refutation of Henry and of Skepticism generally (*Ordinatio* I, dist.3, pt.1, qu.4)

Finally, on the subject of what we can know, I ask whether any sure and genuine truth can be known by the intellect of a wayfarer[1] without the special illumination of the uncreated light.

I argue that no such truth can be known:

From [St. Augustine's] *On the Trinity* IX, c. 6 or 15:[2] "But we gaze upon the indestructible truth by reason of which we may define perfectly what the mind of a human being ought to be according to

---

1 A wayfarer is any person in the present state of life where the effects of original sin must be taken into account.
2 PL 42, 966.

the eternal types." And again, ch.15:[3] "When we accept or reject something correctly, our incontestable conviction arises from other immutable rules above our minds." And again in c.17:[4] "Grasping by simple intelligence the unspeakably beautiful art that lies beyond the penetration of the mind...." And in the same work, c.8 or 18: "In the eternal truth from which all temporal things are made we look on the form, and hence we have within us like a Word the cognition of what we have conceived."

Also in bk. XII, c.2:[5] "But it pertains to higher reason to judge of these corporeal things according to eternal types."

Also in this same book XII, c.14 or 32:[6] "And not only are there immutable types for sensible things positioned in space...." That Augustine here is speaking of the eternal types that are really in God is proved by the fact that he says in the same passage that "few manage to attain to these," but he would not say this if he were speaking of first principles, since the latter are not something few manage to attain but rather something many attain, inasmuch as first principles are common and known to all.

Also in bk. XIV, c.15 or 34,[7] speaking of the unjust human being who "correctly praises and condemns many things found in the customs of mankind," he asks: "By what rules do they judge...?" And at the end he asks: "Where are those rules written except in that book of light...?" This "book of light" is the divine intellect. Therefore, he intends to say that it is in this light that the unjust person sees what justice demands be done. And that person sees this in something or by something impressed on them by this light, just as Augustine says in this same place: "...whence every just law is transferred to the hearts of humans not by passing from one place to another, but by being impressed, as it were, even as the image is transferred from the ring to the wax without leaving the ring." Therefore, we see in that light

by which justice is imprinted on human hearts. Now, this light is the Uncreated Light.

Also in his *Confessions* XII:[8] "If both of us see the truth, you do not see it in me, nor do I see it in you, but both of us see it in that immutable truth which is above the mind." And there are many other places where Augustine's authoritative statements could be found to support this conclusion.

In opposition to this:

Romans 1: "By the creature which is the world the invisible things of God are seen, inasmuch as they are understood through the things which have been made." The "invisible things of God" are these eternal types; therefore, they are apprehended through creatures; therefore, even before these eternal types are seen, we have sure cognition of creatures.

[The opinion of Henry of Ghent:]

One opinion regarding this question maintains that a natural order exists among general notions. Let us discuss two of these which are relevant here, viz. the intention of being and the intention of true.

That being is the first of these intentions is proved from the fourth proposition of *On Causes*[9]: "The first of created things is being." Also in the comment on the first proposition: "Being is of stronger adherence." The reason for this is that entity is something absolute, whereas truth implies a relation to an exemplar. From this it follows that a being can be apprehended under the character of entity without being apprehended under the character of truth. Consequently, that which is true can be known before its truth is known.

Facts about the mind provide a further proof. A being can be grasped by a non-complex thought of it, and in that case the thing which is true is grasped. But the character of truth is grasped only by a thought that combines or separates. Non-complex

3 *Ibid.*
4 PL 42, 967.
5 PL 42, 999.
6 PL 42, 1010.
7 PL 42, 1052.
8 c.25; PL 32, 840.
9 A book by Proclus, the neo-Platonic philosopher of the 5th century C.E.

thought precedes combining and separating.

Now, if we ask about our cognition of a being, i.e. of that which is true, they tell us that the intellect by relying on what is merely natural can think of the true in this sense. The proof is this: It is absurd that a nature exist deprived of its own distinctive function, as Damascene[10] says. The more perfect the nature in question the more absurd it is, as The Philosopher says in *On the Heaven and the Earth* II,[11] where he remarks that it would be a great absurdity for the stars to have the power of progressive movement and still lack the means necessary for such movement. Therefore, since the distinctive operation of the intellect is to know the true, it seems absurd that nature would not have endowed the intellect with what suffices for this function.

But as for cognition of the truth, they tell us that there are two exemplars, one created, the other uncreated. This is in accord with Plato, who mentions in the *Timaios* one exemplar that is made, i.e. created, and one that is not made, i.e. uncreated. The created exemplar is the species[12] of the universal caused by the thing; the uncreated exemplar is the idea in the divine mind. Consequently there are two sorts of conformity to an exemplar and two sorts of truth. One is the conformity to the created exemplar, and it was in this sense that Aristotle maintained that the truths of things are known through their conformity to the intelligible species. Augustine, also, seems to hold this view in *On the Trinity* VIII, c.7,[13] where he maintains that we possess general and specific cognition of things, gathered from sensible items, and in virtue of this we judge of anything we happen to encounter that it is such and such.

But it seems wholly impossible that such an acquired exemplar should give us infallible and completely sure cognition of a thing. The advocates of this opinion give three reasons for such a conclusion. The first is based on the thing from which the exemplar is abstracted; the second, on the subject in which the exemplar exists; and the third, on the exemplar itself.

The first argument runs as follows: The object from which the exemplar is abstracted is itself mutable; therefore, it cannot be the cause of something unchangeable. But it is only in virtue of some immutable character that someone can have sure knowledge of something as truth. An exemplar such as this, then, provides no such knowledge. They claim this to be Augustine's argument in his *83 Questions*, qu.9,[14] where he tells us not to look for truth from the senses because what the senses perceive constantly undergoes change.

The second argument runs as follows: Of itself the soul is changeable and subject to error. Now something which is even more changeable than the soul itself cannot put the soul right or rule it in such a way that it does not err. But the exemplar which exists in the soul is even more mutable than the soul itself. Consequently, such an exemplar does not rule the soul so perfectly that it makes no mistakes. Some special higher influence, then, is required. This, they say, is the argument Augustine uses in *On True Religion*: "The law of all arts...."

The third argument is that only those possess sure and infallible cognition of truth who have that whereby they can distinguish the true from what is like the true, for if they are unable to distinguish the true from the false or from what is like the true, they can wonder whether or not they have made a mistake. Now the true cannot be distinguished from what is like the true by means of the aforementioned exemplar. Therefore, etc.

Proof of the minor: Such a species can either represent itself as a species or, as happens in dreams, present itself as an object. In the latter case, we have falsity; in the former, truth. There is nothing about such a species, then, that suffices to distinguish the case in which it represents itself as itself from the case in which it represents itself as an object, and thus there is nothing sufficient to dis-

---

10 St. John Damascene, leader of the Christian community in Damascus in the 8th century.
11 *De Caelo*, c.8, 290a 29-35.
12 See glossary entry for 'species.'
13 Actually c.4; PL 42, 952.
14 PL 40, 13.

tinguish the true from the false.

From all this they conclude that if human beings can know the infallible truth and possess sure knowledge, this is not because they look on an exemplar derived from the thing by way of the senses, no matter how much such an exemplar may be purified and universalized. Rather it is necessary that they look toward the uncreated exemplar. The way they claim this takes place is the following: God does not have the character of an exemplar in the sense that He is an object known and by looking at Him we can know genuine truth. For God is known only under some general attribute. But God is a means for knowing in as much as He is the pure exemplar and distinctive type for a created essence.

The following example is used to explain how God can be a means for knowing yet not be known: Some sunlight is reflected while other rays come directly from their source. And even though the sun is a means for seeing what is seen in reflected rays, the sun itself is not seen. On the other hand, in the case of what is seen in the rays coming directly from their source, the sun is there both the means of apprehending and what is apprehended. In similar fashion, then, when the Uncreated Light illumines the intellect directly, as it were, this light as seen is the means for seeing the other things in it. In the present state of life, however, this Uncreated Light illumines our intellect indirectly, as it were. Consequently, though unseen itself, it is the means by which our intellect sees.

Now they claim that the uncreated exemplar is related to the act of vision in three ways, viz. as a stimulating light, as a transforming species, and as the character or exemplar which produced a like form [in the intellect]. From this they conclude that a special influence is required. For just as we do not naturally see this essence in itself, neither do we naturally see it as the exemplar of any essence. As Augustine says in *On Seeing God*:[15] It is in his power to be seen. "If He wills it, He is seen; if He does not will it, He is not seen."

Finally, they add that perfect cognition of truth results when the two exemplar species concur in the mind, viz. the created exemplar which inheres in the soul and the uncreated exemplar which has slipped into our mind as illuminating it. The mind conceives the word of perfect truth from those two species combined to form a single means for understanding the thing of which it is [the word].

[Refutation of Henry's opinion and solution of the question:]

(First, I argue against the opinion in itself; secondly, I argue against the basic arguments used to support it or turn them to my advantage. Under the first falls the fourth article, which is a sort of *ad hominem* argument, as well as the third article, which deals with what is really the case. The second includes the first article given here as well as the third and the sixth. The fifth article, then, is the solution to the question.)[16]

Against this opinion in the first [article] I show that these arguments are not a basis for any true opinion, nor are they in accord with the mind of Augustine. Instead they lead to the view of the Academics[17]. In the second [article] I show how the view of the Academics, which seems to follow from these arguments, is false. In the third I answer these arguments insofar as they are inconclusive. In the fourth I argue against the conlusion of this opinion [of Henry's]. In the fifth I solve the question. In the sixth I show how these arguments, insofar as they are Augustine's, prove what Augustine intended to prove rather than what they are here used to prove.

[Article 1: Refutation of the basic arguments Henry uses:]

First, these arguments seem to imply the impossibility of any sure natural cognition. Consider the first. If an object is continually changing, we can have no certitude about it as having the character of immutability. In fact, in that case we cannot have certitude in any light, for there can be no certitude when an object is known in some way other than the way in which it exists. Therefore, there is no

---

15 PL 33, 603.

16 Note found in one ms. and ascribed to Scotus.

17 I.e. the view of the skeptical philosophers, for example Carneades (214 - 129 B.C.E.), who dominated the Academy in the 2nd century B.C.E.

certitude in knowing a changeable thing as unchangeable.

It is also clear that the antecedent of this argument is false, viz. that the items the senses can perceive are continually changing. This is the opinion attributed to Heraclitus[18] in *Metaphysics* IV.[19]

Likewise, if the mutability of the exemplar in our soul makes certitude impossible, then it follows that nothing in the soul could prevent it from erring, for everything existing in such a subject is mutable, even the act of thinking itself. ([Note, perhaps not by Scotus himself:] It follows further that, inasmuch as the act of thinking is even more mutable than the soul in which it exists, it will never be true nor contain truth.)

Likewise, according to this opinion, the created species which inheres in the soul concurs with the species that slips in. But no certitude is possible where something incompatible with certitude concurs. For just as we can infer only a contingent proposition from a necessary and contingent proposition combined, so also a concurrence of what is certain and what is uncertain does not produce sure knowledge.

The same reasoning clearly applies to the third argument. For if the species abstracted from the thing is a concurrent factor in all cognition, and if we cannot judge when such a species represents itself as such and when it represents itself as object, then it makes no difference what concurs with such a species. We shall never have a sure basis for distinguishing the true from what is like the true. These arguments, then, seem to lead to the conclusion that all is uncertain, i.e. the opinion of the Academics.

That such a conclusion is not what Augustine intended I prove from his *Soliloquies* II:[20] "Everyone concedes without any doubt that the proofs of the sciences are most true." Also Boethius says in *De*

hebdomadibus:[21] "A common conception of the mind is what anyone takes to be certain once they have heard it." And The Philosopher in *Metaphysics* II:[22] "First principles are, like the doors to a house, known to everyone, for just as the doors are obvious even though the inside of the house remains hidden, so first principles are known to all."

On the basis of these three authoritative texts the following argument is constructed: Whatever belongs to all the members of a given species[23] is entailed by the specific nature itself. Therefore, since anyone has infallible certitude about the first principles, and further anyone naturally finds the form of the perfect syllogism valid (see *Prior Analytics* I[24]), and moreover the knowledge of the conclusions depends solely upon the obviousness of the first principles and of the syllogistic inference, it follows that anyone can know naturally any conclusion demonstrable from self-evident principles.

Secondly, it is clear that Augustine concedes the certitude of those things known through sense experience. Hence he say in *On the Trinity* XV, c.12 or 32:[25] "Far be it from us to doubt about those things which we learn to be true through our bodily senses, for through these we learn about the heavens, the earth, the sea and all that are in them." If then we are not deceived nor in doubt about the truth of these things, as is obvious, we are sure about things known through the senses; for where doubt and deception are excluded, there we have certitude.

Thirdly, it is clear that in the same place (c.12 or 31) Augustine also concedes that we have certitude regarding our own acts: "A person is alive whether they are asleep or awake, for it is a part of living also to sleep and to see in dreams." Second acts of the soul are always conscious, but one need not always be conscious of the readiness to have these, i.e. of the first acts.[26]

---

18 Heraclitus was one of the earliest Greek cosmologists. He lived in Ephesus in the late 6th century B.C.E.
19 c.5 1010a7-11.
20 Actually I, ch.8; PL32, 877.
21 PL 64, 1311.
22 c.1, 993b 4-5.
23 See glossary entry for 'species/genus.'
24 c.1, 24b 22-24.
25 PL 42, 1075.
26 See Aristotle, *De anima* II, c.5. Scotus's point here is that Augustine makes it clear that the living he is talking about is something one is conscious of engaging in. See glossary entry for 'first/second actuality.'

Augustine says in the same place: "If anyone should say, 'I know that I know or that I live,' that person cannot be in error, no matter how often they reflect back on this first knowledge [i.e. by saying 'I know that I know,' 'I know that I know that I know' and so on]." "And in the same place: "If one says, 'I want to be happy,' how can you say without being impudent, 'Perhaps you are in error'? And here again this applies by reflecting back right to infinity, i.e. 'I know that I want [to be happy]' and so on." Also in the same place: "If anyone says I do not want to make a mistake, will it not be true that this person does not want to make a mistake...?" "And other arguments," he says, "can be found which hold against the Academics, who argue that nothing can be known by human beings." Also in the same place: "Those who have read our *Against the Academics* will not be moved by the many arguments against the perception of truth given by them." Further in the same book, c.15 or 38:[27] "Those things which are known in such a way that they can never slip from the mind but pertain to the nature of the soul itself, of such kind is the knowledge that we are alive..."

Note that there are four kinds of cognitions where we are necessarily certain, viz. (1) items knowable in an unqualified sense, (2) items knowable through experience, (3) our own actions, (4) items known at the present time through the senses. (Those in the first group are obvious; those in the third we conclude are self-evident otherwise we wouldn't know what it was to be self-evident; the second and fourth contain an infinity of self-evident truths, to which are united others drawn from several senses.) An example [of each]: (1) 'A triangle has three angles [equal to two right angles].' (2) 'The moon is eclipsed.' (3) I 'am awake.' (4) 'That is white.' The first and third require the senses merely as an occasion, because even if all the senses erred, there would still [in these cases] be unqualified certitude. The second and fourth hold in virtue of this: Whatever happens frequently through something that is not free, has this something as its natural, *per se* cause. Both in the second and in the fourth cases sometimes a necessary proposition gets added. (Therefore, you may set aside Augustine's authoritative texts until we reach

the second article, which concerns what really is the case, i.e. gives us the solution.)

And so the first article is clear, viz. how [Henry's] arguments are inconclusive and that his view is false and contrary to Augustine.

[Article 2: Refutation of the Academics by showing what is really the case:]

As regards the second article, lest the error of the Academics be repeated in regard to any of those items that can be known, we must see what is to be said about the three types of knowable items mentioned above, viz. whether it is possible to have naturally infallible certitude of (1) self-evident principles and propositions deduced from them, (2) what is known from experience, and (3) our own acts.

[On the certitude of principles and what is deduced from them:]

As to the certitude of principles I have this to say: The terms of a self-evident proposition have the sort of identity in which one evidently and necessarily includes the other. Consequently, the intellect which combines these terms, from the very fact that it grasps those terms, has present to itself the necessary cause, and even the evident cause, of the conformity that act of combining has to those terms which it combines. This conformity, then, the evident cause of which the intellect perceives in the terms, cannot help but be evident to the intellect. That is why the intellect could not apprehend these terms and combine them without having this relationship of conformity arise between the combination and the terms, any more than two white objects could exist without a relationship of similarity arising between them. Now it is precisely this conformity the combination has to the terms that constitutes the truth of the combination. There cannot be, then, a composition of such terms which is not true, and thus there cannot be a perception of that combination and a perception of the terms unless there is a perception of the conformity of the combination to the terms and consequently a perception of truth. For what is first perceived evidently includes the perception of that truth.

---

27 *On the Trinity* XV, c.15, PL 42, 1078.

In *Metaphysics* IV[28] The Philosopher bolsters this argument by a simile. There he points out that the opposite of a first principle such as 'It is impossible that the same thing be and not be,' cannot enter the mind of anyone because then the mind would possess contrary opinions simultaneously. This is indeed true of contrary opinions, that is, ones that formally reject each other, for the opinion that attributes being to something and the opinion that attributes not-being to the same thing formally reject each other.

And so in the question at hand, I argue that there are some thoughts in the mind that reject each other, although they do not do this formally. For if there exists in the intellect a cognition of whole and part, and also the combination of these [as, perhaps, in the proposition 'Every whole is greater than its part'], and if there existed in the intellect the opinion that this combination was false, then, since those terms include as necessary causes the conformity of the combination to the terms, there will exist [in the intellect] cognitions that reject each other – not that they do this formally, but rather one cognition will exist along with the other and yet will be the necessary cause of a cognition opposed to the other, which is impossible. For just as it is impossible for white and black to exist together, since they are formally opposed, so also it is impossible for white to exist together with what is the direct cause of black in such a way that necessarily [the cause's] existing apart from that [which it causes] is not possible without contradiction.

Once we have certitude of first principles, it is clear how one can be certain of the conclusions inferred from such principles, since the perfect syllogism is evident, and the certitude of the conclusion depends solely upon the certitude of the principles and the obviousness of the inference.

But will the intellect not err in its knowledge of principles and conclusions, if all the senses are mistaken about the terms? I reply that, so far as this kind of cognition goes, the senses are not a cause but merely an occasion of the intellect's knowledge, for the intellect is not able to have non-complex cognition [of the terms] except what it gets from the senses. But once it gets this, it can by its own power combine these non-complex cognitions together. And if the complex is by reason of the non-complex terms involved obviously true, the intellect will assent to this complex by its own power and that of the terms, and not by the power of the senses from which it got the terms from outside itself. To give an example: If the notion of *whole* and the notion of *greater than* be taken from the senses and the intellect forms the complex *Every whole is greater than its part*, the intellect by its own power and that of the terms will assent to this proposition without the shadow of doubt. And it will do this not just because it sees those terms united in some thing, i.e. in the way that it assents to *Socrates is white* by seeing the terms to be united in the thing.

Rather, I maintain, if all the senses from which these terms were received were false, or some were false and others true (which is even more deceptive), the intellect would still not make a mistake about such principles, because the terms which are the cause of the truth would always be present to the intellect. And so it would be if the species of whiteness and blackness were impressed miraculously in sleep upon one who was blind from birth and they remained after he awoke. [This person's] intellect could abstract from these and form the complex *White is not black*, and it would not be mistaken about this even if the terms were taken from erring senses, because the formal character of the terms, which is what the intellect ends up with, is a necessary cause of this negative truth.

[On the certitude of what we learn from experience:]

As for what is known by experience, I have this to say: Even though not all the particular cases, but only quite a few, are experienced, and even though the experience is not always repeated but only frequently, still the observer knows infallibly that it is always this way and in all cases. This the observer knows through this proposition reposing in their soul: 'Whatever occurs for the most part by a cause that is not free is the natural effect of that cause.' This proposition is known to the intellect even if the terms are derived from erring senses, because a

28 c.3 1005b 29-32.

non-free cause cannot produce unfreely for the most part an effect opposed to the effect to which it is naturally directed, or to which it is not naturally directed by its form. A chance cause, however, is naturally directed either to produce or not produce the opposite of the chance effect. Consequently, nothing which frequently produces an effect is a chance cause [of that effect], and thus if it is not free it will be a natural cause [of that effect]. But this effect occurs through this cause for the most part. This we learn from experience, because we observe such and such a nature with such and such accidents and then with such and such other accidents, and we discover that, no matter how diverse the accidents it is with, such and such an effect always follows on that nature. Therefore, this effect follows not because of some accident belonging to the nature but rather because of that nature itself.

It should be noted further that sometimes we have experience of a conclusion, such as that the moon is frequently eclipsed, and then assuming that conclusion (because it is in fact the case) we proceed by the method of division to inquire after the cause of this. And sometimes beginning with a conclusion thus experienced we arrive at a principle known through its terms, and then the conclusion, which at first was known only by experience, can through such a principle known through its terms be known with greater certainty, namely that characteristic of the first kind of knowledge since it is known as deduced from a self-evident principle. Thus, for instance, it is a self-evident principle that when an opaque body is placed between a visible object and a light, the transmission of light to such an object is prevented. Now, if it were discovered by the method of division that the earth is such a body interposed between sun and moon, [our conclusion that the moon is frequently eclipsed] would be known with the greatest of certainty by a demonstration that shows why it is the case (because it shows the cause) and not just known by experience in the way it used to be known before the discovery of the principle.

Sometimes, however, we have experience of the principle in such a way that we cannot discover by the method of division any further principle that is known from its terms. Instead we have to stop with something that is true for the most part and whose terms are known to be frequently united, for example that a certain species of herb is hot. Neither do we find any other prior means of demonstrating just why this attribute belongs to this particular subject; rather we have to stop with this as primitive in our knowledge, though known through experience. Now even though the uncertainty and fallibility in such a case is removed by the proposition 'What occurs for the most part as the effect of some non-free cause is the natural effect of that cause,' still this is the very lowest grade of scientific knowledge. Perhaps in this case we do not have knowledge of the actual union of the terms but only of what is apt to be the case. For if the attribute is some absolute thing other than its subject, it might be separated from its subject without contradiction, and the observer would not have knowledge that this is the way it actually is but that this is the way it is naturally apt to be.

[On certitude about our own acts:]

Regarding the third type of knowledge, viz. of our own acts, I say that of many of these we are as sure as we are of the first and self-evident principles, as is clear from *Metaphysics* IV.[29] There The Philosopher says to the arguments of those who say that all that appears is true that they look for proofs of whether we are now awake or asleep. "All these doubts, however, amount to the same thing, for they all think that there is a reason for everything." And he adds: "They seek a reason for things for which there is no reason, for there is no demonstration of a principle of demonstration." Therefore, according to him in that text, that we are awake is as self-evident as is a principle of demonstration. Nor does it matter that it is a contingent matter, for, as we have said elsewhere, contingent propositions get ranked so that some are first and immediate. Otherwise, there would be an infinite regress in contingent propositions or something contingent would follow from a necessary cause, both of which are impossible.

Also, just as our certitude of being awake is like that of self-evident propositions, the same holds

---

29 c.6, 1011a39.

for many other acts in our power, such as 'I am thinking,' or 'I am hearing,' and other such acts which we are performing. For, even if there is no certitude that I see white existing outside or in such a subject or at such a distance (for an illusion can be caused in the medium, or in the organ, or in a number of other ways), still there is certitude that I am seeing, even given that an illusion is occurring in the organ, which seems to be the greatest of all illusions (for instance, when an act of the sort that is naturally apt to be brought about by an object present [to the organ] occurs in the organ but not on account of a present object). In such a case, if the faculty were actually to perform its action, what is called vision would truly be there, whether vision be an action or a passive reception [of something] or both. But if the illusion occurred not in the organ proper but in something near it, something which seems to be the organ, – for instance if an impressing of a species of the sort that is naturally produced by the color white did not occur in the bundle of nerves but in the eye itself, – then there would still be an act of vision, for we would see such a species, or what is apt to be seen in it, because it is sufficiently distant from the organ of sight which resides in that bundle of nerves. This is evident from Augustine in *On the Trinity* XI, c.2[30] where he notes that the left-overs of vision which persist in the eye are seen even after the eyes are closed. It is also evident from The Philosopher when in *On the senses and what is sensed*[31] he notes that the flash of fire produced by violently lifting the eye and transmitted right up to the closed eyelid is seen. Although these are not the most perfect, they are true cases of seeing, for in these cases a sufficient distance intervenes between the species and the principal organ of vision.

[Certitude of Sense Knowledge:]

But how can a person be sure about those things which fall under the acts of the senses, for instance, that something outside is white or hot in the way that it appears to be?

I reply as follows: Regarding such an object, either the same things appear opposite to different senses or they do not appear so but rather all the senses apprehending such an object judge the same about it. If the latter is the case, then we have certitude regarding the item apprehended by the senses in virtue of the aforementioned principle, viz. that where something occurs in most cases as a result of something, the latter is the natural cause of the former, given the latter is not a free cause. Therefore, when the same change in the senses occurs for the most part if the object is present, it follows that the change or species produced is the natural effect of that sort of cause, and thus the external thing will be white or hot or such as it naturally appears to be in virtue of the species which the object for the most part produces.

But if the judgments of the different senses differ in regard to what is seen outside – for example, sight says that the stick which is partly in the water and partly in the air is broken; sight always says that the sun is smaller in size than it really is, and in general that everything seen from a distance is smaller than it is in reality – in such cases we are still sure of what is true and know which sense is in error. This we know by reason of some proposition in the soul, more certain than any sense judgment, together with the concurrent testimony of several of the senses. For there is always some proposition to set the mind or intellect right regarding which acts of the senses are true and which false, a proposition which the senses do not cause but merely occasion in the intellect.

For example, the intellect has the following proposition reposing in it: 'No harder object is broken by contact with something soft which gives way to it.' This proposition is so self-evident in virtue of its terms that the intellect cannot call it in doubt, even if the terms were derived from erroneous senses. Indeed, the opposite of this proposition includes a contradiction. Now both sight and touch say that the stick is harder than the water and that the water gives way to the stick. It follows, therefore, that the stick is not broken in the way that sight judged. Hence in the case of the "broken stick" the intellect judges which sense errs and which does not by something more certain than any act of the senses. Likewise in the other example. No matter how

30 PL 42, 987.
31 *De sensu et sensibilibus*, c.2, 437a23-26.

much the terms are taken from erring senses, the intellect knows that a size that is applied to something that has size is completely equal to itself. But both sight and touch tell us that the same size can be applied to what we see when it is near as is applied to it when it is far away. Therefore, the size that we see close up is equal to that which we see from far away. Thus sight in saying that the latter is smaller errs. This conclusion is inferred from self-evident principles and from the acts of the two senses that apprehend that something is for the most part the case. And so when reason judges that a sense errs, it does so in virtue of two kinds of knowledge. The first is knowledge for which the intellect requires the senses only as an occasion, not as a cause, a knowledge in which it would not be deceived even if all the senses were deceived. The other is a knowledge acquired from one or more senses telling us how things are for the most part, and this is known to be true by reason of the proposition often cited, viz. 'Whatever occurs in most cases....'

[Article 3: Replies to Henry's three main arguments:]

In this third article, using what we have just said, we must reply to those three arguments [of Henry's].

[Note added by Scotus:] Note that cognition of a principle is immutable in the sense that it cannot change from truth to falsity; not in some other way, for example that it is unqualifiedly imperishable. Thus the intelligible species (not the phantasm) is weak, yet it cannot change from a true representation into a false one. And an object, even though it is perishable, still cannot change from a true entity into a false one, and consequently it makes cognition conform to itself or causes cognition to conform to its truth in actual existence, for a true entity, incapable of changing into a false one, contains virtually[32] cognition that is immutably true, i.e. conforms to a true entity.

(Note that according to Augustine what is necessarily true or immutably true is "above the mind," by which he means "with the character of an evident truth,' because [what is necessarily and immutably true] causes this [evidence of its truth] in the mind. As evident such a truth is not subject to the mind so that it could appear either true or false in the way that a probable truth is subject to the mind inasmuch as it is in the power of the mind to make it appear true or false by looking here or there for arguments to prove or disprove it. In this way we must understand the remark that the mind does not make judgments about what is immutably true but about other matters, for it is only in the case of something probable and not in the case of something necessary that asserting it is true, i.e. an act of judgment, lies within the power of the mind. But this does not mean that the mind asserts less perfectly of what is necessary that it is true. According to Aristotle, this assertion can be called a judgment, but Augustine means by 'judgment' something which is in the power of the one judging and not something which is immediately and necessarily determined by something else. And so it is clear how the mind makes a "judgment" about a necessary conclusion, because it is not immediately evident of itself and therefore does not force itself upon the mind as something evident. The mind can even bring up sophistical arguments against the conclusion and on the basis of these dissent from it. This it cannot do in the case of something that is first known, according to *Metaphysics* IV[33] [where Aristotle says,] "Its opposite cannot enter the mind.")

As for [Henry's] first argument, viz. the one based in changes in the object, the antecedent is false, for sensible things are not in continual motion, rather they remain the same for some time. Neither is this Augustine's opinion; rather it is the error of Heraclitus and his disciple Cratylus, who decided not even to speak but just move his finger, as *Metaphysics* IV[34] relates. But even if the antecedent were true, the consequence would still be invalid, for as Aristotle pointed out, we could still be certain of this, that all things are in continuous motion.

32 See glossary entry for 'virtual existence.'
33 c.3, 1005b15.
34 c.5, 1010a7-15.

Nor does this follow: 'If the object is subject to change, then what it produces cannot represent it as not subject to change.' For the mutability in the object is not the reason it produces something; rather the reason is the nature of the mutable object, and, therefore, what it produces represents the nature on its own. Consequently, if the nature, from the fact that it is a nature, is in some unchangeable relationship to something else, that something else, through its exemplar, and the nature itself, through its exemplar, may be represented as immutably united. In that case through those two exemplars that are produced by two mutable things – but not insofar as they are mutable items but rather insofar as they are natures – we can have knowledge of the immutability of their union.

[Question:] Even if something produces but not insofar as it is mutable, how can it have an immutable relationship to something else?

I answer: The relationship is immutable in this sense: the opposite relationship could not exist between the terms, nor could the original relationship fail to exist given the existence of the terms, but if one or both of them are destroyed so is it.

Against this answer: How can we assert that the proposition is necessary if the identity of the terms can be destroyed?

I answer: When a thing does not exist, its identity is not real. Thus, if it is in the intellect, its identity exists as an object of the intellect and is qualifiedly necessary, because in that sort of existence the terms cannot exist without having such an identity. Nevertheless, that identity might not exist [in the intellect], just as one of the terms might not be thought of. Therefore a "necessary proposition" in our intellect is [only necessary] qualifiedly, since it cannot change into something false. The unqualifiedly necessary exists only in the divine intellect, inasmuch as the terms have an identity in an unqualifiedly necessary way in some sort of existence only as existing in that [divine] intellect.

It is also clear that something that does the representing and is in itself subject to change can represent something under the character of immutable, because we find that the divine essence is represented to the intellect under the character of immutable by something completely mutable, whether that is a species or an act. This is evident, too, by the similarity to this case: Something can be represented under the character of infinite by something finite.

As for the second [of Henry's arguments]: I say that in the soul we can think of two sorts of mutability: one from affirmation to negation, and vice versa, such as from not-knowing to knowledge, or from not grasping something to grasping it; the other is sort of from one contrary to another, for example from correctness to error, and vice versa. Now in respect of any objects the soul is subject to change with the first sort of mutability, and nothing formally existing in it can remove that sort of mutability from it. But it is subject to change with the second sort of mutability only in respect of those complexes which are not evident on the basis of the terms. In respect of those which are evident on the basis of the terms it cannot be changed with the second sort of mutability, because, once those terms are apprehended, they are an evident and necessary cause of the conformity to those terms themselves of the combination they have made. Therefore, given that the soul is in an absolute sense subject to changing from correctness to error, it does not follow that "nothing other than itself can set it right"; in the very least it can by the terms it has apprehended be set right in regard to matters about which the intellect cannot err.

As for the third [of Henry's arguments]: I say that if it is to have some appearance [of validity], it would argue against that opinion which denies that there is an intelligible species (which is the view of him who put this argument forward [viz. Henry]), because the species which is able to represent the sensible in dreams as though it were an object would be the phantasm[35], not the intelligible species. Therefore, if the intellect were to use just the phantasm to make the object be present to it, and not any intelligible species, it does not seem that it could discern what is true from what is like the true by anything in which the object is revealed to it. But if we propose that there is a species in the intellect, the argument is invalid, because the intel-

---

35 See glossary entry for 'phantasm.'

lect cannot use that [species in the intellect] to substitute for itself as though for an object because the intellect in fact does not use it in sleep.

You may object that if the phantasm can represent itself as an object, then the intellect can err by reason of this error in the faculty of imagination, or at least, as is the case in dreams or with madmen, the intellect could be put under such restraints that it would not be able to perform its function. To this it can be said that even if the intellect were under restraints when such an error occurs in the faculty of imagination, still the intellect would not make a mistake, simply because at that time it performs no act.

But how will the intellect then know or be sure when the faculty of imagination is not in error, given that its not being in error is required for the intellect not to err? I answer: The following truth reposes in the intellect: A faculty does not err in regard to an object proportioned to it unless it is disordered. Also it is known to the intellect that the faculty of imagination is not disordered during a waking state by a disorder of the sort which would make a phantasm represent itself as an object. This is because it is self-evident to the intellect that what is thinking is awake, and this in such a way that the faculty of imagination is not during the waking state under the restraints that it is under in sleep.

But at this point arises an objection to the aforementioned certitude about our acts, which runs as follows: It seems to me that I am seeing or I am hearing in cases where in fact I am neither seeing nor hearing; therefore there is no certitude about these matters. I answer: It is one thing to show someone who denies a certain proposition that it is true, quite another to show to someone who admits the proposition how it is true. For example, in *Metaphysics* IV[36] The Philosopher does not against someone who denies the first principle [i.e. the law of non-contradiction] rely on the absurdity that [given the first principle were false] opposed opinions would exist simultaneously in the soul (for they would accept that [i.e. that opposed opinions exist simultaneously in the soul] in just the way they would accept the premise [i.e. that the first principle is false]. Rather he relies on other absur-

dities, some that are more obviously [absurd] to them although not in themselves. But he does show those who grant the first principle how this principle is known. For it is known in such a way that "its opposite could not even enter the mind," and he proves this from the fact that "then opposed opinions would be able to exist at the same time." Such a conclusion is in this context more absurd than the assumption [i.e. the denial of the first principle]. This is the way it is in what we are discussing. If there is nothing you will allow to be self-evident, then I do not want to argue with you, because it is obvious that you are being perversely obstinate and are not about to be persuaded. This is apparent from your actions (as The Philosopher argues in *Metaphysics* IV),[37] for if you dream of possessing something nearby, as it were, after you wake up you do not pursue it as you would pursue it had you been that close to getting it when awake. If, however, you admit some proposition as self-evident and that a disordered faculty can err with regard to anything (as is clear in dreams), then for something to be known and known to be self-evident one has to know when a faculty is disordered and when not, and consequently from our own acts we can know that a faculty is well ordered in such a way that what appears to it to be self-evident is in fact self-evident.

I say, then, to the form of this sophistical argument that, just as it appears to the dreamer that he is seeing, so also the opposite of some one self-evident, theoretical principle might appear to that person, and nevertheless it does not follow that that principle is not self-evident. Thus it does not follow that it is not self-evident to hearers that they are hearing, for in respect of both of these it is the disordered faculty which can err, not the well ordered one, and when it is well ordered and when not is self-evident. Otherwise, nothing else could be known to be self-evident, because one would not be able to know what might be self-evident, i.e. whether it is what the intellect would assent to if it were well ordered in this way or what it [when well ordered] would assent to in this way [i.e. as self-evident].

---

36 c.3, 1005a29 – 1006a18.
37 c.5, 1010b3-11.

[Article 4: Refutation of Henry's conclusion:]

In the fourth article I argue against the conclusion of the opinion as follows: What, I ask, is meant by 'sure and genuine truth'? It may mean, on the one hand, infallible truth, on the other hand, a truth which excludes all doubt and deception. We have proved and explained already in the second and third articles that such truth can be obtained by relying on what is merely natural. Or by such truth is meant truth as an attribute of being. In that case, since we can naturally think of being, we can also think of true as it is an attribute of being, and if true also truth by abstraction, for any form that can be thought of as in a subject can be thought of as it is in abstraction from a subject. Or he means truth in still another sense, conformity to an exemplar. If the exemplar in question is taken to be a created one, we have what we seek to prove. But if conformity to an uncreated exemplar is meant, conformity to that can only be grasped by the intellect once that exemplar is apprehended, for a relation can be apprehended only when the term is. Thus it is false to claim that an eternal exemplar is a means of knowing yet is not itself known.

Furthermore, and secondly, a non-complex thought can apprehend definitionally everything which it thinks of in a confused way, by seeking out the definition of the apprehended item by using the method of division. This definitional apprehension seems to be the most perfect that pertains to non-complex thought. Now, from this most perfect cognition of the terms the intellect can most perfectly grasp a principle, and from that principle a conclusion. In this, intellectual cognition seems to be completed in that no cognition of truth beyond those truths we have mentioned seems to be necessary.

Thirdly, either the eternal light, which you say is necessary for having genuine truth, causes something naturally prior to the act or not. If it does, then [it does this] either in the object or in the intellect. [It does not do it] in the object, because the object, inasmuch as it has existence in the intellect, does not have real existence but only intentional existence,[38] and consequently it is incapable of any real accident. If [it does it] in the intellect, then the eternal light brings the intellect to the apprehension of genuine truth only by the mediation of its effect. In that case, the usual opinion seems to claim just as completely that cognition is in an uncreated light as does this position [of Henry's], for the common view claims that cognition is seen in the agent intellect,[39] which is an effect of the uncreated light and a more perfect one than that created accidental light. On the other hand, if it [the eternal light] causes nothing prior to the act, then either the light alone causes the act, or the light along with the intellect and the object. If the light does so alone, then the agent intellect has no function whatever in the apprehension of genuine truth. But this seems absurd, because that is the noblest function of our intellect, and, therefore, the agent intellect, which is the noblest [capacity] in the soul, must concur in some way in this act. ([added note:] Also the act of grasping something with the intellect would not more be said to belong to one person than to any other, and thus the agent intellect would be otiose. This is not to be asserted, since it belongs to the agent intellect "to make all things," just as it belongs to the possible intellect "to be made into all things." Likewise, according to The Philosopher in De Anima III,[40] the agent intellect corresponds in its active character to the possible intellect in its passive character; consequently, the agent intellect relates actively in some way to whatever the possible intellect receives.)

Also the absurdity here inferred follows from the aforesaid opinion in another way. For, according to the one who holds this opinion, any agent using an instrument is incapable of performing an action which exceeds the action of the instrument. Therefore, since the power of the agent intellect could not arrive at a cognition of genuine truth, it follows that the eternal light using the agent intellect could not arrive at an action that apprehends genuine truth and still use the agent intellect as an instrument. And if you say that the uncreated light, operating in conjunction with the intellect and the object, causes this genuine truth, this is the usual opinion which says that the eternal light acting as a

---

38 See glossary entry for 'intentional existence.'
39 See glossary entry for 'agent or active intellect.'
40 c.5, 430a10-14.

"remote cause" causes any sure truth. Consequently, either this opinion [of Henry's] is absurd or it is not at variance with the usual view.

[Article 5: Solution of the question:]

As to the question, then, I say that because of what Augustine has said, one should concede that infallible truths are seen in the eternal rules, where the term 'in' can be taken objectively. There are four ways in which this could be the case: (1) either as in a proximate object, or (2) as in something that contains the proximate object, or (3) as in that in virtue of which the proximate object causes movement, or (4) as in a remote object.

Taking the first meaning, I say that all intelligibles have intelligible existence[41] in virtue of the act of the divine intellect. In these intelligibles all the truths about them shine forth in such a way that an intellect that apprehends them and in virtue of them apprehends the necessary truths about them sees those necessary truths in them as in objects. Now, these [intelligibles] inasmuch as they are secondary objects of the divine intellect, are 'truths,' because they conform to their exemplar, viz. the divine intellect. Also they are a light because they are manifest; and they are immutable there as well as necessary. But they are eternal only in a qualified sense, for eternity is a condition of existence and they have only a qualified existence. This then is the first way in which we can be said to see in the eternal light, i.e. in the secondary object of the divine intellect, which object is truth and an eternal light in the way explained.

In the second meaning, it is similarly clear that the divine intellect contains those truths sort of in the way a book does, as this authoritative text of Augustine's, *On the Trinity* XIV, c.15,[42] says: "Those rules are written in the book of eternal light," i.e. in the divine intellect insofar as it contains those truths. Although this book is not seen, still those truths which are written in that first book are seen. And to this extent our intellect could be said to see

truths in the eternal light, i.e. to see things which are in that book as in something containing the object.

The former of these two senses seems to be what Augustine had in mind in *On the Trinity* XII, c.14,[43] where he says that "the character of square body remains incorruptible and immutable" and so on. But it remains such only as it is a secondary object of the divine intellect.

In opposition to the first meaning, there is a question. If we do not see these truths as they are in the divine intellect (because we do not see the divine intellect itself), how can we be said "to see in the uncreated light" in virtue of the fact that we see in a light of the sort that is only qualifiedly eternal and has existence in the uncreated light as in an intellect apprehending it?

The third meaning gives us an answer to this. These [intelligibles], insofar as they are secondary objects of the divine intellect, have only qualified existence. But something that has only qualified existence, to the precise extent that it exists in this way, does not have any true, real function. If such a function pertains to it at all, it does so only in virtue of something with unqualified existence. Therefore, these secondary objects do not, in an exact sense, cause movement in the intellect except in virtue of the existence of the divine intellect, which is unqualified existence, and through it these secondary objects have qualified existence. Thus we see in a light which is qualifiedly eternal as in a proximate object, but we see in the eternal uncreated light in the third sense, i.e. as in the proximate cause in virtue of which the proximate object causes movement.

We can also be said to see in the eternal light in this third sense inasmuch as this light is the cause of the object itself. For the divine intellect produces by its own act these objects as having intelligible existence and in doing so gives to one object one sort of being and to another another sort, and consequently gives to them their character of being an object. Then through this character of being an object they cause the intellect to take on a sure cog-

---

41 See glossary entry for 'esse objectivum.'
42 Actually ch.14, PL 42, 1011.
43 PL 42, 1011.

nition. And, properly speaking, it could be said that our intellect sees in the light because the light is the cause of the object. This is clear from a simile: we are properly said to think of something in the light of the agent intellect, even though that light is just an active cause, i.e. by its own act it makes the object or is that in virtue of which the object causes movement, or both.

The fact, then, that the divine intellect, the true uncreated light, has a twofold causality, viz. that it produces objects in intelligible being and that it is also that in virtue of which the secondary objects produced actually move the intellect), this fact can unify, as it were, the third sense or way in which we might truly be said to see in the eternal light.

But if someone were to object to these two ways of unifying the third sense that speaks about a cause, on the grounds that then we should rather be said to see in God willing or in God insofar as He is a will, for the divine will is the immediate principle of every [divine] act directed towards something outside [God] – I answer that the divine intellect, insofar as it is in some way prior to the act of the divine will, produces these objects in intelligible existence, and in respect of them it seems to be a purely natural cause, for God is a free cause of only what presupposes as prior to itself in some way the will in the sense of an act of will. Now, just as the intellect as prior to the act of the will produces objects in intelligible existence, so also it seems as a prior cause to cooperate with those intelligibles to produce their natural effect, viz. that, once they are apprehended and combined, they cause an apprehension of a conformity to themselves. Therefore, for the intellect to form some such combination but the combination not to be in conformity to the terms seems to involve a contradiction, although it is possible for [the intellect] not to combine those terms. For, even though God voluntarily cooperates with the intellect's combining or not combining the terms, still, once it has combined them, it seems necessarily to follow from the character the terms get from the divine intellect, which naturally produces those terms in intelligible existence, that the combination [of those terms] is in conformity with those terms.

From all this it is clear why a special illumination is not required in order to see in the eternal rules, for Augustine claims that we see in them only such items which are necessarily true in virtue of the meanings of the terms. In such cases there is the greatest naturalness and necessity, of both the remote and proximate causes, i.e. of both the divine intellect in respect of the objects that cause movement [in the intellect] and of the objects in respect of the truth of the complex that is about them. Furthermore, although the naturalness and necessity leading to the perception of that truth is not so great that the opposite of it includes a contradiction, still there is on the part of the proximate cause, with the remote cause assisting it, a naturalness and necessity since the terms once apprehended and combined are naturally apt to cause the evidence of the conformity of the combination [of the terms] to the terms. And if someone claims that God's cooperation with the terms in producing this effect is just due to His general influence [i.e. something which is due to God's will], or due to something even greater, i.e. a natural necessity working through the terms to produce this effect, in either case it is clear that no special illumination is required.

The assumption as to what Augustine meant is clearly justified by what he says of the philosophers in *On the Trinity* IV, c.35:[44] "Some of them have been able with the penetration of their minds to rise above all creatures and reach at least in some degree the light of immutable truth, and they ridicule many Christians who live by faith alone for not yet being able to do this." What he means is that Christians do not see what they believe in the eternal rules, but philosophers do see many necessarily [true] items in those rules.

He says the same in *On the Trinity* IX, c.6:[45] "Look on the indestructible truth by which we may define, to the extent we can, not what the mind of any human is in fact like but what in accord with the everlasting types it ought to be like," as though he said: Contingents are not seen there, but necessary items are.

Again, in the same work, book IV, c.36,[46] he

---

44 Actually c.15, PL 42, 901-2.
45 PL 42, 966.
46 Actually c.16, PL 42, 902.

argues against those philosophers: "Just because they argue most truly that all that happens in time takes place on account of eternal types, are they, therefore, able to perceive therein how many kinds of animals exist or how many seeds of each there were in the beginning, and so on? ... Have they not sought all these things not by that unchangeable knowledge, but by the history of places and times, and have they not believed the written experience of others?" Consequently, he means that they do not apprehend through eternal rules those contingents, which are known only through the senses or are believed on the basis of historical accounts. And yet special illumination is even more required in the case of what we are to believe than it is in the knowledge of necessarily [true] items. Indeed, special illumination is least needed in the case of the latter; general illumination alone suffices.

Against this interpretation: Why, then, does Augustine say in *On the Trinity* XII, c.14:[47] "It is only for the few to attain by the penetration of their minds to the intelligible types"? Or in *83 Questions*, qu.46:[48] "Only the pure of soul reach them"?

I answer: He does not mean by this purity a freedom from vices, for in *On the Trinity* XIV, c.15[49] he holds that the unjust person sees in the eternal rules what a just person must do. In book IV, the chapter cited above,[50] he maintains that the philosophers saw truth in the eternal reasons even though they lacked faith. And in the same question, he holds that no one can be wise without an apprehension of the ideas (in the sense in which they might allow that Plato was wise). Rather this purity must be interpreted as the elevation of the intellect to the contemplation of these truths as they are in themselves and not as they appear in the phantasm.

Here we must remember that the sensible thing outside causes a confused phantasm, something with only an incidental unity, in the faculty of imagination, and this represents the thing in respect of its quantity, shape, color, and the other sensible accidents. And just as the phantasm represents only confusedly and incidentally, so many perceive only what is an incidental being. Primary truths, on the other hand, are just that in virtue of the terms' very own character, inasmuch as those terms are abstracted from everything that is incidentally combined with them. For this proposition, 'Every whole is greater than its part,' is not primarily true if the "whole" is thought of as in stone or wood, but rather as the whole is abstracted from all that is incidentally combined with it. Thus an intellect which never thinks of a totality except through an incidental concept of it, for example as a totality of stone or of wood, never grasps the genuine truth of this principle, since it never grasps the exact character of the terms in virtue of which it is a truth.

It is only within the power of the few to attain the eternal types, because it is only the few that have a grasp of the essentials, whereas the many grasp things merely in incidental concepts such as those mentioned above. But these few are not said to be distinguished from the others by a special illumination, but by better natural powers, since they have a sharper and more abstractive intellect, or because of more thorough inquiry which enables one person to know those quiddities[51] which an equally talented individual does not discover because he has not conducted an inquiry.

And in this way we can understand Augustine's statement in *On the Trinity* IX, c.6,[52] regarding the person on the mountain who sees the pure light above and the mist below. For whoever grasps nothing but incidental concepts in the way that a phantasm represents such objects, viz. as incidental beings, is like the one in a valley surrounded by mist. But the person who separates out quiddities by grasping them exclusively in essential concepts – and these still reside in the phantasm along with many other connected accidents – this person possesses the phantasm as down below in the mist, while being on the mountain to the extent that they

---

47 PL 42, 1010.
48 PL 40, 30.
49 PL 42, 1052.
50 c.15, PL 42, 901-2.
51 See glossary entry for 'quiddity.'
52 PL 42, 966.

know that truth and see the truth above, i.e. the higher truth which they know in virtue of the uncreated intellect which is the eternal light.

In the final sense we can concede that genuine truths are apprehended in the eternal light as in an object remotely known, for the uncreated light is the first source of things investigated theoretically and the ultimate end of the things investigated for practical purposes. The first theoretical and practical principles are, then, derived from it. Hence the knowledge of all things, both theoretical and practical, which we get through the principles drawn from the eternal light (to the extent that is known), is a more perfect and purer knowledge than that drawn from the principles we find in the sort of things that they deal with. In this sense the theologian has knowledge of everything, as was said in the question on the subject of theology, and theological knowledge is more excellent than any other. It is in this sense that genuine truth is said to be known, because through it we know just the truth, without any non-truth being mixed in, for this is through the first being from which, when we apprehend it, we draw the principles for this kind of knowing. But any other thing from which are drawn principles for knowing the sort of thing those principles deal with is defectively true.

In this sense only God knows genuinely everything, because, as was said on the question of the subject of theology, only He knows everything exclusively through His own essence. Any other intellect can be moved by some other object to the knowing of some truth by virtue of that object. For to know that a triangle has three [angles equal to two right angles] as a kind of participation in God and that it has such a rank in the universe that it expresses more perfectly, as it were, the perfection of God, – this is a nobler way of knowing a triangle has three [angles etc.] than to know this from the character of triangle itself. Similarly, to know that one should live moderately in order to attain the supreme happiness, which consists in attaining to the essence of God in Himself, is a more perfect way of knowing this practical point than to know it through some moral principle, for example that one should live uprightly.

And in this manner Augustine speaks of the uncreated light as known in *On the Trinity* XV, c.27 or 82,[53] where addressing himself he says: "You have seen many things and these you have discerned through that light in which you saw them shining forth to you. Turn your eyes to the light itself and fasten them upon it, if you can, for in this way you will see how the nativity of the Word of God differs from the procession of the Gift of God." And a little later: "This and other things this light has revealed to your inner eyes. What then is the reason with fixed glance you are unable to see the light itself, if it is not indeed your weakness?..."

From all that has been said it is clear how the authoritative texts from Augustine that were used to argue the opposite are to be interpreted, i.e. the texts of Augustine concerning this matter can be explained in terms of one of the aforementioned senses of 'seeing in.'

[Article 6: What Henry's arguments do show:]

As to the sixth article we must see how the three arguments brought forth in favor of the first opinion, insofar as they are taken from Augustine, do prove some truth, although they do not establish that false conclusion for which they were advanced.

Here we have to realize [at this point one ms. says that Scotus stopped writing here but the following has been inserted] that we should not expect genuine truth from sensible things as from a primary and essential cause, for sense knowledge has to do with something incidental, as was said, even though some of the acts of the senses are sure and true. But the quiddities of things are known in virtue of the agent intellect, which as a participation in the uncreated light illumines the phantasms, and from this we get true genuineness. In this manner Henry's first argument is solved, and according to the mind of Augustine it proves nothing more.

To Henry's second argument I say that the soul can change in the sense that it has now one act, now another, on account of the diversity of objects and its own unlimitedness and immateriality in the sense that it can relate to anything whatsoever. Likewise, it can go from acting to not-acting in that it is not always acting. But in respect of first principles, whose truth is known through the terms, and in respect of conclusions evidently deduced from the terms, it cannot change from one contrary into the other, i.e. from true into false. For the rules found in the light of the agent intellect set the intellect right, and the intelligible species itself of the terms, despite being mutable in its being, represents immutably when it represents in the light of the agent intellect. The terms of a first principle are apprehended through two intelligible species and thus their union is obviously true and certain.

As for Henry's third argument, we have to say that it argues against him, because it posits either an intelligible species or a phantasm. But it is ineffective if about an intelligible species representing a quiddity. Now we have to say that as long as the sensory faculties are not obstructed, the sensible species accurately represents the thing. But in sleep the exterior sensory faculties are restrained, and thus the imaginative power, which preserves the sensible species in the diverse flows of humors in the head, apprehends them as things of which they are likenesses, since they have the force of things according to The Philosopher in *On the Motions of Animals*.[54] The third argument concludes nothing more than this.

---

54 c.7, 701b 18-22.

VII.5. NICHOLAS OF AUTRECOURT

IN THE THOUGHT OF NICHOLAS CERTITUDE REDUCES TO THE LAW OF non-contradiction. This reduction in effect raises the standard of knowability and certitude of the absolute necessity of terms, the denial of one of which in conjunction with the other implies a contradiction. Nicholas gives this interpretation of that law:

> In every inference that is reduced immediately to the first principle, the consequent, and the antecedent either as a whole or in part, are factually identical.

Nicholas further infers this thesis: From the fact that some thing is known to be, it cannot be inferred evidently, by evidentness reduced to the first principle, that there is some other thing. It would follow the evident inference rests upon a string of identities.

The full development of such a position (executed in the selection below) carries the principle of separability in its wake: any real distinction implies separability. And across the potential gap between the separable there is no completely safe inference. The role of the principle is clear in Nicholas's *The Universal Treatise*:

> In the same way it can be said that a subject and its distinctive characteristics, so far as pertains to anything that can be considered in the real order, are not distinct because no kind of change can separate them. The same can be said of fire and its heat, of water and its coldness, and similarly of other things in relation to what have for a long time been called the qualities of the elements. (223)

The pattern of reasoning evident in the thought of Nicholas survives the end of medieval philosophy and continues with its force into the work of modern philosophy, including Descartes, Berkeley, and Hume.

VII.5.1. Certainty and the Principle of Non-Contradiction (The second Letter to Bernard)

[In the following selection Nicholas is corresponding with a monk, Bernard of Arezzo, whose idea he had questioned in a previous letter to which Bernard had replied.]

1. Reverend father, brother Bernard, the admirable depth of your subtlety would be duly recognised by me, if I knew you to possess evident cognition of the immaterial substances;[1] and not only if I were really certain, but even if I could convince myself without too strong an effort of belief. And not only if I believed that you have true cognition of the immaterial substances but also if I deemed you to have cognition of those conjoined to matter. And therefore to you, Father, who claim that you have

---

1 Nicholas refers here to Aristotelian "separate substances," for which there is an entry in the glossary.

evident cognition of such sublime objects of knowledge, I wish to lay bare my doubtful and anxious mind, so that you may have the opportunity to lead the way and make me and others partners in your knowledge of such magic things.

2. The first thing that presents itself for discussion is this principle: 'Contradictories cannot be simultaneously true.' Concerning which, two things suggest themselves. The first is that this is the first principle, expounding 'first' negatively as 'than which nothing is prior.' The second is that this principle is first in the affirmative or positive sense as 'that which is prior to any other.'

3. These two statements are proved by means of one argument, as follows: Every certitude we possess is resolved into this principle. And it is itself not resolved into any other in the way a conclusion would into its premise(s). It therefore follows that the principle in question is first by a twofold primacy. This implication is well-known as following from the meaning of the term 'first' according to either of the expositions given. The antecedent is proved with respect to both of its parts. First, as to its first part (to wit, that all our certitude falling short of this certitude is resolved into this principle): Regarding anything proven whatsoever, which falls short of [the evidentness of] this principle, and which you assert you are certain of, I propose this inference: 'It is possible, without any contradiction following therefrom, that it will appear to you to be the case, and yet will not be so. Therefore, you will not be evidently certain that it is the case.' It is clear to me that if I admitted the antecedent to be true, I would [thereby] admit the consequent to be true. And, consequently, I would not in the unqualified sense be evidently certain of that of which I said I was certain. From this it is clear that it is into our said principle that our certitude is resolved. And that it is not itself resolved into another one in the way a conclusion would into its principle is clear from the fact that all [arguments] are resolved into this one, as has been said. And so it follows: 'this one is prior to any other than itself; therefore nothing is prior to it.' And thus it is first with the aforesaid twofold primacy.

4. The third point that presents itself is that a contradiction is the affirmation and negation of one and the same [attribute] ... etc., as the common formula runs.

5. From this I infer a corollary, namely 'The certitude of evidentness that one has in the natural light[2], is certitude in the unqualified sense,' since it is the certitude that is held in virtue of the first principle, which neither is nor can be contradicted by any true law. Therefore, what is proved in the natural light, is proved unqualifiedly. And, thus, just as there is no power which can make contradictories simultaneously true, so there is no power by which it can happen that the opposite of the consequent simultaneously obtains with the antecedent.

6. The second corollary I infer on this score is: 'The certitude of evidentness has no degrees.' For example, if there are two conclusions of each of which we are evidently certain, we are not more certain of one than of the other. For (as has been said) all certitude is resolved into the same first principle. Either, indeed, those conclusions are resolved into the same first principle with equal immediacy – in which case we have no reason for being more certain of one than of the other –, or else one is resolved mediately and the other immediately, and, then, this still is no objection [to my thesis], because, once the reduction to the first principle has been made, we are equally certain of the one as of the other; just as the geometrician claims that he is as certain of a second conclusion as of the first, and similarly of a third one, and so on, – although, because of the plurality of the deductions, he cannot be, on first consideration, as certain of the fourth or third as of the first.

7. The third corollary I infer, on the basis of what has been said, is: 'With the exception of the certitude of faith, there is no other certitude but the certitude of the first principle, or the one that can be resolved to the first principle.' For there is no certitude but that which is not founded on falsity, because: If there were any certitude that could be based on falsity, let us suppose that it is actually based on falsity. Then, since (according to you) that certitude remains, it follows that somebody will be certain of something whose contradictory opposite is true.

---

2 I.e., the natural powers of the mind to discern truth.

8. The fourth corollary is this: 'Every syllogistic scheme is immediately reduced to the first principle,' because the conclusion which has been proved by means of it, either is immediately reduced (and, then, I have made my point), or else mediately; and, then, either there will be an infinite regress, or one must arrive at some conclusion that is immediately reduced to the first principle.

9. The fifth corollary is: 'In every inference that is reduced immediately to the first principle, the consequent, and the antecedent either as a whole or in part, are factually identical,' because, if this were not so, then it would not be immediately evident that the antecedent and the opposite of the consequent cannot simultaneously be true, without contradiction.

10. The sixth corollary is this: 'In every evident inference, reducible to the first principle by as many steps as you please, the consequent is factually identical with the antecedent, or with part of what is signified by the antecedent.' This is shown as follows: Suppose that some conclusion is reduced to the certitude of the first principle by three steps, then in the first consequence, which is evident with the evidentness reduced to the certitude of the first principle, the consequent will be factually identical with the antecedent, or with part of what is signified by the antecedent (in virtue of the fifth corollary); and similarly in the second inference (by the same corollary), and in the third one as well (by the same corollary). And, thus, since in the first inference the consequent is factually identical with the antecedent, or with part of what is signified by the antecedent, and likewise in the second, and similarly in the third, – so it follows, from the first to the last, that in this series of inferences, the last consequent will be factually identical with the first antecedent, or with part of what is signified by the first antecedent.

11. In accordance with these statements, I have laid down elsewhere, among others, this thesis: 'From the fact that some thing is known to be, it cannot be inferred evidently, by evidentness reduced to the first principle, or to the certitude of the first principle, that there is some other thing.' Among other arguments (which were quite numerous) I brought forward this argument: "In such an inference in which from one thing another thing would be inferred, the consequent would not be factually identical with the antecedent, nor with

part of what is signified by the antecedent. It therefore follows that such an inference would not be evidently known with the aforesaid evidentness of the first principle. The antecedent is conceded and posited by the opponent. The implication is plain from the definition of 'contradiction,' which runs 'an affirmation and a negation of one and the same [attribute] ... etc.' Since, then, in this case the consequent is not factually identical with the antecedent, or with part of the antecedent, it is manifest that, assuming the opposite of the consequent, and the antecedent to be simultaneously true, there still would not be an 'affirmation and negation of one and the same [attribute] ... etc.'"

12. But Bernard replies, saying that although in this case there is no formal contradiction, for the reason given, yet there is a virtual contradiction; he calls that contradiction virtual from which a formal one can be evidently inferred.

13. But against this you can argue manifestly, on the basis of the fifth and the sixth of the above corollaries. For in these it has been shown that in every inference either mediately or immediately reducible to the certitude of the first principle, it is necessary that the consequent, – whether the first one given or the last – be factually identical with the antecedent first given, or with part of it.

14. It can also manifestly be refuted on the basis of another argument, namely as follows: He says that, although in an inference in which from one thing another thing is inferred, there is not a formal contradiction, yet there is a virtual one from which a formal one can be evidently inferred. Well, let us propose, for example, the following inference: 'A is; therefore B is.' If, then, from the propositions 'A is' and 'B is not,' a formal contradiction could be evidently inferred, this either would be the case by assuming one or more consequents of one of these propositions, or else of each of these propositions. But whichever way it is, the point is not made. For these consequents would either be in fact identical with their antecedents, or they would not. If identical, then: just as there will not be a formal contradiction between those consequents, because there would not be an affirmation and a negation of one and the same [attribute], – likewise this would not be the case between the antecedents either. Just as, if there is no formal contradiction in saying that a man is and a horse is not, so there would not be a formal contradiction either in

asserting a rational animal to be and a neighing animal not to be; and this for the same reason.

15. If it be said, however, that these consequents differ from their antecedents, then (just as before) the implication is not evidently known, with the evidentness reduced to the certitude of the first principle, because the opposite of the consequent would be compatible with whatever is signified by the antecedent, without contradiction. And if one should say that there is a virtual contradiction from which a formal contradiction can be inferred, we will go on as before. And, thus, it [either] would be an infinite process, or else it will be necessary to say that in an inference that is evident in an unqualified sense, the consequent is identical in its meaning with the antecedent or part of what is signified by the antecedent.

16. What this father has said with regard to this matter, is true, [viz.] that it would not be correct to say that, in an inference which is evident in an unqualified sense, it is required that the opposite of the consequent, and the antecedent contradict. For he says that here is a plain counter-instance: 'Every animal is running; therefore every man is running'; indeed, the contradictory of the consequent, and the antecedent can simultaneously be false, and are, therefore, not opposed as contradictories.

17. In actual fact, however, this by no means impedes [what I am maintaining]. For I do not mean to say that the opposite of the consequent must be the contradictory of the antecedent, for in many inferences the antecedent can signify more than does the consequent, albeit that the consequent signifies part of what is signified by the antecedent, as is the case in the inference that has been put forward: 'There is a house; therefore there is a wall.' And on this account the opposite of the consequent, and the antecedent can be both false. But what I mean to say is that in an evident inference, the opposite of the consequent, and the antecedent, or part of what it signifies, are opposed as contradictories.

18. It is obvious that this is the case in every valid syllogism.[3] For since no term occurs in the conclusion without occurring in the premisses, therefore the opposite of the conclusion, and something of what is signified by the premisses, are opposed as contradictories. So it must also be in every valid enthymeme, because an enthymeme[4] is only conclusive in virtue of some withheld proposition; and thus it is a sort of mental syllogism.

19. Furthermore, as to my main thesis I presented the following argument: "Never, in virtue of any implication, can there be inferred a greater mutual identity between the extreme terms than that which existed between the extremes and the middle term, because the former is only inferred in virtue of the latter. But the opposite of this would happen, if from the fact that one thing is a being, it could evidently be inferred that something else is a being, because the predicate and the subject of the conclusion signify what is in fact identical, whereas they are not in fact identical with the middle term, by which some other thing is posited."

20. But Bernard counter-instances against the proposed rule: "It follows evidently, with the evidentness reduced to the certitude of the first principle, 'There is whiteness; therefore there is some thing else,' because there can only be whiteness if some substrate sustains it in being. Likewise it follows 'A is now for the first time; therefore there was something else [before]'; similarly, 'Fire is brought into contact with the hemp; and there is no impediment; therefore there will be heat.'"

21. To these counter-instances I have elsewhere given many answers. But for the present I claim that if he came up with a thousand such counter-instances, either he would have to admit that they are not to the point, or else, if relevant, yet they argue nothing conclusively against me, since in such inferences as he states, the consequent is in fact identical in its meaning either with the antecedent as a whole, or with part of the antecedent, and, therefore, the argument is not to the point, because in that case I would admit the inferences to be evident, and this would not be inconsistent with my position. But if it should be said that the consequent is not identical with the antecedent, or with part of it, then, too, if I admit the opposite of the consequent, and the

---

3 See glossary entry for 'syllogism.'
4 I.e., a syllogism with a suppressed premise.

antecedent to be simultaneously true, it is patent-ly clear that I am not admitting contradictories, because a contradiction concerns one and the same [attribute] ... etc., even so such an inference is not evident either with the evidentness of the first principle, since, it was said, one speaks of "evidentness of the first principle" when, if to admit that the opposite of the consequent is com-patible with the antecedent would amount to admitting that contradictories are simultaneously true. For although someone who, with regard to this inference 'There is a house; therefore there is a wall,' admits that there is a house and there is not a wall, does not [thereby] admit that contra-dictories are simultaneously true (because the propositions 'There is a house' and 'There is not a wall' are not contradictories, for they can be simultaneously false), – yet he does admit contra-dictories for another reason, [viz.] because some-one who indicates that there is a house indicates that there is a wall; and then the contradiction occurs that there is a wall and that there is not a wall.

22. From this rule, thus made plain to whoever is gifted with intellect, I infer that Aristotle never pos-sessed evident knowledge about any substance other than his own soul – taking "substance" as a thing other than the objects of the five senses, and other than our formal experiences. And this is so, because he would have possessed knowledge of such a thing prior to all discursive thought – which is not true, since they are not perceived intuitively, and [if they were] also rustics would know that there are such things. Nor are they known by dis-cursive thought, namely as inferred from what, prior to any discursive thought, is perceived to be – for from one thing it cannot be inferred that there is another thing, as the above thesis states. And if he did not possess evident knowledge of conjoined substances,[5] a fortiori he had no such knowledge of abstract ones.[6]

23. From this it follows – whether you like it or not, and let they not impute it to me, but to the force of argument! – that Aristotle in his entire nat-ural philosophy and metaphysics possessed such certitude of scarcely two conclusions, and perhaps not even of one. And father Bernard, who would not put himself above Aristotle, possesses an equal amount of certitude, or much less.

24. And not only did Aristotle possess no evident knowledge, but, worse than that, – although I do not hold this as a tenet, I have an argument that I am unable to refute, to prove that he did not even possess probable knowledge. For nobody possesses probable knowledge of a consequent in virtue of an antecedent of which he is not absolutely certain whether the consequent has once obtained simulta-neously with the antecedent. For, if one considers it properly, it is in this way that probable knowledge is acquired. For example, because it was once evi-dent to me that when I put my hand toward the fire, I was hot, therefore it seems probable to me that if I should do it now, I would be hot. But from the rule stated above it follows that it was never evident to anyone that, if these things which are apparent before any discursive thought existed, there should be some other things, that is, which are called sub-stances. From this it follows that we do not possess probable knowledge of their existence. I am not committed to this conclusion. Let anyone who can think up a solution refute this argument.

25. And that we do not possess certitude con-cerning any substance conjoined to matter other than our own soul is clear: When a log or a stone has been pointed out, it will be most clearly deduced that a substance is there, from a belief accepted simultaneously. But this cannot be inferred from a simultaneous belief evidently. For, even if all kinds of things are perceived prior to such discursive thought, it can happen, by some power, namely the divine[7], that no substance is there. Therefore in the natural light it is not evi-dently inferred from these appearances that a sub-stance is there. This inference is apparent from what has been explained above. For it was said that an inference which is evident in the natural light is evident in an unqualified manner, so that it is a contradiction that by some power it could occur that the opposite of the consequent would be com-patible with the antecedent. And if he says that the

---

5 I.e., substances composed of form and matter.
6 I.e., "separate substances," which are forms that can exist without being enmattered.
7 God is "omnipotent," i.e. He can make anything be the case which is logically possible.

inference is evident when it is added to the antecedent that God is not performing a miracle, this is disproved along the same line of argument as is found in a similar case in the first letter to Bernard.[8]

26. Please, Father, take notice of these doubts and give counsel to my lack of wisdom. I believe that I will not be obdurate in evading the truth for which I am grasping with all my strength.

---

8 In the first letter Nicholas has argued that, since it is not evident that only natural causes are operative, the antecedent Bernard proposes will not be evident, and thus it cannot lead to evident knowledge of the consequent.

TOPIC VIII:

VIRTUE AND REASON, SIN AND SEX

TOPIC VIII

VIRTUE AND REASON, SIN AND SEX

THE ETHICAL THEORIES OF MOST OF THE GREEK PHILOSOPHERS HAD
stressed excellence of character (virtue) as the key to having a good life. This
excellence was achieved by doing well what human beings by nature are designed
to do, and in the Platonic, Aristotelian and Stoic schools this meant using one's
thinking capacity (Reason) to direct one's life. Within this area of broad agreement there was considerable diversity on the question of how the passions fitted
into (or not) with a good human life. The Platonists tended to view the bodily passions, particularly sexual lust, as obstacles to a person's achieving a life befitting
their true nature. Aristotle held that habituation of the passions to following the
dictates of reason was a large part of moral excellence, and that the bodily passions were particularly prone to violate the rules of "right reason." The Stoics
believed in developing a kind of imperturbability that rid the person of irrational
passions.

Monotheistic religion tended to see the good life as the righteous life lived in
accord with divine wishes and commands. It introduced the notion of "sin," the
deliberate breaking of divine law. In Islam and Christianity there was a definite
belief in an after-life with rewards for the righteous and punishments for the sinners. In this doctrine Islam and Christianity found an ally in Platonism, which
went so far as to think that the present life as a physical organism could be sur-
mounted by the human soul, providing it turned its attentions to the incorporeal
world, i.e. the world it properly belonged to. This Platonic view that humans are
"fallen" spirits coping with a physical world which is essentially alien to them was
adapted in both Islam and Christianity to the story in *Genesis* of the fall of
mankind through the original disobedience of Adam and Eve and God's consequent punishment of them and the whole human race. But the fit was far from
perfect. The monotheistic religions agreed that God had created human beings as
physical creatures and that therefore mere embodiment could not be considered a
punishment for something that occurred after their creation.

The doctrine of original sin makes it difficult, if not impossible, to argue from
the universality of various aspects of human life to their naturalness to humans,
in the way Aristotelians would certainly have argued. Christian and Islamic theologians often accused Aristotle of confusing the general character of life as it is

in the present state, where we suffer from the effects of divine wrath, with what is natural to humans. It is a short step from this to an ethics which recommends looking beyond this life to a better one after death and doing now whatever is needed to secure that future bliss. As the selection from Al-Ghazali shows, hope and fear with respect to this life to come could be made the motivation for living righteously in the life we have now.

Nevertheless, theologians and teachers in the monotheistic religions usually agreed that many of the moral principles they espoused as commands of God had been adopted on rational grounds by the major Greek thinkers, and that the way of life Greek philosophers had encouraged had much in common with what the Deity would see us follow. In particular, the philosophers' disdain for bodily pleasure, especially sex, was approved. Especially in Christianity, since it was more affected by Platonism, sexual lust was looked on as an unfortunate part of our present condition, and a celibate life spent in repressing it held up as an ideal. The pleasures of sex were an unwelcome intrusion into the Platonic realm of Reason, and once Christian intellectuals like Augustine had decided that God Himself was the source of Reason and Order, indeed that being itself was in proportion to the sort of order Reason recognizes, delight in sexual union would have a difficult time maintaining its legitimacy in Christian ethics.

Both ancient philosophy and the monotheistic religions were prone to defending rules of proper conduct, and the codes they proposed had much in common. But is righteousness or virtue (and conversely sin and vice) just a matter of outward observance (or non-observance) of certain rules or commands? Neither the ancient philosophers nor the adherents of monotheistic religions could answer this affirmatively. Outward behavior had to be the manifestation of the proper intentions and desires before it could be called either virtuous or righteous. In Aristotelian ethics actions which strike a mean between excess and deficiency are the ones the virtuous person would do, but they are not *done virtuously* unless the person performs them with pleasure and out of a love for what is noble. In Christian ethics a person is righteous only if they act out of a love or respect for the God who commands upright behaviour. The reader is invited to reflect on whether this emphasis on the proper inner motivation is compatible with the reliance on "hope and fear" to keep us on the straight and narrow path.

VIII.1. ARISTOTLE

LIKE PLATO BEFORE HIM, ARISTOTLE EMPHASIZES WHAT OVERALL END a person should pursue in their life. His answer is *eudaimonia*, usually translated as happiness, i.e. a person should pursue their own happiness. But happiness, according to Aristotle, lies mostly in activity in accordance with human "excellence," often translated 'virtue.' People, then, should be concerned with developing and maintaining their own virtue, and of course the virtue of their children and friends.

VIII.1.1. Excellence (Virtue) and the Mean
(*Nicomachean Ethics* II)

[Aristotle emphasizes the role of habits in becoming morally virtuous. Morally virtuous persons take pleasure in controlling their actions and feelings so that they avoid the extremes of excess and deficiency and strike an intermediate position, the mean. Only the person who is habituated to noble action will consistently take pleasure in it for its own sake, and only this person is genuinely virtuous.]

Chapter 1

Excellence, then, being of two kinds, intellectual and moral, intellectual excellence in the main owes both its birth and its growth to teaching (for which reason it requires experience and time), while moral excellence comes about as a result of habit, whence also its name is one that is formed by a slight variation from the word for habit.[1] From this it is also plain that none of the moral excellences arises in us by nature; for nothing that exists by nature can form a habit contrary to its nature. For instance the stone which by nature moves downwards cannot be habituated to move upwards, not even if one tries to train it by throwing it up ten thousand times; nor can fire be habituated to move downwards, nor can anything else that by nature behaves in one way be trained to behave in another. Neither by nature, then, nor contrary to nature do excellences arise in us; rather we are adapted by nature to receive them, and are made perfect by habit.

Again, of all the things that come to us by nature we first acquire the potentiality and later exhibit the activity (this is plain in the case of the senses; for it was not by often seeing or often hearing that we got these senses, but on the contrary we had them before we used them, and did not come to have them by using them); but excellences we get by first exercising them, as also happens in the case of the arts as well. For the things we have to learn before we can do, we learn by doing, e.g. people become builders by building and lyre-players by playing the lyre; so too we become just by doing just acts, temperate by doing temperate acts, brave by doing brave acts.

This is confirmed by what happens in states; for legislators make the citizens good by forming habits in them, and this is the wish of every legislator; and those who do not effect it miss their mark, and it is in this that a good constitution differs from a bad one.

Again, it is from the same causes and by the same means that every excellence is both produced and destroyed, and similarly every art; for it is from playing the lyre that both good and bad lyre-players are produced. And the corresponding statement is true of builders and of all the rest; people will be good or bad builders as a result of building well or badly. For if this were not so, there would have been no need of a teacher, but all people would have been born good or bad at their craft. This, then, is the case with the excellences also; by doing the acts that we do in our transactions with other people we become just or unjust, and by doing the acts that we do in the presence of danger, and being habituated to feel fear or confidence, we become brave or cowardly. The same is true of appetites and feelings of anger; some people become temperate and

---

1 *ethike* from *ethos*.

good-tempered, others self-indulgent and irascible, by behaving in one way or the other in the appropriate circumstances. Thus, in one word, states arise out of like activities. This is why the activities we exhibit must be of a certain kind; it is because the states correspond to the differences between these. It makes no small difference, then, whether we form habits of one kind or of another from our very youth; it makes a very great difference, or rather *all* the difference.

Chapter 2

Since, then, the present inquiry does not aim at theoretical knowledge like the others (for we are inquiring not in order to know what excellence is, but in order to become good, since otherwise our inquiry would have been of no use), we must examine the nature of actions, namely how we ought to do them; for these determine also the nature of the states that are produced, as we have said. Now, that we must act according to right reason is a common principle and must be assumed – it will be discussed later, i.e. both what it is, and how it is related to the other excellences. But this must be agreed upon beforehand, that the whole account of matters of conduct must be given in outline and not precisely, as we said at the very beginning that the accounts we demand must be in accordance with the subject-matter; matters concerned with conduct and questions of what is good for us have no fixity, any more than matters of health. The general account being of this nature, the account of particular cases is yet more lacking in exactness; for they do not fall under any art or set of precepts, but the agents themselves must in each case consider what is appropriate to the occasion, as happens also in the art of medicine or of navigation.

But though our present account is of this nature we must give what help we can. First, then, let us consider this, that it is the nature of such things to be destroyed by defect and excess, as we see in the case of strength and of health (for to gain light on things imperceptible we must use the evidence of sensible things); both excessive and defective exercise destroys the strength, and similarly drink or food which is above or below a certain amount destroys the health, while that which is proportionate both produces and increases and preserves it. So too is it, then, in the case of temperance and

courage and the other excellences. For the person who flies from and fears everything and does not stand his ground against anything becomes a coward, and the person who fears nothing at all but goes to meet every danger becomes rash; and similarly the person who indulges in every pleasure and abstains from none becomes self-indulgent, while the person who shuns every pleasure, as boors do, becomes in a way insensible; temperance and courage, then, are destroyed by excess and defect, and preserved by the mean.

But not only are the sources and causes of their origination and growth the same as those of their destruction, but also the sphere of their activity will be the same; for this is also true of the things which are more evident to sense, e.g. of strength; it is produced by taking much food and undergoing much exertion, and it is the strong person that will be most able to do these things. So too is it with the excellences; by abstaining from pleasures we become temperate, and it is when we have become so that we are most able to abstain from them; and similarly too in the case of courage; for by being habituated to despise things that are terrible and to stand our ground against them we become brave, and it is when we have become so that we shall be most able to stand our ground against them.

Chapter 3

We must take as a sign of states the pleasure or pain that supervenes on acts; for the person who abstains from bodily pleasures and delights in this very fact is temperate, while the person who is annoyed at it is self-indulgent, and he who stands his ground against things that are terrible and delights in this or at least is not pained is brave, while the person who is pained is a coward. For moral excellence is concerned with pleasures and pains; it is on account of pleasure that we do bad things, and on account of pain that we abstain from noble ones. Hence we ought to have been brought up in a particular way from our very youth, as Plato says, so as both to delight in and to be pained by the things that we ought; for this is the right education.

Again, if the excellences are concerned with actions and passions, and every passion and every action is accompanied by pleasure and pain, for this reason also excellence will be concerned with pleasures and pains. This is indicated also by the fact that punishment is inflicted by these means; for it is a kind of cure, and it is the nature of cures to be effected by contraries.

Again, as we said but lately, every state of soul has a nature relative to and concerned with the kind of things by which it tends to be made worse or better; but it is by reason of pleasures and pains that persons become bad, by pursuing and avoiding these – either the pleasures and pains they ought not or when they ought not or as they ought not, or by going wrong in one of the other similar ways that reason can distinguish. Hence people even define the excellences as certain states of impassivity and rest; not well, however, because they speak absolutely, and do not say "as one ought" and "as one ought not" and "when one ought or ought not," and the other things that may be added. We assume, then, that this kind of excellence tends to do what is best with regard to pleasures and pains, and badness does the contrary.

The following facts also may show us that they are concerned with these same things. There being three objects of choice and three of avoidance, the noble, the advantageous, the pleasant, and their contraries, the base, the injurious, the painful, about all of these the good person tends to go right and the bad person to go wrong, and especially about pleasure; for this is common to the animals, and also it accompanies all objects of choice; for even the noble and the advantageous appear pleasant.

Again, it has grown up with us all from our infancy; this is why it is difficult to rub off this passion, engrained as it is in our life. And we measure even our actions, some of us more and others less, by pleasure and pain. For this reason, then, our whole inquiry must be about these; for to feel delight and pain rightly or wrongly has no small effect on our actions.

Again, it is harder to fight with pleasure than with anger, to use Heraclitus'[2] phrase, but both art and excellence are always concerned with what is harder; for even the good is better when it is harder. Therefore for this reason also the whole concern both of excellence and of political science is with pleasures and pains; for the man who uses these

well will be good, he who uses them badly bad.

That excellence, then, is concerned with pleasures and pains, and that by the acts from which it arises it is both increased and, if they are done differently, destroyed, and that the acts from which it arose are those in which it actualizes itself – let this be taken as said.

Chapter 4

The question might be asked, what we mean by saying that we must become just by doing just acts, and temperate by doing temperate acts; for if people do just and temperate acts, they are already just and temperate, exactly as, if they do what is grammatical or musical they are proficient in grammar and music.

Or is this not true even of the arts? It is possible to do something grammatical either by chance or under the guidance of another. A person will be proficient in grammar, then, only when they have both done something grammatical and done it grammatically; and this means doing it in accordance with the grammatical knowledge in themself.

Again, the case of the arts and that of the excellences are not similar; for the products of the arts have their goodness in themselves, so that it is enough that they should have a certain character, but if the acts that are in accordance with the excellences have themselves a certain character it does not follow that they are done justly or temperately. Agents also must be in a certain condition when they do them; in the first place they must have knowledge, secondly they must choose the acts, and choose them for their own sakes, and thirdly their actions must proceed from a firm and unchangeable character. These are not reckoned in as conditions of the possession of the arts, except the bare knowledge; but as a condition of the possession of the excellences, knowledge has little or no weight, while the other conditions count not for a little but for everything, i.e. the very conditions which result from often doing just and temperate acts.

Actions, then, are called just and temperate when they are such as the just or the temperate person

---

2 Early Greek cosmologist who lived in Ephesus in the late 6th century B.C.E.

would do; but it is not the person who does these that is just and temperate, but the person who also does them as just and temperate persons do them. It is well said, then, that it is by doing just acts that the just person is produced, and by doing temperate acts the temperate person; without doing these no one would have even a prospect of becoming good.

But most people do not do these, but take refuge in theory and think they are being philosophers and will become good in this way, behaving somewhat like patients who listen attentively to their doctors, but do none of the things they are ordered to do. As the latter will not be made well in body by such a course of treatment, the former will not be made well in soul by such a course of philosophy.

Chapter 5

Next we must consider what excellence [virtue] is. Since things that are found in the soul are of three kinds – passions, faculties, states – excellence must be one of these. By passions I mean appetite, anger, fear, confidence, envy, joy, love, hatred, longing, emulation, pity, and in general the feelings that are accompanied by pleasure or pain; by faculties the things in virtue of which we are said to be capable of feeling these, e.g. of becoming angry or being pained or feeling pity; by states the things in virtue of which we stand well or badly with reference to the passions, e.g. with reference to anger we stand badly if we feel it violently or too weakly, and well if we feel it moderately; and similarly with reference to the other passions.

Now neither the excellences nor the vices are *passions*, because we are not called good or bad on the ground of our passions, but are so called on the ground of our excellences and our vices, and because we are neither praised nor blamed for our passions (for the person who feels fear or anger is not praised, nor is the person who simply feels anger blamed, but the person who feels it in a certain way), but for our excellences and our vices we *are* praised or blamed.

Again, we feel anger and fear without choice, but the excellences are choices or involve choice.

Further, in respect of the passions we are said to be moved, but in respect of the excellences and the vices we are said not to be moved but to be disposed in a particular way.

For these reasons also they are not *faculties*; for we are neither called good nor bad, nor praised nor blamed, for the simple capacity of feeling the passions; again, we have the faculties by nature, but we are not made good or bad by nature; we have spoken of this before.

If, then, the excellences are neither passions nor faculties, all that remains is that they should be *states*.

Thus we have stated what excellence is in respect of its genus.[3]

Chapter 6

We must, however, not only describe it as a state, but also say what sort of state it is. We may remark, then, that every excellence both brings into good condition the thing of which it is the excellence and makes the work of that thing be done well; e.g. the excellence of the eye makes both the eye and its work good; for it is by the excellence of the eye that we see well. Similarly the excellence of the horse makes a horse both good in itself and good at running and at carrying its rider and at awaiting the attack of the enemy. Therefore, if this is true in every case, the excellence of human beings also will be the state which makes human beings good and which makes them do their own work well.

How this is to happen we have stated already, but it will be made plain also by the following consideration of the nature of excellence. In everything that is continuous and divisible it is possible to take more, less, or an equal amount, and that either in terms of the thing itself or relatively to us; and the equal is an intermediate between excess and defect. By the intermediate in the object I mean that which is equidistant from each of the extremes, which is one and the same for all people; by the intermediate relatively to us that which is neither too much nor too little – and this is not one, nor the same for all. For instance, if ten is many and two is few, six is intermediate, taken in terms of the object; for it exceeds and is exceeded by an equal amount; this is

---

3 See glossary entry for 'species/genus.'

intermediate according to arithmetical proportion. But the intermediate relatively to us is not to be taken so; if ten pounds are too much for a particular person to eat and two too little, it does not follow that the trainer will order six pounds; for this also is perhaps too much for the person who is to take it, or too little – too little for Milo,[4] too much for the beginner in athletic exercises. The same is true of running and wrestling. Thus a master of any art avoids excess and defect, but seeks the intermediate and chooses this – the intermediate not in the object but relatively to us.

If it is thus, then, that every art does its work well – by looking to the intermediate and judging its works by this standard (so that we often say of good works of the art that it is not possible either to take away or to add anything, implying that excess and defect destroy the goodness of works of art, while the mean preserves it; and good artists, as we say, look to this in their work), and if, further, excellence is more exact and better than any art, as nature also is, then it must have the quality of aiming at the intermediate. I mean moral excellence; for it is this that is concerned with passions and actions, and in these there is excess, defect, and the intermediate. For instance, both fear and confidence and appetite and anger and pity and in general pleasure and pain may be felt both too much and too little, and in both cases not well; but to feel them at the right times, with reference to the right objects, towards the right people, with the right aim, and in the right way, is what is both intermediate and best, and this is characteristic of excellence. Similarly with regard to actions also there is excess, defect, and the intermediate. Now excellence is concerned with passions and actions, in which excess is a form of failure, and so is defect, while the intermediate is praised and is a form of success; and both these things are characteristics of excellence. Therefore excellence is a kind of mean, since it aims at what is intermediate.

Again, it is possible to fail in many ways (for evil belongs to the class of the unlimited, as the Pythagoreans conjectured, and good to that of the limited), while to succeed is possible only in one way (for which reason one is easy and the other dif-

ficult – to miss the mark easy, to hit it difficult); for these reasons also, then, excess and defect are characteristic of vice, and the mean of excellence; for people are good in but one way, but bad in many.

Excellence, then, is a state concerned with choice, lying in a mean relative to us, this being determined by reason and in the way in which the person of practical wisdom[5] would determine it. Now it is a mean between two vices, that which depends on excess and that which depends on defect; and again it is a mean because the vices respectively fall short of or exceed what is right in both passions and actions, while excellence both finds and chooses that which is intermediate. Hence in respect of its substance and the account which states its essence is a mean, with regard to what is best and right it is an extreme.

But not every action nor every passion admits of a mean; for some have names that already imply badness, e.g. spite, shamelessness, envy, and in the case of actions adultery, theft, murder; for all of these and suchlike things imply by their names that they are themselves bad, and not the excesses or deficiencies of them. It is not possible, then, ever to be right with regard to them; one must always be wrong. Nor does goodness or badness with regard to such things depend on committing adultery with the right woman, at the right time, and in the right way, but simply to do any of them is to go wrong. It would be equally absurd, then, to expect that in unjust, cowardly, and self-indulgent action there should be a mean, an excess, and a deficiency; for at that rate there would be a mean of excess and of deficiency, an excess of excess, and a deficiency of deficiency. But as there is no excess and deficiency of temperance and courage because what is intermediate is in a sense an extreme, so too of the actions we have mentioned there is no mean nor any excess and deficiency, but however they are done they are wrong; for in general there is neither a mean of excess and deficiency, nor excess and deficiency of a mean.

Chapter 7

We must, however, not only make this general

4 A well-known wrestler.
5 I.e., the person who has the virtue of *phronesis*, often translated as prudence.

statement, but also apply it to the individual facts. For among statements about conduct those which are general apply more widely, but those which are particular are more true, since conduct has to do with individual cases, and our statements must harmonize with the facts in these cases. We may take these cases from the diagram. With regard to feelings of fear and confidence courage is the mean; of the people who exceed, they who exceed in fearlessness have no name (many of the states have no name), while the person who exceeds in confidence is rash, and the one who exceeds in fear and falls short in confidence is a coward. With regard to pleasures and pains – not all of them, and not so much with regard to the pains – the mean is temperance, the excess self-indulgence. Persons deficient with regard to the pleasures are not often found; hence such persons also have received no name. But let us call them "insensible."

With regard to giving and taking of money the mean is liberality, the excess and the defect prodigality and meanness. They exceed and fall short in contrary ways to one another: the prodigal exceeds in spending and falls short in taking, while the mean person exceeds in taking and falls short in spending. (At present we are giving a mere outline or summary, and are satisfied with this; later these states will be more exactly determined.) With regard to money there are also other dispositions – a mean, magnificence (for the magnificent person differs from the liberal person; the former deals with large sums, the latter with small ones), an excess, tastelessness and vulgarity, and a deficiency, niggardliness; these differ from the states opposed to liberality, and the mode of their difference will be stated later.

With regard to honour and dishonour the mean is proper pride, the excess is known as a sort of empty vanity, and the deficiency is undue humility; and as we said liberality was related to magnificence, differing from it by dealing with small sums, so there is a state similarly related to proper pride, being concerned with small honours while that is concerned with great. For it is possible to desire small honours as one ought, and more than one ought, and less, and the person who exceeds in his desires is called ambitious, the person who falls short unambitious, while the intermediate person has no name. The dispositions also are nameless, except that that of the ambitious person is called

ambition. Hence the people who are at the extremes lay claim to the middle place; and we ourselves sometimes call the intermediate person ambitious and sometimes unambitious, and sometimes praise the ambitious person and sometimes the unambitious. The reason of our doing this will be stated in what follows; but now let us speak of the remaining states according to the method which has been indicated.

With regard to anger also there is an excess, a deficiency, and a mean. Although they can scarcely be said to have names, yet since we call the intermediate person good-tempered let us call the mean good temper; of the persons at the extremes let the one who exceeds be called irascible, and his vice irascibility, and the person who falls short an inirascible sort of person, and the deficiency inirascibility.

There are also three other means, which have a certain likeness to one another, but differ from one another: for they are all concerned with intercourse in words and actions, but differ in that one is concerned with truth in this sphere, the other two with pleasantness; and of the latter pair one kind is exhibited in giving amusement, the other in all the circumstances of life. We must therefore speak of these too, that we may the better see that in all things the mean is praiseworthy, and the extremes neither praiseworthy nor right, but worthy of blame. Now most of these states also have no names, but we must try, as in the other cases, to invent names ourselves so that we may be clear and easy to follow. With regard to truth, then, the intermediate is a truthful sort of person and the mean may be called truthfulness, while the pretence which exaggerates is boastfulness and the person characterized by it a boaster, and that which understates is mock modesty and the person characterized by it mock-modest. With regard to pleasantness in the giving of amusement the intermediate person is ready-witted and the disposition ready wit, the excess is buffoonery and the person characterized by it a buffoon, while the man who falls short is a sort of boor and his state is boorishness. With regard to the remaining kind of pleasantness, that which is exhibited in life in general, the person who is pleasant in the right way is friendly and the mean is friendliness, while the persons who exceed are obsequious persons if they have no end in view, flatterers if they are aiming at their own advantage, and the person who falls short and is unpleasant in all circumstances is a quarrelsome and surly sort of person.

There are also means in the passions and concerned with the passions; since shame is not an excellence, and yet praise is extended to the modest person. For even in these matters one person is said to be intermediate, and another to exceed, as for instance the bashful person who is ashamed of everything; while he who falls short or is not ashamed of anything at all is shameless, and the intermediate person is modest. Righteous indignation is a mean between envy and spite, and these states are concerned with the pain and pleasure that are felt at the fortunes of our neighbours; the person who is characterized by righteous indignation is pained at undeserved good fortune, the envious person, going beyond him, is pained at all good fortune, and the spiteful person falls so far short of being pained that he even rejoices. But these states there will be an opportunity of describing elsewhere; with regard to justice, since it has not one simple meaning, we shall, after describing the other states, distinguish its two kinds and say how each of them is a mean; and similarly we shall treat also of the rational excellences.

Chapter 8

There are three kinds of disposition, then, two of them vices, involving excess and deficiency and one an excellence, viz. the mean, and all are in a sense opposed to all; for the extreme states are contrary both to the intermediate state and to each other, and the intermediate to the extremes; as the equal is greater relatively to the less, less relatively to the greater, so the middle states are excessive relatively to the deficiencies, deficient relatively to the excesses, both in passions and in actions. For the brave person appears rash relatively to the coward, and cowardly relatively to the rash man; and similarly the temperate person appears self-indulgent relatively to the insensible person, insensible relatively to the self-indulgent, and the liberal person prodigal relatively to the mean person, mean relatively to the prodigal. Hence also the people at the extremes push the intermediate person each over to the other, and the brave person is called rash by the coward, cowardly by the rash person, and correspondingly in the other cases.

These states being thus opposed to one another, the greatest contrariety is that of the extremes to each other, rather than to the intermediate; for these are further from each other than from the intermediate, as the great is further from the small and the small from the great than both are from the equal. Again, to the intermediate some extremes show a certain likeness, as that of rashness to courage and that of prodigality to liberality; but the extremes show the greatest unlikeness to each other; now contraries are defined as the things that are furthest from each other, so that things that are further apart are more contrary.

To the mean in some cases the deficiency, in some the excess is more opposed; e.g. it is not rashness, which is an excess, but cowardice, which is a deficiency, that is more opposed to courage, and not insensibility, which is a deficiency, but self-indulgence, which is an excess, that is more opposed to temperance. This happens from two reasons, one being drawn from the thing itself; for because one extreme is nearer and liker to the intermediate, we oppose not this but rather its contrary to the intermediate. E.g., since rashness is thought liker and nearer to courage, and cowardice more unlike, we oppose rather the latter to courage; for things that are further from the intermediate are thought more contrary to it. This, then, is one cause, drawn from the thing itself; another is drawn from ourselves; for the things to which we ourselves more naturally tend seem more contrary to the intermediate. For instance, we ourselves tend more naturally to pleasures, and hence are more easily carried away towards self-indulgence than towards propriety. We describe as contrary to the mean, then, the states into which we are more inclined to lapse; and therefore self-indulgence, which is an excess, is the more contrary to temperance.

Chapter 9

That moral excellence is a mean, then, and in what sense it is so, and that it is a mean between two vices, the one involving excess, the other deficiency, and that it is such because its character is to aim at what is intermediate in passions and in actions, has been sufficiently stated. Hence also it is no easy task to be good. For in everything it is no easy task to find the middle, e.g. to find the middle of a circle is not for everyone but for him who knows; so, too, any one can get angry – that is easy – or give or spend money; but to do this to the right person, to the right extent, at the right time, with the right aim, and in the right way, *that* is not for everyone, nor is it easy; that is why goodness is both rare and laudable and noble.

Hence he who aims at the intermediate must first depart from what is the more contrary to it, as Calypso advises –

Hold the ship out beyond that surf and spray.

For of the extremes one is more erroneous, one less so; therefore, since to hit the mean is hard in the extreme, we must as a second best, as people say, take the least of the evils; and this is done best in the way we describe.

But we must consider the things towards which we ourselves also are easily carried away; for some of us tend to one thing, some to another; and this will be recognizable from the pleasure and the pain we feel. We must drag ourselves away to the contrary extreme; for we shall get into the intermediate state by drawing well away from error, as people do in straightening sticks that are bent.

Now in everything the pleasant or pleasure is most to be guarded against; for we do not judge it impartially. We ought, then, to feel towards pleasure as the elders of the people felt towards Helen, and in all circumstances repeat their saying; for if we dismiss pleasure thus we are less likely to go astray. It is by doing this, then, (to sum the matter up) that we shall best be able to hit the mean.

But this is no doubt difficult, and especially in individual cases; for it is not easy to determine both how and with whom and on what provocation and how long one should be angry; for we too sometimes praise those who fall short and call them good-tempered, but sometimes we praise those who get angry and call them manly. The person, however who deviates little from goodness is not blamed, whether he do so in the direction of the more or of the less, but only the person who deviates more widely; for *he* does not fail to be noticed. But up to what point and to what extent a person must deviate before they become blameworthy it is not easy to determine by reasoning, any more than anything else that is perceived by the senses; such things depend on particular facts, and the decision

rests with perception. So much, then, makes it plain that the intermediate state is in all things to be praised, but that we must incline sometimes towards the excess, sometimes towards the deficiency; for so shall we most easily hit the mean and what is right.

VIII.1.2. Ethics and Deliberation (*Nicomachean Ethics* III, ch.3)

[Questions of moral excellence arise paradigmatically in situations where we must deliberate about some choice. But we do not deliberate about everything. Aristotle says we deliberate only about possible means to some end we have already accepted.]

Do we deliberate about everything, and is everything a possible subject of deliberation, or is deliberation impossible about some things? We ought presumably to call not what a fool or a madman would deliberate about, but what a sensible person would deliberate about, a subject of deliberation. Now about eternal things no one deliberates, e.g. about the universe or the incommensurability of the diagonal and the side of a square. But no more do we deliberate about the things that involve movement but always happen in the same way, whether of necessity or by nature or from any other cause, e.g. the solstices and the risings of the stars; nor about things that happen now in one way, now in another, e.g. droughts and rains; nor about chance events, like the finding of treasure. But we do not deliberate even about all human affairs; for instance, no Spartan deliberates about the best constitution for the Scythians. For none of these things can be brought about by our own efforts.

We deliberate about things that are in our power and can be done; and these are in fact what is left. For nature, necessity, and chance are thought to be causes,[6] and also thought and everything that depends on people. Now every class of persons deliberates about the things that can be done by their own efforts. And in the case of exact and self-contained sciences there is no deliberation, e.g. about the letters of the alphabet (for we have no doubt how they should be written); but the things that are brought about by our own efforts, but not

---

6 See selection I.1.3.

always in the same way, are the things about which we deliberate, e.g. questions of medical treatment or of money-making. And we do so more in the case of the art of navigation than in that of gymnastics, inasmuch as it has been less exactly worked out, and again about other things in the same ratio, and more also in the case of the arts than in that of the sciences; for we have more doubt about the former. Deliberation is concerned with things that happen in a certain way for the most part, but in which the event is obscure, and with things in which it is indeterminate. We call in others to aid us in deliberation on important questions, distrusting ourselves as not being equal to deciding.

We deliberate not about ends but about what contributes to ends. For doctors do not deliberate whether they shall heal, nor orators whether they shall convince, nor statesmen whether they shall produce law and order, nor does any one else deliberate about his end. Having set the end they consider how and by what means it is to be attained; and if it seems to be produced by several means they consider by which it is most easily and best produced, while, if it is achieved by one only, they consider how it will be achieved by this and by what means this will be achieved, till they come to the first cause, which in the order of discovery is last. For the person who deliberates seems to inquire and analyse in the way described as though they were analysing a geometrical construction (not all inquiry appears to be deliberation – for instance mathematical inquiries – but all deliberation is inquiry), and what is last in the order of analysis seems to be first in the order of becoming. And if we come on an impossibility, we give up the search, e.g. if we need money and this cannot be got; but if a thing appears possible we try to do it. By "possible" things I mean things that might be brought about by our own efforts; and these in a sense include things that can be brought about by the efforts of our friends, since the moving principle is in ourselves. The subject of investigation is sometimes the instruments, sometimes the use of them; and similarly in the other cases – sometimes the means, sometimes the mode of using it or the means of bringing it about. It seems, then, as has been said, that a person is a moving principle of actions; now deliberation is about the things to be done by the agent himself, and actions are for the sake of things other than themselves. For the end cannot be a subject of deliberation, but only what contributes to the ends; nor indeed can the particular facts be a subject of it, as whether this is bread or has been baked as it should; for these are matters of perception. If we are to be always deliberating, we shall have to go on to infinity.

The same thing is deliberated upon and is chosen, except that the object of choice is already determinate, since it is that which has been decided upon as a result of deliberation that is the object of choice. For every one ceases to inquire how he is to act when he has brought the moving principle back to himself and to the ruling part of himself; for this is what chooses. This is plain also from the ancient constitutions, which Homer represented; for the kings announced their choices to the people. The object of choice being one of the things in our own power which is desired after deliberation, choice will be deliberate desire of things in our own power; for when we have decided as a result of deliberation, we desire in accordance with our deliberation.

We may take it, then, that we have described choice in outline, and stated the nature of its objects and the fact that it is concerned with what contributes to the ends.

VIII.2. ST. AUGUSTINE

AUGUSTINE'S PECULIAR BLEND OF BIBLICAL AND GREEK ETHICS was to be the benchmark in the field in Christian thought until Aristotle's ethics was recovered in the thirteenth century, and even then it remained a powerful influence. His emphasis on reason as opposed to the senses and bodily passions shows his deep indebtedness to the Platonists.

VIII.2.1. What is the Supreme Good for Human Beings? (from *The Way of Life of the Catholic Church*)

[The idea of a "supreme good" or "end" that human beings should pursue was present in all the ancient Greek ethical theorists. But in their case that good was usually a way of life or an excellence of character that people could strive for. Augustine pushes the notion in a religious direction by arguing that this supreme good can only be the Divinity Himself.]

Chapter 3

(4) Let us inquire, then, how according to reason human beings ought to live. Certainly, we all wish to live happily. There is no human being who would not assent to this statement almost before it is uttered. However, in my opinion, neither one who lacks what he loves can be called happy, whatever it be, nor one who has what he loves if it be harmful, nor one who does not love what he has although it be the best. For he who desires what he cannot obtain is tormented, and he who has attained what he should not have desired is deceived, while he who does not desire what he should seek to attain is diseased. To souls such as these, there remains nothing but misery, and since misery and happiness are not accustomed to dwell in the same person simultaneously, none of these persons can be happy.

As I see it, however, a fourth alternative remains in which the happy life may be found – when that which is best for a human being is both loved and possessed. For what else is meant by enjoyment but the possession of what one loves? But no one is happy who does not enjoy what is supremely good

for human beings, and whoever does enjoy it is not unhappy. We must possess our supreme good, therefore, if we intend to live happily.

(5) It follows that we must seek to discover what is the supreme good for human beings, and it cannot, of course, be anything inferior to humans themselves; for whoever strives after something inferior to themselves becomes themself inferior. But all human beings are obliged to seek what is best. Therefore, the supreme good for human beings is not inferior to human beings.

Will it then perhaps be something similar to human beings themselves? It might well be so, provided there is nothing superior to human beings that they can enjoy. If, however, we find something that is both more perfect than human beings and which can be attained by the one loving it, who would doubt that they should, in order to be happy, strive to possess this thing, which is more excellent than they themselves who seek it? For if happiness is the possession of a good than which there is no greater, and this is what we call the supreme good, how can a person be said to be happy who has not yet attained their supreme good? Or how can it be called the supreme good if there is something better that they can attain? Such being the case, it follows that one cannot lose it against their will, for no one can be confident of a good they know can be snatched from them even though they wish to keep and cherish it. And if they lack this confidence in the good which they enjoy, how can they, in such fear of loss, be happy?

Chapter 4

(6) Let us, then, attempt to discover what is better than human beings. And this will be very difficult unless we first discuss what human beings them-

selves are. But I do not think I should be expected to give a definition of *human being* here. Rather, it seems to me that since nearly everyone agrees (or at least, and it is sufficient, those with whom I am now dealing agree) that we are composed of body and soul, what should be determined at this point is *what human beings themselves are.* Of the two which I have mentioned, are they body alone or soul alone? For although these are two things, soul and body, and neither could be called a human being were the other not present (for the body would not be a human being if there were no soul, nor would the soul be a human being were there no body animated by it), it might happen, nevertheless, that one of these would be looked upon and be spoken of as a human being.

What do we call "human being," then? Is the human a soul and body like a centaur or two horses harnessed together? Or shall we call him the body alone in the service of a governing soul, as is the case when we give the name *lamp,* not to the vessel and flame together, but to the vessel alone on account of the flame within it? Or shall we say that a human is nothing but the soul, inasmuch as it rules the body, just as we say that the horseman is not the horse and human together, but the human alone from the fact that he guides the horse? This is a difficult problem to solve, or, at any rate, even if its solution were simple, it would require a lengthy explanation involving an expense of time and labor which would not profit us here. For whether it be both body and soul or soul alone that goes by the name of 'human being,' that is not the supreme good for human beings which constitutes the supreme good of the body. But whatever is the highest good either of body and soul together or of the soul alone, that is the supreme good for human beings.

Chapter 5

(7) If we ask what is the supreme good of the body, reason compels us to admit it is whatever causes the body to be at its best. But of all the things that give vigor to the body, none is better nor more important than the soul. Hence, the supreme good of the body is not sensual pleasure, nor absence of pain, nor strength, nor beauty, nor swiftness, nor whatever else is ordinarily numbered among the goods of the body, but the soul alone. For by its very pres-

ence, the soul provides the body with all the things we have enumerated and with that which excels them all besides, namely, life. Therefore, it does not seem to me that the soul is the supreme good for human beings, whether we call a human being soul and body together, or soul alone. For, as reason declares, the greatest good of the body is that which is better than the body and by which the body is given life and vigor, so, too, whether the body and soul together be the human being or the soul alone, we must still find out whether there is anything beyond the soul itself which, when sought after, makes the soul more perfect in its own order. If we can discover some such thing, all of our doubts will be removed, for it will unquestionably merit the name of the supreme good for human beings.

(8) If the body be a human being, it cannot be denied that the supreme good for human beings is the soul. But, surely, when it is a question of morals – when we ask what kind of life we must lead in order to attain happiness – the commandments are not for the body, and we are not concerned with bodily discipline. In a word, good morals pertain to that part of us which inquires and learns, and these are acts of the soul. Therefore, when we are dealing with the attainment of virtue, the question is not one which concerns the body. But if it follows, as it does, that the body when ruled by a virtuous soul is ruled both better and more worthily and is at its best because of the perfection of the soul ruling it rightly, then that which perfects the soul will be the supreme good for human beings even though we call the body a human being. For if at my command the charioteer feeds and properly manages the horses in his care, and enjoys my generosity in proportion as he is obedient to me, who can deny that not only the charioteer but the horses, too, owe their well being to me? And so, whether body alone, or soul alone, or both together be the human being, the important thing, it seems to me, is to discover what makes the soul perfect, for when this is attained, a man cannot but be perfect, or at least much better than if it were lacking to him.

Chapter 6

(9) No one disputes the fact that virtue perfects the soul, but the question might well be asked as to whether virtue can exist by itself or only in the

soul. This is another of those profound questions demanding lengthy discussion, but perhaps a summary will be adequate for our purpose. And I hope that God will grant His assistance, so that, to the extent our weakness of mind permits, we may treat this subject not only clearly but briefly as well.

Whichever it be – whether virtue can exist by itself without the soul, or whether it cannot exist except in the soul – doubtless, the soul seeks after something in order to attain virtue, and this must be either itself, or virtue, or some third thing. If the soul pursues itself in seeking virtue, it pursues something foolish, since the soul itself is foolish before it has acquired virtue. And since the supreme desire of all who seek is to attain what they are seeking, in this case either the soul must not wish to attain what it seeks, and there is nothing more absurd nor perverse than this, or, in pursuing its foolish self, it attains the very foolishness from which it flees. But if, in its desire to attain virtue, it seeks after it, how can it seek what does not exist? Or how can it desire to attain what it already has? Therefore, either virtue is outside the soul, or, if we must reserve the name of virtue only for that disposition or quality of the wise soul which cannot exist except in the soul, it remains that the soul must pursue something else in order that virtue may arise within itself. For neither by pursuing nothing nor by pursuing foolishness can the soul, in my opinion, reach wisdom.

(10) Consequently, this something else, through the seeking of which the soul becomes possessed of virtue and wisdom, is either a wise person or God. But as has been said above, it must be of such a nature that we cannot lose it against our will. Now who would hesitate to admit that a wise person, should we be satisfied to follow after him, can be taken from us, not only against our will, but even in spite of our resistance? Only God remains, therefore. If we follow after Him, we live well; if we reach Him, we live not only well but happily. As for those who may deny that God exists, I cannot concern myself with arguments by which to persuade them, for I am not even sure that we ought to enter into discussion with them at all. To do so, in any event, would necessitate starting out all over again

with a different approach, a different method, and different arguments from those we have taken up at present. I am now concerned only with those who do not deny God's existence and who, besides, acknowledge that He is not indifferent to human affairs. For I cannot believe there is anyone who considers himself religious who does not hold at least that Divine Providence looks after our souls.

VIII.2.2. The Ultimate Good is not to be found in this Life (*On the City of God* XIX, ch.4)

[This passage is one of Augustine's harshest criticisms of the view of human happiness that he had found in the ancient schools of philosophy, particularly among the Stoics.]

What view the Christians hold about the supreme good and the supreme evil, as against the philosophers who have maintained that for them the supreme good is in themselves.

If, then, we are asked what the City of God replies when asked about these several matters, and first what its opinion is about the ultimate good and the ultimate evil, it will reply that the ultimate good is eternal life, and that the ultimate evil is eternal death, and that in order to obtain the one and escape the other we must live rightly. Wherefore it is written: "The just person lives by faith."[1] For neither do we see as yet our good, and therefore must seek it by believing, nor is it in our power of ourselves to live rightly unless he who has given us faith to believe that we must seek help from him shall help us, as we believe in and pray to him. But those who have supposed that the ultimate good and evil are to be found in the present life, placing the ultimate good either in the body or in the soul or in both, or, to speak more explicitly, either in pleasure or in virtue or in both, in repose or in virtue or in both, in pleasure combined with repose or in virtue or in both, in the primary wants of nature or in virtue or in both, all these persons have sought, with a surprising vanity, to be happy in this life and to get happiness by their own efforts. Truth laughed at these people through the words of the prophet: "The Lord knows the

---

1 Habakkuk 2:4; *Romans* 1:17; *Galatians* 3:11; *Hebrews* 10:38.

thoughts of men,"[2] or, as the apostle Paul has set forth this passage: "The Lord knows the thoughts of the wise, that they are vain."[3]

For who, no matter how great his torrent of eloquence, can avail to enumerate the miseries of this life? Cicero lamented them, as best he could, in the *Consolation* on the death of his daughter; but how inadequate was his best! For when, where, how can the so-called primary wants of nature be on such a good footing in this life that they are not tossed about at the mercy of blind accidents? Why, what pain is there, the opposite of pleasure, what turbulence is there, the opposite of repose, that may not assail the wise person's frame? Surely the amputation or weakening of a person's limbs forces his freedom from physical defects to capitulate, ugliness his beauty, illness his health, weariness his strength, sleepiness or sluggishness his agility; now, which of these may not invade the flesh of the wise person? Fitting and harmonious attitudes and movements of the body are also reckoned among the primary wants of nature; but what if some disease makes the limbs quake and tremble? What if a person's spine be so bent that he puts his hands on the ground, which makes of him a quadruped, so to speak? Will not this ruin all beauty and grace whether of bodily pose or of movement?

What of the so-called primary goods of the mind itself, of which the two that are rated first, as means to the grasping and observing of truth, are sensation and intelligence? But how much sensation remains, and of what value, if a person becomes deaf and blind, to say nothing of other defects? And whither will reason and intelligence withdraw, where will they slumber, if a person is crazed by some disease? When the insane say or do many absurd things that are for the most part alien to their own aims and characters, – nay, even opposed to their good aims and characters, – whether we use our imaginations or have them before our eyes, if we reflect on their case as it deserves, we can scarce hold back our tears, or it may be even that we cannot. What shall I say of those who are afflicted by attacks of demons? In what hidden or submerged places do their intellects lurk, when the evil spirit is using their souls and bodies according to its own will? And who is quite sure that this evil cannot befall the wise person in this life? Then what sort of observation of truth is there in this flesh, or how great is it, when, as we read in the truthful book of Wisdom: "The corruptible body weighs down the soul, and the earthly frame lies heavy on a mind that ponders many things?"[4] Furthermore, drive or impulse to act, – if either is the correct Latin word for what the Greeks call *horme,* for that, too, is included among the primary goods of nature, – is not impulse also responsible for those pitiable movements and acts of the insane that shock us, when sensation is distraught and reason is asleep?

Finally, as to virtue itself, which is not among the primary wants of nature, since it is a later addition ushered in by instruction, although it claims the highest place among human goods, what is its activity here but perpetual war with vices, not external vices but internal, not alien but clearly our very own, a war waged especially by that virtue called in Greek *sophrosyne* and in Latin temperance, which bridles the lusts of the flesh lest they win the consent of the mind and drag it into crimes of every sort? For it is not the case that there is no vice when, as the Apostle says: "The flesh lusts against the spirit." For to this vice there is an opposing virtue, when, as the same Apostle says: "The spirit lusts against the flesh. These two," he says, "are opposed one to the other, so that you do not what you would."[5] But what is it that we would do, when we wish to be made perfect by the ultimate good, unless it be that the flesh should not lust against the spirit, and that there should be in us no such vice for the spirit to lust against it? But since we cannot bring that to pass in the present life, however much we may desire it, we can at least with God's help so act that we do not yield to the lust of the flesh against the spirit by failure of the spirit, and we are not dragged with our own consent to the perpetration of sin. Far be it from us, then, so long as we are engaged in this internal war,

---

2 *Psalms* 94:11.
3 1 *Corinthians* 3:20.
4 *Wisdom* 9:15.
5 *Galatians* 5:17.

to hold it true that we have already attained to that happiness which is the goal that we would gain by victory. And who is so wise that he has no battle at all to wage against his lusts?

What of that virtue which is called prudence? Does she not devote all her vigilance to the discrimination of good and evil, so that in pursuing the one and shunning the other no error may creep in? Thus she bears witness herself that we are among evils, that is, that evils are in us; for she teaches us herself that it is an evil to yield to a lust for sin, and a good not to yield to a lust for sin. But that evil to which prudence teaches and temperance causes us not to yield, is neither by prudence nor by temperance banished from this life. What of justice, whose function it is to assign to each person their due, whereby there is located in man himself a certain right order of nature, so that soul is subordinated to God, and flesh to soul, and therefore both soul and flesh to God? Does not justice thereby demonstrate that she is still labouring in her task rather than resting already at the goal of her labours? For the less the soul keeps God clearly in mind in all its activity, the less it is subordinate to God; and the more the flesh lusts against the spirit, the less it is subordinate to the soul. So long, then, as we have in us this weakness, this sickness, this torpor, how shall we dare say that we are already saved, and if not saved, how already blest with that ultimate bliss? Then truly that virtue called fortitude, though combined with however great wisdom, bears witness most convincingly to human ills, for they are what she is required to endure with patience.

Now I am amazed that the Stoic philosophers have the face to argue that these ills are no ills, though they admit that, if they should be so great that the wise person cannot or ought not to endure them, he is compelled to inflict death on himself and depart from this life. But such is the stupid pride of these men who suppose that the supreme good is to be found in this life, and that they can be the agents of their own happiness, that their wise person, – I mean the person whom they describe as such with astounding inanity, – whom, even if he be blinded and grow deaf and dumb, lose the use of his limbs, be tortured with pain, and visited by every other evil of the sort that tongue can utter or fancy conceive, whereby he is driven to inflict death on himself, they do not scruple to call happy. What a happy life, that seeks the help of death to end it! If it be happy, let a person stay in it. How can those things not be evil that vanquish the good that is fortitude, and compel it not only to give way to them but so to rave that it calls the same life happy from which it advises us to escape? Who is so blind as not to perceive that, if it were happy, it would not be a life to escape from? Why, the word 'escape' is an unconcealed admission of weakness in their argument! What ground have they now to keep them, with stiff-necked pride broken, from admitting that it is even a wretched life? Was it not through lack of fortitude, rather than through fortitude, that the famous Cato[6] took his life? For he would not have done it, had he not lacked the fortitude to bear the victory of Caesar. Where, then, is his fortitude? It yielded, it succumbed, it was so far vanquished that he gave up, forsook, escaped from this happy life. Or was it no longer happy? Then it was wretched. How, then, were those not evils that made life wretched and a thing to be escaped from?

And therefore those who admitted that these are evils, as did the Peripatetics[7] and the Old Academics,[8] the sect that Varro[9] defends, speak in a more tolerable manner; but they, too, are sponsors of a surprising error, in that they maintain that amid these evils, even if they be so grave that he who suffers them is obliged to escape by seeking his own death, life is nevertheless happy. "Among evils," says Varro, "are pains and anguish of body, and their evil is the greater in proportion to their severity; and to avoid them one should escape from this life." What life, pray? "This life," he says, "that is beset by so great evils." So it is definitely happy,

---

6 Cato the younger, who committed suicide in 46 B.C.E. when Julius Caesar defeated Pompey to become dictator of Rome.

7 I.e., the Aristotelian school.

8 Skeptics who took over Plato's Academy in the 3rd century B.C.E. Their position is discussed in many of the selections of topic **VII**.

9 Narcus Tarrentius Varro, who lived in the 2nd century C.E. and on whose works Augustine depended for much of his knowledge of ancient philosophy. The doctrines Augustine describes here are those of the Stoics.

then, amid those very evils because of which you say that one must escape from it? Or do you call it happy because you have freedom to escape from these evils by death? What, then, if by some divine judgement you were held among them and were not permitted either to die or ever to be free of them? Then, no doubt, at any rate, you would say that such a life is wretched. So it is not unwretched merely because it is soon abandoned, inasmuch as, if it were everlasting, even you yourself would pronounce it to be wretched. And so it ought not to be judged free from all wretchedness because the wretchedness is brief; or, still more absurdly, because the wretchedness is brief, on that account be even called a state of bliss.

Mighty is the power in these evils that compel a person, and according to these philosophers compel even a wise person, to deprive himself of his own existence as a human being; although they say, and say truly, that the first and greatest commandment of nature is that a person should be brought into harmony with himself and therefore instinctively avoid death, and that he be his own friend in such wise as to be vigorously determined and eager to keep the breath of life and to live on in this union of body and soul. Mighty is the power in these evils that overcome the natural feeling we hear of, by whose working we use every means and bend all our strength and all our endeavours to avoid death, and so completely defeat nature that what was avoided is now longed for, pursued, and, if it may not arrive from some other quarter, inflicted on a person by himself. Mighty is the power in these evils that make fortitude a homicide, if indeed she should still be called fortitude who is overcome by these evils so completely that she not only cannot by her endurance safeguard the human being whom, as virtue, she has undertaken to govern and protect but is herself compelled to go to the length of killing him. The wise person ought, to be sure, to endure even death with firmness, but death that befalls him from an external source. If, then, he is compelled, according to these philosophers, to inflict it on himself, surely they must admit not only that those are evils but that they are in fact intolerable evils that compel him to perpetrate this crime.

The life, then, that is oppressed by the weight of such great and grievous evils or exposed to the chance of them would by no means be termed happy if the people who use that term, – people who, when they are defeated by the increasing pressure of their ills, in the act of inflicting death upon themselves, surrender to misfortune, – would with equal condescension, when they are defeated by sound logic in the attempt to discover a happy life, surrender to the truth, instead of supposing that the enjoyment of the supreme good is a goal to be attained in the mortal state of which they speak. For our very virtues, which are surely the best and most useful attributes of a human being, bear trustworthy witness to life's miseries so much the more, the more strongly they support us against life's dangers, toils and sorrows. For if our virtues are genuine, – and genuine virtues can exist only in those who are endowed with true piety, – they do not lay claim to such powers as to say that persons in whom they reside will suffer no miseries (for true virtues are not so fraudulent in their claims); but they do say that our human life, though it is compelled by all the great evils of this age to be wretched, is happy in the expectation of a future life in so far as it enjoys the expectation of salvation too. For how can a life be happy, if it has no salvation yet? So the apostle Paul, speaking not of persons who lacked prudence, patience, temperance and justice, but of persons who lived in accordance with true piety, and whose virtues were therefore genuine, says: "Now we are saved by hope. But hope that is seen is not hope. For how should a person hope for what he sees? But if we hope for that which we do not see, then we look forward with endurance."[10] As, therefore, we are saved by hope, so it is by hope that we have been made happy; and as we have no hold on a present salvation, but look for salvation in the future, so we look forward to happiness, and a happiness to be won by endurance. For we are among evils, which we ought patiently to endure until we arrive among those goods where nothing will be lacking to provide us ineffable delight, nor will there now be anything that we are obliged to endure. Such is the salvation which in the life to come will itself be also the ultimate bliss. But those philosophers, not believing in

10 *Romans* 8:24,25. On the importance of hope to Islamic faith see selection **VIII.3.1.**

this blessedness because they do not see it, strive to manufacture for themselves in this life an utterly counterfeit happiness by drawing on a virtue whose fraudulence matches its arrogance.

VIII.2.3. How Order pervades everything (from *Concerning Order* II, ch.4-5)

[Order, proportion, harmony – these are the sources of beauty and the mark of the divine in the world. Augustine here develops this Pythagorean and Platonist theme. *Concerning Order* was one of the earliest of Augustine's works, written in the very year of his conversion to Christianity. It is in dialogue form, the participants being Augustine and two pupils, Licentius and Trygetius (who also participated in the dialogue found in selection **VII.1.1**).]

Chapter 4

(11) "But let us get back to order, for Licentius may at any moment be returned to us. For the present, I ask you this question: Does it seem to you that the unwise person acts according to order, no matter what he does? But, mark what snares the question contains. If you say that he acts according to order, then, if even the unwise person always acts according to order, what will become of that definition: *Order is that by which God governs all things that are?* And, if there is no order in the things that are done by the unwise person, then there will be something which order does not embrace. But you are not willing to accept either alternative. See to it, I beg you, lest in your defense of order you throw everything into disorder."

At this point Trygetius answered again, for the other boy was still absent:

"It is easy," he said, "to reply to this dilemma of yours. For the moment, however, I cannot call to mind an analogy by which my opinion ought, I know, to be declared and illustrated. I shall simply state my impression, for you will do what you did a little while ago. Certainly that mention of the darkness has brought us a great deal of light on what has been put forward very obscurely by me. Indeed, the entire life of the unwise, although it is by no means consistent and by no means well regulated by themselves, is, nevertheless, necessarily included in the order of things by Divine Providence. And,

certain places having been arranged, so to speak, by that ineffable and eternal law, it is by no means permitted to be where it ought not to be. Thus it happens that whoever narrow-mindedly considers this life by itself alone is repelled by its enormous foulness, and turns away in sheer disgust. But, if he raises the eyes of the mind and broadens his field of vision and surveys all things as a whole, then he will find nothing unarranged, unclassed, or unassigned to its own place."

(12) "What great and wonderful responses does not God Himself – and, as I am more and more led to believe, also that unfathomable order of things – send to me through you! Verily, you speak things of such import that I cannot understand either how you discern them or how they can be spoken unless they are discerned. And for that reason I believe that they are both true and from on high. Now, you were looking for just one or two illustrations for that opinion of yours. To me there already occur countless illustrations which bring me to complete agreement. What more hideous than a hangman? What more cruel and ferocious than his character? Yet he holds a necessary post in the very midst of laws, and he is incorporated into the order of a well-regulated state; himself criminal in character, he is nevertheless, by others' arrangement, the penalty of evildoers. What can be mentioned more sordid, more bereft of decency, or more full of turpitude than prostitutes, procurers, and the other pests of that sort? Remove prostitutes from human affairs, and you will unsettle everything because of lusts; place them in the position of matrons, and you will dishonor these latter by disgrace and ignominy. This class of people is, therefore, by its own mode of life most unchaste in its morals; by the law of order, it is most vile in social condition.

"And is it not true that in the bodies of animals there are certain members which you could not bear to look at, if you should view them by themselves alone? But the order of nature has designed that because they are needful they shall not be lacking, and because they are uncomely they shall not be prominent. And these ugly members, by keeping their proper places, have provided a better position for the more comely ones. What more agreeable to us – because it was quite an appropriate sight for field and farmyard – than that contest and conflict of the barnyard cock, which we have related in the preceding book? But, what have we ever seen more abject than the deformity of the vanquished one? And yet, by that very deformity was the more perfect beauty of the contest in evidence."

(13) "So it is, I think, with all things, but they have to be seen. Poets have found delight in what they call solecisms and barbarisms. But, by a mere change of name, they chose to call them tropes and metaplasms, rather than refrain altogether from the use of such manifest blunders. Remove these from poems: we shall be wanting their delightful relish. Crowd a great many of them into one passage: I shall loathe the whole passage as sour, malodorous, and rancid. Carry them over into familiar and forensic speech: who will not bid them flee and retreat to the theater? Because order directs and restrains them, it does not suffer them to be in excess in their proper place, or to be anywhere out of place. Unpretentious and seemingly inelegant diction, interspersed in a discourse, brings into bolder relief the fancy flights and the ornate passages. If it is ever by itself alone, you throw it out as worthless. On the other hand, whenever it is lacking, those adornments are not conspicuous – they are not dominant, so to speak, in their own provinces and realms; they are a hindrance to themselves by their own brilliance, and they confuse the whole design."

Chapter 5

"We ought to be truly grateful for the fact of order. Who has not a fear of fallacious arguments or those which, by understatement or overstatement, lead imperceptibly to false judgments? Who does not despise them? And yet, when placed in their proper positions in certain disputations, they have such force that somehow or other deception through them becomes pleasant. And in this, too, will not order have the credit?"

(14) "Now in music, in geometry, in the movements of the stars, in the fixed ratios of numbers, order reigns in such manner that if one desires to see its source and its very shrine, so to speak, he either finds it in these, or he is unerringly led to it through them. Indeed, such learning, if one uses it with moderation – and in this matter, nothing is to be feared more than excess – rears for philosophy a

soldier, or even a captain, so competent that he sallies forth wherever he wishes and leads many others as well, and reaches that ultimate goal, beyond which he desires nothing else, beyond which he neither ought nor can seek anything. Now, from that point, while he is held by human affairs, he reviews and discerns all things in such manner that it by no means troubles him why one man desires to have children and has them not, while another is worried over the excessive fecundity of his wife; or why he who is ready to bestow gifts lavishly is in need of money, while the mean and mangy money-lender sleeps over his buried treasure; or why extravagance spends and wastes an ample inheritance, while the tearful beggar hardly gets a coin all the day; or why undeserved honor exalts a person, and a blameless life passes unobserved in the crowd."

(15) "These and other things in human life drive many people to the impious belief that we are not governed by any order of Divine Providence. Others, however, upright and good, and endowed with splendid mentality – people who can not bring themselves to believe that we are abandoned by God – are so confused by the great obscurity and maze of affairs, so to speak, that they cannot see any order. Seeking to have the most hidden causes laid bare to them, even in poems they frequently bewail their errors. Now, who will easily give them the answer if they should ask only this: Why do the Italians always pray for mild winters, while our own poor Gaetulia[11] is parched with heat, or where will any trace of that order be found among ourselves? For my part, if I can give an advice to my own, insofar as I can see, and incline to an opinion, I think that they are to be instructed in all branches of learning. By no other means can these things be so thoroughly understood that they become clear as day. But, if those people are too slothful or preoccupied with other affairs or dull of understanding, let them provide for themselves a stronghold of faith, so that He, who suffers no one that rightly believes in Him through the mysteries to perish, may by this bond draw them to Himself and free them from these dreadful, entangling evils."

(16) "When the obscurity of things perplexes us, we follow a twofold path: reason, or at least, authority. Philosophy sends forth reason, and it

---

11 A region lying south of the Atlas mountain range.

frees scarcely a few. By itself it compels these not only not to spurn those mysteries, but to understand them insofar as they can be understood. The philosophy that is true – the genuine philosophy, so to speak – has no other function than to teach what is the First Principle of all things – Itself without beginning, – and how great an intellect dwells therein, and what has proceeded therefrom for our welfare, but without deterioration of any kind. Now, the venerated mysteries, which liberate persons of sincere and firm faith – not indiscriminately, as some say; and not harmfully, as many assert – these mysteries teach that this First Principle is one God omnipotent, and that He is tripotent, Father and Son and Holy Spirit. Great, indeed, though it be that so great a God has for our sake deigned to take up and dwell in this body of our own kind, yet, the more lowly it appears, so much the more is it replete with clemency and the farther and wider remote from a certain characteristic pride of ingenious people."

VIII.2.4. The Works of Reason (from *Concerning Order*, chs.11-16)

[In us it is Reason, as opposed to the senses, that recognizes and appreciates the forms of order in the world. The "wise person" is the one who develops this faculty and the sciences that depend on it.]

Chapter 11

(30) "Reason is a mental operation capable of distinguishing and connecting the things that are learned. But, only a rare class of persons is capable of using it as a guide to the knowledge of God or of the soul; either of the soul within us or of the world-soul.[12] This is due to nothing else than the fact that, for anyone who has advanced toward objects of sense, it is difficult to return to himself. Wherefore, although people strive to act entirely with reason in those things which are liable to deceive, yet only a very few know what reason *is*, or what its qualities are. This seems strange, but that is how the matter stands. For the present, however,

it is enough to have said that much, for, even if I should wish to expound the matter to you as it should be understood, my incompetence would be equaled by my arrogance if I should profess that I myself have grasped it already. Nevertheless, insofar as reason has deigned to reveal itself in the things that appear familiar to you, let us now examine it to the best of our ability, in accordance with the demands of the discussion we have undertaken."

(31) "And first of all, let us see in what connection this word which is called *reason* is wont to be used. Of particular interest to us ought to be the fact that *human being* has been defined thus by the ancient philosophers: *A human being is an animal, rational and mortal.* In this definition, when the genus[13] which is called *animal* has been given, then we notice that two distinguishing notes are added. And by those distinguishing notes human beings, I believe, were to be admonished both whither they were to return and what they ought to flee, for, just as the soul's forward movement has fallen down to the things that are mortal, so ought its return be to reason. By the one term, *rational*, humans are distinguished from brute animals; by the other term, *mortal*, they are distinguished from God. Therefore, unless it holds fast to the rational element, it will be a beast; unless it turns aside from the mortal element, it will not be divine.

"But, because very learned men are wont to distinguish keenly and ingeniously between the rational [*rationale*] and the reasonable [*rationabile*], such distinction is by no means to be ignored in view of what we have undertaken. They designate as *rational* whatever uses reason or possesses the faculty of reasoning, but, whatever has been done or spoken according to reason, *that* they call *reasonable*. Accordingly, we could call these baths or our discourse *reasonable*; but, him who constructed the baths, or ourselves who are now discoursing, we could term *rational*. Reason, then, proceeds from a rational soul into reasonable things which are done or spoken."

(32) "I see, therefore, two things wherein the faculty and power of reason can even be brought

---

12 Plato proposed that the whole world is a single living being with a soul, the "world soul." Elsewhere Augustine expresses scepticism about the doctrine.
13 See glossary entry for 'species/genus.'

before the senses: namely, the works of human beings which are seen and their words which are heard. In each case the mind uses a twin messenger, the eye and the ear, according to the needs of the body. Thus, when we behold something formed with well-fitting parts, not absurdly do we say that it appears reasonably [fashioned]. In like manner, when we hear a melody harmonize well, we do not hesitate to say that it sounds reasonably [harmonized]. But, anyone would be laughed at if he should say that something smells reasonably or tastes reasonably or is reasonably tender, unless, perchance, in those things which for some purpose have been contrived by people so to smell, or taste, or glow, or anything else. For instance, if someone, considering the reason why it was done, should say that a place whence serpents are put to flight by pungent odors emits smells reasonably; or that a potion which a physician has prepared is reasonably bitter or sweet; or that the bath which he ordered regulated for a sickly person is reasonably warm or tepid. But no one, entering a garden and lifting a rose to his nose, would venture to say: 'How reasonably sweet it smells!' No, not even if a physician should order him to smell it – indeed in that case, it is said to have been prescribed or offered reasonably, but not to smell reasonably – and still not, because that odor is a natural one. And, even though food be seasoned by a cook, we still may say that it is reasonably seasoned. But, in accordance with accepted usage, it is not said to taste reasonably, whenever without any extrinsic cause it satisfies a momentary craving. But, if he to whom a physician has given a potion should be asked why he ought to think it sweet, then something else is implied as the reason for his thinking so, namely, the nature of his illness, which is not in the sense, but is otherwise present in the body. On the other hand, if one is licking something because he is incited by the stimulus of the palate – if he should be asked why it is sweet, and if he should reply: 'Because it is pleasant' or 'Because I like it,' no one will call it reasonably sweet unless, perhaps, its delight is necessary for something, and what he is chewing has been sweetened for that very purpose."

(33) "In so far as we have been able to investigate, we now detect certain traces of reason in the senses, and, with regard to sight and hearing, we find it in pleasure itself. Other senses, however, usually demand this attribute, not because of the pleasure they afford, but because of something else, for a purposeful act is the characteristic of a rational animal. With regard to the eyes, that is usually called *beautiful* in which the harmony of parts is wont to be called reasonable; with regard to the ears, when we say that a harmony is reasonable and that a rhythmic poem is reasonably composed, we properly call it *sweet*. But, we are not wont to pronounce it reasonable when the color in beautiful objects allures us or when a vibrant chord sounds pure and liquid, so to speak. We must therefore acknowledge that, in the pleasure of those senses, what pertains to reason is that in which there is a certain rhythmic measure."

(34) "Wherefore, considering carefully the parts of this very building, we cannot but be displeased because we see one doorway toward the side and another situated almost, but not exactly, in the middle. In things constructed, a proportion of parts that is faulty, without any compelling necessity, unquestionably seems to inflict, as it were, a kind of injury upon one's gaze. But, the fact that three windows inside, one in the middle and two at the sides, pour light at equal intervals on the bathing place – how much that delights and enraptures us as we gaze attentively is a thing already manifest, and need not be shown to you in many words. In their own terminology, architects themselves call this *design*, and they say that parts unsymmetrically placed are without *design*.

"This is very general; it pervades all the arts and creations of man. Who, indeed, does not see that in songs – and we likewise say that in them there is a sweetness that pertains to the ears – rhythm is the producer of all this sweetness? But when an actor is dancing, although a certain rhythmic movement of his limbs may indeed afford delight by that same rhythm, yet, since to the attentive spectators all his gestures are signs of things, the dance itself is called *reasonable,* because it aptly signifies and exhibits something over and above the delight of the senses. And, even if he should represent a winged Venus and a cloaked Cupid, how skillfully so ever he may depict it by a wonderful movement and posture of the body, he does not seem to offend the eyes, but through the eyes he would offend the mind, to which those signs of things are exhibited. The eyes would be offended if the movements were not graceful, for that pertains to the sense, in which the soul perceives delight precisely because it is united with the body.

"Therefore, delight *of* the sense is one thing; delight *through* the sense is something else. Graceful movement delights the sense, but the timely import of the movement delights the mind alone through the sense. This is more easily noticed in the case of hearing: whatever has a pleasing sound, that it is which pleases and entices the hearing itself. What is really signified by that sound, that is what is borne to the mind, though by the messenger of our hearing. And so, when we hear these lines – '*Why do the suns in the winter rapidly sink in the ocean? What is the hindrance that holds back late-coming nights in the summer?*'[14] – our praise of the meter is one thing, but our praise of the meaning is something else. Neither is it in the same sense of the term that we say: 'It sounds reasonable' and 'It is spoken reasonably.'"

Chapter 12

(35) "There are, then, three classes of things in which that 'something reasonable' is to be seen. One is in actions directed toward an end; the second, in discourse; the third, in pleasure. The first admonishes us to do nothing without purpose; the second, to teach correctly; the last, to find delight in contemplation. The first deals with right living; the other two, with those branches of learning which we are now considering. Now, that which is rational in us, that which uses reason and either produces or seeks after the things that are reasonable – saw that names, or meaningful sounds, had to be assigned to things, so that men might use the sense almost as an interpreter to link them together, inasmuch as they could not perceive one another's minds. For reason was held fast by a certain natural bond in the fellowship of those with whom it possessed reason as a common heritage, since human beings could not be most firmly associated unless they conversed and thus poured, so to speak, their minds and thoughts back and forth to one another. But, they could not hear the words of those not present. Therefore, reason, having carefully noted and discriminated all the sounds of the

mouth and tongue, invented letters. But, it could have done neither of these, if the vast number of things seemed to extend endlessly without any fixed limit. Therefore, the great utility of enumerating was brought to mind by its very necessity. When these two discoveries had been made, then arose the profession of copyists and calculators – the infancy of grammar, so to speak, which Varro calls *literatio*. What it is called in Greek, I do not recall just now."

(36) "When reason had gone further, it noticed that, of those oral sounds which we used in speaking and which it had already designated by letters, there were some which by a varied modulation of the parted lips flowed clear and pure from the throat without any friction; that others acquired a certain kind of sound from the diversified pressure of the lips; and that there were still other sounds which could not issue forth unless they were conjoined with these. Accordingly, it denominated the letters in the order of their exposition: vowels, semivowels, and mutes. In the next place, it took account of syllables. Then, words were grouped into eight classes and forms, and their entire evolvement, purity, and articulation were skillfully and minutely differentiated. Furthermore, not unmindful of numbers and measure, it directed the mind to the different lengths of vocal sounds and syllables, and thereby it discovered that of the time-intervals through which the long and the short syllables were extended, some were double and others were simple. It noted these points as well, and reduced them to fixed rules.

(37) "The science of grammar could now have been complete. But, since by its very name it proclaims that it knows letters[15] – indeed on this account it is called 'literature' in Latin – it came to pass that whatever was committed to letters as worth remembering necessarily pertained to it. And in this way history was added to this science. For, its name is one, but its subject matter is undefined and many-sided, and is filled more with cares than with enjoyment or truth, and more burdensome to grammarians than to the historians themselves. Who, indeed, would tolerate the imputing of ignorance to a man who has not heard that

14 Virgil, *Georgics* 2.481-482.
15 Grammar, derived from *grapho*, to write, and *gramma*, meaning letter.

Daedalus flew, and not the imputing of mendacity to the man who invented the fable; folly to anyone who believed it, and impudence to him who questions anyone about it? Or the case in which I always feel great pity for those of our household who are accused of ignorance if they cannot answer what the name of the mother of Euryalus[16] was, since they, in turn, would not dare to call their questioners vain, absurd, or unduly inquisitive?"

Chapter 13

(38) "When the science of grammar had been perfected and systematized, reason was then reminded to search out and consider the very power by which it produced art, for, by definition, division, and synthesis it not only had made it orderly and syntactical, but also had guarded it against every subtle encroachment of error. How, therefore, would it pass on to other discoveries, unless it first classified, noted, and arranged its own resources – its tools and machines, so to speak – and brought into being that discipline of disciplines which they call *dialectics*?[17] This science teaches both how to teach and how to learn. In it, reason itself exhibits itself, and reveals its own nature, its desires, its powers. It knows what knowledge is; by itself, it not only wishes to make people learned, but also can make them so. Yet, because in the pursuit of the things which are rightly commended as useful and upright, unwise people generally follow their own feelings and habits rather than the very marrow of truth – which indeed only a very exceptional mind beholds – it was necessary that they not only be taught to the extent of their ability, but also frequently and strongly aroused as to their emotions. To the portion of itself which would accomplish this – a portion more replete with lack than with enlightenment, its lap heaped high with charms which it would scatter to the crowd so that the crowd might deign to be influenced for its own good – to this portion, it gave the name of *rhetoric*. And so, the part which is called reasonable in discourse has been advanced to this point by the liberal arts and disciplines."

Chapter 14

(39) "From this point, reason wished to be straightway transported to the most blessed contemplation of things divine. But, lest it fall from on high, it sought steps of ascent and devised an orderly path for itself through the slopes it had already won. It longed for a beauty which it alone could behold by itself without these eyes of ours; but it was impeded by the senses. Therefore, it turned its gaze slightly toward those senses, for they, shouting with noisy importunity that they possessed truth, kept calling it back when it fain would hasten to other things. And it began with the ears, because they claimed as their own the very words from which it had fashioned grammar, dialectic, and rhetoric. But reason, being endowed with the keenest powers of discernment, quickly saw what difference there was between sound itself and that of which it was a symbol. It saw that to the jurisdiction of the ears pertained nothing more than sound, and that this was threefold: sound in the utterance of an animate being, or sound in what breath produces in musical instruments, or sound in what is given forth by percussion. It saw that to the first class pertained actors of tragedy and comedy or stageplayers of this kind, and in fact all who give vocal renditions; that the second class was restricted to flutes and similar instruments; and that to the third class were attributed the cithara, the lyre, cymbals, and everything that would be tonal on being struck."

(40) "Reason saw, however, that this material was of very little value, unless the sounds were arranged in a fixed measure of time and in modulated variation of high and low pitch. It realized that it was from this source that those elements came which it had called *feet* and *accents*, when, in grammar, it was treating of syllables with diligent consideration. And, because in words themselves it was easy to notice the syllabic *longs* and *shorts*, interspersed with almost equal frequency in a discourse, reason endeavored to arrange and conjoin them into definite series. At first it followed the sense of hearing itself in this, and superimposed measured link units, which it called *segments* and *members*. Then, lest the series of feet be carried further than its dis-

16 Cf. Virgil, *Aeneid* 5.294 ff.
17 I.e., logic.

cernment could continue, it set a limit at which *reversion* to the beginning should be made, and, precisely on this account, called it *verse*. But, whatever was not restricted by a definite limit, and yet ran according to methodically arranged feet – that, it designated by the term *rhythm*. In Latin this can be called nothing other than *number*. Thus, poets were begotten of reason. And, when it saw in them great achievements, not in sound alone, but in words also and realities, it honored them to the utmost, and gave them license for whatever reasonable fictions they might desire. And yet, because they took origin from the first of the liberal disciplines, it permitted grammarians to be their critics."

(41) "Reason understood, therefore, that in this fourth step of ascent – whether in particular rhythm or in modulation in general – numeric proportions held sway and produced the finished product. With the utmost diligence it investigated as to what their nature might be, and, chiefly because by their aid it had elaborated all the aforesaid developments, it concluded that they were divine and eternal. From then onwards, it most reluctantly endured their splendor and serenity to be clouded by the material stuff of vocal utterances. And, because whatever the mind is able to see is always present and is acknowledged to be immortal, numeric proportions seemed to be of this nature. But, because sound is something sensible, it flows away into the past and is imprinted on the memory. By a reasonable fiction it was fabled that the Muses were the daughters of Jupiter and Memory. Now, with reason bestowing its favor on the poets, need it be asked what the offspring likewise contained? Since this branch of learning partakes as well of sense as of the intellect, it received the name of *music*."

Chapter 15

(42) "From this stage, reason advanced to the province of the eyes. Scanning the earth and the heavens, it realized that nothing pleased it but beauty; and in beauty, design; and in design, dimensions; and in dimensions, number. It asked itself whether any line or curve or any other form or shape in that realm was of such kind as intelligence comprehended. It found that they were far inferior, and that nothing which the eyes beheld could in any way be compared with what the mind discerned. These distinct and separate realities it also reduced to a branch of learning, and called it *geometry*.

"The movement of the heavens also aroused and invited reason to consider it diligently. And there, too, because of the most constant alternations of the seasons, as well as the fixed and unerring courses of the stars and the regulated spacing of distance, it understood that nothing other than dimension and number held sway. Linking these, also, into an orderly whole by definition and division, it gave rise to *astrology* – a great subject for the God-fearing, but a torment for the curious."

(43) "In all these branches of study, therefore, all things were being presented to reason as numerically proportioned. And they were all the more clearly visible in those dimensions which reason, by reflection and contemplation, beheld as most true; but it used to recall rather the shadows and vestiges of those dimensions in the things that are perceived by the senses. Then, reason gained much courage and preconceived a great achievement; it ventured to prove the soul immortal. It treated diligently of all things. It came to feel that it possessed great power, and that it owed all its power to numerical proportions. Something wondrous urged it on. And it began to suspect that it itself was perhaps the very number by which all things are numbered, or if not, that this number was there whither it was striving to arrive. And he of whom Alypius made mention when we were treating of the Skeptics,[18] grasped with all his might – as if Proteus[19] were in his hands – this number which would be the discloser of universal truth. But, false images of the things which we number drift away from that most hidden something by which we enumerate, snatch our attention to themselves, and frequently make that hidden something slip away even when it has been already in our grasp."

---

18 Cf. *Contra Academicos* 3.5.11.
19 The sea-god who was considered capable of assuming various forms.

Chapter 16

(44) "If a man does not yield to these images, and if he reduces to a simple, true, and certain unity all the things that are scattered far and wide throughout so many branches of study, then he is most deserving of the attribute *learned*. Then, without being rash, he can search after things divine – not merely as truths to be believed, but also as matters to be contemplated, understood, and retained. But, whoever is still a slave to his passions, or is keenly desirous of perishable goods, or even though he flee from these and live a virtuous life, yet if he does not know what pure nothing is, what formless matter is, what a lifeless informed being is, what a body is, what species in a body is, what place and time are, what *in a place* and *at a time* signify, what local motion is, what non-local motion is, what stable motion is, what eternity is, what it is to be neither in a place nor nowhere, what is beyond time and forever, what it is to be nowhere and nowhere not to be, what it is to be never and never not to be – anyone who does not know these matters, and yet wishes to question and dispute about even his own soul – let alone investigating about the Most High God, who is better known by knowing what He is not – such a one will fall into every possible error.

"But then, whoever has grasped the meaning of simple and intelligible numbers will readily understand these matters. Furthermore, anyone of good talents and leisure – through the privilege of age or any kind of good fortune – if he be eagerly devoted to study and if he follow the above-mentioned order of studies in so far as is required, will certainly comprehend such numbers. But since all the liberal arts are learned partly for practical use and partly for the knowledge and contemplation of things, to attain the use of them is very difficult except for some very gifted person who even from boyhood has earnestly and constantly applied himself."

VIII.2.5. Why Adultery is evil (from *On Free Choice* I, iii,6-iv,10)

[This passage illustrates Augustine's emphasis on the "inner" side of actions when it comes to their being right or wrong, good or evil. The example of a slave who unwillingly kills his master is also treated by Abelard in selection **VIII.4.1.**, but very differ-

ently. The dialogue below is between Evodius (*Ev.*), a young student, and Augustine (*Aug.*) himself.]

Augustine: You ask for the cause of our doing evil. First we must discuss what doing evil is. Tell me what you think about this. If you cannot put the whole thing briefly in a few words, at least indicate your opinion by naming some evil deeds one by one.

Evodius: Adultery, homicide, sacrilege. I need mention no more. To enumerate all the others neither time nor my memory would be sufficient. But no one doubts that those I have mentioned are examples of evil deeds.

Aug. Tell me now why you think adultery is evil. Is it because it is forbidden by law?

Ev. It is not evil because it is forbidden by law. It is forbidden by law because it is evil.

Aug. Suppose someone were to press us, stressing the delights of adultery and asking why it is evil and why we think it worthy of condemnation. Do you think that people who wanted not only to believe that adultery is evil but also to know the reason why it is so, would be driven to appeal to the authority of the law? You and I believe without the slightest hesitation that adultery is evil, and I declare that all peoples and nations must believe that too. But our present endeavour is to obtain intelligent knowledge and assurance of what we have accepted in faith. Give this matter your best consideration and tell me the reason why you know that adultery is evil.

Ev. I know it is evil because I should not wish it to be committed with my own wife. Whoever does to another what he would not have done to himself does evil.

Aug. Suppose someone offered his wife to another, being willing that she should be corrupted by him in return for a similar licence allowed him with the other's wife. Would he have done no evil?

Ev. Far from that. He would have done great evil.

Aug. And yet his sin does not come under your general rule, for he does not do what he would not have done to him. You must find another reason to prove that adultery is evil.

Ev. I think it evil because I have often seen men condemned on this charge.

Aug. But are not men frequently condemned for righteous deeds? Without going to other books, think of scripture history which excels all other books because it has divine authority. If we decide that condemnation is a certain indication of evil-doing, what an evil opinion we must adopt of the apostles and martyrs, for they were all thought worthy of condemnation for their faith. If whatever is condemned is evil, it was evil in those days to believe in Christ and to confess the Christian faith. But if everything is not evil which is condemned you must find another reason for teaching that adultery is evil.

Ev. I have no reply to make.

Aug. Possibly the evil thing in adultery is lust. So long as you look for the evil in the outward act you discover difficulties. But when you understand that the evil lies in lust it becomes clear that even if a man finds no opportunity to lie with the wife of another but shows that he desires to do so and would do it if he got the chance, he is no less guilty than if he were caught in the act.

Ev. Nothing is more manifest; and I now see that there is no need of lengthy argument to persuade me that the same is true of homicide, sacrilege and all other sins. For it is clear that lust alone dominates the whole realm of evil-doing.

Aug. You know that lust is also called cupidity?

Ev. I do.

Aug. Do you think there is or is not a difference between cupidity and fear?

Ev. Indeed there is a great difference between them.

Aug. I suppose you think so because cupidity longs for its object while fear avoids its object.

Ev. That is so.

Aug. What if someone kills a person from no desire to get possession of anything but from fear of suffering some evil at their hands? In that case he will not be a homicide?

Ev. He will indeed. Even such a deed is not without a trace of cupidity. He who kills a person from fear desires to live without fear.

Aug. And it is no small good to live without fear?

Ev. It is a great good, but the homicide cannot attain it by his crime.

Aug. I am not seeking what he can attain, but what he desires. Certainly he desires a good thing who desires a life free from fear, and so far his desire is not to be blamed. Otherwise we shall be blaming all lovers of good things. So we are compelled to admit that there can be homicide in which the dominance of evil cupidity is not to be found;

and it will consequently be false to say that it is the dominance of lust which makes all sins evil. In other words there can be homicide which is not a sin.

Ev. If to kill a person is homicide it can sometimes be done without sin. When a soldier kills an enemy, or when a judge or an officer of the law puts a criminal to death, or when a weapon slips out of someone's hand without his will or knowledge, the killing of a person does not seem to me to be a sin.

Aug. I agree, but these are not usually called homicides. But tell me this. A slave kills his master because he feared he would be terribly tortured by him. Do you think he would have to be regarded as one of those who are not to be classed as homicides because they have killed a person?

Ev. His is a very different case from theirs. They act in accordance with the laws, or not contrary to the laws, but no law approves his deed.

Aug. You are reverting again to authority. You must remember that we have undertaken to try to understand what we believe. We believe the laws and must accordingly try if we can to understand whether the law which punishes this deed does not wrongly punish.

Ev. It does not punish wrongly when it punishes a person who willingly and knowingly slays his master. None of these other cases we have mentioned is similar. *Aug.* You remember you recently said that in every evil deed lust prevailed, and that for that very reason it was evil?

Ev. Certainly I remember.

Aug. Did you not also admit that he who desires to live without fear has no evil cupidity?

Ev. That too I remember.

Aug. When our slave kills his master from that motive he does so without any culpable cupidity. So we have not discovered why the deed was evil. We have agreed that all evil deeds are evil for no other reason than that they are committed from lust, that is, wrongful cupidity.

Ev. Now it seems I must admit that he is unjustly condemned. But I should not dare to say so if I had any other answer to give.

Aug. You are persuaded that so great a crime ought to go unpunished before you consider whether the slave desired to be free of fear of his master in order to satisfy his own lusts? To desire to live without fear is characteristic of all people, not only of the good but also of the bad. But there is this difference. The good seek it by diverting their love from things which cannot be had without the risk of losing them. The bad are anxious to enjoy these things with security and try to remove hindrances so as to live a wicked and criminal life which is better called death.

Ev. I am recovering my wits. Now I am glad to have learned what culpable cupidity is, which we also call lust. Evidently it is love of things which one may lose against one's will.

VIII.2.6 Lust, a Penalty for the Original Sin (from *On the City of God* XIV, 15-24)

[Orthodox Christian theology held that the present condition of mankind is in part the result of an original disobedience to God by the first man and woman and God's consequent punishment of all subsequent generations of human beings. It follows that what holds universally of human beings as we now find them might not be something natural to human nature but rather a result of this divine retribution. Augustine, here very much influenced by the negative views of the Platonists with regard to sexual passion, holds that sexual lust and the dependence of human reproduction on it is one of these features of human existence which have resulted from the original sin of disobedience.]

Chapter 15

On the justice of the retribution that was meted out to the first human beings for their disobedience.

Man, as we know, scorned the bidding of God who had created him, who had made him in his own image, who had placed him above the other animals, who had established him in paradise, who had provided him with an abundance of all things and of security, and who had not laden him with commands that were numerous or onerous or difficult but had propped him up for wholesome obedience with one very brief and easy command, whereby he sought to impress upon this creature, for whom free service was expedient, that he was

the Lord. Therefore, as a consequence, just condemnation followed, and this condemnation was such that man, who would have been spiritual even in flesh if he had observed the order, became carnal in mind as well. Moreover, this man who had pleased himself in his pride was then granted to himself by God's justice; yet this was not done in such a way that he was completely in his own power, but that he disagreed with himself and so led, under the rule of the one with whom he agreed when he sinned, a life of cruel and wretched slavery in place of the freedom for which he had conceived a desire. He was willingly dead in spirit and unwillingly destined to die in body; a deserter of the eternal life, he was doomed also to eternal death, unless he were freed by grace. Whoever thinks that condemnation of this sort is either excessive or unjust surely does not know how to gauge the magnitude of wickedness in sinning when the opportunity for not sinning was so ample.

Just as Abraham's obedience is not undeservedly celebrated as great because he was ordered to do a very difficult thing, namely, to slay his son, so in paradise disobedience was all the greater because the command that was given would have involved no difficulty. And just as the obedience of the Second Man[20] is the more laudable because "he became obedient unto death," so the disobedience of the first man is the more abominable because he became disobedient unto death. For where the proposed punishment for disobedience is great and the command of the Creator is easy to obey, who can adequately expound how grave an evil it is not to obey when an easy matter has been ordered by so mighty a power and is attended by the terror of such awful punishment?

To put it briefly then, in the punishment of that sin the requital for disobedience was no other than disobedience. For man's wretchedness consists only in his own disobedience to himself, wherefore, since he would not do what he then could, he now has a will to do what he cannot. In paradise, to be sure, man could not do everything whatsoever even before he sinned, yet, whatever he could not do, he did not have a will to do, and in that way he could do everything that he would. Now, however, as we

---

20 The reference is to Jesus Christ.
21 *Psalms* 144:4.

recognize in his offspring and as holy Scripture attests, "Man has become like vanity."[21] For who can count up all the things that man has a will to do but cannot as long as he is disobedient to himself, that is, as long as his very mind and even his flesh, which is lower, are disobedient to his will? For even against his will his mind is very often agitated and his flesh feels pain, grows old, dies and suffers whatever else we suffer; but we should not suffer all this against our will if our being in every way and in every part gave obedience to our will.

Someone may perhaps protest that the flesh is unable to serve us because of what it suffers. But what difference does it make how this happens? It only matters that through the justice of God, who is our master and to whom we his subjects refused service, our flesh, which had been subject to us, is troublesome by its insubordination, though we by our insubordination to God have succeeded only in being troublesome to ourselves and not to him. For he does not need our service as we need that of the body; so that what we get is punishment for us, but what we did was none for him. Further, the so-called pains of the flesh are pains of the soul that exist in and proceed from the flesh. For what pain or desire does the flesh experience by itself apart from a soul?

When we say that the flesh feels desire or pain, we mean that it is either the person themself, as I have argued, or some part of the soul affected by what the flesh experiences, whether it be harsh and painful or gentle and pleasant. Pain of the flesh is only a vexation of the soul arising from the flesh and a sort of disagreement with what is done to the flesh, just as the pain of the mind that we call grief is a disagreement with the things that have happened to us against our will. But grief is generally preceded by fear, which is also something in the soul and not in the flesh. Pain of the flesh, on the other hand, is not preceded by anything like fear on the part of the flesh that is felt in the flesh before the pain. Pleasure, however, is preceded by a certain craving that is felt in the flesh as its own desire, such as hunger, thirst and the desire that is mostly called lust when it affects the sex organs, though this is a general term applicable to any kind of desire.

Even anger itself, so the ancients defined it, is nothing but a lust for revenge, although at times persons vent their anger even upon inanimate objects, where no effect of vengeance can be felt, and in their rage smash their style or break their reed pen when it writes badly. But even this lust, though rather irrational, is a sort of lust for revenge and something like a shadowy reflection, as it were, of the principle of retribution whereby they who do evil must suffer evil. There is then a lust for revenge, which is called anger; there is a lust for possessing money, which is termed greed; there is a lust for winning at any price, which is termed obstinacy; and there is a lust for bragging, which is termed vainglory. There are many different kinds of lust, of which some have special designations also while others have none. No one, for example, would find it easy to say what the lust to be overlord is called, though, as even civil wars attest, it exercises a very powerful influence in the minds of tyrants.

Chapter 16

On the evil of lust, a term which, though it is applicable to many vices, is especially ascribed to the stirrings of obscene heat.

Therefore, although there are lusts for many things, yet when the term lust is employed without the mention of any object, nothing comes to mind usually but the lust that excites the shameful parts of the body. Moreover, this lust asserts its power not only over the entire body, nor only externally, but also from within. It convulses all of a man when the emotion in his mind combines and mingles with the carnal drive to produce a pleasure unsurpassed among those of the body. The effect of this is that at the very moment of its climax there is an almost total eclipse of acumen and, as it were, sentinel alertness. But surely any friend of wisdom and holy joys, who lives in wedlock but knows, as the Apostle admonished, "how to possess his bodily vessel in holiness and honour, not in the disease of lust like the gentiles who do not know God,"[22] would prefer, if he could, to beget children without this kind of lust. For he would want his mind to be served, even in this function of engendering off-

---

22 1 *Thessalonians* 4:4-5.

spring, by the parts created for this kind of work, just as it is served by the other members, each assigned to its own kind of work. They would be set in motion when the will urged, not stirred to action when hot lust surged.

But not even those who are enamoured of this pleasure are aroused whether to marital intercourse or to the uncleanness of outrageous vice just when it is their will. At times the urge intrudes uninvited; at other times it deserts the panting lover, and although desire is ablaze in the mind, the body is frigid. In this strange fashion lust refuses service not only to the will to procreate but also to the lust for wantonness; and though for the most part it solidly opposes the mind's restraint, there are times when it is divided even against itself and, having aroused the mind, inconsistently fails to arouse the body.

Chapter 17

On the nakedness of the first human beings, which seemed to them base and shameful after they sinned.

It is reasonable then that we should feel very much shamed of such lust, and reasonable too that those members which it moves or does not move by its own right, so to speak, and not in full subjection to our will, should be called pudenda or shameful parts as they were not before man sinned; for we read in Scripture: "They were naked, and not embarrassed."[23] And the reason for this is not that they were unaware of their nakedness, but that their nakedness was not yet base because lust did not yet arouse those members apart from their will, and the flesh did not yet bear witness, so to speak, through its own disobedience against the disobedience of man.

For the first human beings had not been created blind, as the ignorant multitude think, since Adam saw the animals upon which he bestowed names, and of Eve we read: "The woman saw that the tree was good for food and that it was a delight for the eyes to behold.[24]" Accordingly, their eyes were not closed, but they were not open, that is, attentive so as to recognize what a boon the cloak of grace afforded them, in that their bodily members did not know how to oppose their will. When this grace was lost and punishment in kind for their disobedience was inflicted, there came to be in the action of the body a certain shameless novelty, and thereafter nudity was indecent. It drew their attention and made them embarrassed.

This is why Scripture says of them, after they had violated God's command in open transgression: "And the eyes of both were opened, and they discovered that they were naked, and they sewed fig leaves together and made themselves aprons."[25] "The eyes of both," we are told, "were opened," yet not that they might see, since they could see already, but that they might distinguish between the good that they had lost and the evil into which they had fallen. This also explains why the tree itself, which was to enable them to make such a distinction if they laid hands on it to eat its fruit in spite of the prohibition, was named for that fact and called the tree of the knowledge of good and evil. For experience of discomfort in sickness gives a clearer insight into the joys of health as well.

Accordingly, "they realized that they were naked," stripped naked, that is, of the grace that kept nakedness of body from embarrassing them before the law of sin came into opposition with their minds. Thus they learned what they would more fortunately not have known if through belief in God and obedience to his word they had refrained from an act that would compel them to find out by experience what harm unbelief and disobedience could do. Therefore, embarrassed by their flesh's disobedience, a punishment that bore witness to their own disobedience, "they sewed fig leaves together and made themselves aprons (*campestria*)," that is, loin-cloths, a term employed by certain translators. (Moreover, though '*campestria*' is a Latin word, it derives its origin from the practice of young men who used to cover up their pudenda while they exercised in the nude on the so-called campus or field. Hence, those who are so girt are commonly designated as *campestrati*.) Thus

---

23 *Genesis* 2:25.
24 *Genesis* 3:6.
25 *Genesis* 3:7.

modesty, prompted by a sense of shame, covered what was disobediently aroused by lust against a will condemned for disobedience.

Ever since that time, this habit of concealing the pudenda has been deeply ingrained in all peoples, descended, as they are, from the original stock. In fact, certain barbarians do not expose those parts of the body even in the bath but wash with their coverings on. In the dark retreats of India too certain men who practice philosophy in the nude (and hence are called gymnosophists) nevertheless use coverings for their genitals, though they have none for the other parts of the body.

Chapter 18

On the sense of shame in sexual intercourse, whether promiscuous or marital.

Let us consider the act itself that is accomplished by such lust, not only in every kind of licentious intercourse, for which hiding-places are prerequisite to avoid judgement before human tribunals, but also in the practice of harlotry, a base vice that has been legalized by the earthly city. Although in the latter case the practice is not under the ban of any law of this city, nevertheless even the lust that is allowed and free of penalty shuns the public gaze. Because of an innate sense of shame even brothels have made provision for privacy, and unchastity found it easier to do without the fetters of legal prohibition than shamelessness did to eliminate the secret nooks of that foul business.

But this harlotry is called a base matter even by those who are base themselves, and although they are enamoured of it, they dare not make public display of it. What of marital intercourse, which has for its purpose, according to the terms of the marriage contract, the procreation of children? Lawful and respectable though it is, does it not seek a chamber secluded from witnesses? Before the bridegroom begins even to caress his bride, does he not first send outside all servants and even his own groomsmen as well as any who had been permitted to enter for kinship's sake, whatever the tie? And since, as a certain "supreme master of Roman elo-

quence "[26] also maintains, all right actions wish to be placed in the light of day,[27] that is, are eager to become known, this right action also desires to become known, though it still blushes to be seen. For who does not know what goes on between husband and wife for the procreation of children? Indeed, it is for the achievement of this purpose that wives are married with such ceremony. And yet, when the act for the birth of children is being consummated, not even the children that may already have been born from the union are allowed to witness it. For this right action does indeed seek mental light for recognition of it, but it shrinks from visual light. What is the reason for this if not that something by nature fitting and proper is carried out in such a way as to be accompanied also by something of shame as punishment.

Chapter 19

That anger and lust, parts that are stirred in man with such harmful effect that they must be checked and curbed by wisdom, did not exist in that sound state of his being before he sinned.

Here we have the reason why those philosophers too who came closer to the truth admitted that anger and lust are faulty divisions of the soul. They reasoned that these emotions proceed in a confused and disorderly way to engage even in acts that wisdom forbids and that consequently they stand in need of a controlling and rational mind. This third part of the soul, according to them, resides in a sort of citadel to rule the other two parts in order that, as it commands and they serve, justice in a human being may be preserved among all the parts of the soul.

Now as for these two divisions of the soul, those philosophers confess that they are vicious even in a wise and temperate man. It is for this reason that the mind by repression and restraint curbs and recalls them from things that they are wrongly moved to do, but allows them to follow any course that the law of wisdom has sanctioned. Anger, for example, is permitted for the display of a just compulsion, and lust for the duty of propagating off-

26 Cf. Lucan 7.62-63.
27 Cicero, *Tusculanae Disputationes* 2.26.64

spring. But these divisions, I maintain, were not vicious in paradise before man sinned, for they were not set going against a right will in pursuit of anything that made it necessary to check them with the guiding reins, as it were, of reason. For in so far as these emotions are now set going in this way and controlled with more or less ease or difficulty, yet still controlled, by restraint and opposition on the part of those who lead temperate, just and holy lives, this is by no means a healthy state due to nature; it is a morbid condition due to guilt. Moreover, if modesty does not conceal the actions prompted by anger and the other emotions in every word and deed as it does those of lust in which the sexual organs are used, the reason is simply that in other cases the members of the body are not put into operation by the emotions themselves but by the will, after it has consented to them, for it has complete control in the employment of such members. No one who utters a word in anger or even strikes a person could do so if his tongue or hand were not set in motion at the command, so to speak, of his will; and these members can also be set in motion by the same will even when there is no anger. But in the case of the sexual organs, lust has somehow brought them so completely under its rule that they are incapable of activity if this one emotion is lacking and has not sprung up spontaneously or in answer to a stimulus. Here is the cause of shame, here is what blushingly avoids the eye of onlookers; and a man would sooner put up with a crowd of spectators when he is wrongly venting his anger upon another than with the gaze of a single individual even when he is rightly having intercourse with his wife.

Chapter 20

On the utterly absurd indecency of the Cynics.

Those canine philosophers, or Cynics,[28] were not aware of this fact when they expounded a view offensive to human modesty, a view that can only be termed canine, that is, base and shameless. They held that since the act is lawful when it is done with a wife, no one should feel ashamed to do it openly and engage in marital intercourse on any street or square. Nevertheless, our natural sense of shame has been victorious over this heretical notion. There is, to be sure, a tradition that Diogenes once ostentatiously performed such an act because he thought that his school would win more publicity in this way, that is, if its shamelessness was more sensationally impressed upon the memory of mankind. The later Cynics, however, have abandoned any such practice, and modesty has prevailed over error, that is, the instinct among people to feel ashamed before other people has prevailed over the doctrine that people should make it their aim to be like dogs.

Hence I prefer to think that Diogenes and others who reputedly did such a thing rather acted out the motions of lying together before the eyes of people who really did not know what was done under the cloak. I do not believe that there could have been any achievement of such pleasure under the glare of human gaze. For those philosophers did not blush to seem willing to lie together in a place where lust itself would have blushed to rear its head. Even now we see that there are still Cynic philosophers among us. They are the ones who not only wrap themselves in a cloak but also carry a club. Yet none of them dares to behave so, for it would bring down upon any who had dared a shower, if not of stones, at any rate of spittle from the outraged public.

Human nature then doubtless feels shame at this lust, and rightly so. For its disobedience, which subjected the sexual organs to its impulses exclusively and wrested them from control by the will, is a sufficient demonstration of the punishment that was meted out to man for that first disobedience. And it was fitting that this punishment should show itself particularly in that part of the body which engenders the very creature that was changed for the worse through that first great sin. No one can be delivered from the meshes of that sin unless the offence that was committed to the common disaster of all and punished by the justice of God when all men existed in but one, is expiated in each man singly by the grace of God.

---

28 Philosophers in 4th century B.C.E. Athens who believed they were following the true teachings of Socrates in their disregard for many ordinary opinions about what was right and wrong. The word 'cynic' comes from the Greek word for dog.

Chapter 21

That the blessing of increase in human fertility given before sin was not forfeited through transgression but alloyed with the disease of lust.

Far be it then from us to believe that the couple that were placed in paradise would have fulfilled through this lust, which shamed them into covering those organs, the words pronounced by God in his blessing: " Increase and multiply and fill the earth."[29] For it was only after man sinned that this lust arose; it was after man sinned that his natural being retaining the sense of shame but losing that dominance to which the body was subject in every part, felt and noticed, then blushed at and concealed that lust. The nuptial blessing, however, whereby the pair, joined in marriage, were to increase and multiply and fill the earth, remained in force even when they sinned, yet it was given before they sinned, for its purpose was to make it clear that the procreation of children is a part of the glory of marriage and not of the punishment of sin.

There are, nevertheless, in our own day persons who must surely lack knowledge of that former happiness in paradise, for they believe that children could only have been engendered by the means with which they are personally acquainted, that is, by lust, which, as we see, causes embarrassment even to the honourable state of marriage. Some of these people do not merely reject outright but unbelievingly deride the holy Scriptures, in which we read that after sin nakedness caused shame and the organs of shame were covered. Others among them, on the other hand, accept and honour the Scriptures but hold that the words "Increase and multiply" are not to be taken as referring to carnal fertility because some similar statement is also found with reference to the soul: "Thou wilt multiply me with strength in my soul."[30] Relying on this passage, they interpret allegorically the words that follow in *Genesis*: "Both fill the earth and be masters of it."[31] By earth they understand the flesh which the soul fills with its presence and over which

it has greatest mastery when it is multiplied in inner strength, or virtue. But carnal offspring, they maintain, could no more have been born then than now without lust, which arose after man sinned, and which was observed with embarrassment and concealed; and they would not have been born in paradise but only outside it, as in fact happened. For it was after the first couple had been sent away from there that they united to beget children and did beget them.

Chapter 22

On the matrimonial bond as originally established and blessed by God.

I myself, however, have no doubt at all that to increase, multiply and fill the earth in accordance with the blessing of God is a gift of marriage and that God established this institution from the beginning before man's fall by the creation of male and female; the difference in sex is in any case clear enough in the flesh. It was also with this work of God that the blessing itself was connected, for immediately after the Scriptural words: "Male and female he created them," there was added: "And God blessed them, and God said to them: 'Increase and multiply and fill the earth and be masters of it,'" and so on.

Granted that all this can without impropriety be taken in a spiritual sense, yet we cannot understand "male" and "female" as figurative terms referring to any analogy in a single human being on the ground that in that person, as we know, there is one element that rules and another that is ruled. As the bodies of different sex make abundantly clear, it is the height of absurdity to deny that male and female were created as they were to increase, multiply and fill the earth by begetting offspring. For when the Lord was asked whether it was permitted to divorce one's wife on any grounds whatever, since Moses allowed the Israelites to give a bill of divorcement on account of their hardness of heart, his reply did not concern the spirit which commands and the flesh which obeys, or the rational mind which rules and the irra-

---

29 *Genesis* 1:28.
30 *Psalms* 138:3.
31 *Genesis* 1:28.

tional desire which is ruled, or the contemplative virtue which is superior and the active virtue which is subordinate, or the understanding of the mind and the sensation of the body, but it plainly referred to the marriage tie which binds both sexes to one another. In this answer he said: "Have you not read that he who made them from the beginning made them male and female, and said, 'For this reason a man shall leave his father and mother and be joined to his wife, and the two shall become one flesh'? So they are no longer two but one flesh. What therefore God has joined together, let not man put asunder."[32]

There is no doubt then that from the very beginning male and female were fashioned in quite the same way as we see and know two human beings of different sex to be now and that they are called "one" either because of their union or because of the origin of the female, who was created from the side of the male. For the Apostle too invoked this first example, which God instituted as a precedent, to admonish each and every one that husbands should love their wives.

Chapter 23

Whether procreation would have been allowed even in paradise if no one had sinned, or whether the principle of chastity would have fought there against the ardour of lust.

When anyone says that there would have been no copulation or generation if the first human beings had not sinned, does he not imply that man's sin was required to complete the number of saints? For if by not sinning they would have continued to be solitary because, so some think, they could not have produced offspring if they had not sinned, then surely sin was required before there could be not just two but many righteous persons. But if that is too absurd to believe, we must rather believe that even if no one had sinned, a sufficiently large number of saints would have come into existence to populate that supremely happy city – as large a number, that is, as are now being gathered through the grace of God from the multitude of sinners,

and as will be, so long as "the children of this world" beget and are begotten.[33]

This leads to the conclusion that if no sin had been committed, that marriage, being worthy of the happiness of paradise, would have produced offspring to be loved, yet no lust to cause shame. But there is now no example with which to illustrate how this could have been effected. Nevertheless, that is no reason why it should seem incredible that the will, which is now obeyed by so many members, might also have been obeyed in the absence of this lust by that one part as well. Consider how, when we choose, we set our hands and feet in motion to do the things that are theirs to do, how we manage this without any conflict and with all the facility that we see both in our own case and in that of others, especially among workers in all kinds of physical tasks, where a natural capacity that is too weak and slow is fitted for its employment by the application of greater dexterity and effort. May we not similarly believe that those organs of procreation could, like the others, have served mankind by obedience to the decision of the will for the generation of children even if there had been no lust inflicted as punishment for the sin of disobedience?

When in his discussion of the different forms of rule in his work entitled *On the Commonwealth* Cicero drew an analogy for his purpose from human nature, did he not say that the members of the body are ruled like children because of their readiness to obey, whereas the depraved parts of the soul are constrained like slaves by a harsher rule?[34] No doubt, in the order of nature, the soul ranks above the body, yet the soul itself finds it easier to rule the body than to rule itself. Nevertheless, this lust that we are now discussing is something all the more shameful because under its effect the soul neither succeeds in ruling itself so as to have no lust at all nor controls the body completely in such a way that the organs of shame are set in motion by the will rather than by lust. Indeed, if such were the case, they would not be organs of shame.

As things now stand, the soul is ashamed of the body's opposition to it, for the body is subject to it

---

32 *Matthew* 19:4-6.
33 Cf. *Luke* 20:34.
34 Cf. Cicero, *De Re Publica* 3.25.37.

because of its lower nature. When the soul opposes itself in the case of other emotions, it feels less ashamed because when it is vanquished by itself, the soul is its own vanquisher. Although this victory of soul over soul is disorderly and morbid because it is a victory of constituents that should be subject to reason, yet it is a victory of its own constituents and therefore, as was said, a self-conquest. For when the soul vanquishes itself in an orderly fashion and thus subordinates its irrational emotions to the rule of a rational purpose, such a victory is laudable and virtuous, provided that its purpose in turn is subordinate to God. Still, the soul feels less ashamed when it is not obeyed by its own depraved constituents than when its will and bidding are not heeded by the body, which is different from it and inferior to it and has a substance that has no life without it.

But when a curb is imposed by the will's authority on the body's other members, without which those organs that are excited by lust in defiance of the will cannot fulfil their craving, chastity is safeguarded, not because the pleasure of sinning has disappeared, but because it is not allowed to appear. If culpable disobedience had not been punished with disobedience in retribution, then doubtless the marriage in paradise would not have experienced this resistance, this opposition, this conflict of will and lust or, at any rate, the deficiency of lust as against the sufficiency of will; rather, the will would have been obeyed not only by other members of the body but by all alike.

Under those circumstances, the organ created for his work would have sown its seed upon the field of generation, as the hand does now upon the earth. And though I am now hampered by modesty when I wish to treat this subject in greater detail, and am compelled to apologize to chaste ears and to ask their pardon, there would then have been no reason for this to happen. Discussion, free and unencumbered by any fear of obscenity, would range over every aspect that might occur to the thought of anyone who reflected on bodily parts of this sort. There would not even be words that could be called obscene, but all our talk on this subject would be as decent as what we say in speaking about the other members of the body. Accordingly, if anyone

approaches in a wanton spirit what I have written here, let him shun any guilt on his own part, not the natural facts. Let him censure the deeds of his own depravity, not the words of my necessity. Herein I shall very readily be pardoned by the chaste and devout reader or listener as long as I refute the scepticism which relies for argument not on the faith in things unexperienced, but on the perception of things experienced. For these words of mine will give no offence to the reader who is not appalled by the Apostle's censure of the appalling immoralities of the women who "exchanged natural relations for unnatural"[35] especially since I am not, like the Apostle, now bringing up and censuring damnable lewdness. Still, in explaining, as best I can, the working of human generation I try, like him, to avoid the use of lewd terms.

Chapter 24

That if human beings had remained innocent and had earned the right to stay in paradise by their obedience, they would have used their genital organs for the procreation of offspring in the same way as they used the rest, that is, at the discretion of the will.

The Seed of offspring then would have been sown by the man and received by the woman at such time and in such amount as was needed, their genital organs being directed by the will and not excited by lust. For we move at our bidding not only those members which have joints and solid bones, like hands, feet and fingers, but we can at will shake and move, stretch and extend, twist and bend or contract and stiffen even the parts that are slackly composed of soft muscular tissue, like those which the will moves, as far as it can, in the mouth and face. Indeed, even the lungs, which, except for the marrows, are the most delicate of all the internal organs and for that reason are sheltered in the cavity of the chest, are made to function in this way for the purpose of drawing in and expelling the breath and uttering or modulating a sound; for just as bellows serve the will of blacksmiths or organists, so lungs serve the will of anyone who blows out or draws in his breath or speaks or shouts or sings.

---

35 *Romans* 1:26.

I shall not dwell on the natural endowment of certain animals in connexion with the covering that clothes their entire body; suffice it to say that if in any part of it they feel anything that should be driven off, they are able to make it move just at the point where they feel the object and to dislodge with a quiver of their hide not only flies settled upon them but also spears sticking in them. Granted that man does not have this faculty, yet surely it does not follow that the creator was unable to grant it to such animate beings as he chose. Hence man himself too may once have commanded even from his lower members an obedience that by his own disobedience he has lost. For it was not difficult for God to design him in such a way that even what now is moved in his flesh only by lust was then moved only by his will.

Certain human beings too, as we know, have natural endowments that are quite different from those of others and remarkable for their very rarity. They can at will do with their bodies some things that others find utterly impossible to imitate and scarcely credible to hear. For some people can actually move their ears, either one at a time or both together. Other people, without moving their head, can bring all the scalp that is covered with hair to the forefront and then draw it back again at will. Others can swallow an astonishing number of different objects and then, with a very slight contraction of their diaphragm, bring forth, as though from a bag, whatever item they please in perfect condition. Certain people mimic and render so expertly the utterances of birds and beasts, as well as of any other human beings, that it is impossible to tell the difference unless they are seen. Some people produce at will without any stench such rhythmical sounds from their fundament that they appear to be making music even from that quarter. From my own experience I know of a man who used to perspire at will. Certain people are known to weep at will and to shed a flood of tears.

But here is something far more incredible, a spectacle that a large number of our own brethren very recently witnessed. There was a certain presbyter, Restitutus by name, in the parish of the church of Calama.[36] Whenever he pleased (and he used to be asked to do it by those who desired to have a first-hand knowledge of the amazing phenomenon), he would withdraw from his senses to an accompaniment of cries as of some person in distress and lie still exactly like a dead man. In this state he not only was completely insensitive to pinching and pricking but at times was even burned by the application of fire and yet felt no pain except afterwards from the wound. Proof that his body remained motionless, not through deliberate effort, but through absence of feeling was provided by the fact that, like someone deceased, he showed no sign of breathing. Nevertheless, he later reported that he could hear people talking, as though from a distance, if they spoke distinctly enough.

The body then, as we have seen, even now remarkably serves certain people beyond the ordinary limits of nature in many kinds of movement and feeling although they are living our present wretched life in perishable flesh. That being so, what is there to keep us from believing that human members may have served the human will without lust for the procreation of offspring before the sin of disobedience and the consequent punishment of deterioration?

Man therefore was handed over to himself because he forsook God in his self-satisfaction, and since he did not obey God, he could not obey even himself. From this springs the more obvious wretchedness whereby man does not live as he chooses. For if he lived as he chose, he would deem himself happy; but yet he would not be happy even so if he lived an indecent life.

---

36 A Numidian city located south of Hippo and east of Cirta.

VIII.3. AL-GHAZALI

THE FOLLOWING TWO SELECTIONS SHOW AL-GHAZALI'S POWERS of synthesis: while making subtle philosophical distinctions he unites the philosophical insight of ancient thinkers into the Doctrine of the Mean and Islamic religious traditions.

Al-Ghazali offers a doctrine of hope which places it between the two extremes of despair, on the one hand, and self-deceit and wishful thinking on the other. The extremes do not include fear as such; for fear can be a companion and complement of hope. Although the higher kind of life is hope of God, a second but nevertheless good life is fear of God's wrath.

VIII.3.1. Hope (from *The Book of Hope and Fear*)

[This] is the third book of the volume on *The Means of Salvation* of the books of *The Revival of the Religious Sciences*. In the name of God, The Merciful, the Compassionate. Praise be to God whose loving kindness and reward are hoped for, whose strategems and punishment are feared; who keeps alive the hearts of His saints with the breath of hope in Him, so that He may urge them on with the kindnesses of His benefits to alight in His courtyard and to swerve from His house of tribulation which is the abode of His enemies. And with the lashes of threatening and His harsh upbraiding He has driven the faces of those who shun His presence towards the house of His reward and preferment; and he has blocked them from thwarting His leaders and becoming the butt of His wrath and vengeance by leading the different types of His creatures with chains of violence and coercion, and reins of compassion and graciousness, to His Garden.[1] And the blessing be on Muhammad, Master of His prophets and the most elect of His caliphs, and on his family and Companions and relations.

To proceed. Hope and fear are two wings by means of which those who are brought near fly to every commendable station, and two mounts on which every steep ascent of the paths of the next world is traversed. And nothing but the reins of hope will lead to the vicinity of the Merciful and the joy of the Gardens the person who is distant

from hoping and heavy with burdens, who is encompassed with what the heart abhors and with toils of members and limbs. And nothing shall avert from the fire of Gehenna and the painful punishment the person who is encompassed with the blandishments of lusts and the marvels of pleasures except the scourges of threatening and the assaults of violence. Consequently there is nothing for it but an exposition of the essence and merits of them both, as well as the way of arriving at a junction between the two of them, in spite of their polarity and mutual antipathy.

And we join the mention of them in a single book which is comprised of two parts, the first part concerning hope and the second part fear. As for the first part it is made up of an exposition of the essence of hope and an exposition of its merit; and an exposition of the therapy of hope and the way in which hope is induced by it.

Exposition of the essence of hope

Know that hope is among the sum of the stations of the pilgrims and the states of the seekers. And the description *station* is given only when it is permanent and endures, and *state* only when transitoriness is hinted at. Just as yellow is divided into permanent such as the yellow of gold; transitory such as the yellow of fear; and what comes between these two like the yellow of a sick person. Similarly the attributes of the heart follow these divisions and whatever is not permanent is called a state,

---

1 I.e., paradise in the world to come.

because it soon changes, and this is continually happening in any description of the heart.

We are dealing at present with the essence of hope. Hope also comprises state, knowledge, and deed. Knowledge is the cause which produces the state and the state decrees the deed. Hope is the comprehensive name of the three. Its exposition is that everything that confronts you is either what is abhorred or what is desired, and is divided into what is existent at the moment, what has existed in the past, and what is expected in the future. When what has existed in the past occurs to your mind, it is called remembering and recollecting; if what occurs to your mind is existent at the moment, it is called finding and tasting and perceiving. It is called finding because it is a state which you find for yourself. And, if the existence of something in the future occurs to your mind and prevails over your heart, it is called expectation and anticipation. If the thing expected is abhorred, with pain in the heart resulting from it, it is called fear and distress. If it is something desired, with pleasure and relief of heart resulting from the expectation of it and the attachment of the heart to it and the occurrence of its existence to your mind, that relief is hope.

Hence hope is the relief of the heart, because of the expectation of what it esteems desirable. But The desirable thing which is anticipated must have a cause, so, if the expectation of it is on account of the obtaining of the majority of the means to it, the name of hope in relation to it is justified. If that expectation is in spite of the defectiveness of the means and their disorder, the name of self-deceit and stupidity is more justified in relation to the expectation than that of hope. If the means are not specified either as existent or in mutual contradiction, the name of wishful thinking is more justified in relation to the expectation of it, because it is an expectation which is devoid of a cause. And, in any circumstance, the name of hope and fear does not apply to what is determined. For one does not say: I hope for the rising of the sun at the time of sunrise, and I fear its setting at the time of sunset, because that is determined. But one does say: I hope that the rain will fall and I fear lest it should be cut off.

And the Spiritual Directors[2] teach that this present world is the field of the next world, and the heart is as the earth, and faith is as the seed in it, and obedience is conducive to the turning over of the earth and the cleansing of it and the digging of channels and the leading of waters to them; and the heart which is infatuated with this present world and submerged in it is like swampy ground in which the seed does not fructify. And the Day of Resurrection is the day of reaping, and no one reaps except what he has sown, and only he who has sown the seed of faith grows crops. Rarely is faith profitable in company with a vicious heart whose moral traits are tainted just as seed does not fructify in swampy soil. And it is fitting that the hope of the creature for pardon should equal the hope of the owner of the crops.

For everyone who seeks good ground and casts into it seed of first quality which is neither mouldy nor worm-eaten, who thereafter furnishes it with what is necessary to it, that is, the conducting of water to it at appropriate times; who then clears the ground of thorns and weeds and everything that obstructs the growth of the seed or makes it rot; who then sits down and expects from the bounty of God the warding off of thunderbolts and blights, until his crop is mature and he arrives at his goal – his expectation is called hope. And, if he scatters his seed in ground which is baked hard or swampy, which is so elevated that the water does not flow into it, and does not labour one whit in the preparation of the seed – if he then expects a harvest from it, his expectation is called stupidity and self-deceit, not hope. And, if he scatters seed in ground which is good but without water, and proceeds to wait for the waters of the rains where they neither prevail nor are cut off, his expectation is called wishful thinking and not hope. Therefore, the name of hope is legitimate only in relation to the expectation of a thing desired, all of whose means, which come within the choice of the creature, have been facilitated, and only what does not come within his choice remains, and this is the bounty of God in repelling birds and blights.

So when the creature sows the seed of faith and irrigates it with the water of obedience and cleans-

2 Literally, Masters of the Heart; in effect, the Prophet Mohammed, the Caliphs, as well as established teachers of the believers.

es the heart from the thorns of vicious moral traits and expects from the bounty of God his being established in that course until death and the virtue of the Seal[3] that gives access to pardon, such expectation as his is hope in its essence, commendable in itself, and giving him an incentive for perseverance and endurance, in accordance with the means of faith, in perfecting the means of pardon until death. If its preparation with the water of obedience is cut off from the seed of faith, or, if the heart is remiss, filled with moral delinquencies, and obstinately persists in seeking the pleasures of this world, and then expects pardon, its expectation is stupidity and self-deceit. [Muhammad] said: "The fool is he whose soul follows its passions and who desires of God the Garden." And [God] said: "Then there came after them a succession who have wasted the prayer and followed their lusts; so they shall meet error."[4] And He said: "And there came after them a succession who inherited the Book, who lay hold on the chance gain of this present world and say: It will be forgiven us."[5] And God condemned the owner of the garden, when he entered his garden and said: "I do not think that this will ever perish, nor do I think the Hour is coming; and, if I am indeed taken back to my Lord, I shall surely find a better sphere than this."[6]

Therefore, the creature who strives after obedience and recoils from disobedience is right to expect from the bounty of God the completion of blessing[7] and blessing achieves completion only by the entering into the Garden. As for the disobedient person, when he has repented and repaired all that was remiss through shortcoming, it is proper that he should hope to receive repentance. With regard to the reception of repentance, when he has come to abhor disobedience, when sin grieves him and virtue delights him, when he blames himself and reproves [evil] and desires repentance and yearns after it, it is proper that he should hope from God the advancement towards repentance because of his repugnance for disobedience; and his zeal for

repentance is conducive to the cause which may give access to repentance.

And hope is only present after the consolidating of the means and for that reason He said: "But those who have believed and emigrated and striven in the way of God have hope of the mercy of God."[8] His meaning is that these have a right to hope for the mercy of God. He did not intend by it that the existence of hope is exclusive to them, since others also may hope, but he has made exclusive to them the right to hope. As for him who obstinately perseveres in what God abhors, and does not upbraid himself because of it, and does not resolve on repentance and return, his hope of pardon is stupidity, like the hope of the person who has sown seed in swampy ground and made up his mind not to cultivate it by leading water to it and cleansing it of weeds.

Since you are acquainted with the essence of hope and its marks you know that it is a state which knowledge has produced through the setting in motion of the majority of the means, and this state produces zeal to persevere in the remainder of the means in accordance with what is possible. For the man whose seed is fine and whose land is good and who has abundance of water is entitled to his hope, and his legitimate hope will continually urge him towards the oversight of the ground and the cultivation of it and the clearing of all the weeds which grow on it. Thus he will not be remiss in any detail of its cultivation until the time of harvest. This is because hope sets him at the opposite pole from despair, and despair inhibits cultivation. For whoever "knows" that the ground is swampy and that the water will not flow and the seed will not grow, will, doubtless, as a consequence, neglect the oversight of the land and toil in its cultivation.

Hope is a commendable thing, because it is a source of incentive, and despair is reprehensible and is the antithesis of hope, because it distracts from work. Fear is not the antithesis of hope, rather it is a companion to it, as its exposition will bring out.

---

3 I.e., the mark or sign at death with which we face the day of Judgment.
4 *Koran* xix, 60.
5 *Koran* vii, 168.
6 *Koran* xviii, 33-34.
7 *Koran* v, 9.
8 *Koran* ii, 215.

More, it is another source of incentive, impelling along the path of awe just as hope impels along the path of inclination. Hence, the state of hope produces sustained spiritual combat through actions, and perseverance in obedience, however fickle circumstances may be. Among its effects are finding pleasure in unbroken acceptance with God, contentment in private prayer with Him and fondness for deferring to Him. For these states must be manifest to everyone who hopes, whether king or commoner, and so how will that not be manifest to God? If it is not manifest, that will be a pointer to preclusion from the station of hope and descent into the pit of self-delusion and wishful thinking. This then is the exposition of the state of hope and how knowledge produces it and how action is produced from it.

Exposition of the merit of hope and the inclination towards it

Know that action on account of hope is of a higher order than action on account of fear, because the creatures who are nearest to God are those who love Him most, and love dominates hope. This is expressed by two kings, one of whom is served through fear of his punishment and the other through hope of his reward. For this reason what is desiderated, especially at the time of death, has to do with hope and optimism. [God] said: "Do not despair of the mercy of God."[9] Thus He proscribed the root of despair. And [it is recorded] in the traditions about Jacob that God revealed to him saying: "Do you know why I parted Joseph from you? It was because you said: 'I am afraid that the wolf will eat him, while you are neglectful of him.' Why did you fear the wolf and not hope in me? And why did you have regard to the negligence of his brothers and did not have regard to my preserving him?"

Exposition of the therapy of hope and the way in which the state of hope is obtained from it and becomes dominant

Know that two types of persons have need of this therapy; either the person over whom despair has become dominant, so that he has neglected worship; or the person over whom fear has become dominant, and who has been extravagant in his perseverance in worship, so that he has done injury to himself and his family. And these two examples of persons incline away from the equilibrium towards the two extremes of neglect and excess, and so they have need of the treatment which will restore them to the equilibrium.

For the person who is disobedient and self-deceived, who has wishful thoughts of God in company with his evasion of worship and his blind plunging into deeds of disobedience – the therapeutic properties of hope are, in his case, turned into lethal poisons, just as is the case with honey which is a cure for the person who is overcome by cold and a lethal poison to the person who is overcome by heat. More, in the case of the self-deluded person, only the therapeutic properties of fear can be employed and the means which excite it and, for that reason, it is necessary that there should be one to preach to the people; one benevolently disposed who observes the incidence of diseases and treats every disease with its antidote and not with what it has excess of. For what is sought after is the equilibrium, and the goal with respect to all attributes and moral traits, and the optimum state of affairs, is their mean. And, when the mean transgresses upon one of the two extremes, it is treated with what returns it to the mean, not with what would increase its tendency away from the mean.

And the present time is one in which it is not expedient that the means of hope should be employed with most people. Yet an exaggerated employment of threatening, no less, will hardly return them to the highway of truth and the beaten tracks of rectitude. As for the mention of the means of hope it would cause them to perish and would destroy them totally. But when [the means of hope] are less burdensome to the heart and more pleasurable to the appetites, the goal of preaching is no more than to sway hearts [to hope] and make people speak in eulogies, whatever be the reason for their inclining to hope, so that the corrupt increase in corruption and the stubborn in their rebellion through procrastination.

Ali[10] said: "The knowledgeable person is simply

9 *Koran* xxxix, 54.
10 Son-in-law of the Prophet Mohammed who was Caliph from 656-661 C.E.

he who does not make people despair of the mercy of God and does not make them feel secure from the strategems of God."

And we make mention of the means of hope in order that they may be employed in the case of the despairing person or the one who has been overcome by fear, according to the pattern of the Book of God and the Practice of His Messenger. For both embrace hope and fear in union, since these two unite the means of healing with respect to different kinds of sick people, in order that the Knowledgeable, who are the heirs of the prophets, may employ one or other of them according to need, just as the discriminating physician would employ them and not the quack who supposes that everything that has therapeutic value will be salutary to every sick person, whatever may be his condition.

The state of hope becomes dominant by means of two things; the one is reflection, and the other the reciting of the verses [of the *Koran*] and traditions and reports. With respect to reflection a person reflects on all that we have mentioned concerning the different kinds of benefits in *The Book of Gratitude*, until he knows the kindnesses of the blessings of God to His creatures in this world, and the marvels of His wisdom which He has disposed in the constitution of human beings, so that He has furnished for them in this world all that is necessary to them for the maintenance of existence. For example, the means of sustenance and what is needful to them, such as fingers and nails, and what is adornment to them, such as the arching of the eye-brows and the variegation of the colors of the eyes, and the redness of the lips, and other such things by the loss of which the goal aimed at would not be impaired. Only they would miss thereby the attainment of beauty. Since the Divine Providence has not left His creatures deficient in the instances of these minutiae, so that He was not content for His creatures that accessories and refinements in respect of adornment and necessity should pass them by, how will He take pleasure in driving them to everlasting destruction?

Moreover, when He ran over mankind with the eye of a physician, He knew that most people have at their disposal the means of happiness in this world, so that they dislike the translation from this world through death. Even if it were reported that there was never a single instance of a person being chastised after death or that there was no gathering [for Judgement], their distaste would not be nonexistent, unless, doubtless, because the means of grace were predominant. The person who wishes for death is simply a rarity, and then he does not wish for it except in a rare circumstance, and an unexpected and unfamiliar contingency.

Since the condition of most people in this world is one in which well-being and security prevail, the Practice of God does not find a substitute for them. The probability is that the affair of the next world is likewise, for the Framer of this world and the next is One, and He is forgiving, merciful and kind to His creatures, having compassion on them. So, when due reflection is given to this, the means of hope are strengthened thereby.

And also included in reflection is the scrutiny of the wisdom of the Law and its Practice in respect of this-worldly benefits, and the aspect of mercy to the creatures which is in it, so that one of the gnostics used to consider the verse on incurring a debt in the Sura al-Baqra[11] as among the most powerful of the means of hope. So it was said to [the gnostic]. And what is there of hope in it? So he said: This present world in its entirety is small, and the provision for mankind from it is small, and religion is small separated from His provision. And perceive how God revealed concerning it the longest verse (*Koran* ii, 282), that He might guide His creature in the way of being encompassed in the keeping of his religion. And how will his religion not keep him who will not give anything in exchange for it?

The second kind is the reciting of the verses and the traditions, and the material which has to do with hope is beyond definition. With regard to the verses, He said: "Say: O my creatures who have been profligate against yourselves, do not despair of the mercy of God; surely God pardons sins altogether; He is the Forgiving, the Compassionate."[12] And according to the recitation of the Messenger of God: Then do not fret, surely He is the Forgiving, the Compassionate. And He said: "And

11 *Koran* ii, 82.
12 *Koran* xxxix, 54.

the angels celebrate the praise of their Lord, and ask pardon for those upon the earth."[13] And He has recorded that He has prepared the Fire for His enemies and has simply frightened His friends with it. So He said to them: "Above them are overshadowings from the Fire and below them are overshadowings; by means of that God threatens His servants."[14] And He said: "And fear the Fire prepared for unbelievers."[15] And He said: "And I have warned you of a blazing fire; only the most reprobate who has been perfidious and turned renegade will roast in it."[16] He said: "Surely your Lord is forgiving to the people in spite of their wrongdoing."[17]

These are the means by which the relief of hope is induced in the hearts of the fearful and despairing. And, as for the foolish and self-deluded, it is not expedient that they should hear anything of that; no, they are to hear what we shall cite of the means of fear. For the most of people are not made healthy except through fear, just as the bad servant and the naughty boy are not reformed except through the whip and the stick and speech with an explicit threat. But the opposite of that would block up against them the door of health with respect to religion and this world.

VIII.3.2. Fear (from *The Book of Hope and Fear*)

The second part of the book concerning fear

In [this part] is the exposition of the essence of fear, and an exposition of its degrees, and an exposition of the divisions of the objects of fear; and an exposition of the merit of fear, and an exposition of whether fear or hope is the optimum, and an exposition of the therapy of fear, and an exposition of the meaning of the evil of the Seal; and an exposition of the states of those among the prophets and the sound in faith who feared. And let us ask God for good success.

The exposition of the essence of fear

Know that fear is an expression for the suffering of the heart and its conflagration by means of the anticipation of what is abhorred as a future contingency. And this has been made clear in the exposition of the essence of hope. And whoever is intimate with God, whose heart is ruled by truth and who lives in the present through his seeing the majesty of truth perpetually, no longer turns to the future and is possessed of neither fear nor hope. More, his state has become higher than fear or hope, for both of these are reins which preclude the soul from its excursions into laxness. Al-Wasiti[18] has pointed to this in saying: Fear is a veil between God and the creature. Again he said: When the truth makes plain the things which are secret, there remains in them no residue for hope and fear.

And, in general, if the heart of the lover is distracted by fear of separation, while he is viewing his beloved, that would indicate a deficiency of vision, and the goal of the stations is simply constancy of vision. But, for the present, we are to discuss only the initial stations and so we shall say: The state of fear can also be classified in terms of knowledge, state, and action. With regard to knowledge, it is knowledge of the cause which leads to the thing which is abhorred. So that it is as if someone committed a crime against a king, then fell into his hands and feared that he would be put to death as an example, while pardon and escape were possibilities. But the suffering of his heart through fear is in proportion to the strength of his knowledge of the means which would lead to his being put to death, such as the enormity of his crime and the fact that the king in himself is rancorous, wrathful and revengeful, that he is surrounded by such as incite him to take vengeance and is isolated from such as would intercede with him in his case. And this man in his fear was destitute of any merit or virtue that might wipe out the trace of his crime with the king. Hence the know-

13 *Koran* xlii, 3.
14 *Koran* xxxix, 18.
15 *Koran* iii, 126.
16 *Koran* xcii, 14-16.
17 *Koran* xiii, 7.
18 A religious writer who died in 942.

ledge that these means are manifest is a cause of the strength of the fear and the rigour of the suffering of the heart.

And fear is faint in proportion to the weakness of those means. And it may be that fear does not derive from the crime which the person who fears has committed, but is because of the nature of the object feared. As, for example, the person who falls into the claws of the lion, for he fears the lion because of the nature of the lion itself, namely, that, for the most part, it is avid and violent in pouncing on its prey. Even if its pouncing on its prey were within the province of choice, it might seem to the person threatened by it to be due to inborn disposition. Similarly the person who falls into the path of a torrent or into a blazing pit, for he fears the water because it is endowed by nature with the power of flowing and drowning, and likewise fire is endowed with burning. And the knowledge of the means of the thing which is abhorred is the cause which initiates and fans the conflagration and suffering of the heart, and that conflagration is fear. And, similarly, fear of God may sometimes be due to knowledge of God and His attributes, that, if He destroyed the worlds, He would not care and no person would obstruct Him. And sometimes it may be due to the multitude of the sins of the creature through his committing deeds of disobedience; and sometimes it may be due to both of them together. And the strength of his fear will be in proportion to his knowledge of his own defects and his knowledge of the majesty of God and His self-subsistence, and that He will not be asked about what He does, while they will be asked. And the person most filled with fear in respect of His Lord is the man who has most knowledge of himself and his Lord. For that reason Muhammad said: I am the one who fears God most among you. And likewise God said: "Only the knowledgeable among his creatures fear God."[19]

Then, when knowledge is perfected, the majesty of fear and the conflagration of the heart are produced. Then the trace of the conflagration flows from the heart into the body and the members and the attrib-

utes. In the body by means of emaciation and pallidness and fainting and shrieking and weeping, and it may be that in this way bitterness is inhaled and it leads to death; or it goes up to the brain and rots the intelligence; or it intensifies in strength and produces despair and hopelessness.

In the members by restraining them from disobedience and binding them to deeds of obedience by repairing what is defective and making ready for the future. And for that reason it is said: The man who fears is not he who weeps and wipes his eyes; no, it is he who forsakes that on whose account he fears punishment. And Abu l-Qasim al-Hakim[20] said: "Whoever fears anything flees from it, and whoever fears God flees to Him." And it was said to Dhu 'l-Nun[21]: "When is the creature a person who fears?" He said: "When he has brought himself down to the level of the sick man who is abstemious for fear that his sickness may be prolonged."

In the attributes by stifling the lusts and blackening the pleasures, so that the disobediences beloved by him become abhorrent, just as honey becomes abhorrent to the man who desires it, when he knows that there is poison in it. So the lusts are burned up by fear and the members are trained, and self-abasement and humility and submissiveness and lowliness obtain in the heart, and pride, rancour and envy abandon it.

Moreover he is absorbed with concern through his fear and his observing the peril of its sequel, and has no leisure for other than it. And he has no preoccupation but vigilance and self-examination and spiritual combat and conserving breaths and glances and reprehending the soul for the suggestions and footsteps and words [of Satan]. And his condition is that of the man who falls into the claws of a harmful lion. And he does not know whether it will ignore him and he will escape, or it will pounce on him and he will perish. So he will be engrossed outwardly and inwardly with what he fears and there will be no room in him for anything else. This is the state of the person over whom fear has prevailed and gained the mastery. The state of the company of the Companions and Followers[22]

19 *Koran* xxxv, 25.
20 A religious writer who died around 1119-20.
21 Died 861.
22 I.e., companions and followers of the Prophet Mohammed.

was thus. And the strength of vigilance and self-examination and spiritual combat is in proportion to the strength of fear which is the suffering of the heart and its conflagration. And the strength of fear is in proportion to the strength of knowledge of the majesty of God and of His attributes and His actions, and in proportion to the defects of the soul and the perils and terrors which confront it.

And the least of the degrees of fear whose trace is visible in actions is the blocking of access to the forbidden; and the restraint which excludes the forbidden is called abstinence. If its strength increases, it restrains from what directs at it the possibility of the forbidden and hence also from that whose forbiddenness is not a matter of certainty, and that is called piety, since piety is the forsaking of that which one suspects so as to arrive at what one does not suspect. And it may urge a person on to forsake what has no evil in it for fear of what has evil in it, and this is sincere piety. When fully consecrated worship is joined to it, the consequence is that one does not build what he does not inhabit nor gather what he does not eat, nor turn to this world, since he knows that it will abandon him nor expend a single breath except towards God.

This is sincerity and its owner is worthy to be named Sincere. And piety enters into sincerity and abstinence into piety and chastity into abstinence, for it (chastity) is a specialized expression for being cut off from the determinism of lusts. Therefore, fear is effective in the members through restraint and perseverance, and it is in virtue of restraint that it is given the new name of chastity which is refraining from the determinism of lusts. And abstinence is higher than it, since it is more universal, because it is refraining from everything forbidden. And higher than it is piety, since it is the name for refraining from the sum of things forbidden and dubious. And beyond it is the name Sincere and He who is brought near. And the course of the most ultimate rank in relation to what precedes it is from the most general to the most particular, for, when you have mentioned the most particular, you have mentioned the whole. As if you were saying: Mankind, whether Arab or non-Arab, and Arab, whether Quraysh or non-Quraysh, and Quraysh, whether Hashimi[23] or non-Hashimi, and Hashimi,

whether Alid or non-Alid, and Alid, whether Hasani or Husayni; and, when you have mentioned, for example, that a man is Hasani, you have described him totally, and, if you describe him as Alid, you describe him by what is above him – what is more general than he. Similarly when I have said *sincere*, I have said that a man is pious, is abstemious, and is chaste. And there is no need for you to suppose that these numerous names point to numerous dissimilar meanings; for that would reduce you to confusion, just as confusion reigns over whoever seeks different meanings from linguistic variants, where the meanings have not followed the variants. So this is a pointer to the concert of the meanings of fear, and what surrounds it on the higher side, such as the knowledge which determines it, and on the lower side, such as the actions which derive from it through restraint and perseverance.

Exposition of the degrees of fear and its differentiation into power and weakness

Know that fear is commendable. Often it is supposed that all fear is commendable, and that the more powerful and frequent it is the more it is commendable. This is a fallacy. No, fear is the whip of God by which He drives His creatures towards perseverance in knowledge and action, so that by means of both of these they may obtain the rank of nearness to God. And what is most salutary for the beast is that it should not escape the whip, and thus with the boy, but that does not point to the conclusion that excessive beating is commendable. And likewise with fear; it has deficiency and equilibrium, and what is commendable is the equilibrium and the mean.

The person who is deficient in it is he who tends towards effeminate softness which alights on his mind, whenever he hears a verse from the *Koran*, and produces weeping, and the tears overflow and similarly when he sees a cause of terror. And, when that cause is absent from his attention, his heart returns to negligence. So this is a fear which is deficient, of little profit and feeble in utility; just like the slight stick with which the powerful riding-beast is beaten, which gives it no serious pain and

---

23 Al-Ghazali gives here examples of different tribes and groups in the realm of Islam.

does not urge it on to the destination, nor is it salutary for its correction. Such is the fear of all men except the Gnostics and the Knowledgeable. And I do not mean by Knowledgeable those who are stamped with the marks of Scholars or are called by their names; for they, of all men, are the most distant from fear. No, I mean those who are knowledgeable concerning God and His Days and His actions, and that is a thing whose existence is rare at the present time. And, for that reason, al-Fudayl b. 'Iyad[24] said: "When it is said to you: Do you fear God?, keep silence. For, if you say: No, you are an unbeliever; and, if you say: Yes, you are a liar." And he indicated by this that it is fear that restrains the members from deeds of disobedience and binds them to deeds of obedience, and whatever does not take effect in the members is no more than an impulse and a fleeting motion which does not deserve the name of fear.

The extremist is he whose fear is strong and transgresses the limit of the equilibrium, so that it goes out towards hopelessness and despair, and it again is reprehensible, because it stultifies action. Fear may also issue in sickness and weakness and depression and bewilderment and intellectual atrophy. The aim of fear is the same as the aim of the whip which is to incite to action. If it is otherwise, fear is imperfect, because it is deficient in its essence, since its product is ignorance and impotence. Ignorance, because one does not know the sequel of his affair; and, if he knew he would not be afraid, since the thing which is feared is that about which there is doubt. Impotence, because he is exposed to a forbidden thing which he is unable to repel. Therefore, fear is commendable in connection with human deficiencies, and only knowledge is commendable in itself and its essence, together with power and everything by which it is possible to describe God. And that by which it is not possible to describe God is not perfect in its essence and only becomes commendable in connection with a deficiency which is greater than it; just as the enduring of therapeutic pain is commendable, because it is milder than the pain of disease and death. And whatever issues in despair is reprehensible, and fear also may issue in disease, weakness,

depression and bewilderment and intellectual atrophy; it may even issue in death. All that is reprehensible and is to be likened to the beating which kills the boy and the whip which slays the riding-beast or makes it ill or breaks one of its limbs.

The Messenger of God[25] mentioned the means of hope and multiplied them simply in order that he might thereby treat the shock of excessive fear which leads to despair or one of these conditions, and all that is implied with respect to a condition. The commendable part of it is whatever leads to the goal which is intended by it, and whatever comes short of it or goes beyond it is reprehensible. The profit of fear is caution and abstinence and piety and spiritual combat and worship and reflection and recollection, and all the means that bring about union with God. And all of that requires life along with health of body and wholeness of intellect, and whatever impairs these means is reprehensible.

If you say: Whoever fears and dies because of his fear is a martyr, and how can his state be reprehensible? Know that the meaning of his being a martyr is that he possesses a rank in virtue of his death through fear which he would not have attained had he died at that time through a cause other than fear. So that in connection with him it is meritorious, but in connection with the ordering of his survival and the prolongation of his life in obedience to God and the treading of His paths it is not meritorious. No, the person who is making a pilgrimage to God by the path of reflection and spiritual combat and the ascent of the degrees of knowledge possesses at every instant the rank of martyr and martyrs. Were it otherwise the rank of a lad who is killed or the madman whom a lion mauls would be higher than the rank of a prophet or saint who dies a natural death, and this would be absurd. Nor is it proper that this should be supposed. No, the most valued of blessings is prolongation of life in obedience to God, and everything which annuls life or mind or health (for life is impaired when it is impaired) is a loss and deprivation in relation to some conditions, even if some parts of it should have merit in relation to the other conditions, just as martyrdom has merit in relation to what is

---

24 Died 803.
25 I.e., the Prophet Mohammed.

below it, not in relation to the degree of the Pious and the Sincere. So, if fear does not effect action, its existence and non-existence are alike, just as the whip which does not accelerate the movement of the riding-beast. And, if it is effective, it has degrees according as its effects are visible. For, if it is an incentive only to chastity, it is the refraining from the determinism of lusts, so that it possesses a degree. And, if it produces abstinence, it is higher (in degree). And the most ultimate of its degrees is that it should produce the degrees of the Sincere, which is that it should tear one away outwardly and inwardly from what is other than God, so that there remains in him no room for other than God, and this is the most ultimate of its commendable characteristics, and it is accompanied with preservation of health and mind. If it goes beyond this towards the atrophy of mind and health, it is sickness which must be treated, if there is an effectual treatment. And, if it were commendable, its treatment by hope and other means until it passes away would not be necessary. For this reason Sahl[26] used to say to novices who persisted with fasting over a long period: Keep your wits. God has never had a saint who was mentally deficient.

Exposition of the divisions of fear in relation to the object which is feared

Know that fear does not deserve the name except it concerns the expectation of what is abhorred, whether it is abhorred in its essence, such as fire, or because it leads to what is abhorred, as deeds of disobedience are abhorred, because they lead to what is abhorred in the next world; just as the invalid abhors the fruits which do him injury, because they lead to death. So everyone who fears is bound to picture to himself an abhorred thing from one of the two divisions, and the expectation of it grows powerful in his heart, so that his heart is burnt up through his terror of the abhorred thing.

And the station of those who fear is differentiated in accordance with the kind of abhorred things whose dread dominates their hearts. So there are those whose hearts are dominated by what is not essentially abhorred, but abhorred because of what

is outside itself, such as those who are dominated by the fear of death before repentance or a fear of a deficiency of repentance and a breaking of the covenant; or the fear of a diminishing of strength so as not to fulfil the complete demands of God. Or the fear that the tenderness of the heart will pass away and that it will be replaced by hardness; or the fear of inclining away from uprightness; or the fear of the mastery of custom in the following of the familiar lusts; or the fear that God will entrust people to their good works in which they have put their trust, and which they have boasted about among God's creatures. Or the fear of taking God for granted by reason of the multitude of God's favors towards one; or the fear of being distracted from God by other than God; or the fear of being deceived by the regular succession of favors. Or the fear that the defections of one's obedience will be uncovered, where there is revealed to him from God what he did not take into the reckoning. Or the fear that people will persecute one with back-biting, perfidy, dissimulation and premeditated thoughts of evil. Or the fear of one's lack of knowledge of what may happen in the remainder of one's life; or the fear of punishment being brought forward to this world and one's being disgraced before death. Or the fear of being deceived by the blandishments of this world; or the fear that God will scrutinize one's secret heart at a moment when one is heedless of Him. Or the fear of being sealed at death with the Seal of evil; or the fear of the predestination which has been predestined to one from all eternity.

And all these are things which the Gnostics fear and there is that which is particularly advantageous to everyone, which is the treading of the path of caution so as to exclude what leads to the thing feared. And so whoever fears the mastery of custom over him will persevere in weaning himself from custom. And whoever fears that God will scrutinize his secret heart occupies himself with the purifying of his heart from the whisperings of Satan. And thus with the remainder of the divisions; and among those fears the one which most overcomes assurance is the fear of the Seal, for its affair is full of danger. The highest of all the divisions and the one which gives best access to perfection of knowledge is the fear of predestination,[27] because the Seal follows from what has been predestined, and is a branch which springs from it in accordance with the interaction of many causes. So the Seal makes manifest what the eternal decree has predestined in the essence of the Book.

The relation of him who fears the Seal to him who fears predestination is like that of two men in judgement of whom the king has signed a decree, the import of which might be their beheading or the assigning to them of a Ministry. And the decree was not yet delivered to them and the heart of one was tied up with the circumstance of the delivery of the decree and its publication and what it would disclose; and the heart of the other was tied up with the circumstance of the decree of the king, its nature, and what it was that had passed through his mind at the moment of the decree, of mercy or of anger. And this was to turn towards the cause which is a higher activity than to turn towards what is a corollary. And likewise to turn towards the eternal decree in promulgating which the reed-pen flowed is a higher activity than turning towards what is made manifest at the End.

The Prophet pointed to this when he was in the pulpit and clenched his right hand and said: "This is the Book of God in which He has written the people of the Garden with their names and the names of their fathers of which there shall be no increase and no diminution." Then he clenched his left hand and said: "This is the Book of God in which He has written the people of the Fire with their names and the names of their fathers of which there shall be no increase and no diminution." And let the people of bliss do the works of the people of woe, so that it is said: It is as if they were numbered with them; more, they are identical with them. Then God will save them before death, even if it is in the time between two milkings of a she-camel. And let the people of woe do the works of the people of bliss, so that it is said: It is as if they were numbered with them; more, they are identical with them. Then God will extract them before death, even if it is in the time between two milkings of a she-camel. He who is numbered among the blessed is so by the decree of God, as is the reprobate by the decree of God, and works are in the nature of Seals.

And this accords with the division of those who fear into the person who fears his disobedience and Sin, and the one who fears God in Person, because of His attributes and majesty and characteristics which, without a doubt, compel awe. So this fear is the highest in rank, and, for that reason, his fear endures, even if he enters into the obedience of the Sincere. As for the other it is in the target area of self-deception, and the safest part of it is if one perseveres in obedience. So fear of disobedience is the fear of the Sound in Faith, and the fear of God is that of the Unitarians and the Sincere. It is the fruit of knowledge concerning God, and whoever knows Him and knows His attributes, knows from His attributes how He is worthy to be feared apart altogether from sin. More, if the disobedient person knew God as he ought to know Him, he would fear God and would not fear his disobedience. And were it not that He is to be feared in His Person, He would not constrain him to disobedience and smooth its path for him and prepare its means, for the facilitating of the means of disobedience is alienation. And he has not committed disobedience prior to his (present) disobedience in virtue of which he deserves to be constrained to disobedience and to have access to its means. Nor is obedience preceded by merit in virtue of which favour is shown to him for whom obedience is made easy and the path of communion smoothed for him. For the disobedient person has had disobedience decreed to him whether he wills it or not; and thus with the obedient person. And He who exalts Muhammad to the Highest Heaven irrespective of merit which he had acquired prior to its taking place, and abases Abu Jahl in the Lowest Hell irrespective of sin which he had committed prior to its taking place, is worthy to be feared for His attribute of majesty.

For whoever obeys God, obeys because the will to obedience has dominion over him and power comes to him, and, after the creation of the irrevocable will and the complete power, the action comes into being of necessity. And he who is disobedient is so because a powerful and irrevocable will has dominion over him, and the means and power come to him, and the action, in the wake of the will and the power, is of necessity. Would that I knew what it is

---

27 See glossary entry for 'predestination.'

that determines the preferment of this man and his being singled out through the dominion over him of the will to obedience, and what determines the abasement of that man and his alienation through the dominion over him of the impulses of disobedience, and how this is transferred to the creature! But, since the transfer goes back to the eternal decree, irrespective of sin or merit, fear of One who decrees as He wills and legislates as He desires is a resolution with every intelligent person. And beyond this meaning is the secret of predestination whose dissemination is not permissible.

And the understanding of the fear of Him in respect of His attributes is not possible except by parable. Were it not for the permission of the Law, the person of insight would not have dared to mention it. So it has come down in the tradition: Surely God revealed to David: Fear Me as you fear the harmful lion. And this is the parable which lets you understand what is the effect of the meaning, even if it does not acquaint you with its cause. For to be acquainted with its cause is to be acquainted with the secret of predestination, and He does not disclose that except to His "People." And the conclusion to be drawn is that the lion is to be feared not because of the sin which you have previously committed against it, but because of its characteristics, its violence and rapaciousness and arrogance and awfulness, and because it does what it will and does not care. For, if it killed you, its heart would be untouched by compunction, and it would feel no pain at killing you. And, if it left you alone, it would not leave you out of pity for you or to preserve your breath. No, you are in its sight too insignificant for it to notice you, whether dead or alive. More, the killing of a thousand like you and the killing of a gnat are on one plane with it, since that does not impugn the animal kingdom or the power and rapaciousness attributed to it. And the parable has its highest application to God. Whoever knows Him knows with inward sight which is more powerful and trustworthy and transparent than outward sight. He speaks the truth in His saying: These to the Garden and I do not care; and these to the Fire and I do not care. And of the things which compel awe and fear knowledge that He is self-subsistent and that He does not care will suffice you.

As for the second class of those who fear, the thing abhorred is pictured within them, such as the image of the pangs of death and its rigours, or the interrogation of Munkar and Nakir, or the punishment of the grave, or the terror of the resurrection, or the awfulness of the halting-place before God and shame because of the drawing back of the veil, and the interrogation about the smallest details; or the fear of the Bridge and its edge and the manner of crossing over it; or the fear of the Fire and its shackles and terrors, or the fear of being banned from the Garden, the House of Bliss and the enduring Kingdom, and from a diminution of degrees; or the fear of being veiled from God.

And all these means are abhorred in themselves and are, indubitably, to be feared. And the states of those who fear are differentiated according to them; and the highest of them in rank is the fear of alienation and of being veiled from God and this is the fear of the Gnostics. And what comes before this is the fear of the Practitioners and the Sound in Faith and the Ascetics and the body of the people. He whose knowledge is not perfect and whose inner sight is not opened up does not feel the pleasure of union nor the pain of alienation and separation. When it is mentioned to him that the Gnostic does not fear the Fire but fears only the veil, he finds that inwardly repugnant, and marvels at it in his soul. And it may be that he would find repugnant the pleasure of looking at the face of God, the Magnanimous One, were it not that the Law precludes him from being repugnant to it. And his confessing it with the tongue derives from the compulsion of authority, and, were it otherwise, it would not be inwardly vouched for because he knows only the pleasure of the stomach, of sexual intercourse and of the eye (when he looks at colors and fair faces), and, in general, every pleasure in which the beasts are his associates. As for the pleasure of the Gnostics they only attain to it, and its classification and exposition are forbidden to whoever is not a party to it. And whoever is a party to it himself possesses the insight, and so has no need that someone else should expound it to him. The fear of those who fear can be traced to these divisions. Let us ask God for good success through His magnanimity.

VIII.4. ABELARD

VIII.4.1. What Sin and Vice consist in (from *Know Thyself* or *Ethics*)

[Abelard's conception of sin and its relation to such things as lust, evil deeds and vices is usefully contrasted with Augustine's in selections **VIII.2.5. & 6.**, as well as with the selections from Thomas Aquinas which follow.]

Morals concerns vices and virtues

We consider morals to be the vices or virtues of the mind which make us prone to bad or good works. However, there are vices or goods not only of the mind but also of the body, such as bodily weakness or the fortitude which we call strength, sluggishness or swiftness, limpness or being upright, blindness or vision. Hence to distinguish these, when we said "vices" we added "of the mind." Now these vices, that is of the mind, are contrary to the virtues, as injustice is to justice, sloth to constancy, intemperance to temperance.

Of vice of the mind which concerns morals

There are also, however, some vices or good things of the mind which are separate from morals and do not make human life worthy of blame or praise, such as dullness of mind or quickness of thinking, forgetfulness or a good memory, ignorance or learning. Since all these befall the wicked and the good alike, they do not in fact belong to the composition of morality nor do they make life base or honourable. Hence rightly when above we presented "vices of the mind" we added, in order to exclude such things, "which make us prone to bad works," that is, incline the will to something which is not at all fitting to be done or to be forsaken.

The difference between sin and vice inclining to evil

Mental vice of this kind is not, however, the same as sin nor is sin the same as a bad action. For example, to be irascible, that is, prone or ready for the emotion of anger, is a vice and inclines the mind impetuously or unreasonably to do something which is not at all suitable. However, this vice is in the soul, so that in fact it is ready to be angry even when it is not moved to anger, just as the limpness for which a person is said to be lame is in him even when he is not walking limply, because the vice is present even though the action is not. So too nature itself or the constitution of the body makes many prone to lechery just as it does to anger, yet they do not sin in this because that is how they are, but through this they have the material for a struggle so that triumphing over themselves through the virtue of temperance they may obtain a crown. As Solomon said: "The patient person is better than the valiant: and he that ruleth his spirit than he that taketh cities."[1] For religion does not consider it base to be beaten by humans but by vice. The former happens in fact to good people too; in the latter we turn away from good things. The Apostle commends this victory to us, saying: "He will not be crowned except he strive lawfully."[2] Strive, I say, in resisting vices rather than people, lest they entice us into wrongful consent; even if people cease, vices do not cease to assault us, and their attack is so much more dangerous for being more constant and victory is so much more brilliant for being more difficult. But however much people prevail over us, they bring no turpitude into our lives unless after the manner of the vices and having, as it were, converted us to vices they submit us to a shameful consent. When they command our bodies, so long as the mind remains free, true freedom is not in peril and we do not fall into an indecent subjection. For it is shameful to serve vice, not peo-

1 *Proverbs* 16:32.
2 *Timothy* 2:5.

548

ple; subjection to vices soils the soul, bodily servitude does not. For whatever is common to good and bad people alike is of no importance to virtue or vice.

What is mental vice and what is properly said to be sin

And so vice is that by which we are made prone to sin, that is, are inclined to consent to what is not fitting so that we either do it or forsake it. Now this consent we properly call sin, that is, the fault of the soul by which it earns damnation or is made guilty before God. For what is that consent unless it is contempt of God and an offence against him? For God cannot be offended against through harm but through contempt. He indeed is that supreme power who is not impaired by any harm but who avenges contempt of himself. And so our sin is contempt of the Creator and to sin is to hold the Creator in contempt, that is, to do by no means on his account what we believe we ought to do for him, or not to forsake on his account what we believe we ought to forsake. So, by defining sin negatively, that is to say, as not doing or not forsaking what is fitting, we plainly show there is no substance of sin; it subsists as not being rather than being, just as if in defining darkness we say it is the absence of light where light used to be.

But perhaps you will say that the will to do a bad deed is also sin and makes us guilty before God, even as the will to do a good deed makes us just, so that just as virtue consists in a good will, so sin consists in a bad will and not only in not being but also, and like virtue, in being. For just as we please God by willing to do what we believe to please him, so we displease him by willing to do what we believe to displease him and we seem to offend him or hold him in contempt. But I say that if we consider this more carefully, our conclusion should be very different from what it seems. For since we sometimes sin without any bad will and since that bad will when restrained but not extinguished procures a prize for those who resist it and brings the material for a struggle and a crown of glory,[3] it ought not to be called sin so much as a weakness which is now necessary. For consider: there is an innocent man whose cruel lord is so burning with rage against him that with a naked sword he chases him for his life. For long that man flees and as far as he can he avoids his own murder; in the end and unwillingly he is forced to kill him lest he be killed by him. Tell me, whoever you are, what bad will he had in doing this. If he wanted to escape death, he wanted to save his own life. But surely this was not a bad will? You say: not this, I think, but the will he had to kill the lord who was chasing him. I reply: that is well and cleverly said if you can show a will in what you claim. But, as has already been said, he did this unwillingly and under compulsion; as far as he could he deferred injury to life; he was also aware that by this killing he would put his own life in danger. So how did he do willingly what he committed with danger to his own life as well?

If you reply that that too was done out of will, since it is agreed that he was led to this out of a will to avoid death, not to kill his lord, we do not confute that at all but, as has already been said, that will is in no way to be derided as bad through which he, as you say, wanted to evade death, not to kill the lord. And yet although he was constrained by fear of death, he did do wrong in consenting to an unjust killing which he should have undergone rather than have inflicted. In fact he took the sword himself; no power had handed it to him. Whence Truth says: "All that take the sword shall perish by the sword." "He who takes the sword," he says, by presumption, not he to whom it has been granted for the purpose of administering vengeance, "shall perish by the sword," that is, he incurs by this rashness damnation and the killing of his own soul. And so he wanted, as has been said, to avoid death, not to kill the lord. But because he consented to a killing to which he ought not to have consented, this unjust consent of his which preceded the killing was a sin.

If perhaps someone says that he wanted to kill his lord for the sake of avoiding death, he cannot therefore simply infer that he wanted to kill him. For example, if I were to say to someone: "I want you to have my cap for this reason, that you give me five solidi" or "I gladly want it to become yours at that price," I do not therefore concede that I want it to be yours. Moreover if anyone held in prison wants

---

3 Cf. 1 *Peter* 5:4.

to put his son there in his place so that he may seek his own ransom, surely we do not therefore simply concede that he wants to put his own son in prison – something which he is driven to endure with floods of tears and with many sighs? At any rate such a will which consists in great grief of mind is not, I would say, to be called will but rather suffering. That he wills this on account of that is the equivalent of saying that he endures what he does not will on account of the other things which he desires. Thus the sick man is said to want a cauterization or an operation in order to be healed and martyrs to suffer in order to come to Christ or Christ himself in order that we may be saved by his suffering. Yet we are not therefore compelled to concede simply that they want this. On no occasion can there be suffering except where something is done against will nor does anyone suffer where he fulfills his will and gains delight in doing so. Certainly the Apostle who says:[4] "I desire to be dissolved and to be with Christ," that is, to die for the purpose of coming to him, himself observes elsewhere: "We would not be unclothed but clothed upon, that that which is mortal may be swallowed up by life." The blessed Augustine also remembers this thought which the Lord expressed when he said to Peter:[5] "Thou shalt stretch forth thy hands, and another shall gird thee and lead thee whither thou wouldest not." In the weakness which he had assumed of human nature the Lord also said to the Father:[6] "If it be possible, let this chalice pass from me. Nevertheless, not as I will but as thou wilt." His soul naturally dreaded the great suffering of death and what he knew to be painful could not be voluntary for him. Although it is written of him elsewhere:[7] "He was offered because it was his own will," this is either to be understood according to the nature of the divinity in whose will it was that the assumed man should suffer, or 'it was his will' means 'it was his plan' as it does when the Psalmist says:[8] "He hath done all things whatsoever he would." So it is evident that sometimes sin is committed entirely without bad will; it is therefore clear from this that what is sin is not to be called will.

Certainly, you will say, that is so where we sin under constraint, but not where we do so willingly, as for instance if we want to commit something which we know should not be done by us at all. There indeed that bad will and the sin seem to be the same. For example, someone sees a woman and falls into concupiscence and his mind is affected by the pleasure of the flesh, so that he is incited to the baseness of sexual intercourse. Therefore, you say, what else is this will and base desire than sin?

I answer that if that will is restrained by the virtue of temperance but is not extinguished, it remains for a fight and persists in struggling and does not give up even when overcome. For where is the fight if the material for fighting is lacking? Or whence comes the great reward if what we endure is not hard? When the struggle is over, it no longer remains to fight but to receive the reward. Here, however, we strive by fighting, so that elsewhere as winners of the struggle we may receive a crown. But in order that there be a fight, it is evident that there must be an enemy who resists, not one who actually gives up. This surely is our bad will, over which we triumph when we subdue it to the divine will, but we do not really extinguish it, so that we always have it to fight against.

Indeed, what great thing do we for God if we support nothing against our will but rather discharge what we will? And who has thanks for us if in what we say we are doing for him we fulfil our own will? But what, you will say, do we gain before God out of what we do whether willingly or unwillingly? I reply: nothing, certainly, since he considers the mind rather than the action when it comes to a reward, and an action adds nothing to merit whether it proceeds from a good or a bad will, as we shall later show. But when we put his will before our own so as to follow his rather than ours, we obtain great merit with him according to that perfectness of Truth:[9] "I came not to do my own will

4 *Philippians* 1:23.
5 *John* 21:18.
6 *Matthew* 26:39.
7 *Isaiah* 53:7.
8 *Psalms* 113:3.
9 *John* 6:98.

but the will of him that sent me." Exhorting us to this he says:[10] "If any man come to me and hate not his father and mother, yea and his own life also, he is not worthy of me," that is, if he does not renounce their suggestions or his own will and subject himself completely to my precepts. If therefore we are ordered to hate but not to destroy a father, so too our will; we are not to follow it but neither are we to destroy it completely. For he who said:[11] "Go not after thy lusts: but turn away from thy own will," taught us not to fulfil our lusts, but not to be entirely without them. The former is vicious, but the latter is not possible for our weakness. So sin is not lusting for a woman but consenting to lust; the consent of the will is damnable, but not the will for intercourse.

What we have said with respect to lechery, let us consider with respect also to gluttony. Someone passes through another man's garden and seeing delightful fruits he falls into longing for them; however, he does not consent to his longing so as to remove something from there by theft or robbery, even though his mind has been incited to great desire by the pleasure of food. But where desire is, there undoubtedly is will. And so he desires to eat of that fruit in which he is certain there is pleasure. In fact by the very nature of his infirmity he is compelled to desire what he is not allowed to take without the knowledge or the permission of the lord. He represses his desire; he does not extinguish it, but because he is not drawn to consent, he does not incur sin.

Now where does this lead us? It shows, in short, that in such things also the will itself or the desire to do what is unlawful is by no means to be called sin, but rather, as we have stated, the consent itself. The time when we consent to what is unlawful is in fact when we in no way draw back from its accomplishment and are inwardly ready, if given the chance, to do it. Anyone who is found in this disposition incurs the fullness of guilt; the addition of the performance of the deed adds nothing to increase the sin. On the contrary, before God the person who to the extent of his power endeavours to achieve this is as guilty as the person who as far

as he is able does achieve it – just as if, so the blessed Augustine reminds us,[12] he too had also been caught in the act.

Now, although will is not sin and, as we have said, we sometimes commit sins unwillingly, yet some say that every sin is voluntary, and they find a certain difference between sin and will, since will is said to be one thing and what is voluntary is said to be something different, that is, will is one thing but what is committed through the will is another. But if we call sin what we have previously said is properly called sin, that is, contempt of God or consent to that which we believe should be forsaken on God's account, how do we say that sin is voluntary, that is, our own willing to offer the contempt of God which is sin or to become worse or to be made worthy of damnation? For although we may want to do that which we know ought to be punished or for which we may deserve to be punished, we do not, however, want to be punished. Obviously we are wicked in this, that we want to do what is wicked, yet we do not want to submit to the fairness of a just punishment. The punishment which is just is displeasing; the action which is unjust is pleasing. Moreover, it often happens that when we want to lie with a woman whom we know to be married and whose looks have enticed us, yet we by no means want to be adulterous with her – we would prefer that she was unmarried. There are, on the other hand, many men who for their own renown desire the wives of the mighty more keenly because they are married to such men than they would if they were unmarried; they want to commit adultery rather than fornication, that is, to transgress by more rather than by less. There are people who are wholly ashamed to be drawn into consent to lust or into a bad will and are forced out of the weakness of the flesh to want what they by no means want to want. Therefore I certainly do not see how this consent which we do not want to have may be called voluntary with the result, as has been said, that we should, according to some, call every sin voluntary, unless we understand voluntary to exclude the element of necessity, since clearly no sin is unavoidable, or unless we call voluntary that

---

10 *Luke* 14:26.
11 *Ecclesiastes* 18:30.
12 In *De libero arbitrio*, (*On Free Choice*) i. 3, n. 8 (PL 32.1225). See selection **VIII.2.5.**

which proceeds from will. For even if he who killed his lord under constraint did not have the will to kill, yet he did it out of will, since in fact he wanted to avoid or to defer death.

There are people who may be considerably disturbed when they hear us say that the doing of sin adds nothing to guilt or to damnation before God. They object that in the action of sin a certain pleasure may follow which increases the sin, as in sexual intercourse, or in that eating which we mentioned. They would not in fact say this absurdly if they were to prove that carnal pleasure of this sort is sin and that such a thing cannot be committed except by sinning. If they really admit this, it is definitely not lawful for anyone to have this fleshly pleasure. Therefore, spouses are not immune from sin when they unite in this carnal pleasure allowed to them, nor is he who enjoys the pleasurable consumption of his own fruit. Also, all invalids would be at fault who relish sweeter foods to refresh themselves and to recover from illness; they certainly do not take these without pleasure or if they did so, they would not benefit. And lastly the Lord, the creator of foods as well as of bodies, would not be beyond fault if he put into them such flavours as would necessarily compel to sin those who eat them with pleasure. For how would he produce such things for our eating or allow their eating if it were impossible for us to eat them without sin? And how can sin be said to be committed in that which is allowed? For what were at one time unlawful and prohibited acts, if they are later allowed and thus become lawful, are now committed wholly without sin, for example the eating of swine's flesh and many other things formerly forbidden to Jews but now permitted to us. And so when we see Jews converted to Christ also freely eating foods of this sort which the Law had forbidden, how do we defend them from blame if not by our claim that this is now granted to them by God? So if in such eating once forbidden but now conceded to them the concession itself excuses sin and removes the contempt of God, who will say that anyone sins in that which a divine concession has made lawful to

him? If therefore to lie with a wife or even to eat delicious food has been allowed to us since the first day of our creation which was lived in Paradise without sin, who will accuse us of sin in this if we do not exceed the limit of the concession?

Yet again they say that marital intercourse and the eating of delicious food are in fact conceded in such a way that the pleasure itself is not conceded; they should be performed wholly without pleasure. But assuredly if this is so, they are allowed to be done in a way in which they cannot be done at all and it was an unreasonable permission which allowed them to be done in a way in which it is certain that they cannot be done. Besides, by what reason did the law once prescribe marriage so that everyone should leave his seed in Israel or the Apostle urge spouses to pay their debt to one another,[13] if these cannot be done at all without sin? In what way does he speak here of debt where now necessarily there is sin? Or how is one to be compelled to do what in sinning will offend God? It is clear, I think, from all this that no natural pleasure of the flesh should be imputed to sin nor should it be considered a fault for us to have pleasure in something in which when it has happened the feeling of pleasure is unavoidable. For example, if someone compels a religious who is bound in chains to lie between women and if he is brought to pleasure, not to consent, by the softness of the bed and through the contact of the women beside him, who may presume to call this pleasure, made necessary by nature, a fault?

But if you object that, as it seems to some, carnal pleasure in legitimate intercourse is also to be considered a sin, since David says:[14] "For, behold, I was conceived in iniquities," and since the Apostle when he said:[15] "Return together again, lest Satan tempt you for your incontinency" adds:[16] "But I speak this by indulgence, not by commandment," the pressure upon us to say that this carnal pleasure itself is sin seems to come from authority rather than from reason. For it is known that David had been conceived not in fornication but in matrimony and, as they say, indulgence, that is, pardon,

---

13 1 *Corinthians* 7:6.
14 *Psalms* 1:7.
15 1 *Corinthians* 7:5.
16 *Ibid.* 5:6.

does not occur where fault is wholly absent. In my view, however, David's statement that he had been conceived in iniquities or in sins – he did not add whose they were – represents the general curse of original sin by which everyone is subjected to damnation because of the fault of their parents, in accordance with what is written elsewhere: "No one is free from uncleanness nor is the one-day-old child if he is alive upon earth." For as the blessed Jerome[17] has mentioned, and as manifest reason holds, as long as the soul exists in the age of infancy it lacks sin. If therefore it is clean from sin, how is it soiled with the uncleanness of sin unless the former is to be understood with respect to fault, the latter with respect to punishment? One who does not yet see through reason what he should do has no fault arising from contempt of God, but he is not free of the stain of earlier parents and thence he already contracts punishment, but not fault, and he sustains in his punishment what they committed in their fault. So when David says he was conceived in iniquities or in sins, he saw that he was subjected to a general sentence of damnation by virtue of the fault of his own parents and he referred these crimes back less to his immediate parents than to earlier ones.

However, what the Apostle calls indulgence is not to be interpreted, as they want, as if he had meant this indulgence of permission to be the pardon of a sin. In fact what he says, "by indulgence, not by commandment," means "by permission, not by compulsion." For if spouses want and have decided with equal consent, they can abstain altogether from carnal relations and they should not be driven into them by authority. But if they have not taken this decision, they have the indulgence, that is, the permission to turn aside from the more perfect life into the practice of a laxer life. In this place, therefore, the Apostle did not mean by indulgence pardon for sin but permission for a laxer life for the sake of avoiding fornication, so that a lower life might prevent a magnitude of sin and one might be smaller in merits lest one become greater in sins.

Now we have mentioned this lest anyone, wishing perhaps every carnal pleasure to be sin, should say

that sin itself is increased by action when one carries the consent given by the mind into the commission of an act and is polluted not only by shameful consent but also by the blemishes of an action, as if an exterior and corporeal act could contaminate the soul. The doing of deeds has no bearing upon an increase of sin and nothing pollutes the soul except what is of the soul, that is, the consent which alone we have called sin, not the will which precedes it nor the doing of the deed which follows. For even though we will or do what is not fitting, we do not therefore sin, since these things often happen without sin, just as conversely consent occurs without them. This we have already partly shown for the will which lacks consent, in the case of the man who fell into longing for a woman he had seen or for fruit which did not belong to him and yet is not brought to consent, and for evil consent without evil will, in the case of him who killed his lord unwillingly.

Moreover, I think everyone knows how often things that should not be done are done without sin, when, that is, they are committed under coercion or through ignorance, as for example if a woman is forced to lie with another woman's husband or if a man who has been tricked in some way or other sleeps with a woman whom he thought to be his wife or kills in error a man whom he believed he, as a judge, should kill. And so it is not a sin to lust after another's wife or to lie with her but rather to consent to this lust or action. This consent to covetousness the Law calls covetousness when it says:[18] "Thou shall not covet." In fact, what had to be forbidden was not the coveting of what we cannot avoid or in which, as has been said, we do not sin, but the assenting to that. What the Lord said has similarly to be understood:[19] "Whosoever shall look on a woman to lust after her," that is, whosoever shall look in such a way as to fall into consent to lust, "hath already committed adultery in his heart," although he has not committed the deed of adultery, that is, he is already guilty of sin although he is still without its outcome.

If we carefully consider also all the occasions where actions seem to come under a command-

---

17 St. Jerome, a contemporary of Augustine's, and translator of the Bible into Latin.
18 *Deuteronomy* 5:21.
19 *Matthew* 5:28.

ment or a prohibition, these must be taken to refer to the will or to consent to actions rather than to the actions themselves, otherwise nothing relating to merit would be put under a commandment and what is less within our power is less worthy of being commanded. There are in fact many things by which we are restrained from action yet we always have dominion over our will and consent. Behold, the Lord says:[20] "Thou shalt not kill," "Thou shall not bear false witness." If, following the sound of the words, we take these to refer only to the deed, guilt is by no means forbidden nor is fault thereby, but the action of a fault is prohibited. Truly, it is not a sin to kill a man nor to lie with another's wife; these sometimes can be committed without sin. If a prohibition of this kind is understood, according to the sound of the words, to refer to the deed, he who wants to bear false witness or even consents to speaking it, as long as he does not speak it, whatever the reason for his silence, does not become guilty according to the Law. For it was not said that we should not want to bear false witness or that we should not consent to speaking it, but only that we should not speak it. The Law forbids us to marry our sisters or to have sexual intercourse with them, but there is no one who can keep this ordinance, since one is often unable to recognize one's sisters – no one, I mean, if the prohibition refers to the act rather than to consent. And so when it happens that someone through ignorance marries his sister, he is not surely the transgressor of an ordinance because he does what the Law has forbidden him to do? He is not a transgressor, you will say, because in acting ignorantly he did not consent to transgression. Therefore, just as he is not to be called a transgressor who does what is forbidden, but he who consents to that which it is evident has been prohibited, so the prohibition is not to be applied to the deed but to the consent, so that when it is said "do not do this or that" the meaning is "do not consent to do this or that," just as if it were said "do not venture this knowingly."

The blessed Augustine carefully considered this and reduced every commandment or prohibition to charity or cupidity rather than to deeds, saying: "The Law ordains nothing except charity and prohibits nothing except cupidity."[21] Hence also the Apostle says:[22] "All the Law is fulfilled in one word: Thou shalt love thy neighbour as thyself." And again:[23] "Love is the fulfilling of the Law." It does not in fact matter to merit whether you give alms to the needy; charity may make you ready to give and the will may be there when the opportunity is missing and you no longer remain able to do so, whatever the cause preventing you.

It is indeed obvious that works which it is or is not at all fitting to do may be performed as much by good as by bad men who are separated by their intention alone. In fact, as the same Doctor has observed, in the same deed in which we see God the Father and the Lord Jesus Christ we also see Judas the betrayer. The giving up of the Son was certainly done by God the Father; and it was done by the Son and it was done by that betrayer, since both the Father delivered up the Son and the Son delivered up himself, as the Apostle observed, and Judas delivered up the Master. So the betrayer did what God also did, but surely he did not do it well? For although what was done was good, it certainly was not well done nor should it have benefited him. For God thinks not of what is done but in what mind it may be done, and the merit or glory of the doer lies in the intention, not in the deed. In fact the same thing is often done by different people, justly by one and wickedly by another, as for example if two men hang a convict, that one out of zeal for justice, this one out of a hatred arising from an old enmity, and although it is the same act of hanging and although they certainly do what it is good to do and what justice requires, yet, through the diversity of their intention, the same thing is done by diverse men, by one badly, by the other well.

Who, finally, may be unaware that the devil himself does nothing except what he is allowed by God to do, when either he punishes a wicked person for his faults or is allowed to strike a just person in order to purge him or to provide an example of patience? But because on the prompting of his own

---

20 *Deuteronomy* 5:17, 20.
21 *De doctrina christiana,* iii. 10, n. 15 (PL 34.71).
22 *Galatians* 5:14.
23 *Romans* 13:10.

wickedness he does what God allows him to do, so his power is said to be good or even just, while his will is always unjust. For he receives the former from God; the latter he holds of himself.

Moreover, in respect of works, who among the elect can be compared with hypocrites? Who endures or does out of love of God as much as they do out of greed for human praise? Who lastly may not know that what God forbids to be done is sometimes rightly performed or should be done, just as conversely he sometimes ordains some things which, however, it is not at all fitting to do? For consider, we know of some miracles of his that when by them he healed illnesses, he forbade that they should be revealed, as an example, that is, of humility, lest someone who had a similar grace granted to him should perhaps seek prestige. None the less they who had received those benefits did not stop publicizing them in honor, of course, of him who had both worked them and had prohibited their revelation. Of such it was written:[24] "The more he charged them that they should not tell, so much the more did they publish it," etc. Surely you will not judge such men guilty of transgression for acting contrary to the command which they had received and for even doing this knowingly? What will excuse them from transgression if not the fact that they did nothing through contempt of him who commanded; they decided to do this in honour of him. Tell me, I ask you, if Christ ordained what should not have been ordained or if they repudiated what should have been kept? What was good to be commanded was not good to be done. You at any rate will reproach the Lord in the case of Abraham, whom at first he commanded to sacrifice his son and later checked from doing so. Surely God did not command well a deed which it was not good to do? For if it was good, how was it later forbidden? If, moreover, the same thing was both good to be commanded and good to be prohibited – for God allows nothing to be done without reasonable cause nor yet consents to do it – you see that the intention of the command alone, not the execution of the deed, excuses God, since he did well to command what is not a good thing to be done. For God did not urge or command this to be done in order

that Abraham should sacrifice his son but in order that out of this his obedience and the constancy of his faith or love for him should be very greatly tested and remain to us as an example. And this indeed the Lord himself subsequently avowed openly when he said:[25] "Now I know that thou fearest the Lord," as if he were saying expressly: the reason why I instructed you to do what you showed you were ready to do was so that I should make known to others what I myself had known of you before the ages. This intention of God was right in an act which was not right, and similarly, in the things which we mentioned, his prohibition was right which prohibited for this reason, not so that the prohibition should be upheld but so that examples might be given to us weaklings of avoiding vainglory. And so God enjoined what was not good to be done, just as conversely he prohibited what was good to be done; and just as the intention excuses him in the one case, so too in this case it excuses those who have not fulfilled the command in practice. They knew indeed that he had not made the command on this account, that it should be observed, but so that the example that has been mentioned should be set forth. While not violating the will of him who commands, they did not offer contempt to him to whose will they understood that they were not opposed. If therefore we think of deeds rather than the intention, we shall not only see that sometimes there is a will to do something against God's commandment but also that it is done and knowingly so without any guilt of sin. So, when the intention of him to whom the command is made does not differ from the will of the commander, one should not speak of an evil will or an evil action simply because God's commandment is not kept in a deed. Just as intention excuses the commander who commands to be done what is however not at all fitting to be done, so also the intention of charity excuses him to whom the command is made.

To bring the above together in a brief conclusion, there are four things which we have put forward in order carefully to distinguish them from each other, namely the vice of the mind which makes us prone to sinning and then the sin itself which we fixed in

24 *Mark* 7:36.
25 1 *Corinthians* 10:13.

consent to evil or contempt of God, next the will for evil, and [finally] the doing of evil.

Just as, indeed, to will and to fulfil the will are not the same, so to sin and to perform the sin are not the same. We should understand the former to relate to the consent of the mind by which we sin, the latter to the performance of the action when we fulfil in a deed what we have previously consented to. When we say that sin or temptation occurs in three ways, namely in suggestion, pleasure, and consent, it should be understood in this sense, that we are often led through these three to the doing of sin. This was the case with our first parents. Persuasion by the devil came first, when he promised immortality for tasting the forbidden tree. Pleasure followed, when the woman, seeing the beautiful fruit and understanding it to be sweet to eat, was seized with what she believed would be the pleasure of the food and kindled a longing for it. Since she ought to have checked her longing in order to keep the command, in consenting she was drawn into sin. And although she ought to have corrected the sin through repentance in order to deserve pardon, she finally completed it in deed.

And so she proceeded to carry through the sin in three stages. Likewise we also frequently arrive by these same steps not at sinning but at the carrying through of sin, namely by suggestion, that is, by the encouragement of someone who incites us externally to do something which is not fitting. And if we know that doing this is pleasurable, even before the deed our mind is seized with the pleasure of the deed itself and in the very thought we are tempted through pleasure. When in fact we assent to this pleasure through consent, we sin. By these three we come at last to the execution of the sin.

There are those who would like carnal suggestion to be included in the term suggestion, even if there is no person making a suggestion, for instance, if someone on seeing a woman falls into lust for her. But this suggestion, it seems, should really be called nothing other than pleasure. Indeed this pleasure, which has become almost necessary, and others of its kind which, we observed above, are not sin, are called by the Apostle human temptation when he says:[26] "Let no

temptation take hold on you, but such as is human. And God is faithful, who will not suffer you to be tempted above that which you are able; but will also make issue with temptation, that you may be able to bear it." Now, temptation is generally said to be any inclination of the mind, whether a will or consent, to do something which is not fitting. But human temptation, such as carnal concupiscence or the desire for delicious food, is said to be that without which human infirmity can now scarcely or can never survive. He asked to be set free from these who said:[27] "Deliver me from my necessities, O Lord," that is, from these lustful temptations which have now become almost natural and necessary, lest they lead to consent; alternatively, let me really be free of them at the end of this life full of temptations. So, what the Apostle says, "Let no temptation take hold on you, but such as is human," is as an opinion very like saying: "If the mind is inclined by pleasure which is, as we have said, human temptation, let it not lead as far as consent, in which sin consists." He says, as if someone were asking by what virtue of ours we can resist those lusts: "God is faithful who will not suffer you to be tempted," that is as if to say: "Rather than rely on ourselves we should trust in him who, promising help for us, is true in all his promises," that is, he is faithful, so in everything faith should clearly be put in him. Then indeed he does not allow us to be tempted above that which we are able, since he moderates this human temptation with his mercy, so that it does not press us into sin by more than we are able to bear in resisting it. However, he then in addition turns this very temptation to our advantage when he trains us by it, so that eventually when it occurs it can bother us less and so that we should now have less fear of the attack of an enemy over whom we have already triumphed and whom we know how to manage. Every struggle which we have not hitherto experienced is borne more severely and is dreaded more. But when it comes regularly to the victorious, its power and its dread alike vanish.

26 1 *Corinthians* 10:13.
27 *Psalm* 24:17.

Of the suggestions of demons

Suggestions are made not only by men but also by demons, because they too sometimes incite us to sin, less by words than by deeds. By their subtle talent as much as by their long experience they are certainly experts in the nature of things and for this are called demons, that is, knowledgeable; they know the natural powers of things by which human weakness may easily be stirred to lust or to other impulses. Sometimes by God's leave they send some into languor and then provide the remedies for those who beseech them, and when they cease to afflict they are often thought to cure. In Egypt they were in the end allowed through the magicians to do many things marvelously against Moses, in reality by the natural power of things which they knew. They should not be called creators of what they have made so much as compositors; for instance, if anyone, following the example in Virgil, having pounded the flesh of a bull should by his labour bring about from this the making of bees, he should be called not so much a creator of bees as a preparer of nature. And so, by this expertise which they have with the natures of things, demons provoke us to lust or to other passions of the mind, bringing them by every possible stratagem while we are unawares, whether setting them in taste or in bed or placing them by no matter what means inside or outside us. There are certainly many forces in herbs or seeds or in the natures of trees as much as of stones which are suitable for provoking or soothing our minds; those who carefully learn to know them can easily do this.

Why works of sin are punished rather than sin itself

There are also those who are considerably troubled, when they hear us say that a work of sin is not properly called sin or that it does not add anything to increase a sin, as to why a heavier satisfaction is imposed on penitents for doing a deed than for being guilty of a fault. To these I answer first: why do they not chiefly wonder about the fact that sometimes a large penalty of satisfaction is instituted where no fault has occurred? And why ought we sometimes to punish those whom we know to be innocent? For, consider, some poor woman has a suckling baby and lacks clothing adequate to provide for the little one in the cradle and for herself. And so, stirred by pity for the baby she takes him to herself to keep him warm with her own rags, and finally in her weakness overcome by the force of nature, she unavoidably smothers the one she clasps with the utmost love. "Have charity," says Augustine, "and do whatever you wish."[28] However, when she comes before the bishop for satisfaction, a heavy punishment is imposed upon her, not for the fault which she committed but so that subsequently she or other women should be rendered more cautious in providing for such things. Occasionally also it happens that someone is accused by his enemies before a judge, and that a certain imputation is made about him by which the judge knows he is innocent. However, because they insist and demand a hearing at a trial, they commence the suit on the appointed day, produce witnesses, albeit false ones, to convict him whom they accuse. Since the judge can in no way rebut these witnesses with plain reasons, he is compelled by law to recognize them and, having accepted their proof, he punishes the innocent man. Thus he ought to punish him who ought not to be punished. He ought at any rate because he transacts justly according to law what that other man has not deserved.

It is clear from these examples that sometimes a punishment is reasonably inflicted on a person in whom no fault went before. So what is surprising if, where a fault has preceded, the subsequent action increases the punishment with people in this life, not with God in the future? For people do not judge the hidden but the apparent, nor do they consider the guilt of a fault so much as the performance of a deed. Indeed God alone, who considers not so much what is done as in what mind it may be done, truly considers the guilt in our intention and examines the fault in a true trial. Whence he is said to be both the prover of the heart and the reins[29] and to see in the dark.[30] For he particularly sees there

28 *In Epistolam Joannis ad Parthos Tractatus* VII, cap. 8 (PL 35. 2033).
29 *Jeremiah* 20:12.
30 *Matthew* 6:4.

where no man sees, because in punishing sin he considers not the deed but the mind, just as conversely we consider not the mind which we do not see but the deed which we know. Whence often we punish the innocent or absolve the culpable through error or, as we have said, through the compulsion of the law. God is said to be the prover and the judge of the heart and the reins, that is, of all the intentions which come from an affection of the soul or from a weakness or a pleasure of the flesh.

Of spiritual or carnal sins

Since all sins are uniquely of the soul, not of the flesh, there can certainly be fault and contempt of God where knowledge of him and where reason dwell. Yet some sins are called spiritual, some carnal, that is, some come from the vices of the soul, some from the weakness of the flesh. And although concupiscence, like will too, is only of the soul – for we cannot lust after or desire anything except by willing – yet there is said to be concupiscence of the flesh as well as concupiscence of the spirit. "For," the Apostle says,[31] "the flesh lusteth against the spirit and the spirit against the flesh," that is, the soul, by reason of the pleasure which it has in the flesh, seeks some things which, however, it shuns in the judgement of reason, or which it thinks should not be sought.

***

That a multitude of good things is not better than one of the good things

Now, in a deed and in an intention there does not seem to exist a number either of goodnesses or of good things. For when one speaks of a good intention and of a good action, that is, one proceeding from the good intention, the goodness of the intention alone is indicated and the name 'good' does not keep the same meaning so as to enable us to say there are more good things. For example, when we say a man is simple and a saying is simple, we do not therefore grant that these are several simple things, since this name 'simple' is employed differently here and differently there. Let no one urge us, therefore, that when a good action is added to a good intention, good is added to good as if there are more good things for which the reward ought to be enlarged, since, as has been said, we cannot rightly say that they are several good things which the word 'good' does not fit in a single way.

That a work is good by reason of a good intention

In fact we say that an intention is good, that is, right in itself, but that an action does not bear anything good in itself but proceeds from a good intention. Whence when the same thing is done by the same man at different times, by the diversity of his intention, however, his action is now said to be good, now bad, and so it seems to fluctuate around the good and the bad, just as this proposition 'Socrates is seated' or the idea of it fluctuates around the true and the false, Socrates being at one time seated, at another standing. Aristotle says[32] that the way in which this change in fluctuating around the true and the false happens here is not that what changes between being true and being false undergoes anything by this change, but that the subject, that is Socrates, himself moves from sitting to standing or vice versa.

Whence an intention should be said to be good

There are those who think that an intention is good or right whenever someone believes he is acting well and that what he does, is pleasing to God, like the persecutors of the martyrs mentioned by Truth in the Gospel:[33] "The hour cometh that whosoever killeth you will think that he doth a service to God." The Apostle had compassion for the ignorance of such as these when he said: "I bear them witness that they have a zeal for God, but not according to knowledge," that is, they have great fervor and desire in doing what they believe to be pleasing to God. But because they are led astray in this by the zeal or the eagerness of their minds,

---

31 *Galatians* 5:7.
32 *Categories* 5. See selection **VI.2.1.**
33 *John* 16:2.

their intention is in error and the eye of their heart is not simple, so it cannot see clearly, that is, guard itself against error. And so the Lord, in distinguishing works according to right or wrong intention, carefully called the mind's eye, that is, the intention, sound and, as it were, free of dirt so that it can see clearly; or, conversely, dark when he said: "If thy eye be sound thy whole body shall be full of light,"[34] that is, if the intention was right, the whole mass of works coming from it, which like physical things can be seen, will be worthy of the light, that is, good; conversely also. And so an intention should not be called good because it seems to be good but because in addition it is just as it is thought to be, that is, when, believing that one's objective is pleasing to God, one is in no way deceived in one's own estimation. Otherwise even the unbelievers themselves would have good works just like ourselves, since they too, no less than we, believe they will be saved or will please God through their works.

That there is no sin unless it is against conscience

However, if one asks whether those persecutors of the martyrs or of Christ sinned in what they believed to be pleasing to God, or whether they

could without sin have forsaken what they thought should definitely not be forsaken, assuredly, according to our earlier description of sin as contempt of God or consenting to what one believes should not be consented to, we cannot say that they have sinned in this, nor is anyone's ignorance a sin or even the unbelief with which no one can be saved. For those who do not know Christ and therefore reject the Christian faith because they believe it to be contrary to God, what contempt of God have they in what they do for God's sake and therefore think they do well – especially since the Apostle says:[35] "If our heart do not reprehend us, we have confidence towards God?" As if to say: where we do not presume against our conscience our fear of being judged guilty of fault before God is groundless; alternatively, if the ignorance of such men is not to be imputed to sin at all, how does the Lord pray for his crucifiers, saying:[36] "Father, forgive them, for they know not what they do," or Stephen, taught by this example, say in prayer for those stoning him[37]: "Lord, lay not this sin to their charge"? For there seems no need to pardon where there was no prior fault; nor is pardon usually said to be anything other than the remission of a punishment earned by a fault. Moreover, Stephen manifestly calls sin that which came from ignorance.

---

34 *Matthew* 6:22-3; *Luke* 11: 34.
35 1 *John* 3:2.
36 *Luke* 23:34.
37 *Acts* 7:59.

VIII.5. ST. THOMAS AQUINAS

Aquinas was committed to the essential harmony of Aristotelian philosophy with Augustinean theology and ethics. These selections show how he attempted to reconcile the basically naturalistic approach of Aristotle with Augustine's emphasis on accordance with the divine will in the face of the disorder rampant in the soul on account of original sin.

VIII.5.1. Goodness and Badness in outward Acts
(*Summa Theologiae*, 1aIIae, qu.20)

[In this selection Aquinas very carefully sorts through the issues involved in why human acts can be morally good or morally bad, an issue already discussed above in the selections from Augustine and Abelard.]

Question 20: Concerning the goodness and badness of the outward acts of human beings.

Next we turn to goodness and badness as found in outward acts. Here there are six questions:

1. Are goodness and badness found first in the act of the will or in the outward act?

2. Does the goodness or badness of the outward act totally depend on the goodness of the will?

3. Is the goodness, or badness, of the inner act the same as that of the outward act?

4. Does the outward act add some goodness, or badness, beyond that of the inner act?

5. Does a consequent event add some goodness or badness to the outward act?

6. Can the same outward act be both good and bad?

Article 1: Are goodness and badness found first in the act of the will or in the outward act?

On the first question we proceed as follows:

[1] It seems that good and bad are found first in the outward act rather than in the act of the will. For the will gets its goodness from its object, as we said earlier.[1] But the outward act is the object of the inner act of will, for we speak of willing a theft or of willing to give alms. Therefore, good and bad are found first in the outward act rather than in the act of the will.

[2] Further, good belongs first to the end, since things which are directed toward an end get their goodness from their subordination to that end. But an act of the will cannot be an end, as we said earlier.[2] However, an act of some other power can be an end. Therefore, good is found first in an act of another power rather than in an act of the will.

[3] Further, the act of the will relates as a form to the outward act, as we said earlier.[3] But what is formal comes later, for form comes to matter.[4] Therefore, good and bad are found first in the outward act rather than in the act of the will.

But opposed to this is Augustine, who says that

---

1 1aIIae 19,1&2.
2 1aIIae 1,1 ad2.
3 1aIIae 18,6.
4 See glossary entry for 'form/matter.'

"by will we sin and by it we live correctly."[5] Therefore, what is morally good or bad is first found in the will.

Reply: Some outward acts can be called good, or bad, in two senses. In one sense they are called that in virtue of the type of act they are as well as the circumstances surrounding them. For example, giving alms is said to be good as long as the required circumstances are present. In another sense something is said to be good, or bad, on account of its subordination to an end. For example, giving alms in order to show off is bad.

However, since an end is exactly what the will's object is, it is clear that the goodness, or badness, which the outward act has on account of its subordination to an end is first found in the act of the will, and the outward act derives it from there.

But the goodness, or badness, which the outward act possesses in virtue of itself, on account of being the required matter [for the act of will, considered as form] and occurring in the required circumstances, is not derived from the will but more from reason.

Thus, if we consider the outward act's goodness insofar as it exists in the prescription and apprehension of reason, it comes before the goodness of the act of will. But if we consider it insofar as it exists in the performance of a deed, it is consequent on the goodness of the will, which is its source.

To [1], then, we have to say that the outward act is the will's object to the extent that reason sets it before the will as a certain good thing that reason has apprehended and prescribed. In this respect it is good before the act of the will is. But to the extent that that act amounts to the performance of a deed it is an effect of the will and consequent on the will.

To [2], we have to say that the end comes first in the intention, but comes afterwards in the performance.

To [3], we have to say that insofar as the form is received by matter it comes later in the generative process than does the matter, even though it comes earlier by nature. But insofar as it is in the causal agent, it comes earlier in every sense. The will, however, relates to the outward act as its efficient cause, and hence the goodness of the act of the will is the form of the outward act as something existing in a causal agent.

Article 2: Is the goodness, or badness, of the outward act totally dependent on the goodness of the will?

On the second question we proceed as follows:

[1] It seems that the goodness, or badness, of the outward act does totally depend on the will, for in *Matthew* [vii,18] it is said: "A good tree cannot bear bad fruit, nor a bad tree good." According to the *Gloss*[6] we should understand the "tree" to mean the will and the "fruit" to mean the deed. Therefore, it is impossible for the inner will to be good while the outward act is bad, and vice versa.

[2] Further, Augustine says[7] that we sin only through the will. Therefore, if there is no sin in the will, there will be no sin in the outward act. Consequently, the goodness, or badness, of the outward act depends totally on the will.

[3] Further, the good and bad we are talking about are differences of the genus[8] moral act. Now, differences divide the genus in virtue of what it is in itself, according to The Philosopher in his *Metaphysics* [VII,12]. Since, then, an act is moral in virtue of being voluntary, it seems that good and bad apply to an act only as it belongs to the will.

But opposed to this is Augustine, who says that "some things are such that they cannot be rightly done no matter what the apparently good end or good will."[9]

---

5 *Retractationes* I,9.
6 *Glossa ordinaria in loc.* v, 29B.
7 *Retractationes* I,9.
8 See glossary entry for 'species/genus.'
9 *Contra Mendacium* 7.

Reply: We have to say here that, as we just now said [in art.1], goodness or badness in an outward act can be thought of in two ways: one way, in respect of the required material and circumstances; another way, in respect of subordination to an end. The goodness, or badness, which relates to subordination to an end totally depends on the will, while that which arises from the required material or circumstances depends on reason, and the goodness of the will depends on it insofar as the will is directed toward it.

We have to note as well, as we said earlier,[10] that in order for something to be bad a single particular defect suffices, but for it to be unqualifiedly good a single particular good does not suffice, rather it has to be good in all respects. Consequently, if the will is good, both on account of its own object and its end, it follows that the outward act is good. But for the outward act to be good the goodness of the will which comes from intending an end does not suffice. On the other hand, if the will is bad, either from its intending an end or from the act it has willed, it follows that the outward act is bad.

To [1], we have to say that the good will, as signified by the good tree, should be interpreted as getting its goodness both from the act it has willed and from the end it has intended.

To [2], we have to say that someone sins by his will not only when he wills a bad end but also when he wills a bad act.

To [3], we have to say that we call voluntary not just the inner act of the will but also the outward acts inasmuch as they proceed from the will as well as from reason. Consequently, good and bad can be differences of both these sorts of act.

Article 3: Is the goodness, or badness, of the inner act the same as that of the outward act?

On the third question we proceed as follows:

[1] It seems that the goodness, or badness, of the inner act of the will is not the same as that of the outward act, for the source of the inner act is a cognitive or desiring power of the soul, while the source of an outward act is a power which performs a movement. But where we have different sources of action we have different acts. Now it is an act that is the subject of goodness or badness, and the same accident cannot exist in different subjects. Therefore, the goodness of the inner act cannot be the same as that of the outward act.

[2] Further, a virtue is what makes the person who has it good and renders their deed good, as says the *Ethics*.[11] But an intellectual virtue in the power that commands is other than the commanded moral virtue, as is clear in the *Ethics*. Therefore, the goodness of the inner act which belongs to the power that commands is other than the goodness of the outward act which belongs to the commanded power.

[3] Further, a cause cannot be the same as its effect, for nothing is a cause of itself. But the goodness of the inner act is the cause of the goodness of the outward act, and vice versa, as we said [in arts. 1&2]. Therefore, the same goodness cannot belong to both.

But opposed to this is what we showed earlier,[12] that the act of the will relates to the outward act as what is formal. The formal and the material, however, make up a single thing. Therefore, there is a single goodness for the inner and outward acts.

Reply: We have to say, as we said earlier,[13] that the inner act of the will and the outward act, as considered to be in the genus of moral acts, are a single act. But it sometimes happens that an act which serves as a single subject has several types of goodness and badness, and sometimes it has just one. Consequently, we have to say that sometimes the goodness, or badness, of the inner act is the same as that of the outward act, and sometimes they are different.

As we said [in arts. 1&2], these two goodnesses or badnesses, that of the inner act and that of the outward act, are subordinated to each other. Now,

---

10 1aIIae 19,6 ad1.
11 *Nicomachean Ethics* II,6. See selection **VIII.1.1**.
12 1aIIae 18,6.
13 1aIIae 17,4.

in things which are subordinated to something else it happens that sometimes such a thing is good merely from being subordinated to that something else, as for example a bitter drink is good only because it is productive of health. In this case the goodness of health is not other than the goodness of the drink; rather they are one and the same. Sometimes, however, the thing which is subordinated to something else has in itself some type of goodness, even over and above its subordination to the other good thing, as for example a tasty medicine has the good of deliciousness over and above its being productive of health.

Therefore, we have to say that when the outward act is good or bad only on account of its subordination to an end, in that case the goodness and badness of the act of the will, which just by being what it is relates to an end, is completely the same as that of the outward act, which relates to the end by way of the act of the will. But when the outward act gets goodness or badness from itself, i.e. from its material or circumstances, then the goodness of the outward act is one item and the goodness of the will which is due to the end is another. Nevertheless, the goodness of the end flows from the will into the outward act, and the goodness of the material and circumstances flows into the act of the will, as we said before [in arts. 1&2].

To [1], then, we have to say that the argument shows that the inner act and outward act are different considered under a natural genus. Nevertheless, a single thing in the genus of moral acts is made up of items that are different in that way, as we said earlier.[14]

To [2], we have to say, as is said in the *Ethics*,[15] the moral virtues are subordinated to the very acts of those virtues and are like their ends. Practical wisdom, on the other hand, is directed at those things which are for an end, and exists in the reason. On account of this they have to be treated as different virtues. But right reason concerning the end itself of the virtues has no other goodness than the goodness of the virtue, inasmuch as the goodness of rea-

son is shared in by every virtue.

To [3], we have to say that when something derives something from something else as from a univocal causal agent,[16] then what is derived is other than what was in that from which it was derived. For example, when what is hot heats, the heat in the thing doing the heating and the heat in the thing being heated are different in number, although the same in species. But when something derives something from something else by analogy or proportion, then the items are only one in number. For example, from the healthy which is in an animal body is derived the healthy that applies to medicine and urine. Here the health of the medicine and urine is not other than the health of the animal, i.e. than the health which medicine brings about and urine is a sign of. It is in this latter way that the goodness of the outward act is derived from the goodness of the will, and vice versa, i.e. by a subordination of the one to the other.

Article 4: Does the outward act add some goodness, or badness, beyond that of the inner act?

On the fourth question we proceed as follows:

[1] It seems that the outward act does not add any goodness, or badness, beyond that of the inner act, for Chrysostom says[17] that it is the will which is either rewarded for good or condemned for what is bad. However, deeds attest to the will. Therefore, God does not ask for deeds for his own sake, i.e. so that he may know how to judge, but for the sake of others, so that everyone may realize that God is just. But what is bad and what is good should be assessed more by God's judgment than by human judgment. Therefore, the outward act adds nothing to the goodness or badness already given by the inner act.

[2] Further, we already said [in art.3] that the goodness of the inner act is the same as that of the outward act. But increase comes by adding one thing to another. Therefore, the outward act adds no goodness or badness beyond that of the inner

---

14 1aIIae 17,4.
15 *Nicomachean Ethics* VI,12
16 See glossary entry for 'univocal production.'
17 In *Homilies on St. Matthew's Gospel* 19.

act.

[3] Further, the total goodness of a creature adds nothing beyond the divine goodness since it is totally derived from the divine goodness. But sometimes the goodness of the outward act totally derives from the goodness of the inner act, and sometimes vice versa, as we said [in arts. 1&2]. Thus no one of these adds any goodness or badness beyond what the other possesses.

But in opposition to this, every agent intends to pursue good and avoid the bad. Therefore, if no goodness or badness is added by the outward act, it would be useless for the person who has a good will, or a bad will, to do a good deed, or to refrain from doing a bad deed. This is an absurd result.

Reply: It has to be said that, if we are speaking of the goodness the outward act gets from the will for the end, the outward act adds to the goodness only if that will in itself becomes better in doing good things or worse in doing bad things. This, it seems, can happen in three ways. One way is in respect of number; for example, when someone wills to do something for a good end, or for a bad end, and then does not do it but later wills again and does do it, the act of the will is duplicated and thus a double good occurs, or a double bad. Another way is in respect of extent; for example, when someone wills to do something for a good end, or a bad one, but does not carry through on account of some obstacle, while someone else continues the movement of this will right up to finishing the deed, it is clear that this latter will lasts longer in what makes it good, or in what makes it bad, and for that reason is better, or worse. A third way is in respect of intensiveness, for there are some outward acts which on account of their delightfulness, or their painfulness, naturally tend to attract the will, or to repel it. But clearly the more intensely the will inclines toward something good, or something bad, the better, or worse, it is.

On the other hand, if we are speaking of the goodness the outward act gets from the matter and the requisite circumstances, then that act relates to the will as its goal and end, and in this sense it does add to the goodness, or the badness, of the will,

since every tendency or movement gets completed by achieving its end or attaining its goal. Consequently, the will is complete only if, given the opportunity, it does the deed. But if this is impossible and the will is complete to the extent that it would do the deed if it could, the lack of completeness due to the outward act is then involuntary. Since the involuntary, however, in matters of doing good or bad does not deserve either punishment or reward, so neither in the case where a person completely involuntarily fails to carry out a good, or bad, deed does the involuntary element take something away from the reward, or from the punishment.

To [1], we have to say that Chrysostom speaks of the case where the person's will is fulfilled and stops short of the act only through an inability to perform it.

To [2], we have to say that this argument works for the goodness the outward act gets from the will for the end. But the goodness the outward act gets from its material and circumstances is other than the goodness the will gets from its end, not, however other than the goodness the will gets from the willed act itself; rather it relates to this last goodness as its definition and cause, as we said earlier [in arts. 1&2].

To [3], the above clearly provides the solution.

Article 5: Does a consequent event add some goodness or badness to the outward act?

On the fifth question we proceed as follows:

[1] The consequent event seems to add to the goodness or badness of the act, for an effect pre-exists virtually in its cause. But events are consequent on acts as effects on causes. Therefore, they pre-exist virtually in the acts. But anything is judged good or bad on account of its virtue, for a virtue is what "makes good that which has it," according to the *Ethics*.[18] Therefore, the event adds something to the goodness or badness of the act.

[2] Further, the good things that listeners do are some of the effects consequent on a teacher's preaching. But good things of this sort redound to

18 *Nicomachean Ethics* II,6. See selection **VIII.1.1.**

the merit of the preacher, as is clear from this text in *Philippians* [iv:1]: "My dearly beloved and desired brethren, my joy and my crown." Therefore, the consequent event adds something to the goodness, or badness, of the act.

[3] Further, the penalty is not added to unless the fault is increased. Thus *Deuteronomy* [xxv:2]: "The stripes will be in proportion to the amount of sin." But the penalty is added to on account of a consequent event, for *Exodus* [xxi:29] says that "if the ox liked pushing with its horns yesterday and the day before, and its owner was warned but did not shut it up, and then the ox killed a man or a woman, the ox shall be stoned and its owner put to death." Even though the ox had not been shut up, the owner would not have been put to death if the ox had not killed a person. Therefore, the consequent event adds to the goodness or badness of the act.

[4] Further, if someone does something that is normally a cause of death, for example by striking or passing a sentence, and the death does not ensue, then the person incurs no debarment.[19] However, they would have incurred it had the death ensued. Therefore, a consequent event adds to the goodness or badness of the act.

But, in opposition to this, a consequent event does not make an act bad which was good nor one good which was bad. For example, if someone gives alms to a poor person, who then proceeds to misuse them for sinful deeds, this does not detract at all from the person who gave the alms. Likewise, the fact that someone patiently endures a wrong done them does not excuse the person who did the wrong. Therefore, a consequent event does not add to the goodness or badness of an act.

Reply: We have to say that the consequent event is either foreknown or not. If it is, clearly it adds to the goodness or badness of the act, for, when someone who knows that many bad things can be consequent on their deed does not for this reason refrain from the deed, it is clear that their will is all the more deranged.

But if the consequent event is not foreknown, then we need to distinguish different cases. If the

event is consequent on such an act in virtue of what it is to be such an act, and is consequent on it in most cases, then the consequent event does add to the goodness or badness of the act. For it is obvious that within a given type of act an act on which many good things can be consequent is better, and an act on which many bad things tend to be consequent is worse. But if it is consequent only incidentally and in few cases, the consequent event does not add to the goodness or to the badness of the act. For something is not judged by what is incidental to it but only by what belongs to it in virtue of what it is to be that type of thing.

To [1], then, we have to say that the virtue of a cause is assessed by the effects it has in virtue of what it is to be the type of thing it is, and not by the effects which are incidental to it.

To [2], we have to say that the good things listeners do are consequent on the teacher's preaching as effects it has in virtue of the type of thing it is. Thus they redound to the reward of the preacher, especially when the preacher intended them all along.

To [3], we have to say that the event the person is to be punished for is consequent on such a cause in virtue of that cause's being the type of thing it is, and further it is given that it is foreknown. For these reasons the event justifies a penalty.

To [4], we have to say that the argument would work if debarment were consequent on fault. However, it is due not to fault but to fact, out of fear that some failure in the performance of the sacraments might occur.

Article 6: Can the same outward act be both good and bad?

On the sixth question we proceed as follows:

[1] It seems that a single act can be both good and bad, for, as is said in the *Physics* [V,4], "a motion is one when it is continuous." But a single continuous motion can be both good and bad, for example, if someone going to church first does it to show off and then later in order to serve God. Therefore, a single act can be both good and bad.

---

19 I.e., the person is not automatically excluded from taking Holy Orders, as they would be if the death had occurred.

[2] Further, according to The Philosopher in the *Physics* [III,3],[20] "the action and the receiving of it are one act." But the receiving can be good, as was Christ's, while the action is bad, as was that of the Jews [who put Christ to death]. Therefore, one act can be both good and bad.

[3] Further, since a slave is like a tool of the slave's master, the slave's action is the master's action, just as a tool's action is the action of the artisan using it. But it can happen that the slave's action proceeds from the master's good will, and thus is itself good, as well as from the slave's bad will, and thus is bad. Thus the same act can be both good and bad.

But, in opposition to this, contraries cannot exist in the same thing. But good and bad are contraries. Therefore, one single act cannot be both good and bad.

Reply: We have to say that nothing prevents something being a single item inasmuch as it is of one type and being a multiple item inasmuch as it is put in some other type. For example, a continuous surface is a single item inasmuch as it is considered to belong to the genus of quantity, but it is a multiple item inasmuch as it is placed in the genus of color, given it is partly white and partly black. For this reason nothing prevents some act's being a single item inasmuch as it is put in a natural type even though it is not a single thing when put in a moral type, just as we noted occurs but vice versa.[21] For a continuous walking is a single act taken as belonging to a natural type; nevertheless, it can happen that it is many acts when taken as belonging to a moral type, given that the walker's will, i.e. the source of moral acts, changes [during the walk].

Therefore, if an act taken as belonging to a moral type is a single item, it is impossible for it to be both good and bad with a moral goodness and badness. But if it is a single item in virtue of a natural unity and not in virtue of a moral unity, it can be both good and bad.

To [1], then, we have to say that the continuous

motion which proceeds from different intentions is not a single item in virtue of a moral unity even though it is a single item in virtue of a natural unity.

To [2], we have to say that action and the receiving of it belong to a moral type to the extent that they are voluntary, and for this reason inasmuch as there are different wills by which they are called voluntary they are two items morally speaking. Thus it is possible that to one of these good belongs and to the other bad.

To [3], we have to say that the slave's act, to the extent that it proceeds from the slave's will, is not the master's act; rather it is this only to the extent that it proceeds from the master's command. Thus the slave's bad will does not in this way make the master's act bad.

VIII.5.2. Is Pleasure bad? (*Summa Theologiae*, 1a IIae, question 34, art. 1.)

Article 1: Is every pleasure bad?

On this first question we proceed as follows:

[1] It seems that every pleasure is bad, for what destroys practical wisdom and hinders the exercise of reason seems to be bad of itself, since the good for humans consists in being in accord with reason, as Dionysius says.[22] But pleasure destroys practical wisdom and hinders the exercise of reason, and the greater the pleasure the more it does this. Consequently, while enjoying the pleasures of sex, which are the greatest of all pleasures, it is impossible to apprehend anything with the mind, as is said [in the *Nicomachean Ethics* VII,11]. Jerome,[23] too, says that "during the performance of conjugal intercourse the Holy Spirit is not present, even if it is a prophet who is fulfilling his duty to beget." Therefore, pleasure is in itself bad. Therefore every pleasure is bad.

[2] Further, what the virtuous person avoids and someone lacking in virtue pursues seems to be bad in itself and to be avoided, because, as is said [in

---

20 See selection **V.1.3.**
21 1aIIae 18,7 ad 1.
22 *De divinis nominibus* 4.

Nicomachean Ethics X,5], "the virtuous person is a sort of measure and rule for human acts." Also the Apostle says,[24] "The spiritual person judges all things." But children and animals, in whom there is no virtue, pursue pleasures, while the person of moderation avoids them. Therefore, pleasures are in themselves bad and to be avoided.

[3] Further, it is said [in *Nicomachean Ethics* II,3][25] that "virtue and art concern what is difficult and good." But no art is directed toward pleasure. Therefore, pleasure is not something good.

But, in opposition to this, there is what the *Psalms* [xxxvi,4] say, "Delight in the Lord." Since, then, divine authority encourages nothing bad, it seems that not every pleasure is bad.

Reply: We have to say that, as has been noted [by Aristotle in *Nicomachean Ethics* X,1], some have maintained that all pleasures are bad. The reason for this seems to have been that they concentrated only on the sensual and bodily pleasures, which are the more obvious ones, for in other matters as well the ancient philosophers used not to distinguish things accessible by the mind from things accessible by the senses, as has been said [by Aristotle in *De Anima* III,3]. They thought that all bodily pleasures should be declared bad so that human beings, prone as they are to immoderate pleasures, will, by abstaining from those pleasures, achieve the mean which is virtue. Their judgment on this was not without problems.

For, since no one can live without enjoying some sensual and bodily pleasure, if those who teach that all pleasures are bad are caught enjoying some pleasures, human beings will tend toward these pleasures on account of the example of their deeds and overlook their verbal teaching. For in human activities and emotions, where experience is what counts, examples move more than words.

We have to say, then, that some pleasures are good

and some are bad, for pleasure is the rest which the desiring faculty takes in some good it loves and it is consequent on some activity. We can give two arguments for this.

One argument arises in connection with the good which someone rests in and enjoys. For we speak of good and bad in moral matters as meaning what accords with reason or disaccords with it, as we said earlier.[26] This is just like the way in natural things we say something is "natural" meaning it accords with nature, and "unnatural" meaning it disaccords with nature. Consequently, just as in natural things some rests are natural, namely those which accord with nature, like a heavy body resting down below, and some rests are unnatural, namely those which nature rejects, like a heavy body resting up above, so also in moral matters some pleasures are good, i.e. where a higher or lower desire takes its rest in what accords with reason, and some are bad, i.e. where it rests in what disaccords with nature, and with God's law.

The other argument we can give arises in connection with the activities, some of which are bad and some good. Now the pleasures which adhere to these activities are more closely associated with them than are the desires which precede them in time. Consequently, since the desires for good activities are good, and those for bad bad, much more are the pleasures of good activities good and those of bad bad.

To [1], then, we have to say that, as we said earlier,[27] the pleasures which belong to reason's act do not hinder reason, nor do they destroy practical wisdom. Rather it is the pleasures lying outside of reason that do this, and of this sort are bodily pleasures. These certainly hinder the exercise of reason, as we said earlier,[28] either by the contrariness of the desire which takes its rest in what reason rejects, and here we have a morally bad pleasure, or by somehow fettering reason, as in the pleasures of the

---

23 St. Jerome, contemporary of St. Augustine. Actually the quote is from Origen.

24 In 1 *Corinthians* 2:15.

25 See selection **VIII.1.1.**

26 1aIIae 18,5.

27 1aIIae 33,3.

28 *Ibid.*

marriage bed, where, although we have something in accord with reason, it nevertheless hinders the exercise of reason on account of the bodily changes that go along with it. In this case no moral badness follows, just as sleep which also fetters the exercise of reason is not morally bad if it is taken in accord with reason, for reason itself demands that sometimes the exercise of reason be interrupted.

Nevertheless, we say that the sort of fettering of reason that arises from the pleasure taken in the marriage act, even given that it possesses no moral badness since it is neither a mortal nor a venial sin, still arises from a certain moral badness, namely from the sin of the first parents, for in the state of innocence this fettering did not exist, as is clear from things we said in the first part.[29]

To [2], we have to say that a moderate person does not avoid all pleasures but only the excessive ones and those not in accord with reason. That children and animals pursue pleasures does not show that those pleasures are universally bad, because the natural desire in them is from God and it moves toward what is appropriate to them.

To [3], we have to say that not every good has its art, but only those external, producible goods, as we will explain later.[30] The activities and emotions which are in us are the concern more of practical wisdom and virtue than of art. Still there are some arts productive of pleasure, for example, the arts of using spices and of using cosmetics, as has been said [in *Nicomachean Ethics* VII,12].

VIII.5.3. Is Enjoyment in the Thought of Fornication a Sin? (*Summa Theologiae*, 1a IIae, qu.74, art.8)

Is consent to enjoying pleasure a mortal sin?

On the eighth question we proceed as follows:

[1] It seems that consent to enjoying pleasure is not a mortal sin, for consent to enjoying pleasure pertains to the lower reason, which does not turn toward the eternal types, i.e. the divine law, nor, consequently, does it turn away from them. But every mortal sin is a turning away from the divine law. This is clear from the definition Augustine gives of mortal sin,[31] which is found above.

[2] Further, consent to something is bad only because what is consented to is bad. But "what anything is on account of is even more that,"[32] or at least it is not less that. Therefore, what is consented to cannot be less bad than the consent. But pleasure without the deed is not a mortal sin, just a venial sin.[33] Therefore, neither is consent to enjoying the pleasure a mortal sin.

[3] Further, pleasures differ in goodness and badness according to the difference in the activities, as The Philosopher says in the *Ethics*.[34] But the inner thought is one activity and the outward act another, for example in the case of fornication. Therefore, also the pleasure consequent on the inner act of thought differs from the pleasure of fornication in respect of goodness and badness just so much as the inner thought differs from the outward act [in respect of goodness and badness]. Consequently the consents to each also differ in the same way. But an inner thought is not a mortal sin, and so neither is consent to that thought, and consequently neither is consent to enjoying the pleasure.

[4] Further, it is not on account of the pleasure that an outward act of fornication or adultery is a mortal sin, since that pleasure is also found in married sex; rather it is on account of the derangement of the act itself. But the person who consents to enjoying the pleasure does not on that account consent to the derangement of the act. Therefore, it seems this person does not sin mortally.

[5] Further, the sin of murder is more serious than that of mere fornication. But consent to enjoying the pleasure which is consequent on the thought of murder is not a mortal sin. Therefore, much less is consent to enjoying the pleasure consequent on the thought of fornication a mortal sin.

---

29 Ia 98,2. See selection **VIII.5.5.**
30 1aIIae 57,3.
31 *On Free Choice (De libero arbitrio)* I.
32 If X is A on account of Y, then Y is even more A that X is. From Aristotle's *Posterior Analytics* I,2.
33 In Catholic theology those sins are mortal which deserve damnation; the other, lesser sins are "venial".
34 *Nicomachean Ethics* X,5.

[6] Further, according to Augustine[35] the Lord's Prayer is said daily in order to remit venial sins. But Augustine teaches that consent to the enjoyment of a pleasure should be annulled by reciting the Lord's Prayer, for he says that "this is far less a sin than if it be decided to fulfill it in deed, and for this reason we should seek pardon for thoughts like these too, striking our breast and saying 'Forgive us our trespasses.'"[36] Therefore, consent to enjoying a pleasure is a venial sin.

But in opposition to this, a little further on Augustine adds: "The whole of humanity will be damned unless by the grace of the Mediator are forgiven those things which a person has a will to enjoy but no will to perform and are deemed sins of mere thought." But a person is damned only for mortal sin; therefore, consent to enjoying pleasure is a mortal sin.

Reply: We have to say that people have held different views on this, for some have said that consent to enjoying pleasure is not a mortal sin, but only a venial sin, while others have said that it is a mortal sin, and this latter view is more common as well as more probable.

It must be noted that, since every pleasure is consequent on some activity, as is said in the *Ethics*[37] and further every pleasure has an object, any pleasure can be related to two items, namely to the activity on which it is consequent and to the object in which someone takes pleasure. Moreover, it sometimes happens that an activity is the object of the pleasure, just as some other thing might be, because the activity itself can be treated as a good and an end, in which someone who takes pleasure in it rests content. And sometimes the very activity on which the pleasure is consequent is the object of the pleasure, as happens when the desiring power, to which enjoying pleasure belongs, turns back on to the activity itself treating it as a good, for example, when someone thinks and takes pleasure in their thinking itself to the extent that they like to think. On the other hand, sometimes a pleasure consequent on one activity, for example some activ-

ity of thinking, has for its object some other activity which is like the thing that is thought of. In this case a pleasure of this sort derives from a desire not for the thinking but for the activity that is thought of. In this way, then, a person who is thinking about fornication can take pleasure in two things, either in the thinking or in the fornicating the person is thinking of.

Now pleasure in the thinking itself is consequent on an affective tendency toward the thinking itself. But thinking itself, in itself, is not a mortal sin; rather sometimes it is a mere venial sin as when someone thinks idly, and sometimes it is no sin at all as when someone thinks about fornication to some useful end, as when they intend to preach or argue about it. Consequently, an affection for, and a taking pleasure in, the activity of thinking about fornication in this latter way does not fall into the category of mortal sin; rather sometimes it is a venial sin and sometimes not a sin at all. Thus consent to such an enjoyment of pleasure is not a mortal sin either. In this sense the first view is right.

But when the person who is thinking about fornication takes pleasure in the act thought about, this happens because his affection tends toward that act. Hence someone's consenting to enjoying such a pleasure is nothing other than their consenting to their affection's tending toward fornication, for no one takes pleasure in anything except what accords with their desire. But for a person deliberately to choose to have his affection fixed on things which in themselves are mortal sins is a mortal sin. Thus this sort of consent to enjoying the pleasure of a mortal sin is a mortal sin, as says the second view.

To [1], then, we have to say that consent to enjoying pleasure can belong not only to the lower reason but to the higher reason as well, as has been said [art.7]. Nevertheless, even the lower reason itself can turn away from the eternal types, because, even though it does not take its direction from them in the sense of regulating things by reference to them, still it does take its direction from them in the sense that it is regulated by them. In this way it can by turning itself away from them fall

35 *De fide et operibus* 26.
36 *De Trinitate* XII, 12.
37 *Nicomachean Ethics* X,4.

into mortal sin. For acts of lower powers, and even of external bodily parts, can be mortal sins inasmuch as the higher reason, which regulates them by reference to the eternal types, fails to provide direction for them.

To [2], we have to say that consent to a sin which is of a venial type is a venial sin. From this it can be concluded that consent to enjoying the pleasure of idly thinking about fornication is a venial sin. But the pleasure taken in the act of fornication itself is, by the very type of thing it is, a mortal sin. But the fact that before the consent it is only a venial sin is incidental to it since it is due to the incompleteness of the act. This incompleteness is removed by the deliberate consent that affects it later. This change in its nature makes it a mortal sin.

To [3], we have to say that this argument works for the pleasure which has as its object the thinking.

To [4], we have to say that a pleasure which has an outward act for its object necessarily involves approval of the outward act taken in itself, even if on account of a prohibition issued by a superior there is no decision to perform it. Thus, given the act is out of order, as a consequence the pleasure will be too.

To [5], we have to say that the consent to enjoying the pleasure which derives from approval of the contemplated act of murder is also a mortal sin. But this is not true of the consent to enjoying the pleasure which derives from approval of thinking about murder.

To [6], we have to say that the Lord's Prayer should be said to counteract not only venial sins but mortal sins as well.

VIII.5.4. Why Lechery is a sin (*Summa Theologiae*, 2a IIae, qu.153, arts. 2,3,5)

Article 2: Is it impossible for a sexual act to be sinless?

On the second question we proceed as follows:

[1] It seems that no sexual act can be sinless, for only sin seems to constitute an obstacle to virtue. But every sexual act constitutes an especially great obstacle to virtue, for as Augustine says,[38] "I know of nothing that more throws the male mind down from its heights than feminine charms and the touch of their bodies." Therefore, no sexual act seems to be sinless.

[2] Further, wherever we find something excessive that brings about a move away from the good set by reason, that thing is vicious, since virtue is destroyed by excess and deficiency, as it says in the *Ethics*.[39] But in any sexual act there is such an excess of pleasure that it so completely absorbs the mind that during it it is impossible to apprehend anything intellectually, as The Philosopher says,[40] and Jerome[41] says similarly that during that act the prophets' hearts were not touched by the spirit of prophecy. Therefore, no sexual act can be sinless.

[3] Further, a cause is more powerful than its effect. But original sin is transmitted to infants by the lust without which the sexual act is impossible, as is clear through Augustine.[42] Thus no sexual act can be sinless.

But, in opposition to this, Augustine says:[43] "We have a sufficient reply to the heretics if they will just accept that there is no sin where there is nothing done either against nature, or against morals, or against the law." He speaks here of the sexual acts the patriarchs had with their many wives. Therefore, not every sexual act is a sin.

Reply: We have to say that sin in human acts is what goes against the order set by reason. Now this order set by reason demands that everything be directed appropriately toward its end. For that reason there is no sin when by reason a person uses some things for an end and they are appropriately directed in an appropriate way to that end, as long as the end is really something good. Now just as it is really good that a single individual's physical

---

38 *Soliloquies* I,40.
39 *Nicomachean Ethics* II,2. See selection **VIII.1.1**.
40 *Nicomachean Ethics* VII,11.
41 St. Jerome, contemporary of St. Augustine. The reference, however, is to a work by Origen.
42 *De nuptiis et concup.* I,24.
43 *De bono conjug.* 25.

nature be preserved, so also it is an even greater good that the nature of the human species be preserved. And just as the use of food is directed toward the preservation of the life of a single human being, so also the use of sex is directed toward the preservation of the whole human race. Thus Augustine says:[44] "What food is to the health of a human being, sexual intercourse is to the health of the race." Consequently, just as the use of food can be sinless, given it is done in the right way and directed to what contributes to the health of the body, so also the use of sex can be sinless if it is done in the right way and directed toward what contributes to the end of human reproduction.

To [1], then, we have to say that something can create an obstacle to virtue in two ways: One way occurs in so far as it is an obstacle to the ordinary state of virtue, and in this sense only sin creates an obstacle to virtue; in another way it occurs insofar as it creates an obstacle to the perfect state of virtue, and in this sense a virtue can be blocked by something that is not a sin but only a lesser good. It is in this way that the use of a woman throws the mind down not from virtue but from the "heights," i.e. the perfection of virtue. Thus Augustine says:[45] "Just as Martha's occupying herself with serving the saints was good, but even better was Mary's listening to the word of God, so also even though we praise as good Susanna's chastity in marriage, we place higher the good of Anna's widowhood and higher still that of Mary's virginity."

To [2], we have to say, as we said earlier,[46] that the virtuous mean is not a matter of quantity but of what agrees with right reason, and, therefore, the abundance of pleasure involved in a sexual act that is directed in accord with reason does not conflict with the virtuous mean. Besides, how much pleasure the external senses feel, a matter which depends on the state of the body, is not relevant to the question of virtue; what is relevant is how much the inner desire is attached to pleasures of this sort. That reason cannot engage in its free act of consid-

ering spiritual matters when one is experiencing this pleasure does not show that the [sexual] act is contrary to virtue, for it is not contrary to virtue if the act of reason is sometimes interrupted in order to do something that accords with reason; otherwise, it would be against virtue for someone to let themselves go to sleep.

Nevertheless, the fact that sexual lust and pleasure are not subject to the moderating rule of reason does arise from the penalty imposed for the original sin, i.e. insofar as reason rebelled against God it deserves to have its own flesh rebel [against it], as Augustine makes clear.[47]

To [3], we have to say what Augustine says in the same place, "A child is born bound by original sin as though from the daughter of sin, i.e. from the carnal lust which in the reborn is not counted as a sin." Thus it does not follow that the [sexual] act is a sin, but that by that act comes some penalty due to the original sin.

Article 3: Can sexual lechery be a sin?

On the third question we proceed as follows:

[1] It seems that sexual lechery cannot be a sin, for by the sexual act semen is discharged and this is a surplus of nutriment, as The Philosopher makes clear.[48] But no sin can be involved in the discharge of other surpluses; therefore, neither can there by any sin in sexual acts.

[2] Further, anyone can legitimately use as they see fit what is their own. But in the sexual act a person uses only what is their own, except probably in adultery or rape. Therefore, in sexual usings there can be no sin and so lechery of this sort is not a sin.

[3] Further, every sin has a vice that is its opposite. But no vice seems to be opposed to lechery. Therefore, lechery is not a sin.

But, in opposition to this, a cause is more powerful than its effect. But wine is prohibited on account of sexual lechery, according to The

---

44 *De bono conjug.* 16.
45 *De bono conjug.* 16.
46 1aIIae 64,2; 2aIIae 152,2 ad 2.
47 *On the City of God* XIV. See selection **VIII.2.6**.
48 *De gen. anim.* 18.

Apostle who says,[49] "Do not get drunk on wine because from that comes sexual lechery." Therefore, sexual lechery is prohibited.

Further, in *Galatians* [5:19] over-indulgence in sex is listed among the works of the flesh.

Reply: We have to say that the more necessary something is the more the order of reason must be preserved with respect to it, and, consequently, the more vicious it is if the order set by reason is ignored. Now the use of sexual things, as we said [art.2], is very necessary to the common good of preserving the human race. Therefore, in this matter it is especially required to abide by the order set by reason, and consequently if in this matter something is done beyond what the order set by reason demands, it will be vicious. But it is part of the meaning of lechery that it exceeds in sexual matters the order and mode which reason sets, and thus doubtless sexual lechery is a sin.

To [1], then, we have to say, just as The Philosopher says in the same book: "Semen is a surplus which is needed," for it is a surplus left over from the activity of the nutritive faculty but is needed for the work of the generative faculty. The other surpluses from the human body are ones that are not needed and therefore it does not matter how they are discharged as long as social decencies are observed. The discharge of semen is not like this, since it ought to occur in a way that suits it to the end for which it is needed.

To [2], we have to follow The Apostle in saying[50] against sexual lechery: "You have been bought at a great price. Glorify and carry God in your body." Therefore, by using their body in an inordinate way a person through over-indulgence in sex wrongs God, who is the original owner of our body. Thus Augustine too says [*Serm. ad popul.* IX,10]: "God, who governs his servants for their own benefit, not his, orders this, and commands it, so that his temple, which you have begun to be, is not defiled by wanton and illicit pleasures."

To [3], we have to say that since humans are very prone to enjoying pleasures, the opposite of over-indulgence is not often found. Nevertheless, the opposed vice falls under unfeelingness, and it occurs in a person who so dislikes using women that he does not even give his wife what is her due.

Article 5: Concerning the "daughters" of lechery.

[1] It does not seem correct to say that the "daughters" of sexual lechery are blindness of mind, thoughtlessness, rashness, unsteadiness, self-love, hatred of God, attachment to the present world, and abhorrence or despair in respect of the future world, because blindness of mind, thoughtlessness, and rashness pertain to lack of practical wisdom, something which is found in every sin just as practical wisdom is found in every virtue. Therefore, they should not be given as special "daughters" of lechery.

[2] Further, steadiness, as stated earlier,[51] is given as a part of courage. But lechery is not opposed to courage, but rather to moderation. Therefore, unsteadiness is not a "daughter" of over-indulgence in sex.

[3] Further, self-love up to the point of contempt for God is the source of all sin, as Augustine makes clear.[52] Therefore, it should not be given as a "daughter" of over-indulgence in sex.

[4] Further, Isidore gives four such "daughters": obscene language, offensive talk, jesting, and foolish talk. Therefore, the earlier list seems to be superfluous.

But, in opposition to this, there is the authoritative text from Gregory.[53]

Reply: We have to say that, when the lower faculties are powerfully attached to their objects, a consequence is that the higher powers are blocked and deranged in their acts. Now especially in the vice of lechery a lower faculty of desire, namely the faculty that lusts, tends powerfully toward its object, i.e. the pleasurable, on account of the strength of the emotion and the enjoyment. It follows that the

---

49 *Ephesians* 5:18.
50 I *Corinthians* 6:20.
51 2aIIae 128 & 137,3.
52 *De civitate dei* XIV,28.
53 *Moralia* XXXI,45.PL76,621.

higher powers, namely reason and will, are especially deranged by lechery.

Now, when we do things our reason engages in four acts. First, there is mere intellectual apprehension of some end as good; this act is blocked by lechery, as is said in *Daniel* [xiii,56]: "Good looks have deceived you and lust has perverted your heart." The result here is blindness of mind.

The second act is that of taking counsel about what must be done to achieve the end, and this too is blocked by the lust associated with lechery. Thus Terence, speaking of sexual love, says:[54] "This thing in itself admits of neither counsel nor moderation, and you cannot control it by counsel." The result here is rashness, which involves a removal of counsel, as noted above.

The third act is the judgment about what is to be done, and this too is blocked by lechery, for speaking of the sexually lecherous old men Daniel says [xiii,9], "They turned off their minds so that they would not recall just judgments." The result here is thoughtlessness.

The fourth act is reason's command to act, and this too is blocked by lechery. This happens to the extent that the force of lust blocks a person from carrying out what they have decided to do. The result here is unsteadiness. Thus Terence says[55] of someone who declared he would leave his girlfriend, "One false, little tear will undo those words."

On the side of the will there follow two sorts of deranged acts. One is the desire for the end, and this leads to self-love proportional to the pleasure which is inordinately desired. Conversely, hatred of God results from God's forbidding the desired pleasure. On the one hand, then, we have the desire for the things that lead to the end, and this means an attachment to the present world, the one in which the person wishes to enjoy the pleasure; on the other hand, we have despair about the future world, since when a person is too much involved in carnal pleasures they do not care about getting the spiritual ones, rather they scorn them.

To [1], then, we have to say, as says The Philosopher,[56] immoderation most of all destroys practical wisdom.[57] This vice opposed to practical wisdom especially arises from sexual lechery, the paradigm type of immoderation.

To [2], we have to say that steadiness in difficult and terrifying matters is given as a part of courage, but steadiness in abstaining from pleasurable things belongs to self-restraint, and that is given as a part of moderation, as was said earlier.[58] For this reason the unsteadiness which is opposed to self-restraint is given as a "daughter" of lechery. Nevertheless, even the first sort of unsteadiness is caused by lechery inasmuch as it enfeebles a man's heart and renders him effeminate. Hosea [iv:11] says this: "Fornication, wine, and drunkenness take away the heart." And Vegetius says,[59] "The person who experiences less of pleasure in life fears death less." Also it is not necessary, as has often been said, that the "daughters" of a capital sin pertain to the same matters as does the sin.

To [3], we have to say that inasmuch as self-love is a desire for any sort of good for oneself it is the general source of sins. But insofar as it is a particular desire for having for oneself carnal pleasures it is a "daughter" of sexual lechery.

To [4], we have to say that the things Isidore lists are certain deranged external acts which particularly pertain to speech. In speech things can go wrong in four ways. One way is due to the subject matter, and here we find obscene speech, because, as Matthew says [xii:34], "the mouth speaks of what fills the heart," and thus sexually lecherous persons, whose hearts are full of obscene lusts, easily break out into obscene words. A second way is due to the cause, for lechery causes thoughtlessness and rashness and the result is that the person breaks out into words that are lightly and thoughtlessly said, and this is called offensive talk. A third way relates to the end, for the person given to sex-

---

54 *Eunuch* I,1.

55 *Eunuch* I,1.

56 *Nicomachean Ethics* VI 5. See selection **VIII.1.1**.

57 Also translated as "prudence," for example in the Augustine selections.

58 IIa2ae q.143.

59 *De re militari* I, 3.

ual lechery seeks pleasure and directs their words to the enjoyment of pleasure, and as a result they break out into jokes. A fourth way relates to the views expressed by the words; lechery degrades these by causing blindness of mind, and the result is that the person breaks out into foolish talk, expressing with their words a preference above all other things for the pleasures they desire.

VIII.5.5. Sex in the Garden of Eden (*Summa Theologiae* I, qu.98, art.2)

[Aquinas here tries to square an Aristotelian approach which sees sexual reproduction as entirely natural to humans with Augustine's view (in selection VIII.2.6) that sex would have been without lust in the original state of innocence, i.e. before Adam and Eve committed the original sin.]

In the state of innocence would reproduction have taken place through sexual intercourse?

On the second question we proceed as follows:

[1] It seems that in the state of innocence reproduction would not have taken place through sexual intercourse, since, as Damascene says,[60] the first human being was in the earthly paradise "like an angel." But in the future state of the resurrection, when humans will be like angels, "they will neither marry nor be married," as it says in *Matthew* [xxii:30]. Therefore, neither in paradise would reproduction have taken place through sexual intercourse.

[2] Further, the first human beings were fully mature when created. Consequently, if in their case before sin reproduction had occurred through sexual intercourse, they would even in paradise have joined together in carnal union. But this is clearly false from what scripture says.[61]

[3] Further, in carnal union on account of the intensity of the pleasure human beings become most of all like animals. For this reason the self-control by which humans abstain from such pleasures is praised. But it is on account of sin that human beings are compared to animals, as the *Psalms* say:[62] "When they were in honour human beings did not use their minds; they were compared to stupid beasts of burden and became like them." Therefore, before sin there would not have been any carnal union of male and female.

[4] Further, in the state of innocence there would not have been any destruction, but sexual intercourse destroys virginal purity. Therefore, sexual intercourse would not have occurred in the state of innocence.

But in opposition to this, *Genesis* says [i:27 & ii:22] that before sin God made male and female. But God does nothing in vain. Therefore, even if human beings had not sinned, they would have had sexual intercourse, since it is toward that the distinction of the sexes is directed.

Further, *Genesis* [ii:18 & 20] says that the woman was made as a helper for the man. But what she helps with must be reproduction through sexual intercourse, since for any other job it would have been more fitting for the man to be helped by a man than by a woman. Therefore, even in the state of innocence reproduction would have taken place through sexual intercourse.

Reply: We have to say that some of the ancient doctors, when they reflected on the foulness of the lust attending sexual intercourse in the present state, proposed that in the state of innocence reproduction would not have taken place through sexual intercourse. Thus Gregory of Nyssa says[63] that just as the angels have been multiplied without sex by the working of divine power, so in paradise the human race would have multiplied in some other way. He also says that before sin God made male and female because he was thinking of the mode of reproduction that was going to be after the sin which he foresaw would happen.

But this does not make sense, for the things that are natural to human beings are neither withdrawn nor given to them on account of sin. Now it is obvious that in virtue of the animal life that they had

---

60 *De fide orthodoxa* II, 11, (PG94,916). Damascene led the Christian community in Damascus in the 8th century.
61 *Genesis* 4:1.
62 *Psalm* 68: 13, 21.
63 *De hominis opificio* 17, (PG44,189). Gregory lived from c.335 to 395. Was Bishop of Nysssa.

even before sin it was, as we said earlier,[64] natural to human beings to reproduce through sexual intercourse, just as do the rest of the complete animals. The natural organs assigned for this function evidence this fact. For this reason it should not be said that these natural organs would not have been used before sin, no more than we would say that of the other organs.

Therefore, in the present state as regards sexual intercourse two things are to be considered. One is the natural union of male and female for purposes of reproduction, for in every process of reproduction there is required an active power and a passive power. Thus wherever we find a distinction of the sexes, the active power is in the male and the passive power in the female. The order of nature requires that for reproduction male and female come together in sexual intercourse.

The other thing which can be considered is a certain ugliness associated with immoderate lust. This would not have existed in the state of innocence where the lower powers were completely under the control of reason. Augustine says this:[65] "Far be it from us to suspect that it was impossible for the seed of offspring to be sown without the infection of sexual desire; rather the sexual organs could have been set in motion by the same authority of will as the other organs and without all the seductive goading of passion, in peace of mind and body."

To [1], then, we have to say that although in paradise human beings were like angels because of their spiritual minds, nevertheless they had an animal life in respect of their bodies. But after the resurrection human beings will be made like angels both in mind and body. Thus the cases are not similar in the way the argument requires.

To [2], we have to say, as Augustine says,[66] that the first parents did not get to mate in paradise because no sooner was the woman made than they were thrown out of paradise for their sin. Alternatively, it was because they were waiting for the divine authority, who had issued the general command [to be fruitful and multiply], to determine the time of their union.

To [3], we have to say that animals lack reason, and thus human sexual intercourse becomes like that of the animals by the fact that reason cannot moderate the pleasure of sexual intercourse nor the ardor of lust. But in the state of innocence there would have been nothing which reason would not have moderated. This is not because the sensual pleasure would have been less, as some say, for the sensory pleasure would have been all the greater the purer the nature and the more sensitive the body. Rather this is because the force of lust would not have spent itself so inordinately on this sort of pleasure, since it would have been regulated by reason, which is not concerned to lessen sensual pleasure but to keep the force of lust from attaching itself immoderately to pleasure. By "immoderate" here I mean what goes beyond the measure set by reason. A sober person who eats moderately has just as much pleasure as a glutton; it is just that his lust comes to rest less in this sort of pleasure. This is what Augustine's words means. They do not exclude from the state of innocence the greatness of the pleasure but rather ardor of sexual desire and a disturbed mind.

To [4], we have to follow Augustine[67] and say that in that state "without any destruction of purity the husband would have come in the depth of his wife... For then the male semen could be introduced into the wife's uterus without damage to her genitalia, even as now the menstrual flow can be excreted. Just as for giving birth the womb of the female would not have been opened by any pang of pain but by some impulse when the time had arrived, so for impregnation and conception the two sexes would have come together not by sexual desire but by an exercise of the will.

64 Ia, 97,3.
65 On the City of God XIV. See selection VIII.2.6.
66 In Gen. ad litt. IX 4,(PL41,434).
67 On the City of God, XIV, 24. See selection VIII.2.6.

TOPIC IX

THE "DARKNESS WHICH IS BEYOND INTELLECT"

PHILOSOPHY BECOMES MYSTICAL WHEN IN ITS SEARCH FOR FINAL WISDOM and happiness it looks to some experience of union with something that, because it lies beyond all the things of ordinary experience, cannot be literally described by any of the categories by which we understand the world about us. In the West one important form of mystical philosophy emanates from the thought of Plotinus (203-269 C.E.), who while adopting the fundamentals of Platonic philosophy and modifying it with ideas from Aristotle held that Plato's thought ultimately required the positing of The One, something which is the source of all being and intelligibility while lying beyond both. Obviously such a being could not be understood in the way the Platonic Forms were, i.e. by rational insight culminating in definitions; instead, Plotinus held, it was apprehended in an inexpressible vision in which the soul let go of itself and joined its object.

Both Islam and Christianity were very much affected by this line of thought. Plotinus's ideas were proclaimed and developed by the neo-Platonic school of philosophy, the last of the major pagan philosophies, and the writings of such figures as Porphyry, Iamblichus, and Proclus were well known to Christians of late antiquity. Once Islam came into contact with the Christian world of Syria and Egypt it too became familiar with these writings, and they became an inspiration for both metaphysics and mysticism. The Greek Christian Church was always very open to Platonic ideas with their mystical possibilities, but this whole tendency received its Plotinian direction through the writings of someone who probably lived in Syria around 500 C.E. and wrote a series of treatises and letters pretending to have been authored by Dionysius the Areopagite, a person mentioned in *Acts* as having been converted in Athens by St. Paul. This fictitious ascription of their authorship became accepted as fact largely through the work of Maximus the Confessor (6th century), who interpreted them in a way that avoided theological heresy. Pseudo-Dionysius' work had little influence in the Latin West before the ninth century when they were translated by John Scotus Eriugena. The false authorship continued to be accepted and consequently the Dionysian works had much more of an impact than they otherwise would have.

In the West the pantheistic possibilities of Plotinian thought were fully brought out in Eriugena's own rendering of what he took from pseudo-Dionysius. This led to the ecclesiastical condemnation of his work and its consequent lack of influence on the later middle ages. But the mystical side of pseudo-Dionysius could not easily be suppressed, and it continued to be a challenge to the mainstream of scholastic thought and its Aristotelian scientific direction. The paradoxical emphasis on both the total transcendence of the Source of all being and the possibility of the human soul returning in union to that Source had an irresistible attraction for the mystics of the later middle ages like Meister Eckhart.

IX.1. PLOTINUS

IN PLOTINUS'S THOUGHT WE FIND IDEAS FROM BOTH PLATO AND Aristotle worked into a cosmological synthesis that provides ample place for many themes typical of mysticism. Plato's Ideas or Forms become The Intelligence which produces The Soul, which in turn produces the multiplicity of natural things. But beyond this Intelligence, with its multiplicity of Forms, lies a source which cannot be thought of as a being at all, and which Plotinus refers to simply as The One since it is free of all multiplicity. Plotinus encourages each human soul to forsake the sensible realm of things that come and go and turn to what is purely intelligible, and eventually to The One itself which lies beyond all intelligibility. In his disparaging remarks about our bodily existence and sexual love Plotinus echoes Plato; in his insistence that all that is intelligible demands a source that is not intelligible at all but known through a kind of union with it Plotinus articulates a mysticism that goes well beyond his master's thought.

IX.1.1. The One that is the Source of Being (from *Enneads* VI, 9)

[In this selection most of the themes of Plotinian mysticism surface: God lies beyond all being and is entirely formless; it is not possible to say what God is or indeed to know God in the way we know other things; it is necessary for the soul to turn away from its existence in a physical body and concentrate on what is purely intelligible if it is to return to the source from which it ultimately comes.]

I. It is by The One that all beings are beings. This is equally true of those that are primarily beings and those that in some way are simply classed among beings, for what could exist were it not one? Not a one, a thing is not. No army, no choir, no flock exists except it be one. No house, even, or ship exists except as the unit, house, or the unit, ship; their unity gone, the house is no longer a house, the ship is no longer a ship. Similarly quantitative continua would not exist, had they not an inner unity; divided, they forfeit existence along with unity. It is the same with plant and animal bodies; each of them is a unit; with disintegration, they lose their previous nature and are no longer what they were; they become new, different beings that in turn exist only as long as each of them is a unit. Health is contingent upon the body's being coordinated in unity; beauty, upon the mastery of parts by The One; the soul's virtue, upon unification into one sole coherence.

The Soul imparts unity to all things in producing, fashioning, forming, and disposing them. Ought we then to say that The Soul not only gives unity but is unity itself, The One? No. It bestows other qualities upon bodies without being what it bestows (shape, for instance, and Idea, which are different from it); so also this unity; The Soul makes each being one by looking upon The One, just as it makes man by contemplating the Idea, Man, effecting in the man the unity that belongs to Man.

Each thing that is called "one" has a unity proportionate to its nature, sharing in unity, either more or less, according to the degree of its being. The Soul, while distinct from The One, has greater unity because it has a higher degree of being. It is not The One. It is one, but its unity is contingent. Between The Soul and its unity there is the same difference as between body and body's unity. Looser aggregates, such as a choir, are furthest from unity; the more compact are the nearer; The Soul is nearer still, yet – as all the others – is only a participant in unity.

The fact that The Soul could not exist unless it was one should not, really, lead anyone to think it and The One identical. All other things exist only as units, and none of them is The One; body, for instance, and unity are not identical. Besides, The Soul is manifold as well as one even though it is not constituted of parts; it has various faculties – discursive reason, desire, perception – joined together in unity as by a bond. The Soul bestows unity because it has unity, but a unity received from another source.

II. Granted that being is not identical with unity in each particular thing, might not the totality, Being, be identical with unity? Then upon grasping Being, we would hold The One, for they would be the same. Then, if Being is The Intelligence,[1] The One would also be The Intelligence; The Intelligence, as Being and as The One, would impart to the rest of things both being and, in proportion, unity.

Is The One identical with Being as *man* and *one man* are identical? Or is it the number of each thing taken individually? (Just as one object and another joined to it are spoken of as "two," so an object taken singly is referred to as "one.") In the second case, if number belongs to the class of beings, evidently The One will belong in that way, too, and we shall have to discover what kind of being it is. But if unity is no more than a numbering device of the soul, The One has no real existence; but this possibility is eliminated by our previous observation that each object upon losing unity loses existence as well.

Accordingly, we must determine whether being and unity are identical either in each individual object or in their totality.

As the being of each thing consists in multiplicity and The One cannot be multiplicity, The One must differ from Being. Man is animal, rational, and many things besides; and this multiplicity is held together by a bondlike unity. Thus there is a difference between man and unity: man is divisible, unity indivisible. Being, containing all beings, is still more multiple, thus differing from The One even though it is one by participation. Because being possesses life and intelligence, it is not dead. It must be multiple. If it is The Intelligence, it must be multiple – and the more so if it contains the Ideas,

because Ideas, individually and in their totality, are a sort of number and are one only in the way in which the universe is one.

In general, then, The One is the first existent. But The Intelligence, the Ideas,[2] and Being are not the first. Every form is multiple and composite, and consequently something derived because parts precede the composite they constitute.

That The Intelligence cannot be primary should be obvious as well from the following. The activity of The Intelligence consists necessarily in intellection. Intelligence, which does not turn to external objects, contemplates what is superior to it; in turning towards itself it turns towards its origin. Duality is implied if The Intelligence is both thinker and thought; it is not simple, therefore not The One. And if The Intelligence contemplates some object other than itself, then certainly there exists something superior to The Intelligence. Even if The Intelligence contemplates itself and at the same time that which is superior to it, it still is only of secondary rank. We must conceive The Intelligence as enjoying the presence of the Good and The One and contemplating it while it is also present to itself, thinks itself, and thinks itself as being all things. Constituting such a diversity, The Intelligence is far from being The One.

Thus The One is not all things because then it would no longer be one. It is not The Intelligence, because The Intelligence is all things, and The One would then be all things. It is not Being because Being is all things.

III. What then is The One? What is its nature?

It is not surprising that it is difficult to say what it is when it is difficult to say even what being is or what form is, although there knowledge has some sort of approach through the forms. As the soul advances towards the formless, unable to grasp what is without contour or to receive the imprint of reality so diffuse, it fears it will encounter nothingness, and it slips away. Its state is distressing. It seeks solace in retreating down to the sense realm, there to rest as upon a sure and firm-set earth, just as the eye, wearied with looking at small objects,

---

1 "The Intelligence" in Plotinus's thought combines the functions of Plato's Creator "Demiurge" with Aristotle's God who thinks all the forms of nature in thinking itself. See the next selection for Plotinus's own account of this entity.
2 A reference to Plato's Forms. See selection **VI.1.1.**, and also the next selection in this section.

gladly turns to large ones. But when the soul seeks to know in its own way – by coalescence and unification – it is prevented by that very unification from recognizing it has found The One, for it is unable to distinguish knower and known. Nevertheless, a philosophical study of The One must follow this course.

Because what the soul seeks is The One and it would look upon the source of all reality, namely the Good and The One, it must not withdraw from the primal realm and sink down to the lowest realm. Rather must it withdraw from sense objects, of the lowest existence, and turn to those of the highest. It must free itself from all evil since it aspires to rise to the Good. It must rise to the principle possessed within itself; from the multiplicity that it was it must again become one. Only thus can it contemplate the supreme principle, The One.

Having become The Intelligence, having entrusted itself to it, committed itself to it, having confided and established itself in it so that by alert concentration the soul may grasp all The Intelligence sees, it will, by The Intelligence, contemplate The One without employing the senses, without mingling perception with the activity of The Intelligence. It must contemplate this purest of objects through the purest of The Intelligence, through that which is supreme in The Intelligence.

When, then, the soul applies itself to the contemplation of such an object and has the impression of extension or shape or mass, it is not The Intelligence that guides its seeing, for it is not the nature of The Intelligence so see such things. From sensation, rather, and from opinion, the associate of sensation, comes this activity. From The Intelligence must come the word of what its scope is. It contemplates its priors, its own content, and its issue. Purity and simplicity characterize its issue and, even more, its content and, most of all, its priors or Prior.

The One, then, is not The Intelligence but higher. The Intelligence is still a being, while The One is not a being because it is precedent to all being. Being has, you might say, the form of being; The One is without form, even intelligible form.

As The One begets all things, it cannot be any of them – neither thing, nor quality, nor quantity, nor intelligence, nor soul. Not in motion, nor at rest, not in space, nor in time, it is "the in itself uniform," or rather it is the "without-form" preceding

form, movement, and rest, which are characteristics of Being and make Being multiple.

But if The One is not in motion, why is it not at rest? Because rest or motion, or both together, are characteristic of Being. Again, because what is at rest must be so on account of something distinct from it, rest as such. The One at rest would have the contingent attribute, *at rest*, and would be simple no longer.

Let no one object that something contingent is attributed to The One when we call it the first cause. It is to ourselves that we are thereby attributing contingency because it is we who are receiving something from The One while The One remains self-enclosed. When we wish to speak with precision, we should not say that The One is this or that, but revolving, as it were, around it, try to express our own experience of it, now drawing nigh to it, now falling back from it as a result of the difficulties involved.

IV. The chief difficulty is this: awareness of The One comes to us neither by knowing nor by the pure thought that discovers the other intelligible things, but by a presence transcending knowledge. When the soul knows something, it loses its unity; it cannot remain simply one because knowledge implies discursive reason and discursive reason implies multiplicity. The soul then misses The One and falls into number and multiplicity.

Therefore we must go beyond knowledge and hold to unity. We must renounce knowing and knowable, every object of thought, even Beauty, because Beauty, too, is posterior to The One and is derived from it as, from the sun, the daylight. That is why Plato says of The One, "It can neither be spoken nor written about." If nevertheless we speak of it and write about it, we do so only to give direction, to urge towards that vision beyond discourse, to point out the road to one desirous of seeing. Instruction goes only as far as showing the road and the direction. To obtain the vision is solely the work of him who desires to obtain it. If he does not arrive at contemplation, if his soul does not achieve awareness of that life that is beyond, if the soul does not feel a rapture within it like that of the lover come to rest in his love, if, because of his closeness to The One, he receives its true light – his whole soul made luminous – but is still weighted down and his vision frustrated, if he does not rise alone but still carries within him something alien to The One, if he is not yet sufficiently unified, if he has not yet risen far but is still at a distance either because of the obstacles of which we have just spoken or because of the lack of such instruction as would have given him direction and faith in the existence of things beyond, he has no one to blame but himself and should try to become pure by detaching himself from everything.

The One is absent from nothing and from everything. It is present only to those who are prepared for it and are able to receive it, to enter into harmony with it, to grasp and to touch it by virtue of their likeness to it, by virtue of that inner power similar to and stemming from The One when it is in that state in which it was when it originated from The One. Thus will The One be "seen" as far as it can become an object of contemplation. Anyone who still lacks faith in these arguments should consider the following:

V. Those who believe that the world of being is governed by luck or by chance and that it depends upon material causes are far removed from the divine and from the notion of The One. It is not such persons as these that we address but such as admit the exigence of a world other than the corporeal and at least acknowledge the existence of soul. These persons should apply themselves to the study of soul, learning among other things that it proceeds from The Intelligence and attains virtue by participating in the reason that proceeds from The Intelligence. Next they must realize that The Intelligence is different from our faculty of reasoning (the so called rational principle), that reasoning implies, as it were, separate steps and movements. They must see that knowledge consists in the manifestation of the rational forms that exist in The Soul and come to The Soul from The Intelligence, the source of knowledge. After one has seen The Intelligence, which like a thing of sense is immediately perceived (but which, although it transcends the soul, is its begetter and the author of the intelligible world), one must think of it as quiet, unwavering movement; embracing all things and being all things, in its multiplicity it is both indivisible and divisible. It is not divisible as are the ingredients of discursive reason, conceived item by item. Still its content is not confused either: each element is distinct from the other, just as in science the the-

ories form an indivisible whole and yet each theory has its own separate status. This multitude of coexisting beings, the intelligible realm, is near The One. (Its existence is necessary, as reason demonstrates, if one admits The Soul exists, to which it is superior.) It is nevertheless not the supreme because it is neither one nor simple.

The One, the source of all things, is simple. It is above even the highest in the world of being because it is above The Intelligence, which itself, not The One but like The One, would become The One. Not sundered from The One, close to The One, but to itself present, it has to a degree dared secession.

The awesome existent above, The One, is not a being for then its unity would repose in another than itself. There is no name that suits it, really. But, since name it we must, it may appropriately be called "one," on the understanding, however, that it is not a substance that possesses unity only as an attribute. So, the strictly nameless, it is difficult to know. The best approach is through its offspring, Being: we know it brings The Intelligence into existence, that it is the source of all that is best, the self-sufficing and unflagging begetter of every being, to be numbered among none of them since it is their prior.

We are necessarily led to call this "The One" in our discussions the better to designate "partlessness" while we strive to bring our minds to "oneness." But when we say that it is one and partless, it is not in the same sense that we speak of the geometrical point or the numerical unit, where "one" is the quantitative principle which would not exist unless substance, and that which precedes substance and being, were there first. It is not of this kind of unity that we are to think, but simply use such things here below – in their simplicity and the absence of multiplicity and division – as symbols of the higher.

VI. In what sense, then, do we call the supreme The One? How can we conceive of it?

We shall have to insist that its unity is much more perfect than that of the numerical unit or the geometrical point. For with regard to these, the soul, abstracting from magnitude and numerical plurality, stops indeed at that which is smallest and comes to rest in something indivisible. This kind of unity is found in something that is divisible and exists in a subject other than itself. But "what is not in another than itself" is not in the divisible. Nor is it indivisible in the same sense in which the smallest is indivisible. On the contrary, The One is the greatest, nor physically but dynamically.[3] Hence it is indivisible, not physically but dynamically. So also the beings that proceed from it; they are, not in mass but in might, indivisible and partless. Also, The One is infinite not as extension or a numerical series is infinite, but in its limitless power. Conceive it as intelligence or divinity; it is more than that. Here is unity superior to any your thought lays hold of, unity that exists by itself and in itself and is without attributes.[4]

Something of its unity can be understood from its self-sufficiency. It is necessarily the most powerful, the most self-sufficient, the most independent of all. Whatever is not one, but multiple, needs something else. Its being needs unification. But The One is already one. It does not even need itself. A being that is multiple, in order to be what it is, needs the multiplicity of things it contains. And each of the things contained is what it is by its union with the others and not by itself, and so it needs the others. Accordingly, such a being is deficient both with regard to its parts and as a whole. There must be something that is fully self-sufficient. That is The One; it alone, within and without, is without need. It needs nothing outside itself either to exist, to achieve well-being, or to be sustained in existence. As it is the cause of the other things, how could it owe its existence to them? And how could it derive its well-being from outside itself since its well-being is not something contingent but is its very nature? And, since it does not occupy space, how can it need support or foundation? What needs foundation is the material mass which, unfounded, falls. The One is the foundation of all other things and gives them, at one and the same time, existence and location; what needs locating is not self-sufficing.

Again, no principle needs others after it. The principle of all has no need of anything at all. Deficient being is deficient because it aspires to its principle. But if The One were to aspire to any-thing, it would evidently seek not to be The One, that is, it would aspire to that which destroys it. Everything in need needs well-being and preservation. Hence The One cannot aim at any good or desire anything: it is superior to the Good; it is the Good, not for itself, but for other things to the extent to which they can share in it.

The One is not an intellective existence. If it were, it would constitute a duality. It is motionless because it is prior to motion quite as it is prior to thinking. Anyhow, what would it think? Would it think itself? If it did, it would be in a state of ignorance before thinking, and the self-sufficient would be in need of thought. Neither should one suppose it to be in a state of ignorance on the ground that it does not know itself and does not think itself. Ignorance presupposes a dual relationship: one does not know another. But The One, in its aloneness, can neither know nor be ignorant of anything. Being with itself, it does not need to know itself. Still, we should not even attribute to it this presence with itself if we are to preserve its unity.

Excluded from it are both thinking of itself and thinking of others. It is not like that which thinks but, rather, like the activity of thinking. The activity of thinking does not itself think; it is the cause that makes some other being think, and cause cannot be identical with effect. This cause, therefore, of all existing things cannot be any one of them. Because it is the cause of good it cannot, then, be called the Good; yet in another sense it is the Good above all.

VII. If the mind reels at this, The One being none of the things we mentioned, a start yet can be made from them to contemplate it.

Do not let yourself be distracted by anything exterior, for The One is not in some one place, depriving all the rest of its presence. It is present to all those who can touch it and absent only to those who cannot. No person can concentrate on one thing by thinking of some other thing; so he should not connect something else with the object he is thinking of if he wishes really to grasp it. Similarly, it is impossible for a soul, impressed with some-

---

3 The sense here is derived from the Greek word '*dynamis*,' meaning power.
4 The original text throughout the latter part of the paragraph is grievously defective. The translation attempts, out of the textual materials provided, merely to round off the reasoning begun.

thing else, to conceive of The One so long as such an impression occupies its attention, just as it is impossible that a soul, at the moment when it is attentive to other things, should receive the form of what is their contrary. It is said that matter must be void of all qualities in order to be capable of receiving all forms. So must the soul, and for a stronger reason, be stripped of all forms if it would be filled and fired by the supreme without any hindrance from within itself.

Having thus freed itself of all externals, the soul must turn totally inward; not allowing itself to be wrested back towards the outer, it must forget everything, the subjective first and, finally, the objective. It must not even know that it is itself that is applying itself to contemplation of The One.

After having dwelled with it sufficiently, the soul should, if it can, reveal to others this transcendent communion. (Doubtless it was enjoyment of this communion that was the basis of calling Minos[5] "the confidant of Zeus"; remembering, he made laws that are the image of The One, inspired to legislate by his contact with the divine.) If a person looks down on the life of the city as unworthy of him, he could, if he so wishes, remain in this world above. This does indeed happen to those who have contemplated much.

The divinity, it is said, is not outside any being but, on the contrary, is present to all beings though they may not know it. They are fugitives from the divine, or rather from themselves. What they turn from they cannot reach. Themselves lost, they can find no other. A son distraught and beside himself is not likely to recognize his father. But persons who have learned to know themselves will at the same time discover whence they come.

VIII. Self-knowledge reveals to the soul that its natural motion is not, if uninterrupted, in a straight line, but circular, as around some inner object, about a center, the point to which it owes its origin. If the soul knows this, it will move around this center from which it came, will cling to it and commune with it as indeed all souls should but only divine souls do. That is the secret of their divinity, for divinity consists in being attached to the center. One who withdraws from it becomes an ordinary human or an animal.

Is this "center" of our souls, then, the principle we are seeking? No, we must look for some other principle upon which all centers converge and to which, only by analogy to the visible circle, the word 'center' is applied. The soul is not a circle as, say, a geometrical figure. Our meaning is that in the soul and around about it exists the "primordial nature," that it derives its existence from the first existence especially when entirely separate from the body. Now, however, as we have a part of our being contained in the body, we are like a person whose feet are immersed in water while the rest of their body remains above it. Raising ourselves above the body by the part of us that is not submerged, we are, by our own center, attaching ourselves to the center of all. And so we remain, just as the centers of the great circles coincide with that of the sphere that surrounds them. If these circles were material and not spiritual, center and circumference would have to occupy definite places. But since the souls are of the intelligible realm and The One is still above The Intelligence, we are forced to say that the union of the intellective thinking being with its object proceeds by different means. The intellective thinking being is in the presence of its object by virtue of its similarity and identity, and it is united with its kindred with nothing to separate it from them. Bodies are by their bodies kept from union, but the bodiless are not held by this bodily limitation. What separates bodiless beings from one another is not spatial distance but their own differences and diversities: when there is no difference between them, they are mutually present.

As The One does not contain any difference, it is always present and we are present to it when we no longer contain difference. The One does not aspire to us, to move around us; we aspire to it, to move around it. Actually, we always move around it; but we do not always look. We are like a chorus grouped about a conductor who allow their attention to be distracted by the audience. If, however, they were to turn towards their conductor, they would sing as they should and would really be with him. We are always around The One. If we were not, we would dissolve and cease to exist. Yet our gaze does not remain fixed upon The One. When

---

5 In Greek mythology one of the judges set to rule in Hades. He was a paradigm of the fair judge.

we look at it, we then attain the end of our desires and find rest. Then it is that, all discord past, we dance an inspired dance around it.

IX. In this dance the soul looks upon the source of life, the source of The Intelligence, the origin of Being, the cause of the Good, the root of The Soul.

All these entities emanate from The One without any lessening for it is not a material mass. If it were, the emanants would be perishable. But they are eternal because their originating principle always stays the same; not fragmenting itself in producing them, it remains entire. So they persist as well, just as light persists as long as sun shines.

We are not separated from The One, not distant from it, even though bodily nature has closed about us and drawn us to itself. It is because of The One that we breathe and have our being: it does not bestow its gifts at one moment only to leave us again; its giving is without cessation so long as it remains what it is. As we turn towards The One, we exist to a higher degree, while to withdraw from it is to fall. Our soul is delivered from evil by rising to that place which is free of all evils. There it knows. There it is immune. There it truly lives. Life not united with the divinity is shadow and mimicry of authentic life. Life there is the native act of The Intelligence, which, motionless in its contact with The One, gives birth to gods, beauty, justice, and virtue.

With all of these The Soul, filled with divinity, is pregnant; this is its starting point and goal. It is its starting point because it is from the world above that it proceeds. It is its goal because in the world above is the Good to which it aspires and by returning to it there its proper nature is regained. Life here below in the midst of sense objects is for the soul a degradation, an exile, a loss of wings.[6]

Further proof that our good is in the realm above is the love innate in our souls; hence the coupling in picture and story of Eros with Psyche. The soul, different from the divinity but sprung from it, must needs love. When it is in the realm above, its love is heavenly; here below, only commonplace. The heavenly Aphrodite dwells in the realm above; here below, the vulgar, harlot Aphrodite.

Every soul is an Aphrodite, as is suggested in the myth of Aphrodite's birth at the same time as that of Eros. As long as soul stays true to itself, it loves the divinity and desires to be at one with it, as a daughter loves with a noble love a noble father. When, however, the soul has come down here to human birth, it exchanges (as if deceived by the false promises of an adulterous lover) its divine love for one that is mortal. And then, far from its begetter, the soul yields to all manner of excess.

But, when the soul begins to hate its shame and puts away evil and makes its return, it finds its peace.

How great, then, is its bliss can be conceived by those who have not tasted it if they but think of earthly unions in love, marking well the joy felt by the lover who succeeds in obtaining his or her desires. But this is love directed to the mortal and harmful – to shadows – and it soon disappears because such is not the authentic object of our love nor the good we really seek. Only in the world beyond does the real object of our love exist, the only one with which we can unite ourselves, of which we can have a part and which we can intimately possess without being separated by the barriers of flesh.

Anyone who has had this experience will know what I am talking about. He will know that the soul lives another life as it advances towards The One, reaches it and shares in it. Thus restored, the soul recognizes the presence of the dispenser of the true life. It needs nothing more. On the contrary, it must renounce everything else and rest in it alone, become it alone, all earthiness gone, eager to be free, impatient of every fetter that binds below in order so to embrace the real object of its love with its entire being that no part of it does not touch The One.

Then of it and of itself the soul has all the vision that may be – of itself luminous now, filled with intellectual light, become pure light, subtle and weightless. It has become divine, is part of the Eternal that is beyond becoming. It is like a flame. If later it is weighted down again by the realm of sense, it is like a flame extinguished.

---

6 A reference to Plato's *Phaedrus* in which the soul is pictured as having feathered wings with which it can fly up to the outer rim of the universe and catch a glimpse of the eternal Forms.

X. Why does a soul that has risen to the realm above not stay there? Because it has not yet entirely detached itself from things here below. Yet a time will come when it will uninterruptedly have vision, when it will no longer be bothered by body. The part of us that sees is not troubled. It is the other part which, even when we cease from our vision, does not cease from its activity of demonstration, proof and dialectic. But the act and faculty of vision is not reason but something greater than, prior and superior to, reason. So also is the object of the vision. When the contemplative looks upon himself in the act of contemplation, he will see himself to be like its object. He feels himself to be united to himself in the way that the object is united to itself; that is to say, he will experience himself as simple, just as it is simple.

Actually, we should not say, "He will see." What he sees (in case it is still possible to distinguish here the seer and the seen, to assert that the two are one would be indeed rash) is not seen, not distinguished, not represented as a thing apart. The person who obtains the vision becomes, as it were, another being. He ceases to be himself, retains nothing of himself. Absorbed in the beyond he is one with it, like a center coincident with another center. While the centers coincide, they are one. They become two only when they separate. It is in this sense that we can speak of The One as something separate.

Therefore is it so very difficult to describe this vision, for how can we represent as different from us what seemed, while we were contemplating it, not other than ourselves but perfect at-oneness with us?

XI. This, doubtless, is what is back of the injunction of the mystery religions which prohibit revelation to the uninitiated. The divine is not expressible, so the initiate is forbidden to speak of it to anyone who has not been fortunate enough to have beheld it himself.

The vision, in any case, did not imply duality; the persons who saw were identical with what they saw. Hence they did not "see" it but rather were "oned" with it. If only they could preserve the memory of what they were while thus absorbed into The One,

they would possess within themselves an image of what it was.

In that state they had attained unity, nothing within them or without effecting diversity. When they had made their ascent, there was within them no disturbance, no anger, emotion, desire, reason, or thought. Actually, they were no longer themselves; but, swept away and filled with the divine, they were still, solitary, and at rest, not turning to this side or that or even towards themselves. They were in utter rest, having, so to say, become rest itself. In this state they busied themselves no longer even with the beautiful. They had risen above beauty, had passed beyond even the choir of virtues.

They were like those who, penetrating the innermost sanctuary of a temple, leave temple images behind. The images will be the first objects to strike their view upon coming out of the sanctuary, after their contemplation and communion there not with an image or statue but with what they represent. They are but lesser objects of contemplation.

Such experience is hardly a vision. It is a seeing of a quite different kind, a self-transcendence, a simplification, self-abandonment, a striving for union and a repose, an intentness upon conformation. this is the way one sees in the sanctuary. Anyone who tries to see in any other way will see nothing.

By the use of these images, the wise among the soothsayers expressed in riddles how the divinity is seen. A wise priest, reading the riddle, will, once arrived in the realm beyond, achieve the true vision of the sanctuary. One who has not yet arrived there and knows the sanctuary is invisible, is the source and principle of everything, will also know that by hypostasis is hypostasis[7] seen, and that like alone joins like. He will leave aside nothing of the divine the soul is capable of acquiring. If his vision is not yet complete, he will attend to its completion, which, for him who has risen above all, is The One that is above all. It is not the soul's nature to attain to utter nothingness. Falling into evil it falls, in this sense, into nothingness, but still not complete nothingness. And when it reverses direction, it arrives not at something different but at itself. Thus, when it is not in anything else, it is in nothing but itself. Yet, when it is in itself alone and not in being, it is in the supreme.

7 By 'hypostasis' Plotinus means a transcendent source of reality.

We as well transcend Being by virtue of The Soul with which we are united.

Now if you look upon yourself in this state, you find yourself an image of The One.

If you rise beyond yourself, an image rising to its model, you have reached the goal of your journey.

When you fall from this vision, you will, by arousing the virtue that is within yourself and by remembering the perfection that you possess, regain your likeness and through virtue rise to The Intelligence and through wisdom to The One.

Such is the life of the divinity and of divine and blessed persons: detachment from all things here below, scorn of all earthly pleasures, the flight of the lone to the Alone.

IX.1.2. The Intelligence and its Relation to the Soul (from *Enneads* V, 9)

[The ideas (1) that the knowing of a form and the form's own immaterial existence are one and the same, and (2) that the knowledge of a form amounts to the art of producing things with that form come from Aristotle's philosophy. These provide the basis for Plotinus's view that the Platonic Ideas exist as a creative intelligence which has emanated from The One.]

III. We must inquire more closely into the nature of The Intelligence.

It is not unreasonable to identify it simply with authentic essence and existence. Ours, however, must be a more circuitous route: we must decide whether it really exists.

There is something ridiculous, surely, about questioning the existence of The Intelligence, but there are people who do it. So let us inquire whether it really is as we say, whether it is "separate,"[8] whether it is identical with existents, and whether it is the seat of the Ideas.[9] We shall do so right now.

Clearly, everything we call "being" is composite, whether man made it or nature. The man-made, with its metal or stone or wood, is not achieved until skill, by the induction of a form, has turned it into statue or house or bed. The natural, however,

is even more complicated – I mean what we call a "compound," the sort of thing that can be analyzed into constituent elements and form, as a human being, for example, into soul and body, and the human body into the four elements.

Now, finding everything to be made up of materials and a shaping form (of itself the matter of the elements is formless), one naturally asks whence comes the shaping form.

And one has questions of a similar sort about the soul. Is it partless? Is it, on the contrary, composite? Has it something representing matter and something else representing form? Is the intelligence within it the equivalent of the shape of the statue and sculptor giving it shape?

Adopting the same method in regard to the cosmos, one will once more end up with an intelligence and think it the true maker and demiurge.[10] The matter, then, is fire, water, earth, and air. Formation comes from yet another being, The Soul. The Soul it is that gives them their cosmic pattern. But The Intelligence provides them the seminal reasons much as skill gives the soul of the artist norms of performance. For there is an intelligence that is the form of The Soul. And there is The Intelligence that gives the form to The Soul, like the sculptor who gives shape to the statue, still possessing the while all that is given. What it gives to The Soul is neighbor to the true real; what body receives is image and imitation.

IV. But why must one go beyond The Soul? Why not make it the supreme?

First off, The Intelligence is different from The Soul and is its prior; there is no truth in the belief that The Soul begets The Intelligence. How could potentiality become actuality unless cause brought it about? Could chance effect it? Then it might never become actuality. What has to be admitted is that the primal beings are in act, sufficient unto themselves, and perfect. Those that are sequent to them are imperfect and receive what perfection they have from their begetters – as children, imperfect when born, are brought to adulthood by their parents. Produced is to producing principle as matter

---

8 I.e., "separate" from matter.
9 A reference to Plato's Forms. See selection **VI.1.1**.
10 A reference to Plato's Demiurge in the *Timaios*. See selection **VI.1.1**.

is to form and it is brought to perfection by its informing principle. If, further, The Soul is thus changeable while there must be somehow something unchangeable – else time would wear all away – this something must be prior to The Soul. Again, there must be something prior to The Soul since The soul is in the world; there has to be something outside a world that, all body and matter, has nothing enduring about it. Were there not, neither mankind nor the seminal reasons would know either survival or identity.

Arguments such as these make clear that The Intelligence must be prior to The Soul.

V. If words are going to mean anything, 'The Intelligence' must be understood not as intelligence in potency or intelligence evolving (which would, in any case, require another and prior intelligence) but as intelligence in actuality and for all eternity. It does not acquire thoughts; it has thoughts of itself. It thinks of itself and by itself; it is its thoughts. Were its thoughts a reality other than itself, its own reality would not be the object of its thinking and it would be in potency and not in act. We should not separate these realities from one another even though we are so inclined, in thinking, to do so.

What, then, is this that is both the knower and the known?

It is, without doubt, authentically The Intelligence: it thinks beings and they are. It is these beings, for it will perceive them either as being somewhere else or as in itself and as itself. The "somewhere else" is out of the question. Where could it be? So they are itself and the content of itself. They are not things of sense, although that has been suggested. Sense existence is primal in no being. Form inherent in things of sense is imitation of authentic form. Every form that is in anything has come from another form and is its imitation.

What is more, if The Intelligence is "maker of this all," it cannot think these things in order to produce them in this cosmos, for the cosmos would not yet exist. Such beings must exist before the cosmos, must not be typical of other beings, but must

themselves be archetypal. They are the very essence of The Intelligence.

The suggestion might be made that the seminal reasons[11] would suffice here. But then they must be eternal. If eternal, if immune to change, they must exist in The Intelligence such as we have described it – a principle prior to condition, to nature, to soul, for they are contingent existents.

The Intelligence, accordingly, is itself the authentic existents. It is not a knower that knows them as somewhere else. They are not prior to it. They are not after it. Of being it is rather the lawgiver, or – better still – the law. Thus is it true to say that "to be and to think are the same thing," and "in beings that involve no matter, thinker and thought are identical," and "I sought myself" as a being. The theory of reminiscence[12] bears on this as well.

None of the beings is off in space, outside The Intelligence. They all subsist in themselves without end, undergoing no change or decay. It is for this reason that they are real. Things that come and go have only borrowed being; not they, but they on whom they draw are real. Only by such borrowing are sense objects the things we say they are, their substrate having received formation from elsewhere, as bronze from the sculptor's skill or wood from the carpenter's. The skill penetrates them with form and yet remains integrally apart from them, continuing to carry within it the reality of statue or bed. So it is with all corporeal things.

This cosmos of ours characteristically a participant in images itself, shows how copies differ from authentic beings. Against the variability of the first there is the unchanging quality of the second – reposing in themselves, not needing space because not having magnitude, possessing an existence intellective and self-sufficing. Bodies seek their sufficiency in others than their own kind. The Intelligence, sustaining by its wondrous power all that would of themselves fail, seeks no stay anywhere.

VI. Let it be said, then, that The Intelligence is identical with these beings and contains them all,

---

11 This term comes from the Stoics, but in Plotinus it refers to the principles in The Soul which are productive of all sensible things in nature.

12 A reference to Plato's doctrine that the Forms are "recollected" by the human mind while it exists in a body. See especially Plato's *Meno* and *Phaedo*.

not locally but as containing itself and being one with its content.

"All, in it, are one" and yet distinct. It is rather like the way the mind contains many items and branches of knowledge at the same time without any one of them merging into any other; at a given moment each does what is expected of it without involving any of the others, every concept active singly. In this way, but with even greater unity, The Intelligence is every one of the beings and not every one of the beings at the same time because each of the beings is a distinct power. As the genus contains all the species[13] or as the whole contains all the parts, The Intelligence contains all the beings.

The seminal reasons provide an illustration of this. All the properties of a being are, in an undivided state, there as in one kernel – the form of eye and form of hand, for instance, whose difference is manifest only in the bodily organs they subsequently bring into being. Each of the seminal reasons is, with its content, an intelligence which has something spatial (as a liquid) for its matter while it is itself the form complete and is identical with generative soul – the generative soul, for its part, being the image of a higher soul.

Sometimes the name "Nature" is given to this seminal power. Partner to its prior as light is to flame, it both transforms and informs matter, not by push and pull and a working of levers – of which we hear so much – but by bestowal of reasons.

VII. In the rational soul there is knowledge of sense objects (if one must call it "knowledge"; "opinion" would be the better word); it is of later origin than the objects since it is a reflection of them. There is also knowledge – truly knowledge this – of intelligible objects. It comes from The Intelligence and traffics not with things of sense. Truly knowledge, it actually is everything it takes cognizance of. It is its own object and the thought of the object, because The Intelligence is the primal themselves, ever self-present, never compelled to seek or acquire (it is no journeyman as is The Soul), but immobile, the whole of all, not given to thought

that beings should be. It is not by its thinking *god* that god exists. It is not by its thinking *movement* that movement arises. That is why it is not correct to say that "each of these forms is a thought," if one means by it that a thing exists or is made to exist because The Intelligence has thought it. The object of intellection must exist before there is the act of intellection. If it did not, how would The Intelligence come to know it? Certainly not by luck and haphazard.

VIII. If, then, thought here is thought of an object interior to The Intelligence, that interior object is form and form is Idea.

What is Idea? An intelligence or intellective essence. No Idea is different from The Intelligence but is itself an intelligence. The Intelligence in its totality is made up of the Ideas and each of the Ideas is each of the intelligences. In the same way, a science in its totality is made up of theories and each of the theories is a part of the total science, a part that is not spatially separate from its fellows but, in the totality, having its distinctive qualities for all of that.

The Intelligence is in itself. It possesses itself, is itself ever-unchanging abundance. If prior to being, it would be, by its thought and action, the begetter of being. But we are unable to conceive of existence not preceding what knows it. So it were better to say that the beings are the content of its thought, that its actual thought is as proximate to the beings as the act of fire is to fire so that they, in their inmost are as proximate to The Intelligences as they are to their own proper act.

But being also is an act. Hence the act of The Intelligence and the act of being are one sole act – or, better, The Intelligence and Being are one. They are the same nature. The same nature, too, are the beings as the act of The Intelligence and the act of Being. And in this sense the Ideas, too, are the same nature as the idea of Being, its form, and its act. It is only our way of thinking that splits them up. Quite different is The Intelligence that, itself undivided, does not divide up either Being or beings.

13 See glossary entry for 'species/genus.'

IX.2. PSEUDO-DIONYSIUS THE AREOPAGITE

THE UNKNOWN AUTHOR OF THE TREATISES AND LETTERS THAT PRETEND to be by the Dionysius whom St. Paul is reported to have converted in Athens was heavily influenced by the fifth-century neo-Platonist Proclus who in his *Elements of Theology* provided a systematic interpretation of Plotinus's thought. The Dionysian corpus, once the fictitious authorship was accepted in the sixth century as fact, exercised a great deal of influence during the middle ages in both the Latin West and the Greek East, but its strong mystical tendency was more influential in the latter. Pseudo-Dionysius points the believer in a direction leading from "affirmative" theology, through "negative" theology, to the experience of a union with the deity which defies all expression. Like Plotinus, he accepts that the insights of the rational mind are ultimately completed in something that is above intellect and not rationally describable.

IX.2.1. The Transcendent Good (from *The Divine Names*, ch.5)

[The source of all being cannot itself be the things that it is the source of and hence is beyond all being. This Plotinian theme is clearly affirmed below.]

4. ...
But now let me speak about the Good, about that which truly is and which gives being to everything else. The God who is transcends everything by virtue of his power. He is the substantive Cause and maker of being, of subsistence, of existence, of substance, and of nature. He is the Source and the measure of the ages. He is the reality beneath time and the eternity behind being. He is the time within which things happen. He is being for whatever is. He is coming-to-be amid whatever happens. From him who is come eternity, essence and being, come time, genesis, and becoming. He is the being immanent in and underlying the things which are, however they are. For God is not some kind of being. No. But in a way that is simple and indefinable he gathers himself and anticipates every existence. So he is called "King of the ages,"[1] for in him and around him all being is and subsists. He was not.

He will not be. He did not come to be. He is not in the midst of becoming. He will not come to be. No. He is not. Rather, he is the essence of being for the things which have being. Not only things that are but also the essence of what they are come from him who precedes the ages. For he is the age of ages, the "predecessor of the ages."[2]

5. To repeat. Every being and all the ages derive their existence from the Preexistent. All eternity and time are from him. The Preexistent is the source and is the cause of all eternity, of time and of every kind of being. Everything participates in him and none among beings falls away. "He is before all things and in him all things hold together."[3] In short, the existence of anything whatsoever is there in the Preexistent, and is perceived and preserved.

Being precedes the entities which participate in it. Being in itself is more revered than the being of Life itself and Wisdom itself and Likeness to divinity itself. Whatever beings participate in these things must, before all else, participate in Being. More precisely, those absolute qualities of which things have a share must themselves participate in being itself. Consider anything which is. Its being and

---

1 *Timothy* 1:17.
2 *Psalm* 55:19.
3 *Colossians* 1:17.

eternity is Being itself. So therefore God as originator of everything through the first of all his gifts is praised as "He who is." In a surpassing fashion he possesses preexistence and preeminence and he originated being, I mean absolute being, and with that as instrument he founded every type of existent. All the sources of whatever there is both exist and are sources by virtue of their participation in Being. First, they are, and then, they are sources. You could express it this way: Life itself is the source of everything alive; Similarity itself is the source of everything similar, Unity itself of everything unified, Order itself of everything orderly. So it goes, you will find, with all other things which participate in this quality or that, in both or in many. What they have primarily is existence, and this existence ensures for them that they remain and that they are then themselves the source of this or that. It is only because of their participation in Being that they exist themselves and that things participate in them. If they have being as a result of the participation in Being itself, all the more so is this the case with the things which participate in them.

6. The first gift therefore of the absolutely transcendent Goodness is the gift of being, and that Goodness is praised from those that first and principally have a share of being. From it and in it are Being itself, the source of beings, all beings and whatever else has a portion of existence. This characteristic is in it as an irrepressible, comprehensive, and singular feature.

Every number preexists uniquely in the monad and the monad holds every number in itself singularly. Every number is united in the monad; it is differentiated and pluralized only insofar as it goes forth from this one. All the radii of a circle are brought together in the unity of the center which contains all the straight lines brought together within itself. These are linked one to another because of this single point of origin and they are completely unified at this center. As they move a little away from it they are differentiated a little, and as they fall farther they are farther differentiated. That is, the closer they are to the center point, the more they are at one with it and at one with each other, and the more they travel away from it the more they are separated from each other.

7. In the totality of nature all the laws governing each individual nature are gathered together in one unity within which there is no confusion, and in the soul the individual powers providing for all the parts of the body are assembled together as one. So there is nothing absurd in rising up, as we do, from obscure images to the single Cause of everything, rising with eyes that see beyond the cosmos to contemplate all things, even the things that are opposites, in a simple unity within the universal Cause. For that Source is the beginning of everything and from it come Being itself and every kind of being, all source and all end, all life and immortality and wisdom, all order and harmony and power, all maintenance and establishment and arrangement, all intelligence and reason and perception, all quality and rest and motion, all unity and intermingling and attraction, all cohesiveness and differentiation, all definition, and indeed every attribute which by the mere fact of being gives a character thereby to every existing thing.

8. From this same universal Cause come those intelligent and intelligible beings, the godlike angels. From it also come the nature of souls, the nature of everything in the cosmos, together with all the qualities said to subsist in other objects or in our thinking processes. And from it too come those all-holy and most venerable powers which have the most real existence and which have their foundation, so to speak, in the anteroom of the transcendent Trinity. They draw being from it. They exist in it. And from it they derive their godlike being.

Next come the subordinate beings, and these too [receive their being and godlike being] in subordinate status from the same Cause. Below these again are the lowliest beings whose [being and godlike being] comes from this cause, but in the lowliest way. If they are the lowliest, this is in comparison with the other angels since in comparison with us they are above and beyond the world.

And then there are the souls, together with all the other creatures. It is in accordance with the same principle that they too possess being and well-being. They are and are well, and they have this being and this well-being from the Preexistent, in whom they are, in whom they are well, from whom they have their beginning and their protection, toward whom they come as a final goal. He grants the highest measure of existence to those more exalted beings described in scripture as eternal. But beings are never without being which, in turn, comes from the Preexistent. He is not a facet of being. Rather, being is a facet of him. he is not contained in being, but being is contained in him. He does not possess being, but being possesses him. He is the eternity of being, the source and the measure of being. He precedes essence, being, and eternity. He is the creative source, middle and end of all things. That is why scripture applies to the truly Preexistent the numerous attributes associated with every kind of being. To him is properly attributed past, present, and future, came-to-be, coming-to-be, will-come-to-be.[4] All these characteristics, when divinely understood, indicate the complete transcendence of his Being and show him to be the Cause responsible for every mode of being. It is not that he exists here and not there. He does not possess *this* kind of existence and not *that*. No. He is all things since he is the Cause of all things. The sources and goals of all things are in him and are anticipated in him. But he is also superior to them all because he precedes them and is transcendentally above them. Therefore every attribute may be predicated of him and yet he is not any one thing. He has every shape and structure, and yet is formless and beautyless, for in his incomprehensible priority and transcendence he contains the sources, mean terms, and ends of all things and he undefiledly enlightens Being for them in one undifferentiated cause.

The sun, as we know it, is one. It is a single illuminating light, acting upon the essences and the qualities of the many and various things we perceive. It renews them, nourishes them, protects them and perfects them. It establishes the differences between them and it unifies them. It warms them and makes them fruitful. It makes them exist, grow, change, take root, burst forth. It quickens them and gives them life. Each thing therefore has, in its own way, a share of the one and the same sun and the one sun contains within itself as a unity the causes of all the things which participate in it.

All this holds all the more truly with respect to the Cause which produced the sun and which produced everything else. The exemplars of everything preexist as a transcendent unity within It. It brings forth being as a tide of being. We give the name of "exemplar" to those principles which preexist as a unity in God and which produce the essences of things. Theology calls them predefining, divine and good acts of will which determine and create things and in accordance with which the Transcendent One predefined and brought into being everything that is.

9. Now it may be that Clement, the philosopher,[5] uses the term "exemplar" in relation to the more important things among beings, but his discourse does not proceed according to the proper, perfect, and simple naming. Even if we were to concede all this to him, we would still be obliged to remember the scriptural statement, "I did not show these things to you, so that you might follow after them."[6] That is, through the knowledge we have, which is geared to our faculties, we may be uplifted as far as possible to the Cause of everything. We must attribute all things to this Cause and we must regard them as joined together in one transcendental unity. Starting with being and initiating the creative procession of goodness, reaching out to fill all things with being as a gift from itself, rejoicing in all things, it anticipates all things in itself. In its total simplicity it shakes off all duplication and it embraces everything in its transcendent infinity. It is therefore shared indivisibly by all in the same way that one and the same sound is perceived by numerous ears.

10. And so it is that the Preexistent is the Source and the end of all things. He is their Source, for he is their Cause. He is their end, for he is the "for the

---

4 *Revelations* 1:4 & 8.

5 One would think here either of Clement the Apostolic Father (c.100) or Clement of Alexandria (c.150-c.215), but such a reference would lay bare the fiction of ascribing this treatise to the Dionysius St. Paul converted in Athens. However, St. Paul does refer (*Philippians* 4:3) to a co-worker named Clement, and presumably one might suppose the reference is to him.

6 *Hosea* 13:4.

sake of whom." He is the boundary to all things and is the unbounded infinity about them in a fashion which rises above the contradiction between finite and infinite. As was often said, he contains beforehand and created everything in a single act. He is present to all and he is everywhere, according to one and the same and the totality of everything. He proceeds to everything while yet remaining within himself. He is at rest and astir, is neither resting nor stirring and has neither source, nor middle nor end. He is in nothing. He is no thing. The categories of eternity and of time do not apply to him, since he transcends both and transcends whatever lies within them. Eternity itself and beings and the measures of beings and the measured world exist through him and from him.

However, so far as these last topics are concerned, let that suffice which I shall more fittingly say elsewhere.

IX.2.2. How God can be called Wisdom (*The Divine Names*, ch.7)

[God's knowledge of everything other than Himself is really knowledge of Himself, and our knowledge of God must in the end be a kind of "unknowing." Dionysius here seems to delight in the paradoxes his theology compels him to accept.]

Concerning 'wisdom,' 'mind,' 'word,' 'truth,' 'faith'

1. Now, if you will, let us give praise to the good and eternal Life for being wise, for being the principle of wisdom, the subsistence of all wisdom, for transcending all wisdom and all understanding. It is not simply the case that God is so overflowing with wisdom that "his understanding is beyond all measure"[7] but, rather, he actually transcends all reason, all intelligence, and all wisdom. This is something which was marvelously grasped by that truly divine man, my teacher[8] and yours[9] and the

light of our common instructor. For this is what he said: "The foolishness of God is wiser than men."[10] Those words are true not only because all human thinking is a sort of error when compared with the solid permanence of the perfect divine thoughts but also because it is customary for theologians to apply negative terms to God, but contrary to the usual sense of a deprivation. Scripture, for example, calls the all-apparent light "invisible."[11] It says of the One who is present in all things and who may be discovered from all things that he is ungraspable and "inscutable."[12] And here the divine apostle is said to be praising God for his "foolishness," which in itself seems absurd and strange, but uplifts [us] to the ineffable truth which is there before all reasoning. But, as I have often said elsewhere, we have a habit of seizing upon what is actually beyond us, clinging to the familiar categories of our sense perceptions, and then we measure the divine by our human standards and, of course, are led astray by the apparent meaning we give to divine and unspeakable reason. What we should really consider is this: The human mind has a capacity to think, through which it looks on conceptual things, and a unity which transcends the nature of the mind, through which it is joined to things beyond itself. And this transcending characteristic must be given to the words we use about God. They must not be given the human sense. We should be taken wholly out of ourselves and become wholly of God, since it is better to belong to God rather than to ourselves. Only when we are with God will the divine gifts be poured out onto us. therefore let us supremely praise this foolish "Wisdom," which has neither reason nor intelligence and let us describe it as the Cause of all intelligence and reason, of all wisdom and understanding. All counsel belongs to it, from it come all knowledge and understanding, and "in it are hid all the treasures of wisdom and knowledge."[13] From all that has been said above, it follows that the transcendently wise Cause is indeed the subsistence of

---

7 *Psalm* 147:5.
8 The author here pretends to have been instructed by St. Paul.
9 The whole treatise pretends to be addressed to the Timothy to whom St. Paul wrote the letters found in Scripture.
10 1 *Corinthians* 1:25.
11 *Colossians* 1:15; 1 *Timothy* 1:17, 6:16; *Hebrews* 11:27.
12 *Romans* 11:33.
13 *Colossians* 2:3.

absolute wisdom and of the sum total and individual manifestations of wisdom.

2. The intelligent and intelligible powers of the angelic minds draw from Wisdom their simple and blessed conceptions. They do not draw together their knowledge of God from fragments nor from bouts of perception or of discursive reasoning. And, at the same time, they are not limited to perception and reason. Being free from all burden of matter and multiplicity, they think the thoughts of the divine realm intelligently, immaterially, and in a single act. Theirs is an intelligent power and energy, glittering in an unmixed and undefiled purity, and it surveys the divine conceptions in an indivisible, immaterial, and godlike oneness. They become shaped as close as possible to the transcendently wise mind and reason of God, and this happens through the workings of the divine Wisdom.

Human souls also possess reason and with it they circle in discourse around the truth of things. Because of the fragmentary and varied nature of their many activities they are on a lower level than the unified intelligences. Nevertheless, on account of the manner in which they are capable of concentrating the many into the one, they too, in their own fashion and as far as they can, are worthy of conceptions like those of the angels. Our sense perceptions also can properly be described as echoes of wisdom, and even the intelligence of demons, to the extent that it is intelligence, comes from it, though we could more accurately describe this as a falling away from wisdom, since demonic intelligence stupidly has no idea how to obtain what it really wants and indeed does not want it.

I have said already that the divine Wisdom is the source, the cause, the substance, the perfection, the protector, and the goal of Wisdom itself, of mind, of reason, and of all sense perception. How, then, is it that God who is more-than-wise, is praised as wisdom, mind, word, and a knower? If he does not have intellectual activities, how can he possess understanding of conceptual things? How does he have knowledge of sense data when he himself transcends the domain of sense, while scripture, on the other hand, proclaims that he knows everything[14] and that nothing escapes the divine knowledge? But, as I have often said previously, we must interpret the things of God in a way that befits God, and when we talk of God as being without mind and without perception, this is to be taken in the sense of what he has in superabundance and not as a defect. Hence we attribute absence of reason to him because he is above reason; we attribute lack of perfection to him because he is above and before perfection, and we posit intangible and invisible darkness of that Light which is unapproachable[15] because it so far exceeds the visible light. The divine Mind, therefore, takes in all things in a total knowledge which is transcendent. Because it is the Cause of all things it has a foreknowledge of everything. Before there are angels he has knowledge of angels and he brings them into being. He knows everything else and, if I may put it so, he knows them from the very beginning and therefore brings them into being. This, I think, is what scripture means with the declaration, "He knows all things before their birth."[16] The divine mind does not acquire the knowledge of things from things. Rather, of itself and in itself it precontains and comprehends the awareness and understanding and being of everything in terms of their cause. This is not a knowledge of each specific class. What is here is a single embracing causality which knows and contains all things. Take the example of light. In itself it has a prior and causal knowledge of darkness. What it knows about darkness it knows not from another, but from the fact of being light. So too the divine Wisdom knows all things by knowing itself. Uniquely it knows and produces all things by its oneness: material things immaterially, divisible things indivisibly, plurality in a single act. If with one causal gesture God bestows being on everything, in that one same act of causation he will know everything through derivation from him and through their preexistence in him and, therefore, his knowledge of things will not be owed to the things themselves. He will be a leader, giving to each he knowledge it has of itself and of others. Consequently, God does not possess

14 *John* 21:17.
15 1 *Timothy* 6:16.
16 *Daniel* 13:42 (*Susanna* 42).

a private knowledge of himself and a separate knowledge of all the creatures in common. The universal Cause, by knowing itself, can hardly be ignorant of the things which proceed from it and of which it is the source. This, then, is how God knows all things, not by understanding things, but by understanding himself.

Scripture also says that the angels know the things of earth not because these latter may be perceived by the senses but because of the proper capacity and nature inherent in a Godlike intelligence.

3. If God cannot be grasped by mind or sense-perception, if he is not a particular being, how do we know him? This is something we must inquire into.

It might be more accurate to say that we cannot know God in his nature, since this is unknowable and is beyond the reach of mind or of reason. But we know him from the arrangement of everything, because everything is, in a sense, projected out from him, and this order possesses certain images and semblances of his divine paradigms. We therefore approach that which is beyond all as far as our capacities allow us and we pass by way of the denial and the transcendence of all things and by way of the cause of all things. God is therefore known in all things and as distinct from all things. He is known through knowledge and through unknowing. Of him there is conception, reason, understanding, touch, perception, opinion, imagination, name, and many other things. On the other hand he cannot be understood, words cannot contain him, and no name can lay hold of him. He is not one of the things that are and he cannot be known in any of them. He is all things in all things and he is no thing among things. He is known to all from all things and he is known to no one from anything.

This is the sort of language we must use about God, for he is praised from all things according to their proportion to him as their Cause. But again, the most divine knowledge of God, that which comes through unknowing, is achieved in a union far beyond mind, when mind turns away from all things, even from itself, and when it is made one with the dazzling rays, being then and there enlightened by the inscrutable depth of Wisdom.

Still, as I have said already, we must learn about Wisdom from all things. As scripture says, Wisdom has made and continues always to adapt everything.[17] It is the cause of the unbreakable accommodation and order of all things and it is forever linking the goals of one set of things with the sources of another and in this fashion it makes a thing of beauty of the unity and the harmony of the whole.

4. God is praised as "Logos" [word] by the sacred scriptures not only as the leader of word, mind, and wisdom, but because he also initially carries within his own unity the causes of all things and because he penetrates all things, reaching, as scripture says, to the very end of all things.[18] But the title is used especially because the divine Logos is simpler than any simplicity and, in its utter transcendence, is independent of everything. This Word is simple total truth. Divine faith revolves around it because it is pure and unwavering knowledge of all. It is the one sure foundation for those who believe, binding them to the truth, building the truth in them as something unshakably firm so that they have an uncomplicated knowledge of the truth of what they believe. If knowledge unites knower and known, while ignorance is always the cause of change and of the inconsistency of the ignorant, then, as scripture tells us,[19] nothing shall separate the one who believes in truth from the ground of true faith and it is there that he will come into the possession of enduring, unchanging identity. The man in union with truth knows clearly that all is well with him, even if everyone else thinks that he has gone out of his mind. What they fail to see, naturally, is that he has gone out of the path of error and has in his real faith arrived at truth. He knows that far from being mad,[20] as they imagine him to be, he has been rescued from the instability of error and that he has been set free by simple and

---

17 *Psalm* 104:24; *Proverbs* 8:30.
18 *Hebrews* 4:12; *Wisdom* 7:24.
19 *Romans* 8:29, 11:20.
20 *Acts* 26:24.

immutable stable truth. That is why the principle leaders of our divine wisdom die each day for the truth. They bear witness in every word and deed to the single knowledge of the truth possessed by Christians. They prove that truth to be more simple and more divine than every other. Or, rather, what they show is that here is the only true, single, and simple knowledge of God.

IX.2.3. *The Mystical Theology*

[This very short treatise, given here in its entirety, defends the need for both affirmative and negative theology while pointing to the ultimate unknowing in which one is united to the "divine darkness."]

Chapter one: *What is the divine darkness?*

1. Trinity!! Higher than any being,
any divinity, any goodness!
Guide of Christians
in the wisdom of heaven!
Lead us up beyond unknowing and light,
up to the farthest highest peak
of mystic scripture,
where the mysteries of God's Word
lie simple, absolute and unchangeable
in the brilliant darkness of a hidden silence.
Amid the deepest shadow
they pour overwhelming light
on what is most manifest.
Amid the wholly unsensed and unseen
they completely fill our sightless minds
with treasures beyond all beauty.

For this I pray; and, Timothy, my friend, my advice to you as you look for a sight of the mysterious things, is to leave behind you everything perceived and understood, everything perceptible and understandable, all that is not and all that is, and, with your understanding laid aside, to strive upward as much as you can toward union with him who is beyond all being and knowledge. By an undivided and absolute abandonment of yourself and every-

thing, shedding all and freed from all, you will be uplifted to the ray of the divine shadow which is above everything that is.

2. But see to it that none of this comes to the hearing of the uninformed, that is to say, to those caught up with the things of the world, who imagine that there is nothing beyond instances of individual being and who think that by their own intellectual resources they can have a direct knowledge of him who has made the shadows his hiding place.[21] And if initiation into the divine is beyond such people, what is to be said of those others, still more uninformed, who describe the transcendent Cause of all things in terms derived from the lowest orders of being, and who claim that it is in no way superior to the godless, multiformed shapes they themselves have made? What has actually to be said about the Cause of everything is this: Since it is the Cause of all beings, we should posit and ascribe to it all the affirmations we make in regard to beings, and, more appropriately, we should negate all these affirmations, since it surpasses all being. Now we should not conclude that the negations are simply the opposites of the affirmations, but rather that the cause of all is considerably prior to this, beyond privations, beyond every denial, beyond every assertion.

3. This, at least, is what was taught by the blessed Bartholomew.[22] He says that the Word of God is vast and minuscule, that the Gospel is wide-ranging and yet restricted. To me it seems that in this he is extraordinarily shrewd, for he has grasped that the good cause of all is both eloquent and taciturn, indeed wordless. It has neither word nor act of understanding, since it is on a plane above all this, and it is made manifest only to those who travel through foul and fair, who pass beyond the summit of every holy ascent, who leave behind them every divine light, every voice, every word from heaven, and who plunge into the darkness where, as scripture proclaims, there dwells the One who is beyond all things.[23] It is not for nothing that the blessed

---

21 *Psalm* 18:11.
22 Like the other apostles, the Bartholomew of the New Testament (*Matthew* 10:3, *Mark* 3:18, *Luke* 6:14, *Acts* 1:13) was later credited with several apocryphal works.
23 *Exodus* 20:21; cf. *Exodus* 19.

Moses is commanded to submit first to purification and then to depart from those who have not undergone this. When every purification is complete, he hears the many-voiced trumpets. He sees the many lights, pure and with rays streaming abundantly. Then, standing apart from the crowds and accompanied by chosen priests, he pushes ahead to the summit of the divine ascents. And yet he does not meet God himself, but contemplates, not him who is invisible, but rather where he dwells. This means, I presume, that the holiest and highest of the things perceived with the eye of the body or the mind are but the rationale which presupposes all that lies below the Transcendent One. Through them, however, his unimaginable presence is shown, walking the heights of those holy places to which the mind at least can rise. But then he [Moses] breaks free of them, away from what sees and is seen, and he plunges into the truly mysterious darkness of unknowing. Here, renouncing all that he may conceive, wrapped entirely in the intangible and the invisible, he belongs completely to him who is beyond everything. Here, being neither oneself nor someone else, one is supremely united by a completely unknowing inactivity of all knowledge, and knows beyond the mind by knowing nothing.

Chapter two: *How one should be united, and attribute praises, to the Cause of all things who is beyond all things.*

I pray we could come to this darkness so far above light! If only we lacked sight and knowledge so as to see, so as to know, unseeing and unknowing, that which lies beyond all vision and knowledge. For this would be really to see and to know: to praise the Transcendent One in a transcending way, namely through the denial of all beings. We would be like sculptors who set out to carve a statue. They remove every obstacle to the pure view of the hidden image, and simply by this act of clearing aside[24] they show up the beauty which is hidden.

Now it seems to me that we should praise the denials quite differently than we do the assertions. When we made assertions we began with the first things, moved down through intermediate terms until we reached the last things. But now as we climb from the last things up to the most primary we deny all things so that we may unhiddenly know that unknowing which itself is hidden from all those possessed of knowing amid all beings, so that we may see above being that darkness concealed from all the light among beings.

Chapter three: *What are the affirmative theologies and what are the negative?*

In my *Theological Representations*[25] I have praised the notions which are most appropriate to affirmative theology. I have shown the sense in which the divine and good nature is said to be one and then triune, how Fatherhood and Sonship are predicated of it, the meaning of the theology of the Spirit, how these core lights of goodness grew from the incorporeal and indivisible good, and how in this sprouting they have remained inseparable from their co-eternal foundation in it, in themselves, and in each other. I have spoken of how Jesus, who is above individual being, became a being with a true human nature. Other revelations of scripture were also praised in *The Theological Representations*.

In *The Divine Names* I have shown the sense in which God is described as good, existent, life, wisdom, power, and whatever other things pertain to the conceptual names for God.[26] In my *Symbolic Theology*[27] I have discussed analogies of God drawn from what we perceive. I have spoken of the images we have of him, of the forms, figures, and instruments proper to him, of the places in which he lives and of the ornaments he wears. I have spoken of his anger, grief, and rage, of how he is said to be drunk and hungover, of his oaths and curses, of his sleeping and waking, and indeed of all those images we have of him, images shaped by the workings of the symbolic representations of God. And I feel sure that you have noticed how these latter come much more abundantly than what went before, since *The*

---

24 The Greek word here, 'aphairesos,' can mean 'denial' in a logical context.
25 This work has never been known to exist and may be an entirely fictitious treatise.
26 Some of these topics are covered in the two preceding selections from *The Divine Names*.
27 Another unknown treatise that may be entirely fictitious.

Theological Representations and a discussion of the names appropriate to God are inevitably briefer than what can be said in *The Symbolic Theology*. The fact is that the more we take flight upward, the more our words are confined to the ideas we are capable of forming; so that now as we plunge into that darkness which is beyond intellect, we shall find ourselves not simply running short of words but actually speechless and unknowing. In the earlier books my argument traveled downward from the most exalted to the humblest categories, taking in on this downward path an ever-increasing number of ideas which multiplied with every stage of the descent. But my argument now rises from what is below up to the transcendent, and the more it climbs, the more language falters, and when it has passed up and beyond the ascent, it will turn silent completely, since it will finally be at one with him who is indescribable.

Now you may wonder why it is that, after starting out from the highest category when our method involved assertions, we begin now from the lowest category when it involves a denial. The reason is this: When we assert what is beyond every assertion, we must then proceed from what is most akin to it, and as we do so we make the affirmation on which everything else depends. But when we deny that which is beyond every denial, we have to start by denying those qualities which differ most from the goal we hope to attain. Is it not closer to reality to say that God is life and goodness rather than that he is air or stone? Is it not more accurate to deny that drunkenness and rage can be attributed to him than to deny that we can apply to him the terms of speech and thought?

Chapter four: *That the supreme Cause of every possible thing is not itself perceptible.*

So this is what we say. The Cause of all is above all and is not inexistent, lifeless, speechless, mindless. It is not a material body, and hence has neither shape nor form, quality, quantity, or weight. It is not in any place and can neither be seen nor be touched. It is neither perceived nor is it perceptible. It suffers neither disorder nor disturbance and is overwhelmed by no earthly passion. It is not powerless and subject to the disturbances caused by sense perception. It endures no deprivation of light. It passes through no change, decay, division, loss,

no ebb and flow, nothing of which the senses may be aware. None of all this can either be identified with it nor attributed to it.

Chapter five: *That the supreme Cause of every conceptual thing is not itself conceptual.*

Again, as we climb higher we say this: It is not soul or mind, nor does it possess imagination, conviction, speech, or understanding. Nor is it speech *per se*, understanding *per se*. It cannot be spoken of and it cannot be grasped by understanding. It is not number or order, greatness or smallness, equality or inequality, similarity or dissimilarity. It is not immovable, moving, or at rest. It has no power, it is not power, nor is it light. It does not live nor is it life. It is not a substance, nor is it eternity or time. It cannot be grasped by the understanding since it is neither knowledge nor truth. It is not kingship. It is not wisdom. It is neither one nor oneness, divinity nor goodness. Nor is it a spirit, in the sense in which we understand that term. It is not sonship or fatherhood and it is nothing known to us or to any other being. It falls neither within the predicate of nonbeing nor of being. Existing beings do not know it as it actually is and it does not know them as they are. There is no speaking of it, nor name nor knowledge of it. Darkness and light, error and truth – it is none of these. It is beyond assertion and denial. We make assertions and denials of what is next to it, but never of it, for it is both beyond every assertion, being the perfect and unique cause of all things, and, by virtue of its preeminently simple and absolute nature, free of every limitation, beyond every limitation; it is also beyond every denial.

IX.2.4. The Divine Darkness (from the letters of Dionysius)

Letter One
To the monk Gaius
Darkness disappears in the light, the more so as there is more light. Knowledge makes unknowing disappear, the more so as there is more knowledge.

However, think of this not in terms of deprivation but rather in terms of transcendence and then you will be able to say something truer than all truth, namely, that the unknowing regarding God escapes anyone possessing physical light and knowledge of beings: His transcendent darkness remains hidden from all light and concealed from all knowledge. Someone beholding God and understanding what he saw has not actually seen God himself but rather something of his which has being and which is knowable. For he himself solidly transcends mind and being. He is completely unknown and non-existent. He exists beyond being and he is known beyond the mind. And this quite positively complete unknowing is knowledge of him who is above everything that is known.

Letter Five

To Dorotheus, the deacon

The divine darkness is that "unapproachable light"[28] where God is said to live. And if it is invisible because of a superabundant clarity, if it cannot be approached because of the outpouring of its transcendent gift of light, yet it is here that is found everyone worthy to know God and to look upon him. And such a one, precisely because he neither sees him nor knows him, truly arrives at that which is beyond all seeing and all knowledge. Knowing exactly this, that he is beyond everything perceived and conceived, he cries out with the prophet, "Knowledge of you is too wonderful for me; it is high, I cannot attain it."[29]

It is in this sense that one says of the divine Paul that he knew God, for he knew that God is beyond every act of mind and every way of knowing. He says too that "inscrutable are his ways and unsearchable his judgments,"[30] that "his gifts are inexpressible,"[31] and that "his peace passes all understanding,"[32] for he found him who is beyond all things and he knew, in a way surpassing any conception, that the cause of all surpasses all.

---

28 1 *Timothy* 6:16.
29 *Psalm* 139:6.
30 *Romans* 11:33.
31 2 *Corinthians* 9:15.
32 *Philippians* 4:7.

IX.3. JOHN SCOTUS ERIUGENA

ALTHOUGH HE WORKED IN THE WEST (IN THE NINTH-CENTURY kingdom of Charles the Bald), Eriugena was much more influenced by the writings of Greek sources than Latin ones. He translated into Latin the works medieval writers attributed to Dionysius the Areopagite (see preceding section) and thus brought to the West the tradition of mystical thought that originates in Plotinus. But his major work, *Periphyseon*, from which these selections are drawn, is no mere rendering into Latin of the ideas of pseudo-Dionysius; it is an original cosmological synthesis of amazing scope and theological heterodoxy. The work was never well received in medieval Europe and in fact was condemned as heretical. It is consequently difficult to determine exactly how much influence it exercised over later thinkers. It certainly represents an alternative cosmology and metaphysics to the Aristotelianism which came to dominate Western scholasticism after 1200, a cosmology which provides much more of a place to the mystical ideas of the "Divine Darkness" and ultimate unification of everything with God that are typical of the Plotinian tradition.

IX.3.1. Things that are and things that are not
(from *Periphyseon*, bk.I)

[An alternative title for the *Periphyseon* (which means 'Concerning Nature') is *Concerning the divisions of nature,* and this selection shows the appropriateness of this other title, for 'Nature' is considered the general term for everything that either is or is not, and then this class is divided into four groups. That non-beings are included is very distinctive of Eriugena's metaphysics where non-being plays a more basic role than being, in contrast to Aristotle's metaphysics and the mainstream of Greek thought in general.]

NUTRITOR: As I frequently ponder and, so far as my talents allow, ever more carefully investigate the fact that the first and fundamental division of all things which either can be grasped by the mind or lie beyond its grasp is into those that are and those that are not, there comes to mind as a general term for them all what in Greek is called *physis* and in Latin *natura*. Or do you think otherwise?

ALUMNUS: No, I agree. For I too, when I enter

upon the path of reasoning, find that this is so.

N.: Nature, then, is the general name, as we said, for all things, for those that are and those that are not.

A.: It is. For nothing at all can come into our thought that would not fall under this term.

N.: Then since we agree to use this term for the genus,[1] I should like you to suggest a method for its division by differentiations into species; or, if you wish, I shall first attempt a division, and your part will be to offer sound criticism.

A.: Pray begin. For I am impatient to hear from you a true account of this matter.

N.: It is my opinion that the division of Nature by means of four differences results in four species, being divided first into that which creates and is not created, secondly into that which is created and also creates, thirdly into that which is created and does not create, while the fourth neither creates nor is created. But within these four there are two pairs of opposites. For the third is the opposite of the first, the fourth of the second; but the fourth is classed among the impossibles, for it is of its essence that it cannot be. Does such a division seem right to you or not?

---

1 See glossary entry for 'species/genus.'

A.: Right, certainly. But please go over it again so as to elucidate more fully the oppositions within these four forms.

N.: I am sure you see the opposition of the third species to the first – for the first creates and is not created; it therefore has as its contrary that which is created and does not create – and of the second to the fourth, for the second both is created and creates; it therefore has as its contrary in all respects the fourth, which neither creates nor is created.

A.: I see that clearly. But I am much perplexed by the fourth species which you have introduced. For about the other three I should not presume to raise any question at all, because, as I think, the first is understood to be the Cause of all things that are and that are not, Who is God; the second to be the primordial causes; and the third those things that become manifest through coming into being in times and places. For this reason a more detailed discussion which shall take each species individually is required, as I think.

N.: You are right to think so. But in what order we should pursue our path of reasoning, that is to say, which of the species of Nature we should take first, I leave it to you to decide.

A.: It seems to me beyond question that before the others we should say of the first species whatever the light of minds has granted us to utter.

N.: Let it be so. But first I think a few words should be said about the first and fundamental division – as we called it – of all things into the things that are and the things that are not.

A.: It would be correct and wise to do so. For I see no other beginning from which reasoning ought to start, and this not only because this difference is the first of all, but because both in appearance and in fact it is more obscure than the others.

N.: This basic difference, then, which separates all things requires for itself five modes of interpretation:

I. Of these modes the first seems to be that by means of which reason convinces us that all things which fall within the perceptions of bodily sense or within the grasp of intelligence are truly and reasonably said to be, but that those which because of the excellence of their nature elude not only all sense but also all intellect and reason rightly seem not to be – which are correctly understood only of God and matter and of the reasons and essences of all the things that are created by Him. And rightly so: for as Dionysius the Areopagite says, He is the Essence of all things Who alone truly is. "For," says he, "the being of all things is the Divinity Who is above Being." Gregory the Theologian[2] too proves by many arguments that no substance or essence of any creature, whether visible or invisible, can be comprehended by the intellect or by reason as to what it is. For just as God as He is in Himself beyond every creature is comprehended by no intellect, so is He equally incomprehensible when considered in the innermost depths of the creature which was made by Him and which exists in Him; while whatsoever in every creature is either perceived by the bodily sense or contemplated by the intellect is merely some accident to each creature's essence which, as has been said, by itself is incomprehensible, but which, either by quality or by quantity or by form or by matter or by some difference or by place or by time, is known not as to what it is but as to that it is.

That, then, is the first and fundamental mode of division of those things of which it is said that they are and those of which it is said that they are not. For what somehow appears to be a mode of division based upon privations of substances and accidents should certainly not be admitted, in my opinion. For how can that which absolutely is not, and cannot be, and which does not surpass the intellect because of the pre-eminence of its existence, be included in the division of things? – unless perhaps someone should say that the absences and privations of things that exist are themselves not altogether nothing, but are implied by some strange natural virtue of those things of which they are the privations and absences and oppositions, so as to have some kind of existence.

II. Let then the second mode of being and not being be that which is seen in the orders and *differences* of created natures, which, beginning from the intellectual power, which is the highest and is constituted nearest to God, descends to the furthermost degree of the rational and irrational creature, or to speak more plainly, from the most exalted angel to

2 St. Gregory Nazianzen, died 390. One of the early Greek Fathers of the Church.

the furthermost element of the rational and irrational soul – I mean the nutritive and growth-giving
life-principle, which is the least part of the soul in
the general acceptance of the term because it nourishes the body and makes it grow. Here, by a wonderful mode of understanding, each order, *including* the last at the lower end, which is that of bodies and in which the whole division comes to an
end, can be said to be and not to be. For an affirmation concerning the lower order is a negation
concerning the higher, and so too a negation concerning the lower order is an affirmation concerning the higher, and similarly an affirmation concerning the higher order is a negation concerning
the lower, while a negation concerning the higher
order will be an affirmation concerning the lower.
Thus the affirmation of 'man' (I mean, man while
still in his mortal state) is the negation of 'angel,'
while the negation of 'man' is the affirmation of
'angel' and vice versa. For if man is a rational, mortal, risible animal, then an angel is certainly neither
a rational animal nor mortal nor risible; likewise, if
an angel is an essential intellectual motion about
God and the causes of things, then man is certainly not an essential intellectual motion about God
and the causes of things. And the same rule is
found to apply in all the celestial essences until one
reaches the highest order of all. This, however, terminates in the highest negation upward; for its
negation confirms the existence of no higher creature. Now, there are three orders which they call "of
equal rank": the first of these are the Cherubim,
Seraphim, and Thrones; the second, the Virtues,
Powers, and Dominations; the third, the
Principalities, Archangels, and Angels.
Downwards, on the other hand, the last order
merely denies or confirms the one above it, because
it has nothing below it which it might either take
away or establish since it is preceded by all the
orders higher than itself but precedes none that is
lower than itself.

It is also on these grounds that every order of
rational or intellectual creatures is said to be and
not to be; it is in so far as it is known by the orders
above it and by itself; but it is not in so far as it does
not permit itself to be comprehended by the orders
that are below it.

III. The third mode can suitably be seen in those
things of which the visible plenitude of this world

is made up, and in their causes in the most secret
folds of nature, which precede them. For whatsoever of these causes through generation is known as
to matter and form, as to times and places, is by a
certain human convention said to be, while whatsoever is still held in those folds of nature is not
manifest as to form or matter, place or time, and
the other accidents, by the same convention
referred to is said not to be. Clear examples of this
mode are provided over a wide range of experience,
and especially in human nature. Thus, since God in
that first and one man whom He made in His
image established all men at the same time, yet did
not bring them all at the same time into this visible
world, but brings the nature which He considers all
at one time into visible essence at certain times and
places according to a certain sequence which He
Himself knows: those who already are becoming,
or have become visibly manifest in the world are
said to be, while those who are as yet hidden,
though destined to be, are said not to be. Between
the first and third mode there is this difference: the
first is found generically in all things which at the
same time and once for all have been made in their
causes and effects; the third specifically in those
which partly are still hidden in their causes, partly
are manifest in their effects, of which in particular
the fabric of this world is woven. To this mode
belongs the reasoning which considers the potentiality of seeds, whether in animals or in trees or in
plants. For during the time when the potentiality of
the seeds is latent in the recesses of nature, because
it is not yet manifest it is said not to be; but when it
has become manifest in the birth and growth of the
animals or flowers or of the fruits of trees and
plants it is said to be.

IV. The fourth mode is that which, not improbably
according to the philosophers, declares that only
those things which are contemplated by the intellect alone truly are, while those things which in
generation, through the expansions or contractions
of matter, and the intervals of places and motions
of times are changed, brought together, or dissolved, are said not to be truly, as is the case with
all bodies which can come into being and pass
away.

V. The fifth mode is that which reason observes
only in human nature, which, when through sin it

renounced the honour of the divine image in which it was properly substantiated, deservedly lost its being and therefore is said not to be; but when, restored by the grace of the only-begotten Son of God, it is brought back to the former condition of its substance in which it was made after the image of God, it begins to be, and in him who has been made in the image of God begins to live. It is to this mode, it seems, that the Apostle's saying refers: "and He calls the things that are not as the things that are"; that is to say, those who in the first man were lost and had fallen into a kind of non-subsistence God the Father calls through faith in His Son to be as those who are already reborn in Christ. But this too may also be understood of those whom God daily calls forth from the secret folds of nature, in which they are considered not to be, to become visibly manifest in form and matter and in the other conditions in which hidden things are able to become manifest.

Although keener reasoning can discover some modes besides these, yet I think at the present stage enough has been said about these things, unless you disagree.

A.: Quite plainly so. ...

IX.3.2. God as Hyper-being (from *Periphyseon*, bk.I)

[Eriugena takes over from pseudo-Dionysius (see selection IX.2.2) the idea that statements about God proceed through three stages: an affirmative (*kataphatic*), a negative (*apophatic*), and one where God is said to be "more-than" (*hyper-*) whatever was denied in the previous stage. This approach is defended by the claim that all our predicates admit of opposites, but God contains both of any pair of opposites.]

NUTRITOR: ... Here too is something which I see should not be passed over without consideration, and therefore I should like you to tell me whether you understand that anything opposed to God or conceived alongside of Him exists. By 'opposed' I mean either deprived of Him or contrary to Him or related to Him or absent from Him; while by 'conceived alongside of Him' I mean something that is

understood to exist eternally with Him without being of the same essence with Him.

ALUMNUS: I see clearly what you mean. And therefore I should not dare to say that there is either anything that is opposed to Him or anything understood in association with Him which is *heterousion*, that is, which is of another essence that what He is. For opposites by relation[3] are always so opposed to one another that they both begin to be at the same time and cease to be at the same time, whether they are of the same nature, like single to double or 2/3 to 3/2, or of different natures, like light to darkness, or in respect to privation, like death and life, sound and silence. For these are correctly thought to belong to the things which are subject to coming into being and passing away. For those things which are in discord with one another cannot be eternal. For if they were eternal they would not be in discord with one another, since eternity is always like what it is and ever eternally subsists in itself as a single and indivisible unity. For it is the one beginning of all things, and their one end, in no way at discord with itself. For the same reason I do not know of anyone who would be so bold as to affirm that anything is co-eternal with God which is not co-essential with Him. For if such a thing can be conceived or discovered it necessarily follows that there is not one Principle of all things, but two or more, widely differing from each other – which right reason invariably rejects without any hesitation; for from the One all things take their being; from two or more, nothing.

N.: You judge correctly, as I think. If therefore the aforesaid Divine Names are confronted by other names directly opposed to them, the things which are properly signified by them must also of necessity be understood to have contraries opposite to them; and therefore they cannot properly be predicated of God, to Whom nothing is opposed, and with Whom nothing is found to be co-eternal which differs from Him by nature. For right reason cannot find a single one of the names already mentioned or others like them to which *another* name, disagreeing with it, being opposed or differing from it within the same genus, is not found; and what we know to be the case with the names we

3 Eriugena means here correlative terms like 'master/slave,' 'parent/child.'

605

must necessarily know to be so with the things which are signified by them. But since the expressions of divine significance which are predicated of God in Holy Scripture by transference from the creature to the Creator – if, indeed, it is right to say that anything can be predicated of Him, which must be considered in another place – are innumerable and cannot be found or gathered together within the small compass of our reasoning, only a few of the Divine Names can be set forth for the sake of example. Then, God is called Essence, but strictly speaking He is not essence; for to being is opposed not-being.[4] Therefore He is *hyperousios*, i.e. superessential. Agian, He is called Goodness, but strictly speaking He is not goodness; for to goodness wickedness is opposed. Therefore he is *hyperagathos*, that is, more-than-good, and *hyperagathotes*, that is, more-than-goodness. He is called God [*theos* in Greek], but He is not strictly speaking God; for to vision is opposed blindness, and to him who sees, he who does not see. Therefore He is *hypertheos*, that is, more-than-God – for '*theos*' means 'he who sees.' But if you have recourse to the alternative origin of this name, so that you understand '*theos*,' that is, 'God,' to be derived not from the verb '*thoro*,' that is, 'I see,' but from the verb '*theo*,' that is, 'I run,' the same reason confronts you. For to him who runs he who does not run is opposed, as slowness to speed. Therefore He will be *hypertheos*, that is, more-than-running, as it is written: "His word runneth swiftly"; for we understand this to refer to God the Word, Who in an ineffable way runs through all things that are, in order that they may be. We ought to think in the same way concerning Truth; for to truth is opposed falsehood, and therefore strictly speaking He is not truth. Therefore He is *hyperalethes* and *hyperaletheia*, that is, more-than-true and more-than-truth. The same reason must be observed in all the Divine Names. For He is not called Eternity properly, since to eternity is opposed temporality. Therefore He is *hyperaionios* and *hyperaionia*, that is, more-than-eternal and more-than-eternity. Concerning Wisdom also no other eason applies, and therefore it must not be thought that it is predicated of God properly, since against

wisdom and wise are set the fool and folly. Hence rightly and truly He is called *hypersophos*, that is, more-than-wise, and *hypersophia*, that is, more-than-wisdom. Similarly, He is more-than-life because to life is opposed death. Concerning Light it must be understood in the same way; for against light is set darkness. For the present, as I think, enought has been said concerning these matters.

IX.3.3. God's Diffusion into all things (from *Periphyseon*, bk.I)

[Perhaps Eriugena's most daring heresy is that God is the Essence of all the things He creates. This leads inevitably to the view that the real essence of anything is unknowable, i.e. lies beyond the realm of being altogether. It also provides the basis for Eriugena's Plotinian view that ultimately everything must return to God, i.e. the One which lies at the heart of all the multiplicity of things.]

NUTRITOR: God, then, did not exist before He made all things?

ALUMNUS: No, for if He did, the making of all things would be an accident to Him; and if the making of all things were an accident to Him, it would be understood that motion and time were in Him, for He would move Himself to make the things which He had not yet made, and He would precede in point of time His own action, which was neither co-essential with Him nor co-eternal.

N.: Then His action of making is co-eternal with God and co-essential?

A.: So I believe and understand.

N.: Are God and His making, that is, His action, two things, or one simple and indivisible thing?

A.: I see that they are one, for God does not admit number in Himself, since He alone is innumerable and Number without number and Cause of all numbers which surpasses every number.

N.: Therefore it is not one thing for God to be and another to make, but for Him being is the same as making?

A.: I dare not resist this conclusion.

N.: So when we hear that God makes all things we

---

4 "Essence" derives from the Latin verb "*esse*" which means "to be," just as its Greek equivalent "*ousia*" derives from the participle form for the Greek word meaning "to be."

ought to understand nothing else than that God is in all things, that is, that He is the Essence of all things. For only He truly exists by Himself, and He alone is everything which in the things that are is truly said to be. For none of the things that are truly exists by itself, but whatever is understood truly to be in it receives its true being by participation of Him, the One, Who alone by Himself truly is.

A.: Nor would I wish to deny this.

N.: Do you see, then, how true reason completely excludes the category[5] of making from the Divine Nature and attributes it to the things which are mutable and temporal and cannot be without a beginning and an end?

A.: I see this clearly too, and now at last I understand without any doubt that no category applies to God.

N.: What then? Should we not examine in the same way the force of all the verbs which Holy Scripture predicates of the Divine Nature, so as to conclude that nothing else is signified by them but the Divine Essence and More-than-essence, itself, which is simple and immutable and cannot be grasped by any intellect or signification? For instance, when we hear that God wills and loves or desires, sees, hears, and the other verbs which can be predicated of Him, we should simply understand that we are being told of His ineffable Essence and Power in terms which are adapted to our nature, lest the true and holy Christian religion should be so silent about the Creator of all things that it dare not say anything for the instruction of simple minds and in refutation of the subtleties of the heretics who are always lying in wait to attack the truth and labouring to overthrow it and seeking to lead into error those who are less well instructed in it. Therefore to be and to will and to make and to love and to desire and to see and the other things of this sort which, as we said, can be predicated of Him, are not different things for God, but all these are to be accepted as one and the same in Him, and indicate His ineffable Essence in the way in which it allows itself to be signified.

A.: Indeed they are not different. For where there

is true and eternal and indissoluble simplicity by itself, there cannot be anything which is either this and that or which is much and various. But I should like you to tell me more explicitly, so that I may clearly see, how, when I hear that God loves or is loved, I shall understand nothing but His Nature without any motion of lover or beloved. For when I have been shown this I shall have no misgiving at all in reading anywhere or hearing that He wills or desires or is desired, loves or is loved, sees or is seen, seeks or is sought, and likewise that He moves or is moved. For all these must be accepted in one and the same sense. For as will and desire and vision and longing too and motion, when predicated of God, indicate to us one and the same thing, so the verbs, whether they be active or passive or neutral and whatever sense they are uttered, are understood not to disagree with one another by any difference of meaning, in my opinion.

N.: I think you are not deceived in this either, for it is as you think. First, then, take this definition of love: Love is a bond and chain by which the totality of all things is bound together in ineffable friendship and indissoluble unity. It can be defined in this way too: Love is the end and quiet resting place of the natural motion of all things that are in motion, beyond which no motion of the creature extends. These definitions St. Dionysius[6] openly supports in the "Amatory Hymns," saying: "Let us think of love, whether we are speaking of divine or angelic or intellectual or psychic or natural love, as a certain unitive and continuative power which moves the higher things to provide for the lower, and again those of equal form to exercise a close influence upon one another, and those things which are placed lowest to turn to those that are better and are placed above them."

The same author says in the same Hymns: "Since we have given in order the many kinds of love which derive from the One ... let us now ... involve them all together again into the one and all-embracing Love and Father of them all and collect them together from being many, first comprehending in two general virtues all their amatory virtues, over which absolutely commands and rules, from

---

5 See glossary entry for 'category.'

6 I.e., pseudo-Dionysius the Areopagite. Eriugena, like all the Christian medieval thinkers, wrongly believed that the author of the treatises ascribed to Dionysius was the Dionysius of Athens who was converted by St. Paul.

the summit of all things, the immeasurable Cause of all love, towards which also is directed all the love from all things that exist in conformity with the nature of each existent."

The same author says in the same Hymns: "Come now, and gathering these," that is, the virtues of love, "again into one, let us say that there is one simple virtue which moves itself to a unitive mingling of all things from the Best to the lowest of beings and back from that through all things in order to the Best again, spinning itself out from itself through itself towards itself and ever winding itself up again into itself in the same way."

Rightly therefore is God called Love, since He is the Cause of all love and is diffused through all things and gathers all things together into one and involves them in Himself in an ineffable Return, and brings to an end in Himself the motions of love and of the whole creature. Moreover this diffusion of the Divine Nature into all things which are in it and from it is said to be the love of all things, not that what lacks all motion and fills all things at once is diffused in any way, but because it diffuses through all things the rational mind's way of regarding them and moves it, for it is the Cause of the diffusion and motion of the mind to seek Him and to find Him and to understand Him, as far as it is possible to understand one who fills all things in order that they may be, and in the pacific embrace of universal love gathers all things together into the indivisible Unity which is what He Himself is, and holds them inseparably together.

Again, He is said to be loved by all things that were made by Him not because he suffers anything from them – for He alone is impassible – but because all things seek Him and because His beauty draws all things to Himself. For He alone is truly lovable because he alone is the supreme and real Goodness and Beauty. For He Himself is whatever in creatures is understood to be really good and really beautiful and lovable. For as there is no essential good so there is nothing essentially beautiful and nothing essentially lovable apart from Himself alone. Therefore, as that stone which is called the magnet, although by a natural power of its own it attracts to itself the iron which approach-

es it, does not move itself in any way in order to do this nor suffers anything from the iron which it attracts to itself; so the Cause of all things leads back to itself all things that derive from it without any motion of its own but solely by the power of its beauty.

Hence again St. Dionysius says among other things: "But ... why do the theologians call God sometimes Love but at other times Desire, at other times Lovable and Desirable?" He concludes his homily by saying: "Because ... under the one aspect He is moved, under the other He moves." This conclusion the venerable Maximus[7] expounds more fully by saying : "As being Love and Desire God is moved, while as Lovable and Desired He moves to Himself all things which are receptive of love and desire." And this must be explained more clearly still: He is moved as bringing an inseparable bond of love and desire to those who are receptive of them, but moves as attracting through nature the desire of those who are moved towards Him. And again: He moves and is moved as thirsting to be thirsted for and loving to be loved and desiring to be desired. For even this sensible light which fills the whole visible world, while it remains ever immutable although its vehicle, which we call the solar body, revolves in an eternal motion through the intermediate spaces of ether about the earth, nevertheless the light itself, glowing forth from this vehicle as from an inexhaustible source, so pervades the whole world by the immeasurable diffusion of its rays that it leaves no place into which it may move itself, and remains ever immutable. For everywhere in the world it is always full and whole, and it does not depart from any place nor does it seek any place save a certain small part of this lower air about the earth, which it leaves free for the purpose of admitting the earth's shadow which is called night; and yet it moves the gaze of all animals which are sensitive to light and draws them to itself that by it they may see in so far as they can see what they can see; and therefore it is thought to be moved, because it moves the rays of the eyes so that they are moved towards it, that is, it is the cause of the motion of the eyes towards seeing. And do not be surprised to hear that the nature of light, which

---

7 Maximus the Confessor, c.580-662, was one of the earliest writers to make extensive use of the Dionysian corpus and accept their attribution to the Dionysius Paul converted in Athens.

is fire, fills the whole sensible world and is every-where without change. For St. Dionysius also teaches this in his book on the "Celestial Hierarchy," and St. Basil[8] too affirms the same in the "Hexaemeron,"[9] saying that the substance of light is everywhere, but breaks forth by some nat-ural operation in the luminaries of the world whether they be great or small, not only in order to provide illumination but that it may mark off the whole of time into portions by the motions of the celestial bodies.

What shall I say of the skills the wise call the Liberal Arts, which, while they remain in them-selves by themselves complete, whole and immutable, yet are said to be moved when they move the rational mind's way of regarding them to seek them, to find them, and attract it to consider them, so that they too, although, as we said, they are immutable in themselves, yet seem to be moved in the minds of the wise because they move them? And there are many other things in which an obscure likeness of the Divine Power is seen. For it itself is above every likeness and surpasses every example, and while by itself and in itself it is immutably and eternally at rest, yet it is said to move all things since all things through it and in it subsist and have been brought from not-being into being, for by its being, all things proceed out of nothing, and it draws all things to itself. And it is said to be moved because it moves itself to itself.

Therefore God by Himself is Love, by Himself is Vision, by Himself is Motion; and yet He is neither motion nor vision nor love, but More-than-love, More-than-vision, More-than-motion. And He is by Himself Loving, Seeing, Moving; and yet He is not by Himself moving, seeing, loving, because He is More-than-loving, More-than-seeing, More-than-moving. Also, by Himself He is Being-loved and Being-seen and Being-moved; yet He is not by Himself being-moved nor being-seen nor being-loved, because He is More-than-being-loved and More-than-being-seen and More-than-being-moved.

Therefore He loves Himself and is loved by Himself in us and in Himself; and yet He does not love Himself nor is loved by Himself in us or in Himself, but More-than-loves and is loved in us and in Himself. He sees Himself and is seen by Himself in Himself and in us; and yet He does not see Himself nor is seen by Himself in Himself or in us, but More-than-sees and is seen in Himself and in us. He moves Himself and is moved by Himself in Himself and in us; yet He does not move Himself nor is moved by Himself in Himself or in us, because He More-than-moves and is moved in Himself and in us.

And this is the prudent and catholic and salutary profession that is to be predicated of God: that first by the *Cataphatic*, that is, by affirmation, we pred-icate all things of Him, whether by nouns or by verbs, though not properly but in a metaphorical sense; then we deny by the *Apophatic*, that is, by negation, that He is any of the things which by the *Cataphatic* are predicated of Him, only this time not metaphorically but properly – for there is more truth in saying that God is not any of the things that are predicated of Him than in saying that He is; then, above everything that is predicated of Him, His superessential Nature which creates all things and is not created must be superessentially More-than-praised. Therefore that which the Word made Flesh says to His dsciples, "It is not you who speak but the Spirit of your Father that speaks in you," true reason compels us to believe, and say, and understand in the same way with reference to other like things: it is not you who love, who see, who move, but the Spirit of the Father, Who speaks in you the truth about me and My Father and Himself in you, and moves Himself in you that you may desire Me and My Father. If then the Holy Trinity loves and sees and moves Itself in us and in Itself, surely It is loved and seen and moved by Itself after a most excellent mode known to no creature, by which It both loves and sees and moves Itself, and is loved, seen and moved by Itself in Itself and in Its creatures, although It surpasses all that is said about It. For who and what can speak about the Unspeakable, for Whom no proper noun or verb or

8 Died 379. Was one of the early Greek Fathers who were well versed in Greek philosophy.
9 The title means 'six days' and refers to the six days in which *Genesis* says that God created the world. Many authors wrote works with this title, in which they interpreted the *Genesis* account of creation, often importing elements from philosophical and speculative cosmologies.

any proper word is found or exists or can come into existence, and "Who alone possesses immortality and dwells in inaccessible light? For who knows the intellect of the Lord?"

IX.3.4. The Return of the Many to the One (from *Periphyseon*, bk.II)

[Here Eriugena expresses his doctrine of the "Return" in the vocabulary of logic. Where we have had division of Nature into different classes, now we see that all these classes resolve themselves back into the One. The same doctrine receives a metaphysical expression in selection IX.3.9.]

NUTRITOR: Since in the earlier book we spoke briefly of the universal division of universal nature[10] – not as a division of a genus into its species[11] nor of a whole into its parts, for God is not a genus of the creature nor the creature a species of God any more than the creature is the genus of God nor God a species of creature. The same can be said of the whole and its parts, for God is not the whole of the creature nor the creature a part of God any more than the creature is the whole of God or God a part of the creature, although in the loftier contemplation of Gregory the Theologian[12] we who participate in human nature are a part of God because "in Him we live and move and have our being," and in a metaphorical sense God is said to be both genus and whole and species and part since everything which is in Him and comes from Him can honestly and reasonably be predicated of Him, but by a kind of intellectual contemplation of the universe, under which term I include both God and creature – let us now, if you agree, re-examine the same division of nature more broadly.

ALUMNUS: I agree, and it seems very necessary. For unless this subject is opened up by a broader inquiry of the reason it will appear that we have only touched upon it, not discussed it.

N.: This then, as I think, was the fourfold division

of universal nature as we gave it above:[13] first into that form or species – if one may rightly call form or species the First Cause of all things which surpasses every form and species since it is the formless Principle of all forms and species – which creates and is not created. Now we call God the formless Principle so that no one may suppose that He is to be reckoned in the number of the forms while in fact He is the Cause of all forms. For every formed thing seeks Him while in Himself He is infinite and more-than-infinite, for He is the Infinity of all infinities. Therefore, not being constricted or defined by any form, since He is unknowable to every intellect, He is more reasonably called formless than form; for, as has often been said, we can speak more truly about God by negation than by affirmation; secondly into that which is both created and creates; third comes that which is created and does not create; then fourth that which neither creates nor is created.

A.: So indeed was the division made.

N.: Therefore, since in our earlier discourse we have already spoken briefly of the oppositions of these forms of nature – for we considered how the third conflicts with the first, for they confront each other as it were from diametrically opposed positions; for, as we said, the species which is created but does not create is the opposite of that which creates and is not created. Similarly the second form is opposed to the fourth; for the species which is created and creates is the opposite of that which neither is created nor creates.

Now the reason why we say that the universal nature possesses forms is that it is from her that our intelligence is in a manner formed when it attempts to treat of her; for in herself the universal nature does not everywhere admit forms. It certainly is not improper for us to say that she comprises God and creature, and therefore in so far as she is creative she admits no form in herself, but gives multiformity to the nature formed by her – I think we should now consider in what respects they resemble one another, and in what they differ.

A.: The natural order demands that we should

---

10 See above selection **IX.3.1.**
11 See glossary entry for 'species/genus.'
12 St. Gregory Nazianzen, died 390. One of the early Greek Fathers of the Church.
13 I.e., in selection **IX.3.1.**

proceed in no other way.

N.: The second form is similar to the first in that it creates, but dissimilar in that it is created. For the first creates and is not created, while the second both creates and is created. The third takes on a likeness of the second in that it is created, but differs from it in that it creates nothing. For the second both is created and creates, while the third is created and does not create. The third is similar to the fourth in that it does not create, but is dissimilar in that it is created. For the third is created and does not create, while the fourth neither is created nor creates. Furthermore the fourth is similar to the first because it is not created, but *appears to be* remote from it because it does not create. For the first creates and is not created, while the fourth neither creates nor is created. And now that the oppositions and similarities and differences have been stated, I see that we must say a few words about their return and collection by that science which the philosophers call *analytike*.[14]

A.: This too is required by the natural order. For there is no rational division, whether it be of essence into genera or of genus into species and individuals or of the whole into its parts – for which the proper name is partition – or of the universe into those divisions which right reason contemplates therein, that cannot be brought back again by the same stages through which the division had previously ramified into multiplicity, until it arrive at that One which remains inseparably in itself and from which that division took its origin. But I see that it is necessary that first you tell me a little about the etymology of the word *analytike*, for it is not clear to me.

N.: '*Analytike*' comes from the verb '*analuo*' which means 'I resolve' or 'I return'; for '*ana*' stands for 're-,' '*luo*' for 'solve.' Thence comes also the noun 'analysis,' which is similarly rendered 'resolution' or 'return.' But '*analysis*' is properly used in connection with the solution of set problems, while '*analytike*' is used in connection with the return of the division of the forms to the origin of that division. For every division, which is called by the Greeks "*merismos*," seems to be a kind of descent from some finite unity down into an infinite number of individuals, that is to say, from the

most general to the most specific, while every recollection, which is like a return back, starting from the most specific and ascending to the most general, is called '*analytike*.' Thus it is the return and resolution of individuals into forms, of forms into genera, of genera into *ousiai* [essences], of *ousiai* into the Wisdom and Providence with which every division begins and in which every division ends.

A.: You have said enough about the etymology of '*analytike*.' Pass on to other matters.

N.: Let us then make an "analytical" or regressive collection of each of the two pairs of the four forms we have mentioned so as to bring them into a unity. the first, then, and fourth are one since they are understood of God alone. For He is the Principle of all things which have been created by Him, and the end of all things which seek Him so that in Him they may find their eternal and immutable rest. For the reason why the Cause of all things is said to create is that it is from it that the universe of those things which have been created after it and by it proceeds by a wonderful and divine multiplication into genera and species and individuals, and into differentiations and all those other features which are observed in created nature; but because it is to the same Cause that all things that proceed from it shall return when they reach their end, it is therefore called the end of all things and is said neither to create nor to be created. For once all things have returned to it nothing further will proceed from it by generation in place and time and genera and forms since in it all things will be at rest and will remain an indivisible and immutable One. For those things which in the processions of natures appear to be divided and partitioned into many are in the primordial causes unified and one, and to this unity they will return and in it they will eternally and immutably remain.

But this fourth aspect of the universe, which, like the first also, is understood to exist in God alone, will receive a more detailed treatment in its proper place, as far as the Light of Minds shall grant us.

Now what is said of the first and fourth, that is to say, that neither the one nor the other is created since both the one and other are One – for both are predicated of God – will not be obscure, I think, to

---

14 Of which Aristotle's *Prior* and *Posterior Analytics* are the founding texts.

any who use their intelligence aright. For that which has no cause either superior to or equal with itself is created by nothing. For the First Cause of all things is God, whom nothing precedes nor is anything understood to be in conjunction with Him which is not coessential with Him. Do you see, then, that the first and fourth forms of nature have been reduced to a unity?

A.: I see it sufficiently and I understand it clearly. In God, therefore, the first form is not distinct from the fourth. For in Him they are not two things but one; in our contemplation, however, since we form one concept of God from consideration of Him as Beginning and another concept when contemplating Him as End, they appear to be as it were two forms, formed from one and the same simplicity of the Divine Nature as a consequence of the double direction of our contemplation.

N.: You see it correctly. Well, then, ought we not also, in the same way, to reduce the second and the third to a unity? For I think you will not have failed to notice that as the first and the fourth are with reason recognized in the Creator, so are the second and the third in the creature. For the second, as has been said, both is created and creates and is understood to be in the primordial causes of created things, while the third form is created and does not create, and is found in the effects of the primordial causes. Thus the second and third are contained within one and the same genus, namely, created nature, and in it are one. For forms are a unity in their genus. Do you not then see that of these four forms two, namely the first and the fourth, have been resumed into the Creator; and two, I mean the second and the third, into the creature?

A.: I see it clearly and I am filled with wonder at the subtlety of nature. For these two forms are discerned not in God but in our contemplation of Him, and are not forms of God but of our reason, resulting from our double consideration of Him as Beginning and End, nor is it in God that they are reduced to one form but in our contemplation which, in considering the beginning and the end, creates in itself, as it were, two forms of contemplation, and these again, it would seem, it reduces into a single form of contemplation when it begins to consider the simple unity of the Divine Nature. For 'Beginning' and 'End' are not proper names of the Divine Nature but of its relation to the things which are created. For they begin from it and that is why it is called 'Beginning'; and since they end in it so that in it they cease, it is rightly called by the name of 'End.' On the other hand, the other two forms, I mean the second and the third, not only come into being in our contemplation but are also found in the very nature of created things, in which the causes are separated from the effects and the effects are united to the causes because they make one with them in a single genus, I mean, in the creature.

N.: So the four become two.

A.: I do not deny it.

N.: But suppose you join the creature to the Creator so as to understand that there is nothing in the former save Him who alone truly is – for nothing apart from Him is truly called essential since all things that are are nothing else, in so far as they are, but the participation in Him who alone subsists from and through Himself – , will you deny that Creator and creature are one?

A.: It would not be easy for me to deny it. For it seems to me ridiculous to resist this reduction.

N.: So the universe, comprising God and creature, which was first divided as it were into four forms, is reduced again to an indivisible One, being Principle as well as Cause and End.

IX.3.5. The three Motions of the Soul (from *Periphyseon*, bk.II)

['Intellect' (*nous*), 'reason,' and 'sense' are basic concepts in the epistemology of the ancients. Here Eriugena re-interprets these in his own original way so as to incorporate through intellect Plotinian mysticism, through reason Platonic intuition of the Forms, and through sense Aristotelian concepts of genera and species.]

NUTRITOR: Let us begin our reasoning from the words of the venerable Maximus,[15] not making use of continuous extracts from the discourses but availing ourselves of their sense.

---

15 Maximus the Confessor, c.580-662, was one of the earliest writers to make extensive use of the Dionysian corpus and accept their attribution to the Dionysius Paul converted in Athens.

ALUMNUS: Proceed upon the path of reasoning by whatever means you wish.

N.: There are three universal motions of the soul, of which the first is of the mind, the second of the reason, the third of sense. And the first is simple and surpasses the nature of the soul herself and cannot be interpreted, that is, it cannot have knowledge of that about which it moves; "by this motion the soul moves about the unknown God, but, because of His excellence, she has no kind of knowledge of Him from the things that are" as to *what* He is, that is to say, she cannot find Him in any essence or substance or in anything which can be uttered or understood; for He surpasses everything that is and that is not, and there is no way in which He can be defined as to *what* he is.

The second motion is that by which she "defined the unknown" God "as Cause" of all. For she defines God as being Cause of all things; and this motion is within the nature of the soul, "and by it she moves naturally and takes upon herself by the operation of her science all the natural reasons (which are) formative of all things, which subsist as having been eternally made in Him Who is known only as Cause," for He is known because He is Cause, that is, she expresses them in herself through her knowledge of them, and the knowledge itself is *begotten* by the first motion in the second.

The third motion is "composite, and is that by which" the soul "comes into contact with that which is outside her as though by certain signs and re-forms within herself the reasons of visible things." It is called "composite" not because it is not simple in itself as the first and second are simple, but because its first knowledge of the reasons of sensible things does not come from the things themselves. For first the soul receives the phantasies of the things themselves through the exterior sense, which is fivefold because of the number of the corporeal instruments in which and through which it operates, and by gathering them to itself and sorting them out it sets them in order; then, getting through them to the reasons of the things of which they are the phantasies, she moulds them (I mean the reasons) and shapes them into conformity with herself.

And let it not trouble you that a little earlier we defined exterior sense as the phantasy of sensible things while now we teach that it is the means by which the phantasies of those same sensible things reach the interior sense. For this third motion begins to move as a consequence of being informed of the phantasies of exterior things by means of the exterior sense.

For there are two kinds of phantasies, of which the first is that which is born at first of sensible nature in the instruments of the sense and is properly called the image expressed in the senses; while the second is that which is formed next out of this image, and it is this phantasy which properly bears the customary name of exterior sense. And that which comes first is always attached to the body, that which comes after to the soul. And the first, although it is in the sense, is not sensible of itself, but the second is both sensible of itself and received the first.

But when this third motion abandons the phantasies of sensible things and clearly understands the reasons stripped bare of all corporeal imagery and in their own simplicity, it transmits the reasons of visible things freed from every phantasy back to the first motion through the intermediate motion as the simple operation of something which is also itself simple, that is to say (it transmits them as universal reasons by a universal operation. But the first motion itself carries back whatever it perceives from the third through the intermediate, and from that intermediate immediately in the modified forms of created things, to that which, unknown immediately in itself as to *what* it is, is yet known by the fact that it is the cause of all things, and to the principles of all things, that is, to the principal causes which are created by it and in it and distributed by it. That is, it understands that they proceed from God through them into all things that are after them and through them return to Him again.

Therefore the motion of the soul which is purged by action, illumined by knowledge, perfected by the divine word, (the motion) by which she eternally revolves about the unknown God, and understands that God Himself is beyond both her own nature and that of all things, absolutely distinct from everything which can either be said or understood and everything which cannot be said or understood – and yet which somehow exists – , and denies that He is anything of the things that are or of the things that are not and affirms that all things that are predicated of Him are predicated of Him not literally but metaphorically, is called 'nous' by the

Greeks, but by out writers '*intellectus*' [intellect] or '*animus*' [spirit] or '*mens*' [mind]; and it exists substantially, and is understood to be the principal part of the soul. For the essential being of the soul is not other than her substantial motion. For the soul subsists in her motions and her motions subsist in her. For she is by nature simple and indivisible, and is differentiated only by the substantial differences of her motions. Since, according to the tradition handed down by the holy fathers, the celestial essences, which the Divine Oracles also call the celestial and angelic powers, are substantially nothing else but intelligible, eternal and unceasing motions about the Beginning of all things, from Whom and through Whom and in Whom and towards Whom they move and subsist (for the motion of the celestial powers about their Beginning is circular, that is to say, it starts from Him as their Beginning, it passes through Him by means of the created causes, it moves in Him as in the natural laws which are in Him and beyond which it neither wills to stray nor can stray nor can will to stray, and returns to Him as its end, and such a motion exists in the understanding alone; for they understand that they are from Him and that their intellect moves through Him and in Him, and they know for certain that they have no other end than Him), what is to prevent us from understanding in a similar way that human intellects unceasingly revolve about God, seeing that they are from Him and through Him and in Him and for Him (for they revolve in the same intelligible circle), especially as the Divine Oracles declare that man is made in the image of God, which we do not find explicitly said of the angels? However, we are left to infer this from their intellectual nature. Also we read that the celestial powers stand in the presence of God and minister to Him, but the Catholic Faith witnesses that human nature becomes God in the Word of God and sitteth at the right hand of God and reigneth.

But that which the Lord promises to all men generally after the resurrection of all, "They shall be as angels of God in heaven," is to be understood, I think, as a sharing in the same status of nature and as an equality of immortality and as meaning that

they shall lack all corporeal sexuality and every corruptible mode of generation. For it is not unreasonable to believe that man's first state before sin in paradise, that is, in heavenly bliss, was equal and, as it were, of the same nature with that of the angels.[16] For the divine word refers to both these natures, I mean the angelic and the human, when it says: "Who made the heavens in intellect," that is, in order that they might be intelligences[17] in essence and in substance. But since man when he was in honour abandoned his intellect and became equal to the beasts who lack wisdom and was made like them, he withdrew far from his angelic status and fell into the misfortune of this mortal life. But after the Word was made flesh, that is, after God was made man, there is fulfilled what is written in the psalm: "What is man that Thou art mindful of him, or the son of man that Thou visitest him?"; marvelling, that is, at the exaltation of the first state of human nature "Thou madest him," it says, "a little less than the angels," that is, Thou hast permitted him to be made less because of his pride, and Thou hast left him of his own proper will to fall into the disgrace of an irrational life. For by a figure of speech God is said to do what He allows to be done; "Thou hast crowned him with glory and honour and hast set him above the works of Thy hands. Thou hast subjected all things under his feet."

Do you see how deeply human nature has been humiliated in the first man after sin, and how highly, through grace, it has been exalted in the second man, I mean, in Christ? For man is not only restored to the first state of his nature from which he fell, but is even lifted up in his Head, which is Christ, above all the celestial powers. For where sin was abundant grace was more abundant.

If therefore human nature, renewed in Christ, not only attains the angelic status but is even carried up beyond every creature into God, and if it would be impious to deny that that which was done in the Head will be done in the members, what wonder if Human intellects are nothing else but the ineffable and unceasing motions – in those, I mean, who are worthy – about God, in Whom they live and move and have their being? For they have their being

16 Cf. selection **VIII.5.5**.
17 See glosssary entry for 'intelligence.'

through the reasons by which they exist, they move through the reasons of the powers by which they are able to exist well, they live through the reasons by which they exist eternally. Thus they have being and well being and eternal being in God.

A.: Not only do I admit but I also understand that the most excellent motion of the soul about the unknown God beyond every creature is most rightly called, and is, intellect. But how or in what sense the intellect, while confined to the limits of human nature, can ascend above itself and above every creature so as to be able to perform its substantial motions about the unknown God who is far removed from every created nature should, I think be investigated.

N.: In this part of our contemplation which concerns the intellectual and rational substances, when it comes to the question how created nature can ascend beyond itself so as to be able to adhere to the creative Nature, every inquiry of those who study the potentiality of nature fails. For there we see not a reason of nature but the ineffable and incomprehensible excellence of Divine Grace. For in no created substance does there naturally exist the power to surpass the limits of its own nature and directly attain to Very God in Himself. For this is of grace alone, not of any power of nature.

This is why the Apostle confesses that he does not know how he was rapt into paradise, saying: "I know the man was rapt but I do not know how, whether in the body or out of the body." For it is not in the natural motions of the soul that I see in the body or out of the body any power by which I can be rapt into the Third Heaven. But only God knows, and it is only by His grace that I know for certain I was rapt. For no nature can of itself ascend into that place of which the Lord says: "Where I am, there is my servant also." Therefore, just as it passes all intellect how the Word of God descends into man, so it passes all reason how man ascends into God.

A.: Although your reply is brief it is sufficient and clear; so turn your attention to what comes next, the consideration of the second motion of the soul.

N.: The second motion of the soul, as we have said, is that which is contained within the bounds of its nature and defines the Very God as Cause, that is, it knows only this about the God Who is unknown as to what He is, (namely), that He is the Cause of all things that are, and that the primordial causes of all things are eternally created by Him and in Him; and it impresses the knowledge of those causes, when it has understood them, upon the soul herself, whose motion it is, as far as her capacity allows. For as from what is below her the soul receives the images of sensible things, which the Greeks call *phantasiai*, so from what is above her, that is, from the primordial causes, she implants within herself the cognitions which are usually called by the Greeks *theophaneiai* and by the Latins *divinae apparitiones*, and through them, through the first causes, I mean, she receives some motion of God – not that it understands what they are substantially, for this is beyond every motion of the soul – but it has the general knowledge that they are and that they flow forth by an ineffable process into their effects; and this is the motion which is called by the Greeks *logos* or *dynamis*, but by our writers *ratio* [reason] or *virtus* [power], and it is born of the first motion, which is intellect.

For just as a wise artist produces his art from himself in himself and foresees in it the things he is to make, and in a general and causal sense potentially creates their causes before they actually appear, so the intellect *brought forth* from itself in itself its reason, in which it foreknows and causally pre-creates all things which it desires to make. For we say that a plan is nothing else but a concept in the mind of the artist.

The second motion of the soul, then, is the reason, which is understood as a kind of substantial seeing in the mind and a kind of art begotten of it and in it, in which it foreknows and pre-creates the things which it wishes to make; and therefore it is not unreasonably named its form, for the intellect in itself is unknown but begins to become manifest both to itself and to others in its form, which is reason. For just as the Cause of all things cannot in itself be discovered as to what it is either by itself or by anyone else, but somehow comes to be known in its theophanies, so the intellect, which ever revolves about it and is created wholly in its image, cannot be understood as to *what* it is either by itself or by anyone else, but in the reason which is born of it begins to become manifest. But as to my saying that the Cause of all and the intellect are not understood by themselves as to *what* they are, the reason for that will be considered a little later. Concerning the second motion, what it is and whence it takes its origin, enough has been said, I think.

A.: Enough, certainly.

N.: There remains, then, the third motion, which functions in the particular reasons of particular things, which are created simply, that is, as a whole, in the primordial causes; and which, although it takes the beginning of its substantial motion from the phantasies of sensible things which are communicated to it through exterior sense, attains, by the most precise descrimination of all things through their proper reasons, to the most general essences and to the less general genera, then to the species and to the most specific species,[18] that is, the individuals, countless and unlimited, but limited by the immutable proportions of their nature; and this is the motion which in Greek is called *dianoia* or *energeia*, but in Latin *sensus* [sense] or *operatio* [operation] – by '*sensus*' I mean that which is substantial and interior – , which similarly proceeds from the intellect through the reason. For everything which the intellect by its gnostic view of the primordial causes impresses upon its art, that is, its reason, it distributes through the sense which proceeds from it and is called after its operation, into the particular reasons of individual *things*, which were created in the causes primordially and as a whole.

All essences are one in the reason; in sense they are divided into different essences. Therefore reason receives the most unified unity of their principles through the descending intellect; but sense separates that unity by means of differences. Similarly, reason knows through intellect the genera of things after a uniform and simple mode in their universal causes and in themselves; but that most universal simplicity which in itself is indivisible and is liable to no differences and is subject to no accidents and is not extended by spatial intervals and is not composed of any parts and is not varied by any motion through place or time, sense breaks up into the diverse genera and differences and a thousand other things. Those things which from the point of view of reason are one in their genera are the same in different forms as those which, on the other hand, by the operation of sense are differentiated from one another by natural dis-

tinctions. That is to say, the intellect itself through the medium of reason and through the sense which is consubstantial with itself, infallibly investigates and discovers and comprehends by sure rules the manner in which they are divided by their nautral motions under the rule and ordinance and administration of Divine Providence into the manifold differences of nature.

What shall I say of the unlimited number of individuals which, as much as they become multiple by the operation of sense, whether it is sense itself or in nature that they are multiple, so much are they one when by the reason they are considered in their forms under a universal and simple mode?

And to sum up: whatever the soul through her first motion, which is the intellect, knows under one form and as a whole concerning God and the primordial causes she implants, still under one form and as a whole, in her second motion, which is reason; but whatever she receives from the natures that are above her, through the intellect, after it has been formed in the reason, this whole she distributes through sense into the separated genera, into the diverse species, into the multiple individuals, in the effects below, and, to speak more plainly, whatever the human soul, through her intellect in her reason, knows of God and the principles of things as a unity she always retains as a unity; but whatever, through the reason, she perceives to subsist in the causes as one and under a uniform mode, this whole, through sense, she understands as multiple and under a multiform mode in the effects of the causes. But she most clearly knows through her intellect that from the one Cause of all things all things start upon their movement towards multiplicity without abandoning the simplicity of the unity by which they subsist in it eternally and immutably, and move towards it as the end of their whole movement, and end in it.

The three motions of the soul, that is, intellect which is also called her essence, and reason which is called her power, and sense which is called her operation, have been sufficiently discussed, as I think.

A.: Most clearly and abundantly.

---

18 See glossary entry for 'species/genus.'

IX.3.6. The Indefinability of God (from *Periphyseon*, bk.III)

[God, according to Eriugena, lies beyond all the Aristotelian categories, and thus beyond being. There is no "what" which God is, and thus the fact that He does not know *what* He is is no failing on His part and does not show that He does not know Himself. In denying that God has an Essence Eriugena expresses Himself in a heterodox way, but the doctrine that God does not fall into any of the categories and admits of no definition is one most medieval theologians shared.]

ALUMNUS: ... we must return to the consideration of the trinity in which we have been created in the image and likeness of God, and carefully consider whether that image copies throughout all things the likeness of that of which it is the image or whether it is dissimilar in anything, and does not in every respect attain to a perfect image. For so far as it imitates, thus far it is rightly called image; for if it deviates at any point it falls short of the reason of a perfect image.

NUTRITOR: We believe that man was most perfectly created in the image and likeness of God and that in paradise before his sin he fell short of that in nothing except in respect of subject. For God, subsisting through Himself and receiving subsistence from nothing that precedes Him, brought Man in His image and likeness out of nothing into essence, Therefore, once it has been noted that God, being *anarchos*, that is, without beginning, possesses His Essence through Himself, while man, created out of nothing, has a beginning of his creation, not only in the primordial causes in which all things were created at once, but also in the processions into the diverse essences and species, whether intelligible or sensible, all other things which are said and understood of God through the excellence of His Essence are wholly seen in His image through nature and grace. For the Creator Who is invisible and incomprehensible and passes all understanding created His image similar to Himself in all these things. For even our intellect is not known as to what it is in its

essence either by itself or by any other save God Who alone knows *what* He has made; but as concerning its Creator it knows only *that* He is but does not perceive *what* He is, so concerning itself it only determines that it is created, but how or in what substance it is constituted it cannot understand. For if in any way it could understand *what* it is it would necessarily deviate from the likeness of its Creator. For the *prototypon*, that is, the Principle Exemplar, is God through nature, while the image is God through grace. The *prototypon* is diffused through all things, distributing to all things their essence; the image, purified, illumined and perfected by the light of grace, pervades all things, forming a knowledge of them in itself. The *prototypon* penetrates all things that it has made, dividing its gifts to each in the proportion proper for each; the image surveys all things, giving glory to the Bestower of good things for His innumerable gifts which He has bestowed upon all – for some gifts, which are properly called *data* [givens], are substantial, others are added to substance; and as the *prototypon* created His image so that in it He might reveal some knowledge of Himself, so the image made for itself an image in which it might manifest its motions which in themselves are hidden. For the soul is the image of God, the body the image of the soul.

And concerning the other things which are to be understood and declared concerning the similitude of the image anyone who desires fuller knowledge may read the book of St. Gregory Nysseus[19] "On the Image."

A.: These things I readily accept. But I see another difference besides that of substance which appears to divide the image from its Principal Exemplar.

N.: Please tell me what it is.

A.: Does the difference seem to you slight between the nature which knows of itself both *that* it is and *what* it is, and that which knows of itself only *that* it is but does not understand *what* it is? For you will not deny, as I think, that God himself understands of Himself *what* He is, whereas we do not deny that the other essences and substances, which are created, cannot understand of themselves *what* they are lest we should appear impu-

---

19 St. Gregory of Nyssa, born c.335 and died c.395. Bishop of Nyssa and one of the most influential of the early Greek Fathers.

dently to oppose Gregory Nazianzen the Theologian,[20] who declares without hesitation and with sound reasons that no created essence can be defined by itself or by another, even though endowed with reason and intellect, as to *what* it is. Do you see, then, that the dissimilarity between the image and its Principal Exemplar, that is, between the human intellect and God the Creator is not only in respect of subject but also for the reason that the Principal Exemplar itself knows *what* it is, while the image does not understand how to define substantially either itself as to *what* it is or its Exemplar which it copies?

N.: I see that you have been misled by an appearance of true reasoning, and it is not surprising. For unless one has keenly and carefully examined from all sides the things in which you seem to be mistaken, they will be considered as not only likely but true.

A.: Please explain where I am mistaken.

N.: Do you believe that the Divine Essence is infinite or finite?

A.: To hesitate over that would be impious and very foolish, especially as it ought to be believed and understood that it is not Essence but More-than-Essence and the infinite Cause of all essences, and not only infinite but the Infinity of all infinite essence, and More-than-infinity.

N.: You speak correctly and in accordance with catholic doctrine. It is, then, in every respect infinite?

A.: I have granted this and do not regret having granted it but most firmly declare that it is not otherwise.

N.: See that you do not retract.

A.: You need have no fear of that.

N.: So when we ask of this or that, "What is it?", does it not appear to you that we are seeking for nothing else but a substance which either has been defined or is capable of being defined?

A.: Nothing else (but that). For this word 'what,' when it is interrogative, seeks nothing else but that the substance which it seeks be somehow defined.

N.: If, then, no wise man asks of all essence in general *what* it is, since it cannot be defined except in terms of the circumstances which circumscribe

it, so to speak, within limits, I mean place and time, quantity and quality, connection, rest, motion, condition, and the other accidents by which the substance itself, by reason of being subject, unknown and indefinable through itself, is shown only as subsisting, but not as to *what* it is, what persons learned in the discipline of the divine word would presume to inquire of the Divine Substance *what* it is when they understand very well concerning it that it cannot be defined, and is not any of the things that are, and surpasses all things that can be defined?

Hear the Nazianzen: "If ... the accumulation of the things which are both understood and said by us about that" which is being sought "is nothing whatever of the things that exist according to being itself as it is and is spoken of, but if that to which these relate – since it contains them while it is in no way contained by them – is something other than they, then let every soul refrain from rashly rushing into any speech of the matters that concern God" to define Him thereby, "... but let her reverence in silence only the truth of the Divine Essence which is ineffable and beyond understanding and the summit of all science." If, then, there is no one even among the wisest who can know the reasons of the substance of existing things as those reasons were first established, who would dare to find in anything a definition of God?

A.: I would not presume to question this either. For I know that His Substance is altogether infinite.

N.: If, then, God knows of Himself *what* He is, does He not define Himself – for everything which is understood by itself or by another as to *what* it is can be defined by itself or by another – and therefore is not altogether infinite but partially so if by the creature only He cannot be defined whereas by Himself He can be, or, if I may say so, subsists as finite to Himself, infinite to the creature? And if this be admitted, it will necessarily follow that either God is not universally infinite, if it is only by the creature that He does not admit definition and not by Himself; or that, in order to be universally infinite, He does not admit definition at all, either from the creature or from Himself.

A.: I think that the obscurity of this reasoning is

---

20 St. Gregory Nazianzen, died 390. One of the early Greek Fathers of the Church.

impenetrable and were it not that He Who is being sought Himself extends His aid to those who seek Him I could easily believe that there is no way of entering upon it. For if God does not define Himself, or if He could not define Himself, who would deny that ignorance and impotence are admitted into His Nature – ignorance if He does not understand of Himself *what* He is, impotence if He is unable to define His Substance? For He will be seen to be impotent when He can find nothing in which to define Himself.

On the other hand, if He both understands and defines *what* He Himself is, this will show that He is not altogether infinite since only by the creature can He not be defined, because by no means is He understood by it, but by Himself He is both defined and known as to *what* He is.

N.: Do not be troubled but rather be of good heart. For this discussion is drawing us towards an understanding of ourselves, and teaching us the things which it is right to think and understand and declare about our God, He being our Guide. For the more obscure and wearisome it will be thought at the beginning of the inquiry, the more lucid and fruitful it will turn out to be. "For," says St. Augustine, "by some divine providence it cannot be that religious minds who devoutly and seriously seek themselves and their God, that is, the Truth, should lack the ability to find it."

A.: I am not troubled but rather, and with justification, concerned about the obscurity of the problem that confronts us; and I do not think that its solution will be an easy one.

N.: Let us go back, then, to the problems which were debated between us in the first book, and unless I am mistaken, were completely solved.

A.: Please tell me what they are.

N.: Do you remember that it was settled between us to a certainty that none of the categories[21] which are included in the decad can by any means be literally predicated of the Divine Nature?

A.: That was conceded and established beyond question.[22]

N.: We shall not, then, have to work as hard as you think to resolve the difficulty of this problem,

if we look keenly at the valid conclusions of the first book. For their subtle and penetrating usefulness will now be shown to bear most fair and useful fruit.

A.: If this turns out to be the case, it is certainly necessary that we should do so.

N.: It will certainly be so. The train of our reasoning seems to require that we should briefly recall to our memory the categories themselves.

A.: No other way of inquiry suggests itself. But I should like you to recapitulate them in interrogative form.[23]

N.: Consider carefully, then, this order of interrogation: What? How great? Of what kind? In relation to what? In what position? With what possession? Is it in place? Is it in time? Does it act, or is it acted upon? Or if you prefer the Greek terms: *ti?*; *poson?*; *poion?*; *pros ti?*; *keisthai ara?*; *echesthai ara?*; *pou?*; *pote?*; *prattei ara e paschei?*. Of these interrogatives, then, there is none that can properly be asked of God because none of them is understood in Him either by Himself or by any other. For these can properly be considered only in things which are shown to fall within the scope of intellect or sense. For if you ask of God *what* He is will you not be seeking a proper defined substance? And if one should reply that He is this or that, will he not seem to be defining a certain and circumscribed substance? But if anyone were to assert this of Him as a truth, or if He Himself understands this of Himself, He will rightly occupy the first place of the categories which is alloted to certain and defined subjects in which and about which all accidents are associated and contained and thus the first category will be predicated of Him not figuratively but literally. For if the Divine Nature, whether by the intelligible creature or by itself, is understood to be in some defined essence, it is not altogether infinite and uncircumscribed and free from all accident, and therefore is not believed to be truly removed from everything which is said and understood, since it is understood to be within certain limits of a defined nature. For nothing of which it can be predicated or understood as to what it is can overstep the limit of the things that are, but

---

21 See glossary entry for 'category.'

22 See selection **IX.3.3** above.

23 As, in fact, they were first given by Aristotle. See selection **VI.1.1**.

will rightly be considered to be as though a part in a whole, or a whole in its parts, or a species in a genus,[24] or a genus in its species, or individuals in a species, or a species in its individuals, or some collection of all these things out of many into one; and this is far from the simple and infinite truth of the Divine Nature, which is nothing of the things that are. For it is neither whole nor part, although it is called whole and part because by it every whole and every part, and all wholes and all parts are created. Similarly it is neither genus nor form nor species nor individual nor *ousia* [essence], whether the most general or the most specific; and yet all these are predicated of it because from it they receive their ability to subsist. Moreover it is called the totality of all these although by the infinity of its excellence it surpasses the totality of all creation, because by it the total totality is created.

How, therefore, can the Divine nature understand of itself *what* it is, seeing that it is nothing? For it surpasses everything that is, since it is not even being but all being derives from it, and by virtue of its excellence it is supereminent over every essence and every substance. Or how can the infinite be defined by itself in anything or be understood in anything when it knows itself to be above every finite thing and every infinite thing and beyond finitude and infinity? So God does not know of Himself *what* He is because He is not a "what," being in everything incomprehensible both to Himself and to every intellect; and since Truth Itself in intelligible language proclaims in pure intellects that this is most truly said of God, no one of the persons of pious learning or of the adepts in the Divine Mysteries, hearing of God that He cannot understand of Himself *what* He is, ought to think anything else than that God Himself, Who is not a "what," does not know at all in Himself that which He Himself is not. But He does not recognize Himself as being something. Therefore he does not know *what* He Himself is, that is, He does not know that He is a "what," because He recognizes that He is none at all of the things which are known in something and about which it can be said or understood *what* they are. For if He were to recognize Himself in something He would show that He is not in every respect infinite and incomprehensi-

ble and unnameable. Thus He says: "Why do you ask My Name? For it is wonderful." Or is not this Name indeed wonderful, which is above every name, which is unnameable, which is set above every name that is named whether in this world or in the world to come? If, then, He disapproves the asking of His Name because it is unnameable above every name, what if one were to inquire of His Substance, which, were it in any finite thing, would not be without a finite name? But as He subsists in nothing because He is infinite, He lacks all naming because He is unnameable.

For nothing that is understood to be substantially in anything in such a way that it can be literally predicated of it *what* it is exceeds its proportion and measure. For it is enclosed within some proportion by which it is limited and is circumscribed by some measure which it cannot overstep. For if it occupies the lowest place in the nature of things, in which all bodies are contained, it cannot descend further below the measure of its nature because below it there is nothing; and it cannot ascend above it because it is limited to that vital motion from which it receives nourishment and growth, and therefore it is not carried beyond itself. On the other hand, if it subsists at the highest level of all creation, it is necessary that it should be confined within its limits so that it may be recognized as intellectual. For it cannot ascend to any creature above itself because there is seen to be nothing among created things that is higher than itself; likewise it cannot be thrust further down because of the substances that come after it. Finally, if it should occupy a place poised in the midst, it would neither be permitted to fall to the regions below it nor to extend to the regions above, but would hold to its natural position at the centre. And therefore there is no creature, whether visible or invisible, which is not confined in something within the limits of its proper nature by measure and number and weight.

But God understands that he is none of those things but recognizes that He is above all the orders of nature by reason of the excellence of His Wisdom, and below all things by reason of the depth of His Power, and within all things by the inscrutable dispensations of His Providence, and encompasses

---

24 See glossary entry for 'species/genus.'

all things because all things are within Him, and without Him there is nothing. For He alone is the measure and without measure, the number without number, and the weight without weight. And rightly so; for He is not measured or numbered or ordered by anything or by Himself, and He understands that He is not confined by any measure or number or order since in none of these things is he substantially contained, for he alone truly exists in all things, being infinite above all things.

And do not oppose my statement that the order of bodies cannot be extended into the natures that are above it on the ground that we believe that all bodies shall pass into incorporeal qualities and substances. For when this happens they will cease to be bodies. But at present, as long as they are bodies, they cannot overstep either the upper or the lower limits of their nature. But this part of philosophy will be more carefully treated when we come to consider the return of things into their causes. Now, however, let us attend to the topic before us, that is, the proposition that God does not understand *what* He is; and do not be afraid to say openly how it seems to you, whether what we are trying to teach about this seems plausible to you.

A.: I confess that what you have said of this wonderful Divine Ignorance by which God does not understand what He is, although obscure, yet does not seem to be false, but true and likely. For you do not teach that God does not know Himself but only that He does not know *what* He is; and rightly so, because he is not a "what." For He is infinite both to Himself and to all things that are from Him, and therefore there is most clearly and beautifully revealed in this form of ignorance the supreme and ineffable Wisdom. For the foolishness of God is wiser than men.

IX.3.7. The Self-creation of the Divine Darkness
(from *Periphyseon*, bk.III)

[In Eriugena's highly heterodox view of creation all creatures are "theophanies," i.e. the divine non-being making itself appear as a multiplicity of beings. Thus in creation God is making Himself *be*. There is, then, a fundamental identity of creature with the creator. Where orthodox theology treats the "nothing" out of which God creates all things as a purely negative term (there is *not* anything other than God which preceded the creation), Eriugena sees "nothing" as referring to the Creator Himself, since He is the non-being or "darkness" that is the source of all being.]

NUTRITOR: Concerning the simplicity of the Divine Nature we said that that is not to be truly and properly understood in it which is alien from it as not co-essential with it; and since all things are truly and properly understood to be within it – for nothing subsists outside it – it was concluded that it alone is truly and properly in all things, and that nothing truly and properly is what it itself is not.

ALUMNUS: It was.

N.: It follows that we ought not to understand God and the creature as two things distinct from one another, but as one and the same. For both the creature, by subsisting, is in God; and God, by manifesting Himself, in a marvellous and ineffable manner creates Himself in the creature, the invisible making Himself visible, and the incomprehensible comprehensible, and the hidden revealed, and the unknown known, and being without form and species formed and specific, and the superessential essential, and the supernatural natural, and the simple composite, and the accident-free subject to accident, and the infinite finite, and uncircumscribed circumscribed, and the supratemporal temporal, and the Creator of all things created in all things, and the Maker of all things made in all things, and eternal He begins to be, and immobile He moves into all things and becomes in all things all things.

And I am not here speaking of the Incarnation of the Word and His taking of humanness on Himself, but of the ineffable descent of the Supreme Goodness, which is Unity and Trinity, into the things that are so as to make them be, indeed, so as itself to be, in all things from the highest to the lowest, ever eternal, ever made, by itself in itself eternal, by itself in itself made. And while it is eternal it does not cease to be made, and made it does not cease to be eternal, and out of itself it makes itself, for it does not require some other matter which is not itself in which to make itself. Otherwise it would seem to be impotent and imperfect in itself if it were to receive from some other source an aid to its manifestation and perfection. So it is from Himself that God takes the occasions of His theophanies, that is, of the divine apparitions, since all things are from Him and through Him and in Him and for Him. And therefore even that matter from which it is read that He made the world is from Him and in Him, and He is in it in so far as it is understood to have being.

***

A.: ... But I beg you to explain what Holy Theology means by that name of 'nothing' [as it appears in 'God created the world out of nothing.']

N.: I should believe that by that name is signified the ineffable and incomprehensible and inaccessible brilliance of the Divine Goodness which is unknown to all intellects whether human or angelic – for it is superessential and supernatural – , which while it is contemplated in itself neither is nor was nor shall be, for it is understood to be in none of the things that exist because it surpasses all things, but when, by a certain ineffable descent into the things that are, it is beheld by the mind's eye, it alone is found to be in all things, and it is and was and shall be. Therefore so long as it is understood to be incomprehensible by reason of its transcendence it is not unreasonably called "nothing," but when it begins to appear in its theophanies it is said to proceed, as it were, out of nothing into something, and that which is properly thought of as beyond all essence is also properly known in all essence, and therefore every visible and invisible creature can be called a theophany, that is, a divine apparition. For every order of natures from the highest to the lowest, that is, from the celestial essences to the last bodies of this visible world, the more secretly it is understood, the closer it is seen to approach the divine brilliance.

Hence the inaccessible brilliance of the celestial powers is often called by theology "Darkness." Nor is this surprising when even the most high Wisdom itself, which is what they approach, is very often signified by the word 'Darkness.' Hear the Psalmist: "As His Darkness so also is His Light," as though he were saying openly: so great is the splendour of the Divine Goodness that, not unreason-

ably for those who desire to contemplate it and cannot, it shall be turned into darkness. For He alone, as the Apostle says, "possesseth the inaccessible light."

But the further the order of things descends downwards, the more manifestly does it reveal itself to the eyes of those who contemplate it, and therefore the forms and species of sensible things receive the name of "manifest theophanies." Therefore the Divine Goodness which is called "Nothing" for the reason that, beyond all things that are and that are not, it is found in no essence, descends from the negation of all essences into the affirmation of the essence of the whole universe; from itself into itself, as though from nothing into something, from non-essentiality into essentiality, from formlessness into innumerable forms and species. For its first progression into the primordial causes in which it is made is spoken of by Scripture as formless matter: matter because it is the beginning of the essence of things; formless because it comes nearest to the formlessness of the Divine Wisdom.

Now the Divine Wisdom is rightly called formless because it does not turn to any form above itself for its formation. For it is of all forms the undefined exemplar, and while it descends into the various forms of things visible and invisible it looks back to itself as to its formation. Therefore the Divine Goodness, regarded as above all things, is said not to be, and to be absolutely nothing, but in all things it both is and is said to be, because it is the Essence of the whole universe and its substance and its genus and its species[25] and its quantity and its quality and the bond between all things and its position and habit and place and time and action and passion and everything whatsoever that can be understood by whatever sort of intellect in every creature and about every creature. And whosoever shall look carefully into the words of St. Dionysius[26] will find that this is their meaning; ...

Whoever looks into the meaning of these words will find that they teach, indeed proclaim, nothing else but that God is the Maker of all things and is made in all things; and when He is looked for above

---

25 See glossary entry for 'species/genus.'
26 I.e., pseudo-Dionysius the Areopagite, whom medieval thinkers wrongly believed was the Dionysius St. Paul converted in Athens.

all things He is found in no essence – for as yet there is no essence – , but when He is understood in all things nothing in them subsists but Himself alone; and "neither is He this," as he says, "but not that," but He is all. Therefore, descending first from the superessentiality of His Nature, in which He is said not to be, He is created by Himself in the primordial causes and becomes the beginning of all essence, of all life, of all intelligence, and of all things which the gnostic contemplation considers in the primordial causes; then, descending from the primordial causes which occupy a kind of intermediate position between God and the creature, that is, between the ineffable superessentiality which surpasses all understanding and the substantially manifest nature which is visible to pure minds, He is made in their effects and is openly revealed in His theophanies; then He proceeds through the manifold forms of the effects to the lowest order of the whole of nature, in which bodies are contained; and thus going forth into all things in order He makes all things and is made all in all things, and returns into Himself, calling all things back into Himself. And while He is made in all things, He does not cease to be above all things and thus makes all things from nothing, that is, He produces from His Superessentiality essences, from His Supervitality lives, from His Superintellectuality intellects, from the negation of all things which are and which are not the affirmations of all things which are and which are not.

And this is very clearly shown by the return of all things into the Cause from which they proceeded, when all things shall be converted into God as the air into light, when God shall be all in all. Not that even now God is not all in all, but after the sin of human nature and its expulsion from the abode of paradise, when, that is, it was thrust down from the height of the spiritual life and knowledge of the most clear wisdom into the deepest darkness of ignorance, no one unless illuminated by Divine Grace and rapt with Paul into the height of the Divine Mysteries can see with the sight of true understanding how God is all in all, for there intervenes the cloud of fleshly thoughts and darkness of variegated phantasies, and the keenness of the mind is weakened by the irrational passions, and is turned back from the splendours of clear truth and is held in the grasp of the bodily shadows to which it has become accustomed. For it is not to be

believed of the celestial essences which have never abandoned the condition of eternal bliss that they know any other thing in the universal creature except God Himself. For in God and in the primordial causes they behold all things beyond every sense and intellect, since they do not require all the works of nature in order to see the truth, but use only the ineffable grace of the eternal light, and it was to bring human nature back to this vision that the Incarnate Word of God descended, taking it upon Himself after it had fallen in order that He might recall it to its former state, healing the wounds of transgressions, sweeping away the shadows of false phantasies, opening the eyes of the mind, showing Himself in all things to those who are worthy of such a vision.

IX.3.8. Man contains all Creatures (from *Periphyseon*, bk IV).

[Here Eriugena presents his own version of the Plotinian theme that Man is a microcosm in which all creatures are represented. Note that the doctrine that there is no possibility of knowing *what* God is is now applied to Man as well. There is no knowing *what* man is since man is ultimately God and God is beyond all "whats."]

ALUMNUS: We should understand, then, that man has two substances, one that is a genus among the Primordial Causes, and another which is a species among the effects of those Causes.

NUTRITOR: No, I should not say that there were two substances, but one which may be conceived under two aspects. Under one aspect the human substance is perceived as created among the intelligible Causes, under the other as generated among their effects; under the former free from all mutability, under the latter subject to change; under the former simple, involved in no accidents, it eludes all reason and intelligence; under the latter it received a kind of composition of quantities and qualities and whatever else can be understood in relation to it, whereby it becomes apprehensible to the mind. So it is that what is one and the same thing can be thought of as twofold because there are two ways of looking at it, yet everywhere it preserves its incomprehensibility, in the effects as in the causes, and whether it is endowed with accidents or abides in its naked simplicity, under neither set of circumstances is it subject to created sense or intellect nor even the knowledge of itself as to *what* it is.

A.: How can it be, then, that the human mind, as you have been asserting now for some time, possesses a notion by which it knows itself and a discipline by which it learns of itself; and yet, as you now maintain, is not discernible either to itself or to any other creature?

N.: Both assertions have the full support of reason. For the human mind does know itself, and again does not know itself. For it knows *that* it is, but does not know *what* it is. And as we have taught in the earlier books it is this which reveals most clearly the Image of God to be in man. For just as God is comprehensible in the sense that it can be deduced from His creation *that* He is, and incomprehensible because it cannot be comprehended by any intellect whether human or angelic nor even by Himself *what* He is, seeing that He is not a thing but is superessential, so to the human mind it is given to know one thing only, *that* it is — but as to *what* it is no sort of notion is permitted it; and, a fact which is stranger still and to those who study God and man, more fair to contemplate, the human mind is more honoured in its ignorance than in its knowledge; for the ignorance in it of *what* it is is more praiseworthy than the knowledge *that* it is, just as the negation of God accords better with the praise of His Nature than the affirmation and it shows greater wisdom not to know than to know that Nature of Which ignorance is the true wisdom and Which is known all the better for not being known. Therefore the Divine Likeness in the human mind is most clearly discerned when it is only known *that* it is, and not known *what* it is; and, if I may so put it, *what* it is is denied in it and only *that* it is is affirmed. Nor is this unreasonable. For if it were known to be something, then at once it would be limited by some definition, thereby would cease to be a complete expression of the Image of the Creator, Who is absolutely unlimited and contained within no definition, because He is infinite, beyond all that may be said or comprehended, superessential.

A.: How then is every creature made in the knowledge of man, which does not even know of itself *what* it is, and this is thought to be its greatest glory, the mark of a superior nature and indication that it is circumscribed by no finite substance?

N.: I assure you that there is a very strong argument which points to the fact that every creature is created as substance in man. For we are taught by Gregory the Theologian[27] (who touches on this matter in his controversy with those who deny that the Word of God is superessential and maintain that it is contained within some substance and therefore does not transcend all things but is to be counted among their number, seeking thereby to show a distinction between the Substance of the Father and the Substance of the Son), that of the substance of all things we cannot have a definition of *what* it is. So the human replica of the Divine Essence is not bound by any fixed limit any more than the Divine Essence in Whose Image it is made. And it is the same with the attributes by which it is surrounded: its time and place; its differences and properties; its acts and its passions; of these too it can only be understood that they exist but by no means what they are. From this it follows that there is no creature that can be held to possess any other substance but that reason by which it subsists in the Primordial Causes within the Word of God, and thus there can be no definition of *what* it is, seeing that it transcends every substantial definition. There can only be circumstantial definition, which relates to its accidents whereby it proceeds through generation into its proper species, either intelligible or sensible.

A.: Both Holy Scripture and our own reason declare that the human and the angelic nature are either the same or very similar; for both man and angel are held to be, and in fact are, intelligible and rational creatures. And if there is this close correspondence between them it is reasonable to enquire why we are taught that every creature is made in man but not in angel.

N.: There is a good reason for this, I think. For we observe in man not a few things which neither reason understands nor authority transmits to subsist in angel. For instance there is this animal body which, according to Holy Scripture, was attached to the human soul even before the Transgression;

---

27 St. Gregory Nazianzen, died 390. One of the early Greek Fathers of the Church.

there is the fivefold bodily exterior sense; there are the phantasies of sensible objects, which through that sense enter into the soul; there are the perplexity and difficulty which delay the reason's enquiries into the nature of the Universe; the painful industry which it requires to discriminate between vice and virtue; and very many other things of that sort. For that all these things are lacking to the angelic nature while present in [human] nature no truly wise person would deny.

Nevertheless, Augustine in the eighth book of the *City of God*, chapter seven [*sic*], would appear to have taught that the angels have sense, for in that chapter he praises the contemplative power of the great philosophers because "they saw that all forms of mutable things, whereby they are what they are (of what nature soever they be) have their origin from none but Him that truly is and is unchangeable. Consequently neither the body of this universe, the figures, qualities, ordered motion, and elements disposed from heaven down to earth, and whatever bodies are in them, nor any life – whether that which nourishes and conserves, as in the case of trees, or that which has this but also perceives, as in the case of the animals, or that which has all this but also understands, as in the case of man, or that which has no need of the support of nourishment, but conserves, perceives and understands, as in the case of the angels – can have being but from Him who has only simple being."

But I should say that he was here referring to the interior sense. For who does not know that the celestial being is untouched by very many of the parts and motions of nature which are naturally innate in the human being? And of those things which are not innate in it either as substance or happen to it as accident, it is not reasonable to hold that the celestial substance possesses the knowledge. For although the Angels are held to administer this world and every corporeal creature, yet we must by no means suppose they do so through the instrument of the corporeal senses or by movements through space or time or by visible manifestations. Now would it be right to say that it was through some defect in their power that they do not have those accidents which are ours through the shortcomings of a nature which is still subject to variations of space and time. For when they transform their spiritual and invisible bodies into visible apparitions in order to reveal themselves in space

and time to the mortal sense, they accept this accident not for their own sakes, but for the sake of those people of whom they are in charge and to whom they declare the mysteries of God. For with them vision is not exercised through sense nor conditioned by space, nor their knowledge of how they shall act in administering nature conditioned by time, for they eternally transcend all time, and all space in the contemplation of Truth, in which the causes of their administration are present all at once to their sight.

And do not suppose that I am speaking of all celestial essences, – I speak only of the higher orders who stand ever before the face of God and in whom there is no ignorance save that of the Divine Dark which excels every intellect. In fact, the lowest order, the angelic properly so called, through which the higher orders carry out the mandates of divine Providence either in the human mind by means of apparitions or in the other parts of this world, is not yet free from all ignorance, for, as St. Dionysius the Areopagite in his book on the *Celestial Heirarchy* most ingeniously shows, "It is instructed by the higher orders and initiated into knowledge of divine mysteries beyond its ken."

And so not unreasonably are we told to believe and understand that every visible and invisible creature is created in man alone. For no substance has been created which is not understood to subsist in him, no species or difference or property or natural accident is found in nature which either is not naturally in him or of which he cannot have knowledge; and the knowledge of the things which are contained within him excels the things of which it is the knowledge by so much as the nature in which it is constituted excels. For every rational nature is rightly preferred to the irrational and sensible nature because it is closer to God. Wherefore it is also rightly understood that the things of which the knowledge is innate in human nature have their substance in the knowledge of themselves. For where they have the better knowledge of themselves, there they must be considered to enjoy the truer existence. Furthermore, if the things themselves, and the notions of them, are naturally present to man, therefore in man are they universally created, as will no doubt be proved in due course by the Return of all things into man. For why should they all return to him if they did not in some sense partake of his nature, and did not in some manner proceed from him? But about the Return we have promised to speak in its proper place.

IX.3.9. The Return of all things to God (from *Periphyseon*, bk. V)

[The theme given a logical treatment in selection **4** of this section now gets developed as a kind of eschatology (doctrine of last things), which incorporates the overcoming of man's fall from the sexless paradise into the sexually opposed state we all now experience. Contrast this view with those of Augustine and Aquinas in selections **VIII.2.6** and **VIII.5.5**.]

ALUMNUS: We have now been talking long enough about the end of the world, or rather, about its Return into the eternal Causes from which it issued forth. But I should like to have a clearer idea about the consummation of this process.

NUTRITOR: I am surprised that you should ask this, when you yourself just now had no hesitation in defining the end of the world as the Eternal Causes which subsist always without change in the Word of God. And we had already agreed before that of all things that are in motion or at rest, or in mobile rest or stable motion, if I may use such an expression, the beginning does not differ from the end but is one and the same. So it follows that if the principles of the world are the Causes out of which it originated, its ends will lie in the same Causes, and to these it must return. When it has completed its course it will not be brought to nothing but led back to its Causes, and there it will be preserved and rest for all eternity. But if the Word of the Father, in whom all things are made and have their being, is the Cause of all causes both visible and invisible, will not the final end of the world be this Cause of Causes? Shall they not end in Him, when all movement shall find rest in that towards which it moves, and which is none other than the Word of God, an End beyond which the appetite of no creature can reach further? For there is no further goal to be sought or longed for: the common end of the whole creation is the Word of God. Thus both the

beginning and the end of the world are in the Word of God, indeed, to speak more plainly, they are the Word Itself, for It is the manifold end with out end and beginning without beginning, being *anarchos*, save for the Father.

Hence we may make a brief summary of the argument which it has required so much exposition to prove, and define the position thus: All things are from Him and to Him all things return; for He is the Beginning and the End. And this is most clearly the conclusion reached by the Apostle when he says: "Seeing that from Him and through Him and in Him are all things."

It is also very clearly manifest in the five-fold division of all created nature, which, as Maximus[28] in the thirty-seventh chapter of his *Ambigua* says, "is handed down by the authority of the Apostles." For here too we find the Return and the Unification of all things through the same divisions and mustations of the whole creature into the One, and finally into God Himself.

The first division of all natures is that which divides what is created from what is not created, which is God. The second divides created nature into sensible and intelligible.

The third divides the sensible into heaven and earth. The fourth distinguishes Paradise from the habitable globe. The fifth and final division segregates mankind into male and female.

In man every creature is established, both visible and invisible. Therefore he is called the workshop of all, seeing that in him all things which came after God are contained. Hence he is also customarily called the Intermediary, for since he consists of soul and body he comprehends within himself and gathers into one two ultimate extremes of the spiritual and corporeal. That is why the sacred account of the Creation of the Universe introduces him at the end of all, signifying that in him is the consummation of the totality of created nature.

So it is from the unification of the division of man into the two sexes that the Return and unification through all the other divisions will take its start. For in the Resurrection sexual differentiation will be done away, and human nature will be made one, and there will be only man as it would have

---

28 Maximus the Confessor, c.580-662, was one of the earliest writers to make extensive use of the Dionysian corpus and accept their attribution to the Dionysius Paul converted in Athens.

been if man had not sinned.

Next the inhabited globe will be made one with Paradise and there will be only Paradise. Then heaven and earth will be made one, and there will be only heaven. And note here that it is always the lower nature that is transformed into the higher. The sexually differentiated mankind is transformed into man, for sexuality is inferior to humanness; and so the inhabited globe, which is inferior to Paradise, is transformed into Paradise. Earthly bodies, being inferior, will be changed into heavenly bodies. Next, there is a unification of the whole sensible creature, followed by a transformation into the intelligible, so that the universal creature becomes intelligible. Finally the universal creature shall be unified with its Creator, and shall be in Him and with Him One. And this is the end of all things visible and invisible, for all visible things shall pass into intelligibles, and all intelligibles into God Himself. But, as we have often said, this wonderful and ineffable unification does not involve the confusion of the individual essences and substances.

IX.4. IBN TUFAIL

THROUGH A VARIETY OF NEO-PLATONIC TREATISES THE THOUGHT OF
Plotinus had a great impact on the philosophers of Islam, and certainly on Ibn
Sina (Avicenna) who attempted a kind of synthesis of neo-Platonism with
Aristotelian science. Within this context too there was ample room for mysticism.
Ibn Tufail, a learned polymath living in Spain and north Africa in the 12th century, exploited these possibilities in the charming tale told in his *The Journey of
the Soul*, a small portion of which is presented below. In it the mystic experience
is fitted into the context of the cosmology which the Islamic philosophers had
developed on the basis of Greek philosophy and science. The Platonist origins are
evident in the emphasis on unity over multiplicity and the disparagement of the
sensible and material world in comparison with the immaterial essences.

IX.4.1. The Experience of total Self-annihilation
(from *The Journey of the Soul*)

[*The Journey of the Soul* is the story of a man,
named "Hai ibn Yaqzan," who grows from infancy
to adulthood on a deserted island. In the course of
his life he learns by observation and reflection most
of science and philosophy and ultimately trains
himself to have the experience of union with the
source of all existence. At the beginning of the tale
ibn Tufail cannot resist displaying a bit of his learning in natural science while recounting the fanciful
tale of Hai ibn Yaqzan's origins.]

Our virtuous ancestors – may Allah be pleased
with them – have described a certain island of India
which lies below the equator. Since this island has
the fairest climate on Earth and is most advanta-
geously sited and prepared to receive the supreme
light, human beings can be formed there without
parents.

On this island, called by Al Masaudi[1] The Island
of Waq Waq,[2] a tree is to be found which bears
women as its fruit.

The view that the Island of Waq Waq has the best
of all climates is contrary to the view of philosophers and physicians who claim that the Fourth
Region has the fairest weather of all. If the philosophers make this claim for the Fourth Region
because they believe that some geographical condition makes human habitation along the Equator
impossible, then their point of view may be valid.
But if they say that the Fourth Region is the fairest
on Earth because – and most of them do so declare
– they believe that what lies along the Equator is
unbearably hot, then this is a fallacy easy to disprove.

It has been shown by the natural sciences that the
causes of heat are motion or contact with hot bodies or illumination. The natural scientists have also
found that polished, non-transparent bodies accept
illumination best, followed by dense, non-polished
bodies. Transparent bodies of low density do not
under any circumstances accept light. These findings are due to Sheikh Abu Ali and were not published by any of his predecessors. If these propositions are valid, it follows that the sun does not heat
the Earth in the way that hot bodies warm other
bodies in contact with them, since the sun is not
itself hot.

---

1 Abu al Hasan ibn al Masaudi was a geographer, traveller and historian who died about 956 C.E.
2 An island referred to in many stories, said to be situated in the east of the China Sea or above Zanzibar. It was supposed to be inhabited by creatures similar to human beings (females) who cry out "waq waq" and who drop dead if
touched. Other ancient sources mention an Indian tree called the Waq Waq which bears fruit that looks like a human
head suspended by the hair.

Neither can motion be the cause of the Earth's heat, since the Earth is stationary, occupying the same position at sunrise as it did at sunset. It is obvious to the senses, however, that the Earth warms up at sunrise and cools down at sunset.

Nor can it be a question of the air receiving warmth from the sun and transmitting this to the Earth by contact. How could this be so when we find that during the hot period, the air nearest the Earth is hotter than the air higher up? This leaves us with illumination as the only means by which the sun heats the Earth. Heat is always associated with light, as we discover if we concentrate light in a concave mirror and observe that it will set fire to what is near it.

Science has shown convincingly that the sun and the Earth are both spherical, the size of the sun being greater than the size of the Earth. Thus half of the Earth's surface is always receiving illumination from the sun, the point of maximum illumination being at the centre of this area, since this point is farthest from darkness and faces a larger section of the sun. Places on the Earth towards the circumference receive less light and this shades off into darkness when we reach the periphery of the circle which is out of the sun's illumination.

A place on the Earth is at the centre of illumination when the sun is at its zenith exactly overhead, heat being then at its maximum. At a great distance from such a place, the cold would be very great indeed.

Astronomy has ascertained that places on the Equator have the sun directly overhead only twice a year, in the sign of the Ram and the sign of the Balance. For the rest of the year, the sun is to the south for six months and to the north for six months. People in these areas avoid both excessive heat and excessive cold and enjoy a uniform climate.

This subject requires further explanation but this is not what we set out to do. We have brought it to your attention because it is one of the factors which confirms the truth of what has been said about the possibility of human formation, in certain regions, without parents.

Some sources claim that Hai ibn Yaqzan was one of those formed without parents. Others deny this and simply relate what we shall now tell you.

Near the island we spoke of there was another island, very large, fruitful and well populated. This island was owned and ruled over by an extremely proud and jealous man. This king had a sister of exquisite charm and beauty whom he forbade to marry because he had still to find someone he considered worthy and equal. The king also had a relative called Yaqzan and this man married the king's sister in secret but nonetheless lawfully, according to the rules of their sect.

Later she bore Yaqzan a son but fearing that her secret could no longer be kept, she suckled the child for the last time and placed him in a little coffin which she sealed all round. Then, her heart burning with love and with fear for the child, she took him to the seashore accompanied by a group of servants and intimates whom she trusted. There she bade him farewell, saying: "Oh God who has created this child from nothing, sustained him in the darkness of the womb and looked after him till he was completely formed, to you I surrender him now, praying that he may receive Your bounty, because of my fear for this stubborn, mighty and unjust king. Be with him and abandon him not, O most Merciful."

She then cast him into the sea. The tide was high and the strong current carried the child to the coast of the aforementioned island. It so happened that this night had the highest tide of the year and the force of the waves carried the coffin into a wood normally well clear of the sea. The wood was thick with trees, standing in good soil, sheltered from wind and rain and bending the sun's rays gently at sunrise and sunset.

The tide receded, leaving the coffin wedged in the trees. The wind now blew the sand till it built up, forming a barrier which would prevent further access to the sea, even at the highest tide. The nails holding the planks of the coffin together had been loosened when the waves threw it into the wood and the child inside being now hungry began to move and cry. His cries were heard by a doe who had lost her fawn – the fawn had ventured out of its shelter and been carried off by an eagle – and the doe thought the child's cries were the cries of her lost fawn.

The doe traced the sound and standing up with her front hooves on the coffin, she dislodged one of the planks, while the child moaned and groaned inside. The doe bent over the child and comforted him, then succeeded in suckling him with her delicious milk. From then on, she took charge of the child, caring for him and protecting him.

***

[Hai convinces himself of the existence of a necessary being (here ibn Tufail shows the influence of ibn Sina [Avicenna] – see selection **I.2.1-4**) on which all other beings depend for their existence and that he should "imitate" this being. This is referred to here as the "third form of imitation," the others being imitation of the animals and imitation of the heavenly bodies.]

He then started to strive for the third form of imitation. Before the period of his practical approach, he had already discovered by theoretical and intellectual consideration that the qualities of the Being whose existence is necessary are of two types. The first includes the qualities of permanence such as knowledge, power, and wisdom. The second are the negative qualities such as being above and beyond any association with matter and its qualities.

The quality of permanence requires transcendence over matter, since one of the qualities of physical matter is plurality and His essence is not multiple. All His attributes reduce to one, the reality of His essence. So he had to learn to imitate Him in each of these two ways.

Considering first the positive qualities he had to imitate, he realized that they were not many but only one. The awareness by Him of His own essence is not something additional to His essence. His essence *is* His consciousness of His own essence: His knowledge of His essence *is* His essence. If therefore he could come to know His essence, then the knowledge with which he came to know it would not be something distinct from His essence. It would be Him. Thus the third imitation, based on His positive qualities, means simply knowing Him without associating Him with any material or physical qualities. This he would strive to do. And as for the negative qualities, all these reduced simply to transcending the qualities of physical matter.

He began then to try to rid his essence of physical qualities. Much had already been discarded through the exercises he had done in imitation of the heavenly bodies but much still remained. He still employed rotary motion, and this was a cardinal quality of objects. He still exercised kindness to plants and animals, and this again was physical since he used physical senses to see their situation and used physical means to take action. He resolved to cast all this from him, seeing that in its totality it was unworthy of the state he sought.

He continued to cultivate solitude in his cave, head bent, eyes closed, unaware of all sensual objects and bodily forces, struggling only to concentrate on the Being whose existence is necessary. Whenever his imagination produced an image he would strive to banish it with all his might. Sometimes he persisted so intensely in trying to bring his self under control that days would pass during which he neither ate nor even moved.

During such an intense struggle all physical and material things vanished from his mind with one exception – his awareness of himself. Even while witnessing the first Being, the Truth, whose existence is necessary, awareness of himself remained. This disturbed him, for he recognized it as an imperfection in total witnessing, an association within his observation.

He continued to strive for sincerity in witnessing and for the annihilation of his self, and finally achieved it. The heavens and the earth and all that lies between them vanished from his thoughts and his memory. So also did spiritual visions, bodily forces and all the non-material forces which are the essences conscious of that Being which is Truth; and his own essence vanished with them. All became as scattered dust, shrunk, vanished. Only the Truth, the One, the Being whose existence is permanent, remained. As he says through His words, which add nothing to His essence: "For whom is the dominion today? It is for Allah, the One, the victorious!"[3] Though he was ignorant of these words and lacked human speech, he nevertheless understood these words and hearkened to His call. Immersed in this state, he saw what eyes have not seen nor ears heard, neither has human heart experienced.

Do not attach your desires to something that can be described but has not occurred in the human heart. Certain experiences can reach the heart which cannot be described. How much less can a

---

3 *The Koran*, surat Almomin, 16.

state be described which the heart cannot receive, this state being beyond the nature of the heart or its world?

By 'heart' I do not mean the physical heart, nor do I mean the spirit that resides there. What I mean is the form of that spirit which diffuses its powers through the human body. All of these three can be called a 'heart' but the state being indicated could not occur in any of them since description can refer only to what happens in these.

Explaining this state which he had reached is impossible. Any attempt is like someone trying to taste a colour and requiring that black, say, is to be sweet or sour. We shall not leave you, however, entirely without signs which may point to what he saw of the wonders of that stage – but as an analogy only and not as a knock on the door of the truth. The only way to verify that state is to reach it.

Hearken then with the hearing of your heart and stare with the vision of your mind at what I point out to you. Perhaps you will find in it guidance which will lead you on the proper path. I make only one condition: that you do not ask for further verbal description beyond what I am setting down on these pages; because the limits are fine and the strict control of expression on a matter which is beyond being put into words is a dangerous concern.

So, he was annihilated beyond his essence and beyond all other essences and could see within existence nothing but the One, the Living, the Self-subsisting; and he saw what he saw. When he awoke from this state, which is not unlike inebriation, and returned, he again saw other things. He realized that his own essence was no different from the Truth most high and that the reality of his own essence is the essence of Truth. He saw also that that which he had at first thought to be his essence and distinct from the essence of Truth was in reality nothing at all, for there is nothing other than the essence of the Truth.

An analogy would be light from the sun falling on dense bodies and apparently coming from them. In reality, it is nothing but the light of the sun. When the sun vanishes, the light vanishes. The light of the sun however remains intact and is neither reduced by the presence f the object nor increased by its absence. When a body suitable for registering the light of the sun appears, it receives the light. When

that body disintegrates its reception for the light vanishes also and no longer has any meaning. It was apparent to him that the essence of Truth – may He be exalted and glorified – never in any sense becomes multiple. His knowledge of His essence is His essence itself. He could therefore see that whoever acquires the *knowledge* of His essence also acquires His essence. As he had already acquired the knowledge, he had acquired the essence. Now this essence is not acquired except as itself; the act of acquiring it is the essence. He *was* now that essence, as were all the non-material essences which also knew Him. These he had earlier seen as a multiplicity but now knew were one.

This idea of multiplicity had come close to being fixed within him but Allah had responded with His mercy and, through his guidance, his thoughts had been put right. He then understood that such thoughts of multiplicity were generated in him merely because of the dark and impure influence of things physical and sensual. The concept of many and few; of the unit; of combination and collectedness; of separation – all these are merely the qualities of material objects. Nor should the non-material essences be described as one or many – they who, through their innocence of matter, know the Truth, glory and exaltation due to Him. Multiplicity is the contrasting of essences one with another; unity can be achieved only through union. The reality of all this is incomprehensible if we try to use concepts based on the relationship of material objects.

Possibilities for suggesting the real situation are limited in the extreme. If one refers to the non-material essences in the plural, as we have done, this implies that they are a multiplicity. But they are innocent of multiplicity. If one refers to them in the singular, this implies that they are not a unity, and it is impossible for them not to be a unity.

Whoever stops at this stage is like a bat blinded by the sun, which rushes about in its madness and says to itself: "You have gone so into excess with your scrutinizing that you have left the nature of the sane and shed the judgement of reason; a thing must be either one or many." But let the bat control the excesses of his tongue. Let him rather accuse himself of failing to do what Hai ibn Yaqzan did. Though enfolded in the low world of the senses, he used these senses to consider the situation from both points of view. He considered from one point of view and found unbounded multiplicity. He considered from another point of view and found unity. On the two viewpoints he reserved judgement.

The world of the senses is the source of plurality and of singularity, and only within the world of the senses do such concepts have a meaning. The sensory world yields a picture of separation and union, of agreement and disagreement, of accretion and dispersion. Any thoughts he had about the divine world which involved 'all' or 'some' or were capable of being conveyed in language, were necessarily imaginary and did not accord with reality. Only they know, who experience and witness. The real nature of Truth is ascertained only by those who acquire it. As for the saying, "You have left the nature of the sane and have shed the judgement of reason," let us grant the bat this and leave him with his logic and intellect.

For those who speak like this, mind is only the verbal power which examines the individual units in the world of the senses and arrives thereby at a general overall concept. The persons of reason are those who think and reason in this way. Our words are beyond all that. So let him who knows no more than the world of the senses shut his ears and return to his kind, who "know but the other things in the life of this world; but of the end of things they are heedless."[4]

So if you are one of those who can be convinced by the kind of sign and hint I have given as to what the divine world contains, and if you do not attach to our words the common and customary meanings associated with them, then we shall give you more of what Hai ibn Yaqzan saw in the station of the Friends of the Truth.

After he had experienced total annihilation, absorption, true arrival and union, he saw the highest sphere which has no physical body. He saw there an essence innocent of matter which was neither the essence of the One, the Truth, nor was it the essence of the highest sphere; nor was it different from these. It could be compared to the image of the sun as seen in a polished mirror. It is neither the sun nor the mirror nor is it anything other than them. He saw signs of such perfection, glory and

beauty in the essence of that non-material sphere so great as to be beyond description; too fine, too delicate to be clothed in letters or sound. In a state of ultimate pleasure, happiness, gladness and joy, his vision showed him the essence of Truth, glory be to His Majesty.

Just below the sphere just mentioned he saw another, the sphere of the fixed stars. Its essence too, was innocent of matter. This was not the essence of the One, the Truth, nor was it the essence of the highest sphere; nor was it either the same or other than they. It was not unlike a reflection of the sun as it appears in a mirror which has an image reflected on it from another mirror, which is facing the sun. In this essence he saw as much glory, beauty, and pleasure as he had seen in the highest sphere.

At the next sphere, the sphere of Saturn, he saw a non-material essence which was not of the essences he had seen before nor was it different from them. It was like the image of the sun as it appears in a mirror that has received its image from another mirror which in turn has received its image from a mirror facing the sun. In respect of this essence he saw what he had seen in respect of the others, as to glory and pleasure.

He witnessed, for each sphere in turn, a non-material essence which was not of the preceding essences nor was it other than they were. He saw the arrangement as similar to the image of the sun reflected from one mirror to another in a certain glory, beauty, pleasure and joy as no eye has seen and no ear heard and no heart has ever imagined.

He descended finally to the world of creation and decay and saw that all of it was within the bowels of the sphere of the moon. This, he saw, had a non-material essence which was not of, or different from, the essences he had witnessed before. This essence had seventy thousand faces. In each face there were seventy thousand mouths and in each mouth seventy thousand tongues each glorifying and praising unceasingly the essence of the One, the Truth. In this essence, which gave him the impression of multiplicity but was not multiple, he saw such perfection and pleasure as he had seen in the previous ones. This essence appeared as the image from the last mirror in a series, starting with

---

4 *The Koran*, surat Alrum, 7.

a first mirror facing the sun. He then saw a separate essence and had it been permissible to identify individuals among the seventy thousand faces he would have said that this was his own and he was one of them. Had this essence not been brought into being out of non-being he would have said that it was. And had it not been designated to his body at the time of his creation, he would have said that it did not come into being. In this gradation he saw essences not unlike his own, which had belonged to bodies which had been and gone. And he also saw essences that belonged to bodies which were still with him in the world of creation. They were of such quantity that if multiplicity could apply to essences, then their number was infinite. Otherwise they were one. For his own and for all other essences in the same rank he saw beauty, glory and limitless pleasure such as no eye has seen or ear heard or human heart conceived, indescribable and incomprehensible to all but the gnostics [the Sufis] – those who arrive.

He also saw many non-material essences which were like rusted mirrors, tarnished with dirt and turning their faces away from the polished mirrors which reflect the sun. In these essences he saw ugliness and error of unimaginable degree. He saw that they were in unending pain and he heard sighing he could never forget. He saw that they were in torture chambers being burned with the fire of the veil and ripped by saws of attraction and repulsion.

Beside the essences of the tormented ones he saw others which appeared and then disappeared, forming and then vanishing. He concentrated so as to examine this situation closely and understood that it amounted to something very serious – a calamity. It involved forming and reforming, serious (mis)judgements and hurried creations. It involved the creative breath.

Slowly he took hold of himself and his senses returned, as if he were awakening from a faint. As he returned to the world of the senses, his hold on his previous state was lost and the divine world receded; for both cannot be present in the same state. The world of creation and the other world are like a man with two wives; if he pleases one, he angers the other.

IX.5. MEISTER ECKHART

ECKHART WROTE INSPIRATIONAL PIECES IN BOTH LATIN and German as well as scholastic treatises. The following selections are from the former category. In his thought God and Intellect are merged in a non-Plotinian way, but there remains the emphasis on God as the One beyond being and the necessity of emptying the soul of all thoughts of created things if union with God is to be achieved.

IX.5.1. On the Names of God (from the *Commentary on Exodus*)

[Moses Maimonides in his *Guide for the Perplexed* had strongly reinforced the status of "negative theology" that pseudo-Dionysius had championed. (See selection **IX.2.2.**) In this selection Eckhart connects that theme to the familiar scholastic doctrine that God is Existence itself.]

161. As a consequence from what has been said, in the seventh place there is that other name of God, I mean the name "Who is." "He who is sent me."[1] John Damascene in Book 1 says that this is the first name of God,[2] and Thomas gives three beautiful reasons for this in Ia, q.13, a.11.[3]

162. This can be proven in another fashion here by the following four arguments. The first is this: No name is more proper to human being than the name 'human being.' Therefore, no name is more proper to Existence Itself than the name 'existence.' But God is Existence Itself, as we have said.

163. The second argument is this. That name is most proper to a thing which encompasses everything that belongs to and is attributed to it. But Existence Itself has and possesses everything which is proper to God. Therefore, this name 'existence' is the first and most proper of God's names.

The major is explained as follows. Not everything that exists is called 'human being,' nor everything that lives or senses, because all these thing are not proper to human beings, but are shared by other things. But everything which reasons and makes syllogisms is called 'human being,' because reasoning is proper to the thing called 'human being.'

The minor is evident by means of a universal induction, for example as in the text, "From him, through him and in him are all things."[4] The same is clear from the fact that God is everywhere, and from the fact that God is in everything created through power, presence, and essence, totally in each thing – totally within and totally without. Therefore, he is not moved, nor changed, nor corrupted when the hand is cut off, because the whole soul is in the hand in such a way that it is also completely outside the hand. You must not think that existence is not totally in every being, but only some part of existence. A part of existence is no existence and consequently does not give existence, just as a part of a human being is not a human being, and so on. Further, existence belongs to and is attributed to God because he is said to be lasting and eternal, having no cause nor principle, but himself being the cause and principle of all things. The same can be said about everything that is generally spoken about God. All these statements more plainly and clearly appear to belong to God under the name of existence than under the name of 'God.'

164. The minor and major premises of the second

---

1 *Exodus* 3:14.
2 John Damascene was the leader of the Christian community in Damascus in the 8th century. The reference is to his work, *De Fide Orthodoxa (On the Othodox Faith)*, 1.12.
3 The reference is to Thomas Aquinas' *Summa Theologiae*.
4 *Romans* 11:36.

argument are clear, and so the conclusion follows, that is, that of all the names of God 'existence' is the first and proper one. This is why Avicenna very frequently, especially in his *Metaphysics*, speaks of God as "necessary existence."[5] Rabbi Moses[6] and many others rightly do the same. Only God's existence is "necessary existence." Someone might perhaps think that 'existence' [*esse*] is the name of four letters itself, because the term 'existence' has literally four letters and many hidden properties and perfections. It also does not seem "to be derived from an operation nor express any participation." But this is enough.

165. The third argument for the thesis is this. In every being there are three things to consider: genus, species,[7] and *suppositum*.[8] Because a thing is constituted in existence, known and hence named from these three, it follows that any created thing received its name from genus, species, and the distinctiveness of the *suppositum*. For example, Martin truly is and is called an animal by virtue of genus; he is truly called a human being by virtue of species, and he is truly and distinctively called Martin by virtue of the distinctiveness of his *suppositum*. The names taken from the genus and species belong to many others and by nature are common and communicable to other beings besides Martin. Therefore, only the proper name that is taken from the distinctiveness and the idea of the *suppositum* (whatever it is) belongs to Martin and is incommunicable to other beings and proper to Martin alone. In God alone, if we could speak this way about the Godhead, the *suppositum* is totally identical with the nature of the species and genus, and existence is the selfsame simple thing, as Thomas says in the second book of his *Quodlibetal Questions*.[9] Therefore, the term existence is the proper name of God himself. This is what is said in the Psalm: "His name is in the

Selfsame"[10]; and Augustine in the ninth book of the *Confessions* when he discusses Psalm 4 ("In peace in the selfsame"[11]) says: "Oh in peace, Oh in the Selfsame ... You, O Lord, who do not change, are completely the same, because there is no other like you."[12] To say "in the selfsame" three times is important for referring to genus, species and *suppositum*. If someone says that God's name is "the Same," following the Psalm text, "But you are the same"[13] – that is, "the same thing" – then the first part refers to the nature and the second to the *suppositum*.

166. The fourth argument for the main thesis is this. That which is above every name excludes no name, but universally includes all names and in an equally indistinct way. None of these names will consequently be proper to it save that which is above every name and is common to all names. But existence is common to all beings and names, and hence 'existence' is the proper name of God alone.

167. The major is evident from the nature of what is essentially superior which always includes everything that is beneath it totally in itself, even in its least part. Thus, the whole of time and its differences are found in equal fashion in the now of eternity, the past and future no less than the present. The minor is explained thus. What does not participate in existence is not a being or a name. Wisdom, power, and each of these things either are not names or participate in that which is above every name. But that is existence alone. What is without existence does not exist, is not a name, but a false, empty, phony name. It is not a name, because it does not give knowledge. 'Name' [*nomen*] is derived from 'knowledge' [*notitia*] in that it is the mark of some concept in the intellect making that concept known to others. This is why nothing impossible deserves to be called a name or word, as the text says: "No word is impossible with God."[14]

---

5 See the selections in **I.2.**
6 I.e. Moses Maimonides.
7 See glossary entry for 'species/genus.'
8 See glossary entry for '*suppositum*.'
9 Thomas Aquinas, *Qdlb. Qus.* 2.2.4.
10 *Psalm* 33:4.
11 *Psalm* 4:9.
12 *Conf.* 9.4.11.
13 *Psalm* 101:28.
14 *Luke* 1:37.

168. With the major and the minor set forth, the conclusion follows, namely that 'existence' is the proper name of God alone. This is what is said in the Psalm, "You have magnified your holy name above all,"[15] and in Philippians 2, "He has given him a name which is above every name."[16] The twenty-second proposition of the *Book of Causes*[17] says, "The First Cause is above every name by which it is named."

169. According to Avicenna, "the first thing that comes into the intellect" and what is most general in understanding "is being."[18] This is the reason why the metaphysician in treating the primary beings and the first principles of things presupposes being, and why being is and is said to be his subject in that it underlies and is presupposed by everything, even the first act of knowing and grasping. Every noun and word is a mark and sign of a preceding apprehension. Hence the meaning of the passage about "everything that is impossible with God" is that anything whose existence is impossible will not be and is not a "word."

170. Finally, in the eighth place we must take a look at the universal[19] names of God, such as when he is called steadfast, generous, good, wise, and the like. On these you have [what I said above] on the fifteenth chapter concerning the text "Almighty is his name." I still have something to note here, first about affirmative terms, like wise and others, and second about negative ones.

171. Rabbi Moses in [*The Guide for the Perplexed*] 1.59 says: "Nothing is in the Creator but the true, perfectly realized simplicity." Therefore, anyone who "attributes positive denominations to the Creator seen in four ways." First, because the intellect and the apprehension of the one grasping something of this sort about God is "limited." Second, because such a person "makes God participate," that is, he understands him as having parts, and not as perfectly realized simplicity, or else as "participating," that is, he makes him participate and share something with the creature. Third,

because "he apprehends God other than he is"; and fourth, because such a person removes "God's existence from his heart," even if he does not know it.

172. He proves the premises in this chapter with the following words: "The explanation of this matter is that everyone who is limited in apprehending the truth of something grasps some part of its truth, but does not know how to grasp the other part, e.g., as when a person understands that a human being is alive, but not the truth of his rationality. In the Creator there is no multiplicity in the truth of his essence that would enable you to know one part and be ignorant of another. Similarly, one who shares something with someone knows the truth of some substance as it is and attributes the truth of the substance to something else. ... Likewise, one who apprehends a thing otherwise than it really is cannot do this without apprehending something of what it is. Concerning someone who thinks that taste is a quantity, I do not say that he thinks of the thing otherwise than it is, but that he does not know the essence of taste and does not know to what the term applies." Later on he says, "Anyone who attributes a denomination to the Creator ... thinks that the name applies to him. This is not in the nature of things, but is a useless thought, as though one were to use that name about something that did not exist, because there is no being like that."

173. He says, "An example would be of a person who has heard the name 'elephant' and knows that it is something alive. He wants to know its shape and truth, and someone responds who leads him astray, saying 'It is something having one foot and three wings that lives at the bottom of the sea. Its body shines like clear light, its face is like a human face, and sometimes it flies through the air, other times it swims in the sea like a fish.' Such a person would have the wrong idea of an elephant and would be limited in his apprehension; the way he conceived an elephant would be empty, because there is nothing like this among real beings. It is only a privation to

---

15 *Psalm* 137:2.

16 2:9.

17 The *Liber de Causis*, a work long thought to be by Aristotle but really by the 5th-century neo-Platonist Proclus (his *Elements of Theology*), and thus heavily endowed with Plotinian doctrine. Aquinas seems to have been one of the first to realize that the work could not be genuinely Aristotelian.

18 *Metaphysics* 1.2.

19 See glossary entry for 'universal.'

which the name of a being is attributed."[20]

174. This is why he says in another chapter that the sages find it is dangerous, harmful, and unfitting to hear someone piling up words about God even in prayer, due to the imperfection which names and words entail and their distance from God's simplicity. Thus the text of the sage, "God is in heaven, you are upon the earth, therefore let your words be few"; and in Psalm 4 according to another version it says, "Speak in your hearts and on your beds and always be silent."[21] Again, in another Psalm where we have "A hymn is fitting for you, O God,"[22] the text of Rabbi Moses has, "Silence is praise for you," or "To be silent is praise for you." Therefore, he concludes that "our every affirmative apprehension of God ... is defective for drawing near to understanding him. ... Whatever we say of God in praise and exaltation ... diminishes what belongs to him and is a defect," or withdrawal from knowing him. This is how to explain the verse of 1 *Kings* 2: "Do not multiply words to speak lofty things."[23] Rabbi Moses also says, "Let the Creator be praised. In the apprehension of his essence the inquiries of the sciences receive their limit, wisdom is held to be ignorance, and elegance of words is foolishness."[24] The Savior himself says, "When you pray, do not say many words"[25]; and *Proverbs* 10 says, "Where there are many words sin is not lacking."[26]

175. A threefold reason can now again be given for what has been said. The first point is this. Everything which with us is found in things is in them in a formal sense, but in God they are in no way formally found, because they do not inform him, but [they are there] virtually.[27] To grasp these things or to affirm them of God is false and unfitting, just as if we were to call God a circle or changeable. There is no circle or changeableness in God, but rather the idea of the circle and the idea of changeableness. The idea of circle is not a circle itself, nor is the idea of changeableness changeable, just as there is no stone in the soul, but the [intelligible] species[28] of a stone.

176. The second reason is this. Reason in its essence belongs to intellect and to truth, for truth is only in the intellect, not outside it. Therefore, the perfections in exterior things are not true perfections, and to attribute them to God is to apprehend him imperfectly and as not being totally pure Intellect himself, but as being something external, at least with some part of him, as is the case in created intellects.

177. The third reason is this. Existence receives nothing, since it is last, and it is not received in anything, since it is first. But God is existence, "the first and the last."[29] Therefore, nothing is positively received by God nor apprehended truly in him, but it is empty and incorrect. So much for the affirmative names applied to God.

178. In the second place we need to look at what is negatively said about God. The first thing to recognize here is that "a negative statement provides no truth about the thing to which the statement applies" – nor about anything that is in it.[30] Therefore, "from negatives nothing follows,"[31] is known, or established in existence. A twofold question remains. First, according to the saints and doctors in general how is it that negations in the Godhead or in God are true? Hence, even Rabbi Moses himself, as mentioned above, says about the

---

20 This is taken from *The Guide for the Perplexed* 1.60, but in a rather different form from that found in modern versions.

21 *Psalm* 4:5.

22 *Psalm* 64:2.

23 verse 4.

24 *The Guide for the Perplexed* 1.58.

25 *Matthew* 6:5.

26 verse 19.

27 See glossary entry for 'virtual existence.'

28 See glossary entry for 'species.'

29 *Isaiah* 44:6.

30 Maimonides, *The Guide for the Perplexed*, 1:59.

31 From Peter of Spain, *Summulae Logicales*, 4, a favourite logical textbook in the later middle ages.

32 verse 3.

passage in *Exodus* 15 "Almighty is his name"[32]: "Know that a negative proposition concerning the Creator is true; there is nothing doubtful in it, nor does it detract from the Creator's truth in any way. But an affirmative proposition about him is partly equivocal and partly imperfect." Later he says, "we do not have any way to speak about God except through negatives." Further, what is the difference between Moses, Solomon, Paul, John, and the other wise men and any nincompoop whatever in knowing God if the only things they know about him are pure negations?

179. There is still the second question. How do negatives spoken about God differ from affirmatives if the latter posit nothing, and the former, that is, the negatives, do not posit either, but only deny? [In answer to this] know that affirmations of their nature produce knowledge of something that is either the substance of what is being talked about, or what belongs to it, such as a property or an accident. Negations, on the other hand, are not so by nature, but as negative terms they signify only the removal or privation of a perfection. Negation surely takes away the whole of what it finds and posits nothing. Blindness, as Anselm says, does not posit anything more in the eye than it does in the stone.[33] Therefore, the negations that are said of God only show that nothing of what is found in external things and grasped by the senses is in him.

180. To make this clearer, let us look at an example.[34] Someone sees "a person far off," and asks what it is. Somebody answers and says that what he sees and asks about is "a living thing." Someone else responds that what he sees is not metal nor a stone. The first respondent, though he did not fully and exactly say what it was that was seen, still brought something to mind which in some way belongs "to the universe" that one sees. The second, however, who said that what was seen was not a stone, said nothing at all about the substance or anything in the substance, except by way of negation. This is the solution to the second question.

181. As far as both parts of the first question are concerned, we can say that just as a negation in law is not a direct but an indirect proof (e.g., Martin did not commit adultery at Thebes, if he was seen at Athens on that day and at that hour), so in our proposition the manifest works of God prove that he is not material, and therefore it is an evident conclusion that he is free from every imperfection that accompanies the property of matter, such as ignorance, capacity to change, and the like. Because privation necessarily follows possession, and negation is based on affirmation, it can be decisively concluded that something exists in God, whatever it is, that excludes ignorance, capacity to change, and this sort of thing, just as light does darkness and good evil.

182. Here note that "negative names are not attributed to the Creator save in the way in which one denies something of a thing that is not fittingly found in it, for example, when we say that a wall does not see."[35] in the same way we say that the heavens are not "composed of matter and form" found in things that corrupt, and that "the heavens are neither light nor heavy, nor 'made,' nor do they receive passing influences. nor do they have a flavor or odor, or anything of the sort." We say all these things, "because we are ignorant of their nature." As *Wisdom* 9 says, "Who will investigate what is in heaven?"[36] This is the answer to the first part of the first question.

183. As for the second part, know that "whatever you add by way of negative names with respect to the Creator, you come nearer to grasping him and will be closer to him than the person who does not know how to remove from God the perfections and attributes that have been proven to be far from him. It will be a conclusion and advance for knowledge to prohibit and remove from the Creator by way of negative names those things that have been proven to be meaningless when applied to him."[37] Let us give an example. Say there is someone who does not know how to prove that God is not a body. Therefore, when he thinks of God, he imagines him to be a body, having the qualities and properties he

---

33 St. Anselm, *Virginal Conception* 5.
34 From *The Guide for the Perplexed* 1, 58.
35 Ibid.
36 verse 16.
37 *The Guide for the Perplexed* 1, 58.

sees in bodies. Another person knows through demonstration that God is not a body and does not possess the things that are perfections in bodies, and that to posit them in God is impossible because they have many imperfections. There is a third person who knows by demonstration that not only corporeality, but also all matter is far from God, and consequently all the properties of matter, such as corruptibility, the capacity to change, and the like, are also distant from him. Even the things that seem to be perfections in material things, but are really only remedies of imperfections, for example, motion, generation, corruption, alteration, and things of the sort, are not in God in any way. There is a fourth person who knows how to prove universally that nothing that is created or limited or determined to some genus of being is in God. Hence in God himself there is nothing which signifies an end or a limit, like definition, or demonstration, existence from another, the possibility of nonexistence, all changeableness, instability, and anything of the sort.

How great the perfection in knowledge of the second person is in relation to that of the first, the third to the second and the fourth to the third is clear. This is sufficient for the other part of the first question. The stronger the argument by which a person removes these attributes from God, the more perfect he is in divine knowledge. The same holds for one who knows how to deny many such things of him by means of the removal that happens through negative names.

184. Rabbi Moses says, "Therefore, the sages agree that the sciences do not grasp the Creator, and only he himself understands himself. Our understanding in his case is a distancing rather than an approach to grasping him."[38] Hence Plato, as Macrobius says,[39] when "he was inspired to speak about God did not dare to say what he is, but only knew that no one can know what he is." This supports the axiom of Socrates: "I know that I do not know," which is like saying, "The one thing I know about God is that I do not know him." Algazel[40] toward the end of the third tractate of his *Metaphysics* agrees with all this, as do many of the ancient philosophers.

IX.5.2. "God is One"[41] (from *Latin Sermon XXIX.*) *Thirteenth Sunday after Pentecost. On the Epistle (Galatians 3:16-22)*

[*One* is the most basic attribute of God, but Eckhart derives from this that God is first and foremost pure Intellect.]

295. "God," Anselm says "God is that than which nothing better can be thought."[42] Augustine in Book One of *Christian Doctrine* says, "the God of gods is thought of as something than which nothing is better or higher"; and further on, "You can't find anyone who thinks that God is something which has a better."[43] Bernard[44] in the fifth Book of *On Consideration* says, "What is God? That than which nothing better can be thought."[45] In the prologue to the *Natural Questions* Seneca[46] says, "What is God? The totality that you see and the totality that you don't see. His greatness belongs to him in such a way that nothing greater can be conceived."[47]

296. God is infinite in his simplicity and simple by reason of his infinity. Therefore, he is everywhere and everywhere entire. He is everywhere by his infinity, but entire everywhere by reason of his simplcity. God alone flows into all created beings, into their essences; nothing of other beings flows into anything else. God is the inner reality of each thing, and only in the inner reality. He alone "is one."

297. Note that every creature loves the One in

---

38 Maimonides, *Ibid.*
39 *Commentary on the Dream of Scipio*, 1.2.15. Macrobius was a neo-Platonic writer who lived around 400 C.E.
40 I.e., Al-Ghazali.
41 *Galatians 3:20; Deuteronomy 6:4.*
42 *Proslogion 2.* See selection **II.2.1.**
43 1:15-16.
44 St. Bernard of Clairvaux, 12th-century church reformer and theological opponent of Peter Abelard.
45 5.7.15.
46 The Roman Stoic who committed suicide at the command of the Emperor Nero in 65 C.E.
47 1, Preface 13.

God, loves him for the sake of the One and loves him because he "is one." The first reason is that everything that exists loves and seeks God's likeness, and likeness is a kind of unity of certain things. The second reason is that in the One there is never pain, punishment, or distress, nor ability to suffer or die. Third, because all things exist in the One by the very fact that it is the One. Every multiplicity is one and one thing in the One and through the One. Fourth, neither power nor wisdom nor goodness itself, nor even existence, would be loved unless they were united to us and we to them.

298. Fifth, who truly loves can love only one thing, hence to our text "God is one" there follows "You shall love the Lord your God with your whole heart."[48] Certainly, whoever loves something totally does not want it to be more than one. Sixth, because he wishes to be united with what he loves and this is not possible unless it be one. Furthermore, God would not unite anything to himself except because he is one and by reason of being one. Also, by the fact that he is one he necessarily unites all things and unites them in and to himself. Seventh, because the One is indistinct from all things, and here all things and the fullness of existence are found in it by reason of indistinction or unity. Eighth, the One properly refers to what is whole and perfect, and so once again nothing is wanting to it. Ninth, note that the One essentially refers to Existence Itself or to unitary essence, for essence is always one. Union or the ability to be united belongs to it by reason of this unity.

299. On this basis, observe that a person who truly loves God as the One and for the sake of the One and union no longer cares about or values God's omnipotence or wisdom because these are multiple and refer to multiplicity. Nor do they care about goodness in general, both because it refers to what is outside and in things and because it consists in attachment, according to the Psalm text, "It is good for me to adhere to God."[49]

Tenth, note that the One is higher, prior, and simpler than the Good Itself, and it is closer to Existence Itself and to God, or rather according to

its name it is one existence in or with Existence Itself. Eleventh, God is unstintingly rich because "he is one." He is first and supreme by the fact that "he is one." Hence the One descends into each and every thing, always remaining one and uniting what is divided. (This is why six is not twice three, but six times one.)

300. "Hear, Israel, your God is one God." At this point note that unity or the One pertains to and is a property of the intellect alone. Material beings are both one and not one insofar as they have size or at least are composed of form and matter. Immaterial beings, such as intellectual ones, are also not one, either because their essence is not existence, or perhaps rather because their existence is not understanding. They are composed of existence and essence or of existence and understanding. (See the *Book of Causes*,[50] the comment on the last proposition.) And so the text says significantly, "Your God is one God," the God of Israel, a God who sees, a God of those who see, a God who understands and is understood by intellect alone, who is totally intellect.

301. "God is one." This can be taken in two ways. First thus: "God is one," for by the fact that he is one, existence belongs to him, that is, he is his existence, he is pure existence, and he is the existence of all things. Second thus: "Your God is one God," as if nothing else is truly one because nothing created is pure existence and totally intellect. For then it would no longer be creatable. Similarly, in the case of anything whatever I ask whether it has intellect or understanding or not. If not, it is clear that because it lacks intellect, it is not God or the First Cause of all the things ordered to definite ends. If it does have intellect, I ask whether there is any existence besides understanding in it or not. If not, I already have what is simply One, and what is uncreatable, first and the like – and that is God. If it has some existence other than understanding, it is already composed and not simply One. It is very clear then that God is properly alone and that he is intellect or understanding and that he is purely and simply understanding with no other existence. Therefore only God brings things into existence

through intellect because existence is understanding in him alone. Also, only he can be pure understanding – otherwise they would not be creatures, both because understanding is uncreatable and because "existence is the first of created things."[51]

302. On the basis of what has been said, all the things that follow upon the One or unity (equality, likeness, image, relation, and the like) in the universal sense are properly only in God and in the Godhead. Augustine in *True Religion* speaks of "that true equality or likeness."[52]

303. The reason is, first, that they follow upon unity which is proper to God, as was said. Second, because all these things are spoken of as the One in many, the One which is found nowhere and at no time save in intellect. It does not exist, but it is understood. Where existence is not Understanding Itself there is never equality. Only in God is existence the same as Understanding. A third reason is that two things that are alike and equal cannot be likeness itself and equality itself. The same is true for the others. Fourth, in the universe there are never two things completely equal and alike in all things, for then they would not be two or related to each other. Fifth, diversity, deformity, and the like are always found outside intellect, as the Psalm text says: "You are always the self-same."[53] Identity is unity.

304. From what has been said you can understand the way in which one "who adheres to God is one spirit."[54] Intellect properly belongs to God, and "God is one." Therefore, anything has as much of God and of the One and of "One-Existence" with God as it has of intellect and what is intellectual. For God is one intellect and intellect is one God. Nowhere and never do we find God as God save in intellect. In the tenth Book of the *Confessions* Augustine says, "Where I found truth there I found my God, Truth itself."[55] Rise up then to intellect; to be attached to it is to be united to God. To be united, to be one, is to be one with God. "God is one." Every kind of existence that is outside or beyond intellect is a creature; it is creatable, other than God, and is not God. In God there is nothing other.

305. Act and potency are divisions of the existence of all created being. Existence is the first act, the first division; but in the Intellect, in God, there is no division. This is why Scripture always exhorts us to go out of this world, to go out of ourselves, to forget our house and the house of our origin, to go forth from our land and our relations so that we may grow into a great people, so that all nations may be blessed in such a person (see *Genesis* 12:1-3). This best takes place in the region of the intellect where without doubt all things, insofar as they are intellect and not other, are in all things.

IX.5.3. The Intellect perceives God bare of Goodness and Being (*German Sermon 9*)

[Not only is God Intellect but it is intellect which perceives God as He is beneath all the usual attributes theology claims for him.]

"As the morning star through the mist and as the full moon in its days and as the resplendent sun, so did this man shine in the temple of God" (*Wisdom 50:6-7*)

First I shall take the last phrase: "temple of God." What is "God" and what is "temple of God"?

Twenty-four philosophers came together and wanted to discuss what God is. They came at the appointed time and each of them gave his definition. I shall now take up two or three of them. One said: "God is something compared to which all changeable and transitory things are nothing, and everything that has being is insignificant in his presence." The second said: "God is something that is of necessity above being; that in himself needs no one and that all things need." The third said: "God is intellect living in the knowledge of himself alone."

I shall leave aside the first and the last definition and speak about the second, that God is something that of necessity must be above being. Whatever has being, time, or place does not touch God. He is

---

51 *Book of Causes*, prop. 4.
52 30.55.
53 *Psalm* 101:28.
54 1 *Corinthians* 6:17.
55 10.24.35.

above it. God is in all creatures, insofar as they have being, and yet he is above them. That same thing that he is in all creatures is exactly what he is above them. Whatever is one in many things must of necessity be above them. Some masters have gone astray here. The soul is complete and undivided at the same time in the foot and in the eye and in every part of the body. If I take a segment of time, it is neither today nor yesterday. But if I take "now," that contains within itself all time. The "now" in which God made the world is as near to this time as the "now" in which I am presently speaking, and the last day is as near to this "now" as the day that was yesterday.

One authority says: "God is something that works in eternity undivided in himself; that needs no one's help or instrumentality, and remains in himself; that needs nothing and that all things need, and toward which all things strive as to their final end."[56] This end has no limited manner of being. It grows out beyond manner and spreads out into the distance. St. Bernard says: "To love God is a manner without manner." A physician who wants to make a sick person healthy does not have any degree of health [to measure] how healthy he wants to make the sick person. He certainly has a manner by which he wants to make him healthy, but how healthy he wants to make him – that does not have a manner: as healthy as he can! How we should love God has no manner: as much as we at all can, that is, without manner.

Everything works in being; nothing works above its being. Fire cannot work except in wood. God works above being in vastness, where he can roam. He works in nonbeing. Before being was, God worked. He worked being when there was no being. Unsophisticated teachers say that God is pure being. He is as high above being as the highest angel is above a gnat. I would be speaking as incorrectly in calling God a being as if I called the sun pale or black. God is neither this nor that. A master says: "Whoever imagines that he has understood God, if he knows anything, it is not God that he knows."[57] However, in saying that God is not a being and is above being, I have not denied being to God; rather, I have elevated it in him. If I take copper [mixed] with gold, it is still present and is present in a higher manner than it is in itself. St. Augustine says: God is wise without wisdom, good without goodness, powerful without power.[58]

Young masters say in the schools that all being is divided into ten modes of being[59] and they deny them completely of God. None of these modes touches God, but neither does he lack any of them. the first mode, which has the most of being in which all things receive being, is substance; and the last mode, which contains the least of being, is called relation, and in God this is the same as the greatest of all which has the most of being. They have equal images in God. In God the images of all things are alike, but they are images of unlike things. The highest angel and the soul and a gnat have like images in God. God is neither being nor goodness. Goodness adheres to being and is not more extensive. If there were no being, neither would there be goodness. Yet being is purer than goodness. God is neither good nor better nor best of all. Whoever would say that God is good would be treating him as unjustly as though he were calling the sun black.[60]

And yet God says: No one is good but God alone. What is good? Good is that which shares itself. We call a person good who shares with others and is useful. Because of this a pagan master says: A hermit is neither good nor evil in a sense because he does not share and is not useful. God shares most of all. Nothing [else] shares itself out of what is its own, for all creatures are nothing in themselves. Whatever they share they have from another. Nor is it themselves that they give. The sun gives its radiance yet remains where it is; fire gives its heat but remains fire. God, however, shares what is his because what he is, he is from himself. And in all the gifts he gives he always gives himself first of all.

---

56 Eckhart seems to be citing himself here. Similar passages are found in his Latin works.

57 Again Eckhart seems to be citing himself.

58 *On the Trinity* 5.1.2.

59 Eckhart refers here to the ten Aristotelian categories. See glossary entry for 'category' and selection **VI.1.1**.

60 This sentence was used against Eckhart in the bull of condemnation of his teachings drawn up by the church authorities.

He gives himself as God, as he is in all his gifts, to the extent that the person who can receive him is capable. St. James says: "All good gifts flow down from above from the Father of lights."[61]

When we grasp God in being, we grasp him in his antechamber, for being is the antechamber in which he dwells. Where is he then in his temple, in which he shines as holy? Intellect is the temple of God. Nowhere does God dwell more properly than in his temple, in intellect, as the second[62] philosopher said: "God is intellect, living in the knowledge of himself alone," remaining in himself alone where nothing ever touches him; for he alone is there in his stillness. God in the knowledge of himself knows himself in himself.

Now let us understand this in the soul, which has a drop of understanding, a little spark, a sprout. The soul has powers which work in the body. One such power is that through which one digests. It works more at night than during the day. Because of it one gains weight and grows. The soul also possesses a power in the eye, because of which the eye is so delicate and refined that it does not perceive things in the coarse condition in which they exist. They have to be previously sifted and refined in the air and the light. This is because the eye has the soul within it. There is another power in the soul with which it thinks. This power forms things within itself which are not present, so that I know the things as well as if I were seeing them with my eyes; even better. I can call to mind a rose just as well in winter. And with this power the soul works in nonbeing and so follows God who works in nonbeing.

A pagan master says: "The soul that loves God loves him under the coat of goodness."[63] All these words which have been quoted up to now are those of pagan masters, who knew only in a natural light; I have not yet come to the words of sacred masters, who knew in a much higher light. The pagan says: "The soul that loves God perceives him under the coat of goodness." The intellect pulls off the coat from God and perceives him bare, as he is stripped of goodness and of being and of all names.

I said in a lecture that the intellect is nobler than the will, and yet they both belong in this light. A professor in another school said that the will was nobler than the intellect because the will grasps things as they are in themselves, while the intellect grasps things as they are in it.[64] This is true. An eye is nobler in itself than an eye that is painted on a wall. Nevertheless, I say that the understanding is nobler than the will. The will perceived God in the garment of goodness. The understanding perceives God bare, as he is stripped of goodness and being. Goodness is a garment by which God is hidden, and the will perceives God in this garment of goodness. If there were no goodness in God, my will would want nothing of him. If someone wanted to clothe a king on the day when he was to be made king, and if one clothed him in gray attire, such a one would not have clothed him well. I am not happy because God is good. I shall never beg that God make me happy with his goodness because he could not do it. I am happy for this reason alone – because God is of an intellectual nature and because I know this. A master says that God's intellect is that upon which the being of an angel depends completely. One can pose the question: Where is the being of an image most properly? In the mirror or in the object from which it comes? It is more properly in the object from which it comes. The image is in me, from me, to me. As long as the mirror is placed exactly opposite my face, my image is in it. If the mirror were to fall, the image would disappear. An angel's being depends upon this: that the divine understanding in which it knows itself is present to it.

"As the morning star through the mist." I would now like to focus on the little word 'quasi' which means 'as.' Children in school call this an adverb.[65] This is what I focus on in all my sermons. What one can most properly say about God is that he is word and truth. God called himself a word. St. John said: "In the beginning was the Word."[66] He means that

---

61 *James* 1:17.

62 Actually the third.

63 The source of this has not been identified.

64 This is the Franciscan theologian Gonsalvo of Spain, with whom Eckhart debated.

65 Actually '*biwort*,' which is translated here as 'adverb,' can refer to just about any part of speech except to a noun or verb. It can also mean allegory.

one should be an ad-verb [*adverbum* or *biwort*] to the Word [*verbum* or *wort*]. The planet Venus, after which Friday is named, has many names. When it precedes and rises before the sun, it is called the morning star; when it so follows that the sun sets first, it is called an evening star. Sometimes its path is above the sun, sometimes below the sun. In contrast to all the other stars it is always equally near the sun. It never departs farther from, nor approaches nearer to, the sun. It stands for a person who wants always to be near to and present to God in such a way that nothing can separate them from God, neither happiness nor unhappiness, nor any creature.

The sage also says: "as the full moon in its days."[67] The moon rules over all moist nature. The moon is never so near the sun as when it is full and is receiving its light directly from the sun. Because it is closer to the earth than any star, it has two defects: It is pale and spotted, and it loses its light. It is never so powerful as when it is farthest from the earth, because then it causes the ocean to rise the most. The more it wanes, the less it causes it to rise. The more the soul is raised above earthly things, the more powerful it is. Whoever knew but one creature would not need to ponder any sermon, for every creature is full of God and is a book. The person who wants to achieve what we have just spoken about – and this is the whole point of the sermon – should be like the morning star: always present to God, always with him and equally near him, and raised above all earthly things. He should be an "ad-verb" to the Word.

There is one kind of word which is brought forth, like an angel and a human being and all creatures. There is a second kind of word, thought out and not brought forth, as happens when I form a thought. There is yet another kind of word that is not brought forth and not thought out, that never comes forth. Rather, it remains eternally in him who speaks it. It is continually being conceived in the Father who speaks it, and it remains within. The understanding always works internally. The

more refined and immaterial a thing is, the more powerfully it works internally. And the more powerful and refined the understanding is, the more that which it knows is united with it and is more one with it. This is not the case with material things – the more powerful they are, the more they work outside themselves. God's happiness depends on his understanding's working internally, where the Word remains within. There the soul should be an ad-verb and work one work with God in order to receive its happiness in the same inwardly hovering knowledge where God is happy.

That we may be forever an ad-verb to this Word, for this may we receive the help of the Father and the same Word and the Holy Spirit. Amen.

IX.5.4. The "Negation of Negation" (from *German Sermon* 21)

[Unity is the denial of distinction, while distinction is itself a negation of the other. Since God is not distinct from anything, He is this negation of a negation.]

St. Paul says, "One God."[68] *One* is purer than goodness and truth. Goodness and truth do not add anything [to God]; they add something only in the thought. When it is thought, it is added. *One* adds nothing to him as he is before he flows out into the Son and the Holy Spirit. Hence he says, "Friend, draw yourself up higher."[69] A master says: "One is a negation of negation."[70] If I say God is good, this adds something [to him]. *One* is a negation of negation and a denial of denial. What does 'one' mean? 'One' means something to which nothing has been added. The soul receives the Godhead as it is purified in itself, where nothing has been added, not even in thought. *One* is a negation of negation. All creatures have a negation in themselves; one creature denies that it is the other creature. One angel denies that it is some other angel. But God has a negation of negation; he is one and negates everything other, for outside of God is

---

66 *John* 1:1.
67 *Wisdom* 50:6.
68 *Ephesians* 4:6.
69 *Luke* 14:10.
70 Thomas Aquinas, *Quodlibetal Questions* 10.1.1. ad 3, and elsewhere.

nothing. All creatures are in God and are his very Godhead, and this implies an abundance, as I said previously. He is one Father of the whole Godhead. I say "one Godhead" because here nothing is yet flowing out, nor is it touched at all or thought. By negating something of God – say, I negate goodness of him (of course, I cannot really negate anything of him) – by negating something of God, I catch hold of something that he is *not*. It is precisely this that has to be removed. God is one, he is a negation of negation.

IX.5.5. The Attraction of the Soul to the One
(from *The Book of "Benedictus": The Book of Divine Consolation*)

[The attraction of like things to each other is a Dionysian theme which Eckhart here puts to good use in explaining his view of spiritual union with the deity. But Eckhart adds the twist that since likeness implies distinction the soul really "hates" likeness and in its flight to God is trying to eliminate it.]

And as it has already been said about emptiness or nakedness, as the soul becomes more pure and bare and poor, and possesses less of created things, and is emptier of all things that are not God, it receives God more purely, and is more totally in him, and it truly becomes one with God, and it looks into God and God into it, face to face, as it were two images transformed into one. This is what Saint Paul says,[71] and this is what I say now about likeness and about the heat of love; because as one thing becomes more like another, so it hastens always faster toward it, and travels with greater speed, and its course is sweeter and more joyful to it. And the further it goes away from itself and from everything that is not the object of its pursuit, the less like it becomes to itself and to everything that is not that object, and the more it becomes like the object toward which it drives. And because likeness flows from the One and draws and attracts by the power and in the power of the One, this does not pacify or satisfy that which is drawing or that which is being drawn, until they become united into one. Therefore the Lord said through the prophet Isaias and meant that "no likeness, however exalted, and no loving peace will satisfy me, until I shine out myself in my Son,"[72] and until I myself am set on fire and enkindled in the love of the Holy Spirit. And our Lord prayed his Father that we might become one with him and in him,[73] not merely that we should be joined together. Of what this says, and of its truth, we have a plain example and proof even in the external natural order: When fire works, and kindles wood and sets it on fire, the fire diminishes the wood and makes it unlike itself, taking away its coarseness, coldness, heaviness and dampness, and turns the wood into itself, into fire, more and more like to it. But neither the fire nor the wood is pacified or quieted or satisfied with any warmth or heat or likeness until the fire gives birth to itself in the wood, and gives to the wood its own nature and also its own being, so that they both become one and the same unseparated fire, neither less nor more. And therefore, before this may be achieved, there is always smoke, contention, crackling, effort and violence between fire and wood. But when all the unlikeness has been taken away and rejected, then the fie is stilled and the wood is quiet. And I say something else that is true, that nature's hidden power secretly hates likeness as it carries within itself distinction and duality, and nature seeks in likeness the One it loves for its own sake alone in likeness. So the mouth seeks and loves in the wine and from the wine its flavor or its sweetness. If water had the flavor that wine has, the mouth would love the wine no more than the water.

And this is why I have said that the soul hates likeness in likeness and does not love it in itself and for its own sake, but it loves likeness for the sake of the One that is concealed in likeness, and is the true "Father," beginning without beginning, "of all in heaven and on earth."[74] And therefore I say: So long as likeness can still be perceived and appears between fire and wood, there is never true delight or silence or rest or contentment. That is why the

---

71 1 *Colossians* 13:12; 2 *Colossians* 3:18.
72 *Isaiah* 62:1.
73 *John* 17:11.
74 *Ephesians* 4:6 and 3:15.

authorities say: Fire comes about in strife and contention and unrest, and it happens in time; but the birth of the fire and joy is timeless, placeless. It seems to no one that delight and joy are slow or distant. Everything I have now said is signified when our Lord says: "When a woman gives birth to a child she has pain and anguish and sorrow; but when the child is born, she forgets the pain and anguish."[75] Therefore too God says in the gospel and admonishes us that we should pray to the heavenly Father that our joy may be complete;[76] and Saint Philip said: "Lord, show us the Father, and it is enough for us."[77] For 'Father' implies birth, not likeness, and it signifies the One in which all likeness is stilled, and everything is silenced that longs for being.

Now a person may plainly see why and because of what they are unconsoled in all their sorrow, distress and hurt. This all comes from nothing else than that they are far away from God, that they are not emptied of created things, that they are unlike to God, cold toward divine love.

IX.5.6. "On Detachment"

[In praising detachment as the best of virtues Eckhart returns to the deeply Platonic theme that the best life for a human being consists in turning away from this world of the senses and filling oneself with the eternal. Into this frame Eckhart works the typical claim of the mystic that the way to God is through ridding the mind of all its contents; in that way God is "compelled" to enter the soul and fill it.]

I have read many writings both by the pagan teachers and by the prophets and in the Old and the New Law, and I have inquired, carefully and most industriously, to find which is the greatest and best virtue with which a person can most completely and closely conform themselves to God, with which they can by grace become that which God is by nature, and with which a person can come most of all to resemble that image which he was in God,

and between which and God there was no distinction before ever God made created things. And as I scrutinize all these writings, so far as my reason can lead and instruct me, I find no other virtue better than a pure detachment from all things; because all other virtues have some regard for created things, but detachment is free from all created things. That is why our Lord said to Martha: "One thing is necessary,"[78] which is as much as to say: "Martha, whoever wants to be free of care and to be pure must have one thing, and that is detachment."

The teachers have great things to say in praise of love, as had Saint Paul, who says: "Whatever I may practice, if I do not have love, I am worth nothing at all."[79] And yet I praise detachment above all love. First, because the best thing about love is that it compels me to love God, yet detachment compels God to love me. Now it is far greater for me to compel God to come to me than to compel myself to come to God; and that is because God is able to conform himself, far better and with more suppleness, and to unite himself with me than I could unite myself with God. And I prove that detachment compels God to come to me in this way; it is because everything longs to achieve its own natural place. Now God's own natural place is unity and purity, and that comes from detachment. Second, I praise detachment above love because love compels me to suffer all things for God's love, yet detachment leads me to where I am receptive to nothing except God. Now it is far greater to be receptive to nothing except God than to suffer all things for God's love, for man when he suffers has some regard for the created things from which he receives the suffering, but detachment is wholly free of all created things. And that detachment is receptive to nothing at all except God – that I prove in this way: Whatever is to be received must be received by something; but detachment is so close to nothingness that there is nothing so subtle that it can be apprehended by detachment, except God alone. He is so simple and so subtle that he can indeed be apprehended in a detached heart. And so detachment can apprehend nothing except God.

75 *John* 16:21.
76 *John* 15:11.
77 *John* 14:8.
78 *Luke* 10:42.
79 1 *Corinthians* 13:1-2.

The authorities also praise humility above many other virtues. But I praise detachment above all humility, and that is because perfect humility proceeds from annihilation of self. Now detachment approaches so closely to nothingness that there can be nothing between perfect detachment and nothingness. Therefore perfect detachment cannot exist without humility. Now two virtues are better than one. The second reason why I praise detachment above humility is that perfect humility is always abasing itself below all created things, and in this abasement a person goes out of himself toward created things, but detachment remains within itself. Now there can never be any going out of self so excellent that remaining within self is not itself much more excellent. The prophet David said of this: "All the glory of the king's daughter is from her inwardness."[80] Perfect detachment has no looking up to, no abasement, not beneath any created thing or above it; it wishes to be neither beneath nor above, it wants to exist by itself, not giving joy or sorrow to anyone, not wanting equality or inequality with any created thing, not wishing for this or for that. All that it wants is to be. But to wish to be this thing or that, this it does not want. Whoever wants to be this or that wants to be something, but detachment wants to be nothing at all. So it is that detachment makes no claim upon anything.

Now a person could say: "All virtues were most perfectly present in our Lady, so that she must have had perfect detachment." But if detachment is more excellent than humility, why did our Lady single out not her detachment but her humility, when she said: "Because he has regarded the humility of his handmaid"?[81] To this I answer and say that detachment and humility are in God, so far as we can speak of virtues as present in God. Now you must know that it was loving humility that brought God to abase himself into human nature; yet when he became man, detachment remained immovable in itself as it was when he created the kingdoms of heaven and earth, as afterward I intend to say to you. And when our Lord, wishing to become man,

remained immovable in his detachment, our Lady knew well that this was what he desired also from her, and that on that account it was to her humility that he was looking, not to her detachment. So she remained immovable in her detachment, and praised in herself not detachment but humility. And if she had by so much as a word mentioned her detachment, and had said: "He has regarded my detachment," detachment would have been troubled by that, and would not have remained wholly perfect, for there would then have been a going out. There can be no going out, however small, in which detachment can remain unblemished. And so you have the reason why our Lady singled out her humility and not her detachment. The prophet spoke about that: "I shall hear what the Lord God will say in me,"[82] that is, I shall be silent and hear what my God and my Lord may say in me, as if he were to say: "If God wishes to speak to me, let him come in here to me; I do not want to go out."

I also praise detachment above all mercifulness, because mercifulness is nothing else than people's going out of themselves to the shortcomings of their fellow human beings, and through this their heart becomes troubled. But detachment remains free of this, and remains in itself, and allows nothing to trouble it, for nothing can ever trouble a person unless things are not well with them. In a few words, if I regard all virtues, I find not one so much without shortcomings and so leading us to God as detachment.

An authority called Avicenna says: "The excellence of the spirit which has achieved detachment is so great that whatever it contemplates is true, and whatever it desires is granted, and whatever it commands one must obey."[83] And you should know that this is really so; when the free spirit has attained true detachment, it compels God to its being; and if the spirit could attain formlessness, and be without all accidents, it would take on God's properties. But this God can give to no one but to himself; therefore God cannot do more for the spirit that has attained detachment than to give himself to it. And the person who has attained this complete

80 *Psalm* 44:14. Eckhart's translation here is interpretive.
81 *Luke* 1:48.
82 *Psalm* 84:9.
83 *On the Soul* 4.4.

detachment is so carried into eternity that no transient thing can move them, so that they experience nothing of whatever is bodily, and they call the world dead, because nothing earthly has any savor for them. This is what Saint Paul meant when he said: "I live, and yet I do not; Christ lives in me."[84]

Now you may ask what detachment is since it is in itself so excellent. Here you should know that true detachment is nothing else than for the spirit to stand as immovable against whatever may chance to it of joy and sorrow, honour, shame, and disgrace, as a mountain of lead stands before a little breath of wind. This immovable detachment brings a person into the greatest equality with God, because God has it from his immovable detachment that he is God, and it is from his detachment that he has his purity and his simplicity and his unchangeability. And if man is to become equal with God, insofar as a creature can have equality with God, that must happen through detachment. It then draws a person into purity, and from purity into simplicity, and from simplicity into unchangeability, and these things produce an equality between God and the person; and the equality must come about in grace, for it is grace that draws a person away from all temporal things, and makes them pure of all transient things. And you must know that to be empty of all created things is to be full of God, and to be full of created things is to be empty of God.

Now you must know that God has been in this immovable detachment since before the world began, and he still remains so; and you must know that when God created heaven and earth and all created things, that affected his immovable detachment as little as if no creature had ever been made. And I say more: All the prayers and good works that people can accomplish in time move God's detachment as little as if no single prayer or good work were ever performed in time, and yet for this God is never any less gentle or less inclined toward people than if they had never achieved prayer or good works. And I say more: When the Son in his divinity wished to become man, and became man, and suffered his passion, that affected God's immovable detachment as little as if the Son had never become man. Now you may say: "If I hear rightly, all prayers and good works are wasted, because God does not accept them in such a way that anyone could move him through them; and yet people say that God wants to be asked for everything." But here you must pay me good attention, and understand properly, if you can, that God, in his first everlasting glance – if we can think of his first glancing at anything – saw all things as they were to happen, and in that same glance he saw when and how he would make all created things, and when the Son would become man and would suffer. He also saw the smallest prayer and good work that anyone would ever perform, and he took into his regard which prayers and devotion he would or should give ear to. He saw what you will earnestly pray and entreat him for tomorrow; and it will not be tomorrow that he will give ear to your entreaty and prayer, because he has heard it in his everlastingness, before ever you became man. But if your prayer is not insistent and lacks earnestness, it will not be now that God refuses you, because he has refused you in his everlastingness. And so God has looked upon all things in his first everlasting glance, and God does not undertake anything whatever afresh, because everything is something already accomplished.[85] And so God always remains in his immovable detachment, and yet people's prayers and good works are not on this account wasted; for whoever does well will also be well rewarded, whoever does evil will be rewarded accordingly. This is the meaning of what Saint Augustine says in the fifth book of *On the Trinity*, in the last chapter, where he begins: "Yet God ..."[86] which has this sense:

God forbid that anyone would say that God loves anyone in time, because with him nothing is past, and nothing is to come, and he had loved all the saints before ever the world was created, when he foresaw that they would be. And when it comes to pass in time that he in time regards what he has looked upon in eternity, then people think that God has turned to them with a new love; yet it is so that whether God be angry or confer some blessing, it is

---

84 *Galatians* 2:20.
85 See topic IV for discussion of the problems afflicting this view of God's foreknowledge.
86 5.16.17.

we who are changed, and he remains unchangeable, as the light of the sun is painful to sick eyes and good for healthy ones, and yet the light of the sun remains in itself unchangeable.

And he touches on the same meaning in the twelfth book of *On the Trinity*, in the fourth chapter, where he says: "God does not see in temporal fashion, and nothing new happens in his sight."[87] Isidore[88] also means this, in his book about the highest good where he says: "Many people ask what God did before he created heaven and earth, or when did the new will in God, to make created things, come about?"[89] He answers this so: "No new will ever came about in God, because when it was so that the creature was in itself nothing" – of what it now is – "still it was before the world began, in God and in his mind." God did not create heaven and earth in the temporal fashion in which we describe it – "Let there be" – because all created things were spoken in the everlasting Word. We must also deduce this from the Lord's colloquy with Moses, when Moses said to the Lord: "Lord, if Pharaoh asks me who you are, what shall I say to him?" and the Lord said: "Say, 'He who is has sent me,'"[90] which is as much as to say: He who is in himself unchangeable, he has sent me.

Now someone might say: "Did Christ have immovable detachment, even when he said: 'My soul is sorrowful even to death'[91] and did Mary, when she stood beneath the cross – and people tell us much about her lamentations. How can all this be reconciled with immovable detachment?" Here you must know that the authorities say that in every human being there are two kinds of human being: One is called the outer man, which is our sensuality, with the five senses serving him, and yet the other man works through the power of the soul. The second man is called the inner man, which is the person's inwardness. Now you should know that a spiritual person who loves God makes no use in their outer man of the soul's powers except when the five senses require it; and their inwardness pays

no heed to the five senses, except as this leads and guides them, and protects them, so that they are not employed for beastly purposes, as they are by some people who live for their carnal delight, as beasts lacking reason do. Such people deserve to be called beasts rather than human beings. And whatever power the soul possesses, beyond that which it gives to the five senses, it gives wholly to the inner man, and if he has a high and noble object, the soul draws to itself all its powers it had loaned to the five senses. Then the person is called senseless and rapt, for his object is an image which the reason can apprehend, or, it may be, something reasonable which has no image. Yet know that God requires of every spiritual person to love him with all the powers of their soul. Of this he said: "Love your God with your whole heart."[92] But there are people who squander all the soul's powers on the outer man. They are those who apply all their intelligence and reason to perishable goods, and who know nothing about the inner man. Now you must know that the outer man may be active whilst the inner man remains wholly free and immovable. In Christ, too, there was an outer man and an inner man, and also in Our Lady; and whatever Christ and Our Lady may have said about outward affairs, they acted according to the outer man, and the inner man remained in an immovable detachment. And Christ spoke in this sense when he said: "My soul is sorrowful even to death"; and however much Our Lady lamented, and whatever else she may have said, still always her inwardness remained in an immovable detachment. Consider a simile of this: A door, opening and shutting on a hinge. I compare the planks on the outside of the door with the outer man, but the hinge with the inner man. As the door opens and shuts, the outside planks move backwards and forwards, but the hinge remains immovable in one place, and the opening and shutting does not affect it. It is just the same here, if you can understand it rightly.

---

87 Actually 12.7.10.
88 Isidore of Seville, d.636 C.E.
89 *Sentences* 1.8.4.
90 *Exodus* 3:10-14.
91 *Matthew* 26:38.
92 *Deuteronomy* 6:5, etc.

And now I ask, what is the object of this pure detachment? My answer is that neither this nor that is the object of pure detachment. It reposes in a naked nothingness, and I shall tell you why that is: Pure detachment reposes in the highest place. If a person has repose in the highest place, God can work in him according to his whole will. But God cannot work according to his whole will in every person's heart, for though it may be that God is omnipotent, still he cannot work except where he finds or creates a willing cooperation. And I say "or creates" because of Saint Paul, for in him God did not find willing cooperation, but he made Paul willing by the inpouring of grace.[93] So I say: God works according as he finds willingness. He works in one way in human beings, and another in stones. We can find an analogy of this in nature: If someone heats a baker's oven, and puts in one loaf of oats and another of barley and another of rye and another of wheat, there is only one temperature in the oven, but it does not have the same effect upon the different doughs, because one turns into fine bread, another is coarse and a third even coarser. And that is not the fault of the temperature but of the materials, which are not the same. In the same way, God does not work alike in every person's heart; he works as he finds willingness and receptivity. There may be one thing or another in some heart, on which one thing or another God cannot work to bring it up to the highest place. And if the heart is to be willing for that highest place, it must repose in a naked nothingness; and in this there is the greatest potentiality that can be. And when the heart that has detachment attains to the highest place, that must be nothingness, for in this is the greatest receptivity. See an analogy of this in nature. If I want to write on a wax tablet, it does not matter how fine the words may be that are written on the tablet, they still hinder me from writing on it. If I really want to write something, I must erase and eliminate everything that is already there; and the tablet is never so good for me to write on as

when there is nothing on it at all. In the same way, if God is to write on my heart up in the highest place, everything that can be called this or that must come out of my heart, and in that way my heart will have won detachment. And so God can work upon it in the highest place and according to his highest will. And this is why the heart in its detachment has no this or that as its object.

But now I ask: "What is the prayer of a heart that has detachment?" And to answer it I say that purity in detachment does not know how to pray, because if someone prays they ask god to get something for them, or they ask God to take something away from them. But a heart in detachment asks for nothing, nor has it anything of which it would gladly be free. So it is free of all prayer, and its prayer is nothing else than for uniformity with God. That is all its prayer consists in. To illustrate this meaning we may consider what St. Dionysius[94] said about Saint Paul's words, when he said: "There are many of you racing for the crown, but it will be given only to one."[95] All the powers of the soul are racing for the crown, but it will be given only to the soul's being – and Dionysius says: "The race is nothing but a turning away from all created things and a uniting oneself with that which is uncreated."[96] And as the soul attains this, it loses its name and it draws God into itself, so that in itself it becomes nothing, as the sun draws up the red dawn into itself so that it becomes nothing. Nothing else will bring a person to this except pure detachment. And we can also apply to this what Augustine says: "The soul has a secret entry into the divine nature when all things become nothing to it."[97] This entry here on this earth is nothing else than pure detachment. And when this detachment ascends to the highest place, it knows nothing of knowing, it loves nothing of loving, and from light it becomes dark. To this we can also apply what one teacher says: "The poor in spirit are those who have abandoned all thing for God, just as they were his when we did not exist."[98] No one can do this but a heart with

---

93 The reference is to the famous conversion of Paul on the road to Damascus. See *Acts* 9:1-18.

94 I.e., pseudo-Dionysius the Areopagite.

95 1 *Corinthians* 9:24.

96 *Divine Names* 4.9 & 13.3.

97 No passage from Augustine that reads like this has been found.

98 It is not certain whether the reference is to Eckhart himself or some other writer.

pure detachment. We can see that God would rather be in a heart with such detachment than in all hearts. For if you ask me: "What is it God seeks in all things?," then I answer you out of the *Book of Wisdom*, where he says: "In all things I seek rest."[99] Nowhere is there complete rest, except only in the heart that has found detachment. Hence God would rather be there than in other virtues or in any other things. And you should also know that the more people apply themselves to becoming susceptible to the divine inflowing, the more blessed will they be; and whoever can establish themselves in the highest readiness, they will also be in the highest blessedness. Now no one can make himself susceptible to the divine inflowing except through uniformity with God, for as people become uniform with God, to that measure they becomes susceptible to the divine inflowing. And uniformity comes from people's subjecting themselves to God; and the more people subject themselves to created things, the less are they uniform with God. Now a heart that has pure detachment is free of all created things, and so it is wholly submitted to God, and so it achieves the highest uniformity with God, and is most susceptible to the divine inflowing. This is what Saint Paul means when he said: "Put on Jesus Christ."[100] He means through uniformity with Christ, and this putting-on cannot happen except through uniformity with Christ. And you must know that when Christ became man, it was not just a human being he put on himself; he put on human nature. Therefore, do you too go out of all things, and then there will be only what Christ accepted and put on, and so you will have put on Christ.

Whoever now wishes to see properly what is the excellence and the profit of perfect detachment, let him take good heed of Christ's words, when he spoke about his human nature and said to his disciples: "It is expedient for you that I go from you, for if I do not go, the Holy Spirit cannot come to you."[101] This is just as if he were to say: "You have taken too much delight in my present image, so that the perfect delight of the Holy Spirit cannot be yours. So detach yourselves from the image, and unite yourselves to the formless being, for God's spiritual consolation is delicate; therefore he will not offer it to anyone except to those who disdain bodily consolations."

Now, all you reasonable people, take heed! No one is happier than a person who has attained the greatest detachment. No one can accept fleshly and bodily consolations without spiritual damage, "because the flesh longs in opposition to the spirit and the spirit to the flesh."[102] Therefore whoever sows in the flesh inordinate love will reap everlasting death, and whoever in the spirit sows a well-ordered love will from the spirit reap everlasting life.[103] So it is that the sooner a person shuns what is created, the sooner will the creator come to them. So take heed, all you reasonable people! Since the delight we might have in Christ's bodily image deprives us of receptivity for the Holy Spirit, how much more shall we be deprived of God by the ill-ordered delight that we take in transient consolations! So detachment is the best of all, for it purifies the soul and cleanses the conscience and enkindles the heart and awakens the spirit and stimulates our longings and shows us where God is and separates us from created things and unites itself with God.

Now, all you reasonable people, take heed! The fastest beast that will carry you to your perfection is suffering, for no one will enjoy more eternal sweetness than those who endure with Christ in the greatest bitterness. There is nothing more gall-bitter than suffering, and nothing more honey-sweet than to have suffered; nothing disfigures the body more than suffering, and nothing more adorns the soul in the sight of God than to have suffered. The firmest foundation on which this perfection can stand is humility, for whichever mortal crawls here in the deepest abasement, his spirit will fly up into the highest realms of the divinity, for love brings sorrow, and sorrow brings love. And therefore,

99 *Wisdom* 14:11.
100 *Romans* 13:14.
101 *John* 16:7.
102 *Galatians* 5:17.
103 *Galatians* 6:8.

whoever longs to attain to perfect detachment, let him struggle for perfect humility, and so he will come close to the divinity.

That we may all be brought to this, may that supreme detachment help us which is God himself. Amen.

BIOGRAPHIES

PETER ABELARD

Peter Abelard was born in 1079 at Pallet, Brittany; he died in 1142 at the Abbey of Cluny. He studied with a number of teachers: Roscelin and William of Champeaux; the first was an extreme nominalist; the second, an extreme realist. Disagreement with William of Champeaux led Abelard to set up his own school at Melun in 1104. Abelard's reputation as a brilliant teacher and dialectician brought him a large following.

He studied theology under Anselm of Laon beginning in 1113 and returned to Paris in 1116 to teach. There followed the famous love affair with Heloise, their secret marriage, and the castration ordered by her uncle in 1118.

In 1121 Abelard's book *On the Trinity* was condemned. After a brief period as abbot of St. Gildas in his native Brittany, he returned to Paris. Bernard of Clairvaux succeeded in getting his theology condemned at the synod of Sens in 1140. Peter the Venerable of Cluny mediated the dispute and arranged for Abelard to spend his last days in quiet study.

For further reading please consult the following:

Abelard, Peter. *The story of Abelard's adversities: a translation with notes of the Historia calamitatum.* 1954.

Charrier, Charlotte. *Héloïse dans l'histoire et dans la légende.* Paris: H. Champion, 1933.

Tweedale, M. M. *Abailard on Universals.* North-Holland, 1976.

ST. ANSELM

Anselm of Canterbury was born in 1033 at Aosta, in northern Italy. He took up the life of a wandering scholar and eventually settled at the Norman monastery of Bec. Anselm became a monk in 1060, a prior by 1063, and an abbot in 1078. During these years at Bec he wrote his famous works dealing with the existence of God: the *Monologion* and *Proslogion*.

In 1093 he became Archbishop of Canterbury; he died in 1109.

Anselm's famous proof in the *Proslogion* of the existence of God, now called the Ontological Argument, has excited interest from the time it was discovered to the present day.

The reader may wish to consult some of the following works:

Barnes, Jonathan. *The Ontological Argument.* Macmillan, 1972.

Barth, Karl. *Anselm, Fides quaerens intellectum.* München: C. Kaiser, 1931.

Hartshorne, Charles, 1897. *Anselm's discovery: a re-examination of the ontological proof for God's existence.* La Salle, IL: Open Court, 1965.

ST. THOMAS AQUINAS

Thomas Aquinas (1225-1274), born at Rocca Secca in Italy, was the youngest son of Count Landulf of Aquino, who was related to the Emperor and the King of France. He received his first education at the neighbouring Benedictine monastery of Monte Cassino.

In 1239 he proceeded to Naples where he completed his training in the arts and first came into contact with the writings of Aristotle. His brothers vehemently opposed his decision to enter the newly founded Dominican Order and held him prisoner for fifteen months in a vain effort to dissuade him.

He later pursued his studies under Albert the Great, whose pupil he became perhaps at Paris before 1248 and certainly at Cologne from 1248 to 1252. He returned to Paris in 1252 and embarked upon a teaching and writing career that was to occupy the remaining twenty-two years of his life.

From 1252 to 1259 he received his degree in theology, lectured at the Dominican convent of St. Jacques, and composed his early works. In 1259 he was sent to Italy and taught successively at Anagni (1259-1261), Orvieto (1261-1264), Rome (1265-1267), and Viterbo (1268).

In Italy he met his confrere William of Moerbeke,

a skilled translator of Greek philosophical texts, and undertook with him a series of commentaries on Aristotle. At the beginning of 1269 he resumed his teaching in Paris during the most theologically and philosophically turbulent period of the thirteenth century. There he became engaged in the controversy with the Latin Averroists, defended the mendicants against the attacks of the seculars, and upheld his own doctrinal positions against the more traditional views of Etienne Tempier.

In 1272 he was recalled to Naples to found a new *studium generale* at the university and directed the teaching of theology there until the following year. He died on March 7, 1274 at the Cistercian Abbey of Fossanova, between Naples and Rome, on his way to the Ecumenical Council of Lyon.

In 1879 Pope Leo XIII issued the encyclical *Aeterni Patris*, in which he in effect made Aquinas the Doctor *par excellence* of the Catholic Church.

For further reading the following may be consulted:

Copleston, Frederick. *Thomas Aquinas*. London: Search Press, 1976.

D'Arcy, Martin Cyril. *Thomas Aquinas*. London: Oxford University Press, 1944.

ARISTOTLE

Aristotle was born in Stagira in 384 B.C.E. His father was a physician at the court of Philip of Macedonia. At the age of 17 Aristotle went to Athens where he became a pupil in Plato's Academy. And thus began the first of the three great phases of his life. He remained at the Academy for 20 years, from 367 to 347 B.C.E.

The second phase of Aristotle's life began in 347 when he and some companions sailed eastward across the Aegean and settled at Atarneus, a town with which Aristotle had family ties. The ruler of Atarneus was Hermias, a friend both of philosophy and of Macedonia. Aristotle married Hermias's niece, Pythias, who was the mother of his two children, Pythias and Nicomachus. This second phase encompassed 12 years, during which Aristotle undertook the major part of his work upon which his scientific reputation rests.

The third phase opens in 335 when Aristotle returned to Athens and began to teach in the Lyceum. After Alexander died Aristotle again left

Athens, in the spring of 322 when he moved to Chalcis, on the island of Euboea, where his mother's family had property. In the last months of his life he lamented the fact that he had become isolated and cut off. Aristotle died in the autumn of 322.

ST. AUGUSTINE OF HIPPO

Augustine was born in Tagaste in the province of Numidia in 354. His father was a pagan; his mother, a Christian. Augustine was reared as a Christian by his devout mother Monica. In 370 he went to Carthage to study rhetoric, and he there became a Manichean.

In 386 he was baptized a Christian, and in 391 he was ordained a priest; in 396 he became the bishop of Hippo. Augustine died in 430.

Some suggestions for reading on St. Augustine:

Chadwick, Henry. *Augustine*. Oxford; New York: Oxford University Press, 1986.

Clark, Mary T. *Augustine*. Washington, D.C.: Georgetown University Press, 1994.

Kirwan, Christopher. *Augustine*. London; New York: Routledge, 1991.

O'Donnell, James Joseph. *Augustine*. Boston: Twayne Publishers, 1985.

AVERROES (IBN RUSHD)

Averroes (Abu al-Walid Muhammad Ibn Ahmad Ibn Rushd) was born in 1126 in Cordova, Spain, to a distinguished family of jurists; both his grandfather and father occupied posts as judges in that city. He is reported to have studied Islamic jurisprudence and dialectical theology; in 1153 he went to Marrakesh where he was received by the founder of the Almohad dynasty 'Abd al-Mu'min, apparently in connection with the prince's plans to establish a school; and he composed a work on medicine.

The ruler's chief physician ibn Tufail, reported to Averroes that the sovereign had complained to him about the lack of coherence in Aristotle's style, and about the obscurity of Aristotle's aims, and that he had expressed the hope that someone would paraphrase them and make their aims more accessible. Averroes was charged with the task.

Averroes was named judge in Seville in 1169, where he started composing his commentaries, a work that he continued after returning to Cordova in 1171. His commentaries on most of Aristotle's work earned him the title "The Commentator" and his particular kind of Aristotelianism (a mixture, in fact, of Aristotelianism and neo-Platonism) helped later medieval, Christian thought define its own Aristotelianism. He died in 1198.

For further study of Averroes the following may be consulted:

Davidson, Herbert A. "Alfarabi and Avicenna on the Active Intellect." *Viator: Medieval and Renaissance Studies*, III, 1972, 109-178.
Fakhry, Majid. *Islamic occasionalism, and its critique by Averroës and Aquinas*. London: Allen & Unwin, 1958.
Gauthier, Léon. *Ibn Rochd (Averroès)*. Paris: Presses universitaires de France, 1948.
Kogan, Barry S. *Averroes and the Metaphysics of Causation*. State University of New York Press, 1985.

AVICENNA (IBN SINA)

Avicenna (Abu 'Ali al-Husayn ibn Sina) was born in 980 in Afshana, a village in the Kharmaithan district of Bukhara. His father was the governor of the district. While Avicenna was still a child, the family moved to Bukhara, where he received his education and spent the first sustained period of his life. His studies began with the Koran and Arabic literature and continued with Islamic law, logic, and mathematics, as well as the natural sciences and metaphysics.

Avicennna was extraordinarily gifted, and he soon surpassed his teachers. He taught himself medicine and became an accomplished physician by the time he was sixteen. When Avicenna's medical skills helped cure the Samanid sultan of Bukhara, the ruler enrolled him in his service. The ruler died in 997 and with the end of the Samanid dynasty in 999 Avicenna left Bukhara. He remained at various courts in the eastern part of the Caliphate of Baghdad. He died in 1037.

The following are useful for further study.

Afnan, Soheil Muhsin. *Avicenna, his life and works*. London: G. Allen & Unwin, 1958.
Anawati, Georges C. *Saint Thomas D'Aquin, Avicenne et le dialogue Islamo-Chretien*. Cairo: Instito italiano de Cultura, 1975.
Avicenna. *The life of Ibn Sina*; a critical edition and annotated translation. 1974.
Bloch, Ernst. *Avicenna und die Aristotelische Linke*. Berlin: Suhrkamp, 1963.
Davidson, Herbert A. *Proofs for Eternity, Creation, and the Existence of God in Medieval Islamic and Jewish Philosophy*. New York: Oxford University Press, 1987.

BOETHIUS

Anicius Manlius Severinus Boethius was born about 480 into a prominent Roman senatorial family. He was educated in Athens where he acquired the knowledge which later enabled him to translate Greek philosophical writings into Latin.

He took up a political career and came to the attention of Theodoric, the Ostrogoth King who ruled what had been the western part of the Roman Empire. He was appointed consul in 510 and Master of Offices in 522. In 523, for reasons still unknown, he was accused of treason and condemned. After a year spent in prison he was executed.

For further reading the following may be consulted:

Barrett, Helen Marjorie. *Boethius: some aspects of his times and work*. Cambridge: The University Press, 1940.
Boethius, his life, thought and influence, edited by Margaret Gibson. Oxford: B. Blackwell, 1981.
Chadwick, Henry. *Boethius: the consolations of music, logic, theology, and philosophy*. Oxford: Clarendon Press, 1981.

PSEUDO-DIONYSIUS THE AREOPAGITE

Little is known about the author of the treatises which appeared in the early 6th century as works of the Dionysius whom *Acts* says St. Paul converted in Athens in the first century C.E. He or she probably lived in Syria around 500 C.E. At the beginning there were doubts about the authorship of the works, but after Maximus the Confessor in the sixth century interpreted them in an orthodox way their authenticity was not seriously challenged before the Renaissance, and debates about this continued up to the 19th century.

A good recent study is:

Rorem, Paul. *Pseudo-Dionysius: A Commentary on the Texts and an Introduction to Their Influence*. New York, Oxford: Oxford University Press, 1993.

GARLANDUS COMPOTISTA

The identity of the author of the *Dialectica* which some scholars have ascribed to Garlandus the Computist is not known. The doctrines found in the work are consonant with those credited to Roscelin of Compeigne, the notorious "nominalist" of the late eleventh and early twelfth centuries and teacher of Peter Abelard. About all that can be said with certainty is that the work was composed in Roscelin's milieu if not by Roscelin himself.

For further reading the following articles may be consulted:

Henry, D.P. "The Singular Syllogisms of Garlandus Compotista." *Revue internationale de philosophie* 113 (1993): 243-70.
Stump, Eleonore. "Dialectic in the Eleventh and Twelfth Centuries: Garlandus Compotista." *History and Philosophy of Logic* I (1980): 1-18.

AL-GHAZALI

Al-Ghazali was born in Tus, Persia, in 1058. In 1077 he went to Nishapur where he studied with al-Juwayni, the distinguished theologian of the age.

In 1085 Nizam al-Mulk, the vizier of two Seljuk sultans, appointed him to the Nizamiyyah school in Bagdad, one of the most distinguished academic positions of the day. Al-Ghazali underwent a spiritual crisis in 1095 when he found it impossible to lecture. He decided to leave Baghdad. In 1105-1106 the son of Nizam al-Mulk, his former benefactor, convinced him to teach again, and he accepted a position at Hishapur.

Toward the end of his life he retired to his native Tus where he opened a kind of monastery in which he taught Sufism. He died in 1111.

For further reading the following may be consulted:

Ahmed, Mohamed. *Ghazali's theory of virtue*. Albany: State University of New York Press, 1975.

Shehadi, Fadlou. *Ghazali's unique unknowable God; a philosophical critical analysis of some of the problems raised*. Leiden: E. J. Brill, 1964.

HENRY OF GHENT

Henry of Ghent (Henricus Gandavensis, Henricus de Gandavo) was born around 1217. He taught at the University of Paris from 1276-92 and served on the commission that drew up the list of condemned theses issued in 1277. He died in 1293.

For further study the following may be consulted:

Macken, R. (Raymond). *Bibliotheca manuscripta Henrici de Gandavo*. Leuven: University Press; Leiden: E.J. Brill, 1979.
Maurer, Armand. "Henry of Ghent and the Unity of Man," *Medieval Studies* 10 (1948):1-20.
Paulus, J. *Henri de Gand: Essai sur les tendances de sa Metaphysique*. Paris: J.Vrin, 1938.
Schöllgen, Werner. *Das Problem der Willensfreiheit bei Heinrich von Gent und Herveus Natalis*. Hildesheim: H. Gerstenberg, 1975.

IBN TUFAIL (ABUBACER)

Abu Bakr Muhammad ibn Tufail was born around 1100 near Granada in Spain. He was a famous polymath in his day teaching philosophy, mathematics and medicine, as well as writing poetry. He worked first at the court in Granada and then later in the court of the Sultan of the Muwahidin in Morocco. He died in Marrakesh in 1185. His most famous student was Ibn Rushd (Averroes) (*q.v.*).

JOHN DUNS SCOTUS

John Duns Scotus (known as the Subtle Doctor) was born in 1265 at Duns, in Scotland. In 1278 he was taken to the Franciscan friary at Dumfries. He took his vows as a friar in 1281 and was ordained priest in 1291.

He studied at the University of Paris from 1293 to 1296. By 1300 he was lecturing on the *Sentences* at Oxford and by the autumn term of 1302 he had moved to Paris and in 1305 he received the degree of doctor of theology. Two years later he was sent to Cologne to teach; he died there in 1308.

For further reading the following may be consulted:

Boler, John Francis. *Charles Peirce and scholastic realism; a study of Peirce's relation to John Duns Scotus*. Seattle: University of Washington Press, 1963.

Duns Scotus, John, ca. 1266-1308. *A treatise on God as first principle*; a revised Latin text of the *De primo principio* translated into English by A.Wolter, 1966.

Frank, William A. & Wolter, Allan, B. *Duns Scotus, metaphysician*. West Lafayette, IN: Purdue University Press, 1995.

JOHN SCOTUS ERIUGENA

This highly original thinker was born and educated in Ireland (both 'Scotus' and 'Eriugena' mean 'Irish') sometime in the first half of the ninth century. Although Ireland had never been part of the Roman Empire, it had been Christianized in the fifth century and developed an educational system centered on monastic communities where a knowledge of Greek was apparently maintained although it is uncertain just how extensive this was. Eriugena appeared in the France of Charles the Bald around 848 and soon became an important scholar in the Palace School. Charles was very interested in things Greek and set John to work on a translation of the works of pseudo-Dionysius which had come into Charles' possession through his contacts with Byzantium. John undertook this and was so affected by his reading of Dionysius that he was inspired to create his own theology along Dionysian, and thus indirectly Plotinian, lines. This we find in his great work, the *Periphyseon*, published around 867. The doctrine of this work was condemned by the church at the Councils of Vercelli in 1050 and of Rome in 1059 and by a Bull of Pope Honorius III in 1225. Consequently it never had any great standing during the middle ages. We hear nothing of John after 877 and his death date is not known.

MOSES MAIMONIDES

Moses Maimonides (Moshe ben Maimon, 1135-1204) was born in Cordova, Spain. He received his early training in Jewish studies from his father, who was a scholar of some note. In addition, he was instructed in philosophy and in the natural sciences by local Muslim scholars.

With the fall of Cordova to the Almohads in 1148, his father fled with his family and wandered about Spain for over a decade. In 1160 the family settled in Fez, where Maimonides continued studying with Muslim scholars. But, again, the pressure of religious persecution forced the family to leave in 1165. After passing through Acre and Jerusalem, Maimonides settled in al-Fustat (Old Cairo). Here he took up a medical career as a means of livelihood, finally serving as court physician to Saladin.

Maimonides was a communal leader, and much of his time was occupied in answering legal and doctrinal questions addressed to him by Jews in all lands. He died in Cairo and was buried at Tiberias.

Maimonides was the best known Jewish philosopher of the Middle Ages; his *Guide of the Perplexed* is the most important medieval Jewish philosophic work.

For further reading the following may be consulted:

Leaman, Oliver. *Moses Maimonides*. London; New York: Routledge, 1990.

MEISTER ECKHART

Born around 1260, probably near Erfurt in Germany, he was given the name 'John' but won in his own lifetime the honorific title 'Meister' by which he has always been known. He joined the Dominican order early in his life and was eventually sent to Paris to study, probably around 1277, just after the series of condemnations were handed down by Bishop Stephen Tempier of doctrines that went too far in the direction of Aristotelianism. After his studies in Paris he was sent by his Order back to Germany to direct Dominican affairs in Saxony. In the 1320s Eckhart's unusual teachings came to the attention of the church authorities and some of them were pronounced heretical in 1327. Eckhart then went to the papal court in Avignon to defend himself at about the same time that Ockham was there for a similar purpose. A papal tribunal took up the case but did not produce its adverse ruling until March 1329, by which time Eckhart was dead.

NICHOLAS OF AUTRECOURT

Nicholas of Autrecourt was born around 1300 at Autrecourt in the diocese of Verdun. He studied at the Sorbonne between 1320 and 1327. In 1338 he became a canon of the cathedral of Metz.

In 1340 Nicholas was summoned to appear at Avignon to answer charges of heresy for doctrines that had appeared in his *Universal Treatise* and his letters to Bernard of Arezzo. Nicholas fled from Avignon. In 1346 the formal trial was conducted, and Nicholas was sentenced to burn his writing at Paris and to recant many of his published statements, which he did in 1347. It is not known when he died.

For further reading please consult the following:

The Universal Treatise of Nicholas of Autrecourt. Translated by L.A. Kennedy, R.E. Arnold, & A.E. Milward. Milwaukee: Marquette University Press, 1971.

Weinberg, Julius R. *Nicolaus of Autrecourt. A study in fourteenth-century thought.* Princeton, NJ: Princeton University Press, 1948.

PLATO

Plato was born about 428 B.C.E. His family was an ancient one with political connections in high places. He was a follower of Socrates and wrote numerous dialogues in which Socrates figures as the central character. At the age of forty he founded the Academy and directed its affairs until his death. Thereafter the Academy had a continuous life of nine hundred years. Plato died about 348.

PLOTINUS

Plotinus was born in Egypt c.203 C.E. where he studied at the famous school of Alexandria under Ammonius Saccas, among others. He eventually came to Rome and taught there under the patronage of the Emperor Gallienus. His written works were arranged after his death by his devoted pupil Porphyry into six books of nine chapters each and called the *Enneads*. He died in 269 after a life admired for its asceticism and spirituality. Little of Plotinus's work was directly known in the middle ages, although a work called the *Theology of Aristotle* and falsely attributed to Aristotle was

known and consisted of portions of the *Enneads*. In the fifth century Proclus systematised Plotinus's ideas in a work called *Elements of Theology*, and through this work Plotinus's ideas became known to the pseudo-Dionysius and thus had a major impact on Christianity both in the East and West. Proclus's work also circulated as the *Book of Causes (Liber de Causis)* which was also mistakenly thought to be by Aristotle until the middle of the 13th century.

A good introduction to Plotinus is:

Bréhier, Emile. *La philosophie de Plotin, 2ᵉ éd.* Paris: Bovin, 1928. English translation: *Philosophy of Plotinus*, trans. by Joseph Thomas. Chicago: University of Chicago Press, 1958.

PORPHYRY

Porphyry was born in 233 in Tyre, Syria. He came from a distinguished family. He went abroad to continue his studies, going first to Athens and later to Rome where he studied with Plotinus whose teachings he admired and defended. He died in about 304.

For further reading the following may be consulted:

Smith, Andrew. *Porphyry's place in the neo-Platonic tradition; a study in post-Plotinian neo-Platonism.* The Hague: M. Nijhoff, 1974.

SIGER OF BRABANT

Siger was born around the year 1240. He arrived in Paris about 1256. He would have come into a stimulating atmosphere. Aristotle's *On the Soul* was required reading in the Faculty of Arts by 1252, and discussion of that treatise would have prompted the question whether there is only one intellect for all human beings. By 1260 a certain movement, called heterodox Aristotelianism, took shape, and by 1266 Siger was active in this movement. By the time Siger is first mentioned, in 1266, he had already become a master in the Faculty of Arts.

From 1265 to 1270 Siger's first writings make their appearance. The text included in this anthology as selection IV.5.1., *On the Necessity and the Contingency of Causes*, was written around 1272.

Siger came to philosophical maturity at a time when conditions were relatively favourable for a good understanding, a legitimate use, and a fair criticism of Aristotle. Aristotle's scientific and metaphysical works had been forbidden earlier in the century; his logic and ethics, on the other hand, were being read and discussed. *On the Soul* was required reading by 1252, and a more general study of Aristotle was imposed upon students in the Faculty of Arts by 1255.

In 1277, the year of Stephen Tempier's second condemnation, Siger was summoned by Simon du Val, the Chief Inquisitor of France. Siger had by then left Paris, perhaps believing that he would fare better at the more lenient papal Curia. Siger was acquitted of heresy by Pope Nicholas III, but kept under house arrest. Sometime between 1281 and 1284 he was murdered at Orvieto by his demented secretary.

For further reading the following may be consulted:

Mandonnet, P. (Pierre Félix), 1858-1936. *Siger de Brabant et l'averroïsme latin au XIIIme siècle*. Fribourg: Librairie de l'Université, 1899.

Van Steenberghen, Fernand. *Maitre Siger de Brabant*. Louvain Publications Universitaires, 1977.

Wéber, Edouard-Henri. *La Controverse de 1270 à l'Université de Paris et son retentissement sur la pensée de s. Thomas d'Aquin*. Paris: J. Vrin, 1970.

WILLIAM OF OCKHAM

Ockham, born around 1285, became a Franciscan as a youth, was educated in the Franciscan school at Oxford, and later taught at the Franciscan house in London. All his non-political philosophy was written between 1317 and 1324, and consists of both theological and purely philosophical works. Among the latter are commentaries on the logical and physical works of Aristotle as well as his *Summa Logicae*, which transformed the subject of logic. In the second half of his life Ockham became involved in the dispute over poverty in the Franciscan Order and eventually in polemics against the power of the papacy. He died in Munich under the protection of the emperor, Louis the Bavarian, in 1347.

For further reading consult the following:

Adams, Marilyn M. *William Ockham*. 2 vols. Notre Dame, IN: University of Notre Dame Press, 1987.

Leff, Gordon. *William of Ockham; the Metamorphosis of Scholastic Discourse*. Manchester: Manchester University Press, 1975.

Moody, Ernest A. *The Logic of William of Ockham*. New York: Sheed & Ward, 1935.

GLOSSARY

---

absolute:

What does not involve some relation. For example, the colour of something is absolute, while the act of causing something is relational and not absolute. Sometimes the adverb 'absolutely' is used to mean 'without qualification.' See entry for 'qualified/unqualified.'

absolute perfection:

A perfection (*q.v.*) which implies no sort of imperfection or limitation whatsoever and hence must belong to any being which is as perfect as it is possible for a being to be. For example, it might be claimed that knowledge is an absolute perfection whereas sensory knowledge, although certainly a perfection of the things which have it, is not absolute since it implies corporeality and finitude.

absolute term:

In Ockham's logic an absolute term is one which has only a "primary signification," i.e. its meaning consists simply in its having certain things in its extension. Terms for genera and species are all of this sort. Contrasts with 'connotative term' (*q.v.*).

accident:

In a broad sense X is an accident of a subject Y just in case X is a characteristic of Y but not one directly entailed by a definition of what Y is; in a narrower sense X is an accident of Y just in case Y could exist even though it did not have X. In either case the accident's existence is explanatorily posterior to the existence of its subject.

accidental vs. essential order:

An ordering of items by some relationship of priority and posteriority is essential where the posterior items require for their own existence the simultaneous existence of the items prior to them. The ordering is accidental where this is not required, i.e.

where the posterior items can exist even though the items prior to them no longer exist.

aevum:

According to orthodox theology time was created when the angels were, but at that point time was not divided into any days, months, years, etc., since none of the heavenly bodies had yet been created. This undivided time in which the angels originally lived is called the *aevum*.

agent or active intellect:

According to Aristotle our ability to think of abstract forms depends on a mind or aspect of our own mind which is everlastingly active and creates in our possible or passive intellect (*q.v.*) the forms which we understand. Many followers of Aristotle, notably Alexander of Aphrodisias, thought the agent intellect was a single everlasting mind on which all human abstract thought depended.

agent/recipient:

In Latin: *agens/patiens*. The agent is the efficient cause, i.e. the motivating force, bringing about some change. The recipient is the subject in which that change is brought about. Thus a fire heats a piece of wood. The fire is the agent for the heating and the wood the recipient of the process of heating up. Both agent and recipient must have certain powers to interact in this way; the former has "active" powers, the latter "passive" powers.

annihilation:

The destruction of something to nothing, i.e. so that nothing which was part of it remains in existence. This is the opposite of "creation from nothing," where something is produced although earlier nothing that was to be part of it was in existence.

attribute:

Passio in Latin. A character which necessarily belongs to a certain sort of subject but is not mentioned in the definition of that sort of subject. That it belongs to the subject is supposed to logically follow from the definition in the way that having angles equal to two right angles follows from the definition of 'triangle.' Some attributes are coextensive ("convertible") with a certain sort of subject, for example 'capable of laughing' with 'human being,' and also 'one,' 'true' and 'good' with 'being'. (These are the famous "*passiones entis*," attributes of being, which are among the "transcendental" (*q.v.*) terms.)

basis of a relation:

The *primary* bearer of a relation, as opposed to something which bears the relation only indirectly because the basis belongs to it in some way. For example, an object's colour might be the basis for a relation of similarity to some other object, but the object bears the similarity relation only because it has the colour which is the basis for the relation.

being of thought:

In Latin: *ens rationis*. An entity which exists only because certain items are thought of. Contrasted with a "real" or "formal" being, which exists apart from anything's being the content of thought. However, acts of thought themselves are real beings and not beings of thought; a predicate or a syllogism would be, since such do not exist unless there is thought about something.

categorematic term:

A term which has some descriptive meaning such that it is possible to assign to it an extension within the realm of things we talk about. Most of these would be found under one of the Aristotelian categories (*q.v.*). Examples are mainly nouns, adjectives and verbs. Contrasted with 'syncategorematic term' (*q.v.*).

categorical proposition:

An assertion or denial whose overall grammatical form is that of a subject and a predicate, where the association of the predicate to the subject (or the dissociation of the predicate from the subject in the case of denials) is not affected by a modal determination. Categorical propositions are contrasted both with "hypothetical" propositions (*q.v.*), which do not have subject-predicate form but rather combine two sentences with some sort of conjunction like 'or,' 'and,' 'if,' 'because,' 'when,' etc., and with modal propositions where the connection (or disconnection) between subject and predicate is asserted to hold 'necessarily' or 'possibly,' or 'not possibly.' Categorical propositions can have various 'quantities,' viz. 'universal,' 'particular,' or 'singular,' depending on how the subject term is determined by words like 'every,' 'some,' 'no,' etc.

category:

In Aristotelian logic a highest genus (see 'species/genus'), or that genus and all the terms which fall under it. In *Categories* 4 Aristotle listed ten such genera and this list was the accepted one in medieval times. Chief examples are 'substance,' 'quantity,' 'quality,' 'relation.' The classification in Aristotle reflects the idea that each categorematic term typically answers a certain question, e.g. 'What is it?' (substance), 'How much is it?' (quantity), etc.

common sense:

In Aristotelian psychology this is the sensory faculty to which all the "special" senses (sight, hearing, smell, taste and touch) report their data, and which judges of those sensory characteristics which are perceived by more than one of the special senses, e.g. movement, shape, and size.

complex:

In scholastic logic a "complex" is any sort of proposition, where a proposition is always composed out of simpler elements and ultimately out of non-complex terms.

composite and divided senses:

When a sentence contains a modal term (i.e. a term importing necessity or possibility) or some sentence connective (subordinating conjunctions, relative pronouns, etc.) it often admits of a structural ambiguity where in one sense (the composite sense) it should be read as having the overall form of a predicate affirmed or denied of a subject, and in another sense (the divided sense) it should be read as a compound sentence composed from two other sentences somehow connected. Examples:

Ambiguous: Every bachelor is necessarily unmarried.

Comp. sense: That every bachelor is unmarried is necessarily true.

Div. sense: If something is a bachelor, then it is unmarried necessarily (i.e. can never be married).

Ambiguous: Scholars who read books will object to censorship.

Comp. sense: All those scholars who read books will object to censorship.

Div. sense: All scholars read books and they will all object to censorship.

Ambiguous: I did not go to the party because she was there.

Comp. sense: That I went to the party because she was there is not the case.

Div. sense: I did not go to the party, and this was because she was there.

connotative term:

In Ockham's logic a connotative term is one which has both a primary and a secondary signification, i.e. besides its extension it makes reference to something else. This is because, in contrast to an "absolute term"(*q.v.*), it has a nominal definition, i.e. it is possible to express the meaning of a connotative term by spelling out what it says about anything in its extension. For example, 'father' has the nominal definition 'male who has sired offspring.' Its primary signification is all such males; its secondary signification is the offspring.

continuum:

Any whole divisible into parts *ad infinitum*, i.e. where there are no smallest parts, but every part is divisible into still smaller parts.

de re/de dicto:

An ambiguity affecting many modal propositions and which is actually a special case of the "composite/divided sense" ambiguity (*q.v.*). The "*de re*" reading corresponds to the divided sense; the "*de dicto*" reading to the composite sense. In the "*de re*" reading something is said of a thing, while in the "*de dicto*" reading something is said of what a proposition says. For example:

Ambiguous: Every citizen could be mayor.

de re sense: Of anyone it is the case that if they are a citizen they could be mayor.

de dicto: That every citizen is mayor could be the case.

demonstration:

A deductively valid argument from necessarily true premisses to a necessarily true conclusion where the truth of the premisses is certain from the start and explains why the conclusion is true, i.e. the facts related by the premisses are explanatorily prior to the fact related by the conclusion. Also called an *apodictic* argument.

denominative term:

A term which refers to things in virtue of their possessing a feature which is not their quiddity (*q.v.*) or a part of their quiddity. Sometimes any categorematic term (*q.v.*) other than those which say *what* something is, i.e. species and genus terms, is considered denominative.

element:

In Aristotelian physical science an element is the simplest material substance that can exist "separately," i.e. without having to exist *in* something else as its substratum (*q.v.*). Aristotle accepted a traditional view that earth, air, fire and water are elements. To these he added a fifth which served as the matter for the heavenly bodies. Out of these elements all the other physical objects of the world are ultimately composed.

Aristotle's theory claimed that earth, air, fire and water were formed by combining in "prime matter" one opposite from each of the two opposing pairs, warm vs. cold, fluid (wet) vs. dry. Thus fire = warm plus dry; air = warm plus fluid; water = cold plus fluid; and earth = cold plus dry.

eminence:

A perfection (*q.v.*) exists "eminently" in a subject when, even though that subject is not actually characterized by that perfection, it has perfections of a higher sort which would enable it in principle to be the ultimate source for all that perfection in something else. This contrasts with having such perfections "formally," i.e. as real features directly belonging to the subject. A "most eminent being" is one whose perfection is not in this way exceeded by the perfection of some other being.

esse objectivum:

The existence something has merely by being an object of some mental act, state, or power. Contrasted with *esse formale* which is real existence independent of being thought of, willed, desired or whatever. The scholastics speak of different forms of this such as *esse cognitum* (existence as something known), *esse intellectum* (existence as something thought of*)*, *esse volitum* (existence as something willed). All of these are ways of existing "in the soul" but not as some real entity which is a part of or an attribute of the soul.

essential-in-the-first-mode:

In latin: *per se primo modo*. This is a term of art derived from Aristotle's *Posterior Analytics*. X is said to be predicated *per se primo modo* of Y just

in case X is a component of the definition of Y which must itself be predicated of Y if the definition is to be. For example, in 'An animal is an organism,' 'organism' is predicated of 'animal' *per se primo modo* since any definition of what it is to be an animal will have to mention that an animal is a sort of organism. Aristotle contrasts this with something which is predicated *per se secundo modo* of Y. In this latter case Y must occur in the definition of X as a specification of the sort of subject X is required to belong to if it is to belong to anything. For example: in 'A number is even,' 'even' is predicated of 'number' *per se secundo modo*, since any explanation of what it is to be even would have to mention that only numbers are even.

extremes:

The terms which form the subject and the predicate in the conclusion of a syllogism. In this sense the extremes are opposed to the "middle" (*q.v.*). Sometimes the subject and predicate terms of any categorical proposition (*q.v.*) are referred to as the "extremes."

fallacy of accident:

A broad category of mistaken arguments which appear to be valid only because of a hidden ambiguity in one or more of the terms involved.

fallacy of consequent:

An argument which reasons that if A entails B, then B entails A, or at least accepts that B entails A, where in fact all that is true is that A entails B.

fallacy of figure of speech:

A broad category of mistaken arguments which appear to be valid only because of some hidden ambiguity in the phrasing of one or more of the sentences used or some subtle difference in the use of a term in one occurrence from its use in another.

final cause:

That for the sake of which what is caused exists or comes to be. Examples of final causes are the ends to be achieved by actions or products of intentional design. But Aristotle extended the notion so that even where no mind is present to formulate a design there could still be final causes, as in the way bodily organs exist for the sake of certain functions and lower animals behave so as to achieve certain ends. Also sometimes the final cause is a being whose good is served by what is caused, and in the case of motions the terminal state is often treated as the final cause of the motion.

first/second actuality:

In Aristotle's metaphysics a "first actuality" is a sort of readiness, capacity, or disposition to engage in behaviour which manifests that first actuality. The behaviour itself is the "second actuality." For example, a moral virtue is a first actuality in the sense that it is a disposition to engage in morally virtuous behaviour in appropriate circumstances, while that behaviour itself is the second actuality manifesting the virtue. Also the sense in which someone knows something even when they are unconscious is a first actuality, while their actually thinking about what they know is a second actuality.

Form:

In Plato's philosophy the eternal, changeless archetypes on which all physical things are modelled, and which are knowable only by abstract, intellectual thought or intuition. See selection **VI.1.1**.

formality:

John Duns Scotus uses this term to refer to the reality of some aspect of a thing. Sometimes he claims that in the same thing there can be distinct formalities although this distinction is not a distinction of things (*res*), nor does the distinction amount to an unqualified real distinction.

form/matter:

In Aristotelian science all physical objects are thought of as combining a substratum (*q.v.*) with some actuality, analogous to the way a statue combines the material out of which it is composed with the shape the sculptor gives it in creating the statue. The former component is the "matter"; the latter, the "form." The form is accidental to the matter, in the sense that the matter can exist even though it does not have that form, but is essential to the object that combines the matter and the form. The statue, for example, cannot exist without that shape the sculptor gives it. Where the object in question is a substance, the form is referred to as a "substantial form" (*q.v.*). Aristotle and most of his followers thought that there could exist forms that did not exist in any matter. These were called "separated forms" or "separated substances" since they were substances on their own. Such substances were all minds, since only intellectual activity was held not to require some physical organ.

habit:

A fairly permanent dispositional or capacitative state of something (usually something alive). A habit is always a *first* actuality (*q.v.*) as opposed to some activity or on-going behaviour.

homonymous:

In Aristotle things were "homonyms" when the same word was applied to them but not as having the same definition. Thus both the wing of a bird and the wing of a house are called "wing," but the definition of 'wing' in the first use would be something like 'limb used for flying,' whereas in the second use it would be something like 'extension jutting out from the center.' A term is then said to be homonymous if it admits of usages in which one and the same definition of it is not always applicable. Contrasts with 'synonymous.'

hypothetical proposition:

Any proposition constructed out of two or more sentences joined by a coordinating or subordinating conjunction, such as 'and,' 'or,' 'if,' 'when,' 'because,' etc. Hypothetical propositions are often classified by the type of conjunction involved; thus there are disjunctive hypotheticals, temporal hypotheticals, and causal hypotheticals. Contrasted with "categorical propositions" (*q.v.*).

in quid:

Pertaining to what (*quid*) a thing is. See 'quiddity.'

infinity:

In Aristotelian philosophy two sorts of infinity are recognized: actual and potential. An actual infinity occurs extensively when a quantity of things simultaneously in existence is greater than any whole number whatsoever; it occurs intensively when the degree to which some quality or perfection is present exceeds any other degree by a proportion greater than any whole number. A potential infinity occurs when some process of addition or division could go on endlessly. For example, Aristotle thinks space is endlessly divisible and thus potentially infinite; time, on the other hand, is something to which endless additions can be made, and so it too is potentially infinite. Aristotle rejected the possibility of an extensive actual infinity; on the question of an intensive actual infinity he is not clear whether it is possible or not. See *Physics* III, 4-8.

instant of nature:

Some scholastics thought of the "order of nature" (*q.v.*) as analogous to the temporal order with its successive moments or instants, and assigned "instants" in the order of nature corresponding to the ordering of prior to posterior that was supposed to exist there. What "occurs at an earlier instant of nature" is then explanatorily prior to what "occurs at a later instant," even though those instants of nature may all exist at the same time in the temporal order.

intelligence:

A mind which exists as a separate substance, i.e. as a substantial form with its own existence apart from matter.

intention:

In logic and metaphysics an intention is a character or feature that is meant by some categorematic term (*q.v.*) or is considered by an act or thought, and which can be thought to belong to something. A *first intention* is what is meant by a term that is descriptive of things in respects that do not imply that the thing is an object of thought. A *second intention* is what is meant by a term that holds of things only insofar as they are meant or thought of, i.e. it holds only of first intentions. Ockham gives his own explanation of these terms in selection **VI.9.2**.

intentional existence = esse intentionale:

The existence something has merely by being considered by the mind, whether or not it has real existence apart from such consideration. See entry for '*esse objectivum*.'

intrinsic vs. extrinsic cause:

The material cause, i.e. the substratum (*q.v.*), of a thing, and the formal cause, i.e. the actuality which constitutes the quiddity (*q.v.*) of a thing, are called the intrinsic causes of that thing. The efficient, i.e. producing cause and the final cause, i.e. the end for the sake of which the thing exists, are called the extrinsic causes of the thing.

intuitive vs. abstractive cognition:

Intuitive cognition is illustrated by sight where typically what is apprehended is taken to be something existing independently of the act of apprehension. Abstractive cognition is illustrated by imagining where typically the apprehension of the object implies no belief in the independent existence of that object. In late scholastic thought this distinction is applied to strictly intellectual apprehensions as well as sensory cognitions. The intuitive cognition is defined by its tending to cause a judgment that what is apprehended exists, while the abstractive lacks this element.

loci (topoi):

Grounds of inference, many of which do not admit of a formal treatment. The original discussion of these is Aristotle's *De Topicis (Topics)*, but more influential on medieval thinkers were the discussions by Cicero, Themistius, and Boethius which had a more practical orientation than Aristotle's treatment.

middle term:

Every syllogism in the strict sense consists of two premisses and a conclusion which are constructed from three terms. One of these terms appears in both premisses but not in the conclusion; it is called the "middle term." Example:

Some numbers are *even numbers*.
All *even numbers* are divisible by two.
Therefore, some numbers are divisible by two.

natural generation:

The production by some agency operative in the physical world of a new individual substance (*q.v.*) through a temporal process in which pre-existent material of some sort is given a substantial form (*q.v.*) which it did not have before, and the composite that results is a substance of some physical species.

necessity of the consequence/consequent

When a conditional is asserted with some modal word indicating necessity, the whole is often ambiguous as between a composite and a divided sense (*q.v.*), where the former states that the connection between the antecedent and the consequent holds necessarily ("necessity of the consequence") and the latter states that if the antecedent is true then the consequent is not just true but necessarily true ("necessity of the consequent"). For example:

Ambiguous: If John is captain he must be in charge.

nec. of consequence: It is necessarily true that if John is captain he is in charge.

nec. of consequent: If John is captain, then 'John is in charge' states a necessary truth.

obligation:

The scholastics sometimes engaged in disputational contests which were governed by definite rules for questions and responses and where each disputant tried to force their opponent into asserting contradictory propositions. The rules established certain "obligations" on the part of each disputant, i.e. they were forced to respond in certain ways to the inquiries of their opponent.

order of nature:

Contrasted with the "temporal order." Items which are ordered by nature are prior and posterior to each other, i.e. they are arranged in a series in which each is either "before" or "after" or "simultaneous" with any of the others, but the ordering is based on explanatory priority, i.e. one is a pre-requisite for the existence of the other, even though it may not have to exist temporally before the other. Thus the scholastics would say that the fire is prior in the order of nature to the heat and light it produces even though as soon as the fire exists the heat and light exist as well. The fire is prior in the sense that the heat and light exist *because* the fire exists, not vice versa. Duns Scotus gives an explanation of "priority in nature" in selection **III.7.1**, pp.432-433.

passive or possible intellect:

The mind or part of the mind which is not always active and is receptive of the abstracted forms of things through the action on it of the agent or active intellect (*q.v.*) in conjunction with input from sense experience. In some Islamic thinkers, notably Averroes, both the possible and the agent intellect were thought to belong to a single everlasting mind on which all humans depended for their intellectual capacities.

perfection:

Fullness of being. In scholastic metaphysics this translates pretty much into breadth of causal power. The more different types of positive features an entity can cause to exist the more causal power and hence perfection it has. An important principle here is that anything which is the total efficient cause of the existence of something else must have more perfection than the item it causes.

persistent being:

An entity that continues to exist over time but does not extend over time in such a way that its parts come into existence one after the other and are never all in existence at once. For example, a physical object all of whose parts are spatially related rather than temporally related. Contrasted with a "successive being," like a day or year, whose parts are hours or months.

phantasm:

A sensory mental image. Aristotle proposed that these serve as a kind of vehicle for thinking.

possible intellect: See *passive or possible intellect*.

predestination:

According to orthodox theology God has selected from eternity those to whom He will give the grace necessary for salvation. This selection is called "predestination" and the person selected is said to be "predestined."

prime matter:

The substratum common to the elements (*q.v.*) which receives the contrary forms of heat and cold, wetness and dryness, and survives the transformation of one element into another. As the ultimate substratum for the physical world, of itself it is potentially all physical substances but actually none of them.

privation:

The state we find matter in at the start of a process of generation which ends with the full possession of some form by that matter. At the beginning the matter is "deprived" of the form that it will have at the end.

qualified/unqualified:

The "qualified/unqualified" (*haplos*) contrast was frequently deployed by Aristotle when a word commonly had two uses, one with some sort of qualifier or complement, and one without. For example, some thing might be said to "come to be" white, or large, or whatever, and then one speaks of a qualified coming to be. But one can also just say that something comes to be *full stop*, and then what one means is that the thing has come into existence. This would be "unqualified coming to be."

There is also a fallacy of "qualified and unqualified," which is just an argument which depends on thinking that some term is used unambiguously when in fact it varies its meaning between a qualified and an unqualified sense.

quiddity:

The "quiddity" of a thing is what (*quid*) it is to be that thing. The "quiddity" is what is spelled out in a definition of the thing and the term is synonymous with 'essence' in many places. In Avicenna's philosophy the quiddity of anything other than God does not include that thing's existence and hence it is not something whose non-existence is simply self-contradictory.

real relation:

A relation which belongs to a term in respect of some other term independently of those terms being conceived in some way or other. Opposed to a "relation of thought" or "of reason" (*relation rationis*) where the terms are only so related because a mind thinks of those terms in some way. Examples: being a father is a real relation; being predicated is a relation of thought. Real relations require that the terms have real existence (or at least possible real existence) and not just existence in a mind; but relations of thought can hold between items whose only existence is in the mind.

separate substance:

A form that has an existence on its own independent of matter. In Aristotle's philosophy all of these are minds or intellects. In neo-Platonic cosmology they are called Intelligences. Such substances can be neither generated nor destroyed and are to this extent necessary beings.

species:

In ancient and medieval theories of cognition a "species" is a "likeness" of what is perceived by the senses (the "sensible species") or by the mind ("intelligible species") and which by existing in the sensory faculty or in the mind enables those powers to apprehend that of which it is a likeness. In some theories such species also exist in the "medium" between the external object of sensory cognition and the sensory organ.

species/genus:

In Aristotelian philosophy everything which is a definite type of thing, i.e. has a quiddity (*q.v.*), falls into classes each of which can be defined by characteristics essential to all the members of the class and which together belong only to members of that class. When a class of this sort has no sub-classes which can be similarly defined it is a "lowest species" (*infima species*). If such a class does have sub-classes which can be similarly defined it is a "genus" and the sub-classes are its species. Every species which is not a lowest species is thus a genus. But there are genera, the so-called "highest genera," which are not species of any further genus. Often it is not the classes which are treated as species and genera but the predicates whose extensions are those classes, or the characters which are definitive of those classes. See selection **VI.3.1**.

specific difference:

The feature or features which appear in the definition of a species and set it apart from other species of the genus to which it immediately belongs.

substance:

In Aristotelian philosophy a substance is a subject to which characteristics belong and which has a definite essence or quiddity (*q.v.*) but which does not itself exist in another substance. Natural phys-

ical bodies such as organisms, as well as the heavenly bodies, are standard examples. Also the substantial forms (*q.v.*) of these as well as minds that exist without any dependence on bodies are considered substances and better examples of the notion of substance than physical things.

Primary substances are individuals of the above types. *Second* or *secondary substances* are the types themselves, i.e. the species and genera.

Separate or *separated substances* are forms that exist without being in any matter and thus do not take up space. See entry for '*form/matter*.'

substantial/accidental form:

A form is an actuality which gives some character to what it is the form of. In the case of a "substantial form" the character is that by which the thing is what it is, i.e. belongs to some species of being; in the case of an "accidental form" it is that by which the thing has some character that is not definitive of what it is.

substratum:

A subject for items accidental to itself which can persist despite losing any one of those accidents. Substrata are usually substances (*q.v.*) or the material out of which physical substances are composed. These persist despite losing the particular size, shape, colour, etc. that they once had.

successive being:

An entity like a day whose parts exist successively over time. Opposed to "persistent" or "permanent" beings like ordinary physical objects all of whose parts are spatial and exist simultaneously.

supposition:

The way a categorematic term (*q.v.*) as used in a certain sentence "stands for" certain things. The scholastics recognized three general modes of supposition: *personal*: where the term stands for things that are, or have been, or will be, or can be, in what we would call its extension (e.g. 'animal' stands for fish, mammals, insects, etc.); *material*: where the term stands for itself as a word (e.g. the way 'animal' stands for itself in 'Animal has six letters'); *simple*: where the term stands for the concept it engenders in the mind of someone who hears it and understands its meaning (e.g. 'animal' in 'Animal is a concept for which there is a word in all languages'). Ockham explains some of the distinctions within personal supposition in selection **III.8.1**, pp.231-232.

suppositum:

Something which is stood for, i.e. referred to, by a term in a proposition, and thus can be a subject of predication. Often this term is restricted to things which cannot themselves exist in any subject nor in any way be common to many subjects.

syllogism:

Deductive reasoning standardly proceeding from two premisses to a conclusion, in which the validity is a matter of the logical/grammatical form of the sentences involved rather than the particular meanings of the terms involved. "Categorical syllogisms" consist of categorical propositions (*q.v.*) and their validity depends on what we now think of as class logic. For example, this syllogism,

Every star twinkles.
Everything that twinkles is far away.
Therefore, every star is far away.

is valid, and any grammatical substitution on the terms 'star,' 'twinkles,' and 'far away' would also result in a valid syllogism.

"Hypothetical syllogisms" involve at least one proposition which is "hypothetical" in the sense of containing more than one sentence connected by some coordinating or subordinating conjunction. For example, this syllogism,

If a luminous body is far away, it twinkles.
Mars does not twinkle.
Therefore, Mars is not a luminous body that is far away.

is valid, and substitution on 'luminous body,' 'far away,' 'twinkles,' and 'Mars' will result in another valid syllogism.

syncategorematic term:

Terms which do not have any descriptive meaning and thus do not fall under any of the Aristotelian "categories" (*q.v.*). They are terms to which it would not make any sense to assign an extension. Examples are quantifying determiners like 'every,' 'some,' 'no,' etc., as well as conjunctions, prepositions, and many adverbs. Contrasts with 'categorematic term.'

synonymy:

Things are synonymous when they are referred to by the same term in the same sense of that term. This contrasts with their being "homonymous" (*q.v.*). Terms are said to be synonymous when they do not differ in signification. Ockham defines this in his own way in selection **VI.9.3**.

transcendental:

A term whose extension includes things in different categories (*q.v.*) or something, like God, which is not in any category at all. Examples are 'being' and its "attributes": 'one,' 'good,' 'true.'

universal:

Whatever can, at least in principle, be predicated of more than one thing. See Aristotle's definition in *De Interpretatione* 7 (selection **VI.2.2**).

universal vs. particular:

A universal *term* is one that at least in principle can have more than one item in its extension, i.e. be true of more than one thing. A *proposition* is universal when its subject term is a universal term and the predicate is asserted, or denied, of all the items in that terms extension. A proposition is particular when its subject term is a universal term and it claims only that the predicate holds of, or does not hold of, *some* items in the extension of the subject term.

Also 'particular' can mean simply an individual thing, i.e. some thing which is not a whole type of things, whereas 'universal' refers to a type of thing, i.e. something which is or could be common to many things.

univocal production:

A production in which the producer shares the same nature as what is produced, as when fire produces fire. Opposed to "equivocal production" where the producer has a different nature from what it produces.

univocity:

A term is univocal when it applies in the same sense to more than one type of thing. The things in question are then said to possess some feature "univo-cally" rather than "equivocally." For example, it was a question in scholastic metaphysics whether 'being' was a univocal term in its application to things in different categories, i.e. whether, say, substances and qualities possess being univocally or only equivocally. Cf. 'homonymous.'

virtual existence:

Some perfection virtually exists in a cause X just in case X does not really (or formally) have that perfection but can cause it to exist in other things. For example, God does not Himself really have the perfection of corporeality, i.e. God is not (formally) a body, but He can cause other things to be bodies, and thus has that perfection virtually. This contrasts with having the perfection "formally," i.e. as a real feature directly inhering in the subject.

SOURCES

PETER ABELARD

I.3.1

Opera Theologica III, in *Corpus Christianorum, Continuatio Mediaevalis* XIII, ed. E. M. Buytaert & C. J. Mews; Turnholt: Brepols, 1987, pp.511-24. Translation especially for this volume by M.M. Tweedale.

V.3.1

Petri Abaelardi Opera Theologica III, ed. E. M. Buytaert in *Corpus Christianorum, Continuatio Mediaevalis* XII; Turnholt: Brepols, 1969. Book III, 60-2, 69, 88, 115, 136-43, 148-53, 157, 162-4, 166; Book IV, 20, 22-3, 25-6, 33-6, 86, 90. Translation especially for this volume by M.M. Tweedale.

VI.6.1

Peter Abaelards Philosophische Schriften, ed. by B. Geyer in *Beitrage zur Geschichte der Philosophie des Mittelalters*, bd. xxi, Munster i.W., 1919 & 1933; *Logica Ingredientibus, Glossae super Porphyrium* (8,32-32,12). Translation by M.M. Tweedale especially for this volume.

VI.6.2

Op.cit., *Logica "Nostrorum Petitioni Sociorum,"* (530, 30-533, 9). Translation by M.M. Tweedale especially for this volume.

VI.6.3

Op.cit., *Logica Ingredientibus, Glossae super Peri Ermenias*, (365-70, 390-3). Translation by M.M. Tweedale especially for this volume.

VIII.4.1

D.E. Luscombe, *Peter Abelard's Ethics*, Oxford: Clarendon Press, 1971. Selections from *Know thyself (Scito te ipsum)*, translation by D.E. Luscombe, pp.3-41, 53-7.

ST. ANSELM

II.2.1

Anselm of Canterbury, vol.I, ed. and translated by J. Hopkins & H. Richardson; Toronto & New York: Edwin Mellen Press, 1974. pp.93-5.

IV.3.1

Op.cit. vol.II, pp.181-8.

ST. THOMAS AQUINAS

I.5.1

St. Thomas Aquinas: On the Truth of the Catholic Faith (Summa Contra Gentiles) Bk.II; Garden City, NY: Hanover House, 1956; ch.30 (pp.85-90); translation by James F. Anderson.

I.5.2

Op.cit., Bk.I, ch.31.

I.5.3

Op.cit., Bk.I, chs.82 & 83.

II.4.1

St. Thomas Aquinas, Summa Theologiae, New York, London: Blackfriars, with McGraw-Hill Book Company, 1963, vol.2, pp.4-8; translation especially for this volume by M.M. Tweedale.

II.4.2

Op.cit., pp.12-17; translation especially for this volume by M.M. Tweedale.

II.4.3

Divi Thomae Aquinatis Opuscula Philosophica, ed. R.M. Spiazzi; Turin & Rome: Marietti, 1954, p.13. Translation especially for this volume by M.M. Tweedale.

III.5.1

St. Thomas Aquinas, Siger of Brabant, St. Bonaventure: On the Eternity of the World (De Aeternitate Mundi); translation by C. Vollert, L.H.

Kendzierski, P.M. Byrne; Milwaukee: Marquette University Press, 1964, pp.26-7.

III.5.2.
Op.cit., pp.19-25.

IV.4.1
St. Thomas Aquinas, Summa Theologiae, New York, London: Blackfriars, with McGraw-Hill Book Company, 1963, vol.IV, pp.45-51; translation especially for this volume by M.M. Tweedale.

VIII.5.1
Op.cit., vol.XVIII, pp.84-103; translation especially for this volume by M.M. Tweedale.

VIII.5.2
Op.cit., vol. XX, pp.64-9; translation especially for this volume by M.M. Tweedale.

VIII.5.3
Op.cit., vol. XXV, pp.114-21; translation especially for this volume by M.M. Tweedale.

VIII.5.4
Op.cit., vol. XLIII, pp.190-7,198-203; translation especially for this volume by M.M. Tweedale.

VIII.5.5
Op.cit., vol. XIII, pp.154-9; translation especially for this volume by M.M. Tweedale.

ARISTOTLE

I.1.1
The Complete Works of Aristotle, the revised Oxford translation, ed. J. Barnes. Princeton University Press, 1984. vol.II, pp.1600-1; translation by W.D. Ross.

I.1.2
Ibid, p.1603.

I.1.3
Op.cit., vol.I, pp.332-8; translation by R.P. Hardie and R.K. Gaye.

I.1.4
Op.cit., vol.II, pp. 1619-23; translation by W.D. Ross.

II.1.1
Op.cit., vol.I, pp. 432-4; translation by R.P. Hardie and R.K. Gaye.

II.1.2
Ibid, pp. 444-6; translation by R.P. Hardie and R.K. Gaye.

II.1.3
Op.cit., vol.II, pp. 1692-5; translation by W.D. Ross.

III.1.1
Op.cit., vol.I, pp. 418-421; translation by R.P. Hardie and R.K. Gaye.

IV.1.1
Op.cit., vol.I, pp.28-30; translation by J.L. Ackrill.

V.1.1
Op.cit., vol.I, pp.171-2; translation by W.A. Pickard-Cambridge.

V.1.2
Op.cit., vol.II, pp.1603-6; translation by W.D. Ross.

V.1.3
Op.cit., vol.I, pp.344-5; translation by R.P. Hardie and R.K. Gaye.

VI.2.1
Op.cit., vol.I, pp. 3-8; translation by J.L. Ackrill.

VI.2.2
Ibid., pp.27-8; translation by J.L. Ackrill.

VI.2.3
Op.cit., vol.II, pp.1578-9; translation by W.D. Ross.

VI.2.4
Ibid., p.1584; translation by W.D. Ross.

VI.2.5
Ibid., pp.1639-41; translation by W.D. Ross.

VIII.1.1
Op.cit., vol.II, pp.1742-52; translation by W.D. Ross, revised by J.O. Urmson.

VIII.1.2
Ibid., pp.1756-7.

ST. AUGUSTINE OF HIPPO

III.2.1

Basic Writings of St. Augustine, 2 vols., ed. W.J. Oates, New York: Random House, 1948. *The Confessions*, translation by J.G. Pilkington, vol.I, pp.190-202.

III.2.2

Op. cit.; *The City of God*, translation by M. Dods, assisted by G. Wilson, vol.II, pp.194-6.

VII.1.1

St. Augustine: Against the Academics (no.12 of *Ancient Christian Writers*), translation by J.J. O'Meara; Westminster, MD: The New Man Press, and London: Longmans, Green & Co., 1951, pp.91-117.

VII.1.2

Saint Augustine: The City of God against the Pagans (De Civitate Dei contra Paganos), translated by W.M. Green; Loeb Classical Library, 7 vols.; London: Wm. Heinemann Ltd., and Cambridge, MA.: Harvard University Press, 1960-6; vol.iii, pp.531-5.

VII.1.3

Augustine: Earlier Writings (vol.VI of *The Library of Christian Classics*), translated by J.H.S. Burleigh; Philadelphia: The Westminster Press, 1953, pp.144-60.

VIII.2.1

Saint Augustine: The Catholic and Manichaean Ways of Life (vol.56 of *The Fathers of the Church*), translated by D.A. Gallagher & I.J. Gallagher, Washington, DC: The Catholic University of America Press, 1966, pp.5-11.

VIII.2.2

Saint Augustine: The City of God against the Pagans (De Civitate Dei contra Paganos); *op.cit.*, vol.iv, pp.123-39.

VIII.2.3

Divine Providence and the Problem of Evil (De ordine), translated by R.P. Russell, in *Writings of St. Augustine*, vol.1 (in *The Fathers of the Church*); New York: Cima Publishing Co., 1948, pp.286-93.

VIII.2.4

Ibid., pp.308-21.

VIII.2.5

Augustine: Earlier Writings (vol.VI of *The Library of Christian Classics*); *op.cit.*, pp.115-8.

VIII.2.6

Saint Augustine: The City of God against the Pagans (De Civitate Dei contra Paganos); *op.cit.*, vol.iv, pp.345-93.

AVERROES (IBN RUSHD)

I.4.1

Tahafut al-Tahafut. Translation by Simon Van Den Bergh, Unesco Collection of Great Works Arabic Series; London: Luzac & Co. Ltd., 1969, pp.235-41.

I.4.2

Op.cit., pp.316-33.

II.3.1

Op.cit., pp.241-9.

III.3.1

Op.cit., pp.1-36.

AVICENNA (IBN SINA)

I.2.1

G. F. Hourani, "Ibn Sina on Necessary and Possible Existence" in *Philosophical Forum* 4 (1972-3), pp.74-86. Selection on p.76.

I.2.2

Ibid., pp.77-8.

I.2.3

Ibid., pp.79-82.

I.2.4

Ibid., pp.82-4.

VI.7.1

from *Avicenna Latinus: Liber de Philosophia Prima sive Scientia Divina*, 2 vols., ed. S. Van Riet, E. Peeters, Louvain & Leiden: E.J. Brill, 1977, 1980. Translation by M.M. Tweedale especially for this volume.

VI.7.2
from *Logica,* ff.2r-12v in *Opera Philosophica,* Venice 1508; reimpression en fac-simile, Louvain, 1961. Translation by M.M. Tweedale especially for this volume.

BOETHIUS

IV.2.1
Boethius, The Theological Tractates, and The Consolation of Philosophy; translation by H.F. Stewart, E.K. Rand, and S.J. Tester, Loeb 2nd edition, Cambridge, MA, & London: Harvard University Press, 1978, pp.395-435; translation modified somewhat by the editors.

V.2.1
Op.cit., pp.2-31; with some modifications by the editors.

VI.4.1
Five Texts on the Medieval Problem of Universals, translations by Paul Spade, Indianapolis/ Cambridge: Hackett, 1994; pp.20-5.

PSEUDO-DIONYSIUS THE AREOPAGITE

IX.2.1
Pseudo-Dionysius, The Complete Works; New York, Mahwah: Paulist Press, 1987, translation by Colm Luibheid, pp.98-103.

IX.2.2
Op.cit., pp.105-10.

IX.2.3
Op.cit., pp.135-41

IX.2.4
Op.cit., pp.263, 265-6

GARLANDUS COMPOTISTA

VI.5.1
Garlandus Compotista, Dialectica, ed. by L.M. de Rijk; Assen: Van Gorcum, 1959; pp. 3-11. Translation by M.M. Tweedale especially for this volume.

AL GHAZALI

VIII.3.1
The Book of Fear and Hope, translated by W. McKamp; Leiden: E.J. Brill; pp.1-25.

VIII.3.2
Ibid., pp.25-37.

HENRY OF GHENT

I.8.1
Ioannis Duns Scoti Opera Omnia XVIII, ed. P.L. Modric; Vatican: Typis Polyglottis Vaticanis, 1982, note on pp.35-7. Translation by M.M. Tweedale especially for this volume.

III.6.1
Henrici de Gandavo, Opera Omnia V, *Quodlibet I,* ed. R. Macken O.F.M.; Leiden: Leuven University Press & E.J. Brill, 1979; pp.27-46. Translation by M. M. Tweedale especially for this volume.

VII.2.1
Summae Quaestionum Ordinarium, I. Badius, 1520 (reprint in Franciscan Institute Publications, text series no.5, 1953) ff3v-7v; translation by M.M. Tweedale especially for this volume.

IBN TUFAIL (ABUBACER)

IX.4.1
The Journey of the Soul, The Story of Hai bin Yaqzan, as told by Abu Bakr Muhammad bin Tufail, translation by Riad Kocache; London; The Octagon Press, 1982; pp.3-5, 44-50.

JOHN DUNS SCOTUS

I.9.1
Ioannis Duns Scoti Opera Omnia, vol.II, ed. P. C. Balic; Vatican: Typis Polyglottis Vaticanis, 1950, pp.176-9. Adapted from the translation by A. Wolter in *Duns Scotus: Philosophical Writings,* Nelson, 1962, pp.53-5.

I.9.2
Op.cit., pp.151-65, 167-8; pp.39-47, 48-9, in Wolter's translation.

I.9.3

Op.cit., vol. VI, pp.341-9. Translated by M.M. Tweedale especially for this volume.

I.9.4

Op.cit., vol. VI, pp.351-61.Translated by M.M. Tweedale especially for this volume.

I.9.5

Op.cit., vol. VI, pp. 363-9. Translated by M.M. Tweedale especially for this volume.

II.5.1

Adapted from the translation by A. Wolter in *Duns Scotus: Philosophical Writings*, Nelson, 1962, pp.62-8.

II.5.2

Op.Cit., vol. II, pp.206-13. Translated especially for this volume by M.M. Tweedale.

III.7.1

Op.Cit., vol. VII, pp.50-91. Translation by M.M. Tweedale especially for this volume.

IV.6.1

Op.Cit., vol. VI, pp.401-44. Translation by M.M. Tweedale especially for this volume.

V.4.1.

Joanni Duns Scoti Opera Omnia, ed. Vives; Paris, 1891-5, vol.XXII, pp.399-410. Translation by M.M. Tweedale.

VI.8.1

Ioannis Duns Scoti Opera Omnia, vol.VII, ed. P.C. Balic, Vatican: Typis Polyglottis Vaticanis, 1973; pp.391-410. Translation by M.M. Tweedale especially for this volume.

VI.8.2

Op.cit., vol.VII, pp.474-84. Translation by M.M. Tweedale especially for this volume.

VI.8.3

Joanni Duns Scoti Opera Omnia, ed. Vives; Paris, 1891-5, vol.VII, pp.452-62. Translation by M.M. Tweedale especially for this volume.

VII.4.1

Adapted from the translation by A. Wolter in *Duns Scotus: Philosophical Writings*, Nelson, 1962, pp.97-132.

JOHN SCOTUS ERIUGENA

IX.3.1

Eriugena: Periphyseon (The Division of Nature), Montreal, Dumbarton Oaks: Bellarmin, 1987; translation by I.P. Sheldon-Williams, revised by John J. O'Meara; pp.25-30.

IX.3.2

Op.cit., pp.46-8.

IX.3.3

Op.cit., pp.115-21.

IX.3.4

Op.cit., pp.123-7.

IX.3.5

Op.cit., pp.176-83.

IX.3.6

Op.cit., pp.190-207.

IX.3.7

Op.cit., pp.305-11.

IX.3.8

Op.cit., pp.417-21.

IX.3.9

Op.cit., pp.561-3.

MOSES MAIMONIDES

VII.4.1

The Guide for the Perplexed, translated by M. Friedlander; New York: Dover Publications Inc., 1956. Selection on pp.133-8.

VII.4.2

Op.cit., pp.171-6.

VII.4.3

Op.cit., pp.178-89.

VII.4.4
Op.cit., pp.190-9.

MEISTER ECKHART

IX.5.1
Meister Eckhart, Teacher and Preacher, ed. Bernard McGinn; New York, Mahwah, Toronto: Paulist Press, 1986; pp.95-102, translation by B. McGinn.

IX.5.2
Ibid., pp.223-6.

IX.5.3
Op.cit., pp.255-60, translation by Frank Tobin.

IX.5.4
Ibid., p.281.

IX.5.5
Meister Eckhart, The Essential Sermons, Commentaries, Treatises, and Defense, translation and introduction by Edmund Colledge, O.S.A. and Bernard McGinn; London: SPCK, 1981; pp.222-3.

IX.5.6
Ibid., pp.285-94.

NICHOLAS OF AUTRECOURT

VII.5.1
Nicholas of Autrecourt: His Correspondence with Master Giles and Bernard of Arezzo; ed. and translation L.M. de Rijk; Leiden, New York, Koln: E.J. Brill, 1994; pp.59-75.

PLATO

VI.1.1
Plato: The Collected Dialogues, translated by B. Jowett; Princeton, NJ: Princeton University Press, 1961; pp.1161-8, 1178-9.

PORPHYRY

VI.3.1
Five Texts on the Medieval Problem of Universal; translation by Paul Spade; Indianapolis/ Cambridge: Hackett, 1994; pp.1-11.

SIGER OF BRABANT

I.7.1
A Commentary on Necessity; Questions concerning the Metaphysics, ed. A. Maurer; Louvain-La-Neuve: Editions de l'Institut Supérieur de Philosophie, 1983, pp.224-7. Translation by R.N. Bosley.

IV.5.1.
La doctrine de la providence dans les écrits de Siger de Brabant, ed. J.J. Duin, (Phil. med. III); Louvain, 1954. pp.14-44; translation by R.N. Bosley especially for this volume.

VII.3.1
from *A Commentary on Necessity; Questions concerning the Metaphysics,* ed. A. Maurer; Louvain-La-Neuve: Editions de l'Institut Supérieur de Philosophie, 1983, pp.429-31. Translation by R.N. Bosley especially for this volume.

STEPHEN TEMPIER (BISHOP OF PARIS)

I.8.1
Medieval Political Philosophy: A Sourcebook. Edited by Ralph Lerner and Muhsin Mahdi; The Free Press of Glencoe Collier-Macmillan Limited, Canada, 1963. pp. 338-54.

WILLIAM OF OCKHAM

I.10.1
Guillelmi de Ockham Opera Philosophica et Theologica, Opera Theologica IV, ed. G.I. Etzkorn & F.E. Kelley, St. Bonaventure, NY: Franciscan Institute, St. Bonaventure University, 1979; pp.610-22. Translation especially for this volume by M.M. Tweedale.

I.10.2
Ibid., pp.622-40. Translation especially for this volume by M.M. Tweedale.

I.10.3
Ibid., pp.640-50. Translation especially for this volume by M.M. Tweedale.

I.10.4
Ibid., pp.650-61. Translation especially for this volume by M.M. Tweedale.

I.10.5

Op.cit., *Opera Philosophica VI*, ed. S. Brown, 1984, pp.767-9. Translation especially for this volume by M.M. Tweedale.

I.10.6

Ibid., pp.760-2. Translation especially for this volume by M.M. Tweedale.

I.10.7

Ibid., pp.762-7. Translation especially for this volume by M.M. Tweedale.

II.6.1

Op.cit., *Opera Theologica IX*, *Quodlibeta Septem*, ed. J.C. Wey; St. Bonaventure, 1980, pp.738-45; translation especially for this volume by M.M. Tweedale.

II.6.2

Op.cit., pp.755-62; translation especially for this volume by M.M. Tweedale.

II.6.3

Op.cit., pp.766-74; translation especially for this volume by M.M. Tweedale.

III.8.1

Op.cit., *Opera Theologica* VIII: *Quaestiones Variae*, ed. G.I. Etzkorn, F.E. Kelley, J.C. Wey; St. Bonaventure NY: Franciscan Institute, St. Bonaventure University, 1984. Selection on pp.59-97. Translation by M.M. Tweedale especially for this volume.

IV.7.1

Predestination, God's Foreknowledge, and Future Contingents; translation by M.M. Adams and N. Kretzmann; New York: Appleton-Century-Crofts, 1969; pp.71-92.

V.5.1.

Guillelmi de Ockham Opera Philosophica et Theologica, Opera Theologica II: *Ordinatio* I, eds. S.F. Brown and G. Gal; St. Bonaventure, N.Y.: Franciscan Institute, St. Bonaventure Univ., 1970; pp.160-77; translation by M.M. Tweedale.

VI.9.1

Ibid., pp. 177-92. Translation by M.M. Tweedale.

VI.9.2

Op.cit., *Opera Theologica IX*, *Quodlibeta Septem*, ed. J.C. Wey, St. Bonaventure, 1980; pp.469-74. Translation by M.M. Tweedale especially for this volume.

VI.9.3

Ibid., pp.518-23. Translation by M.M. Tweedale especially for this volume.

VI.9.4

Ibid., pp.528-31. Translation by M.M. Tweedale especially for this volume.

VI.9.5

Ibid., pp.531-6. Translation by M.M. Tweedale especially for this volume.

VI.9.6

Ibid., pp.569-74. Translation by M.M. Tweedale especially for this volume.

BIBLIOGRAPHY

Adams, Marilyn McCord. *William Ockham*. Notre Dame, IN: University of Notre Dame Press, 1987.

Armstrong, A.H., ed. *The Cambridge history of later Greek and early medieval philosophy*. London: Cambridge University Press, 1967.

Ayers, Robert H. *Language, logic, and reason in the church fathers: a study of Tertullian, Augustine, and Aquinas*. Hildesheim, New York: Olms, 1979.

Badawi, 'Abd al-Rahman. *Histoire de la philosophie en Islam*. Paris: J. Vrin, 1972.

Bettoni, Efrem. *Duns Scotus*. Washington: Catholic University of America Press, 1961.

Colish, Marcia L. *The mirror of language; a study in the medieval theory of knowledge*. New Haven: Yale University Press, 1968.

Davidson, Herbert A. *Proofs for eternity, creation, and the existence of God in medieval Islamic and Jewish philosophy*. New York: Oxford University Press, 1987.

Dronke, Peter, ed. *A History of twelfth-century Western philosophy*. Cambridge; New York: Cambridge University Press, 1988.

Efros, Israel. *Ancient Jewish philosophy; a study in metaphysics and ethics*. Detroit: Wayne State University Press, 1964.

Fox, Marvin. *Interpreting Maimonides : studies in methodology, metaphysics, and moral philosophy*. Chicago: University of Chicago Press, 1990.

Frank, William A., and Allan B. Wolter. *Duns Scotus, metaphysician*. West Lafayette, IN: Purdue University Press, 1995.

Gilson, Etienne, *History of Christian philosophy in the Middle Ages*. New York: Random House, 1955.

Gilson, Etienne. *The philosophy of St. Thomas Aquinas*. Salem, NH: Ayer Company, 1989.

Goichon, A. M. *The philosophy of Avicenna and its influence on medieval Europe*. Delhi: Motilal Banarsidass, 1969.

Gracia, Jorge J. E. *Introduction to the problem of individuation in the early Middle Ages*. Washington, D.C.: Catholic University of America Press; München: Philosophia Verlag, 1984.

Haren, Michael. *Medieval thought: the western intellectual traditon from antiquity to the thirteenth century*. 2nd ed. Toronto; Buffalo: University of Toronto Press, 1992.

Husik, Isaac. *A history of mediaeval Jewish philosophy*. New York: Meridian Books, 1958, 1940.

Hyman, Arthur. *Philosophy in the Middle Ages; the Christian, Islamic, and Jewish traditions*. Indianapolis: Hackett Pub. Co., 1973.

Klibansky, Raymond. *The continuity of the Platonic tradition during the Middle Ages*. Millwood, NY: Kraus International Publications, 1982.

Knowles, David. *The evolution of medieval thought*. New York: Vintage Books, 1962, 1988.

Kretzmann, N., A. Kenny, and J. Pinborg. *The Cambridge history of later medieval philosophy*. Cambridge: Cambridge University Press, 1982.

Leaman, Oliver. *An introduction to medieval Islamic philosophy*. Cambridge; New York: Cambridge University Press, 1985.

Leaman, Oliver. *Moses Maimonides*. London; New York: Routledge, 1990.

Leff, Gordon. *Medieval thought: St. Augustine to Ockham*. Harmondsworth: Penguin Books, 1958.

Libera, Alain de. *La philosophie médiévale*. Paris: Presses universitaires de France, 1993.

Marenbon, John. *Early medieval philosophy (480-1150): an introduction*. Rev. ed., 2nd ed. London; New York: Routledge, 1988.

Matthews, Gareth B. *Thought's ego in Augustine and Descartes*. Ithaca: Cornell University Press, 1992.

McGinn, Bernard. *The foundations of mysticism*. New York: Crossroad, 1991.

Merlan, Philip. *Monopsychism, mysticism, meta-consciousness; problems of the soul in the neoaristotelian and neoplatonic tradition*. 2nd ed. The Hague: Martinus Nijhoff, 1969.

O'Meara, John Joseph. *Studies in Augustine and Eriugena*. Edited by Thomas Halton. Washington, D.C.: Catholic University of America Press, 1992.

O'Meara, John Joseph. *The young Augustine: an*

introduction to the Confessions of St. Augustine. London; New York: Longman, 1980.

Price, B.B. *Medieval thought: an introduction.* Oxford; Cambridge: Blackwell, 1992.

Rorem, Paul. *Pseudo-Dionysius: A Commentary on the Texts and an Introduction to their Influence.* New York and Oxford: University Press, 1993.

Sharif, Mian Mohammad. *A history of Muslim philosophy.* Wiesbaden: Harrassowitz, 1963-66.

Stern, S.M. *Medieval Arabic and Hebrew thought.* Edited by F.W. Zimmermann. London: Variorum, 1983.

Tachau, Katherine H. *Vision and certitude in the age of Ockham: optics, epistemology, and the foundations of semantics.* Leiden; New York: E.J. Brill, 1988.

Tobin, Frank J. *Meister Eckhart, thought and language.* Philadelphia: University of Pennsylvania Press, 1986.

Weinberg, Julius Rudolph. *A short history of medieval philosophy.* Princeton, NJ: Princeton University Press, 1964.

Wetzel, James. *Augustine and the limits of virtue.* Cambridge; New York: Cambridge University Press, 1992.